Anthony & Berry
Magistrates' Co[

2015

A J Turner
Barrister, Chambers of Adrian Turner, Eastbourne

LexisNexis®

Members of the LexisNexis Group worldwide

United Kingdom	LexisNexis, a Division of Reed Elsevier (UK) Ltd, Lexis House, 30 Farringdon St, London, EC4A 4HH, and London House, 20–22 East London Street, Edinburgh EH7 4BQ
Australia	LexisNexis Butterworths, Chatswood, New South Wales
Austria	LexisNexis Verlag ARD Orac GmbH & Co KG, Vienna
Benelux	LexisNexis Benelux, Amsterdam
Canada	LexisNexis Canada, Markham, Ontario
China	LexisNexis China, Beijing and Shanghai
France	LexisNexis SA, Paris
Germany	LexisNexis GmbH, Dusseldorf
Hong Kong	LexisNexis Hong Kong, Hong Kong
India	LexisNexis India, New Delhi
Italy	Giuffrè Editore, Milan
Japan	LexisNexis Japan, Tokyo
Malaysia	Malayan Law Journal Sdn Bhd, Kuala Lumpur
New Zealand	LexisNexis NZ Ltd, Wellington
Poland	Wydawnictwo Prawnicze LexisNexis Sp, Warsaw
Singapore	LexisNexis Singapore, Singapore
South Africa	LexisNexis South Africa, Durban
USA	LexisNexis, Dayton, Ohio

© Reed Elsevier (UK) Ltd 2014
Published by LexisNexis

This is a Butterworths title

All rights reserved. No part of this publication may be reproduced in any material form (including photocopying or storing it in any medium by electronic means and whether or not transiently or incidentally to some other use of this publication) without the written permission of the copyright owner except in accordance with the provisions of the Copyright, Designs and Patents Act 1988 or under the terms of a licence issued by the Copyright Licensing Agency Ltd, Saffron House, 6–10 Kirby Street, London EC1N 8TS. Applications for the copyright owner's written permission to reproduce any part of this publication should be addressed to the publisher.
Warning: The doing of an unauthorised act in relation to a copyright work may result in both a civil claim for damages and criminal prosecution.

Crown copyright material is reproduced with the permission of the Controller of HMSO and the Queen's Printer for Scotland. Parliamentary copyright material is reproduced with the permission of the Controller of Her Majesty's Stationery Office on behalf of Parliament. Any European material in this work which has been reproduced from EUR-lex, the official European Union legislation website, is European Union copyright.
A CIP Catalogue record for this book is available from the British Library.

ISBN for this volume: 9781405787932

Printed and bound by CPI Group (UK) Ltd, Croydon, CR0 4YY

Visit LexisNexis at http://www.lexisnexis.co.uk

ii

Preface

This year I have continued the task of reforming the structure and style of this work to make it a more informative and navigable handbook for the wide range of magistrates' courts practitioners and advice workers whom it seeks to serve.

The old subdivisions reflected the origins of *Anthony & Berryman's* as a guide written primarily for magistrates, and the jurisdiction of magistrates' courts as it then was. The new structure reflects the work's now broader readership and the contemporary shape of magisterial law. Sections A, B, C and E are as before. Section D has become Criminal Procedure and includes former sections: I Court Room Procedure; J Remands in Custody and on Bail; and L Role of the Justices' Clerk. Section F has become Civil and Miscellaneous Proceedings and includes former sections: D Property in Possession of the Police; F Liquor Licensing; G Betting and Gaming Licensing; H Council Tax; and M Applications to a Justice.

There have been a number of significant developments since the last edition. The Sentencing Council has been particularly active and produced updates 10, 11 and 12 of the Magistrates' Courts Sentencing Guidelines, which deal, respectively, with sexual offences, environmental offences, and fraud and bribery. It has been decades since a year passed without the enactment of a major piece of criminal justice legislation and the offering for 2014 was the Anti-social, Crime and Policing Act 2014. There have now been seven commencement orders, the last of which implemented criminal behaviour orders, which replace 'CrASBOs' and drink banning orders on conviction. The Act's enabling powers to increase fine levels 1 to 5 and to empower magistrates' courts to impose unlimited fines in some cases have been brought into effect, but at the time of going to press they have not been exercised. This is likely to change in the very near future. This and other prospective changes, such as the repeal of civil ASBOs (replaced by a new injunction, with jurisdiction transferred to the county court for adults), are flagged up in the relevant parts of this book.

While the criminal justice system continues to suffer from severe financial cuts, the volume of important case law has certainly not shrunk. Many recent decisions have been noted.

In more detail, changes to Section A Offences include:

— Sentences for knife crimes: *R v Gomes-Monteiro and others* **A[11.15]**
— Child pornography offences: new SC guidelines **A[14.6]**
— Disorderly behaviour: 'insulting' disappears from certain offences

A[14.20]
— Exploitation/control of prostitution: new SC guideline A[29.4]
— Exposure: new SC guideline A[30.3]
— Fraud by false representation, knowledge of falsity: *R v Augunas* A[36.7]
— Fraud: new SC guidelines on fraud by false representation, failing to disclose information, abuse of position and revenue fraud A[36.10]
— Possession of article for use in fraud: past use insufficient – *R v Sakalauskas* A[38.3]
— Possessing, making or supplying articles for use in fraud: new SC guidelines A[38.4]
— Possession, etc, of indecent photographs of children: new SC guideline A[43.9]
— Keeping a brothel for prostitution: new SC guideline A[44.4]
— Making off without payment: meaning of 'making off' – *R v Morris* A[45.6A]
— Non-school attendance: *West Sussex CC v C* A[49.3]
— Sexual assault of a child under 13: new SC guideline A[52.12]
— Sexual assault: new SC guideline A[53.10]
— Benefit and tax credit fraud: new SC guidelines A[54.6]
— Low value shoplifting: mode of trial changes A[57.2]
— Voyeurism: new SC guideline A[68.6]
— Witness intimidation: requirement of actual intimidation – *R v Patrascu* A[69.4]
— Offences under the Dangerous Act 1991: changes made by the Anti-social Behaviour, Crime and Policing Act 2014 A[72]
— Health and safety at work: Annex 3 to CPD XIII Listing and Allocation Practice Direction added A[80 .5]
— Health and safety at work: inclusion of many sentencing decisions in anticipation of the commencement of the power to impose unlimited fines (see the introduction to this preface) A[80.22]
— Immigration offences: membership of particular social group – *R v Evans* A[81.8A]
— Obstructing the highway: many cases on 'reasonable excuse' added to improve coverage of this offence A[85.3]
— Bribery: new SC guidelines A[89.11]

Changes to Section B Sentencing include:

— Victim Personal Statements: relevant part of the Criminal Practice Direction 2014 reproduced B[5.55]–[5.60]
— Orders on conviction: narrative on the order which replaces CrAS-BOs B[8.8]–[8.12]
— Binding over: Section J of the Criminal Practice Directions 2014 reproduced B[10.20]–[10.21]
— Programme requirements in community orders: limits on delegation to probation – *R v Price* B[17.5]
— Defence costs on acquittal: relevant parts of the Practice Direction (Costs in Criminal Proceedings) 2013, as amended, reproduced B[20.16]
— Wasted costs: meaning of 'party' – *R (Singh) v Ealing Magistrates' Court* and limits of discretion – *R (DPP) v Crown Court at Sheffield* B[20.19]

— Costs against third parties: meaning of 'serious misconduct – *R v Applied Language Solutions* **B[20.20A]**

Changes to Section C Road traffic offences include:

— Table of fixed penalty offences: amendments made to reflect changes made to excise licences by the Finance Act 2014 **C[8.9]**
— Overloading: precedents amended to reflect changes to the way in which weight band limits are expressed **C[38.1]**
— Pelican/zebra crossing offences: meaning of 'proceeding' – *Brooks v Blackpool BC* **C[9.10]**
— Temporary or experimental speed limits: validity of variable speed limits – *Castle v Wakefield and Pontefract Magistrates' Court* **C[49.32]**

New Section D Criminal procedure includes the following amendments:

— Court room procedure: restrictions on reporting – *R (A) v Lowestoft Magistrates' Court; JC and another v Central Criminal Court* **D[1B.7]**
— Abuse of process: not to be used to punish inefficiency – *DPP v Gowing* **D[1B.12]**
— Contempt of court – procedure: Part 62 of the Criminal Procedure Rules 2014 reproduced **D[3.7]**
— Role of the justices' clerk/legal adviser: Part 37A of the Criminal Practice Directions 2014 reproduced **D[9]**

New Section F Civil and miscellaneous matters includes the following amendments:

— Warrants to enter premises: a number of cases added to narrative on obligations on the applicant **F[5.1]**
— Warrants to enter premises: subsequent applications for disclosure – *Commissioner of Police for the Metropolis v Bangs* **F[2.24A]**

I am very grateful to the publisher LexisNexis for all the assistance I have received and to my wife, Yelena, for checking my manuscript for typographical errors.

I have endeavoured to state the law as at 30 September 2014, but have been able to add one or two later developments, particular the commencement of criminal behaviour orders on conviction. If there are any inaccuracies in the text I accept full responsibility.

ADRIAN TURNER

Barrister, Chambers of Adrian Turner, Eastbourne

Contents

Table of Statutes

Paragraph references printed in **bold** type indicate where the Statute is set out in part or in full.

Table
of Statutory Instruments

Paragraph references printed in **bold** type indicate where the Statutory Instrument is set out in part or in full.

D

Table of Cases

A

B

C

D

H

I

J

K

L

N

O

R

V

W

Y

Z

Criminal offences dealt with in magistrates' courts

Index to criminal offences and table of maximum penalties

Set out below are a number of maximum penalties for some common offences. If an offence is dealt with more fully in this book the relevant paragraph is stated.

† or + Penalty on summary conviction of an offence triable either way.

* Indicates that the police may issue a fixed penalty ticket

For index and penalties for road traffic offences, see C[1]

Absconding level 5 and 3 months A[10]

Abstracting/using electricity level 5 and/or 6 months A[1] †

Abusive words or behaviour level 5 and 6 months A[21]

Actual bodily harm level 5 and 6 months † A[8]

Affray level 5 and 6 months† A[2] †

Aggravated vehicle-taking level 5 and 6 months A[66]

Air gun in public place (FA 1968, s 22(5)) level 3 forfeiture A[71]

Airports (Aviation Security Act 1982)
false statements relating to baggage, cargo, etc (s 21A) level 5
false statements in connection with identity documents (s 21B) level 5
unauthorised presence in restricted zone (s 21C) level 5
unauthorised presence on board aircraft (s 21D) level 5
intentionally obstructing an authorised person (s 21E(1)(a)) level 5
impersonating an authorised person (s 21E(1)(b)) level 5

Alcohol sale offences level 3 A[3]

Alcohol/tobacco, fraudulently evade duty (See Customs duty) A[4]

Ammunition (FA 1968, s 1) (*See* Firearms) level 5 and 6 months, forfeiture A[36]

Animal cruelty £20,000 and/or 6 months (ss 4 and 8) level 5 and 6 months

(s 9) A[5]

Animals straying on highway level 3

Anti-social behaviour order – breach level 5 and 6 months † A[6], B[8] and B[8.15]

Arson (see Criminal damage)

Article with blade or point in public place (CJA 1988, s 139) level 5 and 6 months † A[11]

Assault (*See* Actual bodily harm, Common assault, Indecent assault, Grievous bodily harm, Wounding)

Assault on police constable or person assisting police constable level 5 and 6 months A[9]

Assault with intent to resist arrest level 5 and 6 months † A[7]

Avoiding customs duty (*See* Customs duty) A[4]

Bail, failure to surrender level 5 and/or 3 months A[10]

Bankrupt (undischarged, obtaining credit) level 5 and 6 months †

Begging level 3

Bladed article/offensive weapon, possession of (CJA 1988, ss 139, 139A and 139AA) level 5 and 6 months † A[11]

Breach of the peace (*See* Insulting words, and *see* B[10] for Binding over) A[21]

Breach of a non-molestation order (Family Law Act 1996, s 42A) level 5 and 6 months † A[46]

Bribery Bribery Act 2010
Bribing another person (s 1) level 5 and/or 6 months † A[89]
Being bribed (s 2) level 5 and/or 6 months † A[89]
Bribery of foreign public officials (s 6) level 5 and/or 6 months † A[89]
Failure of commercial organisations to prevent bribery (s.7) indictable only A[89]

Breach of a protective order (Protection from Harassment Act 1997, s 5) level 5 and/or 6 months † A[46]

Brothel level 3 and 3 months; level 4 and 6 months (second or subsequent offence in relation to a brothel) For **keeping a brothel used for prostitution** see A[44]

Builder's skip
depositing on highway level 3
not complying with a condition level 3
unlit on roadway level 3

Burglary in a dwelling (domestic burglary) level 5 and 6 months † A[12]

Burglary in a building other than a dwelling (non-domestic burglary) level 5 and/or 6 months † A[13]

Car dumping (*See* Litter) A[83]

Child prostitution and pornography (includes possession of extreme photographic images) level 5 and 6 months † A[14]

Children (cruelty to) level 5 and 6 months † A[19]

Chimes level 5 A[34]

Common assault level 5 and 6 months A[15]

Communications network offences Communications Act 2003, s 127 (1) and (2) level 5 and/or 6 months A[16]

Community order, breach of Criminal Justice Act, 2003, schedule 8. For powers of the court see A[17]

Computers (Computer Misuse Act 1990)
unauthorised access to computer material (s 1) level 5 and 6 months
unauthorised access with intent to commit or facilitate further offences (s 2) level 5 and 6 months
unauthorised modification of computer material (s 3) level 5 and 6 months †

Contempt of court level 4 and 1 month I[3]

Controlled drugs Penalty varies with classification of drug A[22]

Copying false instrument level 5 and 6 months † A[40]

Court security officer
assault level 5 and 6 months A[9]
obstruction level 3 A[47]

Criminal damage Penalties vary with value of property A[18]–A[18B]

Crossbow (draw weight 1.4kg or more) (Crossbows Act 1987)
sell or lease to person under 17 level 5 and 6 months, forfeiture
buying or hiring by person under 17 level 3, forfeiture
possession of by person under 17 level 3, forfeiture

Cruelty to animals £20,000 fine and/or 6 months (ss 4 and 8) level 5 and 6 months (s 9) A[5]

Cruelty to a child level 5 and 6 months † A[19]

Customs duty (avoiding) 3 times value of goods or £5,000 and 6 months (**12months)† A[4]

Damaging property Penalty varies with value of damage A[18]–A[18B]

Dangerous dog A[72]

Dangerous drugs (*See* Controlled drugs) A[22]

Dangerous machinery level 5†

Dishonestly handling level 5 and 6 months † A[49]

Disorderly behaviour (Public Order Act 1986, s 5) level 3 A[20]

Displaying indecent matter level 5

Disposal of property in police possession A[66]

Dogs
Dangerous Dogs Act 1991
  breeding or parting with, etc, fighting dogs (s 1(2)) level 5 and 6 months
  fighting dog in public place without muzzle and lead (s 1(2)) level 5 and 6 months
  dog dangerously out of control in public place level 5 and 6 months + (if aggravated offence)
control order (Dogs Act 1871) A[72]
dog worrying livestock level 3 A[73]

Domestic Violence (see breach of a non-molestation order)

Drugs (controlled) Penalty varies with classification of drug A[22]–A[27B]

Drunk in a highway, public place or licensed premises level 2 A[28]

Drunk and disorderly level 3 A[28]

Drunk at, or on the way to, a football match level 2 A[76]

Earnings of prostitution (living on) level 5 and 6 months †

Electricity, abstract/use without authority level 5 and/or
6 months A[1] †

Enclosed premises (found on) level 3 or 3 months (**level 3
only) A[79]

Excessive noise (nuisance order) level 5 A[74]

Exclusion order (licensed premises), breach of level 4 and
1 month B[32]

Exploitation of Prostitution – causing or inciting prostitution
for gain; controlling prostitution for gain (Sexual Offences Act
2003, ss 52, 53) level 5 and 6 months † A[29]

Exposure (Sexual Offences Act 2003, s 66) level 5 and/or
6 months † A[30]

Failure to maintain oneself or a dependant
level 3 or (and, depending on the facts) 3 months (National Assistance Act 1948,
 s 51)
level 4 and 3 months (**level 4 only) (Social Security Administration Act 1992,
 s 105)

False accounting (Theft Act 1968, s 17) level 5 and 6 months †
A[31]

False identity documents (Identity Documents Act 2010, s 6(1))
level 5 and 6 months † A[32]

False instrument, using level 5 and 6 months † A[40]

False statement to obtain social security level 5 and 3 months
(Social Security Administration Act 1992, s 112) A[54]

False representation to obtain benefit level 5 and 6 months †
(Social Security Administration Act 1992, s 111A) A[54]

Firearm (forfeiture for each of the following) (Firearms Act
1968)
air weapon in public place level 5 and 6 months (s 19) A[71]
air weapon (preventing minor from having with him) level 3 (s 24ZA) A[71A]
firearm (other than air weapon) in public place level 5 and 6 months † (s 19) A[33]
purchasing, possession, etc, without certificate level 5 and 6 months † (s 1) A[76]
trespassing in a building level 5 and 6 monthsA[77]
trespassing on land level 4 and 3 months A[77]

Food (selling food not of quality demanded) (Food Safety Act
1990, s 14) £20,000 and 6 months †

Football related offences (may attract a football banning order)
Possession of alcohol whilst entering or trying to enter ground level 3 A[34]
Being drunk in, or whilst trying to enter, ground level 2 A[35]
throwing missile, indecent or racist chanting; going into prohibited areas level 3
 A[34]
unauthorised sale or attempted sale of tickets level 5 A[34]

Forgery level 5 and 6 months † A[78]

Found on enclosed premises level 3 or 3 months (**level 3 only) A[79]

Fraud level 5 and/or 6 months † A[36]–A[39]
fraud by false representation (s 1 (2) (a)) A[36]
fraud by failing to disclose information (s 1 (2) (b)) A[36]
fraud by abuse of position (s 1 (2) (c)) A[36]
banking and insurance fraud, and obtaining credit through fraud, benefit fraud, and revenue fraud A[36]
confidence A[36]
obtaining services dishonestly (s 11) A[37]
possession of articles for fraud (s 6) A[38]
possessing, making or supplying articles for use in fraud (ss 6, 7 and 1) A[38]
making, adapting, supplying or offering to supply articles for fraud (s 7) A[39]

Fraudulently receiving programmes (see Television licence below)

Game (trespassing on land in day time in search of game) level 3; level 5 if 5 or more trespassers (Game Act 1831, s 30) A[86]

Glue sniffing, supplying level 5 and 6 months

Going equipped for theft level 5 and 6 months † A[58]

Grievous bodily harm level 5 and 6 months † A[70]

Gross indecency level 5 and 6 months †

Handling stolen goods level 5 and 6 months † A[40]

Harassing residential occupier (Protection from Eviction Act 1977, s 1) level 5 and 6 months †

Harassment (Protection from Harassment Act 1997, s 2) level 5 and 6 months A[41]

Harassment (Protection from Harassment Act 1997, s 4) level 5 and 6 months † A[41]

Harassment, alarm or distress/disorderly behaviour (Public Order Act 1986, s 5) level 3* A[20]

Health and Safety at Work Act 1974
failure to discharge a duty imposed by ss 2–6 fine not exceeding £20,000 and/or 6 months A[80]
contravention of s 7 fine not exceeding £20,000 and 6 months †
contravention of s 8 fine not exceeding £20,000 and 6 months †
contravention of s 9 fine not exceeding £20,000 †
an offence under s 33(1)(c) fine not exceeding £20,000 and 6 months †
an offence under s 33(1)(d) level 5 fine
an offence under s 33(1)(e), (f) or (g) fine not exceeding £20,000 and 6 months †
an offence under s 33(1)(h) level 5 and/or 6 months
an offence under s 33(1)(i) level 5 †
an offence under s 33(1)(j) fine not exceeding £20,000 and 6 months †
an offence under s 33(1)(k), (l) or (m) fine not exceeding £20,000 and 6 months †
an offence under s 33(1)(n) level 5 fine
an offence under s 33(1)(o) fine not exceeding £20,000 and 6 months †
an offence under the existing statutory provisions for which no other penalty is specified fine not exceeding £20,000 and 6 months † A[80]

Health Act 2006 (See smoking)

Highway
builder's skip (depositing or leaving unlit) level 3
straying animals on level 3
wilful obstruction level 3 A[85]

Housebreaking implements (*See* Going equipped to steal) A[58]

Immigration offences (Immigration Act 1971, ss 24 – 26) A[81]

Income tax evasion (Finance Act 2000, s 144) level 5 and
6 months † A[42]

Indecent photographs of children level 5 and 6 months † A[43]

Indecent display level 5

Insulting magistrate, etc level 4 and 1 month I[3]

Insulting words or behaviour level 5 and 6 months A[21]

Interference with vehicle level 4 and 3 months A[63]

Intoxicating liquor
possessing at, or on the way to, a designated sporting event level 3 and 3 months A[76]
selling outside permitted hours level 3
selling to persons under 18 level 3 and forfeiture of licence (on second or subsequent conviction within 5 years)
selling without a licence level 4 and 6 months; forfeiture of liquor and containers. For a subsequent offence defendant can be disqualified from holding a licence
persistently sell alcohol to persons aged less than 18 years, fine not exceeding £10,000, the holder of a premises licence may have the licence suspended by the court up to three months

Intoxicating substance, supplying level 5 and 6 months

Keeping a brothel used for prostitution (Sexual Offences Act 2003, s 55) level 5 and/or 6 months † A[44]

Kerb crawling level 3 A[82]

Kill, threatening to (Offences Against the Person Act 1861, s 16) level 5 and/or 6 months † A[59]

Landlord and tenant (unlawful eviction or harassment) level 5 and 6 months †

Litter (including car dumping)
(i) Environmental Protection Act 1990 A[83.18]
(ii) Refuse Disposal (Amenity) Act 1978 level 4 and 3 months A[83]

Living on earnings of prostitution level 5 and 6 months †

Loudspeakers level 5 A[74]

Making off without payment level 5 and 6 months † A[45]

Malicious communications level 5 and 6 months

Measuring equipment (false or unjust) level 5 (and 6 months if fraud), and forfeiture (Weights and Measures Act 1985, s 17)

Messages, offensive or threatening level 5 and 6 months (Malicious Communications Act 1988, s(1))

Misbehaviour in court level 4 and 1 month I[3]

Misuse of drugs (*See* Controlled drugs) A[22]–A[27B]

Mobile phones level 3 or level 4 for HGVs and PSVs*

National insurance, failing to pay contributions level 3 plus arrears of contributions for two years

Noise (excessive) A[74]

Noise or nuisance on NHS premises A[74]

Nuisance A[84]

Obscenely exposing person level 3 or 3 months (Vagrancy Act 1824, s 4); level 3 or 14 days (**not imprisonable for offences from a date to be appointed) (Town Police Clauses Act 1847, s 28)

Obstructing highway level 3 A[85]

Obstructing or resisting a police officer (or a person assisting a police officer) level 3 and 1 month A[47]

Offensive weapon and threatening with offensive weapon level 5 and 6 months, forfeiture † A[11]

Payment, making off without level 5 and 6 months † A[45]

Pedlar
trading without certificate (Pedlars Act 1871, s 4) level 1

Poaching (For hunting wild mammals with dogs and hare coursing see the Hunting Act 2004, ss 1–5)
day time offence level 3; level 5 if 5 or more trespassers (Game Act 1831, s 30) A[86]
night time offences level 3; level 4 and 6 months where violence is used or offered
 (Night Poaching Act 1828, ss 1 and 2) or 3 or more being armed (s 9) A[86.9]
pursuing game without a licence level 2 (Game Licence Act 1860, s 4) A[86.23]

Point, article with, in public place (CJA 1988, s 139) level 5 or 6 months + A[11]

Possessing certain false documents level 5 and 6 months † (Forgery etc Act 1981, s 5)

Property (damaging or destroying) Penalty varies with value A[18] to A[18B]

Property (obtaining property by deception) level 5 and 6 months † A[22]

Prostitutes (see also exploitation of prostitution)
living on earnings of level 5 and 6 months †
soliciting by prostitutes level 2/level 3 or Support and Engagement Order A[82.2]

Public telephone (see **Telephone**) (Telecommunications Act 1984 – Communications Act 2003
fraudulent use of (s 42) level 5 and 6 months †
indecent or false telephone calls (s 43) level 5 and 6 months

Racially or religiously aggravated offences
wounding level 5 and 6 months † A[48]
actual bodily harm level 5 and 6 months † A[8.2]
common assault level 5 and 6 months A[8.2]

criminal damage level 5 and 6 months † A[18]

threatening behaviour/intentional harassment alarm or distress level 5 and 6 months + A[21]

disorderly behaviour level 3 A[20]

harassment level 5 and/or 6 months † A[41]

Railway fare evasion

avoid fare level 3 or 3 months A[48]

giving false name or address level 3 or 3 months A[48.2]

Resisting a constable or a person assisting a constable level 3 and 1 month A[47]

Scales (unjust) level 5 (and 6 months if fraud), and forfeiture (Weights and Measures Act 1985, s 17)

School attendance, parent not ensuring (Education Act 1996, s 444) level 3 Aggravated offence level 4 and 3 months A[49] and D[17]

Selling food not of quality demanded (Food Safety Act 1990, s 14) £20,000 and 6 months †

Sexual activity with child level 5 and 6 months † A[52]

Sexual activity in a public lavatory level 5 and 6 months † A[51]

Sexual assault level 5 and 6 months † A[53]

Sex Offenders register – fail to comply with notification requirements level 5 and 6 months † A[50]

Shotgun

purchasing or possessing, etc, without certificate level 5 and 6 months †, forfeiture A[88]

loaded shotgun in a public place level 5 and 6 months +, forfeiture A[33]

Skip

depositing on highway level 3

not complying with condition level 3

unlit level 3

Smuggling 3 times value of goods or £5,000 and 6 months † A[19]

Social security

Dishonest statement/representation for obtaining benefit etc level 5 and/or six months
† (Social Security Administration Act 1992, s 111A) A[54]

false statement/representation to obtain level 5 and 3 months (Social Security Administration Act 1992, s 112) A[54]

persistently refusing or neglecting to maintain oneself or a dependant level 4 and 3 months (**no longer imprisonable for offences from a date to be appointed) (Social Security Administration Act 1992, s 105)

Soliciting by prostitutes level 2/level 3 or Support and Engagement Order A[82.2]

Soliciting women for prostitution level 3 A[82]

Solvent, supplying for intoxication level 5 and 6 months

Smoking (Health Act 2006)

Smoking in a smoke free place (£200 – a fixed penalty of £50 reduced to £30 if paid before the end of 15 days)

Failing to display the required no-smoking signs (£1000 – a fixed penalty of £200 reduced to £150 if paid before the end of 15 days) – this offence is committed by anyone who manages or occupies smoke-free premises or a vehicle

Failing to prevent smoking in a smoke-free place (£2,500 – no fixed penalty) – this offence is committed by anyone who manages or controls smoke-free premises or a vehicle

Sporting event (may attract a football banning order)
football banning order B[32]
intoxicating liquor, possessing at/on the way to level 3 and 3 months A[35]
drunk at/on the way to level 2 A[35]

Squatting in a residential building level 5 and 6 months

Statutory nuisance (noise) A[61]

Stealing level 5 and 6 months † A[57]

Taking motor vehicle or conveyance level 5 and 6 months, disqualification A[65]

Tattooing a minor level 3

Tax credit fraud level 5 and 6 months † (Tax Credits Act 2005, s 35) A[55]

Taxi-touting/soliciting for hire level 4 (Criminal Justice and Public Order Act 1994, s 167) A[56]

Telephone (Telecommunications Act 1984 – Communications Act 2003)

NB: Ss 42, 42A and 43 below were replaced by ss 125–127 of the Communications Act 2003 effective from 25/7/03 by virtue of SI 2003/1900 as amended. A[16]
fraudulent use of public telephone (s 42) level 5 and 6 months †
indecent or false calls (s 43) level 5 and 6 months *

Television licence payment evasion (Communications Act 2003, s 363) level 3 A[61]

[Fraudulently receiving programmes] (Copyright, Designs and Patents Act 1988, s 297) level 5 F[3]

Terrorism offences (Terrorism Act 2000, ss 15–18) level 5 or 6 months†
(Breach of notification provisions under the Counter-Terrorism Act 2008) level 5 or 6 months† See also B[52]

Theft (covers breach of trust; in a dwelling; from the person and from a shop) level 5 and 6 months† A[57]

Threatening to damage or destroy property level 5 and 6 months † A[18A]

Threatening letters level 4

Threats to kill (Offences Against the Person Act 1861, s 16) level 5 and/or 6 months † A[59]

A[1]

Electricity – Abstracting/Use without authority

Charge

A[1.1] Dishonestly uses without due authority, or dishonestly causes to be wasted or diverted, any electricity

Theft Act 1968, s 13

Maximum penalty – Fine level 5 and 6 months. Triable either way.

Crown Court – 5 years' imprisonment and unlimited fine.

Mode of Trial

A[1.2] Consider the SGC Guideline at A[1.4] below.

Legal notes and definitions

A[1.3] Dishonestly. See the notes at A[57.5] onwards.

It is sufficient for the prosecution to establish electricity was used without the authority of the relevant provider (company) and with no intention to pay (*R v McCreadie and Tume* (1993) 157 JP 541).

Sentencing
SC Guideline – Electricity, abstract/use without authority

A[1.4]

OFFENCE SERIOUSNESS (CULPABILITY AND HARM)		
A. IDENTIFY THE APPROPRIATE STARTING POINT		
Starting points based on first time offender pleading not guilty		
Example of nature of activity	**Starting point**	**Range**
Where the offence results in substantial commercial gain, a custodial sentence may be appropriate		
Offence involving evidence of planning and indication that the offending was intended to be continuing, such as using a device to interfere with the electricity meter or re-wiring or to by-pass the meter.	Medium level community order	Band A fine to high level community order
OFFENCE SERIOUSNESS (CULPABILITY AND HARM)		
B. CONSIDER THE EFFECT OF AGGRAVATING AND MITIGATING FACTORS (OTHER THAN THOSE WITHIN EXAMPLES ABOVE)		

Common aggravating and mitigating factors are identified at B[5.2A]. The following may be particularly relevant but **these lists are not exhaustive**
Factor indicating greater degree of harm 1. Risk of danger caused to property and/or life
FORM A PRELIMINARY VIEW OF THE APPROPRIATE SENTENCE, THEN CONSIDER OFFENDER MITIGATION Common factors are identified at B[5.2A] – see also note (c) below
CONSIDER A REDUCTION FOR A GUILTY PLEA
CONSIDER ANCILLARY ORDERS, INCLUDING COMPENSATION
Refer to Part B for available ancillary orders and in particular B[18] **for guidance on compensation.** This may be ordered in respect of any injury loss or damage resulting from the offence. Maximum is £5,000 per offence. It may be ordered in addition to another sentence, or as a substantive penalty by itself. If a monetary penalty is appropriate and the defendant's means are limited, preference must be given to ordering compensation instead of a fine.
DECIDE SENTENCE **GIVE REASONS**

Electricity, abstract/use without authority – factors to be taken into consideration

Key factors

(a) The starting points and sentencing ranges in this guideline are based on the assumption that the offender was motivated by greed or a desire to live beyond his or her means. To avoid double counting, such a motivation should not be treated as a factor that increases culpability.

(b) When assessing the harm caused by this offence, the starting point should be the loss suffered by the victim. In general, the greater the loss, the more serious the offence. However, the monetary value of the loss may not reflect the full extent of the harm caused by the offence. The court should also take into account the impact of the offence on the victim, any harm to persons other than the direct victim, and any harm in the form of public alarm or erosion of public confidence.

(c) The following matters of offender mitigation may be relevant to this offence:

(i) *Offender motivated by desperation or need.* The fact that an offence has been committed in desperation or need arising from particular hardship may count as offender mitigation in exceptional circumstances.

(ii) *Voluntary restitution.* Whether and the degree to which payment for stolen electricity constitutes a matter of offender mitigation will depend on an assessment of the circumstances and, in particular, the voluntariness and timeliness of the payment.

(iii) Impact on sentence of offender's dependency. Many offenders convicted of acquisitive crimes are motivated by an addiction, often to drugs, alcohol or gambling. This does not mitigate the seriousness of the offence, but an offender's dependency may properly influence the type of sentence imposed. In particular, it may sometimes be appropriate to impose a drug rehabilitation requirement or an alcohol treatment requirement as part of a community order or a suspended sentence order in an attempt to break the cycle of addiction and offending, even if an immediate custodial sentence would otherwise be warranted (see **B[2.17]**).

The Court of Appeal gave guidance on the approach to making drug treatment and testing orders, which also applies to imposing a drug rehabilitation requirement in *Attorney General's Reference No 64 of 2003 (R v Boujettif and Harrison) v Sanchez* [2003] EWCA Crim 3514 and *R v Woods and Collins* [2005] EWCA Crim 2065 summarised in the Sentencing Guidelines Council Guideline Judgments Case Compendium (Section (A) Generic Sentencing Principles) available at: sentencingcouncil.judiciary.gov.uk.

A[2]

Affray

Charge

A[2.1] Using or threatening unlawful violence towards another such that the conduct would cause a person of reasonable firmness present at the scene to fear for his personal safety

Public Order Act 1986, s 3

Maximum penalty – Fine level 5 and 6 months. Triable either way. Specified violent offence under Sch 15, Part 1, CJA 2003

Crown Court – 3 years' imprisonment and unlimited fine.

Mode of trial

A[2.2] Consider the SGC Guideline at A[2.15] below.

Legal notes and definitions

A[2.3] The charge. Only one offence is created.

A[2.4] Using or threatening. Where two or more persons use or threaten the violence, it is the conduct of them taken together that must be considered for the purpose of the offence.

A[2.5] Threats. Cannot be made by way of words alone, there must be at least a physical gesture towards someone. For the purposes of s 3(1), the carrying of dangerous weapons by a group of persons can in some circumstances constitute a threat of violence without those weapons being waved or brandished, but the mere possession of a weapon, without threatening circumstances, is insufficient to constitute such a threat. Nor can carrying a concealed weapon itself be such a threat. However, the visible carrying in public of primed petrol bombs by a large number of what is obvious a gang out for no good is clearly capable of constituting a threat of unlawful violence: *I v DPP, M v DPP, H v DPP* [2001] UKHL 10, [2002] AC 285, [2001] 2 All ER 583, [2001] 2 WLR 765.

A[2.6] Person of reasonable firmness need not actually be or be likely to be present at the scene, it is the hypothetical reasonable bystander who has to be put in fear for his personal safety, not just the victim himself (*R v Sanchez* (1996) 160 JP 321, [1996] Crim LR 572, CA). In *R v Plavecz* (2002) it is made clear that an assault does not turn into an affray because it is in a public place. There must be evidence that anyone watching would have been put in fear themselves.

The purpose of the legislation was to address public order. The authorities made it plain that the facts in particular circumstances required careful study before the legal principle was applied. It was difficult to see how, when viewed contextually, the evidence in the instant case, supported the appellant's conviction for affray. The incident had consisted of brief exchanges which were essentially private in nature. Further, there was no realistic possibility of a notional third party entering the premises and fearing for his own safety: *R (on the application of Leeson) v DPP* [2010] EWHC 994 (Admin), 174 JP 367, [2010] 17 LS Gaz R 16. It does not necessarily follow that because a person is present at a location where a gang are carrying petrol bombs there is a threat of violence towards that person; whether the latter is the case will depend on the facts of the actual case: *I v DPP, M v DPP, H v DPP* (above).

A[2.7]–[2.8]   **Violence.** Violence does not include violence justified in law (self-defence or prevention of crime). The violence must be directed towards another, ie not property – such as kicking a door. However, the violence is not restricted to violence causing or intended to cause injury and includes violent conduct such as throwing a missile of a kind capable of causing injury even though it misses or falls short.

A[2.9]   **Intent.** The accused must intend to use or threaten violence or be aware that his conduct may be violent or threaten violence.

A[2.10]–[2.14]   **Intoxication.** See under the offence of violent disorder at A[67]. Affray can be committed in a public or private place.

Sentencing
SC Guideline – Affray

A[2.15]

OFFENCE SERIOUSNESS (CULPABILITY AND HARM)		
A. IDENTIFY THE APPROPRIATE STARTING POINT		
Starting points based on first time offender pleading not guilty		
Examples of nature of activity	**Starting point**	**Range**
Brief offence involving low-level violence, no substantial fear created	Low level community order	Band C fine to medium level community order
Degree of fighting or violence that causes substantial fear	High level community order	Medium level community order to 12 weeks custody
Fight involving a weapon/throwing objects, or conduct causing risk of injury	18 weeks custody	12 weeks custody to Crown Court
OFFENCE SERIOUSNESS (CULPABILITY AND HARM)		
B. CONSIDER THE EFFECT OF AGGRAVATING AND MITIGATING FACTORS (OTHER THAN THOSE WITHIN EXAMPLES ABOVE)		
Common aggravating and mitigating factors are identified at B[5.2A]. The following may be particularly relevant but these lists are not exhaustive:		
Factors indicating higher culpability		*Factors indicating lower culpability*
1. Group action		1. Did not start the trouble
2. Threats		2. Provocation
3. Lengthy incident		3. Stopped as soon as police arrived
Factors indicating greater degree of harm		
1. Vulnerable person(s) present		
2. Injuries caused		

3. Damage to property	
FORM A PRELIMINARY VIEW OF THE APPROPRIATE SENTENCE, THEN CONSIDER OFFENDER MITIGATION Common factors are identified at B[5.2A].	
CONSIDER A REDUCTION FOR A GUILTY PLEA	
CONSIDER ANCILLARY ORDERS, INCLUDING COMPENSATION AND FOOTBALL BANNING ORDER (where appropriate) Refer to Part B for guidance on ancillary orders and in particular B[18] for guidance on compensation.	
DECIDE SENTENCE **GIVE REASONS**	

A[2.16] Domestic violence. For domestic violence offences see SC Definitive Guideline: "Overarching Principles: Domestic Violence".

Alcohol sale offences

Charge

A[3.1] Sale of alcohol to a person who is drunk

Licensing Act 2003, s 141

NB: For the sale of alcohol to a drunk person under s 141 LA 2003, a fixed penalty of £80 is available

A[3.2] Sale of alcohol to children

Licensing Act 2003, s 146

NB: For the sale of alcohol to a person under 18 a fixed penalty of £80 is available for staff under s 146 Licensing Act 2003. Licensees should be the subject of a summons

A[3.3] Allowing the sale of alcohol to children

Licensing Act 2003, s 147

Maximum penalty – level 3 fine for a s 141 offence; level 5 fine for ss 146 and 147 offences

Section 23 of the Violent Crime Reduction Act 2006 created a new offence of persistently selling alcohol to children, which came into force on April 6, 2007. This is committed if, on three or more different occasions within a period of three consecutive months, alcohol is unlawfully sold on the same premises to a person under 18. The offence is summary only and the maximum penalty is a £10,000 fine. **Consult your legal adviser for guidance on the approach to sentencing and the court's powers in relation to liquor licences.**

Legal notes and definitions

A[3.4] The provisions apply to any person who works at the premises in a capacity, whether paid or unpaid, which gives him authority to sell the alcohol concerned (see s,141 (2) for further definitions).

The provisions apply equally to the sale or supply of alcohol in club premises.

Sentencing
SC Guideline – Alcohol sale offences

A[3.5]

OFFENCE SERIOUSNESS (CULPABILITY AND HARM)
A. IDENTIFY THE APPROPRIATE STARTING POINT
Starting points based on first time offender pleading not guilty

Examples of nature of activity	Starting point	Range
Sale to a child (ie a person under 18)/to a drunk person	Band B fine	Band A fine to band C fine

Note: refer to guidance at B[33.24] for approach to fines for offences committed for commercial purposes.

OFFENCE SERIOUSNESS (CULPABILITY AND HARM)

B. CONSIDER THE EFFECT OF AGGRAVATING AND MITIGATING FACTORS (OTHER THAN THOSE WITHIN THE EXAMPLES ABOVE)

Common aggravating and mitigating factors are identified at B[5.2A]. The following may be particularly relevant but **these lists are not exhaustive:**

Factors indicating higher culpability	Factors indicating greater degree of harm
1. No attempt made to establish age	1. Younger child/children
2. Spirits/high level of drink	2. Drunk person causing distress to others
3. Drunk person highly intoxicated	3. Drunk person aggressive
4. Large quantity of alcohol supplied	
5. Sale intended for consumption by group of children/drunk people	
6. Offender in senior or management position	

FORM A PRELIMINARY VIEW OF THE APPROPRIATE SENTENCE, THEN CONSIDER OFFENDER MITIGATION

Common factors are identified at B[5.2A]

CONSIDER A REDUCTION FOR A GUILTY PLEA

CONSIDER ANCILLARY ORDERS, INCLUDING FORFEITURE OR SUSPENSION OF PERSONAL LIQUOR LICENCE

Refer to Part B for available ancillary orders

DECIDE SENTENCE

GIVE REASONS

Sentencing Note: See A[3.3] above.

A[4]

Alcohol/tobacco, fraudulently evade duty

Charge

A[4.1] (1) Knowingly acquiring possession of any of the following goods:

*   goods which have been unlawfully removed from a warehouse or Queen's warehouse;
*   goods which are chargeable with a duty which has not been paid;
*   goods with respect to the importation or exportation of which any prohibition or restriction is for the time being in force under or by virtue of any enactment; or

knowingly concerned in carrying, removing, depositing, harbouring, keeping or concealing or in any manner dealing with any such goods,

with intent to defraud Her Majesty of any duty payable on the goods or to evade any such prohibition or restriction with respect to the goods he shall be guilty of an offence under this section and may be arrested.

OR

(2) In relation to any goods, in any way knowingly concerned in any fraudulent evasion or attempt at evasion:

*   of any duty chargeable on the goods;
*   of any prohibition or restriction for the time being in force with respect to the goods under or by virtue of any enactment; or
*   of any provision of the Customs and Excise Acts 1979 applicable to the goods.

Maximum penalty – Three times the value of the goods or £5,000 fine whichever is the greater and 6 months. Triable either way.

Crown Court – 7 years' imprisonment and unlimited fine.

A[4.2] Drugs – Different penalties will apply in both the magistrates' court and the Crown Court if drugs are involved and in the Crown Court where there is the import or export of counterfeit money. The legal adviser should be consulted. For drugs see A[27B].

Mode of trial

A[4.3] See general notes at D[4] and SGC Guideline at A[4.36] below.

Legal notes and definitions

A[4.4] Offence (1): knowingly and intent to defraud. The possession by a defendant of dutiable goods raises a presumption that they were knowingly in his possession; the intent to defraud may be inferred from the surrounding circumstances: *R v Cohen* [1951] 1 KB 505, [1951] 1 All ER 203, 115 JP 91; *Sayce v Coupe* [1953] 1 QB 1, [1952] 2 All ER 715, 116 JP 552; *Schneider v Dawson* [1960] 2 QB 106,[1959] 3 All ER 584, 124 JP 7.

A[4.5] Offence (2): knowingly concerned. What is required is a specific intent to be knowingly concerned in any fraudulent evasion of a prohibition. Where the case concerns the importation of drugs, to found a conviction the prosecution must establish that, at the time of the offence, the accused intended dishonestly to evade the prohibition and import the drugs by entering UK territorial waters, and knew that they had in fact entered those waters. Merely running the risk of entering UK waters did not suffice: *R v Panayi (No 2)* [1989] 1 WLR 187, 88 Cr App Rep 267, CA. 'Knowingly concerned' involves not merely knowledge of the smuggling operation, but also that the substance is one the importation of which is prohibited. Where the defendant smuggled cannabis into the UK believing it was currency, he could not be convicted of the offence even though he wrongly thought that smuggling currency was prohibited: *R v Taafe* [1984] AC 539, [1984] 1 All ER 747, 148 JP 510, HL. Where, however, a defendant smuggled drugs believing they were pornographic goods, believing correctly that the importation of such goods was prohibited, he was liable to conviction: *R v Ellis* (1987) 84 Cr App Rep 235, [1987] Crim LR 44.

A[4.6] Offence (2): fraudulent evasion or attempt. The prosecution must prove fraudulent conduct in the sense of dishonest conduct deliberately intended to evade the prohibition or restriction with respect to, or the duty chargeable on, goods as the case may be. There is no necessity for the prosecution to prove acts of deceit practised on a customs officer in his presence: *Re A-G's Reference (No 1 of 1981)* [1982] QB 848, [1982] 2 All ER 417.

A[4.7] Duplicity. Offence (2) is an 'activity' offence. Sometimes it will arise in relation to only one transaction and in other cases there will be many giving rise to continuity of activity which may be charged as one offence. Nevertheless s 170 (2) does not permit two different activities to be charged as one offence, see *R v Martin* [1998] 2 Cr App Rep 385, CA.

A[4.8] The prosecution. Must be authorised by HM Revenue and Customs. Neither the police nor a private citizen can instigate proceedings on their own authority.

A[4.9] Death of informant. If the informant (or person authorised by HM Revenue and Customs) dies, is dismissed or is absent then the Revenue and Customs can nominate another person to proceed with the case.

A[4.10] Presumptions against the defendant. The Act is so worded that it gives to the prosecution a number of advantages in presuming certain points to be in the prosecution's favour.

For example, if a defendant claims that the goods were lawfully imported or lawfully unloaded from a ship or aircraft the burden of proving these points rests on the defendant. However, the burden of proof is not to establish his defence beyond all reasonable doubt but to satisfy the magistrates that on the balance of probabilities his defence is true.

A[4.11]–[4.15] Mistake. If the customs officer makes a mistake and undercharges the duty, no offence is committed by a person who pays the duty realising the mistake, provided that he has not given false information or induced the error.

Sentencing
SC Guideline – Alcohol/tobacco, fraudulently evade duty

A[4.16] Refer to the Revenue Fraud guideline at A[36].

A[4.17] Value of goods. The value of the goods, for the purpose of determining the penalty, shall be the price they might reasonably be expected to have fetched on the open market, after duty has been paid, at or about the time of the commission of the offence. See *R v Dosanjh* [1998] 3 All ER 618, [1999] 1 Cr App Rep 371, CA for aggravating features and the use of imprisonment and *R v Howlett* [1999] All ER (D) 777, CA which suggest that cases involving a loss of duty under £10,000 may be dealt with by sentences of under six months' imprisonment.

A[4.18] Financial reporting order. A conviction for an offence under s 170 of the Customs and Excise Management Act 1979 (including attempting, conspiring, inciting, aiding, abetting, counselling or procuring the commission of the offence) is one that is mentioned in s 76(3) of the Serious Organised Crime and Police Act 2005. The court when sentencing or otherwise dealing with an offender convicted on or after 4 May 2007 may also make a financial reporting order.

A[4.19] Appeal. Note that HM Revenue and Customs may appeal any decision of the court including sentence (*Customs and Excise Comrs v Brunt* (1998) 163 JP 161).

A[5]

Animal cruelty

Charges

A[5.1] 1. A person commits an offence if –

(a)   an act of his, or a failure of his to act, causes an animal to suffer;
(b)   he knew, or ought reasonably to have known, that the act, or failure to act, would have that effect or be likely to do so,
(c)   the animal is a protected animal, and
(d)   the suffering is unnecessary.

Animal Welfare Act 2006, s 4(1).

2. A person commits an offence if –

(a)   he is responsible for an animal,
(b)   an act, or failure to act, of another person causes the animal to suffer,
(c)   he permitted that to happen or failed to take such steps (whether by supervising the other person or otherwise) as were reasonable in all the circumstances to prevent that happening, and
(d)   the suffering is unnecessary.

Animal Welfare Act 2006, s 4(2).

3. Fighting etc

A person commits an offence if he –

(a)   causes an animal fight to take place, or attempts to do so;
(b)   knowingly receives money for an animal fight;
(c)   knowingly publicises an animal fight; . . .

Animal Welfare Act 2006, s 8(1).

NB: Offences under (d)–(i) omitted and subsections (2) and (3). Different types of offences are caught by this section including being present at an animal fight. For ease of space not all offences under section 8 have been included in this section.

4. A person commits an offence if –

he does not take such steps as are reasonable in all the circumstances to ensure that the needs of an animal for which he is responsible are met to the extent required by good practice.

Animal Welfare Act 2006, s 9

Maximum penalty

(1)   6 months' imprisonment or a fine not exceeding £20,000 or both – triable only summarily.
(2)   6 months' imprisonment or a fine not exceeding £20,000 or both – triable only summarily.

(3)   6 months' imprisonment or a fine not exceeding £20,000 or both – triable only summarily.

(4)   6 months' imprisonment or a level 5 fine or both – triable only summarily.

Legal notes and definitions

A[5.2] Each of the types of cruelty alleged above are separate offences. The legislation appears designed to catch not only owners or persons in charge of an animal but in specified circumstances any other person "responsible" for an animal (see below). If a defendant causes suffering etc to a number of different animals on the same occasion there does not appear to be any objection to a single charge being preferred eg under s 4 (1). The mutilation of animals is a separate offence covered by s 5 while the docking of animal tails is provided for by s 6 of the AWA 2006.

Animal. Is defined in s 1 and means a vertebrate other than man.

Protected animal. The legislation covers mostly domesticated animals as defined in s 2.

Responsibility for animals. In the AWA 2006:

(1)   References to a person responsible for an animal are to a person responsible for an animal whether on a permanent or temporary basis.

(2)   References to being responsible for an animal include being in charge of it.

(3)   A person who "owns" an animal should always be regarded as being a person who is responsible for it.

(4)   A person should be "treated" as responsible for any animal for which a person under the age of 16 years of whom he has actual care and control is responsible.

Whether suffering unnecessary. In the AWA 2006, the considerations to which it is relevant to have regard when determining for the purposes of this section whether suffering is unnecessary include:

(1)   Whether the suffering could reasonably have been avoided or reduced.

(2)   Whether the conduct which caused the suffering was in compliance with any relevant enactment or any relevant provisions of a licence or code of practice issued under any enactment.

(3)   Whether the conduct which caused the suffering was proportionate to the purpose of the conduct concerned.

(4)   Whether the conduct concerned was in all the circumstances that of a reasonably competent and humane person.

(5)   Nothing in (1)–(4) above applies to the destruction of an animal in an appropriate and humane manner.

Knew or ought reasonably to have known. The prosecution had to establish that the defendant knew or ought reasonably to have known both that his or her act or failure would cause an animal to suffer and that the suffering was unnecessary: *R (on the application of Gray and Gray) v Aylesbury Crown Court, RSPCA (interested party)* [2013] EWHC 500 (Admin), (2013) 177 JP 329.

Difference between 'cruelty' offence (s 4) and the 'welfare' offence (s 9). The difference is whether the animal has suffered unnecessarily and not as to the mental state of the person concerned; s 9(1) sets a purely objective standard: *R (on the application of Gray and Gray) v Aylesbury Crown Court, RSPCA (interested party)* [2013] EWHC 500 (Admin), (2013) 177 JP 32.

A conviction for a s 9 offence will not be bad for duplicity if it is based on the same findings of fact as a conviction for a s 4 offence. There can be no objection to a person being convicted of both offences if the conduct proved in relation to the s 9 offence is wider than the conduct which can be proved to have caused actual suffering to the animal: *R (on the application of Gray and Gray) v Aylesbury Crown Court, RSPCA (interested party)*, above.

Time limits for prosecution.

(a)   Before the end of 3 years beginning with the date of the commencement of the offence, or
(b)   before the end of the period of six months beginning with the date on which evidence which the prosecutor thinks is sufficient to justify the proceedings comes to his knowledge.

A certificate issued under s 31(2) of the AWA 2006 which conformed to the criteria specified in s 31(2) could only be challenged on one of two bases alone: (i) that it constituted a fraud; (ii) that the certificate was plainly wrong. Where it was submitted that a certificate was plainly wrong a challenge should be mounted in relation to the jurisdiction of the court and not as an abuse of the process: *Atkinson v DPP* [2004] EWHC 1457 (Admin), [2004] 3 All ER 971, [2005] 1 WLR 96; see *Lamont-Perkins v RSPCA* immediately below.

Animal Welfare Act 2006, s 31.

Prosecutor. The phrase 'the prosecutor' in s 31 of the AWA 2006 is not limited to a person or body who prosecutes pursuant to a power conferred by some statutory provision but applies to anyone who initiates a prosecution under the Act. Accordingly, s 127 of the MCA 1980 had no application to a prosecution brought under the Animal Welfare Act 2006 where a certificate had been issued under s 31(2): *Lamont-Perkins v Royal Society for the Prevention of Cruelty to Animals* [2012] EWHC 1002 (Admin), (2012) 176 JP 369.

Sentencing
SC Guideline – Animal cruelty

A[5.3]

OFFENCE SERIOUSNESS (CULPABILITY AND HARM)		
A. IDENTIFY THE APPROPRIATE STARTING POINT		
Starting points based on first time offender pleading not guilty		
Examples of nature of activity	**Starting point**	**Range**
One impulsive act causing little or no injury; short term neglect	Low level community order	Band C fine to medium level community order
Several incidents of deliberate ill-treatment/frightening animal(s); medium term neglect	High level community order	Medium level community order to 12 weeks custody

Attempt to kill/torture; animal baiting/conducting or permitting cock-fighting etc; prolonged neglect	18 weeks custody	12–26 weeks custody

OFFENCE SERIOUSNESS (CULPABILITY AND HARM)

B. CONSIDER THE EFFECT OF AGGRAVATING AND MITIGATING FACTORS (OTHER THAN THOSE WITHIN THE EXAMPLES ABOVE)

Common aggravating and mitigating factors are identified at **B[5.2]**. The following may be particularly relevant but these lists are not exhaustive:

Factors indicating higher culpability	*Factors indicating lower culpability*
1. Offender in position of special responsibility	1. Offender induced by others
2. Adult involves children in offending	2. Ignorance of appropriate care
3. Animal(s) kept for livelihood	3. Offender with limited capacity
4. Use of weapon	
5. Offender ignored advice/warnings	
6. Offence committed for commercial gain	
Factors indicating greater degree of harm	
1. Serious injury or death	
2. Several animals affected	

FORM A PRELIMINARY VIEW OF THE APPROPRIATE SENTENCE, THEN CONSIDER OFFENDER MITIGATION

Common factors are identified at **B[5.2A]**

CONSIDER A REDUCTION FOR A GUILTY PLEA

CONSIDER ANCILLARY ORDERS, INCLUDING COMPENSATION

See **Part B** for guidance on available ancillary orders and consult your legal adviser

CONSIDER DISQUALIFICATION FROM OWNERSHIP OF ANIMAL

DECIDE SENTENCE

GIVE REASONS

A[5.4] Deprivation of ownership. If the person convicted of an offence under eg ss 4 or 9 above, is the owner of an animal in relation to which the offence was committed, the court may, instead of or in addition, make an order depriving him of ownership of the animal and for its disposal (Animal Welfare Act 2006, s 33).

Destruction of animal. After conviction the court, if satisfied on the evidence of a veterinary surgeon that it is in the interests of the animal, it may order the animal to be destroyed. The defendant or another person (such as the owner) can be ordered to pay the costs involved. There is a right of appeal to the Crown court except where the court considers that it is in the interests of the animal not to delay the destruction order (Animal Welfare Act 2006, s 37).

Disqualification. The court may disqualify the defendant:

(a)   from owning animals;
(b)   from keeping animals;
(c)   from participating in the keeping of animals; and,

(d) from being party to an arrangement under which he is entitled to control or influence the way in which animals are kept (Animal Welfare Act 2006, s 34).

Such a disqualification must include all the activities specified above: *R (on the application of the RSPCA) v Guildford Crown Court* [2012] EWHC 3392 (Admin), (2013) 177 JP, 154. However, '[10] Under s 3 of the Human Rights Act, legislation must be read, where possible, so as to comply with Convention rights. It may be that in an exceptional case it would be possible to read down the section so as to allow the court a discretion to choose not to apply the disqualification to all the specified acts if that were necessary to protect a Convention right (and, in practice, the right which would be likely to apply would be art 8).' (per Elias LJ)

Alternatively, or additionally, a court may:

(a) disqualify a person from dealing in animals; and/or
(b) disqualify a person from transporting animals and from arranging for the transport of animals.

A disqualification may be imposed in relation to animals generally or in relation to animals of one or more kinds.

If the court decides not to order disqualification it must state its reasons in open court.

The court may specify a period during which no application may be made to terminate the disqualification. If no such period is specified, such an application may be made after the expiry of one year.

The disqualification may be for such period as the court deems fit. If the disqualification order is breached the maximum penalty is a level 5 fine or 51 weeks. The offence is triable summarily only.

Pursuant to s 143 (2) CJA 2003, the court is entitled to have regard to the previous convictions of the offender (as an aggravating factor) for causing unnecessary suffering to an animal. Ten years' disqualification from keeping equine animals upheld on appeal where a farmer had two previous convictions for similar offences: *Anthony Ward v Royal Society for the Prevention of Cruelty to Animals* [2010]) EWHC 347 (Admin).

After the disqualification order has been in force for 12 months the defendant can apply for its removal unless the court specified a different minimum period when imposing the order or a previous application has been refused less than 12 months ago (Animal Welfare Act 2006, s 43).

A[6]

Anti-social behaviour order, breach of

A[6.1] See B[8] and B[8.15].

A[7]

Assault with intent to resist arrest

Charge

A[7.1] Whosoever shall assault any person with intent to resist or prevent the lawful apprehension or detainer of himself or any other person for any offence, shall be guilty of [an offence]

Offences Against the Person Act 1861, s 38

Maximum penalty – Fine level 5 and/or 6 months. Triable either way. Violent specified offence under Sch 15, Part 1, CJA 2003.

Crown Court – 2 years' imprisonment and unlimited fine.

Mode of trial

A[7.2] Consider the SC guideline at A[7.4] below.

Legal notes and definitions

A[7.3] The prosecution must establish:

(1)   That the arrest was lawful.
(2)   An intention by the defendant to resist arrest.
(3)   Knowledge that the person assaulted, who might or might not be a police officer, was a person who was seeking to arrest him.

An honest belief by the defendant that the arrest was unlawful is irrelevant (*R v Lee* (2001) 165 JP 344, CA).

Where the person carrying out the arrest was a police officer, it is not necessary for the prosecution to establish that the defendant knew he/she was a police officer (*R v Brightling* [1991] Crim LR 364).

Sentencing
SC Guideline – Assault with intent to resist arrest

Assault with intent to resist arrest

A[7.4] Offences against the Person Act 1861, section 38

This is a specified offence for the purposes of section 224 of the Criminal Justice Act 2003

Triable either way

Maximum when tried summarily: level 5 and/or 26 weeks' custody

Maximum when tried on indictment: 2 years' custody

Offence range: Fine – 51 weeks' custody

This guideline applies to all offenders aged 18 and older, who are sentenced on or after 13 June 2011. The definitions of 'starting point' and 'first time offender' do not apply for this guideline. Starting point and category ranges apply to all offenders in all cases, irrespective of plea or previous convictions.

Step One
Determining the offence category

The court should determine the offence category using the table below.

Category 1	Greater harm **and** higher culpability
Category 2	Greater harm **and** lower culpability; **or** lesser harm **and** higher culpability
Category 3	Lesser harm **and** lower culpability

The court should determine the offender's culpability and the harm caused, or intended, by reference **only** to the factors identified in the table below (as demonstrated by the presence of one or more). These factors comprise the principal factual elements of the offence and should determine the category.

Factors indicating greater harm

Sustained or repeated assault on the same victim

Factors indicating lesser harm

Injury which is less serious in the context of the offence

Factors indicating higher culpability

Statutory aggravating factors:

Offence racially or religiously aggravated

Offence motivated by, or demonstrating, hostility to the victim based on his or her sexual orientation (or presumed sexual orientation)

Offence motivated by, or demonstrating, hostility to the victim based on the victim's disability (or presumed disability)

Other aggravating factors:

A significant degree of premeditation

Use of weapon or weapon equivalent (for example, shod foot, headbutting, use of acid, use of animal)

Intention to commit more serious harm than actually resulted from the offence

Deliberately causes more harm than is necessary for commission of offence

Leading role in group or gang

Offence motivated by, or demonstrating, hostility based on the victim's age, sex, gender identity (or presumed gender identity)

Factors indicating lower culpability

Subordinate role in group or gang Lack of premeditation

Mental disorder or learning disability, where linked to commission of the offence

---

Step Two
Starting point and category range

Having determined the category, the court should use the corresponding starting points to reach a sentence within the category range below. The starting point applies to all offenders irrespective of plea or previous convictions. A case of particular gravity, reflected by multiple features of culpability in step one, could merit upward adjustment from the starting point before further adjustment for aggravating or mitigating features, set out below.

Offence Category	Starting Point *(Applicable to all offenders)*	Category Range *(Applicable to all offenders)*
Category 1	26 weeks – custody	12 weeks – custody – Crown Court (51 weeks – custody)
Category 2	Medium level community order	Low level community order – High level community order
Category 3	Band B fine	Band A fine – Band C fine

The table below contains a **non-exhaustive** list of additional factual elements providing the context of the offence and factors relating to the offender. Identify whether any combination of these, or other relevant factors, should result in an upward or downward adjustment from the starting point. In some cases, having considered these factors, it may be appropriate to move outside the identified category range.

When sentencing **category 1** offences, the court should consider whether the sentence can be suspended.

Factors increasing seriousness

Statutory aggravating factors:

Previous convictions, having regard to a) the nature of the offence to which the conviction relates and its relevance to the current offence; and b) the time that has elapsed since the conviction

Offence committed whilst on bail

Other aggravating factors include:

Location of the offence

Timing of the offence

Ongoing effect upon the victim

Gratuitous degradation of victim

Failure to comply with current court orders

Offence committed whilst on licence

An attempt to conceal or dispose of evidence

Failure to respond to warnings or concerns expressed by others about the offender's behaviour

Commission of offence whilst under the influence of alcohol or drugs

Established evidence of community impact

Any steps taken to prevent the victim reporting an incident, obtaining assistance and/or from assisting or supporting the prosecution

Offences taken into consideration (TICs)

Factors reducing seriousness or reflecting personal mitigation

No previous convictions **or** no relevant/recent convictions

Single blow

Remorse

Good character and/or exemplary conduct

Determination and/or demonstration of steps taken to address addiction or offending behaviour

Serious medical conditions requiring urgent, intensive or long-term treatment

Isolated incident

Age and/or lack of maturity where it affects the responsibility of the defendant

Mental disorder or learning disability, where not linked to the commission of the offence

Sole or primary carer for dependent relatives

Step Three
Consider any other factors which indicate a reduction, such as assistance to the prosecution

The court should take into account any rule of law by virtue of which an offender may receive a discounted sentence in consequence of assistance given (or offered) to the prosecutor or investigator.

Step Four
Reduction for guilty pleas

The court should take account of any potential reduction for a guilty plea in accordance with section 144 of the Criminal Justice Act 2003 and the *Guilty Plea* guideline.

Step Five
Dangerousness

Assault with intent to resist arrest is a specified offence within the meaning of Chapter 5 of the Criminal Justice Act 2003 and at this stage the court should consider whether having regard to the criteria contained in that Chapter it would be appropriate to award an extended sentence.

Step Six
Totality principle

If sentencing an offender for more than one offence or where the offender is already serving a sentence, consider whether the total sentence is just and proportionate to the offending behaviour.

Step Seven
Compensation and ancillary orders

In all cases, the court should consider whether to make compensation and/or other ancillary orders.

Step Eight
Reasons

Section 174 of the Criminal Justice Act 2003 imposes a duty to give reasons for, and explain the effect of, the sentence.

Step Nine
Consideration for remand time

(Now obligatory.)

A[7.5] **Licensed premises.** If the offence takes place on licensed premises an exclusion order may be made. See **B[32]**.

Assault occasioning actual bodily harm and racially/religiously aggravated assault occasioning ABH

Charge

A[8.1] Assault occasioning actual bodily harm

Offences Against The Person Act 1861, s 47

Maximum penalty – Fine level 5 and 6 months. Triable either way. Violent specified offence under Sch 15, Part 1, CJA 2003.

Crown Court – 5 years' imprisonment and unlimited fine.

A[8.2] Racially or religiously aggravated assault occasioning actual bodily harm

Crime and Disorder Act 1998, s 29

Maximum penalty – Fine level 5 and 6 months. Triable either way. Specified violent offence under Sch 15, Part 1, CJA 2003

Crown Court – 7 years' imprisonment and unlimited fine.

Mode of trial

A[8.3]–[8.4] Consider SC guideline at A[8.31] below. For cases of domestic violence. See SC Definitive Guideline: "Overarching Principles: Domestic Violence".

Owing to the nature of charges of assault it is particularly important that magistrates hear an outline of the facts before making their decision.

Legal notes and definitions

A[8.5]–[8.6] Assault. See under 'Common assault' at A[15].

A[8.7] Intent. The defendant must intend to cause his victim to apprehend immediate and unlawful violence, or be reckless whether such apprehension be caused (*R v Venna* [1976] QB 421, [1975] 3 All ER 788, CA). The offence of assault occasioning actual bodily harm is made out upon proof of an assault together with proof of the fact that actual bodily harm was occasioned by the assault. The prosecution are not obliged to prove that the defendant intended to cause some actual bodily harm or was reckless as to whether such harm would be caused (*R v Savage* [1992] 1 AC 699, [1991] 4 All ER 698, *R v Parmenter* [1991] 4 All ER 698, HL).

In principle it was open to justices to convict on the basis of recklessness even where the prosecution simply alleged a deliberate assault: *D v DPP*

[2005] EWHC 967 (Admin) considered. However, the justices had failed to identify what was the unlawful act of K leading to the assault. Recklessness had only been a possible conclusion if the justices had found that K had thrown a punch, albeit without intending it to land, or was flailing his arms about in an agitated and aggressive manner. The conviction could not stand in the light of the findings of fact made by the justices: *Katsonis v Crown Prosecution Service* [2011] EWHC 1860 (Admin), 175 JP 396.

A[8.8] In *DPP v K (a minor)* [1990] 1 All ER 331, [1990] 1 WLR 1067, a schoolboy who put acid in a hot air dryer recklessly but in a mindless panic rather than with any intention to cause harm was nonetheless guilty of assault. In *DPP v Santra-Bermudez* [2003] EWHC 2908, [2003] All ER (D) 168 (Nov) the offence was made out when a police officer pricked her finger on a needle while carrying out a lawful search of a man who had told her that he had no needles in his pocket.

A[8.9] Actual bodily harm. This is less serious than grievous bodily harm. There need not be permanent injury. Any hurt or injury calculated to interfere with health or comfort can be actual bodily harm, so can an assault causing unconsciousness or an hysterical or nervous condition (*R v Miller* [1954] 2 QB 282, [1954] 2 All ER 529), ie some psychiatric damage and not just distress or panic (*R v Chan-Fook* [1994] 2 All ER 552, [1994] 1 WLR 689, CA). Significant psychological symptoms caused by a series of telephone calls, followed by silence can constitute an assault causing actual bodily harm (*R v Ireland* [1998] AC 147, [1997] 4 All ER 225, HL). Where a victim suffered great pain immediately and for some time thereafter suffered tenderness and soreness, that was sufficient for the court to infer that there was actual bodily harm notwithstanding that no physically discernible injury had been occasioned. This would include the victim's unconsciousness without the appearance of physical injury (*T v DPP* [2004] EWHC 183 (Admin), [2004] All ER (D) 278 (Jan)). Where there is evidence that a blow was struck, the justices are entitled if they see fit to infer that some bodily harm, however slight, has resulted.

Cutting off a substantial part of the victim's hair was capable in law of amounting to an assault which occasioned actual bodily harm (*DPP v Smith (MR)* [2006] EWHC 94 (Admin), [2006] 2 All ER 16).

A[8.10]–[8.15] Racial, religious, disability, sexual orientation or transgender identity aggravation. This means that at the time of committing the offence, or immediately before or after doing so, the offender demonstrates towards the victim of the offence either hostility based on the victim's membership (or presumed membership) of a racial or religious group or their disability or presumed sexual orientation; or, the offence is motivated (wholly or partly) by hostility towards members of a racial or religious group based on their membership of that group, or persons of a particular sexual orientation, transgender identity or disability. See *R v H* [2010] EWCA Crim 1931, 174 CL&J 573, 154 Sol Jo (no 31) 28 which reviews the authorities.

A[8.16] When considering whether an offence was racially motivated for the purposes of the CDA 1998, s 28 (1)(a) in the light of words uttered immediately prior to the offence, the following matters were irrelevant: (i) victim's perception of the words used; (ii) any additional reason unrelated to race, for uttering the words (CDA 1998, s 28(3)(b)); and (iii) the fact that in the defendant's frame of mind at the time he uttered the words, he would have abused anyone by reference to an obvious physical characteristic (*DPP v Woods* [2002] EWHC 85 (Admin), [2002] All ER (D) 154 (Jan)).

However, see A[20.6] for more recent case law.

It is immaterial whether or not the offender's hostility is based, to any extent on any other factor not mentioned above. See A[15.33] for sentencing.

A[8.17] Provocation is not a defence but can be taken into consideration when deciding sentence.

A[8.18]–[8.19] Reasonable force for purposes of self-defence etc. A person may use reasonable force to defend himself, his property or another. Where self-defence is put forward to justify the use of violence, the onus is on the prosecution to disprove the defence beyond reasonable doubt. A person must not use force in attacking or retaliating, or revenging himself. It is permissible to use force not merely to counter an actual attack but to ward off an attack honestly believed to be imminent. The reasonableness or otherwise of the belief is only relevant in ascertaining whether he actually held the belief or not (*Beckford v R* [1988] AC 130, [1987] 3 All ER 425, PC).

Proof that the accused tried to retreat or call off the fight might be a cast-iron method of rebutting the suggestion that he was an attacker or retaliator or trying to revenge himself. It is to be stressed, however, that this is not the only method of doing so, and it depends on the circumstances of the particular case (*R v Bird* [1985] 2 All ER 513, [1985] 1 WLR 816, CA). The common law defence of self defence and the defence under s 3 of the Criminal Law Act 1967, extended to the use of violence against an innocent third party: *R v Hichens* [2011] EWCA Crim 1626, [2011] 2 Cr App Rep 370, [2011] Crim LR 873.

A[8.20] A man who is attacked can defend himself but can only do what is objectively reasonable in the circumstances as the defendant believes them to be. In relation to self defence, prevention of crime or effecting or assisting in the lawful arrest of another, s 76 of the Criminal Justice and Immigration Act 2008 codified the common law. It has subsequently been amended by both the Legal Aid, Sentencing and Punishment of Offenders Act 2012 (which inserted subs(6A)) and the Crime and Courts Act 2013 (which inserted subs(5A), (8A)–(8F). It provides as follows:

(1) This section applies where in proceedings for an offence—

   (a) an issue arises as to whether a person charged with the offence ("D") is entitled to rely on a defence within subsection (2), and

   (b) the question arises whether the degree of force used by D against a person ("V") was reasonable in the circumstances.

(2) The defences are—

   (a) the common law defence of self-defence;

   (aa) the common law defence of defence of property; and

   (b) the defences provided by section 3(1) of the Criminal Law Act 1967 (c 58) or section 3(1) of the Criminal Law Act (Northern Ireland) 1967 (c 18 (NI)) (use of force in prevention of crime or making arrest).

(3) The question whether the degree of force used by D was reasonable in the circumstances is to be decided by reference to

the circumstances as D believed them to be, and subsections (4) to (8) also apply in connection with deciding that question.

(4) If D claims to have held a particular belief as regards the existence of any circumstances—

    (a) the reasonableness or otherwise of that belief is relevant to the question whether D genuinely held it; but

    (b) if it is determined that D did genuinely hold it, D is entitled to rely on it for the purposes of subsection (3), whether or not–

        (i) it was mistaken, or

        (ii) (if it was mistaken) the mistake was a reasonable one to have made.

(5) But subsection (4) (b) does not enable D to rely on any mistaken belief attributable to intoxication that was voluntarily induced.

(5A) In a householder case, the degree of force used by D is not to be regarded as having been reasonable in the circumstances as D believed them to be if it was grossly disproportionate in those circumstances.

(6) In a case other than a householder case, the degree of force used by D is not to regarded as having been reasonable in the circumstances as D believed them to be if it was disproportionate in those circumstances.

(6A) In deciding the question mentioned in subsection (3), a possibility that D could have retreated is to be considered (so far as relevant) as a factor to be taken into account, rather than as giving rise to a duty to retreat.

(7) In deciding the question mentioned in subsection (3) the following considerations are to be taken into account (so far as relevant in the circumstances of the case)—

    (a) that a person acting for a legitimate purpose may not be able to weigh to a nicety the exact measure of any necessary action; and

    (b) that evidence of a person having only done what the person honestly and instinctively thought was necessary for a legitimate purpose constitutes strong evidence that only reasonable action was taken by that person for that purpose.

(8) Subsections (6A) and (7) are not to be read as preventing other matters from being taken into account where they are relevant in deciding the question mentioned in subsection (3).

(8A) For the purposes of this section "a householder case" is a case where—

    (a) the defence concerned is the common law defence of self-defence,

    (b) the force concerned is force used by D while in or partly in a building, or part of a building, that is a dwelling or is forces accommodation (or is both),

    (c)   D is not a trespasser at the time the force is used, and
    (d)   at that time D believed V to be in, or entering, the building
           or part as a trespasser.

(8B) Where—
    (a)   a part of a building is a dwelling where D dwells,
    (b)   another part of the building is a place of work for D or
           another person who dwells in the first part,
    (c)   that other part is internally accessible from the first part,

that other part, and any internal means of access between the two parts,
are each treated for the purposes of subsection (8A) as a part of a
building that is a dwelling.

(8C) Where—
    (a)   a part of a building is forces accommodation that is living
           or sleeping accommodation for D,
    (b)   another part of the building is a place of work for D or
           another person for whom the first part is living or sleeping
           accommodation, and
    (c)   that other part is internally accessible from the first part,

that other part, and any internal means of access between the two parts,
are each treated for the purposes of subsection (8A) as a part of a
building that is forces accommodation.

(8D) Subsections (4) and (5) apply for the purposes of subsection
      (8A)(d) as they apply for the purposes of subsection (3).

(8E) The fact that a person derives title from a trespasser, or has the
      permission of a trespasser, does not prevent the person from being
      a trespasser for the purposes of subsection (8A).

(8F) In subsections (8A) to (8C)—

      "building" includes a vehicle or vessel, and
      "forces accommodation" means service living accommodation
      for the purposes of Part 3 of the Armed Forces Act 2006 by
      virtue of section 96(1)(a) or (b) of that Act.

(9)   This section, except so far as making different provision for
      householder cases, is intended to clarify the operation of the
      existing defences mentioned in subsection (2).

(10) In this section—
    (a)   "legitimate purpose" means—
           (i)   the purpose of self-defence under the common law,
           (ia)   the purpose of defence of property under the
                  common law, or
           (ii)   the prevention of crime or effecting or assisting in
                  the lawful arrest of persons mentioned in the
                  provisions referred to in subsection (2)(b);
    (b)   references to self-defence include acting in defence of
           another person; and
    (c)   references to the degree of force used are to the type and
           amount of force used.

In *Dewar v DPP* [2010] All ER (D) 83 (Jan), DC the CA confirmed that the test for self-defence is twofold ie honest belief in self defence and the force used was reasonable. The CA opined the statutory changes above had made no practical difference to the common law test.

A[8.21] Misadventure. See A[15.8].

A[8.22] Consent and reasonable chastisement. See A[15.10]–A[15.17].

A[8.23]–[8.30] Lawful sport. See A[15.18].

Reduction of charge/alternative verdict. The court cannot reduce this charge to common assault or consider an alternative verdict but, if a separate charge of common assault is preferred, a conviction for that may be possible. The legal adviser should be consulted. See **A[15.31]**.

Sentencing
SC Guideline – Assault occasioning actual bodily harm and Racially/religiously aggravated ABH

Assault occasioning actual bodily harm

Offences against the Person Act 1861 (section 47)

Racially/religiously aggravated ABH

Crime and Disorder Act 1998 (section 29)

A[8.31]–[8.32] These are specified offences for the purposes of section 224 of the Criminal Justice Act 2003

Triable either way

Section 47

Maximum when tried summarily: Level 5 fine and/or 26 weeks' custody

Maximum when tried on indictment: 5 years' custody

Section 29

Maximum when tried summarily: Level 5 fine and/or 26 weeks' custody

Maximum when tried on indictment: 7 years' custody

Offence range: Fine – 3 years' custody

This guideline applies to all offenders aged 18 and older, who are sentenced on or after 13 June 2011. The definitions of 'starting point' and 'first time offender' do not apply for this guideline. Starting point and category ranges apply to all offenders in all cases, irrespective of plea or previous convictions.

Step One
Determining the offence category

The court should determine the offence category using the table below.

Category 1	Greater harm **and** higher culpability
Category 2	Greater harm **and** lower culpability; **or** lesser harm **and** higher culpability
Category 3	Lesser harm **and** lower culpability

The court should determine the offender's culpability and the harm caused, or intended, by reference **only** to the factors identified in the table below (as demonstrated by the presence of one or more). These factors comprise the principal factual elements of the offence and should determine the category.

Factors indicating greater harm

Injury (which includes disease transmission and/or psychological harm) which is serious in the context of the offence (must normally be present)

Victim is particularly vulnerable because of personal circumstances

Sustained or repeated assault on the same victim

Factors indicating lesser harm

Injury which is less serious in the context of the offence

Factors indicating higher culpability

Statutory aggravating factors:

Offence motivated by, or demonstrating, hostility to the victim based on his or her sexual orientation (or presumed sexual orientation)

Offence motivated by, or demonstrating, hostility to the victim based on the victim's disability (or presumed disability)

Other aggravating factors:

A significant degree of premeditation

Use of weapon or weapon equivalent (for example, shod foot, headbutting, use of acid, use of animal)

Intention to commit more serious harm than actually resulted from the offence

Deliberately causes more harm than is necessary for commission of offence

Deliberate targeting of vulnerable victim

Leading role in group or gang

Offence motivated by, or demonstrating, hostility based on the victim's age, sex, gender identity (or presumed gender identity)

Factors indicating lower culpability

Subordinate role in group or gang

A greater degree of provocation than normally expected

Lack of premeditation

Mental disorder or learning disability, where linked to commission of the offence

Excessive self defence

Step Two
Starting point and category range

Having determined the category, the court should use the corresponding starting points to reach a sentence within the category range below. The starting point applies to all offenders irrespective of plea or previous convictions. A case of particular gravity, reflected by multiple features of culpability in step one, could merit upward adjustment from the starting point before further adjustment for aggravating or mitigating features, set out below.

Offence Category	Starting Point (Applicable to all offenders)	Category Range (Applicable to all offenders)
Category 1	Crown Court	Crown Court
Category 2	26 weeks' custody	Low level community order – Crown Court (51 weeks' custody)
Category 3	Medium level community order	Band A fine – High level community order

The table below contains a **non-exhaustive** list of additional factual elements providing the context of the offence and factors relating to the offender. Identify whether any combination of these, or other relevant factors, should result in an upward or downward adjustment from the starting point. In some cases, having considered these factors, it may be appropriate to move outside the identified category range.

When sentencing **category 2** offences, the court should also consider the custody threshold as follows:

- has the custody threshold been passed?
- if so, is it unavoidable that a custodial sentence be imposed?
- if so, can that sentence be suspended?

When sentencing **category 3** offences, the court should also consider the community order threshold as follows:

- has the community order threshold been passed?

Factors increasing seriousness

Statutory aggravating factors:

Previous convictions, having regard to a) the nature of the offence to which the conviction relates and its relevance to the current offence; and b) the time that has elapsed since the conviction

Offence committed whilst on bail

Other aggravating factors include:

Location of the offence

Timing of the offence

Ongoing effect upon the victim

Offence committed against those working in the public sector or providing a service to the public

Presence of others including relatives, especially children or partner of the victim

Gratuitous degradation of victim

In domestic violence cases, victim forced to leave their home

Failure to comply with current court orders

Offence committed whilst on licence

An attempt to conceal or dispose of evidence

Failure to respond to warnings or concerns expressed by others about the offender's behaviour

Commission of offence whilst under the influence of alcohol or drugs

Abuse of power and/or position of trust

Exploiting contact arrangements with a child to commit an offence

Established evidence of community impact

Any steps taken to prevent the victim reporting an incident, obtaining assistance and/or from assisting or supporting the prosecution

Offences taken into consideration (TICs)

Factors reducing seriousness or reflecting personal mitigation

No previous convictions **or** no relevant/recent convictions

Single blow

Remorse

Good character and/or exemplary conduct

Determination and/or demonstration of steps taken to address addiction or offending behaviour

Serious medical conditions requiring urgent, intensive or long-term treatment

Isolated incident

Age and/or lack of maturity where it affects the responsibility of the offender

Lapse of time since the offence where this is not the fault of the offender

Mental disorder or learning disability, where **not** linked to the commission of the offence

Sole or primary carer for dependent relatives

Section 29 offences only: The court should determine the appropriate sentence for the offence without taking account of the element of aggravation and then make an addition to the sentence, considering the level of aggravation involved. It may be appropriate to move outside the identified category range, taking into account the increased statutory maximum.

Step Three
Consider any other factors which indicate a reduction, such as assistance to the prosecution

The court should take into account any rule of law by virtue of which an offender may receive a discounted sentence in consequence of assistance given (or offered) to the prosecutor or investigator.

Step Four
Reduction for guilty pleas

The court should take account of any potential reduction for a guilty plea in accordance with section 144 of the Criminal Justice Act 2003 and the *Guilty Plea* guideline.

Step Five
Dangerousness

Assault occasioning actual bodily harm and racially/religiously aggravated ABH are specified offences within the meaning of Chapter 5 of the Criminal Justice Act 2003 and at this stage the court should consider whether having regard to the criteria contained in that Chapter it would be appropriate to award an extended sentence.

Step Six
Totality principle

If sentencing an offender for more than one offence, or where the offender is already serving a sentence, consider whether the total sentence is just and proportionate to the offending behaviour.

Step Seven
Compensation and ancillary orders

In all cases, the court should consider whether to make compensation and/or other ancillary orders.

Step Eight
Reasons

Section 174 of the Criminal Justice Act 2003 imposes a duty to give reasons for, and explain the effect of, the sentence.

Step Nine
Consideration for remand time

(Now obligatory.)

A[8.33] Licensed premises. An assault committed on licensed premises will enable the court to make an exclusion order. See B[32].

A[8.34] Husband and wife and domestic violence. For cases of domestic violence. See SC Definitive Guideline: "Overarching Principles: Domestic Violence".

A[9]

Assaulting a police constable (or a person assisting the police)
Assaulting a court security officer

Charge

A[9.1] Assaulting a constable in the execution of his duty

or

Assaulting a person assisting a constable in the execution of his duty

Police Act 1996, s 89

and

Assaulting a court security officer in the execution of his duty

Criminal Justice Act 1991, s 78 [from 1 April 2005 contrary to Courts Act 2003, s 57]

Maximum penalty – Fine level 5 and 6 months. Triable only summarily.

Legal notes and definitions

A[9.2] **Assault.** See under Common assault at A[8].

A[9.3] **Constable.** Includes a special constable and any member of the police irrespective of actual rank. Offences against designated and accredited persons acting in the execution of their duty ie community support officer, investigating officer, detention officer or escort officer are catered for under the Police Reform Act 2002, s 46. Assaults carry a maximum penalty of a level 5 fine and/or six months imprisonment.

A[9.4] **Court security officer.** A person appointed by the Lord Chancellor or provided under a contract and designated by the Lord Chancellor as a court security officer (s 51 Courts Act 2003).

A[9.5] **In the execution of his duty.** The constable must be carrying out his duty at the time of the assault. If he goes beyond his duty, for example by catching hold of a person whom he is not arresting, then this offence is not committed by a person resisting him with reasonable force. The line between duty and what lies beyond is not easily discernible. This needs reference to many decided cases in the higher courts – see, for example, *Donnelly v Jackman* [1970] 1 All ER 987, [1970] 1 WLR 562 and *Osman v DPP* (1999) 163 JP 725. Police acting on a reasonable expectation of a breach of the peace are acting within their duty (*Wragg v DPP* [2005] EWHC 1389 (Admin), [2005] All ER (D) 131 (Jun)).

In *R (on the application of Reda) v DPP* [2011] EWHC 1550 (Admin), 175 JP 329, the appellant was walking with other youths past an empty police van when he raised his voice and uttered the words "fuck the police". At the material time there were no members of the public present other than the youths and two police officers who were emerging from a nearby block of flats. The first officer heard the specific words used and decided to arrest the appellant for causing harassment, alarm or distress contrary to s 5 of the Public Order Act 1986. Following his arrest the appellant kicked the police officer on the leg.

The Queen's Bench Division concluded that there were reasonable grounds to suspect that an offence had been or was about to be committed. The offending words were said in a public place and, whilst it could not be established that the police officer had himself seen other people present at the material time, nevertheless he could reasonably proceed on the footing that there were or may have been. Furthermore, the arresting officer's colleague was in hearing distance of what was said and the other youths were present. He could not necessarily have taken it that the other boys would not themselves have been insulted or alarmed by what this appellant was shouting or saying. Accordingly, the officer was acting lawfully in the execution of his duty.

If a constable apprehends on reasonable grounds that a breach of the peace may be committed, he is not only entitled, but is under a duty, to take reasonable steps to prevent that breach occurring. Provided the constable honestly and reasonably forms the opinion that there is a real risk of a breach of the peace in the sense that it is in close proximity both in place and time, then the conditions exist for reasonable preventive action. Accordingly, where police officers stopped a convoy of striking miners whom they believed were intending to demonstrate and form a mass picket at one or more of four collieries in the area, it was held that the police officers acted reasonably and in the execution of their duty by preventing the striking miners from passing through the police cordon and, when they did attempt to force their way through the cordon, were justified in arresting them on the ground that if they proceeded it was feared a breach of the peace would occur at one of the collieries (*Moss v McLachlan* (1984) 149 JP 167, [1985] IRLR 76).

Officers who helped a youth leader eject persons from a youth club and were subsequently assaulted, were in the execution of their duty (*Coffin v Smith* (1980) 71 Cr App Rep 221).

In *R (on the application of Laporte) v Chief Constable of Gloucestershire Constabulary* [2006] UKHL 55, [2007] 2 AC 105, [2007] 2 All ER 529, [2007] 2 WLR 46, persons travelling by coach to a demonstration were stopped, the coaches were prevented from proceeding and were forcibly returned and the protesters were detained on the coaches throughout the return journey. The question arose as to whether this police action, which was short of arrest, was legitimate. The House of Lords held that the common law entitled and bound all police officers and citizens alike to seek to prevent, by arrest or action short of arrest, any breach of the peace occurring in their presence, or which they reasonably believed was about to occur, but where no breach of the peace had yet occurred a reasonable apprehension of an imminent breach was required before any form of preventive action was permissible. The police could not, therefore, take whatever action short of arrest they reasonably judged to be reasonable to prevent a breach of the peace which was not sufficiently imminent to justify arrest. Since there had been no indication of any imminent breach of the peace when the coaches were intercepted and searched, and since the defendant had not considered that such a breach was then likely to occur, the action taken in preventing the claimant from continuing to the demonstration had been an interference with her right to demonstrate at a lawful assembly which was not prescribed by domestic law.

The test of the reasonableness of a constable's action is objective in the sense that it is for the court to decide not whether the view taken by the constable fell within the broad band of rational decisions but whether in the light of what he knew and perceived at the time the court is satisfied that it was reasonable to fear an imminent breach of the peace. Accordingly, although reasonableness of belief is a question for the court, it is to be evaluated without the qualifications of hindsight. The court must restrict itself to considering the reasonableness, in the context of the events, of the constable's assessment of the imminence of a breach of the peace; it is not for the court to form its own assessment of that imminence (*R (on the application of Moos and another) v Commissioner of Police for the Metropolis* [2012] EWCA Civ 12, [2012] All ER (D) 83 (Jan)). The next and critical question for the constable, and in turn for the court, is where the threat is coming from, because it is there that the preventative action must be directed. If there is no real threat, no question of intervention for breach of the peace arises. If the defendant is being so provocative that someone in the crowd, without behaving wholly unreasonably, might be moved to violence, the constable is entitled to ask him to stop and arrest him if he will not. If the threat of disorder or violence is coming from passers-by who are taking that opportunity to react so as to cause trouble, then it is they and not the defendant who should be asked to desist and arrested if they will not (*Redmond-Bate v DPP* (1999) 163 JP 789, [1999] Crim LR 998– constable held not to be acting in the execution of his duty when he required three women preachers to stop preaching from the steps of a cathedral because some of those in the crowd that had gathered were showing hostility towards the preachers and he feared a breach of the peace).

A[9.6] A court security officer shall not be regarded as acting in the execution of his duty unless he is readily identifiable by a badge or uniform (powers of court security officers are found in the Courts Act 2003, s 51(3)).

A[9.7] The burden of proof that the constable was acting in the execution of his duty rests on the prosecution but the prosecution does not have to prove that the defendant knew that the constable was a constable, nor that the defendant knew that the constable was acting in the execution of his duty. The offence may be established even if the court accepts that the defendant (who must take his victim as he finds him) did not know that his victim was a police officer. Where the accused is unaware that his victim is a police officer and believes there are circumstances which would justify the use of reasonable force, eg self-defence, he should have a defence (*Blackburn v Bowering* [1994] 3 All ER 380, [1994] 1 WLR 1324, CA. See also *Ali v DPP* [2009] EWHC 3353 (Admin), 174 JP 149. See A[8.8] for defences).

A[9.8] If a police officer touches a person to draw his attention that contact must be acceptable by ordinary standards and for no longer than necessary to remain within the execution of the officer's duty (*Mepstead v DPP* (1995) 160 JP 475, [1996] Crim LR 111). When a police officer, who was not exercising his common law power, restrained a person, but had no intended or purported to arrest a person at that time, he committed an assault, even if the arrest had been justified. To be lawful arrest: (1) There must be reasonable grounds to suspect that a person had committed an arrestable offence (2) That person had to be informed that he was under arrest, either at the time of the arrest or within a reasonable time thereafter (*Wood v DPP* [2008] EWHC 1056 (Admin)).

Plain clothes officers carrying out a drugs search are not acting in the execution of their duty if they fail to comply with the requirements of s 2(3), PACE 1984 (*Bonner v DPP* [2004] EWHC 2415 (Admin), [2004] All ER (D) 74 (Oct); *R v Bristol* [2007] EWCA Crim 3214, (2007) 172 JP 161).

A police officer exercising a power of entry to premises, pursuant to s 17 of the Police and Criminal Evidence Act 1984, 'in order to save life or limb or serious damage to property', was acting lawfully where he sought to search the occupant based on a reasonable belief that she was in possession of a knife (*Baker v Crown Prosecution Service* [2009] EWHC 299 (Admin), 173 JP 215).

Concern for the welfare of somebody within the premises is not enough. It was clear that Parliament intended that the right of entry by force without warrant should be confined to cases where there is an apprehension that something serious was likely to occur or had occurred within premises (*Syed v DPP* [2010] EWHC 81 (Admin),[2010] 1 Cr App Rep 480, 174 JP 97).

In current times, distinguishing between violence in the home and in the street was long gone. Cases that attempted to do so could not be relied on and were out of date, *Foulkes v Chief Constable of Merseyside* [1998] 3 All ER 705, [1999] 1 FCR 98, CA and *McConnell v Chief Constable of Greater Manchester Police* [1990] 1 All ER 423, [1990] 1 WLR 364, CA are no longer good law. The correct approach was to draw a contrast between the ability of those on the street to go their own way, and in a domestic setting where that might not be possible, *Wragg v DPP* [2005] EWHC 1389 (Admin), [2005] All ER (D) 131 (Jun) applied: *Leon Demetriou v DPP*(2012) 156 Sol Jo (no 18) 31.

Although a pat-down search was authorised by the Criminal Law Act 1967, s 3, a police officer was required by s 2 of the Police and Criminal Evidence Act 1984 to take reasonable steps to bring certain matters to the attention of the person being searched. They included his name and police station, the object of the search and his grounds for proposing to make it. It meant that the officer's search of a defendant on this occasion was unlawful. However, there was a sufficient gap in time between the search of the defendant and an assault by the defendant on H to make the events separate and distinct. What the officer was doing was no more than to prevent harm to a woman in accordance with his common law duty and to prevent her from further contributing to violence. It followed that the justices had been entitled to find that the officer had been acting lawfully in the execution of his duty: *Sobczak v DPP* [2012] EWHC 1319 (Admin), 176 JP 575, 176 CL&J 371.

A[9.9] **Reduction of charge/alternative verdict.** The court cannot reduce this charge to common assault, but if a separate charge for common assault is preferred, a conviction for that offence may be possible.

Sentencing
SC Guideline – Assault on a police constable in the execution of his duty

A[9.10] Assault on a police constable in execution of his duty

Police Act 1996 (section 89)

Triable only summarily

Maximum: Level 5 and/or 26 weeks' custody

Offence range: Fine – 26 weeks' custody

This guideline applies to all offenders aged 18 years and older, who are sentenced on or after 13 June 2011. The definitions of 'starting point' and 'first time offender' do not apply for this guideline. Starting point and category ranges apply to all offenders in all cases, irrespective of plea or previous convictions.

Step One
Determining the offence category

The court should determine the offence category using the table below.

Category 1	Greater harm **and** higher culpability
Category 2	Greater harm **and** lower culpability; **or** lesser harm **and** higher culpability
Category 3	Lesser harm **and** lower culpability

The court should determine the offender's culpability and the harm caused, or intended, by reference **only** to the factors below (as demonstrated by the presence of one or more). These factors comprise the principal factual elements of the offence and should determine the category.

Factors indicating greater harm

Sustained or repeated assault on the same victim

Factors indicating lesser harm

Injury which is less serious in the context of the offence

Factors indicating higher culpability

Statutory aggravating factors:

Offence racially or religiously aggravated

Offence motivated by, or demonstrating, hostility to the victim based on his or her sexual orientation (or presumed sexual orientation)

Offence motivated by, or demonstrating, hostility to the victim based on the victim's disability (or presumed disability)

Other aggravating factors:

A significant degree of premeditation

Use of weapon or weapon equivalent (for example, shod foot, headbutting, use of acid, use of animal)

Intention to commit more serious harm than actually resulted from the offence

Deliberately causes more harm than is necessary for commission of offence

Leading role in group or gang

Offence motivated by, or demonstrating, hostility based on the victim's age, sex, gender identity (or presumed gender identity)

Factors indicating lower culpability

Subordinate role in group or gang Lack of premeditation

Mental disorder or learning disability, where linked to commission of
the offence

Step Two
Starting point and category range

Having determined the category, the court should use the corresponding
starting points to reach a sentence within the category range below. The
starting point applies to all offenders irrespective of plea or previous
convictions. A case of particular gravity, reflected by multiple features of
culpability in step one, could merit upward adjustment from the starting
point before further adjustment for aggravating or mitigating features, set
out below.

Offence Category	Starting Point (Applicable to all offenders)	Category Range (Applicable to all offenders)
Category 1	12 weeks' custody	Low level community order – 26 weeks' custody
Category 2	Medium level community order	Low level community order – High level community order
Category 3	Band B fine	Band A fine – Band C fine

The table below contains a **non-exhaustive** list of additional factual
elements providing the context of the offence and factors relating to the
offender. Identify whether any combination of these, or other relevant
factors, should result in an upward or downward adjustment from the
starting point. In some cases, having considered these factors, it may be
appropriate to move outside the identified category range.

When sentencing **category 1** offences, the court should also consider the
custody threshold as follows:

* has the custody threshold been passed?
* if so, is it unavoidable that a custodial sentence be imposed?
* if so, can that sentence be suspended?

Factors increasing seriousness

Statutory aggravating factors:

Previous convictions, having regard to a) the nature of the offence to
which the conviction relates and its relevance to the current offence;
and b) the time that has elapsed since the conviction

Offence committed whilst on bail

Other aggravating factors include:

Location of the offence

Timing of the offence

Ongoing effect upon the victim

Gratuitous degradation of victim

Failure to comply with current court orders

Offence committed whilst on licence

An attempt to conceal or dispose of evidence

Failure to respond to warnings or concerns expressed by others about
the offender's behaviour

Commission of offence whilst under the influence of alcohol or drugs

Established evidence of community impact

Any steps taken to prevent the victim reporting an incident, obtaining assistance and/or from assisting or supporting the prosecution

Offences taken into consideration (TICs)

Factors reducing seriousness or reflecting personal mitigation

No previous convictions **or** no relevant/recent convictions

Single blow

Remorse

Good character and/or exemplary conduct

Determination and/or demonstration of steps taken to address addiction or offending behaviour

Serious medical conditions requiring urgent, intensive or long-term treatment

Isolated incident

Age and/or lack of maturity where it affects the responsibility of the offender

Lapse of time since the offence where this is not the fault of the offender

Mental disorder or learning disability, where **not** linked to the commission of the offence

Sole or primary carer for dependent relatives

Step Three
Consider any other factors which indicate a reduction, such as assistance to the prosecution

The court should take into account any rule of law by virtue of which an offender may receive a discounted sentence in consequence of assistance given (or offered) to the prosecutor or investigator.

Step Four
Reduction for guilty pleas

The court should take account of any potential reduction for a guilty plea in accordance with section 144 of the Criminal Justice Act 2003 and the *Guilty Plea* guideline.

Step Five
Totality principle

If sentencing an offender for more than one offence, or where the offender is already serving a sentence, consider whether the total sentence is just and proportionate to the offending behaviour.

Step Six
Compensation and ancillary orders

In all cases, courts should consider whether to make compensation and/or other ancillary orders.

Step Seven
Reasons

Section 174 of the Criminal Justice Act 2003 imposes a duty to give reasons for, and explain the effect of, the sentence.

Step Eight
Consideration for remand time

Sentencers should take into consideration any remand time served in relation to the final sentence. The court should consider whether to give credit for time spent on remand in custody or on bail in accordance with ss 240 and 240A of the Criminal Justice Act 2003.

A[9.11] Licensed premises. If the offence takes place on licensed premises an exclusion order may be made. See **B[32]**.

A[10]

Bail, failure to surrender

Charge

A[10.1] Having been released on bail in criminal proceedings fails without reasonable cause to surrender to custody

Bail Act 1976, s 6(1)

or

Having been released on bail in criminal proceedings, and having reasonable cause therefore, has failed to surrender to custody, fails to surrender to custody at the appointed place as soon as after the appointed time as is reasonably practicable

Bail Act 1976, s 6(2).

Maximum penalty – level 5 and/or 3 months' imprisonment (if not committed for sentence).

Crown Court – 12 months' imprisonment or an unlimited fine

Legal notes and definitions

A[10.2] 'Fails without reasonable cause'. The fact that a defendant mistakenly formed the opinion he was required to surrender on a later date does not amount to a 'reasonable cause': *Laidlaw v Atkinson* (1986) The Times, 2 August.

'Surrender to custody'. It has been held: ' . . . if a court provides a procedure which, by some form of direction, by notice or orally, instructs a person surrendering to bail to report to a particular office or to a particular official, when he complies with that direction he surrenders to his bail. Thereafter, albeit he may not be physically restrained, albeit he may be allowed to sit in the court concourse and visit the court canteen, he is in the custody of the court. I have already suggested that he is under an implied, if not an express obligation, not to leave the building without consent until the case is called on. The argument that section 7(2) would have no meaning if that were not the correct construction is one which seems to me to be correct. I emphasise that if a person simply goes to the courthouse and does not report to anybody he has not surrendered to his bail. That is not enough. He has to report to somebody and do whatever he is directed to do, but when he does comply with the procedure which he is directed to follow by the court, then I emphasise that he has surrendered' (per Glidewell LJ in *DPP v Richards* [1988] QB 701). As to the position in the Crown Court, see *R v Evans* [2011] EWCA Crim 2842, [2012] 1 WLR 1192, [2012] 2 Cr App Rep 279, 176 JP 139. In the absence of special arrangements either particular to the court or to the individual case, surrender is accomplished when the defendant presents himself to the custody officers by entering the dock or where a hearing commences at which he is formally identified as present.

Burden of proof on accused. An accused who raises this defence is required to establish it on a balance of probabilities: *R v Carr-Briant* (1943) 107 JP 167.

Procedure. This is regulated by the *Practice Direction (Criminal: Consolidated)* (2002) at paras I 13.4 to I 13.6 as revised in 2004.

Prosecution. See the detailed notes at D[8.82] onwards.

Committal to the Crown Court. In certain circumstances, a magistrates' court may commit to the Crown Court for sentence. See s 6(6) of the Bail Act 1976 and consult your legal adviser for guidance.

Sentencing
Bail, failure to surrender

A[10.3] This guideline and accompanying notes are taken from the SGC's definitive guideline *Fail to Surrender to Bail*, published 29 November 2007.

Key factors

(a) Whilst the approach to sentencing should generally be the same whether the offender failed to surrender to a court or to a police station <u>and</u> whether the offence is contrary to ss 6(1) or 6(2), the court must examine the relevant circumstances.

(b) The following factors may be relevant when assessing the harm caused by the offence:

• Where an offender fails to appear for a first court hearing but attends shortly afterwards, the only harm caused is likely to be the financial cost to the system. Where a case could not have proceeded even if the offender had surrendered to bail, this should be taken into account.

• Where an offender appears for trial on the wrong day but enters a late guilty plea enabling the case to be disposed of to some degree at least, the harm caused by the delay may be offset by the benefits stemming from the change of plea.

• The most serious harm is likely to result where an offender fails to appear for trial, especially if this results in witnesses being sent away. Where it has been possible to conclude proceedings in the absence of the offender, this may be relevant to the assessment of harm caused.

• The level of harm is likely to be assessed as high where an offender fails to appear for sentence and is also seen to be flouting the authority of the court, such as where the avoidance of sentence results in the consequential avoidance of ancillary orders such as disqualification from driving, the payment of compensation or registration as a sex offender. This may increase the level of harm whenever the offender continues to be a risk to public safety.

- Whilst the seriousness of the original offence does not of itself aggravate or mitigate the seriousness of the offence of failure to surrender, the circumstances surrounding the original offence may be relevant in assessing the harm arising from the Bail Act offence.
- The circumstances in which bail to return to a police station is granted are less formal than the grant of court bail and the history of the individual case should be examined. There may be less culpability where bail has been enlarged on a number of occasions and less harm if <u>court</u> proceedings are not significantly delayed.

(c) Where the failure to surrender to custody was "deliberate":
- at or near the bottom of the sentencing range will be cases where the offender gave no thought at all to the consequences, or other mitigating factors are present, and the degree of delay or interference with the progress of the case was not significant in all the circumstances;
- At or near the top of the range will be cases where aggravating factors 1, 2 or 4 are present if there is also a significant delay and/or interference with the progress of the case.

(d) A previous conviction that is likely to be "relevant" for the purposes of this offence is one which demonstrates failure to comply with an order of the court.

(e) Acquittal of the original offence does not automatically mitigate the Bail Act offence.

(f) The fact that an offender has a disorganised or chaotic lifestyle should not normally be treated as offence mitigation, but may be regarded as offender mitigation depending on the particular facts.

(g) A misunderstanding which does not amount to a defence may be a mitigating factor whereas a mistake on the part of the offender is his own responsibility.

(h) Where an offender has literacy or language difficulties, these may be mitigation (where they do not amount to a defence) where potential problems were not identified and/or appropriate steps were not taken to mitigate the risk in the circumstances as known at the time bail was granted.

(i) An offender's position as the sole or primary carer of dependant relatives may be offender mitigation when it is the reason why the offender failed to surrender to custody.

(j) The sentence for this offence should usually be in addition to any sentence for the original offence. Where custodial sentences are being imposed for a Bail Act offence and the original offence at the same time, the normal approach should be for the sentences to be consecutive. The length of any custodial sentence imposed must be commensurate with the seriousness do the offence(s).

(k) If an offence is serious enough to justify the imposition of a community order, a curfew requirement with an electronic monitoring requirement may be appropriate.

In certain circumstances, a magistrates' court may commit to the Crown Court for sentence. **Consult your legal adviser for guidance.**

OFFENCE SERIOUSNESS (CULPABILITY AND HARM)		
A. IDENTIFY THE APPROPRIATE STARTING POINT		
Starting points based on first time offender pleading not guilty		
Examples of nature of activity	**Starting point**	**Range**
Surrenders late on day but case proceeds as planned	Band A fine	Band A fine to band B fine
Negligent or non-deliberate failure to attend causing delay and/or interference with the administration of justice	Band C fine	Band B fine to medium level community order
Deliberate failure to attend causing delay and/or interference with the administration of justice	14 days custody	Low level community order to 10 weeks custody
The type and degree of harm actually caused will affect where in the range the case falls (see note (c) above)		

OFFENCE SERIOUSNESS (CULPABILITY AND HARM)	
B. CONSIDER THE EFFECT OF AGGRAVATING AND MITIGATING FACTORS (OTHER THAN THOSE WITHIN THE EXAMPLES ABOVE)	
Common aggravating and mitigating factors are identified at B[5.2A]. The following may be particularly relevant but **these lists are not exhaustive**	
Factors indicating higher culpability	*Factors indicating lower culpability*
1. Serious attempts to evade justice	Where not amounting to a defence:
2. Determined attempt seriously to undermine the course of justice	1. Misunderstanding
3. Previous relevant convictions and/or breach of court orders or police bail	2. Failure to comprehend bail significance or requirements
Factor indicating greater degree of harm	3. Caring responsibilities – see note (i) above
4. Lengthy absence	*Factor indicating lesser degree of harm*
	4. Prompt voluntary surrender

FORM A PRELIMINARY VIEW OF THE APPROPRIATE SENTENCE, THEN CONSIDER OFFENDER MITIGATION
Common factors are identified at B[5.2A]
CONSIDER A REDUCTION FOR A GUILTY PLEA
DECIDE SENTENCE
GIVE REASONS

In appropriate cases, a magistrates' court may impose one day's detention: MCA 1980, s 135.

Bladed article/offensive weapon, possession of

Charge

A[11.1] Having an article which has a blade (or is sharply pointed) namely a
[. . . . .] in a public place or on school premises [or]

[Has an article with a blade or point or offensive weapon on school premises, unlawfully and intentionally threatens another person with the weapon, and does so in such a way that there is an immediate risk of serious physical harm to that other person]

Criminal Justice Act 1988, s 139 and s 139A [and 139AA]*

Having, without lawful authority or reasonable excuse, an offensive weapon in any public place [or]

[Has an offensive weapon with him in a public place, unlawfully and intentionally threatens another person with the weapon, and does so in such a way that there is an immediate risk of serious physical harm to that other person.]

Prevention of Crime Act 1953, s 1 [and 1A]

Maximum penalty:

(a)   In relation to the 'possession' offences, whether in a public place or on school premises, triable either way: maximum penalty on summary conviction fine level 5 and six months; on indictment four years' imprisonment.

(b)   In relation to the threatening offences, triable either way with the same maximum on indictment, but on summary conviction, fine level 5 or 12 months' imprisonment *and* the court (magistrates or Crown) must pass 'an appropriate custodial sentence' if the offender is aged 16 or over unless there are particular circumstances which relate to the offence or the offender which would make it unjust to do so. The minimum sentences are: offenders aged 16 and 17 – four months' DTO; older offenders six months' imprisonment (or 80% of these minimum terms where the offender pleads guilty).

Crown Court – 4 years' imprisonment (for offences committed on or after 12/2/2007) and unlimited fine

A[11.2] **Mode of trial.** Consider the SGC Guidelines at **A[11.15]** below.

Legal notes and definitions

A[11.3] **General.** The possession of offensive weapons is also controlled by several other statutes. The Crossbows Act 1987 regulates the sale or hire of crossbows to persons under 17 years, and the purchase or possession of crossbows by such persons. The Firearms Act 1968 controls the possession and use of airguns, shotguns and firearms and the possession of articles with blades or sharp points is governed by the Criminal Justice Act 1988 (see **A[5]**).

'Samurai swords' are on the list of prohibited articles. Accordingly, with a number of small exemptions the manufacture, sale, hire and importation of samurai swords is an offence. A later amendment order covered swords with a curved blade of 50 centimetres or more: Criminal Justice Act (Offensive Weapons) (Amendment) Order 2008, SI 2008/973.

A[11.4] Controls are also imposed on the manufacturers of and dealers in or persons who lend or give 'flick-knives' by the Restriction of Offensive Weapons Act 1959 and the Criminal Justice Act 1988 extends such controls to offensive weapons specified by the Home Office such as weapons used in martial arts, stun guns and so-called stealth knives. Selling a knife to a person under the age of 18 is an offence by virtue of amendments brought into force in January 1997. The maximum penalty for contravention of such regulations is a fine on level 5 and 6 months' imprisonment.

A[11.5] Offensive weapon. A police constable may arrest without warrant anyone carrying or suspected of carrying an offensive weapon in a public place. In order to convict the prosecution must first prove that the defendant was in possession of an offensive weapon. An offensive weapon means any article either:

(a)   made or adapted for use for causing injury to the person; or
(b)   intended by the person having it with him for such use by him or by some other person (s 1(4) Prevention of Crime Act 1953).

Articles in category (a), such as knuckle dusters and flick-knives and disguised knives, are always offensive weapons. An article in category (b), such as for example a milk bottle, only becomes an offensive weapon when the person carrying it has the intention of using it to cause injury to the person. The prosecution must prove this intention.

An object which bears all the characteristics of a flick-knife does not cease to be or lose its characteristic as a flick-knife because it has the secondary character of being a lighter. It is just as much an offensive weapon and potentially dangerous as if the lighter function were not there: *R v Vasili* [2011] EWCA Crim 615, [2011] 2 Cr App Rep 56, 175 JP 185.

In relation to category (a), in *Sills v DPP* [2006] EWHC 3383 (Admin), [2006] All ER (D) 165 (Oct), justices had been entitled to conclude that half of a pool cue, which had been unscrewed from its counterpart, and which the defendant maintained he had taken with him to scare off any attacker, was an article adapted for use for causing injury to the person within the meaning of s 1(4) above.

A[11.6] Have with him. The prosecution must prove that the defendant knowingly was "carrying" the offensive weapon with him. 'Carrying' would not include the situation where the accused seized a clasp knife, which he had not been carrying, for instant use on his victim.

A[11.7] Knowledge of possession. The accused must have acquired the weapon knowingly (eg it was not slipped into his pocket unawares) (*R v Cugullere* [1961] 2 All ER 343, [1961] 1 WLR 858, 45, CCA). He still has it if he subsequently forgets it is there (*R v McCalla* (1988) 87 Cr App Rep

372, 152 JP 481, CA; *Bayliss v DPP* [2003] All ER (D) 71 (Feb)) until he or another does something to rid him of it. See below as to forgetfulness and 'good reason'.

A[11.8] In a public place. This includes any highway and any other premises or place to which at the material time the public have or are permitted to have access, whether on payment or otherwise. (*R v Roberts* [2003] EWCA Crim 2753, [2003] All ER (D) 325 (Oct)). In *Harriot v DPP* [2005] EWHC 965 (Admin), (2005) 170 JP 494, the Divisional Court held that a "public place" is not a term of legal art and that the statutory definition under the Prevention of Crime Act 1953 was illustrative not exhaustive. Accordingly, the open area between a bail hostel building and a road, was, on the face of it, private premises.

A[11.9] Bladed article – the prosecution merely has to prove that the accused had an article to which this offence applies and it is then up to the accused to justify its possession. The prosecution has a lesser burden of proof, than in the offence described at **A[64]**. The defendant does not discharge this burden merely by providing an explanation uncontradicted by prosecution evidence if the justices disbelieve his explanation (*Godwin v DPP* (1992) 96 Cr App Rep 244, 157 JP 197). However the prosecution must prove the defendant had knowledge of his possession of the blade (*R v Daubney* (2000) 164 JP 519, CA).

It is suggested that having regard to the legitimate aims of the legislation the legal burden of proof which rests with the accused is ECHR compliant.

Exceptions. This offence does not apply to a folding pocket knife except if the cutting edge of its blade exceeds 3 inches. Folding knife does not include a knife where the blade is secured in the open position by a locking device (*Harris v DPP* [1993] 1 All ER 562, [1993] 1 WLR 82).

A[11.10] School premises includes any land used for the purposes of a school but excludes a dwelling occupied by a person employed at the school.

From **31 May 2007** (England only) by virtue of the Violent Crime Reduction Act 2006, school staff with reasonable grounds for suspecting that a pupil may have possession of a blade or offensive weapon, may search the pupil or his possessions for such articles. The persons authorised to search are a Head teacher or someone authorised by the Head teacher. Similar authority is a available to carry out searches of students in **higher education**.

A[11.11] 'Threatening' offences. The use of the weapon must be unlawful. Therefore, the defences of self-defence, defence of others' or own property, etc, are available. 'Serious physical harm' is defined as 'grievous bodily harm' for the purposes of the Offences Against the Person Act 1861. If a person is found not guilty of the aggravated offence, but it is proved that he committed the relevant possession offence, a conviction can be returned on the latter.

See also A[11.13] below.

A[11.12] Good reason or lawful authority includes cases where the accused had the article with him:

(a)   for use at work;
(b)   for religious reasons (eg a Sikh) but not where the reason was connected with a martial art ancillary to a religious practice (*R v*

Wang [2003] EWCA Crim 3228, [2003] All ER (D) 299 (Dec)); or
(c)   as part of any national costume (eg a Scotsman's dirk).The defendant cannot rely on forgetfulness as constituting a good reason for
having a weapon with him even where at an earlier period he was in
lawful possession of the article (*DPP v Gregson* (1992) 96 Cr App
Rep 240, 157 JP 201); or, in the case of the school offence:
(d)   for educational purposes.

A[11.13] Without lawful authority or reasonable excuse. If the prosecution has established that an offensive weapon was carried in a public place
then the onus shifts to the defendant to prove that lawful authority or
reasonable excuse existed. The degree of proof is not to establish this
beyond all reasonable doubt but that on the balance of probabilities it is
true. The common excuse put forward is that the article was carried for use
in self-defence. As the authority or excuse relates to the reason for carrying
the offensive weapon, not to a use for which it is subsequently employed,
one has to look at the situation when the defendant was carrying it.
Accordingly, fear of being attacked, arising from the experience of friends
and general violence in the neighbourhood, has been held not to be a
reasonable excuse for carrying a metal ball and chain for self-protection.
Self-protection from an actual or imminent attack might provide a 'reasonable excuse'. There would be no excuse or authority for a bouncer at a
dance carrying an offensive weapon.

It might be a reasonable excuse that a person carrying a weapon was at risk
of immediate attack and so carried the weapon for his own defence, but the
1953 Act never intended to sanction the continued carrying of an offensive
weapon. A person under that kind of threat had to seek protection via other
means such as contacting the police. Each case had to be determined on its
own facts and no assistance was to be derived from comparing the facts of
other cases. It remained for a jury to determine how soon and how likely
the anticipated attack had to be to constitute reasonable excuse for carrying
an offensive weapon. Further, there was no authority to support the
proposition that reasonable excuse should be determined subjectively. Nor
was there any basis for importing the self-defence test. Accordingly, when
a defendant claimed he had reasonable excuse it was for him to prove both
belief and the reasonableness of the belief on a balance of probabilities.
Otherwise any defendant could claim that he had been at risk of immediate
attack: see *N v DPP* [2011] EWHC 1807 (Admin), 175 JP 337. The
defendant's state of mind might be relevant to the question as to whether
she had a 'good reason' for possession of a bladed article: *R v Clancy*
[2012] EWCA Crim 8, [2012] 1 WLR 2536, [2012] 2 Cr App Rep 71. This
last decision went too far on the facts. The defendant was no longer at risk
of an immediate attack and the excuse put forward lacked merit or
foundation.

ECHR: In the light of *R v Matthews* [2003] EWCA Crim 813, [2004] QB
690, it is submitted that the imposition of a reverse legal burden on the
accused is proportionate in accordance with art 6(2) of the ECHR.

A[11.13A] Good reason. The words 'good reason' are both very general
words and ordinary words which Parliament must have intended would
normally be applied and interpreted by a jury or other fact-finding tribunal
such as justices: *R v McAuley* [2009] EWCA Crim 2130, [2010] 1 Cr App
Rep 148, 173 JP 585, [2010] Crim LR 336. A fear of attack can constitute
a good reason and it therefore follows that the defendant's state of mind is
not wholly irrelevant; if the court considers that defendant's view of the

facts was wholly unreasonable, for example, because he was drunk or had taken drugs or was suffering from mental illness, it may be unlikely to conclude that the defence has been made out, but it is a matter ultimately for the court to determine: *R v Clancy* [2012] EWCA Crim 8, [2012] 1 WLR 2536, [2012] 2 Cr App Rep 71. Forgetfulness is not sufficient to prevent the state of possession from continuing (see above), but there may be circumstances in which forgetfulness can be relevant to the 'good reason' defence: for instance, if the reason that the defendant forgot that a bladed instrument, usually used for his work, was in his possession was a relevant illness or was occasioned by medication for such an illness: *Bayliss v DPP* (2003) 167 JPN 103. See also: *R v McCalla* (1988) 87 Cr App Rep 372; *DPP v Gregson* (1992) 157 JP 201. In *R v Jolie* [2003] EWCA Crim 1543, [2004] 1 Cr App Rep 44, (2003) 167 JP 313, [2003] Crim LR 730 it was affirmed that forgetfulness does not bring possession to an end; that forgetfulness cannot be a good reason, though it can be part of a good reason; and that the words 'good reason' do not require a judicial gloss. As to when forgetfulness might assist a defendant the court gave the example (in para 16) of a parent who, having bought a kitchen knife and put in the glove compartment of a car out of reach of a child then forgot to retrieve it when he got home; it seemed to the court contrary to Parliament's intention that such a person would be committing an offence the next time he drove the vehicle on a public road. See also *Chahal v DPP* [2010] EWHC 439 (Admin), [2010] 2 Cr App R 5. The defendant was found in possession of a knife. He claimed he had used it at work, put it in his coat, forgotten about it and then, at the time of the offence, when he realised it was in his jacket he decided to return home. The justices accepted that the defendant used the knife at work, but found that the work was of a casual nature, that the defendant did not regularly need the knife for work and, therefore, he did not have a 'good reason' for its possession at the relevant time. The appeal by way of case stated succeeded. The justices had been misled into thinking that the nature of the defendant's work deprived him of the statutory defence. The real question was whether the defendant had genuinely forgotten about the knife and at the time when his recollection was restored whether he continued to have 'good reason for possession of the knife.

A reason may be capable of being a good reason, but fail to amount to a good reason on the facts of the case (see *Mohammed v Chief Constable of South Yorkshire Police* [2002] EWHC 406 (Admin), [2002] All ER (D) 374 (Feb), where the defendant took a meat cleaver to sharpen it but had it in his possession for that purpose for longer than he needed to). It cannot be a good reason to possess a knife that you may wish to commit self harm with it at some time the following day: *R v Bown* [2003] EWCA Crim 1989, [2003] 33 LS Gaz R 27, (2003) 167 JP 429, [2004] Crim LR 67.

A[11.14] A claim by the accused that he did not know that the article in question was an offensive weapon cannot amount to a defence of reasonable excuse (*R v Densu* [1998] 1 Cr App Rep 400, [1998] Crim LR 345, CA). However, forgetfulness that one has unintended possession of an offensive weapon, may be relevant as part of a wider set of circumstances relied on as providing reasonable excuse: *R v Glidewell* (1999) 163 JP 557, CA; *R v Tsap* [2008] EWCA Crim 2580, 173 JP 4; *Chahal v DPP* [2010] EWHC 439 (Admin), [2010] 2 Cr App Rep 33.

The burden on the defendant to show a reasonable excuse was a heavy one where the weapon (a butterfly knife) was offensive per se, but the court still has a wide discretion on the facts (*DPP v Patterson* [2004] All ER (D) 239 (Oct), DC; but see *R v Tsap* immediately above.

Sentencing
SC Guideline – Bladed article/offensive weapon, possession of

A[11.15] These guidelines and accompanying notes are drawn from the Court of Appeal's decision in *R v Celaire and Poulton* [2003] 1 Cr App R (S) 610.*

*No SC guidelines have been issued as yet for the aggravated form of offences added under s 142 of LASPOA 2012 (see **A[11.1]**). For offenders aged 16 years the court must assume an immediate custodial sentence is appropriate, six months for an adult, four months for a youth aged 16 or over, unless it is unjust to do so having regard to all the circumstances of the offence and the offender.

Key factors

(a)   Concurrent sentences may be appropriate if the weapons offence is ancillary to a more serious offence: consecutive sentences may be appropriate if the offences are distinct and independent. See **B[37.22]**.

(b)   When assessing offence seriousness, consider the offender's intention, the circumstances of the offence and the nature of the weapon involved.

(c)   Some weapons are inherently more dangerous than others but the nature of the weapon is not the primary determinant of offence seriousness. A relatively less dangerous weapon, such as a billiard cue or knuckle-duster, may be used to create fear and such an offence may be at least as serious as one in which a more obviously dangerous weapon, such as a knife or an acid spray, is being carried for self-defence or no actual attempt has been made by the offender to use it.

(d)   Nevertheless, the fact that the offender was carrying a weapon which is offensive per se may shed light on his or her intentions.

Significant attention was paid to the guideline during 2008 (which is not limited to the possession of knives) and of the Court of Appeal decision in *R v Povey and other applications* [2008] EWCA Crim 1261. The purpose of this note is to set out the effect of the revised guideline following *Povey*.

* Updated guidance – sentencing for possession of a weapon – knife crime

(1)   The guideline has been strengthened from the previous Court of Appeal decision *R v Celaire and Poulton* and is likely to result in many more offences (committed by adult offenders) crossing the custody threshold.

(2)   In *Povey*, attention was drawn to the recent escalation in offences of this kind and the importance, for the time being, of courts focussing on the purposes of sentencing of reduction of crime (including its reduction by deterrence) and the protection of the public.

(3)   In *Povey*, the Court of Appeal recommended that the Magistrates' Courts Sentencing Guidelines guideline should normally be applied at the most severe end of the appropriate range to reflect current prevalence concerns. This will be likely to lead to more cases being sentenced in the Crown Court.

(4)   When the current concerns have been overcome, courts will be notified that the approach should return to the guideline as published.

(5)   The guideline provides three categories of seriousness:

    (i)   **Level 1** is for the situation where a person has a weapon or bladed article, is not in a "dangerous circumstance" and the weapon or bladed article is not used to threaten or to cause fear; in those circumstances:

        –   applying *Povey*, where the offensive weapon is a knife the starting point would be close to 12 weeks custody for a first time adult offender who has pleaded not guilty;

        –   in relation to an offensive weapon other than a knife, the starting point for a first time adult offender who has pleaded not guilty is a high level community order.

    (ii)   **Level 2** is for the situation where a weapon is in the possession of the offender in "dangerous circumstances" but is not used to threaten or to cause fear; in those circumstances:

        –   applying *Povey*, where the offensive weapon is a knife the starting point for a first time adult offender who has pleaded not guilty is committal to the Crown Court and, therefore, a custodial sentence in excess of 6 months;

        –   in relation to an offensive weapon other than a knife, the starting point for a first time adult offender who has pleaded not guilty is a custodial sentence of 6 weeks.

    (iii)   **Level 3** is for the situation where a weapon is used in dangerous circumstances to threaten or cause fear; in those circumstances, both the starting point and range for a first time adult offender who has pleaded not guilty are for sentencing in the Crown Court and, therefore, in excess of 6 months custody.

"Dangerous circumstances" has not been judicially defined but was used in the previous Court of Appeal judgment in *R v Celaire and Poulton*. In relation to a knife, a circumstance is likely to be dangerous if there is a real possibility it could be used.

In *R v Monteiro* [2014] EWCA Crim 747, [2014] 2 Cr App Rep (S) 483, (2014) 178 JP 200 the Court of Appeal heard together six appeals and applications so that it could determine whether or not the guidance given in *R v Povey* was being followed and applied, and to decide whether or not any further guidance was required. The Court took into account the amendments made on 3 December 2012 by the Legal Aid, Sentencing and Punishment of Offenders Act 2012 (see above).

Lord Thomas CJ recited these statistics and stated these conclusions:

'The statistics

14. In the first nine months of 2013 there were 12,132 offences under s.1 of the 1953 Act and s.139 and s.139A of the CJA 1988 Act. 18 per cent resulted in a caution, 28 per cent resulted in immediate custody. The results have been broadly consistent for the past five quarters; the 28 per cent of cases resulting in custody can be seen as an increase from 18 per cent current before *Povey*, whereas the number of cautions is falling.

15. 813 offences were committed by those between 10 and 15. 43 per cent were given a police caution and 47 per cent a community sentence. Only four per cent were given an immediate custodial sentence.

16. We were provided with statistics for 2013 that showed that out of the 89 over 18s who had pleaded guilty or been convicted of offences under s.139AA of the CJA 1988 or s.1A of the 1953 Act, 49 had been given sentences of immediate custody; three had received a caution; seven community service and 19 a suspended sentence. Three were 18, 16 and 17 year olds; 10 had been sent to immediate custody.

Conclusion

18. First, it is important that the youth court pays the closest attention to the guidance given in *Povey*. Given the prevalence of knife crime among young persons, the Youth Court must keep a very sharp focus, if necessary through the use of more severe sentences, on preventing further offending by anyone apprehended for carrying a knife in a public place and to securing a reduction in the carrying of knives. Such sentences fulfil the principles applicable to the sentencing of such persons as set out in s.142A of the Criminal Justice Act 2003 and the Sentencing Council Guidelines. The appeals of NT and RAB illustrate the very serious consequences that can follow from the carrying of knives by young persons and why it is of great importance that the youth court maintains the sharp focus called for in *Povey* by imposing appropriate sentences that will contribute to preventing further offending and to a reduction in knife crime.

19. Secondly, it is important particularly in relation to knife crime that the guidance given in respect of cautions is aligned to the sentencing practice (as it should be in the light of our observation) in the youth court, the magistrates' court and the Crown Court. There is an urgent need for this to be done.'

OFFENCE SERIOUSNESS (CULPABILITY AND HARM)		
A. IDENTIFY THE APPROPRIATE STARTING POINT		
Starting points based on first time offender pleading not guilty		
Examples of nature of activity	**Starting point**	**Range**
Weapon not used to threaten or cause fear	High level community order	Band C fine to 12 weeks custody* * See observations from *R v Povey* above
Weapon not used to threaten or cause fear but offence committed in dangerous circumstances	6 weeks custody	High level community order to Crown Court* *See observations from *R v Povey* above

Weapon used to threaten or cause fear and offence committed in dangerous circumstances	Crown Court	Crown Court
		*See observations from R v Povey above

OFFENCE SERIOUSNESS (CULPABILITY AND HARM)

B. CONSIDER THE EFFECT OF AGGRAVATING AND MITIGATING FACTORS (OTHER THAN THOSE WITHIN THE EXAMPLES ABOVE)

Common aggravating and mitigating factors are identified at B[5.2A]. The following may be particularly relevant but these lists are not exhaustive:

Factors indicating higher culpability	Factors indicating lower culpability
1. Particularly dangerous weapon	1. Weapon carried only on temporary basis
2. Specifically planned use of weapon to commit violence, threaten violence or intimidate	2. Original possession legitimate eg in course of trade or business
3. Offence motivated by hostility towards minority, individual or group	
4. Offender under influence of drink or drugs	
5. Offender operating in group or gang	
Factors indicating greater degree of harm	
1. Offence committed at school, hospital or other place where vulnerable persons may be present	
2. Offence committed on premises where people carrying out public services	
3. Offence committed on licensed premises	
4. Offence committed on public transport	
5. Offence committed at large public gathering, especially where there may be risk of disorder	

FORM A PRELIMINARY VIEW OF THE APPROPRIATE SENTENCE, THEN CONSIDER OFFENDER MITIGATION

Common factors are identified at B[5.2A]

CONSIDER A REDUCTION FOR A GUILTY PLEA

CONSIDER ANCILLARY ORDERS, INCLUDING COMPENSATION

Consult your legal adviser on guidance for available ANCILLARY ORDERS

CONSIDER DEPRIVATION OF PROPERTY (including weapon)

DECIDE SENTENCE

GIVE REASONS

Domestic burglary

Charge

A[12.1] Entering a dwelling-house (or part of a dwelling-house) as a trespasser with intent to steal therein (or with intent to do unlawful damage)

or

Having entered a dwelling-house (or part of a dwelling-house) as a trespasser stole (or attempted to steal)

Theft Act 1968, s 9(1)(a) and s 9(1)(b) respectively

Maximum penalty – Fine level 5 and 6 months. Triable either way. Specified violent offence under Sch 15, Part 1, CJA 2003 if the offence is committed with intent to (i) inflict GBH on a person; or (ii) do unlawful damage to a dwelling or anything in it.

Crown Court – 14 years' imprisonment or life following a third separate conviction (for burglaries involving a dwelling) and unlimited fine.

Mode of trial or allocation

A[12.2] Aggravated burglary is the commission of a burglary whilst armed with a firearm or other weapon of offence at the time of entry and is triable only at the Crown Court. Crime and Disorder Act 1998, s 51 applies.

A[12.3] Burglary comprising the commission of, or an intention to commit, an offence of rape or grievous bodily harm may only be heard at the Crown Court. Crime and Disorder Act 1998, s 51 applies.

A[12.4] Consult the legal adviser. Where the charge is burglary of a dwelling and the accused has two separate convictions for dwelling house burglaries, the charge may only be heard at the Crown Court (PCC(S) A 2000, s 111). See *R v Webster* [2003] EWCA Crim 3597, [2003] All ER (D) 313 (Nov) for an example of a third offence becoming indictable only. Crime and Disorder Act 1998, s 51 applies.

NB: In *R v Miller* [2010] EWCA Crim 809, [2011] 1 Cr App Rep (S) 7, [2010] Crim LR 648, it was stated that where a burglary has not been charged as burglary of a dwelling, it could not be treated as such for sentencing purposes pursuant to PCC(S)A 2000, s 111.

A[12.5] Otherwise a magistrates' court can try the case unless it is alleged that the defendant used, or threatened, violence to someone in the dwelling-house in which case the Crime and Disorder Act 1998, s 51 applies (*R v McGrath* [2003] EWCA Crim 2062, 167 JP 554, [2004] Crim LR 142, [2003] All ER (D) 397 (Jun)).

A[12.6] Where the offence is triable either way consider the SC Guidelines at A[12.18]–[12.19] below.

Legal notes and definitions

A[12.7]–[12.9] Entering. Whether the defendant can properly be described as entering or having entered the building is a question of fact for the magistrates. They will have to decide whether the accused had made an effective entry into the building (*R v Brown* [1985] Crim LR 212, CA). An effective entry can be made by the burglar putting his hand through a broken shop window and stealing therefrom. It can be sufficient for only a part of the burglar's body to enter the premises.

A[12.10]–[12.14] Building. The offence is committed by one who is lawfully in part of a building but trespasses into another part.

A[12.15] An inhabited vehicle (eg a caravan) or vessel is within the section notwithstanding that the occupant is absent at the time of the offence.

A[12.16] Stealing is dishonestly appropriating another person's property with the intention of permanently depriving the other person of it. See A[79].

A[12.17] Trespass. Accidental trespass would not be an offence. The defendant must know, or be reckless as to whether, he is trespassing (*R v Collins* [1973] QB 100, [1972] 2 All ER 1105, CA). If there is doubt whether the defendant was trespassing, consult the legal adviser.

A[12.18]–[12.19] Third conviction. Where magistrates have before them a defendant who appears to be facing a third time domestic burglary, the case must be committed for trial at Crown Court (see A[12.4]). In all cases of burglary dwelling the court should announce in open court for the record that the defendant has been convicted of a qualifying offence.

Sentencing
SC Guideline – Domestic burglary

Domestic burglary (came into force on 16 January 2012)

A[12.20] This is a serious specified offence for the purposes of s 224 of the Criminal Justice Act 2003 if it was committed with intent to: (a) inflict grievous bodily harm on a person, or (b) do unlawful damage to a building or anything in it.

Triable either way

Maximum when tried summarily: Level 5 fine and/or 26 weeks' custody.

Maximum when tried on indictment: 14 years' custody.

Offence range: Community order – 6 years' custody.

Where sentencing an offender for a qualifying third domestic burglary, the Court must apply s 111 of the Powers of the Criminal Courts (Sentencing) Act 2000 and impose a custodial term of at least three years, unless it is satisfied that there are particular circumstances which relate to any of the offences or to the offender which would make it unjust to do so.

This guideline applies to all offenders aged 18 and older, who are sentenced on or after 16 January 2012. The definitions of 'starting point' and 'first time offender' do not apply for this guideline. Starting point and category ranges apply to all offenders in all cases, irrespective of plea or previous convictions.

Step One
Determining the offence category

The court should determine the offence category using the table below.

Category 1	Greater harm **and** higher culpability
Category 2	Greater harm **and** lower culpability; **or** lesser harm **and** higher culpability
Category 3	Lesser harm **and** lower culpability

The court should determine the offender's culpability and the harm caused, or intended, by reference **only** to the factors below which comprise the principal factual elements of the offence. Where an offence does not fall squarely into a category, individual factors may require a degree of weighting before making an overall assessment and determining the appropriate category range.

Factors indicating greater harm

Theft of/damage to property causing a significant degree of loss to the victim (whether economic, sentimental or personal value)

Soiling, ransacking or vandalism of property

Occupier at home (or returns home) while offender present

Trauma to the victim, beyond the normal inevitable consequence of intrusion and theft

Violence used or threatened against victim

Context of general public disorder

Factors indicating lesser harm

Nothing stolen or only property of very low value to the victim (whether economic, sentimental or personal)

Limited damage or disturbance to property

Factors indicating higher culpability

Victim or premises deliberately targeted (for example, due to vulnerability or hostility based on disability, race, sexual orientation)

A significant degree of planning or premeditation

Knife or other weapon carried (where not charged separately)

Equipped for burglary (for example, implements carried and/or use of vehicle)

Member of a group or gang

Factors indicating lower culpability

Offence committed on impulse, with limited intrusion into property

Offender exploited by others

Mental disorder or disability, where linked to the commission of the offence

Step Two
Starting point and category range

Having determined the category, the court should use the corresponding starting points to reach a sentence within the category range below. The starting point applies to all offenders irrespective of plea or previous convictions.

Where the defendant is dependant on or a propensity to misuse drugs and there is sufficient prospect of success, a community order with a drug rehabilitation requirement under s 229 of the Criminal Justice Act 2003 may be a proper alternative to a short or moderate custodial sentence.

A case of particular gravity, reflected by multiple features of culpability in step one, could merit adjustment from the starting point before further adjustment for aggravating or mitigating features, set out below.

Offence Category	Starting Point *(Applicable to all offenders)*	Category Range *(Applicable to all offenders)*
Category 1	Crown Court	Crown Court
Category 2	1 year's custody	High level community order Crown Court (2 years' custody)
Category 3	High level community order	Low level community order – 26 weeks' custody

The table below contains a **non-exhaustive** list of additional factual elements providing the context of the offence and factors relating to the offender. Identify whether any combination of these, or other relevant factors, should result in an upward or downward adjustment from the starting point. In some cases, having considered these factors, it may be appropriate to move outside of the identified category range.

When sentencing **category 3** offences, the court should consider the custody threshold as follows:

- Has the custody threshold been passed?
- If so is it unavoidable that a custodial sentence be imposed?
- If so, can the sentence be suspended?

Factors increasing seriousness

Statutory aggravating factors:

Previous convictions, having regard to a) the nature of the offence to which the conviction relates and its relevance to the current offence; and b) the time that has elapsed since the conviction*

Offence committed whilst on bail

Other aggravating factors include:

Child at home (or returns home) when offence committed

Offence committed at night

Gratuitous degradation of victim

Any steps taken to prevent the victim reporting an incident, obtaining assistance and/or from assisting or supporting the prosecution

Victims compelled to leave their home (in particular victims of domestic violence) Established evidence of community impact

---

Established evidence of community impact

Commission of offence whilst under the influence of alcohol or drugs

Failure to comply with current court orders

Offence committed whilst on licence

Offences taken into consideration (TICs)

Factors reducing seriousness or reflecting personal mitigation

Offender has made voluntary reparation to the victim

Subordinate role in a group or gang

No previous convictions or no relevant recent convictions

Remorse

Good character and/or exemplary conduct

Determination and/or demonstration of steps taken to address addiction or offending behaviour

Isolated incident

Serious medical conditions requiring urgent, intensive or long-term treatment

Age and/or lack of maturity where it affects the responsibility of the defendant

Lapse of time since the offence where this is not the fault of the offender

Mental disorder or learning disability, where not linked to the commission of the offence

Sole or primary carer for dependent relatives

* Where sentencing an offender for a qualifying third domestic burglary, the Court must apply section 111 of the Powers of the Criminal Courts (Sentencing) Act 2000 and impose a custodial term of at least three years, unless it is satisfied that there are particular circumstances which relate to any of the offences or to the offender which would make it unjust to do so.

Step Three
Consider any other factors which indicate a reduction, such as assistance to the prosecution

The court should take into account any rule of law by virtue of which an offender may receive a discounted sentence in consequence of assistance given (or offered) to the prosecutor or investigator.

Step Four
Reduction for guilty pleas

The court should take account of any potential reduction for a guilty plea in accordance with section 144 of the Criminal Justice Act 2003 and the *Guilty Plea* guideline.

Where a minimum mandatory sentence is imposed under section 111 Powers of Criminal Courts (Sentencing) Act, the discount for an early guilty plea must not exceed 20 per cent.

Step Five
Dangerousness

A burglary offence under section 9 of the Theft Act 1968 is a serious specified offence within the meaning of chapter 5 of the Criminal Justice Act 2003 if it was committed with the intent to (a) inflict grievous bodily harm on a person, or (b) do unlawful damage to a building or anything in it. The court should consider whether having regard to the criteria contained in that chapter it would be appropriate to award imprisonment for public protection or an extended sentence. Where offenders meet the dangerousness criteria, the notional determinate sentence should be used as the basis for the setting of a minimum term.

Step Six
Totality principle

If sentencing an offender for more than one offence or where the offender is already serving a sentence, consider whether the total sentence is just and proportionate to the offending behaviour.

Step Seven
Compensation and ancillary orders

In all cases, the court should consider whether to make compensation and/or other ancillary orders.

Step Eight
Reasons

Section 174 of the Criminal Justice Act 2003 imposes a duty to give reasons for, and explain the effect of, the sentence.

Step Nine
Consideration for remand time

(Now obligatory.)

A[13]

Non-domestic burglary

Charge

A[13.1] Entering a building (or part of a building) as a trespasser with intent to steal therein (or with intent to do unlawful damage)

or

Having entered a building (or part of a building) as a trespasser stole (or attempted to steal)

Theft Act 1968, s 9(1)(a) and s 9(1)(b) respectively

Maximum penalty – Fine level 5 and 6 months. Triable either way. Specified violent offence under Sch 15, Part 1, CJA 2003 if the offence is committed with intent to (i) inflict GBH on a person; or (ii) do unlawful damage to a building or anything in it.

Crown Court – 10 years and unlimited fine.

Mode of trial

A[13.2] Aggravated burglary is the commission of a burglary whilst armed with a firearm or other weapon of offence at the time of entry and is triable only at the Crown Court. Crime and Disorder Act 1998, s 51 applies.

A[13.3] Burglary comprising the commission of, or an intention to commit, an offence of rape or grievous bodily harm may only be heard at the Crown Court. Crime and Disorder Act 1998, s 51 applies.

A[13.4] If the building is a non-dwelling a magistrates' court can try the case unless it is alleged that the defendant used, or threatened, violence to someone in the non-dwelling in which case the Crime and Disorder Act 1998, s 51 applies (*R v McGrath* [2003] EWCA Crim 2062, 167 JP 554, [2004] Crim LR 142, [2003] All ER (D) 397 (Jun)).

A[13.5] Where the offence is triable either way consider the SGC Guideline at A[13.19] below and the general notes at D[4].

Legal notes and definitions

A[13.6] **Entering.** Whether the defendant can properly be described as entering or having entered the building is a question of fact for the magistrates. They will have to decide whether the accused had made an effective entry into the building (*R v Brown* [1985] Crim LR 212, CA). An effective entry can be made by the burglar putting his hand through a broken shop window and stealing therefrom. It can be sufficient for only a part of the burglar's body to enter the premises.

A[13.7]–[13.15] **Building.** The offence is committed by one who is lawfully in part of a building but trespasses into another part. An inhabited vehicle (eg a caravan) or vessel is within the section notwithstanding that the occupant is absent at the time of the offence.

A[13.16] Stealing is dishonestly appropriating another person's property with the intention of permanently depriving the other person of it. See A[79].

A[13.17]–[13.18] Trespass. Accidental trespass would not be an offence. The defendant must know, or be reckless as to whether, he is trespassing (*R v Collins* [1973] QB 100, [1972] 2 All ER 1105, CA). If there is doubt whether the defendant was trespassing, consult the legal adviser.

Sentencing
SC Guideline – Non-domestic burglary

Non-domestic burglary (came into force on 16 January 2012)

A[13.19] This is a serious specified offence for the purposes of section 224 Criminal Justice Act 2003 if it was committed with intent to: (a) inflict grievous bodily harm on a person, or (b) do unlawful damage to a building or anything in it.

Triable either way

Maximum when tried summarily: Level 5 fine and/or 26 weeks' custody.

Maximum when tried on indictment: 10 years' custody.

Offence range: Fine – 5 years' custody.

This guideline applies to all offenders aged 18 and older, who are sentenced on or after 16 January 2012. The definitions of 'starting point' and 'first time offender' do not apply for this guideline. Starting point and category ranges apply to all offenders in all cases, irrespective of plea or previous convictions.

Step One
Determining the offence category

The court should determine the offence category using the table below.

Category 1	Greater harm **and** higher culpability
Category 2	Greater harm **and** lower culpability; **or** lesser harm **and** higher culpability
Category 3	Lesser harm **and** lower culpability

The court should determine the offender's culpability and the harm caused, or intended, by reference **only** to the factors below which comprise the principal factual elements of the offence. Where an offence does not fall squarely into a category, individual factors may require a degree of weighting before making an overall assessment and determining the appropriate category range.

Factors indicating greater harm

Theft of/damage to property causing a significant degree of loss to the victim (whether economic, sentimental or personal value)

Soiling, ransacking or vandalism of property

Victim on the premises (or returns) while offender present

Trauma to the victim, beyond the normal inevitable consequence of intrusion and theft

Violence used or threatened against victim

Context of general public disorder

Factors indicating lesser harm

Nothing stolen or only property of very low value to the victim (whether economic, sentimental or personal)

Limited damage or disturbance to property

Factors indicating higher culpability

Premises or victim deliberately targeted (to include pharmacy or doctor's surgery and targeting due to vulnerability of victim or hostility based on disability, race, sexual orientation and so forth)

A significant degree of planning or premeditation

Knife or other weapon carried (where not charged separately)

Equipped for burglary (for example, implements carried and/or use of vehicle)

Member of a group or gang

Factors indicating lower culpability

Offence committed on impulse, with limited intrusion into property

Offender exploited by others

Mental disorder or disability, where linked to the commission of the offence

Step Two
Starting point and category range

Having determined the category, the court should use the corresponding starting points to reach a sentence within the category range below. The starting point applies to all offenders irrespective of plea or previous convictions.

Where the defendant is dependant on or a propensity to misuse drugs and there is sufficient prospect of success, a community order with a drug rehabilitation requirement under s 229 of the Criminal Justice Act 2003 may be a proper alternative to a short or moderate custodial sentence.

A case of particular gravity, reflected by multiple features of culpability in step one, could merit adjustment from the starting point before further adjustment for aggravating or mitigating features, set out below.

Category 1	Crown Court	Crown Court
Category 2	18 weeks' custody	Low level community order – 51 weeks' custody)
Category 3	Medium level community order	Band B fine – low level – 18 weeks' custody

The table below contains a **non-exhaustive** list of additional factual elements providing the context of the offence and factors relating to the offender. Identify whether any combination of these, or other relevant factors, should result in an upward or downward adjustment from the starting point. In some cases, having considered these factors, it may be appropriate to move outside of the identified category range.

When sentencing **category 2 or 3** offences, the court should consider the custody threshold as follows:

- Has the custody threshold been passed?
- If so is it unavoidable that a custodial sentence be imposed?
- If so, can the sentence be suspended?

Factors increasing seriousness

Statutory aggravating factors:

Previous convictions, having regard to a) the nature of the offence to which the conviction relates and its relevance to the current offence; and b) the time that has elapsed since the conviction

Offence committed whilst on bail

Other aggravating factors include:

Offence committed at night, particularly where staff present or likely to be present

Abuse of a position of trust

Gratuitous degradation of victim

Any steps taken to prevent the victim reporting an incident, obtaining assistance and/or from assisting or supporting the prosecution

Established evidence of community impact

Commission of offence whilst under the influence of alcohol or drugs

Failure to comply with current court orders

Offence committed whilst on licence

Offences taken into consideration (TICs)

Factors reducing seriousness or reflecting personal mitigation

Offender has made voluntary reparation to the victim

Subordinate role in a group or gang

No previous convictions or no relevant recent convictions

Remorse

Good character and/or exemplary conduct

Determination and/or demonstration of steps taken to address addiction or offending behaviour

Isolated incident

Serious medical conditions requiring urgent, intensive or long-term treatment

Age and/or lack of maturity where it affects the responsibility of the defendant

Lapse of time since the offence where this is not the fault of the offender

Mental disorder or learning disability, where not linked to the commission of the offence

Sole or primary carer for dependent relatives

Step Three
Consider any other factors which indicate a reduction, such as
assistance to the prosecution

The court should take into account any rule of law by virtue of which an offender may receive a discounted sentence in consequence of assistance given (or offered) to the prosecutor or investigator.

Step Four
Reduction for guilty pleas

The court should take account of any potential reduction for a guilty plea in accordance with section 144 of the Criminal Justice Act 2003 and the *Guilty Plea* guideline.

Step Five
Dangerousness

A burglary offence under section 9 of the Theft Act 1968 is a serious specified offence within the meaning of chapter 5 of the Criminal Justice Act 2003 if it was committed with the intent to (a) inflict grievous bodily harm on a person, or (b) do unlawful damage to a building or anything in it. The court should consider whether having regard to the criteria contained in that chapter it would be appropriate to award imprisonment for public protection or an extended sentence. Where offenders meet the dangerousness criteria, the notional determinate sentence should be used as the basis for the setting of a minimum term.

Step Six
Totality principle

If sentencing an offender for more than one offence or where the offender is already serving a sentence, consider whether the total sentence is just and proportionate to the offending behaviour.

Step Seven
Compensation and ancillary orders

In all cases, the court should consider whether to make compensation and/or other ancillary orders.

Step Eight
Reasons

Section 174 of the Criminal Justice Act 2003 imposes a duty to give reasons for, and explain the effect of, the sentence.

Step Nine
Consideration for remand time

(Now obligatory.)

Child prostitution and pornography

Charge

A[14.1] Intentionally causes or incites another person (B) to become a prostitute or to be involved in pornography in any part of the world, and either—

(i)   B is under 18, and a does not reasonably believe that B is 18 or over, or

(ii)   B is under 13.

Sexual Offences Act 2003, s 48

Intentionally controls any of the activities of another person (B) relating to B's prostitution or involvement in pornography in any part of the world, and either–

(i)   B is under 18, and A does not reasonably believe that B is over 18, or

(ii)   B is under 13.

Sexual Offences Act 2003, s 49.

Intentionally arranges or facilitates the prostitution or involvement in pornography in any part of the world of another person (B), and either—

(i)   B is under 18, and A does not reasonably believe that B is over 18 or over, or

(ii)   B is under 13.

Sexual Offences Act, 2003, s 50.

Maximum penalty – Fine level 5 and 6 months. Triable either way. Specified sexual offence under Sch 15, Part 2, CJA 2003

Crown Court – 14 years' imprisonment and unlimited fine.

A[14.1A] NB: From 26/1/09, section 63 of the Criminal Justice and Immigration Act 2008 created a new offence of possession of extreme pornographic images.

An image is 'pornographic' if it is of such a nature that it must reasonably be assumed to have been produced solely or principally for the purpose of sexual arousal.

An 'extreme image is one which portrays, in an explicit and realistic way, any of the following –

• an act which threatens a person's life
• an act which results, or is likely to result, in serious injury to a person's anus, breasts or genitals
• an act which involves interference with a human corpse, or
• a person performing an act of intercourse or oral sex with an animal (whether dead or alive),

- and a reasonable person looking at the image would think that any such person or animal was real; and
- the image is grossly offensive, disgusting or otherwise of an obscene character.

An 'image' means a moving or still image (produced by any means); or, data (stored by any means) which is capable of conversion into an image.

Classified films are exempted under s 64. See ss 65 and 66 for defences.

Maximum penalty – Fine level 5 and 6 months. Triable either way. At the moment this is not a specified sexual offence under Sch 15, Part 2 of the CJA 2003.

Crown Court – 3 years' imprisonment and unlimited fine.

NB: (1) Proceedings for an offence may not be instituted in England and Wales except by or with the consent of the Director of Public Prosecutions.

(2) There is currently no SC guideline.

Mode of trial

A[14.2] Consider the **SC Guideline** at A[14.5] below.

Legal notes and definitions

A[14.3] Pornography. For the purposes of ss 48 to 50, a person is involved in pornography if an indecent image of that person is recorded; and similar expressions, and 'pornography', are to be interpreted accordingly (Sexual Offences Act 2003, s 51(1)).

A[14.4] Prostitute. Means a person (A) who, on at least one occasion and whether or not compelled to do so, offers or provides sexual services to another person in return for **payment** or a promise of payment to A or to a third person; and "prostitution" is to be interpreted accordingly (Sexual Offences Act 2003, s 51(2)).

A[14.5] Payment. As in A[14.4] "payment" means any financial advantage, including the discharge of an obligation to pay or the provision of goods or services (including sexual services) gratuitously or at a discount (Sexual Offences Act 2003, s 51(3)).

Sentencing
SC Guideline – Child prostitution and pornography

A[14.6] This guideline is taken from the Sentencing Council's definitive guideline *Sexual Offences*, effective from 1 April 2014.

Causing or inciting child prostitution or pornography
Sexual Offences Act 2003 (section 48)

Controlling a child prostitute or child involved in pornography
Sexual Offences Act 2003 (section 49)

Arranging or facilitating child prostitution or pornography
Sexual Offences Act 2003 (section 50)

Triable either way

Maximum: 14 years' custody

Offence range:	Victim aged under 13	1 – 13 years' custody
	Victim aged 13–15	26 weeks' – 11 years' custody
	Victim aged 16–17	Community order – 7 years' custody

For offences committed on or after 3 December 2012, these are offences listed in Part 1 of Schedule 15B for the purposes of sections 224A (life sentence for second listed offence) of the Criminal Justice Act 2003.

For convictions on or after 3 December 2012 (irrespective of the date of commission of the offence), these are specified offences for the purposes of section 226A (extended sentence for certain violent or sexual offences) of the Criminal Justice Act 2003.

The terms 'child prostitute', 'child prostitution' and 'child involved in pornography' are used in this guideline in accordance with the statutory language contained in the Sexual Offences Act 2003.

STEP ONE
DETERMINING THE OFFENCE CATEGORY

The court should determine which categories of harm and culpability the offence falls into by reference **only** to the tables below.

For offences that involve wide scale commercial and/or international activity sentences above the category range may be appropriate.

Harm	Culpability
Category 1	**A**
• Victims involved in penetrative sexual activity	Directing or organising child prostitution or pornography on significant commercial basis
• Abduction/detention	Expectation of significant financial or other gain
• Violence or threats of violence	Abuse of trust Exploitation of victim(s) known to be trafficked
• Sustained and systematic psychological abuse	Significant involvement in limiting the freedom of the victim(s)
• Victim(s) participated in unsafe/degrading sexual activity beyond that which is inherent in the offence	Grooming of a victim to enter prostitution or pornography including through cultivation of a dependency on drugs or alcohol

Harm	Culpability
• Victim(s) passed around by the offender to other "customers" and/or moved to other brothels	**B**
Category 2	Close involvement with inciting, controlling, arranging or facilitating child prostitution or pornography (where offender's involvement is not as a result of coercion)
Factor(s) in category 1 not present	**C**
	Performs limited function under direction
	Close involvement but engaged by coercion/intimidation/exploitation

STEP TWO
STARTING POINT AND CATEGORY RANGE

Having determined the category, the court should use the corresponding starting points to reach a sentence within the category range below. The starting point applies to all offenders irrespective of plea or previous convictions. Having determined the starting point, step two allows further adjustment for aggravating or mitigating features, set out on the next page.

A case of particular gravity, reflected by multiple features of culpability or harm in step one, could merit upward adjustment from the starting point before further adjustment for aggravating or mitigating features, set out on the next page.

Where there is a sufficient prospect of rehabilitation, a community order with a sex offender treatment programme requirement under section 202 of the Criminal Justice Act 2003 can be a proper alternative to a short or moderate length custodial sentence.

		A	**B**	**C**
Category 1	U 13	**Starting point** 10 years' custody	**Starting point** 8 years' custody	**Starting point** 5 years' custody
		Category range 8 – 13 years' custody	**Category range** 6 – 11 years' custody	**Category range** 2 – 6 years' custody
	13–15	**Starting point** 8 years' custody	**Starting point** 5 years' custody	**Starting point** 2 years 6 months' custody
		Category range 6 – 11 years' custody	**Category range** 4 – 8 years' custody	**Category range** 1 – 4 years' custody
	16–17	**Starting point** 4 years' custody	**Starting point** 2 years' custody	**Starting point** 1 years' custody

		A	B	C
		Category range 3 – 7 years' custody	**Category range** 1 – 4 years' custody	**Category range** 26 weeks' – 2 years' custody
Category 2	U 13	**Starting point** 8 years' custody	**Starting point** 6 years' custody	**Starting point** 2 years' custody
		Category range 6 – 11 years' custody	**Category range** 4 – 9 years' custody	**Category range** 1 – 4 years' custody
	13–15	**Starting point** 6 years' custody	**Starting point** 3 years' custody	**Starting point** 1 years' custody
		Category range 4 – 9 years' custody	**Category range** 2 – 5 years' custody	**Category range** 26 weeks' – 2 years' custody
	16–17	**Starting point** 3 years' custody	**Starting point** 1 year's custody	**Starting point** 26 weeks' custody
		Category range 2 – 5 years' custody	**Category range** 26 weeks' – 2 years' custody	**Category range** High level community order – 1 year's custody

The table below contains a **non-exhaustive** list of additional factual elements providing the context of the offence and factors relating to the offender. Identify whether any combination of these, or other relevant factors, should result in an upward or downward adjustment from the starting point. **In particular, relevant recent convictions are likely to result in an upward adjustment.** In some cases, having considered these factors, it may be appropriate to move outside the identified category range.

When sentencing appropriate category 2 offences, the court should also consider the custody threshold as follows:

- has the custody threshold been passed?
- if so, is it unavoidable that a custodial sentence be imposed?
- if so, can that sentence be suspended?

Aggravating factors	Mitigating factors
Statutory aggravating factors	No previous convictions **or** no relevant/recent convictions
Previous convictions, having regard to a) the nature of the offence to which the conviction relates and its relevance to the current offence; and b) the time that has elapsed since the conviction	Remorse

Aggravating factors	Mitigating factors
Offence committed whilst on bail	Previous good character and/or exemplary conduct*
Other aggravating factors	Age and/or lack of maturity where it affects the responsibility of the offender
Failure to comply with current court orders	Mental disorder or learning disability, particularly where linked to the commission of the offence
Offence committed whilst on licence	* Previous good character/exemplary conduct is different from having no previous convictions. The more serious the offence, the less the weight which should normally be attributed to this factor. Where previous good character/exemplary conduct has been used to facilitate the offence, this mitigation should not normally be allowed and such conduct may constitute an aggravating factor. In the context of this offence, previous good character/exemplary conduct should not normally be given any significant weight and will not normally justify a reduction in what would otherwise be the appropriate sentence.
Deliberate isolation of victim(s)	
Vulnerability of victim(s)	
Threats made to expose victim(s) to the authorities (for example, immigration or police), family/friends or others	
Harm threatened against the family/friends of victim(s)	
Passport/identity documents removed	
Victim(s) prevented from seeking medical treatment	
Victim(s) prevented from attending school	
Food withheld	
Earnings withheld/kept by offender or evidence of excessive wage reduction or debt bondage, inflated travel or living expenses or unreasonable interest rates	
Any steps taken to prevent the victim reporting an incident, obtaining assistance and/or from assisting or supporting the prosecution	
Attempts to dispose of or conceal evidence	
Timescale over which the operation has been run	

STEP THREE
CONSIDER ANY FACTORS WHICH INDICATE A REDUCTION, SUCH AS ASSISTANCE TO THE PROSECUTION

The court should take into account sections 73 and 74 of the Serious Organised Crime and Police Act 2005 (assistance by defendants: reduction or review of sentence) and any other rule of law by virtue of which an offender may receive a discounted sentence in consequence of assistance given (or offered) to the prosecutor or investigator.

STEP FOUR
REDUCTION FOR GUILTY PLEAS

The court should take account of any potential reduction for a guilty plea in accordance with section 144 of the Criminal Justice Act 2003 and the *Guilty Plea* guideline.

STEP FIVE
DANGEROUSNESS

The court should consider whether having regard to the criteria contained in Chapter 5 of Part 12 of the Criminal Justice Act 2003 it would be appropriate to award a life sentence (section 224A) or an extended sentence (section 226A). When sentencing offenders to a life sentence under these provisions, the notional determinate sentence should be used as the basis for the setting of a minimum term.

STEP SIX
TOTALITY PRINCIPLE

If sentencing an offender for more than one offence, or where the offender is already serving a sentence, consider whether the total sentence is just and proportionate to the offending behaviour.

STEP SEVEN
ANCILLARY ORDERS

The court must consider whether to make any ancillary orders. The court must also consider what other requirements or provisions may automatically apply. Further information is included at Annex A on page 153.

STEP EIGHT
REASONS

Section 174 of the Criminal Justice Act 2003 imposes a duty to give reasons for, and explain the effect of, the sentence.

STEP NINE
CONSIDERATION FOR TIME SPENT ON BAIL

The court must consider whether to give credit for time spent on bail in accordance with section 240A of the Criminal Justice Act 2003.

Key factors

A[14.7] Notification requirements. See A[52.15].

A[15]

Common assault and racially/religiously aggravated assault

Charge

A[15.1] Did assault [. . . . .] [by beating]

Contrary to the Criminal Justice Act 1988, s 39.

Maximum penalty – Fine level 5 and 6 months. Triable only by magistrates.

(By virtue of s 10 of the Domestic Violence, Crime and Victims Act 2004, from July 1, 2007 common assault is to become an arrestable offence.)

A[15.2] Racially/religiously aggravated assault

Contrary to the Crime and Disorder Act 1998, s 29.

Maximum penalty – Fine level 5 and 6 months. Triable either way. Specified violent offence under Sch 15, Part 1, CJA 2003.

Crown Court – 2 years' imprisonment and unlimited fine.

Legal notes and definitions

A[15.3] The basic offence is triable only by magistrates but may be alleged as an alternative charge at a trial at the Crown Court if the prosecution chooses with a maximum penalty of £5,000 and 6 months (51 weeks). Racially or religiously aggravated assault is triable either way. The two offences may be tried together in the alternative (*R (CPS) v Blaydon Youth Court* [2004] EWHC 2296 (Admin), 168 JP 638).

A[15.4] Intent. The defendant must intend to cause his victim to apprehend immediate and unlawful violence, or be reckless whether such apprehension be caused (*R v Venna* [1976] QB 421, [1975] 3 All ER 788, CA). 'Reckless' means that the accused foresaw the risk and went on to take it (*R v Cunningham* [1957] 2 QB 396, [1957] 2 All ER 412, CA).

In principle it was open to justices to convict on the basis of recklessness even where the prosecution simply alleged a deliberate assault: *D v DPP* [2005] EWHC 967 (Admin) considered. However, the justices had failed to identify what was the unlawful act of K leading to the assault. Recklessness had only been a possible conclusion if the justices had found that K had thrown a punch albeit, without intending it to land, or was flailing his arms about in an agitated and aggressive manner. The conviction could not stand in the light of the findings of fact made by the justices: *Katsonis v Crown Prosecution Service* [2011] EWHC 1860 (Admin), 175 JP 396.

A[15.5] Assault. Does not require any contact between the two parties, a threatening gesture is enough. Words, however insulting, are probably not an assault but any attempt to commit a battery, even if the blow does not connect, can be an assault. It is not necessary that the other party should receive an actual injury, but there must have been a hostile intent. In modern usage the term assault will now include a battery, ie the actual application of force as opposed to its threatened use, and this is how it is used in most statutes. But if a charge alleges 'did assault and batter' then 'assault' will be taken to mean assault in its pure form and the charge will be as bad as being duplicitous. If anything other than 'did assault' is to be alleged it should be 'did assault by beating' (*DPP v Taylor and Little* (1991)). A reckless act which causes injury will suffice, for example a man who having fallen to the ground when struggling with the police lashed out wildly with his legs, striking the officer and fracturing a bone in his hand, was held to have been properly convicted. Just placing a hand on someone's shoulder to call his attention to something is not an assault. Throwing something at a person, even if it misses, may be an assault.

A[15.6] If a man strikes at another but at such a distance that it would be quite impossible for it to connect then it is not an assault (although it might be an attempt). If the other person is actually touched then it is a battery which includes an assault. Equally a punch to a mother causing her to drop her baby is an assault on the baby (*Haystead v Chief Constable of Derbyshire* [2000] 3 All ER 890, [2000] 2 Cr App Rep 339).

A[15.7] Racially or religiously aggravated. This means that at the time of committing the offence, or immediately before or after doing so, the offender demonstrates towards the victim of the assault, hostility based on the victim's membership (or presumed membership) of a racial/religious group, or the offence is motivated (wholly or partly) by hostility towards members of a racial/ religious group based on their membership of that group. It is immaterial whether or not the offender's hostility is also based on other factor not mentioned above. The prosecution can proceed on one or both limbs and will not need to specify which (*G v DPP; T v DPP* [2004] EWHC 183 (Admin), [2004] All ER (D) 278 (Jan)) (*DPP v Woods* [2002] EWHC 85 (Admin), [2002] All ER (D) 154 (Jan)) The victim's perception of the words used is irrelevant, as is the defendant's frame of mind at the time he uttered the words. This offence may also be aggravated by a motivation towards the victim's disability, sexual orientation or transgender identity but not as a separate offence.

A[15.8] Misadventure. If a horse out of control strikes a person that is not an assault. In an old decision a soldier drilling in the ranks fired his gun as a man was passing unexpectedly and this was held not to be an assault.

A[15.9] Accidental jostling. In a crowd there is not an assault as there is an implied consent to the physical contacts of ordinary life.

A[15.10] Hostile intent. See *Collins v Wilcock* [1984] 1 WLR 1172.

A[15.11]–[15.15] Consent. Consent of the victim is a defence but there are limits to this. The test is whether it is in the public interest to allow the activity complained of. In 1981 the Lord Chief Justice decided consent was irrelevant where two youths settled an argument in a public street by agreeing to have a fight. It was not in the public interest for people to cause each other actual bodily harm for no good reason. A similar principle has been applied by the House of Lords to assault which took place in the course of sado-masochistic activities (*R v Brown* [1992] QB 491, [1992] 2 All ER 552, CA; affd [1994] 1 AC 212, [1993] 2 All ER 75, HL). But see *ADT v United Kingdom* [2000] 2 FLR 697, [2000] Fam Law 797, ECtHR for protection from prosecution for such genuinely 'private' activities.

It is not a defence to assault that the complainant is a teacher at a special needs school and, by taking that job, consents to the risk of being assaulted. Knowledge of the risk does not imply consent to assault: *H v Crown Prosecution Service* [2010] EWHC 1374 (Admin), 174 CL&J 271.

A[15.16] Reasonable chastisement is a defence available to a parent accused of assaulting their child; however the chastisement must be reasonable and moderate. This is assessed by:

(i)   the nature and context of the defendant's behaviour
(ii) the duration
(iii) physical/ mental consequences to the child (injury will make it unlawful)
(iv) age and characteristics of the child

While reasonable chastisement can (depending on the circumstances) justify an assault by beating (but not an offence under ss 18, 20, or 47 of the Offences Against the Person Act 1861, or s 1 of the Children and Young Persons Act 1933), battery of a child causing actual bodily harm cannot be justified in any civil proceedings on the ground that it constituted reasonable punishment (Children Act 2004, s 58).

Consensual activity between husband and wife in the privacy of the matrimonial home was held not to be a proper matter for criminal investigation in *R v Wilson* [1997] QB 47, [1996] 3 WLR 125, CA. Lawful sport would be unimpeachable as being in the public interest and the exercise of a legal right.

A[15.17] Defendants who maintained that they had been engaged in rough and undisciplined horseplay, had not intended any harm, and had thought that the victims were consenting to what had occurred, were entitled to have their defence considered by the court (*R v Muir* (1986) 83 Cr App Rep 375, CA).

A[15.18] An injury inflicted on an opponent by deliberately flouting the rules of the game may form the basis of a criminal prosecution: *R v Billinghurst* [1978] Crim LR 553. Most organised sports have their own disciplinary procedures to uphold their rules and standards of play; criminal prosecutions should, therefore, be brought only in cases that are so grave as to be properly categorised as criminal. If what occurs goes beyond what a player can reasonably be regarded as having accepted by taking part in the sport, this indicates that the conduct will not be covered by the defence of consent; on the other hand, the fact that the play is within the rules and practice of the game and does not go beyond them, will be a firm indication that what has happened is not criminal: *R v Barnes* [2004] EWCA Crim 3246, [2005] 2 All ER 113, [2005] 1 Cr App Rep 507, [2005] Crim LR 381 in which the following guidance was given. It must be borne in mind that in highly competitive sports conduct outside the rules could be expected to occur in the heat of the moment and even if conduct justified not only being penalised but also a warning or even a sending off it still might not reach the threshold level required for it to be criminal. The type of sport, the level at which it was played, the nature of the act, the degree of force used, the extent of the risk of injury and the state of mind of the defendant were all likely to be relevant in determining whether the defendant's actions went beyond the threshold and warranted criminal proceedings.

A[15.19] Self-defence. See A[8.18]–A[8.20].

Self-defence – onus of proof. Once the defendant raises the issue of self-defence the onus is on the prosecution to disprove the defence beyond reasonable doubt.

A[15.20] **Execution of legal process.** An officer of justice acting on a court order can, if he is resisted, use whatever force is necessary to carry out the order of the court.

A[15.21]–[15.30] **Justification or triviality.** In a case of common assault where the information was preferred by or on behalf of the party aggrieved, if the court finds that an assault has been committed but that either it was justified or that it was so trifling as not to merit any punishment, they may dismiss the charge and issue a certificate of dismissal (see OPA 1861, s 44).

A[15.31] **Certificate of dismissal.** If, after hearing such a case, the magistrates decide to dismiss the case the defendant can apply for a certificate of dismissal which will protect him from being subsequently prosecuted or sued for damages for the same assault. It is also worth noting that a defendant who has pleaded not guilty to an offence of an assault of actual bodily harm and the prosecution offer no evidence resulting in a dismissal cannot be then tried for common assault on the same facts (*R v G (Autrefois Acquit)* [2001] EWCA Crim 1215, [2001] 1 WLR 1727).

A[15.32] **Provocation.** This is not a defence but may be put forward to mitigate the penalty.

Sentencing
SC Guideline – Common assault and racially/religiously aggravated common assault

A[15.33] Common Assault

Criminal Justice Act 1988 (section 39)

Racially/religiously aggravated common assault

Crime and Disorder Act 1998 (section 29)

Racially/religiously aggravated assault is a specified offence for the purposes of section 224 of the Criminal Justice Act 2003

Section 39

Triable only summarily

Maximum: Level 5 and/or 26 weeks' custody

Section 29

Triable either way

Maximum when tried summarily: Level 5 fine and/or 26 weeks' custody

Maximum when tried on indictment: 2 years' custody

Offence range: Discharge – 26 weeks' custody

This guideline applies to all offenders aged 18 and older, who are sentenced on or after 13 June 2011. The definitions of 'starting point' and 'first time offender' do not apply for this guideline. Starting point and category ranges apply to all offenders in all cases, irrespective of plea or previous convictions.

Step One
Determining the offence category

The court should determine the offence category using the table below.

Category 1	Greater harm **and** higher culpability
Category 2	Greater harm **and** lower culpability; **or** lesser harm **and** higher culpability
Category 3	Lesser harm **and** lower culpability

The court should determine the offender's culpability and the harm caused, or intended, by reference **only** to the factors below (as demonstrated by the presence of one or more). These factors comprise the principal factual elements of the offence and should determine the category.

Factors indicating greater harm

Injury (which includes disease transmission and/or psychological harm) which is serious in the context of the offence (must normally be present)

Victim is particularly vulnerable because of personal circumstances

Sustained or repeated assault on the same victim

Factors indicating lesser harm

Injury which is less serious in the context of the offence

Factors indicating higher culpability

Statutory aggravating factors:

Offence motivated by, or demonstrating, hostility to the victim based on his or her sexual orientation (or presumed sexual orientation)

Offence motivated by, or demonstrating, hostility to the victim based on the victim's disability (or presumed disability)

Other aggravating factors:

A significant degree of premeditation

Threatened or actual use of weapon or weapon equivalent (for example, shod foot, headbutting, use of acid, use of animal)

Intention to commit more serious harm than actually resulted from the offence

Deliberately causes more harm than is necessary for commission of offence

Deliberate targeting of vulnerable victim

Leading role in group or gang

Offence motivated by, or demonstrating, hostility based on the victim's age, sex, gender identity (or presumed gender identity)

Factors indicating lower culpability

Subordinate role in group or gang

A greater degree of provocation than normally expected

Lack of premeditation

Mental disorder or learning disability, where linked to commission of the offence

Excessive self defence

Step Two
Starting point and category range

Having determined the category, the court should use the corresponding starting points to reach a sentence within the category range below. The starting point applies to all offenders irrespective of plea or previous convictions. A case of particular gravity, reflected by multiple features of culpability in step one, could merit upward adjustment from the starting point before further adjustment for aggravating or mitigating features, set out below.

Offence Category	Starting Point (Applicable to all offenders)	Category Range (Applicable to all offenders)
Category 1	High level community order	Low level community order – 26 weeks' custody
Category 2	Medium level community order	Band A fine – High level community order
Category 3	Band A fine	Discharge – Band C fine

The table below contains a **non-exhaustive** list of additional factual elements providing the context of the offence and factors relating to the offender. Identify whether any combination of these, or other relevant factors, should result in an upward or downward adjustment from the starting point. In some cases, having considered these factors, it may be appropriate to move outside the identified category range.

When sentencing **category 1** offences, the court should also consider the custody threshold as follows:

- has the custody threshold been passed?
- if so, is it unavoidable that a custodial sentence be imposed?
- if so, can that sentence be suspended?

When sentencing **category 2** offences, the court should also consider the community order threshold as follows:

- has the community order threshold been passed?

Factors increasing seriousness

Statutory aggravating factors:

Previous convictions, having regard to a) the nature of the offence to which the conviction relates and its relevance to the current offence; and b) the time that has elapsed since the conviction

Offence committed whilst on bail

Other aggravating factors include:

Location of the offence

Timing of the offence

Ongoing effect upon the victim

Offence committed against those working in the public sector or providing a service to the public

---

Presence of others including relatives, especially children or partner of the victim

Gratuitous degradation of victim

In domestic violence cases, victim forced to leave their home

Failure to comply with current court orders

Offence committed whilst on licence

An attempt to conceal or dispose of evidence

Failure to respond to warnings or concerns expressed by others about the offender's behaviour

Commission of offence whilst under the influence of alcohol or drugs

Abuse of power and/or position of trust

Exploiting contact arrangements with a child to commit an offence

Established evidence of community impact

Any steps taken to prevent the victim reporting an incident, obtaining assistance and/or from assisting or supporting the prosecution

Offences taken into consideration (TICs)

Factors reducing seriousness or reflecting personal mitigation

No previous convictions **or** no relevant/recent convictions

Single blow

Remorse

Good character and/or exemplary conduct

Determination and/or demonstration of steps taken to address addiction or offending behaviour

Serious medical conditions requiring urgent, intensive or long-term treatment

Isolated incident

Age and/or lack of maturity where it affects the responsibility of the offender

Lapse of time since the offence where this is not the fault of the offender

Mental disorder or learning disability, where **not** linked to the commission of the offence

Sole or primary carer for dependent relatives

Section 29 offences only: The court should determine the appropriate sentence for the offence without taking account of the element of aggravation and then make an addition to the sentence, considering the level of aggravation involved. It may be appropriate to move outside the identified category range, taking into account the increased statutory maximum.

Step Three
Consider any other factors which indicate a reduction, such as assistance to the prosecution

The court should take into account any rule of law by virtue of which an offender may receive a discounted sentence in consequence of assistance given (or offered) to the prosecutor or investigator.

Step Four
Reduction for guilty pleas

The court should take account of any potential reduction for a guilty plea in accordance with section 144 of the Criminal Justice Act 2003 and the *Guilty Plea* guideline.

Step Five
Dangerousness

Inflicting grievous bodily harm/unlawful wounding and racially/religiously aggravated GBH/unlawful wounding are specified offences within the meaning of Chapter 5 of the Criminal Justice Act 2003 and at this stage the court should consider whether having regard to the criteria contained in that Chapter it would be appropriate to award an extended sentence

Step Six
Totality principle

If sentencing an offender for more than one offence, or where the offender is already serving a sentence, consider whether the total sentence is just and proportionate to the offending behaviour.

Step Seven
Compensation and ancillary orders

In all cases, the court should consider whether to make compensation and/or other ancillary orders.

Step Eight
Reasons

Section 174 of the Criminal Justice Act 2003 imposes a duty to give reasons for, and explain the effect of, the sentence.

Step Nine
Consideration for remand time

(Now obligatory.)

A[16]

Communications network offences

Charge

A[16.1] A person is guilty of an offence if he—

(a)   sends by means of a public electronic communications network a message or other matter that is grossly offensive or of an indecent, obscene or menacing character; or

(b)   causes any such matter to be so sent

Communications Act 2003, s 127(1)

A person is guilty of an offence if he—

(a)   sends by means of a public electronic communications network, a message that he knows to be false,

(b)   causes such a message to be sent; or

(c)   persistently makes use of a public electronic communications network

Communications Act 2003, s 127(2)

Maximum penalty – level 5 fine and/or six months. Triable summarily only.

Legal notes and definitions

A[16.2]–[16.6] Elements of the offence. In *DPP v Collins* [2006] UK 40, [2006] 4 All ER 602, [2006] 1 WLR 2223, (2006) 170 JP 712, [2007] 1 Cr App R 5, [2007] Crim LR 98 the House of Lords held that the purpose and elements of the offence under s 127(1)(a) were as follows. The object was to prohibit the use of a service provided and funded by the public for the benefit of the public, for the transmission of communications that contravened the basic standards of society. The proscribed act was the sending of the message of the proscribed character by the defined means, and the offence was complete when the message was sent. It was for the court, applying the standards of an open and just multiracial society and taking account of the context and all relevant circumstances, to determine as a question of fact whether a message was grossly offensive. It was necessary to show that the defendant intended his words to be grossly offensive to those to whom the message related, or that he was aware that they might be taken to be so. Although s 127(1)(a) interfered with the right to freedom of expression under art 10 of the Convention, it went no further than was necessary in a democratic society for achieving the legitimate objective of preventing the use of the public electronic communications network for attacking the reputations and rights of others.

In *Chambers v DPP* [2012] EWHC 2157 (Admin), [2013] 1 All ER 149, [2013] 1 Cr App Rep 1 the defendant was a registered user of Twitter and 'tweeted' in his own name. When he learned of the closure of an airport owing to adverse weather conditions he tweeted '... You've got a week and a bit to get your shit together otherwise I am blowing the airport sky high!!' This was posted onto the public time line, which meant it was available to be read by about 600 Twitter followers of the defendant. The conviction was quashed by the Divisional Court. At the time the tweet was posted it was a 'message' within s 127, but on an objective assessment there was no proper basis for concluding that the tweet constituted or included a message of a menacing character. There was no evidence that any Twitter follower of the defendant, or anyone else who may have seen the tweet, had found it to be menacing or even slightly alarming. 'The message must be credible as an immediate threat to the mind of an ordinary person of normal stability and courage . . . it is difficult to imagine a serious threat in which warning of it is given to a large number of tweet "followers" in ample time for the threat to be reported and extinguished' (per Lord Judge CJ at paras 30 and 31). His Lordship added this regarding the mental element of the offence. No different test applied to 'menacing' messages than those which were 'grossly offensive'. The mental element is satisfied 'if the offender is proved to have been aware or to have recognised the risk at the time of sending the message that it may create fear or apprehension in any reasonable member of the public who reads or sees it. We would merely emphasise that, even expressed in these terms, the mental element of the offence is directed exclusively to the state of the mind of the offender, and that if he may have intended the message as a joke, even if a joke in bad taste, it is unlikely that the mens rea required before conviction for the offence of sending a message of a menacing character will be established' (at para 37).

Sentencing
SC Guideline – Communications network offences

A[16.7]

OFFENCE SERIOUSNESS (CULPABILITY AND HARM)		
A. IDENTIFY THE APPROPRIATE STARTING POINT		
Starting points based on first time offender pleading not guilty		
Sending grossly offensive, indecent, obscene or menacing messages (s 127(1))		
Examples of nature of activity	**Starting point**	**Range**
Single offensive, indecent, obscene or menacing call of short duration, having no significant impact on receiver	Band B fine	Band A fine to band C fine
Single call where extreme language used and substantial distress or fear caused to receiver	Medium level community order	Low level community order to 12 weeks custody
Single call where extreme language used and substantial distress or fear caused to receiver; OR One of a series of similar calls as described in box above	6 weeks custody	High level community order to 12 weeks custody
Sending false message/persistent use of communications network for purpose of causing annoyance, inconvenience or needless anxiety (s 127(2))		
Examples of nature of activity	**Starting point**	**Range**

Persistent silent calls over short period to private individual, causing inconvenience or annoyance	Band B fine	Band A fine to band C fine
Single hoax call to public or private organisation resulting in moderate disruption or anxiety	Medium level community order	Low level community order to high level community order
Single hoax call resulting in major disruption or substantial public fear or distress; OR One of a series of similar calls as described in box above	12 weeks custody	High level community order to 18 weeks custody

OFFENCE SERIOUSNESS (CULPABILITY AND HARM)
B. CONSIDER THE EFFECT OF AGGRAVATING AND MITIGATING FACTORS (OTHER THAN THOSE WITHIN EXAMPLES ABOVE) Common aggravating and mitigating factors are identified at B[5.2A]
FORM A PRELIMINARY VIEW OF THE APPROPRIATE SENTENCE, THEN CONSIDER OFFENDER MITIGATION Common aggravating are identified at B[5.2A]
CONSIDER A REDUCTION FOR A GUILTY PLEA
CONSIDER ANCILLARY ORDERS, INCLUDING COMPENSATION **Refer to B[18] for guidance on compensation** Consult your legal adviser on guidance for availability of ANCILLARY ORDERS
DECIDE SENTENCE **GIVE REASONS**

Community order, breach of

Charge

A[17.1] That the offender has failed without reasonable excuse to comply with any of the requirements of a community order made on x date by x court. Contrary to Criminal Justice Act 2003, Sch 8.

Legal notes and definitions

A[17.2] See [B17.17].

Burden and standard of proof. The burden is on the prosecutor; the standard of proof is beyond a reasonable doubt (*West Yorkshire Probation Board v Boulter* [2005 [EWHC 2342 (Admin), (2005) 169 JP 601).

Reasonable excuse. A community order takes effect when it is imposed and it remains in full force and effect until and unless it is quashed on appeal or revoked or amended by order of the court. Although the concept of "reasonable excuse" is broad there is no statutory provision which automatically suspends the operation of a community order pending an appeal against it (or the conviction on which it is based). It is not therefore a reasonable excuse for a defendant to fail to carry out the community order despite the lodging of a notice of appeal (*West Midlands Probation Board v Sutton Coldfield Magistrates' Courts* [2005] EWHC 15 (Admin)).

Failed. An offender who "fails to keep in touch" with his responsible officer in accordance with such instructions as he may from time to time be given by that officer, in the absence of documentary or supporting evidence to explain the failure, provided within a specified period of time eg 7 days, breaches the terms of the community order (*Richards v National Probation Service* [2007] EWHC 3108 (Admin)).

Sentencing
SC Guideline – Community order, breach of

A[17.3] These notes are taken from the Sentencing Council's definitive guideline *New Sentences: CJA 2003* published 16 December 2004.

Options in breach proceedings:

When dealing with breaches of community orders for offences committed after 4 April 2005, the court must either:

• amend the terms of the original order so as to impose more onerous requirements. The court may extend the duration of particular requirements within the order, but it cannot extend the overall length of the original order (NB: s 38 of the Criminal Justice and Immigration Act 2008 reduces from 40 hours to 20 hours the minimum period of unpaid work that can be imposed on breach, provided that the order did not previously contain an unpaid work requirement); or

- **fine,** by ordering the offender to pay a fine of an amount not exceeding £2,500; or
- **revoke the original order and proceed to sentence for the original offence.** Where an offender has wilfully and persistently failed to comply with an order made in respect of an offence that is not punishable by imprisonment, the court can impose of to six months custody (CJA, Sch 8, para 9(1)(c)).

NB: revocation and re-sentence: in the case of an offence triable either way this does not include committal to the Crown Court for sentence pursuant to s 3 PCC (S) Act 2000 (*R v Jordan* [1998] Crim LR 353).

Approach to breach proceedings:

- having decided that a community order is commensurate with the seriousness of the offence, the primary objective when sentencing for breach of requirements is to ensure that those requirements are completed;
- a court sentencing for breach must take account of the extent to which the offender has complied with the requirements of the original order, the reasons for the breach, and the point at which the breach has occurred;
- if increasing the onerousness of requirements, sentencers should take account of the offender's ability to comply and should avoid precipitating further breach by overloading the offender with too many or conflicting requirements;
- there may be cases where the court will need to consider re-sentencing to a differently constructed community order in order to secure compliance with the purposes of the original sentence, perhaps where there has already been partial compliance or where events since the sentence was imposed have shown that a different course of action is likely to be effective;
- where available, custody should be the last resort, reserved for those cases of deliberate and repeated breach where all reasonable efforts to ensure that the offender complies have failed.

Where the original order was made by the Crown court, breach proceedings must be commenced in that court, unless the order provided that any failure to comply with its requirements may be dealt with a magistrates' court. **Consult your legal adviser for further guidance when dealing with breach of a community order made in the Crown Court.**

A[18]

Damage to property

Criminal damage (including by fire (arson)) and racially/ religiously aggravated criminal damage

Charge

A[18.1] Without lawful excuse destroyed (or damaged) property namely [. . . . .] belonging to [. . . . .] intending to destroy (or damage) it or being reckless as to whether such property would be destroyed or damaged

Criminal Damage Act 1971, s 1

NB: Where the damage is under £500 and not normally over £300 a fixed penalty of £90 is available

A[18.2] Maximum penalty and venue for trial – Where the damage or destruction is caused by fire (arson) the offence is triable either way without regard to the value of the damage caused and the maximum penalty is a fine on level 5 and 6 months' imprisonment. If it is alleged in the charge that the accused intended to endanger life, or was reckless as to whether life would be endangered, the offence is triable only on indictment and is punishable in the Crown Court with life imprisonment. Where the offence involves racial aggravation it will always be an either way offence (see below).

Offences of arson (s 1(3)) or where life is endangered (s 1(2)) are specified violent offences under Sch 15, Part 1, CJA 2003. See B[16.5] for guidance.

A[18.3] The plea before venue procedure only applies to criminal damage allegations in excess of £5,000 (*R v Kelly* [2001] RTR 45, CA). If the value is ascertained as £5,000 or under the court must proceed to summary trial and the sentence will be restricted to a maximum of a level 4 fine and/or 3 months' imprisonment – or 6 months for two offences (*R v Gwynn* [2002] EWCA Crim 2951, [2003] All ER (D) 318 (Dec)).

A[18.4] Where the defendant does not indicate a guilty plea and it is unclear to the court whether the value of the damage is more than £5,000 or not the court must decide whether the value is more or less than that sum (it is not necessary to decide what the value is, simply whether it is above £5,000). If the court decides that the value of the damage exceeds £5,000 (and it may hear representations from the prosecution and defence to assist in arriving at a decision) then the offence is triable either way as in the preceding paragraph. Likewise if the court reaches a decision that the value of the damage does not exceed £5,000 the offence is triable summarily, as above. In those cases where the court is unable to decide whether the value is more or less than £5,000 the accused must be told that if he wishes he may consent to be tried summarily, and if he does he will be so tried and will be liable to a maximum penalty on level 4 and 3 months (level 5 and 6 months in a case of aggravated vehicle taking). If the accused then consents, the trial will proceed summarily.

A[18.5] If he does not consent, the court proceeds as for an ordinary either way offence, with the plea before venue and mode of trial procedure as is appropriate.

A[18.6] Assessing the value of the damage. Unless the damage was caused by fire, or racial aggravation was involved, where property has been destroyed the mode of trial depends upon its value. This means what it would probably have cost to buy in the open market at the material time. See (*R (on application of DPP) v Prestatyn Magistrates' Courts* [2002] All ER (D) 421 (May)) for further guidance

A[18.7] If the allegation is one of damage (excluding damage caused by fire) the mode of trial depends upon the value of the damage. If, immediately after the damage was caused, the property was capable of repair (eg a car windscreen) then the value of the damage is the lesser of: (a) what would probably have been the market price for the repair of the damage immediately after the damage was caused (this would, for example, not include the cost of repairing further deterioration since the offence); or (b) what the property would probably have cost to buy in the open market at the material time, whichever is the less. Thus, if it would cost more to repair the property than its probable market value, then the value of the damage for the purposes of deciding the venue of trial would be the probable market price. If, immediately after the damage was caused, the property was beyond repair (eg a shattered crystal decanter) then the value for trial purposes is its probable cost in the open market at the time of the offence.

A[18.8] The use of the word 'probable' in the Act indicates that the court must make up its mind in the light of the available information.

A[18.9] Multiple offences. Where an accused is charged with a series of offences of damage or destruction the offences are only triable either way if their aggregate value is in excess of £5,000.

A[18.10]–[18.15] Mode of trial considerations. See SC Guidelines at A[18.32] below.

Charge

A[18.16] Racially/religiously aggravated criminal damage

Crime and Disorder Act 1998, s 30

Maximum penalty – level 5 and 6 months' imprisonment. Triable either way. **Crown Court** – 14 years' imprisonment and unlimited fine.

A[18.17] Racially/religiously aggravated. This means that at the time of committing the offence, of immediately before or after doing so, the offender demonstrates towards the victim's property hostility based on the victim's membership (or presumed membership) of a racial or religious group (see *Parry v DPP* [2004] EWHC 3112 (Admin), [2004] All ER (D) 335 (Dec) for guidance on immediacy); or the offence is motivated (wholly or partly) by hostility towards members of a racial or religious group based on their membership of that group. In *DPP v M* [2004] EWHC 1453 (Admin), [2004] All ER (D) 358 (May) the term 'bloody foreigners' was held to be a group defined by nationality and was hostile. In *R v Rogers*

[2007] UKHL 8, it was decided that the term "foreigners" could constitute a racial group within the meaning of s 28(4) of the Crime and Disorder Act 1998. Whether the evidence in any particular case, taken as a whole, proved that the offender's conduct demonstrated hostility to such a group, or was motivated by such hostility, was a question of fact for the court.

A[18.18] The victim's perceptions of the words used is irrelevant here, as is the fact that the defendant would have used those words to anyone with the victim's characteristics (*DPP v Woods* [2002] EWHC 85 (Admin), [2002] All ER (D) 154 (Jan)).

It is immaterial whether the offender's hostility is also based to any extent on any other factor not mentioned above.

Legal notes and definitions

A[18.19] Without lawful excuse. It is a defence if the defendant proves he had a lawful excuse for destroying or damaging the property. He only has to establish that this defence is probably true, he does not have to establish it beyond reasonable doubt. Section 5(2) provides that, inter alia, the following can be lawful excuses:

(a)   that at the time he destroyed or damaged the property he believed that a person or persons entitled to consent to the destruction or damage had given consent; or that person or persons would have consented if he or they had known of the destruction or damage and the circumstances; or

(b)   that at the time he destroyed or damaged the property he believed that property belonging to himself or another was in immediate need of protection and that the adopted or proposed means of protection were reasonable in all the circumstances.

Provided that the defendant honestly held such a belief, it is immaterial whether the belief was justified or not (even if the defendant was drunk) (*Jaggard v Dickinson* [1981] QB 527, [1980] 3 All ER 716, [1981] 2 WLR 118, 72 Cr App Rep 33, [1980] Crim LR 717, 124 Sol Jo 847). See *R v Mitchell* [2003] EWCA Crim 2188, [2004] RTR 224, [2004] Crim LR 139, [2003] All ER (D) 99 (Aug) on possible defences to removing a wheel clamp.

Individuals facing charges for criminal damage and aggravated trespass arising out of their actions in protesting against the war in Iraq could not argue that they were using **reasonable force** to prevent the commission of a crime under s 3 of the Criminal Law Act 1967, nor that the activities of the activities of the Crown at military bases were unlawful (*R v Jones* [2006] UKHL 16).

The destruction of badger traps were not justified under s 5(2)(b) because the defendants did not cause the damage in order to protect property belonging to themselves or another person (*Currie v DPP* [2006] EWHC AER (D) 429 (Nov)).

A[18.20] Destroy or damage. Where a defendant was initially unaware that he had done an act that in fact set in train events which, by the time he became aware of them, would make it obvious to anyone who troubled to give his mind to them that they presented a risk that property belonging to another would be damaged, he would be guilty if he did not try to prevent or reduce the damage because he gave no thought to the possibility of such a risk or having done so he decided not to prevent or reduce the risk. An example would be the man who, unawares, drops a lighted cigarette down a chair and later, on discovering the chair is smouldering, leaves the room not caring whether the chair catches light or not.

A[18.21] Property is defined at length in s 10(1). It means property of a tangible nature and includes money. It also includes wild creatures which have been tamed or are ordinarily kept in captivity. It does not include mushrooms, fungus, flowers, fruit or foliage of a plant, shrub or tree which are growing wild on any land.

A[18.22] Damage. Defendants who had painted graffiti on a pavement with a water-soluble whitewash in the expectation that the graffiti would be washed away by rainwater, were guilty especially since expense and inconvenience had been caused to the local authority which removed the marks before it rained. 'Damage' may be used in the sense of mischief to property. The 'temporary functional derangement' of a police officer's cap by the defendant's stamping on it constituted damage although it could be pushed back into shape. Accordingly the erasure of a computer program on a plastic circuit card was damage and although it could be restored, this necessitated time, labour and expense (*Cox v Riley* (1986) 83 Cr App Rep 54, [1986] Crim LR 460). A computer 'hacker' who obtains unauthorised entry to a computer system and makes alterations impairing its proper use can be convicted of criminal damage, although the damage to the magnetic particles in the disk are not perceptible without using the computer. Tangible property has been damaged even though the damage itself is not tangible. Impairment of usefulness does not require breaking, cutting or removal of a part: *R v Whiteley* [1991] Crim LR 436.

A[18.23] Belonging to another person (s 10(2)). In addition to an ordinary owner this includes a person who had the custody or control of the property, or a proprietary right or interest in the property (except for an equitable interest arising only from an agreement to transfer or grant an interest), or who had a charge on the property.

A[18.24] As far as trust property is concerned, it can be treated for the purposes of this offence as belonging to any person having the right to enforce the trust (s 10(3)).

A[18.25]–[18.30] Intending. The court must decide whether the defendant intended the damage by considering all the evidence and drawing from it such inferences as appear proper in the circumstances.

A[18.31] Reckless. A person is reckless with respect to:

(a)   a circumstance when he is aware of a risk, that it exists or will exist;
(b)   a result, when he is aware of a risk that it will occur; and
(c)   it is, in the circumstances known to him, unreasonable to take the risk (*R v G* [2003] UKHL 50, [2004] 1 AC 1034, [2003] 4 All ER 765, HL).

For a more recent example of the application of the test of recklessness see *Booth v Crown Prosecution Service* [2006] EWHC 192 (Admin), (2006) 170 JP 305, QBD.

Sentencing
SC Guideline – Arson (criminal damage by fire)

A[18.32] Where offence committed in a domestic context, refer to SC Definitive Guideline: "Overarching Principles: Domestic Violence".

OFFENCE SERIOUSNESS (CULPABILITY AND HARM)		
A. IDENTIFY THE APPROPRIATE STARTING POINT		
Starting points based on first time offender pleading not guilty		
Examples of nature of activity	**Starting point**	**Range**
Minor damage by fire	High level community order	Medium level community order to 12 weeks custody
Moderate damage by fire	12 weeks custody	6 to 26 weeks custody
Significant damage by fire	Crown Court	Crown Court

OFFENCE SERIOUSNESS (CULPABILITY AND HARM)
B. CONSIDER THE EFFECT OF AGGRAVATING AND MITIGATING FACTORS (OTHER THAN THOSE WITHIN EXAMPLES ABOVE)
Common aggravating and mitigating factors are identified at B[5.2A]. The following may be particularly relevant but **these lists are not exhaustive**

Factors indicating higher culpability	*Factors indicating lower culpability*
1. Revenge attack	1. Damage caused recklessly
Factors indicating greater degree of harm	
1. Damage to emergency equipment	
2. Damage to public amenity	
3. Significant public or private fear caused eg in domestic context	

FORM A PRELIMINARY VIEW OF THE APPROPRIATE SENTENCE, THEN CONSIDER OFFENDER MITIGATION
Common factors are identified at B[5.2A]
CONSIDER A REDUCTION FOR A GUILTY PLEA
CONSIDER ANCILLARY ORDERS, INCLUDING COMPENSATION
Refer to B[18] for guidance on compensation.
DECIDE SENTENCE
GIVE REASONS

SC Guideline – Criminal damage – other than by fire)
SC Guideline – Racially or religiously aggravated criminal damage

Racially or religiously aggravated damage: Refer to **B[5.2B]** for further guidance

Where offence committed in a domestic context, refer to SC Definitive Guideline: "Overarching Principles: Domestic Violence".

OFFENCE SERIOUSNESS (CULPABILITY AND HARM)
A. IDENTIFY THE APPROPRIATE STARTING POINT

Starting points based on first time offender pleading not guilty		
Examples of nature of activity	**Starting point**	**Range**
Minor damage eg breaking small window; small amount of graffiti	Band B fine	Conditional discharge to band C fine
Moderate damage eg breaking large plate-glass or shop window; widespread graffiti	Low level community order	Band C fine to medium level community order
Significant damage up to £5,000 eg damage caused as part of a spree	High level community order	Medium level community order to 12 weeks custody
Damage between £5,000 and £10,000	12 weeks custody	6 to 26 weeks custody
Damage over £10,000	Crown Court	Crown Court

OFFENCE SERIOUSNESS (CULPABILITY AND HARM)

B. CONSIDER THE EFFECT OF AGGRAVATING AND MITIGATING FACTORS (OTHER THAN THOSE WITHIN EXAMPLES ABOVE)

Common aggravating and mitigating factors are identified at B[5.2A]. The following may be particularly relevant but **these lists are not exhaustive**

Factors indicating higher culpability	*Factors indicating lower culpability*
1. Revenge attack	1. Damage caused recklessly
2. Targeting vulnerable victim	2. Provocation
Factors indicating greater degree of harm	
1. Damage to emergency equipment	
2. Damage to public amenity	
3. Significant public or private fear caused eg in domestic context	

FORM A PRELIMINARY VIEW OF THE APPROPRIATE SENTENCE

IF OFFENDER CHARGED AND CONVICTED OF THE RACIALLY OR RELIGIOUSLY AGGRAVATED OFFENCE, INCREASE THE SENTENCE TO REFLECT THE ELEMENT

Common factors are identified at B[5.2B]

CONSIDER OFFENDER MITIGATION

Common factors are identified at B[5.2A]

CONSIDER A REDUCTION FOR A GUILTY PLEA

CONSIDER ANCILLARY ORDERS, INCLUDING COMPENSATION

Refer to B[18] for guidance on compensation.

DECIDE SENTENCE

GIVE REASONS

A[18A]

Threatening to destroy or damage property

(Criminal Damage Act 1971, s 2(a))

Charge

A[18A.1] Without lawful excuse made to [. . . . .] a threat to destroy (or damage) property belonging to that other person (or belonging to a third person), intending that the other person would fear it would be carried out

Maximum penalty – Fine level 5 and 6 months. Triable either way.

The legal notes and definitions relating to the previous offence at **A[18]** also apply here, except for the reference to compensation and mode of trial. The threats can be spoken or in writing.

Crown Court – 10 years' imprisonment and unlimited fine.

A[18A.2] The gist of the offence under both parts of s 2 is the threat; the nature of the threat has to be considered objectively so that it does not matter what the person threatened thought was embraced within the threat or whether he feared the threat would be carried out, though the prosecution must prove that the defendant intended that the person threatened would fear that the threat would be carried out: *R v Cakmak* [2002] EWCA Crim 500, [2002] 2 Cr App Rep 158, [2002] Crim LR 581.

A[18B]

Possessing anything with intent to destroy or damage property

(Criminal Damage Act 1971, s 3(a))

Charge

A[18B.1] Had in his custody (or under his control) a [...............] intending without lawful excuse to use it to destroy (or damage) property belonging to another person

Maximum penalty – Fine level 5 and 6 months. Triable either way.

The legal notes and definitions relating to offence no 1 at **A[18]** also apply here except for mode of trial.

Crown Court – 10 years' imprisonment and unlimited fine.

A[19]

Cruelty to a child

Charge

A[19.1] Having responsibility for a child or young person under the age of 16 and wilfully assaulting, ill-treating, neglecting, abandoning, or exposing him in a manner likely to cause him unnecessary suffering or injury to health

Children and Young Persons Act 1933, s 1, as amended

Maximum penalty – Fine level 5 and 6 months. Triable either way. Specified violent offence under Sch 15, Part 1, CJA 2003.

Crown Court – 10 years' imprisonment and unlimited fine.

Mode of trial

A[19.2] Consider the **SC guideline** at A[19.32] below.

A[19.3] All or any of the types of cruelty listed in the charge above can be included in a single information but on conviction one penalty must cover the lot.

A[19.4] The offence of cruelty can only be committed by a person over the age of 16.

A[19.5] Reasonable punishment. In relation to this offence, battery cannot be justified on the ground that it constituted reasonable punishment: Children Act 2004, s 58.

A[19.6] A child. Means someone under 14 years of age.

A[19.7] A young person. Means for this offence someone aged 14 or 15 years.

A[19.8] Wilfully. Offences under s 1(1) are not offences of strict liability, thus the prosecution need to prove a deliberate or reckless act or failure: a genuine lack of appreciation through stupidity, ignorance or personal inadequacy will be a good defence. The offence is not to be judged by the objective test of what a reasonable parent would have done: *R v Sheppard* [1981] AC 394, [1980] 3 All ER 899, 72 Cr App Rep 82. That the parents acted in the deluded belief that the children were possessed by spirits is not mitigation and does not reduce the culpability of the offences: *R v P* (2007) Times 17 March, CA.

A[19.9]–[19.15] Assaulting. See under the charge of 'Common assault', at A[15].

A[19.16] Ill-treating. Actual assault or battery need not be proved. Bullying or frightening or any course of conduct calculated to cause unnecessary suffering or injury to health will suffice.

A[19.17] Neglecting. Means omitting to take such steps as a reasonable parent would take and can include failing to apply for state benefits. Failure to obtain medical care can amount to neglect. It is a question of fact which the magistrates have to determine in each case.

A[19.18] Abandoning. Means leaving the child to his fate. In one case a child was carefully packed in a hamper and sent by train to the father's address and although the child came to no harm it was held that the child had been abandoned: *R v Boulden* (1957) 41 Cr App Rep 105.

A[19.19] In another case a child had been left on his doorstep and the father knew he was there and permitted the child to remain there during an October night for six hours. It was held that he had abandoned the child: *R v White* (1871) LR 1 CCR 311, 36 JP 134.

A[19.20] Leaving children at a youth court has been held not to be an offence under this section: *R v Whibley* [1938] 3 All ER 777, 102 JP 326.

A[19.21] Exposing. It is not necessary to prove that the defendant intended to cause suffering or injury to health. The requisite is that the defendant exposed the child or young person in a manner which was likely to cause unnecessary suffering or injury to health.

A[19.22] In a manner likely to cause him unnecessary suffering or injury to health. This part of the offence must be proved in addition to wilfully assaulting, ill-treating, neglecting, abandoning or exposing as set out in the charge.

A[19.23] Presumption of guilt. A parent or person legally liable to maintain a child or young person will be presumed to have neglected the child or young person in a manner likely to cause injury to health if he has failed to provide adequate food, clothing, medical aid or lodging. If the parent has been unable to provide any of these things he will still be presumed to have neglected him if he fails to apply for them under state benefits. (However the prosecution must still establish that this neglect was 'wilful'.)

A[19.24] Dealing with the children. As the defendant is almost always over the age of 18, this offence is usually tried in the adult court.

A[19.25]–[19.30] Either before the charge is heard in the adult court or concurrently it is often the practice that the ill-treated child or young person is brought before the family proceedings court as in need of care and the family proceedings court can make a care order placing the child or young person in the care of a local authority.

A[19.31] The court may direct that nothing may be published or broadcast which would identify any child concerned; the legal adviser should be consulted.

Sentencing
SC Guideline – Cruelty to children

A[19.32] This guideline and accompanying notes are taken from the Sentencing Council's definitive guideline *Overarching Principles: Assaults on children and Cruelty to a child* published February 2008 and coming into force for persons sentenced on or after 3 March 2008

For cases of domestic violence. See SC Definitive Guideline: 'Overarching Principles: Domestic Violence'.

*The court <u>must</u> inform the defendant that the Independent Safeguarding Authority (now the Disclosure and Barring Service constituted under the Protection of Freedoms Act 2012) will automatically ban him/her from working with children and/or vulnerable adults. As the court has no role in the decision if the defendant needs any further advice he/she should consult a solicitor.

Key factors

(a)   The same starting point and sentencing range is proposed for offences which might fall into the four categories (assault; ill-treatment or neglect; abandonment; and, failure to protect). These are designed to take into account the fact that the victim is particularly vulnerable, assuming an abuse of trust or power and the likelihood of psychological harm, and designed to reflect the seriousness with which society as a whole regards these offences.

(b)   As noted above, the starting points have been calculated to reflect the likelihood of psychological harm and this cannot be treated as an aggravating factor. Where there is an especially serious physical or psychological effect on the victim, even if unintended, this should increase the sentence.

(c)   The normal sentencing starting point for an offence of child cruelty should be a custodial sentence. The length of that sentence will be influenced by the circumstances in which the offence took place.

(d)   However, in considering whether a custodial sentence is the most appropriate disposal, the court should take into account any available information concerning the future care of the child.

(e)   Where the offender is the sole or primary carer of the victim or other dependants, this potentially should be taken into account for sentencing purposes, regardless of whether the offender is male or female. In such cases, an immediate custodial sentence may not be appropriate.

(f)   The most relevant areas of personal mitigation are likely to be:
• Mental illness/depression
• Inability to cope with the pressures of parenthood
• Lack of support
• Sleep deprivation
• Offender dominated by an abusive or stronger partner
• Extreme behavioural difficulties in a child, often coupled with lack of support
• Inability to secure assistance or support services in spite of every effort having been made by the offender

Some of the factors identified above, in particular sleep deprivation, lack of support and an inability to cope, could be regarded as an inherent part of caring for children, especially when a child is very young and could be put forward as mitigation by most carers charged with an offence of child cruelty. It follows that, before being accepted as mitigation, there must be evidence that these factors were present to a high degree and had an identifiable and significant impact on the offender's behaviour.

This is a serious offence for the purposes of the public protection provisions in the Criminal Justice Act 2003. Refer to B[16.5] and consult legal adviser for guidance

OFFENCE SERIOUSNESS (CULPABILITY AND HARM)

A. IDENTIFY THE APPROPRIATE STARTING POINT

Starting points based on first time offender pleading not guilty

Examples of nature of activity	Starting point	Range
(i) Short term neglect or ill-treatment. (ii) Single incident of short-term abandonment. (iii) Failure to protect a child from any of the above.	12 weeks custody	Low level community order to 26 weeks custody
(i) Assault(s) resulting in injuries consistent with ABH. (ii) More than one incident of neglect or ill-treatment (but not amounting to long-term behaviour. (iii) Single incident of long-term abandonment OR regular incidents of short-term abandonment (the longer the period of long-term abandonment or the greater the number of incidents of short-term abandonment, the more serious the offence). (iv) Failure to protect a child from any of the above.	Crown Court	26 weeks to Crown Court
(i) Series of assaults (the more serious the individual assaults an the longer the period over which they are perpetrated, the more serious the offence. (ii) Protracted neglect or ill-treatment (the longer the period of ill-treatment or neglect and the longer the period over which it takes place, the more serious the offence). (iii) Failure to protect a child from any of the above.	Crown	Crown Court
(i) Serious cruelty over a period of time.	Crown Court	Crown Court

(ii) Serious long-term neglect.		
(iii) Failure to protect a child from any of the above.		

OFFENCE SERIOUSNESS (CULPABILITY AND HARM)

B. CONSIDER THE EFFECT OF AGGRAVATING AND MITIGATING FACTORS (OTHER THAN THOSE WITHIN THE EXAMPLES ABOVE)

Common aggravating and mitigating factors are identified at B[5.2A]. The following may be particularly relevant but these lists are not exhaustive

Factors indicating higher culpability	*Factor indicating lower culpability*
1. Targeting one particular child from family.	1. Seeking medical help or bringing the situation to the notice of the authorities.
2. Sadistic behaviour.	
3. Threats to prevent the victim from reporting the offence.	
4. Deliberate concealment of the victim from the authorities.	
5. Failure to seek medical help.	

FORM A PRELIMINARY VIEW OF THE APPROPRIATE SENTENCE, THEN CONSIDER OFFENDER MITIGATION

Common factors are identified at B[5.2A]

CONSIDER A REDUCTION FOR A GUILTY PLEA

CONSIDER ANCILLARY ORDERS, INCLUDING COMPENSATION

Consult your legal adviser on guidance for available ANCILLARY ORDERS

Refer to B[18] for guidance on compensation.

DECIDE SENTENCE

GIVE REASONS

A[19.33] Available sentences. See Table A at B[4.1].

If two or more children are concerned in the same occasion then all of them can be included in one charge and if this is done then only one penalty can be imposed for the one collective charge and not a penalty for each child (s 14). If the prosecution has brought a separate charge for each child, then a separate penalty can be ordered for each charge.

A[19.34] As mentioned above, if in the case of an individual child one information is laid alleging assault, ill-treatment, neglect, etc, only one penalty may be imposed.

A[20]

Disorderly behaviour
(harassment, alarm or distress)
Racially/religiously aggravated disorderly
behaviour
(harassment, alarm or distress)

Charges

A[20.1] Using threatening or abusive words or behaviour or disorderly behaviour (or displaying any writing, sign or other visible representation which is threatening or abusive) within the hearing or sight of a person likely to be caused harassment, alarm or distress thereby

Public Order Act 1986, s 5

Maximum penalty – Fine level 3. Triable only by magistrates.

NB: A fixed penalty of £80 is available for a s 5 offence of disorderly behaviour

A[20.2] Racially or religiously aggravated threats, threatening or abusive or disorderly behaviour.

Crime and Disorder Act 1998, s 31

Maximum penalty – Fine level 4. Triable only by magistrates.

Legal notes and definitions

A[20.3] This offence is designed to deal with such cases as groups of youths persistently shouting abuse and obscenities, rowdy behaviour in the street late at night, hooligans causing disturbances in the common parts of flats, banging on doors, knocking over dustbins and throwing items downstairs.

A[20.3A] Harassment; alarm; distress. Distress by its very nature involved an element of emotional disturbance or upset. The same could not be said of harassment. A person could be seriously harassed without any emotional disturbance or upset (*Southard v DPP* [2006] All ER (D) 101 (Nov), distinguishing on the facts *R v DPP* [2006] All ER (D) 250 (May)).

Taking a photograph of the complainant; transferring the photograph onto a computer followed by a posting of the same on the internet with the words "C'mon I'd love to eat you! We're the Covance Cannibals" held to amount to *intentional harassment* etc where the complainant was shown a hard copy some five months later (*S v DPP* judgment delivered February 8, 2008).

A[20.4] The charge. Only one offence is created. However, the racially/religiously aggravated offence can be heard at the same time as alternative offences (*R (CPS) v Blaydon Youth Court* (2004)).

A[20.5] Threatening; abusive; ECHR. See A[21] and A[21.5].

The principles governing the relationship between s 5 and article 10 could be summarised as follows. The starting point was the importance of the right to freedom of expression, but it was recognised that legitimate protest could be offensive, at least to some. The justification for interference had to be convincingly established and the restrictions in art 10(2) were to be construed narrowly. The justification for invoking the criminal law was the threat to public order and was for the Crown to establish. If the line between legitimate freedom of expression and a threat to public order was crossed, freedom of speech would not be impaired by 'ruling out' threatening, abusive speech: *Abdul v DPP* [2011] EWHC 247 (Admin), 175 JP 190, [2011] Crim LR 553.

See further, A[20.17], below.

A[20.5A] Disorderly. A court is entitled to conclude that walking naked through a town centre violates public order and is thus 'disorderly': *Gough v DPP* [2013] EWHC 3267 (Admin), (2013) 177 JP 669.

A[20.6] Racially/religiously aggravated. This means that at the time of committing the offence, or immediately before or after doing so, the offender demonstrates towards the victim of the offence, hostility based on the victim's membership (or presumed membership) of a racial or religious group, or the offence is motivated (wholly or partly) by hostility towards members of a racial or religious group based on their membership of that group.

Use of the words 'bloody foreigners' and 'go back to your own country' was capable of amounting to racially aggravated abuse (*R v Rogers* [2007] UKHL 8). The court should focus on whether the alleged remark had been made, whether it was a remark which demonstrated racial hostility, and whether s 28(1)(a) or (b) was engaged. On the facts found it was impossible to say whether the offence was motivated in part by racial hostility or by something quite different, namely the defendant's removal from hospital premises: see *R (on the application of the Director of Public Prosecutions) v Dykes* [2008] EWHC 2775 (Admin), (2009) 173 JP 88.

In *Kendall v South East Essex Magistrates' Court* [2008] All ER (D) 356 (Jun) it was open to justices to conclude that the defendant had been aware that posters which he had put on an advertising pillar, and which displayed the words "illegal, immigrant, murdered, scum" had conveyed the message that black people who committed crimes like murder were "scum".

Having regard to the language of s 28(1)(b) of the CDA 1998, if there is no evidence of racial or religious motivation there could be no conviction. See (*DPP v Howard* [2008] All ER (D) 88 (Feb)). Where a charge is brought under s 28(1)(a), the test is objective and the prosecution do not have to prove motive, simply the relevant behaviour: *Jones v DPP* [2010] EWHC 523 (Admin), [2010] 3 All ER 1057, 174 JP 278.

A[20.7] It is immaterial whether or not the offender's hostility is also based, to any extent, on any other factor not mentioned above, nor is the victim's perception nor the defendant's usual usage of the words uttered relevant (*DPP v Woods* [2002] EWHC 85 (Admin), [2002] All ER (D) 154 (Jan)).

A[20.8] Another person. The defendant's behaviour must be within the hearing or sight of a person likely to be caused harassment etc. The prosecution must identify the person who was likely to have been alarmed etc though he need not be called as a witness. In *Chambers and Edwards v DPP* [1995] Crim LR 896 demonstrators made it difficult for a surveyor to carry out his work. Although the surveyor was in no fear for his safety, his annoyance and inconvenience were sufficient to meet the requirements of the section. For further developments see *R (on the application of Reda) v DPP* [2011] EWHC 1550 (Admin) at A[9.5]. In *Harvey v DPP* [2011] EWHC 3992 (Admin), 176 JP 265, [2012] Crim LR 553, commonplace swear words used by the appellant were capable of causing police officers to experience harassment, alarm or distress. Much would depend on the facts, but where a witness was silent on the point, it would be wrong to draw inferences. Accordingly, there was no evidence whereby the justices could have concluded that either police officer had been caused or was likely to have been caused harassment, alarm or distress. As for a group of young people who gathered during the exchanges, the words uttered were commonplace swear words in contrast to the far more offensive terms used in the case of *Taylor v DPP* [2006] EWHC 1202 (Admin), 170 JP 485, 170 JPN 856. It was wrong to infer, in the absence of evidence of evidence from any of them, that one or more persons would have experienced harassment, alarm or distress. As for neighbours and people in the adjoining flats, there was no evidence that anybody other than the group of young people was within earshot. If there had been evidence, for example, of apparently frightened neighbours leaning out of windows or of similar passers-by within earshot, that might have formed the basis of a finding that such persons were caused alarm or distress.

A[20.9] *Vigon v DPP* (1997) 162 JP 115, [1998] Crim LR 289 – A concealed camera in a changing cubicle is capable of being disorderly [and insulting] behaviour.

A[20.10] Intent. The accused must intend his words or behaviour etc to be, or be aware that his words etc may be threatening, abusive, or intend his behaviour to be or is aware that it may be disorderly.

A[20.11]–[20.15] Visible Representation. *Norwood v DPP* [2003] EWHC 1564 (Admin), [2003] Crim LR 888 set out the four elements that need to be proved in such a case, namely: (1) a fact – display by a defendant of a visible representation; (2) a value judgment that the representation is threatening, abusive or insulting; (3) a fact – that the defendant either intended, or was aware that it might be, threatening, abusive or insulting; and (4) a mixed fact and value judgment – that the display was within sight of a person likely to be caused, harassment, alarm or distress by it.

A[20.16] Intoxication. See under the offence of violent disorder, at A[67]. Disorderly conduct may be committed in a public or private place. For offences committed in dwelling-houses see under the offence of threatening behaviour below, at A[21].

A[20.17] Defences. Where the accused proves

(a) that he had no reason to believe that there was any person within hearing or sight who was likely to be caused harassment, alarm or distress, or

(b) that he was inside a dwelling and had no reason to believe that the words or behaviour used, or the writing, sign or other visible representation displayed, would be heard or seen by a person outside that or any other dwelling, or

(c) that his conduct was reasonable,

he must be acquitted. He does not have to establish his defence beyond a reasonable doubt, but only on the balance of probabilities.

It was stated in *Norwood v DPP*, above, that '[20 . . . in this statutory context, whatever the nature of the burden cast on the defence, it is, in any event, hard to find much of a role for any of the s 5(3) defences, directed, as they are, to an objective assessment by the court of the reasonableness of the accused's conduct. That is because the essentials of the basic s 5 offence require the court to be satisfied as to the accused's subjective state of mind, namely that he intended that the representation should be, or was aware that it might be, threatening, abusive or insulting. See eg *DPP v Clarke* (1991) 94 Cr App Rep 359, per Nolan LJ. If the s 5(3) burden on the defence is to be "read down" to an evidential burden so as to make it Convention compliant, with the result of casting upon the prosecution the burden of disproving it, it would be harder to find any sensible role for s 5(3) . . . '.

The defence of reasonable conduct is to be viewed objectively: *DPP v Clarke* (1991) 156 JP 267. In a case involving the defacement of the American flag (the defendant's own property) near the gate of an RAF base, in the course of a protest against the use of weapons of mass destruction and American military policy including the national missile defence system, it was held that the court had to presume that the defendant's conduct was protected by art 10 unless and until it was established that a restriction on her freedom was strictly necessary. While the district judge had been entitled to find that there was a pressing social need in a multicultural society to prevent the denigration of objects of veneration and symbolic importance for one social group, the next stage was to assess whether or not interference, by means of prosecution, with the defendant's right to free expression by using her own property to convey a lawful message, was a proportionate response to that aim, and the fact that the defendant could have demonstrated in other ways was only one factor to be taken into account when determining the overall reasonableness of the defendant's behaviour and the state's response to it: *Percy v DPP* [2001] EWHC Admin 1125, (2001) 166 JP 93, [2002] Crim LR 835.

A[20.18] **Power of arrest.** Police powers of arrest under what was s 5 of the Public Order Act 1986 are now governed by s 24 of the Police and Criminal Evidence Act 1984 as substituted by Part 3, s 110 of the Serious Organised Crime and Police Act 2005.

For the police to justify an arrest a constable has to show two things: first, under the Police and Criminal Evidence Act 1984, s 24(2), that he had reasonable grounds for suspecting that an offence had been committed and that H was guilty of it; second, that he had reasonable grounds for believing that it was necessary to arrest H to allow the prompt and effective investigation of the offence, as per s 24(4) and s 24(5)(e): see *Hayes v Chief Constable of Merseyside* [2011] EWCA Civ 911, [2012] 1 WLR 517, [2011] 2 Cr App Rep 434.

Sentencing

A[20.19] **Domestic violence.** See SC Definitive Guideline: "Overarching Principles: Domestic Violence".

Available sentences. See Table C at B[4.3].

These offences are is not imprisonable and therefore sentences such as detention in a young offender institution are *not* available.

SC Guideline – (1) Disorderly behaviour (harassment, alarm or distress) (2) Racially or religiously aggravated disorderly behaviour

OFFENCE SERIOUSNESS (CULPABILITY AND HARM)		
A. IDENTIFY THE APPROPRIATE STARTING POINT		
Starting points based on first time offender pleading not guilty		
Examples of nature of activity	**Starting point**	**Range**
Shouting, causing disturbance for some minutes	Band A fine	Conditional discharge to band B fine
Substantial disturbance caused	Band B fine	Band A fine to band C fine

OFFENCE SERIOUSNESS (CULPABILITY AND HARM)

B. CONSIDER THE EFFECT OF AGGRAVATING AND MITIGATING FACTORS (OTHER THAN THOSE WITHIN THE EXAMPLES ABOVE)

Common aggravating and mitigating factors are identified at B[5.2A]. The following may be particularly relevant but **these lists are not exhaustive**

Factors indicating higher culpability	*Factors indicating lower culpability*
1. Group action	1. Stopping as soon as police arrvied
2. Lengthy incident	2. Brief/minor incident
	3. Provocation
Factors indicating greater degree of harm	
1. Vulnerable person(s) present	
2. Offence committed at school, hospital or other place where vulnerable persons may be present	
3. Victim providing public service	

FORM A PRELIMINARY VIEW OF THE APPROPRIATE SENTENCE

IF OFFENDER CHARGED AND CONVICTED OF THE RACIALLY OR RELIGIOUSLY AGGRAVATED OFFENCE, INCREASE THE SENTENCE TO REFLECT THIS ELEMENT

Refer to B[5.2B] for guidance

CONSIDER OFFENDER MITIGATION

Common factors are identified at B[5.2A]

CONSIDER A REDUCTION FOR A GUILTY PLEA

CONSIDER ANCILLARY ORDERS, INCLUDING COMPENSATION AND FOOTBALL BANNING ORDER (where appropriate)

Consult your legal adviser on guidance for available ANCILLARY ORDERS

DECIDE SENTENCE

GIVE REASONS

A[20.20] **Bind over.** See the amended Consolidated Criminal Practice Direction and associated notes at **[B10]** onwards.

A[21]

(1) Threatening behaviour
(2) Racially or religiously aggravated threatening behaviour
(3) Disorderly behaviour with intent to cause harassment, alarm or distress
(4) Racially or religiously aggravated disorderly behaviour with intent to cause harassment, alarm or distress

Charge 1

A[21.1] Using towards another threatening, abusive or insulting words or behaviour (or distributing or displaying to another person any writing, sign or other visible representation being threatening, abusive or insulting) intending to cause that other person to believe that immediate unlawful violence would be used against him or another by any person, or to provoke the immediate use of unlawful violence by that person or another or whereby that other person was likely to believe that such violence would be used or it was likely that such violence would be provoked

Public Order Act 1986, s 4(1)

Maximum penalty – Fine level 5 and 6 months. Triable only by magistrates.

Charge 2

A[21.2] A person is guilty of an offence if with intent to cause a person harassment, alarm and distress, he

(a)   uses threatening, abusive or insulting words or behaviour, or
(b)   displays any writing, sign or visible representation which is threatening, abusive or insulting,

thereby causing that or another person harassment, alarm or distress

Public Order Act 1986, s 4A

Maximum penalty – Fine level 4 and 6 months. Triable only by magistrates.

Charge 3

A[21.3] Using towards another threatening, abusive or insulting words or behaviour etc which was racially or religiously aggravated.

Crime and Disorder Act 1998, s 31

Maximum penalty – see Charge 4 below.

Charge 4

A[21.4] Intentional harassment alarm or distress etc which is racially or religiously aggravated.

Crime and Disorder Act 1998, s 31

Maximum penalty – Fine level 5 and 6 months' imprisonment. Triable either way. Specified violent offence under Sch 15, Part 1, CJA 2003.

Crown Court – 2 years' imprisonment and unlimited fine.

Legal notes and definitions

A[21.5] Although s 4(1) creates only one offence, that offence may be committed in four different ways. Common to all four is the requirement that the accused must intend or be aware that his words or behaviour are or may be threatening, abusive or insulting, and must be directed to another person: see *Winn v DPP* (1992) 156 JP 881. The words 'uses towards another person' mean that threatening words must be addressed directly to another person who is present and either in earshot or aimed at as being putatively in earshot: *Atkin v DPP* (1989) 153 JP 383, [1989] Crim LR 581, DC. It is inappropriate to use the words 'another person' in an information charging an offence under s 4 because the person in whom the belief that unlawful violence would be used has to be the same person as the person threatened, abused or insulted: see *Loade v DPP* (1990) 90 Cr App Rep 162.

Threatening; abusive; insulting. (The following comments are based on repealed legislation but still seem applicable.) The High Court has described these as being 'all very strong words'. If the evidence shows that the words or behaviour used fell short of being abusive, insulting or threatening but merely annoying then the case should be dismissed. The words 'f . . . off' shouted at a police officer who was trying to prevent a breach of the peace have been held to be 'insulting'. Shouting encouragement to a gang throwing stones at another gang is sufficient for a conviction under this section. See *Hammond v DPP* [2004] EWHC 69 (Admin), [2004] All ER (D) 50 (Jan) and *Percy v DPP* [2001] EWHC 1125 (Admin), 166 JP 93, [2002] Crim LR 835, [2001] All ER (D) 387 (Dec). Insulting words or an insulting sign should cause harassment, alarm or distress to another not just strong disagreement.

A[21.5A] ECHR. In *Dehal v DPP* [2005] EWHC 2154 (Admin), (2005) 169 JP 581, the defendant had entered a Sikh Temple and affixed a notice to a notice board which, inter alia, described the president of the Temple as a hypocrite. The Administrative Court held that in order to justify the interference with a right to freedom of expression as set out in art 10 of the ECHR, the prosecution had to demonstrate that the prosecution was being brought in pursuance of a legitimate aim and that the prosecution was the minimum necessary response to that aim. Accordingly, the prosecution of the defendant had not been a proportionate response to his conduct. However, there were indications in *Bauer v DPP* [2013] EWHC 634 (Admin), [2013] WLR 3616, (2013) 177 JP 177 by the same judge (Moses LJ) at para 40 that the imposition of such a burden on the prosecution might be open to question, and it is submitted that it is difficult to reconcile with the well established line of authority that it is not for courts to question how prosecutorial discretion is exercised.

A[21.6] Violence does not include violence justified by law (eg self-defence or prevention of crime). The violence apprehended must be immediate which does not mean 'instantaneous' but connotes proximity in time and causation (*R v Horseferry Road Metropolitan Stipendiary Magistrate, ex p Siadatan* [1991] 1 QB 260, [1991] 1 All ER 324). Where the defendant threatened to shoot the complainant coupled with a shooting gesture with his hand, the combination of the hand gesture together with his loud and threatening language satisfied the test of 'immediacy' (*Liverpool v DPP* [2008] EWHC 2540 (Admin), [2008] All ER (D) 50 (Oct)). For what is included under the offence of violent disorder see **A[67]**.

A[21.7] Intent. The accused must *intend* his words or behaviour etc to be, or be aware that his words etc may be, threatening, abusive or insulting and intend the apprehension of unlawful violence etc. It does not have to be shown what the other person in fact believed; it has to be shown that the defendant had the intention to cause that person to believe. This can be proved by any admissible evidence and it is not necessary for the person to whom the threats or insulting behaviour were directed to give evidence: *Swanston v DPP* (1996) 161 JP 203.

In order to ensure that an arrest is lawful the defendant must be warned first about his conduct. This warning is not however part of the offence and so a case can still be determined where the arrest was not lawful (*DPP v Chippendale* [2004] EWHC 464 (Admin), [2004] All ER (D) 308 (Jan)).

Where an appellant had struggled whilst restrained by nightclub doormen, a magistrates' court was entitled to convict him under s 4(1) of the Public Order Act 1986 on the basis that he had intended to cause the doormen to believe that he would use unlawful violence against them if they released him: *Knight v DPP* [2012] EWHC 605 (Admin), 176 JP 177.

By contrast, a court erred in concluding that the appellant had intended to cause his victim to believe that unlawful violence would be used against him, where the appellant had approached the victim in such a way that the victim had not realised that he was about to be attacked: *Hughes v DPP* [2012] EWHC 606 (Admin), [2012] All ER (D) 180 (Jan). The appellant should have been charged with assault by beating.

A[21.8] Intoxication. See under the offence of violent disorder at **A[67]**.

A[21.9] Threatening etc behaviour may be committed in a public or private place. If the threatening etc words or behaviour are used inside a dwelling-house, the offence can only be committed if the other person is not inside that or another dwelling-house, but parts of a dwelling not occupied as a person's house or living accommodation do not count as a dwelling for this purpose, eg the shop underneath the owner's flat; a laundry used by the residents of a block of flats: *Ian Norman Levine v DPP* [2010] May 6, 2010, QBD. A tent, caravan, vehicle, vessel or other temporary or movable structure may be a dwelling for this purpose where it is occupied as a person's house or as other living accommodation. A police cell could not be classified as a dwelling or living accommodation for the purposes of s 4A (2) of the Public Order Act 1986 (*R v Francis* [2007] EWCA Crim 3323).

A[21.10]–[21.15] Racial/religious aggravation. See **A[20.6]**. Words such as 'jungle bunny', 'black bastard' and 'wog' will be a racial aggravation regardless of the fact that the defendant may have some other reason to abuse the victim (*DPP v McFarlane* [2002] EWHC 485 (Admin), [2002] All ER (D) 78 (Mar)). Use of the words "bloody foreigners" and "go back to your own country" was capable of being racially aggravated abuse

(*R v Rogers* [2007] UKHL 8).

May often be sent to Crown Court for sentence and will usually result in a custodial sentence (*R v Miller* [1999] 2 Cr App Rep (S) 392, [1999] Crim LR 590, CA and *R v White* [2001] EWCA Crim 216 [2001] 1 WLR 1352, [2001] Crim LR 576).

Police officers are also entitled to the protection of the courts. See *Re Emma Lisa Jacobs* (2001) where a sentence of 3 months' imprisonment was upheld.

Sentencing
SC Guideline – (1) Threatening behaviour (2) Racially or religiously aggravated threatening behaviour

A[21.16] (Section 4A disorderly behaviour and the racially/religiously aggravated SC guideline is at **A[21.17]** below)

Domestic violence. See SC Definitive Guideline: "Overarching Principles: Domestic Violence"

OFFENCE SERIOUSNESS (CULPABILITY AND HARM)		
A. IDENTIFY THE APPROPRIATE STARTING POINT		
Starting points based on first time offender pleading not guilty		
Examples of nature of activity	Starting point	Range
Fear or threat of low level immediate unlawful violence such as push, shove or spit	Low level community penalty	Band B fine to medium level community order
Fear or threat or medium level immediate unlawful violence such as punch	High level community order	Low level community order to 12 weeks custody
Fear or threat of high level immediate unlawful violence such as use of weapon; missile thrown; gang involvement	12 weeks custody	6 to 26 weeks custody
OFFENCE SERIOUSNESS (CULPABILITY AND HARM)		
B. CONSIDER THE EFFECT OF AGGRAVATING AND MITIGATING FACTORS (OTHER THAN THOSE WITHIN EXAMPLES ABOVE)		
Common aggravating and mitigating factors are identified at B[5.2A]. The following may be particularly relevant but **these lists are not exhaustive**		
Factors indicating higher culpability		*Factors indicating lower culpability*
1. Planning		1. Impulsive action
2. Offender deliberately isolates victim		2. Short duration
3. Group action		3. Provocation
4. Threat directed at victim because of job		
5. History of antagonism towards victim		
Factors indicating greater degree of harm		

1. Offence committed at school, hospital or other place where vulnerable victims may be present	
2. Offence committed on enclosed premises such as public transport	
3. Vulnerable victim(s)	
4. Victim needs medical help/counselling	

FORM A PRELIMINARY VIEW OF THE APPROPRIATE SENTENCE

IF OFFENDER CHARGED AND CONVICTED OF THE RACIALLY OR RELIGIOUSLY AGGRAVATED OFFENCE, INCREASE THE SENTENCE TO REFLECT THE ELEMENT

Common factors are identified at B[5.2B]

CONSIDER OFFENDER MITIGATION

Common factors are identified at B[5.2A]

CONSIDER A REDUCTION FOR A GUILTY PLEA

CONSIDER ANCILLARY ORDERS, INCLUDING COMPENSATION AND FOOTBALL BANNING ORDER (where appropriate)

Refer to B[18] **for guidance on compensation.**

DECIDE SENTENCE

GIVE REASONS

SC Guideline – (3) Disorderly behaviour with intent etc (4) Racially or religiously aggravated threatening behaviour with intent etc

A[21.17] (Section 4 threatening behaviour and the racially/religiously aggravated SC guideline is at **A[21.16]** above)

Domestic violence. See SC Definitive Guideline: "Overarching Principles: Domestic Violence"

OFFENCE SERIOUSNESS (CULPABILITY AND HARM)		
A. IDENTIFY THE APPROPRIATE STARTING POINT		
Starting points based on first time offender pleading not guilty		
Examples of nature of activity	**Starting point**	**Range**
Threats, abuse or insults made more than once but on same occasion against the same person eg while following down the street	Band C fine	Band B fine to low level community order
Group action or deliberately planned action against targeted victim	Medium level community order	Low level community order to 12 weeks custody
Weapon brandished or used or threats against vulnerable victim – course of conduct over longer period	12 weeks custody	High level community order to 26 weeks custody
OFFENCE SERIOUSNESS (CULPABILITY AND HARM)		

B. CONSIDER THE EFFECT OF AGGRAVATING AND MITIGATING FACTORS (OTHER THAN THOSE WITHIN EXAMPLES ABOVE)	
Common aggravating and mitigating factors are identified at B[5.2A].The following may be particularly relevant but **these lists are not exhaustive**	
Factors indicating higher culpability	*Factors indicating lower culpability*
1. High degree of planning	1. Very short period
2. Offender deliberately isolates victim	2. Provocation
Factors indicating greater degree of harm	
1. Offence committed in vicinity of victim's home	
2. Large number of people in vicinity	
3. Actual or potential escalation into violence	
4. Particularly serious impact on victim	

FORM A PRELIMINARY VIEW OF THE APPROPRIATE SENTENCE
IF OFFENDER CHARGED AND CONVICTED OF THE RACIALLY OR RELIGIOUSLY AGGRAVATED OFFENCE, INCREASE THE SENTENCE TO REFLECT THE ELEMENT
Common factors are identified at B[5.2B]
CONSIDER OFFENDER MITIGATION
Common factors are identified at B[5.2A]
CONSIDER A REDUCTION FOR A GUILTY PLEA
CONSIDER ANCILLARY ORDERS, INCLUDING COMPENSATION AND FOOTBALL BANNING ORDER (where appropriate)
Refer to B[18] for guidance on compensation.
DECIDE SENTENCE
GIVE REASONS

A[21.18] Bind over. See the amended Consolidated Criminal Practice Direction and associated notes at B[10] onwards.

A[22]

Drugs

A[22.1] The misuse of drugs is made unlawful by the Misuse of Drugs Act 1971, which introduced the term 'controlled drugs' (ie drugs, the use of which is controlled by the Act). The second schedule of the Act allocates controlled drugs to Classes A, B or C and maximum penalties vary according to the class to which a controlled drug belongs.

A[22.2] The second schedule can be varied by an order in council. Magistrates will be able to ascertain full details from their legal adviser; the following table sets out the class of some of the commoner controlled drugs.

A[22.3] The sections mentioned below are sections of the Act.

A[22.4] Class A

Cocaine, heroin, LSD, morphine, opium, ecstasy (MDMA), *methylamphetamine (crystal meth) remifentanil and dihydroetrophine.

*Reclassified for offences on or after 18/1/07.

A[22.5] Class B

Amphetamines, codeine, dexedrine, methadrine, some derivatives of morphine, preludin and for offences committed on or after 26 January 2009 cannabis and cannabis resin has been reclassified as a Class B drug.

A[22.6] Class C

Lucofen, mandrax and villescon, Gammahydroxy-butyrate (GHB) and zolpidem.

The text below concerns two drug offences which seem likely to be among the most frequently committed offences created by the Act. These are the offences created by the Misuse of Drugs Act 1971, ss 5(2) and 5(3).

A[23]

Drugs – class A – failure to attend initial/ remain for initial assessment

(Drugs Act 2005)

Charge

A[23.1] A person who, by virtue of s 9 (2) of the Drugs Act 2005, without good cause—

(a)   fails to attend an initial drugs assessment at the specified time and place, or

(b)   attends the assessment at the specified time and place but fails to remain for its duration

shall be guilty of an offence.

Drugs Act 2005, s 12

Maximum penalty. A person guilty of an offence under s 12 is liable on summary conviction to a punishment not exceeding 3 months or to a level 4 fine or both.

Legal notes and definitions

A[23.2] If a person fails to attend an initial assessment at the specified time and place, any requirement imposed on him by virtue of s 10(2) ie a "follow-up assessment" ceases to have effect.

Sentencing
SC Guideline – Drugs – class A – fail to attend/remain for initial assessment

A[23.3]

OFFENCE SERIOUSNESS (CULPABILITY AND HARM)		
A. IDENTIFY THE APPROPRIATE STARTING POINT		
Starting points based on first time offender pleading not guilty		
Examples of nature of activity	**Starting point**	**Range**
Failure to attend at the appointed place and time	Medium level community order	Band C fine to high level community order
OFFENCE SERIOUSNESS (CULPABILITY AND HARM)		
B. CONSIDER THE EFFECT OF AGGRAVATING AND MITIGATING FACTORS (OTHER THAN THOSE WITHIN EXAMPLES ABOVE)		
Common aggravating and mitigating factors are identified at B[5.2A]. The following may be particularly relevant but these lists are not exhaustive		
Factor indicating higher culpability	*Factors indicating lower culpability*	

| 1. Threats or abuse to assessor or other staff | 1. Offender turns up but at wrong place and time or fails to remain for duration of appointment |
| | 2. Subsequent voluntary contact to rearrange appointment |

FORM A PRELIMINARY VIEW OF THE APPROPRIATE SENTENCE, THEN CONSIDER OFFENDER MITIGATION

Common factors are identified at B[5.2A]

CONSIDER A REDUCTION FOR A GUILTY PLEA

CONSIDER ANCILLARY ORDERS

Refer to Part B for guidance on available ancillary orders

DECIDE SENTENCE

GIVE REASONS

A[24]

Drugs – class A – fail/refuse to provide a sample

Charge

A[24.1] A person who by virtue of this section, fails without good cause to give any sample which may be taken from him shall be guilty of an offence.

Police and Criminal Evidence Act 1984, s 63B

Maximum penalty. A person guilty of an offence under s 63B is liable on summary conviction to a punishment not exceeding 3 months or to a level 4 fine or both.

Sentencing
SGC Guideline – Drugs – class A – fail/refuse to provide a sample

A[24.2]

OFFENCE SERIOUSNESS (CULPABILITY AND HARM)		
A. IDENTIFY THE APPROPRIATE STARTING POINT		
Starting points based on first time offender pleading not guilty		
Examples of nature of activity	**Starting point**	**Range**
Refusal where reasonable suspicion that misuse of class A drug caused or contribute to offence	Medium level community order	Band C fine to high level community order
OFFENCE SERIOUSNESS (CULPABILITY AND HARM)		
B. CONSIDER THE EFFECT OF AGGRAVATING AND MITIGATING FACTORS (OTHER THAN THOSE WITHIN EXAMPLES ABOVE)		
Common aggravating and mitigating factors are identified at B[5.2A]. The following may be particularly relevant but **these lists are not exhaustive**		
Factor indicating higher culpability	*Factors indicating lower culpability*	
1. Threats or abuse to staff	1. Subsequent voluntary with drug workers	
	2. Subsequent compliance with testing on charge	
FORM A PRELIMINARY VIEW OF THE APPROPRIATE SENTENCE, THEN CONSIDER OFFENDER MITIGATION		
Common factors are identified at B[5.2A]		
CONSIDER A REDUCTION FOR A GUILTY PLEA		
CONSIDER ANCILLARY ORDERS		
Refer to Part B for guidance on available ancillary orders		

DECIDE SENTENCE
GIVE REASONS

A[25]

Possession of a controlled drug

(Misuse of Drugs Act 1971, s 5(2))

Charge

A[25.1] Having a quantity of a controlled drug, namely [. . . . .], in his possession

Maximum penalty

Class A	level 5 and 6 months
Class B	£2,500 and 3 months
Class C	£1,000 and 3 months

Court can order forfeiture but see 'Forfeiture' below.

Crown Court -

Class A	7 years and fine
Class B	5 years and fine
Class C	2 years and fine

Triable either way in respect of any class of drug although see A[25.3] below.

Mode of trial

A[25.2] See the SC guidelines below.

A[25.3] Possession of Class A drugs – see **SC Guideline** at **A[25.16]** below.

It should be noted that the Powers of Criminal Courts (Sentencing) Act 2000, s 110 makes provision for the imposition of a minimum seven-year custodial sentence on 18-year-olds and above who have been convicted of a third Class A drug trafficking offence.

A[25.4] Possession of class B or C drugs – see SC Guideline at **A[25.16]** below.

Legal notes and definitions

A[25.5] Quantity. The charge should state the quantity involved. If it is a diminutive quantity consult the legal adviser. Scrapings from a pocket can be enough. A few droplets in a tube only discernible microscopically are not enough; the court must be satisfied that there is sufficient there to amount to something. If the quantity is very small it may be relevant to the question of the accused's knowledge that it was in his possession.

A[25.6] Expert examination. The court should be satisfied that an expert has confirmed that the substance is the controlled drug alleged. In a contested case this would have to be proved by the prosecution or admitted by the defendant.

A[25.7] Possession. The Act does not contain a definition of 'possession' but the nature of possession has received extensive consideration in case law, in particular by the House of Lords in *R v Lambert* [2001] UKHL 37, [2002] 2 AC 545, [2001] 3 All ER 577, [2001] 3 WLR 206 (see below).

Possession embraces both a factual and a mental element.

The factual element is control. Section 37(3) provides that for the purposes of the Act the things which a person has in his possession shall be taken to include anything subject to his control which is in the custody of another. In *R v Wright* (1975) 119 Sol Jo 825 a distinction was made between mere physical custody of an object, and its possession for the commission of an offence. The defendant was given a container and told to throw it away, which he did instantly: he could not be convicted although he suspected it might contain drugs. A person having given directions to a supplier, following which he receives a parcel containing a drug through his letter-box, becomes the possessor of the drug once the parcel is put through the letter-box: *R v Peaston* [1979] Crim LR 183. If a person smokes cannabis resin he must have cannabis resin in his possession at the time of smoking: *Chief Constable of Cheshire Constabulary v Hunt* (1983) 147 JP 567. Once a controlled drug has been consumed and has changed in character, the consumer could not then be said to be 'in possession' of it, though it might be evidence of possession immediately before he consumed it: *Hambleton v Callinan* [1968] 2 QB 427, [1968] 2 All ER 943, 132 JP 461.

The mental element. The mental element in offences contrary to s 5 was exhaustively considered by the House of Lords in *R v Lambert*, above from which the following propositions are derived.

The prosecution must prove:

(a)   the defendant was in possession of something;
(b)   the defendant knew he was in possession of that something; and
(c)   the thing which the defendant possessed was a controlled drug.

Lack of knowledge. The prosecution is not required to prove that the defendant knew that the thing which he possessed was a controlled drug but if the prosecution have adduced sufficient evidence to prove (a)–(c), s 28(2), (3) post, stipulates the way in which lack of knowledge etc can be a defence in proceedings. To bring himself within the provisions of s 28 (2), (3) the defendant must satisfy an evidential burden of adducing evidence which is sufficient to raise the issue of knowledge. If sufficient evidence is adduced to raise the issue, it will be for the prosecution to show beyond reasonable doubt that the defence is not made out by the evidence.

Quantity is of importance in two respects when determining whether or not an accused person has a controlled drug in his possession. First, is the quantity sufficient to enable a court to find as a matter of fact that it amounts to something? If it is visible, tangible and measurable, it is certainly something. The question is one of fact for the commonsense of the tribunal. Secondly, quantity may be relevant to the issue of knowledge. If the quantity in custody or control is minute, the question arises – was it so minute that it cannot be proved that the accused knew he had it? If knowledge cannot be proved, possession is not established: *R v Boyeson* [1982] AC 768, [1982] 2 All ER 161, 146 JP 217, HL. See also *R v Colyer*

[1974] Crim LR 243 (minute quantity) and *R v Ashton Rickardt* [1977] Crim LR 424. As to aggregating several amounts of a drug, see *R v Bayliss and Oliver* [1978] Crim LR 361. As to conviction for possessing a lesser amount than charged, see *R v Peevey* (1973) 57 Cr App Rep 554, CA.

Mere presence in the same vehicle as cannabis, even if someone had said there was cannabis in the car, is not sufficient to prove possession: *R v Strong* and *R v Berry* [1989] 10 LS Gaz R 41, CA.

Once the prosecution proves that the defendant had control of a box which he was delivering on his motor cycle and knew it contained something, which was in fact the drug alleged, he has the onus of bringing himself within the provisions of s 28(3): see *R v McNamara* (1988) 87 Cr App Rep 246, 152 JP 390 approved in *R v Lambert*, above.

A[25.7A] Controlled drug. Where an experienced drug user admits possession of a substance which he himself identifies as a controlled drug, that admission and identification are sufficient to provide prima facie evidence of the nature of the substance and of unlawful possession of a controlled drug: see *R v Chatwood* [1980] 1 All ER 467, [1980] 1 WLR 874. It is important that the prosecution should prove possession of the drug as charged: see *Muir v Smith* [1978] Crim LR 293 where the prosecution failed as it could not be ascertained whether the substance was cannabis or herbal cannabis.

A[25.8] Defences. Each of the following defences is expressly provided by the Act, but a defendant is also entitled to rely on other common law defences (see **A[25.8A]** below).

(a)   Authorised by regulation (s 7). After consulting the Advisory Council on the Misuse of Drugs, the Home Secretary is empowered to introduce regulations exempting certain persons (eg doctors, dentists, veterinary surgeons, pharmacists) and controlled drugs (in certain circumstances) from the scope of this offence.

or

(b)   Knowing or suspecting it was a controlled drug, the defendant took possession of it to prevent another person from committing or continuing to commit an offence with it; and further that as soon as possible after taking possession of it he took all reasonable steps to destroy it or to deliver it to a person lawfully entitled to take it (s 5(4)(a)).

or

(c)   Knowing or suspecting it was a controlled drug, the defendant took possession of it to deliver it to a person lawfully entitled to it and as soon as possible he took all reasonable steps to deliver it to that person (s 5(4)(b)).

or

(d)   The defendant neither knew nor suspected, nor had reason to suspect, the existence of any fact (except whether the article was a controlled drug, see (e) below) which the prosecution must prove if the defendant is to be convicted (s 28(2)); eg he did not know he possessed anything (this is where quantity might be relevant). Possession is not dependent on the accused's *recollection* that he has it. Where a man had knowingly placed some cannabis in his wallet and had later forgotten it was there, he was still in possession of it. Of course it would be otherwise if a third party had slipped it in his pocket unawares so that he never knew it was there (*R v Martindale* [1986] 3 All ER 25, [1986] 1 WLR 1042, CA). [Where the defendant knew he possessed something but denies he knew it was a controlled drug the next defence ((e) below) is appropriate.]

or

(e)   In cases where the prosecution must prove that the substance or product was the controlled drug alleged in the charge and has done so, the defendant shall not be acquitted by reason only of proving that he neither knew or suspected that the substance was the particular drug alleged but shall be acquitted if he proves either:

(i)   that he neither believed nor suspected nor had reason to suspect that the substance or product was *any kind* of controlled drug, ie not just that it was not the controlled drug referred to in the charge; or

(ii)   that he believed it to be a controlled drug and that he also believed the circumstances were such that he would not be committing any offence (s 28(3)).

A[25.8A] Common law defence of necessity. In *R v Quayle and other appeals; Attorney General's Reference (No 2 of 2004)* [2005] EWCA Crim 1415, [2006] 1 All ER 988, the Court of Appeal held that the common law defence of necessity was not available for individuals who contended that they genuinely and reasonably believed that the cultivation, production, importation and possession of cannabis had been necessary to avoid them suffering serious pain or injury by reason of their medical condition.

A[25.9] Burden of proof upon the defendant. A defendant relying upon one of the above defences does not have to establish it beyond reasonable doubt. He need only establish it was more probable than not (see **ECHR (A[25.10])** below)

A[25.10] ECHR. In the light of *R v Lambert* [2001] UKHL 37, [2002] 2 AC 545, it appears that the imposition of a legal burden of proof on the accused may be disproportionate to a fair trial as required by art 6(2) ECHR. Accordingly, the MDA 1971 should be read as imposing an evidential burden on the accused ie the accused only bears the burden of raising the defence. Once raised it is for the prosecution to negative the defence beyond a reasonable doubt.

A[25.11]–[25.15] Cannabis. Means the whole or any part of the plant except cannabis resin or the separated mature stalk, fibre produced from the mature stalk or the seed.

Sentencing

SC Sentencing Guideline

Possession of a controlled drug
Misuse of Drugs Act 1971 (section 5(2))

A[25.16]

This guideline applies to all offenders aged 18 years and older, who are sentenced on or after 27 February 2012. The definitions of 'starting point' and 'first time offender' do not apply for this guideline. Starting point and category ranges apply to all offenders in all cases, irrespective of plea or previous convictions. **Triable either way**

Class A

Maximum: 7 years' custody

Offence range: Fine – 51 weeks' custody

Class B

Maximum: 5 years' custody

Offence range: Discharge – 26 weeks' custody

Class C

Maximum: 2 years' custody

Offence range: Discharge – Community order

Step One
Determining the offence category

The court should identify the offence category based on the class of drug involved.

Category 1	Class A drug
Category 2	Class B drug
Category 3	Class C drug

Step Two
Starting point and category range

The court should use the table below to identify the corresponding starting point. The starting point applies to all offenders irrespective of plea or previous convictions. The court should then consider further adjustment within the category range for aggravating or mitigating features, set out on the opposite page.

Where the defendant is dependent on or has a propensity to misuse drugs and there is sufficient prospect of success, a community order with a drug rehabilitation requirement under section 209 of the Criminal Justice Act 2003 can be a proper alternative to a short or moderate length custodial sentence.

Offence category	Starting point (applicable to all offenders)	Category range (applicable to all offenders)
Category 1 (class A)	Band C fine	Band A fine – 51 weeks' custody
Category 2 (class B)	Band B fine	Discharge – 26 weeks' custody
Category 3 (class C)	Band A fine	Discharge – medium level community order

The table below contains a **non-exhaustive** list of additional factual elements providing the context of the offence and factors relating to the offender. Identify whether any combination of these, or other relevant factors, should result in an upward or downward adjustment from the starting point. **In particular, possession of drugs in prison is likely to result in an upward adjustment.** In some cases, having considered these factors, it may be appropriate to move outside the identified category range.

Where appropriate, consider the custody threshold as follows:

*   has the custody threshold been passed?
*   if so, is it unavoidable that a custodial sentence be imposed?
*   if so, can that sentence be suspended?

Where appropriate, the court should also consider the community threshold as follows:

*   has the community threshold been passed?

Factors increasing seriousness

Statutory aggravating factors:

Previous convictions, having regard to a) nature of the offence to which conviction relates and relevance to current offence; and b) time elapsed since conviction

Offence committed on bail

Other aggravating factors include:

Possession of drug in prison

Presence of others, especially children and/or non-users

Possession of drug in a school or licensed premises

Failure to comply with current court orders

Offence committed on licence

Attempts to conceal or dispose of evidence, where not charged separately

Charged as importation of a very small amount

Established evidence of community impact

Factors reducing seriousness or reflecting personal mitigation

No previous convictions **or** no relevant or recent convictions

Remorse

Good character and/or exemplary conduct

Offender is using cannabis to help with a diagnosed medical condition

Determination and/or demonstration of steps having been taken to address addiction or offending behaviour

Serious medical conditions requiring urgent, intensive or long-term treatment

Isolated incident

Age and/or lack of maturity where it affects the responsibility of the offender

Mental disorder or learning disability

Sole or primary carer for dependent relatives

Step Three
Consider any factors which indicate a reduction, such as assistance to the prosecution

The court should take into account sections 73 and 74 of the Serious Organised Crime and Police Act 2005 (assistance by defendants: reduction or review of sentence) and any other rule of law by virtue of which an offender may receive a discounted sentence in consequence of assistance given (or offered) to the prosecutor or investigator.

Step Four
Reduction for guilty pleas

The court should take account of any potential reduction for a guilty plea in accordance with section 144 of the Criminal Justice Act 2003 and the *Guilty Plea* guideline.

Step Five
Totality principle

If sentencing an offender for more than one offence, or where the offender is already serving a sentence, consider whether the total sentence is just and proportionate to the offending behaviour.

Step Six
Ancillary orders

In all cases, the court should consider whether to make ancillary orders.

Step Seven
Reasons

Section 174 of the Criminal Justice Act 2003 imposes a duty to give reasons for, and explain the effect of, the sentence.

Step Eight
Consideration for remand time

(Now obligatory.)

A[25.17] Available sentences (Class A, B and C drugs). See Table A at B[4.1].

A[25.18] Forfeiture (s 27). The court can order the controlled drugs, or anything proved to relate to the offence, to be forfeited and either destroyed or otherwise dealt with as the court may order. However, if a person claims to be owner of the drug or item to be forfeited, or to be otherwise interested in it, he must first be given an opportunity to show cause why a forfeiture order should not be made.

A[26]

Supplying or offering to supply a controlled drug
Possessing a controlled drug with intent to supply it to another

(Misuse of Drugs Act 1971, ss 4(3) and 5(3))

Charge

A[26.1] 1. (a) To supply or offer to supply a controlled drug to another; or (b) to be concerned in the supplying of a controlled drug to another; or (c) to be concerned in the making to another of an offer to supply a controlled drug.
2. Having in his possession a quantity of [. . . . . .] a controlled drug of Class [. . . . . .] with intent to supply it to another person

Maximum penalty –

Class A	£5,000 and 6 months
Class B	£5,000 and 6 months
Class C	£2,500 and 3 months

Court can order forfeiture, but see 'Forfeiture' above.

Crown Court –

Class A	Life imprisonment and fine
Class B	14 years and fine
Class C	14 years and fine

Triable either way in respect of any class of drug but see A[25.3]

Mode of trial

A[26.2] See SC Guideline at A[26.5] below.

Legal notes and definitions

A[26.3] The notes in respect of the previous offence at A[25] also apply here except that the defences numbered (b) and (c) in A[25.8] are not applicable.

A[26.4] Intent to supply to another person. In deciding whether or not the defendant had this intention, the court must consider all the evidence drawing such inferences from it as appear proper in the circumstances. An involuntary keeper of drugs can be guilty of supply (*R v Panton* [2001] 19 LS Gaz R 36, CA).

In *R v Wright* [2011] EWCA Crim 1180, [2011] 2 Cr App Rep 168, there was no suggestion that W had intended to supply the immature cannabis plants which he had produced and was in possession of at the material time. The core offence was the production of cannabis under s 4 and the seriousness of that offence depended, inter alia, on whether the cannabis was being grown for W's own use or for supply to others. That question could be resolved within the sentencing process for the offence of production, if necessary by a Newton hearing. It had been unnecessary therefore to add a count of possession with intent to supply in order to determine the purpose for which the cannabis was being produced.

The prosecution only has to establish that the accused was in possession of the controlled drug as charged with the necessary intent; the accused will not be able to avail himself of the defences in s 28(2) or 28(3)(b)(ii) where he believed the substance to be a different drug from that alleged by the prosecution as it is not necessary for the prosecution to prove which controlled drug it was to obtain a conviction. The only purpose of specifying the class of drug in the particulars of the offence is that that factor affects the sentence which can be passed on conviction: *R v Leeson* [2000] 1 Cr App Rep 233, 164 JP 224, [2000] Crim LR 195.

A[26.4A] Supply. 'Supply' covers a wide range of transactions, of which a feature common to all of those transactions is a transfer of physical control of a drug from one person to another: *R v Delgado* [1984] 1 All ER 449, [1984] 1 WLR 89, 148 JP 431, CA; but the transfer must be for the purposes of the transferee: *R v Maginnis* [1987] AC 303,[1987] 1 All ER 907. Where a defendant intends to supply drugs to a courier, even a commercial courier, for eventual supply to a person outside the jurisdiction, there is no contravention of s 4(1) (ante) since there is no intention to supply for the purposes of the transferee (the courier) and the offence does not have extraterritorial effect: *R v Hussain (Shabbir)* [2010] EWCA Crim 970, [2011] QB 1, [2010] 2 WLR 808, [2010] 2 Cr App R 11.

A person in unlawful possession of a controlled drug which has been deposited with him for safe keeping has the intent to supply that drug to another if his intention is to return the drug to the person who deposited it with him: *R v Maginnis*, above. However, 'supply' in s 4(2)(a) implies an act designed to benefit the recipient and does not cover the deposit of a controlled drug with someone for safe keeping: *R v Dempsey* (1985) 82 Cr App Rep 291, 150 JP 213.

Evidence of large amounts of money in the possession of the defendant or an extravagant life style prima facie explicable only if derived from drug dealing is admissible in cases of possession of drugs with intent to supply if it is of probative significance to an issue in the case: *R v Morris* [1995] 2 Cr App Rep 69, 159 JP 1 and see *R v Lucas* [1995] Crim LR 400, CA. Moreover, the finding of money, whether in the home of the defendant or perhaps, more cogently, in the possession of the defendant when away from his home, and in conjunction with a substantial quantity of drugs, is capable of being relevant to the issue of whether there is proved an intent to supply: *R v Grant* [1996] 1 Cr App Rep 73.

A[26.4B] Offer to supply. It is an offence to offer to supply a controlled drug even though the substance in the defendant's possession is not such a drug (but not if the offence charged is supplying): *Haggard v Mason* [1976] 1 All ER 337, 140 JP 198. The offence is complete when the offer to supply a controlled drug is made, regardless of whether the offeror intends to carry the offer into effect by actually supplying the drug: *R v Goddard* [1992] Crim LR 588. Whether the words spoken and the circumstances in which they were uttered amounted to an offer is a question of fact having regard to the effect of the words and any relevant circumstances apparent to the offeree. An offer once made cannot be withdrawn, any attempt to withdraw may only be relevant to the issue whether there was an offer in the first place. There is no need for the offer to meet the specificity as to date and time of delivery of the civil law and it does not matter whether the offeror or the offeree took the initiative: *R v Prior* [2004] EWCA Crim 1147, [2004] Crim LR 849.

A[26.4C] Aggravation of offence of supply of controlled drug. A new s 4A was added to the Misuse of Drugs Act 1971 by the Drugs Act 2005, s 1. This section applies if –

(a)   a court is considering the seriousness of an offence under s 4(3) of the 1971 Act, and

(b)   at the time the offence was committed the offender had attained the age of 18 years.

If **either** of the following conditions is met the court must treat the fact that the condition is met as an aggravating factor ie a factor that increases the seriousness of the offence and when giving its reasons in open court must state that the offence is so aggravated. The conditions are:

(a)   the offence was committed on or in the vicinity of school premises at the relevant time;

(b)   in connection with the commission of the offence the offender used a courier who, at the time the offence was committed, was under the age of 18 years.

A[26.4D] Defences and ECHR. See A[25.9] onwards and (*R v Lambert* [2001] 1 All ER 1014, [2001] 2 WLR 211, CA; affd sub nom R v Lambert [2001] UKHL 37, [2002] 2 AC 545, [2001] 3 All ER 577) and Misuse of Drugs Act 1971, s 28.

Sentencing

SC Sentencing Guideline

Supplying or offering to supply a controlled drug
Misuse of Drugs Act 1971 (section 4(3))

Possession of a controlled drug with intent to supply it to another
Misuse of Drugs Act 1971 (section 5(3))

A[26.5]

Triable either way unless the defendant could receive the minimum sentence of seven years for a third drug trafficking offence under section 110 Powers of Criminal Courts (Sentencing) Act 2000 in which case the offence is triable only on indictment.

Class A

Maximum: Life imprisonment

Offence range: Community order – 16 years' custody

A class A offence is a drug trafficking offence for the purpose of imposing a minimum sentence under section 110 Powers of Criminal Courts (Sentencing) Act 2000

Class B

Maximum: 14 years' custody and/or unlimited fine

Offence range: Fine – 10 years' custody

Class C

Maximum: 14 years' custody and/or unlimited fine

Offence range: Fine – 8 years' custody

Step One
Determining the offence category

The court should determine the offender's culpability (role) and the harm caused (quantity/type of offender) with reference to the tables below.

In assessing culpability, the sentencer should weigh up all the factors of the case to determine role. Where there are characteristics present which fall under different role categories, the court should balance these characteristics to reach a fair assessment of the offender's culpability.

In assessing harm, quantity is determined by the weight of the product. Purity is not taken into account at step 1 but is dealt with at step 2. Where the offence is **street dealing** or **supply of drugs in prison by a prison employee**, the quantity of the product is less indicative of the harm caused and therefore the **starting point is not based on quantity.**

Where the operation is on the most serious and commercial scale, involving a quantity of drugs significantly higher than category 1, sentences of 20 years and above may be appropriate, depending on the role of the offender.

Culpability demonstrated by offender's role

One or more of these characteristics may demonstrate the offender's role. These lists are not exhaustive.

LEADING role:

• directing or organising buying and selling on a commercial scale;
• substantial links to, and influence on, others in a chain;
• close links to original source;
• expectation of substantial financial gain;
• uses business as cover;
• abuses a position of trust or responsibility, for example prison employee, medical professional.

SIGNIFICANT role:

• operational or management function within a chain;
• involves others in the operation whether by pressure, influence, intimidation or reward;
• motivated by financial or other advantage, whether or not operating alone;
• some awareness and understanding of scale of operation;

- supply, other than by a person in a position of responsibility, to a prisoner for gain without coercion.

LESSER role:

- performs a limited function under direction;
- engaged by pressure, coercion, intimidation;
- involvement through naivety/exploitation;
- no influence on those above in a chain;
- very little, if any, awareness or understanding of the scale of operation;
- if own operation, absence of any financial gain, for example joint purchase for no profit, or sharing minimal quantity between peers on non-commercial basis.

Category of harm

Indicative quantity of drug concerned (upon which the starting point is based):

Category 1

- heroin, cocaine – 5kg;
- ecstasy – 10,000 tablets;
- LSD – 250,000 squares;
- amphetamine – 20kg;
- cannabis – 200kg;
- ketamine – 5kg.

Category 2

- heroin, cocaine – 1kg;
- ecstasy – 2,000 tablets;
- LSD – 25,000 squares;
- amphetamine – 4kg;
- cannabis – 40kg;
- ketamine – 1kg.

Category 3

Where the offence is selling directly to users* ('street dealing'), the starting point is not based on a quantity,

OR

where the offence is supply of drugs in prison by a prison employee, the starting point is not based on a quantity – see shaded box on page 232,

OR

- heroin, cocaine – 150g;
- ecstasy – 300 tablets;
- LSD – 2,500 squares;
- amphetamine – 750g;
- cannabis – 6kg;
- ketamine – 150g.

Category 4

- heroin, cocaine – 5g;
- ecstasy – 20 tablets;
- LSD – 170 squares;
- amphetamine – 20g;

- cannabis – 100g;
- ketamine – 5g;

OR

where the offence is selling directly to users* ('street dealing') the starting point is not based on quantity – go to category 3.

*Including test purchase officers

Step Two
Starting point and category range

Having determined the category, the court should use the corresponding starting point to reach a sentence within the category range below. The starting point applies to all offenders irrespective of plea or previous convictions. The court should then consider further adjustment within the category range for aggravating or mitigating features, set out on page 236. In cases where the offender is regarded as being at the very top of the 'leading' role it may be justifiable for the court to depart from the guideline.

Where the defendant is dependent on or has a propensity to misuse drugs and there is sufficient prospect of success, a community order with a drug rehabilitation requirement under section 209 of the Criminal Justice Act 2003 can be a proper alternative to a short or moderate length custodial sentence.

For **class A** cases, section 110 of the Powers of Criminal Courts (Sentencing) Act 2000 provides that a court should impose a minimum sentence of at least seven years' imprisonment for a third class A trafficking offence except where the court is of the opinion that there are particular circumstances which (a) relate to any of the offences or to the offender; and (b) would make it unjust to do so in all the circumstances.

CLASS A	Leading role	Significant role	Lesser role
Category 1	Starting point	Starting point	Starting point
	14 years' custody	10 years' custody	7 years' custody
	Category range	Category range	Category range
	12 – 16 years' custody	9 – 12 years' custody	6 – 9 years' custody
Category 2	Starting point	Starting point	Starting point
	11 years' custody	8 years' custody	5 years' custody
	Category range	Category range	Category range
	9 – 13 years' custody	6 years 6 months' – 10 years' custody	3 years 6 months' – 7 years' custody
Category 3	Starting point	Starting point	Starting point
	8 years 6 months' custody	4 years 6 months' custody	3 years' custody
	Category range	Category range	Category range
	6 years 6 months' – 10 years' custody	3 years 6 months' – 7 years' custody	2 – 4 years 6 months' custody

CLASS A	Leading role	Significant role	Lesser role
Category 4	Starting point	Starting point	Starting point
	5 years 6 months' custody	3 years 6 months' custody	18 months' custody
	Category range	Category range	Category range
	4 years 6 months' – 7 years 6 months' custody	2 – 5 years' custody	High level community order – 3 years' custody

CLASS B	Leading role	Significant role	Lesser role
Category 1	Starting point	Starting point	Starting point
	8 years' custody	5 years 6 months' custody	3 years' custody
	Category range	Category range	Category range
	7 – 10 years' custody	5 – 7 years' custody	2 years 6 months' – 5 years' custody
Category 2	Starting point	Starting point	Starting point
	6 years' custody	4 years' custody	1 year's custody
	Category range	Category range	Category range
	4 years 6 months' – 8 years' custody	2 years 6 months' – 5 years' custody	26 weeks' – 3 years' custody
Category 3	Starting point	Starting point	Starting point
	4 years' custody	1 year's custody	High level community order
	Category range	Category range	Category range
	2 years 6 months' – 5 years' custody	26 weeks' – 3 years' custody	Low level community order – 26 weeks' custody
Category 4	Starting point	Starting point	Starting point
	18 months' custody	High level community order	Low level community order
	Category range	Category range	Category range
	26 weeks' – 3 years' custody	Medium level community order – 26 weeks' custody	Band B fine – medium level community order

CLASS C	Leading role	Significant role	Lesser role
Category 1	Starting point	Starting point	Starting point
	5 years' custody	3 years' custody	18 months' custody
	Category range	Category range	Category range

CLASS C	Leading role	Significant role	Lesser role
	4 – 8 years' custody	2 – 5 years' custody	1 – 3 years' custody
Category 2	**Starting point**	**Starting point**	**Starting point**
	3 years 6 months' custody	18 months' custody	26 weeks' custody
	Category range	**Category range**	**Category range**
	2 – 5 years' custody	1 – 3 years' custody	12 weeks' – 18 months' custody
Category 3	**Starting point**	**Starting point**	**Starting point**
	18 months' custody	26 weeks' custody	High level community order
	Category range	**Category range**	**Category range**
	1 – 3 years' custody	12 weeks' – 18 months' custody	Low level community order – 12 weeks' custody
Category 4	**Starting point**	**Starting point**	**Starting point**
	26 weeks' custody	High level community order	Low level community order
	Category range	**Category range**	**Category range**
	High level community order – 18 months' custody	Low level community order – 12 weeks' custody	Band A fine – medium level community order

The table below contains a **non-exhaustive** list of additional factual elements providing the context of the offence and factors relating to the offender. Identify whether any combination of these, or other relevant factors, should result in an upward or downward adjustment from the starting point. In some cases, having considered these factors, it may be appropriate to move outside the identified category range.

For appropriate **class B** and **C** ranges, consider the custody threshold as follows:

- has the custody threshold been passed?
- if so, is it unavoidable that a custodial sentence be imposed?
- if so, can that sentence be suspended?

For appropriate **class B** and **C** ranges, the court should also consider the community threshold as follows:

- has the community threshold been passed?

Factors increasing seriousness

Statutory aggravating factors:

Previous convictions, having regard to a) nature of the offence to which conviction relates and relevance to current offence; and b) time elapsed since conviction (see shaded box at page 234 if third drug trafficking conviction)

Offender used or permitted a person under 18 to deliver a controlled drug to a third person

Offender 18 or over supplies or offers to supply a drug on, or in the vicinity of, school premises either when school in use as such or at a time between one hour before and one hour after they are to be used

Offence committed on bail

Other aggravating factors include:

Targeting of any premises intended to locate vulnerable individuals or supply to such individuals and/or supply to those under 18

Exposure of others to more than usual danger, for example drugs cut with harmful substances

Attempts to conceal or dispose of evidence, where not charged separately

Presence of others, especially children and/or non-users

Presence of weapon, where not charged separately

Charged as importation of a very small amount

High purity

Failure to comply with current court orders

Offence committed on licence

Established evidence of community impact

Factors reducing seriousness or reflecting personal mitigation

Involvement due to pressure, intimidation or coercion falling short of duress, except where already taken into account at step 1

Supply only of drug to which offender addicted

Mistaken belief of the offender regarding the type of drug, taking into account the reasonableness of such belief in all the circumstances

Isolated incident

Low purity

No previous convictions **or** no relevant or recent convictions

Offender's vulnerability was exploited

Remorse

Good character and/or exemplary conduct

Determination and/or demonstration of steps having been taken to address addiction or offending behaviour

Serious medical conditions requiring urgent, intensive or long-term treatment

Age and/or lack of maturity where it affects the responsibility of the offender

Mental disorder or learning disability

Sole or primary carer for dependent relatives

Step Three
Consider any factors which indicate a reduction, such as assistance to the
prosecution

The court should take into account sections 73 and 74 of the Serious
Organised Crime and Police Act 2005 (assistance by defendants: reduction
or review of sentence) and any other rule of law by virtue of which an
offender may receive a discounted sentence in consequence of assistance
given (or offered) to the prosecutor or investigator.

Step Four
Reduction for guilty pleas

The court should take account of any potential reduction for a guilty plea
in accordance with section 144 of the Criminal Justice Act 2003 and the
Guilty Plea guideline.

For class A offences, where a minimum mandatory sentence is imposed
under section 110 Powers of Criminal Courts (Sentencing) Act, the
discount for an early guilty plea must not exceed 20 per cent.

Step Five
Totality principle

If sentencing an offender for more than one offence, or where the offender
is already serving a sentence, consider whether the total sentence is just and
proportionate to the offending behaviour.

Step Six
Confiscation and ancillary orders

In all cases, the court is required to consider confiscation where the Crown
invokes the process or where the court considers it appropriate. It should
also consider whether to make ancillary orders.

Step Seven
Reasons

Section 174 of the Criminal Justice Act 2003 imposes a duty to give reasons
for, and explain the effect of, the sentence.

Step Eight
Consideration for remand time

(Now obligatory.)

A[26.6]–[26.9] Available sentences (Class A, B and C drugs). See Table
A at B[4.1].

A[26.10]–[26.11] Custodial sentence. See B[2].

A[26.12]–[26.15] "Crack Houses" – Closure orders – S 2 Anti-Social
Behaviour Act 2003

Closure orders. For more detailed guidance see JCS Good Practice Guide
(Closure Notices and Orders dated November 2006 ref: 54.0022.q).

For the closure of premises associated with persistent disorder or nuisance
see **Part 1A of the Anti-Social Behaviour Act 2003** at A[84.37] onwards.

(For closure orders for premises used for activities related to certain **sexual
offences** see ss 22 and 22 and schedule 2 of the Policing and Crime Act 2009

which added a new Part 2A to the Sexual Offences Act 2003. These provisions came into force on **1 April 2010**.)

Within 48 hours of the serving of a closure notice an application must be made to a magistrates' court. If satisfied that:

(a)   the premises have been used for the production or supply of a class 'A' drug;

(b)   that use is associated with disorder or serious public nuisance; and

(c)   the order is necessary to prevent reoccurrence,

the court can order closure of the premises for a period no longer than 3 months.

An application can be to extend the closure order for up to a further three months pursuant to s 5(4) of the 2003 Act; but a closure order may not exceed a total of six months: s 5(5). The court should simply ask whether it had been proved that an extension was necessary and proportionate to prevent the occurrence of further disorder or nuisance; and if so how long the extension should be (*R (on the application of Smith)v Snaresbrook Crown Court* [2008] EWHC 1282 (Admin)).

Closure order applications are civil proceedings. Although closure order applications should be dealt with as a matter of urgency in *R (on the application of Turner v Highbury Corner Magistrates' Court and Commissioner of the Metropolis (Interested Party)* [2005] EWHC 2568 (Admin), [2006] 1 WLR 220, it was decided that the general power of a magistrates' court to grant an adjournment co-existed with the limited and specific power granted under s 2(6) of the Anti-Social Behaviour Act 2003. Accordingly, an adjournment of more than 14 days could be granted where the court was satisfied that there was a need for such an adjournment consonant with the interests of justice (*Metropolitan Police Comr v Hooper* [2005] EWHC 340 (Admin) explained).

The standard of proof applicable to making an order under s 2(3)(a) and (b) of the 2003 Act was the civil standard of proof, namely on a balance of probabilities (*Chief Constable of Merseyside v Harrison* [2006] EWHC 1106 (Admin), [2006] 3 WLR 171).

For general guidance on disclosure of evidence in s 2 applications and observations on the admissibility of and weight to be accorded to hearsay evidence see *R (on the application of Cleary) v Highbury Corner Magistrates' Court and the Comr of Police of the Metropolis and the Secretary of State for the Home Department* [2006] EWHC 1869 (Admin), (2006) Times, 12 September; and more recently *R (on the application of Errington) v Metropolitan Police Authority* (2007) 171 JP 89.

When applying for a closure order it was not necessary for the police and local authority to demonstrate they had first considered and/or tried other less draconian methods first, so as to comply with the ECHR, article 8. Further, it was not possible to adjust the terms of a closure order to exclude visitors from the premises but to allow an occupier to remain there: *Leary v Chief Constable of the West Midlands Police* [2012] EWHC 639 (Admin), 176 CL&J 143.

On a true construction of the Act, the requirement of s 2(3)(b) of disorder or serious nuisance had to derive from the drug use required by s 2(3)(a). The purpose of the legislation was to grant powers to deal with 'crack houses' and it followed that the disturbance(s) required by s 2(3)(b) had to be linked to the drug use referred to in s 2(3)(a). The Act was intended to deal with a present and continuing situation. An order might be obtained if there was a short hiatus in the disorder, although not if the disorder had permanently ceased. Historical evidence was therefore admissible if relevant to a continuing situation (*Chief Constable of Cumbria Constabulary v Wright* [2006] EWHC 3574 (Admin)). In *Dumble v Metropolitan Police Commissioner* [2009] All ER (D) 66 (Feb) for the purposes of s 2(3)(b) the justices were entitled to consider the ongoing nature of disorder and violence at the appellant's premises including the 'few' incidents which had taken place immediately prior to the making of the application. On the facts, the legitimate aim of preventing crime and disorder was a trump card overriding the appellant's Art 8 ECHR rights.

An offence in contravention of the order is punishable summarily by 6 months' imprisonment or a level 5 fine (ss 2 and 4 of the Anti-Social Behaviour Act 2003).

For the closure of '**noisy premises**' see s 40 of the ABA 2003 at **A[84.7]** onwards.

A[26.16] Appeal. Section 6 of the Anti-Social Behaviour Act 2003 states that an appeal against a decision or order must be brought before the end of the period of 21 days beginning with the day on which the order or decision is made. Section 6(1) has been interpreted to mean that an appellant has 21 days from the date of the order or decision to issue the notice of appeal. Further, there was no power to extend the time for appeal under s 6(2): *Hampshire Police Authority v Smith* [2009] EWHC 174 (Admin), 173 JP 207.

A[26.17] Costs. A magistrates' court has jurisdiction to make an award of costs between the parties under s 64 of the Magistrates' Courts Act 1980: *R (on the application of Taylor) v Comr of the Metropolitan Police* [2009] EWHC 264 (Admin), 173 JP 121.

A[26.18] Community sentence. See B[3].

A[26.19] Forfeiture. See A[25.18].

A[26.20] Drug trafficking. For the power of the Crown Court to make a confiscation order in respect of the proceeds of drug trafficking offences, see B[19].

A[27]

Drugs – Cultivation of Cannabis Plant
Drugs – Production of a controlled drug

(Misuse of Drugs Act 1971, s 6(2))
(Misuse of Drugs Act 1971, s 4(2)(a) or (b))

Charge

A[27.1] On X date at . . . . the accused unlawfully cultivated cannabis

On X date at . . . . unlawfully produced a controlled drug (namely . . . .); or was concerned in the production of a controlled drug (namely . . . .)

Maximum penalty –

Fine level 5 and/or 6 months imprisonment. Triable either way.

Crown Court

–   Class A: Life imprisonment and unlimited fine
–   Class B: 14 years' imprisonment and unlimited fine
–   Class C: 14 years' imprisonment and unlimited fine

A[27.2] This offence is subject to s 7 (authorisation of activities otherwise unlawful) and s 28 (proof of lack of knowledge etc to be a defence in proceedings for certain offences.

Mode of trial

A[27.3] See SC Guideline at A[27.4] below.

Legal notes and definitions

A[27.3A] **Produce and be concerned in production.** 'Produce', where the reference is to producing a controlled drug, means producing it by manufacture, cultivation or any other method, and 'production' has a corresponding meaning: s 37(1) of the Misuse of Drugs Act 1971.

Conversion from one form of a drug to another can amount to production: *R v Russell* (1991) 94 Cr App Rep 351, CA. The preparation of plants so as to discard the parts which are not usable for the drug and to put together those which are amounts to 'production' of cannabis: *R v Harris* [1996] 1 Cr App Rep 369, [1996] Crim LR 36, CA. Making an infusion out of B-Caapi and Chacruna amounts to 'producing' a controlled drug (DMT) by making a 'preparation': *R v Aziz* [2012] EWCA Crim 1063, [2012] Crim LR 801. See further para 5 of Pt 1 (Class A) to Sch 2, post, which provides ' . . . any preparation or other product containing a substance or product for the time being specified in any of the paragraphs 1 to 4 above [is a Class A controlled drug]'.

There must be established some identifiable participation in the process of producing a controlled drug before a person can be convicted: *R v Farr* [1982] Crim LR 745, CA.

Sentencing

SC Sentencing Guideline

Production of a controlled drug
Misuse of Drugs Act 1971 (section 4(2)(a) or (b))

A[27.4]

Triable either way unless the defendant could receive the minimum sentence of seven years for a third drug trafficking offence under section 110 Powers of Criminal Courts (Sentencing) Act 2000 in which case the offence is triable only on indictment.

Class A

Maximum: Life imprisonment

Offence range: Community order – 16 years' custody

A class A offence is a drug trafficking offence for the purpose of imposing a minimum sentence under section 110 Powers of Criminal Courts (Sentencing) Act 2000

Class B

Maximum: 14 years' custody

Offence range: Discharge – 10 years' custody

Class C

Maximum: 14 years' custody

Offence range: Discharge – 8 years' custody

Cultivation of cannabis plant
Misuse of Drugs Act 1971 (section 6(2))

Maximum: 14 years' custody

Offence range: Discharge – 10 years' custody

Step One
Determining the offence category

The court should determine the offender's culpability (role) and the harm caused (output or potential output) with reference to the tables below.

In assessing culpability, the sentencer should weigh up all of the factors of the case to determine role. Where there are characteristics present which fall under different role categories, the court should balance these characteristics to reach a fair assessment of the offender's culpability.

In assessing harm, output or potential output is determined by the weight of the product or number of plants/scale of operation. For production offences, purity is not taken into account at step 1 but is dealt with at step 2.

Where the operation is on the most serious and commercial scale, involving a quantity of drugs significantly higher than category 1, sentences of 20 years and above may be appropriate, depending on the role of the offender.

Culpability demonstrated by offender's role

One or more of these characteristics may demonstrate the offender's role. These lists are not exhaustive.

LEADING role:

- directing or organising production on a commercial scale;
- substantial links to, and influence on, others in a chain;
- expectation of substantial financial gain;
- uses business as cover;
- abuses a position of trust or responsibility.

SIGNIFICANT role:

- operational or management function within a chain;
- involves others in the operation whether by pressure, influence, intimidation or reward;
- motivated by financial or other advantage, whether or not operating alone;
- some awareness and understanding of scale of operation.

LESSER role:

- performs a limited function under direction;
- engaged by pressure, coercion, intimidation;
- involvement through naivety/exploitation;
- no influence on those above in a chain;
- very little, if any, awareness or understanding of the scale of operation;
- if own operation, solely for own use (considering reasonableness of account in all the circumstances).

Category of harm

Indicative output or potential output (upon which the starting point is based):

Category 1

- heroin, cocaine – 5kg;
- ecstasy – 10,000 tablets;
- LSD – 250,000 tablets;
- amphetamine – 20kg;
- cannabis – operation capable of producing industrial quantities for commercial use;
- ketamine – 5kg.

Category 2

- heroin, cocaine – 1kg;
- ecstasy – 2,000 tablets;
- LSD – 25,000 squares;
- amphetamine – 4kg;
- cannabis – operation capable of producing significant quantities for commercial use;
- ketamine – 1kg.

Category 3

- heroin, cocaine – 150g;
- ecstasy – 300 tablets;
- LSD – 2,500 squares;
- amphetamine – 750g;*
- cannabis – 28 plants;*
- ketamine – 150g.

Category 4

- heroin, cocaine – 5g;
- ecstasy – 20 tablets;
- LSD – 170 squares;
- amphetamine – 20g;
- cannabis – 9 plants (domestic operation);*
- ketamine – 5g.

---

*   With assumed yield of 40g per plant

Step Two
Starting point and category range

Having determined the category, the court should use the corresponding starting point to reach a sentence within the category range below. The starting point applies to all offenders irrespective of plea or previous convictions. The court should then consider further adjustment within the category range for aggravating or mitigating features, set out on page 243. In cases where the offender is regarded as being at the very top of the 'leading' role it may be justifiable for the court to depart from the guideline.

Where the defendant is dependent on or has a propensity to misuse drugs and there is sufficient prospect of success, a community order with a drug rehabilitation requirement under section 209 of the Criminal Justice Act 2003 can be a proper alternative to a short or moderate length custodial sentence.

For **class A** cases, section 110 of the Powers of Criminal Courts (Sentencing) Act 2000 provides that a court should impose a minimum sentence of at least seven years' imprisonment for a third class A trafficking offence except where the court is of the opinion that there are particular circumstances which (a) relate to any of the offences or to the offender; and (b) would make it unjust to do so in all the circumstances.

CLASS A	Leading role	Significant role	Lesser role
	Starting point	**Starting point**	**Starting point**
	14 years' custody	10 years' custody	7 years' custody
	Category range	**Category range**	**Category range**
	12 – 16 years' custody	9 – 12 years' custody	6 – 9 years' custody
Category 2	**Starting point**	**Starting point**	**Starting point**
	11 years' custody	8 years' custody	5 years' custody
	Category range	**Category range**	**Category range**
	9 – 13 years' custody	6 years 6 months' – 10 years' custody	3 years 6 months' – 7 years' custody

CLASS A	Leading role	Significant role	Lesser role
Category 3	Starting point	Starting point	Starting point
	8 years 6 months' custody	5 years' custody	3 years 6 months' custody
	Category range	Category range	Category range
	6 years 6 months' – 10 years' custody	3 years 6 months' – 7 years' custody	2 – 5 years' custody
Category 4	Starting point	Starting point	Starting point
	5 years 6 months' custody	3 years 6 months' custody	18 months' custody
	Category range	Category range	Category range
	4 years 6 months' – 7 years 6 months' custody	2 – 5 years' custody	High level community order – 3 years' custody

CLASS B	Leading role	Significant role	Lesser role
Category 1	Starting point	Starting point	Starting point
	8 years' custody	5 years 6 months' custody	3 years' custody
	Category range	Category range	Category range
	7 – 10 years' custody	5 – 7 years' custody	2 years 6 months' – 5 years' custody
Category 2	Starting point	Starting point	Starting point
	6 years' custody	4 years' custody	1 year's custody
	Category range	Category range	Category range
	4 years 6 months' – 8 years' custody	2 years 6 months' – 5 years' custody	26 weeks' – 3 years' custody
Category 3	Starting point	Starting point	Starting point
	4 years' custody	1 year's custody	High level community order
	Category range	Category range	Category range
	2 years 6 months' – 5 years' custody	26 weeks' – 3 years' custody	Low level community order – 26 weeks' custody
Category 4	Starting point	Starting point	Starting point
	1 year's custody	High level community order	Band C fine
	Category range	Category range	Category range

CLASS B	Leading role	Significant role	Lesser role
	High level community order – 3 years' custody	Medium level community order – 26 weeks' custody	Discharge – medium level community order

CLASS C	Leading role	Significant role	Lesser role
Category 1	**Starting point**	**Starting point**	**Starting point**
	5 years' custody	3 years' custody	18 months' custody
	Category range	**Category range**	**Category range**
	4 – 8 years' custody	2 – 5 years' custody	1 – 3 years' custody
Category 2	**Starting point**	**Starting point**	**Starting point**
	3 years 6 months' custody	18 months' custody	26 weeks' custody
	Category range	**Category range**	**Category range**
	2 – 5 years' custody	1 – 3 years' custody	High level community order – 18 months' custody
Category 3	**Starting point**	**Starting point**	**Starting point**
	18 months' custody	26 weeks' custody	High level community order
	Category range	**Category range**	**Category range**
	1 – 3 years' custody	High level community order – 18 months' custody	Low level community order – 12 weeks' custody
Category 4	**Starting point**	**Starting point**	**Starting point**
	26 weeks' custody	High level community order	Band C fine
	Category range	**Category range**	**Category range**
	High level community order – 18 months' custody	Low level community order – 12 weeks' custody	Discharge – medium level community order

The table below contains a **non-exhaustive** list of additional factual elements providing the context of the offence and factors relating to the offender. Identify whether any combination of these, or other relevant factors, should result in an upward or downward adjustment from the starting point. In some cases, having considered these factors, it may be appropriate to move outside the identified category range.

Where appropriate, consider the custody threshold as follows:

• has the custody threshold been passed?
• if so, is it unavoidable that a custodial sentence be imposed?

- if so, can that sentence be suspended?

Where appropriate, the court should also consider the community threshold as follows:

- has the community threshold been passed?

Factors increasing seriousness

Statutory aggravating factors:

Previous convictions, having regard to a) nature of the offence to which conviction relates and relevance to current offence; and b) time elapsed since conviction (see shaded box at page 241 if third drug trafficking conviction)

Offence committed on bail

Other aggravating factors include:

Nature of any likely supply

Level of any profit element

Use of premises accompanied by unlawful access to electricity/other utility supply of others

Ongoing/large scale operation as evidenced by presence and nature of specialist equipment

Exposure of others to more than usual danger, for example drugs cut with harmful substances

Attempts to conceal or dispose of evidence, where not charged separately

Presence of others, especially children and/or non-users

Presence of weapon, where not charged separately

High purity or high potential yield

Failure to comply with current court orders

Offence committed on licence

Established evidence of community impact

Factors reducing seriousness or reflecting personal mitigation

Involvement due to pressure, intimidation or coercion falling short of duress, except where already taken into account at step 1

Isolated incident

Low purity

No previous convictions **or** no relevant or recent convictions

Offender's vulnerability was exploited

Remorse

Good character and/or exemplary conduct

Determination and/or demonstration of steps having been taken to address addiction or offending behaviour

Serious medical conditions requiring urgent, intensive or long-term treatment

Age and/or lack of maturity where it affects the responsibility of the offender

Mental disorder or learning disability

Sole or primary carer for dependent relatives

Step Three
Consider any factors which indicate a reduction, such as assistance to the prosecution

The court should take into account sections 73 and 74 of the Serious Organised Crime and Police Act 2005 (assistance by defendants: reduction or review of sentence) and any other rule of law by virtue of which an offender may receive a discounted sentence in consequence of assistance given (or offered) to the prosecutor or investigator.

Step Four
Reduction for guilty pleas

The court should take account of any potential reduction for a guilty plea in accordance with section 144 of the Criminal Justice Act 2003 and the *Guilty Plea* guideline.

For class A offences, where a minimum mandatory sentence is imposed under section 110 Powers of Criminal Courts (Sentencing) Act, the discount for an early guilty plea must not exceed 20 per cent.

Step Five
Totality principle

If sentencing an offender for more than one offence, or where the offender is already serving a sentence, consider whether the total sentence is just and proportionate to the offending behaviour.

Step Six
Confiscation and ancillary orders

In all cases, the court is required to consider confiscation where the Crown invokes the process or where the court considers it appropriate. It should also consider whether to make ancillary orders.

Step Seven
Reasons

Section 174 of the Criminal Justice Act 2003 imposes a duty to give reasons for, and explain the effect of, the sentence.

Step Eight
Consideration for remand time

(Now obligatory.)

A[27A]

Drugs – Permitting premises to be used

(Misuse of Drugs Act 1971, s 8)

Charge

A[27A.1] Being the occupier or concerned in the management of premises at . . . . on X date knowingly permits or suffers the following activity:

(a)   producing or attempting to produce a controlled drug in contravention of section 4(1);

(b)   supplying or attempting to supply a controlled drug to another in contravention of section 4(1), or offering to supply a controlled drug in contravention of section 4(1);

(c)   preparing opium for smoking;

(d)   smoking cannabis, cannabis resin or prepared opium.

Maximum penalty – Fine level 5 and/or 6 months. Triable either way.

Crown Court

–   Class A: 14 years' imprisonment and unlimited fine
–   Class B: 14 years' imprisonment and unlimited fine
–   Class C: 14 years' imprisonment and unlimited fine

Legal notes and definitions

A[27A.2] Occupier, concerned in the management of premises and knowingly permits. 'Occupier' includes anyone in occupation of premises whose degree of occupation was such that he could exclude anyone likely to commit an offence under the Act: *R v Tao* [1977] QB 141, [1976] 3 All ER 65, 140 JP 596. The fact that one person can be identified as an occupier, even if enjoying a legal title or tenancy, does not preclude the application of that description to another person: *R v Coid* [1998] Crim LR 199.

If a person is exercising control over premises, running them or managing them, the fact that he is not lawfully in possession of them is irrelevant: *R v Josephs* and *R v Christie* (1977) 65 Cr App Rep 253.

To establish the offence of permitting the prosecution must prove: (i) knowledge, actual or by closing ones eyes to the obvious, that dealing in controlled drugs is taking place; and (ii) unwillingness to prevent it, which can be inferred from failure to take steps readily available to prevent it. A defendant's belief that he has taken reasonable steps is irrelevant; it is not for the defendant to judge his own conduct: *R v Brock* (1991) 165 JP 331, CA. The commission of the offence requires the actual smoking of cannabis; mere tentative permission to smoke cannabis is insufficient: *R v Auguste* [2003] EWCA Crim 3929, [2004] 4 All ER 373, [2004] 1 WLR 917, [2004] Cr App Rep 173.

Mode of trial

A[27A.3] See SC Guideline at A[27A.4] below.

Sentencing

SC Sentencing Guideline

Permitting premises to be used
Misuse of Drugs Act 1971 (section 8)

A[27A.4]

Triable either way unless the defendant could receive the minimum sentence of seven years for a third drug trafficking offence under section 110 Powers of Criminal Courts (Sentencing) Act 2000 in which case the offence is triable only on indictment.

Class A

Maximum: 14 years' custody

Offence range: Community order – 4 years' custody

A class A offence is a drug trafficking offence for the purpose of imposing a minimum sentence under section 110 Powers of Criminal Courts (Sentencing) Act 2000

Class B

Maximum: 14 years' custody

Offence range: Fine – 18 months' custody

Class C

Maximum: 14 years' custody

Offence range: Discharge – 26 weeks' custody

Step One
Determining the offence category

The court should determine the offender's culpability and the harm caused (extent of the activity and/or the quantity of drugs) with reference to the table below.

In assessing harm, quantity is determined by the weight of the product. Purity is not taken into account at step 1 but is dealt with at step 2.

Category 1	Higher culpability **and** greater harm
Category 2	Lower culpability **and** greater harm; **or** higher culpability **and** lesser harm
Category 3	Lower culpability **and** lesser harm

Factors indicating culpability (non-exhaustive)

Higher culpability:

Permits premises to be used primarily for drug activity, for example crack house

Permits use in expectation of substantial financial gain

Uses legitimate business premises to aid and/or conceal illegal activity, for example public house or club

Lower culpability:

Permits use for limited or no financial gain

No active role in any supply taking place

Involvement through naivety

Factors indicating harm (non-exhaustive)

Greater harm:

Regular drug-related activity

Higher quantity of drugs, for example:

- heroin, cocaine – more than 5g;
- cannabis – more than 50g.

Lesser harm:

Infrequent drug-related activity

Lower quantity of drugs, for example:

- heroin, cocaine – up to 5g;
- cannabis – up to 50g.

Step Two
Starting point and category range

Having determined the category, the court should use the table below to identify the corresponding starting point to reach a sentence within the category range. The starting point applies to all offenders irrespective of plea or previous convictions. The court should then consider further adjustment within the category range for aggravating or mitigating features, set out over the page.

Where the defendant is dependent on or has a propensity to misuse drugs and there is sufficient prospect of success, a community order with a drug rehabilitation requirement under section 209 of the Criminal Justice Act 2003 can be a proper alternative to a short or moderate length custodial sentence.

For **class A** cases, section 110 of the Powers of Criminal Courts (Sentencing) Act 2000 provides that a court should impose a minimum sentence of at least seven years' imprisonment for a third class A trafficking offence except where the court is of the opinion that there are particular circumstances which (a) relate to any of the offences or to the offender; and (b) would make it unjust to do so in all the circumstances.

Class A

Offence category	Starting point (applicable to all offenders)	Category range (applicable to all offenders)
Category 1	2 years 6 months' custody	18 months' – 4 years' custody
Category 2	36 weeks' custody	High level community order – 18 months' custody
Category 3	Medium level community order	Low level community order – high level community order

Class B

Offence category	Starting point (applicable to all offenders)	Category range (applicable to all offenders)
Category 1	1 year's custody	26 weeks' – 18 months' custody
Category 2	High level community order	Low level community order – 26 weeks' custody
Category 3	Band C fine	Band A fine – low level community order

Class C

Offence category	Starting point (applicable to all offenders)	Category range (applicable to all offenders)
Category 1	12 weeks' custody	High level community order – 26 weeks' custody*
Category 2	Low level community order	Band C fine – high level community order
Category 3	Band A fine	Discharge – band C fine

*When tried summarily, the maximum penalty is 12 weeks' custody.

The table below contains a **non-exhaustive** list of additional factual elements providing the context of the offence and factors relating to the offender. Identify whether any combination of these, or other relevant factors, should result in an upward or downward adjustment from the starting point. In some cases, having considered these factors, it may be appropriate to move outside the identified category range.

Where appropriate, consider the custody threshold as follows:

•   has the custody threshold been passed?
•   if so, is it unavoidable that a custodial sentence be imposed?
•   if so, can that sentence be suspended?

Where appropriate, the court should also consider the community threshold as follows:

•   has the community threshold been passed?

Factors increasing seriousness

Statutory aggravating factors:

Previous convictions, having regard to a) nature of the offence to which conviction relates and relevance to current offence; and b) time elapsed since conviction (see shaded box at page 247 if third drug trafficking conviction)

Offence committed on bail

Other aggravating factors include:

Length of time over which premises used for drug activity

Volume of drug activity permitted

Premises adapted to facilitate drug activity

Location of premises, for example proximity to school

Attempts to conceal or dispose of evidence, where not charged separately

Presence of others, especially children and/or non-users

High purity

Presence of weapons, where not charged separately

Failure to comply with current court orders

Offence committed on licence

Established evidence of community impact

Factors reducing seriousness or reflecting personal mitigation

Involvement due to pressure, intimidation or coercion falling short of duress

Isolated incident

Low purity

No previous convictions **or** no relevant or recent convictions

Offender's vulnerability was exploited

Remorse

Good character and/or exemplary conduct

Determination and/or demonstration of steps having been taken to address addiction or offending behaviour

Serious medical conditions requiring urgent, intensive or long-term treatment

Age and/or lack of maturity where it affects the responsibility of the offender

Mental disorder or learning disability

Sole or primary carer for dependent relatives

Step Three
Consider any factors which indicate a reduction, such as assistance to the prosecution

The court should take into account sections 73 and 74 of the Serious Organised Crime and Police Act 2005 (assistance by defendants: reduction or review of sentence) and any other rule of law by virtue of which an offender may receive a discounted sentence in consequence of assistance given (or offered) to the prosecutor or investigator.

Step Four
Reduction for guilty pleas

The court should take account of any potential reduction for a guilty plea in accordance with section 144 of the Criminal Justice Act 2003 and the *Guilty Plea* guideline.

For class A offences, where a minimum mandatory sentence is imposed under section 110 Powers of Criminal Courts (Sentencing) Act, the discount for an early guilty plea must not exceed 20 per cent.

Step Five
Totality principle

If sentencing an offender for more than one offence or where the offender is already serving a sentence, consider whether the total sentence is just and proportionate to the offending behaviour.

Step Six
Confiscation and ancillary orders

In all cases, the court is required to consider confiscation where the Crown invokes the process or where the court considers it appropriate. It should also consider whether to make ancillary orders.

Step Seven
Reasons

Section 174 of the Criminal Justice Act 2003 imposes a duty to give reasons for, and explain the effect of, the sentence.

Step Eight
Consideration for remand time

(Now obligatory.)

A[27B]

Fraudulent evasion of a prohibition by bringing into or taking out of the UK a controlled drug

(Misuse of Drugs Act 1971, section 3) (Customs and Excise Management Act 1979, section 170)

Charge

A[27B.1] A on the . . . . day of . . . . was knowingly concealed in concealing goods, that is to say a quantity of a controlled drug, namely . . . with intent to evade the prohibition on importation of the said goods then in force pursuant to section 3 of the Misuse of Drugs Act 1971

Maximum penalty – Three times the value of the goods or £5,000 fine whichever is the greater and 6 months. Triable either way.

Crown Court – 7 years' imprisonment and unlimited fine.

A[27B.2] Knowingly concerned. See para A[4.5], above, for detailed consideration of the meaning of 'knowingly concerned'.

Mode of trial

A[27B.3] See SC Guideline at A[27B.4] below.

Sentencing

SC Sentencing Guideline

Fraudulent evasion of a prohibition by bringing into or taking out of the UK a controlled drug
Misuse of Drugs Act 1971 (section 3)
Customs and Excise Management Act 1979
(section 170(2))

A[27B.4]

Triable either way unless the defendant could receive the minimum sentence of seven years for a third drug trafficking offence under section 110 Powers of Criminal Courts (Sentencing) Act 2000 in which case the offence is triable only on indictment.

Class A

Maximum: Life imprisonment

Offence range: 3 years 6 months' – 16 years' custody

A class A offence is a drug trafficking offence for the purpose of imposing a minimum sentence under section 110 Powers of Criminal Courts (Sentencing) Act 2000

Class B

Maximum: 14 years' custody and/or unlimited fine

Offence range: 12 weeks' – 10 years' custody

Class C

Maximum: 14 years' custody and/or unlimited fine

Offence range: Community order – 8 years' custody

Step One
Determining the offence category

The court should determine the offender's culpability (role) and the harm caused (quantity) with reference to the tables below.

In assessing culpability, the sentencer should weigh up all the factors of the case to determine role. Where there are characteristics present which fall under different role categories, the court should balance these characteristics to reach a fair assessment of the offender's culpability.

In assessing harm, quantity is determined by the weight of the product. Purity is not taken into account at step 1 but is dealt with at step 2.

Where the operation is on the most serious and commercial scale, involving a quantity of drugs significantly higher than category 1, sentences of 20 years and above may be appropriate, depending on the role of the offender.

Culpability demonstrated by offender's role

One or more of these characteristics may demonstrate the offender's role. These lists are not exhaustive.

LEADING role:

- directing or organising buying and selling on a commercial scale;
- substantial links to, and influence on, others in a chain;
- close links to original source;
- expectation of substantial financial gain;
- uses business as cover;
- abuses a position of trust or responsibility.

SIGNIFICANT role:

- operational or management function within a chain;
- involves others in the operation whether by pressure, influence, intimidation or reward;
- motivated by financial or other advantage, whether or not operating alone;
- some awareness and understanding of scale of operation.

LESSER role:

- performs a limited function under direction;
- engaged by pressure, coercion, intimidation;
- involvement through naivety/exploitation;

- no influence on those above in a chain;
- very little, if any, awareness or understanding of the scale of operation;
- if own operation, solely for own use (considering reasonableness of account in all the circumstances).

Category of harm

Indicative quantity of drug concerned (upon which the starting point is based):

Category 1

- heroin, cocaine – 5kg;
- ecstasy – 10,000 tablets;
- LSD – 250,000 squares;
- amphetamine – 20kg;
- cannabis – 200kg;
- ketamine – 5kg.

Category 2

- heroin, cocaine – 1kg;
- ecstasy – 2,000 tablets;
- LSD – 25,000 squares;
- amphetamine – 4kg;
- cannabis – 40kg;
- ketamine – 1kg.

Category 3

- heroin, cocaine – 150g;
- ecstasy – 300 tablets;
- LSD – 2,500 squares;
- amphetamine – 750g;
- cannabis – 6kg;
- ketamine – 150g.

Category 4

- heroin, cocaine – 5g;
- ecstasy – 20 tablets;
- LSD – 170 squares;
- amphetamine – 20g;
- cannabis – 100g;
- ketamine – 5g.

Step Two
Starting point and category range

Having determined the category, the court should use the corresponding starting point to reach a sentence within the category range below. The starting point applies to all offenders irrespective of plea or previous convictions. The court should then consider further adjustment within the category range for aggravating or mitigating features, set out over the page. In cases where the offender is regarded as being at the very top of the 'leading' role it may be justifiable for the court to depart from the guideline.

Where the defendant is dependent on or has a propensity to misuse drugs and there is sufficient prospect of success, a community order with a drug rehabilitation requirement under section 209 of the Criminal Justice Act 2003 can be a proper alternative to a short or moderate length custodial sentence.

For **class A** cases, section 110 of the Powers of Criminal Courts (Sentencing) Act 2000 provides that a court should impose a minimum sentence of at least seven years' imprisonment for a third class A trafficking offence except where the court is of the opinion that there are particular circumstances which (a) relate to any of the offences or to the offender; and (b) would make it unjust to do so in all the circumstances.

CLASS A	Leading role	Significant role	Lesser role
Category 1	**Starting point**	**Starting point**	**Starting point**
	14 years' custody	10 years' custody	8 years' custody
	Category range	**Category range**	**Category range**
	12 – 16 years' custody	9 – 12 years' custody	6 – 9 years' custody
Category 2	**Starting point**	**Starting point**	**Starting point**
	11 years' custody	8 years' custody	6 years' custody
	Category range	**Category range**	**Category range**
	9 – 13 years' custody	6 years 6 months' – 10 years' custody	5 – 7 years' custody
Category 3	**Starting point**	**Starting point**	**Starting point**
	8 years 6 months' custody	6 years 6 months' – 10 years' custody	4 years 6 months' custody
	Category range	**Category range**	**Category range**
	6 years' custody	5 – 7 years' custody	3 years 6 months' – 5 years' custody
Category 4	Where the quantity falls below the indicative amount set out for category 4 on the previous page, first identify the role for the importation offence, then refer to the starting point and ranges for possession or supply offences, depending on intent.		
	Where the quantity is significantly larger than the indicative amounts for category 4 but below category 3 amounts, refer to the category 3 ranges above.		

CLASS B	Leading role	Significant role	Lesser role
Category 1	**Starting point**	**Starting point**	**Starting point**
	8 years' custody	5 years 6 months' custody	4 years' custody
	Category range	**Category range**	**Category range**
	7 – 10 years' custody	5 – 7 years' custody	2 years 6 months' – 5 years' custody
Category 2	**Starting point**	**Starting point**	**Starting point**
	6 years' custody	4 years' custody	2 years' custody
	Category range	**Category range**	**Category range**
	4 years 6 months' – 8 years' custody	2 years 6 months' – 5 years' custody	18 months' – 3 years' custody

CLASS B	Leading role	Significant role	Lesser role
Category 3	**Starting point**	**Starting point**	**Starting point**
	4 years' custody	2 years' custody	1 year's custody
	Category range	**Category range**	**Category range**
	2 years 6 months' – 5 years' custody	18 months' – 3 years' custody	12 weeks' – 18 months' custody
Category 4	Where the quantity falls below the indicative amount set out for category 4 on the previous page, first identify the role for the importation offence, then refer to the starting point and ranges for possession or supply offences, depending on intent. Where the quantity is significantly larger than the indicative amounts for category 4 but below category 3 amounts, refer to the category 3 ranges above.		

CLASS C	Leading role	Significant role	Lesser role
Category 1	**Starting point**	**Starting point**	**Starting point**
	5 years' custody	3 years' custody	18 months' custody
	Category range	**Category range**	**Category range**
	4 – 8 years' custody	2 – 5 years' custody	1 – 3 years' custody
Category 2	**Starting point**	**Starting point**	**Starting point**
	3 years 6 months' custody	18 months' custody	26 weeks' custody
	Category range	**Category range**	**Category range**
	2 – 5 years' custody	1 – 3 years' custody	12 weeks' – 18 months' custody
Category 3	**Starting point**	**Starting point**	**Starting point**
	18 months' custody	26 weeks' custody	High level community order
	Category range	**Category range**	**Category range**
	1 – 3 years' custody	12 weeks' – 18 months' custody	Medium level community order – 12 weeks' custody
Category 4	Where the quantity falls below the indicative amount set out for category 4 on the previous page, first identify the role for the importation offence, then referto the starting point and ranges for possession or supply offences, depending on intent. Where the quantity is significantly larger than the indicative amounts for category 4 but below category 3 amounts, refer to the category 3 ranges above.		

The table below contains a **non-exhaustive** list of additional factual elements providing the context of the offence and factors relating to the offender. Identify whether any combination of these, or other relevant factors, should result in an upward or downward adjustment from the starting point. In some cases, having considered these factors, it may be appropriate to move outside the identified category range.

For appropriate **class** C ranges, consider the custody threshold as follows:

- has the custody threshold been passed?
- if so, is it unavoidable that a custodial sentence be imposed?
- if so, can that sentence be suspended?

Factors increasing seriousness

Statutory aggravating factors:

Previous convictions, having regard to a) nature of the offence to which conviction relates and relevance to current offence; and b) time elapsed since conviction

Offender used or permitted a person under 18 to deliver a controlled drug to a third person

Offence committed on bail

Other aggravating factors include:

Sophisticated nature of concealment and/or attempts to avoid detection

Attempts to conceal or dispose of evidence, where not charged separately

Exposure of others to more than usual danger, for example drugs cut with harmful substances

Presence of weapon, where not charged separately

High purity

Failure to comply with current court orders

Offence committed on licence

Factors reducing seriousness or reflecting personal mitigation

Lack of sophistication as to nature of concealment

Involvement due to pressure, intimidation or coercion falling short of duress, except where already taken into account at step 1

Mistaken belief of the offender regarding the type of drug, taking into account the reasonableness of such belief in all the circumstances

Isolated incident

Low purity

No previous convictions **or** no relevant or recent convictions

Offender's vulnerability was exploited

Remorse

Good character and/or exemplary conduct

Determination and/or demonstration of steps having been taken to address addiction or offending behaviour

Serious medical conditions requiring urgent, intensive or long-term treatment

Age and/or lack of maturity where it affects the responsibility of the offender

Mental disorder or learning disability

Sole or primary carer for dependent relatives

Step Three
Consider any factors which indicate a reduction, such as assistance to the prosecution

The court should take into account sections 73 and 74 of the Serious Organised Crime and Police Act 2005 (assistance by defendants: reduction or review of sentence) and any other rule of law by virtue of which an offender may receive a discounted sentence in consequence of assistance given (or offered) to the prosecutor or investigator.

Step Four
Reduction for guilty pleas

The court should take account of any potential reduction for a guilty plea in accordance with section 144 of the Criminal Justice Act 2003 and the *Guilty Plea* guideline.

For class A offences, where a minimum mandatory sentence is imposed under section 110 Powers of Criminal Courts (Sentencing) Act, the discount for an early guilty plea must not exceed 20 per cent.

Step Five
Totality principle

If sentencing an offender for more than one offence, or where the offender is already serving a sentence, consider whether the total sentence is just and proportionate to the offending behaviour.

Step Six
Confiscation and ancillary orders

In all cases, the court is required to consider confiscation where the Crown invokes the process or where the court considers it appropriate. It should also consider whether to make ancillary orders.

Step Seven
Reasons

Section 174 of the Criminal Justice Act 2003 imposes a duty to give reasons for, and explain the effect of, the sentence.

Step Eight
Consideration for remand time

(Now obligatory.)

Drunkenness

Charges

A[28.1] 1 Being found drunk in any highway, public place, or on licensed premises

Licensing Act 1872, s 12

Maximum penalty – Fine level 2.

A[28.2] 2 In a public place namely [. . . . .] was guilty while drunk of disorderly behaviour

Criminal Justice Act 1967, s 91

Maximum penalty – Fine level 3.

NB: A fixed penalty of £80 is available

Legal notes and definitions

A[28.3] Found. Means 'ascertained to be', not 'discovered'.

Lawfulness of arrest.

Police were called to a disturbance in a private garden at 4am. A police officer led the defendant by the arm out of the garden onto a public path. The defendant continued to disturb the peace and was arrested. Placing the events in context and taking a common sense approach, the officer, in acting as he had done, had acted in conformity with the general accepted standards of conduct. A conviction for drunk and disorderly was upheld (*McMillan v Crown Prosecution Service* [2008] EWHC 1457 (Admin), [2008] All ER (D) 142 (May)).

A[28.4] Drunk. Typical evidence of drunkenness is strong smell of drink, falling over, swaying, stumbling, showing evidence of a lack of co-ordination, slurred thick speech, rapid pulse, redness in the face, glazed expression, drowsiness or semi-coma and no evidence of any other cause for these symptoms. A person exhibiting these symptoms as a result of 'glue sniffing' is not drunk for the purposes of this offence or the offence of being drunk and disorderly.

The offence is constituted by the state of drunkenness. The inability of the defendant to take care of himself may permit a constable to arrest the defendant. On a charge of being drunk and disorderly it is the disorderly behaviour that normally provides the trigger for an arrest without warrant (*H v DPP* [2005] EWHC 2459 (Admin), 170 JP 4).

A[28.5] Disorderly. The term 'drunk and disorderly' should be given its natural and ordinary meaning. It was a question of fact and degree whether or not the accused had exhibited 'disorderly behaviour' (*Carroll v DPP* [2009] All ER (D) 35 (Mar), 173 JP 285).

A[28.6] Public place. Includes buildings and any place to which the public has access whether on payment or otherwise, as well as buses or taxis. The entrance hall of a block of flats where admission was controlled by an intercom and a security lock was not a public place (*Williams v DPP* [1992] Crim LR 503).

A[28.7] 'Licensed premises'. Means premises in respect of which a premises licence has effect: Licensing Act 2003, s 193. A licensee cannot be convicted of being found drunk on his own licensed premises after the house has closed because the premises are then his private place: *Lester v Torrens* (1877) 2 QBD 403, 41 JP 821.

Sentencing

A[28.8] NB: There is no published guideline for being drunk in a highway. Consider whether a fine or discharge is appropriate?

SC Guideline – Drunk and disorderly in a public place

A[28.9]

OFFENCE SERIOUSNESS (CULPABILITY AND HARM)		
A. IDENTIFY THE APPROPRIATE STARTING POINT		
Starting points based on first time offender pleading not guilty		
Examples of nature of activity	**Starting point**	**Range**
Shouting, causing disturbance for some minutes	Band A fine	Conditional discharge to band B fine
Substantial disturbance caused	Band B fine	Band A fine to band C fine
OFFENCE SERIOUSNESS (CULPABILITY AND HARM)		
B. CONSIDER THE EFFECT OF AGGRAVATING AND MITIGATING FACTORS (OTHER THAN THOSE WITHIN EXAMPLES ABOVE)		
Common aggravating and mitigating factors are identified at B[5.2A]. The following may be particularly relevant but **these lists are not exhaustive**		
Factors indicating higher culpability	*Factors indicating lower culpability*	
1. Offensive words or conduct involved	1. Minor and non-threatening	
2. Lengthy incident involved	2. Stopped as soon as police arrived	
3. Group action		
Factors indicating greater degree of harm		
1. Offence committed at school, hospital or other place where vulnerable persons may be present		
2. Offence committed on public transport		
3. Victim providing public service		
FORM A PRELIMINARY VIEW OF THE APPROPRIATE SENTENCE, THEN CONSIDER OFFENDER MITIGATION		
Common factors are identified at B[5.2A]		
CONSIDER A REDUCTION FOR A GUILTY PLEA		
CONSIDER ANCILLARY ORDERS, INCLUDING COMPENSATION AND FOOTBALL BANNING ORDER (where appropriate)		
Refer to **Part B** for guidance on available ancillary orders		

DECIDE SENTENCE
GIVE REASONS

A[29]

Exploitation of prostitution

Charges

A[29.1] 1. Intentionally causes or incites another person to become a prostitute in any part of the world, and does so for or in the expectation of gain for himself or a third person.

Sexual Offences Act 2003, s 52.

Maximum penalty – level 5 and/or 6 months' imprisonment. Triable either way.

Specified sexual offence under Sch 15, Part 2, CJA 2003.

Crown Court – 7 years' imprisonment or an unlimited fine.

NB: A new s 51A of the 2003 Act has been added by the Policing and Crime Act 2009. From **1 April 2010** this makes it an offence for a person in a street or public place to solicit another (B) for the purposes of obtaining B's sexual services as a prostitute. References to a person is a street or public place include a person in a vehicle in a street or public place. The offence is a summary only offence carrying a maximum level 3 fine.

A[29.2] 2. Intentionally controls any of the activities of another person relating to that person's prostitution in any part of the world, and does so for or in the expectation of gain for himself or a third person.

Sexual Offences Act 2003, s 53.

Maximum penalty – level 5 and/or 6 months' imprisonment. Triable either way.

Specified sexual offence under Sch 15, Part 2, CJA 2003.

Crown Court – 7 years' imprisonment or an unlimited fine.

NB: A new s 53A of the 2003 Act has been added by the Policing and Crime Act 2009. From **1 April 2010** this makes it an offence to pay for the services of a prostitute subjected to force etc. The offence is a summary only offence carrying a maximum level 3 fine.

Mode of trial

A[29.3] See SC Guideline at A[29.4] below.

Note

Where an offender has profited from his or her involvement in the prostitution of others, the court should consider making a confiscation order approximately equivalent to the profits enjoyed. Such an order may be made only in the Crown Court.

Sentencing
Magistrates' Court Sentencing Guidelines – Exploitation
of prostitution

A[29.4] This guideline is taken from the Magistrates' Court Sentencing Guidelines, effective from 1 April 2014.

Causing or inciting prostitution for gain
Sexual Offences Act 2003 (section 52)

Controlling prostitution for gain
Sexual Offences Act 2003 (section 53)

Triable either way

Maximum: 7 years' custody

Offence range: Community order – 6 years' custody

For convictions on or after 3 December 2012 (irrespective of the date of commission of the offence), these are specified offences for the purposes of section 226A (extended sentence for certain violent or sexual offences) of the Criminal Justice Act 2003.

The terms 'prostitute' and 'prostitution' are used in this guideline in accordance with the statutory language contained in the Sexual Offences Act 2003.

STEP ONE
DETERMINING THE OFFENCE CATEGORY

The court should determine which categories of harm and culpability the offence falls into by reference only to the tables below.

Harm	Culpability
Category 1	**A**
• Abduction/detention	Causing, inciting or controlling prostitution on significant commercial basis
• Violence or threats of violence	Expectation of significant financial or other gain
• Sustained and systematic psychological abuse	Abuse of trust
• Individual(s) forced or coerced to participate in unsafe/degrading sexual activity	Exploitation of those known to be trafficked
• Individual(s) forced or coerced into seeing many 'customers'	Significant involvement in limiting the freedom of prostitute(s)
• Individual(s) forced/coerced/deceived into prostitution	Grooming of individual(s) to enter prostitution including through cultivation of a dependency on drugs or alcohol
Category 2	**B**

Harm	Culpability
Factor(s) in category 1 not present	Close involvement with prostitute(s), for example control of finances, choice of clients, working conditions, etc (where offender's involvement is not as a result of coercion)
	C
	Performs limited function under direction
	Close involvement but engaged by coercion/intimidation/exploitation

STEP TWO
STARTING POINT AND CATEGORY RANGE

Having determined the category, the court should use the corresponding starting points to reach a sentence within the category range on the next page. The starting point applies to all offenders irrespective of plea or previous convictions. Having determined the starting point, step two allows further adjustment for aggravating or mitigating features, set out on the next page.

A case of particular gravity, reflected by multiple features of culpability or harm in step one, could merit upward adjustment from the starting point before further adjustment for aggravating or mitigating features, set out on the next page.

Where there is a sufficient prospect of rehabilitation, a community order with a sex offender treatment programme requirement under section 202 of the Criminal Justice Act 2003 can be a proper alternative to a short or moderate length custodial sentence.

	A	B	C
Category 1	**Starting point** 4 years' custody	**Starting point** 2 years 6 months' custody	**Starting point** 1 years' custody
	Category range 3– 6 years' custody	**Category range** 2 – 4 years' custody	**Category range** 26 weeks' – 2 years' custody
Category 2	**Starting point** 2 years 6 months' custody	**Starting point** 1 year's custody	**Starting point** Medium level community order
	Category range 2 – 5 years' custody custody	**Category range** High level community order – 2 year's custody	**Category range** Low level community order – High level community order

The table below contains a **non-exhaustive** list of additional factual elements providing the context of the offence and factors relating to the offender. Identify whether any combination of these, or other relevant factors, should result in an upward or downward adjustment from the starting point. **In particular, relevant recent convictions are likely to result** in an upward adjustment. In some cases, having considered these factors, it may be appropriate to move outside the identified category range.

When sentencing appropriate **category 2 offences**, the court should also consider the custody threshold as follows:

- has the custody threshold been passed?
- if so, is it unavoidable that a custodial sentence be imposed?
- if so, can that sentence be suspended?

Aggravating factors	Mitigating factors
Statutory aggravating factors	No previous convictions **or** no relevant/recent convictions
Previous convictions, having regard to a) the nature of the offence to which the conviction relates and its relevance to the current offence; and b) the time that has elapsed since the conviction	Remorse
Offence committed whilst on bail	Previous good character and/or exemplary conduct*
Other aggravating factors	Age and/or lack of maturity where it affects the responsibility of the offender
Failure to comply with current court orders	Mental disorder or learning disability, particularly where linked to the commission of the offence
Offence committed whilst on licence	Demonstration of steps taken to address offending behaviour

Aggravating factors	Mitigating factors
Deliberate isolation of prostitute(s)	* Previous good character/exemplary conduct is different from having no previous convictions. The more serious the offence, the less the weight which should normally be attributed to this factor. Where previous good character/exemplary conduct has been used to facilitate the offence, this mitigation should not normally be allowed and such conduct may constitute an aggravating factor.
Threats made to expose prostitute(s) to the authorities (for example, immigration or police), family/friends or others	
Harm threatened against the family/friends of prostitute(s)	
Passport/identity documents removed	
Prostitute(s) prevented from seeking medical treatment	
Food withheld	
Victim(s) prevented from attending school	
Food withheld	
Earnings withheld/kept by offender or evidence of excessive wage reduction or debt bondage, inflated travel or living expenses or unreasonable interest rates	
Any steps taken to prevent the reporting of an incident, obtaining assistance and/or from assisting or supporting the prosecution	
Attempts to dispose of or conceal evidence	
Prostitute(s) forced or coerced into pornography	
Timescale over which operation has been run	

STEP THREE
CONSIDER ANY FACTORS WHICH INDICATE A REDUCTION, SUCH AS ASSISTANCE TO THE PROSECUTION

The court should take into account sections 73 and 74 of the Serious Organised Crime and Police Act 2005 (assistance by defendants: reduction or review of sentence) and any other rule of law by virtue of which an offender may receive a discounted sentence in consequence of assistance given (or offered) to the prosecutor or investigator.

STEP FOUR
REDUCTION FOR GUILTY PLEAS

The court should take account of any potential reduction for a guilty plea in accordance with section 144 of the Criminal Justice Act 2003 and the *Guilty Plea* guideline.

STEP FIVE
DANGEROUSNESS

The court should consider whether having regard to the criteria contained in Chapter 5 of Part 12 of the Criminal Justice Act 2003 it would be appropriate to award an extended sentence (section 226A).

STEP SIX
TOTALITY PRINCIPLE

If sentencing an offender for more than one offence, or where the offender is already serving a sentence, consider whether the total sentence is just and proportionate to the offending behaviour.

STEP SEVEN
ANCILLARY ORDERS

The court must consider whether to make any ancillary orders. The court must also consider what other requirements or provisions may automatically apply. Further information is included on page 303.

STEP EIGHT
REASONS

Section 174 of the Criminal Justice Act 2003 imposes a duty to give reasons for, and explain the effect of, the sentence.

STEP NINE
CONSIDERATION FOR TIME SPENT ON BAIL

The court must consider whether to give credit for time spent on bail in accordance with section 240A of the Criminal Justice Act 2003.

A[29.5] Closure orders: see [B53].

A[30]

Exposure

Charge

A[30.1] Intentionally exposes his genitals, and he intends that someone will see them and be caused alarm or distress.

Sexual Offences Act 2003, s 66.

Maximum penalty – level 5 and/or 6 months' imprisonment. Triable either way.

Specified sexual offence under Sch 15, Part 2, CJA 2003.

Crown Court – 2 years' imprisonment and unlimited fine.

Mode of trial

A[30.2] See SGC Guideline and Notes at A[30.3] below.

Sentencing
Magistrates' Court Sentencing Guidelines – Exposure

A[30.3] This guideline is taken from the Magistrates' Court Sentencing Guidelines, effective from 1 April 2014.

Exposure
Sexual Offences Act 2003 (section 66)

Triable either way

Maximum: 2 years' custody

Offence range: Fine – 1 year's custody

For convictions on or after 3 December 2012 (irrespective of the date of commission of the offence), this is a specified offence for the purposes of section 226A (extended sentence for certain violent or sexual offences) of the Criminal Justice Act 2003.

STEP ONE
DETERMINING THE OFFENCE CATEGORY

The court should determine the offence category using the table below.

Category 1	Raised harm **and** raised culpability
Category 2	Raised harm **or** raised culpability
Category 3	Exposure **without** raised harm or culpability factors present

The court should determine culpability and harm caused or intended, by reference only to the factors below, which comprise the principal factual elements of the offence. Where an offence does not fall squarely into a category, individual factors may require a degree of weighting before making an overall assessment and determining the appropriate offence category.

Factors indicating raised harm	Factors indicating raised culpability
Victim followed/pursued	Specific or previous targeting of a particularly vulnerable victim
Offender masturbated	Abuse of trust
	Use of threats (including blackmail)
	Offence racially or religiously aggravated
	Offence motivated by, or demonstrating, hostility to the victim based on his or her sexual orientation (or presumed sexual orientation) or transgender identity (or presumed transgender identity)
	Offence motivated by, or demonstrating, hostility to the victim based on his or her disability (or presumed disability)

STEP TWO
STARTING POINT AND CATEGORY RANGE

Having determined the category, the court should use the corresponding starting points to reach a sentence within the category range on the next page. The starting point applies to all offenders irrespective of plea or previous convictions. Having determined the starting point, step two allows further adjustment for aggravating or mitigating features, set out on the next page.

A case of particular gravity, reflected by multiple features of culpability or harm in step one, could merit upward adjustment from the starting point before further adjustment for aggravating or mitigating features, set out on the next page.

Where there is a sufficient prospect of rehabilitation, a community order with a sex offender treatment programme requirement under section 202 of the Criminal Justice Act 2003 can be a proper alternative to a short or moderate length custodial sentence.

Category 1	**Starting point** 26 weeks' custody
	Category range 12 weeks' – 1 year's custody
Category 2	**Starting point** High level community order
	Category range Medium level community order – 26 weeks' custody
Category 3	**Starting point** Medium level community order

Category range Band A fine – High level community order

The table below contains a **non-exhaustive** list of additional factual elements providing the context of the offence and factors relating to the offender. Identify whether any combination of these, or other relevant factors, should result in an upward or downward adjustment from the starting point. **In particular, relevant recent convictions are likely to result in an upward adjustment.** In some cases, having considered these factors, it may be appropriate to move outside the identified category range.

When sentencing **category 2 offences**, the court should also consider the custody threshold as follows:

•   has the custody threshold been passed?
•   f so, is it unavoidable that a custodial sentence be imposed?
•   if so, can that sentence be suspended?

When sentencing **category 3 offences**, the court should also consider the community order threshold as follows:

Aggravating factors	Mitigating factors
Statutory aggravating factors	No previous convictions or no relevant/recent convictions
Previous convictions, having regard to a) the nature of the offence to which the conviction relates and its relevance to the current offence; and b) the time that has elapsed since the conviction	Remorse
Offence committed whilst on bail	Previous good character and/or exemplary conduct*
Other aggravating factors	Age and/or lack of maturity where it affects the responsibility of the offender
Location of offence	Mental disorder or learning disability, particularly where linked to the commission of the offence
Timing of offence Any steps taken to prevent the victim reporting an incident, obtaining assistance and/or from assisting or supporting the prosecution	Demonstration of steps taken to address offending behaviour
Failure to comply with current court orders	* Previous good character/exemplary conduct is different from having no previous convictions. The more serious the offence, the less the weight which should normally be attributed to this factor. Where previous good character/exemplary conduct has been used to facilitate the offence, this mitigation should not normally be allowed and such conduct may constitute an aggravating factor.
Offence committed whilst on licence	
Commission of offence whilst under the influence of alcohol or drugs Presence of others, especially children	

STEP THREE
CONSIDER ANY FACTORS WHICH INDICATE A REDUCTION, SUCH AS ASSISTANCE TO THE PROSECUTION

The court should take into account sections 73 and 74 of the Serious Organised Crime and Police Act 2005 (assistance by defendants: reduction or review of sentence) and any other rule of law by virtue of which an offender may receive a discounted sentence in consequence of assistance given (or offered) to the prosecutor or investigator.

STEP FOUR
REDUCTION FOR GUILTY PLEAS

The court should take account of any potential reduction for a guilty plea in accordance with section 144 of the Criminal Justice Act 2003 and the *Guilty Plea* guideline.

STEP FIVE
DANGEROUSNESS

The court should consider whether having regard to the criteria contained in Chapter 5 of Part 12 of the Criminal Justice Act 2003 it would be appropriate to award an extended sentence (section 226A).

STEP SIX
TOTALITY PRINCIPLE

If sentencing an offender for more than one offence, or where the offender is already serving a sentence, consider whether the total sentence is just and proportionate to the offending behaviour.

STEP SEVEN
ANCILLARY ORDERS

The court must consider whether to make any ancillary orders. The court must also consider what other requirements or provisions may *automatically* apply. Further information is included on page 303.

STEP EIGHT
REASONS

Section 174 of the Criminal Justice Act 2003 imposes a duty to give reasons for, and explain the effect of, the sentence.

STEP NINE
CONSIDERATION FOR TIME SPENT ON BAIL

The court must consider whether to give credit for time spent on bail in accordance with section 240A of the Criminal Justice Act 2003.

False accounting

Charge

A[31.1] Dishonestly and with a view to gain for himself or another or with intent to cause loss to another—

(a) destroys, defaces, conceals or falsifies any account or any record or document made or required for any accounting purpose; or

(b) in furnishing information for any purpose produces or makes use of any account, or any such record or document as aforesaid, which to his knowledge is or may be misleading, false or deceptive in any material particular.

Theft Act 1968, s 17

Maximum penalty – Fine level 5 and/or 6 months' imprisonment.

Crown Court – 7 years' imprisonment and unlimited fine.

Mode of trial

A[31.2] See general notes at D[4] and SC Guidelines below.

Legal notes and definitions

A[31.3] 'Gain' and 'loss'. These terms are defined in s 34(2)(a) of the Theft Act as:

'"gain" and "loss" are to be construed as extending only to gain or loss in money or other property, but as extending to any such gain or loss whether temporary or permanent; and–

(i) "gain" includes a gain by keeping what one has, as well as a gain by getting what one has not; and

(ii) "loss" includes a loss by not getting what one might get, as well as a loss by parting with what one has;'

The use of falsified bills of exchange with a view to securing a bank's forbearance from enforcing repayment of existing debts does not constitute falsification with a view to 'gain' within the meaning of this section, *R v Golechha* [1989] 3 All ER 908, [1989] 1 WLR 1050, CA.

This section applies generally to the falsification of accounting documents for the purpose of obtaining financial gain or causing financial loss. It does not require that such gain or loss should in fact result. It is to be contrasted to the statutory scheme under s 111A of the Social Security Administration Act 1992 where the mischief aimed at is not falsification of documents but dishonest failure by a recipient of public benefits to notify the relevant authority of a change of circumstances which would make a difference to the computation of his benefit: *R v Lancaster* [2010] EWCA Crim 370, [2010] 3 All ER 402, [2010] 2 Cr App R 7, [2010] Crim LR 776.

A[31.3A] 'Accounting purpose' and 'material particular'. In *Re A-G's Reference (No 1 of 1980)* [1981] 1 All ER 366, [1981] 1 WLR 34 it was held, on the facts of that reference, that a personal loan proposal form was a document 'required for any accounting purpose'. A claim form submitted in respect of a home insurance policy may be a document made or required for an accounting purpose in that the insurance company may use the form as a basis for keeping its accounting records, but the court must receive some evidence that it is in fact used for this purpose and the court cannot draw its own conclusion from the nature and form of the claim form: *R v Sundhers* [1998] Crim LR 497, CA. A court is entitled, however, without any further direct evidence of the accounting practices of the lender, to conclude that an application for a mortgage or a loan made to a commercial institution is a document required for an accounting purpose: *R v O and B* [2010] EWCA Crim 2233, [2011] 2 All ER 656, [2011] 1 WLR 2936, [2011] 2 Cr App R 33(in this regard not following *Sundhers*). See also *R v Manning* [1999] QB 980, [1998] 4 All ER 876, [1998] 2 Cr App Rep 461, CA (court entitled to conclude that insurance cover note an accounting document as it set out on the document what was owed by the client), and *Re Baxter* [2002] All ER (D) 218 (Jan), (2002) JPN 99 (a certificate, included in an application pack for an investment scheme, by which an insurance company purportedly stood behind the investment programme concerned could be regarded as a document made or required for an accounting purpose, but another document that was a general solicitation, any response to which would have resulted in the issue of accounting documents, could not be so regarded).

Although the document itself must be made or required for an accounting purpose, the material particular in question does not have to be one which is directly connected with the accounting purpose of the document: *R v Mallett* [1978] 3 All ER 10.

A[31.4]–[31.7] The offence information and guidelines on fraud – banking and insurance fraud, and obtaining credit through fraud, benefit fraud, revenue fraud and confidence – can now be found at **A[36.10]** and **A[36.11]**.

A[32]

False identity documents

Charge

A[32.1] Have in his possession or under his control, without reasonable excuse—

(a)   an identify document that is false,
(b)   an identity document that was improperly obtained,
(c)   an identity document that relates to someone else,
(d)   any apparatus, article or material which, to his knowledge, is or has been specially designed or adapted for he making of false identify documents or to be used in the making of such documents, or
(e)   any article or material which, to his knowledge, is or has been specially designed or adapted to be used in the making of such documents.

Identity Documents Act 2010, s 6(1)*

Maximum penalty – Fine level 5 and/or 6 months' imprisonment.

Crown Court – 2 years' imprisonment and unlimited fine.

*NB: From 21 January 2011 this legislation repealed the Identity Cards Act 2006.

Mode of trial

A[32.2] See the SC Guideline below.

Defences

A[32.2A] Section 31(1) of the Immigration and Asylum Act 1999 provides a defence to certain offences, including those under ss 4 and 6 of the Identity Documents Act 2010, based on Art 31(1) of the United Nations Convention relating to the Status of Refugees. It states:

(1)   It is a defence for a refugee charged with an offence to which this section applies to show that, having come to the United Kingdom directly from a country where his life or freedom was threatened (within the meaning of the Refugee Convention), he–
    (a)   presented himself to the authorities in the United Kingdom without delay;
    (b)   showed good cause for his illegal entry or presence; and
    (c)   made a claim for asylum as soon as was reasonably practicable after his arrival in the United Kingdom.

The term 'refugee' bears its Convention meaning, namely:

'a refugee is a person who has left his own country owing to a well-founded fear of being persecuted for reasons of race, religion, nationality, membership of a particular social group or political opinion.'

Provided that the defendant can adduce sufficient evidence in support of his claim to refugee status to raise the issue, the prosecution bears the burden of proving to the usual standard that he is not in fact a refugee. Different considerations apply, however, in relation to the other matters which have to be established under s 31(1). The burden, here, is legal rather than merely evidential.

The defence is qualified, however, by s 32(2). This provides:

'If, in coming from the country where his life or freedom was threatened, the refugee stopped in another country outside the United Kingdom, subsection (1) applies only if he shows that he could not reasonably have expected to be given protection under the Refugee Convention in that other country.'

See further, **A[81.8A]**, below.

In *R v MV* [2010] EWCA Crim 2400, [2011] 1 Cr App Rep 432, the appellant had come into the UK on a flight from Italy. Given his inability to say whether his flight had stopped during his journey from Somalia and to account for where he had spent one and a half days, a jury could have inferred that he had in all probability remained in Italy. Even if no legal advice had been given regarding the availability of a defence under s 31 of the Immigration and Asylum Act 1999, there was no reasonable prospect of that defence succeeding.

The absence of words in what was subsection (5) of s 25 of the Identity Cards Act 2006, such as are found in subsection (1) of s 25, indicates that a defendant who does not know or believe that a document is false cannot of itself, per se, amount to a reasonable excuse (even for an offence under what is now s 6(1)). However, lack of knowledge or belief might be relevant to a defence of reasonable excuse. The defence is found in various statutory contexts and it is par excellence a matter for the jury whether or not a reasonable excuse has been established. A judge ought to withdraw that issue from the jury only if no reasonable jury could conclude on the facts alleged that the explanation was capable of constituting a reasonable excuse. Nothing in s 25 suggested that honest belief in the genuineness of the document is a factor which the jury is obliged to ignore. Accordingly, the defendant was entitled to rely upon her genuine belief that the document was valid while contending that she had a reasonable excuse for having the false passport in her possession: see *R v Unah* [2011] EWCA Crim 1837, 175 JP 391, [2011] 30 LS Gaz R 24.

Sentencing
SC Guideline – False identity documents

A[32.3] Note: possession of a false identity document with an improper intention of using it is an indictable only offence (Identity Documents Act 2010, s 4(1)). The maximum penalty is 10 years' imprisonment and an unlimited fine.

OFFENCE SERIOUSNESS (CULPABILITY AND HARM)
A. IDENTIFY THE APPROPRIATE STARTING POINT

Starting points based on first time offender pleading not guilty		
Examples of nature of activity	**Starting point**	**Range**
Single document possessed	Medium community order	Band C fine to high level community order
Small number of documents, no evidence of dealing	12 weeks custody	6 weeks custody to Crown Court
Considerable number of documents possessed, evidence of involvement in larger operation	Crown Court	Crown Court

OFFENCE SERIOUSNESS (CULPABILITY AND HARM)

B. CONSIDER THE EFFECT OF AGGRAVATING AND MITIGATING FACTORS (OTHER THAN THOSE WITHIN EXAMPLES ABOVE)

Common aggravating and mitigating factors are identified at B[5.2A]. The following may be particularly relevant but **these lists are not exhaustive**

Factors indicating higher culpability	*Factor indicating lower culpability*
1. Clear knowledge that documents false	1. Genuine mistake or ignorance
2. Number of documents possessed (where not in offence descriptions above)	
Factors indicating greater degree of harm	
1. Group activity	
2. Potential impact of use (where not in offence descriptions above)	

FORM A PRELIMINARY VIEW OF THE APPROPRIATE SENTENCE, THEN CONSIDER OFFENDER MITIGATION

Common factors are identified at B[5.2A]

CONSIDER A REDUCTION FOR A GUILTY PLEA

DECIDE SENTENCE

GIVE REASONS

Firearm, carrying in a public place

Charge

A[33.1] Without lawful authority or reasonable excuse having in a public place (a loaded shotgun), (a firearm loaded or not and ammunition suitable for use in the said firearm) (an air weapon loaded or not) or (an imitation firearm)

Firearms Act 1968, s 19

Maximum penalty -

Firearm: Fine level 5 and 6 months and forfeiture. Triable either way.

Air weapon: Fine level 5 and/or 6 months and forfeiture. Triable only by magistrates.

Crown Court – 7 years' imprisonment and unlimited fine (12 months for imitation firearm).

Where the offence is committed in respect of certain, specified firearms or ammunition the court must pass an 'appropriate custodial sentence' of at least the 'required minimum term' (three years for offenders aged under 18, five years for older offenders) unless the court is of the opinion that there are 'exceptional circumstances relate to the offence or to the offender which justify its not doing so': Firearms Act 1968, s 51A.

Mode of trial

A[33.2] See the SC Guideline below.

Legal notes and definitions

A[33.3] 'Public place' and 'has with him'. Public place 'includes any highway, premises or place to which the public at the material time has access whether on payment or otherwise': Firearms Act 1968, s 57(4). In *Anderson v Miller* [1976] Crim LR 743, the space behind a counter in a shop was held to be a public place.

To prove that the accused had with him a firearm the prosecution must establish more than mere possession, namely that the accused had a close physical link and immediate control over the firearm; but it is not necessary to establish that he had been carrying it: *R v Kelt* [1977] 3 All ER 1099, 142 JP 60 and see *R v Pawlicki* and *R v Swindell* [1992] 1 WLR 827, [1992] Crim LR 584, CA.

A[33.4] Without lawful authority or reasonable excuse. The Firearms Act 1968 expressly places on the defendant the burden of proving that he had lawful authority or reasonable excuse. He only has to prove that on the balance of probabilities he had lawful authority or reasonable excuse. He does not have to prove this beyond all reasonable doubt.

(a)   A certificate for a firearm was not in itself lawful authority under the Firearms Act 1968, s 19, for the holder of the certificate to have the firearm and ammunition for it in a public place.

(b)   The mistaken belief by the holder of an invalid firearm certificate that it was valid and that it was lawful authority under the Firearms Act 1968, s 19 was not capable of being a reasonable excuse and therefore a defence under that section

(*R v Jones* [1995] QB 235, [1995] 3 All ER 139, CA).

A[33.5] ECHR. Having regard to the legitimate aims of the legislation, it is suggested that the shifting of the legal burden of proof to the accused is necessary and proportionate in ECHR terms.

A[33.6] Shotgun. Although the firearm need not be loaded a shotgun must be loaded to establish this offence. A shotgun is a smooth bore gun whose barrel is 24 inches or longer with a bore not exceeding two inches and which is not a revolver nor has an illegal magazine, not being an air gun.

A[33.7] Air weapon. An air weapon may be loaded or not to establish this offence. An air weapon is an air gun, air rifle or an air pistol of a type which has not been declared by the Home Office to be specially dangerous (see **A[76.7]**).

A[33.8] Firearm. This is defined by s 57(1) of the Firearms Act 1968 as:

(1)   In this Act, the expression 'firearm' means a lethal barrelled weapon of any description from which any shot, bullet or other missile can be discharged and includes–

    (a)   any prohibited weapon, whether it is such a lethal weapon as aforesaid or not; and

    (b)   any component part of such a lethal or prohibited weapon; and

    (c)   any accessory to any such weapon designed or adapted to diminish the noise or flash caused by firing the weapon.

'Lethal weapon' includes a weapon not designed to kill or inflict injury but capable of doing so if misused: *Read v Donovan* [1947] KB 326, [1947] 1 All ER 37, 111 JP 46 (signal pistol); *Moore v Gooderham* [1960] 3 All ER 575, 124 JP 513 (air gun); *R v Thorpe* [1987] 2 All ER 108, [1987] 1 WLR 383 (revolver powered by compressed carbon dioxide); *R v Singh* [1989] Crim LR 724 (flare launcher).

A[33.9] An imitation firearm which is so constructed or adapted as to be readily convertible into a firearm is to be treated as a firearm even though it has not been so converted: *Castle v DPP* (1998) The Times, April 3. A starting pistol which could be adapted for firing bullets if the barrel was drilled was held to be a firearm in *R v Freeman* [1970] 2 All ER 413, [1970] 1 WLR 788, CA.

In *R v Bewley* [2012] EWCA Crim 1457, [2013] 1 All ER 1, [2013] 1 WLR 137 the weapon in question was a starting pistol, which was originally designed to fire blank cartridges. A 2cm hole had been drilled into the solid barrel and the top of the hammer had been broken off. A senior forensic scientist was able to fire it by placing it in a vice, inserting a specially selected lead pellet and using a mallet and punch to strike the firing pin. The judge ruled that the pistol was a lethal-barrelled weapon from which a missile '(could) be discharged', but the Court of Appeal quashed the conviction. Although the Firearms Act 1982 had not amended the Firearms Act 1968, the two had to be construed as creating a single code. It was the clear legislative intention of the 1982 Act to exclude from the 1968 Act imitation firearms which could only be readily convertible into firearms by equipment or tools not in common use.

A[33.9A] Imitation firearm. An imitation firearm means anything which has the appearance of being a firearm (other than any weapon designed or adapted for the discharge of any noxious liquid, gas or other thing) whether or not it is capable of discharging any shot, bullet or other missile: Firearms Act 1968, s 57(4). The test is whether the thing looked like a firearm at the time when the accused had it for that purpose: *R v Morris and King* (1984) 149 JP 60, 79 Cr App Rep 104, CA. Two fingers inside the defendant's pocket cannot constitute possession of an imitation firearm under s 17(2) of the Act: *R v Bentham* [2005] UKHL 18, [2005] 2 All ER 65, HL.

A[33.10] An offence is committed whether the firearm is loaded or not but the defendant must have with him ammunition suitable for use in that firearm.

Sentencing
SC Guideline – Firearm, carrying in a public place

A[33.11]

OFFENCE SERIOUSNESS (CULPABILITY AND HARM)
A. IDENTIFY THE APPROPRIATE STARTING POINT
Starting points based on first time offender pleading not guilty

Examples of nature of activity	Starting point	Range
Carrying an unloaded air weapon	Low level community order	Band B fine to medium level community order
Carrying loaded air weapon/imitation firearm/unloaded shotgun without ammunition	High level community order	Medium level community order to 26 weeks custody (air weapon) Medium level community order to Crown Court (imitation firearm, unloaded shotgun)
Carrying loaded shotgun/carrying shotgun or any other firearm together with ammunition with it	Crown Court	Crown Court

OFFENCE SERIOUSNESS (CULPABILITY AND HARM)
B. CONSIDER THE EFFECT OF AGGRAVATING AND MITIGATING FACTORS (OTHER THAN THOSE WITHIN EXAMPLES ABOVE)
Common aggravating and mitigating factors are identified at B[5.2A]. The following may be particularly relevant but **these lists are not exhaustive**

Factors indicating higher culpability	*Factors indicating lower culpability*
1. Brandishing the firearm	1. Firearm not in sight
2. Carrying firearm in a busy place	2. No intention to use forearm
3. Planned illegal use	3. Firearm to be used for lawful purpose (not amounting to a defence)
Factors indicating greater degree of harm	
1. Person or people put in fear	
2. Offender participating in violent incident	

FORM A PRELIMINARY VIEW OF THE APPROPRIATE SENTENCE, THEN CONSIDER OFFENDER MITIGATION
Common factors are identified at B[5.2A]
CONSIDER A REDUCTION FOR A GUILTY PLEA
CONSIDER ANCILLARY ORDERS, INCLUDING COMPENSATION, FORFEITURE OR SUSPENSION OF PERSONAL LIQUOR LICENCE AND FOOTBALL BANNING ORDER (where appropriate)
Refer to B[18] for guidance on compensation and **Part B** for guidance on available ancillary orders
DECIDE SENTENCE
GIVE REASONS

A[33.12] Available sentences. See Table A at B[4.1] (firearms) and Table B at B[4.2] (air weapons).

A[33.13] Forfeiture. The court can order the firearm (imitation, or shotgun or air weapon) to be forfeited to the police or to be disposed of as the court thinks fit. The court can also cancel any firearm or shotgun certificate held by the defendant.

A[34]

Football related offences

(For other related drunkenness offences see A[35] below)

Charges

A[34.1] 1 Being a person at a regulated football match and throwing anything at or towards (the playing area, or any area adjacent to the playing area to which spectators are not generally admitted) (any area in which spectators or other persons are or may be present) without lawful authority or lawful excuse

Football (Offences) Act 1991, s 2

A[34.2] 2 Taking part at a regulated football match in chanting of an indecent or racialist nature

Football (Offences) Act 1991, s 3

A[34.3] 3 At a regulated football match going onto the playing area, or any area adjacent to the playing area to which spectators are not generally admitted, without lawful authority or lawful excuse

Football (Offences) Act 1991, s 4

Maximum penalty (for each offence) – Fine level 3.

A[34.4] 4 Being an unauthorised person, did sell, or offer or expose for sale, a ticket for a designated football match in any public place or place to which the public has access or, in the course of a trade or business, in any other place.

Criminal Justice and Public Order Act 1994, s 166.

Maximum penalty – Fine level 5.

Legal notes and definitions

A[34.5] The creation of these offences follows the recommendations of the Taylor report into the Hillsborough Disaster. They can be committed only in respect of matches in England and Wales.

A[34.6] Designated football matches for the purposes of the Football (Offences) Act 1991. The Football (Offences) (Designation of Football Matches) Order 2004, SI 2004/2410, as amended, designates football matches for the purpose of this Act. A designated football match is an association football match in which one or both of the participating teams represents a club which is for the time being a member (whether a full or associate member) of the Football League, the Football Association Premier League, the Football Conference, the Scottish Football League or the Welsh Premier League, or whose home ground is for the time being situated outside England and Wales, or represents a country or territory. A designated match is also an association football match in competition for the Football Association Cup (other than in a preliminary or qualifying round).

A[34.6A] Designated football match (ticket touting). The Ticket Touting (Designation of Football Matches) Order 2007, SI 2007/790 designates the following matches:

(1)   an association football match played in England and Wales in which one or both of the participating teams represents:

    (a)   a club which is for the time being a member (whether a full or associate member) of the Football League, the Football Association Premier League, the Football Conference or the League of Wales;

    (b)   a club whose home ground is for the time being situated outside England and Wales; or

    (c)   a country or territory.

(2)   an association football match played outside England and Wales involving:

    (a)   a national team appointed by the Football Association to represent England or appointed by the Football Association of Wales to represent Wales;

    (b)   a team representing a club which is for the time being a member (whether a full or associate member) of the Football League, the Football Association Premier League, the Football Conference or the League of Wales;

    (c)   a team representing any country or territory whose football association is for the time being a member of FIFA, where:

        (i)   the match is part of a competition or tournament organised by, or under the authority of, FIFA or UEFA, and

        (ii)   the competition or tournament is one in which a team referred to in sub-paragraph (a) is eligible to participate or has participated; or

    (d)   a team representing a club which is for the time being a member (whether a full or associate member) of, or affiliated to, a national football association which is a member of FIFA, where:

        (i)   the match is part of a competition or tournament organised by, or under the authority of, FIFA or UEFA, and

        (ii)   the competition or tournament is one in which a club referred to in sub-paragraph (b) is eligible to participate or has participated.

A[34.7] In addition, the match must take place on a ground occupied by a Football (or Premier) League Club or which is designated under the Safety of Sports Grounds Act 1975.

A[34.8] **Being or taking part at.** The offence may be committed in a period beginning two hours before the start of the match or, if earlier, two hours before the time it is advertised to start and ending one hour after the end of the match. Where a match is postponed or cancelled, the period includes the two hours before and one hour after the advertised starting time.

A[34.9] **Without lawful authority or lawful excuse.** The defendant must establish this but he only has to establish that his defence is probably true, he does not have to establish it beyond reasonable doubt.

A[34.10] Charge 1: Throwing an object. The prosecution only has to prove that the object was thrown, not that a particular person was aimed at or caused alarm or distress thereby.

A[34.11]–[34.14] Charge 2: Indecent or racialist chanting. 'Chanting' means the repeated uttering of any words or sounds alone or with one or more others. 'Racialist nature' means consisting of or including matter which is threatening, abusive or insulting to a person by reason of his colour, race, nationality (including citizenship) or ethnic or national origins, whether alone or in concert with one or more others. In *DPP v Stoke on Trent Magistrates' Court* [2003] EWHC 1593 (Admin), [2003] 3 All ER 1086, for example, 'Paki' was racially offensive.

Sentencing
SC Guideline – Football ground offences

A[34.15]

OFFENCE SERIOUSNESS (CULPABILITY AND HARM)		
A. IDENTIFY THE APPROPRIATE STARTING POINT		
Starting points based on first time offender pleading not guilty		
Examples of nature of activity	**Starting point**	**Range**
Being drunk in, or whilst trying to enter, ground (see A[35]).	Band A fine	Conditional discharge to band B fine
Going onto playing or other prohibited area Unauthorised sale or attempted sale of tickets	Band B fine	Band A fine to band C fine
Throwing missile Indecent or racist chanting	Band C fine	Band B fine to medium level community order
Possession of alcohol whilst entering or trying to enter ground (see A[35]).	Band C fine	Band B fine to high level community order
OFFENCE SERIOUSNESS (CULPABILITY AND HARM)		
B. CONSIDER THE EFFECT OF AGGRAVATING AND MITIGATING FACTORS (OTHER THAN THOSE WITHIN THE EXAMPLES ABOVE)		
Common aggravating and mitigating factors are identified at B[5.2A]. The following may be particularly relevant but **these lists are not exhaustive**		
Factors indicating higher culpability		
1. Commercial ticket operation; potential high cash value; counterfeit tickets		
2. Inciting others to misbehave		
3. Possession of large quantity of alcohol		
4. Offensive language or behaviour (where not an element of the offence)		
Factor indicating greater degree of harm		

1. Missile likely to cause serious injury eg coin, glass, bottle or stone	
FORM A PRELIMINARY VIEW OF THE APPROPRIATE SENTENCE, THEN CONSIDER OFFENDER MITIGATION Common factors are identified at B[5.2A]	
CONSIDER A REDUCTION FOR A GUILTY PLEA	
CONSIDER ANCILLARY ORDERS, INCLUDING COMPENSATION AND FOOTBALL BANNING ORDER Refer to **Part B** and consult your legal adviser on guidance for available ancillary orders	
DECIDE SENTENCE **GIVE REASONS**	

A[34.16] Available sentences. See Table C at B[4.3].

A[34.17] In addition to any sentence it may impose, the court will normally make a **football banning order** (at B[41]). These orders prevent the defendant from attending football matches in England and Wales or outside England and Wales under s 10 of the Act, if the court is satisfied, on conviction of a relevant offence, that there are reasonable grounds for believing that such an order will help prevent disorder at football matches (*R (on the application of Brown) v Inner London Crown Court* [2003] EWHC 3194 (Admin), [2003] All ER (D) 256 (Dec)). If the court is not so satisfied, it must state that fact in open court and give its reasons. Those reasons will be recorded in the court register.

Football-related offences: Sporting events (control of alcohol etc)

Charges

A[35.1] 1(a) Being the operator (or hirer) (or his servant or agent) knowingly causing or permitting intoxicating liquor to be carried on a public service vehicle which was being used for the principal purpose of carrying passengers for the whole or part of a journey to or from a designated sporting event

OR

(b) Possessing intoxicating liquor whilst on such a vehicle

OR

(c) Being drunk on such a vehicle

Sporting Events (Control of Alcohol etc) Act 1985, 1(2), 1(3) and 1(4) (See para A[35.4] for like offences in respect of drivers and keepers of, and passengers on, minibuses.)

A[35.2] 2 (a) Possessing intoxicating liquor (or an article specified by the Act namely [. . . . .]) at a time during the period of a designated sporting event when in an area of a designated sports ground from which the event might have been directly viewed (or while entering or trying to enter such an event)

OR

(b) Being drunk in a designated sports ground at a time during the period of a designated sporting event (or, being drunk while entering or trying to enter such an event)

Sporting Events (Control of Alcohol etc) Act 1985, 2(1) and 2(2)

OR

(c) Possessing an article to which s 2A of the Sporting Events (Control of Alcohol etc) Act 1985 applies:

(i) at any time during the period of a designated sporting event when he is in any area of a designated sports ground from which the event may be directly viewed, or

(ii) while entering or trying to enter a designated sports ground at any time during the period of a designated sporting event at the ground.

Sporting Events (Control of Alcohol etc) Act 1985, s 2A

Maximum penalties –

Offences under   s 1(2) (or 1A(2)) – Fine level 4

ss 1(3), 1A(3), 2(1), 2A(1) – Fine level 3 and 3 months
ss 1(4), 1A(4), and 2(2) – Fine level 2.

Legal notes and definitions

A[35.3] These offences were created in an attempt to deal with rowdy behaviour at football matches primarily where teams belonging to the Football (or Premier) League are involved (including their reserve and youth teams) but generally not at games exclusively concerning 'non-league' or amateur clubs. In addition, the Act provides for a total ban on the sale of alcohol at such matches although there is the opportunity for the club to apply to the relevant local authority for an order modifying this prohibition (see Section F).

A[35.4] **Public service vehicle** means a motor vehicle adapted to carry more than eight passengers for hire or reward. (For this and the definition of 'operator' see the Public Passenger Vehicles Act 1981, s 181.) This offence also applies to a person who knowingly causes or permits intoxicating liquor to be carried in these circumstances on a railway passenger vehicle which he has hired. The Sporting Events (Control of Alcohol etc) Act 1985, s 1A makes provision for offences similar to those under s 1(a), (b) and (c) for drivers and keepers of a minibus, ie not a public service vehicle, but one which is adapted to carry more than eight passengers, and is being used for the principal purpose of carrying two or more passengers for the whole or part of a journey to or from a designated sporting event.

A[35.5] **Designated sports grounds and sporting events.** The Sports Grounds and Sporting Events (Designation) Order 2005, SI 2005/3204, as amended, designates the following:

(1) Grounds
Any sports ground in England or Wales.
(2) Classes of Sporting Events
(a) Association football matches in which one or both of the participating teams represents a club which is a member (whether a full or associate member) of the Football League, the Football Association Premier League, the Football Conference National Division, the Scottish Professional Football League or Welsh Premier League, or whose home ground is situated outside England and Wales, or represents a country or territory.
(b) Association football matches in competition for the Football Association Cup (other than in a preliminary or qualifying round).
(c) Association football matches at a sports ground outside England and Wales in which one or both of the participating teams represents a club which is for the time being a member (whether a full or associate member) of the Football League, the Football Association Premier League, the Football Conference National division, the Scottish Professional Football League or Welsh Premier League, or represents the Football Association or the Football Association of Wales.

A[35.6] **Period of the event.** The prohibitions apply to a period beginning two hours before the start of the event or, if earlier, two hours before the time it is advertised to start and ends one hour after the end of the event. Where a match is postponed or cancelled, the period includes the two hours before and one hour after the advertised start of the event. A shorter restricted period starting 15 minutes before and ending 15 minutes after the event applies to private boxes overlooking the ground.

A[35.7] Exceptions. Apart from those clubs or matches not covered by the designation, eg games exclusively concerning 'non-league' clubs, the Sporting Events (Control of Alcohol etc) Act 1985 does not apply to matches where all competitors take part without reward *and* all spectators are admitted free of charge.

A[35.8] Prohibited articles. As well as intoxicating liquor this includes any article capable of causing injury to a person struck by it being a bottle, can or other portable container (including such a container when crushed or broken) which is for holding *any* drink and which when empty is of a kind normally discarded or returned to the supplier, or part of such a container eg a beer glass. Thus a vacuum flask containing tea would be exempt. Also exempted are containers for holding medicinal products.

A[35.9] Prohibited articles also include under s 2A any article or substance whose main purpose is the emission of a flare for purposes of illuminating or signalling (as opposed to igniting or heating) or the emission of smoke or visible gas, eg distress flares, fog signals, pellets for fumigating, but not matches, lighters, or heaters; fireworks are also prohibited. It is a defence if the accused proves that he was in possession of an article under s 2A with lawful authority.

A[35.10]–[35.15] Designated sports ground. These are the home grounds of all Football Association clubs (ie not necessarily just those clubs in the Football (or Premier) League) including any ground used occasionally or temporarily by such a club, Wembley Stadium and any ground used for any international association match. However, it should be noted that all the restrictions apply only to a designated sporting event and so where, for example, a boxing match is held on a Football League ground the provisions of the Act do not apply.

Sentencing

A[35.16] SC Guideline – Football ground offences – see A[34.15] above.

A[35.17] For the power to make banning orders on persons convicted of certain offences in relation to football matches see B[41].

Fraud
(a) Fraud by false representation (s 1(2)(a))
(b) Fraud by failing to disclose information
(s 1(2)(b))
(c) Fraud by abuse of position (s 1(2)(c))

Charges

A[36.1] (1)

(a)   Dishonestly makes a false representation, and intends, by making the representation—
    (i)   to make a gain for himself or another, or
    (ii)   to cause loss to another or to expose another to a risk of loss.

Fraud Act 2006, s 1(2)(a)

A[36.2] (1)

(b)   Dishonestly fails to disclosed to another person information which he is under a legal duty to disclose, and intends, by failing to disclose that information—
    (i)   to make a gain for himself or another, or
    (ii)   to cause loss to another or to expose another to a risk of loss.

Fraud Act 2006, s 1(2)(b)

A[36.3] (1)

(c)   Occupies a position in which he is expected to safeguard, or not to act against, the financial interests of another person, dishonestly abuses that position, and intends, by means of the abuse of that position—
    (i)   to make a gain for himself or another, or
    (ii)   to cause loss to another or to expose another to a risk of loss.

Fraud Act 2006, s 1(2)(c)

A[36.4] **Maximum penalty** – Fine level 5 and 6 months. Triable either way.

Crown Court – 10 years and unlimited fine.

Mode of Trial

A[36.5] Consider first the notes at D[4]. In general, offences of fraud should be tried summarily except for the presence of one or more of the following factors (not an exhaustive list):

(a)   breach of trust by a person in a person of substantial authority or in whom a high degree of trust has been placed;
(b)   there has been sophisticated hiding or disguising of the offence;

(c)   the offence has been committed by an organised gang;
(d)   the victim was particularly vulnerable;
(e)   there is unrecovered property of high value.

Legal notes and definitions

A[36.6] **Fraud by false representation: s 1(2)(a).** This offence is further defined in s 2 of the Act. The effect is to create a very broad offence which consists of lying for economic purposes. This is a "conduct crime". There is no requirement that a gain or anything else should have been obtained, or that a loss should have been caused, or that any risk of loss should have been created. Note, however, the words 'intends by'. It is a matter of fact in each case whether the required causative link between the intention and the false representation has been established: *R v Gilbert* [2012] EWCA Crim 2392, [2012] All ER (D) 251, where G was party to providing false information to open a bank account, but it was not suggested that she was party to a subsequent scheme to obtain computer equipment by means of post-dated cheques drawn on that account which were subsequently stopped, causing a loss of £130,000 to the supplier. The need to be sure of the above causative link had not been properly addressed and the conviction was, therefore, quashed.

A magistrates' court was correct to find a case to answer against the appellant who was alleged to have committed fraud by false representation. There was overwhelming evidence that the appellant had had another person impersonate him for the purposes of sitting a theory driving test: *Idrees v DPP* [2011] All ER (D) 156 (Feb), QBD.

A[36.7] **Dishonesty.** There is no statutory definition. It is suggested that the test of dishonesty for is: (a) whether the accused's actions were dishonest according to the ordinary standards of reasonable and honest people and, if so, (b) whether the accused himself had realised that his actions were, according to those standards, dishonest (*R v Ghosh* [1982] QB 1053, [1982] 2 All ER 689, CA).

Representation. A representation is "false" if it is untrue or misleading and the person making it knows that it is, or might be, untrue or misleading. The term "representation" is widely defined as any representation as to fact or law, including a representation as to the state of the mind of –

(a)   the person making the representation, or
(b)   any other person.

In *Government of the United Arab Emirates v Allen* [2012] EWHC 1712 (Admin), [2012] 1 WLR 3419, the defendant, a British national, obtained a mortgage from a bank in the United Arab Emirates. The loan was for a period of 20 years, repayable by monthly instalments to be debited from the defendant's credit card account held with the bank. As security, the defendant provided the bank with an undated cheque in a sum approximately equal to the loan amount. Some 19 months later, the defendant defaulted on her loan payments and the bank presented the cheque for payment, but it 'bounced'. The defendant returned to the UK and thereafter was convicted in her absence in the UAE of an offence of issuing an uncovered cheque. The UAE sought her extradition, but this was refused on the basis that the 'dual criminality' requirement was not satisfied since the default on a loan agreement supported by the security of an undated cheque could not of itself amount to an offence in the United Kingdom of fraud by false representation contrary to s 2 of the Fraud Act 2006 (the UK offence relied on by the UAE). This decision was upheld on appeal. A 'representation' for the purposes of s 2 had to be capable of being expressed as a statement of the past or present, and did not include a simple promise of future action. While the issue of a post-dated cheque can convey an implied representation of existing fact – see *R v Gilmartin* [1983] QB 953 – it was necessary to consider the commercial context and what a reasonable person would have understood from the defendant's conduct in so doing. The defendant's contractual promises to the bank were not representations for the purposes of s 2. By agreeing to provide an undated cheque as security against a default on her loan, the defendant had not thereby impliedly represented that her current financial circumstances were such as to be able to say with confidence that in the event of that contingency occurring, at any time during the term of the loan, the cheque would in the ordinary course be met. Furthermore, there was no basis for concluding that the defendant had made any implied representation as to her financial circumstances which continued at the time when the cheque was presented. The only representation which could be inferred from the defendant's conduct was that she intended, at the time the loan agreement had been entered into, to honour its terms, but it was not alleged that such representation had been false.

A representation may be express or implied and is wide enough to include deceiving a mechanical device such as a machine (s 2(5)).

Knowing a representation is, or might be, misleading. The test is subjective, ie it is what the accused knows is or may be misleading and not what a reasonable person in his position would have known or suspected. ' . . . the safest course for a judge to adopt is to pose to the jury the question for them in words as close as possible to those of the statute. Elaboration will rarely assist. It may be that some direction as to the consequences of an accused wilfully shutting his eyes to the obvious may be required, but rarely will more be needed': *R v Augunas* [2013] EWCA Crim 2046, [2014] 1 Cr App Rep 240 (per McCombe LJ at para 19).

Gain and loss. See s 5 of the Act. The terms are defined in the same terms as s 24 of the Theft Act 1968 and are to be construed as extending only to gain or loss in money or other property, but as extending to any such gain or loss whether temporary or permanent; and –

(i)   "gain" includes a gain by keeping what one has, as well as gain by getting what one has not; and

(ii)   "loss" includes a loss by not getting what one might get, as well as loss by parting with what one has.

A[36.8] Fraud by failing to disclose information: s 1(2)(b). This offence is further defined in s 3 of the Act. The section is narrower than s 1(2)(a) above, but there is some overlap between the two types of offence.

Dishonesty. There is no statutory definition. See A[36.7] above.

Gain and loss. Defined in A[36.7] above.

Legal duty. There is no statutory definition. The Law Commission report on Fraud (Law Com No 276, Cm 5560, 2002) explained the concept of legal duty as:

'7.28 . . . Such a duty may derive from statute (such as the provisions governing company prospectuses), from the fact that the transaction in question is one of the utmost good faith (such as a contract of insurance), from the express or implied terms of a contract, from the custom of a particular trade or market, or from a fiduciary relationship between the parties (such as that of agent and principal).

7.29 For this purpose there is a legal duty to disclose information not only if the defendant's failure to disclose it gives the victim a cause of action for damages, but also if the law gives the victim a right to set aside any change in his or her legal position to which he or she may consent as a result of the non-disclosure. For example, a person in a fiduciary position has a duty to disclose material information when entering into a contract with his or her beneficiary, in the sense that a failure to make such disclosure will entitle the beneficiary to rescind the contract and to reclaim any property transferred under it.'

It is no defence to claim a lack of knowledge as to the duty to disclose; nevertheless, the accused may claim a lack of **dishonesty**.

A[36.9] **Fraud by abuse of position: s 1(2)(c).** This offence is further defined in s 4 of the Act. It is the most controversial of the three forms of fraud and was criticised in Parliament as a "catch all provision that will be a nightmare of judicial interpretation". The section is intended to criminalise the secret profiteer such as the wine waiter selling his own bottles passing them off as a belonging to the restaurant (a form of cheat): see *R v Doukas* [1978] 1 All ER 1071. There is no legal requirement for the conduct to be "secret" and the government also emphasised that the potential for s 4 to combat legacy fraud with an expectation that charities will benefit to the tune of £2–3 million per annum.

Abuse. There is no statutory definition.

Dishonesty. There is no statutory definition. See **A[36.7]** above.

Position. The Law Commission report on Fraud (Law Com No 276, Cm 5560, 2002) explained the meaning of 'position' as:

'7.38 The necessary relationship will be present between trustee and beneficiary, director and company, professional person and client, agent and principal, employee and employer, or between partners. It may arise otherwise, for example within a family, or in the context of voluntary work, or in any context where the parties are not at arm's length. In nearly all cases where it arises, it will be recognised by the civil law as imposing fiduciary duties, and any relationship that is so recognised will suffice. We see no reason, however, why the existence of such duties should be essential. This does not of course mean that it would be entirely a matter for the fact-finders whether the necessary relationship exists. The question whether the particular facts alleged can properly be described as giving rise to that relationship will be an issue capable of being ruled upon by a judge and, if the case goes to the jury, of being the subject of directions.'

The breadth of the offence gives rise to the potential for all sorts of civil law disputes within the family or employment to become issues of criminal law. As elsewhere the element of **dishonesty** may prove crucial.

A[36.10] Update 12 of the Magistrates' Court sentencing guidelines took in the new definitive guideline of the Sentencing Council on fraud, bribery and money laundering. The same kind of fraud may be charged in a number of ways and the guidelines reflect this. The categories are: fraud by false representation, failing to disclose information and by abuse of position; possessing, making or supplying articles for use in fraud; revenue fraud; benefit fraud; money laundering; bribery; and corporate offences fraud, bribery and money laundering.

The guidelines on fraud by false representation, failing to disclose information and by abuse of position; and revenue fraud are reproduced below. (There are separate guidelines for corporate offenders which are not reproduced since cases are rarely heard in the magistrates' court.)

Fraud

Fraud by false representation, fraud by failing to disclose information, fraud by abuse of position
Fraud Act 2006 (section 1)

Triable either way

Conspiracy to defraud
Common law

Triable on indictment only

Maximum: 10 years' custody

Offence range: Discharge – 8 years' custody

False accounting
Theft Act 1968 (section 17)

Triable either way

Maximum: 7 years' custody

Offence range: Discharge – 6 years and 6 months' custody

STEP ONE
DETERMINING THE OFFENCE CATEGORY

The court should determine the offence category with reference to the tables below. In order to determine the category the court should assess **culpability** and **harm**.

Culpability demonstrated by one or more of the following:

A – High culpability
A leading role where offending is part of a group activity Involvement of others through pressure, influence
Abuse of position of power or trust or responsibility
Sophisticated nature of offence/significant planning
Fraudulent activity conducted over sustained period of time
Large number of victims
Deliberately targeting victim on basis of vulnerability

B – Medium culpability	
Other cases where characteristics for categories A or C are not present	
A significant role where offending is part of a group activity	
C – Lesser culpability	
Involved through coercion, intimidation or exploitation	
Not motivated by personal gain	
Peripheral role in organised fraud	
Opportunistic 'one-off' offence; very little or no planning	
Limited awareness or understanding of the extent of fraudulent activity	

Where there are characteristics present which fall under different levels of culpability, the court should balance these characteristics to reach a fair assessment of the offender's culpability.

Harm is initially assessed by the actual, intended or risked loss as may arise from the offence.

The values in the table below are to be used for **actual** or **intended** loss only.

Intended loss relates to offences where circumstances prevent the actual loss that is intended to be caused by the fraudulent activity.

> **Risk of loss** (for instance in mortgage frauds) involves consideration of both the likelihood of harm occurring and the extent of it if it does. Risk of loss is less serious than actual or intended loss. Where the offence has caused risk of loss but no (or much less) actual loss the normal approach is to move down to the corresponding point in the next category. This may not be appropriate if either the likelihood or extent of risked loss is particularly high.

Harm A – Loss caused or intended		
Category 1	£500,000 or more	Starting point based on £1 million
Category 2	£100,000 – £500,000 or Risk or category 1 harm	Starting point based on £300,000
Category 3	£20,000 – £100,000 or Risk of category 2 harm	Starting point based on £50,000
Category 4	£5,000 – £20,000 or Risk of category 3 harm	Starting point based on £12,500
Category 5	Less than £5,000 or Risk of category 4 harm	Starting point based on £2,500
Risk of category 5 harm, move down the range within the category		

Harm B – Victim impact demonstrated by one or more of the following:
The court should then take into account the level of harm caused to the victim(s) or others to determine whether it warrants the sentence being moved up to the corresponding point in the next category or further up the range of the initial category.
High impact – move up a category; if in category 1 move up the range
Serious detrimental effect on the victim whether financial or otherwise, for example substantial damage to credit rating
Victim particularly vulnerable (due to factors including but not limited to their age, financial circumstances, mental capacity)
Medium impact – move upwards within the category range
Considerable detrimental effect on the victim whether financial or otherwise

Lesser impact – no adjustment
Some detrimental impact on victim, whether financial or otherwise

STEP TWO
STARTING POINT AND CATEGORY RANGE

Having determined the category at step one, the court should use the appropriate starting point (as adjusted in accordance with step one above) to reach a sentence within the category range in the table below. The starting point applies to all offenders irrespective of plea or previous convictions.

Where the value is larger or smaller than the amount on which the starting point is based, this should lead to upward or downward adjustment as appropriate.

Where the value greatly exceeds the amount of the starting point in category 1, it may be appropriate to move outside the identified range.

TABLE 1

Section 1 Fraud Act 2006

conspiracy to defraud

Maximum: 10 years' custody

	A	B	C
Category 1 £500,000 or more	**Starting point** 7 years' custody	**Starting point** 5 years' custody	**Starting point** 3 years' custody
Starting point based on £1 million	**Category range** 5 – 8 years' custody	**Category range** 3 – 6 years' custody	**Category range** 18 months' – 4 years' custody
Category 2 £100,000–£500,000	**Starting point** 5 years' custody	**Starting point** 3 years' custody	**Starting point** 18 months' custody
Starting point based on £300,000	**Category range** 3 – 6 years' custody	**Category range** 18 months' – 4 years' custody	**Category range** 26 weeks' – 3 years' custody
Category 3 £20,000 - £100,000	**Starting point** 3 years' custody	**Starting point** 18 months' custody	**Starting point** 26 weeks' custody
Starting point based on £50,000	**Category range** 18 months' – 4 years' custody	**Category range** 26 weeks' – 3 years' custody	**Category range** Medium level community order – 1 year's custody
Category 4 £5,000- £20,000	**Starting point** 18 months' custody	**Starting point** 26 weeks' custody	**Starting point** Medium level community order
Starting point based on £12,500	**Category range** 26 weeks' – 3 years' custody	**Category range** Medium level community order – 1 year's custody	**Category range** Band B fine – High level community order
Category 5 Less than £5,000	**Starting point** 36 weeks' custody	**Starting point** Medium level community order	**Starting point** Band B fine

	A	B	C
Starting point based on £2,500	**Category range** High level community order – 1 year's custody	**Category range** Band B fine – 26 weeks' custody	**Category range** Discharge – Medium level community order

TABLE 2

Section 17 Theft Act 1968: false accounting

Maximum: 7 years' custody

	A	B	C
Category 1 £500,000 or more	**Starting point** 5 years 6 months' custody	**Starting point** 4 years' custody	**Starting point** 2 years 6 months' custody
Starting point based on £1 million	**Category range** 4 years' – 6 years 6 months' custody	**Category range** 2 years 6 months' – 5 years' custody	**Category range** 15 months' – 3 years 6 months' custody
Category 2 £100,000–£500,000	**Starting point** 4 years' custody	**Starting point** 2 years 6 months' custody	**Starting point** 15 months' custody
Starting point based on £300,000	**Category range** 2 years 6 months' – 5 years' custody	**Category range** 15 months' – 3 years 6 months' custody	**Category range** 26 weeks' – 2 years 6 months' custody
Category 3 £20,000 - £100,000	**Starting point** 2 years 6 months' custody	**Starting point** 15 months' custody	**Starting point** High level community order
Starting point based on £50,000	**Category range** 15 months' – 3 years 6 months' custody	**Category range** High level community order – 2 years 6 months' custody	**Category range** Low level community order – 36 weeks' custody
Category 4 £5,000- £20,000	**Starting point** 15 months' custody	**Starting point** High level community order	**Starting point** Low level community order
Starting point based on £12,500	**Category range** High level community order – 2 years 6 months' custody	**Category range** Low level community order – 36 weeks' custody	**Category range** Band B fine – Medium level community order
Category 5 Less than £5,000	**Starting point** 26 weeks' custody	**Starting point** Low level community order	**Starting point** Band B fine
Starting point based on £2,500	**Category range** Medium level community order – 36 weeks' custody	**Category range** Band B fine – Medium level community order	**Category range** Discharge – Low level community order

The table below contains a non-exhaustive list of additional factual elements providing the context of the offence and factors relating to the offender.

Identify whether any combination of these or other relevant factors should result in an upward or downward adjustment from the sentence arrived at so far.

Consecutive sentences for multiple offences may be appropriate where large sums are involved.

Factors increasing seriousness	Factors reducing seriousness or reflecting personal mitigation
Statutory aggravating factors	No previous convictions **or** no relevant/recent convictions
Previous convictions, having regard to a) the nature of the offence to which the conviction relates and its relevance to the current offence; and b) the time that has elapsed since the conviction	Remorse
Offence committed whilst on bail	Good character and/or exemplary conduct
Other aggravating factors	Little or no prospect of success
Steps taken to prevent the victim reporting or obtaining assistance and/or from assisting or supporting the prosecution	Serious medical conditions requiring urgent, intensive or long-term treatment
Attempts to conceal/dispose of evidence	Age and/or lack of maturity where it affects the responsibility of the offender
Established evidence of community/wider impact	Lapse of time since apprehension where this does not arise from the conduct of the offender
Failure to comply with current court orders	Mental disorder or learning disability
Offence committed on licence	Sole or primary carer for dependent relatives
Offences taken into consideration	Offender co-operated with investigation, made early admissions and/or voluntarily reported offending
Failure to respond to warnings about behaviour	Determination and/or demonstration of steps having been taken to address addiction or offending behaviour
Offences committed across borders	Activity originally legitimate
Blame wrongly placed on others	

STEP THREE
CONSIDER ANY FACTORS WHICH INDICATE A REDUCTION, SUCH AS ASSISTANCE TO THE PROSECUTION

The court should take into account sections 73 and 74 of the Serious Organised Crime and Police Act 2005 (assistance by defendants: reduction or review of sentence) and any other rule of law by virtue of which an offender may receive a discounted sentence in consequence of assistance given (or offered) to the prosecutor or investigator.

STEP FOUR
REDUCTION FOR GUILTY PLEAS

The court should take account of any potential reduction for a guilty plea in accordance with section 144 of the Criminal Justice Act 2003 and the *Guilty Plea* guideline.

STEP FIVE
TOTALITY PRINCIPLE

If sentencing an offender for more than one offence, or where the offender is already serving a sentence, consider whether the total sentence is just and proportionate to the overall offending behaviour.

STEP SIX
CONFISCATION, COMPENSATION AND ANCILLARY ORDERS

The court must proceed with a view to making a confiscation order if it is asked to do so by the prosecutor or if the court believes it is appropriate for it to do so.

Where the offence has resulted in loss or damage the court must consider whether to make a compensation order.

If the court makes both a confiscation order and an order for compensation and the court believes the offender will not have sufficient means to satisfy both orders in full, the court must direct that the compensation be paid out of sums recovered under the confiscation order (section 13 of the Proceeds of Crime Act 2002).

The court may also consider whether to make ancillary orders. These may include a deprivation order, a financial reporting order, a serious crime prevention order and disqualification from acting as a company director.

STEP SEVEN
REASONS

Section 174 of the Criminal Justice Act 2003 imposes a duty to give reasons for, and explain the effect of, the sentence.

STEP EIGHT
CONSIDERATION FOR TIME SPENT ON BAIL

The court must consider whether to give credit for time spent on bail in accordance with section 240A of the Criminal Justice Act 2003.

Revenue fraud

Fraud
Conspiracy to defraud (common law)

Triable on indictment only

Fraud Act 2006 (section 1)

Triable either way

Maximum: 10 years' custody

Offence range: Low level community order – 8 years' custody

False accounting
Theft Act 1968 (section 17)

Fraudulent evasion of VAT; False statement for VAT purposes; Conduct amounting to an offence
Value Added Tax Act 1994 (section 72)

Fraudulent evasion of income tax
Taxes Management Act 1970 (section 106A)

Fraudulent evasion of excise duty; Improper importation of goods
Customs and Excise Management Act 1979 (sections 50, 170 and 170B)

Triable either way

Maximum: 7 years' custody

Offence range: Band C fine – 6 years and 6 months' custody

Fraud
Cheat the public revenue (common law)

Triable on indictment only

Maximum: Life imprisonment

Offence range: 3 – 17 years' custody

STEP ONE
DETERMINING THE OFFENCE CATEGORY

The court should determine the offence category with reference to the tables below. In order to determine the category the court should assess **culpability** and **harm**.

The level of culpability is determined by weighing up all the factors of the case to determine the offender's role and the extent to which the offending was planned and the sophistication with which it was carried out.

A – High culpability
A leading role where offending is part of a group activity Involvement of others through pressure, influence
Abuse of position of power or trust or responsibility
Sophisticated nature of offence/significant planning
Fraudulent activity conducted over sustained period of time

Large number of victims
B – Medium culpability
Other cases where characteristics for categories A or C are not present
A significant role where offending is part of a group activity
C – Lesser culpability
Involved through coercion, intimidation or exploitation
Not motivated by personal gain
Peripheral role in organised fraud
Opportunistic 'one-off' offence; very little or no planning
Limited awareness or understanding of the extent of fraudulent activity

Where there are characteristics present which fall under different levels of culpability, the court should balance these characteristics to reach a fair assessment of the offender's culpability.

Category 1
£50 million or more Starting point based on £80 million
Category 2
£10 million–£50 million Starting point based on £30 million
Category 3
£2 million–£10 million Starting point based on £5 million
Category 4
£500,000–£2 million Starting point based on £1 million
Category 5
£100,000–£500,000 Starting point based on £300,000
Category 6
£20,000–£100,000 Starting point based on £50,000
Category 7
Less than £20,000 Starting point based on £12,500

STEP TWO
STARTING POINT AND CATEGORY RANGE

Having determined the category at step one, the court should use the appropriate starting point to reach a sentence within the category range in the table below. The starting point applies to all offenders irrespective of plea or previous convictions.

Where the value is larger or smaller than the amount on which the starting point is based, this should lead to upward or downward adjustment as appropriate.

Where the value greatly exceeds the amount of the starting point in category 1, it may be appropriate to move outside the identified range.

TABLE 1

Section 1 Fraud Act 2006

Conspiracy to defraud (common law)

Maximum: 10 years' custody

	A	B	C
Category 4 £500,000 or more	**Starting point** 7 years' custody	**Starting point** 5 years' custody	**Starting point** 3 years' custody
Starting point based on £1 million	**Category range** 5 – 8 years' custody	**Category range** 3 – 6 years' custody	**Category range** 18 months' – 4 years' custody
Category 5 £100,000– £500,000	**Starting point** 5 years' custody	**Starting point** 3 years' custody	**Starting point** 18 months' custody
Starting point based on £300,000	**Category range** 3 – 6 years' custody	**Category range** 18 months' – 4 years' custody	**Category range** 26 weeks' – 3 years' custody
Category 6 £20,000 - £100,000	**Starting point** 3 years' custody	**Starting point** 18 months' custody	**Starting point** 26 weeks' custody
Starting point based on £50,000	**Category range** 18 months' – 4 years' custody	**Category range** 26 weeks' – 3 years' custody	**Category range** Medium level community order – 1 year's custody
Category 7 Less than £20,000	**Starting point** 18 months' custody	**Starting point** 36 weeks' custody	**Starting point** Medium level community order
Starting point based on £12,500	**Category range** 36 weeks' – 3 years' custody	**Category range** Medium level community order – 1 year's custody	**Category range** Low level community order – High level community order

TABLE 2

Section 17 Theft Act 1968: False Accounting

Section 72(1) Value Added Tax Act 1994: Fraudulent evasion of VAT

Section 72(3) Valued Added Tax Act 1994: False statement for VAT purposes

Section 72(8) Value Added Tax Act 1994: Conduct amounting to an offence

Section 106(a) Taxes Management Act 1970: Fraudulent evasion of income tax

Section 170(1)(a)(i), (ii), (b), 170(2)(a), 170B

Customs and Excise Management Act 1979: Fraudulent evasion of excise duty

Section 50(1)(a), (2)

Customs and Excise Management Act 1979: Improper importation of goods

Maximum: 7 years' custody

Harm	A	B	C
Category 4 £500,000 or more	**Starting point** 5 years 6 months' custody	**Starting point** 4 years' custody	**Starting point** 2 years 6 months' custody
Starting point based on £1 million	**Category range** 4 years' – 6 years 6 months' custody	**Category range** 2 years 6 months' – 5 years' custody	**Category range** 15 months' – 3 years 6 months' custody
Category 5 £100,000–£500,000	**Starting point** 4 years' custody	**Starting point** 2 years 6 months' custody	**Starting point** 15 months' custody
Starting point based on £300,000	**Category range** 2 years 6 months' – 5 years' custody	**Category range** 15 months' – 3 years 6 months' custody	**Category range** 26 weeks' – 2 years 6 months' custody
Category 6 £20,000 - £100,000	**Starting point** 2 years 6 months' custody	**Starting point** 15 months' custody	**Starting point** High level community order
Starting point based on £50,000	**Category range** 15 months' – 3 years 6 months' custody	**Category range** High level community order – 2 years 6 months' custody	**Category range** Low level community order – 36 weeks' custody
Category 7 Less than £20,000	**Starting point** 15 months' custody	**Starting point** 26 weeks' custody	**Starting point** Low level community order
Starting point based on £12,500	**Category range** High level community order – 2 years 6 months' custody	**Category range** Medium level community order – 15 months' custody	**Category range** Band C fine – High level community order

TABLE 3

Cheat the Revenue (common law)

Maximum: Life imprisonment

Where the offending is on the most serious scale, involving sums significantly higher than the starting point in category 1, sentences of 15 years and above may be appropriate depending on the role of the offender. In cases involving sums below £2 million the court should refer to Table 1.

Harm	A	B	C
Category 1 £50 million or more	**Starting point** 12 years' custody	**Starting point** 8 years' custody	**Starting point** 6 years' custody
Starting point based on £80 million	**Category range** 10 – 17 years' custody	**Category range** 7 – 12 years' custody	**Category range** 4 – 8 years' custody
Category 2 £10 million–£50 million	**Starting point** 10 years' custody	**Starting point** 7 years' custody	**Starting point** 5 years' custody
Starting point based on £30 million	**Category range** 8 – 13 years' custody	**Category range** 5 – 9 years' custody	**Category range** 3 – 6 years' custody

Harm	A	B	C
Category 3 £2 million–£10 million	Starting point 8 years' custody	Starting point 6 years' custody	Starting point 4 years' custody
Starting point based on £5 million	Category range 6 – 10 years' custody	Category range 4 – 7 years' custody	Category range 3 – 5 years' custody

The table below contains a non-exhaustive list of additional factual elements providing the context of the offence and factors relating to the offender.

Identify whether any combination of these or other relevant factors should result in any further upward or downward adjustment from the starting point.

> Consecutive sentences for multiple offences may be appropriate where large sums are involved.

Factors increasing seriousness	Factors reducing seriousness or reflecting personal mitigation
Statutory aggravating factors	No previous convictions **or** no relevant/recent convictions
Previous convictions, having regard to a) the nature of the offence to which the conviction relates and its relevance to the current offence; and b) the time that has elapsed since the conviction	Remorse
Offence committed whilst on bail	Good character and/or exemplary conduct
Other aggravating factors	Little or no prospect of success
Involves multiple frauds	Serious medical conditions requiring urgent, intensive or long-term treatment
Number of false declarations	Age and/or lack of maturity where it affects the responsibility of the offender
Attempts to conceal/dispose of evidence	Lapse of time since apprehension where this does not arise from the conduct of the offender
Failure to comply with current court orders	Mental disorder or learning disability
Offence committed on licence	Sole or primary carer for dependent relatives
Offences taken into consideration	Offender co-operated with investigation, made early admissions and/or voluntarily reported offending
Failure to respond to warnings about behaviour	Determination and/or demonstration of steps having been taken to address addiction or offending behaviour

Factors increasing seriousness	Factors reducing seriousness or reflecting personal mitigation
Blame wrongly placed on others	Activity originally legitimate
Damage to third party (for example as a result of identity theft)	
Dealing with goods with an additional health risk	
Disposing of goods to under age purchasers	

STEP THREE
CONSIDER ANY FACTORS WHICH INDICATE A REDUCTION, SUCH AS ASSISTANCE TO THE PROSECUTION

The court should take into account sections 73 and 74 of the Serious Organised Crime and Police Act 2005 (assistance by defendants: reduction or review of sentence) and any other rule of law by virtue of which an offender may receive a discounted sentence in consequence of assistance given (or offered) to the prosecutor or investigator.

STEP FOUR
REDUCTION FOR GUILTY PLEAS

The court should take account of any potential reduction for a guilty plea in accordance with section 144 of the Criminal Justice Act 2003 and the *Guilty Plea* guideline.

STEP FIVE
TOTALITY PRINCIPLE

If sentencing an offender for more than one offence, or where the offender is already serving a sentence, consider whether the total sentence is just and proportionate to the overall offending behaviour.

STEP SIX
CONFISCATION, COMPENSATION AND ANCILLARY ORDERS

The court must proceed with a view to making a confiscation order if it is asked to do so by the prosecutor or if the court believes it is appropriate for it to do so.

Where the offence has resulted in loss or damage the court must consider whether to make a compensation order.

If the court makes both a confiscation order and an order for compensation and the court believes the offender will not have sufficient means to satisfy both orders in full, the court must direct that the compensation be paid out of sums recovered under the confiscation order (section 13 of the Proceeds of Crime Act 2002).

The court may also consider whether to make ancillary orders. These may include a deprivation order, a financial reporting order, a serious crime prevention order and disqualification from acting as a company director.

STEP SEVEN
REASONS

Section 174 of the Criminal Justice Act 2003 imposes a duty to give reasons for, and explain the effect of, the sentence.

STEP EIGHT
CONSIDERATION FOR TIME SPENT ON BAIL

The court must consider whether to give credit for time spent on bail in accordance with section 240A of the Criminal Justice Act 2003.

Fraud: obtaining services dishonestly

Charge

A[37.1] (1) Obtains services for himself or another—

(a)   by a dishonest act, and
(b)   in breach of subsection (2)

(2)

(a)   the services are made available on the basis that payment has been, is being or will be made for or in respect of them,

(b)   obtains them without any payment having been made for or in respect of them or without payment having been made in full, and

(c)   when he obtains them, he knows—

　　　(i)   that they are being made available on the basis as described in paragraph (a), or

　　　(ii)   that they might be

but intends that payment will not be made, or will not be made in full.

Fraud Act 2006, s 11.

Maximum penalty – Fine level 5 and/or 6 months. Triable either way

(**NB:** Until repealed by the CJA 2003, the general limit on a magistrates' court is to impose imprisonment up to a maximum of six months for one offence: s 78 PCC (S) Act 2000.)

Crown Court – five years and an unlimited fine.

Mode of trial

A[37.2] Consider first the notes at D[4]. In general, offences of obtaining services dishonestly should be tried summarily except for the presence of one or more of the following factors (not an exhaustive list):

(a)   breach of trust by a person in position of substantial authority or in whom a high degree of trust has been placed;

(b)   there has been a sophisticated hiding or disguising of the offence;

(c)   the offence has been committed by an organised gang;

(d)   the victim was particularly vulnerable;

(e)   there is unrecovered property of high value.

Legal notes and definitions

A[37.3] Services. As with the 1978 Act it applies only to services for which payment is required. There must be an act and an obtaining of the service.

Intention. The new offence is wider than the old offence in that it can cover obtaining services through a wholly automated process; however, it is narrower than the old offence because the defendant must intend to avoid payment which presents problems if D knows that the bank will pay.

Act. The new offence extends well beyond the machine 'deception' offences, to encompass eg cases where the defendant climbs a wall to watch a football match without paying the entrance fee (even though not deceiving the provider of the service directly); this is because the defendant is obtaining a service which is provided on the basis that people will pay for it.

As under the Theft Acts 1968 and 1978, an application for a bank account or credit card will only be caught if the service is to be paid for (see *R v Sofroniou* [2003] EWCA Crim 3681).

Dishonesty. There is no statutory definition. See **A[36.7]** above.

Sentencing
Fraud – Obtaining Services Dishonestly (Fraud Act 2006, s 11)

A[37.4] Triable either way:

Maximum when tried summarily: Level 5 fine and/or 6 months

Maximum when tried on indictment: 5 years

The offence of **obtaining services dishonestly** may be committed in circumstances that otherwise could be charged as an offence contrary to s 1 of the Fraud Act 2006 or may be more akin to *making off without payment*, contrary to s 3 of the Theft Act 1978.

For this reason, it has not been included specifically within any of the guidelines for fraud, and one of the following approaches should be used:

* where it involves conduct which can be characterised as a fraud offence (such as obtaining credit through fraud or payment card fraud), the court should apply the guideline for the relevant type of fraud (see **A[31]** and **A[36]**); or

* where the conduct could be characterised as *making off without payment* (where an offender, knowing that payment on the spot for any goods supplied or service done is required or expected, dishonestly makes off without having paid and with intent to avoid payment), the guideline for that offence should be used: **A[21.16]**.

A[38]

Possession of articles for fraud

Charge

A[38.1] The defendant [person] had in his possession or under this control any article for use in the course of or in connection with any fraud

Fraud Act 2006, s 6.

Maximum penalty – Fine level 5 and/or 6 months. Triable either way.

(**NB:** until repealed by the CJA 2003, the general limit on a magistrates' courts sentencing powers is six months imprisonment for a single offence: s 78 PCC(S)A 2000).

Crown Court – 5 years' imprisonment and unlimited fine.

An on-line introduction to the legislation can be found on **Crimeline** (see issue 203, crimeline.info).

Mode of trial

A[38.2] Consider first the general notes at D[4]. In general, offences of possessing articles for fraud should be tried summarily except for the presence of one or more of the following factors (not an exhaustive list):

(a)   offence committed by a person in a position of substantial authority or in whom a high degree of trust has been placed;
(b)   sophisticated offence or disguising of the offence;
(c)   the offence has been committed by an organised gang;
(d)   targeting of a vulnerable victim;
(e)   property acquired of high value (or would have been).

Legal notes and definitions

A[38.3] This is another very wide offence. It was created in order to meet concerns that the s 25 of the Theft Act 1968 offence of going equipped, was outdated in relation to its application to modern fraud cases eg given that many frauds are now perpetrated from home computers. Unlike s 25, there is no requirement to prove that the relevant articles were carried or used outside the defendant's "place of abode".

When the words 'or cheat' (repealed by this Act) appeared in the offence of going equipped for theft in s 25 of the Theft Act 1968, they were interpreted as follows. In *R v Rashid* [1977] 2 All ER 237, 141 JP 305, because of a misdirection to the jury, the defendant was held to have been wrongly convicted of possession of bread and tomatoes with which he intended to make sandwiches for sale to passengers on a train on which he was a steward. In that case the Court of Appeal, in an obiter dicta, expressed the view that on the facts of the case there was probably no obtaining by deception and that it was not appropriate to exalt a breach of contractual duty owed to the defendant's employers into a criminal offence. But *R v*

Rashid, was distinguished in *R v Doukas* [1978] 1 All ER 1061, where a wine waiter in an hotel was held to have been properly convicted of having with him his own wine which he dishonestly intended to sell to customers as property of his employers. In the latter case it was held that it had to be assumed that the hypothetical customer against whom the intended deception was to be practised was reasonably honest and intelligent, and that it was unlikely that any customer to whom the true situation was made clear would willingly make himself a party to what was a fraud by the waiter on his employer. See also *R v Corboz* [1984] Crim LR 629 and *R v Whiteside* and *R v Antoniou* [1989] Crim LR 436, CA.

Article. Includes "any program or data held in electronic form" – Fraud Act 2006, s 8. The offence is designed to combat the growing menace of computer programs used to generate credit card numbers and blank utility bills.

Intention. It is not necessary to prove intended use in a particular fraud. The Crown must prove that the defendant had a general intention that the article be used by someone for a fraudulent purpose (as with the interpretation of intent in going equipped: see *R v Ellames* [1974] 3 AER 130. The article must, however, be with the defendant for the purpose or intention that it will be used for fraud then or in the future. It is insufficient that the article may have been used for fraud in the past: *R v Sakalauskas* [2013] EWCA Crim 2278, (2014) 178 JP 30(applying *Ellames*).

Possession or control. It is submitted that the said terms will be construed analogous to offences under eg the Misuse of Drugs Act 1971 (see **A[25.7]**).

Sentencing
Fraud – Possessing, making or supplying articles for use in fraud

Possession of articles for use in frauds
Fraud Act 2006 (section 6)

A[38.4]–[38.6]

Triable either way

Maximum: 5 years' custody

Offence range: Band A fine – 3 years' custody

Making or supplying articles for use in frauds
Fraud Act 2006 (section 7)

Triable either way

Maximum: 10 years' custody

Offence range: Band C fine – 7 years' custody

STEP ONE
DETERMINING THE OFFENCE CATEGORY

The court should determine the offence category with reference to the tables below. In order to determine the category the court should assess **culpability** and **harm**.

> The level of **culpability** is determined by weighing up all the factors of the case to determine the offender's role and the extent to which the offending was planned and the sophistication with which it was carried out.

Culpability demonstrated by one or more of the following:

A – High culpability
A leading role where offending is part of a group activity Involvement of others through pressure, influence
Involvement of others through pressure, influence
Abuse of position of power or trust or responsibility
Sophisticated nature of offence/significant planning
Fraudulent activity conducted over sustained period of time
Articles deliberately designed to target victims on basis of vulnerability
B – Medium culpability
Other cases where characteristics for categories A or C are not present
A significant role where offending is part of a group activity
C – Lesser culpability
Performed limited function under direction
Involved through coercion, intimidation or exploitation
Not motivated by personal gain
Opportunistic 'one-off' offence; very little or no planning
Limited awareness or understanding of the extent of fraudulent activity

Where there are characteristics present which fall under different levels of culpability, the court should balance these characteristics to reach a fair assessment of the offender's culpability.

Harm

This guideline refers to preparatory offences where no substantive fraud has been committed. The level of **harm** is determined by weighing up all the factors of the case to determine the harm that would be caused if the article(s) were used to commit a substantive offence.

Greater harm
Large number of articles created/supplied/in possession
Article(s) have potential to facilitate fraudulent acts affecting large number of victims
Article(s) have potential to facilitate fraudulent acts involving significant sums Use of third party identities
Offender making considerable gain as result of the offence
Lesser harm
All other offences

STEP TWO
STARTING POINT AND CATEGORY RANGE

Having determined the category at step one, the court should use the appropriate starting point to reach a sentence within the category range in the table below. The starting point applies to all offenders irrespective of plea or previous convictions.

Section 6 Fraud Act 2006: Possessing articles for use in fraud

Maximum: 5 years' custody

	Culpability		
	A	**B**	**C**
Greater	**Starting point** 18 months' custody	**Starting point** 36 weeks' custody	**Starting point** High level community order
	Category range 36 weeks' custody – 3 years' custody	**Category range** High level community order – 2 years' custody	**Category range** Medium level community order – 26 weeks' custody
Lesser	**Starting point** 26 weeks' custody	**Starting point** Medium level community order	**Starting point** Band B fine
	Category range High level community order – 18 months' custody	**Category range** Low level community order – 26 weeks' custody	**Category range** Band A fine – Medium level community order

Section 7 Fraud Act 2006: Making or adapting or supplying articles for use in fraud

Maximum: 10 years' custody

	Culpability		
	A	**B**	**C**
Greater	**Starting point** 4 years 6 months' custody	**Starting point** 2 years 6 months' custody	**Starting point** 1 year's custody
	Category range 3 – 7 years' custody	**Category range** 18 months' – 5 years' custody	**Category range** High level community order – 3 years' custody
Lesser	**Starting point** 2 years' custody	**Starting point** 36 weeks' custody	**Starting point** Medium level community order
	Category range 26 weeks' – 4 years' custody	**Category range** Low level community order – 2 years' custody	**Category range** Band C fine – 26 weeks' custody

The table below contains a non-exhaustive list of additional factual elements providing the context of the offence and factors relating to the offender.

Identify whether any combination of these or other relevant factors should result in an upward or downward adjustment from the sentence arrived at so far.

Consecutive sentences for multiple offences may be appropriate where large sums are involved.

Factors increasing seriousness	Factors reducing seriousness or reflecting personal mitigation
Statutory aggravating factors	No previous convictions **or** no relevant/recent convictions
Previous convictions, having regard to a) the nature of the offence to which the conviction relates and its relevance to the current offence; and b) the time that has elapsed since the conviction	Remorse
Offence committed whilst on bail	Good character and/or exemplary conduct
Other aggravating factors	Little or no prospect of success
Steps taken to prevent the victim reporting or obtaining assistance and/or from assisting or supporting the prosecution	Serious medical conditions requiring urgent, intensive or long-term treatment
Attempts to conceal/dispose of evidence	Age and/or lack of maturity where it affects the responsibility of the offender
Established evidence of community/wider impact	Lapse of time since apprehension where this does not arise from the conduct of the offender
Failure to comply with current court orders	Mental disorder or learning disability
Offence committed on licence	Sole or primary carer for dependent relatives
Offences taken into consideration	Offender co-operated with investigation, made early admissions and/or voluntarily reported offending
Failure to respond to warnings about behaviour	Determination and/or demonstration of steps having been taken to address addiction or offending behaviour
Offences committed across borders	Activity originally legitimate
Blame wrongly placed on others	

STEP THREE
CONSIDER ANY FACTORS WHICH INDICATE A REDUCTION, SUCH AS ASSISTANCE TO THE PROSECUTION

The court should take into account sections 73 and 74 of the Serious Organised Crime and Police Act 2005 (assistance by defendants: reduction or review of sentence) and any other rule of law by virtue of which an offender may receive a discounted sentence in consequence of assistance given (or offered) to the prosecutor or investigator.

STEP FOUR
REDUCTION FOR GUILTY PLEAS

The court should take account of any potential reduction for a guilty plea in accordance with section 144 of the Criminal Justice Act 2003 and the *Guilty Plea* guideline.

STEP FIVE
TOTALITY PRINCIPLE

If sentencing an offender for more than one offence, or where the offender is already serving a sentence, consider whether the total sentence is just and proportionate to the overall offending behaviour.

STEP SIX
CONFISCATION, COMPENSATION AND ANCILLARY ORDERS

The court must proceed with a view to making a confiscation order if it is asked to do so by the prosecutor or if the court believes it is appropriate for it to do so.

Where the offence has resulted in loss or damage the court must consider whether to make a compensation order.

If the court makes both a confiscation order and an order for compensation and the court believes the offender will not have sufficient means to satisfy both orders in full, the court must direct that the compensation be paid out of sums recovered under the confiscation order (section 13 of the Proceeds of Crime Act 2002).

The court may also consider whether to make ancillary orders.

STEP SEVEN
REASONS

Section 174 of the Criminal Justice Act 2003 imposes a duty to give reasons for, and explain the effect of, the sentence.

STEP EIGHT
CONSIDERATION FOR TIME SPENT ON BAIL

The court must consider whether to give credit for time spent on bail in accordance with section 240A of the Criminal Justice Act 2003.

Making, adapting, supplying or offering to supply articles for fraud

Charge

A[39.1] The defendant [person] makes, adapts, supplies or offers to supply any article –

(a)   knowing that it is designed or adapted for use in the course of or in connection with fraud, or

(b)   intending it to be used to commit, or assist in the commission of, fraud

Fraud Act 2006, s 7.

Maximum penalty – Fine level 5 and/or 12 months. Triable either way.

(**NB:** Until repealed by the CJA 2003, the general limit on a magistrates' court to impose imprisonment is six months for a single offence (s 78 PCC(S)A 2000)).

Crown Court – 10 years' imprisonment and an unlimited fine.

Mode of trial

A[39.2] Consider first the general notes at D[4]. In general, offences of making/adapting articles etc for fraud should be tried summarily except for the presence of one or more of the following factors (not an exhaustive list):

(a)   offence committed by a person in a position of substantial authority or in whom a high degree of trust has been placed;

(b)   sophisticated offence or disguising of the offence;

(c)   the offence has been committed by an organised gang;

(d)   targeting of a vulnerable victim;

(e)   property acquired or high value (or would have been).

Legal notes and definition

A[39.3] This offence is aimed at, amongst others, the manufacturers of the 'black boxes' (which caused electricity meters to under-record consumption) in the well-known case of *R v Hollinshead* [1985] AC 975. The defendants in that case were convicted of conspiracy to defraud at common law (still preserved under the Fraud Act 2006). It would no longer be necessary to rely on the common law in such a case.

Parliament has created numerous specific offences to tackle similar behaviour see eg Communications Act 2003, s 126; Mobile Telephones (Reprogramming) Act 2002, s 2; but this is a valuable general offence wide enough to catch eg software manufacturers producing programmes designed for criminal purposes.

It is not clear what the difference is, if any, between 'in the course of' (s 7(1)(a)) and 'in the commission of' (s 7(1)(b)).

A[39.4] Article. Includes any "program or data held in electronic form" – Fraud Act 2006, s 8.

Makes. It is submitted that the term would be accorded its ordinary dictionary meaning.

Adapts. It is submitted that the term would be accorded its ordinary dictionary meaning.

Supplies. It is submitted that the term will be given its ordinary everyday meaning similar to eg under the Misuse of Drugs Act 1971. The offence does not appear to require proof of payment or reward. 'Supply' connotes more than a mere transfer of physical control of some chattel or object from one person to another. There is an additional concept namely that of enabling the recipient to apply the thing transferred for his own nefarious desires or purposes (see *R v Maginnis* [1987] AC 303, HL).

Offers to supply. It is inappropriate to introduce civil notions of offer and acceptance. The offence lies in the making of the offer to supply any article, It is submitted, therefore, that an offer to supply can be made by words or conduct.

Knowledge. Means actual knowledge. Mere suspicion would not appear to be sufficient for the purposes of s 7.

Intention. The accused must intend the article to be used to commit, or assist in the commission of the fraud.

Sentencing
Fraud – Making, adapting, supplying or offering to supply articles for fraud (Fraud Act 2006, s 7)

A[39.5] Triable either way:

Maximum when tried summarily: Level 5 fine and/or 6 months.

Maximum when tried on indictment: 10 years.

See the relevant guideline at **A[38.4]** onwards.

A[40]

Handling stolen goods

Charge

A[40.1] Handled stolen goods, namely [. . . . .], knowing or believing them to have been stolen

Theft Act 1968, s 22

Maximum penalty – Fine level 5 and 6 months. Triable either way.

Crown Court – 14 years' imprisonment and unlimited fine.

Mode of trial

A[40.2] Consider the SC Guidelines below.

Legal notes and definitions

A[40.3] The prosecution must prove that the goods were:

(a)   stolen; or
(b)   obtained by deception; or
(c)   obtained by blackmail.

Also that the defendant knew or believed the goods had been obtained by one of those methods (see below).

A[40.4] Handling. A person handles stolen goods if, otherwise than in the course of the stealing, knowing or believing them to be stolen goods he:

(a)   dishonestly receives the goods; or
(b)   dishonestly undertakes in the retention, removal, disposal or realisation of the goods by or for the benefit of another; or
(c)   dishonestly assists in the retention, removal, disposal or realisation of the goods by or for the benefit of another; or
(d)   arranges to do (a) or (b) or (c).

Thus a defendant who has not himself personally handled goods can be convicted for this offence.

A[40.5] Otherwise than in the course of the stealing. If a person handles goods he has stolen subsequent to the theft he may be guilty of both theft and handling, though normally theft and handling will be alternative charges: see *R v Dolan* [1976] Crim LR 145 and *R v Sainthouse* [1980] Crim LR 506. See also *R v Pitham and Hehl* [1977] Crim LR 285, where the defendants were convicted of handling, having been taken to a house and sold furniture by the thief who thereby appropriated furniture left in his care: their buying was nevertheless not 'in the course of the stealing'.

In the ordinary case where there is no evidence that the defendant was the thief, the prosecution is not required to prove affirmatively that the defendant was not the thief, because handling the goods 'otherwise than in the course of the stealing' is not an essential ingredient of the offence. However, where the defendant is in possession of stolen goods so recently after they are stolen that the inevitable inference is that he is the thief then, if he is charged only with handling, the words 'otherwise than in the course of the stealing' are relevant since the prosecution can only prove the offence of handling if it proves affirmatively that the defendant was not the thief: *R v Cash* [1985] QB 801, [1985] 2 All ER 128, CA.

A[40.6] Forms of handling. 'Assists' means helping or encouraging amongst other things; there must be either affirmative or circumstantial evidence of help or encouragement: *R v Coleman* (1985) 150 JP 175, [1986] Crim LR 56. Something must be done by the defendant; a mere failure to act, where no duty to act existed in law, does not amount to an offence: *R v Burroughes* [2000] All ER (D) 2032, CA.

The words 'by or for the benefit of another person', 'govern retention', 'removal', 'disposal' and 'realisation', and should be included in the charge where retention, removal, disposal or realisation is alleged: *R v Sloggett* [1972] 1 QB 430, [1971] 3 All ER 264, 135 JP 539. If the accused knows that the stolen goods are hidden on his property, mere failure to reveal their presence does not in itself amount to assisting in their retention but would afford strong evidence of providing accommodation for the goods which may amount to assisting in their retention: *R v Brown* [1970] 1 QB 105, [1969] 3 All ER 198, 133 JP 592. Merely using stolen goods in the possession of another does not constitute the offence of assisting in their retention, because something must be done by the offender, and done intentionally and dishonestly, for the purpose of enabling the goods to be retained: *R v Kanwar* [1982] 2 All ER 528, 146 JP 283; *R v Sanders* [1982] Crim LR 695.

'Realisation' merely involves the exchange of the goods for money; and he who pays is just as much involved in the realisation as he who receives the payment: *R v Deakin* [1972] 3 All ER 803, 137 JP 19. A person who has bona fide acquired goods for value does not commit an offence of dishonestly undertaking the disposal or realisation of stolen property for the benefit of another if when he sells the goods he knows or believes them to be stolen, because it is the purchase, not the sale, which is for the purchaser's benefit: *R v Bloxham* [1983] 1 AC 109, [1982] 1 All ER 582, 146 JP 201.

The word 'another' in s 22(1) cannot be construed to embrace a co-accused on the same charge: *R v Gingell* (1999) 163 JP 648, [2000] 1 Cr App Rep 88, CA.

'Arranges' does not cover the situation where the goods are not yet stolen: *R v Park* [1988] Crim LR 238.

A[40.7] Goods. Includes money and every kind of property except land. The term also includes things severed from land by stealing.

A[40.8] Knowledge or belief. Mere suspicion which does not amount to knowledge or belief is not sufficient to justify conviction. The state of the defendant's mind must be judged subjectively, ie what did *this* defendant know, or believe, not what did he suspect.

A[40.9] The term 'belief' connotes its ordinary meaning of holding something to be true.

A[40.10] In *R v Hall* (1985) 81 Cr App R 260, the Lord Chief Justice presided in a court which gave some examples of what might amount to knowledge and what might amount to belief. A man might be said to *know* that goods were stolen when he was told by someone with first-hand knowledge, such as the thief, that such was the case. *Belief* was something short of knowledge. It might be said to be the state of mind of a person who said to himself: 'I cannot say I know for certain that those goods are stolen, but there can be no other reasonable conclusion in the light of all the circumstances of all I have heard and seen.' It was enough for belief even if the person said to himself: 'Despite all that I have seen and heard, I refuse to believe what my brain tells me is obvious.'

A[40.11] What was insufficient was a mere suspicion: 'I suspect that these goods may be stolen but on the other hand they may not be stolen.' That state of mind does not fall within the words 'knowing or believing'. [Contrast the intention under s 22 with an offence under say, s 329 of the Proceeds of Crime Act 2002 (acquisition, use and possession of criminal property). In *Hogan v DPP* [2007] EWHC 978 (Admin), [2007] All ER (D) 253 (Feb) once a defendant raise the issue that consideration had been paid in respect of criminal property in his possession it was for the prosecution to prove to the criminal standard that the consideration paid was not adequate.]

Sentencing
SC Guideline – Handling stolen goods

A[40.12] These guidelines are drawn from the Court of Appeal's decision in *R v Webbe* [2001] EWCA Crim 1217, [2002] 1 Cr App Rep (S) 22.

OFFENCE SERIOUSNESS (CULPABILITY AND HARM)		
A. IDENTIFY THE APPROPRIATE STARTING POINT		
Starting points based on first time offender pleading not guilty		
Examples of nature of activity	**Starting point**	**Range**
Property worth less than £1,000 acquired for offender's own use	Band B fine	Band B fine to low level community order
Property worth less than £1,000 acquired for re-sale; or	Medium level community order	Low level community order to 12 weeks custody
Property worth more than £1,000 acquired for offender's own use; or		Note: the custody threshold is likely to be passed if the offender has a record of dishonesty offences
Presence of at least one aggravating factor listed below – regardless of value		
Sophisticated offending; or	12 weeks custody	6 weeks custody to Crown Court
Presence of at least two aggravating factors listed below		
Offence committed in context of a business; or	Crown Court	Crown Court

Offender acts as organiser/distributor of proceeds of crime; or		
Offender makes himself available to other criminals as willing to handle the proceeds of thefts or burglaries; or		
Offending highly organised, professional; or		
Particularly serious original offence, such as armed robbery		

OFFENCE SERIOUSNESS (CULPABILITY AND HARM)

B. CONSIDER THE EFFECT OF AGGRAVATING AND MITIGATING FACTORS (OTHER THAN THOSE WITHIN THE EXAMPLES ABOVE)

Common aggravating and mitigating factors are identified at B[5.2A]. The following may be particularly relevant but **these lists are not exhaustive**

Factors indicating higher culpability	*Factors indicating lower culpability*
1. Closeness of offender to primary offence. Closeness may be geographical, arising from presence at or near the primary offence when it was committed, or temporal, where the handler instigated or encouraged the primary offence beforehand, or, soon after, provided a safe haven or route for disposal.	1. Little or no benefit to offender.
2. High level of profit made or expected by offender.	2. Voluntary restitution to victim.
Factors indicating greater degree of harm	*Factors indicating lower degree of harm*
1. Seriousness of the primary offence, including domestic burglary.	1. Low value of goods.
2. High value of goods to victim, including sentimental value.	
3. Threats of violence or abuse of power by offender over others, such as adult commissioning criminal activity by children, or a drug dealer pressurising addicts to steal in order to pay for their habit.	

FORM A PRELIMINARY VIEW OF THE APPROPRIATE SENTENCE, THEN CONSIDER OFFENDER MITIGATION

Common factors are identified at B[5.2A]

CONSIDER A REDUCTION FOR A GUILTY PLEA

CONSIDER ANCILLARY ORDERS, INCLUDING RESTITUTION AND COMPENSATION

Refer to **Part B** and consult your legal adviser on guidance for available ancillary orders

CONSIDER DEPRIVATION OF PROPERTY

DECIDE SENTENCE

GIVE REASONS

A[41]

Harassment

Harassment – putting people in fear of violence
Racially or religiously aggravated harassment –
putting people in fear of violence
Harassment – without violence
Racially or religiously aggravated harassment –
non violent

Charges

A[41.1] 1 Did pursue a course of conduct on two or more occasions, causing another to fear that violence would be used against him, which he knew or ought to have known would cause that other person to fear violence would be used against him

Protection from Harassment Act 1997, s 4

Maximum penalty – Fine level 5 and 6 months. Triable either way. Specified violent offence under Sch 15, Part 1, CJA 2003.

Crown Court – 5 years' imprisonment and unlimited fine.

A[41.2] 2 Racially/religiously aggravated course of conduct on two or more occasions causing fear of violence etc

Crime and Disorder Act 1998, s 32

Maximum penalty – Fine level 5 and 6 months. Triable either way. Sch 15, Part 1, CJA 2003 does not identify this offence as a "specified violent offence". This would appear to be a drafting error given the classification of the basic offence under s 4 PHA 1997 above. The SGC Guideline (below) recognises this offence as a specified violent offence.

Crown Court – 7 years' imprisonment and unlimited fine.

A[41.3] 3 Did pursue a course of conduct amounting to harassment of another which he knew or ought to have known amounted to harassment

Protection from Harassment Act 1997, s 2

Maximum penalty – Fine level 5 and 6 months summary only.

A[41.3A] 3A Did pursue a course of conduct which amounted to stalking and either:

(a) caused another (B) to fear, on at least two occasions, that violence would be used against B, or

(b) caused B serious alarm or distress which had a substantial adverse effect on B's usual day-to-day activities, knowing that the course of conduct would cause B so to fear on each of those occasions or would cause B such alarm or distress.

Protection from Harassment Act 1997, s 4A

Maximum penalty – Fine level 5 and 6 months. Triable either way. Specified violent offence under CJA 2003, Sch 15, Pt 1.

Crown Court – 5 years' imprisonment and unlimited fine.

A[41.3B] 3B Did pursue a course of conduct amounting to harassment of another and the acts or omissions involved in that court of conduct were ones associated with stalking, which he knew or ought to have known amounted to harassment of that person.

Protection from Harassment Act 1997, s 2A

Maximum penalty – Fine level 5 and 6 months summary only.

A[41.4] 4 Racially/religiously aggravated conduct amounting to harassment of another etc

Crime and Disorder Act 1998, s 32

Maximum penalty – Fine level 5 and 6 months. Triable either way.

Crown Court – 2 years' imprisonment and unlimited fine.

A[41.5] **Harassment of a person in his home.** In response to animal rights protests and the like the Serious Organised Crime and Police Act 2005 amended the Protection from Harassment Act 1997 to make it an offence to harass two or more persons with the intention of persuading them not to do something they are required or entitled to do, or to do something they are not required to do. A course of conduct may involve conduct on just one occasion for each victim if there is more than one.

Section 126 of the Act adds s 42A to the Criminal Justice and Police Act 2001 and creates an offence of harassment of a person in his home. Punishable with fine level 4 and 6 months (**the maximum term of imprisonment may be subject to alteration under s 280(2) CJA 2003). Triable only by magistrates.

Mode of trial

A[41.6] Consider the SC Guidelines below.

Note that the Crown Court can bring in an alternative verdict under the Protection from Harassment Act 1997, s 2 or s 2A, but magistrates cannot.

Legal notes and definitions

A[41.7] It has been held that the 'course of conduct' under s 4 must be a course of conduct amounting to harassment under s 1: *R v Curtis* [2010] EWCA Crim 123, [2010] 3 All ER 849, [2010] WLR 2770, [2010] Crim LR 638; followed in *R v Widdows* [2011] EWCA Crim 1500, (2011) 175 JP 345. These decisions were followed, with reluctance, in *R v Haque*

[2011] EWCA Crim 1871, [2012] 1 Cr App R 5, [2011] Crim LR 962. The result of this is that a prosecution under s 4 requires, in addition to the elements expressly set out: (a) proof of harassment; (b) that the conduct was targeted at an individual; and (c) that it was calculated to produce the consequence of alarm or distress.

Course of conduct denotes actions taking place on at least two occasions. In the case of a s 4 offence the victim must have been put in fear that violence would have been used against him on at least two of those occasions (*Caurti v DPP* [2002] EWHC 867 (Admin), [2002] Crim LR 131). The fewer the incidents and the wider apart they are spread, the less likely it is that a finding of harassment can reasonably be made (*Lau v DPP* [2000] 1 FLR 799, [2000] Fam Law 610). In *Pratt v DPP* [2001] EWHC 483 (Admin), (2001) 165 JP 800 incidents three months apart were said to be borderline, while in *Kelly v DPP* [2002] All ER (D) 177 (Jun) nine telephone calls all within five minutes amounted to a course of conduct even though the victim listened to them as recorded messages at the same time. A threat to harm a person's dog may be inferred to be a threat directed at them (*R v DPP* [2001] EWHC 17 (Admin), (2001) 165 JP 349).

Events between May 2005 and November 2005 constituted a "course of conduct" and could not be regarded as one continuous episode of intimidation (*Buckley v CPS* [2008] All ER (D) 06 (Jan)). At least one of the incidents relied on by the prosecution must have occurred within the 6 month limitation period for summary proceedings (*DPP v Baker* (2004) 169 JP 140, [2004] All ER (D) 28 (Nov), DC).

Conduct which may begin with what is or may be a legitimate inquiry (in this case by telephone) may become harassment within the meaning of section 1, by reason of the manner of its being pursued and its persistence: see *DPP v Hardy* [2008] EWHC 2874 (Admin), 173 JP 10. A series of six incidents, over the course of nine months during a volatile relationship with aggression on both sides, could not on the facts be described as a course of conduct and giving rise to an offence under s 4(1): *R v Curtis* [2010] EWCA Crim 123, [2010] 3 All ER 849, [2010] 1 Cr App Rep 457. See also *R v Widdows* [2011] EWCA Crim 1500, [2011] 2 FLR 869, [2011] Fam Law 937.

Two or more complainants. See A[41.5] above. **Two or more complainants** may be named in one charge under **s 2** and such a charge is not necessarily bad for duplicity: see *DPP v Dunn* (2008) 165 JP 130. For a **s 4** offence, the interpretation is slightly narrower in that the course of conduct complained of must cause at least one of the complainants to fear, on at least two occasions, that violence will be used against him, as opposed to another: see *Caurti v DPP* [2002] EWHC 867 (Admin), [2002] Crim LR 131.

A[41.8] **Knows or ought to have known.** In the case of the defendant this means that he will be presumed to have that knowledge if a reasonable person in possession of the same information would think the course of conduct would amount to harassment or cause the other person to fear violence would be used against him. The defendant's mental disorder (paranoid schizophrenia) was not to be considered as a relevant condition of the hypothetical reasonable man under s 1(2) or to be taken into account when assessing whether the defendant's conduct was reasonable under s 1(3)(c); both s 1(2) and s 1(3) involved objective test: *R v Colohan* [2001] EWCA Crim 1251, [2001] Crim LR 845.

A[41.8A] The basic offence of stalking, contrary to s 2A, consists of:

(a)   pursuing a course of conduct in breach of s 1(1); and
(b)   the course of conduct amounts to stalking.

A person's course of conduct amounts to stalking of another person if:

(a)   it amounts to harassment of that person;
(b)   the acts or omissions involved are ones associated with stalking; and
(c)   the person whose course of conduct it is knows or ought to know
       that the course of conduct amounts to harassment of the other
       person.

Subsection (3) provides the following examples of acts or omissions which,
in particular circumstances, are ones associated with stalking:

(a)   following a person;
(b)   contacting, or attempting to contact, a person by any means;
(c)   publishing any statement or other material:
       (i)   relating or purporting to relate to a person; or
       (ii)   purporting to originate from a person,
(d)   monitoring the use by a person of the internet, email or any other
       form of electronic communication;
(e)   loitering in any place (whether public or private);
(f)   interfering with any property in the possession of a person;
(g)   watching or spying on a person.

A[41.8B] The aggravated offence of stalking, contrary to s 4A, consists of
a course of conduct which:

(a)   amounts to stalking by 'A'; and
(b)   either:
       (i)   causes another ('B') to fear, on at least two occasions, that
               violence will be used against B; or
       (ii)   causes B serious alarm or distress which has a substantial
               adverse effect on B's usual day-to-day activities,

and A knows or ought to know that A's course of conduct will cause B so
to fear on each of those occasions or (as the case may be) will cause such
alarm or distress.

For the purposes of s 4A:

(a)   A ought to know that A's course of conduct will cause B to fear that
       violence will be used against B on any occasion if a reasonable
       person in possession of the same information would think the course
       of conduct would cause B so to fear on that occasion; or
(b)   A ought to know that A's course of conduct will cause B serious
       alarm or distress which has a substantial adverse effect on B's usual
       day-to-day activities if a reasonable person in possession of the same
       information would think the course of conduct would cause B such
       alarm or distress.

A[41.8C] Defences. Section 4A(4) provides the same three defences as
s 1(3)and s 4(3), which are considered at A[4.10], below.

A[41.9] Racial aggravation. See A[8.10] and A[15.7].

May be heard together with a harassment charge as an alternative (*R (CPS)
v Blaydon Youth Court* [2004] EWHC Admin 2296, (2004) 168 JP 638).

A[41.10] Defences. The Protection from Harassment Act 1997, s 1 gives
three possible defences if the defendant can show:

(a)   his course of conduct was pursued for the purposes of preventing or detecting crime;
(b)   that it was pursued under an enactment or rule of law;
(c)   that in the particular circumstances the course of conduct was reasonable and in the case of a s 4 offence that it was reasonable for the protection of himself or another or his or another's property.

'Purpose' is not a wholly subjective test. The purpose does not have to be 'reasonable' but it must be 'rational'.

> 'Before an alleged harasser can be said to have had the purpose of preventing or detecting crime, he must have sufficiently applied his mind to the matter. He must have thought rationally about the material suggesting the possibility of criminality and formed the view that the conduct said to constitute harassment was appropriate for the purpose of preventing or detecting it. If he has done these things, then he has the relevant purpose. The court will not test his conclusions by reference to the view which a hypothetical reasonable man in his position would have formed. If, on the other hand, he has not engaged in these minimum mental processes necessary to acquire the relevant state of mind, but proceeds anyway on the footing that he is acting to prevent or detect crime, then he acts irrationally. In that case, two consequences will follow. The first is that the law will not regard him as having had the relevant purpose at all. He has simply not taken the necessary steps to form one. The second is that the causal connection which section 1(3)(a) posits between the purpose of the alleged harasser and the conduct constituting the harassment, will not exist. The effect of applying a test of rationality to the question of purpose is to enable the court to apply to private persons a test which would in any event apply to public authorities engaged in the prevention or detection of crime as a matter of public law. It is not a demanding test, and it is hard to imagine that Parliament can have intended anything less.' (per Lord Sumption SCJ in *Hayes v Willoughby* [2013] UKSC 17, [2013] 1 WLR 935, at para 15)

It is not reasonable to pursue a course of conduct which is in breach of a court injunction designed to prevent it: *DPP v Selvanayagam* (1999) Times, 23 June, DC. As to the relevance of mental illness to 'reasonable', see A[41.8], above.

A[41.11] In our view, the standard of proof is on a preponderance of probabilities: *R v Carr-Briant* [1943] KB 607, [1943] 2 All ER 156, 107 JP 167, *R v Dunbar* [1958] 1 QB 1, [1957] 2 All ER 737, [1957] 3 WLR 330. It is arguable, however, that it will be held that the ECHR requires s 1(3) to be 'read down' to imposed only an evidential burden on the defendant.

Sentencing
SC Guideline – 1 Harassment – putting people in fear of violence
SC Guideline – 2 Racially or religiously aggravated harassment – putting people in fear of violence

A[41.11A] (For offences 3 and 4 see A[41.12] below).

Where offence committed in a domestic context, see SC Definitive Guideline: "Overarching Principles: Domestic Violence"

IDENTIFY DANGEROUS OFFENDERS		
This is a specified offence for the purposes of the public protection provisions in the Criminal Justice Act 2003. Refer to B[16.5] and consult legal adviser for guidance		
OFFENCE SERIOUSNESS (CULPABILITY AND HARM)		
A. IDENTIFY THE APPROPRIATE STARTING POINT		
Starting points based on first time offender pleading not guilty		
Examples of nature of activity	**Starting point**	**Range**
A pattern of two or more incidents of unwanted contact	6 weeks custody	High level community order to 18 weeks custody
Deliberate threats, persistent action over a longer period; or Intention to cause fear of violence	18 weeks custody	12 weeks custody to Crown Court
Sexual threats, vulnerable person targeted	Crown Court	Crown Court

OFFENCE SERIOUSNESS (CULPABILITY AND HARM)	
B. CONSIDER THE EFFECT OF AGGRAVATING AND MITIGATING FACTORS (OTHER THAN THOSE WITHIN EXAMPLES ABOVE)	
Common aggravating and mitigating factors are identified at B[5.2A]. The following may be particularly relevant but **these lists are not exhaustive**	
Factors indicating higher culpability 1. Planning	*Factors indicating lower culpability* 1. Limited understanding of effect on victim
2. Offender ignores obvious distress	2. Initial provocation
3. Visits in person to victim's home or workplace	
4. Offender involves others	
5. Using contact arrangements with a child to instigate offence	
Factors indicating greater degree of harm 1. Victim needs medical help/counselling	
2. Physical violence used	
3. Victim aware that offender has history of using violence	
4. Grossly violent or offensive material sent	
5. Children frightened	
6. Evidence that victim changed lifestyle to avoid contact	

FORM A PRELIMINARY VIEW OF THE APPROPRIATE SENTENCE
IF OFFENDER CHARGED AND CONVICTED OF THE RACIALLY OR RELIGIOUSLY AGGRAVATED OFFENCE, INCREASE THE SENTENCE TO REFLECT THIS ELEMENT
Refer to B[5.2B] for guidance
CONSIDER OFFENDER MITIGATION

Common factors are identified at B[5.2A]
CONSIDER A REDUCTION FOR A GUILTY PLEA
CONSIDER MAKING A RESTRAINING ORDER
CONSIDER ANCILLARY ORDERS, INCLUDING COMPENSATION   Refer to B[18] for guidance on compensation.
DECIDE SENTENCE
GIVE REASONS

SC Guideline – 3 Harassment – without violence
SC Guideline – 4 Racially or religiously aggravated harassment – without violence

A[41.12] (For offences 1 and 2 see A[41.11] above).

Where offence committed in a domestic context, see SC Definitive Guideline: "Overarching Principles: Domestic Violence"

OFFENCE SERIOUSNESS (CULPABILITY AND HARM)		
A. IDENTIFY THE APPROPRIATE STARTING POINT		
Starting points based on first time offender pleading not guilty		
Examples of nature of activity	**Starting point**	**Range**
Small number of incidents	Medium level community order	Band C fine to high level community order
Constant contact at night, trying to come into workplace or home, involving others	6 weeks custody	Medium level community order to 12 weeks custody
Threatening violence, taking personal photographs, sending offensive material	18 weeks custody	12 to 26 weeks custody
OFFENCE SERIOUSNESS (CULPABILITY AND HARM)		
B. CONSIDER THE EFFECT OF AGGRAVATING AND MITIGATING FACTORS (OTHER THAN THOSE WITHIN EXAMPLES ABOVE)		
Common aggravating and mitigating factors are identified at B[5.2A]. The following may be particularly relevant but **these lists are not exhaustive**		

Factors indicating higher culpability	Factors indicating lower culpability
1. Planning	1. Limited understanding of effect on victim
2. Offender ignores obvious distress	2. Initial provocation
3. Offender involves others	
4. Using contact arrangements with a child to instigate offence	
Factors indicating greater degree of harm	
1. Victim needs medical help/counselling	
2. Action over a long period of time	
3. Children frightened	
4. Use or distribution of photographs	

FORM A PRELIMINARY VIEW OF THE APPROPRIATE SENTENCE
IF OFFENDER CHARGED AND CONVICTED OF THE RACIALLY OR RELIGIOUSLY AGGRAVATED OFFENCE, INCREASE THE SENTENCE TO REFLECT THIS ELEMENT Refer to B[5.2B] for guidance
CONSIDER OFFENDER MITIGATION Common factors are identified at B[5.2A]
CONSIDER A REDUCTION FOR A GUILTY PLEA
CONSIDER MAKING A RESTRAINING ORDER
CONSIDER ANCILLARY ORDERS, INCLUDING COMPENSATION Refer to B[18] for guidance on compensation.
DECIDE SENTENCE
GIVE REASONS

A[41.13] Restraining orders. On conviction pursuant to s 5(1) of the Protection from Harassment Act 1997 as amended, from **30 September 2009**, restraining orders can be issued for any offence rather than just offences covered by ss 2 or 4 of the 1997 Act. The order can be made for a determinate or indeterminate period of time.

On acquittal by virtue of s 5A of the Protection from Harassment Act 1997 (as inserted by s 12 of the Domestic Violence, Crime and Victims Act 2004). Again restraining orders can be issued for any offence on acquittal, not just for offences covered by the PHA 1997. The order can be made for a determinate or indeterminate period of time. This legislation came into force on **30 September 2009**. The legislation states that the court 'may', if it considers it necessary to do so to protect a person from harassment by the defendant . . . make an order. Despite a declaration that that legislation complies with the European Convention of Human Rights difficulties arise eg what is the evidential basis and standard for making an order?

In *R v Major* [2010] EWCA Crim 3016, [2011] 1 Cr App Rep 322, [2011] 2 Cr App Rep (S) 139, it was held that s 5A(1) of the Act was inserted to deal with those cases where there is clear evidence that the victim needs protection but there is insufficient evidence to convict of the particular charges before the court. The victim need not have been blameless and the court's added powers avoided the need for alternative proceedings to protect the victim, added costs and delay. The fact that a criminal court was unsure that the alleged conduct amounted to harassment did not mean that there was no risk of future harassment. Even though the required criminal standard of proof might not have been met, a retraining order was a civil order and the civil standard of proof applied. (2) A restraining order made on acquittal is not a sentence. However, the requirements of s 174(1) of the Criminal Justice Act 2003 and the Consolidated Criminal Practice Direction at III.31.4 should be applied (see now Part 50 of the CPR 2012). Accordingly, a court imposing a restraining order should state in open court, its reasons for doing so. In the instant case, while there may have been good reason for making the order, it was not apparent from the Judge's remarks as to whether or not the order was justified. *R v Major* was followed just two weeks later in *R (on the application of Gonzales) v Folkestone Magistrates' Court* [2010] EWHC 3428 (Admin), 175 JP 453.

In the case of a prison sentence a copy of the order should be sent to the prison. Any order should be specific and name parties protected by it (*R v Mann* (2000) 144 Sol Jo LB 150, CA).

Section 5 and Sch 1 of the Interpretation Act 1978 provide that when the word appears in a statute, unless a contrary intention appears "person" includes a body of persons corporate or unincorporated. If there is evidence to indicate that there is a real fear of actual harassment or violence in the future, a restraining order can therefore be imposed in appropriate circumstances either to protect a limited company or its employees. However, in this particular case, the practical sense of the imposition of the order had to be balanced against the failure of the Crown, which had not originally intended applying for restraining orders, to adduce any evidence that there was actual harassment or anything close to it or any perceived danger from anything said or done by any particular defendant to put anybody in fear of violence (*R v Buxton* [2010] EWCA Crim 2923, [2011] 1 WLR 857, [2011] Bus LR 448).

In *R v Debnath* [2005] EWCA Crim 3472, the Court of Appeal stated that when considering whether or not to make a restraining order the following principles applied: (i) the purpose of a restraining order was to prohibit particular conduct with a view to protecting the complainant from further offences; (ii) the order had to be clear and in precise terms so that there could be no doubt as to what the defendant was prohibited from doing; (iii) the order had to be practical in its terms; (iv) when considering the terms, or the extent of an order, the court had to have regard to the issue of proportionality; and (v) the power to vary or discharge an order was an important safeguard and the Court of Appeal would be unlikely to interfere with the order where an application could be made to the court that made the order for its variation or discharge.

Under s 12 above gives any person mentioned in a restraining order the right to make representations in court if an application is made to vary or discharge an order.

In *R v K* [2011] EWCA Crim 1843, 175 JP 378, a restraining order was quashed because at the hearing no consideration appeared to have been given to the provisions of either s 5A of the 1997 Act or the Criminal Procedure Rules 2010. The serious nature of a restraining order was underpinned by the provisions of Part 50 of the Criminal Procedure Rules 2010 which identified the steps which had to be taken in order to ensure that any person to whom any such order was directed was given a proper opportunity to understand what was being proposed and why and to make representations at a hearing. In the instant case, no procedural steps were taken either before or after the Crown offered no evidence, and the limited evidence before the court could not provide a sound evidential basis upon which to make the restraining order. See also *R v Trott* [2011] EWCA Crim 2395, 175 JP 458.

Income tax evasion

Charge

A[42.1] Being knowingly concerned in the fraudulent evasion of income tax by him or another person.

Finance Act 2000, s 144

Maximum penalty – Fine level 5 and 6 months' imprisonment †

Crown Court – 7 years' imprisonment and unlimited fine.

Mode of trial

A[42.2] See general notes at D[4] and SC Guideline below.

Sentencing

A[42.3] Refer to guidelines *Fraud – banking and insurance fraud and obtaining credit through fraud, benefit fraud and revenue fraud* at A[36.10].

Indecent photographs of children

Charges

A[43.1] Did take or make an indecent photograph of a child or

Distribute or show such photographs or

Possess such photographs with a view to distribution or

Publish an advertisement conveying that the advertiser distributes or shows such photographs.

Protection of Children Act 1978, s 1

Possession of indecent photograph of child

Criminal Justice Act 1988, s 160

Possession of a prohibited image of a child

Coroners and Justice Act 2009, s 62**

Maximum penalty – Fine level 5 and/or 6 months' imprisonment. Triable either way. Specified sexual offence under Sch 15, Part 2, CJA 2003.

Crown Court – 10 years' imprisonment (3 years if committed before 11/01/2001) and unlimited fine. **(3 years' imprisonment and unlimited fine for an offence under s 62 above.)

Mode of Trial

A[43.2] Consider the SC guideline at A[43.8] below. Possession of indecent photographs of children may be tried in the magistrates' court but the court must have regard to an ascending level of seriousness as set out at A[43.8] below.

Legal Notes and definitions

A[43.3] Indecent photographs or pseudo-photographs. The section makes it an offence to make an indecent photograph, pseudo photograph, copy, negative or data stored on a computer disc. A person who downloads indecent images of children from an internet site and prints or saves them is also making an indecent photograph (*R v Smith, R v Jayson* [2002] EWCA Crim 683, [2003] 1 Cr App Rep 212, CA).

The offence of possession under s 160(1) is not committed unless the defendant knows that he has the photographs in his possession: *Atkins v DPP* [2000] 2 All ER 425, [2000] 1 WLR 1427, [2000] 2 Cr App Rep 248, DC.

'Possession' means physically in one's custody or under one's physical control. A defendant is not in 'possession' of indecent images which he has deleted from his computer, if he cannot retrieve or gain access to them as he no longer has custody or control of them. Whether he is able to retrieve items deleted from the recycle bin will depend on a finding of fact about his computer skills and ownership of the requisite software. There may also be practical reasons why an accused is not charged with possession at the time when he viewed the images until he deleted them: *R v Porter* [2006] EWCA Crim 560, [2007] 2 All ER 625, [2006] 1 WLR 2633, [2006] 2 Cr App R 25. See also *R v Rowe* [2008] EWCA Crim 2712, 172 JP 585, considered at A[43.7], below. Problems can be resolved if the indictment addresses the deletion issue by alleging possession of the indecent image over a period covering either the date of the deletion (if it can be established) or between the dates when the defendant assumed control of the computer and the date when the images were found. If that were done, it would not be the end of the case as it would be open to the defendant to advance any of the statutory defences provided in s 160(2), and, if convicted, if the defendant had truly tried to rid himself of the material, that would be likely to provide substantial mitigation: *R v Leonard* [2012] EWCA Crim 277, [2012] 2 Cr App Rep 138, 176 CL&J 466.

'Pop-ups' that occur when a computer user visits particular websites are made by the user and not the website designer; and in 'pop-up' cases the offence of possession is committed where: (a) the images stored there are of persons under age and are of an indecent nature; and (b) the defendant was the person responsible for accessing the images, and he knew that such material would then be automatically stored to the hard drive and that his browsing would or could access illegal images, or be likely to do so: *R v Harrison* [2007] EWCA Crim 2976, [2008] 1 Cr App R 29.

From 8 July 2008, the meaning of "photograph" in s 7(4) of the Protection of Children Act 1978 was extended by the Criminal Justice and Immigration Act 2008 to include:

> (4A) (a)a tracing or other image, whether made by electronic or other means (of whatever nature) –
>
> (i) which is not itself a photograph or pseudo-photograph, but
>
> (ii) which is derived from the whole or part of a photograph or pseudo-photograph (or a combination of either or both); and
>
> (b) data stored on a computer disc or by other electronic means which is capable of conversion into an image within paragraph (a);
>
> and subsection (8) applies in relation to such an image as it applies in relation to a pseudo-photograph.

A[43.4] Indecent photographs or pseudo-photographs: marriage etc. From April 6, 2010, ss 62–69 of the Coroners and Justice Act 2009 came into force. Section 69 amends s 1A of the Protection of Children Act 1978 and s 160A of the Criminal Justice Act 1988 to insert a reference to 'pseudo-photograph'.

The age of the child is a material consideration for the court in determining whether the photograph of the child was in fact indecent: *R v Owen* [1988] 1 WLR 134, 86 Cr App Rep 291, CA. To convict a person of taking an indecent photograph, it must be proved that the defendant took the photograph deliberately and intentionally. If so satisfied, the court must then decide whether the photograph was indecent by applying the recognised standards of propriety, but for this purpose the circumstances in which the photograph was taken and the motivation of the taker are irrelevant: *R v Graham-Kerr* [1988] 1 WLR 1098, 153 JP 171, CA. Articles 8 and 10 of the European Convention on Human Rights do not require a reconsideration of the interpretation of s 1 of the 1978 Act as the exceptions in art 8(2) and 10(2) apply as the Act is there for the prevention of crime, for the protection of morals, and in particular for the protection of children from being exploited, which is a matter necessary in a democratic society: *R v Smethurst* [2001] EWCA 772, 165 JP 377, [2001] Crim LR 657, [2002] 1 Cr App Rep 50.

A[43.5] Evidence. It is for the court to decide on the evidence as a whole whether a child in a photograph was under age at the material time (*R v Land* [1999] QB 65, [1998] 1 All ER 403, CA).

Child includes 16 and 17 year olds: Sexual Offences Act 2003, s 45.

A[43.6] Distribution. A person distributes an indecent photograph if he parts with possession of it, or exposes or offers it to another person.

Section 1(1)(b) ("to distribute or show") created an offence of strict liability, in which it was not necessary for the prosecution to prove the defendant's knowledge that a CD which he had given to another person, had contained indecent images at the time of his parting with possession. That section was subject only to the statutory defences, in which knowledge was in issue (*R v P* [2006] All ER (D) 238 (Oct).

A[43.7] Knowledge. Deletion of files may be directly relevant to the accused's lack of knowledge of possession of the material particularly where specialist software would be needed to recover the deleted files (*R v Rowe* [2008] EWCA Crim 2712, 172 JP 585).

A[43.8] Defences. Section 1(4) of the Protection of Children Act 1978 provides that it is a defence for a person to prove that he had a legitimate reason for possessing, distributing or showing the photographs, or that he had not himself seen the photographs and did not know or have cause to suspect them to be indecent.

The above defences are limited to persons who distribute or are in possession of such material for a legitimate reason (eg the police) or an individual who was ignorant of and had no reason to believe that he was in possession of or distributing indecent material or in the case of simple possession, who received it unsolicited and gets rid of it with reasonable promptness. No statutory defence is available for the person who creates the material or advertises its availability. It is also not a defence that a person did not know nor had any cause to suspect that the photograph depicted persons who were 16 years or older: *R v Land* [1998]) 1 All ER 403, [1998] 3 WLR 322, [1998] 1 Cr App Rep 301.

In respect of 16 and 17 year olds specific defences are provided that the defendant can show:

(a)　the child was 16 or over or they were married or in an enduring family relationship;

(b)　there was consent or a reasonable belief the child consented;

(c)　the photograph is not of the child and another person other than the defendant.

Whilst the 1978 Act does not impede an accused from engaging in sexual intercourse with a person who is aged 17, he is not permitted to make such a person the subject of pornography. The defence does not apply to a 'one night stand' as a defence which includes a 'brief sexual relationship' would diminish the protection provided and would risk the re-introduction of issues as to the circumstances in which the photograph was taken and the motivation for taking or making it. The legislation strikes the balance between keeping interference by the State in the private lives of individuals to the minimum and maintaining under the law maximum protection for children from sexual abuse and exploitation: *R v M* [2011] EWCA Crim 2752, [2012] Crim LR 789.

There is also a defence for those involved in law enforcement activities.

Sentencing
SC Guideline – Indecent photographs of children

A[43.9] This guideline is taken from the SC's definitive guideline *Sexual Offences Act 2003* effective from 1 April 2014.

Triable either way

Maximum: 10 years' custody

Offence range: Community order – 9 years' custody

For section 1 offences committed on or after 3 December 2012, this is an offence listed in Part 1 of Schedule 15B for the purposes of section 224A (life sentence for second listed offence) of the Criminal Justice Act 2003.

For convictions on or after 3 December 2012 (irrespective of the date of commission of the offence), these are specified offences for the purposes of section 226A (extended sentence for certain violent or sexual offences) of the Criminal Justice Act 2003.

STEP ONE
DETERMINING THE OFFENCE CATEGORY

The court should determine the offence category using the table below.

	Possession	Distribution*	Production**
Category A	Possession of images involving penetrative sexual activity	Sharing images involving penetrative sexual activity	Creating images involving penetrative sexual activity
	Possession of images involving sexual activity with an animal or sadism	Sharing images involving sexual activity with an animal or sadism	Creating images involving sexual activity with an animal or sadism
Category B	Possession of images involving non-penetrative sexual activity	Sharing of images involving non-penetrative sexual activity	Creating images involving non-penetrative sexual activity
Category C	Possession of other indecent images not falling within categories A or B	Sharing of other indecent images not falling within categories A or B	Creating other indecent images not falling within categories A or B

*   Distribution includes possession with a view to distributing or sharing images.

**   Production includes the taking or making of any image at source, for instance the original image. Making an image by simple downloading should be treated as possession for the purposes of sentencing.

In most cases the intrinsic character of the most serious of the offending images will initially determine the appropriate category. If, however, the most serious images are unrepresentative of the offender's conduct a lower category may be appropriate. A lower category will not, however, be appropriate if the offender has produced or taken (for example photographed) images of a higher category.

STEP TWO
STARTING POINT AND CATEGORY RANGE

Having determined the category, the court should use the corresponding starting points to reach a sentence within the category range below. The starting point applies to all offenders irrespective of plea or previous convictions. Having determined the starting point, step two allows further adjustment for aggravating or mitigating features, set out on the next page.

Where there is a sufficient prospect of rehabilitation, a community order with a sex offender treatment programme requirement under section 202 of the Criminal Justice Act 2003 can be a proper alternative to a short or moderate length custodial sentence.

	Possession	Distribution	Production
Category A	**Starting point** 1 year's custody	**Starting point** 3 years' custody	**Starting point** 6 years' custody
	Category range 26 weeks' – 3 years' custody	**Category range** 2 – 5 years' custody	**Category range** 4 – 9 years' custody
Category B	**Starting point** 26 weeks' custody	**Starting point** 1 year's custody	**Starting point** 2 years' custody
	Category range High level community order – 18 months' custody	**Category range** 26 weeks' – 2 years' custody	**Category range** 1 – 4 years' custody
Category C	**Starting point** High level community order	**Starting point** 13 weeks' custody	**Starting point** 18 months' custody
	Category range Medium level community order – 26 weeks' custody	**Category range** High level community order – 26 weeks' custody	**Category range** 1 – 3 years' custody

The table below contains a **non-exhaustive** list of additional factual elements providing the context of the offence and factors relating to the offender. Identify whether any combination of these, or other relevant factors, should result in an upward or downward adjustment from the starting point. **In particular, relevant recent convictions are likely to result in an upward adjustment. In some cases, having considered these factors, it may be appropriate to move outside the identified category range.**

When sentencing appropriate **category B or C offences,** the court should also consider the custody threshold as follows:

- has the custody threshold been passed?
- if so, is it unavoidable that a custodial sentence be imposed?
- if so, can that sentence be suspended?

Aggravating factors	Mitigating factors
Statutory aggravating factors	No previous convictions **or** no relevant/recent convictions
Previous convictions, having regard to a) the nature of the offence to which the conviction relates and its relevance to the current offence; and b) the time that has elapsed since the conviction	Remorse
Offence committed whilst on bail	Previous good character and/or exemplary conduct[*]
Other aggravating factors	Age and/or lack of maturity where it affects the responsibility of the offender
Failure to comply with current court orders	Mental disorder or learning disability, particularly where linked to the commission of the offence
Offence committed whilst on licence	Demonstration of steps taken to address offending behaviour
Age and/or vulnerability of the child depicted	
Discernable pain or distress suffered by child depicted	
Period over which images were possessed, distributed or produced	
High volume of images possessed, distributed or produced	
Placing images where there is the potential for a high volume of viewers	
Collection includes moving images	
Attempts to dispose of or conceal evidence	
Abuse of trust	
Child depicted known to the offender	
Active involvement in a network or process that facilitates or commissions the creation or sharing of indecent images of children	
Commercial exploitation and/or motivation	
Deliberate or systematic searching for images portraying young children, category A images or the portrayal of familial sexual abuse	
Large number of different victims	
Child depicted intoxicated or drugged	

[*]   Age and/or vulnerability of the child should be given significant weight. In cases where the actual age of the victim is difficult to determine sentencers should consider the development of the child (infant,

pre-pubescent, post-pubescent).

* Previous good character/exemplary conduct is different from having no previous convictions. The more serious the offence, the less the weight which should normally be attributed to this factor. Where previous good character/exemplary conduct has been used to facilitate the offence, this mitigation should not normally be allowed and such conduct may constitute an aggravating factor.

STEP THREE
CONSIDER ANY FACTORS WHICH INDICATE A REDUCTION, SUCH AS ASSISTANCE TO THE PROSECUTION

The court should take into account sections 73 and 74 of the Serious Organised Crime and Police Act 2005 (assistance by defendants: reduction or review of sentence) and any other rule of law by virtue of which an offender may receive a discounted sentence in consequence of assistance given (or offered) to the prosecutor or investigator.

STEP FOUR
REDUCTION FOR GUILTY PLEAS

The court should take account of any potential reduction for a guilty plea in accordance with section 144 of the Criminal Justice Act 2003 and the *Guilty Plea* guideline.

STEP FIVE
DANGEROUSNESS

The court should consider whether having regard to the criteria contained in Chapter 5 of Part 12 of the Criminal Justice Act 2003 it would be appropriate to award a life sentence (section 224A) or an extended sentence (section 226A). When sentencing offenders to a life sentence under these provisions, the notional determinate sentence should be used as the basis for the setting of a minimum term.

STEP SIX
TOTALITY PRINCIPLE

If sentencing an offender for more than one offence, or where the offender is already serving a sentence, consider whether the total sentence is just and proportionate to the overall offending behaviour.

STEP SEVEN
ANCILLARY ORDERS

The court must consider whether to make any ancillary orders. The court must also consider what other requirements or provisions may automatically apply. Further information is included on page 303.

STEP EIGHT
REASONS

Section 174 of the Criminal Justice Act 2003 imposes a duty to give reasons for, and explain the effect of, the sentence.

STEP NINE
CONSIDERATION FOR TIME SPENT ON BAIL

The court must consider whether to give credit for time spent on bail in accordance with section 240A of the Criminal Justice Act 2003.

A[43.10] Available sentences. See Table A at B[4.1].

A[43.11] Forfeiture.

Section 5 of the 1978 Act has been amended by s 39 of the Police and Justice Act 2006 to specifically provide for the forfeiture of indecent photographs and pseudo-photographs.

A[43.12] Notification requirements. See A[52.15]. Requirements apply even on the making of a conditional discharge (*R v Longworth* [2004] EWCA Crim 2145, [2005] 1 Cr App Rep (S) 419, (2004) Times, 17 August).

A[44]

Keeping a brothel used for prostitution

Charge

A[44.1] Did keep, or to manage, or act or assist in the management of, a brothel to which people resort for practices involving prostitution (whether or not also for other practices)

Sexual Offences Act 1956, s 33A

Maximum penalty – Fine level 5 and/or 6 months. Triable either way. Specified sexual offence under Sch 15, Part 2, CJA 2003

Crown Court – 7 years' imprisonment and unlimited fine.

Section 33A was inserted by s 55 of the Sexual Offences Act 2003. The Sexual Offences Act 1956 also provides offences of: keeping a brothel (s 33); letting premises for use as brothel (s 34); tenant permitting premises to be used as a brothel (s 35); and tenant permitting premises to be sued for prostitution (s 36). These offences are summary only. The maximum penalty is a fine level 3 and three months, or, for second or subsequent conviction, a fine level 4 and six months.

Mode of trial

A[44.2] Consider the **SC Guideline** at A[44.4] below. Note, where an offender has profited from his or her involvement in the prostitution of others, the courts should always consider making a confiscation order approximately equivalent to the profits enjoyed. Such an order can only be made in the Crown Court.

Legal notes and definitions

A[44.3] Brothel. A brothel is a place where people of opposite sexes are allowed to resort for illicit intercourse, whether the women are common prostitutes or not: *Winter v Woolfe* [1931] 1 KB 549, 95 JP 20. A house occupied by one woman and used by her for prostitution but not allowed by her to be used by other women for a like purpose, is not a brothel: *Singleton v Ellison* [1895] 1 QB 607, 59 JP 119. However, the facts justified a finding that premises were used as a brothel where two women, one being the tenant and occupier both used the premises for prostitution: *Gorman v Standen, Palace-Clark v Standen* [1964] 1 QB 294, [1963] 3 All ER 627, 128 JP 28. On other facts it has been held that two flats in one building, separately let to prostitutes, did not justify a finding that the building was used as a brothel: *Strath v Foxon* [1956] 1 QB 67, [1955] 3 All ER 398, 119 JP 581; but a block of flats, inhabited by different women and used by them for prostitution was held, on the facts, to be a brothel: *Durose v Wilson* (1907) 71 JP 263; and where there was use by three prostitutes in separate rooms, separately let to them, in such proximity as to constitute a 'nest' of prostitutes, it was held that the premises were a brothel: *Donovan v Gavin*

[1965] 2 QB 648, [1965] 2 All ER 611, 129 JP 404. Similarly where premises were used by a team of different prostitutes, but no more than one used the premises each day, the premises were held to constitute a brothel: *Stevens v Christy* (1987) 151 JP 366, [1987] Crim LR 503.

Assisting in the management. Evidence of normal sexual intercourse provided on the premises is not essential to prove a charge of assisting in the management of a brothel; it is sufficient to prove that more than one woman offered herself as a participant in physical acts of indecency for the sexual gratification of men: *Kelly v Purvis* [1983] QB 663, [1983] 1 All ER 525, 76 Cr App Rep 165. Women in a massage parlour, who not only performed lewd acts, but also discussed the nature of the acts to be performed and negotiated the terms of payment for their services, were held to be assisting in the management of a brothel: *Elliott v DPP* (1989) Times, 19 January, DC. To establish the offence of assisting in the management it is not necessary to show that the defendant exercised some sort of control over the management, nor is it necessary to show there was a specific act of management for that would be acting in the management: *Jones and Wood v DPP* (1992) 156 JP 866.

Prostitution. Has the same meaning as give by s 51(2) of the Sexual Offences Act 2003.

Sentencing
SC Guideline – Keeping a brothel used for prostitution

A[44.4] This guideline is taken from the SC's definitive guideline *Sexual Offences Act 2003* effective from 1 April 2014.

Triable either way

Maximum: 7 years' custody

Offence range: Community order – 6 years' custody

The terms 'prostitute' and 'prostitution' are used in this guideline in accordance with the statutory language contained in the Sexual Offences Act 2003.

STEP ONE
DETERMINING THE OFFENCE CATEGORY

The court should determine which categories of harm and culpability the offence falls into by reference **only** to the tables below.

Harm		Culpability
Category 1	• Under 18 year olds working in brothel	A
	• Abduction/detention	Keeping brothel on significant commercial basis Involvement in keeping a number of brothels
	• Violence or threats of violence	Expectation of significant financial or other gain
	• Sustained and systematic psychological abuse	Abuse of trust

Harm		Culpability
	• Those working in brothel forced or coerced to participate in unsafe/degrading sexual activity	Exploitation of those known to be trafficked
	• Those working in brothel forced or coerced into seeing many 'customers'	Significant involvement in limiting freedom of those working in brothel
	• Those working in brothel forced/coerced/deceived into prostitution	Grooming of a person to work in the brothel including through cultivation of a dependency on drugs or alcohol
	• Established evidence of community impact	**B**
Category 2	Factor(s) in category 1 not present	Keeping/managing premises
		Close involvement with those working in brothel, for example control of finances, choice of clients, working conditions, etc (where offender's involvement is not as a result of coercion)
		C
		Performs limited function under direction
		Close involvement but engaged by coercion/intimidation/exploitation

STEP TWO
STARTING POINT AND CATEGORY RANGE

Having determined the category, the court should use the corresponding starting points to reach a sentence within the category range on the next page. The starting point applies to all offenders irrespective of plea or previous convictions. Having determined the starting point, step two allows further adjustment for aggravating or mitigating features, set out on the next page.

A case of particular gravity, reflected by multiple features of culpability or harm in step one, could merit upward adjustment from the starting point before further adjustment for aggravating or mitigating features, set out on the next page.

Where there is a sufficient prospect of rehabilitation, a community order with a sex offender treatment programme requirement under section 202 of the Criminal Justice Act 2003 can be a proper alternative to a short or moderate length custodial sentence.

	A	B	C
Category 1	**Starting point** 3 – 6 years' custody	**Starting point** 2 – 5 years' custody	**Starting point** High level community order – 18 months' custody
	Category range 5 – 8 years' custody	**Category range** 3 – 6 years' custody	**Category range** 18 months' – 4 years' custody
Category 2	**Starting point** 3 years' custody	**Starting point** 12 months' custody	**Starting point** Medium level community order
	Category range 2 – 5 years' custody	**Category range** 26 weeks' – 2 years' custody	**Category range** Low level community order – High level community order

The table below contains a **non-exhaustive** list of additional factual elements providing the context of the offence and factors relating to the offender. Identify whether any combination of these, or other relevant factors, should result in an upward or downward adjustment from the starting point. **In particular, relevant recent convictions are likely to result in an upward adjustment. In some cases, having considered these factors, it may be appropriate to move outside the identified category range.**

When sentencing appropriate **category 1 offences,** the court should also consider the custody threshold as follows:

* has the custody threshold been passed?
* if so, is it unavoidable that a custodial sentence be imposed?
* if so, can that sentence be suspended?

Aggravating factors	Any steps taken to prevent those working in brothel reporting an incident, obtaining assistance and/or from assisting or supporting the prosecution
Statutory aggravating factors	Attempts to dispose of or conceal evidence
Previous convictions, having regard to a) the nature of the offence to which the conviction relates and its relevance to the current offence; and b) the time that has elapsed since the conviction	Those working in brothel forced or coerced into pornography
Offence committed whilst on bail	Timescale over which operation has been run
Other aggravating factors	**Mitigating factors**
Failure to comply with current court orders	No previous convictions or no relevant/recent convictions
Offence committed whilst on licence	Remorse
Deliberate isolation of those working in brothel	Previous good character and/or exemplary conduct[*]
Threats made to expose those working in brothel to the authorities (for example, immigration or police), family/ friends or others	Age and/or lack of maturity where it affects the responsibility of the offender

Harm threatened against the family/friends of those working in brothel	Mental disorder or learning disability, particularly where linked to the commission of the offence
Passport/identity documents removed	Demonstration of steps taken to address offending behaviour
Those working in brothel prevented from seeking medical treatment	
Food withheld	
Those working in brothel passed around by offender and moved to other brothels	
Earnings of those working in brothel withheld/kept by offender or evidence of excessive wage reduction or debt bondage, inflated travel or living expenses or unreasonable interest rates	

  *   Previous good character/exemplary conduct is different from having no previous convictions. The more serious the offence, the less the weight which should normally be attributed to this factor. Where previous good character/exemplary conduct has been used to facilitate the offence, this mitigation should not normally be allowed and such conduct may constitute an aggravating factor.

STEP THREE
CONSIDER ANY FACTORS WHICH INDICATE A REDUCTION, SUCH AS ASSISTANCE TO THE PROSECUTION

The court should take into account sections 73 and 74 of the Serious Organised Crime and Police Act 2005 (assistance by defendants: reduction or review of sentence) and any other rule of law by virtue of which an offender may receive a discounted sentence in consequence of assistance given (or offered) to the prosecutor or investigator.

STEP FOUR
REDUCTION FOR GUILTY PLEAS

The court should take account of any potential reduction for a guilty plea in accordance with section 144 of the Criminal Justice Act 2003 and the *Guilty Plea* guideline.

STEP FIVE
TOTALITY PRINCIPLE

If sentencing an offender for more than one offence, or where the offender is already serving a sentence, consider whether the total sentence is just and proportionate to the overall offending behaviour.

STEP SIX
ANCILLARY ORDERS

The court must consider whether to make any ancillary orders. The court must also consider what other requirements or provisions may automatically apply. Further information is included on page 303.

STEP SEVEN
REASONS

Section 174 of the Criminal Justice Act 2003 imposes a duty to give reasons for, and explain the effect of, the sentence.

STEP EIGHT
CONSIDERATION FOR TIME SPENT ON BAIL

The court must consider whether to give credit for time spent on bail in accordance with section 240A of the Criminal Justice Act 2003.

A[45]

Making off without payment

Charge

A[45.1] Knowing that payment on the spot for certain goods supplied [or service done] was required or expected dishonestly made off without having paid as required or expected and with intent to avoid payment of the amount due

Theft Act 1978, s 3

A[45.2] Maximum penalty – Fine level 5 and 6 months. Triable either way.

Crown Court – 2 years and unlimited fine.

Mode of trial

A[45.3] Consider the SC Guideline at A[45.8] below.

Legal notes and definitions

A[45.4] The basis of this offence is dishonesty. Dishonesty can be inferred from the surrounding circumstances. It is an offence whether the advantage is obtained for the defendant or for someone else.

A[45.5] Dishonesty. The test of dishonesty is (a) whether the accused's actions were dishonest according to the ordinary standards of reasonable and honest people and, if so, (b) whether the accused himself had realised that his actions were, according to those standards, dishonest (*R v Ghosh* [1982] QB 1053, [1982] 2 All ER 689, CA).

A[45.6] Payment on the spot includes payment at the time of collecting goods on which work has been done, or in respect of which a service has been provided, eg collecting one's car from a garage after repair.

A[45.6A] Making off. 'Making off' involves a departure from the spot where payment is required: *R v Brooks* (1983) 76 Cr App Rep 66. In the case of a taxi, payment might be made while sitting in the taxi or standing by the window. Payment might be requested whilst the fares are still in the cab and at this stage the fares might be disputed. The fact that the taxi driver then drives off to a police station, or somewhere else, locking the door, does not mean that when the defendant runs off he could not be making off without having paid, dishonestly intending to avoid payment. It is the time at which he makes off which is critical at which he had to have formed the intention to avoid payment. But to apply the words too literally would be to misunderstand the legislation. Thus, if a passenger were to explain (honestly) to the taxi driver that he had to enter his house in order to obtain the fare, the moment for payment would be deferred for him to do so. A decision not to return to the taxi would mean that, from that moment, the passenger is making off without payment. See *R v Morris* [2013] EWCA Crim 436, [2013] 2 Cr App R 9, [2013] RTR 22.

A breach of contract by the party claiming payment may mean that the defendant may not have been in a situation in which he was bound to pay or even tender the money and, thus, cannot be charged with making off: *Troughton v Metropolitan Police* [1987] Crim LR 138.

A[45.7] With intent to avoid payment of the amount due. This means with intent *never* to pay the sum due. An intent merely to defer or delay payment is not enough for a 'making off' offence (*R v Allen* [1985] 1 All ER 148, [1985] 1 WLR 50, CA; affd [1985] AC 1029, [1985] 2 All ER 641, HL).

Sentencing
SC Guideline – Making off without payment

Key factors

A[45.8] The key factors are set out below:

(a)   The starting points and sentencing ranges in this guideline are based on the assumption that the offender was motivated by greed or a desire to live beyond his or her means. To avoid double counting, such a motivation should not be treated as a factor that increases culpability.

(b)   When assessing the harm caused by this offence, the starting point should be the loss suffered by the victim. In general, the greater the loss, the more serious the offence. However, the monetary value of the loss may not reflect the full extent of the harm caused by the offence. The court should also take into account the impact of the offence on the victim, any harm to persons other than the direct victim, and any harm in the form of public alarm or erosion of public confidence.

(c)   The following matters of offender mitigation may be relevant in this offence:

   (i)   *Offender motivated by desperation or need.* The fact that an offence has been committed in desperation or need arising from particular hardship may count as offender mitigation in exceptional circumstances.

   (ii)   *Voluntary return of stolen property.* Whether and the degree to which the return of stolen property constitutes a matter of offender mitigation will depend on the assessment of the circumstances, and, in particular, the voluntariness and timeliness of the return.

   (iii)   *Impact on sentence of offender's dependency.* Many offenders convicted of acquisitive crimes are motivated by an addiction, often to drugs, alcohol or gambling. This does not mitigate the seriousness of the offence, but an offender's dependency may properly influence the type of sentence imposed. In particular, it may sometimes be appropriate to impose a drug rehabilitation requirement or an alcohol treatment requirement as part of a community order or a suspended sentence order in an attempt to break the cycle of addiction and offending, even if an immediate custodial sentence would otherwise be warranted (See B[2.17]. The Court of Appeal gave guidance on the approach to making drug treatment and testing orders, which also applies to imposing a drug rehabilitation requirement in *Attorney General's Reference No 64 of 2003 (R v Boujettif and*

Harrison) v Sanchez [2003] EWCA Crim 3514 and *R v Woods and Collins* [2005] EWCA Crim 2065 summarised in the Sentencing Council's Guideline Judgments Case Compendium (Section (A) Generic Sentencing Principles) available at: sentencingcouncil.judiciary.gov.uk.

OFFENCE SERIOUSNESS (CULPABILITY AND HARM)		
A. IDENTIFY THE APPROPRIATE STARTING POINT		
Starting points based on first time offender pleading not guilty		
Examples of nature of activity	**Starting point**	**Range**
Single offence committed by an offender acting alone and with evidence of little or no planning, goods or services worth less than £200	Band C fine	Band A fine to high level community order
Offence displaying one or more of the following: – offender acting in unison with others – evidence of planning – offence part of a 'spree' – intimidation of victim – goods or services worth £200 or more	Medium level community order	Low level community order to 12 weeks custody
OFFENCE SERIOUSNESS (CULPABILITY AND HARM)		
B. CONSIDER THE EFFECT OF AGGRAVATING AND MITIGATING FACTORS (OTHER THAN THOSE WITHIN EXAMPLES ABOVE)		
Common aggravating and mitigating factors are identified at B[5.2A]		
FORM A PRELIMINARY VIEW OF THE APPROPRIATE SENTENCE, THEN CONSIDER OFFENDER MITIGATION		
Common factors are identified at B[5.2A]. See also "Key factors" above.		
CONSIDER A REDUCTION FOR A GUILTY PLEA		
CONSIDER ANCILLARY ORDERS, INCLUDING COMPENSATION		
Refer to B[18] for guidance on compensation and **Part B** for available ancillary orders		
DECIDE SENTENCE		
GIVE REASONS		

Protective order, breach of

Charges

A[46.1] 1 Without reasonable excuse the defendant breached the terms of his restraining order in that he [specify] thereby making him guilty of an offence.

Protection from Harassment Act 1997, s 5(5).

2. Without reasonable excuse the defendant breached the terms of his non-molestation order in that he [specify] thereby making him guilty of an offence.

Family Law Act 1996, s 42A(1).

Maximum penalty – (in either case) Fine level 5 and 6 months. Triable either way. Specified violent offence under Sch 15, Part 1, CJA 2003.

Crown Court – 5 years' imprisonment and unlimited fine.

Mode of trial

A[46.2] Consider the SC Guideline at A[46.4] below.

Legal notes and definitions

A[46.3] **Non-molestation – duplicity.** An information couched in the form of a s 1 offence (ie it referred to a 'course of conduct') and alleging this to be in breach of the terms of a restraining order, contrary to s 5(5) and (6), was held not to be bad for duplicity in *McCaskill v DPP* [2005] EWHC 3208 (Admin), (2006) 170 JP 301.

Harassment – terms of order. An order under s.5 must identify by name those who are protected by it (*R v Mann* [2000] The Times, April 11, CA).

Interpretation. The interpretation of ordinary words in a court order is a question of fact; the criminal context is not a reason for giving a narrow or strained meaning to words which bear their ordinary meaning, and the application of that meaning to the facts is a matter for the fact-finding tribunal: *R v Evans* [2004] EWCA Crim 3102, (2005) 169 JP 129, [2005] 1 Cr App Rep 546, [2005] Crim LR 654 (parking a car so that it blocked in the van of somebody visiting the complainants' property was held to breach a restraining order that prohibited the defendant from 'abusive action' towards the complainants).

Sentencing
Sentencing Council – Protective order, breach of

A[46.4] This guidelines and accompanying notes are taken from the SC's definitive guideline *Breach of a Protective Order*, published 7 December 2006.

Where the conduct is particularly serious, it would normally be charged as a separate offence. These starting points are based on the premise that the activity has either been prosecuted separately as an offence or is not of a character sufficient to justify prosecution of it as an offence in its own right.

For cases of domestic violence. See SC Definitive Guideline: "Overarching Principles: Domestic Violence".

Aims of sentencing

(a)   The main aim of sentencing for breach of a protective order (which would have been imposed to protect a victim from future harm) should be to achieve future compliance with that order.

(b)   The court will need to assess the level of risk posed by the offender. Willingness to undergo treatment or accept help may influence sentence.

Key factors

(a)   The nature of the conduct that caused the breach of the order. In particular, whether the conduct was direct or indirect, although it is important to recognise that indirect contact is capable of causing significant harm or anxiety.

(b)   There may be **exceptional cases** where the nature of the **breach** is **particularly serious** but has not been dealt with by a separate offence being charged. In those cases the **risk** posed by the offender and the **nature of the breach** will be particularly significant in determining the response.

(c)   The nature of the original conduct or offence is relevant in so far as it allows a judgement to be made on the level of harm caused to the victim by the breach, and the extent to which that harm was intended.

(d)   The sentence following a breach is for the breach alone and must avoid punishing the offender again for the offence or conduct as a result of which the order was made.

(e)   It is likely that all breaches of protective orders will pass the threshold for a community sentence. Custody is the starting point where violence is used. Non-violent conduct may also cross the custody threshold where a high degree of harm or anxiety has been caused.

(f)   Where an order was made in civil proceedings, its purpose may have been to cause the subject of the order to modify behaviour rather than to imply that the conduct was especially serious. If so, it is likely to be disproportionate to impose a custodial sentence if the breach of the order did not involve threats or violence.

(g)   In some cases where a breach might result in a short custodial sentence but the court is satisfied that the offender genuinely intends to reform his or her behaviour and there is a real prospect of rehabilitation, the court may consider it appropriate to impose a sentence that will allow this. This may mean imposing a suspended sentence order or a community order (where appropriate with a requirement to attend an accredited domestic violence programme).

OFFENCE SERIOUSNESS (CULPABILITY AND HARM)

A. IDENTIFY THE APPROPRIATE STARTING POINT		
Starting points based on first time offender pleading not guilty		
Examples of nature of activity	**Starting point**	**Range**
Single breach involving no/minimal direct contact	Low level community order	Band C fine to medium level community order
More than one breach involving no/minimal contact or some direct contact	Medium level community order	Low level community order to high level community order
Single breach involving some violence and/or significant physical or psychological harm to the victim	18 weeks custody	13 weeks to 26 weeks custody
More than one breach involving some violence and/or significant physical or psychological harm to the victim	Crown Court	26 weeks custody to Crown Court
Breach (whether one or more) involving significant physical violence or psychological harm to the victim	Crown Court	Crown Court

OFFENCE SERIOUSNESS (CULPABILITY AND HARM)	
B. CONSIDER THE EFFECT OF AGGRAVATING AND MITIGATING FACTORS (OTHER THAN THOSE WITHIN EXAMPLES ABOVE)	
Common aggravating and mitigating factors are identified at B[5.2A]. The following may be particularly relevant but **these lists are not exhaustive**	
Factors indicating higher culpability	*Factors indicating lower culpability*
1. Proven history of violence or threats by the offender	1. Breach occurred after a long period of compliance
2. Using contact arrangements with a child to instigate offence	2. Victim initiated contact
3. Offence is a further breach, following earlier breach proceedings	
4. Offender has history of disobedience to court orders	
5. Breach committed immediately or shortly after order made	
Factors indicating greater degree of harm	
1. Victim is particularly vulnerable	
2. Impact on children	
3. Victim is forced to leave home	

FORM A PRELIMINARY VIEW OF THE APPROPRIATE SENTENCE, THEN CONSIDER OFFENDER MITIGATION
Common factors are identified at B[5.2A]

CONSIDER A REDUCTION FOR A GUILTY PLEA

CONSIDER ANCILLARY ORDERS
Refer to B[18] for guidance on compensation and **Part B** for available ancillary orders

```
                    DECIDE SENTENCE
                    GIVE REASONS
```

Variation

A[46.5] Variation of restraining order. Where a restraining order has been made for a specified period of time, on a true construction of s 5(4), a court had power to vary a restraining order by extending the expiry date of the order (*DPP v Kevin Hall* [2005] EWHC 2612 (Admin), [2006] 3 All ER 170). The refusal by a magistrates' court to vary or discharge a restraining order on an application under s 5(4) was not subject to a right of appeal to the Crown Court as such an order was not a sentence (or "order") for the purposes of s 108 MCA 1980 (*R (on the application of Lee) v Leeds Crown Court* [2006] All ER (D) 18 (Oct). The same argument was canvassed in *R v Bradfield* [2006] All ER (D) 394 (Nov) in relation to s 9 of the Criminal Appeal Act 1968 but the Court of Appeal did not find it necessary to decide the point. The case of *Lee*, therefore, remains good law).

A[47]

Obstructing or resisting a constable in the execution of his duty
Obstructing a court security officer in the execution of his duty

Charges

A[47.1] 1 Resisting a constable in the execution of his duty

A[47.2] 2 Resisting a person assisting a constable in the execution of his duty

A[47.3] 3 Wilfully obstructing a constable in the execution of his duty

A[47.4] 4 Wilfully obstructing a person assisting a constable in the execution of his duty

Police Act 1996, s 89(2)

Maximum penalty – Fine level 3 and one month.

A[47.5] 5 Wilfully obstructing a court security officer in the execution of his duty

Courts Act 2003, s 57

Maximum penalty – Fine level 3.

Legal notes and definitions

A[47.6] The offences of resisting and wilfully obstructing will usually involve some other activity than an assault on the police or a court security officer (which would constitute a different charge). A person exercising their right to silence does not commit the offence of obstructing a police officer.

A[47.7] **Resisting.** Means striving against, opposing or trying to impede. For the intention which the defendant must have to commit the offence see A[9] (police assault).

A[47.8] **Wilfully.** A person wilfully obstructs a police constable in the execution of his duty if he deliberately does an act which, though not necessarily 'aimed at' or 'hostile to' the police, in fact prevents a constable from carrying out his duty or makes it more difficult for him to do so, and if he knows and intends (whether or not that is his predominant intention) that his conduct will have that effect; the motive with which the act is committed is irrelevant unless it constitutes a lawful excuse for the obstruction: *Lewis v Cox* [1985] QB 509, [1984] 3 All ER 672, 148 JP 601. It is immaterial that the defendant does not appreciate that his action amounted to obstruction: *Moore v Green* [1983] 1 All ER 663. A person cannot obstruct a police officer in the execution of his duty when he reasonably believes that he is not a police officer: *Ostler v Elliott* [1980] Crim LR 584.

A[47.9] **Obstructing.** A person who simply gave drivers of motor cars notice of a 'police trap' was held not guilty of obstruction under an enactment replaced by this sub-section: *Bastable v Little* [1907] 1 KB 59, 71 JP 52. But, where cars when warned of a police trap are being driven at an illegal speed, the person so warning may be convicted of obstruction: *Betts v Stevens* [1910] 1 KB 1, 73 JP 486. In *R (on the application of DPP) v Glendinning* [2005] EWHC Admin 2333, (2005) 169 JP 649 it was re-affirmed that a conviction for obstruction required evidence that there were vehicles that were speeding or were likely to speed at the location of the speed trap.

A person's mere refusal to answer a constable's questions which, in the circumstances, he was not legally obliged to answer, is not caught by the section: *Rice v Connolly* [1966] 2 QB 414, [1966] 2 All ER 649, 130 JP 322, but in *Ricketts v Cox* (1981) 74 Cr App Rep 298, [1982] Crim LR 184, it was held that a defendant who was abusive, uncooperative and positively hostile to police officers, using obscene language calculated to provoke and antagonise the officers, was guilty of obstruction.

Running off to avoid apprehension amounts to an act that is capable of constituting the wilful obstruction of a police officer: *Sekfall, Banamira and Ouham v DPP* [2006] EWHC 894 (Admin), (2006) 170 JP 393. While it is lawful for a third party to advise a suspect of his right not to answer questions put to him by a police officer, if the third party by his abusive, persistent and unruly behaviour, acts in a way that goes well beyond the exercise of his legal rights and prevents communication between the officer and the suspect, or makes it more difficult, he will be guilty of obstructing the police: see *Green v DPP* (1991) 155 JP 816, DC. In *Ingleton v Dibble* [1972] 1 QB 480, [1972] 1 All ER 275, 136 JP 155, it was held that there was a distinction between a refusal to act (as in *Rice v Connolly*, above) and the doing of some positive act, and that it was not necessary to show, where the obstruction consists of a positive act, that it must be unlawful independently. It was held that the driver of a motor car who drank whisky after being asked to take a breath test with the object and effect of frustrating the procedure under ss 2 and 3 of the Road Safety Act 1967 was guilty of obstructing the police, and in *R v Britton* [1973] Crim LR 375 a similar action with a bottle of beer led to a conviction for the common law misdemeanour of attempting to defeat the due course of justice.

A private citizen can never have a lawful excuse for interfering with an arrest by a police officer which is lawful: *Hills v Ellis* [1983] QB 680, [1983] 1 All ER 667.

A person who shouted, outside a public house, outside 'permitted hours', that the police were waiting to enter, was rightly convicted: *Hinchliffe v Sheldon* [1955] 3 All ER 406, 120 JP 13.

Failure to accord entry to police officers acting under s 4 of the Road Traffic Act 1988 may be a wilful obstruction: *Lunt v DPP* [1993] Crim LR 534.

A[47.10] **Constable.** A constable includes a special constable and member of the police force of any rank however high. Offences against designated and accredited persons acting in the execution of their duty ie community support officer, investigating officer, detention officer and escort officer are catered for by the Police Reform Act 2002, s 46. Wilful obstruction carries on conviction imprisonment of one month or a level 3 fine.

A[47.11] **In the execution of his duty.** See A[9.5], where this topic is considered in detail in relation to the offence of assaulting a constable acting in the execution.

If as a finding of fact/law the constable was not acting in the course of his duty then the charge must be dismissed. Once it had been established that the initial arrest of the accused was unlawful, and provided he did not unreasonable force in resisting the arrest, the accused could not be guilty of resisting other police officers who were bona fide assisting the first officer in the unlawful arrest (*Cumberbatch v Crown Prosecution Service* [2009] EWHC 3353 (Admin), 174 JP 149).

A[47.12] This type of defence sometimes raises difficult questions of law as to whether, for example, a constable had a right to be on private premises when not in possession of a search warrant, or whether a constable had a right to detain a person without there being in force a warrant for arrest. See *James and Chorley v DPP* (1997) 161 JP 89, [1997] Crim LR 831 where a defendant had ceased driving thus ending a constable's right to arrest for driving whilst disqualified. His friend did not obstruct the constable by preventing an arrest as the arrest was not lawful.

A[47.13] The burden of proof that the constable was acting in the execution of his duty rests on the prosecution (*Redmond-Bate v DPP* (1999) 163 JP 789, [1999] Crim LR 998).

A[47.14] **Police officer and court security officer.** See A[9.4] for definitions.

Sentencing
SC Guideline – Obstruct/resist a constable in the execution of duty

A[47.15]

OFFENCE SERIOUSNESS (CULPABILITY AND HARM)		
A. IDENTIFY THE APPROPRIATE STARTING POINT		
Starting points based on first time offender pleading not guilty		
Examples of nature of activity	**Starting point**	**Range**
Failure to move when required to do so	Band A fine	Conditional discharge to band B fine
Attempt to prevent arrest or other lawful police action; or giving false details	Band B fine	Band A fine to band C fine
Several people attempting to prevent arrest or other lawful police action	Low level community order	Band C fine to medium level community order
OFFENCE SERIOUSNESS (CULPABILITY AND HARM)		
B. CONSIDER THE EFFECT OF AGGRAVATING AND MITIGATING FACTORS (OTHER THAN THOSE WITHIN EXAMPLES ABOVE)		

Common aggravating and mitigating factors are identified at B[5.2A]. The following may be particularly relevant but **these lists are not exhaustive**

Factors indicating higher culpability	*Factors indicating lower culpability*
1. Premeditated action	1. Genuine mistake or misjudgement
2. Aggressive words/threats	2. Brief incident
3. Aggressive group action	

FORM A PRELIMINARY VIEW OF THE APPROPRIATE SENTENCE, THEN CONSIDER OFFENDER MITIGATION
Common factors are identified at B[5.2A]
CONSIDER A REDUCTION FOR A GUILTY PLEA
CONSIDER ANCILLARY ORDERS
Refer to B[18] for guidance on compensation and **Part B** for available ancillary orders
DECIDE SENTENCE
GIVE REASONS

A[48]

Railway fare evasion

Charge 1

A[48.1] Failure to give name and address following a failure to produce a valid ticket

Regulation of Railways Act 1889, s 5(1)

Maximum penalty – Fine level 2 (Railway Company or London Transport)

Charge 2

A[48.2] Travelling on a railway without having previously paid the fare with the intention of avoiding payment

OR

Having paid a fare knowingly and wilfully travelling beyond the distance paid for without previously paying for an additional distance with the intention of avoiding additional fare

OR

Giving a false name and address following a failure to pay

Regulation of the Railways Act 1889, s 5(3)(a), (b), and (c) respectively

Maximum penalty – Fine level 3 or 3 months (Railway Company or London Transport).

Byelaws. All railway operators and Railtrack have adopted the Framework Railway Byelaws. Penalty for a breach of a byelaw is a level 3 fine.

Legal notes and definitions

A[48.3] A fare must be paid to the railway authority or one of its employees.

The request for a traveller's name and address must be made by an officer of the railway operator.

A[48.4]–[48.6] Intention. A person travelling with a return ticket of another person may be rightly convicted for travelling without having paid his fare, and with intent to avoid payment: *Langdon v Howells* (1879) 4 QBD 337, 43 JP 717; *London, Midland and Scottish Rly Co v Greaver* [1937] 1 KB 367, [1936] 3 All ER 333, 100 JP 511.

Payment of fare means payment to the railway company, or to their servant or agent. The intent to avoid payment thereof is proved by travelling on a non-transferable ticket issued to someone else. It is not necessary to show that the offender knew the ticket was non-transferable. The transferor is guilty of aiding and abetting him in the commission of the offence: *Reynolds v Beasley* [1919] 1 KB 215, 83 JP 35.

Proof of intent to defraud is not required; there need only be proof of intent to avoid payment: *Browning v Floyd* [1946] KB 597, [1946] 2 All ER 367, 110 JP 308. A dishonest intention is not necessarily imported and an offence is committed if a passenger travels or attempts to travel intending not to pay what, in fact, turns out to be the proper fare: see *Covington v Wright* [1963] 2 QB 469, [1963] 2 All ER 212. But there must be proof of intent to avoid payment and the burden of proof remains throughout on the prosecution: *R v Steane* [1947] KB 997, [1947] 1 All ER 813, 111 JP 387.

'His fare' means the fare by the train and for the class of carriage in which the passenger travels; so a person travelling in a first-class carriage with a second-class ticket, and fraudulently intending to avoid payment of first-class fare, may be convicted for travelling 'without having previously paid his fare': *Gillingham v Walker* (1881) 45 JP 470. In such circumstances, the passenger may be convicted on proof that he declined to pay the excess fare demanded: *Noble v Killick* (1891) 60 LJMC 61.

The intent to avoid payment refers in point of time to the period of travel and this continues at least until the traveller reaches the ticket barrier: *Bremme v Dubery* [1964] 1 All ER 193, 128 JP 148; *Murphy v Verati* [1967] 1 All ER 861. There is no reason for importing the adverb 'permanently' into s 5(3)(a); an intention not to pay the proper fare unless and until he was tracked down and payment requested is sufficient to constitute an intent to avoid payment: *Corbyn v Saunders* [1978] 2 All ER 697, 142 JP 458.

A[48.7] Travelling. This includes the time between leaving the railway carriage and proceeding to the exit barrier. Thus an offence is committed if a passenger decides to avoid the fare at that stage of the journey.

A[48.8] Wilfully. This means deliberately.

Sentencing
SC Guideline – Railway fare evasion

A[48.9]

OFFENCE SERIOUSNESS (CULPABILITY AND HARM)		
A. IDENTIFY THE APPROPRIATE STARTING POINT		
Starting points based on first time offender pleading not guilty		
Examples of nature of activity	**Starting point**	**Range**
Failing to produce ticket or failure to pay fare on request	Band A fine	Conditional discharge to band B fine
Travelling on railway without having paid the fare or knowingly and wilfully travelling beyond the distance paid for, with intent to avoid payment	Band B fine	Band A fine to band C fine
OFFENCE SERIOUSNESS (CULPABILITY AND HARM)		
B. CONSIDER THE EFFECT OF AGGRAVATING AND MITIGATING FACTORS (OTHER THAN THOSE WITHIN EXAMPLES ABOVE)		
Common aggravating and mitigating factors are identified at B[5.2A]. The following may be particularly relevant but **these lists are not exhaustive**		
Factor indicating higher culpability		

1. Offensive or intimidating language or behaviour towards railway staff	
Factor indicating greater degree of harm	
1. High level of loss caused or intended to be caused	
FORM A PRELIMINARY VIEW OF THE APPROPRIATE SENTENCE, THEN CONSIDER OFFENDER MITIGATION	
Common factors are identified at B[5.2A]	
CONSIDER A REDUCTION FOR A GUILTY PLEA	
CONSIDER ANCILLARY ORDERS INCLUDING COMPENSATION	
Refer to B[18] for guidance on compensation and Part B for available ancillary orders	
DECIDE SENTENCE	
GIVE REASONS	

A[48.10]   See Table B at B[4.2] for available sentences.

School non-attendance

Charge 1

A[49.1] Being the parent of a child [identify] of compulsory school age and who is a registered pupil at a school [specify], [identify child] failed to attend regularly at the school.

Education Act 1996, s 444(1).

Maximum penalty – Level 3 fine.

Charge 2

A[49.2] Being the parent of a child [identify] of compulsory school age and who is a registered pupil at a school namely [specify], knowing that the child [identify] is failing to attend regularly at that school, fails without justification to cause the child to do so.

Education Act 1996, s 444 (1A).

Maximum penalty – Level 4 fine and/or 3 months.

Legal notes and definitions

A[49.3] "Compulsory school age" and "school" is defined by Education Act 1996, s 8.

"Registered pupil" in relation to a school, means a person registered as a pupil at the school in the register kept under the Education Act 1996, s 434.

"Parent" is defined by Education Act 1996, s 576.

Subject to the defences set out in s 444(1), the offence is one of strict liability; which does not contravene article 6(2) of the ECHR (*Barnfather v Islington Education Authority* [2003] 1 WLR 2318). Where the parent asserted that the child was receiving a suitable education outside of school, the burden lay on the parent to prove that defence albeit on a balance of probabilities: *Oxford County Council v L* (unreported) 3/3/10, DC.

It is a defence to a charge under s 444(1A) for the defendant to prove that he had a reasonable justification for his failure to cause the child to attend regularly at the school: s 444(1B). A child shall not, however, be taken to have failed to attend regularly at the school at any time if the parent proves that at that time the child was prevented from attending by reason of sickness or any unavoidable cause (discussed below): s 444(2A).Therefore, if 'unavoidable cause' is raised it should be considered first because if it is made out there can be no conviction of under s 444(1) or s 444(1A): *A County Council v C* [2013] EWHC 1757, (2013) 177 JP 567.

In *Islington London Borough Council v TD* [2011] EWHC 990 (Admin), it was held that the Education Act created two distinct offences and two distinct defences for non-school attendance. It was a defence that the child was prevented from attending regularly by reason of sickness, or any unavoidable cause. "Unavoidable cause" had to be in relation to the child and had to be something in the nature of an emergency. On the facts there was no question of something in the nature of an emergency that stopped the child from going to school and the fact that P was unable to persuade the child to go to school was not a defence. The magistrates had applied the wrong test. The fact that P had done all she reasonably could do to ensure the child's attendance went to mitigation only. See also *West Sussex County Council v C*, above (the mother's chaotic lifestyle could not constitute an 'unavoidable cause'). See further *Jenkins v Howells* [1949] 2 KB 218, (1949) 113 JP 292.

A[49.3A] If, on the trial of an offence under subsection (1A), the court finds the defendant not guilty of that offence but is satisfied that he is guilty of an offence under subsection (1), the court may find him guilty of that offence: Education Act 1996, s 444(8B). It is not obligatory to convict of an offence under subsection (1) although as a general proposition, if the offence under subsection (1A) is not made out, magistrates ought to convict of an offence under subsection (1) because it is an absolute offence; none the less the interests of justice may dictate to the contrary: *R (P) v Liverpool City Magistrates' Court* [2006] EWHC 887 (Admin), 170 JP 453. See also *West Sussex County Council v C*, above. Though the child concerned had attained 16 and the mother was on benefits, remitting the case with a direction to convict of the lesser offence was 'far from being pointless'. The mother had another child whose education was being seriously disrupted.

Sentencing
SC Guideline – School non-attendance

A[49.4]

OFFENCE SERIOUSNESS (CULPABILITY AND HARM)		
A. IDENTIFY THE APPROPRIATE STARTING POINT		
Starting points based on first time offender pleading not guilty		
Examples of nature of activity	**Starting point**	**Range**
Short period following previous good attendance (s 444(1))	Band A fine	Conditional discharge to band A fine
Erratic attendance for a long period (s 444(1))	Band B fine	Band B fine to low level community order
Colluding in and condoning non-attendance or deliberately instigating non-attendance (s 444(1A))	Medium level community order	Low level community order to high level community order
OFFENCE SERIOUSNESS (CULPABILITY AND HARM)		
B. CONSIDER THE EFFECT OF AGGRAVATING AND MITIGATING FACTORS (OTHER THAN THOSE WITHIN EXAMPLES ABOVE)		
Common aggravating and mitigating factors are identified at B[5.2A]. The following may be particularly relevant but **these lists are not exhaustive**		
Factors indicating higher culpability		*Factors indicating lower culpability*
1. Parental collusion (s 444(1) only)		1. Parent unaware of child's whereabouts
2. Lack of parental effort to ensure attendance (s 444(1) only)		2. Parent tried to ensure attendance

3. Threats to teachers and/or officials	3. Parent concerned by child's allegations of bullying/unable to get school to address bullying
4. Refusal to co-operate with school and/or officials	
Factors indicating greater degree of harm	
1. More than one child	
2. Harmful effect on other children in family	

FORM A PRELIMINARY VIEW OF THE APPROPRIATE SENTENCE, THEN CONSIDER OFFENDER MITIGATION

Common factors are identified at B[5.2A]

CONSIDER A REDUCTION FOR A GUILTY PLEA

CONSIDER ANCILLARY ORDERS, INCLUDING PARENTING ORDER

Refer to B[18] for guidance on compensation and Part B for available ancillary orders

DECIDE SENTENCE

GIVE REASONS

A[50]

Sex offenders register – fail to comply with notification requirements

Charge

A[50.1] A person commits an offence if he—

(a)   fails, without reasonable excuse, to comply with section 83 (1), 84 (1), 84 (4) (b), 85 (1), 87 (4) or 89 (2) (b) or any requirement imposed by regulations made under section 86 (1); or

(b)   notifies to the police, in purported compliance with section 83 (1), 84 (1) or 95 (1) or any requirement imposed by regulations made under section 86 (1), any information which he knows to be false.

Sexual Offences Act 2003, s 91 (1).

Maximum penalty – Fine level 5 and 6 months. Triable either way.

Crown Court – 5 years' imprisonment and unlimited fine

Mode of trial

A[50.2] See SC Guideline at A[50.4] below.

Legal notes and definitions

A[50.3] As to the obligation to register see A[52.15] and A[53.16].

Sentencing
SC Guideline – Sex offenders register – fail to comply with notification requirements

A[50.4]

OFFENCE SERIOUSNESS (CULPABILITY AND HARM) A. IDENTIFY THE APPROPRIATE STARTING POINT Starting points based on first time offender pleading not guilty		
Examples of nature of activity	**Starting point**	**Range**
Negligent or inadvertent failure to comply with requirements	Medium level community order	Band C fine to high level community order
Deliberate failure to comply with requirements OR Supply of information known to be false	6 weeks custody	High level community order to 26 weeks custody
Conduct as described in box above AND	18 weeks custody	6 weeks custody to Crown Court

Long period of non-compliance OR Attempts to avoid detection		

OFFENCE SERIOUSNESS (CULPABILITY AND HARM)
B. CONSIDER THE EFFECT OF AGGRAVATING AND MITIGATING FACTORS (OTHER THAN THOSE WITHIN EXAMPLES ABOVE)
Common aggravating and mitigating factors are identified at B[5.2A]. The following may be particularly relevant but **these lists are not exhaustive**

Factor indicating higher culpability	*Factor indicating lower culpability*
1. Long period of non-compliance (where not in the examples above)	1. Genuine misunderstanding
Factors indicating greater degree of harm	
1. Alarm or distress caused to victim	
2. Particularly serious original offence	

FORM A PRELIMINARY VIEW OF THE APPROPRIATE SENTENCE, THEN CONSIDER OFFENDER MITIGATION
Common factors are identified at B[5.2A]
CONSIDER A REDUCTION FOR A GUILTY PLEA
CONSIDER ANCILLARY ORDERS, INCLUDING PARENTING ORDER
Refer to **Part B** for guidance on available ancillary orders
DECIDE SENTENCE
GIVE REASONS

Note. An offender convicted of this offence will always have at least one relevant previous conviction for the offence that resulted in the notification requirements being imposed. The starting points and ranges take this into account; any other previous convictions should be considered in the usual way. See A[52.15] and A[53.16].

A[51]

Sexual activity in a public lavatory

Charge

A[51.1] The accused was in a lavatory to which the public or a section of the public has or were permitted to have access, whether on payment or otherwise; that he intentionally engaged in an activity and, the activity was sexual.

Sexual Offences Act 2003, s 71.

Maximum penalty – Fine level 5 and 6 months.

Legal Notes and definitions

A[51.2] For the purposes of s 71, an activity is sexual if a reasonable person would, in all the circumstances but regardless of any person's purpose, consider it to be sexual.

Sentencing
SC Guideline – Sexual activity in a lavatory

A[51.3] This guideline and accompanying notes are taken from the SC's definitive guideline *Sexual Offences Act 2003* published 30 April 2007.

Key factors

(a)   This offence is committed where an offender intentionally engages in sexual activity in a public lavatory. It was introduced to give adults and children the freedom to use public lavatories for the purpose for which they are designed, without the fear of being an unwilling witness to overtly sexual behaviour of a kind that most people would not expect to be conducted in public. It is primarily a public order offence rather than a sexual offence.

(b)   When dealing with a repeat offender, the starting point should be a low level community order with a range of Band C fine to medium level community order. The presence of aggravating features may suggest that a sentence above the range is appropriate.

(c)   This guideline may be relevant by way of analogy to conduct charged as the common law offence of outraging public decency; the offence is triable either way and has a maximum penalty of a level 5 and/or 6 months' imprisonment when tried summarily.

OFFENCE SERIOUSNESS (CULPABILITY AND HARM)
A. IDENTIFY THE APPROPRIATE STARTING POINT
Starting points based on first time offender pleading not guilty

---

Examples of nature of activity	Starting point	Range
Basic offence as defined in the Act, assuming no aggravating or mitigating factors	Band C fine	Band C fine
Offence with aggravating factors	Low level community order	Band C fine to medium level community order

OFFENCE SERIOUSNESS (CULPABILITY AND HARM)

B. CONSIDER THE EFFECT OF AGGRAVATING AND MITIGATING FACTORS (OTHER THAN THOSE WITHIN EXAMPLES ABOVE)

Common aggravating and mitigating factors are identified at B[5.2A]. The following may be particularly relevant but **these lists are not exhaustive**

Factors indicating higher culpability	
1. Intimidating behaviour/threats of violence to member(s) of the public	
2. Blatant behaviour	

FORM A PRELIMINARY VIEW OF THE APPROPRIATE SENTENCE, THEN CONSIDER OFFENDER MITIGATION

Common factors are identified at B[5.2A]

CONSIDER A REDUCTION FOR A GUILTY PLEA

CONSIDER ANCILLARY ORDERS, INCLUDING COMPENSATION

Refer to B[18] for guidance on compensation and **Part B** for available ancillary orders

DECIDE SENTENCE

GIVE REASONS

A[52]

Sexual offences against children

A. Children aged under 13

Charge

A[52.1] (1) Intentionally touching a child under 13 in a sexual manner

Sexual Offences Act 2003, s 7

Maximum penalty – Fine level 5 and 6 months. Triable either way. Specified sexual offence under Sch 15, Part 2, CJA 2003.

Crown Court – 14 years' imprisonment and unlimited fine.

(2) Intentionally causing or inciting a child under 13 to engage in sexual activity

Sexual Offences Act 2003, s 8

Maximum penalty – Fine level 5 and 6 months. Triable either way. Specified sexual offence under Sch 15, Part 2, CJA 2003. Triable only on indictment if the activity involved penetration.

B. Children aged under 16 – defendants aged 18 or over**

Charge

A[52.2] (3) Intentionally touching a child (B) in a sexual manner and:

(i)   B is under 16 and the defendant did not reasonably believe that B was 16 or over; or
(ii)   B is under 13.

Sexual Offences Act 2003, s 9

Maximum penalty – Fine level 5 and 6 months. Triable either way. Specified sexual offence under Sch 15, Part 2, CJA 2003. Triable only on indictment if the activity involved penetration.

(4) Intentionally causing or inciting a child (B) to engage in sexual activity and:

(i)   B is under 16 and the defendant did not reasonably believe that B was 16 or over; or
(ii)   B is under 13.

Sexual Offences Act 2003, s 10

Maximum penalty – Fine level 5 and 6 months. Triable either way. Specified sexual offence under Sch 15, Part 2, CJA 2003. Triable only on indictment if the activity involved penetration

(5) Intentionally engaging in sexual activity when a child (B) is present or in place where B can observe the activity and:

(i)   B is under 16 and the defendant did not reasonably believe that B was 16 or over; or
(ii)   B is under 13.

Sexual Offences Act 2003, s 11

(6) For the purpose of obtaining sexual gratification, intentionally cause a child (B) to watch a third person or an image of that person engaging in a sexual activity and:

(i)   B is under 16 and the defendant did not reasonably believe that B was 16 or over, or
(ii)   B is under 13.

Sexual Offences Act 2003, s 12

Maximum penalty – Fine level 5 and 6 months. Triable either way. Specified sexual offence under Sch 15, Part 2, CJA 2003.

** The offences under ss 9–12 can also be committed by offenders aged under 18, but the maximum penalty on indictment is then reduced to five years.

A[52.3] Further offences against children (excluding familial offences). The Sexual Offences Act 2003 additionally creates offences of: arranging or facilitating commission of a child sex offence (s 14); meeting a child following sexual grooming (s 15); and abuse of a position sexual activity (s 16), causing or inciting sexual activity (s 17), sexual activity in the presence of a child (s 18) and causing a child to watch a sexual act (s 19).

A[52.4] Sexual activity. An activity is sexual if a reasonable person would conclude:

(a)   whatever the circumstances or purpose, it is because of its nature sexual; or
(b)   because of its nature it may be sexual and because of the circumstances and or purpose it is sexual (s 78).

In relation to (b), two distinct questions should be identified for the court/jury (both of which must be answered in the affirmative to find the defendant guilty), namely: (i) whether they, as reasonable people, consider that the touching, in the particular circumstances before them, because of its nature, may be sexual; and (ii) whether they, as 12 reasonable people, consider that the touching, in view of its circumstances, or the purpose of any person in relation to it, or both, was in fact sexual. In relation to the first question, evidence as to the circumstances before and after the touching, and evidence of the purpose of any person in relation to that touching is irrelevant. However, in most cases, the answer will be same whether the two-stage approach is adopted or whether the matter is looked at as a whole: *R v H* [2005] EWCA Crim 732, [2005] 2 All ER 859, [2005] 2 Cr App R 9, [2005] Crim LR 735.

Touching. This includes touching with any part of the body, with anything else, through anything and in particular touching amounting to penetration (s 79). If, whether intoxicated or otherwise, the touching is unintentional the offence is not committed. Thus, to flail about resulting in unintended touching, objectively sexual, does not make out the offence. However, the offence under s 3 is not an offence of 'specific intent', since purpose is not an element that falls under consideration. Therefore, voluntary intoxication preventing the defendant from intending to touch is not available as a defence: *R v Heard* [2007] EWCA Crim 125, [2008] QB 43, [2007] 3 All ER 306, [2007] 3 WLR 475, [2007] 1 Cr App R 37.

Legal notes and definitions

A[52.5] Causing or inciting. The following propositions are derived from the case of *R v Grout* [2011] EWCA Crim 299, (2011) 175 JP 209, [2011] 1 Cr App R 38, [2011] Crim LR 584.

(a)   Section 8(1) creates two basic offences. The first is intentionally causing a child to engage in sexual activity. The second is intentionally inciting a child to engage in sexual activity. Intentional incitement means the intentional seeking by encouragement or persuasion to bring something about, namely the child engaging in sexual activity, though it is unnecessary to prove that the defendant intended that sexual activity should take place.

(b)   The offences are not concerned with whether the defendant engages in sexual activity.

(c)   There is no definition of 'activity'. (For the purposes of the appeal it was accepted that it could embrace conversation or text or other messages.)

(d)   The questions to be considered when deciding whether or not a particular 'activity' is 'sexual' were set out in *R v H* (see A[52.4], above).

(e)   Because s 8 creates two, if not four (by reason of the higher penalties prescribed for cases within s 8(2)), offences a charge must be drawn with particular care to avoid duplicity.

The offence under s 8 can be committed by a person who, with the requisite intention, makes a statement which in specific terms directly incites a child or children under the age of 13 to engage in sexual activity; it does not matter that it is not possible to identify any specific or identifiable person to whom the statement was addressed because the criminality is directed at the incitement: *R v Jones* [2007] EWCA Crim 1118, [2008] QB 460, [2007] 4 All ER 112, [2007] 3 WLR 907, [2007] 2 Cr App Rep 267 (where the defendant left explicit messages on trains, etc, seeking girls aged between 8 and 13 for sex, offering payment and including a contact text number).

A[52.6] Sexual gratification. The sexual gratification need not be taken immediately. It can extend to a longer term plan to obtain further or greater sexual gratification in the form of the eventual working out of a particular sexual fantasy or activity involving the child. The purpose may involve both short-term and long-term sexual gratification; immediate or deferred, or immediate and deferred gratification: *R v Abdullahi* [2006] EWCA Crim 2060, [2007] 1 WLR 225, [2007] 1 Cr App R 14, [2007] Crim LR 184 at para 117.

Defences

A[52.7] Consent is not a defence to any of the charges. Where the victim is aged 13-16, it must additionally be proved that the defendant did not reasonably believe that the victim was 16 or over. A mistake as to age is otherwise relevant only to sentence.

Section 73 of the Sexual Offences Act 2003 provides exceptions to aiding, abetting and counselling the offences under (inter alia) ss 7 and 9 where the person acts for one of the four stated purposes, eg to protect the child from sexually transmitted infection, and not for the purpose of obtaining sexual gratification.

Evidence

A[52.8] Competence. A court may not refuse to admit the evidence of a child complainant by reason of age only. The court should assess whether the child is capable of giving intelligible testimony either by watching a video of the child or by questioning the complainant themselves: *DPP v M* [1998] QB 913, [1997] 2 All ER 749. See *R v Barker* [2011] Crim LR 233, (2010) Times, 5 February in which comprehensive guidance was given in relation to the statutory test of competence prescribed by s 53 of the Youth Justice and Criminal Evidence Act 1999. Where the issue is raised, it is for the party calling a witness to establish competence to the civil standard.

A[52.9] Special measures. See section D[6.13A].

Privacy and anonymity

A[52.10] Privacy: clearing the court. The magistrates can order the court to be cleared (except for those directly concerned with the case and the press) whilst the child or young person is testifying: Children and Young Persons Act 1933, s 37 as amended.

A[52.11] Anonymity of victim. The general prohibition on revealing the identity of the victim of a sexual offence applies (see **A[53.11]**). In the case of persons under 18 the existing power under s 39 of the Children and Young Persons Act 1933 (as amended) is preserved. The court may direct that any press, radio or television report of the case must not reveal the name, address, school or identity of any child or young person concerned in the proceedings including the defendant. However, such an order must be clear as to precisely what is prohibited: *Briffet v DPP* [2001] EWHC 841 (Admin), (2001) 166 JP 66, sub nom *Briffett and Bradshaw v Crown Prosecution Service* [2002] EMLR 203 and should be in writing: *Re BBC Litigation Department* [2002] All ER (D) 69 (Apr), CA. This topic is considered in detail at D[1B.7].

It has been doubted whether an order under s 39 can embrace reporting in digitised or other form not in existence when s 39 was enacted: *MXB v East Sussex Hospitals NHS Trust* [2012] EWHC 32769, (2012) 177 JP 177.

A decision to vary reporting restrictions in relation to a young offender pursuant to the Children and Young Persons Act 1933, s 39 was quashed as the proper test had not been applied and inadequate reasons had been given to justify the variation. In deciding whether to impose reporting restrictions under s 39, a court had to balance the welfare of the child, the public interest and the requirements of the ECHR, art 10, and to restrict publication if the factors were evenly balanced. Prior to conviction, the former is likely to prevail. After conviction, the defendant's age and the gravity of the crime are likely to be particularly relevant: *R (on the application of Y) v Aylesbury Crown Court, Crown Prosecution Service and Newsquest Media Group Ltd* [2012] EWHC 1140 (Admin), [2012] Crim LR 893.

Sentencing
*SC Guideline – Sexual assault and Sexual assault of a
child under 13*

A[52.12] These guidelines are taken from the SC's definitive guideline
Sexual Offences Act 2003 effective from 1 April 2014.

Triable either way

Maximum: 14 years' custody

Offence range: Community order – 9 years' custody

For offences committed on or after 3 December 2012, this is an offence
listed in Part 1 of Schedule 15B for the purposes of section 224A (life
sentence for second listed offence) of the Criminal Justice Act 2003.

For convictions on or after 3 December 2012 (irrespective of the date of
commission of the offence), this is a specified offence for the purposes of
section 226A (extended sentence for certain violent or sexual offences) of
the Criminal Justice Act 2003.

STEP ONE
DETERMINING THE OFFENCE CATEGORY

The court should determine which categories of harm and culpability the
offence falls into by reference **only** to the tables below.

Harm		Culpability	
Category 1	• Severe psychological or physical harm	**A**	
	• Abduction	Significant degree of planning	
	• Violence or threats of violence	Offender acts together with others to commit the offence	
	• Forced/uninvited entry into victim's home	Use of alcohol/drugs on victim to facilitate the offence	
Category 2	• Touching of naked genitalia or naked breast area	Grooming behaviour used against victim	
	• Prolonged detention/sustained incident	Previous violence against victim	
	• Additional degradation/humiliation	Abuse of trust	
	• Child is particularly vulnerable due to extreme youth and/or personal circumstances	Offence committed in course of burglary	
Category 3	Factor(s) in categories 1 and 2 not present	Sexual images of victim recorded, retained, solicited or shared	
		Deliberate isolation of victim	

Harm		Culpability
		Commercial exploitation and/or motivation
		Offence racially or religiously aggravated
		Offence motivated by, or demonstrating, hostility to the victim based on his or her sexual orientation (or presumed sexual orientation) or transgender identity (or presumed transgender identity)
		Offence motivated by, or demonstrating, hostility to the victim based on his or her disability (or presumed disability)
		B
		Factor(s) in category A not present

STEP TWO
STARTING POINT AND CATEGORY RANGE

Having determined the category, the court should use the corresponding starting points to reach a sentence within the category range on the next page. The starting point applies to all offenders irrespective of plea or previous convictions. Having determined the starting point, step two allows further adjustment for aggravating or mitigating features, set out on the next page.

A case of particular gravity, reflected by multiple features of culpability or harm in step one, could merit upward adjustment from the starting point before further adjustment for aggravating or mitigating features, set out on the next page.

Where there is a sufficient prospect of rehabilitation, a community order with a sex offender treatment programme requirement under section 202 of the Criminal Justice Act 2003 can be a proper alternative to a short or moderate length custodial sentence.

	A	B
Category 1	**Starting point** 6 years' custody	**Starting point** 4 years' custody
	Category range 4 – 9 years' custody	**Category range** 3 – 7 years' custody
Category 2	**Starting point** 4 years' custody	**Starting point** 2 years' custody
	Category range 3 – 7 years' custody	**Category range** 1 – 4 years' custody
Category 3	**Starting point** 1 year's custody	**Starting point** 26 weeks' custody
	Category range 26 weeks' – 2 years' custody	**Category range** High level community order – 1 year's custody

The table below contains a **non-exhaustive** list of additional factual elements providing the context of the offence and factors relating to the offender. Identify whether any combination of these, or other relevant factors, should result in an upward or downward adjustment from the starting point. **In particular, relevant recent convictions are likely to result in an upward adjustment.** In some cases, having considered these factors, it may be appropriate to move outside the identified category range.

Aggravating factors	Commission of offence whilst under the influence of alcohol or drugs
Statutory aggravating factors	Victim encouraged to recruit others
Previous convictions, having regard to a) the nature of the offence to which the conviction relates and its relevance to the current offence; and b) the time that has elapsed since the conviction	**Mitigating factors**
Offence committed whilst on bail	No previous convictions **or** no relevant/recent convictions
Other aggravating factors	Remorse
Specific targeting of a particularly vulnerable child	Previous good character and/or exemplary conduct[*]
Blackmail or other threats made (where not taken into account at step one)	Age and/or lack of maturity where it affects the responsibility of the offender
Location of offence	Mental disorder or learning disability, particularly where linked to the commission of the offence
Timing of offence	
Use of weapon or other item to frighten or injure	
Victim compelled to leave their home, school, etc	
Failure to comply with current court orders Offence committed whilst on licence	
Exploiting contact arrangements with a child to commit an offence	
Presence of others, especially other children	
Any steps taken to prevent the victim reporting an incident, obtaining assistance and/or from assisting or supporting the prosecution	
Attempts to dispose of or conceal evidence	

[*] Previous good character/exemplary conduct is different from having no previous convictions. The more serious the offence, the less the weight which should normally be attributed to this factor. Where previous good character/exemplary conduct has been used to facilitate the offence, this mitigation should not normally be allowed and such conduct may constitute an aggravating factor.

In the context of this offence, previous good character/exemplary conduct should not normally be given any significant weight and will not normally justify a reduction in what would otherwise be the appropriate sentence.

STEP THREE
CONSIDER ANY FACTORS WHICH INDICATE A REDUC-
TION, SUCH AS ASSISTANCE TO THE PROSECUTION

The court should take into account sections 73 and 74 of the Serious Organised Crime and Police Act 2005 (assistance by defendants: reduction or review of sentence) and any other rule of law by virtue of which an offender may receive a discounted sentence in consequence of assistance given (or offered) to the prosecutor or investigator.

STEP FOUR
REDUCTION FOR GUILTY PLEAS

The court should take account of any potential reduction for a guilty plea in accordance with section 144 of the Criminal Justice Act 2003 and the *Guilty Plea* guideline.

STEP FIVE
DANGEROUSNESS

The court should consider whether having regard to the criteria contained in Chapter 5 of Part 12 of the Criminal Justice Act 2003 it would be appropriate to award a life sentence (section 224A) or an extended sentence (section 226A). When sentencing offenders to a life sentence under these provisions, the notional determinate sentence should be used as the basis for the setting of a minimum term.

STEP SIX
TOTALITY PRINCIPLE

If sentencing an offender for more than one offence, or where the offender is already serving a sentence, consider whether the total sentence is just and proportionate to the overall offending behaviour.

STEP SEVEN
ANCILLARY ORDERS

The court must consider whether to make any ancillary orders. The court must also consider what other requirements or provisions may automatically apply. Further information is included on page 303.

STEP EIGHT
REASONS

Section 174 of the Criminal Justice Act 2003 imposes a duty to give reasons for, and explain the effect of, the sentence.

STEP NINE
CONSIDERATION FOR TIME SPENT ON BAIL

The court must consider whether to give credit for time spent on bail in accordance with section 240A of the Criminal Justice Act 2003.

A[52.13] For other sexual offences involving children, see Part 3A of the definitive guidance of the Sentencing Guidelines Council on offences under the Sexual Offences Act 2003, issued in April 2007. Custody for at least six months is appropriate for forms of contact more serious than contact not involving touching the genitalia of either the defendant or the victim.

A[52.14] Sexual Offences Act 2003 (**Part 2**). Under r 42.3 of the CPR 2014, on conviction the court must explain the notification requirements to the defendant.

(a)   **notify the police** within the next three days (or if in custody or otherwise detained, within three days of release) of his name, any other names he uses, his date of birth and his home address;

(b)   **notify the police** of any change of name or home address within 14 days of any change;

(c)   **notify the police** of any address where he resides or stays for 14 days or longer. This means either 14 days at a time, or a total of 14 days in any 12-month period;

(d)   **notify the police** of an intention to leave the UK for a period of 24 hours or longer, at least 24 hours prior to departure of the particulars of the journey;*

(e)   **notify the police** of his national insurance number.

*See the Sexual Offences Act 2003 (Notification Requirements) (England and Wales) Regulations 2012, SI 2012/1876). These Regulations amend the Sexual Offences Act 2003 (Travel Notification Requirements) Regulations 2004, SI 2004/1220 ('the 2004 Regulations') and introduce new notification requirements under the Sexual Offences Act 2003 ('the 2003 Act').

Part 2 of the 2003 Act imposes notification requirements on offenders convicted of certain sex offences. These offenders are called 'relevant offenders'. The 2003 Act requires relevant offenders to notify certain personal information to the police, both at the outset and periodically thereafter (and to notify certain changes of circumstances). These Regulations amend the 2004 Regulations and impose new notification requirements on relevant offenders.

In *R v Longworth*, January 26, 2006, the House of Lords held that for persons convicted before May 1, 2004, the notification requirements under the Sex Offenders Act 1997 do not arise if an order of **absolute** or **conditional discharge** is made. In some cases this means that a notification requirement will arise on conviction but where sentencing is adjourned, will cease on the imposition of an absolute or conditional discharge. Persons conditionally discharged after May 1, 2004 are subject to the notification requirements of the 2003 legislation.

The Sexual Offences Act 2003 (Amendment of Schedules 3 and 5) Order 2007 (SI 2007/296) amended the primary legislation. Section 80 of the 2003 Act now provides that if a person is convicted, found not guilty by reason of insanity or cautioned for an offence listed in Sch 3 to the Act, or found to be under a disability and to have done the act charged against him in respect of such an offence, then that person is subject to the notification requirements of Part 2 of the Act.

For observations on the appropriate level of sentence for failing to comply with the notification requirements see *R v Bickerton* [2007] EWCA Crim 2884, [2007] All ER (D) 230 (Nov).

A[52.15] Provision has been made for the review of indefinite notification requirements by the insertion of ss 91A–91F of the Sexual Offences Act 2003, inserted by SI 2012/1883.

A[52.16] **Sexual offences prevention order** may be applied for separately under Part II of the Sexual Offences Act 2003. The application is a civil matter (*B v Chief Constable of Avon and Somerset Constabulary* [2001] 1 All ER 562, [2001] 1 WLR 340) or made on conviction. See A[53.17]. The police may also apply independently for a **Risk of Sexual Harm Order.**

Sexual assault

Charge

A[53.1] Intentionally touching another person (B) in a sexual manner without B's consent and without reasonable belief that B consents

Sexual Offences Act 2003, s 3

Maximum penalty – Fine level 5 and 6 months. Triable either way. Specified sexual offence under Sch 15, Part 2, CJA 2003.

Crown Court – 10 years' imprisonment and unlimited fine.

Mode of trial

A[53.2] Consider first the general notes at D[4] and the SC definitive guidance set out at A[52.14] above.

Legal notes and definitions

A[53.3] Touching and sexual manner. See A[52.4] above.

A[53.4] An accused's explanation for the assault, whether or not it reveals a sexual motive, is admissible to support or negative that the touching was sexual and was so intended by the accused: *R v Court* [1989] AC 28, [1988] 2 All ER 221, HL. See also *R v H* [2005] EWCA Crim 732, [2005] 2 All ER 859 (grabbing a girl's tracksuit bottoms coupled with the request 'Do you fancy a shag?').

A[53.5] Defences. Consent of the alleged victim is a defence except if obtained by force or fraud. A reasonable belief that the person consents is a defence, as would be non-intentional touching. The defence that voluntary intoxication had rendered a defendant unable to form the intent to touch is not open to him: *R v Heard* [2007] EWCA Crim 125. See further para A[52.3] above.

Consent is not a defence if the victim is aged under 16: see A[52.7] above.

A[53.6] Special measures. See section D[6.13A].

A[53.7] Privacy and anonymity. See A[52.11] above.

A[53.8] Sentencing. See A[52.12] above.

A[53.9] Sexual Offences Act 2003 (Sch 3) Under r 42.3 of the CPR 2014, on conviction the court must explain the notification requirements to the defendant.

Depending upon the nature of the conviction, on conviction, including a conditional discharge, the court must require the defendant to:

(a)   notify the police within the next three days (or if in custody or otherwise detained, within three days of release) of his name, any other names he uses, his date of birth and his home address;

(b)   notify the police of any change of name or home address within 14 days of any change;

(c)   notify the police of any address where he resides or stays for 14 days or longer. This means either 14 days at a time, or a total of 14 days in any 12-month period;

(d)   notify the police of an intention to leave the UK for a period of 24 hours or longer, at least 24 hours prior to departure of the particulars of the journey;

(e)   notify the police of his national insurance number.

In the case of a conviction under s 3 or s 13 (sexual assault or sexual assault of a child under 13) notification is mandatory for any custodial sentence of at least 12 months or where the victim is under 18. Otherwise any custodial sentence or community sentence of 12 months or a mental health detention will trigger notification in the case of an adult offender.

Juvenile offenders. Where the offender is under 18 years these provisions will apply to a person identified as having parental responsibility.

Order for absolute or conditional discharge. See A [52.15] and *R v Longworth*, January 26, 2006, HL.

See A[52.15] for amendments to the Sexual Offences Act 2003 by reason of the Sexual Offences Act 2003 (Amendment of Schedules 3 and 5) Order 2007 (SI 2007/296).

A[53.10] Sexual Offences prevention order may be applied for separately under Part II of the Sexual Offences Act 2003. The application is a civil matter (*B v Chief Constable of Avon and Somerset Constabulary* [2001] 1 All ER 562, [2001] 1 WLR 340). In civil proceedings, the judgment whether it is necessary to make an order is the criminal standard, proof beyond a reasonable doubt: *Cleveland Police v Haggas* [2009] EWHC 3231 (Admin), [2010] 3 All ER 506. Alternatively where on conviction the court is satisfied it is necessary to protect the public from serious sexual harm from the defendant an order may be made prohibiting the defendant from prescribed activities for a period not less than 5 years. Similar to anti-social behaviour orders, given the fact that breach of an order is punishable by a sentence of up to five years, there was a need for the terms of the order to be clear and precise (*R v H* [2006] EWCA Crim 1470, [2006] All ER (D) 87 (Jun); *R v Emery* [2007] EWCA Crim 2469). Similarly in *R v R* [2007] EWCA Crim 1603 it was held that a sexual offences prevention order should be (a) clear and readily intelligible in its terms; (b) specific as to time and place; (c) and, no wider than necessary to restrain the particular harm which it was feared the defendant might cause.

The Sexual Offences Act 2003 (amendment of Schedules 3 and 5) Order 2007 (SI 2007/296) added eight offences to those offences which may lead to a person being made subject to a sexual offences prevention order.

It was not a pre-condition to the making of a sexual offences prevention order that the court should be satisfied that the defendant would also qualify for an extended sentence, life imprisonment or imprisonment for public protection (*R v Richards* [2006] All ER (D) 338 (Oct)).

The following, additional, general guidance on the making and terms of sexual offences prevention orders in criminal cases has been given by the Court of Appeal in *R v Smith* [2011] EWCA Crim 1772, [2012] 1 WLR 1316, [2012] 1 Cr App Rep (S) 468, [2011] Crim LR 967.

(1)   A SOPO must be tailored to the prevention of Sch 3 offences; it might not prohibit unusual or socially disapproved sexual behaviour unless such was likely to lead to the commission of Sch 3 offences.

(2)   A convicted person might be subject to at least three other relevant regimes: a notification requirement; disqualification from working with children; and licence on release from prison. A SOPO is unnecessary if it merely duplicates another regime, and a SOPO must not interfere with such a regime.

(3)   (Following *R v Bolton* [2010] EWCA Crim 1177 and *R v Longman (Mark)* [2010] EWCA Crim 2046) a SOPO is generally inappropriate, because it is unnecessary, if an indefinite sentence is being imposed; by contrast an order might plainly be necessary for determinate or extended sentences, where licence conditions have a defined and limited life, and a SOPO can extend beyond the licence period.

(4)   A SOPO must operate in tandem with the notification requirement; it must not conflict with such a requirement, and it is improper to impose a SOPO which amounts in effect to no more than a notification requirement and runs for a longer period.

(5)   Subject to the above, there is no reason why a SOPO should not run for longer than a notification requirement if the circumstances so require; conversely, a SOPO for a definite period can be made alongside an indefinite notification requirement.

(6)   In the case of offences involving the use of the internet, the Court drew these conclusions:

(a)   a blanket prohibition on computer use or internet access is impermissible;

(b)   a formulation restricting internet use to job search, study, work, lawful recreation and purchases, while having its attractions, suffers from the same flaw that the legitimate use of the internet extends beyond such spheres of activity;

(c)   a prohibition on possession of a computer without notifying the police carries the problem that numerous devices have computer functions and internet access;

(d)   there are fewer difficulties about a prohibition from internet access without filtering software, though this can give rise to problems of uncertainty and policing;

(e)   of the formulations so far devised the one which is likely to be most effective is to require a readable internet history to be submitted to inspection on request;

(f)   where the risk consists of or includes the use of chat lines, etc, to groom young people, it may be appropriate to include a prohibition on communicating via the internet with any young person known or believed to be under the age of 16; prohibitions on contact with children under 18 might be justified for offences committed under ss 16-19 and 25 and 26 of SOA 2003;

(g)   prohibitions on contact with children must, however, be necessary; multiple prohibitions just in case the offending might progress from, for example, downloading child pornography are not legitimate.

(7)   In the case of offences concerning children within the offender's family:

(a)   any order should ordinarily be subject to any order made in family proceedings;

(b) where it is necessary to impose a prohibition on contact with children, it is essential to include a saving for incidental contact such as is inherent in everyday life, otherwise, for example, an offender committed an offence if he was dealt with by a 15-year-old at a shop checkout.

(8) Prohibitions from taking part in activities which might bring an offender into contact with children must be justified as required beyond the restrictions placed on the offender by the Independent Safeguarding Authority. The prosecution should be required to justify this.

(9) It is essential that there should be a written draft properly considered in advance of the sentencing hearing. This should normally be served on the court and the defence at least two days in advance.

It is primarily the responsibility of prosecution counsel to put before the court provisions which go no further than are necessary and proportionate to provide for the protection of children and other vulnerable persons in the future. If there is a question of what are the appropriate provisions that should be included in a particular SOPO, or argument as to the extent to which the prohibitions should be imposed, it is essential that the court is referred to the leading authorities, so that the court is able to judge for itself what is appropriate: *R v Jackson* [2012] EWCA Crim 2602, (2013) 177 JP 147.

In *R v Brown* [2011] EWCA Crim 1223, the final provision of the Sexual Offences Prevention Order made against B read as follows: 'Save where to do so is inadvertent or unavoidable, not to possess any images of a child under the age of 16 years unless the prior permission of that child's parents or guardian has been obtained'. It was decided that the said restriction would, for example, serve to criminalise the continued possession of a daily newspaper which happened to have an inoffensive photograph of a child in it unless it was disposed of straight away upon realisation that such a photograph was in the newspaper. It was not adequate to rely upon the good sense of prosecutors in cases of this type so that very widely drafted prohibitions could be incorporated into such orders. The Court of Appeal regarded that prohibition as being far too widely drafted and proposed to delete it.

Where there was a discrepancy between the terms of a sexual offences prevention order announced by the court and the order issued by the court administration, the appellant was subject to the order announced in court: *R v P* (2012) May 10, CA.

The police may also apply independently for a **risk of sexual harm order**. In *Metropolitan Police Comr v Ebanks* [2012] All ER (D) 45 (Jul), DC, it was decided that the standard of proof on an application for a risk of sexual harm order under the Sexual Offences Act 2003, s 123(4) was the criminal standard of proof. It appears the penny seems to have dropped with the higher courts. Unlike eg restraining orders under ss 4–5 PHA 1997, (see *R v Major* [2010] EWCA Crim 3016, [2011] 1 Cr App Rep 322, [2011] 2 Cr App Rep (S) 139) the standard of proof clearly is the criminal standard. The sooner the CA revisits its decision in *Major* et al, the better.

Sentencing
SC Guideline – Sexual assault

A[53.10A] This guideline is taken from the SC's definitive guideline *Sexual Offences Act 2003* effective from 1 April 2014.

Triable either way

Maximum: 10 years' custody

Offence range: Community order – 7 years' custody

For convictions on or after 3 December 2012 (irrespective of the date of commission of the offence), this is a specified offence for the purposes of section 226A (extended sentence for certain violent or sexual offences) of the Criminal Justice Act 2003.

STEP ONE
DETERMINING THE OFFENCE CATEGORY

The court should determine which categories of harm and culpability the offence falls into by reference **only** to the tables below.

Harm		Culpability
Category 1	• Severe psychological or physical harm	**A**
	• Abduction	Significant degree of planning
	• Violence or threats of violence	Offender acts together with others to commit the offence
	• Forced/uninvited entry into victim's home	Use of alcohol/drugs on victim to facilitate the offence
Category 2	• Touching of naked genitalia or naked breasts	Abuse of trust
	• Prolonged detention/sustained incident	Previous violence against victim
	• Additional degradation/humiliation	Offence committed in course of burglary
	• Victim is particularly vulnerable due to personal circumstances*	Recording of offence
Category 3	Factor(s) in categories 1 and 2 not present	Commercial exploitation and/or motivation
		Offence racially or religiously aggravated
		Offence motivated by, or demonstrating, hostility to the victim based on his or her sexual orientation (or presumed sexual orientation) or transgender identity (or presumed transgender identity)
		Offence motivated by, or demonstrating, hostility to the victim based on his or her disability (or presumed disability)
		B

Harm	Culpability
	Factor(s) in category A not present

STEP TWO
STARTING POINT AND CATEGORY RANGE

Having determined the category, the court should use the corresponding starting points to reach a sentence within the category range on the next page. The starting point applies to all offenders irrespective of plea or previous convictions. Having determined the starting point, step two allows further adjustment for aggravating or mitigating features, set out on the next page.

A case of particular gravity, reflected by multiple features of culpability or harm in step one, could merit upward adjustment from the starting point before further adjustment for aggravating or mitigating features, set out on the next page.

Where there is a sufficient prospect of rehabilitation, a community order with a sex offender treatment programme requirement under section 202 of the Criminal Justice Act 2003 can be a proper alternative to a short or moderate length custodial sentence.

	A	B
Category 1	**Starting point** 4 years' custody	**Starting point** 2 years 6 months' custody
	Category range 3 – 7 years' custody	**Category range** 2 – 4 years' custody
Category 2	**Starting point** 2 years' custody	**Starting point** 1 year's custody
	Category range 1 – 4 years' custody	**Category range** High level community order – 2 years' custody
Category 3	**Starting point** 26 weeks' custody	**Starting point** High level community order
	Category range High level community order – 1 year's custody	**Category range** Medium level community order – 26 weeks' custody

The table below contains a **non-exhaustive** list of additional factual elements providing the context of the offence and factors relating to the offender. Identify whether any combination of these, or other relevant factors, should result in an upward or downward adjustment from the starting point. **In particular, relevant recent convictions are likely to result in an upward adjustment.** In some cases, having considered these factors, it may be appropriate to move outside the identified category range.

When sentencing appropriate **category 2 or 3 offences**, the court should also consider the custody threshold as follows:

*   has the custody threshold been passed?
*   if so, is it unavoidable that a custodial sentence be imposed?
*   if so, can that sentence be suspended?

Aggravating factors	Any steps taken to prevent those working in brothel reporting an incident, obtaining assistance and/or from assisting or supporting the prosecution
Statutory aggravating factors	Attempts to dispose of or conceal evidence
Previous convictions, having regard to a) the nature of the offence to which the conviction relates and its relevance to the current offence; and b) the time that has elapsed since the conviction	Commission of offence whilst under the influence of alcohol or drugs
Offence committed whilst on bail	**Mitigating factors**
Other aggravating factors	No previous convictions or no relevant/recent convictions
Specific targeting of a particularly vulnerable victim	Remorse
Blackmail or other threats made (where not taken into account at step one)	Previous good character and/or exemplary conduct[*]
Location of offence	Mental disorder or learning disability, particularly where linked to the commission of the offence
Timing of offence	Demonstration of steps taken to address offending behaviour
Use of weapon or other item to frighten or injure	
Victim compelled to leave their home (including victims of domestic violence)	
Failure to comply with current court orders	
Offence committed whilst on licence	
Exploiting contact arrangements with a child to commit an offence	
Presence of others, especially children	

[*] Previous good character/exemplary conduct is different from having no previous convictions. The more serious the offence, the less the weight which should normally be attributed to this factor. Where previous good character/exemplary conduct has been used to facilitate the offence, this mitigation should not normally be allowed and such conduct may constitute an aggravating factor.

STEP THREE
CONSIDER ANY FACTORS WHICH INDICATE A REDUCTION, SUCH AS ASSISTANCE TO THE PROSECUTION

The court should take into account sections 73 and 74 of the Serious Organised Crime and Police Act 2005 (assistance by defendants: reduction or review of sentence) and any other rule of law by virtue of which an offender may receive a discounted sentence in consequence of assistance given (or offered) to the prosecutor or investigator.

STEP FOUR
REDUCTION FOR GUILTY PLEAS

The court should take account of any potential reduction for a guilty plea in accordance with section 144 of the Criminal Justice Act 2003 and the *Guilty Plea* guideline.

STEP FIVE
DANGEROUSNESS

The court should consider whether having regard to the criteria contained in Chapter 5 of Part 12 of the Criminal Justice Act 2003 it would be appropriate to award an extended sentence (section 226A).

STEP SIX
TOTALITY PRINCIPLE

If sentencing an offender for more than one offence, or where the offender is already serving a sentence, consider whether the total sentence is just and proportionate to the overall offending behaviour.

STEP SEVEN
ANCILLARY ORDERS

The court must consider whether to make any ancillary orders. The court must also consider what other requirements or provisions may *automatically* apply. Further information is included on page 303.

STEP EIGHT
REASONS

Section 174 of the Criminal Justice Act 2003 imposes a duty to give reasons for, and explain the effect of, the sentence.

STEP NINE
CONSIDERATION FOR TIME SPENT ON BAIL

The court must consider whether to give credit for time spent on bail in accordance with section 240A of the Criminal Justice Act 2003.

A[54]

Social security benefit, false statement/ representation to obtain

Charges

A[54.1] 1. The accused, for the purpose of obtaining any benefit or other payment under the relevant social security legislation whether or himself or some other person, or for any other purpose connected with that legislation –

(a)   makes a statement or representation which he knows to be false; or
(b)   produces or furnishes, or knowingly causes or knowingly allows to be produced or furnished, any document or information which he knows to be false in a material particular.

Social Security Administration Act 1992, s 112(1).

Maximum penalty – Fine level 5 and 3 months

2. The accused dishonestly –

(a)   makes a statement or representation or;
(b)   produces or furnishes, or causes or allows to be produced or furnished, any document or information which is false in a material particular;

With a view to obtaining any benefit or other payment or advantage under the relevant social security legislation (whether for himself or for some other person).

Social Security Administration Act 1992, s 111A.

Maximum penalty – Fine level 5 and 6 months. Triable either way.

Crown Court – 7 years' imprisonment and unlimited fine.

As to further offences under ss 111A and 112, see A[54.3] below.

Mode of trial

A[54.2] For charge 2 consider the SC definitive guidance set out at A[54.5] below.

More serious charges may well be charged under the Fraud Act 2006.

Legal notes and definitions

A[54.3] Charge 2 requires proof of dishonesty unlike charge 1. For the definition of dishonesty see A[60.5].

The provisions of ss 111A or 112 do not apply in any case where the benefit or other payment or advantage is or relates to, or the failure to notify relates to, tax credit (see Tax Credits Act 2002, s 35 and A[55]).

Sections 111A and 112 create a number of further offences concerning failure to notify a change in circumstances affecting entitlement to benefit. The same maximum penalties apply. The essential difference, again, is the added element of dishonesty in the s 111A offences.

The change of circumstances must have made a difference to the amount of benefit which the recipient was entitled to claim: *R v Passmore* [2007] EWCA Crim 2053, [2008] 1 Cr App Rep 165, 171 JP 519. Where a defendant has more than one new source of income arising from her gaining employment, eg working tax credits and child tax credits, all those sources are disclosable if at the time each would have made a difference to the computation of the defendant's entitlement to benefit. But if there had been disclosure of one source which extinguished liability, there would be no requirement to notify further sources: *London Borough of Croydon v Shanahan* [2010] EWCA Crim 98, 174 JP 172.

A[54.4] Under s 112 the offence is committed where there is a false representation made which the person making the claim knows to be false; the proof of intent to defraud is not necessary (*Clear v Smith* [1981] 1 WLR 399, HL). The offence under s 112 does not require proof of dishonesty. However, "constructive knowledge" ie that the defendant neglected to make such inquiries as a reasonable and prudent person would make (as distinct from deliberately closing one's eyes to an obvious means of knowledge) is insufficient to found liability (*Flintshire County Council v Reynolds* [2006] EWHC 195 (Admin), 170 JP 73).

In *Pearson v Greenwich Borough Council.* [2008] All ER [D] 256 (Jan), the accused owned two properties. A council tax form required the accused to provide details of the name and address of the property for which he sought to receive a council tax reduction. The subsequent allegation was that he had made representations that he only owned one property for the purposes of obtaining benefit. The charge failed because the accused's omission did not necessarily mean he had made representations to the effect that he only owned one house.

By virtue of s 116(2) of the 1992 Act, a prosecution could be started at any time from 3 months or 12 months, whichever period last expired. The time limits for an offence under s 112 had been satisfied where it had been brought within 12 months even thought there had been some evidence available for a prosecution within three months, as the offence was a continuing offence and the investigations were ongoing: *Bennett v Secretary of State for Work and Pensions* [2012] EWHC 371 (Admin), 176 JP 181.

A[54.5] Causes or Allows. The word 'causes' suggests that the defendant did something that 'caused' the recipient of the benefit not to report a change of circumstances (alternatively, the defendant could be guilty of aiding and abetting an offence under s 111A(1A)). The word 'allows' normally means there has to be some act that the defendant could have taken which could have resulted in the recipient of benefit discharging his/her liability to report. The one exception might be where the defendant is aware of circumstances that he knew affected the recipient's entitlement to benefit (*R v Tilley* [2009] EWCA Crim 1426, 173 JP 393).

Sentencing
SC Guideline – Benefit fraud

A[54.6] Update 12 of the Magistrates' Court sentencing guidelines took in the new definitive guideline of the Sentencing Council on fraud, bribery and money laundering. The same kind of fraud may be charged in a number of ways and the guidelines reflect this. The categories are: fraud by false representation, failing to disclose information and by abuse of position; possessing, making or supplying articles for use in fraud; revenue fraud; benefit fraud; money laundering; bribery; and corporate offences fraud, bribery and money laundering. The guidelines on benefit fraud are reproduced below.

Dishonest representations for obtaining benefit etc
Social Security Administration Act 1992 (section 111A)

Tax Credit fraud
Tax Credits Act 2002 (section 35)

False accounting
Theft Act 1968 (section 17)

Triable either way

Maximum: 7 years' custody

Offence range: Discharge – 6 years 6 months' custody

False representations for obtaining benefit etc
Social Security Administration Act 1992 (section 112)

Triable summarily only

Maximum: Level 5 fine and/or 3 months' custody

Offence range: Discharge – 12 weeks' custody

Fraud by false representation, fraud by failing to disclose information, fraud by abuse of position
Fraud Act 2006 (section 1)

Triable either way

Conspiracy to defraud
Common law

Triable on indictment only

Maximum: 10 years' custody Offence range:

Discharge – 8 years' custody

STEP ONE
DETERMINING THE OFFENCE CATEGORY

The court should determine the offence category with reference to the tables below. In order to determine the category the court should assess **culpability** and **harm**.

> The level of **culpability** is determined by weighing up all the factors of the case to determine the offender's role and the extent to which the offending was planned and the sophistication with which it was carried out.

Culpability demonstrated by one or more of the following:

A – High culpability
A leading role where offending is part of a group activity Involvement of others through pressure, influence
Involvement of others through pressure, influence
Abuse of position of power or trust or responsibility
Sophisticated nature of offence/significant planning
B – Medium culpability
Other cases where characteristics for categories A or C are not present
Claim not fraudulent from the outset
A significant role where offending is part of a group activity
C – Lesser culpability
Involved through coercion, intimidation or exploitation
Performed limited function under direction

Where there are characteristics present which fall under different levels of culpability, the court should balance these characteristics to reach a fair assessment of the offender's culpability.

Harm – Amount obtained or intended to be obtained
Category 1 £500,000–£2 million Starting point based on £1 million
Category 2 £100,000–£500,000 Starting point based on £300,000
Category 3 £50,000–£100,000 Starting point based on £75,000
Category 4 £10,000–£50,000 Starting point based on £30,000
Category 5 £2,500–£10,000 Starting point based on £5,000
Category 6 Less than £2,500 Starting point based on £1,000

STEP TWO
STARTING POINT AND CATEGORY RANGE

Having determined the category at step one, the court should use the appropriate starting point to reach a sentence within the category range in the table below. The starting point applies to all offenders irrespective of plea or previous convictions.

Where the value is larger or smaller than the amount on which the starting point is based, this should lead to upward or downward adjustment as appropriate.

Where the value greatly exceeds the amount of the starting point in category 1, it may be appropriate to move outside the identified range.

TABLE 1

Section 111A Social Security Administration Act 1992: Dishonest representations to obtain benefit etc

Section 35 Tax Credits Act 2002: Tax Credit fraud

Section 17 Theft Act 1968: False accounting

Maximum: 7 years' custody

Harm	Culpability		
	A	**B**	**C**
Category 1 £500,000 or more	**Starting point** 5 years 6 months' custody	**Starting point** 4 years' custody	**Starting point** 2 years 6 months' custody
Starting point based on £1 million	**Category range** 4 years' – 6 years 6 months' custody	**Category range** 2 years 6 months' – 5 years' custody	**Category range** 15 months' – 3 years 6 months' custody
Category 2 £100,000– £500,000	**Starting point** 4 years' custody	**Starting point** 2 years 6 months' custody	**Starting point** 1 year's custody
Starting point based on £300,000	**Category range** 2 years 6 months' – 5 years' custody	**Category range** 15 months' – 3 years 6 months' custody	**Category range** 26 weeks' – 2 years 6 months' custody
Category 3 £50,000– £100,000	**Starting point** 2 years 6 months' custody	**Starting point** 1 year's custody	**Starting point** 26 weeks' custody
Starting point based on £75,000	**Category range** 2 years' – 3 years 6 months' custody	**Category range** 26 weeks' – 2 years 6 months' custody	**Category range** High level community order – 36 weeks' custody
Category 4 £10,000–£50,000	**Starting point** 18 months' custody	**Starting point** 36 weeks' custody	**Starting point** Medium level community order
Starting point based on £30,000	**Category range** 36 weeks' – 2 years 6 months' custody	**Category range** Medium level community order – 21 months' custody	**Category range** Low level community order – 26 weeks' custody
Category 5 £2,500–£10,000	**Starting point** 36 weeks' custody	**Starting point** Medium level community order	**Starting point** Low level community order
Starting point based on £5,000	**Category range** Medium level community order – 18 months' custody	**Category range** Low level community order – 26 weeks' custody	**Category range** Band B fine – Medium level community order
Category 6 Less than £2,500	**Starting point** Medium level community order	**Starting point** Low level community order	**Starting point** Band A fine
Starting point based on £1,000	**Category range** Low level community order – 26 weeks' custody	**Category range** Band A fine – Medium level community order	**Category range** Discharge – Band B fine

TABLE 2

Section 112 Social Security Administration Act 1992: False representations for obtaining benefit etc

Maximum: Level 5 fine and/or 3 months' custody

	Culpability		
	A	**B**	**C**
Category 5 Above £2,500	**Starting point** High level community order	**Starting point** Medium level community order	**Starting point** Low level community order
Starting point based on £5,000	**Category range** Medium level community order – 12 weeks' custody	**Category range** Band B fine – High level community order	**Category range** Band A fine – Medium level community order
Category 6 Less than £2,500	**Starting point** Medium level community order	**Starting point** Band B fine	**Starting point** Band A fine
Starting point based on £1,000	**Category range** Low level community order – High level community order	**Category range** Band A fine – Band C fine	**Category range** Discharge – Band B fine

TABLE 3

Section 1 Fraud Act 2006

Conspiracy to defraud (common law)

Maximum: 10 years' custody

	Culpability		
Harm	**A**	**B**	**C**
Category 1 £500,000 or more	**Starting point** 7 years' custody	**Starting point** 5 years' custody	**Starting point** 3 years' custody
Starting point based on £1 million	**Category range** 5 – 8 years' custody	**Category range** 3 – 6 years' custody	**Category range** 18 months' – 4 years' custody
Category 2 £100,000–£500,000	**Starting point** 5 years' custody	**Starting point** 3 years' custody	**Starting point** 15 months' custody
Starting point based on £300,000	**Category range** 3 – 6 years' custody	**Category range** 18 months' – 4 years' custody	**Category range** 26 weeks' – 3 years' custody
Category 3 £50,000–£100,000	**Starting point** 3 years' custody	**Starting point** 15 months' custody	**Starting point** 36 weeks' custody
Starting point based on £75,000	**Category range** 2 years 6 months' – 4 years' custody	**Category range** 36 weeks' – 3 years' custody	**Category range** 26 weeks' – 1 year's custody
Category 4 £10,000–£50,000	**Starting point** 21 months' custody	**Starting point** 1 year's custody	**Starting point** High level community order

Harm	Culpability		
	A	**B**	**C**
Starting point based on £30,000	**Category range** 1 year's – 3 years' custody	**Category range** High level community order – 2 years' custody	**Category range** Low level community order – 26 weeks' custody
Category 5 £2,500–£10,000	**Starting point** 1 year's custody	**Starting point** High level community order	**Starting point** Medium level community order
Starting point based on £5,000	**Category range** High level community order – 2 years' custody	**Category range** Low level community order – 26 weeks' custody	**Category range** Band C fine – High level community order
Category 6 Less than £2,500	**Starting point** High level community order	**Starting point** Low level community order	**Starting point** Band B fine
Starting point based on £1,000	**Category range** Low level community order – 26 weeks' custody	**Category range** Band B fine – Medium level community order	**Category range** Discharge – Band C fine

The table below contains a non-exhaustive list of additional factual elements providing the context of the offence and factors relating to the offender.

Identify whether any combination of these or other relevant factors should result in an upward or downward adjustment from the sentence arrived at so far.

Consecutive sentences for multiple offences may be appropriate where large sums are involved.

Factors increasing seriousness	Factors reducing seriousness or reflecting personal mitigation
Statutory aggravating factors	No previous convictions **or** no relevant/recent convictions
Previous convictions, having regard to a) the nature of the offence to which the conviction relates and its relevance to the current offence; and b) the time that has elapsed since the conviction	Remorse
Offence committed whilst on bail	Good character and/or exemplary conduct
Other aggravating factors	Serious medical condition requiring urgent, intensive or long term treatment
Claim fraudulent from the outset	Legitimate entitlement to benefits not claimed
Proceeds of fraud funded lavish lifestyle	Little or no prospect of success
Length of time over which the offending was committed	Age and/or lack of maturity where it affects the responsibility of the offender
Number of false declarations	Lapse of time since apprehension where this does not arise from the conduct of the offender

Factors increasing seriousness	Factors reducing seriousness or reflecting personal mitigation
Attempts to conceal/dispose of evidence	Mental disorder or learning disability
Failure to comply with current court orders	Sole or primary carer for dependent relatives
Offence committed on licence	Offender co-operated with investigation, made early admissions and/or voluntarily reported offending
Offences taken into consideration	Determination and/or demonstration of steps having been taken to address addiction or offending behaviour
Failure to respond to warnings about behaviour	Offender experiencing significant financial hardship or pressure at time fraud was committed due to **exceptional** circumstances
Blame wrongly placed on others	
Damage to third party (for example as a result of identity theft)	

STEP THREE
CONSIDER ANY FACTORS WHICH INDICATE A REDUCTION, SUCH AS ASSISTANCE TO THE PROSECUTION

The court should take into account sections 73 and 74 of the Serious Organised Crime and Police Act 2005 (assistance by defendants: reduction or review of sentence) and any other rule of law by virtue of which an offender may receive a discounted sentence in consequence of assistance given (or offered) to the prosecutor or investigator.

STEP FOUR
REDUCTION FOR GUILTY PLEAS

The court should take account of any potential reduction for a guilty plea in accordance with section 144 of the Criminal Justice Act 2003 and the *Guilty Plea* guideline.

STEP FIVE
TOTALITY PRINCIPLE

If sentencing an offender for more than one offence, or where the offender is already serving a sentence, consider whether the total sentence is just and proportionate to the overall offending behaviour.

STEP SIX
CONFISCATION, COMPENSATION AND ANCILLARY ORDERS

The court must proceed with a view to making a confiscation order if it is asked to do so by the prosecutor or if the court believes it is appropriate for it to do so.

Where the offence has resulted in loss or damage the court must consider whether to make a compensation order.

If the court makes both a confiscation order and an order for compensation and the court believes the offender will not have sufficient means to satisfy both orders in full, the court must direct that the compensation be paid out of sums recovered under the confiscation order (section 13 of the Proceeds of Crime Act 2002).

The court may also consider whether to make ancillary orders.

STEP SEVEN
REASONS

Section 174 of the Criminal Justice Act 2003 imposes a duty to give reasons for, and explain the effect of, the sentence.

STEP EIGHT
CONSIDERATION FOR TIME SPENT ON BAIL

The court must consider whether to give credit for time spent on bail in accordance with section 240A of the Criminal Justice Act 2003.

A[55]

Tax credit fraud

Charge

A[55.1] The accused was knowingly concerned in any fraudulent activity undertaken with a view to obtaining payments of a tax credit by him or any other person.

Tax Credits Act 2002, s 35.

Maximum penalty – Fine level 5 and 6 months. Triable either way.

Crown Court – 7 years' imprisonment and unlimited fine.

Mode of trial

A[55.2] Consider first the general notes at D[4] and the SC definitive guidance set out at A[54.6] above.

More serious charges may well be charged under the Fraud Act 2006.

Legal notes and definitions

A[55.3] Administrative penalties may be levied under ss 31–34 in respect of incorrect statements, failure to comply with requirements and failure by employer to make correct payments.

In order to prove 'fraudulent activity' for the purposes of s 35, an offender had to behave in a manner calculated to achieve false benefits payments. A passive receipt of funds and a deliberate failure to notify the benefits agency of an overpayment, while dishonest, fell short of fraudulent activity: *R v Nolan; R v Howard* [2012] EWCA Crim 671, [2012] All ER (D) 43 (Apr).

Sentencing

A[55.4] Offences under s 35 of the Tax Credit Act 1992 are included within the SC Guideline on benefit fraud, which is reproduced at A[54.6], above.

A[56]

Taxi-touting/soliciting for hire

Charge

A[56.1] The accused, in a public place, solicited persons to hire vehicles to carry them as passengers.

Criminal Justice and Public Order Act 1994, s 167.

Maximum penalty – Fine level 4

Legal notes and definitions

A[56.2] No offence is committed where soliciting persons to hire licensed taxis is permitted by a scheme under the Transport Act 1985, s 10.

It is a defence for the accused to show (on a balance of probabilities) that he was soliciting for passengers to be carried at separate fares by public service vehicles for public service vehicles on behalf of the holder of a PSV operator's licence for those vehicles whose authority he had at the time of the alleged offence.

"Public place" includes any highway and any other premises or place to which at the material time the public have or are permitted to have access (whether on payment or otherwise); "Public service vehicle" and "PSV operator's licence" have the same meaning as in Part II of the Public Passengers Act 1981 (Criminal Justice and Public Order Act 1994, s 167(5))

Sentencing
SC Guideline – Taxi-touting/soliciting for hire

A[56.3] **Note:** refer to B[33.24] for approach to fines for offences committed for commercial purposes.

OFFENCE SERIOUSNESS (CULPABILITY AND HARM)		
A. IDENTIFY THE APPROPRIATE STARTING POINT		
Starting points based on first time offender pleading not guilty		
Examples of nature of activity	**Starting point**	**Range**
Licensed taxi-driver touting for trade (ie making approach rather than waiting for a person to initiate hiring)	Band A fine (see Note above)	Conditional discharge to band A fine and consider disqualification from driving 1–3 months
PHV licence held but touting for trade rather than being booked through an operator; an accomplice to touting	Band B fine (see Note above)	Band A fine to Band C fine and consider disqualification from driving 3–6 months

No PHV licence held	Band C fine (see Note above)	Band B fine to medium level community order and disqualification from driving 6–12 months

OFFENCE SERIOUSNESS (CULPABILITY AND HARM)

B. CONSIDER THE EFFECT OF AGGRAVATING AND MITIGATING FACTORS (OTHER THAN THOSE WITHIN EXAMPLES ABOVE)

Common aggravating and mitigating factors are identified at B[5.2A]. The following may be particularly relevant but **these lists are not exhaustive**

Factors indicating higher culpability	*Factor indicating lower culpability*
1. Commercial business/large-scale operation	1. Providing a service when no licensed taxi available
2. No insurance/invalid insurance	
3. No driving licence and no MOT	
4. Vehicle not roadworthy	
Factors indicating greater degree of harm	
1. Deliberately diverting trade from taxi rank	
2. PHV licence had been refused/offender ineligible for licence	

FORM A PRELIMINARY VIEW OF THE APPROPRIATE SENTENCE, THEN CONSIDER OFFENDER MITIGATION

Common factors are identified at B[5.2A]

CONSIDER A REDUCTION FOR A GUILTY PLEA

CONSIDER ANCILLARY ORDERS

Refer to B[18] for guidance on compensation and **Part B** for available ancillary orders

CONSIDER DISQUALIFICATION FROM DRIVING AND DEPRIVATION OF PROPERTY

DECIDE SENTENCE

GIVE REASONS

A[57]

Theft

(Covers (1) Theft – breach of trust (2) Theft – person (3) Theft – shop (4) Theft – dwelling

Charge

A[57.1] Stealing

Theft Act 1968, s 1(1)

Maximum penalty – Fine level 5 and/or 6 months. Triable either way, except for low value shoplifting (see below).

Crown Court – 7 years' imprisonment and unlimited fine.

Motor vehicles. See A[77].

Theft, going equipped for. See A[58].

NB: A fixed penalty of £90 is available for theft from a shop but only where the goods are under £200, and not normally where the goods are over £100

Mode of trial

A[57.2] Consider first the general notes at D[4] and the SC Guidelines at A[57.37] onwards below.

Section 176 of the Anti-social Behaviour, Crime and Policing Act 2014 inserted new s 22A of the Magistrates' Court Act 1980 to make 'low value shoplifting' triable only summarily, but where the accused is an adult and appears before the court before the summary trial of the offence begins, the court must give him the opportunity to elect Crown Court trial and, if he so elects, he must be sent to the Crown Court for trial. The preservation of the right to elect may lead one to question the administrative benefits of this reform; only in very rare circumstances would magistrates decline jurisdiction. The answer, however, appears to be this. The right to elect applies only where the accused appears before the summary trial begins. Otherwise, the offence is summary for all purposes (save those mentioned below). Thus, the written plea of guilty procedure under the Magistrates' Courts Act 1980, s 12, can be invoked; or the court can proceed to try the defendant in his absence without a prior mode of trial procedure (and thereby avoiding the need to issue an arrest warrant before conviction).

'Low-value shoplifting' is defined as theft of goods where the value does not exceed £200, the goods were being offered for sale in shop or any other premises, stall, vehicle or place from which there is carried on a trade or business, and at the time the accused was or was purporting to be a customer or potential customer of the person offering the goods for sale.

The value of the goods is defined as the price at which they were being offered for sale at the time. In our view this requires a clear verbal or written representation as to the price. Where a person is charged on the same occasion with two or more offences of low-value shoplifting the reference to the value is a reference to the aggregate of the values involved.

A person convicted of low-value shoplifting may not appeal against conviction to the Crown Court on the ground that the convicting court was mistaken as to whether the offence was one of low-value shoplifting.

These provisions apply to secondary parties as well as principal offenders.

Amendments to the Criminal Attempts Act 1981 and the Police and Criminal Evidence Act 1984 preserve, respectively, the ability to charge an offence of attempt and the inclusion of low-value shoplifting in any reference to an 'indictable offence'.

Legal notes and definitions

A[57.3] Theft or **stealing** means dishonestly appropriating property belonging to another person with the intention of permanently depriving the other person of it. It does not matter whether the purpose of the theft was gain or not. Nor does it matter if the theft was for the benefit of the defendant or another person.

A[57.4] The prosecution does not have to prove that the property was appropriated without the owner's consent. However, if the defendant believed he had the owner's consent that could be relevant in deciding whether the defendant acted dishonestly.

1 Dishonestly

A[57.5] The appropriation can be dishonest even though the defendant was willing to pay for the property.

A[57.6] The general test of dishonesty is: first, whether the accused's actions were dishonest according to the ordinary standards of reasonable and honest people and second, if so, whether the accused himself had realised that his actions were, according to those standards, dishonest. Thus a genuine belief by the accused that he was morally justified in acting as he did is no defence if he knew that ordinary people would consider such conduct to be dishonest (*R v Ghosh* [1982] QB 1053, [1982] 2 All ER 689, CA).

A[57.7] The Theft Act 1968 provides that appropriation in the following circumstances is not 'dishonest':

(a)   if the defendant believed he had the legal right to deprive the other of the property, either for himself or a third party; or
(b)   if the defendant believed the other person would have consented had the other person known of the appropriation and the circumstances of the appropriation; or
(c)   if the defendant believed the person to whom the property belonged could not be discovered by taking reasonable steps (but this defence is not available if the property came to the defendant as a trustee or a personal representative).

2 Appropriates

A[57.8] Any assumption of the rights of an owner amounts to appropriation. If the defendant came by the property (innocently or otherwise) without stealing it and later assumed a right to it by keeping it or dealing with it as an owner, he has appropriated it. An appropriation may occur even though the owner has consented to the property being taken (*R v Hinks* [2001] 2 AC 241, [2000] 4 All ER 833, HL).

A[57.9] The following are examples of dishonest appropriation:

(a)   a parent whose child has brought home someone else's property and who retains the property; or

(b)   a person who has found property (but see (1)(c) above); or

(c)   a person who has acquired property through another person's mistake and has taken advantage of the error; or

(d)   a person who switches price labels in a supermarket in order to obtain the goods at a price lower than the original marked price.

A[57.10]–[57.15] Repentance. It is important in some cases to appreciate the moment when the offence is complete. Sometimes, for example, the shoplifter decides either to put the goods back or to pay for them. Once the offence is completed such action is evidence of repentance only and may affect the sentence, but it does not establish innocence.

A[57.16] Acquiring in good faith. If the defendant in good faith gave value for the property and later found that the vendor (or other person from whom he acquired the property) had no right to the goods, then the defendant is not guilty of theft in the event of his keeping or disposing of the property.

3 Property

A[57.17] Includes money, stocks and shares, bills of exchange, insurance policies and all kinds of goods and property.

Nothing in the 1968 Act suggested that what would otherwise constitute or be regarded as 'property' for the purposes of the Act ceased to be so because its possession or control was, for whatever reason, unlawful or illegal or prohibited. The criminal law was concerned with keeping the Queen's peace, not vindicating individual property rights: *R v Smith* [2011] EWCA Crim 66, [2011] 1 Cr App Rep 379, [2011] Crim LR 719.

A[57.18] Land. Land or anything forming part of land cannot be stolen except in the following circumstances:

(a)   dishonest appropriation by trustees, personal representatives, liquidators of companies, persons holding a power of attorney and certain similar persons; or

(b)   dishonest appropriation of something forming part of land by a person not in possession of the land (eg removing soil); or

(c)   dishonest appropriation by tenants of fixtures let to be used with land.

A[57.19] Attempting the impossible. A person may be guilty of an attempt to steal even though the facts are such that the commission of the offence of theft is impossible, for example by placing one's hand into an empty pocket.

A[57.20] Things growing wild. If mushrooms, flowers, fruit or foliage from a plant which is growing wild are picked, that only amounts to theft if it is done for reward, or for sale or any other commercial purpose.

A[57.21] Wild creatures. Appropriating a wild creature can only amount to theft if it has been reduced into the possession of someone else who has not lost or abandoned such possession of the creature; or if someone else is in the course of reducing it into his possession.

4 Belonging to another

A[57.22] The property must be treated as belonging to anyone having possession or control of it or having any proprietary right or interest in it. Petrol ceases to belong to another when it is put in a vehicle's petrol tank at a self-service filling station (this accounts for the offence under s 3 of the Theft Act 1978 – see A[45]). When goods in a supermarket are for convenience or hygiene bagged, weighed and priced by an assistant they remain the property of the supermarket until paid for, and may therefore be the subject of the theft:*Davies v Leighton* [1978] Crim LR 575.

Where items were left by unknown donors outside a charity shop and were then dishonestly appropriated, while it could not be said that the charity had acquired possession or assumed control simply by reason of the items being left in close proximity, it was open to the court to infer that the items had not been abandoned; the donors had attempted to effect delivery but it would not be complete until the charity took up possession and, until then, the donors had not given up ownership; if, alternatively, the items had been placed in bins provided by the charity near their shop premises, the court could conclude that the bins were controlled by the charity with the result that anything put in them belonged to the charity in addition to the donors: *R (Ricketts) v Basildon Magistrates' Court* [2010] EWHC 2358, [2011] 1 Cr App R 15.

A[57.23] Trust property. Must be treated as belonging to anyone having a right to enforce the trust. An intention to defeat the trust shall be treated as an intention to deprive the person entitled to enforce the trust of the property.

A[57.24] Being entrusted with property. If a defendant (eg the treasurer of a holiday fund or Christmas club) has received property and is under an obligation to retain it or deal with it in a particular way, the property shall be treated as belonging to the beneficiary and not to the defendant.

A[57.25]–[57.30] Getting property by mistake. If the defendant obtained property by a mistake on the part of another person, and is under a legal (as opposed to a moral or social) obligation to restore it, then the property must be treated as belonging to the other person.

A[57.31] If the court considers the defendant formed an intention not to restore the property, he must be deemed to have intended to deprive the other person of the property.

5 With the intention of permanently depriving

A[57.32] The court must be satisfied that the defendant had this intention; or alternatively that he intended treating the property as his own to dispose of regardless of the owner's rights. The court must decide the defendant's intention by considering all the evidence and drawing from it such inferences as appear proper in the circumstances.

An offer, not to return a person's car to him in exactly the same condition that it had been when it was removed from his possession and control, but to sell his property back to him, and to make its return subject to a condition or conditions inconsistent with his right to possession of his own property fell within the definition of s 6(1): See *R v Raphael* [2008] EWCA Crim 1014.

In *R v Vinall* [2011] EWCA Crim 6252, [2012] 1 Cr App Rep 400, 175 JP 517 on a charge of robbery the judge should have invited the jury to consider whether the subsequent abandonment of D's bicycle was evidence from which it could be inferred that when the appellants appropriated the bicycle they intended to treat the bicycle as their own to dispose of regardless of D's rights. If such a direction had been given, an explicit direction would also have been required explaining that an intention formed only upon abandonment of the bicycle at the bus shelter was inconsistent with and fatal to the robbery count. In the absence of a proper direction the verdicts were unsafe. The jury was discharged from reaching a verdict on count 2. This was not a case in which the court should substitute a conviction for theft or taking a pedal cycle as those alternatives were not left to the jury.

A[57.33] **Borrowing or lending.** Can be used to establish that the defendant had the intention of permanently depriving the owner if, and only if, the borrowing or lending were for a period and the circumstances of the case make it equivalent to an outright taking or disposal. Ordinary borrowing or lending would not have this effect.

A[57.34] **Reduction of the charge (motor vehicles).** If the property is a motor vehicle a magistrates' court cannot reduce the charge of theft to one of 'taking a conveyance', see A[65].

A[57.35] **Proof of stealing one article enough.** If the charge alleges the theft of several articles, the court can convict of theft if it decides that only one of the articles was stolen. The announcement of decision and court register should make the decision clear.

A[57.36] **Partnership property.** A partner can be convicted of stealing property which he and another or other partners own.

Sentencing
(1) SC Guideline: Theft – breach of trust

A[57.37] Maximum when tried summarily: Level 5 and/or 6 months.

Maximum when tried on indictment: 7 years.

OFFENCE SERIOUSNESS (CULPABILITY AND HARM)		
A. IDENTIFY THE APPROPRIATE STARTING POINT		
Starting points based on first time offender pleading not guilty		
Examples of nature of activity	Starting point	Range
Theft of less than £2,000	Medium level community order	Band B fine to 26 weeks custody
Theft of £2,000 or more but less than £20,000 OR Theft or less than £2,000 in breach of a high degree of trust	18 weeks custody	High level community order to Crown Court

Theft of £20,000 or more OR Theft of les than £20,000 in breach of a high degree of trust	Crown Court	Crown Court

OFFENCE SERIOUSNESS (CULPABILITY AND HARM)

B. CONSIDER THE EFFECT OF AGGRAVATING AND MITIGATING FACTORS (OTHER THAN THOSE WITHIN EXAMPLES ABOVE)

Common aggravating and mitigating factors are identified at B[5.2A]. The following may be particularly relevant but **these lists are not exhaustive**

Factors indicating higher culpability 1. Long course of offending 2. Suspicion deliberately thrown on others 3. Offender motivated by intention to cause harm or out of revenge	

FORM A PRELIMINARY VIEW OF THE APPROPRIATE SENTENCE, THEN CONSIDER OFFENDER MITIGATION

Common factors are identified at B[5.2A]

CONSIDER A REDUCTION FOR A GUILTY PLEA

CONSIDER ANCILLARY ORDERS

Refer to B[18] for guidance on compensation and **Part B** for available ancillary orders.

DECIDE SENTENCE

GIVE REASONS

(2) SC Guideline: Theft – dwelling

A[57.37A] Triable either way.

Maximum when tried summarily: Level 5 and/or 6 months.

Maximum when tried on indictment: 7 years.

OFFENCE SERIOUSNESS (CULPABILITY AND HARM)

A. IDENTIFY THE APPROPRIATE STARTING POINT

Starting points based on first time offender pleading not guilty

Examples of nature of activity	Starting point	Range
Where the effect on the victim is particularly severe, or the stolen property is of high value (defined as more than £2,000 (including sentimental value to the victim) although this will depend on an assessment of all the circumstances of the particular case), or substantial consequential loss results thereby, a sentence higher than the range into which the offence would fall may be appropriate.		
Theft in a dwelling not involving a vulnerable victim.	Medium level community order	Band B fine to 18 weeks custody
Theft from a vulnerable victim	18 weeks custody	High level community order to Crown Court

(A 'vulnerable victim' is a person targeted by the offender because it is likely that he or she is unlikely or unable to resist the theft. The exploitation of a vulnerable victim indicates a high level of culpability and will influence the category of seriousness into which the offence falls).		
Theft from a vulnerable victim (as defined above) involving intimidation or the use or threat of force (falling short of robbery) or the use of deception.	Crown Court	Crown Court

OFFENCE SERIOUSNESS (CULPABILITY AND HARM)

B. CONSIDER THE EFFECT OF AGGRAVATING AND MITIGATING FACTORS (OTHER THAN THOSE WITHIN EXAMPLES ABOVE)

Common aggravating and mitigating factors are identified at B[5.2A]. The following may be particularly relevant but **these lists are not exhaustive**

Factors indicating higher culpability 1. Offender motivated by intention to cause harm or out of revenge	
Factors indicating greater degree of harm 1. Intimidation or face to face confrontation with victim [except where this raises the offence into a higher sentencing range]. 2. Use of force, or threat of force, against victim (not amounting to robbery) [except where this raises the offence into a higher sentencing range]. 3. Use of deception [except where this raises the offence into a higher sentencing range]. 4. Offender takes steps to prevent the victim from reporting the crime or seeking help.	

FORM A PRELIMINARY VIEW OF THE APPROPRIATE SENTENCE, THEN CONSIDER OFFENDER MITIGATION

Offender Mitigation

(i) Return of stolen property – *Will depend on an assessment of the circumstances and, in particular, the voluntariness and timeliness of the return*

(ii) Impact of sentence on offender's dependency – *Where an offence is moti-vated by an addiction (often to drugs, alcohol or gambling) this does not miti-gate the seriousness of the offence, but a dependency may influence the type of sentence imposed. In particular, it may sometimes be appropriate to impose a drug rehabilitation requirement, an alcohol treatment requirement (for depen-dent drinkers) or an activity or supervision requirement including alcohol spe-cific information, advice and support (for harmful and hazardous drinkers) as part of a community order or suspended sentence order in an attempt to break the cycle of addiction and offending, even if an immediate custodial sentence would otherwise be warranted.*

(iii) *The fact that an offence has been committed in desperation or need aris-ing from particular hardship may count as offender mitigation in exceptional circumstances.*

CONSIDER A REDUCTION FOR A GUILTY PLEA
CONSIDER ANCILLARY ORDERS
Refer to B[18] for guidance on compensation and **Part B** for available ancillary orders.
DECIDE SENTENCE
GIVE REASONS

(3) SC Guideline: Theft – person

A[57.37B]   Triable either way.

Maximum when tried summarily: Level 5 and/or 6 months.

Maximum when tried on indictment: 7 years.

OFFENCE SERIOUSNESS (CULPABILITY AND HARM)		
A. IDENTIFY THE APPROPRIATE STARTING POINT		
Starting points based on first time offender pleading not guilty		
Examples of nature of activity	**Starting point**	**Range**
Where the effect on the victim is particularly severe, or the stolen property is of high value (defined as more than £2,000 (including sentimental value to the victim) although this will depend on an assessment of all the circumstances of the particular case), or substantial consequential loss results thereby, a sen-tence higher than the range into which the offence would fall may be appropri-ate.		
Theft in a dwelling not involving a vulnerable victim.	Medium level community order	Band B fine to 18 weeks custody
Theft from a vulnerable victim (A 'vulnerable victim' is a person targeted by the offender because it is likely that he or she is unlikely or unable to re-sist the theft. The exploi-tation of a vulnerable victim indicates a high level of culpability and will influence the cat-egory of seriousness into which the offence falls).	18 weeks custody	High level community order to Crown Court

Theft involving the use or threat of force (falling short of robbery) against a vulnerable victim as described above.	Crown Court	Crown Court

OFFENCE SERIOUSNESS (CULPABILITY AND HARM)

B. CONSIDER THE EFFECT OF AGGRAVATING AND MITIGATING FACTORS (OTHER THAN THOSE WITHIN EXAMPLES ABOVE)

Common aggravating and mitigating factors are identified at B[5.2A]. The following may be particularly relevant but **these lists are not exhaustive**

Factors indicating higher culpability 1. Offender motivated by intention to cause harm or out of revenge	
Factors indicating greater degree of harm 1. Intimidation or face to face confrontation with victim [except where this raises the offence into a higher sentencing range]. 2. Use of force, or threat of force, against victim (not amounting to robbery) [except where this raises the offence into a higher sentencing range]. 3. High level of inconvenience caused to victim, eg replacing house keys, credit cards etc.	

FORM A PRELIMINARY VIEW OF THE APPROPRIATE SENTENCE, THEN CONSIDER OFFENDER MITIGATION

Offender Mitigation

(i) Return of stolen property – *Will depend on an assessment of the circumstances and, in particular, the voluntariness and timeliness of the return.*

(ii) Impact of sentence on offender's dependency – *Where an offence is motivated by an addiction (often to drugs, alcohol or gambling) this does not mitigate the seriousness of the offence, but a dependency may influence the type of sentence imposed. In particular, it may sometimes be appropriate to impose a drug rehabilitation requirement, an alcohol treatment requirement (for dependent drinkers) or an activity or supervision requirement including alcohol specific information, advice and support (for harmful and hazardous drinkers) as part of a community order or suspended sentence order in an attempt to break the cycle of addiction and offending, even if an immediate custodial sentence would otherwise be warranted.*

(iii) *The fact that an offence has been committed in desperation or need arising from particular hardship may count as offender mitigation in exceptional circumstances.*

CONSIDER A REDUCTION FOR A GUILTY PLEA

CONSIDER ANCILLARY ORDERS

Refer to B[18] for guidance on compensation and **Part B** for available ancillary orders.

DECIDE SENTENCE

GIVE REASONS

(4) SC Guideline: Theft – shop

A[57.37C] Triable either way.

Maximum when tried summarily: Level 5 and/or 6 months.

Maximum when tried on indictment: 7 years.

OFFENCE SERIOUSNESS (CULPABILITY AND HARM)		
A. IDENTIFY THE APPROPRIATE STARTING POINT		
Starting points based on first time offender pleading not guilty		
Examples of nature of activity	**Starting point**	**Range**
Little or no planning or sophistication and goods stolen of low value.	Band B fine	Conditional discharge to low level community order
Low level intimidation or threats or some planning eg a session of stealing on the same day or going equipped or some related damage.	Low level community order	Band B fine to medium level community order
Significant intimidation or threats or use of force resulting in slight injury or very high level of planning or significant related damage.	6 weeks custody	High level community order to Crown Court
Organised gang/group and intimidation or the use or threat of force (short of robbery).	Crown Court	Crown Court

OFFENCE SERIOUSNESS (CULPABILITY AND HARM)	
B. CONSIDER THE EFFECT OF AGGRAVATING AND MITIGATING FACTORS (OTHER THAN THOSE WITHIN EXAMPLES ABOVE)	
Common aggravating and mitigating factors are identified at B[5.2A]. The following may be particularly relevant but **these lists are not exhaustive**	
Factors indicating higher culpability 1. Child accompanying offender is involved or aware of theft. 2. Offender is subject to a banning order that includes the store targeted. 3. Offender motivated by intention to cause harm or out of revenge. 4. Professional offending.	
Factors indicating greater degree of harm 1. Victim particularly vulnerable (eg small independent shop). 2. Offender targeted high value goods.	

FORM A PRELIMINARY VIEW OF THE APPROPRIATE SENTENCE, THEN CONSIDER OFFENDER MITIGATION
Offender Mitigation
(i) Return of stolen property – *Will depend on an assessment of the circumstances and, in particular, the voluntariness and timeliness of the return.*

(ii) Impact of sentence on offender's dependency – *Where an offence is motivated by an addiction (often to drugs, alcohol or gambling) this does not mitigate the seriousness of the offence, but a dependency may influence the type of sentence imposed. In particular, it may sometimes be appropriate to impose a drug rehabilitation requirement, an alcohol treatment requirement (for dependent drinkers) or an activity or supervision requirement including alcohol specific information, advice and support (for harmful and hazardous drinkers) as part of a community order or suspended sentence order in an attempt to break the cycle of addiction and offending, even if an immediate custodial sentence would otherwise be warranted.*

(iii) *The fact that an offence has been committed in desperation or need arising from particular hardship may count as offender mitigation in exceptional circumstances.*

CONSIDER A REDUCTION FOR A GUILTY PLEA

CONSIDER ANCILLARY ORDERS

Refer to B[18] for guidance on compensation and **Part B** for available ancillary orders.

DECIDE SENTENCE

GIVE REASONS

A[57.38] Structure of the sentencing decision. See B[3.6].

A[57.39] Compensation. This may be ordered up to £5,000 either as part of a wider sentence or by itself as a substantive penalty. The court may deprive the defendant of any property in his possession when arrested if it was used, or intended for use, in the commission of a crime.

A[57.40] Motor vehicles. If the property was a motor vehicle (defined as a mechanically propelled vehicle intended or adapted for use on a road) the court may disqualify but there is no endorsement or penalty points.

A[58]

Theft, going equipped for

Charge

A[58.1] Having, when not at his place of abode, an article, namely a [
. . . .], for use in the course of burglary or theft

Theft Act 1968, s 25

Maximum penalty – Fine level 5 and 6 months. Triable either way.

Crown Court – 3 years' imprisonment and unlimited fine.

Motor vehicles. If the defendant intended to steal or take a motor vehicle the offence is not endorsable nor are penalty points applicable but disqualification may be ordered.

Mode of trial

A[58.2] See the SC Guideline at A[58.8] below.

Legal notes and definitions

A[58.3] **Theft** includes taking a conveyance without the owner's consent: Theft Act 1968, s 25(5).

A[58.4] The words 'or cheat' were removed from this offence by the Fraud Act 2006. For the offence of possession of articles for fraud, see A[38], above.

A[58.5] If the article was made or adapted for use in committing a burglary or theft, the court can treat that as evidence that the defendant had the article with him for such use: Theft Act 1968, s 25(3).

A[58.6] The offence can be committed by day or night. The offence cannot take place at the defendant's place of abode: s 25(1). It must be proved that he had the articles with him for the purpose of using them in connection with burglary or theft, though it is not necessary for the prosecution to prove that the defendant intended to use them himself: *R v Ellames* [1974] 3 All ER 130, 138 JP 682. An intention to use the item if the opportunity arose would be sufficient to convict the accused, but it would not be sufficient where he had not actually decided whether to use the item if the opportunity presented itself: *R v Hargreaves* [1985] Crim LR 243, CA.

A[58.7] More than one article may be specified in the charge without offending the rule against duplicity.

Sentencing
SC Guideline – Theft, going equipped for

A[58.8]

OFFENCE SERIOUSNESS (CULPABILITY AND HARM)		
A. IDENTIFY THE APPROPRIATE STARTING POINT		
Starting points based on first time offender pleading not guilty		
Examples of nature of activity	**Starting point**	**Range**
Possession of items for theft from shop or of vehicle	Medium level community order	Low level community order to high level community order
Possession of items for burglary, robbery	High level community order	Medium level community order to Crown Court

OFFENCE SERIOUSNESS (CULPABILITY AND HARM)
B. CONSIDER THE EFFECT OF AGGRAVATING AND MITIGATING FACTORS (OTHER THAN THOSE WITHIN EXAMPLES ABOVE)
Common aggravating and mitigating factors are identified at B[5.2A]. The following may be particularly relevant but **these lists are not exhaustive**

Factors indicating higher culpability	
1. Circumstances suggest offender equipped for particularly serious offence	
2. Items to conceal identify	

FORM A PRELIMINARY VIEW OF THE APPROPRIATE SENTENCE, THEN CONSIDER OFFENDER MITIGATION
Common factors are identified at B[5.2A]

CONSIDER A REDUCTION FOR A GUILTY PLEA

CONSIDER ANCILLARY ORDERS
Refer to B[18] for guidance on compensation and **Part B** for available ancillary orders

CONSIDER DISQUALIFICATION FROM DRIVING AND DEPRIVATION OF PROPERTY

DECIDE SENTENCE
GIVE REASONS

A[59]

Threats to kill

Charge

A[59.1] Without lawful excuse makes to another a threat intending that that other would fear it would be carried out, to kill that other or a third person

Offences Against the Person Act 1861, s 16

Maximum penalty – Fine level 5 and 6 months. Triable either way. Specified violent offence under Sch 15, Part 1, CJA 2003.

Crown Court – 10 years' imprisonment and unlimited fine.

An allegation must particularise only one threat; there is no offence of making multiple threats to kill: *R v Marchese* [2008] EWCA Crim 389, [2009] 1 WLR 992, [2008] 2 Cr App R 12, [2008] Crim LR 797.

Mode of trial

A[59.2] See the SC Guideline at A[59.5] below.

Legal notes and definitions

A[59.3] **Lawful excuse.** Making a threat where it is for the prevention of crime or self-defence can amount to a defence if it is reasonable in the circumstances to make such a threat. Once the issue is raised by the defence the onus is on the prosecution to prove that there was no lawful excuse, beyond a reasonable doubt (*R v Cousins* [1982] 2 All ER 115, CA).

A[59.4] **Person.** A foetus in utero is not a person distinct from its mother; therefore a threat to cause the mother to have a miscarriage is not an offence under s 16. However, a threat to kill a child after its birth when it is still in foetus does amount to an offence under s 16 (*R v Tait* [1989] 3 All ER 682, CA).

Sentencing
SC Guideline – Threats to kill

A[59.5] Where committed in a domestic context, see SC Definitive Guideline: "Overarching Principles: Domestic Violence".

OFFENCE SERIOUSNESS (CULPABILITY AND HARM)		
A. IDENTIFY THE APPROPRIATE STARTING POINT		
Starting points based on first time offender pleading not guilty		
Examples of nature of activity	**Starting point**	**Range**

One threat uttered in the heat of the moment, no more than fleeting impact on victim	Medium level community order	Low level community order to high level community order
Single calculated threat or victim fears that threat will be carried out	12 weeks custody	6 to 26 weeks custody
Repeated threats or visible weapon	Crown Court	Crown Court

OFFENCE SERIOUSNESS (CULPABILITY AND HARM)

B. CONSIDER THE EFFECT OF AGGRAVATING AND MITIGATING FACTORS (OTHER THAN THOSE WITHIN EXAMPLES ABOVE)

Common aggravating and mitigating factors are identified at B[5.2A]. The following may be particularly relevant but **these lists are not exhaustive**

Factors indicating higher culpability	*Factor indicating lower culpability*
1. Planning	1. Provocation
2. Offender deliberately isolates victim	
3. Group action	
4. Threat directed at victim because of job	
5. History of antagonism towards victim	
Factors indicating greater degree of harm	
1. Vulnerable victim	
2. Victim needs medical help/counselling	

FORM A PRELIMINARY VIEW OF THE APPROPRIATE SENTENCE, THEN CONSIDER OFFENDER MITIGATION

Common factors are identified at B[5.2A]

CONSIDER A REDUCTION FOR A GUILTY PLEA

CONSIDER ANCILLARY ORDERS, INCLUDING COMPENSATION AND FOOTBALL BANNING ORDER (where appropriate)

Refer to B[18] for guidance on compensation and **Part B** for available ancillary orders

DECIDE SENTENCE

GIVE REASONS

A[60]

Trade mark, unauthorised use of etc

Charge

A[60.1] (1) With a view to gain for himself or another, or with intent to cause loss to another, and without the consent of the proprietor—

(a)   applies to goods or their packaging a sign identical to, or likely to be mistaken for, a registered trade mark, or

(b)   sells or lets for hire, offers or exposes for sale or hire or distributes goods which bear, or the packaging of which bears, such a sign, or

(c)   has in his possession, custody or control in the course of a business any such goods with a view to the doing of anything, by himself or another, which would be an offence under paragraph (b).

Trade Marks Act 1994, s 92(1)

(2) With a view to gain for himself or another, or with intent to cause loss to another, and without the consent of the proprietor—

(a)   applies a sign identical to, or likely to be mistaken for, a registered trade mark to material intended to be used—

     (i)   for labelling or packaging goods,

     (ii)   as a business paper in relation to goods, or

     (iii)   as advertising goods, or

(b)   uses in the course of a business material bearing such a sign for labelling or packaging goods, as a business paper in relation to goods, or for advertising goods, or

(c)   has in his possession, custody or control in the course of a business any such material with a view to the doing of anything, by himself or another, which would be an offence under paragraph (b).

Trade Marks Act, 1994, s 92(2)

(3) With a view to gain for himself or another, or with intent to cause loss to another, and without the consent of the proprietor—

(a)   makes an article specifically designed for or adapted for making copies of a sign identical to, or likely to be mistaken for, a registered trade mark, or

(b)   has such an article in his possession, custody or control in the course of a business,

Knowing or having reason to believe that it has been, or is to be, used to produce goods, or material for labelling or packaging goods, as a business paper in relation to goods, or for advertising goods.

Trade Marks Act 1994, s 92(3)

Maximum penalty – Fine level 5 and 6 months' imprisonment+.

Crown Court – 10 years' imprisonment and unlimited fine.

Mode of trial

A[60.2] See the SC Guideline at A[60.5] below.

Legal notes and definitions

A[60.3] Defences. A criminal offence under s 92 cannot be committed unless there is a civil infringement of a trade mark (see ss 10–12); the civil defences will not apply in every case. Once a defence has been raised it is for the prosecution to disprove it (*R v Johnstone* [2003] UKHL 28; *R v Isaac* [2004] EWCA Crim 1082, 168 JP 417).

Section 92(4) provides that a person does not commit an offence unless –

(a)   the goods are goods in respect of which the trade mark is registered, or

(b)   the trade mark has a reputation in the UK and the use of the sign takes or would take unfair advantage of, or is or would be detrimental to, the distinctive character or repute of the trade mark.

The validity of the registration of a trade mark cannot be tried in criminal proceedings. If there is a challenge to the validity, the court must adjourn to allow that challenge to be determined against the trademark owner; albeit, not where the challenge is made late or is frivolous (*R v Johnstone* [2003] 3 All ER 884).

Section 92(5) provides that it a defence to show that the accused believed on reasonable grounds that the use of the sign in the manner in which it was used, or was to be used, was not an infringement of the registered trade mark.

The burden of proof rests with the accused to establish the defence on a balance of probabilities (*R v Johnstone* [2003] 3 All ER 884).

It was held in *Torbay Council v Singh* [1999] 2 Cr App Rep 451, [1999] 163 JP 744 that to establish criminal liability for offences under this section it was not necessary for the prosecution to prove knowledge or intent to infringe a registered trademark; the statutory defence related to a reasonable belief that the manner of use of a sign did not infringe the registered trademark and it presupposed an awareness of the registration. This view was doubted, however, in *R v Johnstone*, above (which concerned 'bootleg' CDs that bore the names of the performers and those performers had previously registered their names as trademarks).

'Section 92(5) is concerned to provide a defence where the person charged has a reasonable belief in the lawfulness of what he did. Those who act honestly and reasonably are not to be visited with criminal sanctions. It makes no sense to confine this defence to cases where the defendant is aware of the existence of the registered trade mark and exclude altogether those cases where the defendant is not. Section 92(5) provides a defence where the defendant believes on reasonable grounds his use of the sign does not infringe a registered trade mark of whose existence he is aware. It would be extraordinary if the subsection does not equally furnish a defence in the stronger case where the reason why the defendant believes his use of the sign does not infringe a registered trade mark is that he reasonably believes no relevant trade mark is registered. Section 92(5) is to be interpreted as including the latter case as well as the former' (per Lord Nicholls at para 43).

A[60.4] Companies. For offences committed by partnerships and bodies corporate see s 101.

Sentencing
SC Guideline – Trade mark, unauthorised use of

A[60.5] *This may be an offence for which it is appropriate to combine a fine with a community order. Consult your legal adviser for further guidance.

OFFENCE SERIOUSNESS (CULPABILITY AND HARM)		
A. IDENTIFY THE APPROPRIATE STARTING POINT		
Starting points based on first time offender pleading not guilty		
Examples of nature of activity	**Starting point**	**Range**
Small number of counterfeit items	Band C fine	Band B fine to low level community order
Larger number of counterfeit items but no involvement in wider operation	Medium level community order, plus fine*	Low level community order to 12 weeks custody, plus fine*
High number of counterfeit items or involvement in wider operation eg. Manufacture or distribution	12 weeks custody	6 weeks to Crown Court
Central role in large-scale operation	Crown Court	Crown Court
OFFENCE SERIOUSNESS (CULPABILITY AND HARM)		
B. CONSIDER THE EFFECT OF AGGRAVATING AND MITIGATING FACTORS (OTHER THAN THOSE WITHIN EXAMPLES ABOVE)		
Common aggravating and mitigating factors are identified at B[5.2A]. The following may be particularly relevant but **these lists are not exhaustive**		
Factors indicating higher culpability	*Factor indicating lower culpability*	
1. High degree of professionalism	1. Mistake or ignorance about provenance of goods	
2. High level of profit		
Factor indicating greater degree of harm		
1. Purchasers at risk of harm eg from counterfeit drugs		
FORM A PRELIMINARY VIEW OF THE APPROPRIATE SENTENCE, THEN CONSIDER OFFENDER MITIGATION		
Common factors are identified at B[5.2A]		
CONSIDER A REDUCTION FOR A GUILTY PLEA		
CONSIDER ANCILLARY ORDERS		
Refer to B[18] for guidance on compensation and **Part B** for available ancillary orders		
Consider ordering forfeiture and destruction of the goods		

DECIDE SENTENCE
GIVE REASONS

A[61]

TV licence payment evasion

Charge

A[61.1] Installation or use of a television receiver without a licence.

Communications Act 2003, s 363(2)

Has a television receiver in his possession or under his control who –

(a) intends to install or use it in contravention of subsection (1), or
(b) knows, or has reasonable grounds for believing, that another person intends to install or use it in contravention of that subsection.

Communications Act 2003, s 363(3)

NB: The Wireless Telegraphy Act 1949, was repealed by the Wireless Telegraphy Act 2006. See ss 8 and 35 for further provision concerning the use of television and wireless apparatus.

Maximum penalty – Fine level 3.

Legal notes and definitions

A[61.2] The charge should allege either that the apparatus was used or was installed.

A[61.3] Using should be given its natural and ordinary meaning. This might create problems for enforcing authorities. They would if necessary have to persuade the court to draw the inference that the apparatus in question had been used by the defendant during the relevant period. If, for example, a television set in working order was found in the sitting-room of a house occupied by the defendant, it would not be difficult for a court to draw the necessary inference in the absence of some credible explanation by the defendant to the effect that it was not being used (*Rudd v Secretary of State for Trade and Industry* [1987] 2 All ER 553, [1987] 1 WLR 786, HL) and (*Whiley v DPP* [1995] Crim LR 39) in respect of a radio scanner.

A[61.4] A user does not have to be an owner or hirer. Therefore where a set belonged to a husband but the wife switched it on, she was convicted of using it (*Monks v Pilgrim* [1979] Crim LR 595).

A[61.5] Licence. Applies to the person named on the licence, his family and domestic staff living with him on the premises. The prosecution does not have to prove that the defendant did not have a valid licence (see s 101 MCA 1980).

A[61.6] Applies to the premises named on the licence. Also covers members of family living away as full-time students at educational establishments using a portable television set (black and white or colour as described in the licence) in any other place provided:

(a) they normally reside at the licence holder's address; and
(b) the equipment is powered by internal batteries; and

(c)   is not permanently installed.

There are concessions for touring caravans.

A[61.7] Duration. Normally one year. If the licence is paid for by a subsequently dishonoured cheque, it continues in force until it is properly revoked. It may be short-dated if it is not renewed immediately on the expiry of the previous licence.

A[61.8] A licence is required where a television set is used to receive BBC, ITV, satellite or cable television programmes, whether or not it is used for other purposes such as a home computer.

A[61.9]–[61.14] Concessions and exemptions are made under regulations for particular categories of persons. The number of sets that may be used on the same or different premises is also regulated by secondary legislation.

Sentencing
SC Guideline – TV licence payment evasion

A[61.15]

OFFENCE SERIOUSNESS (CULPABILITY AND HARM)		
A. IDENTIFY THE APPROPRIATE STARTING POINT		
Starting points based on first time offender pleading not guilty		
Examples of nature of activity	**Starting point**	**Range**
Up to 6 months unlicensed use	Band A fine	Band A fine
Over 6 months unlicensed use	Band B fine	Band A fine to band B fine
OFFENCE SERIOUSNESS (CULPABILITY AND HARM)		
B. CONSIDER THE EFFECT OF AGGRAVATING AND MITIGATING FACTORS (OTHER THAN THOSE WITHIN EXAMPLES ABOVE)		
Common aggravating and mitigating factors are identified at B[5.2A]. The following may be particularly relevant but **these lists are not exhaustive**		
Factors indicating lower culpability		
1. Accidental oversight or belief licence held		
2. Confusion of responsibility		
3. Licence immediately obtained		
FORM A PRELIMINARY VIEW OF THE APPROPRIATE SENTENCE, THEN CONSIDER OFFENDER MITIGATION		
Common factors are identified at B[5.2A]		
CONSIDER A REDUCTION FOR A GUILTY PLEA		
CONSIDER ANCILLARY ORDERS		
Refer to **Part B** for guidance on available ancillary orders		
DECIDE SENTENCE		
GIVE REASONS		

VAT evasion

Charge

Being knowingly concerned in, or in the taking of steps with a view to, the fraudulent evasion of VAT by him or any other person.

Value Added Tax Act, s 72(1)

Maximum penalty – Fine level 5 and/or 6 months' imprisonment.

Crown Court – 7 years' imprisonment and unlimited fine.

Mode of trial

A[62.1] See general notes at D[4] and SC Guideline at A[36.10] below.

Legal notes and definitions

A[62.2] Evasion of VAT. Includes a reference to the obtaining of –

(a)   the payment of a VAT credit; or
(b)   a refund under ss 35, 36 or 40 of this Act or s 22 of the 1983 Act; or
(c)   a refund under any regulations made by virtue of s 13 (5); or
(d)   a repayment under s 39;

and any reference in those subsections to the amount of VAT shall be construed –

(i)   in relation to VAT itself or a Vat credit, as a reference to the aggregate of the amount (if any) falsely claimed by way of credit for input tax and the amount (if any) by which output tax was falsely understated, and
(ii)   in relation to a refund or repayment falling within paragraph (b), (c) or (d) above, as a reference to the amount falsely claimed by way of refund or repayment.

A[62.3] Knowingly. Can include "deliberately looking the other way" (*Ross v Moss* [1965] 2 QB 396, (1965) 129 JP 537).

Evasion. Means a deliberate non-payment when payment is due. There is no need therefore for the Crown to prove an intention permanently to deprive (*R v Dealy* [1995] 1 WLR 658).

Sentencing
VAT evasion

A[62.4] See the SC definitive guidance on revenue fraud, reproduced at A[36.10] above.

A[63]

Vehicle interference

Charge

A[63.1] Interfered with a motor vehicle or anything carried in or on the same with the intention that an offence of theft of the said motor vehicle or part of it or of anything carried in or on the said motor vehicle or an offence of taking and driving it away without consent should be committed

Criminal Attempts Act 1981, s 9(1)

Maximum penalty – Fine level 4 and/or 3 months.

Legal notes and definitions

A[63.2] This offence applies to trailers. A trailer means a vehicle drawn by a motor vehicle.

A[63.3] Interfere. It will be for the court to decide whether a particular activity amounts to interference; simply keeping a vehicle under observation in the hope that an opportunity will arise to commit an offence would not be interference. In many cases the alleged activity would support a charge of attempting to steal which, unlike this offence is triable either way but this offence may be easier to prove because of the provision regarding 'intent'.

A[63.4] Intent. There must be evidence of an intention to commit theft of the vehicle, trailer, any parts of them or anything carried in or on them, or to commit the offence of unauthorised taking of the vehicle or trailer. The prosecution does not have to prove precisely which of these offences the accused intended. In some cases, for example, the prosecution would be unable to prove whether the intention was to take the vehicle, steal it, or steal goods from inside it.

A[63.5] Motor vehicle. Means a mechanically propelled vehicle intended or adapted for use on the road.

Sentencing
SC Guideline – Vehicle interference

A[63.6]

OFFENCE SERIOUSNESS (CULPABILITY AND HARM)		
A. IDENTIFY THE APPROPRIATE STARTING POINT		
Starting points based on first time offender pleading not guilty		
Examples of nature of activity	Starting point	Range
Trying door handles; no entry gained to vehicle; no damage caused	Band C fine	Band A fine to low level community order

| Entering vehicle, little or no damage caused | Medium level community order | Low level community order to high level community order |
| Entering vehicle with damage caused | High level community order | Medium level community order to 12 weeks custody |

OFFENCE SERIOUSNESS (CULPABILITY AND HARM)

B. CONSIDER THE EFFECT OF AGGRAVATING AND MITIGATING FACTORS (OTHER THAN THOSE WITHIN EXAMPLES ABOVE)

Common aggravating and mitigating factors are identified at B[5.2A]. The following may be particularly relevant but **these lists are not exhaustive**

| *Factor indicating higher culpability*
1. Targeting vehicle in dark/isolated location | |
| *Factors indicating greater degree of harm*
1. Emergency services vehicle
2. Disabled driver's vehicle
3. Part of series | |

FORM A PRELIMINARY VIEW OF THE APPROPRIATE SENTENCE, THEN CONSIDER OFFENDER MITIGATION

Common factors are identified at B[5.2A]

CONSIDER A REDUCTION FOR A GUILTY PLEA

CONSIDER ANCILLARY ORDERS, INCLUDING COMPENSATION

Refer to B[18] for guidance on compensation and **Part B** for available ancillary orders

CONSIDER DISQUALIFICATION FROM DRIVING

DECIDE SENTENCE

GIVE REASONS

A[63.7] See Table B at B[4.2] for available sentences.

Vehicle licence/registration fraud

Charge

A[64.1] Forging, or fraudulently altering, or fraudulently using, or fraudulently lending, or fraudulently allowing to be used by another person any of the following: a vehicle licence; a trade licence; a nil licence; a registration mark; a registration document; and a trade plate (including a replacement trade plate)

Vehicle Exercise and Registration Act 1994, s 44

Maximum penalty – Fine level 5 (for fines see B[33]).

Crown Court – Unlimited fine and 2 years' imprisonment. Triable either way.

Mode of trial

A[64.2] See the SC Guideline at **A[64.4]** below.

Note: Custody only available in Crown Court.

Legal notes and definitions

A[64.3] **Forgery.** The definition of forgery in the Forgery and Counterfeiting Act 1981, s 1, should be applied. Accordingly a person charged under s 44 with forgery of a licence will be guilty of an offence if (i) he made a false licence; (ii) with the intent that he or another should use it to include another to accept it as genuine; and (iii) by reason of so accepting it to do or not to do some act, to his own or another's prejudice as a result of such acceptance of the false licence as genuine in connection with the performance of any duty: *R v Macrae* (1993) 159 JP 359, [1994] Crim LR 363. In *Clifford v Bloom* [1977] RTR 351, where the terminal letter on registration plates was altered, 'forges' was defined as the making of a false registration mark upon a number plate with the intention that it should be regarded as genuine.

A[64.3A] **Fraudulently using.** The offence of fraudulently using a vehicle licence is only committed where there is evidence that the vehicle was being or had been used on a public road while displaying the offending licence. Accordingly, exhibiting an altered licence on private land, with an intention to use the vehicle with the licence in future, is insufficient to constitute an offence: *R v Johnson (Tony)* (1994) 158 JP 788, [1995] RTR 15, [1995] Crim LR 250, CA.

A[64.4] **Fraudulently.** In *R v Terry* [1984] AC 374, [1984] 1 All ER 65, 78 Cr App Rep 101 'fraudulently' was given a wide meaning, following *Welham v DPP* [1961] AC 103, [1960] 1 All ER 805, 124 JP 280, not confined to economic loss but including the purpose of deceiving a police officer into thinking a motor car was properly licensed.

Sentencing
SC Guideline – Vehicle licence/registration fraud

A[64.5]

OFFENCE SERIOUSNESS (CULPABILITY AND HARM)		
A. IDENTIFY THE APPROPRIATE STARTING POINT		
Starting points based on first time offender pleading not guilty		
Examples of nature of activity	**Starting point**	**Range**
Use of unaltered licence from another vehicle	Band B fine	Band B fine
Forged licence bought for own use, or forged/altered for own use	Band C fine	Band C fine
Use of number plates from another vehicle; or licence/number plates forged or altered for sale to another	High level community order	Medium level community order to Crown Court Note: custody only available in Crown Court

OFFENCE SERIOUSNESS (CULPABILITY AND HARM)	
B. CONSIDER THE EFFECT OF AGGRAVATING AND MITIGATING FACTORS (OTHER THAN THOSE WITHIN EXAMPLES ABOVE)	
Common aggravating and mitigating factors are identified at B[5.2A]. The following may be particularly relevant but **these lists are not exhaustive**	
Factors indicating higher culpability	*Factors indicating lower culpability*
1. LGV/PSV/LGV/taxi etc	1. Licence/registration mark from another vehicle owned by defendant
2. Long-term fraudulent use	2. Short-term use
Factors indicating greater degree of harm	
1. High financial gain	
2. Innocent victim deceived	
3. Legitimate owner inconvenienced	

FORM A PRELIMINARY VIEW OF THE APPROPRIATE SENTENCE, THEN CONSIDER OFFENDER MITIGATION
Common factors are identified at B[5.2A]
CONSIDER A REDUCTION FOR A GUILTY PLEA
CONSIDER ANCILLARY ORDERS
Refer to B[18] for guidance on compensation and **Part B** for available ancillary orders
CONSIDER DISQUALIFICATION FROM DRIVING AND DEPRIVATION OF PROPERTY (including vehicle)

DECIDE SENTENCE
GIVE REASONS

Vehicle taking, without consent

Charge

A[65.1] Without the consent of the owner or other lawful authority taking a conveyance, namely a [. . . . .] for his own use (or for another person's use)

Theft Act 1968, s 12(1)

Note – It is also an offence to drive a conveyance, or allow oneself to be carried in or on it, if one knows the conveyance has been taken without such authority; the penalty for such offences is the same as for the offence of unauthorised taking.

Maximum penalty – Fine level 5 and 6 months. Triable only by magistrates.

Motor vehicles. The defendant may be disqualified but no endorsement or penalty points are applicable.

Legal notes and definitions

A[65.2] Pedal cycles. The Theft Act 1968, s 12(5) applies a special provision if the conveyance is a pedal cycle. The maximum penalty is a fine up to level 3.

A[65.3] If the circumstances amounted to theft and theft is alleged, the notes at A[57.3] will apply.

A[65.4] Taking. An offence is committed if the conveyance is taken. 'Driving away' does not have to be proved but there must be evidence of some movement and that the vehicle was used as a conveyance. Accordingly, the moving of a motor car round the corner as a practical joke to lead the owner to believe it had been stolen was not an offence as it was not established that anyone rode inside it (*R v Stokes* [1983] RTR 59, [1982] Crim LR 695, CA). But where a defendant allowed a vehicle to roll down a hill by climbing in it and releasing the handbrake, he was guilty of the offence (*R v Bow* [1977] RTR 6, 64 Cr App Rep 54, CA). It would be otherwise if he did not get inside the vehicle. It is not a defence that the conveyance was stolen, as opposed to being taken. Nor is it a defence that the vehicle had been previously taken (*DPP v Spriggs* [1994] RTR 1, 157 JP 1143, [1993] Crim LR 622).

The offence does not require the propelling of the conveyance 'in its own element'; thus a conviction was upheld where a defendant had loaded an inflatable rubber dinghy on a trailer which he then drove away: *R v Pearce* [1973] Crim LR 321.

A[65.5] Conveyance. Means a conveyance constructed or adapted for carrying one or more persons by land, water or air. It does not include a conveyance which can only be controlled by a person not carried in or on it.

A[65.6] Motor vehicle. A motor vehicle is a mechanically propelled vehicle intended or adapted for use on a road.

A[65.7] Owner. Includes a person in possession of the conveyance under a hiring or hire-purchase agreement.

A[65.8] Owner's consent. Where the owner is induced by fraud to part with possession of his vehicle, no offence under this section has been committed (*Whittaker v Campbell* [1984] QB 318, [1983] 3 All ER 582). The owner has in fact consented even though in the civil law he may have a remedy against the fraudster.

A[65.9] No offence was committed where consent was obtained by a false pretence as to the destination and purpose of the journey (*R v Peart* [1970] 2 QB 672, [1970] 2 All ER 823, CA). Nor where consent of an owner to allow a vehicle to be hired was obtained by the fraudulent misrepresentation of the hirer as to his identity and the holding of a full driving licence.

A[65.10] Reduction of charge from theft of conveyance. If a defendant is tried in a magistrates' court for stealing a conveyance, the court cannot reduce the charge to this offence of taking the conveyance.

A[65.11]–[65.15] Time Limits. Like many summary road traffic offences, proceedings may be commenced within six months of the day the prosecution had knowledge of the offence subject to an overall time limit of three years from the commission of the offence.

A[65.16] Successful defence. If the court is satisfied the defendant acted in the belief that he had lawful authority, or that the owner would have consented if the owner knew the circumstances, then he must be acquitted. The defendant only has to raise the defence. The absence of lawful authority or the owner's consent is an essential ingredient of the offence and it remains the prosecutor's duty to prove the allegation beyond a reasonable doubt.

A[65.17] Aggravated vehicle-taking. See A[66].

Sentencing
SC Guideline – Vehicle taking, without consent

A[65.18]

OFFENCE SERIOUSNESS (CULPABILITY AND HARM)		
A. IDENTIFY THE APPROPRIATE STARTING POINT		
Starting points based on first time offender pleading not guilty		
Examples of nature of activity	Starting point	Range
Relative's vehicle; exceeding authorised use of eg. employer's vehicle; retention of hire car beyond return date	Low level community order	Band B fine to medium level community order
As above with damage caused to lock/ignition; or stranger's vehicle involved but no damage caused	Medium level community order	Low level community order to high level community order

Taking vehicle from private premises; causing damage to eg. lock/ignition of stranger's vehicle	High level community order	Medium level community order to 26 weeks custody

OFFENCE SERIOUSNESS (CULPABILITY AND HARM)
B. CONSIDER THE EFFECT OF AGGRAVATING AND MITIGATING FACTORS (OTHER THAN THOSE WITHIN EXAMPLES ABOVE)
Common aggravating and mitigating factors are identified at B[5.2A]. The following may be particularly relevant but **these lists are not exhaustive**

Factors indicating greater degree of harm	*Factor indicating lower culpability*
1. Vehicle later burnt	1. Misunderstanding with owner
2. Vehicle belonging to elderly/disabled person	*Factor indicating lesser degree of harm*
3. Emergency services vehicle	1. Offender voluntarily returned vehicle to owner
4. Medium to large goods vehicle	
5. Passengers carried	

FORM A PRELIMINARY VIEW OF THE APPROPRIATE SENTENCE, THEN CONSIDER OFFENDER MITIGATION
Common factors are identified at B[5.2A]
CONSIDER A REDUCTION FOR A GUILTY PLEA
CONSIDER ANCILLARY ORDERS, INCLUDING COMPENSATION
Refer to B[18] for guidance on compensation and **Part B** for available ancillary orders
CONSIDER DISQUALIFICATION FROM DRIVING
DECIDE SENTENCE
GIVE REASONS

A[65.19] Available sentences. See Table B at B[4.2].

A[65.20] Disqualification may be ordered in the case of a motor vehicle (no points available).

A[66]

(1) Vehicle-taking (aggravated) – damage caused to property other than the vehicle in accident or damage caused to the vehicle (ss 12A(2)(c) and (d))
(2) Vehicle-taking (aggravated) – dangerous driving or accident causing injury (ss 12A(2)(a) and (b))

Charges

A[66.1] Taking a mechanically propelled vehicle without the owner's consent or other lawful authority (or driving, or allowing oneself to be carried in or on it, knowing it to have been taken without the owner's consent etc) and at any time after it had been unlawfully taken (whether by him or another) and before it was recovered:

(a)   the vehicle was driven dangerously on a road or other public place;
(b)   owing to the driving of the vehicle, an accident occurred by which injury was caused to any person;
(c)   owing to the driving of the vehicle an accident occurred by which damage was caused to any property, other than the vehicle;
(d)   damage was caused to the vehicle.

Theft Act 1968, s 12A(1)

Maximum penalty – Fine level 5 and 6 months' imprisonment. Specified violent offence under Sch 15, Part 1, CJA 2003 if the offence involves an accident causing the death of any person.

Mandatory disqualification for one year and endorsement. Penalty points 3–11.

Crown Court – 2 years' imprisonment (14 years where death has been caused) and unlimited fine.

Mode of trial

A[66.2] See the SC Guideline at A[66.16] and A[66.17] below.

Where no allegation is made other than damage to property or the vehicle concerned, the offence is triable only before magistrates where the total value of the damage concerned does not exceed £5,000 (*R v Kelly* [2001] RTR 45, CA). The value of the damage to property other than the vehicle involved in the offence is what it would probably have cost to buy the property in the open market at the time of the offence. The value of the damage to the vehicle taken is assessed in a similar manner to that where property has been damaged. Otherwise the offence is triable either way.

A[66.3]–[66.4] For the procedure where it is not clear whether the damage is above or below £5,000, see A[18.4].

Legal notes and definitions

A[66.5] Mechanically propelled vehicle ie a vehicle intended or adapted for use on a road. This includes, inter alia, a Mantis City electric scooter (*DPP v King* [2008] EWHC 447 (Admin), 172 JP 401).

A[66.6] Vehicle recovered ie when it is restored to its owner or to other lawful possession or custody.

A[66.7] Owner includes a person in possession under a hiring or hire-purchase agreement.

A[66.8] Dangerous driving ie driven in a way which falls far below what would be expected of a competent and careful driver and it would be obvious to a competent and careful driver that driving the vehicle in that way would be dangerous.

A[66.9] Road or public place. See C[22.5], C[22.6].

A[66.10] Defence. The defendant is not guilty of this offence if he proves that, as regards any such proven driving, injury or damage as the offence refers to, either:

(a)   that the driving accident or damage occurred before he committed the basic offence ; or
(b)   that he was neither in, nor on, nor in the immediate vicinity of the vehicle when that driving etc occurred: Theft Act 1968, s 12A(3).

The standard of proof is on a balance of probabilities: *R v Carr-Briant* (1943) 107 JP 167.

A[66.11]–[66.15] Reduction of charge/alternative verdict. The court may find the defendant guilty of the basic offence if it decides to dismiss the aggravated version. (*H v Liverpool City Youth Court* [2001] Crim LR 897)

Sentencing
SC Guideline – Vehicle taking (aggravated) – Damage caused to property etc – ss 12A(2)(c) and (d)

A[66.16] Must endorse and disqualify for at least 12 months

Must disqualify for at least two years if offender has had two or more disqualifications for periods of 56 days or more in preceding 3 years – consult your legal adviser for further guidance

If there is a delay in sentencing after conviction, consider interim disqualification

OFFENCE SERIOUSNESS (CULPABILITY AND HARM)		
A. IDENTIFY THE APPROPRIATE STARTING POINT		
Starting points based on first time offender pleading not guilty		
Examples of nature of activity	**Starting point**	**Range**

Relative's vehicle; exceeding authorised use of eg. employer's vehicle; retention of hire car beyond return date; minor damage to taken vehicle	Medium level community order	Low level community order to high level community order
Greater damage to taken vehicle and/or moderate damage to another vehicle and/or property	High level community order	Medium level community order to 12 weeks custody
Vehicle taken as part of burglary or from private premises; severe damage	18 weeks custody	12 to 26 weeks custody (Crown Court if damage over £5,000)

OFFENCE SERIOUSNESS (CULPABILITY AND HARM)

B. CONSIDER THE EFFECT OF AGGRAVATING AND MITIGATING FACTORS (OTHER THAN THOSE WITHIN EXAMPLES ABOVE)

Common aggravating and mitigating factors are identified at B[5.2A]. The following may be particularly relevant but **these lists are not exhaustive**

Factors indicating greater degree of harm	Factors indicating lower culpability
1. Vehicle deliberately damaged/destroyed	1. Misunderstanding with owner
2. Offender under influence of alcohol/drugs	2. Damage resulting from actions of another (where this does not provide a defence)

Factors indicating greater degree of harm	
1. Passengers carried	
2. Vehicle belonging to elderly or disabled person	
3. Emergency services vehicle	
4. Medium to large goods vehicle	
5. Damage caused in moving traffic accident	

FORM A PRELIMINARY VIEW OF THE APPROPRIATE SENTENCE, THEN CONSIDER OFFENDER MITIGATION

Common factors are identified at B[5.2A]

CONSIDER A REDUCTION FOR A GUILTY PLEA

CONSIDER ANCILLARY ORDERS, INCLUDING COMPENSATION

Refer to B[18] for guidance on compensation and **Part B** for available ancillary orders

DECIDE SENTENCE

GIVE REASONS

SC Guideline – Vehicle taking (aggravated) – Dangerous driving or accident causing injury – ss 12A(2)(a) and (b)

A[66.17] Must endorse and disqualify for at least 12 months

Must disqualify for at least two years if offender has had two or more disqualifications for periods of 56 days or more in preceding 3 years – consult your legal adviser for further guidance

If there is a delay in sentencing after conviction, consider interim disqualification

OFFENCE SERIOUSNESS (CULPABILITY AND HARM)		
A. IDENTIFY THE APPROPRIATE STARTING POINT		
Starting points based on first time offender pleading not guilty		
Examples of nature of activity	**Starting point**	**Range**
Taken vehicle involved in single incident of bad driving where little or no damage or risk of personal injury	High level community order	Medium level community order to 12 weeks custody
Taken vehicle involved in incident(s) involving excessive speed or showing off, especially on busy roads or in built-up area	18 weeks custody	12 to 26 weeks custody
Taken vehicle involved in prolonged bad driving involving deliberate disregard for safety of others	Crown Court	Crown Court
OFFENCE SERIOUSNESS (CULPABILITY AND HARM)		
B. CONSIDER THE EFFECT OF AGGRAVATING AND MITIGATING FACTORS (OTHER THAN THOSE WITHIN EXAMPLES ABOVE)		
Common aggravating and mitigating factors are identified at B[5.2A]. The following may be particularly relevant but **these lists are not exhaustive**		
Factors indicating greater degree of harm 1. Disregarding warnings of others 2. Evidence of alcohol or drugs 3. Carrying out other tasks while driving 4. Carrying passengers or heavy load 5. Tiredness 6. Trying to avoid arrest 7. Aggressive driving, such as driving much too close to vehicle in front, inappropriate attempts to overtake, or cutting in after overtaking		
Factors indicating greater degree of harm 1. Injury to others 2. Damage to other vehicles or property		
FORM A PRELIMINARY VIEW OF THE APPROPRIATE SENTENCE, THEN CONSIDER OFFENDER MITIGATION		
Common factors are identified at B[5.2A]		
CONSIDER A REDUCTION FOR A GUILTY PLEA		
CONSIDER ORDERING DISQUALIFICATION UNTIL APPROPRIATE DRIVING TEST PASSED		
CONSIDER ANCILLARY ORDERS, INCLUDING COMPENSATION		

A[66.17] Criminal offences dealt with in magistrates' courts

Refer to B[18] for guidance on compensation and **Part B** for available ancillary orders

DECIDE SENTENCE

GIVE REASONS

A[67]

Violent disorder

Charge

A[67.1] Being one of three or more persons present together and using or threatening unlawful violence so that the conduct taken together is such as would cause a person of reasonable firmness present at the scene to fear for his personal safety

Public Order Act 1986, s 2(1)

Maximum penalty – Fine level 5 and 6 months. Triable either way. Specified violent offence under Sch 15, Part 1, CJA 2003.

Crown Court – 5 years' imprisonment and unlimited fine.

Mode of trial

A[67.2] Cases of violent disorder should generally be considered for trial on indictment. See SC Guideline at **A[67.10]** below.

Legal notes and definitions

A[67.3] The charge. Only one offence is created.

A[67.4] Three or more persons. The defendants need not be using or threatening violence simultaneously. The term 'present together' meant no more than being present in the same place at the same time; the prosecution are not required to prove a common purpose among those using or threatening violence: *R v NW* [2010] EWCA Crim 404, [2010] 2 Cr App Rep 54, [2010] Crim LR 723.

A[67.5] Violence does not include violence justified by law (eg self-defence or prevention of crime) but apart from that includes violent conduct towards property or persons and is not restricted to conduct causing or intended to cause injury or damage but includes any other violent conduct (for example, throwing at or towards a person a missile of a kind capable of causing injury which does not hit or falls short).

A[67.6] Person of reasonable firmness need not actually be or be likely to be, present at the scene. See A[2.6].

A[67.7] Intent. A person may be guilty only if he intends to use or threaten violence, or is aware that his conduct may be violent or threaten violence.

A[67.8] Intoxication. A person whose awareness is impaired by intoxication shall be taken to be aware of that of which he would be aware if not intoxicated, unless he shows that his intoxication was not self-induced, or that it was caused solely by the taking of a substance in the course of medical treatment. 'Intoxication' may be caused by drink, drugs or other means.

A[67.9] Violent disorder may be committed in a public or private place.

Sentencing
SC Guideline – Violent disorder

A[67.10]

OFFENCE SERIOUSNESS (CULPABILITY AND HARM)
A. IDENTIFY THE APPROPRIATE STARTING POINT Starting points based on first time offender pleading not guilty
These offences should normally be dealt with in the Crown Court. However, there may be rare cases involving missile violence or threats of violence leading to no or minor injury, with few people involved and no weapon or missiles, in which a custodial sentence within the jurisdiction of a magistrates' court may be appropriate.

A[67.11] Available sentences. See Table A at B[4.1].

A[68]

Voyeurism

Charge

A[68.1] For the purpose of obtaining sexual gratification, observed another person doing a private act, and he knows that the other person does not consent to being observed for sexual gratification.

Sexual Offences Act 2003, s 67(1)

Operates equipment with the intention of enabling another to observe, for sexual gratification, a third person (B) doing a private act and know that B does not consent to his operating equipment with that intention.

Sexual Offences Act 2003, s 67(2)

Maximum penalty – Fine level 5 and 6 months. Triable either way. Specified sexual offence under Sch 15, Part 2, CJA 2003.

Crown Court – 2 years' imprisonment and unlimited fine.

Mode of trial

A[68.2] See the SC Guideline at A[68.5] below.

Legal notes and definitions

A[68.3] The purpose of obtaining sexual gratification forms part of the relevant act; thus, where a defendant was unfit to plead and the jury had to determine whether or not he had committed the relevant act, it was necessary for the jury to find both deliberate observation and the purpose of sexual gratification: *R v B* [2012] EWCA Crim 770, [2012] 3 All ER 1093, [2013] 1 WLR 499.

For the purpose of this offence 'private act' means an act carried out in a place which, in the circumstances, would reasonably be expected to provide privacy, and the person's genitals, buttocks or breasts are exposed or covered only in underwear; or the person is using a lavatory; or the person is doing a sexual act that is of a kind not ordinarily done in public (the offence does not extend solely to 'ogling male breasts'): *R v Bassett* [2008] EWCA Crim 1174.

A[68.4] Definitions. See the notes at the end of the SC guideline at A[68.5] below.

"Private Act" and "structure" are defined by s 68.

There must be a private act in order for offences of voyeurism to be committed. Section 68 is then concerned to bring within the meaning of the private act those parts of the body for which people conventionally expect or normally expect privacy. The clear intention of Parliament therefore was to mean the female "breast" or breasts" and not the male breast (see the notes to A[68.5] below)

"Observes" and "image" are further defined by s 79.

For "consent" see s 74.

Sentencing

A[68.5] In accordance with s 80 of and Sch 3 to the Sexual Offences Act 2003, automatic notification requirements apply upon conviction to an offender aged 18 or over where:

(1)   a victim was under 18; or
(2)   a term of imprisonment or a community sentence of at least 12 months is imposed.

For notification requirements generally, see A[52.15].

NB: A community order with a requirement to carry out 120 hours unpaid work was not a community sentence of at least 12 months for the purposes of Sch 3 and therefore the offender was not subject to the notification requirements of the legislation (*R v Odam* [2008] EWCA Crim 1087).

Sentencing
SC Guideline – Voyeurism

A[68.6] This guideline is taken from the SC's definitive guideline *Sexual Offences Act 2003* effective from 1 April 2014.

Triable either way

Maximum: 2 years' custody

Offence range: Fine – 18 months' custody

For convictions on or after such date (irrespective of the date of commission of the offence), these are specified offences for the purposes of section 226A (extended sentence for certain violent or sexual offences) of the Criminal Justice Act 2003.

STEP ONE
DETERMINING THE OFFENCE CATEGORY

The court should determine the offence category using the table below.

Category 1	Raised harm **and** raised culpability
Category 2	Raised harm **or** raised culpability
Category 3	Voyeurism **without** raised harm or culpability factors present

The court should determine culpability and harm caused or intended, by reference **only** to the factors below, which comprise the principal factual elements of the offence. Where an offence does not fall squarely into a category, individual factors may require a degree of weighting before making an overall assessment and determining the appropriate offence category.

Factors indicating raised harm	Factors indicating raised culpability
Image(s) available to be viewed by others	Significant degree of planning

Factors indicating raised harm	Factors indicating raised culpability
Victim observed or recorded in their own home or residence	Image(s) recorded
	Abuse of trust
	Specific or previous targeting of a particularly vulnerable victim
	Commercial exploitation and/or motivation
	Offence racially or religiously aggravated
	Offence motivated by, or demonstrating, hostility to the victim based on his or her sexual orientation (or presumed sexual orientation) or transgender identity (or presumed transgender identity)
	Offence motivated by, or demonstrating, hostility to the victim based on his or her disability (or presumed disability)

STEP TWO
STARTING POINT AND CATEGORY RANGE

Having determined the category, the court should use the corresponding starting points to reach a sentence within the category range on the next page. The starting point applies to all offenders irrespective of plea or previous convictions. Having determined the starting point, step two allows further adjustment for aggravating or mitigating features, set out on the next page.

A case of particular gravity, reflected by multiple features of culpability or harm in step one, could merit upward adjustment from the starting point before further adjustment for aggravating or mitigating features, set out on the next page.

Where there is a sufficient prospect of rehabilitation, a community order with a sex offender treatment programme requirement under section 202 of the Criminal Justice Act 2003 can be a proper alternative to a short or moderate length custodial sentence.

Category 1	**Starting point** 26 weeks' custody
	Category range 12 weeks' – 18 months' custody
Category 2	**Starting point** High level community order
	Category range Medium level community order – 26 weeks' custody
Category 3	**Starting point** Medium level community order
	Band A fine – High level community order

The table below contains a **non-exhaustive** list of additional factual elements providing the context of the offence and factors relating to the offender. Identify whether any combination of these, or other relevant factors, should result in an upward or downward adjustment from the starting point. **In particular, relevant recent convictions are likely to result in an upward adjustment.** In some cases, having considered these factors, it may be appropriate to move outside the identified category range.

When sentencing **category 2 offences**, the court should also consider the custody threshold as follows:

* has the custody threshold been passed?
* if so, is it unavoidable that a custodial sentence be imposed?
* if so, can that sentence be suspended?

When sentencing **category 3 offences**, the court should also consider the community order threshold as follows:

* has the community order threshold been passed?

Aggravating factors	Any steps taken to prevent victim reporting an incident, obtaining assistance and/or from assisting or supporting the prosecution
Statutory aggravating factors	Attempts to dispose of or conceal evidence
Previous convictions, having regard to a) the nature of the offence to which the conviction relates and its relevance to the current offence; and b) the time that has elapsed since the conviction	**Mitigating factors**
Offence committed whilst on bail	No previous convictions **or** no relevant/recent convictions
Other aggravating factors	Remorse
Location of offence	Previous good character and/or exemplary conduct[*]
Timing of offence	Age and/or lack of maturity where it affects the responsibility of the offender
Failure to comply with current court orders	Mental disorder or learning disability, particularly where linked to the commission of the offence
Offence committed whilst on licence	Demonstration of steps taken to address offending behaviour
Distribution of images, whether or not for gain	
Placing images where there is the potential for a high volume of viewers	
Period over which victim observed	
Period over which images were made or distributed	

[*] Previous good character/exemplary conduct is different from having no previous convictions. The more serious the offence, the less the weight which should normally be attributed to this factor. Where previous good character/exemplary conduct has been used to facilitate the offence, this mitigation should not normally be allowed and such conduct may constitute an aggravating factor.

STEP THREE
CONSIDER ANY FACTORS WHICH INDICATE A REDUCTION, SUCH AS ASSISTANCE TO THE PROSECUTION

The court should take into account sections 73 and 74 of the Serious Organised Crime and Police Act 2005 (assistance by defendants: reduction or review of sentence) and any other rule of law by virtue of which an offender may receive a discounted sentence in consequence of assistance given (or offered) to the prosecutor or investigator.

STEP FOUR
REDUCTION FOR GUILTY PLEAS

The court should take account of any potential reduction for a guilty plea in accordance with section 144 of the Criminal Justice Act 2003 and the *Guilty Plea* guideline.

STEP FIVE
DANGEROUSNESS

The court should consider whether having regard to the criteria contained in Chapter 5 of Part 12 of the Criminal Justice Act 2003 it would be appropriate to award an extended sentence (section 226A).

STEP SIX
TOTALITY PRINCIPLE

If sentencing an offender for more than one offence, or where the offender is already serving a sentence, consider whether the total sentence is just and proportionate to the overall offending behaviour.

STEP SEVEN
ANCILLARY ORDERS

The court must consider whether to make any ancillary orders. The court must also consider what other requirements or provisions may automatically apply. Further information is included on page 303.

STEP EIGHT
REASONS

Section 174 of the Criminal Justice Act 2003 imposes a duty to give reasons for, and explain the effect of, the sentence.

STEP NINE
CONSIDERATION FOR TIME SPENT ON BAIL

The court must consider whether to give credit for time spent on bail in accordance with section 240A of the Criminal Justice Act 2003.

Witness intimidation

Charge 1

A[69.1] Did intimidate [. . . . .] knowing or believing [
. . . .] is assisting an investigation/is a witness or potential
witness in proceedings with the intention that the investigation/course of
justice would be interfered/perverted/obstructed

Criminal Justice and Public Order Act 1994, s 51(1)

See Charge 2 for penalty.

Charge 2

A[69.2] Did harm or threaten with harm [. . . . .] intending
to harm him knowing or believing that [. . . . .] has assisted in
an investigation or has given evidence in proceedings for an offence because
he believes/ knows that assistance or evidence was given

Criminal Justice and Public Order Act 1994, s 51(2)

Maximum penalty – Fine level 5 and 6 months. Triable either way.

Crown Court – maximum 5 years' imprisonment.

Note that similar offences carrying the same maximum penalty may now be
charged under the Criminal Justice and Police Act 2001, ss 39 and 40.
These offences are specifically aimed at incidents not covered by CJPOA
1994, s 51 and cover both civil and criminal proceedings.

Mode of trial

A[69.3] See the SC Guideline at A[69.11] below.

Legal notes and definitions

A[69.4] A person does an act to another person with the intention of
intimidating/harming not only when it is done directly but also when it is
done to a third party with the same intention. The threat may be at a
distance, eg over the telephone: *DPP v Mills* [1997] QB 300, [1996] 3 WLR
1093.

In *R v Patrascu* [2004] EWCA Crim 2417, [2014] 4 All ER 1066, [2005]
1 WLR 3344, [2005] 1 Cr App R 35 it was held that 'to intimidate'
normally means 'to put someone in fear', another meaning is 'to force to or
deter from some action by threats of violence'. However, the person
intended to be intimidated must in fact be intimidated: *R v ZN* [2013]
EWCA Crim 989, [2013] 4 All ER 331, [2013] 1 WLR 3900, [2013] 2 Cr
App R 25 (not following *Patrascu* in this respect). (If the victim is
sufficiently steadfast not to be intimidated a charge of attempt remains
possible.)

It was not enough to describe the defendant's behaviour as objectively intimidating, but rather, there had to have been an act that had intimidated and had been intended to intimidate the victim: *R v Mahmood* [2007] EWCA Crim 13. The requirement of actual intimidation is inconsistent, however, with *Patrascu*, and it is submitted that the former authority is to be preferred on this point.

A[69.5] Harm may be financial/physical to a person or property.

A[69.6] Intention. The intention or motive required for the two charges need not be the only or predominant motive or intention with which the act is done or threatened. A threat to harm a witness relayed via a third party constitutes an offence under this section. If a threat to harm a witness takes place within one year after the trial the prosecution do not have to prove a connection between the threat and the trial: *A-G's Reference (No 1 of 1999)*. If the prosecution can prove the act/threat and the defendant's knowledge/belief in the circumstances then the resultant motive/intention shall be presumed unless the contrary is proven.

A[69.7] Knowingly and ECHR. Section 51(7) of the CJPOA 1994 provides that if the defendant knowingly commits an act of intimidation it will be presumed that the defendant intended to interfere with the course of justice unless otherwise proven. The fact that the legislation imposes a reverse burden of proof on the defence is both justiciable and proportionate in ECHR terms having regard to the stated aims of the legislation and *Attorney General's Reference (No 1 of 2004)* [2004] EWCA Crim 1025, [2004] 1 WLR 2111.

A[69.8] Witness includes jurors or potential jurors in the Crown Court.

A[69.9] Investigation into an offence means an investigation by police or such other person charged with the duty of investigating offences or charging offenders. The prosecution must prove that there was an investigation under way, not merely that the defendant believed there to be one: *R v Singh* [2000] 1 Cr App Rep 31, [1999] Crim LR 681, CA.

A[69.10] Offence includes an alleged or suspected offence.

Sentencing
SC Guideline – Witness intimidation

A[69.11] Where offence committed in a domestic context, see SC Definitive Guideline: "Overarching Principles: Domestic Violence".

OFFENCE SERIOUSNESS (CULPABILITY AND HARM) A. IDENTIFY THE APPROPRIATE STARTING POINT Starting points based on first time offender pleading not guilty		
Examples of nature of activity	**Starting point**	**Range**
Sudden outburst in chance encounter	6 weeks custody	Medium level community order to 18 weeks custody

Conduct amounting to a threat; staring at, approaching or following witnesses; talking about the case; trying to alter or stop evidence	18 weeks custody	12 weeks custody to Crown Court
Threats of violence to witnesses and/or their families; deliberately seeking out witnesses	Crown Court	Crown Court

OFFENCE SERIOUSNESS (CULPABILITY AND HARM)

B. CONSIDER THE EFFECT OF AGGRAVATING AND MITIGATING FACTORS (OTHER THAN THOSE WITHIN EXAMPLES ABOVE)

Common aggravating and mitigating factors are identified at B[5.2A]. The following may be particularly relevant but these lists are not exhaustive

Factors indicating higher culpability	
1. Breach of bail conditions	
2. Offender involves others	
Factors indicating greater degree of harm	
1. Detrimental impact on administration of justice	
2. Contact made at or in vicinity of victim's home	

FORM A PRELIMINARY VIEW OF THE APPROPRIATE SENTENCE, THEN CONSIDER OFFENDER MITIGATION

Common factors are identified at B[5.2A]

CONSIDER A REDUCTION FOR A GUILTY PLEA

CONSIDER ANCILLARY ORDERS, INCLUDING COMPENSATION

Refer to B[18] for guidance on compensation and **Part B** for available ancillary orders

DECIDE SENTENCE

GIVE REASONS

A[70]

Wounding/causing grievous bodily harm, and racially/religiously aggravated grievous bodily harm and malicious wounding

(Offences Against the Person Act 1861, s 20; Crime and Disorder Act 1998, s 29)

Charges

A[70.1] Unlawfully and maliciously inflicting grievous bodily harm

A[70.2] Unlawfully and maliciously wounding

Offences against the Person Act 1861, s 20

Maximum penalty – Fine level 5 and 6 months. Triable either way. Specified violent offence under Sch 15, Part 1, CJA 2003.

Crown Court – 5 years and unlimited fine.

Racially/religiously aggravated offences.

Maximum penalty – Fine level 5 and 6 months. Triable either way. Specified violent offence under Sch 15, Part 1, CJA 2003.

Crown Court – 7 years and unlimited fine.

Mode of trial

A[70.3] For cases of domestic violence. See SC Definitive Guideline: "Overarching Principles: Domestic Violence".

A[70.4] See the SC Guideline at A[70.20] below

Legal notes and definitions

A[70.5] Intent. 'Maliciously' means intentionally or recklessly (*R v Mowatt* [1968] 1 QB 421, [1967] 3 All ER 47, CA) and 'recklessly' means that the accused foresaw the particular risk and yet went on to take it (*R v Cunningham* [1957] 2 QB 396, [1957] 2 All ER 412, CCA). In offences under the Offences Against The Person Act 1861, s 20 what must be intended or foreseen is that some physical harm might occur, not necessarily amounting to grievous bodily harm or wounding. An intention to frighten is not enough. (*DPP v A* [2000] All ER (D) 1247). In *Re Dica* (5 May 2004, unreported), CA it was held that where a person, knowing he suffers from a serious sexual disease, infects another through consensual sex (but not deliberately intending to pass on the disease) he will be guilty of the offence, so long as the victim did not consent to the risk of infection. An honest belief in an informed consent will amount to a defence (*R v Konzani* [2005] EWCA Crim 706, [2005] All ER (D) 292 (Mar)).

In principle it was open to justices to convict on the basis of recklessness even where the prosecution simply alleged a deliberate assault: *D v DPP* [2005] EWHC 967 (Admin) considered. However, the justices had failed to identify what was the unlawful act of K leading to the assault. Recklessness had only been a possible conclusion if the justices had found that K had thrown a punch albeit, without intending it to land, or was flailing his arms about in an agitated and aggressive manner. The conviction could not stand in the light of the findings of fact made by the justices: *Katsonis v Crown Prosecution Service* [2011] EWHC 1860 (Admin), 175 JP 396.

A[70.6] Grievous bodily harm. Means really serious bodily harm. The injuries caused do not have to be permanent or dangerous, but they have to be more severe than actual bodily harm. (See A[8].)

A[70.7] Provocation is no defence, but can be taken into account when sentencing.

A[70.8] Racial/religious aggravation (See A[8.7].)

A[70.9] Misadventure (See A[8.8].)

A[70.10] Consent (See A[8.10]–A[8.17].)

A[70.11]–[70.15] Self-defence etc (See A[8.18]–A[8.20].)

A[70.16] Lawful sport (See A[15.18].)

A[70.17] Trespasser on property (See A[15.21]–A[15.30].)

A[70.18] Execution of legal process (See A[8.24].)

A[70.19] Reduction of charge/alternative verdict. The court cannot reduce this charge to a less serious one (eg actual bodily harm or common assault); but if a separate charge for a lesser offence has been preferred there could be a conviction for that. Consult a legal adviser and A[15.31] on the effect of a dismissal for common assault.

Sentencing
SC Guideline – Wounding/causing grievous bodily harm and Racially/religiously aggravated GBH/Unlawful wounding

Grievous bodily harm

Inflicting grievous bodily harm/Unlawful wounding

Offences against the Person Act 1861 (section 20)

Racially/religiously aggravated GBH/Unlawful wounding

Crime and Disorder Act 1998 (section 29)

A[70.20] These are specified offences for the purposes of section 224 of the Criminal Justice Act 2003

Triable either way

Section 20

Maximum when tried summarily: Level 5 fine and/or 26 weeks' custody

Maximum when tried on indictment: 5 years' custody

Section 29

Maximum when tried summarily: Level 5 fine and/or 26 weeks' custody

Maximum when tried on indictment: 7 years' custody

Offence range: Community order – 4 years' custody

This guideline applies to all offenders aged 18 and older, who are sentenced on or after 13 June 2011. The definitions of 'starting point' and 'first time offender' do not apply for this guideline. Starting point and category ranges apply to all offenders in all cases, irrespective of plea or previous convictions.

Step One
Determining the offence category

The court should determine the offence category using the table below.

Category 1	Greater harm **and** higher culpability
Category 2	Greater harm **and** lower culpability; **or** lesser harm **and** higher culpability
Category 3	Lesser harm **and** lower culpability

The court should determine the offender's culpability and the harm caused, or intended, by reference **only** to the factors below (as demonstrated by the presence of one or more). These factors comprise the principal factual elements of the offence and should determine the category.

Factors indicating greater harm

Injury (which includes disease transmission and/or psychological harm) which is serious in the context of the offence (must normally be present)

Victim is particularly vulnerable because of personal circumstances

Sustained or repeated assault on the same victim

Factors indicating lesser harm

Injury which is less serious in the context of the offence

Factors indicating higher culpability

Statutory aggravating factors:

Offence motivated by, or demonstrating, hostility to the victim based on his or her sexual orientation (or presumed sexual orientation)

Offence motivated by, or demonstrating, hostility to the victim based on the victim's disability (or presumed disability)

Other aggravating factors:

A significant degree of premeditation

Use of weapon or weapon equivalent (for example, shod foot, headbutting, use of acid, use of animal)

Intention to commit more serious harm than actually resulted from the offence

Deliberately causes more harm than is necessary for commission of offence

Deliberate targeting of vulnerable victim

Leading role in group or gang

Offence motivated by, or demonstrating, hostility based on the victim's age, sex, gender identity (or presumed gender identity)

Factors indicating lower culpability

Subordinate role in a group or gang

A greater degree of provocation than normally expected

Lack of premeditation

Mental disorder or learning disability, where linked to commission of the offence

Excessive self defence

Step Two
Starting point and category range

Having determined the category, the court should use the corresponding starting points to reach a sentence within the category range below. The starting point applies to all offenders irrespective of plea or previous convictions. A case of particular gravity, reflected by multiple features of culpability in step one, could merit upward adjustment from the starting point before further adjustment for aggravating or mitigating features, set out below.

Offence Category	Starting Point (Applicable to all offenders)	Category Range (Applicable to all offenders)
Category 1	Crown Court	Crown Court
Category 2	Crown Court	Crown Court
Category 3	High level community order	Low level community order – Crown Court (51 weeks' custody)

The table below contains a **non-exhaustive** list of additional factual elements providing the context of the offence and factors relating to the offender. Identify whether any combination of these, or other relevant factors, should result in an upward or downward adjustment from the starting point. In some cases, having considered these factors, it may be appropriate to move outside the identified category range.

When sentencing **category 3** offences, the court should also consider the custody threshold as follows:

* has the custody threshold been passed?
* if so, is it unavoidable that a custodial sentence be imposed?
* if so, can that sentence be suspended?

Factors increasing seriousness

Statutory aggravating factors:

Previous convictions, having regard to a) the nature of the offence to which the conviction relates and its relevance to the current offence; and b) the time that has elapsed since the conviction

Offence committed whilst on bail

Other aggravating factors include:

Location of the offence

Timing of the offence

Ongoing effect upon the victim

Offence committed against those working in the public sector or providing a service to the public

Presence of others including relatives, especially children or partner of the victim

Gratuitous degradation of victim

In domestic violence cases, victim forced to leave their home

Failure to comply with current court orders

Offence committed whilst on licence

An attempt to conceal or dispose of evidence

Failure to respond to warnings or concerns expressed by others about the offender's behaviour

Commission of offence whilst under the influence of alcohol or drugs

Abuse of power and/or position of trust

Exploiting contact arrangements with a child to commit an offence

Established evidence of community impact

Any steps taken to prevent the victim reporting an incident, obtaining assistance and/or from assisting or supporting the prosecution

Offences taken into consideration (TICs)

Factors reducing seriousness or reflecting personal mitigation

No previous convictions **or** no relevant/recent convictions

Single blow

Remorse

Good character and/or exemplary conduct

Determination and/or demonstration of steps taken to address addiction or offending behaviour

Serious medical conditions requiring urgent, intensive or long-term treatment

Isolated incident

Age and/or lack of maturity where it affects the responsibility of the offender

Lapse of time since the offence where this is not the fault of the offender

Mental disorder or learning disability, where **not** linked to the commission of the offence

Sole or primary carer for dependent relatives

Section 29 offences only: The court should determine the appropriate sentence for the offence without taking account of the element of aggravation and then make an addition to the sentence, considering the level of aggravation involved. It may be appropriate to move outside the identified category range, taking into account the increased statutory maximum.

Step Three
Consider any other factors which indicate a reduction, such as
assistance to the prosecution

The court should take into account any rule of law by virtue of which an offender may receive a discounted sentence in consequence of assistance given (or offered) to the prosecutor or investigator.

Step Four
Reduction for guilty pleas

The court should take account of any potential reduction for a guilty plea in accordance with section 144 of the Criminal Justice Act 2003 and the *Guilty Plea* guideline.

Step Five
Dangerousness

Inflicting grievous bodily harm/unlawful wounding and racially/religiously aggravated GBH/unlawful wounding are specified offences within the meaning of Chapter 5 of the Criminal Justice Act 2003 and at this stage the court should consider whether having regard to the criteria contained in that Chapter it would be appropriate to award an extended sentence.

Step Six
Totality principle

If sentencing an offender for more than one offence, or where the offender is already serving a sentence, consider whether the total sentence is just and proportionate to the offending behaviour.

Step Seven
Compensation and ancillary orders

In all cases, the court should consider whether to make compensation and/or other ancillary orders.

Step Eight
Reasons

Section 174 of the Criminal Justice Act 2003 imposes a duty to give reasons for, and explain the effect of, the sentence.

Step Nine
Consideration for remand time

(Now obligatory.)

A[71]

Air guns

Charge

A[71.1] Being a person under 18 having with him an air weapon or ammunition

Firearms Act 1968, s 22(4)

Maximum penalty – Fine level 3 or any other adjudication to which a young person is liable, bearing in mind the offence is not punishable with imprisonment.

Forfeiture of the air weapon or ammunition can be ordered.

Legal notes and definitions

A[71.2] **Possession**, a close physical link and immediate control over the firearm but not necessarily that he had been carrying it. It is not an offence where he is under the supervision of someone of or over 21 years.

A[71.3] **Air weapon** means an air rifle, air gun or air pistol of a type which has not been declared to be specially dangerous in rules made by the Home Office. See *Street v DPP* [2004] EWHC 86 (Admin), (2004) Times, 23 January, [2004] All ER (D) 70 (Jan) where a low powered ball bearing gun was included in the definition.

A[71.4] **Public place** includes any highway or premises or place to which at the material time the public had access whether for payment or otherwise.

A[71.5] It is not an offence for a person of 14 or over to have with him an air weapon on private premises with the consent of the occupier.

Section 23(1) provides that it is not an offence under s 22(4) for a person to have with him an air weapon or ammunition while he is under the supervision of a person of or over the age of 21; but where a person has with him an air weapon on any premises in circumstances where he would be prohibited from having it with him but for this subsection, it is an offence for the person under whose supervision he is to allow him to use it for firing any missile beyond those premises. In proceedings against a person this offence it shall be a defence for him to show that the only premises into or across which the missile was fired were premises the occupier of which had consented to the firing of the missile (whether specifically or by way of a general consent): Firearms Act 1968, s 23(1A).

A[71.6] He does not commit an offence if he is engaged in target practice as a member of a club approved by the Home Office or if the weapon and ammunition are being used at a shooting gallery where only air weapons or miniature rifles of 0.23 calibre or less are used (Firearms Act 1968, s 23(2)).

Sentencing

A[71.7] No SC guideline. For available sentences see Table C at B[4.3].

A[71.8] Fines. See B[33].

Air guns

Charge

A[71A.1] (1) It is an offence for a person in possession of an air weapon to fail to take reasonable precautions to prevent any person under the age of eighteen from having the weapon with him.

(2) Subsection (1) does not apply where by virtue of section 23 of this Act (see A[71.5], above) the person under the age of eighteen is not prohibited from having the weapon with him.

Firearms Act 1968, s 24ZA

Maximum penalty – Fine level 3 or any other adjudication to which a young person is liable, bearing in mind the offence is not punishable with imprisonment.

Forfeiture of the air weapon or ammunition can be ordered.

Legal notes and definitions

A[71A.2] In proceedings for an offence under subsection (1) it is a defence to show that the person charged with the offence—

(a)   believed the other person to be aged eighteen or over; and
(b)   had reasonable ground for that belief.

A person shall be taken to have shown the matters specified in subsection (3) if—

(a)   sufficient evidence of those matters is adduced to raise an issue with respect to them; and
(b)   the contrary is not proved beyond a reasonable doubt.

Sentencing

A[71A.3] No SC guideline. For available sentences see Table C at B[4.3].

Dangerous dogs

Offences under the Dangerous Dogs Act 1991

A[72.1] Being the owner (person for the time being in charge) of a dog which on [. . . . .] was dangerously out of control in a public place namely [. . . . .] (and which injured a person or assistance dog)

Dangerous Dogs Act 1991, s 3

Maximum penalty Non-aggravated offences: Fine level 5 and 6 months' imprisonment. Triable only summarily.

Aggravated offences: 14 years if a person dies as a result of being injured; 5 years in other cases where a person is injured; 3 years where an assistance dog is killed. Triable either way.

Significant amendments to the 1991 Act were made by the Anti-social Behaviour, Crime and Policing Act 2014, ss 106 and 107. In particular, the offence was extended to private places (subject to a householder defence), and maximum penalties were increased for aggravated offences.

Legal notes and definitions

A[72.2] Owner. Includes, where the dog is owned by a person who is less than 16 years old, the head of the household of which that person is a member. In *L v CPS* [2010] EWHC 341 (Admin), (2010) 174 JP 209 the appellant, who had charge of a dog but was not the owner, handed the lead to another person while he tied his shoe lace and that other person deliberately released the dog, which proceeded to bite somebody. It was held that the appellant remained in charge of the dog. The short and temporary transfer did not prevent this. The appellant had the right and power to take the dog back any time and was able to control it since the dog responded to his commands.

In proceedings for an offence under s 3(1) it is a defence for the accused to prove that the dog was at the material time in charge of a person whom he reasonably believed to be a fit and proper person to be in charge of it: s 3(2). A contention, however, that different members of a family looked after a dog at different times fell well outside the ambit of the s 3(2) defence, which was intended to cover situations such as a dog being left with a neighbour for a period of time: *R v Huddart* [1999] Crim LR 568.

Natural justice requires that the known owner of the dog be notified of any prosecution where a conviction will result in the destruction of the dog: *R v Trafford Magistrates' Court, ex p Riley* (1995) 160 JP 418, DC.

A[72.3] Standard of liability. Section 3(1) creates an offence of strict liability. Nevertheless, liability is not absolute. As has been seen, s 3(2) makes available a defence in certain circumstances to an owner of a dog placed in the charge of another. Also, there must be some causal connection between having charge of the dog and the prohibited state of affairs that has arisen. Section 3(1) requires proof by the prosecution of an act or omission of the defendant (with or without fault) that to some (more than minimal) degree caused or permitted the prohibited state of affairs to come about: *R v Robinson-Pierre* [2013] EWCA Crim 2396, 178 JP 45 (explaining *R v Bezzina* [1994] 1 WLR 1057, 158 JP 671) (In Robinson-Pierre the dog was in a public place only as a result of escaping from the house when police broke down the door executing a search warrant. The offence under s 3(1) can now be committed in private, as well as public, places. It is submitted, however, that this has no bearing on the principles established by the case).

The behaviour of the dog in that it bit a person and the fact that it was not controlled by its handler when on a lead was ample evidence of the dog being dangerously out of control in a public place (*R v Gedminintaite and Collier* [2008] EWCA Crim 814).

A[72.4] Householder cases. The extension of the law to private places was accompanied by a 'householder' defence mirroring the provisions of s 76(8B) to 8(F) of the Criminal Justice and Immigration Act 2008 (use of force at place of residence).

A person is not guilty of the offence under s 3(1) in a case which is a householder case, defined as a case where:

(a) the dog is dangerously out of control while in or partly in a building, or part of a building, that is a dwelling (or forces accommodation, or both); and

(b) at that time the person to whom the dog is dangerously out of control is in, or entering, the building or part as a trespasser and the defendant (if present at that time) believed that person to be in, or entering, the building or part as a trespasser. The reasonableness of the defendant's belief is relevant to the question as to whether he genuinely held it, but if it is determined the belief was genuine D may rely on it whether or not it was mistaken or, if mistaken, the mistake was a reasonable one. The defendant cannot, however, rely on a mistaken belief attributable to voluntary intoxication: s 3(1B).

A[72.5] Dangerously out of control. This term is partly defined by s 10(3), which provides: 'For the purposes of this Act a dog shall be regarded as dangerously out of control on any occasion on which there are grounds for reasonable apprehension that it will injure any person or assistance dog, whether or not it actually does so, but references to a dog injuring a person or assistance dog or there being grounds for reasonable apprehension that it will do so do not include references to any case in which the dog is being used for a lawful purpose by a constable or a person in the service of the Crown'.

Section 10(3) sets an objective standard of reasonable apprehension, not related to the state of mind of the dog owner; it is no defence that the owner had no realisation that his dog might behave in such a way: see *R v Bezzina* [1994] 1 WLR 1057, 158 JP 671. Where injury in fact results there must have been, immediately before, reasonable apprehension that injury would occur: *Rafiq v DPP* (1997) 161 JP 412. Note, however, that s 10(3) does not provide an exhaustive definition and the court is entitled to go back to the straightforward words of s 3: *R v Gedminitaite and Collier* [2008] EWCA Crim 814, 172 JP 413.

'Assistance dog' has the meaning given to it by the Equality Act 2010, s 173(1) (dog trained to assist the blind, deaf or persons with certain disabilities).

A[72.6]–[72.7] Sentencing. The following guidelines are effective from 20 August 2012. They predate the significant changes made by the Anti-social, Crime and Policing Act 2014 (which are described above). The 2014 Act repealed s 3(3) (which became redundant following the extension of the s 3(1) offence to private places).

The 2014 Act also amended the criteria for determining whether or not a dog would constitute a danger to public safety. The changes are noted at A[72.10] and A[72.14].

Sentencing

SC Sentencing Guideline

A[72.8]

This guideline applies to all offenders aged 18 years and older, who are sentenced on or after 20 August 2012. The definitions of 'starting point' and 'first time offender' do not apply for this guideline.

Owner or person in charge of a dog dangerously out of control in a public place, injuring any person
Dangerous Dogs Act 1991 (section 3(1))

Owner or person in charge allowing a dog to be in a private place where the dog is not permitted to be, injuring any person
Dangerous Dogs Act 1991 (section 3(3)(a))

Triable either way

Maximum: 2 years' custody

Offence range: Discharge – 18 months' custody

Step One
Determining the offence category

The court should determine the offence category using the table below.

Category 1	Greater harm **and** higher culpability
Category 2	Greater harm **and** lower culpability; **or** lesser harm **and** higher culpability
Category 3	Lesser harm **and** lower culpability

The court should determine culpability and harm caused or intended, by reference **only** to the factors below, which comprise the principal factual elements of the offence. Where an offence does not fall squarely into a category, individual factors may require a degree of weighting before making an overall assessment and determining the appropriate offence category.

Factors indicating greater harm

Serious injury (which includes disease transmission and/or psychological harm)

Sustained or repeated attack

Victim is a child or otherwise vulnerable because of personal circumstances

Factor indicating lesser harm

Minor injury

Factors indicating higher culpability

Statutory aggravating factors:

Offence racially or religiously aggravated

Offence motivated by, or demonstrating, hostility to the victim based on his or her sexual orientation (or presumed sexual orientation)

Offence motivated by, or demonstrating, hostility to the victim based on the victim's disability (or presumed disability)

Other aggravating factors:

Failure to respond to warnings or concerns expressed by others about the dog's behaviour

Goading, or allowing goading, of dog

Dog used as weapon or to intimidate victim

Offence motivated by, or demonstrating, hostility based on the victim's age, sex, gender identity (or presumed gender identity)

Factors indicating lower culpability

Attempts made to regain control of dog and/or intervene

Provocation of dog without fault of the offender

Evidence of safety or control measures having been taken

Mental disorder or learning disability, where linked to the commission of the offence

Step Two
Starting point and category range

Having determined the category, the court should use the corresponding starting points to reach a sentence within the category range below. The starting point applies to all offenders irrespective of plea or previous convictions. A case of particular gravity, reflected by multiple features of culpability or harm in step 1, could merit upward adjustment from the starting point before further adjustment for aggravating or mitigating features, set out on the next page.

Offence Category	Starting Point *(Applicable to all offenders)*	Category Range *(Applicable to all offenders)*
Category 1	26 weeks' custody	Medium level community order – Crown Court (18 months' custody)
Category 2	Medium level community order	Band B fine – 26 weeks' custody
Category 3	Band B fine	Discharge – Band C fine

The table below contains a **non-exhaustive** list of additional factual elements providing the context of the offence and factors relating to the offender. Identify whether any combination of these, or other relevant factors, should result in an upward or downward adjustment from the starting point. In some cases, having considered these factors, it may be appropriate to move outside the identified category range.

When sentencing **category 1 or 2** offences, the court should also consider the custody threshold as follows:

- has the custody threshold been passed?
- if so, is it unavoidable that a custodial sentence be imposed?
- if so, can that sentence be suspended?

When sentencing **category 2** offences, the court should also consider the community order threshold as follows:

- has the community order threshold been passed?

Factors increasing seriousness

Statutory aggravating factors:

Previous convictions, having regard to a) the nature of the offence to which the conviction relates and its relevance to the current offence; and b) the time that has elapsed since the conviction

Offence committed whilst on bail

Other aggravating factors include:

Injury to another animal(s)

Location of the offence

Ongoing effect upon the victim and/or others

Failure to take adequate precautions to prevent dog escaping

Allowing person insufficiently experienced or trained, to be in charge of dog

Ill treatment or failure to ensure welfare needs of dog, where not charged separately

Dog known to be prohibited

Lack or loss of control of dog due to influence of alcohol or drugs

Offence committed against those working in the public sector or providing a service to the public

Established evidence of community impact

Failure to comply with current court orders

Offence committed whilst on licence

Factors reducing seriousness or reflecting personal mitigation

No previous convictions **or** no relevant/recent convictions

Isolated incident

No previous complaints against, or incidents involving, the dog

Remorse

Good character and/or exemplary conduct

Evidence of responsible ownership

Determination and/or demonstration of steps taken to address addiction or offending behaviour

Serious medical conditions requiring urgent, intensive or long-term treatment

Age and/or lack of maturity where it affects the responsibility of the offender

Mental disorder or learning disability, where not linked to the commission of the offence

Sole or primary carer for dependent relatives

Step Three
Consider any factors which indicate a reduction, such as assistance to the prosecution

The court should take into account sections 73 and 74 of the Serious Organised Crime and Police Act 2005 (assistance by defendants: reduction or review of sentence) and any other rule of law by virtue of which an offender may receive a discounted sentence in consequence of assistance given (or offered) to the prosecutor or investigator.

Step Four
Reduction for guilty pleas

The court should take account of any potential reduction for a guilty plea in accordance with section 144 of the Criminal Justice Act 2003 and the *Guilty Plea* guideline.

Step Five
Compensation and ancillary orders

In all cases, the court should consider whether to make a compensation order and/or other ancillary orders.

Compensation order

The court should consider compensation orders in all cases where personal injury, loss or damage has resulted from the offence[1]. The court must give reasons if it decides not to award compensation in such cases.

Other ancillary orders available include:

Disqualification from having custody of a dog

The court **may** disqualify the offender from having custody of a dog[2]. The test the court should consider is whether the offender is a fit and proper person to have custody of a dog.

Destruction order/contingent destruction order

In any case where the offender is not the owner of the dog, the owner must be given an opportunity to be present and make representations to the court.

The court **shall** make a destruction order unless the court is satisfied that the dog would not constitute a danger to public safety[3].

In reaching a decision, the court should consider the relevant circumstances which include:

- the incident – what degree of harm was caused by the dog's behaviour?
- past behaviour of the dog – is this an isolated incident or have there been previous warnings or incidents? and
- owner's character – is the owner a fit and proper person to own this particular dog?

If the court is satisfied that the dog would not constitute a danger to public safety, it **shall** make a contingent destruction order imposing certain available conditions[4]. A contingent destruction order should specify the measures to be taken by the owner for keeping the dog under proper control, which include:

- muzzling;
- keeping on a lead;
- neutering in appropriate cases; and
- excluding it from a specified place[5].

Where the court makes a destruction order, it **may** order the offender to pay what it determines to be the reasonable expenses of destroying the dog and of keeping it pending its destruction[6].

Step Six
Totality principle

If sentencing an offender for more than one offence, or where the offender is already serving a sentence, consider whether the total sentence is just and proportionate to the offending behaviour.

Step Seven
Reasons

Section 174 of the Criminal Justice Act 2003 imposes a duty to give reasons for, and explain the effect of, the sentence.

Step Eight
Consideration for remand time

(Now obligatory.)

---

[1]   Powers of Criminal Courts (Sentencing) Act 2000, s 130.
[2]   Dangerous Dogs Act 1991, s 4(1)(b).
[3]   Dangerous Dogs Act 1991, s 4(1)(a).
[4]   Dangerous Dogs Act 1991, s 4A(4).
[5]   Dangerous Dogs Act 1991, s 4A(5).
[6]   Dangerous Dogs Act 1991, s 4(4)(b).

A[72.8A]

For structure of the sentencing decision see also B[3.6].

Owner or person in charge of a dog dangerously out of control in a public place
Dangerous Dogs Act 1991 (section 3(1))

Owner or person in charge allowing a dog to be in a private place where the dog is not permitted to be, which makes a person fear injury
Dangerous Dogs Act 1991 (section 3(3)(b))

Triable summarily only

Maximum: 26 weeks' custody

Offence range: Discharge – 26 weeks' custody

Step One
Determining the offence category

The court should determine the offence category using the table below.

Category 1	Greater harm **and** higher culpability
Category 2	Greater harm **and** lower culpability; **or** lesser harm **and** higher culpability
Category 3	Lesser harm **and** lower culpability

The court should determine culpability and harm caused or intended, by reference **only** to the factors below, which comprise the principal factual elements of the offence. Where an offence does not fall squarely into a category, individual factors may require a degree of weighting before making an overall assessment and determining the appropriate offence category.

Factors indicating greater harm

Presence of children or others who are vulnerable because of personal circumstances

Injury to another animal(s)

Factors indicating lesser harm

Low risk to the public

Factors indicating higher culpability

Statutory aggravating factors:

Offence racially or religiously aggravated

Offence motivated by, or demonstrating, hostility to the victim based on his or her sexual orientation (or presumed sexual orientation)

Offence motivated by, or demonstrating, hostility to the victim based on the victim's disability (or presumed disability)

Other aggravating factors:

Failure to respond to warnings or concerns expressed by others about the dog's behaviour

Goading, or allowing goading, of dog

Dog used as weapon or to intimidate victim

Offence motivated by, or demonstrating, hostility based on the victim's age, sex, gender identity (or presumed gender identity)

Factors indicating lower culpability

Attempts made to regain control of dog and/or intervene

Provocation of dog without fault of the offender

Evidence of safety or control measures having been taken

Mental disorder or learning disability, where linked to the commission of the offence

Step Two
Starting point and category range

Having determined the category, the court should use the corresponding starting points to reach a sentence within the category range below. The starting point applies to all offenders irrespective of plea or previous convictions. A case of particular gravity, reflected by multiple features of culpability or harm in step 1, could merit upward adjustment from the starting point before further adjustment for aggravating or mitigating features, set out on the next page.

Offence Category	Starting Point (Applicable to all offenders)	Category Range (Applicable to all offenders)
Category 1	Medium level community order	Band C fine – 26 weeks' custody
Category 2	Band B fine	Band A fine – Low level community order
Category 3	Band A fine	Discharge – Band B fine

The table below contains a **non-exhaustive** list of additional factual elements providing the context of the offence and factors relating to the offender. Identify whether any combination of these, or other relevant factors, should result in an upward or downward adjustment from the starting point. In some cases, having considered these factors, it may be appropriate to move outside the identified category range.

When sentencing **category 1** offences, the court should also consider the custody threshold as follows:

- has the custody threshold been passed?
- if so, is it unavoidable that a custodial sentence be imposed?
- if so, can that sentence be suspended?

When sentencing **category 1 or 2** offences, the court should also consider the community order threshold as follows:

- has the community order threshold been passed?

Factors increasing seriousness

Statutory aggravating factors:

Previous convictions, having regard to a) the nature of the offence to which the conviction relates and its relevance to the current offence; and b) the time that has elapsed since the conviction

Offence committed whilst on bail

Other aggravating factors include:

Location of the offence

Ongoing effect upon the victim and/or others

Failure to take adequate precautions to prevent dog escaping

Allowing person insufficiently experienced or trained, to be in charge of dog

Ill treatment or failure to ensure welfare needs of dog, where not charged separately

Dog known to be prohibited

Lack or loss of control of dog due to the influence of alcohol or drugs

Offence committed against those working in the public sector or providing a service to the public

Established evidence of community impact

Failure to comply with current court orders

Offence committed whilst on licence

Factors reducing seriousness or reflecting personal mitigation

No previous convictions or no relevant/recent convictions

Isolated incident

No previous complaints against, or incidents involving, the dog

Remorse

Good character and/or exemplary conduct

Evidence of responsible ownership

Determination and/or demonstration of steps taken to address addiction or offending behaviour

Serious medical conditions requiring urgent, intensive or long-term treatment

Age and/or lack of maturity where it affects the responsibility of the offender

Mental disorder or learning disability, where not linked to the commission of the offence

Sole or primary carer for dependent relatives

Step Three
Consider any factors which indicate a reduction, such as assistance to the prosecution

The court should take into account sections 73 and 74 of the Serious Organised Crime and Police Act 2005 (assistance by defendants: reduction or review of sentence) and any other rule of law by virtue of which an offender may receive a discounted sentence in consequence of assistance given (or offered) to the prosecutor or investigator.

Step Four
Reduction for guilty pleas

The court should take account of any potential reduction for a guilty plea in accordance with section 144 of the Criminal Justice Act 2003 and the *Guilty Plea* guideline.

Step Five
Compensation and ancillary orders

In all cases, the court should consider whether to make a compensation order and/or other ancillary orders.

Compensation order

The court should consider compensation orders in all cases where personal injury, loss or damage has resulted from the offence[1]. The court must give reasons if it decides not to award compensation in such cases.

Other ancillary orders available include:

Disqualification from having custody of a dog

The court **may** disqualify the offender from having custody of a dog[2]. The test the court should consider is whether the offender is a fit and proper person to have custody of a dog.

Destruction order/contingent destruction order

In any case where the offender is not the owner of the dog, the owner must be given an opportunity to be present and make representations to the court.

The court **may** make a destruction order[3]. Alternatively, it **may** make a contingent destruction order imposing certain available conditions[4]. A contingent destruction order should specify the measures to be taken by the owner for keeping the dog under proper control, which include:

*   muzzling;
*   keeping on a lead;
*   neutering in appropriate cases; and
*   excluding it from a specified place[5].

In reaching a decision, the court should consider the relevant circumstances which include:

*   the incident – what degree of harm was caused by the dog's behaviour?
*   past behaviour of the dog – is this an isolated incident or have there been previous warnings or incidents? and
*   owner's character – is the owner a fit and proper person to own this particular dog?

Where the court makes a destruction order, it **may** order the offender to pay what it determines to be the reasonable expenses of destroying the dog and of keeping it pending its destruction[6].

Step Six
Totality principle

If sentencing an offender for more than one offence, or where the offender is already serving a sentence, consider whether the total sentence is just and proportionate to the offending behaviour.

Step Seven
Reasons

Section 174 of the Criminal Justice Act 2003 imposes a duty to give reasons for, and explain the effect of, the sentence.

Step Eight
Consideration for remand time

(Now obligatory.)

Possession of a prohibited dog
Dangerous Dogs Act 1991 (section 1(3))

Breeding, selling, exchanging or advertising a prohibited dog
Dangerous Dogs Act 1991 (section 1(2))

Triable only summarily

Maximum: 26 weeks' custody

Offence range: Discharge – 26 weeks' custody

Step One
Determining the offence category

The court should determine the offence category using the table below.

Category 1	Greater harm **and** higher culpability
Category 2	Greater harm **or** higher culpability
Category 3	**Neither** greater harm **nor** higher culpability

The court should determine culpability and harm caused or intended, by reference **only** to the factors below, which comprise the principal factual elements of the offence. Where an offence does not fall squarely into a category, individual factors may require a degree of weighting before making an overall assessment and determining the appropriate offence category.

Factors indicating greater harm

Injury to person

Injury to another animal(s)

Factors indicating higher culpability

Possessing a dog known to be prohibited

Breeding from a dog known to be prohibited

Selling, exchanging or advertising a dog known to be prohibited

Offence committed for gain

Dog used to threaten or intimidate

Permitting fighting

Training and/or possession of paraphernalia for dog fighting

Step Two
Starting point and category range

Having determined the category, the court should use the corresponding starting points to reach a sentence within the category range below. The starting point applies to all offenders irrespective of plea or previous convictions. A case of particular gravity, reflected by multiple features of culpability or harm in step 1, could merit upward adjustment from the starting point before further adjustment for aggravating or mitigating features, set out on the next page.

Offence Category	Starting Point *(Applicable to all offenders)*	Category Range *(Applicable to all offenders)*
Category 1	Medium level community order	Band C fine – 26 weeks' custody*
Category 2	Band C fine	Band A fine – Medium level community order
Category 3	Band A fine	Discharge – Band B fine

* Imprisonment is not available if the provisions of s 1(7) of the Dangerous Dogs Act 1991 apply

The table below contains a **non-exhaustive** list of additional factual elements providing the context of the offence and factors relating to the offender. Identify whether any combination of these, or other relevant factors, should result in an upward or downward adjustment from the starting point. In some cases, having considered these factors, it may be appropriate to move outside the identified category range.

When sentencing **category 1** offences, the court should also consider the custody threshold as follows:

• has the custody threshold been passed?
• if so, is it unavoidable that a custodial sentence be imposed?
• if so, can that sentence be suspended?

When sentencing **category 1 or 2** offences, the court should also consider the community order threshold as follows:

• has the community order threshold been passed?

Factors increasing seriousness

Statutory aggravating factors:

Previous convictions, having regard to a) the nature of the offence to which the conviction relates and its relevance to the current offence; and b) the time that has elapsed since the conviction

Offence committed whilst on bail

Other aggravating factors include:

Presence of children or others who are vulnerable because of personal circumstances

Ill treatment or failure to ensure welfare needs of dog, where not charged separately

Established evidence of community impact

Failure to comply with current court orders

Offence committed whilst on licence

Factors reducing seriousness or reflecting personal mitigation

No previous convictions **or** no relevant/recent convictions

Unaware that dog was prohibited type despite reasonable efforts to identify type

Evidence of safety or control measures having been taken by owner

Prosecution results from owner notification

Remorse

Good character and/or exemplary conduct

Evidence of responsible ownership

Determination and/or demonstration of steps taken to address addiction or offending behaviour

Serious medical conditions requiring urgent, intensive or long-term treatment

Age and/or lack of maturity where it affects the responsibility of the offender

Lapse of time since the offence where this is not the fault of the offender

Mental disorder or learning disability

Sole or primary carer for dependent relatives

Step Three
Consider any factors which indicate a reduction, such as assistance to the prosecution

The court should take into account sections 73 and 74 of the Serious Organised Crime and Police Act 2005 (assistance by defendants: reduction or review of sentence) and any other rule of law by virtue of which an offender may receive a discounted sentence in consequence of assistance given (or offered) to the prosecutor or investigator.

Step Four
Reduction for guilty pleas

The court should take account of any potential reduction for a guilty plea in accordance with section 144 of the Criminal Justice Act 2003 and the *Guilty Plea* guideline.

Step Five
Ancillary orders

In all cases, the court should consider whether to make any ancillary orders.

Ancillary orders available include:

Disqualification from having custody of a dog

The court **may** disqualify the offender from having custody of a dog[7]. The test the court should consider is whether the offender is a fit and proper person to have custody of a dog.

Destruction order/contingent destruction order

The court **shall** make a destruction order unless the court is satisfied that the dog would not constitute a danger to public safety[8].

In reaching a decision, the court should consider the relevant circumstances which include:

- danger to the public – what is the potential risk of harm posed by the dog?
- behaviour of the dog – have there been any warnings or incidents involving the dog? and
- owner's character – is the owner a fit and proper person to own this particular dog?

If the court does not make a destruction order, the court **shall** make a contingent destruction order providing that unless the dog is exempted from the prohibition within two months it shall be destroyed[9].Statutory procedures and conditions automatically apply to exempted dogs and no other conditions can be imposed[10].Where the offender is the owner of the dog, it would not normally be appropriate to make a contingent destruction order in conjunction with a disqualification order.

Furthermore, the court **must not** transfer ownership of the dog to another[11].

Where the court makes a destruction order, it **may** order the offender to pay what it determines to be the reasonable expenses of destroying the dog and of keeping it pending its destruction[12].

Step Six
Totality principle

If sentencing an offender for more than one offence, or where the offender is already serving a sentence, consider whether the total sentence is just and proportionate to the offending behaviour.

Step Seven
Reasons

Section 174 of the Criminal Justice Act 2003 imposes a duty to give reasons for, and explain the effect of, the sentence.

Step Eight
Consideration for remand time

(Now obligatory.)

---

1   Section 130 Powers of Criminal Courts (Sentencing) Act 2000.
2   Section 4(1)(b) of the Dangerous Dogs Act 1991.
3   Section 4(1)(a) of the Dangerous Dogs Act 1991.
4   Section 4A(4) of the Dangerous Dogs Act 1991.
5   Section 4A(5) of the Dangerous Dogs Act 1991.
6   Section 4(4)(b) of the Dangerous Dogs Act 1991.
7   Section 4(1)(b) of the Dangerous Dogs Act 1991.
8   Section4(1)(a) of the Dangerous Dogs Act 1991.
9   Section 4A(1) of the Dangerous Dogs Act 1991.
10   The Dangerous Dogs Compensation and Exemption Schemes Order 1991 SI 1991/1744 (as amended by The Dangerous Dogs Compensa-

tion and Exemption Schemes (Amendment) Order 1991, SI 1991/2297).

[11] Section 1(2)(b) of the Dangerous Dogs Act 1991.

[12] Section 4(4)(b) of the Dangerous Dogs Act 1991.

A[72.9] Available sentences. See Table B at B[4.2]; for aggravated offences see Table A at B[4.1]. In *R v Cox* (2004) Times, 20 February, CA a sentence of 3 months was upheld for an aggravated offence where a pack of dogs attacked a child resulting in hospitalisation.

A[72.10]–[72.14] Order for destruction. Before making a destruction order the court must consider ss 4(1A)(a), 4A(4) and 4A(5) – see A[72.15] below. Where a person is convicted of an offence under s 3(1) the court may order the destruction of the dog and must do so in the case of an aggravated offence, unless the court is satisfied the dog does not constitute a danger to public safety. In deciding whether or not a dog would constitute a danger to public safety, the court must consider the dog's temperament and past behaviour, and whether the owner or the person for the time being in charge of the dog, is a fit and proper person to be in charge of the dog; the court may also consider any other relevant circumstances: Dangerous Dogs Act 1991, s 4(1B). A court should not make an order for destruction without giving the dog's owner an opportunity to be heard (*R v Ealing Magistrates' Court, ex p Fanneran* (1995) 160 JP 409, 8 Admin LR 351). Any person having custody of the dog may be required to deliver it up to a person appointed by the court to undertake its destruction which will be suspended pending the determination of any appeal. Note that disobedience of a court order to deliver up for destruction is a criminal offence. The maximum penalty under these provisions is a level 5 fine.

A[72.15] Order for contingent destruction. Section 4(1A) of the Dangerous Dogs Act 1991 allows for a contingent destruction order even if a mandatory or discretionary order is appropriate. For example, the court may order that the dog will be destroyed unless the owner keeps it under proper control, and that it was to be muzzled and on a lead at all times in any public place. The legal principles were outlined in *R v Flack* [2008] EWCA Crim 204, [2008] 2 Cr App Rep (S) 395; *R v Grant David Robert Davies* [2010] EWCA Crim 1923, 174 CL&J 574.

The Crown Court had no power to impose conditions when it made contingent destruction orders under the Dangerous Dogs Act 1991, s 4A in relation to two pit bull terriers, the possession of which was prohibited under s 1 of the Act: *R (on the application of Sandhu) v Isleworth Crown Court* [2012] EWHC 1658 (Admin), 176 JP 537, 176 CL&J 339.

A[72.16] Additional powers. A person convicted under s 3(1) may be ordered to keep the dog under proper control or failing that the dog shall be destroyed. The court may also specify measures for keeping the dog under proper control such as muzzling, keeping on a lead or excluding the dog from entering specific places. The court may also order a male dog to be neutered.

A[72.17] Disqualification. Whether or not there is an order for destruction of the dog the court may disqualify the person convicted (ie not necessarily the owner) for having custody of a dog for a period specified in the order. A person disqualified for having custody of a dog may apply to the court after one year to terminate the disqualification having regard to his character, conduct and any other circumstances (*R v Holland* [2002]

EWCA Crim 1585, [2002] All ER (D) 113 (Jun), CA). Where an application is refused, no further application can be considered for a further year. Costs may be awarded.

Note there is no power to make a disqualification order under s 4(1)(b) that would allow for a single dog to be kept, nor is there power to attach other conditions (*R v Haynes* [2004] EWCA Crim 390, (2004) Times, 27 February, [2004] All ER (D) 235 (Mar), CA).

A[72.18] Having custody of a dog in contravention of a disqualification is an offence, maximum penalty a fine on level 5.

A[72.19] **Right to appeal to the Crown Court.** A person convicted of an offence has an automatic right to appeal to the Crown Court against his conviction, sentence or any order made. In addition, where an order has been made for the destruction of a dog owned by a person other than the offender, then, unless the order was one which the court was required to make the owner may appeal to the Crown Court against the destruction order.

Other offences

A[72.20] The Dangerous Dogs Act 1991 creates a number of offences in connection with 'fighting dogs' which are defined as pit bull terriers, Japanese Tosas and other dogs specified by the Secretary of State. It is unlawful to breed, sell, exchange, advertise for sale or to make a gift of such a dog. Accordingly, these dogs will decline in numbers with the effluxion of time. Those persons who already possess such dogs must obtain a certificate of exemption and comply with the stringent conditions attached thereto. It is an offence for an owner to have such a dog which is not registered, or to abandon it. The most common charge is for the owner or person for the time being in charge of such a dog to allow it to stray or to be in a public place without being muzzled and kept on a lead: maximum penalty 6 months' imprisonment and a level 5 fine – triable only by magistrates. It should be noted that a dog 'of the type known as a pit bull terrier' is not to be taken as being synonymous with the definition breed (*R v Crown Court at Knightsbridge, ex p Dunne* [1993] 4 All ER 491, [1994] 1 WLR 296). The provisions relating to destruction and disqualification apply as for 'aggravated offences' under s 3 of the 1991 Act. Except that where no destruction order is made in the case of a designated dog, the court must order that unless a certificate of exemption is obtained for the dog within two months of the date of the order the dog shall be destroyed. If a certificate is not obtained the court has a discretion to extend the two-month period.

Control or destruction order

(Dogs Act 1871, as amended)

A[72.21] As an alternative to prosecution under the Dangerous Dogs Act 1991 the pre-existing civil remedy under the Dogs Act 1871 is still available and is not confined to public places nor where the dog has injured a person, but is determined by where the dog resides (*R (on the application of Shufflebottom) v Chief Constable of Greater Manchester Police* [2003]

EWHC 246 (Admin), 167 JP 153). The introduction of a national jurisdiction under the Courts Act 2003 means that the case could be heard at any venue within England and Wales. In practice, jurisdiction will usually be exercised by reference to residence or where the cause of action arose.

Legal notes and definitions

A[72.22] Application for dangerous dog to be kept under control or destroyed.

Application may be made to a magistrates' court for an order that the dog be destroyed or kept under proper control by the owner. The magistrates may in their discretion make a destruction order without the option of a control order. A dog is not allowed his 'one bite' although in most cases a control order is sufficient for the first transgression. Costs can be awarded by the court to the successful party.

A[72.23] The proceedings must be in the form of a **complaint** and not as an **information** for an offence.

A[72.24] The court must be satisfied (a) that the dog *is* dangerous and (b) that it *is* not kept under proper control. The dog need not be dangerous to mankind. It is sufficient if it is proved that the dog injured cattle or chased sheep. It need not be proved that the owner knew his dog was dangerous. Moreover the dog need not be dangerous by temperament if he is shown to have been dangerous on one occasion. Evidence of the temperament of the animal, however, is admissible if it shows the likelihood of its being dangerous on a particular occasion. The correct approach is for the justices to ask themselves whether on the facts the behaviour of the dog showed that it had a dangerous disposition (*Briscoe v Shattock* [1999] 1 WLR 432, 163 JP 201, [1999] Crim LR 396).

A[72.25]–[72.30] Change of ownership. If the owner of the dog establishes in court that he is no longer the owner of the dog but has made a bona fide transfer of the dog to some other person no order can be made against him for the dog's destruction or its proper control; but the order can be made against the new owner provided that a complaint is made against the new owner within six months from the date of the cause of the complaint.

A[72.31] Procedure at the hearing. If the **complaint** is accompanied by an **information** alleging some additional offence (such as worrying livestock) then the **information** should be dealt with first and the **complaint** afterwards. The legal adviser should be consulted in such cases.

A[72.32] Control order. The court may specify the measures to be taken for keeping the dog under proper control, whether by muzzling, keeping on a lead, excluding it from specified places, or otherwise. Where the dog is male, the court may order it to be neutered if thereby it would be less dangerous.

A[72.33] Destruction order. Any person having custody of the dog may be required to deliver it up to a person appointed by the court to undertake its destruction which will be suspended pending the determination of any appeal.

A[72.34] Disqualification. A court which makes a destruction order may disqualify the owner for having custody of a dog for a period specified in the order. Disqualification may also be imposed on conviction of an offence of failure to comply with a court order (either to keep the dog under proper control or deliver it up for destruction), maximum penalty a fine on level 3.

A[72.35] A person disqualified for having custody of a dog may apply to the court after one year to terminate the disqualification having regard to his character, conduct and any other circumstances. Where an application is refused, no further application can be considered for a further year. Costs may be awarded.

A[72.36] Disobedience of a court order for control or to deliver up for destruction is a criminal offence, maximum penalty a fine on level 3.

A[72.37] Having custody of a dog in contravention of a disqualification is an offence, maximum penalty a fine on level 5.

A[72.38] Right of appeal to the Crown Court. If an order is made for control or destruction, the owner can appeal to the Crown Court. Appeal against conviction and sentence for the criminal offences lie to the Crown Court in the normal way.

A[73]

Dog worrying livestock

Charge

A[73.1] Being the owner of (or being in charge of) a dog worrying livestock namely [. . . . .] on agricultural land situated at [. . . . .]

Dogs (Protection of Livestock) Act 1953, s 1, as amended

Maximum penalty – Fine level 3.

Legal notes and definitions

A[73.2] A dog's owner or the person in charge of a dog commits an offence if the dog worries livestock on agricultural land. A prosecution for livestock worrying can only be brought by or with the consent of the chief officer of the police, or by the occupier of the agricultural land or the owner of the livestock.

A[73.3] Worrying livestock means:

(a) attacking livestock; or
(b) chasing livestock in such a way as may reasonably be expected to cause injury or suffering to the livestock, or abortion or loss or diminution in their produce; or
(c) being at large in a field where there are sheep except a dog owned by or in the charge of the occupier or the owner of the sheep or a person authorised by them or a police dog, guide-dog, trained sheep dog, working gun dog or pack of hounds.

Livestock is extensively defined by s 3 of the Act and means cattle, sheep, goats, swine, horses or poultry.

A[73.4] Possible lines of defence

(a) That the livestock were trespassing and the dog in question was owned by or in the charge of the occupier of the land on which the livestock were trespassing or the dog was in the charge of a person authorised by the occupier of the land. This defence is not available if the dog was deliberately set on the livestock.
(b) The owner of the dog is not liable if at the time of the attack on the livestock the dog was in the custody of a person whom the owner considered to be a fit and proper person to have charge of the dog.
(c) That the worrying took place on land that was not agricultural land. A street or a private garden is not therefore agricultural land and some moors and heaths are excluded from the definitions of agricultural land.
(d) That the Ministry of Agriculture, Fisheries and Food has directed that this offence shall not apply to the land in question.

A[73.5] No SC guideline. For structure of the sentencing decision see B[3.6].

A[73.6] Fines. See B[33.16].

A[73.7] Compensation. This may be ordered up to a maximum of £5,000 on each charge, eg for the loss of livestock, either as part of a wider sentence or by itself as a substantive penalty. If the offender's means are limited and a monetary penalty is appropriate, preference must be given to ordering compensation instead of a fine.

Excessive noise

(Prosecution)

A[74.1] Problems caused by noise amounting to a nuisance, eg caused by noisy neighbours, are dealt with by proceedings for a nuisance order, see A[84].

Causing a noise or disturbance on National Health Service premises is now an offence contrary to s 119 of the Criminal Justice and Immigration Act 2008. By s 120 a constable or 'authorised person' may remove persons causing a noise or disturbance from NHS premises.

Maximum penalty – Fine level 3.

Night time charge

A[74.2] Operating a loudspeaker in a street between 9 pm and 8 am

Control of Pollution Act 1974, s 62

Maximum penalty – Fine level 5 (and a further fine not exceeding £50 for each day on which the offence continues after the conviction). The notes which follow only apply to proceedings brought under the Control of Pollution Act 1974, s 62 and magistrates should confirm with their legal adviser that the proceedings are in fact being brought under that Act.

Legal notes and definitions

A[74.3] In certain circumstances loudspeakers are exempt from prosecutions as follows:

(a)   those used by the police, fire, ambulance, water authority or local authority;

(b)   those used for communicating with a vessel to direct it or any other vessel;

(c)   those forming part of the public telephone system;

(d)   those fitted to vehicles solely for the entertainment of persons in the vehicle or for communicating with persons in the vehicle or for giving warning to other vehicles if the loudspeaker forms part of the vehicle's horns or warning system but all such loudspeakers fitted to vehicles must not operate so loudly that they give reasonable cause for annoyance to persons in the vicinity or the exemption is forfeited;

(e)   transport undertakings may use loudspeakers off the highways to make announcements to passengers, prospective passengers and staff;

(f)   a travelling showman may use a loudspeaker on his fairground;

(g)   loudspeakers may be used in an emergency.

Except for the above exemptions there is a complete ban on the use of loudspeakers in a street between 9 pm and 8 am.

A[74.4] Loudspeaker. Includes a megaphone and any other device for amplifying sound.

A[74.5] Street. Means any highway, road, footway, square or court which is for the time being open to the public.

Day time charge

A[74.6] Operating a loudspeaker in a street between 8 am and 9 pm for the purpose of advertising an entertainment, a trade or a business

Control of Pollution Act 1974, s 62

Maximum penalty – Fine level 5 (and a further fine not exceeding £50 for each day on which the offence continues after the conviction).

Legal notes and definitions

A[74.7] See under this heading at A[74.3].

A[74.8] Defences. It is permissible to use a loudspeaker in a street between the hours of 8 am and 9 pm except as outlined above for advertising. However, there is an exception to this ban on advertising in the following circumstances. Where the loudspeaker is:

(a) fixed to a vehicle conveying a perishable commodity for human consumption; and
(b) is used solely to inform the public (otherwise than by words) that the commodity is on sale from the vehicle; and
(c) is so operated as not to give reasonable cause for annoyance to persons in the vicinity,

it may be operated between the hours of noon and 7 pm on the same day. This is the provision, for example, under which ice cream vans are allowed to use chimes to advertise their wares.

Sentencing

A[74.9] No SC Guideline.

Noise amounting to a statutory nuisance. If a noise is persistent and seriously affects persons in an area then the local authority may serve a noise abatement notice or the person affected can lay a complaint alleging that the noise or vibration amounts to a statutory nuisance. See A[84].

Offences relating to unfair or prohibited commercial practices

Offences

A[75.1] (From 26/5/08 s 1 of the Trade Description Act 1968 offences were repealed and replaced by a series of new offences contrary to the Consumer Protection from Unfair Trading Regulations 2008.)

Offence 1: Commercial practice contrary to professional diligence

(1) A trader is guilty of an offence if –

(a)   he knowingly or recklessly engages in a commercial practice which contravenes the requirements of professional diligence under regulation 3 (3) (a); and

(b)   the practice materially distorts or is likely to materially distort the commercial behaviour of the average consumer with regard to the product under regulation 3 (3) (b).

Regulation 8 of the Consumer Protection from Unfair Trading Regulations 2008

Offence 2: Commercial practice which is misleading

A trader is guilty of an offence if he engages in a commercial practice which is a misleading action under regulation 5 otherwise than by reason of the commercial practice satisfying the condition in regulation 5 (3) (b).

Regulation 9 of the Consumer Protection from Unfair Trading Regulations 2008

Offence 3: Commercial practice – misleading omission

A trader is guilty of an offence if he engages in a commercial practice which is a misleading omission under regulation 6.

Regulation 10 of the Consumer Protection from Unfair Trading Regulations 2008

Offence 4: Commercial practice – aggressive practice

A trader is guilty of an offence if he engages in commercial practice which is aggressive under regulation 17.

Regulation 11 of the Consumer Protection from Unfair Trading Regulations 2008

Offence 5: Banned commercial practices – contravenes schedule 1 (except paragraphs 11 and 28)

A trader is guilty of an offence if he engages in a commercial practice set out in any of the paragraphs 1 to 10, 12 to 27 and 29 to 31 of Schedule 1.

Regulation 12 of the Consumer Protection from Unfair Trading Regulations 2008

Maximum penalty in each case – Fine statutory maximum (currently £5,000 per offence). Triable either way.

Crown Court – 2 years' imprisonment and unlimited fine.

Mode of trial

A[75.2] See general notes at D[4].

What the justices must consider when determining mode of trial is whether or not the custody threshold is crossed; the test is not whether a custodial sentence is 'highly likely' but whether, on the facts, it should be open to the sentencing court to impose a custodial sentence: *Price v Cheshire East Borough Council* [2012] EWHC 2927 (Admin), (2012) 176 JP 697.

Legal notes and definitions

A[75.3] General. This is a detailed piece of legislation. A detailed three-part commentary to the 2008 regulations can be found at (2008) 172 JPN 516, 536 and 560 respectively.

Time limits for prosecution. These are provided for by regulation 14 and are similar to the repealed Trade Descriptions Act 1968.

Offences committed by bodies of persons. See regulation 15

A[75.4] Mens rea – regulation 8. Creates the only one of the five offence provisions which includes an element of mens rea. Regulation 8(2) defines the term "recklessly". It is submitted that it will suffice if the prosecution can show that the defendant trader did not have regard to the truth or falsity of his statement even though it cannot be shown that he was deliberately closing his eyes to the truth, or that he had any kind of dishonest mind.

A[75.5] Defences. Offence due to the act or default of another person – regulation 16 (applies to prosecutions under regulations 9–12).

Due diligence offence – regulation 17 (applies to prosecutions under regulations 9–12).

Innocent publication of advertisement – regulation 18 (applies to prosecutions under regulations 9–12).

A[75.6]–[75.7] Definitions. Commercial practice: "Any act, omission, course of conduct, representation or commercial communication (including advertising and marketing), by a trader, which is directly connected with the promotion, sale or supply of a product to or from consumers, whether occurring before, during or after a commercial transaction (if any) in relation to a product".

Consumer: "Any individual who in relation to a commercial practice is acting for purposes which are outside his business".

Product: "Any goods or service and includes immovable property, rights and obligations".

Transactional decision: "Any decision taken by a consumer, whether it is to act or to refrain from acting, concerning (a) whether, how and on what terms to purchase, make payment in whole or in part for, retain or dispose of a product; or (b) whether, how and on what terms to exercise a contractual right in relation to a product".

Trader: "Any person who in relation to a commercial practice is acting for purposes relating to his business (including acting in the name of or on behalf of a trader)".

Sentencing

A[75.8] Compensation. This may be ordered up to £5,000 either as part of a wider sentence or by itself as a substantive penalty. If the offender's means are limited and a monetary penalty is appropriate, preference must be given to ordering compensation instead of a fine.

A[75.9] Crown Court. Prison is appropriate only where there has been a deliberate dishonesty. Prison has been upheld in cases involving dishonest dealers eg traders who deliberately "clock" motor vehicles.

A[75.10] Fines. See B[33].

Firearm (purchasing etc without certificate)

Charge

A[76.1] Purchasing or acquiring or possessing a firearm (or ammunition) without certificate

Firearms Act 1968, s 1

For shotguns see A[71].

Maximum penalty – Fine level 5 and 6 months and forfeiture. Triable either way.

Crown Court – 5 years' imprisonment and unlimited fine.

Mode of trial

A[76.2] See general notes at D[4].

Legal notes and definitions

A[76.3] **Purchasing, acquiring and wrongly possessing.** These are three separate offences and the charge should only include one of these allegations. Possession can include where a person has a firearm in his custody for another for the purpose of cleaning it, and is not restricted to physical possession but includes proprietary control (*R v Pawlicki and Swindells* [1992] 3 All ER 902, [1992] 1 WLR 827, CA). More than one person can control a firearm at the same time (*R v Hall-Chung* [2002] EWCA Crim 3088, [2003] All ER (D) 113 (Feb)). 'Acquire' means hire, accept as a gift or borrow: Firearms Act 1968, s 58(4).

A[76.4] **Excessive ammunition.** It is also an offence to have in one's possession more ammunition than the quantity authorised by a firearms certificate.

A[76.5] **Certificate.** This is granted by the police. It may specify conditions. Failure to observe such conditions is an offence. The certificate may bear a photograph of the holder and, unless revoked or cancelled, remains in force for the period specified which may be up to three years.

A[76.6] **Firearm.** This is defined by s 57(1) of the Firearms Act 1968 as:

(1)   (1)In this Act, the expression 'firearm' means a lethal barrelled weapon of any description from which any shot, bullet or other missile can be discharged and includes–

     (a)   any prohibited weapon, whether it is such a lethal weapon as aforesaid or not; and

     (b)   any component part of such a lethal or prohibited weapon; and

     (c)   any accessory to any such weapon designed or adapted to diminish the noise or flash caused by firing the weapon'.

'Lethal weapon'. This includes a weapon not designed to kill or inflict injury but capable of doing so if misused: *Read v Donovan* [1947] KB 326, [1947] 1 All ER 37, 111 JP 46 (signal pistol); *Moore v Gooderham* [1960] 3 All ER 575, 124 JP 513 (air gun); *R v Thorpe* [1987] 2 All ER 108, [1987] 1 WLR 383 (revolver powered by compressed carbon dioxide); *R v Singh* [1989] Crim LR 724 (flare launcher).

An imitation firearm which is so constructed or adapted as to be readily convertible into a firearm is to be treated as a firearm even though it has not been so converted. However, in *R v Bewley* [2012] EWCA Crim 1457, [2013] 1 All ER 1, [2013] 1 WLR 137 the weapon in question was a starting pistol, which was originally designed to fire blank cartridges. A 2cm hole had been drilled into the solid barrel and the top of the hammer had been broken off. A senior forensic scientist was able to fire it by placing it in a vice, inserting a specially selected lead pellet and using a mallet and punch to strike the firing pin. The judge ruled that the pistol was a lethal-barrelled weapon from which a missile '(could) be discharged', but the Court of Appeal quashed the conviction. Although the Firearms Act 1982 had not amended the Firearms Act 1968, the two had to be construed as creating a single code. It was the clear legislative intention of the 1982 Act to exclude from the 1968 Act imitation firearms which could only be readily convertible into firearms by equipment or tools not in common use. The capacity to discharge a missile by conversion (the need for extraneous tools in the present case amounted to a conversion) was now restricted to only imitation weapons which could be converted without any special skill or equipment or tools not in common use. On the facts this weapon did not fall within s 57(1). Nor was it a component part of 'such a lethal or prohibited weapon' within s 57(1)(b). If a starting pistol did not fall within the definition of firearm in s 57(1) no part of it could do so.

A[76.7] Excepted firearms under s 1 apply to every firearm except:

(a)   a shot gun within the meaning of the Act, that is to say a smooth-bore gun (not being an air gun) which–
    (i)   has a barrel not less than 24 inches in length and does not have any barrel with a bore exceeding 2 inches in diameter;
    (ii)   either has no magazine or has a non-detachable magazine incapable of holding more than two cartridges; and
    (iii)   is not a revolver gun; and
(b)   an air weapon (that is to say, an air rifle, air gun or air pistol which does not fall within s 5(1) and which is not of a type declared by rules made by the Secretary of State under s 53 of this Act to be specially dangerous).

A gun which has been adapted to have such a magazine as is mentioned in (a)(ii) above shall not be regarded as falling within that provision unless the magazine bears a mark approved by the Secretary of State for denoting that fact and that mark has been made, and the adaptation has been certified in writing as having been carried out in a manner approved by him, either by one of the two companies mentioned in s 58(1) of the Act or by such other person as may be approved by him for that purpose.

Shot guns and air weapons may be 'firearms', however, for the purpose of other offences under the Act: see A[77.8], below.

A[76.8]   Ammunition. Means ammunition for any firearm as defined above. It also means grenades, bombs and other similar missiles. It also includes ammunition containing or adapted to contain any noxious liquid, gas or other noxious thing.

Section 1(4), however, makes the following exceptions:

(a)   cartridges containing five or more shot, none of which exceeds 36 inch in diameter;

(b)   ammunition for an air gun, air rifle or air pistol; and

(c)   blank cartridges not more than one inch in diameter measured immediately in front of the rim or cannelure of the base of the cartridge.

A[A76.8A] **Mental element.** Section 1 is to be construed strictly and proof of mens rea is unnecessary: *R v Howells* [1977] QB 614, [1977] 3 All ER 417, 141 JP 641. It is immaterial that the accused did not know the nature of the article in his possession: *R v Hussain* [1981] 2 All ER 287, [1981] 1 WLR 416; *R v Waller* [1991] Crim LR 381, CA approved in *R v Vann and Davis* [1996] Crim LR 52, CA, or that possession of a container was for a matter of minutes without opportunity to discover that it contained a firearm: *R v Steele* [1993] Crim LR 298, CA.

A[76.9] **Exemptions.** If a defence is raised that a weapon or ammunition is not covered by the Act the legal adviser should be consulted.

A[76.10]–[76.15] Certain persons and organisations are exempted from having to hold firearms certificates such as the following:

(a)   A registered dealer and his staff, an auctioneer, carrier or warehouseman in the course of his business, a licensed slaughterer in respect of his slaughtering instruments, ships and aircraft (Firearms Act 1968, ss 8–10 and 13).

(b)   A person may carry a firearm or ammunition for another person who does hold a firearms certificate if he is acting under that other person's instructions and if that other person is to use the firearm or ammunition for sporting purposes only. Sporting purposes does not include the shooting of rats (Firearms Act 1968, s 11(1)). **NB:** If the person carrying the firearm etc is under 18 years, the other person must be 18 years or over.

(c)   Members of rifle clubs, miniature rifle clubs and cadet corps in possession of Home Office approval do not require certificates for club or corps activities such as drilling or target practice (Firearms Act 1968, s 11(3) and Firearms (Amendment) Act 1988, s 15).

(d)   A certificate is not necessary for weapons at a miniature rifle range if the miniature rifles do not exceed 0.23 calibre or if the weapons are air guns, air rifles or air pistols which have not been declared as dangerous by the Home Office (Firearms Act 1968, s 11(4)).

(e)   Persons participating in a theatrical performance or rehearsal or in producing a film may have a firearm without a certificate (Firearms Act 1968, s 12).

(f)   Starters aged 18 years or over at athletic meetings may have a firearm without a certificate (different rules for persons aged under 18 years apply for blank-firing weapons): Firearms Act 1968, s 11(2).

(g)   A person who has obtained a permit from the police may have a firearm and ammunition, as authorised by that permit without holding a firearms certificate. The permit will usually be for short periods such as one month to allow, for example, the next of kin of the holder of a firearms certificate time to sell the weapons and ammunition after the holder has died (Firearms Act 1968, s 7).

(h)   A person may borrow a shotgun or, if under 18 years, a rifle from the occupier of private premises (which includes land) and use it on those premises in the occupier's presence (Firearms Act 1968, s 11(5) and Firearms (Amendment) Act 1988, s 16).

(i)   A person visiting Great Britain may have in his possession a firearm or shotgun without a certificate where he has been granted a visitor's permit. Such permits are granted by the police and may continue in force for up to 12 months (Firearms (Amendment) Act 1988, s 17).

(j)   A person temporarily in Great Britain purchasing weapons for export (Firearms (Amendment) Act 1988, s 18).

(k)   Museums granted a licence by the Secretary of State (Schedule to the Firearms (Amendment) Act 1988, para.1).

A[76.16] Degree of proof. A defendant wishing to establish one of the above exemptions does not have to satisfy the court beyond reasonable doubt; he need only satisfy the court that on the balance of probabilities his defence is true. Having regard to the legitimate aims of the above legislation, the shifting of the legal burden to the accused is necessary and proportionate in ECHR terms.

A[76.17] Antique firearms. The legislation does not apply to an antique firearm sold, transferred, purchased, acquired or possessed as a curiosity or ornament (Firearms Act 1968, s 58(2)). See *Bennett v Brown* (1980) 71 Cr App Rep 109.

Sentencing

A[76.18] No SC guideline.

Structure of the sentencing decision. See B[3.6].

Should the case be committed for sentence? (*R v Gent* [2002] EWCA Crim 943 [2002] All ER (D) 46 (Apr)) 2 years' imprisonment for possession of a sawn-off shotgun.

A[76.19] Available sentences. See Table A at B[4.1].

R v Charles [2004] EWCA Crim 1977, [2005] 1 Cr App Rep (S) 253 – 5 years when coupled with a siege and threats to the police.

A[76.20] Custodial sentence. See B[2]. See *R v Clarke* [1997] 1 Cr App Rep (S) 323, CA on the use of imprisonment.

A[76.21] Community sentence. See B[3].

A[76.22] Fines. See B[33].

A[76.23] Forfeiture. The court can order the firearm and ammunition to be forfeited to the police or disposed of as it thinks fit.

A[76.24] The court can cancel any firearm or shotgun certificate held by the defendant.

Firearm (trespassing in a building and on land)

Charges

A[77.1] 1 Whilst having a firearm or imitation firearm with him, entering or being in any building or part of a building, as a trespasser and without reasonable excuse

Firearms Act 1968, s 20(1)

Maximum penalty –

Firearm: Fine level 5 and 6 months and forfeiture. Triable either way.

Air weapon or imitation firearm: Fine level 5 and 6 months and forfeiture. Triable only by magistrates.

Crown Court – 7 years' imprisonment and unlimited fine.

A[77.2] 2 Whilst having a firearm or imitation firearm with him entering or being on any land as a trespasser and without reasonable excuse

Firearms Act 1968, s 20(2)

Maximum penalty – Fine level 4 and 3 months and forfeiture.

Mode of trial

A[77.3] See general notes at D[4].

Legal notes and definitions

A[77.4] Trespasser. The court must be satisfied that the defendant was a trespasser which means that the defendant was personally within the domain of another person without his consent.

A[77.5] Land. The Act provides that 'land' includes 'land covered by water'.

A[77.6] With him. The prosecution must establish more than mere possession, namely, a close physical link and immediate control over the firearm, but not necessarily that he had been carrying it (*R v Kelt* [1977] 3 All ER 1099, [1977] 1 WLR 1365, CA). In the context of an offence under s 18 of the Act a defendant was said not to have a firearm with him when it was 2 or 3 miles away (*R v Bradish* [2004] EWCA Crim 1340, 148 Sol Jo LB 474, [2004] All ER (D) 40 (Apr), CA).

A[77.7] Reasonable excuse. The onus of establishing reasonable excuse for his presence, when a trespasser, in a building and in possession of a firearm rests on the defendant. He does not have to prove reasonable excuse beyond all reasonable doubt. He has only to prove that on the balance of probabilities he had reasonable excuse. For ECHR, see A[33.5] above.

A[77.8] Firearm. Means any lethal barrelled weapon of any description from which any shot, bullet or other missile can be discharged. A lethal weapon includes one capable of inflicting injury although not designed to do so, eg a signal pistol. An imitation firearm which is so constructed or adapted as to be readily converted into a firearm is to be treated as a firearm even though it has not been so converted. The Court of Appeal has ruled that a starting pistol which could be adapted to fire bullets if the barrel was drilled was a firearm. In this case the barrel was partly drilled: *R v Freeman* [1970] 2 All ER 413, [1970] 1 WLR 788. However, in *R v Bewley* [2012] EWCA Crim 1457, [2013] 1 All ER 1, [2013] 1 WLR 137 the weapon in question was a starting pistol, which was originally designed to fire blank cartridges. A 2cm hole had been drilled into the solid barrel and the top of the hammer had been broken off. A senior forensic scientist was able to fire it by placing it in a vice, inserting a specially selected lead pellet and using a mallet and punch to strike the firing pin. The judge ruled that the pistol was a lethal-barrelled weapon from which a missile '(could) be discharged', but the Court of Appeal quashed the conviction. Although the Firearms Act 1982 had not amended the Firearms Act 1968, the two had to be construed as creating a single code. It was the clear legislative intention of the 1982 Act to exclude from the 1968 Act imitation firearms which could only be readily convertible into firearms by equipment or tools not in common use. The capacity to discharge a missile by conversion (the need for extraneous tools in the present case amounted to a conversion) was now restricted to only imitation weapons which could be converted without any special skill or equipment or tools not in common use. On the facts this weapon did not fall within s 57(1). Nor was it a component part of 'such a lethal or prohibited weapon' within s 57(1)(b). If a starting pistol did not fall within the definition of firearm in s 57(1) no part of it could do so.

A[77.9] Shotguns and air weapons count as firearms for the purpose of this offence. An air weapon is an air rifle, air gun or air pistol of a type which has not been declared by the Home Office to be specially dangerous. Nevertheless, an air gun as a species of weapon is not, as a matter of law, a lethal weapon; the prosecution must prove that fact, either by expert evidence or by evidence of someone who has seen the gun fired and can indicate not only that it did work but what its observed effect was when it was fired: *Grace v DPP* (1988) 153 JP 491, DC. However, air rifles which had been tested and classified as in normal working order and capable of killing small vermin or of being used in target practice were held to have been properly found to be lethal barrelled weapons: *Castle v DPP* (1998) Times 3 April.

A[77.9A] Imitation firearm. An imitation firearm means anything which has the appearance of being a firearm (other than any weapon designed or adapted for the discharge of any noxious liquid, gas or other thing) whether or not it is capable of discharging any shot, bullet or other missile: s 57(4) of the Firearms Act 1968. The test is whether the thing looked like a firearm at the time when the accused had it for that purpose: *R v Morris and King* (1984) 149 JP 60, 79 Cr App Rep 104, CA. Two fingers inside the defendant's pocket cannot constitute possession of an imitation firearm under s 17(2) of the Act: *R v Bentham* [2005] UKHL 18, [2005] 2 All ER 65, HL.

Sentencing

A[77.10]–[77.15] No SC guideline but see A[33].

Structure of the sentencing decision. See B[3.6].

A[77.16] Available sentences. See Table A at B[4.1] (firearms) and Table B at B[4.2] (air weapons and trespass on land).

A[77.17] Forfeiture. The court can order the weapon and ammunition to be forfeited to the police or disposed of as the court thinks fit.

A[77.18] The court can also cancel any firearm or shotgun certificate held by the defendant.

A[78]

Forgery

Charge

A[78.1] 1 Unlawfully making a false instrument with the intention that he (or another) should use it to induce somebody to accept it as genuine, and, by reason of so accepting it to do, or not to do, some act to that person's or some other person's prejudice

Forgery and Counterfeiting Act 1981, s 1

A[78.2] 2 Unlawfully using a false instrument, which is and which he knows or believes to be false, with the intention of inducing somebody to accept it as genuine, as above

Forgery and Counterfeiting Act 1981, s 3

A[78.3] 3 Unlawfully using a copy of a false instrument, which is and which he knows or believes to be false, as above

Forgery and Counterfeiting Act 1981, s 4

Maximum penalty – Fine level 5 and 6 months. Triable either way.

Crown Court – 10 years' imprisonment and unlimited fine.

Mode of trial

A[78.4] Consider first the general guidelines at D[4]. In general, forgery offences should be tried summarily except for the presence of one or more of the following factors:

(a)   breach of trust by a person in a position of substantial authority or in whom a high degree of trust has been placed;
(b)   there has been a sophisticated hiding or disguising of the offence;
(c)   the offence has been committed by an organised gang;
(d)   the victim was particularly vulnerable;
(e)   there is unrecovered property of high value.

Legal notes and definitions

A[78.5] Instrument. Means any document whether of a formal or informal character, any stamp issued or sold by the Post Office, any Inland Revenue stamp and any disk, tape, soundtrack or other device on or in which information is recorded, or is stored by mechanical, electronic or other means.

A[78.6] The term 'false' is extensively defined in s 9 of the Forgery and Counterfeiting Act 1981. The essence of forgery is that the document must tell a lie about itself and not merely tell a lie. It was held in *R v*

Warneford and Gibbs [1994] Crim LR 753, CA that any 'lie in the document must relate to the actual circumstances of the making of the document (and) a lie about other facts, extraneous to the document, does not suffice'. However, the Court of Appeal in *A-G's Reference (No 1 of 2000)* [2001] 1 Cr App Rep 218, [2001] Crim LR 127, CA, while agreeing with the above remarks, regarded that case as coming to the wrong conclusion on the facts and held that a tachograph record sheet would be false for the purposes of s 9(1)(g) if it was a document which required, before it could be made or altered, that a set of circumstances should exist or should have existed and those circumstances did not or had not existed (the false circumstance was that the record was being made during a period when there wrongly purported to be a second driver who was driving).

Where a defendant had stolen a cheque, opened a building society account in a name similar to that of the payee, paid the cheque into it and subsequently withdrew money from the account by completing a withdrawal form in the name in which he had opened the account, it was held that as the withdrawal form purported to be signed by the person who had opened the account, and had in that respect been accurate, it had not told a lie about itself and the defendant had not been guilty of forgery by making a false instrument under s 9(1)(h): *R v More* [1987] 3 All ER 825, [1987] 1 WLR 1578.

A[78.7] Make. A person makes a false instrument if he alters it so as to make it false in any respect, whether or not it is false in some other respect apart from that alteration. There is no further element of dishonesty required.

A[78.8] Intention. In *R v Tobierre* [1986] 1 All ER 346, [1986] 1 WLR 125, CA for an offence under s 3, it was held that the prosecution must prove both that the accused intended to induce somebody to accept the forgery as genuine *and* intended that by so doing he should act, or not act, to that person's or some other person's prejudice. In some cases, the demonstrated existence of a claim of right at the time when the false document was used may negative an intent to cause another to act to his prejudice; but where, in relation to the submission of a false expenses invoice by beneficiaries of a trust fund to the trustee, the evidence showed both an intention to induce the trustees to accept the false invoice as genuine, and an intention to cause them by reason of so accepting it to authorise and execute a cheque, which in the circumstances it was not their duty to do, both elements of the mens rea were present: *A-G's Reference (No 1 of 2002)* [2002] EWCA Crim 1768, [2002] 3 All ER 840, [2003] 1 Cr App Rep 131, [2002] Crim LR 844.

A[78.9] Prejudice. An act or omission intended to be induced is to be regarded as being to a person's prejudice only if it is one which *will* result (and not merely which has the *potential* to result (*R v Garcia* (1987) 87 Cr App Rep 175, [1988] Crim LR 115, CA):

(a)   in his temporary or permanent loss of property;
(b)   in his being deprived of the opportunity to earn remuneration, or greater remuneration;
(c)   in his being deprived of an opportunity to gain a financial advantage otherwise than by way of remuneration; or would result in someone being given an opportunity;
(d)   to earn remuneration, or greater remuneration from him; or
(e)   to gain a financial advantage from him otherwise than by way of remuneration; or

(f)   would be the result of his having accepted a false instrument as genuine, or a copy of a false instrument as a copy of a genuine one, in connection with the performance of a duty.

An act which a person has an enforceable duty to do and an omission to do an act which a person is not entitled to do shall be disregarded for the purposes of the Forgery and Counterfeiting Act 1981, s 10(2). Where the defendant had submitted forged documents in support of an application for housing benefit, although the contents of the documents were true, the local authority did not have an enforceable duty to pay the benefit as he was required to provide the evidence required by the Housing Benefit (General) Regulations 1987: *R v Winston* [1998] 1 Cr App Rep 337, 162 JP 775, [1998] Crim LR 81, DC.

Sentencing

A[78.10] No SC guideline.

A[78.11]–[78.15] Structure of the sentencing decision. See B[3.6].

A[78.16] Available sentences. See Table A at B[4.1].

A[78.17] Compensation. This may be ordered up to £5,000 either as part of a wider sentence or by itself as a substantive penalty. If the offender's means are limited and a monetary penalty is appropriate, preference must be given to ordering compensation instead of a fine.

Found on enclosed premises

Charge

A[79.1] Being found in or upon any dwelling-house, warehouse, out-house, or in any enclosed yard, garden or area for an unlawful purpose

Vagrancy Act 1824, s 4

Maximum penalty – For a first offence fine level 3 or 3 months. For a subsequent offence the accused may sometimes be committed to the Crown Court as an incorrigible rogue for sentence.

**For an offence committed from a date to be appointed, the power to impose imprisonment will be repealed by the CJA 2003, Sch 25. In addition the power to commit the offender as an incorrigible rogue to the Crown Court will be repealed by the CJA 2003, Sch 37, Part 9.

Legal notes and definitions

A[79.2] Found. For an offence to be made out an individual had to be found, which meant that he had to be **seen** or **discovered**, with an unlawful purpose in mind at the time he was so found: *L v CPS* [2007] EWHC1843 (Admin).

A[79.3] Enclosed. The yard may still rate as being enclosed even if there is access through spaces in surrounding buildings, an archway, open gate, etc but does not include a room within a building (*Talbot v DPP* [2000] 1 WLR 1102, 164 JP 169, sub nom Talbot v Oxford City Magistrates' Court [2000] 2 Cr App Rep 60).

A[79.4] Yard. Would not include a very large area, such as a shipyard or railway sidings, the essential feature of a yard is that it should be a relatively small area ancillary to a building.

Area. There was no evidence that a university campus amounted to an 'enclosed area' within the terms of the section in *Akhurst v Enfield Magistrates' Court* [2009] EWHC 806 (Admin), 173 JP 499.

A[79.5] Unlawful purpose. Means that the defendant was there for the purpose of committing a criminal offence. In deciding whether the defendant had such a purpose, the court must consider all the evidence drawing such inferences from it as appear proper in the circumstances. "Unlawful purpose" meant that an individual was about to commit a criminal offence. Hiding from the police in order to escape detection for a criminal offence which had already occurred could not constitute an unlawful purpose: *L v CPS* [2007] EWHC 1843 (Admin).

Sentencing

A[79.6] No SC guideline. For structure of the sentencing decision. See B[3.6].

A[79.7] Available sentences. See Table B at B[4.2].

A[79.8] Committal for sentence. For a subsequent offence, as long as the previous offence was **not** dealt with by absolute or conditional discharge the court may commit the defendant to the Crown Court for sentence on bail or in custody as an incorrigible rogue. The Crown Court can impose imprisonment for up to one year. **For offences committed on or after a date to be appointed the power to imprison or commit for sentence has been repealed.

A[79.9] Even if there is no previous conviction for a similar offence but there is evidence of previous convictions under the Vagrancy Act 1824, then this procedure may still be available to the magistrates. **See **A[79.1]** above.

Health and safety at work

Charges

A[80.1] Did fail to comply with an improvement or prohibition notice (specified)

Health and Safety at Work Act 1974, s 33(1)(g)

A[80.2] Did fail to comply with an order of the court to remedy (specified)

Health and Safety at Work Act 1974, s 33(1)(o)

Maximum penalty – Fine £20,000 and 6 months. Triable either way.

Crown Court – 2 years' imprisonment and unlimited fine.

A[80.3] Did fail to comply with a duty specified in the Health and Safety at Work Act 1974, ss 2–6 (for example), under s 3(1) did fail to conduct an undertaking in such a way as to ensure, so far as is reasonably practicable, that persons not in your employment, who may be affected thereby, were not exposed to risks to their health and safety.

Health and Safety at Work Act 1974, s 33(1A)

Maximum penalty – Fine £20,000 and 6 months. Triable either way.

Crown Court – Unlimited fine.

A[80.4] Other breaches of the Act or Regulations

See the new Sch 3A to the Health and Safety at Work Act 1974 as added by Sch 1 to the Health and Safety (Offences) Act 2008.

Mode of trial

A[80.5] Section 85 of the Legal Aid, Sentencing and Punishment of Offenders Act 2012 prospectively enables magistrates' courts to impose unlimited fines. In anticipation of this, the following annex has been added to the Criminal Practice Directions 2014:

'CPD XIII Annex 3

CASES INVOLVING VERY LARGE FINES IN THE MAGIS-TRATES' COURT

(1)   This Annex applies when s.85 Legal Aid, Sentencing and Punishment of Offenders Act 2012 comes into force and the magistrates' court has the power to impose a maximum fine of any amount.

(2)   An authorised DJ (MC) must deal with any allocation decision, trial and sentencing hearing in the following types of cases which are triable either way:

    (a)   Cases involving death or significant, life changing injury or a high risk of death or significant, life-changing injury;

    (b)   Cases involving substantial environmental damage or polluting material of a dangerous nature;

    (c)   Cases where major adverse effect on human health or quality of life, animal health or flora has resulted;

    (d)   Cases where major costs through clean up, site restoration or animal rehabilitation have been incurred;

    (e)   Cases where the defendant corporation has a turnover in excess of £10 million but does not exceed £250 million, and has acted in a deliberate, reckless or negligent manner;

    (f)   Cases where the defendant corporation has a turnover in excess of £250 million;

    (g)   Cases where the court will be expected to analyse complex company accounts;

    (h)   High profile cases or ones of an exceptionally sensitive nature.

(3)   The prosecution agency must notify the justices' clerk where practicable of any case of the type mentioned in paragraph 2 of this Annex, no less than 7 days before the first hearing to ensure that an authorised DJ (MC) is available at the first hearing.

(4)   The justices' clerk shall contact the Office of the Chief Magistrate to ensure that an authorised DJ (MC) can be assigned to deal with such a case if there is not such a person available in the courthouse. The justices' clerk shall also notify a Presiding Judge of the Circuit that such a case has been listed.

(5)   Where an authorised DJ (MC) is not appointed at the first hearing the court shall adjourn the case. The court shall ask the accused for an indication of his plea, but shall not allocate the case nor, if the accused indicates a guilty plea, sentence him, commit him for sentence, ask for a pre sentence report or give any indication as to likely sentence that will be imposed. The justices' clerk shall ensure an authorised DJ (MC) is appointed for the following hearing and notify the Presiding Judge of the Circuit that the case has been listed.

(6)   When dealing with sentence, section 3 of the Powers of Criminal Courts (Sentence) Act 2000 can be invoked where, despite the magistrates' court having maximum fine powers available to it, the offence or combination of offences make it so serious that the Crown Court should deal with it as though the person had been convicted on indictment.

(7)   An authorised DJ (MC) should consider allocating the case to the Crown Court or committing the accused for sentence.'

A[80.6] Offences having an impact on the public at large and breaches of licensing requirements (for example in relation to asbestos, explosives or nuclear plant) may indicate trial on indictment.

Legal notes and definitions

A[80.7] The Health and Safety at Work Act 1974 imposes general duties on employers towards their employees, self-employed persons, persons connected with premises other than employees and articles and substances for use at work in ss 2–6. Most prosecutions are now brought under these sections.

A[80.8] Specific offences are detailed in the Health and Safety at Work Act 1974, s 33.

A[80.9] Offences by bodies corporate. Where an offence committed by a body corporate is proved to have been committed with the consent or connivance of or attributable to neglect by a director, manager, secretary or other officer of the company, he as well as the company shall be guilty of that offence and may be proceeded against.

A[80.10]–[80.15] Prosecution by inspectors. An inspector if authorised by the enforcement authority may prosecute before a magistrates' court.

A[80.16] Power to order remedial action. Where it appears to the court that the defendant can remedy matters they may in addition to or instead of a punishment order him within a given time to remedy the matters complained of (s 42).

A[80.17] Work means work as an employee, or self-employed person. Regulations may extend the meaning of work to include at work.

A[80.18] Article for use at work, means any plant designed for use or operation by persons at work and any article designed for use as a component in any such plant.

Defences

A[80.19] Typical prosecutions involve breaches of duty to safeguard health and safety so far as **is reasonably practicable as well as specific requirements under regulations.** It is therefore a common defence that an employer has safe systems of work and has done all that was reasonably practicable to avoid a breach of duty.

(1) Although s 2 is concerned with ensuring safety and s 3 with ensuring an absence of risk to safety, the language of the statute signified that these two concepts are one and the same thing. It was also implicit from the leading decision in *R v Chargot Ltd (t/a Contract Services)* [2007] EWCA Crim 3032, [2008] 2 All ER 1077, [2008] ICR 517; affd [2008] UKHL 73, [2009] 2 All ER 645, [2009] 1 WLR 1. In each section the obligation is qualified by the words 'so far as is reasonably practicable'. An offence under s 2 is committed if there is a relevant risk to the safety of an employee and the defendant has not taken such steps as are reasonably practicable to avoid it; whilst an offence under s 3 is committed if there is a relevant risk to the safety of a non-employee who may be affected by the conduct of the undertaking and the defendant has not taken such steps as are reasonably practicable to avoid that. In the case of each section, s 40 places on the defendant a reverse onus of proof (on the balance of probabilities) on the issue of reasonable practicability.

(2)   The offence in s 2 or s 3 lies in the failure to ensure safety so far as reasonably practicable, ie in exposure to risk of injury, not in the doing of actual injury. Causation of the injury, therefore, is not an ingredient of either offence: *R v Chargot*; *R v EGS Ltd* [2009] EWCA Crim 1942 followed.

(3)   The risks with which both sections are concerned are those relating to the activities of the defendant. Although it will sometimes be necessary to address the source of a risk, the introduction of a separate test of 'derivation' is more likely to confuse than to illuminate. The jury should be asked to concentrate on two central issues:

(i)   exposure to risk and

(ii)   (assuming the issue is raised) whether it was reasonably practicable to avoid it.

(4)   Foreseeability of risk (strictly foreseeability of danger) is relevant to the question whether a risk to safety exists. That accords with the ordinary meaning of risk, as is demonstrated by the concept of a risk assessment, which is itself an exercise in foresight. Whether a material risk exists or not is a jury question and the foreseeability (or lack of it) of some danger or injury is a part of the enquiry: *Baker v Quantum Clothing Group Ltd* [2011] UKSC 17, [2011] 4 All ER 223, [2011] 1 WLR 1003 followed. Nonetheless, the Crown is not required to prove that the accident which occurred was foreseeable. The sections impose, in effect, a duty on employers to think deliberately about things which are not obvious. In most cases, absent the sort of time factor which obtained in *Baker v Quantum*, it is likely that consideration of foreseeability will add little to the question whether there was a risk. In most cases, the principal relevance of foreseeability will be whether the employer took all reasonably practicable precautions to avoid that material risk: *R v Tangerine Confectionary Ltd*; *R v Veolia ES (UK) Ltd* [2011] EWCA Crim 2015, 176 JP 349.

ECHR. This is a legal rather than an evidential burden on the defendant and the reverse burden of proof is compatible with the presumption of innocence under the ECHR (*R v Davies* [2002] EWCA Crim 2949, [2002] All ER (D) 275 (Dec), sub nom *Davies v Health and Safety Executive* [2003] IRLR 170, 147 Sol Jo LB 29;*R v Chargot Ltd (t/a Contract Services)* [2007] EWCA Crim 3032, [2008] 2 All ER 1077, [2008] ICR 517; affd [2008] UKHL 73, [2009] 2 All ER 645, [2009] 1 WLR 1).

Sentencing

A[80.20] No SC guideline, but the Sentencing Guidelines Council (as it was then called) issued definitive guidelines on corporate manslaughter and health and safety offences involving death. The guidance states, in relation to the latter, that the appropriate fine will seldom be less than £100,000. Accordingly, fatal accident cases will almost invariably be committed to the Crown Court for sentence.

Aggravating and mitigating factors. Factors which may aggravate an offence are:

•   a deliberate or reckless breach of the law rather than carelessness;

•   action or lack of action prompted by financial motives-profit or cost saving;

•   disregarding warnings from a regulatory authority or the workforce;

•   an awareness of the specific risks likely to arise from action taken;

- lack of co-operation with a regulatory authority;
- serious extent of damage resulting from offence (but lack of actual damage does not render the offence merely technical; it is still serious if there is risk);
- previous offences of a similar nature;
- death or serious injury or ill health of humans has been a consequence of the offence;
- animal health or flora affected.

Factors in mitigation may include:

- the offender's minor role with little personal responsibility;
- genuine lack of awareness or understanding of specific regulations;
- an isolated lapse.

There may be some offender mitigation:

- prompt reporting;
- ready co-operation with regulatory authority;
- good previous record;
- timely guilty plea.

Costs

A[80.21] The prosecution will normally claim the costs of investigation and presentation. These may be substantial and can incorporate time and activity expended on containing and making the area safe.

Fines – factors and procedure

A[80.22] When dealing with a breach of the health and safety legislation and determining the level of fine and costs to impose on a corporate defendant, it was held in *R v F Howe and Son (Engineers) Ltd* [1999] 2 All ER 249, 163 JP 359, [1999] 2 Cr App Rep (S) 37, [1999] Crim LR 238, CA, that the court should have regard to the following propositions:

(a) In assessing the gravity of the breach, the court should consider how far short of the appropriate standard the defendant fell in failing to meet the reasonably practicable test.
(b) Generally, where death is the consequence of a criminal act, it is regarded as an aggravating feature of the offence – the penalty should reflect public disquiet at the unnecessary loss of life.
(c) The size of a company and its financial strength or weakness cannot affect the degree of care that is required in matters of safety.
(d) Particular aggravating factors will include:
  (i) a failure to heed warnings;
  (ii) deliberately profiting financially from a failure to take necessary health and safety steps or specifically running a risk in order to save money.
(e) Particular mitigating factors will include:
  (i) prompt admission of responsibility and a timely guilty plea;
  (ii) steps to remedy deficiencies after they are drawn to the defendant's attention;
  (iii) good safety record.
(f) Where a defendant company is in a position to pay the whole of the prosecution costs in addition to the fine, there is no reason in principle for the court not to make an order accordingly – the costs do not need to be scaled down so as not to exceed the fine .

The above guidelines also apply to the level of fines in food safety cases: *R v Crestdane Ltd* [2012] EWCA Crim 958, [2013] 1 Cr App Rep (S) 102, [2012] Crim LR 980(fines totalling £51,000, costs £2,700 and a prohibition order upheld, despite the likely permanent closure of the business caused by the latter).

The Court of Appeal has recommended that when the Health and Safety Executive commences proceedings, it should list in writing for the assistance of the court not merely the facts of the case, but the aggravating features, as set out in *R v F Howe and Son (Engineers) Ltd*, which it says exist in the particular case. That document should be served upon the court and upon the defendants for the latter to consider. If the defendants plead guilty they should submit a similar document outlining the mitigating features that the court is to take into account. If by the time the matter comes to court there is agreement between the parties as to which are the relevant mitigating and aggravating factors that the court should take into account, and the plea is upon an agreed basis, that agreed basis should be put into writing so that there is no doubt what is the proper basis upon which the court should pass sentence: *R v Friskies Petcare Ltd* [2000] 2 Cr App Rep (S) 401, [2000] Lexis Citation 06, CA.

The standards are the same for both the public and the private sectors, but when it comes to the imposition of penalties there are particular considerations pertinent to public sector organisations that may call for a moderation of the penalty: *Milford Haven Port Authority* [2000] 2 Cr App R (S) 423, CA.

The standards of health and safety must be the same for small businesses as well as large businesses; if a small business engages in work that involves a high level of risk it must carry out the same level of risk assessment as a large business: *R v George Robertson Graham* [2009] EWCA Crim 2846, [2010] 2 Cr App R (S) 48.

However, In determining the appropriate level of fine a balance may have to be struck between a fitting expression of censure and the counter-productive effect of imposing too great a penalty on an already under-funded organisation: see *R v Yorkshire Water Services Ltd* [2001] EWCA Crim 2635, [2002] 2 Cr App R (S) 37; *R v Clifton Steel Ltd* [2007] EWCA Crim 1537, [2008] 1 Cr App R (S) 58.

Fines – examples

A[80.23] The following examples illustrate the approach of the Court of Appeal.

In *R v Avon Lippiatt Hobbs (Contractors) Ltd* [2003] EWCA Crim 627, [2003] 2 Cr App R (S) 71 fines totalling £250,000 were reduced to £150,000 where, in the course of tunnelling under a road using an impact mole, gas pipes were struck and there was an explosion some hours later that destroyed a house and badly burned an employee).

In *R v Yorkshire Sheeting and Insulation Ltd* [2003] EWCA Crim 458, [2003] 2 Cr App Rep (S) 548 a £100,000 fine was reduced to £55,000 where inadequate safety precautions resulted in a roof sheeter falling through an unprotected roof light, but none of the aggravating factors identified in Howe, save death, was present).

In *R v P & O (Irish Sea Ltd)* [2004] EWCA Crim 3236, [2005] 2 Cr App R (S) 21 fines totalling £300,000 were reduced to £225,000 where a pedestrian employee was killed by driver of a stacker truck during unloading from a ferry, but apart from this there were no significant aggravating factors and there were numerous mitigating factors).

In *R v Jarvis Facilities Ltd* [2005] EWCA Crim 1409, [2006] 1 Cr App R (S) 44 a fine was reduced from £400,000 to £275,000 where a rail junction with a speed limit of 25 mph should have been physically closed owing to the removal of a section of rail on a diversionary route through the junction, but the signaller had no means of knowing this, a freight train was diverted down the route and it derailed, though remained upright; while public service cases would often be treated more seriously, the sentencer had overestimated the actual risk generated.

In *R v Transco plc* [2006] EWCA Crim 838, [2006] 2 Cr App R (S) 111 a fine was reduced from £1m to £250,000 where the company pleaded guilty to failing to discharge a duty of care under s 3 of the Health and Safety at Work Act 1974; it had been called to a building after a leak from a fractured gas main escaped causing gas to enter the building; it identified the source of the leak and dealt with the fracture and ventilated the building; it then allowed residents to return, but, half an hour later, one resident lit a cigarette which ignited gas and he died of his injuries a few days later. It transpired that a void 2m high above his ceiling had filled with gas which had seeped into the room after it had been ventilated; however, the flats were unusually constructed and, apparently, in breach of building regulations. However, the case did not involve systematic fault but merely a mistake by one or more individuals handling an emergency; the guilty plea was promptly entered; and there was no question of cost cutting or profit motives, and the company's safety record was generally good.

In *R v Balfour Beatty Rail Infrastructure Ltd* [2006] EWCA Crim 1586, [2007] 1 Cr App Rep (S) 370 it was noted, inter alia, that the sentencing court could take a more serious view where there was a significant public element involved (fine reduced from £10m to £7.5m on the ground of disparity with the fine imposed on another company responsible for maintenance of the same track).

Where, however, the breach consisted of a one-off failure to build into temporary arrangements safety procedures which were properly observed in the company's normal arrangements, and there was no suggestion of a culture of disregarding health and safety or cutting corners to save costs, and the company pleaded guilty at the first opportunity, a fine of £150,000 was quite disproportionate to the low level of culpability and was reduced to £60,000: *R v AGC Automotive UK Ltd* [2007] EWCA Crim 3396, [2008] 2 Cr App R (S) 26.

In *R v TDG (UK) Ltd* [2008] EWCA Crim 1963, [2009] 1 Cr App R (S) 81 a man was fatally crushed by a rolling trailer, owing to its independent brake not being applied by the driver. Systematic failures of long standing had contributed to the accident and the potential danger was extreme, but there had been no question of putting profit first, significant steps had since been taken to remedy the failures and the company had pleaded guilty at the first opportunity; therefore, the fine was reduced from £325,000 to £275,000.

For a case involving a specialist asbestos removal contractor, see *R v LCH Contracts Ltd* [2009] EWCA Crim 902, [2009] 2 Cr App Rep (S) 665; such a contractor should know the dangers from asbestos better than most, but where workmen from the principal contractor had caused the problems by interfering with correctly bagged waste, the company's record was generally good and none of the aggravating factors in *Howe* was present, £70,000 was excessive and did not bear a proper relationship to the fine of £150,000 imposed on the principal contractor; therefore, the total was reduced to £40,000. Conversely, where the health and safety failings were due to ignorance and did not cause or contribute to the death, attention should focus on the extent to which the breach jeopardised general safety aspects: *R v Wilson & Mainprize* [2004] EWCA Crim 2086, [2005] 1 Cr App R (S) 64.

In *R v Merlin Attractions Operations Ltd* [2012] EWCA Crim 2670, [2013] 2 Cr App Rep (S) 240, the Court of Appeal upheld a fine of £350,000 and costs of £145,000. The company owned Warwick Castle. An elderly visitor tripped over the low parapet wall of a bridge leading to the castle and fell head first into the dry moat, a drop of 13.5ft, causing fatal injuries. While there had been 20m visitors to the castle without prior incident, the company had never carried out a mandatory risk assessment and the bridge was an obvious danger.

In *R v Palmer and Harvey McClane Ltd* [2012] EWCA Crim 993, [2013] 1 Cr App R (S) 189 a company required an employee to work in a freezer, but failed to provide him with appropriate footwear. After a period of time the employee suffered nerve damage to both fingers and feet. The effects on his health were likely to be permanent and a civil claim was settled in his favour for £34,500. The failure extended over several years, but the Court of Appeal concluded that the fine of £75,000 was too large and reduced the fine to £50,000 (the costs were £10,906).

Immigration offences

Charges

A[81.1] 1 Illegal entry and similar offences by a person who is not a British citizen

Immigration Act 1971, s 24

Maximum penalty – Triable summary only. Fine level 5 or 6 months' imprisonment

A[81.2] 2 Assisting unlawful entry to a member state, assisting an asylum seeker to enter the UK and entry to the UK in breach of an exclusion or deportation order.

Immigration Act 1971, s 25, 25A, 25B

Maximum penalty – Fine level 5 and 6 months. Triable either way.

Crown Court – Unlimited fine and/or 14 years' imprisonment.

A[81.3] 3 Possession of false passports, work permits, registration cards etc and other offences in connection with the administration of the Act.

Immigration Act 1971, s 26, 26A

Maximum penalty – Triable summary only. Level 5 and 6 months.

NB: The Nationality, Immigration and Asylum Act 2002 created a large number of related offences under the Act with effect from 10 February 2003. If charged under s 26A they are punishable with a maximum of ten years' imprisonment and a fine unless they only involve possession without reasonable excuse when the maximum penalty is two years' imprisonment and a fine. Both offences are triable either way carrying on summary conviction a fine level 5 and 6 months imprisonment.

Mode of trial

A[81.4] See general notes at D[4] and sentencing below for further guidance, although many cases will be most appropriately dealt with at Crown Court (*R v Uluc* [2001] EWCA Crim 2991 [2001] All ER (D) 273 (Dec)).

Legal notes and definitions

A[81.5] A person commits an offence of knowingly remaining beyond the time limit of a limited leave to stay on the day when he first knows that the time limit of his leave has expired. He continues to commit the offence (Immigration Act 1971, s 24(1)(b)(i)) throughout any period he is in the United Kingdom thereafter.

A[81.6] Extended time limits for prosecution. The normal time limit for laying an information for a summary offence is 6 months. However in cases charged under s 28(1)(a) (knowingly entering the United Kingdom in breach of a deportation order), s 28(1)(c)(having lawfully entered the United Kingdom remains without leave beyond the time allowed), s 26(1)(c) (making a false representation to an immigration officer) or 26(1)(d) (altering any relevant certificate, work permit or passport) an information relating to the offence may in England and Wales be tried by a magistrates' court if it is laid within six months after the commission of the offence, or if it is laid within three years after the commission of the offence and not more than two months after the date certified by a police officer above the rank of chief superintendent to be the date on which evidence sufficient to justify proceedings came to the notice of the police.

A[81.7] Search warrants. In the case of offences of illegal entry (s 24(1)(a)), obtaining leave to enter or remain by deception (s 24(1)(aa)) and remaining beyond a time-limited leave or failing to observe conditions of leave (s 24(1)(b)) may all be the subject of an arrest without warrant by a constable or immigration officer with reasonable grounds to suspect an offence has been committed. A justice of the peace may grant a warrant of entry of search to premises if satisfied by written information on oath that a person suspected of one of the above offences is to be found on those premises.

Immigration and Asylum Act 1999, s 7

A[81.8] An immigration officer is a person appointed by the Secretary of State or may be employed as a revenue and customs officer.

Facilitating entry is not an offence if it is done otherwise than for gain or by a bona fide organisation whose purpose is assisting asylum claimants.

Illegal entrant is not confined to persons who have actually entered the country but includes those seeking to enter (*R v Eyck* [2000] 3 All ER 569, [2000] 1 WLR 1389, CA).

Defence based on art 31 of the United Nations Convention relating to the Status of Refugees

A[81.8A] It is a defence for a refugee charged with one of the offences listed below to show that, having come to the UK directly from a country to which his life or freedom was threatened, he:

(a)   presented himself to the authorities in the UK without delay;
(b)   showed good cause for his illegal entry or presence; and
(c)   made a claim for asylum as soon as was reasonably practicable after his arrival in the UK.

A refugee is defined by the Convention, Article 1.A(2) as any person who 'owing to a well-founded fear of being persecuted for reasons of race, religion, nationality, membership of a particular social group or political opinion, is outside the country of his nationality and is unable or, owing to such fear, is unwilling to avail himself of the protection of that country; or, who, not having a nationality and being outside the country of his former habitual residence . . . is unable or, owing to such fear, is unwilling to return to it . . . '. The Convention meaning is adopted by the Immigration and Asylum Act 1999, s 31(6).

The meaning of 'particular social group' was considered in *R v Evans* [2013] EWCA Crim 125, [2013] 1 Cr App R 34. It was held that there was no basis in logic or the evidence for either of the following collection of individuals to come within the term: (a) migrants of Jamaican origin returning to Jamaica after residing in the US, Canada or UK; or (b) persons deported back to Jamaica from any of those countries.

If the refugee stopped in another country en route to the UK the above defence is only available if he shows that he could not reasonably have expected to be given protection under the Convention in that other country: Immigration and Asylum Act 1999, s 31(1) and (2).

The burden on the refugee to establish his refugee status is an evidential burden only; once he has adduced sufficient evidence to raise the issue the prosecution bears the burden of proving beyond reasonable doubt that he is not a refugee. The burden of proving the other matters that must be established under s 31(1) is, however, the legal burden.

The offences are any offence or attempt to commit an offence under:

(a)   the Forgery and Counterfeiting Act 1981, Part I;
(b)   the Identity Cards Act 2006, s 25(1);
(c)   the Immigration Act 1971, s 24A; and
(d)   the 1971 Act, s 26(1).

Section 31 supersedes the interpretation of art 31 in *R v Uxbridge Magistrates' Court, ex p Adimi* [2001] QB 667, [1999] 4 All ER 520, [2000] 3 WLR 434, DC. The focus is now on the terms of the section, and not on art 31 as interpreted in *ex p Adimi: R (Hussain) v Secretary of State for the Home Department* [2001] EWHC Admin 555. Accordingly, there can be no legitimate expectation that the CPS will have regard to art 31 as, in instituting a prosecution, the CPS is required to apply the domestic law: *R (Pepushi) v Crown Prosecution Service* [2004] EWHC 798 (Admin), [2004] TLR 279. The disparity between the scope of art 31(1) and the scope of s 31 of the 1999 Act cannot be made good by a free-standing defence under art 31(1); it is not permissible for the courts effectively to add to the list of the offences set out in s 31. However, where a defendant faced two factually indistinguishable charges, only one of which was within the scope of s 31, once the statutory defence had been made out it was an abuse of process to proceed further on the other charge: *R v Asfaw* [2008] UKHL 31, [2008] 1 AC 1061, [2008] 3 All ER 775, [2008] 2 WLR 1178. Section 31 is not to be read as limited to offences attributable to a refugee's illegal entry into or presence in this country, but provides immunity, if the other conditions are fulfilled, from the imposition of criminal penalties for offences attributable to the attempt of a refugee to leave the country in the continuing course of a flight from persecution even after a short stopover in transit: *R v Asfaw* (above).

See further, *R v Mateta* [2013] EWCA Crim 1372, [2013] All ER (D) 19 (Aug) (several convictions quashed despite guilty pleas; the defendants had either not been advised as to the s 31 defence or advised that it was unavailable on the facts when in fact s 31 defences would probably have succeeded).'

Sentencing

A[81.9] No SC guideline. For structure of the sentencing decision. See B[3.6].

A[81.10]–[81.15] Available sentences. See Table A at B[4.1] (either way offences) and Table B at B[4.2] (summary offences).

A[81.16] Immigration offences generally attract sentences in excess of the powers of magistrates' courts. Numerous examples are contained in para 3.306 of *Stone's Justices' Manual* and readers are advised to consult this narrative for guidance on sentencing levels for the various offences that can arise in connection with illegal immigration, etc.

A[81.17] Bail See D[8].

It may be the case that some asylum seekers face charges before the criminal courts. In these circumstances, the courts have no powers under immigration and asylum legislation to bail or detain them. Where the criminal proceedings have to be adjourned for any reason, magistrates are advised that defendants who are also asylum seekers should have their applications for bail under the Bail Act 1976 considered by the courts in the same way as any other defendant. Where the case proceeds to sentence, the courts have no additional powers to exercise in relation to the offender's immigration status, save for making a recommendation for deportation under the Immigration Act 1971, s 3(6), where this is appropriate.

Soliciting for prostitution

Charges

A[82.1] In a street or public place did solicit another for the purpose of obtaining that other's sexual services as a prostitute

Sexual Offences Act 2003, s 51A

Maximum penalty – Fine level 3

A further offence, with the same maximum penalty, is provided by s 53A of the 2003 Act of paying for sexual services of a prostitute subjected to force, etc. It is irrelevant whether or not the defendant knew or ought to have been aware of the force/other exploitation.

Legal notes and definitions

A[82.2] 'Street' has the meaning given by s 1(4) of the Street Offences Act 1959. The accused must have given some indication, by act or word, that he required the other's sexual services as a prostitute: *Darroch v DPP* (1990) 90 Cr App Rep 378, 154 JP 844. 'Prostitute' means a person who, on at least one occasion and whether or not compelled to do so, offers or provides sexual services to another for payment or a promise of payment either to the prostitute or another; 'payment' means any financial advantage: Sexual Offences Act 2003, s 51.

A single act on foot of soliciting for prostitution within a recognised area cannot amount in law to the common law offence of public nuisance: *DPP v Fearon* [2010] EWHC 340 (Admin), [2010] 2 Cr App Rep 169, 174 JP 145.

Sentencing

A[82.3] There is no SC guideline.

Ancillary orders

A[82.4] ASBOs are often made for this offence, Alternatively, offenders can be bound over where a future breach of the peace is apprehended.

A[83]

Litter

(including dumping articles and car dumping)

A[83.1] Under the general term of **litter** there are three different offences: car dumping, dumping objects other than vehicles, and depositing general litter.

Charge 1

A[83.2] **Without lawful authority abandoning on land in the open air or on land forming part of a highway a motor vehicle**

Refuse Disposal (Amenity) Act 1978, s 2(1)(a)

Maximum penalty – Fine level 4 and 3 months' imprisonment. May be dealt with by a fixed penalty notice.

A removal charge can also be imposed if the local authority applies.

Legal notes and definitions

A[83.3] It is also an offence to abandon on such land a part of a motor vehicle if the vehicle was brought to that land and there dismantled and some part of the vehicle abandoned there.

A[83.4] **Motor vehicle.** This is defined in the Act as a mechanically propelled vehicle intended or adapted for use on roads whether or not it is in a fit state for such use. It includes a trailer, a chassis or body with or without wheels appearing to have formed part of a motor vehicle or trailer and anything attached to a motor vehicle or trailer.

A[83.5] **Burden of proof.** If the vehicle (or part of a vehicle) was left on the land in such circumstances or for such a period that it may be reasonably assumed that the defendant had abandoned it then he shall be deemed to have abandoned the vehicle (or part of a vehicle) unless he can prove the contrary. The degree of proof required of the defendant is not such as is necessary to establish this point beyond all reasonable doubt but only such as establishes that on the balance of probabilities it is true. Give the stated aims of the legislation and the fact that the reason for leaving [abandoning] the vehicle may peculiarly be within the knowledge of the accused, it is suggested that the shifting of the legal burden of proof to the accused is both necessary and proportionate and therefore ECHR compliant.

A[83.6] **Land.** The land must be land in the open air or land which forms part of the highway.

Sentencing

A[83.7] No SC guideline.

Prison will rarely be appropriate but a fine will in most cases need to be such as to reflect the seriousness of the offence.

A[83.8] On application by police or local authority, a removal charge can also be imposed.

A[83.9] Disqualification from driving. See C[5.45].

Charge 2

A[83.10] Without lawful authority abandoning on land in the open air (or on land forming part of the highway) property namely [. . . . .] which he brought to the land for the purpose of abandoning it there

Refuse Disposal (Amenity) Act 1978, s 2(1)(b)

Maximum penalty – Fine level 4 and 3 months' imprisonment.

Legal notes and definitions

A[83.11]–[83.14] Although this offence does not apply to motor vehicles it does apply to a part of a motor vehicle which was dismantled elsewhere and then brought and abandoned.

A[83.15] Land. Means land in the open air or land forming part of a highway.

Sentencing

A[83.16] No SC guideline.

A[83.17] Disqualification from driving. See C[5.45].

Charge 3

A[83.18] Throwing down (or dropping or depositing) [in a public open place] [in a place to which this section applies] and there leaving certain articles namely [. . . . .] in such circumstances as to tend to lead to defacement by litter

Environmental Protection Act 1990, s 87

Maximum penalty – Fine level 4.

Legal notes and definitions

A[83.19] The charge should allege one or other of the following:

A[83.20] Throwing down; dropping; depositing. If two or more of these words are included in the charge then it may be defective.

A[83.21] Public open place. Means a place in the open air to which the public are entitled or permitted to have access without payment. Any covered place open to the air on at least one side and available for public use is to be treated as a public open place. An enclosed telephone kiosk is not an open space (*Felix v DPP* [1998] Crim LR 657).

A[83.22] Place to which the section applies. Includes publicly maintained highways and motorways, local authority open spaces, certain Crown lands and land belonging to certain designated statutory undertakers and educational establishments. Also included is land designated by a local authority as a 'litter control area', eg a shopping mall.

A[83.23] Time limit. Proceedings must be commenced within six months of the litter being thrown down or dropped or deposited. If litter is left for a considerable period then the time limit of six months still commences from the time the litter was deposited.

A[83.24] Leaving. No offence is committed if the litter is not left; thus prompt clearing up can be a defence.

A[83.25]–[83.30] Consent of the owner. If the owner, occupier or person having control of the place consented to the depositing of the litter then no offence is committed.

Sentencing

A[83.31] No SC guideline.

Aggravating factors to which the court may have regard may include the defacement by litter, but also the nature of the litter and any resulting risk of injury to persons or animals or of damage to property.

A[83.32] Whatever the circumstances the fine will usually need to be such as to reflect the prevalence of the offence in an area.

A[83.33] Fines. See B[33].

A[83.34] Disqualification from driving. See C[5.45].

A[84]

Nuisance

A[84.1] In addition to the remedies which the law affords in respect of nuisances in civil proceedings before the county court and the High Court, local authorities and private persons may bring proceedings for the abatement or restriction of a statutory nuisance before the magistrates' court. Further see **A6** and **A[74]**.

Statutory nuisance

(Environmental Protection Act 1990, s 79)

A[84.2] The following matters constitute statutory nuisances where they are such as to be prejudicial to health or a nuisance:

(a)

(a)   the state of any premises;

(b)   the emission of smoke from premises;

(c)   the emission of fumes or gases from private dwellings;

(d)   any dust, steam, smell or other effluvia arising on industrial, trade or business premises;

(e)   any accumulation or deposit;

(f)   the manner or keeping in such a place of any animal;

(fa)   any insects emanating from relevant industrial, trade or business premises and being prejudicial to health or a nuisance;

(fb)   artificial light emitted from premises so as to be prejudicial to health or a nuisance;

(g)   noise emitted from premises;

(ga)   noise that is prejudicial to health or a nuisance and is emitted from or caused by a vehicle; and also

(h)   any other matter declared by any enactment to be a statutory nuisance.

A[84.3] **Prejudicial to health.** The expressions 'prejudicial to health' and 'injurious or likely to cause injury to health' are aimed at the effect on people's health of filthy or unwholesome premises and the like: in particular, the risk of disease or illness. There is nothing in s 79 to suggest that the powers were intended to protect against the danger of accidental physical injury; accordingly, premises that are in such a state as to create the likelihood of accident causing personal injury are not as a matter of law capable of giving rise to a statutory nuisance within s 79 (1)(a): *R v Bristol City Council, ex p Everett* [1999] 2 All ER 193, [1999] 1 WLR 1170, CA. The powers in this section are directed to the presence of some feature which in itself is prejudicial to health in that it is the source of possible infection or disease or illness such as dampness, mould, dirt or evil-smelling accumulations or the presence of rats. They do not extend to the arrangement of rooms otherwise not in themselves insanitary so as to be prejudicial to health, such as where the nearest facility for washing hands after use of a lavatory required access through kitchen or use of the kitchen sink: *Birmingham City Council v Oakley* [2001] 1 All ER 385, [2000] 3 WLR 1936, HL.

Evidence given by experts about the condition of premises is sufficient by itself, in the absence of evidence relating to the health and medical condition of the tenant, to establish a prima facie case that premises were prejudicial to health and a statutory nuisance: *O'Toole v Knowsley Metropolitan Borough Council* [1999] LS Gaz R 36.

The powers in this provision do not extend to a lack of adequate sound insulation for which there is a separate statutory code under which local authorities have express powers and, in serious cases, duties to deal with sound insulation: *R (Vella) v Lambeth Borough Council* [2005] TLR 533, QBD.

Traffic noise from vehicles, machinery or equipment in the street which renders premises to be in such a state as to be prejudicial to health or a nuisance does not constitute a statutory nuisance within the meaning of s 79(1)(a) because s 79(1)(ga) subject to the limitations in s 79(6A), deals directly with vehicle noise: *Haringey London Borough Council v Jowett* (1999) 78 P & CR D24, [1999] EGCS 64.

A[84.4] Noise. This includes vibration: Environmental Protection Act 1990, s 79(7). It is wrong for justices to refuse to convict of an offence under s 80(4) and (5) merely on the basis that no reliable acoustic measurement evidence has been adduced; however, where the evidence of the environmental enforcement officer is that the nuisance was 'marginal' justices are perfectly entitled to say that they are not sure and to acquit: *Lewisham Borough Council v Hall* [2002] EWHC 960 (Admin), [2002] All ER (D) 83 (May), [2002] JPN 378.

A[84.5] Exceptions are made to the definitions of a statutory nuisance given above. These include activities of the armed forces, smoke emissions covered by the Clean Air Acts (excluding bonfires), dark smoke from trade or industrial premises, smoke and steam from steam locomotives and noise from aircraft.

A[84.6] Premises. Includes land and any vessel (except one powered by steam reciprocating engines).

Proceedings by the local authority

(Environmental Protection Act 1990, s 82)

A[84.7] The local authority must from time to time cause its area to be inspected to detect the existence of any statutory nuisance and, where a complaint has been made, take such steps as are reasonably practicable to investigate the complaint (s 79).

They may also require premises subject to a premises licence on a temporary event notice to close for up to 24 hours if they believe noise from the premises is causing a public nuisance. Contravention is punishable by 3 months' imprisonment and/or a £20,000 fine (Anti Social Behaviour Act 2003, s 40).

A[84.8] Abatement notice. Where the local authority are satisfied that a statutory nuisance exists or is likely to occur or reoccur, the local authority must serve a notice requiring abatement or prohibiting or restricting its occurrence and if the means of abatement are required by the local authority the description of any steps necessary for this purpose and any times within which the required action is to be taken (*R v Falmouth and Truro Port Health Authority, ex p South West Water Services* [2001] QB 445, [2000] 3 All ER 306, [2000] All ER (D) 429, CA). The consent of the Secretary of State or the Environment Agency is not required prior to the issue of an abatement notice by a local authority: *R (on the application of Ethos Recycling Ltd v Barking and Dagenham Magistrates' Court* [2009] EWHC 2885 (Admin).

In *R (on the application of Mohuddin Khan) v Isleworth Crown Court and the London Borough of Hillingdon* [2011] EWHC 3164 (Admin), 176 JP 6, there was no dispute as to the facts of the nuisance itself, nor was there any dispute that the claimant was not at the premises. It was also accepted that the dog (the cause of the nuisance) did not belong to him. The Crown Court considered that the claimant should have made sensible arrangements to collect his post while he was absent from the relevant premises. It concluded that he was therefore responsible for the nuisance and dismissed an appeal from the magistrates' court. It as held that the claimant was not 'the person responsible' for the nuisance. He was not the person 'to whose act, default or sufferance the nuisance was attributable'. That person was manifestly another person whose dog it was, and who was plainly in control of the dog at all material times. The abatement notice should in the ordinary way have been served on him and he should have been prosecuted for its breach. Despite the claimant's failure to make a better arrangement to collect his post from the said premises, that failure could not properly deprive him of an opportunity to raise a cast iron point had he appealed to the magistrates' court.

A[84.9] Appeal. The person served with the notice may appeal within 21 days to the magistrates' court. These are civil proceedings by way of complaint and the court is unable to impose a criminal penalty (*Hounslow London Borough Council v Thames Water Utilities Ltd* [2004] All ER (D) 94 (Feb)).

A[84.10]–[84.15] Offence. Contravention of or failure to comply with the terms of a notice without reasonable excuse is an offence triable only by magistrates. The maximum penalty is a fine of £5,000 and £500 per day for each day the offence continues after conviction. For an offence on industrial, trade or business premises the fine is £20,000.

A[84.16] Defence. It is a defence for the defendant to prove that the best practicable means were used to prevent, or to counteract the effects of, the nuisance. However, the defence is not available:

(a)   in the case of a nuisance falling within paragraph (a), (d), (e), (f), (fa) or (g) of A[84.2] above except where the nuisance arises on industrial, trade or business premises;

(b)   in the case of a nuisance falling within paragraph (fb) of section A[84.2] above except where:

    (i)   the artificial light is emitted from industrial, trade or business premises; or

    (ii)   the artificial light (not being light to which sub-paragraph (i) applies) is emitted by lights used for the purpose only of illuminating an outdoor relevant sports facility;

(c)   in the case of a nuisance falling within paragraph (ga) of A[84.2] above except where the noise is emitted from or caused by a vehicle, machinery or equipment being used for industrial, trade or business purposes;

(d)   in the case of a nuisance falling within paragraph (b) of A[84.2] above except where the smoke is emitted from a chimney; and

(e)   in the case of a nuisance falling within paragraph (c) or (h) of A[84.2] above.

Certain other defences are available where it is alleged that the activity is in conformity with consents or notices under control of pollution legislation.

A[84.17] If the defendant raises the defence of reasonable excuse under s 80(4) and (6) then it is for the prosecution to satisfy the court beyond reasonable doubt that the excuse was not reasonable: *Polychronakis v Richards and Jerrom Ltd* [1998] JPL 588, [1998] Env LR 347. 'Reasonable excuse' does not include matters that should have been raised on an appeal challenging the validity of the notice, unless there has been some special reason for not entering an appeal: *A Lambert Flat Management Ltd v Lomas* [1981] 2 All ER 280, [1981] 1 WLR 898. Mitigating factors, such as loud reggae music playing to celebrate a birthday, do not amount to a reasonable excuse if other ingredients of a nuisance are established: *Wellingborough Borough Council v Gordon* (1990) 155 JP 494.

A[84.18] Appeal. A person convicted of an offence may appeal against conviction and sentence to the Crown Court in the usual way.

Complaint by person aggrieved by a statutory nuisance

(Environmental Protection Act 1990, s 82)

A[84.19] A private individual may complain to the local authority about an alleged statutory nuisance and it will be the duty of the authority to take such steps as are reasonably practicable to investigate the complaint and if they consider it appropriate to serve an abatement notice as described above (Environmental Protection Act 1990, s 79).

A[84.20] However, a person may also lay a complaint before the magistrates on the ground that he is aggrieved by the existence of a statutory nuisance. Proceedings are normally brought against the person responsible for the nuisance; where he cannot be found it will be the owner or occupier of the premises.

A[84.21] Notice of intention to bring proceedings and the matters complained of should be served not less than 3 days before, in respect of noise, and 21 days before, in respect of any other allegation.

A[84.22] Magistrates' order. If the court is satisfied that the alleged nuisance exists or that, although abated, it is likely to reoccur, the court must make either one or both of the following orders:

(a)   to abate the nuisance, within a time specified in the order, and to execute any works necessary for that purpose;

(b)   prohibiting a recurrence of the nuisance, and requiring the defendant, within a time specified in the order, to execute any works necessary to prevent the recurrence.

The court may also impose a fine not exceeding £5,000 (level 5).

A[84.23] Where the nuisance renders premises unfit for human habitation, the order may prohibit their use for this purpose until the court is satisfied they are fit for such use.

A[84.24] Offence. See A[74.9] for private premises.

A[84.25]–[84.30] Defence. See A[84.16]–A[84.17]. The 'best practicable means' defence is not available for a nuisance which is such as to render the premises unfit for human habitation.

A[84.31] Costs. Where the alleged nuisance is proved to have existed at the making of the complaint then, whether or not at the date of the hearing it still exists or is likely to recur, the court shall order the defendant to pay the complainant's proper costs. Such costs should include costs incurred in establishing that a statutory nuisance existed (*Hollis v Dudley Metropolitan Borough Council* [1998] 1 All ER 759, [1999] 1 WLR 642).

Such proceedings are not civil in nature. Any award of costs therefore cannot be made under 64 of the Magistrates' Courts Act 1980: see s 50 of the Magistrates' Courts Act 1980 and s 82(2) of the Environmental Protection Act 1990. The combined effect of those two provisions was that s 82 must be read as if the word 'information' is substituted for 'complaint' in subsection (1). The power to award costs in favour of a successful defendant, other than by a wasted costs order when an information is dismissed, is to be found only in s 16(1) of the Prosecution of Offences Act 1985: *R (on the application of DeSouza) v Croydon Magistrates' Court* [2012] EWHC 1362 (Admin), 176 JP 624.

A[84.32] Local authority. Where a person has been convicted of failing to comply with an order the court, after allowing the local authority an opportunity to be heard, may direct the authority to do anything which the person convicted was required to do by the order. Similarly, where the defendant cannot be found the court may direct the local authority to do that which it would have ordered him to do.

Noise Act 1996

A[84.33] **See the amendments as a result of s 84 and schedule, 1 to the Clean Neighbourhoods and Environment Act 2005 which applies to licensed premises with a penalty (after service of the relevant notice under para 4A of a fine not exceeding **level 5**.

If a warning notice has been served under this Act, in respect of noise emitted from premises, any person who is responsible for such a breach is liable to a fine not exceeding **level 3**.

A[84.34] Defence. It is open to the defendant to show he has reasonable excuse.

A[84.35] Forfeiture. Magistrates may direct the forfeiture of any equipment related to a noise conviction.

A[84.36] Before doing so the court must have regard:

(a)   to the value of the equipment; and
(b)   to the likely financial and other effects on the offender of the making of the order.

*"Closure of premises associated with persistent disorder or nuisance" –
Part 1A of the Anti-Social Behaviour Act 2003*

A[84.37] In some communities there are particular premises that are a
constant focus for severe anti-social behaviour, making the lives of those
living nearby a misery. Premises closure orders are designed to offer
immediate respite via the temporary closure of premises for up to three
months where the person occupying those premises is responsible for:

- Significant and persistent disorder or
- Persistent serious nuisance to a community.

These procedures should only be used as a last resort and not as an eviction
tool or fast-track procedure to eviction. An order can be made by a relevant
police force and/or local authorities. Once a premises closure order has
been made, the police or the local authority must apply to a magistrates'
court for authority to continue the order for up to three months.

The application must be heard by the magistrates' court not later than 48
hours after the notice was served in pursuance of s 11A(7)(a) of the
2003 Act. The magistrates' court may adjourn for a period of not more
than 14 days to enable the owner, occupier, or any other person with an
interest in the premises to show cause why a Part 1A closure order should
not be made.

In adjourning the case the magistrates' court may direct that the closure
order shall continue. Analogous to closure orders associated with 'crack
houses' under s 2 of the 2003 Act, it is submitted that magistrates have a
general discretion to adjourn closure order proceedings beyond the 14 days
period in accordance with the Magistrates' Courts Act 1980.

The definition of 'premises' is a neutral term and applies to privately-owned
properties (including owner-occupied or privately rented properties). The
following premises are covered under the legislation: Flats and apartments,
common areas adjacent to houses or flats, garages and sheds, factories,
pubs and clubs, public buildings, community centres, halls and even car
parks.

The police and local authorities assessing the need to issue a closure
order must have reasonable grounds for believing that:

- at any time in the preceding three months a person had engaged in
  anti-social behaviour on the premises; and
- that the use of the premises is associated with significant and
  persistent disorder or persistent serious nuisance to members of the
  public.

The closure order gives a power to close a property completely or partially
for a maximum of up to three months and to prevent access by any person,
even those with rights of abode or ownership. Orders may be discharged
when problems associated with the premises have been addressed. No
property should remain empty longer than is necessary. There are provisions to extend or discharge the order on application.

It will be up to the courts to define 'significant and persistent disorder' or
'persistent and serious nuisance'.

There is a right of appeal against the making of an order or decision to the
Crown Court.

Breach of a closure order is an offence carrying six months' imprisonment and/or a fine of £5,000 on summary conviction.

Obstructing the highway

Charge

A[85.1] Without lawful authority or excuse wilfully obstructing the free passage along a highway

Highways Act 1980, s 137

Maximum penalty – Fine level 3.

Legal notes and definitions

A[85.2] This offence can be committed in a number of different ways apart from leaving a motor vehicle. It should not be confused with the offence of causing an unnecessary obstruction on a road with a motor vehicle or with a breach of parking regulations. See C[36].

A[85.3] The correct approach for magistrates dealing with an offence of obstruction is as follows:

(a)   Was there an obstruction? Unless within the *de minimis* rule, any stopping on the highway is prima facie an obstruction.

(b)   Was it wilful, ie deliberate?

(c)   Have the prosecution proved that the obstruction was without lawful authority or excuse? Lawful authority includes permits and licences granted under statutory provision; lawful excuse embraces activities otherwise lawful in themselves which may or may not be reasonable in all the circumstances, including the length of time the obstruction continues, the place where it occurs, the purpose for which it is done and whether it does in fact cause an actual obstruction as opposed to a potential obstruction (*Hirst and Agu v Chief Constable of West Yorkshire* (1986) 85 Cr App Rep 143, 151 JP 304).

It was stated in *Dixon v Atfield* [1975] 3 All ER 265, [1975] 1 WLR 1171 that the broad interpretation of 'reasonable excuse' applied in the case of a temporary obstruction did not apply to a permanent obstruction; ie the longer an obstruction exists the more likely it will be found unreasonable. (The defendant erected a bollard on the pavement outside his shop to protect his property and customers from vehicles mounting the footpath – since this was meant to be permanent the case was remitted to the justices with a direction to convict.)

The test of whether a particular use of a highway, eg, by a vehicle, amounts to an obstruction is whether such use is unreasonable having regard to all the circumstances including its duration, position and purpose, and whether it causes an actual, as opposed to a potential, obstruction: *Nagy v Weston* [1965] 1 All ER 78, 129 JP 104.

Although, as noted above, the de minimis principle applies to obstruction cases, the principle is reserved for cases of fractional obstructions: *Torbay*

Borough Council v Cross (1995) 159 JP 682 (displays of goods on the pavement outside a shop projecting by no more than 5% of the total width of the pavement held to be an obstruction which did not satisfy the de minimis principle).

A defendant selling hot dogs from a van parked in a line of parked vehicles in a busy street was properly convicted; as soon as his van turned itself into a shop it ceased to make a reasonable use of the road: *Pitcher v Lockett* [1966] Crim LR 283); applied in *Waltham Forest London Borough Council v Mills* [1980] RTR 201, [1980] Crim LR 243, where it was held that the selling of refreshments from a mobile snack bar on the highway was an unreasonable user.

The placing of shopping trolleys in three parallel rows outside a supermarket was held to constitute an unreasonable user because of the performance of the obstruction, the substantial nature of it, and its denial to the public of free access over the whole of the highway: *Devon County Council v Gateway Foodmarkets Ltd* (1990) 154 JP 557, DC.

Where a club tout approached groups of pedestrians on four occasions and on each of those occasions the free passage of other people using the highway was obstructed to an extent that members of the public passing were forced to step into the roadway, it was held that it was such an unreasonable use of the highway as to amount to an obstruction: *Cooper v Metropolitan Police Comr* (1985) 82 Cr App Rep 238.

An unauthorised encroachment restricting access to any part of the highway is such an obstruction and the prosecution is not obliged to allege or prove that any particular person was incommoded: see *Wolverton UDC v Willis* [1962] 1 All ER 243, 126 JP 84. Similarly, the display for sale of garden produce on a grass verge adjacent to a footpath, which formed part of the highway, was held to be an unreasonable user and, therefore, an obstruction, notwithstanding that the display did not encroach on the footpath itself and there was no evidence of anyone being inconvenienced: *Hertfordshire County Council v Bolden* (1986) 151 JP 252.

If stopping on a highway is merely part and parcel of reasonably passing and re-passing, it is not obstruction; to stand juggling with lighted firesticks, however, is not part and parcel of one's right to pass and re-pass, nor is it a user ancillary to that right: *Waite v Taylor* 149 JP 551, [1985] LS Gaz R 1092.

As to the application of s 131 to peaceful picketing in accordance with s 134 of the Industrial Relations Act 1971 (now s 220 of the Trade Union and Labour Relations Act (Consolidation) Act 1992), see *Broome v DPP* [1974] 1 All ER 314, 138 JP 105.

A[85.4]   Highway. A highway means the whole or part of a highway. Only a part of a highway needs to be obstructed to commit this offence and the highway, available to the general public, may be a wide road or a narrow passageway, only suitable for pedestrians. Bridges and tunnels used by the public are also highways.

Sentencing

A[85.5] No SC guideline. This offence carries a fine only. See B[33.10]–B[33.15].

Poaching

1 Day time offence

A[86.1] Trespassing by entering or being in the day time upon any land in search or pursuit of game, or woodcocks, snipes or conies

Game Act 1831, s 30, as amended

Maximum penalty – Fine level 3. Triable only by magistrates.

Note – Where it is alleged that there were five or more persons together trespassing in pursuit of game the maximum penalty is a fine set at level 4 for each defendant, or level 5 where they are armed and any of them uses violence, etc.

For hunting wild mammals with dogs and hare coursing see ss 1–5 of the Hunting Act 2004.

Legal notes and definitions

A[86.2]–[86.4] A prosecution must be commenced within three calendar months after the commission of the offence (Game Act 1831, s 41). The charge creates only one offence, that of trespass, and the summons may refer to pursuit of more than one species.

A[86.5] Day time commences at the beginning of the last hour before sunrise and concludes at the expiration of the first hour after sunset (s 34).

A[86.6]–[86.7] Game means hares, pheasants, partridges, grouse, heath or moor game, and black game (s 2).

A[86.8] Hunting. This offence does not apply to hunting or coursing in fresh pursuit of deer, hare, or fox (Game Act 1831, s 35). **NB:** By virtue of the Hunting Act 2004, Sch 3, the words, "to any person hunting or coursing upon any land with hounds or greyhounds, and being in pursuit of any deer, hare or fox already started upon any other land, nor" have been repealed.

A[86.8A] Disqualification from driving. See C[5.45].

2 Night time offences

A[86.9] (a) Unlawfully taking or destroying any game or rabbits by night in any land, open or enclosed or by night unlawfully entering or being on any land, whether open or enclosed, with any gun, net, engine, or other instrument for the purpose of taking or destroying game

Night Poaching Act 1828, s 1, as amended

Maximum penalty – Fine level 3 (offence under s 2 where violence is offered to gamekeepers etc with the weapons described in charge (b) the maximum is a fine on level 4 and 6 months). Triable only by magistrates.

A[86.10]–[86.15] (b) Three or more persons together by night unlawfully entering or being on any land, whether open or enclosed, for the purpose of taking or destroying game or rabbits, any of such persons being armed with gun, cross bow, firearms, bludgeon or any other offensive weapon

Night Poaching Act 1828, s 9, as amended

Maximum penalty – Fine level 4 and 6 months. Triable only by magistrates.

Legal notes and definitions

A[86.16] Claim of right. See above at A[86.3].

A[86.17] Game includes hares, pheasants, partridges, grouse, heath or moor game, black game and bustards (Night Poaching Act 1828, s 13).

A[86.18] Land includes public roads, highways, or paths, or the sides thereof or at the opening, outlets, or gates, from any such land into any such road, highway or path.

A[86.19] Charge. Section 1 creates two offences and any information must allege only one offence.

A[86.20] Unlawfully entering or being. (See above.) This offence does not relate to the taking or destroying of rabbits.

A[86.21] Night time commences at the expiration of the first hour after sunset and concludes at the beginning of the last hour before sunrise.

A[86.22] Three or more together. It is not necessary for all the persons actually to enter provided they are associated together on a common purpose, some entering while others remain near enough to assist.

A[86.22A]–[86.30] Disqualification from driving. See C[5.45].

Sentencing

A[86.31] No SC guideline.

Where the police have arrested a person for an offence under the Night Poaching Act 1828 or Game Act 1831 they may search him and may seize and detain any game or rabbits, or any gun or cartridges or other ammunition, or any nets, traps, snares or other devices of a kind used for the killing or taking of game or rabbits, which are found in his possession: Poaching Prevention Act 1862, s 2.

A[86.32] If convicted the court may order any of these items to be forfeited (whether or not the offence of which he was convicted concerned that game, rabbit etc) (Game Laws Amendment Act 1960, s 4).

A[86.32A] Disqualification from driving. See C[5.45].

A[88]

Shotgun (purchasing etc without shotgun certificate)

Charge

A[88.1] Possessing, or purchasing or acquiring a shotgun without holding a shotgun certificate

Firearms Act 1968, s 2(1)

Maximum penalty – Fine level 5 and 6 months. Triable either way.

Crown Court – 5 years' imprisonment and unlimited fine.

Mode of trial

A[88.2] See general notes at D[4].

Legal notes and definitions

A[88.3] Purchasing, possessing, acquiring. These are three separate offences and the charge should only allege one of these. See A[76], above.

A[88.4] Shotgun. Means a smooth bore gun with a barrel of 24 inches or longer with a bore not exceeding two inches and which is not a revolver nor has an illegal magazine, which is not an air gun.

A[88.5] Certificate. This is granted by the police and it may contain conditions. Failure to observe the conditions is an offence which is also triable either way punishable on summary conviction by a fine of level 5 and/or 6 months' imprisonment; the offence carries five years on indictment and an unlimited fine (Firearms Act 1968, s 2(2)). The police can revoke the certificate if they are satisfied that it entails danger to public safety or peace.

A[88.6] Exemptions. These include visitors to Great Britain who are holders of a visitor's shotgun permit; persons using shotguns on occasions and at places approved by the police; a person who borrows a shotgun and uses it on the lender's private premises, in the presence of the lender; persons holding a Northern Ireland firearm certificate which authorises holders to possess shotguns. See also A[76.9].

A[88.7] ECHR. The degree of proof required from the defendant is to establish that on the balance of probabilities he was exempt. He does not have to establish this beyond reasonable doubt. Having regard to the legitimate aims of the legislation it is suggested that the imposition of a legal burden on the accused is necessary and proportionate so as to accord with art 6(2) of the ECHR.

Sentencing

A[88.8] No SC guideline. For structure of the sentencing decision see B[3.6].

A[88.9] Available sentences. See Table A at B[4.1].

A[88.10] Forfeiture. The court can order the shotgun to be forfeited to the police or disposed of as it thinks fit.

A[88.11] The court can also cancel any firearm or shotgun certificate held by the defendant.

A[89]

General bribery offences

Charges

A[89.1] The following charges are available:

1. Bribing another person, or purchasing
Bribery Act 2010, s 1
Maximum penalty – Fine level 5 and 6 months. Triable either way.
Crown Court – 10 years' imprisonment and unlimited fine.*

2. Offences relating to being bribed
Bribery Act 2010, s 2
Maximum penalty – Fine level 5 and 6 months. Triable either way.
Crown Court – 10 years' imprisonment and unlimited fine.*

3. Bribery of foreign officials
Bribery Act 2010, s 6
Maximum penalty – Fine level 5 and 6 months. Triable either way.
Crown Court – 10 years' imprisonment and unlimited fine.*

4. Failure of commercial organisation to prevent bribery
Bribery Act 2010, s 7
Maximum penalty – Indictable only
Crown Court – Unlimited fine.

*The maximum penalties above relate to individuals only.

No proceedings for an offence under this Act may be instituted in England and Wales except by or with the consent of—

(a)   the Director of Public Prosecutions,
(b)   the Director of the Serious Fraud Office, or
(c)   the Director of Revenue and Customs Prosecutions

A[89.2] **1. Offences of bribing another person**

(1)   A person ("P") is guilty of an offence if either of the following cases applies.
(2)   Case 1 is where—
    (a)   P offers, promises or gives a financial or other advantage to another person, and
    (b)   P intends the advantage
        (i)   to induce a person to perform improperly a relevant function or activity, or
        (ii)   to reward a person for the improper performance of such a function or activity.
(3)   Case 2 is where—
    (a)   P offers, promises or gives a financial or other advantage to another person, and
    (b)   P knows or believes that the acceptance of the advantage would itself constitute the improper performance of a relevant function or activity.

(4)   In case 1 it does not matter whether the person to whom the advantage is offered, promised or given is the same person as the person who is to perform, or has performed, the function or activity concerned.

(5)   In cases 1 and 2 it does not matter whether the advantage is offered, promised or given by P directly or through a third party.

2. Offences relating to being bribed

(1)   A person ("R") is guilty of an offence if any of the following cases applies.

(2)   Case 3 is where R requests, agrees to receive or accepts a financial or other advantage intending that, in consequence, a relevant function or activity should be performed improperly (whether by R or another person).

(3)   Case 4 is where—
   (a)   R requests, agrees to receive or accepts a financial or other advantage, and
   (b)   the request, agreement or acceptance itself constitutes the improper performance by R of a relevant function or activity.

(4)   Case 5 is where R requests, agrees to receive or accepts a financial or other advantage as a reward for the improper performance (whether by R or another person) of a relevant function or activity.

(5)   Case 6 is where, in anticipation of or in consequence of R requesting, agreeing to receive or accepting a financial or other advantage, a relevant function or activity is performed improperly—
   (a)   by R, or
   (b)   by another person at R's request or with R's assent or acquiescence.

(6)   In cases 3 to 6 it does not matter—
   (a)   whether R requests, agrees to receive or accepts (or is to request, agree to receive or accept) the advantage directly or through a third party,
   (b)   whether the advantage is (or is to be) for the benefit of R or another person.

(7)   In cases 4 to 6 it does not matter whether R knows or believes that the performance of the function or activity is improper.

(8)   In case 6, where a person other than R is performing the function or activity, it also does not matter whether that person knows or believes that the performance of the function or activity is improper.

3. Bribery of foreign public officials

(1)   A person ("P") who bribes a foreign public official ("F") is guilty of an offence if P's intention is to influence F in F's capacity as a foreign public official.

(2)   P must also intend to obtain or retain—
   (a)   business, or
   (b)   an advantage in the conduct of business.

(3)   P bribes F if, and only if—
   (a)   directly or through a third party, P offers, promises or gives any financial or other advantage—
      (i)   to F, or
      (ii)   to another person at F's request or with F's assent or acquiescence, and
   (b)   F is neither permitted nor required by the written law applicable to F to be influenced in F's capacity as a foreign public official by the offer, promise or gift.

(4)   References in this section to influencing F in F's capacity as a foreign public official mean influencing F in the performance of F's functions as such an official, which includes—
    (a)   any omission to exercise those functions, and
    (b)   any use of F's position as such an official, even if not within F's authority.

(5)   "Foreign public official" means an individual who—
    (a)   holds a legislative, administrative or judicial position of any kind, whether appointed or elected, of a country or territory outside the United Kingdom (or any subdivision of such a country or territory)
    (b)   exercises a public function—
        (i)   for or on behalf of a country or territory outside the United Kingdom (or any subdivision of such a country or territory), or
        (ii)   for any public agency or public enterprise of that country or territory (or subdivision), or
    (c)   is an official or agent of a public international organisation.

(6)   "Public international organisation" means an organisation whose members are any of the following—
    (a)   countries or territories,
    (b)   governments of countries or territories
    (c)   other public international organisations,
    (d)   a mixture of any of the above.

(7)   For the purposes of subsection (3)(b), the written law applicable to F is—
    (a)   where the performance of the functions of F which P intends to influence would be subject to the law of any part of the United Kingdom, the law of that part of the United Kingdom,
    (b)   where paragraph (a) does not apply and F is an official or agent of a public international organisation, the applicable written rules of that organisation,
    (c)   where paragraphs (a) and (b) do not apply, the law of the country or territory in relation to which F is a foreign public official so far as that law is contained in—
        (i)   any written constitution, or provision made by or under legislation, applicable to the country or territory concerned, or
        (ii)   any judicial decision which is so applicable and is evidenced in published written sources.

(8)   For the purposes of this section, a trade or profession is a business.

Mode of trial

A[89.3] See general notes at D[4].

Legal notes and definitions

A[89.4] The Bribery Act 2010 received Royal Assent on 8 April 2010 and came into force on 1 July 2011. Amendments by virtue of the Bribery Act 2010 (Consequential Amendments) Order 2011 reflect the abolition of the following offences:

(1)   The common law offences of bribery and embracery.
(2)   The Public Bodies Corrupt Practices Act 1889.
(3)   The Prevention of Corruption Act 1906.
(4)   The Prevention of Corruption Act 1916.

Section 1: Offences of bribing another person

A[89.5] Makes it an offence for a person ('P') to offer, promise or give a financial or other advantage to another person in one of two cases:

- Case 1 applies where P intends the advantage to bring about the improper performance by another person of a relevant function or activity or to reward such improper performance.
- Case 2 applies where P knows or believes that the acceptance of the advantage offered, promised or given in itself constitutes the improper performance of a relevant function or activity.

'Improper performance' is defined at ss 4 and 5 of the Bribery Act 2010. In summary, this means performance which amounts to a breach of an expectation that a person will act in good faith, impartially, or in accordance with a position of trust. The offence applies to bribery relating to any function of a public nature, connected with a business, performed in the course of a person's employment or performed on behalf of a company or another body of persons. Therefore, bribery in both the public and private sectors is covered.

For the purposes of deciding whether a function or activity has been performed improperly the test of what is expected is a test of what a reasonable person in the UK would expect in relation to the performance of that function or activity. Where the performance of the function or activity is not subject to UK law (for example, it takes place in a country outside UK jurisdiction) then any local custom or practice must be disregarded – unless permitted or required by the written law applicable to that particular country. Written law means any written constitution, provision made by or under legislation applicable to the country concerned or any judicial decision evidenced in published written sources.

By way of illustration, in order to proceed with a case under Bribery Act 2010, s 1 based on an allegation that hospitality was intended as a bribe, the prosecution would need to show that the hospitality was intended to induce conduct that amounts to a breach of an expectation that a person will act in good faith, impartially, or in accordance with a position of trust. This would be judged by what a reasonable person in the UK thought. So, for example, an invitation to foreign clients to attend a Six Nations match at Twickenham as part of a public relations exercise designed to cement good relations or enhance knowledge in the organisation's field is extremely unlikely to engage s 1 as there is unlikely to be evidence of an intention to induce improper performance of a relevant function.

Section 2: Offences relating to being bribed

A[89.6] This section defines the offence of bribery as it applies to the recipient or potential recipient of the bribe, who is called R. It distinguishes four cases, namely Case 3 to Case 6.

In Cases 3, 4 and 5 there is a requirement that R "requests, agrees to receive or accepts" an advantage, whether or not R actually receives it. This requirement must then be linked with the "improper performance" of a relevant function or activity. As with section 1, the nature of this function or activity is addressed in section 3, and "improper performance" is defined in section 4. The link between the request, agreement to receive or acceptance of an advantage and improper performance may take three forms:

- R may intend improper performance to follow as a consequence of the request, agreement to receive or acceptance of the advantage (Case 3, in subsection (2));
- requesting, agreeing to receive or accepting the advantage may itself amount to improper performance of the relevant function or activity (Case 4, in subsection (3));
- alternatively, the advantage may be a reward for performing the function or activity improperly (Case 5, in subsection (4)).

In Cases 3 and 5, it does not matter whether the improper performance is by R or by another person. In Case 4, it must be R's requesting, agreeing to receive or acceptance of the advantage which amounts to improper performance, subject to subsection (6).

In Case 6 (subsection (5)) what is required is improper performance by R (or another person, where R requests it, assents to or acquiesces in it). This performance must be in anticipation or in consequence of a request, agreement to receive or acceptance of an advantage. Subsection (6) is concerned with the role of R in requesting, agreeing to receive or accepting advantages, or in benefiting from them, in Cases 3 to 6. First, this subsection makes it clear that in Cases 3 to 6 it does not matter whether it is R, or someone else through whom R acts, who requests, agrees to receive or accepts the advantage (subsection (6)(a)). Secondly, subsection (6) indicates that the advantage can be for the benefit of R, or of another person (subsection (6)(b)).

Subsection (7) makes it clear that in Cases 4 to 6, it is immaterial whether R knows or believes that the performance of the function is improper. Additionally, by subsection (8), in Case 6 where the function or activity is performed by another person, it is immaterial whether that person knew or believed that the performance of the function is improper.

Section 3: Function or activity to which bribe relates

A[89.7] This section defines the fields within which bribery can take place, in other words the types of function or activity that can be improperly performed for the purposes of sections 1 and 2. The term "relevant function or activity" is used for this purpose.

The purpose of the section is to ensure that the law of bribery applies equally to public and to selected private functions without discriminating between the two. Accordingly the functions or activities in question include all functions of a public nature and all activities connected with a business, trade or profession. The phrase "functions of a public nature" is the same phrase as is used in the definition of "public authority" in section 6(3)(b) of the Human Rights Act 1998 but it is not limited in the way it is in that Act. In addition, the functions or activities include all activities performed either in the course of employment or on behalf of any body of persons: these two categories straddle the public/private divide.

Not every defective performance of one of these functions for reward or in the hope of advantage engages the law of bribery. Subsections (3) to (5) make clear that there must be an expectation that the functions be carried out in good faith (condition A), or impartially (condition B), or the person performing it must be in a position of trust (condition C).

Subsection (6) provides that the functions or activities in question may be carried out either in the UK or abroad, and need have no connection with the UK. This preserves the effect of section 108(1) and (2) of the Anti-terrorism, Crime and Security Act 2001 (which is repealed by the Act).

Section 4: Improper performance to which bribe relates

A[89.8] Section 4 defines "improper performance" as performance which breaches a relevant expectation, as mentioned in condition A or B (subsections (3) and (4) of section 3 respectively) or any expectation as to the manner in which, or reasons for which, a function or activity satisfying condition C (subsection (5) of section 3) will be performed. Subsection (1)(b) states that an omission can in some circumstances amount to improper "performance".

Subsection (3) addresses the case where R is no longer engaged in a given function or activity but still carries out acts related to his or her former function or activity. These acts are treated as done in performance of the function or activity in question.

Section 5: Expectation test

A[89.9] Section 5 provides that when deciding what is expected of a person performing a function or activity for the purposes of sections 3 and 4, the test is what a reasonable person in the UK would expect of a person performing the relevant function or activity. Subsection (2) makes it clear that in deciding what a reasonable person in the UK would expect in relation to functions or activities the performance of which is not subject to UK laws, local practice and custom must not be taken into account unless such practice or custom is permitted or required by written law. Subsection (3) defines what is meant by "written law" for the purposes of this section.

Section 6: Bribery of a foreign public official

A[89.10] Section 6 creates a stand alone offence of bribery of a foreign public official. The offence is committed where a person offers, promises or gives a financial or other advantage to a foreign public official with the intention of influencing the official in the performance of his or her official functions. The person offering, promising or giving the advantage must also intend to obtain or retain business or an advantage in the conduct of business by doing so. However, the offence is not committed where the official is permitted or required by the applicable written law to be influenced by the advantage.

A 'foreign public official' includes officials, whether elected or appointed, who hold a legislative, administrative or judicial position of any kind of a country or territory outside the UK. It also includes any person who performs public functions in any branch of the national, local or municipal government of such a country or territory or who exercises a public function for any public agency or public enterprise of such a country or territory, such as professionals working for public health agencies and officers exercising public functions in state-owned enterprises. Foreign public officials can also be an official or agent of a public international organisation, such as the UN or the World Bank.

Sections 1 and 6 may capture the same conduct but will do so in different ways. The policy that founds the offence at section 6 is the need to prohibit the influencing of decision making in the context of publicly funded business opportunities by the inducement of personal enrichment of foreign public officials or to others at the official's request, assent or acquiescence.

Such activity is very likely to involve conduct which amounts to 'improper performance' of a relevant function or activity to which section 1 applies, but, unlike section 1, section 6 does not require proof of it or an intention to induce it. This is because the exact nature of the functions of persons regarded as foreign public officials is often very difficult to ascertain with any accuracy, and the securing of evidence will often be reliant on the co-operation of the state any such officials serve. To require the prosecution to rely entirely on section 1 would amount to a very significant deficiency in the ability of the legislation to address this particular mischief. That said, it is not the Government's intention to criminalise behaviour where no such mischief occurs, but merely to formulate the offence to take account of the evidential difficulties referred to above. In view of its wide scope, and its role in the new form of corporate liability at section 7, the Government offers the following further explanation of issues arising from the formulation of section 6.

Local law. For the purposes of section 6 prosecutors will be required to show not only that an 'advantage' was offered, promised or given to the official or to another person at the official's request, assent or acquiescence, but that the advantage was one that the official was not permitted or required to be influenced by as determined by the written law applicable to the foreign official.

In seeking tenders for publicly funded contracts Governments often permit or require those tendering for the contract to offer, in addition to the principal tender, some kind of additional investment in the local economy or benefit to the local community. Such arrangements could in certain circumstances amount to a financial or other 'advantage' to a public official or to another person at the official's request, assent or acquiescence. Where, however, relevant 'written law' permits or requires the official to be influenced by such arrangements they will fall outside the scope of the offence. So, for example, where local planning law permits community investment or requires a foreign public official to minimise the cost of public procurement administration through cost sharing with contractors, a prospective contractor's offer of free training is very unlikely to engage section 6. In circumstances where the additional investment would amount to an advantage to a foreign public official and the local law is silent as to whether the official is permitted or required to be influenced by it, prosecutors will consider the public interest in prosecuting. This will provide an appropriate backstop in circumstances where the evidence suggests that the offer of additional investment is a legitimate part of a tender exercise.

Hospitality, promotional, and other business expenditure. Bona fide hospitality and promotional, or other business expenditure which seeks to improve the image of a commercial organisation, better to present products and services, or establish cordial relations, is recognised as an established and important part of doing business and it is not the intention of the Act to criminalise such behaviour. The Government does not intend for the Act to prohibit reasonable and proportionate hospitality and promotional or other similar business expenditure intended for these purposes. It is, however, clear that hospitality and promotional or other similar business expenditure can be employed as bribes.

In order to amount to a bribe under section 6 there must be an intention for a financial or other advantage to influence the official in his or her official role and thereby secure business or a business advantage. In this regard, it may be in some circumstances that hospitality or promotional expenditure in the form of travel and accommodation costs does not even amount to 'a financial or other advantage' to the relevant official because it is a cost that would otherwise be borne by the relevant foreign Government rather than the official him or herself.

Where the prosecution is able to establish a financial or other advantage has been offered, promised or given, it must then show that there is a sufficient connection between the advantage and the intention to influence and secure business or a business advantage. Where the prosecution cannot prove this to the requisite standard then no offence under section 6 will be committed. There may be direct evidence to support the existence of this connection and such evidence may indeed relate to relatively modest expenditure. In many cases, however, the question as to whether such a connection can be established will depend on the totality of the evidence which takes into account all of the surrounding circumstances. It would include matters such as the type and level of advantage offered, the manner and form in which the advantage is provided, and the level of influence the particular foreign public official has over awarding the business. In this circumstantial context, the more lavish the hospitality or the higher the expenditure in relation to travel, accommodation or other similar business expenditure provided to a foreign public official, then, generally, the greater the inference that it is intended to influence the official to grant business or a business advantage in return.

The standards or norms applying in a particular sector may also be relevant here. However, simply providing hospitality or promotional, or other similar business expenditure which is commensurate with such norms is not, of itself, evidence that no bribe was paid if there is other evidence to the contrary; particularly if the norms in question are extravagant. Levels of expenditure will not, therefore, be the only consideration in determining whether a section 6 offence has been committed. But in the absence of any further evidence demonstrating the required connection, it is unlikely, for example, that incidental provision of a routine business courtesy will raise the inference that it was intended to have a direct impact on decision making, particularly where such hospitality is commensurate with the reasonable and proportionate norms for the particular industry; e.g. the provision of airport to hotel transfer services to facilitate an on-site visit, or dining and tickets to an event.

Sentencing

A[89.11] There are separate guidelines for corporate defendants. These are not reproduced since such cases are rarely heard in the magistrates' court.

Bribery

Bribing another person
Bribery Act 2010 (section 1)

Being bribed
Bribery Act 2010 (section 2)

Bribery of foreign public officials
Bribery Act 2010 (section 6)

Triable either way

Maximum: 7 years' custody

Offence range: Discharge – 8 years' custody

STEP ONE
DETERMINING THE OFFENCE CATEGORY

The court should determine the offence category with reference to the tables below. In order to determine the category the court should assess **culpability** and **harm**.

The level of culpability is determined by weighing up all the factors of the case to determine the offender's role and the extent to which the offending was planned and the sophistication with which it was carried out.

Culpability demonstrated by one or more of the following:

A – High culpability
A leading role where offending is part of a group activity
Involvement of others through pressure, influence
Abuse of position of significant power or trust or responsibility
Intended corruption (directly or indirectly) of a senior official performing a public function Intended corruption (directly or indirectly) of a law enforcement officer
Sophisticated nature of offence/significant planning
Offending conducted over sustained period of time
Motivated by expectation of substantial financial, commercial or political gain
B – Medium culpability
All other cases where characteristics for categories A or C are not present
A significant role where offending is part of a group activity
C – Lesser culpability
Involved through coercion, intimidation or exploitation
Not motivated by personal gain
Peripheral role in organised fraud
Opportunistic 'one-off' offence; very little or no planning
Limited awareness or understanding of the extent of fraudulent activity

Where there are characteristics present which fall under different levels of culpability, the court should balance these characteristics to reach a fair assessment of the offender's culpability.

Harm is assessed in relation to any impact caused by the offending (whether to identifiable victims or in a wider context) and the actual or intended gain to the offender.

Harm demonstrated by one or more of the following factors:

Category 1	• Serious detrimental effect on individuals (for example by provision of substandard goods or services resulting from the corrupt behaviour)
	• Serious environmental impact
	• Serious undermining of the proper function of local or national government, business or public services
	• Substantial actual or intended financial gain to offender or another or loss caused to others
Category 2	• Significant detrimental effect on individuals
	• Significant environmental impact
	• Significant undermining of the proper function of local or national government, business or public services
	• Significant actual or intended financial gain to offender or another or loss caused to others
	• Risk of category 1 harm
Category 3	• Limited detrimental impact on individuals, the environment, government, business or public services
	• Risk of category 2 harm
Category 4	• Risk of category 3 harm

Risk of harm involves consideration of both the likelihood of harm occurring and the extent of it if it does. Risk of harm is less serious than the same actual harm. Where the offence has caused risk of harm but no (or much less) actual harm, the normal approach is to move to the next category of harm down. This may not be appropriate if either the likelihood or extent of potential harm is particularly high.

STEP TWO
STARTING POINT AND CATEGORY RANGE

Having determined the category at step one, the court should use the appropriate starting point (as adjusted in accordance with step one above) to reach a sentence within the category range in the table below. The starting point applies to all offenders irrespective of plea or previous convictions.

Where the value is larger or smaller than the amount on which the starting point is based, this should lead to upward or downward adjustment as appropriate.

Section 1 Bribery Act 2010: Bribing another person

Section 2 Bribery Act 2010: Being bribed

Section 6 Bribery Act 2010: Bribery of foreign public officials

Maximum: 10 years' custody

	A	B	C
Category 1	**Starting point** 7 years' custody	**Starting point** 5 years' custody	**Starting point** 3 years' custody
	Category range 5 – 8 years' custody	**Category range** 3 – 6 years' custody	**Category range** 18 months' – 4 years' custody
Category 2	**Starting point** 5 years' custody	**Starting point** 3 years' custody	**Starting point** 18 months' custody
	Category range 3 – 6 years' custody	**Category range** 18 months' – 4 years' custody	**Category range** 26 weeks' – 3 years' custody
Category 3	**Starting point** 3 years' custody	**Starting point** 18 months' custody	**Starting point** 26 weeks' custody
	Category range 18 months' – 4 years' custody	**Category range** 26 weeks' – 3 years' custody	**Category range** Medium level community order – 1 year's custody
Category 4	**Starting point** 18 months' custody	**Starting point** 26 weeks' custody	**Starting point** Medium level community order
	Category range 26 weeks' – 3 years' custody	**Category range** Medium level community order – 1 year's custody	**Category range** Band B fine – High level community order

The table below contains a non-exhaustive list of additional factual elements providing the context of the offence and factors relating to the offender.

Identify whether any combination of these or other relevant factors should result in an upward or downward adjustment from the starting point.

Consecutive sentences for multiple offences may be appropriate where large sums are involved.

Factors increasing seriousness	Factors reducing seriousness or reflecting personal mitigation
Statutory aggravating factors	No previous convictions **or** no relevant/recent convictions
Previous convictions, having regard to a) the nature of the offence to which the conviction relates and its relevance to the current offence; and b) the time that has elapsed since the conviction	Remorse
Offence committed whilst on bail	Good character and/or exemplary conduct
Other aggravating factors	Little or no prospect of success

Factors increasing seriousness	Factors reducing seriousness or reflecting personal mitigation
Steps taken to prevent the victim reporting or obtaining assistance and/or from assisting or supporting the prosecution	Serious medical conditions requiring urgent, intensive or long-term treatment
Attempts to conceal/dispose of evidence	Age and/or lack of maturity where it affects the responsibility of the offender
Established evidence of community/wider impact	Lapse of time since apprehension where this does not arise from the conduct of the offender
Failure to comply with current court orders	Mental disorder or learning disability
Offence committed on licence	Sole or primary carer for dependent relatives
Offences taken into consideration	Offender co-operated with investigation, made early admissions and/or voluntarily reported offending
Failure to respond to warnings about behaviour	
Offences committed across borders	
Blame wrongly placed on others	
Pressure exerted on another party	
Offence committed to facilitate other criminal activity	

STEP THREE
CONSIDER ANY FACTORS WHICH INDICATE A REDUCTION, SUCH AS ASSISTANCE TO THE PROSECUTION

The court should take into account sections 73 and 74 of the Serious Organised Crime and Police Act 2005 (assistance by defendants: reduction or review of sentence) and any other rule of law by virtue of which an offender may receive a discounted sentence in consequence of assistance given (or offered) to the prosecutor or investigator.

STEP FOUR
REDUCTION FOR GUILTY PLEAS

The court should take account of any potential reduction for a guilty plea in accordance with section 144 of the Criminal Justice Act 2003 and the *Guilty Plea* guideline.

STEP FIVE
TOTALITY PRINCIPLE

If sentencing an offender for more than one offence, or where the offender is already serving a sentence, consider whether the total sentence is just and proportionate to the overall offending behaviour.

STEP SIX
CONFISCATION, COMPENSATION AND ANCILLARY OR-DERS

The court must proceed with a view to making a confiscation order if it is asked to do so by the prosecutor or if the court believes it is appropriate for it to do so.

Where the offence has resulted in loss or damage the court must consider whether to make a compensation order.

If the court makes both a confiscation order and an order for compensation and the court believes the offender will not have sufficient means to satisfy both orders in full, the court must direct that the compensation be paid out of sums recovered under the confiscation order (section 13 of the Proceeds of Crime Act 2002).

The court may also consider whether to make ancillary orders. These may include a deprivation order, a financial reporting order, a serious crime prevention order and disqualification from acting as a company director.

STEP SEVEN
REASONS

Section 174 of the Criminal Justice Act 2003 imposes a duty to give reasons for, and explain the effect of, the sentence.

STEP EIGHT
CONSIDERATION FOR TIME SPENT ON BAIL

The court must consider whether to give credit for time spent on bail in accordance with section 240A of the Criminal Justice Act 2003.

Sentencing

Index to sentencing

Violent Offender Order* B[51]

Youth Rehabilitation Order B[50]

YRO requirements (Sch 1, Pt 1 CJ & IA 2008) B[50.4] onwards)
The details are to be found in Schedule 1 of the Act and the relevant paragraph to the
Schedule is indicated below in each of the available requirements:
(1)   Intensive supervision and surveillance requirement
(2)   Activity requirement (paras 6–8)
(3)   Supervision requirement (para 9)
(4)   Unpaid work requirement for those aged 16–17 years when convicted
(para 10)
(5)   Programme requirement (para 11)
(6)   Attendance centre requirement (para 12)
(7)   Prohibited activity requirement (para 13)
(8)   Curfew requirement (para 14)
(9)   Exclusion requirement (para 15)
(10)   Residence requirement (para 16)
(11)   Local authority residence requirement (paras 17 and 19)
(12)   Fostering requirement (paras 4, 18–19)
(13)   Mental health treatment requirement (paras 20–21)
(14)   Drug treatment/drug testing requirement (paras 22–23)
(15)   Intoxicating substance treatment requirement (para 24)
(16)   Education requirement (para 25)
(17)   Electronic monitoring requirement (para 26)
Breach of a YRO requirement B[50.23]
Commission of further offence B[50.24]
Application to revoke B[50.25]
Amendment B[50.26]

*The Anti-social Behaviour, Crime and Policing Act 2014
prospectively replaces these orders.

**Significant changes to supervision after release are pro-
spectively made by the Offender Rehabilitation Act 2014.

B[1]

Remission to another court

B[1.1] If the following conditions are met a magistrates' court may remit an offender to another magistrates' court (Powers of Criminal Courts (Sentencing) Act 2000, s 10). The conditions are:

(a)   The court proposing to remit has convicted the offender of an offence which is punishable by either imprisonment or disqualification.

(b)   The offender has attained 18 years of age.

(c)   The court to which the convicting court proposes to remit has convicted the offender of another such offence but has not sentenced him nor committed him to the crown court to be dealt with.

(d)   The receiving court consents to the remission.

B[1.2] The offender may be remitted on bail or in custody. He is not required to consent to the remission nor has he any right of appeal against it.

B[1.3] Juveniles. A magistrates' court which has found a juvenile offender (under 18) guilty of an offence must remit the juvenile to a youth court unless satisfied that it is undesirable to do so (Powers of Criminal Courts (Sentencing) Act 2000, s 8) and must exercise that power unless it is of the opinion that the case is one which can properly be dealt with by means of:

(a)   an absolute or conditional discharge;

(b)   a fine.

B[1.4] The court to which he is remitted will normally be the youth court for the area in which he resides. If the court finding the juvenile guilty is itself a youth court it may remit to another youth court or deal with him as it thinks fit.

Remittal to an adult court

B[1.5] If a juvenile attains the age of 18 before trial in the youth court or after conviction but before sentence the youth court may remit for trial or sentence to the adult court in the same petty sessions area. The remittal may be on bail or in custody.

There is power for a magistrates' court to remit a youth to the youth court for trial where an adult co-accused pleads guilty: Magistrates' Courts Act 1980, s 29(2). Where a youth is sent to the Crown Court for trial with an adult, similar power is now provided: Crime and Disorder Act 1998, Sch 3, para 13 (overturning the effect of the decision in *R (W) v Leeds Crown Court* [2011] EWHC 2326 (Admin), (2012) 175 JP 367, [2012] 1 Cr App R 13, [2012] Crim LR 160.

Transfer of criminal proceedings

B[1A.1] Where a person appears or is brought before a magistrates' court –

(a)   to be tried by the court for an offence, or
(b)   for the court to inquire into the offence as examining justices,

the court may transfer the matter to another magistrates' court (MCA 1980, s 27A as inserted by Courts Act 2003, s 46).

The court may transfer the matter before or after beginning the trial or inquiry. If the magistrates' court transfers before hearing all of the evidence and the parties the court to whom the case has been transferred must, in effect, hear the evidence and the parties again. The power to transfer must be exercised in accordance with any directions given under Courts Act 2003, s 30(3).

B[1A.2] It would appear that the consent of the magistrates' court to which the proceedings are to be transferred is not a legal requirement. Good practice suggests that the court to whom the case has been transferred should be contacted prior to transfer. (See JCS document: 'Guidance on the use of s 27A MCA 1980'; ref 54.004, Intel October 2008.)

Custodial sentences*

---

* Significant changes to supervision after release are prospectively made by the Offender Rehabilitation Act 2014.

B[2.1] There are three main forms of custodial sentence: imprisonment, detention in a young offender institution and detention and training orders. By virtue of the CJA 2003, sentences of custody plus and intermittent custody will be available nationally from a date to be appointed. Assuming the provisions of the CJA 2003 are implemented, the new sentencing disposals will only apply to offences committed on or after the operative date.

B[2.2] Imprisonment (at B[37]) is confined to defendants over the age of 21 years (**18 years). The minimum period is 5 days (**14 days) and the maximum is that fixed by statute. There is one other form of imprisonment – the suspended sentence.

B[2.3] Detention in a young offender institution (at B[25]) is the equivalent of imprisonment for those under 21. The minimum age is 18 years for both males and females. (**From a date to be appointed sentences of detention in a YOI will be replaced by imprisonment for offences committed on or after the operative date.)

B[2.4] The general minimum for 18–21 year old offenders is 21 days. In the case of detention in a young offender institution imposed for breach of a supervision order made on release from such an institution a term not exceeding 30 days may be imposed. (**B[2.2] will apply to offences committed on or after the appointed date.)

B[2.5] The maximum term is generally the maximum term that an adult could receive for the offence. The maximum is 12 months for two indictable offences.

B[2.6] Detention and training orders. are available for 12 to 17 year old offenders inclusive. The court may order a period of 4, 6, 8, 10, 12, 18 or 24 months, half of which will be detention in a training centre and half of which will be supervised in the community. The offence must carry a sentence of four months or more were an adult to be charged with a similar offence. Accordingly, a detention and training order is not available in the case of a youth convicted of an offence of criminal damage where the damage alleged is below £5,000 (*Pye v Leeds Youth Court* [2006] EWHC 2527 (Admin), [2006] All ER (D) 16 (Oct)).

B[2.7] Presence of the accused. If the proceedings were instituted by an information followed by summons, or by a written charge, the court shall not in absence impose a custodial sentence or order that a suspended sentence shall take effect; in any other case, where such a sentence or order is imposed or made, the offender must be brought before the court before he begins to serve the sentence and the sentence will not be effective until this happens: Magistrates' Courts Act 1980, s 11(3), (3A) and (5).

B[2.8] Restrictions on imposing custodial sentences. A person shall not be sentenced to a custodial sentence (immediate or suspended) unless he is legally represented. The exceptions to this are:

(a)   representation was made available to him for the purposes of the proceedings under Part 1 of the Legal Aid, Sentencing and Punishment of Offenders Act 2012 but was withdrawn because of his conduct or because it appeared that his financial resources were such that he was not eligible for such representation;

(b)   he applied for such representation and the application was refused because it appeared that his financial resources were such that he was not eligible [for such representation; or

(c)   having been informed of his right to apply for such representation and having had the opportunity to do so, he refused or failed to apply: Powers of Criminal Courts (Sentencing) Act 2000, s 83.

B[2.9] A court may not pass a custodial sentence in any form on an offender of any age unless it is satisfied that:

(a)   the offence, or the combination of the offence and one or more offences associated with it, was so serious that neither a fine alone nor a community sentence can be justified for the offence; or

(b)   the offender fails to express a required willingness to comply with a requirement in a community order; or

(c)   the offender fails to comply with an order for pre-sentence drug testing (CJA 2003, s 161(2));

(d)   in the case of an offender aged under 18, the court must obtain a pre-sentence report. The pre-sentence report must be in writing and cannot be given orally. (For older offenders, see **B[2.22]**, below. For mentally disordered persons, see **B[2.23]**, below.)

B[2.10]–[2.15] In forming such an opinion a court must take into account all such information about the circumstances of the offence (including any associated offences and any aggravating or mitigating factors) as is available to it, which will almost invariably include information in a pre-sentence report (see below). A court may also take into account any information about the offender which is before it. The court may take into account previous convictions and previous failures to respond to sentences when assessing the seriousness of current offending.

B[2.16] Exceptionally ((b) above) the court may impose a custodial sentence where the defendant refuses to give his consent to a requirement in a community order proposed by the court which requires his consent.

B[2.17] Apart from the exceptional case, the court must state in open court that it is of the opinion that either one or other of the criteria (a), (b) or (c) apply and why it is of that opinion. In any case, the court must explain to the offender in ordinary language why it is imposing a custodial sentence on him.

Even where the custody threshold is reached the court should take into account:

•   the clear intention of the threshold test is to reserve custody as a punishment for the most serious offences;

- passing the custody threshold does not mean that a custodial sentence should be deemed inevitable; custody can still be avoided in light of personal mitigation or where there is a suitable intervention in the community which provides sufficient restriction (by way of punishment) while addressing the rehabilitation of the offender to prevent future crime. However, where the offence would otherwise appear to warrant a term of imprisonment within the Crown Court's jurisdiction, it is for the Crown Court to make that judgement;
- the approach to the imposition of a custodial sentence should be as follows:

    (a)   Has the custody threshold been passed?

    (b)   If so, is it unavoidable that a custodial sentence be imposed?

    (c)   If so, can that sentence be suspended? (Sentencers should be clear that they would have imposed a custodial sentence if the power to suspend had not been available.)

    (d)   If not, impose a sentence which takes immediate effect for the shortest possible term commensurate with the seriousness of the offence (CJA 2003, s 153(2)).

Length of custodial sentences

B[2.18] A custodial sentence passed by a court shall be for such term (not exceeding the permitted maximum) as in the opinion of the court is commensurate with the seriousness of the offence, or a combination of the offence and other offences associated with it.

B[2.19] In determining sentence the court must have regard to the guidelines set by the Sentencing Guidelines Council and, if it departs from those guidelines, the court must state its opinion and reasons in open court and give an explanation to the offender in ordinary language.

B[2.20] In forming an opinion on the appropriate length of sentence the court must take into account all such information about the circumstances of the offence (including any associated offences and any aggravating or mitigating factors) as is available to it (such as a pre-sentence report).

Section 108 of the Legal Aid, Sentencing and Punishment of Offenders Act 2012 inserted s 240ZA of the Criminal Justice Act 20031 in place of s 240. The effect is to disapply the discretion to withhold credit for time on remand in custody for the offence or a related offence; instead, such time is to be calculated and applied administratively. There are three exceptions, however, where credit for time on remand in custody does not apply, namely:

(a)   if, on any day on which the offender was remanded in custody in connection with the offence, the offender was also detained in connection with any other matter, that day is not to count as time served;

(b)   a day counts as time served in relation to only one sentence, and only once in relation to that sentence;

(c)   a day does not to count as time served as part of any period of 28 days served by the offender before automatic release.

Consecutive and concurrent sentences, where a prisoner has not been released between serving such sentences, are counted as one sentence for the purpose of deducting remand time.

For the purpose of crediting time on remand in custody, a suspended sentence is to be treated as a sentence of imprisonment when it takes effect and is to be treated as imposed by the order under which it takes effect.

The 2003 Act provisions on credit for time on remand apply to any sentence of imprisonment, whether it is: an original sentence of imprisonment; one imposed for breach/revocation of a community order; one imposed by way of activation of a suspended sentence; one imposed in default of payment of a sum adjudged to be paid by way of a conviction; one imposed for want of sufficient distress to satisfy any sum of money; or one imposed for failure to be or abstain from doing anything required to be done or left undone.

It was previously the position that a suspended sentence should not be imposed in a case where the offender had spent time on remand in custody which was equivalent to any immediate term of imprisonment which could be imposed (which is now beyond question), but that the court might nonetheless make a community order. The removal of the discretion to withhold credit when re-sentencing for breach of such an order may result in reconsideration of the latter, though an order for the rehabilitation of the offender may remain open even in a case where the offender has already spent more time on remand in custody than any term of imprisonment which the offence merits.

Sections 21 and 22 of the Criminal Justice and Immigration Act 2008 introduced new provisions which apply to offenders on bail subject to a qualifying curfew condition, defined as a condition to remain at one or more specified places for a total of not less than nine hours in any given day combined with an electronic monitoring condition. In summary, such offenders were entitled, subject to exceptions made by rules, and subject to the court's discretion to withhold credit on interests of justice grounds, to have half the period spent on such curfew count towards any sentence of imprisonment imposed for the offence.

Significant changes were made by the s 109 of the Legal Aid, Sentencing and Punishment of Offenders Act 2012. Principally, the changes were:

(a)   a new method of calculating the 'credit period';
(b)   the enactment of exceptions;
(c)   the removal of the 'interests of justice' discretion to withhold credit.

The credit period is calculated by taking the following, five steps:

(1)   Add–
        The number of days on which the offender's bail was subject to the relevant conditions, including the first whether the condition applied for the whole of the day or not, but excluding the last if the offender spends the last part of it in custody.
(2)   Deduct–
        Any of the above days on which the offender was subject to an electronically monitored curfew requirement in connection with any other sentence including on release under home detention curfew) or temporarily released from prison in relation to another sentence.
(3)   Deduct–
        From the remaining days, the number of days during that remainder on which the offender has broken either or both of the relevant conditions.
(4)   Divide–
        The result by two.
(5)   Round up–

If necessary, to the nearest round number.

A day of the credit period counts as time served in relation to only one sentence and only once in relation to that sentence.

A day of the credit period is not to count as time served as part of any period of 28 days served by the offender before automatic release. (This prevents any shortening of any recall made under s 255B of the 2003 Act where the maximum length of the recall is 28 days.)

If a curfew is not accompanied by an electronic tag the statutory conditions are not met and a court is entitled to refuse to give credit for the curfew period even though it qualified in terms of length and the defendant complied with it; there might, however, be circumstances where some allowance should be made, for example, where there are two defendants for sentence who have been subject to curfews but for some reason only one defendant has been electronically tagged.

The court needs to know the exact number of days of the curfew since it is for the court to work out and announce the number of days to be credited.

In passing a detention and training order on a juvenile offender the [youth] court must also take into account any time spent on secure remand when fixing the length of sentence, and time spent on remand must be calculated and announced at time of sentence in cases of imprisonment.

Pre-sentence report

B[2.21] This means a report in writing which is made by a probation officer (or social worker) with a view to assisting the court in determining the most suitable method of dealing with an offender and contains such information as to such matters as may be prescribed by the Secretary of State.

B[2.22] Before forming an opinion on the necessity for, and appropriate length of, a custodial sentence the court should obtain a pre-sentence report. Although a custodial sentence is not invalidated by the court's failure to obtain such a report, magistrates will no doubt continue to wish to meet the statutory requirement in all cases where an offender is in jeopardy of losing his liberty despite the 'let out' clause 'unless the court is of the opinion that it is unnecessary to obtain a pre-sentence report' (see **B[2.9]** above).

Mentally disordered offenders

B[2.23] Where the offender is, or appears to be, mentally disordered, the court must, unless in the circumstances of the case it appears unnecessary to do so, obtain a medical report made orally or in writing by a doctor approved under the Mental Health Act 1983 as having special experience in the diagnosis or treatment of mental disorder.

B[2.24] Where a court is considering a custodial sentence in such circumstances it must consider:

(a)   any information before it which relates to his mental condition (whether given in a medical report, a pre-sentence report or otherwise); and

(b)   the likely effect of such a sentence on that condition and on any treatment which may be available for it.

Community sentences

B[3.1] The Criminal Justice Act 2003 introduced the concept of a 'community order', ie a sentence which consists of or includes one or more requirements: see B[17.35]. This generic community order only applies to defendants over 18 years.

B[3.2] A court may not impose a community sentence unless:

(a)   the offence is punishable with imprisonment (s 150A CJA 2003);

(b)   it is of the opinion that the offence was serious enough to warrant such a sentence taking into account all such information about the circumstances of the offence (including any associated offences or any aggravating or mitigating factors) as is available to it;

(c)   the particular order or orders comprising or forming part of the sentence are such as in the opinion of the court is, or taken together are, the most suitable for the offender taking into account any information about the offender which is before it (such as a pre-sentence report, see below);

(d)   the restrictions on liberty imposed by the order or orders are such as in the opinion of the court are commensurate with the seriousness of the offence, or the combination of the offence and other offences associated with it, taking into account information about the circumstances etc as in (a) above.

Note that there will still be cases where the community threshold has been passed but a fine or discharge is still an appropriate penalty (see s 148(5) CJA 2003).

B[3.3]–[3.4] When considering seriousness of the current offence or offences previous convictions and previous failures to respond to court orders may be taken into account.

Pre-sentence report

B[3.5] Before forming an opinion as to the suitability for an offender of one or more of the above orders, the court should obtain and consider a pre-sentence report unless it is of the opinion that it is unnecessary to obtain one.

B[3.6] An adult community order must specify an end date of not more than 3 years after commencement when all requirements must be completed. Individual requirements, aside from supervision, may be specified to be completed in a shorter period than that of the overall order.

The sentencing decision

B[3.7]

SENTENCING FORM FOR PSR

A: PRE-SENTENCE ASSESSMENT STAGE

DATE: [   ]   1a) **DEFENDANT:** [   ]

b) **D.O.B:** [   ]   c) **ADDRESS:** [   ]

2. **CUSTODY:** [   ]   **BAIL:** [   ]

3. **CHARGES:** [   ]

4. **GUIDELINE SENTENCE:**   Fine/discharge [   ]   Community [   ]   Custody [   ]   Commit for Sentence [   ]

5. **OFFENCE FACTORS INFLUENCING ASSESSMENT**

a) Aggravating factors: [   ]

b) Mitigating factors: [   ]

c) Culpability   intentional [   ]   reckless [   ]

knew likely outcome [   ]   negligent [   ]

d) Harm caused/risked: [   ]

6. **OFFENDER FACTORS INFLUENCING ASSESSMENT**

[   ]

7. **SERIOUSNESS** (sentencing range justified by offence and offending factors)   **L   M   H**

Fine/discharge (no **PSR**) [   ]   Community (serious enough) [   ] [   ] [   ]

Custody (so serious) [   ]   Commit to Crown Court (too serious) [   ]

8. **MAIN (1) AND SECONDARY (2) PURPOSE(S) OF SENTENCE**

Punishment [   ]   Rehabilitation [   ]   Reduction in crime/ deterrence [   ]

Protection of public [   ]   Reparation [   ]

9. **REPORT TYPE:**   Fast [   ]   Standard [   ]   Due: [   ]

B: SENTENCING STAGES

10. FACTORS ARISING FROM REPORT
Including, if appropriate, a) why you have reached a different conclusion from the indications of seriousness and purpose already given, or b) why you are departing from the proposals in the report.

11. SENTENCE TO BE IMPOSED (referring to reasons)

12. CREDIT FOR GUILTY PLEA
Record a) the extent of credit given and reasons for it, or b) what the sentence would have been if a timely guilty plea had been entered. (NB: Do not double count credit)

13. ANCILLARY ORDERS
Details of compensation (or reasons for not awarding it), plus other ancillary orders.

14. REASONS FOR DEPARTING FROM SENTENCING COUNCIL GUIDELINES

15. EXPLAIN SENTENCE USING APPROPRIATE PRONOUNCEMENTS

B[4]

Sentencing tables

B[4.1] See the following pages for the sentencing tables.

B[4.1] **Table A** Available sentences for either way offences punishable with imprisonment on summary conviction are shaded. See Index to sentencing for paragraph references.

Right-hand annotations:

- Restrictions on custodial sentences: offence 'so serious' etc, pre-sentence report, legal representation
- *Under 15-year-old: court must specify the offender is persistent
- Community Order / Offence 'serious enough' / pre-sentence report / See **B[17]** onwards
- † when in force and initially to be piloted in certain areas
- **Offenders aged 18–24 years only

Age	10	11	12	13	14	15	16	17	18	19	20	21 & over
Imprisonment												■
Suspended with requirements												■
Detention in young offender institution (can be suspended)									■	■	■	
Detention Training Order*			*	*	*	■	■	■				
Detention (One Day)									■	■	■	■
Community Order with requirements (CJA 2003, s 177)									■	■	■	■
Unpaid work									■	■	■	■
Activity requirement									■	■	■	■
Programme requirement									■	■	■	■
Prohibited Activity requirement									■	■	■	■
Curfew requirement									■	■	■	■
Exclusion requirement									■	■	■	■
Residence requirement									■	■	■	■
Foreign travel prohibition requirement									■	■	■	■
Mental Health Treatment requirement									■	■	■	■
Drug Rehabilitation requirement									■	■	■	■
Alcohol Treatment requirement									■	■	■	■
Alcohol abstinence and monitoring requirement†									■	■	■	■
Supervision requirement									■	■	■	■
Attendance Centre requirement**	■	■	■	■	■	■	■	■	**	**	**	**
Referral to a Youth Offender Panel	■	■	■	■	■	■	■	■				

u-14 max £250, 14–17 £1,000 see **B[18]** and **B[34]**

Medical recommendation

*PSR re: dangerousness for youths normally obtained

Court to give reasons

Youth Rehabilitation Order

Offence "serious enough"

Pre-sentence report required

See **B[50.3]** onwards

Fine

Compensation/Deprivation Order

Discharge (Abs/Cond)

Hospital Order

Guardianship Order

Committal for Sentence PCC(S)A 2000, s 3 or 4 (adult offenders) PCC(S)A 2000, s 3C (youths)*

Deferred Sentence with requirements

Reparation Order

Youth Rehabilitation Order with requirements

Activity requirement

Supervision requirement

Unpaid Work requirement (16-17 year olds only)

Programme requirement

Attendance Centre requirement

Prohibited activity requirement

Curfew requirement

Exclusion requirement

Residence requirement

Foreign travel prohibition requirement

Local Authority Residence requirement

Mental Health Treatment requirement

Drug Treatment requirement

Intoxicating Substance Treatment requirement

Education requirement

B[4.2] **Table B** Available sentences for purely summary offences punishable with imprisonment are shaded. See Index to sentencing for paragraph references.

Top annotations:
- Restrictions on custodial sentences: offence 'so serious' etc, pre-sentence report, legal representation
- *Under 15-year-old: court must specify the offender is persistent
- Community Order / Offence 'serious enough' / pre-sentence report / See B[17] onwards
- † when in force and initially to be piloted in certain areas
- **Offenders aged 18–24 years only

Age	10	11	12	13	14	15	16	17	18	19	20	21 & over
Imprisonment												
Suspended with requirements												
Detention in young offender institution (can be suspended)												
Detention Training Order*			*	*	*							
Detention (One Day)												
Community Order with requirements (CJA 2003, s 177)												
Unpaid work												
Activity requirement												
Programme requirement												
Prohibited Activity requirement												
Curfew requirement												
Exclusion requirement												
Residence requirement												
Foreign travel prohibition requirement												
Mental Health Treatment requirement												
Drug Rehabilitation requirement												
Alcohol Treatment requirement												
Alcohol abstinence and monitoring requirement†												
Supervision requirement												
Attendance Centre requirement**									**	**	**	**
Referral to a Youth Offender Panel												

Column headings (top):

- u-14 max £250, 14–17 £1,000 see B[18] and B[34]
- Medical recommendation
- Court to give reasons
- Youth Rehabilitation Order
- Offence "serious enough"
- Pre-sentence report required
- See B[50.3] onwards

Row labels (bottom):

- Fine
- Compensation/Deprivation Order
- Discharge (Abs/Cond)
- Hospital Order
- Guardianship Order
- Committal for Sentence
- PCC(S)A 2000, s 6 (committal for sentence in certain cases where offender committed in respect of another offence)
- Deferred Sentence with requirements
- Reparation Order
- Youth Rehabilitation Order with requirements
- Activity requirement
- Supervision requirement
- Unpaid Work requirement (16–17 year olds only)
- Programme requirement
- Attendance Centre requirement
- Prohibited activity requirement
- Curfew requirement
- Exclusion requirement
- Residence requirement
- Local Authority Residence requirement
- Mental Health Treatment requirement
- Drug Treatment requirement
- Intoxicating Substance Treatment requirement
- Education requirement

B[4.3] **Table C** Available sentences for purely summary offences not carrying imprisonment are shaded. See Index to sentencing for paragraph references.

Age	10	11	12	13	14	15	16	17	18	19	20	21 & over	
Imprisonment													
Suspended with requirements													
Detention in young offender institution (can be suspended)													
Detention Training Order													
Detention (One Day)													
Community Order with requirements (CJA 2003, s 177)													
Unpaid work													
Activity requirement													
Programme requirement													
Prohibited Activity requirement													
Curfew requirement													
Exclusion requirement													
Residence requirement													
Mental Health Treatment requirement													
Drug Rehabilitation requirement													
Alcohol Treatment requirement													
Supervision requirement													
Attendance Centre requirement**													

Community Order
The power is restricted to imprisonable offences

See **B[17]** onwards

*Offenders aged 18–24 years only

**Discretionary referral conditions must apply, See B[48] onwards and s 17 PCC(S)A 2000 u-14 max £250, 14–17 £1,000 see B[18] and B[34]

Medical recommendation

Court to give reasons

Youth Rehabilitation Order The power is restricted to imprisonable offences See B[50.3] onwards

- Referral to a Youth Offender Panel
- Fine
- Compensation/Deprivation Order
- Discharge (Abs/Cond)
- Hospital Order
- Guardianship Order
- Committal for Sentence
- Deferred Sentence with requirements
- Reparation Order
- Youth Rehabilitation Order with requirements
- Activity requirement
- Supervision requirement
- Unpaid Work requirement (16–17 year olds only)
- Programme requirement
- Attendance Centre requirement
- Prohibited activity requirement
- Curfew requirement
- Exclusion requirement
- Residence requirement
- Local Authority Residence requirement
- Mental Health Treatment requirement
- Drug Treatment requirement
- Intoxicating Substance Treatment requirement
- Education requirement

B[4.4] Table D Available sentences according to age of offender are shaded. See Index to sentencing for paragraph references.

Notes / legend:

- Restrictions on custodial sentences: offence 'so serious' etc, pre-sentence report, legal representation
- *Under 15-year-old: court must specify the offender is persistent
- Community Order Offence 'serious enough' pre-sentence report See B[17] onwards
- † when in force and initially to be piloted in certain areas
- **Offenders aged 18–24 years only u-14 max £250, 14–17 £1,000 see B[18] and B[34]

Age	10	11	12	13	14	15	16	17	18	19	20	21 & over
Imprisonment												▓
Suspended with requirements											▓	▓
Detention in young offenders institution (can be suspended)[1]									▓	▓	▓	
Detention Training Order[1,2] *			▓	▓	▓	▓	▓	▓				
Detention (One Day)[1]									▓	▓	▓	▓
Community Order with requirements (CJA 2003, s 177)									▓	▓	▓	▓
Unpaid work									▓	▓	▓	▓
Activity requirement									▓	▓	▓	▓
Programme requirement									▓	▓	▓	▓
Prohibited Activity requirement									▓	▓	▓	▓
Curfew requirement									▓	▓	▓	▓
Exclusion requirement									▓	▓	▓	▓
Residence requirement									▓	▓	▓	▓
Foreign travel prohibition requirement									▓	▓	▓	▓
Mental Health Treatment requirement									▓	▓	▓	▓
Drug Rehabilitation requirement									▓	▓	▓	▓
Alcohol Treatment requirement									▓	▓	▓	▓
Alcohol abstinence and monitoring requirement†									▓	▓	▓	▓
Supervision requirement									▓	▓	▓	▓
Attendance Centre requirement**									**	**	**	**
Fine	▓	▓	▓	▓	▓	▓	▓	▓	▓	▓	▓	▓
Compensation/Deprivation Order[3]	▓	▓	▓	▓	▓	▓	▓	▓	▓	▓	▓	▓

Column headers:

- Medical recommendation
- Either way offences
- Court to give reasons
- Youth Rehabilitation Order
- Offence "serious enough"
- Pre-sentence report required
- See B[50.3] onwards

Row labels:

- Discharge (Abs/Cond)
- Hospital Order[1,2]
- Guardianship Order[1,2]
- Committal for Sentence PCC(S)A 2000, ss 3 and 4
- Deferred Sentence with requirements
- Reparation Order[2]
- Youth Rehabilitation Order with requirements
- Activity requirement
- Supervision requirement
- Unpaid Work requirement (16–17 year olds only)
- Programme requirement
- Attendance Centre requirement
- Prohibited activity requirement
- Curfew requirement
- Exclusion requirement
- Residence requirement
- Local Authority Residence requirement
- Mental Health Treatment requirement
- Drug Treatment requirement
- Intoxicating Substance Treatment requirement
- Education requirement

(a)　Sentences marked with [1] can only be imposed if the offence is punishable with imprisonment when committed by an adult over 21 years.

(b)　As far as offenders under 18 are concerned, a magistrates' court (as opposed to a youth court) cannot impose any of the penalties marked with a [2]. The magistrates' court must remit such juveniles on bail or in care to a youth court which will usually be the youth court for the area in which he lives.

(c)　[3] Under PCC(S)A 2000, s 143: see B[34]

**　Available up to the age of 25 in cases of default in payment of money where the court would have the power to commit to prison

The process of sentencing

Introduction

B[5.1] Sentencing is not and never will be an exact science; only rarely could a group of sentencers agree that a particular sentence was exactly right and, even if they did, they would probably be agreeing only that it was right to show a particular level of leniency. The prerogative of saying what is 'right' in terms of sentencing levels belongs to the Sentencing Council who aim to promote consistency in sentencing and guidance in respect of offences or offenders in a particular category.

However, a degree of vagueness might be thought to be inevitable when there are so many variables to be considered before a sentencing decision is reached. Not only should this fact not discourage a proper study of the subject of sentencing, but it should positively encourage it and the area of study most profitable to the lay magistrate is that of the process of sentencing, the route to be followed in order to reach a sentence which, if it cannot be said to be exactly right, at least is unlikely to be disturbed on appeal if the offender's circumstances remain the same. The framework for a structured sentencing decision is given at B[3.7]. This is amplified and explained in paragraphs 1–8 which follow. Determination of guilt and the factual basis for the sentencing decision is dealt with in Section I court procedure.

Sentencing structure
Magistrates' Courts Sentencing Guidance – Definitive Guideline

B[5.2] Section 172 of the Criminal Justice Act 2003 places a statutory obligation on courts to follow Sentencing Council sentencing guidelines. In general, a court's reasons for departing from sentencing guidelines would be specific to the offence and offenders under consideration. A court which had departed from the guidelines essentially because it considered that they needed reconsideration had erred: *R v Heathcote-Smith (Benjamin) and Melton (Christopher Timothy)* [2011] EWCA Crim 2846, [2012] 2 Cr App Rep (S) 133, [2012] Crim LR 304.

1. Offence seriousness (culpability and harm)
A Identify the appropriate starting point
Consider which of the examples of offence activity corresponds most closely to the circumstances of the case to identify the appropriate **starting point**
Starting points are based on a **first time offender pleading guilty**
Refer to the following where the starting point is, or the **range** includes, a:
(i) fine – B[33]
(ii) community order – B[17]
(iii) custodial sentence – B[2]
Refer to B[5.7] below for the meaning of the terms "starting point", "range" and "first time offender"

B Consider the effect of aggravating and mitigating factors
Move up or down from the starting point to reflect aggravating or mitigating factors that affect the seriousness of the offence to reach a provisional sentence
Common aggravating and mitigating factors are set out below at B[2A] below; relevant factors are also identified in the individual offence guidelines to be found in **Section A** of this book. **These lists are not exhaustive.**
Do not double-count any aggravating or mitigating factors in the description of the activity used to reach the starting point/
The **range** is the bracket into which the provisional sentence will normally fall but the court is not precluded from going outside the range where the facts justify it.
Previous convictions which aggravate the seriousness of the current offence may take the provisional sentence beyond the range, especially if there are significant other aggravating factors present.
2. Form a preliminary view of the appropriate sentence, then consider offender mitigation
Matters of offender mitigation may include remorse and admissions to police in interview
3. Consider a reduction for a guilty plea
Apply the sliding scale reduction for a guilty plea to punitive elements of the sentence – see B[5.46] below.
Application of the reduction may take the sentence below the range in some cases
4. Consider ancillary orders including compensation
Refer to B[18] for compensation and section B generally for available ancillary orders.
Consider compensation in every case where the offending has resulted in personal injury, loss or damage – give reasons if order not made. See B[18].
5. Decide sentence
Give reasons
Review the total sentence to ensure that it is proportionate to the offending behaviour and properly balanced.
Give reasons for the sentence passed, including any ancillary orders.
State if the sentence has been reduced to reflect a guilty plea; indicate what the sentence would otherwise have been.
NB: By law, criminal courts are obliged **to follow** SC guidance. Explain ie give reasons, if the sentence is of a different kind or outside the range indicated in the guidelines.

List of aggravating and mitigating factors

B[5.2A] (Taken from the SGC Guideline "Overarching Principles: Seriousness")

Aggravating factors

Factors indicating higher culpability:

- Offence committed while on bail for other offences
- Failure to respond to previous sentences
- Offence was racially or religiously aggravated
- Offence motivated by, or demonstrated hostility to the victim based on his or her sexual orientation (or presumed sexual orientation)
- Offence motivated by, or demonstrating, hostility based on the victim's disability (or presumed disability)

- Previous conviction(s), particularly where a pattern of repeat offending is disclosed
- Planning of an offence
- An intention to commit more serious harm than actually resulted from the offence
- Offenders operating in groups or gangs
- "Professional" offending
- Commission of the offence for financial gain (where this is not inherent in the offence itself)
- High level of profit from the offence
- An attempt to conceal or dispose of evidence
- Failure to respond to warnings or concerns expressed by others about the offender's behaviour
- Offence committed while on licence
- Offence motivated by hostility towards a minority group, or a member or members of it
- Deliberate targeting of vulnerable victim(s)
- Commission of an offence while under the influence of alcohol or drugs
- Use of a weapon to frighten or injure victim
- Deliberate and gratuitous violence or damage to property, over and beyond what is needed to carry out the offence
- Abuse of power
- Abuse of position of trust

Factors indicating a more than usually serious degree of harm:

- Multiple victims
- An especially serious physical or psychological effect on the victim, even if unintended
- A sustained assault or repeated assaults on the same victim
- Victim is particularly vulnerable
- Location of the offence (for example, in an isolated place)
- Offence is committed against those working in the public sector or providing a service to the public
- Presence of others eg relatives, especially children or partner of the victim
- Additional degradation of the victim (eg taking photographs of a victim as part of a sexual offence)
- In property offences, high value (including sentimental value) of property to the victim, or substantial consequential loss (eg where the theft of equipment causes serious disruption to the victim's life or business)

Mitigating factors

Factors indicating lower culpability:

- A greater degree of provocation than normally expected
- Mental illness or disability
- Youth or age, where it affects the responsibility of the individual defendant
- The fact that the offender played only a minor role in the offence

Offender mitigation

- Genuine remorse
- Admissions to police in interview
- Ready co-operation with authorities

Aggravation related to race, religion, disability or sexual orientation

B[5.2B]   Racial or religious aggravation – statutory provisions

(1)   Sections 29 to 32 of the Crime and Disorder Act 1998 create specific racially or religiously aggravated offences which have higher maximum penalties than the non-aggravated versions of those offences. The individual offence guidelines (see **Part A**) indicate whether there is a specifically aggravated form of the offence.

(2)   An offence is racially or religiously aggravated for the purposes of ss 29–32 of the Act if the offender demonstrates hostility towards the victim based on his or her membership (or presumed membership) of a racial group, or if the offence is racially or religiously motivated: s 28 CDA 1998.

(3)   For all other offences, s 145 of the CJA 2003 provides that the court must regard racial or religious aggravation as an aggravating factor.

(4)   The court should not treat an offence as racially or religiously aggravated for the purposes of s 145 where a racially or religiously aggravated form of the offence was charged but resulted in an acquittal: *R v McGillivray* [2005] EWCA Crim 604. The court should not normally treat an offence as racially or religiously aggravated if a racially or religiously form of the offence was available but was not charged: *R v O'Callaghan* [2005] EWCA Crim 317. **Consult your legal adviser for further guidance in these situations.**

Aggravation related to disability, sexual orientation or transgender identity – statutory provisions

(5)   Under s 146 of the CJA 2003, the court must treat as an aggravating factor the fact that:

    –   an offender demonstrated hostility towards the victim based on his or her sexual orientation or disability (or presumed sexual orientation, transgender identity or disability); or

    –   the offence was motivated by hostility towards persons who are of a particular sexual orientation, transgender or who have a particular disability.

Approach to sentencing

(6)   A court should not conclude that offending involved aggravation relating to race, religion, disability, sexual orientation or transgender without first putting the offender on notice and allowing him or her to challenge allegation.

(7)   When sentencing any offence where such aggravation is found to be present, the following approach should be followed. This applies both to the specific racially or religiously aggravated offences under the CDA 1998 and to offences which are regarded as aggravated under s 145 or 146 of the CJA 2003 (*R v Kelly and Donnelly* [2001] EWCA Crim 1751):

    •   sentencers should first determine the appropriate sentence, leaving aside the element of aggravation relating to race, religion etc but taking into account al other aggravating and mitigating features;

    •   the sentence should then be increased to take account of the aggravation related to race, religion, disability or sexual orientation'

- the increase may mean that a more onerous penalty of the same type is appropriate, or that the threshold for a more severe type of sentence is passed;
- the sentencer must state in open court that the offence was aggravated by reason of race, religion, disability or sexual orientation;
- the sentencer should state what the sentence would have been without that element of aggravation.

(8) The extent to which the sentence is increased will depend on the seriousness of the aggravation. The following factors could be taken as indicating a high level of aggravation:

Offender's intention
- The element of aggravation based on race, religion etc was planned
- The offence was part of a pattern of offending by the offender
- The offender was a member of, or was associated with, a group promoting hostility based on race, religion, disability or sexual orientation
- The incident was deliberately set up to be offensive or humiliating to the victim or to the group of which the victim is a member

Impact on the victim or others
- The offence was committed in the victim's home
- The victim was providing a service to the public
- The timing or location of the offence was calculated to maximise the harm or distress it caused
- The expressions of hostility were repeated or prolonged
- The offence caused fear and distress throughout a local community or more widely
- The offence caused particular distress to the victim and/or the victim's family

(9) At the lower end of the scale, the aggravation may be regarded as less serious if:
- It was limited in scope or duration
- The offence was not motivated by hostility on the basis of race, religion, disability or sexual orientation, and the element of hostility or abuse was minor or incidental.

(10) In these guidelines, the specific racially or religiously aggravated offences under the CDA 1998 are addressed on the same page as the "basic offence"; the starting points and ranges indicated on the guidelines (see Part A) relate to the "basic" (ie non-aggravated) offence. The increase for the element of racial or religious aggravation may result in a sentence above the range; this will not constitute a departure from the guideline for which reasons must be given.

1 The offence

B[5.3] An important principle of sentencing is that a sentence should not be more severe than is warranted by the seriousness of the offence and other offences associated with it. When considering the seriousness of the current offence or offences, previous convictions and failures to respond to previous sentences may be taken into account where relevant. Custodial sentences are reserved primarily for offenders who have committed an offence 'so serious' that only a custodial sentence can be justified for it, and community sentences are only available where the offence is 'serious enough' to warrant such a sentence.

The Purposes of Sentencing

B[5.4] In respect of adults, the Criminal Justice Act 2003 sets out the objectives of sentencing as punishment, the reduction of crime (including deterrence), reforms and rehabilitation, protection of the public and reparation.

B[5.5] A custodial sentence may also be imposed where the offender has refused to consent to a drug testing order or certain conditions requiring consent (see B[2.9]).

B[5.6] Otherwise any sentence imposed will generally be commensurate with the seriousness of the offence, although the court, having considered all the mitigation, may take this into account in mitigating an offender's sentence.

Determining seriousness

B[5.7] Meaning of 'range', 'starting point' and 'first time offender'. As in previous editions, and consistent with other SGC guidelines, these guidelines are for a first time offender convicted after a trial. The guidelines provide a starting point based on an assessment of the seriousness of the offence and a range within which the sentence will normally fall in most cases.

B[5.8] The facts. The court must be satisfied that the facts of the offence or offences for which sentence is to be passed have been proved or agreed.

In determining the seriousness of an offence the court must take into account all information about the circumstances of the offence, any aggravating or mitigating factors as are available to it, and information in a pre-sentence report. The court must consider the offender's culpability and any harm or potential harm caused by the offence.

B[5.9] Associated offence. In considering whether an offence is 'serious enough' to warrant a community sentence, or 'so serious' that only a custodial sentence can be justified, the court may consider the combination of the offence and other offences associated with it. An 'associated offence' is in essence another offence for which the offender is to be sentenced at that time or is to be taken into consideration. Whether it is appropriate for offences to be TIC'd see *R v Lavery* [2008] EWCA Crim 2499, [2009] 3 All ER 295.

B[5.10]–[5.15] Guidance on the seriousness of offences and aggravating and mitigating features is to be found at B[5.2] and B[5.2A] above.

B[5.16] Parliament also gives broad guidance to the courts by prescribing the maximum penalties available. For example, many minor offences are punishable only by a fine on level 1 (max £200) and level 5 (max £5,000). Other, more serious, offences are also punishable with imprisonment of up to 6 (**12) months.

2 Mitigation

B[5.17] There are two particular objectives of mitigation: to draw to the attention of the court any factors relevant to mitigating the seriousness of the offence, and to highlight mitigation personal to the offender.

B[5.18] The first consideration for the court in determining sentence is the seriousness of the offence. The seriousness of the offence will generally determine whether the court must impose a custodial sentence or if the offence warrants the making of a community sentence, a fine or discharge.

B[5.19] In addressing the seriousness of the offence, the circumstances of the offence should be examined to see whether they disclose any mitigating circumstances. Guidance on what may amount to a mitigating (or aggravating) feature of an offence is given by the Sentencing Guidelines Council (see www.sentencing-guidelines.gov.uk) and B[5.2] and B[5.2A] above.

B[5.20] The seriousness of the offence including culpability and harm considerations will broadly determine which range of sentencing options is open to the court: custody, community, financial or a discharge. Where the court is concerned with a violent or sexual offence and is considering a custodial sentence to protect the public, the personal circumstances and history will become relevant. However, personal mitigation is usually more relevant at the second stage when the general level of seriousness has been determined, where mitigation will affect the final choice of sentence and the impact it will have on the offender. While no sentence may be more severe than is justified by the defendant's offence, personal mitigation may serve to reduce the punishment or suggest that a more individualised approach may be appropriate. In forming an opinion, whether a particular community order or orders comprising a community sentence is or are the most suitable for the offender, the court may take into account any information about the offender which is before it. Mitigating factors which have commonly been considered by the courts are referred to under 'Consideration of sentences' at B[5.36]–B[5.48].

3 Availability of sentences

B[5.21] Available sentences are determined by the maximum penalties prescribed by Parliament and by the court's assessment of the gravity of the offence.

As mentioned above the maximum penalty for an offence is fixed by statute as being a fine, or a fine and custody. Some sentences and orders of the court are available only where an offence is punishable in the case of an adult with imprisonment (the defendant himself does not need to be liable to imprisonment). A comparison of Tables A and C at B[4.1] and B[4.3] will make this apparent. Furthermore some sentences are only available to offenders of a certain age – see B[1.5].

B[5.22] By a systematic process of noting whether an offence is punishable with imprisonment and the age of the offender, the sentencing options available to the court can be narrowed progressively.

B[5.23] Criminal Justice Act 2003. This further categorises sentences and orders into four broad divisions: discharges (instead of sentencing), financial, community and custodial. In addition there are orders providing for the medical treatment of mentally disturbed offenders.

B[5.24] Discharges (absolute/conditional). These are available to all offenders and for all offences where the court is satisfied that having regard to the circumstances of the offence and the offender it is inexpedient to inflict punishment. See B[31].

B[5.25]–[5.31] Financial penalties. These include fines (B[33]), compensation (B[18]) and deprivation of property (B[34]) and are available to all offenders and for all offences.

B[5.32] Community orders (adults). The court may only impose a community sentence which consists of one or more requirements where the offence carries imprisonment and the court considers the offence, or a combination of the offence and other 'associated offences' to be 'serious enough' to warrant such a sentence. The fact that an offence is 'serious enough' does not mean that the court must pass a community sentence, only that it may do so (see B[17.35] onwards).

B[5.33] Custodial sentences (see B[2]). The custodial sentences available to the magistrates are imprisonment and for offenders under 21, detention in a young offender institution (**to be replaced by a sentence of imprisonment from a date to be appointed by virtue of the CJA 2003) and detention and training orders for offenders aged 12 to 17 inclusive. They are only available where statute defines an offence as being punishable with imprisonment.

B[5.34] A custodial sentence may generally only be imposed where the offence or a combination of the offence and 'associated offences' is 'so serious' that neither a community penalty nor a fine cannot be justified for it. The court will usually find it helpful to consider the nature and extent of the defendant's criminal culpability and the nature and extent of any injury or damage caused to the victim (*R v Howells* [1999] 1 All ER 50, [1999] 1 WLR 307, CA). However, although this criterion may be satisfied the court may nevertheless, in the case of a mentally ill defendant, make a hospital or guardianship order.

B[5.35] Exceptionally a custodial sentence may be imposed where the offender has refused to consent to a drug testing order and certain conditions in a community order requiring consent ie a willingness to comply with the requirements.

4 Consideration of sentences

B[5.36] When the court has ascertained the range of sentences appropriate for the seriousness of the offence, it must then proceed to select the particular sentence appropriate for the case. In this task it will be assisted by its appreciation of the seriousness of the offence but also by mitigation personal to the offender, any pre-sentence report and the court's objective in sentencing.

B[5.37] Mitigation. Nothing shall prevent a court from mitigating an offender's sentence by taking into account any such matters as, in the opinion of the court, are relevant in mitigation of sentence. Mitigating factors which have commonly been considered by courts include the following.

B[5.38] 1 Youth of the offender. This may operate as mitigation and will usually indicate a lower level of sentence (eg a smaller fine or shorter period of custody) than would be appropriate otherwise. The mitigating effect of youth, however, may be cancelled out by other factors, such as a record of previous convictions which is serious having regard to the offender's age, or which shows a proclivity for crime beyond what one would expect for his age.

B[5.39] 2 **Older offenders** who have not previously offended would receive credit for a previously blameless life especially when receiving a more serious penalty such as a community sentence or custody.

B[5.40]–[5.45] 3 **Effect of previous convictions.** Previous convictions must be taken into account and may make an offence more serious although this will depend upon the nature of the offence and the time elapsed since conviction. Within the range of sentences appropriate to the seriousness of the offence good character is almost always strong mitigation and the worse an offender's previous record is, the less 'discount' he can expect for good character. Occasionally, the record of previous convictions may show a significant gap since the last conviction and might be taken as evidence of a genuine effort to keep out of trouble. The record may also show that the present offence is out of character, for example, when a man with a long record of petty theft appears on a charge of indecent assault.

B[5.46] 4 **Plea of guilty.** Revised definitive guidance (Reduction in Sentence for a Guilty Plea) was handed down by the Sentencing Guidelines Council in 2007 and applies to all cases sentenced on or after 23 July 2007 (see www.sentencing-guidelines.gov.uk).

A plea of guilty will nearly always attract a sentencing discount of between 10% and 33% depending upon the stage of proceedings and the circumstances that the indication of plea was given. Remorse or contrition will mitigate the sentence particularly when there is real evidence of it. A ready admission of guilt, a willingness to assist the police, and voluntary efforts to make compensation can all be interpreted as evidence of contrition. Particularly in cases involving sexual offences a plea of guilty will spare witnesses, especially young persons, from the ordeal of giving evidence, even though the law now provides more sympathetic means for the reception of such evidence. Where the court does reduce or does not reduce the sentence because of the circumstances and stage at which the guilty plea is entered it must state in open court the reasons for its decision.

Where the prosecution case is overwhelming, it may not be appropriate to give the full reduction that would otherwise be given. Whilst there is a presumption in favour of the full reduction being given where a plea has been indicated at the first reasonable opportunity, the fact that the prosecution case is overwhelming without relying on admissions from the defendant may be a reason justifying a lower reduction should be given. The recommended reduction of 20% is likely to be appropriate. Reasons must be given.

The question whether or not a defendant has pleaded guilty at the first available opportunity was an issue which depended on the [youth] court's assessment at the time of sentencing as to whether or not it would have been proper for the defendant to have entered a guilty plea before he had viewed a CCTV recording of the incident (*R (on the application of H) v Bromley Youth Court* [2006] All ER (D) 266 (Oct)).

Annex 1 to the revised SGC definitive guidance states that the critical time for determining the reduction for a guilty plea is the **first reasonable opportunity** for the defendant to have indicated a willingness to plead guilty. This opportunity will vary with a wide range of factors and the court will need to make a judgment on the particular facts of the case before it. The first reasonable opportunity may be the first time that a defendant appears before the court and has the opportunity to plead guilty; but the court may consider that it would have been reasonable to have expected an indication of willingness even earlier, perhaps whilst under interview.

In *R v Caley* [2012] EWCA Crim 2821, (2013) 177 JP 111, 2013] Crim LR
342[, the Court of Appeal gave the following guidance on of the application
of the Sentencing Council guidelines on credit for pleading guilty.

First reasonable opportunity

Some limited narrowing of the spectrum of possibilities as to the point
of first reasonable opportunity could be achieved in the interests of
greater consistency. The right way for courts to deal with admissions in
interview was not by treating them as essential in every case to according
the maximum one-third reduction for guilty plea. Rather, the variable
circumstances of such admissions were best dealt with not by percentage
adjustments prescribed in advance, but by recognising them as a factor
tending towards downwards adjustment to the sentence passed, to be
assessed in the ordinary way by the judge along with other aggravating
and mitigating factors, but before adjustment for plea of guilty. Absent
particular considerations individual to the case, the first reasonable
opportunity for the defendant to indicate (not necessarily enter) his plea
of guilty, if that was his mind, was not the PCMH. The first reasonable
opportunity was normally either at the magistrates' court or immediately on arrival in the Crown Court – whether at a preliminary hearing
or by way of a locally-approved system for indicating plea through the
defendant's solicitors. There would ordinarily be some, but limited,
difference in public benefits between the two stages of the magistrates' Court and the first arrival in the Crown Court, but for practical
reasons, either could properly ordinarily attract the maximum percentage reduction of one third provided for by the guideline. The possibility
adverted to in the guideline that an indication at the magistrates' court
might attract a reduction of 33% and an indication at the first
Crown Court hearing 30%, was not generally reflected in practice as
experience had developed it over the years and, given the minimal
distinction, was likely to be an unlooked-for complication. A plea of
guilty at a PCMH would ordinarily not be significantly different from a
plea notified shortly after it. Whatever the exact procedure in different
courts in for fixing trial windows or dates, that was clearly the stage at
which the guideline contemplated a reduction of about a quarter.

Overwhelming strong cases

The cautious terms of the guideline in relation to limiting the reduction
in sentence for plea of guilty where the case against the defendant was,
irrespective of any admission, overwhelming, were deliberate and wise.
The various public benefits which underlay the practice of reducing
sentence for plea of guilty applied just as much to overwhelming cases as
to less strong ones. Judges ought to be wary of concluding that a case
was 'overwhelming' when all that was seen was evidence which was not
contested. Even when the case was very strong indeed, some defendants
would elect to force the issue to trial, as was their right. It could not be
assumed that defendants would make rational decisions or ones which
were born of any inclination to co-operate with the system, but those
who did merited recognition. When contemplating withholding a reduction for plea of guilty in a very strong case, it was often helpful to reflect
on what might have been the sentences if two identical defendants had

faced the same 'overwhelming' case and one had pleaded guilty and the other had not. In any event, the guideline made clear that normally at least a one-fifth reduction ought to be made, however 'overwhelming' the evidence. It could be particularly tempting for courts to avoid reduction in sentence for a plea of guilty when the statutory maximum sentence was low, or there was other inhibition and the resulting sentence was felt to be insufficient. However tempting, that had to be resisted.

Following a 'Newton' hearing

It was neither necessary nor possible to attempt to lay down a rule as to what, if any, reduction for plea should survive an adverse Newton finding. It would depend on all the circumstances of the case, including the extent of the issue determined, on whether lay witnesses had had to give evidence and on the extra public time and effort that had been involved. Some cases involved little more than an assertion in mitigation which the judge was not minded to accept at face value, so that the defendant was given an opportunity to give evidence about it, often there and then. In that case, the reduction ought normally to be less than it would have been if the false assertion had not been made, but significant reduction for plea of guilty would normally survive. Other cases might be ones where something akin to a full trial had to take place, with full preparation by the Crown, lay witnesses having to be called and considerable court time taken up. In such a case, the reduction for plea of guilty which survived was likely to be very small and might be none at all. In between there might be a considerable range of situations. Those had to be left to the informed judgment of the sentencing judge.

Residual flexibility

Notwithstanding that the general approach set out was essential to an understanding by defendants and their advisers, it did not altogether remove the scope of the judge to treat an individual case individually. However, the necessary residual flexibility which had thus to remain did not extend to suggesting an investigation in every case of the savings which had or had not actually ensued. The rationale of the reduction for plea of guilty lay in the incentive provided, not in an enquiry after the fact into what would or might have happened if a different course had been taken. If that kind of enquiry were necessary in every case, the administration of justice would not be made more efficient, but would unnecessarily be complicated, slowed and made more expensive.

B[5.47] 5 Loss of employment etc. An offender must generally be taken to have foreseen the normal consequences of conviction and so factors such as distress to his family, loss of job, pension, good character, etc will usually have little mitigating value. Where consequences follow which could not reasonably have been foreseen, for example, where the offence was unconnected with the offender's employment but he nevertheless finds himself dismissed, or where the offence was committed on the spur of the moment under provocation with no opportunity to consider the consequences, some allowance may be made if those consequences turn out to be disastrous. The person who is especially vulnerable must be expected to take special care. So, for example, the person whose employment depends upon his having a driving licence must be expected to take particular care not to commit endorsable offences. People such as doctors, nurses and solicitors, from whom a high ethical standard is expected, must expect the consequences of conviction for an offence which amounts to a breach of those standards and cannot claim professional disciplinary action in mitigation.

B[5.48] Unrepresented defendant. The court has a duty itself to seek out mitigating factors before finally arriving at a sentence. It should be especially careful not to assume that there are none in the case of the inarticulate unrepresented defendant.

5 The totality of sentencing

B[5.49] The Sentencing Council laid down a definitive guideline ('Totality') which applies to all offenders, whose cases are dealt with on or after **11 June 2012**. The reader is also recommended to consult the section dealing with 'Offences Taken Into Consideration'. The principle of totality comprises two elements:

(1)   All courts, when sentencing for more than a single offence, should pass a total sentence which reflects all the offending behaviour before it and is just and proportionate. This is so whether the sentences are structured as concurrent or consecutive. Therefore, concurrent sentences will ordinarily be longer than a single sentence for a single offence.

(2)   It is usually impossible to arrive at a just and proportionate sentence for a multiple offending simply by adding together notional single sentences. It is necessary to address the offending behaviour, together with the factors personal to the offender as a whole.

Concurrent/consecutive sentences. There is no inflexible rule governing whether sentences should be structured as concurrent or consecutive components. The overriding principle is that the overall sentence must be just and proportionate. Space precludes some examples which are set out in the SC Guideline. The reader is invited to consult the SC website where necessary.

6 Choice of sentence

B[5.50] The deliberations of the court will have brought into focus more than one form of sentence. For example, it may be that the offence is 'serious enough' to warrant a community sentence. The pre-sentence report may have considered a range of community orders. The probation officer will have considered the seriousness of the offence and have proposed a sentence which is commensurate with the seriousness of the offence and takes into account the circumstances of the offender. The court will need to be clear that the sentence adequately reflects the seriousness of the offence while (in the case of a community penalty) also being the most suitable for the offender. It does not mean that if an offence is serious enough to warrant a community sentence that is the only sentence which may be imposed. If there is mitigation which allows the court to impose a fine then the fine must reflect the seriousness of the offence and the financial circumstances of the offender.

B[5.51] The advice of the legal adviser will be essential to ensure that all the statutory criteria which must be satisfied before sentence can be passed and the correct ancillary orders made.

B[5.52] The good chairman will have noted during the hearing such matters as applications for costs, or forfeiture of drugs. Liability for endorsement and disqualification will also have occupied attention and after the substantive sentence has been agreed by (at least) a majority of the justices, the chairman will deal with each of these matters in turn. Save in the simplest cases, the chairman will make a written note of the total decision so that no error or omission is made.

7 Statement accompanying the sentence

B[5.53] The Criminal Justice Act 2003, s 174 (as amended by s 64 of the Legal Aid, Sentencing and Punishment of Offenders Act 2012, from a date to be appointed) requires a court to give reasons for and explain the effect of its sentence

The requirement of Article 6 of the European Convention on Human Rights means that reasons should be given. Indeed the effect, not to say the benefit, of a sound sentencing decision can sometimes be lost because the defendant does not understand the reasoning behind it, or because the public do not.

B[5.54] When a particular sentence falls within the Sentencing Guidelines Council guidance for the kind of offence and offender – when it is the sort of sentence the defendant probably expected to receive – there will seldom be justification for garnishing the reasons. However, when the court imposes a sentence which might be unexpected the reasons for this departure from normal sentencing habits might be fuller. Likewise, when different types of sentence are imposed on co-accused whose circumstances may appear to be similar. The needs of the public as well as those of the defendant and any victim of his offence should be borne in mind. A structured approach to the sentencing decision, consultation with the clerk and a careful note will assist the chairman when giving reasons

Victim Personal Statement

B[5.55]–[5.60] The Consolidated Practice Direction 2014 [2013] EWCA Crim 1361 provides as follows:

'F.1 Victims of crime are invited to make a statement, known as a Victim Personal Statement ('VPS'). The statement gives victims a formal opportunity to say how a crime has affected them. It may help to identify whether they have a particular need for information, support and protection. The court will take the statement into account when determining sentence. In some circumstances, it may be appropriate for relatives of a victim to make a VPS, for example where the victim has died as a result of the relevant criminal conduct. The Code of Practice for Victims of Crime, the revised version of which was published in the summer of 2013 and will come into force shortly, gives further information about victims' entitlements within the criminal justice system, and the duties placed on criminal justice agencies when dealing with victims of crime.

F.2 When a police officer takes a statement from a victim, the victim should be told about the scheme and given the chance to make a VPS. The decision about whether or not to make a VPS is entirely a matter for the victim; no pressure should be brought to bear on their decision, and no conclusion should be drawn if they choose not to make such a statement. A VPS or an updated VPS may be made (in proper s.9 form, see below) at any time prior to the disposal of the case. It will not normally be appropriate for a VPS to be made after the disposal of the case; there may be rare occasions between sentence and appeal when an update to the VPS may be necessary, for example, when the victim was injured and the final prognosis was not available at the date of sentence. However, VPS after disposal should be confined to presenting up to date factual material, such as medical information, and should be used sparingly.

F.3 If the court is presented with a VPS the following approach, subject to the further guidance given by the Court of Appeal in *R v Perkins; Bennett; Hall* [2013] EWCA Crim 323, [2013] Crim L.R. 533, should be adopted:

(a)   The VPS and any evidence in support should be considered and taken into account by the court, prior to passing sentence.

(b)   Evidence of the effects of an offence on the victim contained in the VPS or other statement must be in proper form, that is a witness statement made under section 9 of the Criminal Justice Act 1967 or an expert's report; and served in good time upon the defendant's solicitor or the defendant, if he is not represented. Except where inferences can properly be drawn from the nature of or circumstances surrounding the offence, a sentencing court must not make assumptions unsupported by evidence about the effects of an offence on the victim.

(c)   In all cases it will be appropriate for a VPS to be referred to in the course of the sentencing hearing and/or in the sentencing re-marks. Subject to the court's discretion, the contents of the VPS may be summarised and in an appropriate case even read out in open court.

(d)   The court must pass what it judges to be the appropriate sentence having regard to the circumstances of the offence and of the offender, taking into account, so far as the court considers it appropriate, the impact on the victim. The opinions of the victim or the victim's close relatives as to what the sentence should be are therefore not relevant, unlike the consequences of the offence on them. Victims should be advised of this. If, despite the advice, opinions as to sentence are included in the statement, the court should pay no attention to them.

For cases involving sexual offences see also B[18] regarding the relevance of the victim's views to any compensation order that may be imposed.

Guidance on victim personal and family impact statements was given in *R v Perkins* [2013] EWCA Crim 323, [2013] Crim LR 533. The following extract from the judgment stresses the fundamental principles.

'[9] Without suggesting any amendments or additions to the current Practice Direction, a number of its aspects need emphasis:

"(a) The decision whether to make a statement must be made by the victims personally. They must be provided with information which makes it clear that they are entitled to make a statement, but, as the Guide to Police Officers and Investigators underlines, no pressure, either way, should be brought to bear on their decision. They are entitled to make statements, and they are equally entitled not to do so. They should be informed of their right, and allowed to exercise it as they wish: in particular the perception should not be allowed to emerge that if they chose not to do so the court may misunderstand or minimise the harm caused by the crime.

(b) When the decision whether or not to make a statement is being made, it should be clearly understood that the victim's opinion about the type and level of sentence should not be included. Again that is entirely consistent with the Guide to Police Officers and Investigators. If necessary, victims must be assisted to appreciate that the court is required to pass the appropriate sentence, in accordance with decisions of this court, and definitive guidelines issued by the Sentencing Guidelines Council or the Sentencing Council, and make a judgment based on all the facts of the case, including both the aggravating and the mitigating features.

(c) The statement constitutes evidence. That is the basis on which it is admitted. It must therefore be treated as evidence. It must be in a formal witness statement, served on the Defendant's legal advisors in time for the Defendant's instructions to be taken, and for any objection to the use of the statement, or part of it, if necessary, to be prepared. In *Perkins*, the statement was handed over far too late in the process, and indeed we are concerned that some of the submissions from counsel in these cases suggest that a somewhat haphazard and slovenly approach to the time when the statement is served may have developed, at any rate in some parts of the country.

(d) Just because the statement is intended to inform the sentencing court of specific features of the consequences of the offence on the victim, responsibility for presenting admissible evidence remains with the prosecution.

(e) It follows that the statement may be challenged, in cross-examination, and it may give rise to disclosure obligations, and indeed as the case of *Hall* underlines, may be used, after conviction, to deploy an argument that the credibility of the victim is open to question."'

Reasons for, and explanation of, sentences

B[5.61] Section 174 of the Criminal Justice Act 2003 requires the following.

The court must state in open court, in ordinary language and in general terms, the court's reasons for deciding on the sentence.

The court must explain to the offender in ordinary language:

(a)   the effect of the sentence;
(b)   the effects of non-compliance with any order that the offender is required to comply with and that forms part of the sentence;
(c)   any power of the court to vary or review any order that forms part of the sentence; and
(d)   the effects of failure to pay a fine, if the sentence consists of or includes a fine.

Particular duties of the court in complying with the above are:

(a)   To identify any definitive sentencing guidelines relevant to the offender's case and:
       (i)   explain how the court discharged any duty imposed on it by s 125 of the Coroners and Justice Act 2009 (duty to follow guidelines unless satisfied it would be contrary to the interests of justice to do so);
       (ii)   where the court was satisfied it would be contrary to the interests of justice to follow the guidelines, state why.
(b)   Where, as a result of taking into account any matter referred to in s 144(1) (guilty pleas), the court imposes a punishment on the offender which is less severe than the punishment it would otherwise have imposed, the court must state that fact.
(c)   Where the offender is under 18 and the court imposes a sentence that may only be imposed in the offender's case if the court is of the opinion mentioned in:
       (i)   s 1(4)(a)–(c) of the Criminal Justice and Immigration Act 2008 and s 148(1) of this Act (youth rehabilitation order with intensive supervision and surveillance or with fostering); or
       (ii)   s 152(2) of this Act (discretionary custodial sentence), the court must state why it is of that opinion.

Other requirements to give reasons include:

(a)   a decision not to activate a suspended sentence on the commission of a further offence;
(b)   a finding of special reasons not to endorse or disqualify from driving; and
(c)   a decision not to award compensation in a case where the court is empowered to make such an award.

B[5.62] It is generally inadvisable to deliver a lecture or homily or offer any other words of worldly wisdom to a defendant who is being sentenced. Research has shown that most prisoners cannot remember even a short time after sentence much of what the judge said and even whether he said anything at all.

8 Pronouncement of sentence

B[5.63] The chairman should announce the sentence(s) in a way which leaves no one in court in any doubt as to the court's decision. In the following pages each possible sentence is considered and a form of words is provided as a guide to the way in which the sentence may be announced. It is not suggested that the chairman should read the sentence from this book but that a glance at the wording suggested here will assist in ensuring that all the necessary legal points have been covered. Where an offender is to be sentenced for more than one offence it is advised that each sentence is related to each offence by description. It is bad practice to sentence in such terms as, 'For the first offence you will be fined £50. For the second offence you will be fined £100 and your licence endorsed. For the third offence etc.' Bear in mind that the offender has no idea of the order in which offences appear on the list and therefore has no way of relating the penalties to the offences if they are announced in this fashion. The better practice is exemplified as follows: 'For the burglary and theft at Jackson's, the butchers, you will go to prison for 20 days; for using the credit card to obtain a camera from Browns, you will go to prison for 15 days which will be in addition to the first sentence, which means you will go to prison for a total of 35 days.' Whenever there are several sentences to be announced, the chairman should totalise the effect of them, that is, the total amount of a monetary penalty, the total period of imprisonment or of disqualification should be stated. Words such as concurrent or consecutive need not be used if other words are used which make it clear what the total effect of the sentence is, as in the example above.

B[5.64] When offences have been taken into consideration in arriving at a sentence that fact should be stated as a preamble to the sentence.

B[5.65] Where relevant the chairman should announce by how much the sentence has been reduced by virtue of the defendant's guilty plea.

B[6]

Multiplicity of charges

B[6.1] Sometimes a defendant faces more than one charge stemming from the same circumstances and while this is generally unobjectionable there are occasions when the court feels that the prosecution is having two bites at the cherry. Some courts impose the appropriate penalty on one charge and mark the other 'No separate penalty'. Another practice is to decide the appropriate penalty and divide it between the two offences but this may result in penalties which appear inadequately low.

It may be improper to charge or enter a conviction for more than one offence arising from the same facts. Before the magistrates can decide whether to convict or not to convict on the second information they must inquire into the matter to determine the facts. There is no statutory provision which allows a defendant in the magistrates' court to be convicted of a lesser offence than that with which he is specifically charged. The practice in magistrates' courts is for both the greater and the lesser offence to be charged but if the greater charge is made out, it is not open to the magistrates' court to convict of both offences as the double conviction is of itself unfair. The right course is for the court to adjourn the lesser charge at the end of the trial but before conviction. In the event of a successful appeal relating to the aggravated offence, and that appeal succeeding on the footing that the aggravating element was not made out, a conviction on the lesser offence might thereafter properly be recorded against the defendant: *R (Dyer) v Watford Magistrates' Court* [2013] EWHC 547 (Admin), 177 JP 265 expressly declining to follow *DPP v Gane* (1991) 155 JP 846, [1991] Crim LR 711 and *R (CPS) v Blaydon Youth Court* [2004] EWHC 2296 (Admin), 168 JP 638, [2005] Crim LR 495.

Power to review decisions – criminal and civil proceedings

(MCA 1980, s 142)

B[7.1] Section 142 of the Magistrates' Courts Act 1980 empowers magistrates' courts 'to re-open cases to rectify mistakes etc'. It is concerned with criminal cases only (for civil cases see **B[7.6]**, below). It enables the court to:

(a)   vary or rescind a sentence or other order imposed or made when dealing with; and

(b)   where a person is convicted, to direct that the case should be heard again by different justices,

in either case where it appears to the court that it would be in the interests of justice to do so.

Varying or rescinding sentences or other orders on conviction

B[7.2] Where the court can vary or rescind a sentence or order, the court may exercise its power under this section on application by a party or on its own initiative. The procedure to be followed for variation of a sentence by a party is prescribed by rules of court and an application must be in writing except that the court may allow an application to be made orally and may extend any time limit. The court may not exercise the power in the defendant's absence unless it makes the variation proposed by the defendant or he has had an opportunity to make representations at a hearing (whether or not he in fact attends): see the Criminal Procedure Rules, r 42.2.

The court has power to vary or rescind a sentence or order and may substitute some other sentence or order (*R v Sheffield City Justices, ex p Foster* (1999) Times, 2 November. If, however, the decision has already been subject to an appeal to a higher court, the power to reopen no longer applies. Likewise, a magistrates' court had no power to quash a conviction and order a rehearing under s 142(2) where the justices had agreed to state a case for the opinion of the High Court: see *R (on the application of Rhodes-Presley) v Worcestershire Magistrates' Court* [2008] EWHC 2700 (Admin), [2008] All ER (D) 92 (Nov).

It was inappropriate for magistrates to exercise their powers under s 142 to increase a sentence originally imposed some 20 months earlier. There had to be finality of proceedings and a power of rectification had to be exercised speedily after the date of the original sentence: see *R (on the application of Trigger) v Northampton Magistrates' Court (Northamptonshire Probation Trust and Northamptonshire Crown Prosecution Service, Interested Parties)* [2011] EWHC 149, (2011) 175 JP 101.

B[7.3] The provisions may operate against a defendant, for example where the court has omitted to impose penalty points or an endorsable road traffic offence. Note, however, the power does not extend to overturning an acquittal (*R v Gravesend Justices, ex p Dexter* [1977] Crim LR 298). The power is directed towards sentences or other orders; it had no bearing on convictions which had been entered by way of procedural irregularity (*R (on the application of D) v Sheffield Youth Court* [2008] EWHC 601 (Admin), [2008] All ER (D) 70 (Mar)).

B[7.4] When the court alters a sentence or order under this procedure, and substitutes another, that other sentence or order will take effect from the date of the first sentence or order, unless the court otherwise directs.

Note the power under the Magistrates Courts Act 1980, s 142 does not extend to civil proceedings (*R (on the application of Mathialagam) v Southwark London Borough Council* [2004] EWCA Civ 1689, [2004] All ER (D) 179 (Dec)). Nor does s 142 have any bearing on criminal convictions which had been entered by way of procedural irregularity (*R (on the application of D) v Sheffield Youth Court* [2008] EWHC 601 (Admin), [2008] All ER (D) 70 (Mar).

Re-opening convictions

B[7.5] Nothing in this section operates to prevent a court acting under its common law powers to amend a plea from 'guilty' to 'not guilty' at any time before final adjudication: see *S (an infant) v Manchester City Recorder* [1971] AC 481, [1969] 3 All ER 1230, 134 JP 3; to hear and adjudicate upon a (summary) case wrongly committed for trial (*Bannister v Clarke* [1920] 3 KB 598, 85 JP 12); to commit for trial following an acquittal for an offence triable only on indictment (*R v West* [1964] 1 QB 15, [1962] 2 All ER 624, 126 JP 352); to re-try a case where some irregularity has vitiated the proceedings (*R v Marsham, ex p Pethick Lawrence* [1912] 2 KB 362, 76 JP 284); or, generally, to deal with a matter when the hearing or sentence was a nullity (*R v Norfolk Justices, ex p DPP* [1950] 2 KB 558, [1950] 2 All ER 42, 114 JP 312; *R v Warwick Quarter Sessions, ex p Patterson* (1971) 115 Sol Jo 484).

The purpose of s 142 is to rectify mistakes. It is generally to be regarded as a slip rule and the power under the section cannot be extended to cover situations beyond those akin to a mistake. It was confirmed in *R (on the application of Williamson) v City of Westminster Magistrates' Court* [2012] EWHC 1444 (Admin), [2012] 2 Cr App Rep 299, [2012] Crim LR 975 that the power to re-open proceedings under s 142 was not to be given a broad interpretation. Section 142 was designed to deal with an obvious mischief: namely the waste of time, energy and resources in correcting clear mistakes made in magistrates' courts by using appellate or review proceedings. It was not a power equivalent to an appeal to the Crown Court or the High Court, nor was it a general power of review. Accordingly, it is wrong to employ s 142(2) as a method by which a defendant can obtain a rehearing in circumstances where he could not appeal to the Crown Court by reason of his unequivocal plea of guilty: *R v Croydon Youth Court, ex p DPP* [1997] 2 Cr App Rep 411. See also *Zykin v CPS* [2009] EWHC 1469 (Admin), (2009) 173 JP 361. This section does not empower a court to re-open a plea of guilty where the court had failed to conduct the mode of trial procedure under s 24 of the Magistrates' Courts Act 1980. Nothing in *S v Recorder of Manchester* (above) suggests that in allowing a change of plea, the court is exercising a power under s 142 or that the power to accept a change of plea extends to a power to re-open, contrary to the wishes of a defendant, a conviction based on an unequivocal plea of guilty previously entered and accepted: *R (D) v Sheffield Youth Court* [2008] EWHC 601 (Admin), 172 JP 576.

There may be circumstances where s 142 can be used to allow an unequivocal plea of guilty to be set aside – eg offence unknown to law or impropriety by the prosecution – but the alleged incompetence of the defendant's own legal adviser, even if established, provides no analogy with prosecution fraud. Nor is s 142 a power equivalent to an appeal or a general review; accordingly, once the court has returned a guilty verdict the defendant is not entitled to make further submissions with a view to persuading the court to change its mind and substitute a not guilty verdict: *DPP v Chajed* [2013] EWHC 188 (Admin), (2013) 177 JP 350, [2013] Crim LR 603.

When exercising its discretion as to whether the interests of justice require a rehearing, the court must act on proper judicial grounds; accordingly, the late arrival at court of a defendant was held not to be a proper ground for refusing a rehearing: *R v Camberwell Green Magistrates' Court, ex p Ibrahim* (1984) 148 JP 400. While delay in making an application under s 142 is always likely to be harmful and is a factor to be taken into account, justices should not reject an application on that ground alone and must consider judicially all the relevant circumstances: *R v Ealing Magistrates' Court, ex p Sahota* (1997) 162 JP 73. See also *R (on the application of Blick) v Doncaster Magistrates' Court* [2008] EWHC 2698 (Admin), 172 JP 651, where it was held the magistrates' court had been wrong to take the question of whether the accused had acted 'with all due diligence' as the primary test, and that 'the inconvenience of the court can never outweigh the interests of justice' (at para 19). However, in *R v Gwent Magistrates' Court, ex p Carey* (1996) 160 JP 613, it was held that justices were entrusted with a broad discretion and were entitled to take into account the fact that the defendant failed to appear through his own fault and that the witnesses would be inconvenienced by ordering a re-trial. The justices could also properly take into account the fact that the defendant was not being deprived of a fair trial by way of appeal in the Crown Court.

Civil proceedings

B[7.6] There are three criteria to be satisfied before an order made by a magistrates' court in its civil jurisdiction can be set aside:

(a) there must be a genuine and arguable dispute as to the defendant's liability to the order in question;

(b) the order must be made as a result of a substantial procedural error, defect or mishap; and

(c) the application to the justices for the order to be set aside must be made promptly after the defendant learns that it has been made or has notice that an order may have been made: *R (London Borough of Newham) v Stratford Magistrates' Court* [2008] EWHC 125 (Admin), 173 JP 30.

In proceedings for a liability order to recover non-domestic rates, where justices had made an order unaware of an application to adjourn, they had jurisdiction to set aside their order. Although there was no express statutory provision, the justices had not exhausted their jurisdiction where they had failed to exercise a judicial discretion whether to proceed or adjourn:

Liverpool City Council v Pleroma Distribution Ltd [2003] 04 LS Gaz R 33.

Although magistrates of their own motion might correct a clear mistake by
the court itself going to the basis of its jurisdiction, or the fairness of the
proceedings, they do not have a general power to set aside their own
decision merely because of the existence of grounds which might support an
application for judicial review. However, it might be sensible, where there
had for example been an obvious mistake or where a party had failed to
attend through no fault of his own, such as a traffic accident, for all parties
to agree to rehear the matter and thereby avoid the expense and delay of
judicial review: *R (Mathialagan) v Southwark London Borough Council*
[2004] EWCA Civ 1689, [2004] All ER (D) 179 (Dec), 169 JPN 26.

B[7A]

Action plan orders

(PCC(S) Act 2000, ss 69–72)

Reports

B[7A.1] Sections 69–72 of the 2000 Act have been repealed by the Criminal Justice and Immigration Act 2008. Action plan orders were replaced by the Youth Rehabilitation Order. See **B[50]** onwards.

B[8]

Anti-social behaviour orders (ASBOs)*

(Crime and Disorder Act 1998, ss 1–4)

> * The Anti-social Behaviour, Crime and Policing Act 2014 prospectively
> replaces civil ASBOs with jurisdiction transferred to the county court for
> adults and the youth court for those under 18.

Limitations

B[8.1] Civil Applications – Can only be applied for by either:

(i)   the relevant local authority;
(ii)   the police;
(iii)   the British Transport Police; or
(iv)   a recognised housing association or action trust.

B[8.2] Age limits – May be made for a person aged 10 years or over.

B[8.3] Maximum/minimum period – An order must be for a minimum
period of 2 years, but it is inappropriate to make an order for an indefinite
period (*R v Vittles* [2004] EWCA Crim 1089, [2004] All ER (D) 334
(May)).

B[8.4] The application – The application is to a magistrates' court by way
of complaint. If the respondent is under 18 years of age the justices
constituting the court should normally be qualified to sit in the youth court.
There are dispensations for interim orders or if it is not practicable to
constitute a bench contributing to a delay in hearing the case (*Practice
Direction (Magistrates' Courts: Anti-Social Behaviour Orders: Composition of Benches)* 24 February 2006, BLD 2702060704). A separate
application must be made in respect of each named individual. The
defendant will receive a summons with a copy of the written application.
Due to the severe sanction for breach a criminal standard of proof is
required (*R v Manchester Crown Court, ex p McCann* [2001] 1 WLR 358,
sub nom R v Crown Court at Manchester, ex p McCann 165 JP 225, [2001]
02 LS Gaz R 40, 144 Sol Jo LB 287; affd sub nom R (on the application of
McCann) v Crown Court at Manchester [2001] EWCA Civ 281 [2001]
4 All ER 264, [2001] 1 WLR 1084, 165 JP 545). Even though the
proceedings are civil in nature, the court may rely upon facts which
previously formed the basis of criminal prosecutions (*S v Poole Borough Council* [2002] EWHC 244 (Admin), [2002] All ER (D) 143 (Feb));
*R (on the application of the Chief Constable of Mercia Constabulary) v
Boorman* [2005] EWHC Admin 2559).

B[8.4A] Hearsay evidence – The procedure for admitting hearsay evidence is governed by rr 50.6–50.8 of the Criminal Procedure Rules 2014.

B[8.5] The order and its terms – may be made against a person who it has
been proved has acted in an anti-social manner (that is in a manner that
caused or was likely to cause harassment, alarm or distress, to one or more

persons not in the same household as himself) and an order is necessary to prevent further anti-social acts. It may prohibit further anti-social acts described in the order, necessary to protect relevant persons. The terms of the ASBO must be clear and commensurate with the risk they seek to guard against (*R v McGrath* [2005] EWCA Crim 353, [2005] All ER (D) 81 (May)). A curfew may be a legitimate condition so long as it was preventive and protective (*R (on the application of Lonergan) v Lewes Crown Court and Secretary of State for the Home Department (interested party)* [2005] EWHC 457 (Admin), [2005] All ER (D) 382 (Mar)).

The reference to behaviour 'likely to cause' harassment, alarm or distress in s 1(1) of the 1998 Act permitted police witnesses to give evidence that there were potential victims present who were caused harassment, alarm or distress. However, s 1(1)(a) of the Act was not made out where it could not be shown that a potential victim was present (*R (on the application of Gosport Borough Council) v Fareham Magistrates' Court* (2007) 171 JP 102).

Guidance – For a more detailed commentary the reader should consult: *Anti-Social Behaviour Orders: a guide for the judiciary* (3rd edn, JSB).

Judicial guidance – In *R v Boness, R v Bebbington* [2005] EWCA Crim 2395, [2006] 1 Cr App Rep (S) 690, the Court of Appeal ruled as follows:

(1)   An ASBO had to be precise and capable of being understood by the offender. It followed that the court should ask itself, before making an order, whether the terms of the order were clear so that the defendant would know precisely what it was that he was prohibited from doing (it would be wrong to make an ASBO against an offender who by reason of mental health would not have the capacity to understand or comply with the terms of the order: *R (on the application of Cooke) v Director of Public Prosecutions* [2008] EWHC 2703 (Admin), 172 JP 596).

(2)   There must be evidence of anti-social behaviour (see *R (on the application of Mills) v Birmingham Magistrates' Court* [2005] EWHC 2732 (Admin), (2005) 170 JP 237). Evidence of later behaviour showing a propensity to behave in an anti-social manner was capable of being relevant, to the question of whether the defendant acted in an anti-social manner at the times and at places alleged in a section complaint. Post-complaint behaviour was also relevant to whether an order was necessary to protect persons from further anti-social acts: see *Birmingham City Council v Dixon* [2009] EWHC 761(Admin), 173 JP 233. Following a finding that the defendant had acted in an anti-social manner (whether or not the act constituted a criminal offence), the test for making an order that prohibited the offender from doing something was one of necessity (see *R v W; R v F* [2006] EWCA Crim 686). [In that context, the prohibition on associating with a named individual, who was not the subject of an ASBO with a reciprocal prohibition on association, was held to be lawful in *Hills v Chief Constable of Essex Police* [2006] EWHC 2633 (Admin)].

(3)   Each separate order prohibiting a person from doing a specified thing had to be necessary to protect persons from further anti-social acts by him. Accordingly, any order had to be tailor-made for the individual defendant, not designed on a word processor for use in every case.

(4)   The purpose of an order was preventative, not to punish. The use of an ASBO to punish a defendant was unlawful.

(5)   Where the ASBO was being sought as ancillary to a criminal sentence or disposal, the court should not allow itself to be diverted by a defendant's representative at the sentencing stage in the hope that the court might make such an order as an alternative to prison or other sanction. It might be better for the court to decide the substantive sentence and then move on to consider whether an ASBO should be made or not after sentence has been pronounced, albeit at the same hearing [subject to the power of the court to adjourn consideration of an ASBO to a later date (Crime and Disorder Act 1998, s 1C as amended)].

(6)   The court should not impose an order which prohibited a defendant from committing a specified criminal offence, if the sentence which could be passed following conviction for the offence should be a sufficient deterrent. It followed that an ASBO should not be used merely to increase the sentence of imprisonment which a defendant was liable to receive. Whilst different considerations might apply where the maximum sentence was a fine, the court had still to go through all the steps to ensure that the order was necessary. [In that context, a prohibition on carrying knives or bladed articles in a public place was held to be lawful in *Hills v Chief Constable of Essex* supra, as the order was intended to cover behaviour not caught by s 139 Criminal Justice Act 1988, namely the carrying of knives or bladed articles with a blade of less than three inches in a public place.]

(7)   The corollary to (6) above was that a court should be reluctant to impose an order which prohibited a defendant from committing a specified criminal offence. The aim of an ASBO was to prevent anti-social behaviour, by enabling action to be taken before the anti-social behaviour it was designed to prevent was to take place.

(8)   The terms of the order had to be proportionate in the sense that they had to be commensurate with the risk to be guarded against. That was particularly important where an order might interfere with a defendant's right under the European Convention of Human Rights.

B[8.6] Statutory defence – to an application is available namely that the behaviour complained of was reasonable in the particular circumstances.

B[8.7] Interim Orders – For guidance on ex parte applications *see R (on the application of Manchester City Council) v Manchester Magistrates' Court* (2005) Times, 8 March, [2005] All ER (D) 103 (Feb). Interim orders may be made pending the determination of an order if the court considers it just. An application may be made without notice if the justices are satisfied that it is necessary. The court itself may direct that notice be served on the defendant and refuse to make an order without notice (*R (Kenny) v Leeds Magistrates* [2003] EWHC 2963 (Admin), [2004] 1 All ER 1333, [2003] All ER (D) 104 (Dec; affd sub nom R (on the application of M) v Secretary of State for Constitutional Affairs and Lord Chancellor* [2004] EWCA Civ 312, [2004] All ER (D) 345 (Mar)). See also *R (on the application of M) v Secretary of State for Constitutional Affairs and Lord Chancellor* [2004] EWCA Civ 312, [2004] All ER (D) 345 (Mar), CA.

There is no presumption that an order against publicity will be made on an interim order against a juvenile but age is an important consideration (*R (on the application of K) v Knowsley Metropolitan Borough Council* [2004] EWHC 1933 (Admin), 168 JP 461, sub nom Keating v Knowsley Metropolitan Borough Council* [2004] All ER (D) 383 (Jul)).

B[8.8] Orders on conviction – Part 2 of the Anti-social Behaviour, Crime and Policing Act 2014 (ABCPA 2014) replaced anti-social behaviour orders on conviction (CRASBOs) with 'criminal behaviour orders' (CBO) (with saving and transitional provisions in respect of ASBOs, individual support orders and drink banning orders on conviction made before these orders were repealed: see s 33).

Three significant differences between the new and old regimes are: the court cannot make an order of its motion – the prosecutor must apply for it (normally this will be at the instigation of the police or local authority); the order may contain requirements as well as prohibitions; and if the proceedings are adjourned and the defendant fails to appear, the court can hear the proceedings in his absence (provided he has had adequate notice).

B[8.9] Grounds and pre-conditions – There are two conditions. The first condition is that the court is satisfied, beyond reasonable doubt, that the offender has engaged in behaviour that caused or was likely to cause harassment, alarm or distress to any person (s 22(3)). The second condition is that the court considers that making the order will help in preventing the offender from engaging in such behaviour (ABCPA 2014, s 22(4)).

A CBO can only be made as an order ancillary to a sentence for the offence or an order of conditional discharge (ABCPA 2014, s 22(6)). It cannot, therefore, accompany an absolute discharge or a bind over to keep the peace.

Where the offender will be under the age of 18 at the time of the application, the police or local authority must consult the youth offending team (YOT) and inform the prosecutor of the YOT's views (ABCPA 2014, s 22(8)). This does not, however, give the YOT a power of veto over the making of an application. It is no more than an obligation to consult.

B[8.10] Procedure – Procedure is governed by Part 50 of the Criminal Procedure Rules 2014. The respondent must be given an opportunity to consider what order is proposed and the evidence relied upon in support and to make representations at a hearing (r 50.2).

Rule 50.3 provides (so far as is relevant to CBOs):

'Application for behaviour order and notice of terms of proposed order: special rules

(2)   . . . the prosecutor must serve a notice of intention to apply for such an order on—
    (a)   the court officer;
    (b)   the defendant against whom the prosecutor wants the court to make the order; and
    (c)   any person on whom the order would be likely to have a significant adverse effect,

as soon as practicable (without waiting for the verdict).

(3)   A notice under paragraph (2) must—
    (a)   summarise the relevant facts;
    (b)   identify the evidence on which the prosecutor relies in support;
    (c)   attach any written statement that the prosecutor has not already served; and

    (d)   specify the order that the prosecutor wants the court to make.

(4)   A defendant served with a notice under paragraph (2) must—

    (a)   serve written notice of any evidence on which the defendant relies on—

        (i)   the court officer, and

        (ii)   the prosecutor,

    (b)   in the notice, identify that evidence and attach any written statement that has not already been served.

(7)   Where the prosecutor wants the court to make an anti-social behaviour order or a criminal behaviour order, the rules about special measures directions in Part 29 (Measures to assist a witness or defendant to give evidence) apply, but—

    (a)   the prosecutor must apply when serving a notice under paragraph (2); and

    (b)   the time limits in rule 29.3(a) do not apply.'

The court cannot proceed in the offender's absence unless it is satisfied that he has had adequate notice of the time and place of the adjourned hearing, but this does not apply to the making of an interim order (ABCPA 2014, s 23(6), s 26(3)).

B[8.11] Evidence and publicity – Section 23 of ABCPA 2014 provides that the court may consider evidence led by both parties and it does not matter whether the evidence would have been admissible in the proceedings in which the offender was convicted.

As to the procedure for admitting hearsay evidence, see CPR rr 50.6–50.8.

Section 31 of ABCPA 2014 applies the special measures directions of the Youth Justice and Criminal Evidence Act 1999 to CBO proceedings.

Section 49 of the Children and Young Persons Act 1933 (restrictions on reports of proceedings in which children and young persons are concerned) is disapplied to CBO proceedings involving youths, but s 39 does apply and this gives the court the discretion to prohibit the publication of certain information which would identify the child or young person.

B[8.11A] Requirements, duration, variation and discharge of orders – A CBO may contain prohibitions and/or requirements. If a CBO includes a requirement it must specify the person responsible for supervising compliance; this may be an individual or an organisation (ABCPA 2014, s 24(1)). The court must receive evidence on the enforceability and suitability of the requirement from the individual or, in the case of an organisation, an individual representing that organisation (ABCPA 2014, s 24(2)). As to guidance on the terms of orders see para B[8.5] above, but note this predates the 2014 Act.

Section 25 of ABCPA 2014 governs duration. A CBO takes effect on the day it is made unless the offender is already subject to a CBO, in which case the court can direct that the order will commence on the expiry of the earlier order. If the subject is under 18 years of age the order must be for a fixed period in the range one to three years. In the case of an adult, the order must be for a fixed term of at least two years or of indefinite duration. Section 26 of ABCPA 2014 provides that If the court adjourns the hearing for a CBO it can make an interim order if it thinks it just to do so which will last until the final hearing or until further order.

Section 27 of ABCPA 2014 governs variation or discharge. Either the offender or the prosecution may apply for variation or discharge. Where a previous application has been dismissed, that party cannot make a further application without the consent of the court or the agreement of the other party. The power to vary includes power to include additional prohibitions or requirements.

Section 28 of ABCPA 2014 provides for the review of orders every 12 months in the case of under-18 offenders.

B[8.12] Variation or discharge of civil orders – of a civil order may only be done within the first two years with the consent of both parties.

In *Leeds City Council v G* [2007] EWHC 1612 (Admin), (2007) Times, 11 September, the Administrative Court held that a magistrates' court did have jurisdiction under s 1(8) of the Crime and Disorder Act 1998 to *vary* a *civil order* by extending the duration of the original order beyond the minimum period ie two years. The Administrative Court did have some misgivings because there is no appeal from any variation. The protection for the defendant is that if the variation seeks more stringent conditions than the original order (including the length of the order), sufficient material would have to be put before the court which, by reference to the normal burden and standard of proof, justifies the extension in order to achieve the statutory objective. Further, the applicant will need to persuade the magistrates that it is appropriate to vary an order rather than make an application for a new anti-social behaviour order. See *James v Birmingham City Council* below.

The misgivings of the Administrative Court regarding a right of appeal were confirmed in *R (on the application of Langley) v Preston Crown Court* [2008] EWHC 2623 (Admin), [2009] 3 All ER 1026 where it was held that there was no right of appeal to the Crown Court against the **variation** of a 'stand-alone' order pursuant to s 1(8) of the 1998 Act. It is submitted that the decision is wrong. Section 4 confers a right of appeal because by analogy the term 'variation' has been interpreted or defined as if it were a fresh order of the court. For the moment, the above decisions are binding and must be followed.

Variation of an ASBO under s 1(8) does not require proof of a fresh act of anti-social behaviour. The court was entitled, in the exercise of its discretion, to consider a variation even if the applicant had the option of applying for a fresh ASBO. A complaint to vary must simply be made within six months from an event or circumstance which it is alleged renders the original order inappropriate for one reason or another. On a purposive construction of s 1(8) the question is whether it is necessary to vary the order to protect the public: *James v Birmingham City Council* [2010] EWHC 282 (Admin), 174 JP 250.

B[8.13] Breach of an order – will result in the commission of a criminal offence triable either way. The order commences when announced in court and not when reduced in writing (*Walkling v DPP* (2004) Independent, 26 January). Repeated and deliberate breaches will indicate committal to Crown Court for sentence (*R v Braxton* [2004] EWCA Crim 1374, [2005] 1 Cr App Rep (S) 167).

Breach of an order – commission of a criminal offence – s 8(2) CDA 1998
– Although there is nothing inherently wrong by passing a consecutive
sentence for breach of an anti-social behaviour order, if the new offence is
derived from the same course of conduct, broadly speaking concurrent
sentences should be imposed (*R v Lawson* [2006] EWCA Crim 2674,
[2006] All ER (D) 61 (Mar)).

Breach – collateral attack on validity of the order or its terms: In *W v DPP*
[2005] EWCA Civ 1333, it was decided that an ASBO was to be treated as
a valid order unless and until it was varied or declared invalid. The Court
of Appeal said it was open to a magistrates' court considering an allegation
of a breach of an order to determine whether the original order was ultra
vires and therefore not a valid order. In *DPP v T* [2006] EWHC 728
(Admin), [2006] 3 All ER 471; sub nom *CPS v T* (2006) 170 JP 470, the
Divisional Court reached a slightly different conclusion. The Divisional Court made reference to the normal rule that an order of the court
was to be obeyed unless and until it was set aside. The Court noted that the
person against whom an ASBO was made had had a full opportunity to
challenge that order on appeal or to apply to vary it. The policy consideration that a magistrates' court had jurisdiction to determine issues of the
validity of a byelaw or an administrative decision was wholly absent when
the issue was the validity of an order of the court. It was open to a
magistrates' court to consider whether the provision lacked sufficient clarity
to warrant a finding that the defendant's conduct did not amount to a
breach of the order; or that the lack of clarity provided him with a
reasonable excuse; or whether, assuming a breach was established, it was
appropriate in the circumstances not to impose any penalty for the breach.

Breach – reasonable excuse – Section 1(10) of the CDA 1998 makes it a
criminal offence to breach an ASBO in the following terms: 'If without
reasonable excuse a person does anything which he is prohibited from
doing by an anti-social behaviour order, he is guilty of an offence'. The Act
only imposes an evidential burden of the defendant, the legal burden rests
with the prosecution to prove that the defendant acted without reasonable
excuse (*R v Charles* [2009] EWCA Crim 1570, [2010] 4 All ER 553, [2010]
1 Cr App Rep 38).

In the context of an ASBO, ignorance, forgetfulness or misunderstanding,
whether arising from an error as to the terms of the order or lack of
knowledge of where the defendant was at the material time, might be
capable of constituting a defence of reasonable excuse (*R v Nicholson*
[2006] EWCA Crim 1518, 170 JP 573)).

Section 1(10) did not require the Crown to prove a specific mental element
on the part of a defendant at the time he committed an act which
constituted a breach of an ASBO. However, if the defence of reasonable
excuse was raised, the state of mind of the accused would usually be
relevant and could, if the circumstances warranted, be taken into account
in determining whether the Crown had proved there was no reasonable
excuse. The burden of so proving lay with the Crown: *R v Charles* [2009]
EWCA Crim 1570, [2010] 4 All ER 553, [2010] 1 Cr App Rep 38. In this
case the Judge was entitled to conclude that there was no reasonable excuse
as the risk was obvious and JB had actually foreseen it. The alarm and
distress had not been an accident but was caused by JB's reckless conduct
in breaching the ASBO: *JB v DPP* [2012] EWHC 72 (Admin), [2012] 1
WLR 2357, [2012] 2 Cr App Rep 9.

SGC Guideline – Anti-social behaviour order, breach of

B[8.14] Triable either way

Maximum when tried summarily: Level 5 and/or 6 months

Maximum when tried on indictment: 5 years or an unlimited fine

Note: A conditional discharge is not available as a sentence for this offence

OFFENCE SERIOUSNESS (CULPABILITY AND HARM)		
A. IDENTIFY THE APPROPRIATE STARTING POINT		
Starting points based on first time offender pleading not guilty		
Examples of nature of activity	**Starting point**	**Range**
Breach where no harassment, alarm or distress was caused or intended	Low level community order	Band B fine to medium level community order
Breach involving a lesser degree of actual or intended harassment, alarm or distress than in the box below, or where such harm would have been likely had the offender not been apprehended	6 weeks custody	Medium level community order to 26 weeks custody
Breach involving serious actual or intended harassment, alarm or distress	26 weeks custody	Custody threshold to Crown Court
OFFENCE SERIOUSNESS (CULPABILITY AND HARM)		
B. CONSIDER THE EFFECT OF AGGRAVATING AND MITIGATING FACTORS (OTHER THAN THOSE WITHIN EXAMPLES ABOVE)		
Common aggravating and mitigating factors are identified at B[5.2A]. The following may be particularly relevant but **these lists are not exhaustive**		
Factors indicating higher culpability	*Factors indicating lower culpability*	
1. Offender has a history of disobedience to court orders	1. Breach occurred after a long period of compliance	
2. Breach was committed immediately or shortly after the order was made	2. The prohibition(s) breached was not fully understood especially where an interim order was made without notice	
3. Breach was committed subsequent to earlier breach proceedings arising from the same order		
4. Targeting of a person the order was made to protect or a witness in the original proceedings		
Factor indicating greater degree of harm		
1. Involvement of vulnerable/young persons		
FORM A PRELIMINARY VIEW OF THE APPROPRIATE SENTENCE, THEN CONSIDER OFFENDER MITIGATION		
Common factors are identified at B[5.2A]		

| CONSIDER A REDUCTION FOR A GUILTY PLEA |
| CONSIDER ANCILLARY ORDERS, INCLUDING FORFEITURE AND DESTRUCTION OF DRUG |
| Refer to B[18] for guidance on compensation and Part B for available ancillary orders |
| DECIDE SENTENCE |
| GIVE REASONS |

B[8.14A] Previous convictions. For the purposes of this guideline a 'first time offender' is one who does not have a previous conviction for breach of an ASBO.

Key factors

B[8.15] (a) An ASBO may be breached in a very wide range of circumstances and may involve one or more terms not being complied with. The examples given below are intended to illustrate how the scale of the conduct that led to the breach, taken as a whole, might come within the three levels of seriousness:

No harm caused or intended – in the absence of intimidation or the causing of fear or violence, breaches involving being very drunk or begging at this level, as may prohibited use of public transport or entry into a prohibited area, where there is no evidence that harassment, alarm or distress was caused or intended.

Lesser degree of harm caused or intended – examples may include lesser degree of threats or intimidation, the use of seriously abusive language, or causing more than minor damage to property.

Serious harm caused or intended – breach at this level of seriousness will involve the use of violence, significant threats or intimidation or the targeting of individuals or groups of people in a manner that leads to a fear of violence.

(b) The suggested starting points are based on the assumption that the offender has the level of culpability.

(c) In the most serious cases, involving repeat offending and a breach causing serious harassment together with the presence of several aggravating factors, such as the use of violence, a sentence beyond the highest range will be justified.

(d) When imposing a community order, the court must ensure that the requirements imposed are proportionate to the seriousness of the breach, compatible with each other, and also with the prohibitions of the ASBO if the latter is to remain in force. Even where the threshold for a custodial sentence is crossed, a custodial sentence is not inevitable.

(e) An offender may be sentenced for more than one offence of breach, which occurred on different days. While consecutive sentences may be imposed in such cases, the overall sentence should reflect the totality principle.

B[8.15A] Sentencing of Young Offenders. The normal approach is that the penalty is scaled down to reflect both reduced culpability (for example, due to a lesser ability to foresee the consequences of actions) and the more onerous effects of punishments on their education and personal development. For the same reasons, the sentencing framework differs significantly depending on the age of the young offender. Space does not permit a full discussion of the SAP advice. See **paragraphs 52–69** of the advice.

B[8.16] The court may not impose a conditional discharge following a breach.

B[8.17] Reporting restrictions – see E[2.4].

Attendance centre orders (adults only)

(Powers of Criminal Courts (Sentencing) Act 2000, s 60; Criminal Justice Act 2003, s 177)

B[9.1] Jurisdiction – Offence must be punishable with imprisonment (even though the individual offender may not be).

B[9.2] Age limits – 18 to under 25 years (25 years old also when used as a fine default power).

B[9.3] Maximum period – 12 hours unless the court thinks that would be inadequate in which event the maximum periods are:

Offender aged 18 to under 25: 36 hours

Note – A further order may be made during the currency of a previous one, in which case the period of the later order may be determined as above without regard to the unexpired part of the previous order.

B[9.4] Minimum period – 12 hours.

B[9.5] Availability. Court must have been notified of the availability of a centre for persons of the offender's age and sex.

B[9.6] Regard must be paid to the accessibility of the centre to the offender.

B[9.7] Juveniles. A magistrates' court may not make this order against a juvenile but must remit him to a youth court.

B[9.8] Community sentences. Note the restrictions on imposing a community sentence, see B[3].

Ancillary orders

B[9.9] Anti-social behaviour orders B[8]

Binding over orders

Compensation at B[18]

Costs at B[20]

Deprivation of property and forfeiture at B[34]

Disqualification from driving at C[5]

Endorsement of driving licence at C[5]

Legal aid contribution order at I[7]

Restitution orders B[39]

How to announce

B[9.10]–[9.15] We shall order you to attend the attendance centre at [................] for a total of [................] hours starting on [................]. You will be given a copy of the order which will show the date and time of your first attendance. After that you will attend as directed by the officer in charge. You will make up the period of [................] hours by attending on Saturday afternoons (or as the case may be) for two (or three, as the case may be) hours at a time. If you arrive late the officer in charge may not count that day's attendance. If you fail to attend without a very good excuse, or if you fail to carry out the officer's instructions properly, he will bring you back here and we shall deal with you. Do you understand?

General considerations

B[9.16] The aims of the attendance centre have been described by the Home Office as follows:

(a)   to vindicate the law by imposing loss of leisure, a punishment that is generally understood by offenders;

(b)   to bring the offender for a period under the influence of representatives of the authority of the state; and

(c)   to teach the offender constructive use of leisure and to guide him, on leaving, towards organisations or activities where he may use what he has learned. Centres usually require attendance for three-hour periods on alternate Saturday afternoons. Only one period of attendance may be required in any one day. The court must take into account the availability of suitable transport and the journey time from home to the centre. A distance of 15 miles or a 90–minutes journey would be the limit.

B[9.17] The court must announce for how many hours the defendant must attend. The court should also tell the defendant the date, time and place of the first attendance.

B[10]

Binding over

B[10.1] There have been significant developments to the making of binding over orders following amendments to the *Consolidated Criminal Practice Direction* which for the sake of completeness is set out below at B[10.21]. The following notes therefore must be read in the light of that Practice Direction.

B[10.2] **Maximum period** – None, but the Practice Direction suggests generally not longer than 12 months.

B[10.3] **Minimum period** – None, but consistent with community orders generally not less than six months.

Ancillary orders

B[10.4] Costs at B[20]. It would appear that there is no power to award costs where a defendant is bound over under the court's inherent powers where the substantive charge is withdrawn or dismissed.

How to announce

B[10.5] We are going to order you to enter a recognisance – that is a binding promise – that you will refrain from the following conduct or activity for the next [*period*]. [Court to specify the specific conduct or activity from which the individual must refrain.]

The amount of that recognisance will be [*amount*] and that means that if you repeat the kind of conduct or activity we have heard about today, during the next [*period*] we will order you to pay that amount. Do you understand? Do you agree to making that promise and to guaranteeing to pay the [*amount*] if you break that promise?

Age limits – None. However, a refusal to enter a recognisance (see below) will result in imprisonment and as those under 21 [**18] may not be imprisoned the court would be powerless to enforce an order to enter into a recognisance.

General considerations

B[10.6] One or more sureties may also be required if the court thinks fit. This order is commonly and conveniently referred to as a binding over order but this tends to disguise its real form. The court orders the defendant to enter a recognisance in terms chosen by the court as to the duration and amount. The defendant or his legal representative must be given an opportunity to address the court in order not to breach Article 6 rights (*Hooper v UK* (2004) Times, 19 November, [2004] All ER (D) 254 (Nov), ECtHR). If the defendant so agrees, he is said to be bound over to keep the peace. If he refuses to enter the recognisance the only course left to the court is to send him to prison from which he will be released after a term fixed by the court of up to six months or when he enters the recognisance, whichever is the sooner. Great care should therefore be exercised before making such an order especially if there is any possibility of refusal to comply with it. An order to be of good behaviour should be avoided as it is imprecise and may breach the ECHR (*Hashman and Harrup v United Kingdom* (1999) 30 EHRR 241, [2000] Crim LR 185, 8 BHRC 104, ECtHR).

NB: The defendant's consent is not required if the binding over order is made as an ancillary penalty to a criminal sentence (*R v Crown Court at Lincoln, ex p Jude* [1997] 3 All ER 737). This case must be read against the Consolidated Practice Direction set out below.

B[10.7] Before a court has any power to order a person to enter a recognisance to keep the peace, it must have grounds for believing that there is a possibility of a future breach of the peace.

B[10.8] Sometimes the court is asked to make this order by an applicant who has taken out a summons for that purpose. In addition to this, the court may on its own initiative consider the need to make the order when dealing with an offender. Moreover, a witness or complainant may also be ordered to enter a recognisance. Whenever the court takes the initiative it should explain to the person concerned what it has in mind to do and offer an opportunity to address the court before it is decided whether to make the order or not.

B[10.9]–[10.15] The procedure for binding over a complainant or witness must be followed punctiliously, and if this is in contemplation, the advice of the legal adviser should be followed.

B[10.16] There is no power generally to impose any conditions, and an order must be specific as to the conduct or activity which the individual must refrain from repeating. Also it appears that there may be a condition not to possess, carry or use firearms or as part of a community order (Firearms Act 1968, s 21(3)).

B[10.17] Breach of the order will be dealt with by forfeiting the recognisance, or any part of it. The defendant may be given time to pay and in default, after a means inquiry, he may be committed to prison, as if he owed a fine.

Binding over a parent

B[10.18] Either a magistrates' court or a youth court may require the parent of a young person (or an 18-year-old who was 17 when the proceedings commenced) who has been found guilty of an offence to enter a recognisance to take proper care of him and to exercise proper control over him. The court must exercise these powers where the juvenile has not attained 16 years if it is satisfied, having regard to the circumstances of the case, that it would be desirable in the interests of preventing the juvenile from committing further offences. If the court does not exercise the powers it must say so and give its reasons in open court. The court's duty to bind over the parent is replaced by a power where the juvenile has attained 16 years. In such a case the maximum amount of the recognisance is £1,000 and the maximum period is three years or until a young person attains 18, whichever is the shorter.

B[10.19] The parent must consent to the order. An unreasonable refusal is punishable by a fine of up to £1,000. A parent may appeal to the Crown Court against the bind over.

Consolidated Criminal Practice Direction 2014

B[10.20]–[10.21] Section J of the CCPD provides:

'J: BINDING OVER ORDERS AND CONDITIONAL DISCHARGES

J.1 This direction takes into account the judgments of the European Court of Human Rights in *Steel v United Kingdom* (1999) 28 EHRR 603, [1998] Crim. L.R.893 and in *Hashman and Harrup v United Kingdom* (2000) 30 EHRR 241, [2000]Crim. L.R. 185. Its purpose is to give practical guidance, in the light of those two judgments, on the practice of imposing binding over orders. The direction applies to orders made under the court's common law powers, under the Justices of the Peace Act 1361, under section 1(7) of the Justices of the Peace Act 1968 and under section 115 of the Magistrates' Courts Act 1980. This direction also gives guidance concerning the court's power to bind over parents or guardians under section 150 of the Powers of Criminal Courts (Sentencing) Act 2000 and the Crown Court's power to bind over to come up for judgment. The court's power to impose a conditional discharge under section 12 of the Powers of Criminal Courts (Sentencing) Act 2000 is also covered by this direction.

Binding over to keep the peace

J.2 Before imposing a binding over order, the court must be satisfied so that it is sure that a breach of the peace involving violence, or an imminent threat of violence, has occurred or that there is a real risk of violence in the future. Such violence may be perpetrated by the individual who will be subject to the order or by a third party as a natural consequence of the individual's conduct.

J.3 In light of the judgment in *Hashman*, courts should no longer bind an individual over "to be of good behaviour". Rather than binding an individual over to "keep the peace" in general terms, the court should identify the specific conduct or activity from which the individual must refrain.

Written order

J.4 When making an order binding an individual over to refrain from specified types of conduct or activities, the details of that conduct or those activities should be specified by the court in a written order, served on all relevant parties. The court should state its reasons for the making of the order, its length and the amount of the recognisance. The length of the order should be proportionate to the harm sought to be avoided and should not generally exceed 12 months.

Evidence

J.5 Sections 51 to 57 of the Magistrates' Courts Act 1980 set out the jurisdiction of the magistrates' court to hear an application made on complaint and the procedure which is to be followed. This includes a requirement under section 53 to hear evidence and the parties, before making any order. This practice should be applied to all cases in the magistrates' court and the Crown Court where the court is considering imposing a binding over order. The court should give the individual who would be subject to the order and the prosecutor the opportunity to make representations, both as to the making of the order and as to its terms. The court should also hear any admissible evidence the parties wish to call and which has not already been heard in the proceedings. Particularly careful consideration may be required where the individual who would be subject to the order is a witness in the proceedings.

J.6 Where there is an admission which is sufficient to found the making of a binding over order and / or the individual consents to the making of the order, the court should nevertheless hear sufficient representations and, if appropriate, evidence, to satisfy itself that an order is appropriate in all the circumstances and to be clear about the terms of the order.

J.7 Where there is an allegation of breach of a binding over order and this is contested, the court should hear representations and evidence, including oral evidence, from the parties before making a finding. If unrepresented and no opportunity has been given previously the court should give a reasonable period for the person said to have breached the binding over order to find representation.

Burden and standard of proof

J.8 The court should be satisfied so that it is sure of the matters complained of before a binding over order may be imposed. Where the procedure has been commenced on complaint, the burden of proof rests on the complainant. In all other circumstances, the burden of proof rests upon the prosecution.

J.9 Where there is an allegation of breach of a binding over order, the court should be satisfied on the balance of probabilities that the defendant is in breach before making any order for forfeiture of a recognisance. The burden of proof shall rest on the prosecution.

Recognisance

J.10 The court must be satisfied on the merits of the case that an order for binding over is appropriate and should announce that decision before considering the amount of the recognisance. If unrepresented, the individual who is made subject to the binding over order should be told he has a right of appeal from the decision.

J.11 When fixing the amount of recognisance, courts should have regard to the individual's financial resources and should hear representations from the individual or his legal representatives regarding finances.

J.12 A recognisance is made in the form of a bond giving rise to a civil debt on breach of the order.

Refusal to enter into a recognisance

J.13 If there is any possibility that an individual will refuse to enter a recognisance, the court should consider whether there are any appropriate alternatives to a binding over order (for example, continuing with a prosecution). Where there are no appropriate alternatives and the individual continues to refuse to enter into the recognisance, the court may commit the individual to custody. In the magistrates' court, the power to do so will derive from section 1(7) of the Justices of the Peace Act 1968 or, more rarely, from section 115(3) of the Magistrates' Courts Act 1980, and the court should state which power it is acting under; in the Crown Court, this is a common law power.

J.14 Before the court exercises a power to commit the individual to custody, the individual should be given the opportunity to see a duty solicitor or another legal representative and be represented in proceedings if the individual so wishes. Public funding should generally be granted to cover representation. In the Crown Court this rests with the Judge who may grant a Representation Order.

J.15 In the event that the individual does not take the opportunity to seek legal advice, the court shall give the individual a final opportunity to comply with the request and shall explain the consequences of a failure to do so.

Antecedents

J.16 Courts are reminded of the provisions of section 7(5) of the Rehabilitation of Offenders Act 1974 which excludes from a person's antecedents any order of the court "with respect to any person otherwise than on a conviction".

Binding over to come up for judgment

J.17 If the Crown Court is considering binding over an individual to come up for judgment, the court should specify any conditions with which the individual is to comply in the meantime and not specify that the individual is to be of good behaviour.

J.18 The Crown Court should, if the individual is unrepresented, explain the consequences of a breach of the binding over order in these circumstances.

Binding over of parent or guardian

J.19 Where a court is considering binding over a parent or guardian under section 150 of the Powers of Criminal Courts (Sentencing) Act 2000 to enter into a recognisance to take proper care of and exercise proper control over a child or young person, the court should specify the actions which the parent or guardian is to take.

Security for good behaviour

J.20 Where a court is imposing a conditional discharge under section 12 of the Powers of Criminal Courts (Sentencing) Act 2000, it has the power, under section 12(6) to make an order that a person who consents to do so give security for the good behaviour of the offender. When making such an order, the court should specify the type of conduct from which the offender is to refrain.

Committal for sentence of dangerous adult offenders

B[11.1] Where an adult offender is convicted of a specified offence within the meaning of s 224 of the Criminal Justice Act 2003 and it appears to the court that the criteria for the imposition of an extended sentence under s 226A of the Criminal Justice Act 2003 would be met, the court must commit the offender in custody or on bail to the Crown Court for sentence: Powers of Criminal Courts (Sentencing) Act 2000, s 3A(1) and (2). The criteria referred to above are:

(a)   at the time the offence was committed, the offender had been convicted of an offence listed in Schedule 15B to the 2003 Act; or

(b)   if the court were to impose an extended sentence of imprisonment, the term it would specify as the appropriate custodial term would be at least four years.

This does not, however, prevent the court from committing for sentence under s 3 of the 2000 Act (see below) where the provisions of that section are satisfied: Powers of Criminal Courts (Sentencing) Act 2000, s 3A(5).

The Crown Court may then deal with the offender in any way in which it could deal with him if he had just been convicted on indictment.

In reaching the above decision the court is not bound by any indication of sentence given during mode of trial; nor may its decision be challenged on the ground that it is inconsistent with such an indication.

Provision is made for the committal for sentence of other offences where a specified offence is committed under this power (see **B[11.13]** below).

Committal to the Crown Court for sentence (other than as a 'dangerous offender')

B[11.2] On conviction of an offence triable either way, the offender may be committed in custody or on bail to the Crown Court for sentence under s 3 of the Powers of Criminal Courts (Sentencing) Act 2000. It is unnecessary for justices to state their reasons for committing for sentence since the person so committed will have an opportunity to make full representations to the sentencing court: *R (on the application of Jermyn) v Wirral Magistrates Court* [2001] Crim LR 45, [2000] All ER (D) 1478, DC.

B[11.3] The court must be of opinion that the offence or the combination of the offence and one or more offences associated with it was so serious that the Crown Court should, in the court's opinion, have the power to deal with the offender in any way it could deal with him if he had been convicted on indictment or, in the case of a violent or sexual offence, that a sentence of imprisonment for term longer than the court has power to impose is necessary to protect the public from serious harm. The terms 'associated with it', 'violent offence', 'sexual offence' and 'serious harm' are all defined in s 161 of the Powers of Criminal Courts (Sentencing) Act 2000.

In considering the seriousness of any offence for this purpose, the court may take into account any previous convictions of the offender or any failure of his to respond to previous sentences. If such an offence was committed while the offender was on bail, the court must treat the fact that it was committed in those circumstances as an aggravating factor: Powers of Criminal Courts (Sentencing) Act 2000, s 151(2).

B[11.4] Where the court is minded to commit the offender for sentence it should first invite representations from the defence and, if it proceeds to commit, it should make clear its opinion when doing so, although this is not binding on the Crown Court.

Guidance on committal for sentence

B[11.5] Where an offender, or his representative, indicates, in accordance with s 17A(6) of the Magistrates' Courts Act 1980, that he would plead guilty if the offence were to proceed to trial the offender may be committed to the Crown Court for sentence if the court is of such opinion as is referred to above (see **B[11.3]**): Powers of Criminal Courts (Sentencing) Act 2000, s 3(2). Guidance on committal for sentence following an indicated guilty plea was given in *R v Warley Magistrates' Court, ex p DPP* [1998] 2 Cr App Rep 307, 162 JP 559, [1998] Crim LR 684, CA. The National Mode of Trial Guidelines and the Magistrates' Courts Sentencing Guidelines are likely to be of the greatest assistance. Magistrates must also have regard to the discount to be granted on a plea of guilty. If the court is of the opinion that the gravity of the offence requires committal for sentence whatever the mitigation may be, it should be prepared to commit for sentence without seeking a pre-sentence report or hearing full mitigation, though a brief submission in opposition to committal may be allowed. If the facts are disputed and, on the defendant's version, the powers of the magistrates' court would be adequate, the court should proceed to hold a '*Newton*' hearing.

If the court considers that a restriction order under the Mental Health Act 1983 is appropriate, it will commit the offender for trial or sentence to the Crown Court as it does not itself possess this power. Similarly, justices may commit a defendant to the Crown Court for sentence if they are of the opinion that, while imprisonment would not be appropriate, the offence was so serious that a larger fine is merited that they have power to impose: *R v North Essex Justices, ex p Lloyd* (2000) 165 JP 117, DC.

There may be no committal for sentence, however, under s 3 of the Powers of Criminal Courts (Sentencing) Act 2000 for offences of criminal damage if the value involved is small: Magistrates' Courts Act 1980, s 33(1).

Committal for sentence following acceptance of summary trial

B[11.6] The opinion that the offence or offences are so serious as to require committal to the Crown Court may be formed after jurisdiction has been accepted and, it would seem, that opinion is not dependent on information showing the offence or offences to be more serious than they were originally thought to be received after the decision to try the case summarily was made: see *R v Sheffield Crown Court and Sheffield Stipendiary Magistrate, ex p DPP* (1994) 158 JP 334, 15 Cr App Rep (S) 768, [1994] Crim LR 470; *R v Dover Magistrates' Court, ex p Pamment* (1994) 158 JP 665, 15 Cr App Rep (S) 778, [1994] Crim LR 471; *R v North Sefton*

Magistrates' Court, ex p Marsh [1994] Crim LR 865, 159 JP 9, (1994) 16 Cr App Rep (S) 401. Nevertheless, justices must still apply their minds to the matters which they are required by s 19(3) of the Magistrates' Courts Act 1980 to consider before deciding to accept summary jurisdiction: *R v Flax Bourton Magistrates, ex p Customs and Excise Comrs* (1996) 160 JP 481, [1996] Crim LR 907.

Previous convictions are now taken into account in mode of trial, but this does not prevent the court from exercising its power to commit for sentence under s 3 of the Powers of Criminal Courts (Sentencing) Act 2000 following a conviction.

B[11.7] A defendant may not be committed for sentence where he has been given a legitimate expectation that the case will be dealt with summarily: *R v North Essex Justices, ex p Lloyd* (2000) 165 JP 117, DC. Such an indication may be given expressly, or it may be given impliedly by, for example, adjourning for a pre sentence report or other inquiries without openly preserving the option of committal for sentence. A sentencing indication (however given) will not bind a subsequent bench, however, if it was so unreasonable to be perverse: see *R (on the application of Nicholas) v Chester Magistrates' Court* [2009] EWHC 1504 (Admin), 173 JP 542; and *R (on the application of Harrington) v Bromley Magistrates Court* [2007] EWHC 2896 (Admin), [2007] All ER (D) 199 (Nov). See also *Thornton v CPS* [2010] 2 Cr App Rep (S) 434, [2010] Crim LR 514, 174 CL&J 109, [2010] All ER (D) 48 (Feb) (indication not binding where the court failed to have regard to the sentencing guidelines, contrary to the duty imposed by s 172 of the Criminal Justice Act 2003).

Committal for sentence of either offences following an indication of guilty pleas where they are related to offences sent for trial

B[11.8] If the court does not form the opinion that its powers are insufficient but sends the offender to the Crown Court for trial for one or more 'related' offences (see below), it may also commit him to the Crown Court to be dealt with in accordance with the provisions of s 5(1) of the Powers of Criminal Courts (Sentencing) Act 2000: Powers of Criminal Courts (Sentencing) Act 2000, s 4(2). Section 5 provides that the Crown Court may deal with the offender in any way in which it could have dealt with him if he had just been convicted of the offence on indictment before the court. This is subject, however, to the exception stated below.

Where the court does commit the offender to the Crown Court to be dealt with, but it does not state that, in its opinion, it does have power so to commit him under s 3(2) of the Powers of Criminal Courts (Sentencing) Act 2000, the provisions of s 5 of the 2000 Act will not apply unless he is convicted before the Crown Court of one or more of the related offences: Powers of Criminal Courts (Sentencing) Act 2000, s 4(4).Where the provisions of s 5 do not apply, the Crown Court's powers to deal with the offender are limited to those of the magistrates' court: Powers of Criminal Courts (Sentencing) Act 2000, s 4(5).

Meaning of 'related'

B[11.9] For the purposes of a committal for sentence on the indication of a guilty plea under s 4 of the 2000 Act, one offence is related to another if, were they both to be prosecuted on indictment, the charges for them could be joined in the same indictment: Powers of Criminal Courts (Sentencing) Act 2000, s 4(7). Charges for any offences may be joined in the same indictment if those charges are founded on the same facts, or form or are a part of a series of offences of the same or a similar character: Criminal Procedure Rules 2013, r 14.2. Where the magistrates' court makes a mistake and instead of committing under s 3(2) commits under s 4 in circumstances where there are no related offences and does not state that it had power to commit under s 3(2) of the 2000 Act, the powers of the Crown Court are limited to those of the magistrates' court: Powers of Criminal Courts (Sentencing) Act 2000, s 5(2) and see *R v Sallis* [2003] EWCA Crim 233, [2003] 2 Cr App Rep (S) 394.

Effect of mistake in recording the basis of committal

B[11.10] Where issues concerning jurisdiction to commit for sentence arise, what matters is the power that was actually used rather than the power that was recorded as being used.

'In our judgment, provided the power of the magistrates' court to commit for sentence was properly exercised in respect of one or more either way offences in accordance with section 3 of the 2000 Act, a mistake in recording the statutory basis for a committal of summary only offences does not invalidate the committal. The principle is that thereafter the Crown Court must abide by the sentencing powers available to the magistrates' court in relation to the summary only offences. If that principle is not followed, then the sentences must be reduced to sentences which fall within the jurisdiction of the magistrates.' (Per Lord Judge CJ in *R v Ayhan* [2011] EWCA Crim 3184, [2012] 1 WLR 1775, [2012] 1 Cr App Rep 391, at para 22.)

Committal on a mistaken view of the facts

B[11.11] Where following plea before venue an offender is committed to the Crown Court for sentence, but before he is sentenced it is discovered that the decision to commit for sentence was taken on the wrong view of the facts, the proper approach will be to allow the offender to make an application to change his plea. If such an application is allowed, the Crown Court may then remit the case to the magistrates' court so that the matter may be considered on a proper view of the facts for the purposes of s 3 of the Powers of Criminal Courts (Sentencing) Act 2000: *R v Crown Court at Isleworth, ex p Buda* [2000] Crim LR 111, [2000] 1 Cr App Rep (S) 538.

Other error in committal

B[11.12] Where a case was erroneously committed to the Crown Court for sentence (the prior consent of the DPP, which was a prerequisite to the prosecution, had not been obtained by that stage, though it was given subsequently), it was unnecessary for the judge to use s 66 of the Courts Act 2003 to exercise the powers of district judge and re-commit the offender; the judge should instead have considered whether it was Parliament's intention that such a failure rendered the proceedings a nullity (however, the judge had been entitled to use his powers under s 66): *R v Ashton, R v Draz, R v O'Reilly* [2006] EWCA Crim 794, [2006] Crim App Rep 231.

Bail or custody

B[11.13] When a person who has been on bail pleads at the plea before venue, the practice should normally be to continue bail, even if it is anticipated that a custodial sentence will be imposed by the Crown Court, unless there are good reasons for remanding the defendant in custody. If the defendant is in custody, then after entering a plea of guilty at the plea before venue, it will be unusual, if the reasons for remanding in custody remain unchanged, to alter the position: *R v Rafferty* [1999] 1 Cr App Rep 235, (1998) 162 JP 353, [1998] Crim LR 433.

Other powers of committal to the Crown Court for sentence

B[11.14] These arise where the offender is committed for sentence for another offence in accordance with any of the following:

- Powers of Criminal Courts (Sentencing) Act 2000, ss 3–4A (committal for sentence for offences triable either way);
- Powers of Criminal Courts (Sentencing) Act 2000, ss 13(5) (conditionally discharged person convicted of further offence);
- Criminal Justice Act 2003, Sch 12, para 11 (offender convicted during operational period of suspended sentence)

Powers of Criminal Courts (Sentencing) Act 2000, s 6

B[11.15] The powers of the Crown Court for offences committed under this provision are limited to those of the magistrates' court: see s 7 of the 2000 Act; see also *R v Bateman; R v Doyle* [2012] EWCA Crim 2518, [2013] 1 WLR 1710, [2013] 2 Cr App Rep (S) 174 – the exception made by s 7(2), namely committal of a person to be dealt with by the Crown Court in respect of a suspended sentence, refers to a suspended sentence imposed by the magistrates' court. Therefore, where offences were committed to the Crown Court for sentence because they were committed during the currency of a Crown Court suspended sentence, the Crown Court's powers were limited to those of the magistrates' court for those further offences.

In relation to these powers as well as the major power to commit for sentence, if the magistrates' court commits to the Crown Court for sentence, then if the offence on which it commits is an indictable offence, it may also commit the offender to be dealt with in respect of any other offence whatsoever in respect of which it has itself power to deal with him. If the offence is on the other hand a summary offence, it may also commit him for sentence if that offence is imprisonable or disqualifiable, or it may commit him in respect of any suspended sentence of imprisonment which it would itself have power to deal with. The committing court must not itself exercise any sentencing powers or duties but must leave them to the Crown Court; it may however impose an interim driving disqualification if that is appropriate: Road Traffic Offenders Act 1988, s 26(1).

A further power of committal to the Crown Court for sentence arises where a court convicts a person who, having been released on bail in criminal proceedings fails without reasonable cause to surrender to custody, and the court thinks that the circumstances of the offence are such that greater punishment should be inflicted for that offence than the court has power to inflict: Bail Act 1976, s 6(6).

B[17]

Community Orders (adults only)

B[17.1] The power to impose a community sentence is restricted to imprisonable offences.

Sections 147–150 of the Criminal Justice Act 2003 define community orders and the restrictions that apply to them. Any requirements imposed must be the most suitable for the offender and must be commensurate and proportionate with the seriousness of the offending. The court may take account of time spent on remand before sentence.

The court must set the end date for completion of all requirements (not later that three years from sentence), but may set different dates for different requirements. If a supervision requirement is included it must be for the full length of the order. The court must impose an electronic monitoring requirement with a curfew or exclusion requirement and may do so for various requirements.

Schedule 16 to the Courts and Crime Act 2013 prospectively inserts new s 177(2A) and (2B) in the Criminal Justice Act 2003. These provisions will require the court to include in a community order at least one requirement imposed for the purpose of punishment, or a fine for the offence for which the community order is made, or both, unless there are exceptional circumstances which:

(a)   relate to the offence or to the offender;
(b)   would make it unjust in all the circumstances for the court to impose a punitive requirement in the particular case; and
(c)   would make it unjust in all the circumstances for the court to impose a fine for the offence concerned.

These amendments will not have retrospective effect.

B[17.2] SGC guidelines provide that the seriousness of the offence should be the initial factor in determining which requirements to include in a community order. It establishes three sentencing ranges within the community order band based on offence seriousness (low, medium and high), and identifies non-exhaustive examples of requirements that might be appropriate in each.

LOW	MEDIUM	HIGH
Offences only just cross community order threshold, where a discharge or fine is inappropriate	Offences that obviously fall within the community order band	Offences only just fall below the custody threshold or the custody threshold is crossed but a community order is more appropriate in the circumstances

In general, only one requirement will be appropriate and the length may be curtailed if additional requirements are necessary		More intensive sentences which combine two or more requirements may be appropriate
Suitable requirements might include:	Suitable requirements might include:	Suitable requirements might include:
40–80 hours unpaid work	80–150 hours unpaid work	150–300 hours unpaid work
Curfew requirement eg up to 12 hours per day for a few weeks (see electronic monitoring below)	Curfew requirement eg up to 12 hours per day for 2–3 months (see electronic monitoring below)	Activity requirement up to the maximum of 60 days
Exclusion requirement, without electronic monitoring for a few months (see electronic monitoring below)	Exclusion requirement lasting in the region of 6 months (see electronic monitoring below)	Curfew requirement up to 12 hours per day for 4–6 months (see electronic monitoring below)
Prohibited activity requirement	Prohibited activity requirement	Exclusion order lasting in the region of 12 months (see electronic monitoring below)
Attendance centre requirement (where available)		

Note: Electronic monitoring. The court must usually impose an electronic monitoring requirement where it makes a community order consisting of a curfew or exclusion requirement, and may do so in all other cases (CJA 2003, s 173(3), (4)). Electronic monitoring should be used with the primary purpose of promoting and monitoring compliance with other requirements, in circumstances where the punishment of the offender and/or the need to safeguard the public and prevent re-offending are the most important concerns.

Permissible requirements

(1) Unpaid work requirement

B[17.3] This is a requirement that the offender must perform unpaid work in accordance for the number of hours specified in the order such work at such times as he may be instructed by the responsible officer. Unless revoked, a community order imposing an unpaid work requirement remains in force until the offender has worked under it for the number of hours specified in it. The work required to be performed under an unpaid work requirement of a community order or a suspended sentence order must be performed during a period of twelve months.

The number of hours which a person may be required to work under an unpaid work requirement must be specified in the relevant order and must be in the aggregate–

(a)   not less than 40, and
(b)   not more than 300.

The court may not impose an unpaid work requirement in respect of an offender unless after hearing (if the court thinks necessary) an appropriate officer, the court is satisfied that the offender is a suitable person to perform work under such a requirement.

Where the court makes orders in respect of two or more offences of which the offender has been convicted on the same occasion and includes unpaid work requirements in each of them, the court may direct that the hours of work specified in any of those requirements is to be concurrent or consecutive. However the total number of hours must not exceed the maximum of 300 hours.

(2) Activity requirement

B[17.4] An activity requirement means a requirement that the offender must do either or both of the following-

(a)   present himself to a person or persons specified in the relevant order at a place or places so specified on such number of days as may be so specified and comply with instructions given by, or under the authority of, the person in charge of that place.

(b)   participate in activities specified in the order on such number of days as may be so specified.

The specified activities may consist of or include reparation, for example contact between the offender and victims affected by their offences.

A court may not include an activity requirement in a relevant order unless it has consulted either an officer of a local probation board or a member of a youth offending team, and it is satisfied that it is feasible to secure compliance with the requirement.

A court may not include an activity requirement in a relevant order if compliance with that requirement would involve the co-operation of a person other than the offender and the offender's responsible officer, unless that other person consents to its inclusion.

The aggregate of the number of days specified must not exceed 60.

A place specified in a requirement for the offender's attendance must be either,

(a)   a community rehabilitation centre, or

(b)   a place that has been approved by the local probation board for the area in which the premises are situated as providing facilities suitable for persons subject to activity requirements.

A requirement to participate in activities operates to require the offender,

(a)   to participate in activities on the number of days specified in the order in accordance with instructions given by his responsible officer, and

(b)   while participating, to comply with instructions given by, or under the authority of, the person in charge of the activities.

(3) Programme requirement

B[17.5] This requirement involves the offender in participation in an accredited programme in accordance with this section on the number of days specified in the order.

Accreditation is by the Secretary of State, and a programme means a systematic set of requirements.

A requirement to attend a programme requirement operates to require the offender,

(a)   in accordance with instructions given by the responsible officer, to participate in the accredited programme that is from time to time specified by the responsible officer at the place that is so specified at the place specified in the order on the number of days specified in the order, and

(b)   while at that place, to comply with instructions given by, or under the authority of, the person in charge of the programme.

The court cannot leave it to the probation officer to decide whether or not the defendant should attend a programme. The amendments to s 202 made by the Legal Aid, Sentencing and Punishment of Offenders Act 2012 give the responsible officer a wide discretion as to the appropriate programme to follow and the place where it must be undertaken, but they do not relieve the court of the duty to specify that an accredited programme needs to be undertaken and to specify the number of days: *R v Price* [2013] EWCA Crim 1283, [2014] 1 Cr App R (S) 36.

4 *Prohibited activity requirement*

B[17.6] This means a requirement that the offender must refrain from participating in activities specified in the order—

(a)   on a day or days so specified, or
(b)   during a period so specified.

A court may not include a prohibited activity requirement in a relevant order unless it has consulted, either an officer of a local probation board or a member of a youth offending team.

The statute provides that the requirements that may be included in a relevant order include a requirement that the offender does not possess, use or carry a firearm within the meaning of the Firearms Act 1968.

(5) *Curfew requirement*

B[17.7] A curfew requirement is a requirement that the offender must remain, for periods specified in the relevant order, at a place so specified. It may specify different places or different periods for different days, but may not specify periods which amount to less than two hours or more than sixteen hours in any one day.

The order may not exceed a period of twelve months beginning with the day on which it is made. For youths and curfew orders see B[50.12].

Before making a relevant order imposing a curfew requirement, the court must obtain and consider information about the place proposed to be specified in the order (including information as to the attitude of persons likely to be affected by the enforced presence there of the offender). An electronic monitoring requirement must be made unless it requires the co-operation of a third party which is not forthcoming.

(6) *Exclusion requirement*

B[17.8] An exclusion requirement, is a provision prohibiting the offender from entering a place named in the order for a specified period of not more than two years.

An exclusion requirement,

(a)   may provide for the prohibition to operate only during the periods specified in the order, and

(b)   may specify different places or areas for different periods or days.

Subject to limited exceptions, the court must impose an electronic monitoring requirement where

it makes a community order with an exclusion requirement.

It is not the objective of an exclusion requirement to punish an offender, nor is it possible to use the means of an exclusion requirement to force an offender already in the UK not to enter the UK – there is no power of expulsion: *R (on the application of Dragoman) v Camberwell Green Magistrates' Court* [2012] EWHC 4105 (Admin), (2013) 177 JP 372.

(7) Residence requirement

B[17.9] This is a requirement that, during a period specified in the relevant order, the offender must reside at a place specified in the order.

If the order makes provision, a residence requirement does not prohibit the offender from residing, with the prior approval of the responsible officer, at a place other than that specified in the order.

Before making a community order containing a residence requirement, the court must consider the home surroundings of the offender.

7A Foreign Travel Prohibition requirement

B[17.9A] This means a requirement prohibiting the offender from travelling, on a day or days, or for a period specified in the order:

(a)   to any country or territory outside the British Isles specified or described in the order;

(b)   to any country or territory outside the British Isles other than a country or territory specified or described in the order; or

(c)   to any country or territory outside the British Isles.

The specified days or period cannot fall outside/extend beyond 12 months beginning with the day on which the order was made.

(8) Mental health treatment requirement

B[17.10] This requires the offender to submit, during periods specified in the order, to treatment by or under the direction of a registered medical practitioner or a chartered psychologist (or both, for different periods) with a view to the improvement of the offender's mental condition.

The treatment required must be one of the following kinds of treatment as may be specified in the relevant order:

(a)   treatment as a resident patient in an independent hospital or care home within the meaning of the Care Standards Act 2000 or a hospital within the meaning of the Mental Health Act 1983, but not in hospital premises where high security psychiatric services within the meaning of that Act are provided;

(b)   treatment as a non-resident patient at such institution or place as may be specified in the order;

(c)   treatment by or under the direction of such registered medical practitioner or chartered psychologist (or both) as may be so specified;

The nature of the treatment may not be specified in the order except as mentioned in (a), (b) or (c) above.

A court may not by virtue of this section include a mental health treatment requirement in an order unless-

(a)   the court is satisfied, that the mental condition of the offender–
        (i)   is such as requires and may be susceptible to treatment, but
        (ii)   is not such as to warrant the making of a hospital order or guardianship order within the meaning of the Mental Health Act 1983;
(b)   the court is also satisfied that arrangements have been or can be made for the treatment intended to be specified in the order (including arrangements for the reception of the offender where he is to be required to submit to treatment as a resident patient); and
(c)   the offender has expressed his willingness to comply with such a requirement.

While the offender is under treatment as a resident patient in pursuance of a mental health requirement, his responsible officer shall carry out the supervision of the offender to such extent only as may be necessary for the purpose of the revocation or amendment of the order.

(9) Mental health treatment at place other than that specified in order

B[17.11] Where the medical practitioner or chartered psychologist, treating the offender in pursuance of a mental health treatment requirement, is of the opinion that part of the treatment can be better or more conveniently given in or at an institution or place which-

(a)   is not specified in the relevant order, and
(b)   is one in or at which the treatment of the offender will be given by or under the direction of a registered medical practitioner or chartered psychologist,

he may, with the consent of the offender, make arrangements for him to be treated accordingly.

These arrangements as are mentioned may provide for the offender to receive part of his treatment as a resident patient in an institution or place notwithstanding that the institution or place is not one which could have been specified for that purpose in the relevant order.

Where any such arrangements are made for the treatment of an offender the medical practitioner or chartered psychologist by whom the arrangements are made shall give notice in writing to the offender's responsible officer giving details of the place and the treatment provided.

(10) Drug rehabilitation requirement

B[17.12] A drug rehabilitation requirement means a requirement that during a period specified in the order the offender must submit to treatment by or under the direction of a specified person having the necessary qualifications or experience with a view to the reduction or elimination of the offender's dependency on or propensity to misuse drugs.

During that period he must provide samples for the purpose of ascertaining whether he has any drug in his body.

A court may not impose a drug rehabilitation requirement unless-

(a)   it is satisfied–
        (i)   that the offender is dependent on, or has a propensity to misuse, drugs, and
        (ii)   that his dependency or propensity is such as requires and may be susceptible to treatment,

(b)   it is also satisfied that arrangements have been or can be made for the treatment intended to be specified in the order (including arrangements for the reception of the offender where he is to be required to submit to treatment as a resident),

(c)   the requirement has been recommended to the court as being suitable for the offender either by an officer of a local probation board or by a member of a youth offending team, and

(d)   the offender expresses his willingness to comply with the requirement.

The treatment and testing period must be no more than three years and must be treatment as a resident in such institution or place as may be specified in the order, or treatment as a non-resident place, as may be so specified.

The nature of the treatment may not be specified in the order except as mentioned in paragraph (a) or (b) above.

A community order imposing a drug rehabilitation requirement must provide that the results of tests carried out on any samples provided by the offender in pursuance of the requirement to a person other than the responsible officer are to be communicated to the responsible officer.

(10A) *Drug rehabilitation requirement: provision for review by court*

B[17.13] A community order imposing a drug rehabilitation requirement may (and must if the treatment and testing period is more than 12 months),

(a)   provide for the requirement to be reviewed periodically at intervals of not less than one month,

(b)   provide for each review of the requirement to be made, at a hearing held for the purpose by the court responsible for the order (a "review hearing"),

(c)   require the offender to attend each review hearing,

(d)   provide for the responsible officer to make to the court responsible for the order, before each review, a report in writing on the offender's progress under the requirement, and

(e)   provide for each such report to include the test results communicated to the responsible officer and the views of the treatment provider as to the treatment and testing of the offender.

References to the court responsible for a community order or suspended sentence order imposing a drug rehabilitation requirement are:

(a)   where a court is specified in the order, to that court;
(b)   in any other case, to the court by which the order is made.

Where the area specified in a community order is not the area for which the court acts, the court may, if it thinks fit, include in the order provision specifying a magistrates' court which acts for the area specified in the order.

(10B) Periodic review of drug rehabilitation requirement

B[17.14] At a review hearing the court may, after considering the responsible officer's report, amend the community order, so far as it relates to the drug rehabilitation requirement but only if the offender expresses his willingness to comply with the requirement as amended.

Nor may the court amend any requirement or provision of the order while an appeal against the order is pending, except with the consent of the offender.

If the offender fails to express his willingness to comply with the drug rehabilitation requirement as proposed to be amended by the court, the court may, revoke the community order and deal with him, for the offence in respect of which the order was made. If the court decides to re-sentence it must take into account the extent to which the offender has complied with the requirements of the order, and may impose a custodial sentence (where the order was made in respect of an offence punishable with such a sentence) notwithstanding anything in section CJA 2003 s 152(2). In the case of a juvenile who has attained the age of 18 the court's powers are to do either or both of the following,

(a)   to impose a fine not exceeding £5,000 for the offence in respect of which the order was made;
(b)   to deal with the offender for that offence in any way in which the court could deal with him if it had just convicted him of an offence punishable with imprisonment for a term not exceeding twelve months.

If at a review hearing the court, after considering the responsible officer's report, is of the opinion that the offender's progress under the requirement is satisfactory, the court may so amend the order as to provide for each subsequent review to be made by the court without a hearing.

If at a review without a hearing the court, after considering the responsible officer's report, is of the opinion that the offender's progress under the requirement is no longer satisfactory, the court may require the offender to attend a hearing of the court at a specified time and place.

At that hearing the court, after considering that report, may:-

(a)   exercise the powers conferred by this section as if the hearing were a review hearing, and
(b)   so amend the order as to provide for each subsequent review to be made at a review hearing.

(11) Alcohol treatment requirement

B[17.15] This is a requirement that the offender submits during a specified period to treatment by or under the direction of a specified person having the necessary qualifications or experience with a view to the reduction or elimination of the offender's dependency on alcohol.

The court may not impose an alcohol treatment requirement in respect of an offender unless it is satisfied that he is dependent on alcohol, and his dependency is such as requires and may be susceptible to treatment. Arrangements must be made for the treatment intended to be specified in the order (including arrangements for the reception of the offender where he is to be required to submit to treatment as a resident).

A court may not impose an alcohol treatment requirement unless the offender expresses his willingness to comply with its requirements.

The treatment required by an alcohol treatment requirement for any particular period must be,

(a)   treatment as a resident in such institution or place as may be specified in the order,

(b)   treatment as a non-resident in or at such institution or place, and at such intervals, as may be so specified, or

(c)   treatment by or under the direction of such person having the necessary qualification or experience as may be so specified;

but the nature of the treatment shall not be specified in the order except as mentioned in paragraph (a), (b) or (c) above.

(11A) *Alcohol abstinence and monitoring requirement*

B[17.15A] Section 76 of the Legal Aid, Sentencing and Punishment of Offenders Act 2012 (LASPOA 2012) inserts new s 212A in the Criminal Justice Act 2003 which adds alcohol abstinence and monitoring to the list of requirements that can be included in a community order. For this purpose, the Legal Aid, Sentencing and Punishment of Offenders Act 2012 (Alcohol Abstinence and Monitoring Requirements) Piloting Order 2014, SI 2014/1777, brought s 76 into force in relation to the South London local justice area.

(12) *Supervision requirement (excludes juvenile offenders)*

B[17.16] A supervision requirement is a requirement that, during the relevant period, the offender must attend appointments with the responsible officer or another person determined by the responsible officer, at such time and place as may be determined by the officer.

The purpose for which a supervision requirement may be imposed is that of promoting the offender's rehabilitation.

For these purposes the relevant period means the period for which the community order remains in force.

B[17.17] Breach of a requirement

See also A[17]. Under national standards an offender will be given one warning and then returned to court following a subsequent breach. It is open to probation to allege in the information both the original warning before the breach proceedings and the subsequent breach after the warning: *West Yorkshire Probation Board v Robinson and Tinker* [2009] EWHC 2468 (Admin). The court's powers are contained in Sch 8 Criminal Justice Act 2003. On breach of a requirement the court must deal with the offender by:

(a)   making the original order more onerous;

(b)   imposing a fine of up to £2,500; or

(c)   revoking the order and dealing with the offender for the original offence (in the case of wilful and persistent failure to comply, the court may impose custody for a non-imprisonable offence.

Crown Court orders may contain a direction that breaches are dealt with in the magistrates' court or reserved to itself.

B[17.18] Revocation

The offender or responsible officer may apply to revoke the order and the court if satisfied it is in the interests of justice may revoke and or deal with the original offence, giving credit for any part of the order already completed. For the procedure see Part 44 of the Criminal Procedure Rules 2012.

It would be wrong in principle to resentence the offender where the revocation was on the grounds of ill health (*R v Bishop* [2004] EWCA Crim 2956, [2004] All ER (D) 116 (Dec)).

Compensation order

(Powers of Criminal Courts (Sentencing) Act 2000,
ss 130–138)

B[18.1] Compensation order. Either as a sentence in its own right or in addition to another sentence, the court may order the defendant to pay compensation to a person who has suffered as a consequence of the defendant's crime.

A court must consider making a compensation order in any case where this section empowers it do so: s 130(2A) of the PCCSA 2000.

Compensation orders are intended to be used in simple, straightforward cases where no great amount is at stake. A compensation order can only be made when sentence is being passed and, therefore, cannot be made when committing for sentence or deferring sentence. The court shall give its reasons, on passing sentence, if it does not make a compensation order where it is empowered to do so. Examples of such reasons will be the defendant's lack of means, or that the loss is difficult to quantify (see below).

Surcharge. It is normally obligatory for the court to require payment of a surcharge – of an amount determined in accordance with the Criminal Justice Act 2003 (Surcharge) Order 2012, SI 2012/1696 – as part its of its sentence. Where, however, the court considers it would be appropriate to make a compensation order, but the offender has insufficient means to pay both the surcharge and appropriate compensation, the court must reduce the amount of the surcharge (if necessary to nil): Criminal Justice Act 2003, s 161A.

Note: the term "fine" does not include any road fund or excise offence committed under the Vehicle Excise and Registration Act 1994 (C[47]) because the legislation provides for payment of an "excise penalty".

B[18.2] For what may compensation be ordered? For any personal injury, loss or damage (or to make payments for funeral expenses or bereavement in respect of a death resulting from any such offence, other than a death due to an accident arising out of the presence of a motor vehicle on a road – (ie the only such situation likely to arise in a magistrates' court, death arising from careless driving, not being covered)) resulting from the offence or any offences taken into consideration. Personal injury need not be physical injury, compensation may be ordered for terror or distress caused by the offence *(Bond v Chief Constable of Kent* [1983] 1 All ER 456, [1983] 1 WLR 40).

B[18.3] In the case of an offence under the Theft Act 1968, if the property is recovered but is damaged, a compensation order may be made against the defendant no matter how the damage was caused provided it was caused while the property was out of the owner's possession.

Exceptions

B[18.4] Exceptions include:

(a)   Loss caused to the dependants of a victim who has died (except funeral expenses etc in the circumstances referred to above).

(b)   Injury, loss or damage due to an accident arising out of the presence of a motor vehicle on a road except compensation may be awarded:

    (i)   for damage caused to a motor vehicle stolen or taken without the owner's consent but not damage caused by the vehicle, eg to another car on the road; and

    (ii)   in cases where the defendant's use of the vehicle was uninsured and no compensation is payable under the Motor Insurers' Bureau scheme (see **C[33.18]–C[33.22]**).

The amounts ordered under (i) and (ii) may include payment to cover loss of a 'no claims' bonus.

B[18.5] Proof of loss. As a result of amendments made to the law in 1982 it was considered that the approach to establishing the amount of the loss was not so strict as it was formerly. However, in 1985 the judges of the Divisional Court reaffirmed that (unless the amount was admitted by the accused at the outset) it was the duty of the prosecution to establish the loss and its amount, and make it clear to the defendant by means of evidence. If, after this, there was any real dispute as to the loss suffered by the victim, a compensation order should not be made and the victim should be left to resort to civil remedies to obtain compensation (*R v Horsham Justices, ex p Richards* [1985] 2 All ER 1114, [1985] 1 WLR 986)); followed in *R v Stapylton (Ben)* [2012] EWCA Crim 728, [2012] All ER (D) 84 (Apr). However where the exact loss cannot be ascertained but finding the minimum loss was a simple task that latter sum may be ordered (*R v Brazil* [2004] EWCA Crim 1975, [2004] All ER (D) 348 (Jun)).

Fixing the amount

B[18.6] The following need to be taken into account when fixing the amount:

(a)   The amount of the loss should be established after proof or agreement.

(b)   Where the loss is not determined the court cannot fix an arbitrary amount at a figure below that which is in dispute. Either the lowest amount admitted should be adopted or no order made at all.

(c)   Compensation for personal injury may be ascertained having regard to guidelines issued by the Criminal Injuries Compensation Board (see **B[18.19]**).

(d)   The maximum compensation that may be awarded is £5,000* for each offence against each defendant. For the maximum where offences are to be taken into consideration the legal adviser should be consulted.

    *This limit is prospectively removed by para 8(1) of Sch 16 to the Courts and Crime Act 2013.

(e)   Having ascertained what the loss is, and what the maximum amount is that can be ordered, the court must have regard to the defendant's ability to pay. He may be allowed to pay by instalments but generally such instalments should not extend beyond two years (*R v Olliver and Olliver* (1989) 11 Cr App Rep (S) 10, 153 JP 369,

[1989] Crim LR 387, CA), a case in the Crown Court where a large sum was to be paid) although in the magistrates' courts simple straightforward orders will probably be paid within a shorter period. Judicial guidance suggests that magistrates' court orders should be paid within a short period of time, preferably 13 weeks and 52 weeks should be regarded as the maximum period for repayment. Where the defendant is of limited means and would be unable to pay both compensation and a fine, preference must be given to the award of compensation. Neither *R v Olliver and Olliver* nor *R v Yehou* [1997] 2 Cr App Rep (S) 48 was authority for the proposition that there was an outer limit for the period of repayment of a compensation order. Under s 130(4) of the Powers of Criminal Courts (Sentencing) Act 2000, a court making a compensation order must ask whether it is appropriate. That requires an enquiry into whether the compensation order will be oppressive or an undue burden given the offender's means; whether realistically the offender can be expected to repay in the terms proposed and whether the compensation order accords with the nature of the offence and the nature of the offender. In neither case was the order an undue burden. Under s 133 of the PCCSA 2000, if there was a change in financial circumstances of either of the appellants, they could apply for a variation or discharge of the order: *R v Ganyo* [2011] EWCA Crim 2491, [2012] 1 Cr App Rep (S) 650, 176 JP 396. With respect, *Ganyo* is wrong. The CA overlooked the Sentencing Council guidelines which recommend maximum periods for repayment in comity with *Olliver* and *Yehou* above,

(f)   If the defendant cannot afford to pay for the whole amount of the loss, then this lower amount, which he can afford, must be ordered.

(g)   The circumstances in which a court may subsequently vary a compensation order are limited. Accordingly, an unrealistically high order for compensation may result in the defendant being committed to prison for default; this is wrong in principle (see B[18.17]–B[18.18] 'appeal and review').

B[18.7] Making an order. When deliberating whether to make an order, the court should bear in mind that the wealthy offender should never be allowed to buy his way out of prison by offering compensation. Also, the court should be wary of an accused mitigating for a suspended sentence on the basis of extravagant promises to pay compensation.

B[18.8] On the other hand, when a custodial sentence is imposed, compensation should be ordered only if the offender has the means to pay immediately or out of existing resources. He should not have to face the payment of compensation upon his discharge from a custodial sentence unless it is clear that he will then have the means to pay, eg he has savings or by being able to return to gainful employment immediately.

B[18.9] The court should announce the amount of compensation for each offence and against each defendant. Where there are competing claims for compensation, the court may make an order for one compensatee in preference to another, eg a private individual in preference to a financial institution (*R v Amey* [1983] 1 All ER 865, [1983] 1 WLR 345, CA).

B[18.10]–[18.15] In all cases where a compensation order is contemplated, the legal adviser should be consulted.

B[18.16] Compensation and deprivation orders. Where a court makes a deprivation order (see B[34]) in a case where a person has suffered personal injury, loss or damage, but a compensation order for the full loss cannot be made because of the offender's inadequate means, it may direct that the proceeds arising from the disposal of the forfeited goods be paid to the victim to make good the deficiency. The amount to be paid is a sum not exceeding the amount of compensation that the court would have ordered were it not for the offender's lack of means. See also B[19] for confiscation orders.

Appeal and review

B[18.17] The entitlement of the victim is suspended for 21 days to allow the defendant time to appeal if he wishes, or until after the appeal is heard. But the enforcement of the order against the offender is not suspended; the obligation to pay arises immediately. Accordingly, where an appeal is successful, the court will have to repay to the appellant any monies that he has already paid.

B[18.18] At any time before the order has been fully complied with, the court may discharge or reduce the order:

(a)   if a civil court determines an amount of damage or loss less than that stated in the order; or
(b)   if the property or part of it is subsequently recovered; or
(c) . where the defendant's means are insufficient to satisfy in full the compensation order and a confiscation order made in the same proceedings; or
(d)   where the defendant has suffered a substantial reduction in his means which was unexpected at the time the compensation order was made, and his means seem unlikely to increase for a considerable period.

The permission of the Crown Court is required where it made the original order, if the magistrates' court contemplates the action at (c) or (d).

Guidelines for compensation for personal injury

B[18.19] Guidelines were to be found originally in Home Office circular 53/1993 for the assistance of magistrates. They were prepared by the Criminal Injuries Compensation Board (now renamed the Criminal Injuries Compensation Authority) and reflect the level of damages which would be awarded in the civil courts for the injuries described. The Criminal Injuries Compensation Authority has no power to compensate for injuries attracting compensation under £1,000 and therefore guidelines for some of the more minor injuries commonly encountered in the magistrates' court are reproduced at B[18.21]–B[18.23].

B[18.20] In each example the victim is assumed to be in the age bracket 20–35 years but the age of the victim may materially affect the assessment, cf for example, the psychological effect of an assault on an elderly victim as opposed to a youth. Scarring is particularly problematical and reference should be made to the full circular for this and other injuries not referred to in the list below. Before making an award magistrates must also take into account the defendant's ability to pay any order made.

Type of injury

B[18.21]

Less serious injury including:		Suggested award
Graze	depending on size	up to £50
Bruise	depending on size	up to £75
Black eye		£100
Cut (without permanent scarring)	depending on size and whether stitched	£75–£500
Sprain	depending on loss of mobility	£100–£1,000
Loss of a tooth (not a front tooth)	depending on position of tooth and age of victim	£250–£500
Minor injury	causing reasonable absence from work of about 3 weeks	£550–£850

B[18.22]

More serious injury		
Loss of a front tooth		£1,000
Nasal	undisplaced fracture of the nasal bone (see note)	£750
Nasal	displaced fracture of the bone requiring manipulation under general anaesthetic (see note)	£1,000
Nasal	not causing fracture but displaced septum requiring a sub-mucous resection (see note)	£1,750

B[18.23] NB: Assuming that after the appropriate treatment there is no visible deformity of the nose and no breathing problem. If either of these factors is present, an increased award is appropriate and the amount of the increase will depend on the severity of the remaining problems. It is not uncommon for a fractured nasal bone to be manipulated and for the patient thereafter to have breathing problems which after some months require a sub-mucous resection – in this situation the suggested award would be £2,000 assuming full recovery after a second operation.

Confiscation orders

B[19.1] The prosecutor may ask the magistrates' court to commit the offender to the Crown Court so that a confiscation order may be made. The court must comply with such a request and may also commit any other offence for which he stands to be sentenced (PCA 2002, s 10).

For case law on the enforcement of confiscation orders, see *R (on the application of Johnson) v Birmingham Magistrates' Court and CPS* [2012] EWHC 596 (Admin), 176 JP 298.

B[20]

Costs

B[20.1] The award of costs is the exercise of a judicial discretion and any decision must always be made after taking each case on its merits, hearing each party and taking proper account of the law. As a general rule, the successful party in any proceedings can expect to be reimbursed for the costs he has incurred in conducting the proceedings. In civil proceedings, a successful party can receive his costs from the other party. Under the Litigants in Person (Costs and Expenses, Magistrates' Courts) Order 2001 an individual who has been successful in civil proceedings may also benefit from an order for costs to cover work done by him in connection with the case and any resultant expenses or losses. In criminal proceedings, according to the circumstances of the particular case, it may be possible for costs to be awarded either against the unsuccessful party or from central funds, which are monies provided by Parliament to defray the costs of criminal proceedings.

Criminal proceedings

(Prosecution of Offences Act 1985, ss 16–19)

B[20.2] See Part 76 of the CPR 2013. In a criminal case, the court's duty is firstly to consider the appropriate sentence. If that is a fine, the offender's means so far as they are known to the court must be taken into account. It is wrong in principle to reduce a fine in order to accommodate an order for costs. Costs should never be awarded as a disguised penalty and the offender's means should be taken into account as above (*R v Nottingham Magistrates' Court, ex p Fohmann* (1986) 84 Cr App Rep 316, 151 JP 49). The costs awarded should be proportionate to the level of any fine (*Nedic v South Staffordshire Council* [2005] EWHC 1481 (Admin), [2005] All ER (D) 182 (Jun)).

B[20.2A] The following sections must be read in the light of *Practice Direction (Costs in Criminal Proceedings)* CLW/10/32/26, unreported, July 30, 2010.

Prosecution costs

B[20.3] **Central funds.** See Part 76 of the CPR 2012. Almost all criminal prosecutions are conducted by the Crown Prosecution Service or a public authority such as the Trading Standards Department of a local authority. The funding for these prosecutions is provided by national or local revenues, and so there is no power to award the costs of the prosecution to these authorities out of central funds, even where the prosecution is successful. This avoids the wasteful practice of transferring moneys from one public fund to another.

B[20.4] **Private prosecutors.** See Part 76 of the CPR 2013. The court may, in a case where an indictable offence is concerned, order the costs of the prosecutor to be paid out of central funds whether the prosecution is successful or not. An indictable offence includes an offence triable either way and also offences of criminal damage where the damage is under

£5,000 and is therefore triable only summarily. This provision does not apply to public authorities such as the CPS and local authorities (POA 1985, s 17(2)).

B[20.5] There is no power to order costs from central funds to a prosecutor for purely summary offences. The costs to be awarded would normally be such amounts as the court considers reasonably sufficient to compensate the prosecutor for any expenses properly incurred by him and can include the costs of compensating a witness for the expense, trouble or loss of time properly incurred in his attendance at court. The amount payable to witnesses in respect of travelling expenses and loss of earnings is fixed by regulations and witnesses' expenses are dealt with in the clerk's office. A witness may be reimbursed even if he did not actually give evidence, if he was properly called to do so. Witnesses may be called, for example, in anticipation of a trial only to find that there is a last minute guilty plea. The cost of investigating offences is not included.

B[20.6] Making an order for the costs of a private prosecutor. The court may fix the amount to be paid to the prosecutor out of central funds at the hearing where the prosecutor is in agreement, or in any other case the amount of the costs can be assessed afterwards by the central taking officer.

B[20.7] Reducing the amount of the prosecutor's order. Where the court is prepared to order the prosecutor's costs out of central funds but is of the opinion that there are circumstances that make it inappropriate to order the full amount of costs, eg where the defendant is convicted of some offences and acquitted of others, the court can assess what in its opinion would be just and reasonable, and specify that amount.

B[20.8] Ordering the accused to pay the prosecution costs. See Part 76 of the CPR 2013. Where a person has been convicted of an either way or purely summary offence, the court can order the accused to pay to the prosecutor (the Crown Prosecution Service, a public authority or a private prosecutor) such costs as it considers just and reasonable. The amount of the costs is specified by the court at the hearing and cannot be left to be assessed later. In general the principle applied to fines imposition (**B[33.16]**) should be applied and should be in keeping with the level of the fine (*R v Northallerton Magistrates' Court, ex p Dove* [2000] 1 Cr App Rep (S) 136, 163 JP 657, [1999] Crim LR 760). In *R (on the application of Middleton) v Cambridge Magistrates' Court* [2012] EWHC 2122 (Admin), 176 JP 569, it was held that there was no requirement for there to be an arithmetical relationship between a fine and the costs sought. In fact, there might well be situations where the fine and costs imposed differed. However, that did not mean that a prosecution could not be brought because it was too expensive as the requirements of justice had to be kept in mind. That being said, the costs imposed should not be grossly disproportionate to the maximum penalty for the offence committed. The instant court could not ignore the fact that the maximum sentence for the offences M had committed was at the lowest level. Notwithstanding the delays because of M's failure to plead guilty at the earliest opportunity, and the inherent complexities, the costs awarded to the prosecution (£6,871) were grossly disproportionate to the fine imposed and could not be sustained as just and reasonable.

An order for costs can include sums expended as part of the investigation but only where the prosecutor has incurred liability for those costs to a third party e.g. an accountancy report, and where the report formed part of the case presented at court. In such a case the court need only be satisfied that it is just and reasonable for the defendant to pay those costs: *Balshaw v Crown Prosecution Service* [2009] EWCA Crim 470, [2009] 2 Cr App Rep 95.

B[20.9] **Monetary penalty not exceeding £5.** Where, on conviction of an offence, the court orders payment of any sum as a fine, penalty, forfeiture or compensation not exceeding £5, the court shall not order the accused to pay the prosecution costs unless in the particular circumstances of the case it considers it right to do so.

B[20.10]–[20.15] **Youths.** Where a person aged under 18 years is convicted of an offence before a magistrates' (or youth) court and he is ordered to pay the costs, the amount that is ordered shall not exceed the amount of any fine that is properly imposed on him. This restriction does not apply if a parent is made responsible for paying the fine etc (see B[33.95]).

Defence costs on acquittal: ss 16 and 16A of the Prosecution of Offences Act 1985

B[20.16] Defence costs may be awarded from central funds where a charge is not proceeded with or is dismissed. Such an order shall be for payment of such amount as the court considers reasonably sufficient to compensate the defendant for any expenses properly incurred by him in the proceedings: s 16(6). Where the court considers that there are circumstances that make it inappropriate for the accused to recover the full amount mentioned above, an order must be for the payment of such lesser amount as the court considers just and reasonable: s 16(6A). Legal costs may only be awarded, however, where the defendant is an individual and, in the case of Crown Court trials (but not appeals to the Crown Court), only where the defendant was financially ineligible for legal aid: s 16A.

The Practice Direction (Costs in Criminal Proceedings) 2013, [2013] EWCA Crim 1632 (as amended by Practice Direction (Criminal Proceedings: Costs) (No 2) [2014] EWCA Crim 1570) summarises the relevant principles and provides:

> '2.1.1 Where an information laid before a justice of the peace charging a person with an offence is not proceeded with or a magistrates' court dealing summarily with an offence dismisses the information the court may make a defendant's costs order. An order under section 16 of the Act may also be made in relation to breach of bind-over proceedings in a magistrates' court or the Crown Court: regulation 14(4) of the General Regulations. Whether to make such an order is a matter in the discretion of the court in the light of the circumstances of each particular case. A defendant's costs order should normally be made unless there are positive reasons for not doing so, for example, where the defendant's own conduct has brought suspicion on himself and has misled the prosecution into thinking that the case against him was stronger than it was. Where the defendant has been acquitted on some counts but convicted on others the court may make an order that only part of the costs be paid: see paragraphs 2.2.1 and 2.2.2 below. The court when declining to make a costs order should explain, in open court, that the reason for not making an order does not involve any suggestion that the defendant is guilty of any criminal conduct but the order is refused because of the positive reason that should be identified: *Hussain v*

32p1222a

2222

United Kingdom (2006) 43 EHRR 437. Where the court considers that it would be inappropriate that the defendant should recover all of the costs properly incurred, either the amount allowed must be specified in the order or the court may describe to the appropriate authority the reduction required.

2.1.2 In respect of proceedings in a magistrates' court commenced on or after 1 October 2012 legal costs (sums paid for advocacy, litigation services or experts' fees) may only be allowed to a defendant who is an individual. Where legal costs may be allowed, if the court fixes the amount to be paid under section 16(6C) of the Act or under sections 62A(4) or 135A(4) of the Extradition Act 2003 it must calculate any amounts allowed in respect of legal costs in accordance with the rates and scales prescribed by the Lord Chancellor. If the court does not fix the amount of costs to be paid out of central funds, the costs will be determined by the appropriate authority in accordance with the General Regulations and any legal costs allowed will be calculated at the prescribed rates and scales.'

When refusing to make an order or refusing an order for costs the court must give its reason: see *Dowler v Merseyrail* [2009] EWHC 558 (Admin). See also *R (on the application of Elliott Spiteri) v Basildon Crown Court* [2009] EWHC 665 (Admin), 173 JP 327.

B[20.16A] The Practice Direction provides:

'1.4.1 If the court does not fix the amount of costs to be paid out of central funds, the costs will be determined in accordance with the General Regulations by the appropriate authority. The appropriate authority will calculate the amount payable in respect of legal costs at such rates and scales as are prescribed by the Lord Chancellor. Where the court makes a defendant's costs order, or an order in favour of a private prosecutor, but is of the opinion there are circumstances which make it inappropriate that the person in whose favour the order is made should recover the full amount of the costs, the court may assess the lesser amount that would in its opinion be just and reasonable, and specify that amount in the order. If the court is not in a position to specify the amount payable, the judge may make remarks which the appropriate authority will take into account as a relevant circumstance when determining the costs payable.

1.4.2 In respect of proceedings commenced on or after 1 October 2012 legal costs (sums paid for advocacy, litigation services or experts' fees) may only be included in a defendant's costs order to a defendant who is an individual and only in proceedings in a magistrates' court, appeals against conviction or sentence from a magistrates' court to the Crown Court, relevant Crown Court proceedings after 27 January 2014 (as to which see paragraph 1.4.3 below) and appeals to the Court of Appeal (i) against a verdict of not guilty by reason of insanity, (ii) against a finding under the Criminal Procedure (Insanity) Act 1964 that the appellant is under a disability or that he did the act or made the omission charged or (iii) under section 16A of the Criminal Appeal Act 1968 (inserted by section 25 of the Domestic Violence, Crime and Victims Act

2004) (appeals against order made in cases of insanity or unfitness to plead).

1.4.3 After 27 January 2014 legal costs may be included in a defendant's costs order, provided that the defendant is an individual, in relevant proceedings in the Crown Court if the Director of Legal Aid Casework has made a determination of financial ineligibility in relation to that defendant. The relevant proceedings are those in which the accused has been sent by a magistrates' court to the Crown Court for trial, where a bill of indictment has been preferred (under section 2(2)(b) of the Administration of Justice (Miscellaneous Provisions) Act 1933) or following an order for a retrial made by the Court of Appeal or the Supreme Court.

...

1.4.4 Where legal costs may be allowed, if the court fixes the amount to be paid to a defendant under section 16(6C) of the Act (inserted by section 62 of and paragraph 2(2) of Schedule 7 to the Legal Aid, Sentencing and Punishment of Offenders Act 2012) or under sections 62A(4) or 135A(4) of the Extradition Act 2003 (inserted by paragraphs 15 and 18 respectively of Schedule 7 to the 2012 Act) it must calculate any amounts to be allowed in respect of legal costs in accordance with rates and scales prescribed by the Lord Chancellor.

1.4.5 Crim PR r 76.2(6), (7) contains general rules about the amount of an award of costs that apply subject to any statutory limitation.'

B[20.17]–[20.18] A publicly aided defendant can only claim those costs which cannot be covered by the representation order, eg his travelling expenses to court.

In *Re Patel and a defendant's costs order* [2012] EWCA Crim 1508, [2012] All ER (D) 115 (Jul), it was decided that whilst the court had jurisdiction to re-open its decision to make a defendant's costs order, as the court had been unaware that the defendant and his solicitors had agreed to remove a cap on fees, which increased the fees retrospectively, it was appropriate to let the assessment by the determining officer take its course.

Costs unnecessarily or improperly incurred (s 19 of the Prosecution of Offences Act 1985)

B[20.19] Where the court is satisfied that one party to criminal proceedings has incurred costs as a result of an unnecessary or improper act or omission, it may order the party responsible to pay the additional costs thereby incurred whatever the final result of the case. This includes the whole of the defence costs where a private prosecutor instituted proceedings knowing an identical prosecution brought by CPS on the same ground had been dismissed without challenge (*Oddy v Bug Bugs Ltd* [2003] All ER (D) 156 (Nov)). This enables the court to mark its displeasure at the unreasonable behaviour of a party, eg where one party has put the other to unnecessary expense by requiring an adjournment when they should have been ready to proceed. Before making such an order both parties should be invited to make representations to the court and the court should determine the sum to be paid.

For the purposes of s 19 of the Act, no distinction could be drawn between the Crown Prosecution Service and the police. The 'party' on the other side from the defendant in such a case was the Crown. 'Improper' did not necessarily connote some grave impropriety. It was intended to cover an act or omission which would not have occurred if the party concerned had conducted his case properly. If the act giving rise to the application consisted of someone on the prosecution side not conducting the case properly and it caused the defendant to incur additional costs, the discretion arose. A single mistake was enough to trigger the court's discretion to make an order. However, s 19(1) of the Act conferred a discretion and the court was not bound to make an order in every case of a mistake causing costs to be incurred. If there was a satisfactory explanation for the mistake, the court might decide that it would not be just to make any order: R *(on the application of Singh) v Ealing Magistrates Court* [2014] EWHC 1443 (Admin), [2014] All ER (D) 174 (May).

The court is not entitled to use s 19 at the end of the trial as a means of impugning the decision to prosecute – if such a decision is to be challenged it must be by way of an application to stay the proceedings as an abuse of process, or, exceptionally, by way of judicial review: *R (DPP) v Crown Court at Sheffield* [2014] EWHC 2014 (Admin).

In *R (on the application of the DPP) v Bury Magistrates' Court* [2007] All ER (D) 208 (Dec) if was held that a court was entitled to make a costs order against the prosecution where it had failed to comply with a court order that it should serve its witness evidence on the defence by a specified date. As the prosecution had given no explanation for its failure there had been a breach of the Criminal Procedural Rules 2013.

A wasted costs order in favour of a legally aided defendant must be limited to the amount which falls to be paid to the legal representatives under the legal aid scheme. It is not permissible to include an amount by way of compensation for work reasonably done in the case which will otherwise not fall to be remunerated (as in the case of work done by way of preparation for a hearing at which the prosecution offered no evidence, where the decision to offer no evidence should have been made earlier and where the fees payable to the defence under the graduated fee scheme would be the same as if the decision had been made when it should have been, ie at an earlier hearing): *R v Fitzgerald* [2012] 3 Costs LR 437, Central Criminal Court (HH Judge Gordon).

As to procedure, see the Practice Direction (Costs in Criminal Proceedings) 2013, 4.1.

Costs against legal representatives: s 19A of the Prosecution of Offences Act 1985

B[20.20] See Part 76 of the CPR 2014. The magistrates may disallow or order a legal representative to meet the whole or any part of any costs incurred by a party as a result of any improper, unreasonable or negligent act or omission of the representative or, where the conduct occurred after the incurring of the costs, the court considers it is unreasonable for the party to pay. Such orders are not common and the court must follow a detailed procedure before ordering costs against a legal representative. If such an order is contemplated, the legal adviser must be consulted.

As to procedure, see the Practice Direction (Costs in Criminal Proceedings) 2013, 4.2.

Costs against third parties

B[20.20A] Section 19B of the Prosecution of Offences Act 1985 (inserted by s 98 of the Courts Act 2003) empowers a criminal court to make costs orders against a third party where it has been guilty of serious misconduct. If such an order is contemplated, the legal adviser must be consulted. See Part 76 of the CPR 2012.

An isolated failure to provide an interpreter when under a contract to do so does not amount to 'serious misconduct'. However, a court is entitled to view successive non-attendance of an individual interpreter or successive failures in system as so amounting: *R v Applied Language Solutions Ltd* [2013] EWCA Crim 326, [2013] 1 WLR 3820, [2013] 2 Cr App R 169.

Miscellaneous provisions

B[20.21] Medical reports. In criminal proceedings, where the court has required a medical practitioner to make a report to the court orally or in writing, for the purpose inter alia of determining the most suitable method of dealing with the offender, his costs may be ordered to be paid from central funds.

B[20.22] Interpreters. In any criminal proceedings provision is made for the payment of interpreters from central funds.

B[20.23] Proceedings for breach or revocation of community orders including youth community orders etc. In appropriate circumstances a magistrates' court may now make an award of costs against the offender in breach proceedings where the breach is admitted or found proved.

Civil proceedings

(Magistrates' Courts Act 1980, s 64)

B[20.24] On hearing a complaint (eg concerning a dangerous dog), the court may order the defendant to pay to the successful complainant such costs as it thinks just and reasonable and, where the complaint is dismissed, the complainant may similarly be ordered to pay the defendant's costs (see the case law and principles discussed in detail in section F[2.20]).

B[20.25]–[20.30] In civil cases, it is not usual to order one party to pay or contribute towards the other's costs if both are publicly funded, but there is no reason why an order for costs should not be paid against a party who is not publicly funded where the successful party is so aided, so that the legal aid fund will receive the benefit of the order.

B[20.31] Applications. There is no power to award costs where proceedings are begun by way of an application (eg an application under the Police (Property) Act 1897).

Costs may be awarded under s 64 in favour of a person who has an interest in premises and appears to oppose the making of a closure order under s 2 of the Anti-social Behaviour Act 2003.

Deferment of sentence

(Powers of Criminal Courts (Sentencing) Act 2000, ss 1A–1F)

Limitations

B[21.1] The offender must consent, and undertake to comply with any requirements the court considers appropriate to impose during the period of deferment.

B[21.2] Deferment may be used only once in respect of any one offence.

B[21.3] The court must be satisfied that it is in the interests of justice to defer sentence, having regard to the nature of the offence and the character and circumstances of the offender.

B[21.4] There are no limitations as to age or the nature of the offence. The court may have regard to the defendant's conduct after conviction (including if appropriate any reparation made by him) and any change in his circumstances. The court may impose requirements as to the offender's conduct during the deferment and appoint an appropriate supervisor with their consent.

*Paragraph 5 of Sch 16 to the Crime and Courts Act 2013 prospectively inserts new s1ZA in the Powers of Criminal Courts (Sentencing) Act 2000 with the effect that the requirements of a deferred sentence may include restorative justice requirements.

Ancillary orders

B[21.5]–[21.7] None, because this is not a final disposal of the case, except that a restitution order may be made.

General considerations

B[21.8] This power of the court might be less confusing if it were referred to as deferment of sentencing. There is no question, contrary to what is sometimes believed, that the court decides upon a sentence but postpones announcing it in case it changes its mind.

B[21.9] Only exceptionally may a custodial sentence be imposed after deferment; it is advised that where an offender is liable to be ordered to serve a suspended sentence it will rarely be appropriate to defer sentencing him for the offence which he has committed during the operational period.

B[21.10]–[21.15] Deferment is appropriate when some event may occur in the near future which, according to whether it occurred or not, would influence the court when imposing a sentence. It may be, for example, that the offender has an uncertain chance of employment upon which voluntary compensation depends. There should always be some reason for deferment which can be stated so that the offender knows what is expected of him and may, as he thinks fit, take steps to improve his situation from a sentencing point of view. Great care should be exercised, however, not to use this power as a threat or coercion or to give an offender an opportunity to buy his way out of prison by making compensation (especially if he may do so by resorting to further offences).

B[21.16] The concern of a victim of the offence should be borne in mind when considering deferment; one effect of deferment, for example, may be to postpone the day when compensation is ordered.

B[21.17] The maximum period for which sentencing may be deferred is six months. The defendant cannot be remanded. A summons or warrant may be issued if he fails to appear on the date for sentencing specified by the court.

Sentence after the period of deferral. The deferred sentence did not represent part of the sentence which was imposed at the end of the period of deferment. Section 204(3) of the Criminal Justice Act 2003 provided that the period with regard to curfew requirements runs from the date of the making of the community order. The six-month curfew condition of the deferred sentence was a factor which needed to be taken into account at the point of sentence when determining the community requirements of the order and the length of any requirement: *R v Saeed Ali* [2011] EWCA Crim 2747, 176 JP 1.

B[21.18] The court will obviously wish to be informed at the end of the period of deferment whether the offender has done what it was hoped he would do, or whether the event has taken place which was the reason for the deferment. In many cases it will be convenient to ask the supervising officer to report, but in some cases only the offender or a third party will be able to satisfy the court. It is advised that the court when deferring sentence makes clear arrangements at that time as to how such information is to be provided.

B[21.19] The court might consider that a conditional discharge for six months but imposed immediately would achieve the court's objectives. It is not necessary, but may be desirable, that the same magistrates should impose the sentence as those who deferred sentence. Provided the requirement and reasons for deferment are explicitly stated, the legal adviser will note them and bring them to the attention of the sentencing court.

B[21.20] The offender can be returned to court if the supervisor has reported to the court that the offender has failed to comply with one or more requirements in respect of which an offender gave an undertaking (s 1B(2)(c)). The can issue a summons or warrant for the offender to appear before it (s 1B(3)).

B[21.21] If the offender commits an offence during the period of deferment, the court convicting him of that offence may deal with the deferred case even though the period of deferment has not expired. Section 1C sets out the powers of the Crown Court and magistrates' courts in these cases. If the original sentence was deferred by a Crown Court, it must be a Crown Court that passes sentence for both offences. The power to commit to the Crown Court for sentence under s 3 PCC(S)A 2000 is retained by s 1D(2)(b) PCC(S)A 2000**.

B[23]

Deportation

[23.1]

. . . a person who is not a British citizen shall be . . . liable to deportation from the United Kingdom if, after he has attained the age of seventeen, he is convicted of an offence for which he is punishable with imprisonment and on his conviction is recommended for deportation by a court

Immigration Act 1971, s 3(6)

NB: Section 32 of the UK Borders Act 2007 provides that the Secretary of State must make a deportation order in respect of foreign national prisoners who meet one of the two conditions set out in s 32 of the Act and are not then covered by the exceptions covered in s 33. This does not affect the power of the court to make a recommendation for deportation as outlined below.

NB: In cases to which the 2007 Act applies, it is no longer necessary or appropriate for a court to make a recommendation for deportation: *R v Kluxen* [2010] EWCA Crim 1081, [2010] Crim LR 657, 174 CL&J 380.

B[23.2] Recommendation. A magistrates' court cannot order deportation, but it can make a recommendation to the Home Secretary for the deportation of the convicted person. In sentencing the offender the court does not have to take into account what might happen in the offender's own country if he is returned (*R v Ukoh* [2004] EWCA Crim 3270, [2005] All ER (D) 58 (Jan)).

B[23.3] Not a British citizen. The following categories of citizens cannot be deported:

(a)   British citizens;
(b)   Commonwealth citizens having a right of abode in the United Kingdom;
(c)   Commonwealth citizens not included in (b) and citizens of the Republic of Ireland provided in either case they were such citizens at the time of the coming into force of the Immigration Act 1971 and were ordinarily resident in the United Kingdom and at the time of conviction had been ordinarily resident in the United Kingdom and Islands for the last five years.

B[23.4] The following may be deported:

(a)   Commonwealth citizens not included in (b) or (c) above;
(b)   aliens;
(c)   aliens being citizens of countries which are members of the European Community.

B[23.5] Age of seventeen. A person shall be deemed to have obtained the age of 17 at the time of his conviction, if on consideration of any available evidence he appears to have done so to the court.

B[23.6] Convicted. Means found to have committed the offence.

B[23.7] Punishable with imprisonment. This means punishable with imprisonment in the case of a person over 21 years even though the defendant himself may not be liable to imprisonment.

Criteria for making a recommendation

General considerations

B[23.8] The court. In deciding whether to make a recommendation for deportation the court may consider:

(a)   Would the offender's continued presence in the United Kingdom be detrimental? In considering this the court might take account of:
   (i)   the seriousness of the crime, eg a simple offence of shoplifting would not merit such a recommendation;
   (ii)   the length of the defendant's criminal record.

The court should not consider:

(b)   A recommendation for deportation does not engage the Convention rights of a defendant. Accordingly, it is no longer necessary for a sentencing court considering the making of a recommendation for deportation to take account of the possible impact of the recommendation on the defendant's family and dependents (*R v Nelson Carmona* [2006] 2 Cr App R (S) 662).

(c)   The consequences to the offender of his being returned to his own country, eg persecution. This is generally a matter for the Home Secretary (*R v Jelk* [2002] EWCA Crim 184 [2002] All ER (D) 200 (Jan)).

(d)   The fact that the offender is in receipt of social security.

See generally *R v Bouchereau* 30/77 [1978] QB 732, [1981] 2 All ER 924n, ECJ.

B[23.9]–[23.15] Home Secretary's considerations. In considering a recommendation the Home Secretary takes into account:

(a)   the nature of the offence;
(b)   the length of time the offender has spent in this country;
(c)   the offender's criminal record;
(d)   the strength of his connections with this country, his personal history and domestic circumstances (eg if the offender's wife or children are citizens of this country and resident here, it might be a great hardship to them to order deportation of the offender);
(e)   any compassionate feature that may be present;
(f)   any representation made by the offender.

B[23.16] The Home Secretary will not normally deport an offender sentenced to borstal training (now abolished and replaced by youth custody), or detention, or a first offender unless the offence was very grave or other offences were taken into consideration.

Citizens of EC countries

B[23.17] Before recommending the deportation of a national of a country in the EC the court must have regard to Community laws. Article 48 of the Treaty makes the following relevant provisions:

1   Freedom of movement for workers shall be secured within the Community by the end of the transitional period at the latest.

2   Such freedom of movement shall entail the abolition of any discrimination based on nationality between workers of the member states as regards employment, remuneration and other conditions of work and employment.

3   It shall entail the right, subject to limitations justified on grounds of public policy, public security or public health:
   (a)   to accept offers of employment actually made;
   (b)   to move freely within the territories of member states for this purpose;
   (c)   to stay in the member state for the purpose of employment in accordance with the provisions governing the employment of nationals of that said state laid down by law, regulation or administrative action;
   (d)   to remain in the territory of a member state after having been employed in that state subject to conditions which shall be embodied in implementing regulations which shall be drawn up by the Commission.

4   The provisions of this Article shall not apply to employment in the public service.

B[23.18] With regard to the references in paragraph 3 above to public policy or security, a directive has been issued (No. 64/221) which states:

(1)   Measures taken on grounds of public policy or public security shall be based exclusively on the conduct of the individual concerned.

(2)   Previous criminal convictions shall not themselves constitute grounds for the taking of such measures.

B[23.19] The European Court of Justice has ruled:

(a)   that any action affecting the rights of persons covered by article 48 to enter and reside freely in a member state under the same conditions as nationals of that state constituted a 'measure' for the purposes of the directive quoted above;

(b)   that a recommendation for deportation by a court of a member state according to its national law was such an action (ie the 'action' referred to in (a) above);

(c)   that the directive must be interpreted to mean that previous convictions are relevant only in so far as the circumstances which gave rise to them are evidence of personal conduct constituting a present threat to the requirements of public policy;

(d)   that the justification for restricting free movement provided in article 48 (above) presupposed the existence of a genuine and sufficiently serious threat affecting one of the fundamental interests of society additional to the disturbance of order which any infringement of the law involved.

See guidance handed down in *R v Secretary of State for the Home Department, ex p Santillo* [1981] 2 All ER 897.

B[23.20] It should be noted that not all EC nationals come within the ambit of the directive. In practice it covers those who come to the United Kingdom to take or seek work, to set up in business or in a self-employed capacity or to receive services for money, eg medical, educational or business.

Procedure

B[23.21] There should be a full inquiry into the case before a recommendation is made. A person who is likely to be the subject of an order must be given seven clear days' notice of what may happen to him. The defendant should have legal representation. Solicitors should be asked to address the court specifically on the possibility of a recommendation for deportation being made. In the case of an **EU National** the court must give reasons for making a recommendation as to deportation (*R v Secretary of State for the Home Department, ex p Dannenburg* [1984] 2 All ER 481, (1984) 148 JP 321).

B[23.22] What should not be done is to add a sentence as if by an afterthought at the end of observations about any sentence of imprisonment.

EC national within the scope of article 48

B[23.23] The recommendation can only be based on the grounds of public policy, public security or public health. The offender must be informed of the grounds on which the recommendation is based. A short statement in writing should be given to the offender and also attached to the written recommendation (see **B[23.21]** above). It should include some indication of the extent to which the current and previous criminal convictions of the defendant have been taken into account and the light which such conviction or convictions threw on the likely nature of the defendant's personal conduct in the future. Of particular importance will be the court's assessment of the gravity of the conduct and the likelihood of reoffending.

EC national to which article 48 does not apply

B[23.24] It is desirable that the same procedure be followed.

Aliens (see generally *R v Nazari* [1988] QB 631, [1988] 2 WLR 1005, sub nom R v Kuxhaus [1988] 2 All ER 705, 56 P & CR 229, CA).

B[23.25]–[23.30] Similarly reasons, not necessarily in writing, should be given.

B[23.31] The effect of a recommendation. Where the court makes a recommendation and the defendant is not sentenced to imprisonment or is not liable to be detained in any other way he will be detained under the Immigration Act 1971 until he is deported. The court may, however, order his release subject to such restrictions as to residence and/ or to reporting to the police as it may direct.

Detention for one day at the court or at a police station

(Magistrates' Courts Act 1980, s 135)

B[24.1] Magistrates may order the detention of a defendant aged 18 years or more in the precincts of the court house or at a police station for any period until 8 pm on the day of the hearing; but the offence must be punishable with imprisonment or alternatively the detention must be an alternative to payment of a fine. The magistrates should announce at what time the defendant can be released, taking into account that the defendant should be given the opportunity of returning home that day.

Detention and training orders

(Powers of the Criminal Courts (Sentencing) Act 2000, s 100)

B[25.1] Detention and training orders (DTO) are the sole custodial sentence available to the courts which may be imposed on a young person aged under 18. Age is generally determined at the time of conviction rather than at sentence. The order is available in the youth court only and not the adult court. The DTO is a rehabilitative order and not simply a young offender's prison.

B[25.2] Where a DTO is a likely sentence the Youth Offending Team (YOT) will make contact with the Youth Justice Board before the court hearing to establish if accommodation is available.

B[25.3] All the restrictions outlined at B[37] and contained in s 152 CJA 2003 apply to the detention and training order because it is defined as a custodial sentence.

B[25.4] Before making an order the court must be satisfied that the following additional circumstances pertain:

(a)   the offender is not less than 12 years of age when the offence for which he is to be dealt with is found proved;

(b)   where the offender is under the age of 15 years at the time of conviction the courts must be of the opinion that he is a persistent young offender. Note this is 15 years old at the time of conviction (*R v Thomas* (2004) although *R v LM* [2002] EWCA Crim 3047, [2002] All ER (D) 35 (Dec) suggests that a non-persistent offender who is under the age of 15 when a non-grave offence is committed cannot receive a DTO even when 15 at date of conviction.

This is not the same definition as a persistent offender for the purposes of monitoring speed of case throughput (*R v Charlton* (2000) 164 JP 685, CA). Where there has been a series of offences on separate occasions the offender may be persistent (*R v Smith* (2000) 164 JP 681, [2000] Crim LR 613, CA). For the purposes of determining whether an offender under the age of 15 at the time of conviction is a 'persistent offender', the court may have regard to earlier offences for which he has been cautioned by the police: *R v D* [2000] Crim LR 867, CA. The court may also have regard to offences committed after the present offence: *R v Cawthorn* [2001] Crim LR 51, (2000) Times, 27 October, CA. Persistent offending does not necessarily involve persistent appearances before a court: *R v Charlton*, above. A series of offences committed over only two days may be sufficient to qualify an offender as persistent, even though he has no previous convictions: *R v Andrew Smith* (2000) 164 JP 681, CA. However, two reprimands for dissimilar offences and three robberies committed on the same occasion within a minute or so of each other could not be characterised as 'persistent offending': *R v L* [2012] EWCA Crim 1336, [2013] 1 Cr App R (S) 56.

B[25.5] Where the court passes a detention and training order it must state in open court that it is of the opinion that the above conditions are satisfied.

B[25.6] Length of the order. The term of a detention and training order (DTO) may only be made up of terms of 4, 6, 8, 10, 12, 18 or 24 months. However the court may not exceed the maximum term the Crown Court could impose for the offence on an offender aged 21. This means that the youth court must be careful when dealing with a case of summary criminal damage (maximum three months' imprisonment) making the DTO unavailable (see *Pye v Leeds Youth Court* [2006] All ER (D) 16 (Oct)) and cases involving other summary offences where the maximum sentence for an adult offender will generally be less than six months. Another exception to this is an offence under the Bail Act where the maximum penalty is currently three months.

B[25.7] In assessing the length of sentence the court must give credit for a timely guilty plea. The level of credit will generally depend on the time the plea of guilty is entered. **Sentencing Guideline Council** guidance suggests up to a third for a timely guilty plea, reducing to roughly 10% for a plea entered on the date set for trial. In rare circumstances credit for plea can be withheld altogether. Magistrates should consult their legal adviser before determining to withhold any credit for a plea of guilty (see *R v Barber* [2006] EWCA Crim 162, [2006] 2 Cr App Rep (S) 539).

The court must also take into account in deciding the overall the length of the DTO any time spent on remand in custody (*R v B* [2000] Crim LR 870). See also *R (on the application of A) v The Governor of Huntercombe Young Offenders' Institute and the Secretary of State for the Home Department* [2006] EWHC 2544 (Admin).

B[25.8] Consecutive orders may be made provided that the overall term does not exceed 24 months. Note that an aggregate term of more than the statutory maximum** may be imposed on the same occasion for summary only offences (*C v DPP* [2001] EWHC 453 (Admin), [2002] 1 Cr App Rep (S) 189, [2001] Crim LR 671). For indictable and either way offences each offence must be one of the specified terms above, although when aggregated it may come to an unspecified term of, for example, 6+ 8+ 10 = 24 months.

B[25.9] Half the order will be served in a secure establishment and half will be the subject of supervision under a member of the Young Offender Team: Powers of Criminal Courts (Sentencing) Act 2000, s 103. Where, however, the term is for less than 12 months the period of supervision is three months from the offender's release: Criminal Justice Act 2003, s 256B (prospectively amended by the Offender Rehabilitation Act 2014 to apply only to those aged under 18 on their date of release – older offenders will be subject to the same period of supervision as adult offenders).

B[25.10] Breach of supervision. Supervision takes place throughout the order, but if a supervision order is breached the offender may be detained for a period not exceeding the shorter of three months or the period beginning with the date of the offender's failure and ending with the last day of the term of the detention and training order. For the purposes of the legislation above a failure that is found to have occurred over two or more days is to be taken to have occurred on the first of those days; the remainder of the term of the DTO; or may be fined up to the maximum of level 3. Offenders brought before the court for further offending during the period of supervision may be dealt with for the new offence as well as the remainder of the existing order.

B[25.11] See *R v Ganley* [2000] All ER (D) 594, [2001] 1 Cr App Rep (S) 60, CA for general guidance on the use of the order.

Detention in a young offender institution

(Powers of the Criminal Courts (Sentencing) Act 2000, s 96)

B[26.0] **Section 96 will be repealed by the Criminal Justice and Courts Services Act 2000, Sch 7 from a date to be appointed. Section 96 will, in effect, be replaced by the provisions to be found in Chapter 3 (ss 181–195 inclusive) of the CJA 2003. This will make available prison sentences, and suspended sentences for offenders aged 18 years or more at the date of conviction (not sentence). It is likely the new regime will only apply to offences committed on or after the operative date ie from a date to be appointed. See B[37] onwards.

There are currently transitory provisions making suspended sentence available for offenders aged 18–20 years inclusive. However, see *R v Campbell* [2006] EWCA Crim 726, [2006] All ER (D) 137 (Mar).

General

B[26.1] Imprisonment is not available for offenders under the age of 21 years. The main custodial provision for these offenders is detention in a young offender institution. This is subject to the criteria restricting the use of custodial sentences imposed by the Powers of the Criminal Courts (Sentencing) Act 2000.

B[26.2] As with all custodial sentences the court must explain:

(a) how long the defendant will spend in custody;
(b) how long after release he will be liable to recall; and
(c) how long after release he will be subject to supervision.

Limitations

B[26.3] Imprisonable offence. The offence of which the offender is found guilty must be punishable with imprisonment in the case of a person aged 21 or over.

B[26.4] Age of offender. The minimum age for male and female offenders is 18 years. In either case the offender must be under 21 years.

B[26.5] Criteria for imposing a custodial sentence. The court must be of the opinion:

(a) that the offence, or the combination of the offence and any other offences associated with it, was so serious that only such a sentence can be justified for the offence;
(b) where the offence is a violent or sexual offence, that only such a sentence would be adequate to protect the public from serious harm from the offender.

B[26.6] Other circumstances in which custody may be imposed. Nothing in paragraphs (a) and (b) above prevents the court imposing a custodial sentence on an offender who refuses to consent to a community sentence proposed by the court which requires his willingness to comply with a proposed requirement. A court may also impose custody for a wilful and persistent breach of a community order.

B[26.7] So serious. See B[37.6]. The court must take account of all the information about the circumstances of the offence including any aggravating or mitigating factors as are available to it.

B[26.8] Associated offence. An offence of which the offender has been convicted in the same proceedings or for which he is sentenced at the same time, or an offence taken into consideration.

B[26.9] Violent offence. An offence which leads, or is intended or likely to lead, to a person's death or to physical injury to a person, and includes an offence which is required to be charged as arson.

B[26.10]–[26.15] Sexual offence under the Sexual Offences Act 2003. It does not include offences relating to prostitution. Nor does it include offences in public lavatories.

B[26.16] Protection from serious harm. This refers to protecting members of the public from death or serious personal injury, whether physical or psychological, occasioned by further such offences committed by the offender.

B[26.17] Pre-sentence report. Except where the court considers it unnecessary to do so, the court must obtain and consider a pre-sentence report before forming an opinion on:

(a) whether the offence etc was so serious;
(b) (violent or sexual offence) only custody would be adequate to protect the public etc;
(c) the length of term commensurate with the offence;
(d) (violent or sexual offence) the length of term necessary to protect the public etc.

B[26.18] In all cases where a court is contemplating sentencing a defendant to custody for the first time a report should be obtained: *R v Gillette* (1999) Times, 3 December, CA.

B[26.19] Failure to obtain pre-sentence report. Does not invalidate the sentence but the appeal court must obtain and consider such a report if the court below was not justified in forming an opinion that a report was unnecessary.

B[26.20] Mentally disordered offender. Where an offender is or appears to be mentally disordered, ie suffering from a mental disorder within the meaning of the Mental Health Act 1983, the court must additionally obtain and consider a medical report before passing a custodial sentence unless the court considers it unnecessary to do so. The court must take any such information into account and consider the likely effect of any custodial sentence on his condition and any treatment for it. Failure to obtain a medical report does not invalidate any sentence but one must be obtained and considered by an appeal court.

B[26.21] Legal representation. The offender must first be given the opportunity to be legally represented unless he has failed to take up the offer of legal representation or has been refused legal representation based on financial grounds. Note that the requirement is not that he should be represented, but that he should have an opportunity to be.

B[26.22] Offenders under 18 years. A magistrates' court (as opposed to a youth court) cannot commit defendants aged under 18 years to custody. Such juveniles must be remitted on bail or in local authority accommodation to a youth court which will usually be the youth court for the area in which they reside.

Passing sentence

B[26.23]–[26.24] Maximum length of sentence. Twelve months or the maximum term of imprisonment available for the offence, whichever is the lesser term, six months if suspended.

B[26.25]–[26.30] Minimum length of sentence. 21 days over 18 years of age, 14 days if suspended except for detention imposed where an offender has breached a supervision order made on his release. See B[26.39].

B[26.31] Consecutive terms. Detention in a young offender institution may be ordered to be consecutive to an existing period of detention or, if more than one period of detention is imposed on the same occasion, one period of detention may be ordered to be consecutive to another so, however, that the offender will not be liable to a period of more than 12 months in total. If a longer period is ordered the excess period will be treated as remitted.

B[26.32] Length of custodial sentence. Shall be for a term which is commensurate with the seriousness of the offence or the combination of the offence and other offences associated with it or, in the case of a violent or sexual offence, for such longer term as is necessary to protect the public from serious harm from the offender. The court may suspend the sentence for an operational period of 2 years maximum, see **B[37.60]**.

B[26.33] Committal to Crown Court. The longest term of detention available to a magistrates' court in respect of an offender for a single indictable or either way offence is six months. However, in certain circumstances a magistrates' court may commit offenders aged 18 years to the Crown Court for sentence under s 3 Powers of Criminal Courts (Sentencing) Act 2000** (see **B[16]**).

Reasons for decisions

B[26.34] It is the duty of the court to state in open court:

(a)   that it is of the opinion that either or both of paragraphs (a) and (b) at B[26.35] apply:

(b)   that it is of the opinion that in the case of a violent or sexual offence it is necessary to pass a longer term than is commensurate with the seriousness of the offence to protect the public from serious harm from the offender;

(c)   why it is of that opinion;

and in all cases to explain to the offender in open court and in ordinary language why it is passing a custodial sentence on him or such longer term.

How to announce

B[26.35] We have decided to pass a sentence of detention in a young offender institution on the defendant and we are of the opinion that:

(a) the offence (or the combination of the offence and other associated offence(s) namely [. . . . .]) was so serious that only such a sentence can be justified for the offence; and/or

(b) this is a violent/sexual offence and only such a sentence would be adequate to protect the public from serious harm from him

because [*then explain why either or both of the paragraphs apply*]. (Violent/sexual offence): We are also passing a sentence of detention for a term longer than is commensurate with the seriousness of the offence as this is necessary to protect the public from serious harm from him because [*give reasons*].

Accordingly [*addressing the defendant*] you will be sent to a young offender institution for [*state period*]. On release you will be subject to supervision for [*state how long*] and you will be subject to recall to detention for the next [*state time*] and this is because [*explain in ordinary language why he is receiving a custodial sentence and, where applicable, why he is receiving a term longer than is commensurate with the seriousness of the offence*].

Note – If there is more than one offence it should be clearly stated what the total period of detention is to be.

Ancillary orders

B[26.36] Compensation at B[18]

Costs at B[20]

Disqualification at C[5]

Endorsement at C[5]

Deprivation of property and forfeiture at B[34]

Restitution order at B[39]

Early release

B[26.37] An offender subject to a term of detention in a young offender institution for 12 months or less will be automatically released after he has served one half of the term. In determining the period that has been served, time spent on remand in custody or secure accommodation is to be taken into account. However, additional days may be imposed under the prison rules where the offender has been guilty of disciplinary offences.

B[26.38] Supervision following release. An offender who is released and is under 22 years will be under the supervision of a probation officer or social worker for a period of three months or until he attains the age of 22 years, whichever is the shorter period.

B[26.39]–[26.45] Failure to comply with requirements as to supervision is punishable by custody of up to 30 days or a fine of up to £1,000.

B[26.46] Further offences. Where an offender commits an imprisonable offence before he would (but for his release) have served his sentence in full, the court which deals with him for the later offence may return him to custody for the whole or part of the period which begins with the making of the order of return and is equal in length to the period between the date of commission of the new offence and the date of expiry of the original term.

B[31]

Discharge (absolute or conditional)

(Powers of Criminal Courts (Sentencing) Act 2000, s 12)

Limitations

B[31.1]

Absolute	–	None.
Conditional	–	minimum period, none,
	–	maximum period, three years.

B[31.2] Special consideration. Before making either of these orders the court must be of opinion, having regard to the circumstances including the nature of the offence and the character of the offender, that it is inexpedient to inflict punishment.

Unless there are exceptional circumstances a magistrates' court (which includes a youth court), may not make an order for conditional discharge in respect of an offence committed within two years of a final warning (CDA 1998, s 66(4)).

B[31.3] Before making an order for conditional discharge the court must explain to the offender in ordinary language that if he commits another offence during the period of discharge he will be liable to be sentenced for the offence for which the conditional discharge is given. This is the court's duty and only in the most exceptional circumstances may it be delegated to another person, eg the accused's lawyer.

Ancillary orders

B[31.4]–[31.6] Compensation at B[18]

Costs at B[20]

Disqualification at C[5]

Endorsement at C[5]

Deprivation of property and forfeiture at B[34]

Restitution at B[39]

Legal note

B[31.7] A defendant who is convicted of an offence while subject to a Crown Court conditional discharge may be committed to the Crown Court to be sentenced for the offence for which the conditional discharge was originally ordered, under the Powers of Criminal Courts (Sentencing) Act 2000, s 13(5). He may also be committed to be dealt with for the new offence, under Powers of Criminal Courts (Sentencing) Act 2000, s 6 (*R v Penfold* (1995) 16 Cr App Rep (S) 1016, [1995] Crim LR 666, CA).

General considerations

B[31.8] It is most important to note that only after the court has decided that it is inexpedient to inflict punishment because of all the circumstances may it make an order for discharge. But magistrates are specifically empowered to make a deprivation order or order for costs and compensation where appropriate: Power of Criminal Courts (Sentencing) Act 2000, s 12(7) as amended. Disqualification and endorsement may be ordered where appropriate.

B[31.9] This is not a conviction for the purposes of the Sex Offenders Act 1997.

B[31.10]–[31.15] No conditions or requirements may be added to either of these orders.

B[31.16] Period of conditional discharge. This must always commence on the pronouncement of sentence. There is no provision to make this period consecutive to any other period.

B[32]

Exclusion orders

Licensed Premises (Exclusion of Certain Persons) Act 1980

B[32.1] This Act will be repealed and replaced by drinking banning orders (on conviction) when ss 6–8 of the Violent Crime Reduction Act 2006 is brought into force). (At the time of going to press, these provisions had been implemented only in certain specified local justice areas: see SI 2010/469, arts 2(a), 4, Sch; and SI 2010/2541, arts 2(a), 4, Sch).

When a person is convicted of an offence (of whatever nature) which was committed on licensed premises and the court which convicts him is satisfied that when he committed the offence he resorted to violence, or offered or threatened violence, the court may make an exclusion order prohibiting him from entering those licensed premises or any other licensed premises which the court may specify in the order. Such an order is made in addition to any sentence imposed, including a discharge.

"Licensed premises" for this purpose means those in respect of which a premises licence under the Licensing Act 2003 has been granted by the relevant local authority authorising the supply of alcohol (within the meaning of s 14 of that Act) for consumption on the premises.

The court must state the period during which the defendant is to be excluded; the minimum period is three months and the maximum is two years. Any person who is subject to such an order and is in the specified premises otherwise than with the express consent of the licensee or one of his staff is guilty of an offence punishable with a fine on level 4 and one months' imprisonment.

Thus, a person convicted of breach of an exclusion order who is also the subject of a suspended sentence (which might be imposed for the offence which gave rise to the exclusion order) will be in jeopardy of having to serve that additional sentence. Courts would probably want to make this point to the defendant both in fairness to him and also perhaps the better to enforce the order. At the time of convicting a person for breach of an exclusion order the court may also determine whether to revoke the order or vary it by deleting the name of any specified premises.

B[32.2] The licensee or his staff may expel from his premises any person whom he reasonably suspects of having entered in breach of an exclusion order and a constable shall at the request of the licensee or his staff, help to expel anyperson whom the constable reasonably suspects of being present in breach of such an order.

B[32A]

Drinking Banning Orders

B[32A.1] A substantial part of Chapter I, Part 1 of the Violent Crime Reduction Act 2006 (drinking banning orders) was brought into force on 31 August 2009.

An application may be made by a chief officer of police (including the British Transport Police) or a local authority (after consultation with each other). Application is by way of complaint to a magistrates' court (s 3) or a county court (s 4). The proceedings are therefore classified as civil proceedings: s 3.

The subject of the order must be at least 16 years of age and since 31 August 2009 engaged in criminal or disorderly behaviour while under the influence of alcohol. If the complaint is proved the court must consider whether an order is necessary to protect others from behaviour of the same kind while under the influence of alcohol.

Rules of court have been made governing the forms and procedure which must be adhered to in relation to orders under sections 3 and 9 of the 2006 respectively: see the Magistrates' Courts (Drinking Banning Orders) Rules 2009, SI 2009/2937 and the Criminal Procedure Rules 2011, r 50.2 onwards.

Driving banning orders on conviction were repealed by the Anti-social Behaviour, Crime and Policing Act 2014.

Order and its terms

B[32A.2] An order may contain such prohibitions as are necessary to protect the public from criminal or disorderly behaviour from the subject of the order while under the influence of alcohol. The prohibitions may include entering premises with a premises licence or club premises licence authorising the sale of alcohol. The individual may not be prohibited from entering a place where he lives, works, attends for education, training or medical treatment or is legally obliged to attend: s 1.

The duration of the order may be between two months and two years although different prohibitions may have effect for different periods: s 2.

The order may provide for the order or any prohibition or provision to cease to have effect at an earlier date if the subject completes a specified approved course and he consents to its inclusion. If it does so the order must specify the date on which the order or prohibition will case to have effect. This will be at least half-way through the original period specified by the court. The court must be satisfied that a place on a specified approved course if available.

The court must explain the terms of the order and if it does not include or offer attendance at an approved course the court must state its reasons in open court: s 2.

Variation or discharge

B[32A.3] Either party may apply by complaint for variation or discharge. The order may not be extended to last longer than two years and may not be discharged before the specified period is half-way through the original term unless the police/local authority consents: see s 5.

Interim order

B[32A.4] An interim order may be made if the court considers it just to do so. An application may be made without notice or be heard in the absence of the subject with the leave of the justices' clerk if he considers that such a procedure is **necessary**. An interim order may last for up to four weeks although there is provision to extend such an order: s 9. It is suggested that a copy of an order made should be served on the offender preferably by personal service by the police/local authority to ensure that the subject is aware of the terms of the order and the sanctions for non-compliance (see breach proceedings below).

Breach proceedings

B[32A.5] Breach of an order without reasonable excuse is punishable on summary conviction with a fine of up to £2,500 (£1,000 in respect of a youth aged 16–17 years). A conditional discharge on breach is not available.

If breach proceedings are brought in the youth court, the list of persons entitled to be present has been expanded to include 'one person authorised by a relevant authority'. Reporting restrictions under s 49 CYPA 1933 do not apply but the court may make an order under s 33 CYPA 1933 (or s 45 YJCEA 1999 when in force) and if the court imposes a reporting restriction or declines to make an order it should give its reasons: see s 11.

Appeal

B[32A.6] An appeal against a full order from the magistrates' court lies to the Crown Court: s 10. No appeal lies against the making of an interim order. There does not appear to be a right of appeal to the Crown Court against the variation or discharge of a full order.

Fines

*For 'Assessment of Fines: Sentencing Process' see B[33A]
below*
Limitations

B[33.1] Offences. The court may fine for any criminal offence.

Surcharge. See B[33.4] below.

B[33.2] Maximum fine. The power of magistrates' courts (unlike that of
the Crown Court) to impose a fine is entirely controlled by statute.
Therefore the maximum fine for the offence may not be exceeded.

B[33.3] The maximum fine for the vast majority of offences which are
only triable by magistrates is expressed as being on one of five levels, each
level representing a monetary limit. (The maximum for most offences
triable either way is expressed as the 'statutory maximum' or 'prescribed
sum'.)

Level 1: maximum fine is £200

Level 2: maximum fine is £500

Level 3: maximum fine is £1,000

Level 4: maximum fine is £2,500

Level 5: maximum fine is £5,000

(Either way offences: prescribed sum is £5,000.)

**Sections 85 and 86 of the Legal Aid, Sentencing and Punishment of
Offenders Act 2012 provide, respectively, for the removal of the £5,000
limit and power to increase other fines. While the enabling powers were
brought into force by SI 2014/1291, they are yet to be exercised.

B[33.4] This is known as the standard scale of fines and it has been
devised as an attempt to rationalise the maximum amounts of fines and to
provide a simple means of increasing them in inflationary times.

Victims surcharge. By virtue of the Criminal Justice Act 2003, s 161A(1)
and secondary legislation, for offences committed on or after **1 April 2007**
where a court requires an offender to pay a fine and/or costs, or by
requiring the offender to pay a fine and compensation and/or costs, it must
order the offender to pay a victims surcharge of £15. Where the means of
the offender are such that he has insufficient income to pay a fine, costs
and/or a surcharge in addition to *compensation*, the court may give
precedence to the compensation order by making no order for the payment
of the surcharge. In other words, the court gives priority to the compensation order.

Where the court proposes a fine and/or costs, but the offender has limited means, it is permissible to give priority to the surcharge by reducing the level of the fine and/or costs, but not the surcharge.

A surcharge is not payable where the court is imposing a fine or back duty in relation to a vehicle excise prosecution. This is because the vehicle excise legislation provides for payment of an "excise penalty".

*As of **1 October 2012** the following provisions apply in the magistrates' court (SI 2012/1696):

Offender aged 18 or over when offence committed	Offender aged under 18 when offence committed	Incorporated and unincorporated companies etc
(a) Conditional discharge at a flat rate of £15 (b) Fine at 10% of the fine value, rounded up or down to the nearest pound, with a minimum amount of £20 and a maximum amount of £120 (c) Community order at a flat rate of £60 (d) Suspended sentence of imprisonment or detention in a young offenders' institution at– (i) £80 for a sentence of 6 months and below; and (ii) £100 for a sentence of over six months but not more than 12 months	(a) Conditional discharge at a flat rate of £10 (b) Fine at a flat rate of £15 (c) Youth rehabilitation order at a flat rate of £15 (d) Referral order at a flat rate of £15	(a) Conditional discharge at a flat rate of £15 (b) Fine at 10% of the fine value, rounded up or down to the nearest pound with a minimum amount of £20 and a maximum amount of £120

Mixed disposal. Where the defendant is dealt with in different ways (so for example a fine in relation to one offence and custody in relation to another) only one surcharge (whichever is the higher) will be paid.

Transitional provisions:

(1)   An offender is dealt with by a court for more than one offence, and at least one of the offences was committed either side of the 1 October 2012 implementation date. In such cases, the surcharge will be payable if the person is fined, at a rate of £15 as specified by the 2007 Order.

(2)   A court deals with an adult offender for more than one offence, and at least one of those offences was committed when under 18, the surcharge will be payable at the rate for under 18s.

Juveniles

B[33.5] Offender under 14 (a child). Maximum fine is the amount in the statute creating the offence or £250, whichever is less.

B[33.6] Offender 14 to under 18 (young person). Maximum fine is the amount in the statute creating the offence or £1,000, whichever is less.

Parental responsibility for payment

B[33.7] In the case of a person under 16 the court must order the parent or guardian to pay unless either he cannot be found or the court is satisfied that it would be unreasonable to order the parent to pay having regard to the circumstances of the case. Provided the parent has been given the opportunity to attend court, an order for payment may be made against him in his absence. If he is present, he must be given the opportunity of making representations about whether he should be ordered to pay.

B[33.8] Before exercising its power to make an order that a parent should pay a financial order in respect of an offence committed by a child the court must be satisfied that it is reasonable to do so. Before making an order a parent or guardian should be given the opportunity of being heard (PCC(S)A 2000, s 137(4)).

B[33.9] Where the offender is aged 16 or 17, and it would not be unreasonable to do so, the court has a power to make the parent responsible for the financial order.

B[33.10]–[33.15] Where a local authority has parental responsibility for a child in their care or accommodated by them, the local authority is responsible for payment, unless it has done everything reasonably and properly expected of it to protect the public from the young offender (*D v DPP* (1995)).

Determining the amount of any fine

B[33.16] Introduction. The amount of a fine must reflect the **seriousness** of the offence (CJA 2003, s 164(2)). The court must also take into account the **financial circumstances** of the offender; this applies whether it has the effect of increasing or reducing the fine (CJA 2003, s 164(1) and (4)). The **aim** is for the fine to have an equal impact on offenders with different financial circumstances; it should be a hardship but should not force the offender below a reasonable "subsistence" level.

Fine Bands. For the purposes of the SGC offence guidelines, a fine is normally based on one of three bands, that is Bands A, B or C (see on for Bands D and E). The selection of the relevant band, and the position of the individual offence within that band, is determined by the **seriousness** of the offence.

Starting points based on first time offender pleading not guilty

	Starting point	**Range**
Fine Band A	50% of relevant weekly income	25%–75% of relevant weekly income
Fine Band B	100% of relevant weekly income	75%–125% of relevant weekly income
Fine Band C	150% of relevant weekly income	125%–175% of relevant weekly income

Fine band starting point and ranges. Each fine band has a starting point and a range. Some guidelines are expressed as a single fine band (eg see careless driving at C[25]). Other guidelines the range may encompass more than one fine band (eg see drunk and disorderly at A[28]).

Multiple offences. The starting point and ranges indicated in the individual offence guidelines assume that the offender is being sentenced for a single offence. Where an offender is being sentenced for multiple offences, the overall sentence must be just and appropriate having regard to the totality of the offending; the court should not simply aggregate the sentences considered suitable for the individual offences. The court's assessment of the totality of the offending may result in an overall sentence above the range indicated by the individual offences, including, where permitted, a sentence of a different type (see CJA 2003, ss 148(1) and 152(2)).

Where an offender is to be fined for two or more offences that arise out of the **same incident**, it will often be appropriate to impose on the most serious offence a fine which reflects the totality of the offending where this can be achieved within the maximum for that offence. "no separate penalty" should be imposed for other offences.

Ancillary orders – order of priority. Where **compensation** is being ordered, that will need to be attributed to the relevant offence as will any necessary **ancillary** orders.

Where the offender does not have sufficient means to pay the total financial penalty, the order of priority is compensation, surcharge, fine and then costs.

Offences not included in the SGC guidelines. Where an offence is not included in this or any other SGC guideline, it may assist in determining sentence to consider the starting points and ranges indicated for offences that are of a similar level of seriousness.

B[33.17] Definition of relevant weekly income. The **seriousness** of an offence determines the choice of fine band and the position of the offence within the range for that band. The offender's **financial circumstances** are taken into account by expressing that position as a proportion of the offender's **relevant weekly income**.

Where an offender is in receipt of income from employment or is self-employed **and** that income is more than £110 per week after deduction of tax and national insurance (or equivalent where the offender is self-employed), the actual income is the **relevant weekly income**.

Where the offender's only source of income is state benefit (including where there is relatively low additional income as permitted by the benefit regulations) or the offender is in receipt of income from employment or is self-employed but the amount of income after deduction of tax and national insurance is £110 or less, the **relevant weekly income is deemed to be £110.** Additional information about this approach is set out below. In calculating relevant weekly income, no account should be taken of tax credits, housing benefit, child benefit or similar.

B[33.18] Determining relevant weekly income – means Information and no reliable information. Under s 95 of the Courts Act 2003 (which amends s 20A of the Criminal Justice Act 1991) it is an offence for a defendant to fail to provide means information to the court when charged. The best way for the court to receive that information is on the standard *Means Form* which should be issued to all defendants so that if they are found guilty the court can impose a fine appropriate to the offender's means and ability to pay.

Where an offender has failed to provide information, or the court is not satisfied that it has been given sufficient reliable information, it is entitled to make such determination as it thinks fit regarding the financial circumstances of the offender (CJA 2003, s 164(5)). Any such determination should be clearly stated on the court records for use in any subsequent variation or enforcement proceedings. A record should also be made of the applicable fine band and the court's assessment of the position of the offence within that band based on the seriousness of the offence.

Where there is **no information** on which a determination can be made, the court should proceed on the basis of an **assumed relevant weekly income of £400**. This is derived from national median pre-tax earnings; a gross figure is used as, in the absence of financial information from the offender, it is not possible to calculate appropriate deductions.

Where there is some information that tends to suggest a significantly lower or higher income than the recommended £400 default sum, the court should make a determination based on that information. A court is empowered to remit a fine in whole or in part if the offender subsequently provides information as to means (CJA 2003, s 165(2)). The assessment of offence seriousness and, therefore, the appropriate fine band and the position of the offence within that band is **not** affected by the provision of this information.

B[33.18A] Approach to offenders on low income (including state benefit). An offender whose primary source of income is state benefit will generally receive a base level of benefit (eg job seekers' allowance, a relevant disability benefit or income support) and may also be eligible for the supplementary benefits depending on his or her individual circumstances (such as child tax credits, housing benefit, council tax benefit and similar. If **relevant weekly income** were defined as the amount of benefit received, this would usually result in higher fines being imposed on offenders with a higher level of need; in most circumstances that would not properly balance the seriousness of the offence with the financial circumstances of the offender. While it might be possible to exclude from the calculation any allowance above the basic entitlement of a single person, that could be complicated and time consuming. Similar issues can arise where the offender is in receipt of a low earned income since this may trigger eligibility for means related benefits such as working tax credits and housing benefit depending on the particular circumstances. It will not always be possible with any confidence whether such a person's financial circumstances are significantly different from those of a person whose primary source of income is state benefit.

For those reasons, a simpler and fairer approach to cases involving offenders in receipt of low income (whether primarily earned or as a result of benefit) is to identify an amount that is **deemed** to represent the offender's relevant weekly income. While a precise calculation is neither possible nor desirable, it is considered that an amount that is approximately half-way between the base rate for job seekers' allowance and the net weekly income of an adult earning the minimum wage for 30 hours per week represents a starting point that is both realistic and appropriately; that is **currently £110**. The calculation is based on a 30 hour working week in recognition of the fact that many of those on a minimum wage do not work a full 37 hour week and that lower minimum wage rates apply to younger people. It is expected that this figure will remain in use until 31 March 2011. Future revisions of the guideline will update the amount in accordance with current benefit and minimum wage levels.

B[33.19] Assessment of financial circumstances. While the initial consideration for the assessment of a fine is the offender's relevant weekly income, the court is required to take account of the offender's **financial circumstances** more broadly. An offender's financial circumstances may have the effect of increasing or reducing the amount of the fine; however they are **not** relevant to the assessment of offence seriousness. They should be considered separately from the selection of the appropriate fine band and the court's assessment of the position of the offence band within the range for that band.

B[33.20] **Out of the ordinary expenses.** In deciding the proportions of relevant weekly income that are the starting point and ranges for each fine band, account has been taken of reasonable living expenses. Accordingly, no further allowances should normally be made for these. In addition, no allowance should normally be made where the offender has dependants. Outgoings will be relevant to the amount of the fine only where the expenditure is **out of the ordinary** and **substantially** reduces the ability to pay a financial penalty so that the requirement to pay a fine based on the standard approach would lead to undue hardship.

Example: Court determines offence seriousness is a Band A fine. Defendant's relevant weekly income is £600 per week. Defendant pleads guilty at the first availability opportunity. The court determines to take into account out of the ordinary expenditure of £50 per week.

Fine = 50% of £600–£300 less a one-third discount for plea = £200 less £50 for out of the ordinary expenses = a total fine of £150.

Unusually low outgoings

Where the offender's living expenses are substantially lower than would normally be expected, it may be appropriate to adjust the amount of the fine to reflect this. This may apply, for example, where an offender does not make any financial contribution towards his or her own living costs.

B[33.21] Savings

Where an offender has savings these will not normally be relevant to the assessment of the amount of a fine although they may influence the decision on time to pay. However, where an offender has substantial savings, the court may consider it appropriate to adjust the amount of the fine to reflect this.

B[33.22] Household has more than one source of income. Where the household of which the offender is a part has more than one source of income, the fine should normally be based on the income of the offender alone. However, where the offender's part of the income is very small (or the offender is wholly dependent on the income of another), the court may have regard to the extent of the householder's income and assets which will be available to meet any fine imposed on the offender (*R v Engen* [2004] EWCA Crim 1536).

B[33.23] Potential earning capacity. Where there is reason to believe that an offender's potential earning capacity is greater than his or her current income, the court may wish to adjust the amount of the fine to reflect this (*R v Little* (unreported) 14 April 1976, CA). This may apply, for example, where an unemployed offender states an expectation to gain paid employment within a short time. The basis for the calculation of fine should be recorded in order to ensure that there is a clear record for use in variation or enforcement proceedings.

High income offenders. Where the offender is in receipt of a very high income, affine based on a proportion of relevant weekly income may be disproportionately high when compared with the seriousness of the offence.

In such cases, the court should adjust the fine to an appropriate level; as a general indication, in most cases the fine for a first time offender pleading not guilty **should not exceed** 75% of the maximum fine.

B[33.24] Offence committed for "commercial" purposes. Some offences are committed with the intention of gaining a significant commercial benefit. These often occur, where, in order to carry out an activity lawfully, a person has to comply with certain processes which may be expensive. They include, for example, "taxi-touting" (where unauthorised persons seek to operate as taxi drivers) and "fly-tipping" (where the cost of lawful disposal is considerable). In some of these cases, a fine based on the standard approach set out above may not reflect the level of financial gain achieved or sought through the offending. Accordingly:

(a)   where the offender has generated income or avoided expenditure to a level that can be calculated or estimated, the court may wish to consider that amount when determining the financial penalty;

(b)   where it is not possible to calculate or estimate that amount, the court may wish to draw on information from the law enforcing authorities about the general costs of operating within the law.

B[33.25] Reduction for a guilty plea. Where a guilty plea has been entered, the amount of the fine should be reduced by an appropriate proportion. See B[5.46].

Announcing the fine and time to pay

B[33.26] Time to pay. When a fine is announced, unless payment can be made forthwith, in the case of an adult offender the court should normally make a collection order. The same applies in the youth court where a parent or guardian has been made responsible for the payment of the fine. In those cases where the juvenile is made responsible it is recommended that fixing time for payment should be deferred by the youth court and responsibility delegated to the fines officer.

B[33.27] An immediate committal to prison in default of payment can only be ordered in the four types of cases mentioned below. In other cases the court must announce (and cause to be entered in the register) the time allowed for payment. This may be a fixed period, eg 14 days, or it may be an order that the defendant pays by instalments.

B[33.28] The court, when imposing a fine, should establish if the defendant is an existing defaulter. If he/she is in default of an existing order the court is normally obliged to make either a deductions of earnings order (if working) or a deductions from benefits order (if claiming benefits). If the offender is not in default of an existing order the court may make these orders with the defendant's consent. In either case the court should make a reserve payment order in case the order fails ie payment in full within 10 working days. In the case of a **compensation order** see B[33.29] below.

B[33.29] Costs and compensation. Costs against a defendant in criminal cases and compensation are normally enforceable in the same way as a fine. However, on imposition it is now **mandatory** that an attachment/deduction order should be considered where the offender is liable to pay compensation as part of the financial imposition. If the attachment/deduction order is subsequently made it should be applied to the whole sum adjudged to be paid.

B[33.30] Limited companies. In law a company is a person. Therefore a fine imposed against a company can only be enforceable against the company and not against any of its officials. For non-payment of a fine a distress warrant can be issued against the company and its property seized and sold to meet the fine and any costs involved in conducting the sale.

B[33.31] Payment of the fine can sometimes be enforced in the High Court or county court. Consult the legal adviser. In certain circumstances the appropriate officer (the collecting officer, in this case the Area Director) may apply to the High Court to have a company wound up under the Insolvency Act 1986.

B[33.32] Partnership firm. The conviction will have been against the partners personally and fines can be enforced against them personally in the usual way.

B[33.33] Searching. The court may order the defendant to be searched and any money found used to pay the fine, compensation and costs. If there is a balance this must be returned to the defendant.

B[33.34] Such money must not be taken if the court is satisfied that the money does not belong to the defendant or if the loss of money would be more injurious to his family than his detention.

B[33.35] Fine supervision order. Instead of the court fixing the time to pay or ordering fixed instalments, it may decide that the defendant is so incompetent or feckless that he will not put aside the money to meet the fine. In such circumstances the court can make a supervision order placing the defendant under the care of some person (often a probation officer) whose duty is not to collect the fine or decide the rate of payments, but to persuade the offender to pay so as to keep out of prison. When making such an order the rate of payment should be fixed by the court.

B[33.36] Imposing a fine and suspended imprisonment. If an offence is punishable both by a fine and imprisonment, a fine and a suspended prison sentence can be imposed.

B[33.37] Fine and immediate imprisonment. This combination is appropriate where the defendant has made a substantial profit from the offence. Generally, however, a fine should be imposed with an immediate custodial sentence only when the defendant has resources from which to pay the fine despite his imprisonment. The situation should be avoided which saddles a discharged prisoner with a fine. Generally offenders who profit from crimes are subject to the Proceeds of Crime Act 2002 confiscation provisions.

Procedure for enforcing fines

B[33.38] Enforcement of a fine. This should begin the moment it is imposed with a fines collection order. The chairman of the court should never invite an application for time to pay. The court should always inquire how much can be paid immediately (if the defendant cannot pay in full) and should consider requiring even a small sum to be paid forthwith. It is usually better to fix any reserve payment order by reference to the offender's pay day rather than seven days from the date of his conviction. On a first default the fines officer must make an attachment of earnings order or apply for an attachment of benefit unless it is impracticable or inappropriate. Thereafter once a fines collection order has been made the fines officer has a wide range of powers but the court still has a role to play in many cases (see Courts Act 2003, Sch 5).

On default the fines officer can impose the following steps:

- Clamping of the offender's car
- Registration of the fine with the Register of Fines and Judgments
- Warrant of control
- Attachment of Earnings
- Deductions from Benefit
- Transfer the case to the civil courts for enforcement where it is cost effective to do so

If the fines officer clamps a car and wants to sell the vehicle he will have to first seek the permission of the court. The fines officer will have to have the case listed and go before the court to seek permission.

There is a new power for the fines officer to transfer cases for enforcement without referring them back to the court. This can be used where the court receives new information on the whereabouts of the offender and it is necessary to transfer for enforcement purposes.

If the fines officer considers that the above disposals are insufficient to recover payment he will refer the matter back to court, for example, to increase the fine or to impose imprisonment in default.

Immediate enforcement

B[33.39] When a fine is imposed the court can use the following methods to enforce immediate payment, if there is a good reason not to make a collection order.

B[33.40] 1 Search. The court can order the defendant to be searched for money to meet the fine. See above.

B[33.41]–[33.45] 2 Immediate committal to prison. In the circumstances listed below the court may order imprisonment forthwith for a period determined in accordance with the following scale:

An amount not exceeding £200	7 days
An amount exceeding £200 but not exceeding £500	14 days
An amount exceeding £500 but not exceeding £1,000	28 days
An amount exceeding £1,000 but not exceeding £2,500	45 days
An amount exceeding £2,500 but not exceeding £5,000	3 months
An amount exceeding £5,000 but not exceeding £10,000	6 months
An amount exceeding £10,000	12 months

B[33.46] It must be borne in mind that these are the maximum periods applicable, the court is not obliged to impose the maximum period in default. In other words, the number of days in default should be proportionate to the sum outstanding eg if the sum imposed was £520 and nothing has been paid, pro rata 15 days (rather than 28 days) should be ordered to be served in default of payment.

B[33.47] If part payments have been made then the period of imprisonment is calculated by taking the period of imprisonment considered appropriate for the whole sum and reducing that period by the proportion which the part payment bears to the original sum due. For example, if a defendant is fined £600 and over a period pays £400, the maximum period of imprisonment for that balance is one-third of 28 days in band 4. Where a defendant is fined at one time for several offences, each fine must be calculated separately and the periods of imprisonment may be made consecutive. However, it is not appropriate to fix consecutive terms of imprisonment in respect of fines imposed for several offences arising out of the same incident. In every case where several fines are outstanding the court must look realistically at the total situation.

NB: Where several fines are ordered to run consecutive to each other the total number of days in default should not exceed the statutory maximum. For example, if four separate fines of £240 are ordered to run consecutive to each other the total number of days in default should not exceed the statutory maximum outlined in B[33.40] above ie 28 days.

B[33.48] The above table applies to monetary penalties (ie fines, costs and compensation) and not to civil orders eg arrears of maintenance for which the maximum period is six weeks. Nor does it apply to the community charge for which the maximum period is three months. (It may be convenient to mention here that periods of imprisonment for more than one amount of unpaid community charge may not be made consecutive.)

B[33.49] An immediate committal to prison can only be ordered in the following cases:

(a)   if the offence is punishable with imprisonment and the defendant appears to the court to have sufficient means to pay immediately; or
(b)   if it appears to the court that the defendant is unlikely to remain at an address in the United Kingdom long enough for the fine to be enforced by other methods; or
(c)   if the defendant is already serving a prison or detention sentence; or
(d)   if the defendant is being sent to prison or detention on the same or another charge.

Note, however, that s 82(1)(c) of the Magistrates' Courts Act 1980 (power to impose imprisonment in default of payment of any sum adjudged to be paid on conviction where the court imposes immediate imprisonment or detention for that or another offence, or the offender is already a serving prisoner) does not apply to the surcharge in consequence of the insertion of s 82(1A) of the MCA 1980 by s 179 of the Anti-social Behaviour, Crime and Policing Act 2014. Section 135 of the MCA 1980 was not, however, amended. Consequently, on the occasion the offender is convicted, or subsequently, the court retains the power to order short-term detention in default.

B[33.50] The court should announce its reasons (that is, (a), (b), (c) or (d) above) for making an immediate committal to prison and these reasons should be entered in the court register and on the committal warrant. Failure to comply may result in a challenge to the decision by judicial review (*R v Oldham Justices, ex p Cawley* [1997] QB 1, [1996] 1 All ER 464). If the defendant has second thoughts about paying and tenders payment to the court staff, the police or the prison officials he is entitled to be released. If only part of the fine is paid then he is entitled to a proportionate remission of the prison sentence. This applies even if he offers part payment after he has served a part of the prison sentence. A committal order, forthwith or suspended, will be inappropriate for a single mother with very little income, trying her best to balance her financial obligations (*R (on the application of Stokes) v Gwent Magistrates' Court*

[2001] EWHC 569 (Admin), [2001] All ER (D) 125 (Jul)). A defaulter's human rights may be breached if he is not offered legal representation (*Best v UK* (2005) Times, 10 March).

B[33.51] The period of imprisonment for non-payment can be concurrent with or consecutive to another sentence already being served; or if more than one fine is being enforced, the periods of imprisonment for non-payment can be consecutive to each other subject to the overall restrictions on the aggregate length of sentences. Consult the legal adviser.

B[33.52] 3 Suspended committal order. The court can order a committal to prison under the scale at B[33.40] to be suspended for a definite period of time during which the defendant has to find the money for the fine or it may suspend the prison sentence whilst he pays instalments at a rate decided by the court (usually weekly, fortnightly or monthly). Such a suspended committal order can only be ordered if the case falls into one of the categories listed at B[33.49] as (a), (b), (c), or (d). If more than one fine is being enforced in this way, the periods of imprisonment for non-payment can be concurrent with or consecutive to each other subject to the overall restrictions on the aggregate length of sentence (at B[33.40]). The defendant may apply subsequently to the court to vary the terms of the postponement. Where the defendant subsequently defaults in payment of the order, the court must give him notice that the warrant of commitment falls to be issued. Magistrates should adjourn hearing a warrant for committal case if they know that the defendant has not been served with proceedings (*R v Doncaster Justices, ex p Hannan* (1998) 163 JP 182, [1998] 32 LS Gaz R 30). He then has an opportunity to make representations orally or in writing as to why the warrant should not issue. Consult the legal adviser.

B[33.53] 4 Detention for one day or overnight at a police station. The court can order the defendant to be detained for the remainder of the day within the precincts of the court or police station but must be released at a time which will allow him to get home the same day or at the latest by 8 p.m. The release time should be announced by the court. Similarly, overnight detention authorises the police to arrest the defendant and keep him until 8 a.m. on the morning following his arrest or if he is arrested between midnight and 8 o'clock in the morning, until 8 o'clock in the morning of the day on which he is arrested. The effect of this is to wipe out the fine.

B[33.54] 5 Warrant of control. The magistrates can issue a warrant of control which orders the seizure of the defendant's property to meet the unpaid fine. Such an order may be suspended on terms that the defaulter pays as ordered by the court.

B[33.55]–[33.60] 6 Supervision order. This means placing the defendant under supervision, usually of the probation officer, see B[33.34].

B[33.61] 7 Fixing a means inquiry. When imposing a fine etc the court may fix a date on which the offender must appear in court for a means inquiry if at that time any part of the monetary penalty remains unpaid.

Enforcement as a result of a referral by the fines officer

B[33.62] If the defendant fails to pay the fine or other enforcement has failed, the fines officer will arrange for the issuing of a summons or warrant to bring the defendant back before the court who will conduct a means inquiry to investigate the defendant's ability to pay the fine and may demand that the defendant produce documentary evidence of his financial resources, eg pay slips, account books, post office savings book, bank statements etc. The defendant must produce a statement of means either before the inquiry or during the inquiry by a specified date and failure to produce such a statement is punishable with a fine up to level 3 if directed by the court and level 2 if directed by the fines officer.

Additionally the court may discharge a fines collection order and revert to its standard powers following an appeal against a decision of the fines officer to vary terms or take action by the use of alternative sanctions (including wheel clamping).

B[33.63] **Increase in fine.** Where the defendant is in default on a collection order, the sum due consists of or includes a fine, and the fines officer has referred the default to a magistrates' court either as an alternative to the issue of a further steps notice or after taking any of the further steps described in B[33.38], above, if the court is satisfied that the default is due to the defendant's wilful refusal or culpable neglect it may increase the fine (but not any other sum which is due) by 50%: Courts Act 2003, Sch 5, para 42A and the Fines Collection Regulations 2006, SI 2006/501, reg 3.

Remission. A fine (but only a fine) may be remitted in whole or in part if the court thinks it is just to do so having regard to a change in circumstances which has occurred since the conviction. A magistrates' court may not, however, remit the whole or any part of a fine imposed by, or sum due under a recognizance forfeited by, the Crown Court or Court of Appeal or Supreme Court, without the consent of the Crown Court. Where a fine is remitted this automatically remits the surcharge to the level it would have been if the fine had not included the remitted amount.

B[33.64]–[33.65] For compensation see B[18].

B[33.66] At a means inquiry magistrates can enforce payment by the following methods:

B[33.67] 1 **Attachment orders.** If the magistrates are satisfied that the defendant is being paid earnings they may make an attachment order directing that the employer make deductions from the defendant's wages and remit them to the court. If the magistrates have this course in mind they should first consult the legal adviser and/or direct that the defendant completes a means form as the court must obtain certain details about the defendant and his employment.

B[33.68] 2 **Warrant of control.** See above.

B[33.69] 3 **Search.** See B[33.32].

B[33.70]–[33.75] 4 **Immediate committal to prison.** The magistrates can order an immediate committal to prison for a specified period according to the scale set out at B[33.40]. For calculation of the term in default see B[33.47]. Immediate committal to prison can only be ordered if:

(a) the offence for which he has been fined is also punishable with imprisonment and the defendant appears to the court to have the means to pay immediately; or

(b)   the court is satisfied that the default is due to the offender's wilful refusal or culpable neglect and the court has considered or tried all other methods of enforcement and it appears to the court that they are inappropriate or unsuccessful.

Culpable neglect cannot be found where a defaulter has no capital or income to pay a fine. Nor should the assumption be made that someone else will pay the fine (*R (on the application of McDonough) v Wigan Magistrates' Court* [2004] EWHC 3272 (Admin), [2005] All ER (D) 304 (Feb)).

A high threshold has to be crossed before making a finding of *wilful refusal* (*R (on the application of Louis) v Ealing Magistrates' Court* [2009] EWHC 521 (Admin), 173 JP 248, [2009] All ER (D) 215 (Feb)).

B[33.76] The test in s 82(4) of the MCA 1980 was that the court had to have regard to other methods of enforcement; it was not obliged to have tried them all: *R (Johnson) v Birmingham Magistrates' Court and CPS* [2012] EWHC 596 (ADMIN).

The other methods referred to are warrants of control, application to the High Court or county court for enforcement, supervision, attachment of earnings and, if under 21, attendance centre.

B[33.77] 5 **Detention for one day or overnight at a police station.** See B[33.53].

B[33.78] 6 **Suspended committal to prison.** The court can order a suspended committal to prison for a period in accordance with the scale on at B[33.40]. This imprisonment can then be suspended for a definite period of time during which the defendant must pay the fine or alternatively the court may direct that the defendant shall pay at so much per week or month. Such a suspended committal can only be ordered if the offence for which the defendant was fined is punishable with imprisonment and the defendant appears to have sufficient means to pay; or the court is satisfied that the default is due to the offender's wilful refusal or culpable neglect and the court has considered all the other methods of enforcement and it appears that they are inappropriate or unsuccessful. See above.

B[33.79] 7 **Supervision order.** See B[22.35].

B[33.80] 8 **Deduction from benefit.** After a means inquiry has been made the court may request the Department of Works and Pensions to make payments towards a fine or compensation direct from the offender's benefit, subject to any right of review or appeal he may have.

B[33.81] 9 **Transfer to High Court or county court.** If the defendant is a holder of shares or has certain kinds of assets, enforcement can sometimes be transferred to the High Court or county court. Consult the legal adviser.

B[33.82] **Defendant already in prison.** If a defendant, who has not paid part or the whole of a fine, is serving a sentence of imprisonment or is confined in a detention centre a committal warrant can be issued without any means inquiry taking place. The clerk will give notice to the debtor who may appear or make written representations.

B[33.83] **Curfew and community service orders.** Where the court has power to issue a warrant of commitment, it may instead make a community service or curfew order provided it has been notified by the Secretary of State that arrangements for implementing the order are available in the relevant area: Crime (Sentences) Act 1997, s 35. These powers are prospectively repealed and replaced, respectively, by Part 7 of Sch 37 to, and s 300 of, the Criminal Justice Act 2003.

Fines imposed by Central Criminal Court and Crown Court

B[33.84] These fines are payable to and enforceable by magistrates' courts.

B[33.85] The whole fine or part of it can be remitted only with the consent of the higher court.

B[33.85A] When calculating the period of default sentence under s 15 of the Criminal Justice (International Co-Operation) Act 1990, interest was to be included: *R (on the application of the CPS) v. City of London Magistrates' Court* [2007] All ER (D) 302 (Jul).

Defendants aged 18 to 21

B[33.86]–[33.90] The above provisions can also be employed in respect of defendants in this age group except that an order of detention in default of payment should only be ordered if a supervision order has already been tried or the court is satisfied that a supervision order is either undesirable or impracticable. These considerations must be noted on any commitment warrant (*R v Oldham Justices, ex p Cawley* [1997] QB 1, [1996] 1 All ER 464 and *R v Stockport Justices, ex p Conlon* [1997] 2 All ER 204, 161 JP 81).

B[33.91] If the court has available to it an attendance centre for defaulters to the age of 25, the court can send the defendant for up to 36 hours in all in default of payment.

B[33.92] The clerk should be consulted as to the exact number of hours that the defendant should attend at the attendance centre.

Defendants aged 10 to 17

B[33.93] Maximum fine. Children under 14, £250; young persons, 14 or over, £1,000, or, in either case the lesser sum applicable in the case of an adult (Powers of the Criminal Courts (Sentencing) Act 2000, s 135).

B[33.94] Costs. The costs ordered must not exceed the amount of the fines unless a parent or guardian is ordered to pay.

B[33.95] Parental liability to pay. The child's parent or guardian must be ordered to pay the fine and costs unless he cannot be found or the court considers it would be unreasonable to order him to pay. In the case of a young person the court has a power to order the parent to pay. If the parent or guardian does not pay, enforcement takes place in the adult court as described at B[33.7]–B[33.10].

Enforcement

B[33.96] The power to make a fines supervision order or an attachment of earnings order is available in the case of juveniles. In addition, where the court is satisfied that the juvenile has had the money to pay but has refused or neglected to pay it may make an order requiring:

(a)   the parent to enter a recognisance to ensure that the defaulter pays the fine or balance; or

(b)   the court may transfer the debt to the parent in which case further enforcement, if necessary, would be taken as if the fine has been imposed on that parent.

B[33.97] The parent must, according to the statute, consent before an order may be made for him to enter into a recognisance. The parent's consent is not required for the responsibility for the fine to be transferred to him provided the court is satisfied in all the circumstances that it is reasonable to make the order.

B[33.98] If an attendance centre is available for persons of the debtor's class or description, he may be ordered to attend, up to the age of 25 years.

B[33.99] The powers mentioned under this heading must be exercised after a means inquiry. An order transferring the debt to the parent may be made in his absence provided he has been given adequate notice of the proceedings; if he is present, he must be given the opportunity of speaking to the court before such an order is made.

B[33A]

Assessment of Fines: Sentencing Process

Sentencing guidelines

B[33A.1] Assessment of fines

1. DECIDE THAT A FINE IS APPROPRIATE
2. OFFENCE SERIOUSNESS **A. IDENTIFY THE APPROPRIATE STARTING POINT** In the offence guidelines, the starting point is identified as band A, B or C Each fine band provides a **starting point** and a **range** related to the **seriousness** of the offence expressed as a proportion of the offender's **relevant weekly income** – see B[33.16].
2. OFFENCE SERIOUSNESS **B. CONSIDER THE EFFECT OF AGGRAVATING AND MITIGATING FACTORS** **Move up or down from the starting point** to reflect aggravating or mitigating factors that affect the **seriousness** of the offence – this will usually be within the indicated range for the fine band but the court is not precluded from going outside the range where the facts justify it.
3. CONSIDER OFFENDER MITIGATION The court may consider it appropriate to make a further adjustment to the starting point in the light of any matters of offender mitigation.
4. FORM A VIEW OF THE POSITION OF THE OFFENCE WITHIN THE RANGE FOR THE FINE BAND THEN TAKE INTO ACCOUNT THE OFFENDER'S FINANCIAL CIRCUMSTANCES Require the offender to provide a statement of **financial circumstances**. Obtain further information through questioning if necessary. Failure to provide the information when required is an offence. The provision of financial information does not affect the seriousness of the offence or, therefore, the position of the offence within the range for the applicable fine band. The initial consideration for the assessment of the fine is the offender's **relevant weekly income** – see B[33.17]. However, the court must take account of the offender's financial circumstances more broadly. These may have the effect of increasing or reducing the amount of the fine – see B[33.18]–B[33.23]. Where the court has insufficient information to make a proper determination of the offender's financial circumstances, it may make such determination as it thinks fit – see B[33.18].
5. CONSIDER A REDUCTION FOR A GUILTY PLEA Reduce the fine by the appropriate proportion – see B[5.46].
6. CONSIDER ANCILLARY ORDERS, INCLUDING COMPENSATION Must consider compensation in every case where the offending has resulted in personal injury, loss or damage – give reasons if order not made – see B[18].
7. CONSIDER A REDUCTION FOR A GUILTY PLEA **GIVE REASONS**

The resulting fine must reflect the seriousness of the offence and must take into account the offender's financial circumstances

Consider the proposed total financial penalty, including compensation, victims surcharge and costs. Where there are insufficient resources to pay the total amount, the order of priority is compensation, surcharge, fine, costs.

Must give reasons for the sentence passed, including any ancillary orders.

Must state if the sentence has been reduced to reflect ca guilty plea; indicate what the sentence would otherwise have been.

Must make a collection order unless this would be impracticable or inappropriate – see B[33.38] onwards above.

B[34]

Deprivation of property and forfeiture

(Powers of Criminal Courts (Sentencing) Act 2000, s 143)

B[34.1] Any court which has convicted a person of an offence and

(a) is satisfied
    (a) that any property
    (b) which has been lawfully seized from him or was in his possession or under his control at the time when he was apprehended for the offence or when a summons in respect of it was issued
    (c) has been used for the purposes of committing, or facilitating the commission of any offence or was intended to be used for that purpose

or

(b) the offence (or an offence taken into consideration) consists of unlawful possession of property in the circumstances of (ii) above

may make an order to deprive him of that property.

B[34.2] Property. Does not include land. For applications under the Proceeds of Crime Act 2002 see F[5.47]. It was held under previous legislation that a deprivation order was not available in respect of property which appeared to be the proceeds of earlier offences: *R v Neville* (1987) 9 Cr App R (S) 222, [1987] Crim LR 585, CA; see, however, *R v Farrell* (1988) 10 Cr App R (S) 74 in which an offender's 'working capital' for future drugs dealing was held to be properly forfeited.

B[34.3] Possession. Usually means physical possession but can include a legal right to possession. If there is any dispute the legal adviser should be consulted.

B[34.4] Facilitating. This includes the taking of any steps after the offence has been committed to dispose of property which is the subject of the crime or to avoid apprehension or detection. The property need not have been used personally by the defendant provided he intended it be used for criminal purposes, even by another.

B[34.5] The effect of an order. The accused is deprived of his rights in the property which passes into the possession of the police. Accordingly, the true owner retained the full rights including a right to possession. The owner had a right to bring civil proceedings for conversion. The orders under PCCSA 2000, s 143 made by the magistrates' court provided no defence to the police to that right, unless possibly there was a public policy defence (*Chief Constable of Merseyside Police v Owens* [2012] EWHC 1515 (Admin), 176 CL&J 353 considered): *O'Leary International Ltd v Chief Constable of North Wales and CPS* [2012] EWHC 1516 (Admin), 176 JP 514, 176 CL&J 370.

The provisions of the Police Property Act 1897 (at **A[66]**) apply and a person may claim the property provided that he satisfies the court that either:

(a)   he had not consented to the offender having possession; or
(b)   he did not know, and had no reason to suspect, that the property was likely to be used for the purpose of committing an offence.

B[34.6] If no successful claim is made the property will be sold and the proceeds disposed of in the same way as described at **A[66]**.

B[34.7] Sentencing. The court may make an order under this section in respect of the property whether or not it also deals with the offender in respect of the offence in any other way, and may combine the making of the order with an absolute or conditional discharge.

B[34.8] Under previous legislation it was stated that an order depriving a defendant of property should not be made for the purpose of realising assets to pay fines or compensation (*R v Kingston-upon-Hull Stipendiary Magistrates, ex p Hartung* [1981] RTR 262, 72 Cr App Rep 26).

B[34.9] In considering whether to make a deprivation order the court shall have regard:

(a)   to the value of the property; and
(b)   to the likely financial and other effects on the offender of the making of the order (together with any other order the court is contemplating) (see *Trans Berckx BVBA v North Avon Magistrates' Court* [2011] EWHC 2605 (Admin), DC);
(c)   any representations of the parties (*R v Ball* [2002] EWCA Crim 2777, [2003] 2 Cr App Rep (S) 92).

B[34.10]–[34.15] But where the offence has resulted in a person suffering personal injury, loss or damage and the court has not been able to make a compensation order because of the defendant's lack of means, the proceeds of sale resulting from a deprivation order may be used for compensation.

B[34.16] This order only takes effect after a period of six months in order to allow a person to make a claim under the Police Property Act 1897.

B[34.17] Motor vehicles. Where a person has committed an offence under the Road Traffic Act 1988 which is imprisonable, eg driving with excess alcohol or whilst disqualified, the Road Traffic Act 1991 provides that the vehicle concerned is to be regarded as used for the purpose of committing the offence. Accordingly, the offender runs the risk of the court, after considering all relevant factors, depriving him of his vehicle. The significant use of a motor vehicle (manoeuvring to strike and injure a victim) justified the forfeiture of a motor car in *R v Norman* [2007] EWCA Crim 624.

B[34.18] Disqualification for any offence: See **C[5.45]**.

B[34.19] Other provisions for forfeiture. Formerly the provisions described here were confined to offences punishable with at least 2 years' imprisonment, but now they are available without regard to maximum penalty and so will overlap with some existing forfeiture powers, eg

forfeiture of controlled drugs and firearms and the Customs and Excise
Management Act 1979. See for example *Customs and Excise Comrs v
Newbury* [2003] EWHC 702 (Admin), [2003] 2 All ER 964.

B[35]

Guardianship order

(Mental Health Act 1983, s 37)

Limitations

B[35.1]–[35.2] The offence must be punishable in the case of an adult with imprisonment. Where a court would have power to make an order on conviction, and the court is satisfied that the accused did the act or made the omission charged, the court may, if it thinks fit, make the order without convicting him: Mental Health Act 1983, s 37(3). It follows that as there is no requirement for a trial, the provisions of s 20 of the Magistrates' Courts Act 1980 (procedure where summary trial appears more suitable for an offence triable either way) do not apply. However, the circumstances in which it will be appropriate to exercise this power will be very rare and will usually require the consent of those acting for the accused if he is under a disability so that he cannot be tried: *R v Lincolnshire (Kesteven) Justices, ex p O'Connor* [1983] 1 All ER 901, [1983] 1 WLR 335. Magistrates may still proceed to act under subsection (3) even where the defendant has elected to go for trial by jury: *R v Ramsgate Justices, ex p Kazmarek* (1984) 149 JP 16, but not where the offence is triable only on indictment: *R v Chippenham Magistrates' Court, ex p Thompson* (1995) 160 JP 207.

B[35.3] The minimum age for a guardianship order is ten.

B[35.4]–[35.5] The conditions for the making of an order are that the court is satisfied on the written or oral evidence of two registered medical practitioners, at least one of whom must be approved by the Secretary of State as having special experience in the diagnosis and treatment of mental disorder, that the offender is suffering from mental disorder and, in the case of an offender who has attained the age of 16 years, that the mental disorder is of a nature or degree which warrants his reception into guardianship, and the court is of the opinion, have regard to all the circumstances of the case including the nature of the offence and the character and antecedents of the offender, and to the other available methods of dealing with him, that the most suitable method of disposal is by means of making a guardianship order.

A guardianship order cannot be made unless the relevant authority or person is willing to receive the offender into guardianship: Mental Health Act 1983, s 37(6).

Where a court is minded to make a guardianship order it may request the local social services authority to inform the court whether it or any other person approved by it is willing to receive the offender into guardianship and to give such information as it reasonably can about how it or the other person could be expected to exercise guardianship powers: Mental Health Act 1983, s 39A.

Ancillary orders

B[35.6]–[35.16] Compensation at B[18]

Costs at B[20]

Disqualification at C[5]

Endorsement at C[5]

Deprivation of property and forfeiture at B[34]

Restitution at B[39]

General considerations

B[35.17] Effect of guardianship order. A guardianship order confers on the authority or person named in it as guardian the same powers as guardianship under Part II of the Mental Health Act 1983. These are set out in s 8 and, in outline, are: to determine place of residence; to require attendance for treatment, occupation, education or training; and to require access to the patient in any place of residence for a doctor, social worker or other person specified.

B[35.18] Normally it will lapse after six months, but the mental specialists can recommend an extension when it will be extended for a further six months. After that the order can be extended for one-year periods or until the mental health authorities consider it safe to grant the defendant a discharge.

B[35.19] As the defendant has now become a patient and not a prisoner his discharge from guardianship can be made on the advice of the mental specialist in charge of his case.

B[35.20] The defendant need not wait for the mental specialist to act, but can apply for his discharge at any time during the first six months of the guardianship order or on any occasion when the order is renewed.

B[35.21] The defendant's nearest relative can make application once a year to the Mental Health Review Tribunal for his release.

B[36]

Hospital order

(Mental Health Act 1983, s 37)

Criteria

B[36.1] The relevant conditions are the same as for the making of a guardianship order (see B[35.4], above) except that the court must also be satisfied that the mental disorder is treatable: Mental Health Act 1983, s 37(2)(a)(i). The court must also be satisfied that on the evidence of the approved clinician who would have responsibility for the offender's case or some other person representing the managers of the hospital that arrangements have been made for his admission to that hospital within the period of 28 days beginning with the date of the making of such an order; the court may, pending his admission within that period, give such directions as it thinks fit for his conveyance to and detention in a place of safety: Mental Health Act 1983, s 37(4).

General considerations

B[36.2]–[36.5] Legal representation should be offered to the defendant, or he should be recommended to consult a solicitor if the court is considering a hospital order.

In limited circumstances it is open to a defendant tried in a magistrates' court to plead **insanity**. There are limits on the availability of this defence. For a review of the authorities and procedures see *R (on the application of Singh) v Stratford Magistrates' Court* [2006] EWHC 1582 (Admin). The judgment also discusses the nature and limitations of the availability of an order under s 37 MHA 1983. It is advisable to consult the legal adviser.

B[36.6] Effect of a hospital order. The court does not fix the period that the defendant has to stay in hospital. The date of his release will be decided by the hospital authorities.

B[36.7] Normally the hospital order lapses after six months but it can be renewed for a further six months on the recommendation of the mental specialist in charge of the case, and thereafter the order can be renewed for one-yearly periods. The procedure is that the responsible mental specialist examines the patient and sends a report to the mental health authorities, which can be the hospital managers, who may then act on the recommendation to retain or discharge the patient. Thus the patient can be discharged at any time without reference back to the sentencing court.

B[36.8] The defendant, once a mental patient, can apply for his discharge at any time after the first six months of the order or whenever it is proposed to extend the order. For these reasons the order is in the discretion of the court and custody may still be dictated by public policy considerations (*R v Nafel* (2004)).

B[36.9] The defendant's nearest relative can apply for his discharge once a year to the Mental Health Review Tribunal.

B[36.10]–[36.15] Including a restriction clause in a hospital order (Mental Health Act 1983, s 41). If the defendant is 14 or more and was convicted (as opposed to having 'done the act'), and the magistrates consider a court restriction should be imposed on his release, he can be committed to the Crown Court for sentence pursuant to PCC(S)A 2000, s 3. [**It would appear that this power will no longer be available on or after a date to be appointed unless the committal for sentence is made immediately after the entering of a plea or the offence is a specified offence and the defendant is committed for sentence on the basis that he is a dangerous offender: see **B[16]**]).

B[36.16] The Crown Court can make a hospital order, and include in it a restriction upon the date of release either for a specified period of time or indefinitely.

B[36.17] The magistrates can commit the defendant to prison pending his appearance at the Crown Court or, if satisfied that a vacancy is available at a mental hospital, can order him to be detained there pending his appearance at the Crown Court.

B[36.18] If the Crown Court includes a restriction clause the defendant cannot be discharged by the mental specialist or allowed out of the specified hospital without the consent of the Home Secretary.

B[36.19] The Home Secretary may at any time refer the case to a Mental Health Review Tribunal for their advice, but does not have to accept the advice if he considers that discharge of the patient is not in the public interest.

B[36.20] If the Home Secretary does decide that the patient should be discharged from the mental hospital, he has powers to impose conditions for the discharge such as the place of residence, a scheme of supervision and the liability to recall if a lapse occurs.

B[36.21] Remand for report on accused's mental condition (s 35). Where a doctor satisfies the court that there is reason to suspect that the accused suffers from one or other of several mental disorders and

(a) the accused has been convicted of an offence punishable on summary conviction with imprisonment or 'did the act' or has consented to this course of action; and
(b) it is otherwise impracticable to obtain medical reports; and
(c) arrangements have been made for his reception into a hospital;

the court may remand the accused in a hospital for up to 28 days. There may be further such remands for a total period of up to 12 weeks.

Interim hospital order (s 38)

B[36.22] Provision is made by s 38 of the Mental Health Act 1983 for the making of an interim hospital order for the purpose of establishing whether or not a convicted person is suitable to be the subject of a hospital order. The conditions are virtually the same as for the making of a full hospital order. One difference is that one of the reporting doctors must be employed at the hospital where the offender is to be detained.

An interim order can last for up to 12 weeks and can then be renewed for periods of up to 28 days subject to an overall limit of 12 months. The defendant need not be present at renewal hearings provided he is legally represented and his legal representative is given an opportunity of being heard.

Imprisonment

(Powers of Criminal Courts (Sentencing) Act 2000, s 78**)

Limitations

B[37.1] (a) **Imprisonable offence.**

B[37.2] (b) **Presence of offender.** If the proceedings were instituted by an information followed by a summons, or by a written charge, the court shall not in absence impose a custodial sentence or order that a suspended sentence shall take effect; in any other case, where such a sentence or order is imposed or made, the offender must be brought before the court before he begins to serve the sentence and the sentence will not be effective until this happens: Magistrates' Courts Act 1980, s 11(3), (3A) and (5).

B[37.3] (c) **Age limit.** Defendant must be 21 or over**. For offenders under 21 the appropriate custodial sentence would be detention in a young offender institution**.

B[37.4] **Criteria for imposing a custodial sentence.** The court must be of the opinion that the offence, or the combination of the offence and any other offence associated with it, is so serious that neither a fine nor a community sentence can be a justified penalty for it.

B[37.5] **Other circumstances in which custody may be imposed.** Nothing in paragraph (a) above prevents the court imposing a custodial sentence on an offender who refuses to consent to a community sentence proposed by the court which requires his consent. A court may also impose custody for a wilful and persistent breach of a community order.

B[37.6] **So serious.** Courts should always bear in mind that criminal sentences were in almost every case intended to protect the public whether by punishing the offender or reforming him, or deterring him and others, or all of those things. The sentence imposed should be no longer than is commensurate with the seriousness of the offence (Criminal Justice Act 2003, s 153). The court must take account of all the information about the circumstances of the offence including any aggravating or mitigating factors as is available to it.

In *R v Mills* [2002] EWCA Crim 26 [2002] 2 Cr App Rep (S) 51, the Lord Chief Justice said that imprisonment was often unnecessary for non-violent crimes of dishonesty committed by mothers caring for young families. In *R v Kefford* [2002] EWCA Crim 519, [2002] Crim LR 432 this principle is extended to those persons with no previous convictions convicted of economic crimes.

B[37.7]–[37.15] **Associated offence.** An offence of which the offender has been convicted in the same proceedings or for which he is sentenced at the same time, or an offence taken into consideration.

B[37.16] Pre-sentence report. A magistrates' court, unless it considers it unnecessary to do so, must obtain and consider a pre-sentence report before forming an opinion on:

(a)   whether the offence etc was so serious;
(b)   the length of term commensurate with the offence.

In all cases where a court is contemplating sentencing a defendant to prison for the first time, other than a very short period, it should be the inevitable practice that a pre-sentence report is obtained (*R v Gillette* (1999) Times, 3 December, CA).

B[37.17] Failure to obtain pre-sentence report. Does not invalidate the sentence but the appeal court must obtain and consider such a report if the court below was not justified in forming the opinion that a report was not necessary (Criminal Justice Act 2003, s 156).

B[37.18] Mentally disordered offender. Where an offender is or appears to be mentally disordered, ie suffering from a mental disorder within the meaning of the Mental Health Act 1983, the court must additionally obtain and consider a medical report before passing a custodial sentence unless the court considers it unnecessary to do so. The court must take any such information into account and consider the likely effect of any custodial sentence on his condition and any treatment for it. Failure to obtain a medical report does not invalidate any sentence but one must be obtained and considered by an appeal court (Criminal Justice Act 2003, s 157).

B[37.19] Legal representation. The offender, who has not previously been imprisoned, must first be given the opportunity to be legally represented unless he has been refused legal aid for financial reasons. Note the requirement is not that he should be represented but that he should have the opportunity to be.

Reasons for decisions

B[37.20] It is the duty of the court to state in open court that it is of the opinion that either or both of paragraph B[37.4] and B[37.2] above apply and why it is of that opinion and in all cases (including where a custodial sentence has been imposed following the offender's refusal to comply with a proposed requirement in a community sentence) explain to the offender in open court and in ordinary language why it is passing a custodial sentence on him or, if applicable, why imprisonment is for a longer term than would normally be commensurate with the seriousness of the offence.

B[37.21] Suspended sentences. All these limitations apply equally to suspended sentences.

General considerations

B[37.22] Consecutive sentences. If the defendant is sentenced to immediate or suspended imprisonment on each of two or more offences the terms will run concurrently unless the court orders they are to run consecutively. Consecutively means that one term of imprisonment follows another.

B[37.23] When a magistrates' court sentences an offender for two or more offences it may order that one sentence runs consecutively to the other. In addition (when sentencing for one or more offences) the court may order that a term of imprisonment shall be consecutive to a term already being served by the defendant. In such a case the term imposed should be stated to be consecutive to the total period to which the defendant is subject.

B[37.24] The total period of two or more consecutive sentences imposed on the same occasion by a magistrates' court must not exceed 6 months, unless two or more of the offences are triable either way, when the total period may not exceed 12 months. If the defendant is convicted of two offences, the former being an offence triable either way and the latter which is purely summary, the maximum total remains as 6 months. If the court orders a suspended prison sentence to take effect, it can order that sentence to take effect consecutively to a period of imprisonment for the later offence, even though the total period will exceed the above limits. When a previously suspended sentence is ordered to be served it should normally be made consecutive to a sentence imposed for the later offence. Minimum sentence is 14 days if the sentence is suspended.

B[37.25]–[37.30] Where several offences arise out of one incident consecutive sentences should not be imposed but the incident should be looked at as a whole and one appropriate period fixed. The same principle would apply to a series of offences committed against the same person over a relatively short period, eg an employee who falsifies a weekly claim for expenses.

B[37.31] Consecutive sentences are appropriate where, although there is a single incident, there is more than one offence but they do not arise as a matter of course from the principal offence. For example, the burglar who attacks a householder who discovers him, or an assault on a police officer effecting an arrest for another offence. Offences committed on bail should normally attract a consecutive sentence where imprisonment is appropriate as offending on bail is an aggravating factor.

B[37.32] When consecutive sentences are imposed the court should pay particular regard to the total period and reduce it if it is excessive; this is especially the rule to follow with young offenders and those receiving a first custodial sentence. One method of adjusting the total period in such cases is to consider concurrent rather than consecutive sentences.

B[37.33] Multiple offences. When sentencing a defendant for several offences it is best to refer to the nature of each offence and the sentence and to state the total time to be served. To say 'For the first offence you will go to prison for two months, for the second two months consecutive, for the third two months concurrent . . . ' can be quite meaningless. Some chairmen prefer to begin with what is perhaps the most important aspect of the sentence first: 'You will go to prison for a total of 6 months. That is made up of two months for stealing the watch, a further two months for stealing the camera . . . etc.'

B[37.34] When consecutive sentences are being considered the total period should be reviewed and reduced if it is excessive.

B[37.35] Period of imprisonment. Great care must be exercised in determining the period of imprisonment, especially if it is to be suspended. The length of a custodial sentence must not exceed a term justified by the seriousness of the offence(s) and where there is appropriate mitigation, may be shorter.

B[37.36] Magistrates' courts tend to consider sentences in units of months and the commonest terms are 3, 6 (and where appropriate) 9 and

12 months. It should be remembered that there is a complete discretion within the range available for a particular offence. It may be that for some offenders receiving a custodial sentence for the first time, a sentence of 7 or 14 days would be a salutary lesson, but with no other sentencing objective.

B[37.37] Magistrates should reserve the maximum period available for an offence for those cases which are the worst type of case they would deal with.

B[37.38] Offences of attempt will not usually attract the same period as would the completed offence.

B[37.39] Credit for time on remand. Section 108 of the Legal Aid, Sentencing and Punishment of Offenders Act 2012 inserted s 240ZA of the Criminal Justice Act 20031 in place of s 240. The effect is to disapply the discretion to withhold credit for time on remand in custody for the offence or a related offence; instead, such time is to be calculated and applied administratively. There are three exceptions, however, where credit for time on remand in custody does not apply, namely:

(a)   if, on any day on which the offender was remanded in custody in connection with the offence, the offender was also detained in connection with any other matter, that day is not to count as time served;

(b)   a day counts as time served in relation to only one sentence, and only once in relation to that sentence;

(c)   a day is not to count as time served as part of any period of 28 days served by the offender before automatic release. (This prevents remand time from shortening any recall under s 255B of the Criminal Justice Act 2003 where the maximum length of the recall is 28 days.)

Consecutive and concurrent sentences, where a prisoner has not been released between serving such sentences, are counted as one sentence for the purpose of deducting remand time.

For the purpose of crediting time on remand in custody, a suspended sentence is to be treated as a sentence of imprisonment when it takes effect and is to be treated as imposed by the order under which it takes effect.

The 2003 Act provisions on credit for time on remand apply to any sentence of imprisonment, whether it is: an original sentence of imprisonment; one imposed for breach/revocation of a community order; one imposed by way of activation of a suspended sentence; one imposed in default of payment of a sum adjudged to be paid by way of a conviction; one imposed for want of sufficient distress to satisfy any sum of money; or one imposed for failure to be or abstain from doing anything required to be done or left undone.

B[37.39A] Credit for time spent on qualifying bail curfew. Sections 21 and 22 of the Criminal Justice and Immigration Act 2008 introduced new provisions which apply to offenders on bail subject to a qualifying curfew condition, defined as a condition to remain at one or more specified places for a total of not less than nine hours in any given day combined with an electronic monitoring condition.

In summary, such offenders were entitled, subject to exceptions made by rules, and subject to the court's discretion to withhold credit on interests of justice grounds, to have half the period spent on such curfew count towards any sentence of imprisonment imposed for the offence.

Significant changes were made by the s 109 of the Legal Aid, Sentencing and Punishment of Offenders Act 2012. Principally, the changes were:

(a)   a new method of calculating the 'credit period';
(b)   the enactment of exceptions;
(c)   the removal of the 'interests of justice' discretion to withhold credit.

The credit period is calculated by taking the following, five steps:

(1)   Add–
The number of days on which the offender's bail was subject to the relevant conditions, including the first whether the condition applied for the whole of the day or not, but excluding the last if the offender spends the last part of it in custody.

(2)   Deduct–
Any of the above days on which the offender was subject to an electronically monitored curfew requirement in connection with any other sentence (including on release under home detention curfew) or temporarily released from prison in relation to another sentence.

(3)   Deduct–
From the remaining days, the number of days during that remainder on which the offender has broken either or both of the relevant conditions.

(4)   Divide–
The result by two.

(5)   Round up–
If necessary, to the nearest round number.

A day of the credit period counts as time served in relation to only once sentence and only once in relation to that sentence.

A day of the credit period is not to count as time served as part of any period of 28 days served by the offender before automatic release.

If a curfew is not accompanied by an electronic tag, the statutory conditions are not met and a court is entitled to refuse to give credit for the curfew period even though it qualified in terms of length and the defendant complied with it; there might, however, be circumstances where some allowance should be made, for example, where there are two defendants for sentence who have been subject to curfews but for some reason only one defendant has been electronically tagged: *R v Barrett* [2009] EWCA Crim 2213, [2010] 1 Cr App Rep (S) 572, [2010] Crim LR 159. See also *Rv Sherif* [2008] EWCA Crim 2653, [2009] 2 Cr App Rep (S) 235, [2008] All ER (D) 203 (Nov), and *R v Rudie Aaron Monaghan* [2009] EWCA Crim 2699, [2010] 2 Cr App R (S) 50.

B[37.40]–[37.45] Suspended sentences (Criminal Justice Act 2003, s 189).

The maximum prison term which can be suspended was increased by the Legal Aid, Sentencing and Punishment of Offenders Act 2012 to two years, though magistrates' courts continue to be subject to the normal limits of six months, or 12 months where the court is dealing with two or more offences triable either way. The minimum term which can be suspended is 14 days or, in the case of offenders aged 18–20, 21 days. For offenders aged 18–20 the form of custody is detention in a young offender institution.

The operational period of a suspended sentence is a minimum of six months and a maximum of two years.

B[37.46] When the court suspends a sentence, it may impose one or more requirements for the offender to undertake in the community. The requirements are identical to those available for community orders.

If the offender **fails** to comply with a community requirement or commits a further offence, the court must either activate the suspended sentence in full or in part unless it is unjust to do so; or amend the order so as to:

(a) extend the period during which the offender is subject to community requirements;
(b) make the community requirements more onerous;
(c) may order the offender to pay a fine not exceeding £2,500; or
(d) extend the operational period (CJA 2003, Sch 12, para 8).

If the suspended sentence was imposed by the **Crown Court,** magistrates should consult their legal adviser. The courses open to the justices may vary according to whether the breach is by reason of re-offending or by breaching the terms of the community requirements).

NB: In *West Yorkshire Probation Service v Cruickshanks* [2010] EWHC 615 (Admin), 174 JP 305 it was held that the Probation Service could not enforce an unpaid work requirement under a suspended sentence order following expiration of the operational period of the order. This means that the Probation Service should be alive to laying breaches during the currency of the order. Levenson LJ, who gave the judgment of the court was also of the view that there was no power to extend the operational period once it had expired.

B[37.47]–[37.49] There are many similarities between suspended sentences and community orders; requirements can be imposed on the offender and the court can respond to breach by sending him or her to custody. The crucial difference is that a suspended sentence is a custodial sentence; it may be imposed **only** where the court is satisfied that the custodial threshold has been passed and that it is not appropriate to impose a community order, fine or other non-custodial disposal.

A further difference is the approach to any breach; while sentencing for breach of a community order, the primary objective is to ensure that the requirements of the order are complied with. When responding to breach of a suspended sentence, the **statutory presumption** is that the custodial sentence will be activated.

In *R v Levesconte* [2011] EWCA Crim 2754, [2012] 2 Cr App Rep (S) 80, 176 JP 204 it was held that the sentencer was not entitled to treat the fact that the offence was committed during the operational period of the suspended sentence as a factor justifying the increase of the second sentence, not at least in circumstances where the suspended sentence was activated in full. To take that factor into account again was to increase the sentence referable to that fact beyond the maximum for which the defendant had been at risk. The court recognised that the same argument may not apply where the suspended sentence is not fully implemented. The decision in *Levesconte* misconstrues s 143(2) of the CJA 2003. A strict application of its principles can lead to the same overall length of sentence being imposed for either the activation of a suspended sentence in full or in part.

B[37.50] Detailed guidance regarding suspended sentence and the appropriate response to breaches is set out in the Sentencing Guidelines Council guideline *New Sentences: Criminal Justice Act 2003*. The guideline emphasises that:

- a custodial sentence that is suspended should be for the same term that would have applied if the sentence was to be served immediately;
- the time for which a sentence is suspended should reflect the length of the sentence; up to 12 months might normally be appropriate for a suspended sentence of up to 6 months;
- the imposition of a custodial sentence is both punishment and a deterrent; to ensure that the overall terms of the sentence are commensurate with offence seriousness, requirements imposed as part of the sentence should generally be less onerous than if a custodial order had been imposed;
- a court wishing to impose onerous or intensive requirements should reconsider whether a community sentence might be more appropriate (refer to section **B[17]**);
- where an offender has breached a suspended sentence, there is a presumption that the suspended custodial term will be activated in full or in part. Relevant considerations will include the extent to which (if any) the offender complied with the requirements, and the circumstances of the breach;
- when the court imposes a suspended sentence, it may also order that the sentence be reviewed periodically at a review hearing (CJA 2003, s 191).

In *R v Finn* [2012] EWCA Crim 881, the 29 year old appellant had 36 convictions for 86 different offences. In February 2010 he was sentenced to 9 months' imprisonment, suspended for two years, for one offence of affray and one offence of possession of a bladed article. He was sentenced to an 18-month supervision order with an unpaid work requirement of 140 hours.

In January 2012, he was sentenced to six months' imprisonment for one offence of shop theft committed in November 2011. In addition, on that occasion the Recorder activated the full nine month suspended sentence, making a total sentence of 15 months. He appealed against the activation of all nine months of the suspended sentence. The Court of Appeal held:

> In the circumstances of this particular case, we do not believe that the judge erred in principle in concluding that it was not unjust to impose the suspended sentence in full. We recognise that some judges might have given the appellant modest credit for the unpaid work he had carried out, but that is not the test. A suspended sentence order must be complied with in full; non-compliance risks activation of the suspended sentence in full. In those circumstances, a defendant such as the appellant in the present case, who does not comply with the terms of the suspended sentence order, only has himself to blame if non-compliance leads to activation of the suspended sentence in full.

B[37.51] **Suspended sentence and fine.** For many offences it is possible to impose a fine as well as a suspended term of imprisonment. Courts must consider a fine but care should be taken in deciding such matters. If the defendant pays the monetary part of the penalty and then after a further offence is ordered to serve the prison sentence he may feel that he has been sentenced twice for his offence. On the other hand, if he is given a suspended sentence and avoids conviction during the operational period he may feel he has got away with it. Some would argue that the court ordering the suspended sentence to take effect would reduce the period because the monetary penalty had been paid, but this is neither a logical nor legally attractive argument. A careful explanation from the chairman emphasising the dual obligations of a single sentence is recommended. If the defendant defaults on the monetary part of his penalty he will be liable to imprisonment in accordance with the scale at B[33.40], not to the sentence which has been suspended.

Ancillary orders

B[37.52] Compensation at B[18]

Costs at B[20]

Disqualification at C[5]

Endorsement at C[5]

Deprivation of property and forfeiture at B[34]

Restitution order at B[39]

Early release**

B[37.53]–[37.54] A person subject to a term of imprisonment for less than 12 months will automatically be released after he has served one half of the term. The Offender Rehabilitation Act 2014 prospectively changes this to place any person who was an adult when released from a sentence of longer than one day and less than two years to be on licence until the expiry of the sentence and then under supervision until the end of 12 months from the date of release.

B[37.55] When sentencing for the new offence, the court can take into account the fact that it was committed in breach of a home detention curfew as an aggravating factor. In *R v Teasdale* [2003] Crim LR 657, CA it is made clear that if a defendant commits an offence while on licence form prison and it is dealt with under s 116 of the PCC(S)A, the court should take into account any period of custody served following an administrative recall and deduct it from the maximum available under s 116. If the defendant is a short term prisoner, a double period could be deducted as the defendant would be entitled to release half way through the term.

Parenting order

(Crime and Disorder Act 1998, ss 8–10; Anti-social Behaviour Act 2003, ss 19–28)

B[37A.1] Criteria. In any court proceedings where:

(a)   a child safety order is made in respect of the child;

(b)   an anti-social behaviour order or sex offender order is made in respect of a child or young person;

(c)   a child or young person is convicted of an offence; or

(d)   a person is convicted of an offence under s 443 (failure to comply with school attendance order) or s 444 (failure to secure regular attendance at school of registered pupil) of the Education Act 1996,

and the court is satisfied that the relevant condition is fulfilled, it may make a parenting order in respect of person who is a parent or guardian of the child or young person or, as the case may be, the person convicted of the offence under s 443 or 444 of the 1996 Act.

B[37A.2] Offenders under 16. Where a person under the age of 16 is convicted of an offence, the court by or before which he is so convicted, if it is satisfied that the relevant condition is fulfilled, shall make a parenting order, and if it is not so satisfied, shall state in open court that it is not and why it is not: Crime and Disorder Act 1998, s 9(1).

B[37A.3] Cases of exclusion from school and truancy. The Anti-social Behaviour Act 2003 introduced parenting contracts in cases of exclusion from school and truancy, and parenting orders in cases of exclusion. In relation to the latter, the exclusion must be on disciplinary grounds (whether for a fixed period or permanently), and such conditions as may be prescribed by regulations must be satisfied. Subject to the above, a local education authority can apply in accordance with the Magistrates' Courts (Parenting Orders) Regulations 2004 to the magistrates' court for a parenting order and the court may make such an order if it is satisfied that such an order would be desirable in the interests of improving the behaviour of the pupil: Anti-social Behaviour Act 2003, s 20.

In making its decision the court must take into account any refusal by the parent to enter into a parenting contract or, if the parent has entered into such a contract, and failure to comply with its requirements. The requirements and consequence of breach specified below in relation to parenting orders made under the Crime and Disorder Act 1998 apply also to orders made under the 2003 Act.

B[37A.4] Parenting contracts for criminal conduct and anti-social behaviour. The Anti-social Behaviour Act 2003 also introduced parenting contracts and parenting orders in respect of criminal conduct and anti-social behaviour, following a reference to a youth offending team. Where a child has been so referred, the team may enter into the contract with a parent or it may apply in accordance with the 2004 regulations to the court for a parenting order. The court may make the latter if it is satisfied that the child or young person has engaged in criminal conduct or anti-social behaviour and an order would be desirable in the interests of preventing the child in engaging in further such conduct: Anti-social Behaviour Act 2003, s 26. In making its decision the court must take into account any refusal by the parent to enter into a parenting contract or, if the parent has entered into such a contract, any failure to comply with its requirements. The requirements and consequences of breach specified below in relation to parenting orders made under the Crime and Disorder Act 1998 apply also to orders made under the 2003 Act.

B[37A.5] The 'relevant condition'. The relevant condition is that a parenting order would be desirable in the interests of preventing:

(i)   in a case falling within **B[37A.1]** (a) or (b), any repetition of the kind of behaviour which led to the child safety order, anti-social behaviour order or sex offender order being made;

(ii)   in a case falling within paragraph (c), the commission of any further offence by the child or young person;

(iii)   in a case falling within paragraph (d) above, the commission of any further offence under s 443 or 444 of the Education Act 1996.

A parenting order is an order which requires the parent:

(i)   to comply, for a period not exceeding 12 months, with such requirements as are specified in the order; and

(ii)   to attend, for a concurrent period not exceeding three months and not more than once in any week, such counselling or guidance sessions as may be specified in directions given by the responsible officer: Crime and Disorder Act 1998, s 8(4).

However, the court need not include the last mentioned requirement in any case where a parenting order has been made in respect of the parent on a previous occasion.

A counselling or guidance session may be or may include a residential course, provided that the court is satisfied as to the likely effectiveness of such a course (as compared with a non-residential course) to prevent repetition of the kind of behaviour or the commission of a further offence and provided that any interference with family life likely to occur from attendance at the course is proportionate in all the circumstances: Crime and Disorder Act 1998, s 8(7A).

A court shall not make a parenting order unless it has been notified by the Secretary of State that arrangements for implementing such orders are available in the area in which it appears to the court that the parent resides or will reside and the notice has not been withdrawn.

B[37A.6] Duty to obtain and consider information. Before making a parenting order in a case within **B[37A.1]** paragraph (a), in a case falling within paragraph (b) or (c) where the person concerned is under the age of 16, or in a case falling within paragraph (d) where the person to whom the offence related is under that age, a court must obtain and consider information about the person's family circumstances and the likely effect of the order on those circumstances.

B[37A.7] Duty to explain. Before making a parenting order, a court must explain to the parent in ordinary language:

(i)   the effect of the order and of the requirements proposed to be included in it;

(ii)   the consequences which may follow if he fails to comply with any of those requirements; and

(iii)   that the court has power to review the order on the application either of the parent or of the responsible officer: Crime and Disorder Act 1998, s 9(7).

B[37A.8] Requirements that may be specified. The requirements that may be specified in a parenting order under s 8(4)(a) of the Crime and Disorder Act 1998 are those which the court considers desirable in the interests of preventing any such repetition or, as the case may be, the commission of any such further offence.

Requirements specified in, and directions given under, a parenting order shall, so far as practicable, be such as to avoid any conflict with the parent's religious beliefs, and any interference with the times, if any, at which he normally works or attends an educational establishment.

B[37A.9] Discharge and variation. If while a parenting order is in force it appears to the court which made it, on the application of the responsible officer or the parent, that it is appropriate to do so, the court may make an order discharging the parenting order or varying it by cancelling any provision included in it, or by inserting in it any provision that could have been included in the order if the court had then had power to make it and were exercising the power. Where an application for the discharge of a parenting order is dismissed, no further application for its discharge shall be made by any person except with the consent of the court which made the order: Crime and Disorder Act 1998, s 9(50, (6).

B[37A.10] Penalty for non-compliance. If while a parenting order is in force the parent without reasonable excuse fails to comply with any requirement included in the order, or specified in directions given by the responsible officer, he shall be liable on summary conviction to a fine not exceeding level 3 on the standard scale: Crime and Disorder Act 1998, s 9(7).

B[37A.11] Meaning of 'responsible officer'. References above to a responsible officer mean one of the following who is specified in the order, namely a probation officer, a social worker of a local authority social services department, and member of a youth offending team: Crime and Disorder Act 1998, s 8(8).

B[37A.12] Right of appeal. An appeal shall lie to the High Court against the making of a parenting order by virtue of B[37A.1] (a) above, and to the Crown Court against the making of a parenting order by virtue of paragraph (b): Crime and Disorder Act 1998, s 10(1). On such an appeal the High Court or the Crown Court may make such orders as may be necessary to give effect to its determination of the appeal and may also make such incidental or consequential orders as appear to it to be just.

In relation to parenting orders made under the Anti-social Behaviour Act 2003, appeals lie to the Crown Court.

A person in respect of whom a parenting order is made by virtue of B[37A.1] paragraphs (c) or (d) above shall have the same right of appeal against the making of the order as if the order were a sentence passed on him for the offence.

Reparation order

(Powers of Criminal Courts (Sentencing) Act 2000, s 73)

Limitations

B[38.1] May only be made in the Youth Court. The offence involved need not be serious enough to merit a community penalty.

B[38.2] A reparation order may not be made if the court proposes to pass a custodial sentence or to make a youth rehabilitation order or a referral order.

Maximum periods

B[38.3] A reparation order may not require the offender to work for more than 24 hours in all, or to make reparation to any person without the consent of that person.

B[38.4] The reparation must be made within three months of the making of the order.

Reports

B[38.5] The order does not require a full pre-sentence report (PSR) but before making a reparation order the court must obtain and consider a report indicating:

(a)   the type of work that is suitable for the offender; and
(b)   the attitude of the victim or victims to the requirements proposed to be included in the order.

General consideration

B[38.6]–[38.7] A reparation order should be considered in less serious cases where the court wishes to

* take into account the feelings and wishes of the victims of crime; and
* prevent the young offender from committing further offences by confronting him with the consequences of his criminal behaviour, and allowing him to make some amends.

B[38.8] Reparation can be in the form of direct or indirect reparation. The court will require a report setting out the reparation activities appropriate, such as writing a letter of apology or meeting the victim in person to apologise, repairing criminal damage for which the young person has been responsible, cleaning graffiti, and working on an environmental or other community project.

B[38.9]–[38.15] Reparation carried out under a reparation order should be reparation in kind rather than financial reparation. Courts are already able to make a compensation order if they believe that financial reparation is appropriate.

Reasons

B[38.16] The court must give reasons if it does not make an order where it has power to do so.

Breach of the order

B[38.17] The responsible officer will instigate breach proceedings.

B[38.18] The powers available to the court are:

(a)   fine up to level 3 or,
(b)   revoke and re-sentence for the original offence; or
(c)   in the case of an order made by the Crown Court the magistrates can commit the offender on bail or in custody until he can be brought up or appear before the Crown Court.

Restitution order

(Powers of Criminal Courts (Sentencing) Act 2000, s 148)

B[39.1] Where goods have been stolen and a person is convicted of any offence with reference to the theft (whether or not the stealing is the gist of his offence) or such an offence is taken into consideration the court may make a restitution order.

B[39.2] Stolen includes obtaining by deception or blackmail.

B[39.3] Restitution. The court:

(a) may simply order the defendant to restore the goods to the person entitled to them whether or not any application is made for restitution; or

(b) (where an application has been made) order the delivery over of any goods directly or indirectly representing the proceeds of the stolen goods; or

(c) where money was taken from the possession of the accused on his apprehension, order its payment to the aggrieved,

but the beneficiary of the restitution must not receive more than the value of the original goods, a matter particularly to note when a combination of orders under (b) and (c) is made.

B[39.4] Innocent purchasers. Sometimes the thief has sold the goods to an innocent purchaser. The goods will be restored to the owner but the court may also order the defendant to pay out of any monies in his possession when apprehended a sum to the innocent third party up to the amount he paid for the goods.

B[39.5] Making a restitution order. Can be made on conviction of the offender whether or not sentencing is otherwise deferred.

B[39.6] Evidence. In the opinion of the court the relevant facts must sufficiently appear from the evidence at the trial, or available documents (ie witness statements, depositions or other documents which were made for use and would have been admissible as evidence in the proceedings) together with any other admissions made.

B[41]–B[46]

Football banning orders

(Football Spectators Act 1989, ss 14 and 22 and Football (Disorder) Act 2000)

Criminal orders

B[41.1] A banning order means an order made under Part II of the Football Spectators Act 1989 which:

(a)   in relation to regulated football matches in the UK, prohibits the person who is subject to the order from entering any premises for the purpose of attending such matches; and

(b)   in relation to football matches outside the UK, requires that person to report to a police station in accordance with Part II.

B[41.2] A **regulated football match** is an association football match (whether in the United Kingdom or elsewhere) which is a prescribed match or a match of a prescribed description.

The Football Spectators (Prescription) Order 2004, SI 2004/2409, as amended, provides:

'3.(1) An association football match (in England and Wales) described in paragraphs (2) or (3) shall be a regulated football match for the purposes of Part II of the 1989 Act.

(2) A regulated match is an association football match in which one or both of the participating teams represents–

(a)   a club which is for the time being a member (whether a full or associate member) of the Football League, the Football Association Premier League, the Football Conference, the Welsh Premier League or the Scottish Professional Football League;

(b)   a club whose home ground is situated outside England and Wales; or

(c)   a country or territory.

(3) A regulated football match is an association football match played in the Football Association Cup (other than in a preliminary or qualifying round).

4.(1) An association football match (outside England and Wales) described in paragraph (2) shall be a regulated football match for the purposes of Part II of the 1989 Act.

(2) A regulated match is an association football match involving-

(a)   a national team appointed by the Football Association to represent England or appointed by the Football Association of Wales to represent Wales;

(b)   a team representing a club which is for the time being a member (whether a full or associate member) of the Football League, the Football Association Premier League, the Football Conference, the Welsh Premier League, the Scottish Professional Football League;

(c)   a team representing any country or territory whose football association is for the time being a member of FIFA, where–

  (i)   the match is part of a competition or tournament organised by, or under the authority of, FIFA or UEFA, and

  (ii)   the competition or tournament is one in which a team referred to in sub-paragraph (a) above is eligible to participate or has participated; or

(d)   a team representing a club which is for the time being a member (whether a full or associate member) of, or affiliated to, a national football association which is a member of FIFA, where–

  (i)   (the match is part of a competition or tournament organised by, or under the authority of, FIFA or UEFA, and

  (ii)   the competition or tournament is one in which a club referred to in sub-paragraph (b) above is eligible to participate or has participated.

B[41.3] Failure to comply with a banning order is a criminal offence triable only by magistrates with a maximum penalty on level 5 and six months' imprisonment.

B[41.4] **Relevant offence** means:

(1) An offence in the Football Spectators Act 1989, Sch 1 which includes:

(a)   an offence under the Sporting Events (Control of Alcohol etc) Act 1985, s 2;

(b)   offences under the Public Order Act 1986, s 5 and Part III (racial hatred or sexual orientation);

(c)   an offence involving the threat or use of violence to a person or property: this includes an offence under Public Order Act 1986, s 4(1)(a) (*R v O' Keefe* (2004))

(d)   offences under the Football (Offences) Act 1991.

See Football Spectators Act 1989, Sch 1 (as amended) for an exhaustive list.

B[41.5] Offences (b)–(d) must be committed during a period relevant to a designated football match at any premises while the accused was at, or was entering or leaving or trying to enter or leave, the premises. Therefore a defendant convicted of a public order offence on a train travelling away from a match he had been refused entry to was on a factual basis not related to a football match (*R v Smith* [2002] EWCA Crim 683, [2003] 1 Cr App Rep 212).

There is, however, no need to prove in a criminal case the civil requirements that the defendants caused or contributed to violence or disorder: s 14B (*R (on the application of Brown) v Inner London Crown Court* [2003] EWHC 3194 (Admin), [2003] All ER (D) 256 (Dec)).

B[41.6] **Relevant period.** A period beginning 24 hours before the start of the match or, if earlier, 24 hours before the time it is advertised to start or the time at which spectators are first admitted to the premises, and ends 24 hours after the end of the match. Where a match is postponed or cancelled, the period includes the 24 hours before and 24 hours after the advertised start of the event. Regulated football match' for the purposes of these offences and those described below (a)–(d) is described above.

B[41.7] (2) The following offences committed on a journey to or from a designated football match where the court makes a declaration that the offence related to football matches:

(a) offences under (b) and (c) above;
(b) drunkenness;
(c) an offence under the Sporting Events (Control of Alcohol etc) Act 1985, s 1;
(d) driving whilst unfit or over the prescribed limit of alcohol: Road Traffic Act 1988, ss 4 and 5

"Related to a football match" is to be given its ordinary meaning (*DPP v Beaumont* [2008] EWHC 523 (Admin); *R v Arbery and Mobley* [2008] EWCA Crim 702).

In *R v Pakes; R v Cartwright* [2010] EWCA Crim 2803, [2011] 2 Cr App Rep (S) 54, 175 JP 33, it was decided that the spark which caused the violence was related to football, that is a match between two Championship sides. From what occurred it was clear that there was hostility between two sets of rival supporters. It mattered not that one of the appellants did not go to an area of the West Midlands looking for trouble; the fact that he became caught up in the hostility which erupted between two rival sets of fans was sufficient.

Where violence arose out of a racial incident between two sets of football supporters outside a London pub and not in relation to the match or matches, the offences could not be said to be "football-related" and banning orders under s 14A were quashed on appeal (*R v Arbery and Mobley* supra; *R v Craig Mabee* [2007] EWCA Crim 3230).

For the court to make a 'declaration of related to', an offence of affray had to be committed in the circumstances stipulated by Schedule 1. Further, there had to be reasonable grounds to believe that the making of a banning order would help to prevent violence or disorder at or in connection with any regulated football matches. In the present case, the court did not so determine and the evidence showed only that the affray arose out of the fact that the defendants were drunk, rather than that it had any connection to football: *R v Doyle; R v Wise; R v Wise* [2012] EWCA Crim 995, 176 JP 337, 176 CL&J 322.

B[41.8] The prosecution must normally give five days' notice of its intention to seek a declaration that the offence related to football matches.

B[41.9] (3) Offences under paras (a) and (c) committed on journeys to designated matches played outside the United Kingdom.

B[41.10]–[41.15] (4) 'Corresponding offences' committed in countries designated from time to time by the Secretary of State.

B[41.16] Therefore an order can be made in respect of a relevant offence whether committed in the United Kingdom or abroad, and the restriction order will apply to designated matches both domestically and internationally.

B[41.17] Offences committed abroad. Where the relevant offence was committed abroad the court may, on information being laid, issue a summons or warrant to bring the offender before the court to consider whether to make a restriction order.

B[41.18] Criterion. The court must make a football banning order in relation to the offender if satisfied that there are reasonable grounds to believe that it would help to prevent violence or disorder at or in connection with regulated football matches. Repetition and propensity are not required for the making of an order under s 14A, and the court is entitled to take into account and to give weight to the question of deterrence: *R (on the application of White) v Crown Court at Blackfriars* [2008] EWHC 510 (Admin), (2008) 172 JP 321. See also *R v Lewis Cash Curtis* [2009] EWCA Crim 1225, [2010] 1 Cr App R (S) 193 where a banning order was upheld even though the behaviour was an isolated first incident in the case of the defendant. If it does not make an order the court must state in open court its reasons for not being satisfied an order was required: see r 50.2 of the Criminal Procedure Rules 2013.

It is important that courts who are considering the rather complex provisions of the Football Spectators Act 1989 should have in mind the nature of the regime for which it provides. It should also address its mind to the differences between the consequences of a football banning order on the one hand and a prohibited activities requirement attached either to a suspended sentence or a community order on the other. They are not to be treated as equivalents.

There is some difference between the two kinds of order as to sanction. Disobedience to a football banning order is itself an offence, whereas disobedience to a prohibited activity requirement is not. But there is ample sanction for disobedience to a prohibited activity requirement because if it is attached to a suspended sentence the suspended sentence can be activated for breach, and if it is attached to a community order then on breach the court can re-sentence for the original offence and that may well involve loss of liberty. The principal difference between the two forms of order lies in the regime which exists. There is quite a sophisticated regime for the co-ordination of intelligence relating to those who are subject to football banning orders. Where such an order is in contemplation, courts who are addressing the test of whether making an order would help to prevent violence or disorder ought to have in mind the extent of the regime as well of course as its potentially draconian effect: *R v Boggild* [2011] EWCA Crim 1928, 175 CL&J 502, (2011) Times, 5 September.

B[41.19]–[41.20] Procedure. Since 6 April 2007, amendments to the primary legislation have been made to allow a court to remand an offender where proceedings are adjourned under s 14A Football Spectators Act 1989.

May only be made in addition to a sentence (which includes a community rehabilitation order and an order for conditional or absolute discharge) imposed in respect of the offence of which the accused was convicted. The court must:

(a)   certify that the offence is a relevant offence where appropriate;
(b)   specify the police station in England and Wales at which the person must report initially;
(c)   explain to the person the effect of the order in ordinary language;
(d)   give a copy of the order to the defendant, and send copies to the Football Banning Orders Authority and the Chief Executive of the Football Association, the specified police station and, if appropriate, the relevant prison governor. The relevant authority is currently

based at: UK Football Policing Unit, Football Banning Orders Authority, PO Box 51997, London, SW9 6TN. The Chief Executive of the Football Association is currently based at: Football Association, 25 Soho Square, London, W1D 4FA.

B[41.21] Duration. Where the person receives an immediate prison sentence but not other forms of detention the mandatory period is a maximum of 10 years and a minimum of 6 years. In any other football case the maximum is 5 years and the minimum three years. In a non-football-related offence, the period is between two and three years.

B[41.22] Effect. The person is under a duty to report initially to the police station specified in the order within five days of the making of the order and thereafter to report to a police station specified when notified by the Banning Orders Authority. Note a banning order is not a punishment for the purposes of ECHR Art 7 (*Gough v Chief Constable of Derbyshire* [2001] EWHC 554 (Admin), [2002] QB 459; affd sub nom *Gough v Chief Constable of Derbyshire Constabulary* [2002] EWCA Civ 351, [2002] 2 All ER 985).

B[41.22A] Further obligatory requirements. A banning order must require the person subject to the order to give notification within seven day to the enforcing authority of the events listed below within seven days beginning with the day of occurrence:

(a)   a change of any of his names;
(b)   the first use by him after the making of the order of a name for himself that was not disclosed by him at the time of making the order;
(c)   a change of his home address;
(d)   his acquisition of a temporary address;
(e)   a change of his temporary address or ceasing to have one;
(f)   his becoming aware of the loss of his travel authorisation;
(g)   receipt by him of a new travel authorisation;
(h)   an appeal by him in relation to the order;
(i)   an application by for him for the termination of the order;
(j)   an appeal against the making of a declaration of relevance in respect of an offence of which he has been convicted.

A banning order must impose a requirement as to the surrender in accordance with Part II of the Football Spectators Act 1989, in connection with regulated football matches outside the UK, of the travel authorisation of the person subject to the order.

Provision is made by s 19 of the Football Spectators Act 1989 for the making of further requirements by the enforcing authority, ie the Football Banning Order Authority. When a person subject to a banning order reports initially at the police station, the officer responsible for the station may make such requirements of that person as are determined by the enforcing authority to be necessary or expedient for giving effect to the banning order, so far as relating to regulated football matches outside the UK. If, in relation to any such match, the enforcing authority is of the opinion that requiring any person subject to a banning order to report is necessary or expedient to reduce the likelihood of violence or disorder at or in connection with the match, the authority must give that person a written notice to report to the police station specified at the specified time and to surrender his travel authorisation. The notice may also include additional requirements.

The enforcing authority is also empowered by notice to impose additional requirements in the case of any regulated football match.

A notice under s 19 may not require reporting/surrender of travel authorisation except with the control period. The notice must require the recipient to state where he intends to stay or has stayed for one night or more during the control period.

B[41.23] Exemption may be granted from reporting in respect of a particular match either an application to the Banning Orders Authority or in cases of urgency to the police. Exemption might be granted, for example, to cover a stay in hospital or the funeral of a close relative.

B[41.24] Application to terminate. The person subject to the order may apply to the court to terminate the order after two-thirds of the period determined has expired.

B[41.25]–[41.30] The court will have regard to the person's character, his conduct since the order was made, the nature of the offence which led to it and any other circumstances of the case.

B[41.31] Further application may not be made within six months of a refusal.

B[41.32] Appeal is to the Crown Court against the making of a banning order or a refusal to award compensation (see below). Prosecutors can now appeal to the Crown Court against the refusal of a magistrates' court to make a banning order on conviction of a "*relevant offence*" (s 14A(5A) Football Spectators Act 1989). These relevant offences are listed in schedule 1 to the Football Spectators Act 1989.

B[41.33] Civil applications. In addition to its imposition as a result of a football-related conviction, a banning order may be imposed by a magistrates' court in accordance with a civil procedure, following a complaint by the police. The requirement that applications by complaint could only be made by the Chief Constable of the area where the individual resides was removed by the Violent Crime Reduction Act 2006. Applications can be made by any Chief Constable including the Chief Constable of the British Transport Police and the Director of Public Prosecutions.

The Violent Crime Reduction Act 2006 removed the statutory time limit of 27 August 2007 for making an application on complaint for a football banning order on complaint under s 14B Football Spectators Act 1989. Also, the power of summary detention by a police constable (as distinct from arrest) under s 21A of the 1989 Act has been removed.

The court must be satisfied that the person who is the subject of the complaint has at any time caused or contributed to any violence or disorder in the United Kingdom or elsewhere, and that there are reasonable grounds to believe that making a banning order would help to prevent violence or disorder at or in connection with any regulated football matches. This is a civil order and not a sentence (*Gough v Chief Constable of Derbyshire* [2001] EWHC 554 (Admin), [2002] QB 459; affd sub nom *Gough v Chief Constable of Derbyshire Constabulary* [2002] EWCA Civ 351, [2002] 2 All ER 985).

B[41.34] If, during a control period when international bans are activated, a police officer has reasonable grounds for suspecting that a person before him or her has caused or contributed to any violence or disorder in the United Kingdom or elsewhere, and for believing that imposing a banning order on that person would help to prevent violence or disorder at or in connection with any regulated football matches, the officer may, with the authorisation of an inspector of police, give the person a notice in writing requiring him or her to appear before a magistrates' court within 24 hours and in the meantime not to leave England and Wales. The magistrates' court will then treat the notice as an application for a banning order under the new civil procedure. Section 14B of the 1989 Act was further amended by the Violent Crime Reduction Act 2006 so that magistrates' Courts are now empowered to remand a respondent when adjourning proceedings on complaint.

B[41.35] Appeal. The respondent may appeal to the Crown Court against the making by a magistrates' court of a banning order on complaint (s 14D Football Spectators Act 1989).

B[41.36] Compensation Where a notice has been issued by a police officer under these powers and a court subsequently refuses to impose a banning order, the court may order compensation up to £5000 to be paid to that person out of central funds if it is satisfied that the notice should not have been given in the first place, that the person has suffered loss as a result of the notice, and that it is appropriate to order the payment of compensation in respect of that loss. There is no statutory definition of the word refuse and so presumably if the police seek to withdraw the proceedings the right to compensation is lost although the right to apply for legal costs remains.

B[41.37] Length of order The minimum civil order has been altered by the Violent Crime Reduction Act 2006. The minimum order will last for three years and the maximum five years.

B[47]

Forfeiture or suspension of personal liquor licence

(Licensing Act 2003, s 129)

B[47.1] Where an offender who holds a personal licence to supply alcohol is charged with a "relevant offence", he or she is required to produce the licence to the court, or inform the court of its existence, no later than his or her first court appearance.

"Relevant offences" are listed in Sch 4 of the Licensing Act 2003 and are set out below.

Where the offender is convicted the court may order forfeiture of the licence or suspend it for up to 6 months pursuant to s 129 (2) LA 2003. When deciding whether to order forfeiture or suspension, the court may take account of the offender's previous convictions for "relevant offences" (s 129 (3)).

Whether or not forfeiture or suspension is ordered, the court is required to notify the licensing authority of the offender's conviction and the sentence imposed.

B[47.2] "Relevant offence"

These include:

- An offence under the Licensing Act 2003
- An offence under the Firearms Act 1968
- Theft – s 1 Theft Act 1968
- Burglary – s 9 Theft Act 1968
- Abstracting electricity – s 13 Theft Act 1968
- Handling stolen goods – s 22 Theft Act 1968
- Going equipped for theft etc – s 25 Theft Act 1968
- Production of a controlled drug – s 4(2) Misuse of Drugs Act 1971
- Supply of a controlled drug – s 4(3) Misuse of Drugs Act 1971
- Possession with intent to supply – s 5(3) Misuse of Drugs Act 1971
- Evasion of duty – s 170 Customs and Excise Management Act 1979 (except s 170(1)(a))
- Driving/attempting to drive while unfit through drink or drugs – s 4 RTA 1988
- In charge of a motor vehicle when unfit through drink or drugs – s 4 RTA 1988
- Driving/attempting to drive with excess alcohol – s 5 RTA 1988
- In charge of a vehicle with excess alcohol – s 5 RTA 1988
- Unauthorised use of a trade mark where the goods in question are or include alcohol – ss 92(1) and 92(2) Trade Marks Act 1994
- Sexual assault – s 3 SOA 2003
- Exploitation of prostitution – ss 52 and 53 SOA 2003
- Exposure – s 66 SOA 2003
- Voyeurism – s 67 SOA 2003
- A violent offence, being any offence which leads, or is intended to lead, to death or to physical injury

B[48]–B[49]

Referral order

(Powers of Criminal Courts (Sentencing) Act 2000, s 16)

Limitations

B[48.1] Although an order can be made by an adult magistrates' court it is recommended that offenders aged 10–17 years should normally be remitted from a magistrates' court to the youth court to be dealt with, including the imposition of a referral order.

B[48.2] Age limits – Person in respect of whom the order is made must be under 18.

B[48.3] Maximum period – 12 months.

B[48.4] Minimum period – 3 months.

B[48.5] Consent – Consent of offender not required.

Ancillary orders

B[48.6] Compensation at B[18]

Costs at B[20]

Disqualification at C[5]

Endorsement at C[5]

Deprivation of property and forfeiture at B[34]

Parenting order B[37A]

Restitution at B[39]

General considerations

B[48.7] Where a youth aged 10–17 years is before a court for an offence where neither the offence nor a connected offence is one for which the sentence is fixed by law eg murder; the court is not proposing to impose a custodial sentence or make a hospital order (within the meaning of the Mental Health Act 1983); and, the court is not proposing to discharge the youth absolutely or conditionally, if referral is available, the court must, if the compulsory referral conditions are satisfied, or may, if the discretionary referral conditions are satisfied, sentence the youth for the offence by ordering him to be referred to a youth offender panel.

Referral is available within England and Wales following notification from the Secretary of State. The relevant youth offender panel will be located in the area in which the youth resides or will reside.

Connected offence. An offence is connected with another if the youth falls to be dealt with at the same time as he is dealt with for the other offence whether or not he is convicted of the offences at the same time by or before the same court.

Compulsory referral conditions. The offence is punishable with imprisonment and the offender pleaded guilty to the offence and to any connected offence and he has never been convicted by or before a court in the UK of any other than the offence and the connected offence or convicted by or before a court in another member State of any offence: Powers of Criminal Courts (Sentencing) Act 200, s 17(1).

Discretionary referral conditions. The compulsory referral conditions are not satisfied in relation to the offence and the offender pleaded guilty to the offence or, if the offender is being dealt with by the court for the offence and any connected offence, to at least one of those offences: Powers of Criminal Courts (Sentencing) Act 200, s 17(2).

Previous conviction. A conviction resulting in the imposition of a conditional discharge is not a conviction for the purposes of the referral conditions.

Appropriate officer. A member of a youth offending team; an officer of a local probation board; or an officer of a provider of probation services.

Attendance of parent or guardian. On making a referral order, the court may order a parent or guardian (which includes a representative of a local authority where the youth is being looked after by that authority), to attend meetings of the youth offender panel.

Prohibited orders

B[48.8] Where a court makes a referral order in respect of an offence it may not deal with him for the offence in any of the prohibited ways. In respect of a connected offence, the court must either make a referral order or an absolute discharge and may not deal with the offence in any of the prohibited ways.

The prohibited ways are:

(a)   a community sentence;
(b)   a fine;
(c)   a reparation order;
(d)   a conditional discharge;
(e)   a bind over; and
(f)   binding over of parent or guardian.

Where the compulsory referral conditions are satisfied the court may not defer sentence but its power of remission to another court, adjournment, committal to the Crown Court or under the mental health legislation are unaffected.

Variation and discharge

B[48.9] Courts have a discretion to discharge referral orders early on application for good behaviour.

Likewise, courts have the option of extending the term of the referral order for up to three months, on application and, at the recommendation of the youth offender panel, eg, in cases of breach. Note the extension cannot exceed the overall maximum of 12 months.

B[48.10] Breach. The young offender may be referred back to the court for a revocation of the order if he fails to attend the panel, fails to agree a contract or fails to comply with the terms of the contract.

On receiving a report of a breach the court must summons or issue a warrant for the appearance of the juvenile.

On his appearance they must consider if the panel was right to refer the breach back. If they decide it was not then the order continues.

If a breach is proved, the court may revoke the order and deal with the original offence in any way it could have done, other than making a referral order.

When dealing with the youth, the court must have regard to:

(i)   the circumstances of his referral back to the court; and
(ii)   the extent of his compliance, if any, with the terms of his referral contract.

Appeal. On a breach, where the court revokes the referral order and deals with the youth for the original offence(s), he may appeal to the Crown Court against the sentence.

There is also power to extend the period of the referral order for offences committed before and during the currency of the order. This may be done once only and must not extend the order beyond the 12 month maximum.

The Youth Rehabilitation Order

B[50.1] The youth rehabilitation order (YRO) was introduced by the Criminal Justice and Immigration Act 2008 for offenders aged under 18. It is a single generic community sentence. It replaced action plan, supervision, intensive supervision, curfew and exclusion orders, and prospectively replaces attendance centre orders. It also replaced community orders in relation to 16 and 17-year-olds (for which provision was made by the Criminal Justice Act 2003, but was never implemented).

YROs are also subject to the restrictions that apply to the making of community sentences generally.

The definitive guideline of the Sentencing Guidelines Council 'Overarching Principles – Sentencing Youths' contains guidance at paragraph 10 on the availability, making and treatment of breach of YROs.

Requirements which may be included: CJ & IA 2008, s 1

B[50.2] When imposing a YRO the court is able to choose one or more requirements from the following 'menu':

- an activity requirement (B[50.6]);
- a supervision requirement (B[50.7]);
- if the offender is aged 16 or 17, an unpaid work requirement (B[50.8]);
- a programme requirement (B[50.9]);
- an attendance centre requirement (B[50.10]);
- a prohibited activity requirement (B[50.11]);
- a curfew requirement (B[50.12]);
- an exclusion requirement (B[50.13]);
- a residence requirement (B[50.14]);
- a local authority residence requirement (B[50.15]);
- a mental health treatment requirement (B[50.17], B[50.18]);
- a drug treatment requirement (B[50.19]);
- an intoxicating substance treatment requirement (B[50.20]);
- an education requirement ([B[50.21]).

Electronic monitoring: CJ & IA 2008, Sch 1, Pt 1, para 2

B[50.3] A YRO may also impose an electronic monitoring requirement and must do so if the YRO imposes a curfew or exclusion requirement unless, in the circumstances of the particular case, the court is satisfied that it would be inappropriate to do so, or it is not practicable to do so either because a third party whose co-operation would be required does not consent or the relevant arrangements for electronic monitoring are not available in the relevant local justice area.

Intensive supervision and fostering: CJ & IA 2008, s 1(3), (4)

B[50.4] A YRO may include intensive supervision and surveillance ('an extended activity requirement', where the number of days exceeds the normal limit of 90 up to a maximum of 180) or a fostering requirement, subject to certain sentencing threshold and other conditions, namely:

(a)   the offence or offences are punishable with imprisonment;
(b)   the offence or the combination of the offence and offences associated with it is so serious that, but for these provisions, a custodial sentence would be appropriate or, if the offender is aged under 12 at the time of conviction, would have been appropriate if he had been aged 12 or older; and
(c)   if the offender is aged 12-15 years, he is a persistent offender.

These restrictions do not, however, prevent the making of a YRO with intensive supervision and surveillance if the offender has failed to comply with an order under s 161(2) of the Criminal Justice Act 2003 (pre-sentence drug testing).

In the case of a fostering requirement, the court must additionally be satisfied that the behaviour which constituted the offence was due to a significant extent to the circumstances in which the offender was living and that the imposition of a fostering requirement would assist in the offender's rehabilitation: CJ & IA 2008, Sch 1, Pt 1, para 4. See further B[50.16], below.

An extended activity requirement must be accompanied by a supervision requirement and a curfew requirement (and accordingly an electronic monitoring requirement, as above): CJ & IA 2008, Sch 1, Pt 1, para 3. It cannot, however, be accompanied by a fostering requirement: CJ & IA 2008, Sch 1, Pt 1, para 4. Subject to this, before a court makes a YRO containing two or more requirements, or two or more YROs in relation to associated offences, it must consider whether the requirements to be imposed are mutually compatible: CJ & IA 2008, Sch 1, Pt 1, para 29.

The court must also ensure, as far as practicable, that any requirement avoids any conflict with the offender's religious beliefs, or interference with his work or education, or any conflict with the requirements of any other YRO to which he may be subject: CJ & IA 2008, Sch 1, Pt 1, para 29.

Duration: CJ & IA 2008, Sch 1, Pt 1, paras 30, 32

B[50.4A] A YRO takes effect on the day after the day on which it was made, unless the offender is subject to a detention and training order in which case the court may direct that the YRO will take effect when the period of supervision under the DTO begins or on the expiry of the term of the DTO.

A youth rehabilitation order must specify a date, 'the end date', not more than three years after the date on which the order takes effect, by which all the requirements in it must have been complied with. If a youth rehabilitation order imposes two or more different requirements, the order may also specify a date by which each of those requirements must have been complied with; and the last of those dates must be the same as the end date. In the case of a youth rehabilitation order with intensive supervision and surveillance, the end date must not be earlier than six months after the date on which the order takes effect. Unless revoked, a youth rehabilitation order imposing an unpaid work requirement remains in force until the offender has worked under it for the number of hours specified in it.

B[50.4B] There are provisions dealing with specifying the local justice area in which the offender resides or will reside, providing copies of the order and empowering the Secretary of State by order, inter alia, to enable or require courts to provide for periodic review of the order.

(1) Intensive supervision and surveillance requirement

B[50.5] The order may be used for juveniles where the following criteria apply:

(a)   the offence or offences are punishable with imprisonment;
(b)   the offence or the combination of the offences associate with it are so serious that, but for these provisions, a custodial sentence would be appropriate, or if the offender is under 12 at the time of conviction, would have been appropriate if he had been aged 12 or more); and
(c)   if the offender was aged 12–15 years, he is a persistent offender.

The restrictions outlined above do not apply if the offender has failed to comply with an order for pre-sentence drug testing pursuant to s 161(2) of the CJA 2003.

The court may include one or more of the other requirements (with the exception of fostering) set out below subject to the caveat that the requirements must be proportionate to the seriousness of the offence or offences.

The court may in addition make an extended activity requirement of up to 180 days. If it does so it <u>must</u> also impose a supervision requirement with electronic monitoring.

Copies of the order must be served on the offender ant other person involved with the order: CJ & IA 2008, Sch 2, para 24.

(2) Activity requirement

B[50.6] The offender must do any or all of the following:

(a)   participate, on such days as may be specified, in activities at the place or places specified by presenting himself at the place specified or to a specified person in accordance with instructions given by the responsible officer and comply with such instructions given by, or under the authority of, the person in charge of that activity;
(b)   participate in activity, or activities, specified in the order on such number of days so specified;
(c)   participate in one or more residential exercises for a continuous period or periods compromising such number of days as specified;
(d)   engage in activities in accordance with instructions of the responsible officer on such number of days as may be specified.

As far as requirement (c) above is concerned, the <u>consent</u> of a parent or guardian of the offender must be obtained.

Specified activities may include *reparation*, direct or indirect, or as directed by the responsible officer.

Before making an order the court should consult either an officer of the local probation board or a member of a youth offending team. The court must be satisfied that the activities to be specified can be made under arrangements that exist in the local justice area in which the offender resides and that it is feasible to secure compliance with those requirements. Where compliance with an activity involves the co-operation of a person other than the offender and/or the responsible officer, that person's consent must be obtained.

The aggregate number of days upon which a juvenile may be required to comply with directions must not exceed 90 unless the 'custody' criteria are satisfied (see B[50.3]) when the total number of days permitted is 180: CJ & IA 2008, s 1(4)(a)–(c).

(3) Supervision requirement

B[50.7] When a youth court makes a supervision requirement the effect is to place the juvenile under the supervision of the responsible officer or another person determined by him for the relevant period. The "relevant period" for these purposes means the period for which the order remains in force ie for up to three years. The purpose of the requirement is to promote the offender's rehabilitation.

(4) Unpaid work requirement (16 and 17 year old offenders only)

B[50.8] This is a requirement that the offender must perform unpaid work in accordance for the number of hours specified in the order, at such times as he may be instructed by the responsible officer. Unless revoked, an unpaid work requirement remains in force until the offender has completed the number of hours specified.

The number of hours which a person may be required to work under an unpaid work requirement must be specified in the relevant order and must be in the aggregate:

(a)   not less than 40, and
(b)   not more than 240.

The court may not impose an unpaid work requirement in respect of an offender unless after hearing (if the court thinks necessary) from an appropriate officer, the court is satisfied that the offender is a suitable person to perform work under such a requirement.

Where the court makes orders in respect of two or more offences of which the offender has been convicted on the same occasion and includes unpaid work requirements in each of them, the court may direct that the hours of work specified in any of those requirements is to be concurrent or consecutive. However the total number of hours must not exceed the maximum of 240 hours.

(5) Programme requirement

B[50.9] This requirement involves the offender's participation in a systematic set of activities specified in the order, on such number of days as may be specified. The court may not include a programme requirement unless:

(a)   the proposed programme has been recommended to the court as being suitable for the offender by an officer of a local probation board or a youth offending team or a provider of probation services; and

(b)   the programme is available at the specified place.

Where compliance with an activity involves the co-operation of a person other than the offender and/or the responsible officer, that person's consent must be obtained.

The programme requirement means the offender must:

(a)   in accordance with instructions given by the responsible officer, participate in the programme at the place specified in the order on the number of days specified in the order; and

(b)   while at that place, comply with instructions given by, or under the authority of, the person in charge of the programme.

(6) Attendance centre requirement

B[50.10] This is a requirement to attend at an attendance centre for any period on any occasion at the beginning of the period and, during that period, to engage in occupations, or receive instruction, under the supervision of and in accordance with instructions given by, or under the authority of the officer in charge of the centre.

The aggregate number of hours will depend on the age of the offender:

(a)   offender aged 16 or over at the time of conviction: not less than 12 and not more than 36 hours.

(b)   offender aged 14 or over but under 16 at the time of conviction: not less than 12 and not more than 24 hours

(c)   offender aged under 14 at the time of conviction: not more than 12 hours.

The court must have been notified of the availability of a centre for persons of the offender's age and sex. Regard must be paid to the accessibility of the centre to the offender.

(7) Prohibited activity requirement

B[50.11] This requires the offender to refrain from participating in activities specified in the order on a day or days so specified <u>or</u> during a period so specified.

The court must first consult either a provider of probation services such as an officer of a local probation board or a member of a youth offending team. One requirement which may be included in an order is that the offender is not to possess, use or carry a firearm within the meaning of the Firearms Act 1968. It is recommended that the court should consult first with its legal adviser before including such a requirement.

(8) Curfew requirement

B[50.12] A curfew requirement is a requirement that the offender must remain, for periods specified in the relevant order, at a place so specified. It may specify different places or different periods for different days, but may not specify periods which amount to less than two hours or more than sixteen hours in any one day.

The order may not exceed a period of 12 months beginning with the day on which it first takes effect. The court must also make an electronic monitoring requirement unless the court considers it inappropriate to do so in the particular circumstances of the case or the court is prevented from doing so eg it is not practicable to secure the co-operation of a person other than the offender: see CJ & IA 2008, Sch 1, para 26.

Before making a relevant order imposing a curfew requirement, the court must obtain and consider information about the place proposed to be specified in the order (including information as to the attitude of persons likely to be affected by the enforced presence there of the offender).

(9) Exclusion requirement

B[50.13] An exclusion requirement is a provision prohibiting the offender from entering a place named in the order for a specified period of not more than three months.

An exclusion requirement:

(a)   may provide for the prohibition to operate only during the periods specified in the order; and
(b)   may specify different places or areas for different periods or days.

The court must also make an electronic monitoring requirement unless the court considers it inappropriate to do so in the particular circumstances of the case or the court is prevented from doing so eg it is not practicable to secure the co-operation of a person other than the offender: see CJ & IA 2008, Sch 1, para 26.

(10) Residence requirement

B[50.14] This requirement is only applicable to offenders aged 16 or over at the time of conviction.

Residence means that, during a period specified in the relevant order, the offender must reside with an individual or at a place specified in the order. If the court proposes to specify residence with a named individual, that person's consent must first be obtained.

If the order makes specific provision, a residence requirement does not prohibit the offender from residing, with the prior approval of the responsible officer, at a place other than that specified in the order.

Before making a YRO containing a residence requirement, the court must consider the home surroundings of the offender.

A court may not specify a hostel or other institution as the place where an offender must reside, except on the recommendation of an officer of a local probation board, or a provider of probation services, a local authority social worker or a member of a youth offending team.

(11) Local authority residence requirement

B[50.15] Local authority residence means that, during a period specified in the relevant order, the offender must reside in accommodation provided by or on behalf of a local authority specified in the order.

The court must be satisfied that the behaviour which constituted the offence was due to a significant extent to the circumstances in which the offender was living, and that the imposition of such a requirement will assist in his rehabilitation.

The court must first consult with the local authority and a parent or guardian of the offender (unless it is not practicable to do so) and the local authority that is to receive the offender (if different). The order may stipulate that the offender is not to reside with a person specified in the order.

The order must specify the local authority in whose area the offender resides or is to reside.

Any period specified in the order as a period for which the offender must reside in accommodation provided by or on behalf of a local authority must not exceed six months, and it must not include any period after the offender attains 18 years of age.

A youth court may not include a *local authority residence requirement* in a YRO unless the offender is legally represented or funding by the Legal Services Commission has been withdrawn because of the offender's conduct; or, having been informed of his right to apply for such representation, has refused or failed to apply.

A local authority has power to place an offender with a local authority foster patent where a local authority residence requirement is imposed: CJ & IA 2008, Sch 2, Pt 2, para 18.

(12) Fostering requirement

B[50.16] During a period specified in the relevant order, the offender must reside with a local authority foster parent.

The specified period of fostering must end no later 12 months beginning with the date on which the requirement takes effect but must not include any period after the offender has attained 18 years of age. An 18-month period may be substituted following breach proceedings: CJ & IA 2008, Sch 2, paras 8 and 16.

The requirement must specify the local authority that is to place the offender with a local authority foster parent under s 23(2)(a) of the Children Act 1989. The authority so specified must be the local authority in whose area the offender resides or is to reside.

If at any time during that period the responsible officer notifies the offender that no suitable local authority foster parent is available, and that he proposes or has applied for the revocation or amendment of the YRO, the fostering requirement is, until the determination of that application, to be taken as requiring the offender to reside in accommodation provided by or on behalf of the a local authority.

Such a requirement cannot be made unless the court has been notified by the Secretary of State that arrangements for placing the offender with a local authority foster parent are available in the relevant local authority area.

(13) Mental health treatment requirement

B[50.17] This requires the offender to submit, during periods specified in the order, to treatment by or under the direction of a registered medical practitioner or a chartered psychologist (or both, for different periods) with a view to the improvement of the offender's mental condition.

The treatment required must be one of the following kinds of treatment as may be specified in the relevant order:

(a)   treatment as a resident patient in an independent hospital or care home within the meaning of the Care Standards Act 2000 or a hospital within the meaning of the Mental Health Act 1983, but not in hospital premises where high security psychiatric services within the meaning of that Act are provided;

(b)   treatment as a non-resident patient at such institution or place as may be specified in the order;

(c)   treatment by or under the direction of such registered medical practitioner or chartered psychologist (or both) as may be so specified;

The nature of the treatment may not be specified in the order except as mentioned in (a), (b) or (c) above.

A court may not by virtue of this section include a mental health treatment requirement in an order unless–

(a)   the court is satisfied, that the mental condition of the offender–
   (i)   is such as requires and may be susceptible to treatment, but
   (ii)   is not such as to warrant the making of a hospital order or guardianship order within the meaning of the Mental Health Act 1983;

(b)   the court is also satisfied that arrangements have been or can be made for the treatment intended to be specified in the order (including arrangements for the reception of the offender where he is to be required to submit to treatment as a resident patient); and

(c)   the offender has expressed his willingness to comply with such a requirement.

While the offender is under treatment as a resident patient in pursuance of a mental health requirement, his responsible officer shall carry out the supervision of the offender to such extent only as may be necessary for the purpose of the revocation or amendment of the order.

B[50.18] **Mental health treatment at place other than that specified in order** Where the medical practitioner or chartered psychologist, treating the offender in pursuance of a mental health treatment requirement, is of the opinion that part of the treatment can be better or more conveniently given in or at an institution or place which–

(a)   is not specified in the relevant order, and

(b)   is one in or at which the treatment of the offender will be given by or under the direction of a registered medical practitioner or chartered psychologist,

he may, with the consent of the offender, make arrangements for him to be treated accordingly.

These arrangements as are mentioned may provide for the offender to receive part of his treatment as a resident patient in an institution or place notwithstanding that the institution or place is not one which could have been specified for that purpose in the relevant order.

Where any such arrangements are made for the treatment of an offender the medical practitioner or chartered psychologist by whom the arrangements are made shall give notice in writing to the offender's responsible officer giving details of the place and the treatment provided.

(14) Drug treatment/drug testing requirement

B[50.19] A drug rehabilitation requirement means a requirement that during a period specified in the order the offender must submit to treatment by or under the direction of a specified person having the necessary qualifications or experience with a view to the reduction or elimination of the offender's dependency on or propensity to misuse drugs.

During that period he must provide samples for the purpose of ascertaining whether he has any drug in his body (a drug testing requirement).

A drug testing requirement may not be made unless the court has been notified that arrangements for implementing drug-testing are in force in the local justice area where the offender resides. The offender must also express his willingness to comply with the order.

Where a requirement is imposed the court must specify for each month the minimum number of occasions on which samples are to be provided. The court may also specify at which, and the circumstances in which, the responsible officer or treatment provider may require samples and descriptions of the samples that may be required.

A court may not impose a drug rehabilitation requirement unless-

(a)   it is satisfied—
   (i)   that the offender is dependent on, or has a propensity to misuse, drugs, and
   (ii)   that his dependency or propensity is such as requires and may be susceptible to treatment;
(b)   it is also satisfied that arrangements have been or can be made for the treatment intended to be specified in the order (including arrangements for the reception of the offender where he is to be required to submit to treatment as a resident);
(c)   the requirement has been recommended to the court as being suitable for the offender either by an officer of a local probation board (or provider of probation services) or by a member of a youth offending team; and
(d)   the offender expresses his willingness to comply with the requirement.

The treatment and testing period is the period specified in the YRO and will be treatment either as a resident in such institution or place as may be specified in the order, or treatment as a non-resident place, as may be so specified.

A YRO imposing a drug rehabilitation requirement must provide that the results of tests carried out on any samples provided by the offender in pursuance of the requirement to a person other than the responsible officer are to be communicated to the responsible officer.

(15) Intoxicating substance treatment requirement

B[50.20] This is a requirement that the offender submits during a specified period or periods to treatment by or under the direction of a specified person having the necessary qualifications or experience with a view to the reduction or elimination of the offender's dependency on or propensity to misuse intoxicating substances.

Intoxicating substances are defined as alcohol or other substance or product (other than a drug) which is, of the fumes of which are, capable of being inhaled or otherwise used for the purpose of causing intoxication.

The court may not impose an alcohol treatment requirement in respect of an offender unless it is satisfied that he is dependent on or has a tendency to misuse intoxicating substances, and his dependency is such as requires and may be susceptible to treatment. Arrangements must be made for the treatment intended to be specified in the order (including arrangements for the reception of the offender where he is to be required to submit to treatment as a resident).

The court must be satisfied that arrangements have been or can be made for the treatment intended and the requirement must have been recommended to the court as suitable for the offender by a member of the youth offending team, an officer of the local probation service or a provider of probation services.

A court may not impose an alcohol treatment requirement unless the offender expresses his willingness to comply with its requirements.

The treatment required by an intoxicating substance treatment requirement for any particular period must be,

(a) treatment as a resident in such institution or place as may be specified in the order; or
(b) treatment as a non-resident in or at such institution or place, and at such intervals, as may be so specified;

but the nature of the treatment shall not be specified in the order except as mentioned in paragraph (a) or (b) above.

(16) Education requirement

B[50.21] The offender must comply during a period or periods specified in the order with approved education arrangements. These may be arrangements made for the offender's education n by his parent or guardian and approved by the local education authority specified in the order. The authority should be the local education authority for the area in which the offender resides.

The court must consult with the local education authority and be satisfied that arrangements exist for the offender to receive sufficient full-time education suitable for his age, ability, aptitude and special education needs (if any).

The court must be satisfied that the requirement is necessary for securing the good conduct of the offender or for preventing the commission of further offences. Any period specified in the YRO cannot include a period once the offender has ceased to be of compulsory school age.

(17) Electronic monitoring requirement

B[50.22] This requirement must normally be added to a curfew or exclusion requirement and may be added to other requirements.

Before making the order arrangements for electronic monitoring must be available in the local justice area proposed to be specified in the order and the order must make provision for making a person responsible for the monitoring of the offender.

The period for monitoring the offender's compliance with other requirements will be specified in the order or determined by the responsible officer in accordance with the relevant requirement. Accordingly, where the responsible officer is to determine when an electronic monitoring is to take effect, he must notify the offender, the monitoring person and any other person whose co-operation is required to ensure that monitoring takes place. The consent of any such person is required and the requirement may not be included in the order without that consent.

Breach of a requirement or order (Sch 2, CJIA 2008)

B[50.23] If at any time while a relevant order is in force in respect of an offender it appears on information to a justice of the peace acting for the local justice area concerned that the offender has failed to comply with any of the requirements, the justice may:

(a)　issue a summons requiring the offender to appear at the place and time specified in it; or

(b)　if the information is in writing and on oath, issue a warrant for his arrest.

If the offender is aged 18 or over breach proceedings will normally commence in an adult magistrates' court. Offenders aged under 18 will appear before a youth court (see *R v Uxbridge Youth Court, ex p Howard* (1998) 162 JP 327).

If it is proved that the offender has failed without reasonable excuse to comply with any of the requirements, the court may deal with the offender in respect of the failure in one of the following ways (the legislation prescribes **must** deal with him in one of the following ways if the relevant order is in force):

(a)　a fine not exceeding £2,500;

(b)　by amending the YRO requirements so as to add to or substitute any requirement imposed by the order. However, this may not include an extended activity requirement or fostering requirement if the original order did not already contain such a requirement. Where the original requirement included a fostering and this is substituted by a new fostering requirement the order may run for 18 months (as opposed to the original 12) beginning with the date on which the original requirement first took effect;

(c)　except where the order was made by the Crown Court without a direction (see infra), revoke the order and re-sentence the offender in any way in which the court could have dealt with the offender for that offence (had the offender been before that court to be dealt with for it).

Where the court amends the order to impose a new requirement, any such requirement must be capable of being complied with before the end date. However, the court may substitute a later date as the end date of up to six months from the original end date provided this power has not been exercised previously.

Where the original order did not contain an unpaid work requirement and the court imposes such a requirement, the minimum number of hours that may be imposed is reduced from 40 to 20.

When dealing with the original offence(s) under (c) above, the court shall take into account the extent to which the offender has complied with the requirements of the relevant order. A person so sentenced may appeal to the Crown Court against that sentence.

In the case of an offender who has wilfully and persistently failed to comply with the requirement(s) of a YRO, and the court is dealing with him under (c) above, the court may impose an intensive supervision and surveillance requirement without regard to the fact that the court is not dealing with the offender for an offence that is punishable with imprisonment nor need it form the opinion that the offence is so serious that it would (but for the statutory restrictions) merit a custodial sentence. Where the court does revoke and re-sentence on breach for any offence not punishable with imprisonment, the court is deemed to have power to deal with the offender for the offence by imposing a detention and training order for a term not exceeding four months: CJIA 2008, Sch 2, paras 12–14.

Where the Crown Court makes a YRO it may include in the order a direction that further proceedings relating to the order be in a youth court or other magistrates' court: CJ & IA 2008, Sch 1, para 36. This gives the youth court or magistrates' court all the powers on breach set out above. However, the court may instead commit the offender in custody or on bail to the Crown Court to be dealt with: CJ & IA 2008, Sch 2, para 7.

Commission of further offence

B[50.24] An offender who is convicted and sentenced of a further offence while subject to a YRO, a youth court may revoke that order and re-sentence the offender for the original offence. That power extends to a YRO made in the Crown Court where the Crown Court has directed that breaches may be dealt with in a youth court. If the court revokes the order and re-sentences, it must take into account the extent to which the offender has complied with the order.

The court must not revoke and re-sentence unless it is in the interests of justice to do so, having regard to the circumstances that have arisen since the YRO was made.

Where a youth court is authorised to deal with a Crown Court order, it may nonetheless commit the offender back to the Crown Court in custody or on bail. **Section 6 of the Powers of Criminal Courts Act 2000 will require amendment to enable a youth court to be able to commit for sentence any summary offence committed during the currency of a YRO requirement.

Application to revoke (Sch 2, Pt 5)

B[50.25] Where a relevant order made by a youth court or adult magistrates' court is in force and, and on the application of the responsible officer, it appears to the court that, having regard to circumstances that have arisen since the order was made, it would be in the interests of justice for the order to be revoked, or for the offence to be dealt with in some other way for the original offence, the court may:

(a)   revoke the order; or
(b)   revoke the order, and deal with the offender for the offence in respect of which the order was made, in any way in which he could have been dealt with for the original offence.

An application to revoke may be based on the offender making good progress or responding satisfactorily to a supervision requirement as the case may be.

If the offender is over 18 the application will be heard in the adult magistrates' court; if under 18, in a youth court.

If an application to revoke is refused (dismissed), no further application may be brought within three months except with the consent of the appropriate court: CJIA 2008, Sch 2, Part 3, para 11(7).

In dealing with an offender for the original offence, the court shall take into account the extent to which the offender has complied with the requirements of a YRO. A person so dealt with may appeal to the Crown Court against that sentence.

Unless the application is made by the offender, the court shall summons the offender to appear before the court, and if he does not appear, may issue a warrant for his arrest.

Amendment

B[50.26] Where an offender has or proposes to change residence from one local justice area to another, at any time while the order is in force, a youth or an adult magistrates' court for the local justice area named in the order, may transfer the relevant order.

On the application of an eligible person, the same court may amend an order by cancelling or inserting any of the requirements in the order (either in addition to or in substitution for any of its requirements) that the court could include if it were then making the order (although see treatment requirements below).

As with breach or revocation applications, the procedural requirements for the issue of summonses or warrant are required to be followed unless the application is to cancel a requirement of an order, reducing the period of an order, reducing the period of any one requirement, or transferring the order to a new local justice area. Natural justice dictates that notice of the amendment should be given to the offender.

In either case where the original order contains a specific area requirement (for example, a curfew requirement), or a programme requirement, the court must not make an amendment that would prevent the offender from complying with that requirement. In such circumstances, the court must substitute a similar requirement within the new area.

Where the court amends by including a new requirement, the new requirement must be capable of being complied with before the end of the order. In the case of a fostering requirement that substitutes a new fostering requirement it may run for a period of 18 months beginning with the date on which the original requirement first had effect.

An order containing an unpaid work requirement may, on the application of the offender or the responsible officer, be amended by extending the period of 12 months during which the order must be complied with. Such an order should only be extended if it is in the interests of justice to do so having regard to circumstances that have arisen since the order was made.

Treatment requirements. The court may not impose a treatment requirement such as mental health treatment, drug treatment or drug testing *by
way of amendment* unless the offender has expressed his willingness to
comply with the requirement.

B[51]

Violent Offender Order

B[51.1] Part VII of the Criminal Justice & Immigration Act 2008, ie ss 98–117, created the Violent Offender Order (VOO). The legislation came into force on 3 August 2009.

A VOO may be made against an offender aged 18 years or more on the application of a chief officer of police. The application is made by way of complaint to a magistrates' court. The proceedings rank as civil proceedings.

The application may be made against an offender convicted of manslaughter, soliciting, conspiracy or attempted murder, corresponding offences under legislation relating to the armed forces, causing GBH or wounding with intent (s 18 OPA 1861) or offences contrary to s 20 OPA 1861 (inflicting or causing GBH).

A VOO when made contains prohibitions, restrictions and conditions intended to protect the public from serious violent harm. The order must be for a minimum duration of two years and a maximum of five years unless renewed or discharged: s 98(1)(b).

Qualifying Offender (s 99)

B[51.2] A person is a qualifying offender if he is aged 18 years or more, has been convicted of a qualifying offence (see above) and received either a custodial sentence of 12 months or more, a hospital order, a supervision order (within the meaning of the Criminal Procedure (Insanity) Act 1964) or found not guilty by way of insanity.

A person is also a qualifying offender if convicted of an equivalent offence or offences and has been dealt with in an equivalent fashion according to the law of any country outside England and Wales: s 99(4).

Application (ss 100–101)

B[51.3] Application is made by complaint via a chief officer of police. The application should specify that the chief officer believes since the date of conviction or finding of insanity etc that the offender has acted in such a way as to give reasonable cause to believe that it is necessary for a VOO to be made in respect of him.

The court may make the order if satisfied that the conditions are met, but in determining whether an order is **necessary** the court must have regard to whether the offender would, at any time while such an order is in force, be subject under any other enactment to any measures that would operate to protect the public from the risk of serious violent harm caused by him.

A VOO cannot come into force while an offender is serving a custodial sentence, is on licence, subject to a hospital or supervision order (see above); nevertheless the order may be sought and made at any time.

Prohibitions, conditions restrictions (s 102) and notification requirements (ss 107–112)

B[51.4] The order may contain specific terms which prevent an offender from going to specified premises or places at any time or specified times, attending any specified event, or having contact with any specified individual.

A person subject to a VOO or interim order is under a duty to notify the police of his name, address, national insurance number and any plans to travel abroad. An offender must comply with the notification requirement within 3 days of the order coming into force. There is also a periodic duty to notify the police of a change of circumstances, make periodic reports and notify any plans to travel outside the UK.

Variation, discharge and renewal (s 103)

B[51.5] A full order may be varied, discharged or renewed on application by way of complaint to a magistrates' court. An order may not be discharged within the first two years unless both the offender and police consent.

Interim orders (s 104)

B[51.6] An interim order may be made where the court is not in a position to make a final determination but the person concerned is a qualifying offender and the court considers that it would be likely to be make a full order and that it is desirable to act to provide the public with immediate protection. As with full orders the VOO will not come into effect while the offender is serving a custodial sentence etc. An interim order ceases to have effect at the end of the specified period subject to any application to vary or discharge the order. There is no provision to extend an interim order. A fresh application would have to be made.

Notice provisions and appeals (ss 105–106)

B[51.7] An application for a full or interim order, discharge, variation or renewal may not be heard unless the court is satisfied that the person concerned has been given reasonable notice of the application. An appeal lies to the Crown Court against the making of an order, interim order, renewal or variation, or a refusal to make or the discharge of an order.

Breach of a VOO (s 113)

B[51.8] Section 113 makes it an offence to fail without reasonable excuse to comply with the terms of the order or with the notification requirements, or notifying false information. The offences are triable either way and punishable summarily to a £5,000 fine, 6 months custody or both. On indictment the offence carries an unlimited fine and/or five years' imprisonment. Unlike ASBOs there is nothing to prevent a court from imposing a conditional discharge for a breach of the order.

Jurisdiction for breach proceedings to be commenced lies with the court in the area where the offender resides or is found: s 113(8).

Foreign Travel Restriction Order

B[52.1] Schedule 5 of the Counter-Terrorism Act 2008 authorises a chief officer of police to apply by way of <u>complaint</u> to a magistrates' court for a foreign travel restriction order. An order can only be sought against a person who is already subject to a notification requirement (see ss 41–45 and Sch 4 of the 2008 Act). The legislation came into force on 1 October 2009.

An order places restrictions on where the person concerned may travel outside the UK. The court may make an order where it is satisfied that the person's behaviour since being dealt with for the original offence makes it necessary for an order to be made to prevent him from taking part in terrorism activity outside the UK (Sch 5, para 2(3)).

A foreign travel restriction order must have effect for a fixed term not exceeding 6 months (Sch 5, para 7(1)). Although proceedings are instituted by way of complaint and therefore the procedures are essentially civil in nature, the imposition of criminal sanctions means that the criminal standard of proof applies to the application: see case law under B[8.4].

There are provisions relating to variation, renewal or discharge: Sch 5, para 8. There is no provision to make an interim order. Failure without reasonable excuse to comply with an order is an offence triable either way carrying an unlimited fine and/or five years' imprisonment on conviction on indictment: Sch 5, para 15(2). On summary conviction the offence carries six months' imprisonment and/or a fine not exceeding £5,000. The magistrates' court may not impose a conditional discharge: Sch 5, para 15(4)(a).

Closure Order (specified prostitution offences)*

---

*   Section 115 of the Anti-social Behaviour, Crime and Policing Act 2014 prospectively extends the closure powers in PART 2A of the Sexual Offences Act 2003, and s 116 gives power to require hotel owners, operators or managers to give information about guests where there is reasonable belief that the premises have been or will be used for child sexual exploitation or conduct preparatory thereto.

B[53.1] Part 2A of the Sexual Offences Act 2003 was inserted by the Policing and Crime Act 2009.

The provisions outlined below came into force on 1 April 2010. Section 136B of the SOA 2003 permits a police officer, not below the rank of superintendent, to authorise a closure order in relation to premises which are being used for certain activities; those activities are associated with "specified prostitution or pornography offences" as defined by the Act. The police must have consulted the local authority first.

If a closure order has been issued, a constable must apply under SOA 2003, s 136D to a magistrates' court for a closure order.

A closure order is an order that the premises (or part of the premises) in respect of which the order is made are closed to all persons for such period not exceeding 3 months as is specified in the order.

The application must be heard by the magistrates' court not later than 48 hours after the notice was served by the police in pursuance of SOA 2003, s 136C(3)(a).

The magistrates' court may adjourn the hearing for a closure order for a period of not more than 14 days to enable any of the following to show why a closure order should not be made: (a) an occupier of the premises; (b) a person who has control of or responsibility for the premises; (c) any other person who has an interest in the proceedings (see SOA 2003, s136B(7)(b)).

If the application is adjourned the magistrates' court may order that the closure order continues in effect until the end of the period of the adjournment.

Closure order applications are civil proceedings. Although closure order applications should be dealt with as a matter of urgency, it is submitted that, analogous to crack house orders (see A[26.12]), a magistrates' court has a general power to grant a further adjournment under the MCA 1980, s 54: see R *(on the application of Turner v Highbury Corner Magistrates' Court and Commissioner of the Metropolitan Police Comr (Interested Party)* [2005] EWHC 2568.

B[53.2] A magistrates' court may make a closure order if satisfied three criteria have been made out:

(1)   That the premises have been used, during the period 3 months ending on the day the closure order was issued by the police, for specified prostitution offences (except if only one person obtained all of the sexual services in question, whether or not on a single occasion) or for specified pornography offences.

(2)   That the closure order is necessary to prevent the premises being used for one or other of the above activities.

(3)   Reasonable steps have been taken to consult the relevant local authority and to establish the identity of any person (see SOA 2003, s 136B(7)(b) above); and, there has been compliance by the police with SOA 2003, s 136C(3)(d) ie a copy of the notice was given to the persons mentioned in s 136B(7)(b) of the SOA 2003.

B[53.3] **Enforcement and offences.** Enforcement is to be found in SOA 2003, s 136F. A person who obstructs a constable or an authorised person acting under s 136C(3) or (4) or s 136F(2) or (4) of the SOA 2003 commits an offence. The offence is summary only carrying a maximum penalty of 6 months' imprisonment (51 weeks if the CJA 2003 is brought into force) and/or a maximum fine of £5,000 (level 5).

B[53.4] **Extension, variation and discharge.** This is catered for by SOA 2003, ss 136H–J. On application a closure order may be extended for a further period of 3 months but a closure order cannot exceed 6 months in total. This would not prevent the police from making a fresh application for a closure order. There is provision for any of the person mentioned in SOA 2003, s 136B(7)(b) to apply for the order to be discharged.

B[53.5] **Appeal.** Any of the above mentioned may appeal to the Crown Court. The appeal must be lodged before the end of 21 days beginning with the day on which the order or decision was made: SOA 2003, s 136K.

B[53.6] There are miscellaneous provisions covering costs or compensation associated with the making of such orders eg see SOA 2003, s 136M. Magistrates would be well advised to consult their legal adviser.

Domestic violence protection notice

Power to issue

B[54.1] Sections 24–30 of the Crime and Security Act 2010 came fully into effect on 8 March 2014. These provisions include the power for an authorising officer to issue a domestic violence protection notice to an alleged perpetrator of domestic violence, and the power for a magistrates' court, on an application made by complaint by a constable, to make a domestic violence protection order.

Contents and service of a domestic violence protection notice

B[54.2] A DVPN must state—

(a)   the grounds on which it has been issued,

(b)   that a constable may arrest P without warrant if the constable has reasonable grounds for believing that P is in breach of the DVPN,

(c)   that an application for a domestic violence protection order under section 27 will be heard within 48 hours of the time of service of the DVPN and a notice of the hearing will be given to P (see B[55] below).

(d)   that the DVPN continues in effect until that application has been determined, and

(e)   the provision that a magistrates' court may include in a domestic violence protection order.

A DVPN must be in writing and must be served on P personally by a constable. On serving P with a DVPN, the constable must ask P for an address for the purposes of being given the notice of the hearing of the application for the domestic violence protection order.

Breach and enforcement of a DVPN

B[54.3] A person arrested for a breach of a DVPN must be held in custody and brought before the magistrates' court which will hear the application for the DVPO under s 27 (see below)—

(a)   before the end of the period of 24 hours beginning with the time of the arrest, or

(b)   if earlier, at the hearing of that application.

If the person is brought before the court and the hearing is adjourned the court may remand the person.

In calculating when the period of 24 hours mentioned above ends, Christmas Day, Good Friday, any Sunday and any day which is a bank holiday in England and Wales under the Banking and Financial Dealings Act 1971 are to be disregarded.

No penalty is prescribed for breach of an order under the 2010 legislation. Breach of a magistrates' court order (other than for payment of money) is provided for by s 63 of the Magistrates' Courts Act 1980. Where breach of an order is established (to the criminal standard it is submitted) the maximum penalty is:

(a)   a fine not exceeding £50 for every day during which P is in default or a sum not exceeding £5,000;

(b)   committal to custody until he has remedied his default or for a period not exceeding 2 months.

B[55]

Domestic violence protection order

Application for a domestic violence protection order

B[55.1] Sections 24-30 of the Crime and Security Act 2010 came fully into effect on 8 March 2014. These provisions include the power for an authorising officer to issue a domestic violence protection notice to an alleged perpetrator of domestic violence, and the power for a magistrates' court, on an application made by complaint by a constable, to make a domestic violence protection order.

Conditions for and contents of a DVPO

B[55.2] The court may make a DVPO if two conditions are met.

The first condition is that the court is satisfied on the balance of probabilities that P has been violent towards, or has threatened violence towards, an associated person.

The second condition is that the court thinks that making the DVPO is necessary to protect that person from violence or a threat of violence by P.

Before making a DVPO, the court must, in particular, consider—

(a)   the welfare of any person under the age of 18 whose interests the court considers relevant to the making of the DVPO (whether or not that person is an associated person), and

(b)   any opinion of which the court is made aware—

      (i)   of the person for whose protection the DVPO would be made, and

      (ii)   in the case of provision included by virtue of subsection (8), of any other associated person who lives in the premises to which the provision would relate.

But the court may make a DVPO in circumstances where the person for whose protection it is made does not consent to the making of the DVPO.

A DVPO must contain provision to prohibit P from molesting the person for whose protection it is made. Provision required to be included may be expressed so as to refer to molestation in general, to particular acts of molestation, or to both.

If P lives in premises which are also lived in by a person for whose protection the DVPO is made, the DVPO may also contain provision—

(a)   to prohibit P from evicting or excluding from the premises the person for whose protection the DVPO is made

(b)   to prohibit P from entering the premises,

(c)   to require P to leave the premises, or

(d)   to prohibit P from coming within such distance of the premises as may be specified in the DVPO.

A DVPO must state that a constable may arrest P without warrant if the constable has reasonable grounds for believing that P is in breach of the DVPO.

A DVPO may be in force for—

(a)   no fewer than 14 days beginning with the day on which it is made,
(b)   no more than 28 days beginning with that day.

A DVPO must state the period for which it is to be in force.

Breach and Enforcement of a DVPO

B[55.3] A person arrested by virtue of section 28(9) for a breach of a DVPO must be held in custody and brought before a magistrates' court within the period of 24 hours beginning with the time of the arrest.

If the matter is not disposed of when the person is brought before the court, the court may remand the person.

In calculating when the period of 24 hours mentioned in subsection (1) ends, Christmas Day, Good Friday, any Sunday and any day which is a bank holiday in England and Wales under the Banking and Financial Dealings Act 1971 are to be disregarded.

There are further provisions about remand to be found in s 30 of the 2010 Act.

No penalty is prescribed for breach of an order under the 2010 legislation. Breach of a magistrates' court order (other than for payment of money) is provided for by s 63 of the Magistrates' Courts Act 1980. Where breach of an order is established (to the criminal standard it is submitted) the maximum penalty is:

(a)   a fine not exceeding £50 for every day during which P is in default or a sum not exceeding £5,000; or
(b)   committal to custody until he has remedied his default or for a period not exceeding 2 months.

Road traffic offences

C[1]

Index and penalties for road traffic offences

Maximum fines and the standard scale

C[1.1]

MCA 1980,	The statutory maximum fine on summary	£5,000
s 32(9);	conviction of an offence triable either way,	
Interpretation	being the prescribed sum under the Magis- trates'	
Act 1978, s 32,	Court Act 1980,	
Sch 1		
CJA 1982,	The standard scale giving maximum fines on an adult on conviction for a summary offence:	
	s 37(2)	

level 1	£200
level 2	£500
level 3	£1,000
level 4	£2,500
level 5	£5,000

C[1.2] The following table contains an alphabetical list of the road traffic offences dealt with in this book, together with some others included to provide the maximum penalty. Readers will wish to note the penalties recommended in the Magistrates' Association National Sentencing Guidelines.

C[1.3] Speed/distance chart. See C[2]

C[1.4] Stopping distances. See C[3]

C[1.5] Endorsement codes. See C[6]

C[1.6]

Offences and endorsement code	Standard scale	Licence and penalty points	para
Abandoning a motor vehicle	level 4+3 months		
Accident, failing to give particulars AC 20	level 5+6 months	E 5–10	C[32]
Report AC 20	level 5+6 months	E 5–10	C[32]
stop after AC 10	level 5+6 months	E 5–10	C[31]
Bicycle			
defective brakes riding	level 3		
Careless	level 3		
Dangerous	level 4		
Inconsiderate	level 3		
two persons on	level 1		
when unfit through drink	level 3		
Brakes, defective			
on private vehicle CU 10 §	level 4	E*3	C[9]
on goods vehicle CU 10 §	level 5	E*3	C[9]
on bicycle	level 3		
Breath test, refusing DR 70	level 3	E 3–11	C[24]
Car door, opening to cause			
injury or danger §	level 3		C[37]
Car dumping	level 4 + 3 months	104	A[60]
Careless driving CD 10	level 5	E 3–9	C[25]
Common land, driving on §	level 3		
Dangerous condition			
using private vehicle in CU 20 §	level 4	E*3 (D) – see C[10]	C[10]
using goods vehicle in CU 20 §	level 5	E*3 (D) – see C[10]	C[10]
Dangerous load			
on private vehicle CU 50 §	level 4	E*3	
on goods vehicle CU 50 §	level 5	E*3	
Dangerous position, leaving			
motor vehicle in MS 10 §	level 3	E 3	
Date of birth, failing to give	level 3		
Defective tyre			
private vehicle CU 30 §	level 4	E*3	C[53]
goods vehicle CU 30 §	level 5	E*3	C[53]
Driver, failing to give particulars of date of birth	level 3		
Driving			
Careless CD 10	level 5	E 3–9	C[25]

Offences and endorsement code	Standard scale	Licence and penalty points	para
causing death by careless or inconsiderate driving †(from **18/8/08**)	level 5 + 12 months	E 3–11	C[16A]
dangerous†DD 40	level 5 + 6 months	D 3–11	C[16]
causing death by driving: unlicensed, disqualified or uninsured† (from **18/8/08**)	level 5 + 12 months	D 3–11	C[16B]
causing serious injury by dangerous driving	level 5 + 12 months	D 3–11	C[16C]
disqualified BA 10	level 5 + 12 months	E 6	C[19]
drink, under influence of DR 20	level 5 + 6 months	D 3–11	C[20]
excess alcohol DR 10	level 5 + 6 months	D 3–11	C[22]
excessive periods on footpath, common land, etc	level 4		
(RT Act) §	level 3		
Without			
due care and attention CD 10	level 4 / 5 for offences on or after 24/9/07	E 3–9	C[25]
insurance IN 10 §	level 5	E 6–8	C[33]
Keeping vehicle which does not meet insurance requirements (RTA, s 144A)	level 3		
licence (excise)	£1,000 or 5 times duty		C[47]
reasonable consideration CD 20	level 5 for offences on or after 24/9/07	E 3–9	C[46]
test certificate			
(private)	level 3		C[51]
(goods)	level 4		C[51]
Drunk in charge DR 50	level 4 + 3 months	E 10	C[21]
Excess alcohol			
driving DR 10	level 5 + 6 months	D 3–11	C[20]
in charge DR 40	level 5 + 3 months	E 10	C[21]
Excise licence			
making false statement to obtain	level 5		
using/keeping vehicle without	level 3 or 5 times duty		C[47]
Eyesight, driving with defective MS 70	level 3	E 3	
Failing to comply with traffic sign §	level 3	+ 3	C[52]
(constable or traffic warden on traffic duty) TS 40 §	level 3	E 3	
Give			
name and address to	level 5	E 5–10	C[31]

Index and penalties for road traffic offences C[1.6]

Offences and endorsement code	Standard scale	Licence and penalty points	para
police AC 20	+ 6 months		
particulars after accident AC 20	level 5 + 6 months	E 5–10	C[31]
specimen of			
breath DR 70	level 3	E 4	C[24]
blood/urine/breath			
driving or attempting DR 30	level 5 + 6 months	D 3–11	C[24]
in charge DR 60	level 4 + 3 months	E 10	C[24]
statement by owner	level 3		
Produce			
driving licence	level 3		C[17]
insurance certificate	level 3		C[17]
test certificate	level 3		C[17]
wear seat belt (front §)	level 2		C[48]
(rear §)	level 2 (child)		
report accident AC 20	level 5 + 6 months	E 5–10	C[31]
sign driving licence	level 3		
stop (a mechanically propelled vehicle when required to do so: s 163 RTA 1988)	level 5		
after accident AC 10	level 5 + 6 months	E 5–10	C[31]
at school crossing TS 60	level 3	E 3	
False declaration to obtain excise licence †	level 5		
False statement to obtain			
driving licence	level 4		
Insurance	level 4		
Footpath, driving on			
(Highways Act 1835, s 72)	level 2		
Forging, etc			
insurance certificate	level 5		
test certificate †	level 5		
Front seat, carrying child in §	level 3		C[48]
Getting on to vehicle to be carried	level 1		
Heavy goods vehicle			
driving without LGV licence	level 3		
overloading §	level 5		C[38]
parking on verge, etc §	level 3		
using without plating certificate	level 3		
using without test certificate	level 4		
Holding on to vehicle to be towed or carried	level 1		

Offences and endorsement code	Standard scale	Licence and penalty points	para
Hours, driving for excessive number	level 4		
Insecure load			
private vehicle CU 50 §	level 4	E*3	
goods vehicle CU 50 §	level 5	E*3	
Insurance			
using without, causing or permitting IN 10 §	level 5	E 6–8	C[33]
failing to produce certificate	level 3		C[17]
false statement to obtain	level 4		
Jay walking	level 3		
Licence			
driving otherwise than in accordance with LC 10 §	level 3	E 3–6	C[18]
excise, keeping/using vehicle without	level 3 or 5 times duty		C[47]
failing to produce for endorsement	level 3		
failing to produce to constable	level 3		C[17]
LGV, driving otherwise than in accordance with	10 units		C[19]
obtaining while disqualified	level 3		
Lights, driving or parking			
without §	level 4 (goods vehicle etc)		C[34]
	level 3 (other)		
(Breach of requirements as to control of vehicle, Mobile Telephone etc)	level 4 if committed in respect of a good vehicle or a vehicle adapted to carry more than 8 persons, otherwise level 3	E 3 (for offence committed on or after 27/2/07 prosecuted under s 41D RTA 1988)	
[Currently] Mobile Telephone§			
Motor cyclists not wearing helmet §	level 2		C[35]
Neglecting policeman's directions			
driver TS 40 §	level 3	E 3	
Pedestrian	level 3		
Obstruction, causing			
unnecessary §	level 4 (goods vehicle etc)		C[36]
	level 3 (other)		

Offences and endorsement code	Standard scale	Licence and penalty points	para
Opening door to cause danger or injury §	level 4 (goods vehicle)		C[37]
	level 3 (other)		
One way street, driving in wrong direction §	level 3	E 3	C[52]
Overloading §	level 5		C[38]
Owner failing to identify driver	level 3	E 6	
Parking			
heavy vehicle on footpath,	level 3		
on offside at night §	level 4 (goods vehicle etc)		
on yellow lines §	level 3		
breach of regulations for			
on street parking places §	level 2		
(abuse of parking for the disabled) §	level 3		
off street parking places	level 2		
(abuse of parking for the disabled)	level 3		
failure to pay initial or excess charge	level 2 + amount unpaid		
interfering with meter with intent to defraud	level 3		
Pedal cycle, see Bicycle			
Pedestrian			
failing to comply with direction of constable on traffic duty	level 3		
Pedestrian crossing			
not giving precedence PC 20 §	level 3	E 3	C[39]
overtaking within limits PC 20 §	level 3	E 3	C[39.10]
Stopping within limits PC 30 §	level 3	E 3	C[40]
Provisional licence holder			
Reasonable consideration			
driving without CD 20	level 5	E 3–9	C[46]
Record of hours, failing to keep	level 4		
Refusing blood/urine/breath specimen			
in charge DR 60	level 4 + 3 months	E 10	C[23]
driving DR 30	level 5 + 6 months	D 3–11	C[23]
Riding bicycle, see Bicycle			
Road fund licence			
keeping/using without	level 3 or 5 times duty		C[47]
fail to display §	level 1		
false statement to obtain †	level 5		

Offences and endorsement code	Standard scale	Licence and penalty points	para
Seat belt, failure to wear (front §)	level 2		C[48]
(rear §)	level 2 (child in rear seat)		
School crossing, fail to stop			
at TS 60	level 3	E 3	
Silencer, defective §	level 4 (goods vehicle etc)		
	level 3 (other)		
Speeding SP 30 §	level 3	E 3–6(FP3) [2–6 under the Road Safety Act 2006]	C[49]
motorway SP 50 §	level 4	E 3–6(FP3) [2–6 under the Road Safety Act 2006]	C[49]
Speed assessment equipment detection devices	level 4 if committed on a special road, otherwise level 3	E 3–6 (FP3) from a date to be appointed under the Road Safety Act 2006	C[38A]
Stealing (or attempt) vehicle †			
NE 99	level 5 + 6 months	D (discretionary)	A[57], A[65]
Steering, defective			
private vehicle CU 40 §	level 4	E*3	C[50]
goods vehicle CU 40 §	level 5	E*3	
Taking motor vehicle			
without consent			
NE 99	level 5	D (discretionary)	A[57], A[65]
(Theft Act 1968, s 12) Aggravated Vehicle Taking UT 50	6 months	D	A[3]
	Level 5		
(Theft Act 1968, s 12A)	6 months		
Tampering with motor vehicle	level 3 +		A[63]

Offences and endorsement code	Standard scale	Licence and penalty points	para
	3 months		
Test certificate §			
using etc vehicle without	level 3		C[51]
using goods vehicle without	level 4		C[51]
failing to produce	level 3		C[17]
Traffic sign, non compliance			
with §	level 3	E 3	C[52]
Tyre, defective			
private vehicle CU 30 §	level 4	E*3	C[53]
goods vehicle CU 30 §	level 5	E*3	C[53]
Waiting on yellow lines §	level 3		

D   means that the offence attracts an obligatory disqualification.

E   means that the offence attracts an obligatory endorsement; in all such cases disqualification is discretionary.

*   The defendant in cases thus marked is not liable to an endorsement if he satisfies the court that he did not know of the defect and had no reasonable cause to suspect that it was present.

+   Endorsable only if the sign is a traffic light (TS 10), double white lines (TS 20), Stop (TS 30), no entry sign or failure to comply with a green arrow traffic sign, abnormal load failing to observe procedure at railway crossing (TS 50), or vehicle contravening height restriction (TS 50).

†   Triable either way.

§   The prosecution may offer a fixed penalty instead of prosecuting in the normal way. See [8].

C[2]

Speed and distance chart

C[2.1] An approximate guide to the distance covered by a vehicle moving at a constant speed is that half the number of miles per hour is roughly the number of yards per second, eg 30 mph = 15 yds per second. The following table is more accurate than that and the distances are expressed in feet. But it must be borne in mind that the distance given will be covered only by a vehicle travelling at the speed given for the whole of the distance, ie at a constant speed. The table cannot therefore be used in the case of a vehicle slowing down or accelerating.

Miles per hour	Feet per second
20	29
30	44
40	59
50	73
60	88
70	103
80	117
90	132
100	146

C[3]

Braking distances

(Taken, with permission, from the Highway Code)

C[3.1] The following braking table appears in the Highway Code. It must be taken as a guide only since no information is given with it as to whether a vehicle with disc or servo assisted brakes, or any particular tyres could improve upon these figures. It is submitted that the court can take judicial notice of the table and may form part of the cross-examination of a witness including the defendant. Moreover, the table, like any other part of the Highway Code, is embraced by the Road Traffic Act 1988, s 38(7) which states:

A failure on the part of a person to observe a provision of the Highway Code shall not of itself render that person liable to criminal proceedings of any kind, but any such failure may in any proceedings (whether civil or criminal and including proceedings under the Traffic Acts . . .) be relied upon by any party to the proceedings as tending to establish or negative any liability which is in question in those proceedings.

C[4]

Shortest stopping distances – in feet

[4.1]

On a dry road, a good car with good brakes and tyres and an alert driver
will stop in the distances shown. Remember these are shortest stopping
distances. Stopping distances increase greatly with wet and slippery
roads, poor brakes and tyres and tired drivers.

Mph	Thinking distance		Braking distance		Overall stopping distance	
	m	ft	m	ft	m	ft
20	6	20	6	20	12	40
30	9	30	14	45	23	75
40	12	40	24	80	36	120
50	15	50	38	125	53	175
60	18	60	55	180	73	240
70	21	70	75	245	96	315

C[5]

Endorsement and disqualification

C[5.1] The Traffic legislation imposes on the courts an obligation to endorse the licence of any person convicted of certain offences. In the case of a convicted person who does not hold a driving licence this acts as an order to endorse any licence which he may obtain during the period when the endorsement is effective. An endorsement means that particulars of the offence and sentence will be recorded in code (as to which see C[6]) on the defendant's licence, unless it is a foreign licence. In the case of a foreign licence, the order for endorsement should be made (subject to there being special reasons for not making it, see below) and the clerk will notify the DVLA. The court must order endorsement unless it decides after hearing sworn evidence (which may be no more than the evidence given during the trial of the offence) that there are special reasons for not doing so.

C[5.2] Special reasons. This has become a term of art; it has a significance which is determined by law rather than by the ordinary meaning of the words. In order to avoid endorsement or compulsory disqualification the defendant must give to the court at least one specific reason why he should not be penalised by endorsement (or disqualification in cases where that is mandatory) and that reason must meet all of the following criteria:

(a)   it must be a mitigating or extenuating circumstance;
(b)   it must not amount to a legal defence to the charge;
(c)   it must be directly connected with the circumstances in which the offence was committed, and not relate solely to the circumstances of the offender;
(d)   it should be a factor which the court ought properly to take into consideration when deciding the sentence (*R v Wickins* (1958) 42 Cr App Rep 236, 122 JP 518, CCA).

C[5.3] Case law has provided very many examples of circumstances under which may, and other circumstances which may not, be accepted as special reasons and some circumstances (eg the distance driven by the defendant) may be accepted or rejected according to the offence with which he is charged. For this reason examples are not set out here since they may confuse rather than clarify the position. Magistrates are recommended always to consult the legal adviser before reaching any final decision on this question.

C[5.4] Disqualification. Disqualification is mandatory for certain offences. In every case where the court can order an endorsement it has the discretion also to disqualify. Thus it can be seen how important it may be for a defendant to persuade the court that there are special reasons for not endorsing, because if he is successful and the court does not order endorsement, it may not disqualify. In cases where disqualification is mandatory, eg dangerous driving and drinking and driving offences, the defendant may submit special reasons for not disqualifying while conceding the endorsement.

C[5.5] For offences of theft of vehicles, going equipped to steal vehicles and taking vehicles without consent, the court may disqualify even though there is no power to impose penalty points. Disqualification may also be imposed for offences of assault involving a motor vehicle and, indeed, where following a motoring incident one driver follows another and assaults him the power to disqualify will arise (*R v Rajesh Patel* (1994) 16 Cr App Rep (S) 756, [1995] Crim LR 440, CA). A discretionary disqualification may not be imposed where the defendant is also liable to be disqualified under the penalty points provisions (see below).

There is a discretionary power to disqualify for any offence under PCC(S) Act 2000, s 146. See C[5.45].

C[5.6] Length of disqualification: s 34 RTOA 1988. A minimum period of disqualification must, in the absence of special reasons, be imposed in the following cases:

driving with excess alcohol/whilst unfit	One year; three years where second offence within 10 years
refusing to supply a specimen	One year; three years where second offence within 10 years
dangerous driving	One year
causing serious injury by dangerous driving	Two years
causing death by careless or inconsiderate driving	One year; three years
causing death by driving: unlicensed, disqualified or uninsured drivers	One year; three years
using vehicle in a dangerous condition	Six months if second conviction within three years of a conviction for any such offence (s 34(4B) RTOA 1988)

In relation to any offence which carries obligatory disqualification by virtue of s s 34 of, and Sch 3 to, RTOA 1988, the minimum term of disqualification rises from one year to two years where the defendant has, within the three years preceding the commission of the offence, been banned more than once for a fixed period of 56 days or more: s 34(4) RTOA. For this purpose, interim disqualifications and bans imposed under s 147 of the Powers of Criminal Courts (Sentencing) Act 2000, for theft of a motor vehicle, for an offence under s 12 or 25 of the Theft Act 1968 and for offences of attempting to commit any of the above shall be disregarded: s 34(4A) RTOA 1988.

Dangerous driving also carries a mandatory disqualification until a test is passed.

C[5.7] There is a tendency for magistrates to think of disqualification in units of say, 6, 12, 18 and 24 months. Research has shown that the longer the period of disqualification the more it is likely to be disobeyed. Moreover, the driver who is disqualified, say for two years, will probably decide within a few weeks that he will ignore the ban. There is, therefore, a strong case for short-term disqualifications especially, for example, for bad cases of careless driving and young men charged with driving licence offences (see below for disqualification under the penalty points system).

C[5.8] Disqualification starts on the day on which the order is made and that day counts as one full day of the disqualification.

C[5.9] Disqualification for life. Such a disqualification will be rare. Only where there are exceptional circumstances should a disqualification for life be imposed (*R v Rivano* (1993) 14 Cr App Rep (S) 578, 158 JP 288, CA), for example, where there is psychiatric evidence that the driver would indefinitely be a danger to the public if allowed to drive (*R v King* [1993] RTR 245, 13 Cr App Rep (S) 668, CA) or evidence of many previous convictions which indicated the same possibility (*R v Buckley* (1994) 15 Cr App Rep (S) 695, [1994] Crim LR 387, CA).

The penalty points system

C[5.10]–[5.15] Persons convicted of certain offences must be disqualified from driving, eg for driving with excess alcohol. A court has a discretion to disqualify any person who has been convicted of an endorsable offence and will do so where the particular offence with which it is dealing is serious. The person who persistently commits minor endorsable offences may therefore escape these mandatory or discretionary disqualifications but will be caught by the disqualification imposed under the penalty points system. This provides in essence that where a person accumulates 12 or more penalty points over a three-year period, he must generally be disqualified for a minimum period.

C[5.16] Penalty points. Every endorsable offence attracts a number of penalty points varying from 2 to 11. Some offences (including careless driving, uninsured use of a vehicle and failing to stop or report after an accident) give the court a discretion to attach a number of penalty points within a range, so indicating the court's view of the relative gravity of the offence. The choice of the number of penalty points in these cases will on occasion determine whether a disqualification must be imposed. For example, Brian A Driver has already accumulated 8 penalty points and is convicted of careless driving for which anything from 3 to 9 penalty points may be awarded. If the court imposes 3 points, Driver escapes disqualification because he does not reach a total of 12; but if the court imposes more than 3 then he must be disqualified, subject to his proving mitigating circumstances amounting to exceptional hardship.

C[5.17] When a driver is convicted of a single endorsable offence his licence will be endorsed with the number of penalty points appropriate to that offence, or with a number within the appropriate range. However, where he is convicted of a number of offences committed on the same occasion (which is not the same as saying on the same day) the number of points to be endorsed will usually be the number for the offence attracting the highest number. For example, if in addition to his careless driving conviction (3–9 penalty points) Brian A Driver is also convicted of driving whilst disqualified (6 penalty points) and driving in a play street (2 penalty points) then his endorsement will show at least 6 penalty points, that being the highest figure. If the court decides to endorse 8 penalty points for the careless driving (that being a number within the range for that offence) then the endorsement would show 8 penalty points. It is these 8 penalty points which count towards disqualification, not the total number for the three offences.

C[5.18] Two things will be evident from this in the normal situation:

(a)   although every endorsable offence has a penalty points value, the endorsement relating to that offence may show a higher number; and

(b)   when a conviction relates to a number of offences committed on the same occasion the number of penalty points which count towards disqualification is the number relating to the offence with the highest number of penalty points.

C[5.19] However, the court may if it thinks fit decide to accumulate the points for offences committed on the same occasion. If it does so it must state its reasons in open court and enter them in the register.

Note that the court should not order penalty points to be endorsed if it orders the offender to be disqualified in respect of any offence of which he has been convicted on that occasion (*Martin v DPP* [2000] RTR 188, [2000] 2 Cr App Rep (S) 18, 164 JP 405, [2000] Crim LR 320).

Penalty points to be taken into account

C[5.20] There is a general misconception as to the law and practice following the decision in *Jones v Chief Constable of West Mercia Police Authority* (2000) 165 JP 6. A totting ban is usually for not less than 6, 12 or 24 months which is substantially longer than the majority of discretionary bans. Accordingly, the starting point is to calculate the number of points to be taken into account and to determine whether the offender tots. As the court in *Jones* indicated the usual practice is to impose a totting ban without reference to the seriousness or triviality of the offence (as provided for by s 35 of the Offenders Act). Only in an exceptional case will the court first consider if it wishes to impose a discretionary disqualification bearing in mind the seriousness of the offence and previous offences. If a discretionary disqualification is imposed any existing points remain on the licence. If discretionary disqualification is not appropriate the court imposes points and goes on to consider the totting-up procedure.

The effect of the decision in *Jones* above was nullified by the introduction of the Magistrates' Courts Sentencing Guidelines – see page 185, para 12 which clearly states that if the court is considering discretionary disqualification but D would be liable to totting up if further points were imposed the court should go down the totting up route not the discretionary ban route. This plugged the *Jones* 'gap' whereby some courts were being persuaded to impose short discretionary bans in the absence of exceptional hardship thus circumventing the totting up.

Subject to there being grounds for mitigation, disqualification is incurred when the number of penalty points to be taken into account reaches or exceeds 12. The following penalty points are to be taken into account at the time of conviction:

(a)   those endorsed at the time of that conviction. Where a person is made the subject of a mandatory or discretionary disqualification no penalty points for the offence for which he was disqualified will be taken into account, for the purpose of imposing an additional disqualification under the penalty points provisions;

(b)   those endorsed previously in respect of any offence committed within three years of the present offence, except where a disqualification under the penalty points provisions has been ordered, in which case the court is only concerned with the penalty points incurred since that disqualification.

C[5.21] Therefore, only a disqualification under the penalty points provisions will have the effect of 'wiping clean' any points previously incurred.

Period of disqualification

C[5.22] Once a defendant becomes liable for disqualification under this scheme he may be disqualified for any period at the court's discretion, but this discretion is limited by the fixing of minimum periods. These minimum periods are as follows:

(a)   six months if no previous disqualification is to be taken into account;
(b)   one year if one previous disqualification is to be taken into account; and
(c)   two years if there is more than one such disqualification.

C[5.23] For a prior disqualification to be taken into account it must have been imposed within three years of the latest offence which has brought the offender's total of penalty points up to 12. Such disqualification may have been imposed:

(a)   for an offence for which it was obligatory (eg driving with excess alcohol); or
(b)   for an offence for which it was optional (eg a bad case of careless driving); or
(c)   for 12 or more penalty points;

and must have been for a period of 56 days or more and was not imposed for stealing a motor vehicle, taking without consent or going equipped for theft.

Mitigating grounds

C[5.24] When a defendant becomes liable to disqualification under this procedure he may claim that there are grounds for mitigating the normal consequences of conviction and if the court finds such grounds it may reduce the minimum period to which the offender is liable or it may decide not to disqualify. In either event it must state its reasons which will be recorded. The court's discretion, however, is limited. It may not take into account:

(a)   any circumstances which are alleged to make the offence (or any of them) not a serious offence;
(b)   the fact that disqualification would cause hardship (but it may take account of exceptional hardship);
(c)   any circumstances which have been taken into account during the previous three years so as to avoid or reduce disqualification.

The case of *Miller v DPP* [2004] EWHC 595 (Admin), [2004] 17 LS Gaz R 30, [2004] All ER (D) 477 (Mar) suggests that where there has been excessive delay (over 2 years) in sentencing the defendant this is a proper ground for reducing the length of a disqualification under RTOA 1988, s 35(1).

C[5.25]–[5.30] So, for example, Mr Zimmer is liable to disqualification but successfully avoids it by pleading that being disabled a disqualification would cause exceptional hardship because his specially adapted vehicle is his only means of getting to work. If he is convicted and attracts a totting disqualification again within three years he is unable to put forward that ground for avoiding disqualification but once three years have passed, that ground is resurrected and may be used again.

C[5.31] Under the penalty points scheme only one disqualification is imposed irrespective of the number of offences. In the event of an appeal against any one or more of the offences, the disqualification will be treated as having been imposed on each offence and in any event the Crown Court has the power to alter sentences imposed by the magistrates' court for several offences even if there is only an appeal against the sentence on one offence.

C[5.32] Summary. Upon conviction of certain offences the court must order endorsement unless either there are special reasons (although the Road Traffic Offenders Act 1988 uses the plural it has always been treated as the singular) for not doing so, or in the case of some offences under the Road Vehicles (Construction and Use) Regulations 1986, the defendant did not know of and had no reason to suspect the condition of the vehicle. These offences are noted in the table at C[1.6].

C[5.33] No disqualification may be ordered unless it is for an endorsable offence (except for offences of theft, going equipped to steal vehicles and taking vehicles without consent). Some few offences carry a compulsory order for disqualification and this must be imposed by the court unless there are special reasons for not doing so.

C[5.34] The term 'special reasons' has a very narrow meaning, in particular, hardship to the defendant is excluded from consideration.

C[5.35] A period of disqualification takes effect immediately. This includes disqualification for 12 or more penalty points. Only one period of disqualification is ordered under the penalty points scheme irrespective of the number of offences. The three year period during which penalty points are to be counted runs between dates of offence, not conviction. The three year period during which, the circumstances once used as mitigating grounds for not disqualifying under the penalty points system may not be used again, is measured between dates of their original use and the present conviction.

C[5.36] Where appeal against sentence is lodged, the court may suspend the effect of disqualification until the appeal is *heard*. This should not be done automatically but only after careful consideration.

Disqualification until passes a test

C[5.37] The court *must* disqualify an offender until he passes an extended driving test where:

(a)   he is convicted of an offence of dangerous driving; or
(b)   in the Crown Court, the offences of manslaughter, causing death by dangerous driving or causing death by careless driving whilst under the influence of drink or drugs; or
(c)   the court orders him to be disqualified until a test of competence is passed, having convicted him of an offence involving obligatory disqualification under s 34 or he is disqualified under s 35 of the RTOA 1988.

C[5.38] The court has a *discretion* to disqualify until an ordinary test of competence is passed where the offender has been convicted of any offence involving obligatory endorsement. The defendant is entitled to drive but must display L plates and be supervised. In cases where the court is exercising its discretion it must have regard to the safety of road users and an order is inappropriate as a punishment, but is suitable for the following cases:

(a)   for people who are growing aged or infirm, or show some incompetence in the offence which needs looking into. In addition a licence may be revoked by the Secretary of State on medical grounds and a provisional licence issued for the sole purpose of a road reassessment;

(b)   where the defendant is disqualified for a long period for the offence and there is doubt about his ability to drive at the expiry of the disqualification period;

(c)   where the manner of the defendant's driving suggests a threat to the safety of other road users (*R v Miller* (1993) 15 Cr App Rep (S) 505, [1994] Crim LR 231, CA). See the Road Traffic Offenders Act 1988, s 36;

(d)   it is not usually appropriate in the cases of passengers in vehicles taken without the owner's consent (*R v Wiggins* [2001] RTR 37, CA).

The onus is on the defendant charged with driving whilst disqualified when not having completed a retest to show he held a provisional licence and was complying with the conditions of that licence (*DPP v Barker* (2004) 168 JP 617, [2004] All ER (D) 246 (Oct), DC).

Interim disqualification

C[5.39] A magistrates' court may impose an interim disqualification on a person where:

(a)   it commits him to the Crown Court for sentence or remits his case to another magistrates' court; or

(b)   it defers or adjourns his case before passing sentence (including a transfer to another magistrates' court post conviction). An interim order of disqualification may continue until the defendant is finally dealt with subject to a limit of six months and any subsequent order of disqualification will be reduced by the period of the interim order.

Disqualification by the Crown Court

C[5.40]–[5.44] Where the Crown Court either convicts or sentences a person who was convicted by a magistrates' court of an offence punishable with at least two years' imprisonment it may disqualify the defendant for an unlimited period if it is satisfied that a motor vehicle was used (whether by him or by an accomplice) to commit or to facilitate the commission of the offence.

C[5.45] Disqualification for any offence. This is a power to disqualify a person from driving instead of or as an addition to dealing with him in any other way and it applies to any criminal offence (PCC(S)A 2000, s 146). Certain non endorsable offences recommend themselves for such a penalty including kerb crawling, unlawful tipping and driving off road unlawfully. See *R v Doick* [2004] EWCA Crim 139, [2004] 2 Cr App Rep (S) 203 for guidance when coupled with custody. The power should not be used arbitrarily but could be used where a vehicle was driven to an affray (*R v Clift* [2004] EWCA Crim 3139, [2005] RTR 147, [2004] All ER (D) 400 (Nov)) or when used in connection with the fraudulent evasion of duty on cigarettes (*R v Skitt* [2004] EWCA Crim 3141, [2004] All ER (D) 401 (Nov)).

The effect of endorsement on new drivers

C[5.46] Drivers within the first two years of first passing a driving test are in a probationary period. If, during that period, such a driver accumulates 6 or more penalty points on his licence the DVLA will automatically revoke his driving licence when it is sent to them or they are notified by the court.

C[5.47] This is not a disqualification but the new driver will only be entitled to hold a provisional licence until he passes a retest, which will restore his previous entitlements. Revocation will occur whether the penalty points are added following a conviction by a court or following a fixed penalty.

C[5.48] Points accumulated before the test was taken will count, unless they were committed more than three years before the current offence (*R (on the application of Adebowale) v Secretary of State for Transport* [2004] EWHC 1741 (Admin), [2004] All ER (D) 335 (Jun)). Points accumulated after the test is passed will count if the *offence* is within two years of the date on which the test was passed. In *R v Damien Joseph Edmunds* [2000] 2 Cr App Rep (S) 62, CA the Court of Appeal reduced the points imposed from 6 to 5 to avoid the defendant from losing his full licence on the grounds that he lived in a rural area without public transport. It is submitted that the Court's basis for so doing was not what Parliament intended when introducing changes to the law on endorsement for new drivers.

C[5.49] If in any proceedings for an offence committed in respect of a motor vehicle it appears to the court that the accused may be suffering from any relevant disability or prospective disability (within the meaning of Part III of the Road Traffic Act 1988), the court **must** notify the Secretary of State.

There must be sufficient material before the court, even if only by way of something said in mitigation, suggesting that the defendant is suffering from a relevant disability or a prospective disability, before the court can properly refer the matter to the Secretary of State. A good example is alcoholism or epilepsy (see *R v Chichester JJ, ex p Crouch* (1981) 146 JP 26). Note that the court has no discretion in the matter. It is advisable to consult the legal adviser.

C[6]

Driving licence codes

C[6.1] Offences and the sentences imposed therefor are recorded on driving licences in code. The codes are reproduced below by permission of the Department of the Environment.

Endorsement code

C[6.2] Causing or permitting

Offences as coded below, but with zero changed to 4, eg IN 10 becomes IN 14.

Inciting

Offences as coded below, but with zero changed to 6, eg DD 30 becomes DD 36.

Periods of time

Periods of time are signified as follows: D = days; M = months; Y = years.

Code	Accident offences
AC 10	Failing to stop after an accident.
AC 20	Failing to give particulars or to report an accident within 24 hours.
AC 30	Undefined accident offence.
	Disqualified driver
BA 10	Driving whilst disqualified by order of court.
BA 20	Driving whilst disqualified by reason of age (obsolete).
BA 30	Attempting to drive whilst disqualified by order of court.
	Careless driving
CD 10	Driving without due care and attention.
CD 20	Driving without reasonable consideration for other road users.
CD 30	Driving without due care and attention or without reasonable consideration for other road users (primarily for use by Scottish courts).
CD 40	Causing death by careless driving when unfit through drink.
CD 50	Causing death by careless driving when unfit through drugs.
CD 60	Causing death by careless driving with alcohol level above the limit.
CD 70	Causing death by careless driving, then failing to supply specimen for analysis.
CD 71	Causing death by careless driving, then failing to supply a specimen for drug analysis.
CD 80	Causing death by careless or inconsiderate driving.
CD 90	Causing death by driving: unlicensed, disqualified or uninsured drivers.

Code	Accident offences
	Construction and use offences
CU 10	Using a vehicle with defective brakes.
CU 20	Causing or likely to cause danger by reason of use of unsuitable vehicle or using a vehicle with parts or accessories (excluding brakes, steering or tyres) in a dangerous condition.
CU 30	Using a vehicle with defective tyres.
CU 40	Using a vehicle with defective steering.
CU 50	Causing or likely to cause danger by reason of load or passengers.
CU 60	Undefined failure to comply with Road Vehicles (Construction and Use) Regulations 1986.
CU 80	Breach of requirements as to control of vehicle, mobile telephones etc
	Reckless driving
DD 30	Reckless driving (obsolete).
DD 40	Dangerous driving.
DD 60	Manslaughter or culpable homicide while driving a vehicle.
DD 70	Causing death by reckless driving (obsolete).
DD 80	Causing death by dangerous driving.
	Drink or drugs
DR 10	Driving or attempting to drive with alcohol concentration above limit.
DR 20	Driving or attempting to drive while unfit through drink.
DR 30	Driving or attempting to drive then refusing to supply a specimen for laboratory testing.
DR 40	In charge of a vehicle with alcohol concentration above limit.
DR 50	In charge of a vehicle when unfit through drink.
DR 60	In charge of a vehicle then refusing to supply a specimen for laboratory testing.
DR 61	In charge of a vehicle then refusing to supply a specimen for drug analysis.
DR 70	Failing to provide specimen for breath test (roadside).
DR 80	Driving or attempting to drive when unfit through drugs.
DR 90	In charge of a vehicle when unfit through drugs.
	Insurance offences
IN 10	Using a vehicle uninsured against third party risks.
	Licence offences
LC 10	Driving without a licence (obsolete).
LC 20	Driving otherwise than in accordance with a licence.
LC 30	Driving after making a false declaration about fitness when applying for a licence.
LC 40	Driving a vehicle having failed to notify a disability.
LC 50	Driving after a licence has been revoked or refused on medical grounds.
	Miscellaneous offences
MS 10	Leaving a vehicle in a dangerous position.
MS 20	Unlawful pillion riding.
MS 30	Playstreet offences.

Code	Accident offences
MS 40	Driving with uncorrected defective eyesight or refusing to submit to a test. (Obsolete code, see now MS 70 and MS 80.)
MS 50	Motor racing on the highway.
MS 60	Offences not covered by other codes.
MS 70	Driving with uncorrected defective eyesight.
MS 80	Refusing to submit to eyesight test.
MS 90	Failure to give information as to identity of driver in certain cases.
	Motorway offences
MW 10	Contravention of Special Road Regulations (excluding speed limits). Road Traffic Regulation Act 1984
	Non-endorsable offences
NE 98	Disqualification under Powers of Criminal Courts (Sentencing) Act 2000, s 146
NE 99	Disqualification under Criminal Justice Act 1972, s 24 and Powers of Criminal Courts (Sentencing) Act 2000, s 147 (and for offences of unauthorised taking see A[77]).
	Pedestrian crossings
PC 10	Undefined contravention of Zebra, Pelican and Puffin Pedestrian Crossing Regulations and General Directions 1997 (primarily for use by Scottish courts).
PC 20	Contravention of Zebra, Pelican and Puffin Pedestrian Crossing Regulations and General Directions 1997 with moving vehicle.
PC 30	Contravention of Zebra, Pelican and Puffin Pedestrian Crossing Regulations and General Directions 1997 with stationary vehicle.
	Provisional licence offences (obsolete, see now LC 20)
PL 10	Driving without 'L' plates.
PL 20	Not accompanied by a qualified person.
PL 30	Carrying a person not qualified.
PL 40	Drawing an unauthorised trailer.
PL 50	Undefined failure to comply with conditions of a provisional licence.
	Speed limits
SP 10	Exceeding goods vehicle speed limit.
SP 20	Exceeding speed limit for type of vehicle (excluding goods or passenger vehicles).
SP 30	Exceeding statutory speed limit on a public road.
SP 40	Exceeding passenger vehicle speed limit.
SP 50	Exceeding speed limit on a motorway.
SP 60	Undefined speed limit offence.
	Traffic directions and signs
TS 10	Failing to comply with traffic light signals.
TS 20	Failing to comply with double white lines.
TS 30	Failing to comply with a 'stop' sign.
TS 40	Failing to comply with directions of a constable or traffic warden.
TS 50	Failing to comply with a traffic sign (excluding 'stop' signs, traffic lights or double white lines).

Code	Accident offences
TS 60	Failing to comply with a school crossing patrol sign.
TS 70	Undefined failure to comply with a traffic direction or sign.
	Theft or unauthorised taking (obsolete (except UT 50), see now NE 99)
UT 10	Taking and driving away a vehicle without consent or an attempt thereat (primarily for use by Scottish courts).
UT 20	Stealing or attempting to steal a vehicle.
UT 30	Going equipped for stealing or taking a vehicle.
UT 40	Taking or attempting to take a vehicle without consent; driving or attempting to drive a vehicle knowing it to have been taken without consent, allowing oneself to be carried in or on a vehicle knowing it to have been taken without consent.
UT 50	Aggravated taking of a vehicle.
	Special codes
TT 99	Disqualification for accumulating 12 or more penalty points.
NSP	(No separate penalty.) Where court does not impose penalty points for minor offences committed at the same time as a more serious one.

C[7]

Sentence code

C[7.1] The sentence is represented by four characters, eg G 02 Y (community rehabilitation order two years). The first letter indicates the nature of the sentence, the middle two numbers (0 always precedes what would otherwise be a single figure) and the final letter indicate the period of the sentence, if any, as hours (H), days (D), months (M), or years (Y). Apart from the special code TT 99 which indicates a disqualification under the penalty points procedure there is no code to represent disqualification because this appears in a special column on the licence. In the case of an absolute discharge there is no period so the code J 000 is used.

C[7.2] The first letter of the code indicates the sentence as follows:

A   imprisonment

B   detention in a place approved by the Secretary of State

C   suspended sentence of imprisonment

E   conditional discharge

F   bound over

G   community rehabilitation

H   supervision order (youth court)

I   no separate penalty

J   absolute discharge

K   attendance centre

M   community punishment order

P   young offender institution

S   compensation

T   hospital or guardianship order

W   care order

C[8]

Fixed penalties

C[8.1] For some time it has been possible to avoid the expense of court proceedings for some criminal and motoring offences by the expedient of the prosecution offering the defendant a 'fixed penalty ticket'. If he accepts the offer he pays the required sum and the matter is settled, otherwise he is summoned to court and the matter proceeds in the usual way.

C[8.2] In the interests of relieving the burden on the courts of having to deal with many minor motoring cases, the fixed penalty system (formerly almost exclusively confined to motoring offences) has been greatly extended to cover a wide range of offences. These are noted in the index at C[1.6] and include a number of offences which carry an endorsement.

C[8.3] A summary of the procedure is as follows:

Offering the fixed penalty

C[8.4] When a constable observes that a 'fixed penalty' offence has been committed, he must decide whether it is endorsable or not.

C[8.5] Non-endorsable offences. He may give the fixed penalty ticket to the driver or affix it to the vehicle if the driver is not present. In the case of criminal offences the offender must be present and at least 18 years old.

C[8.6] Endorsable offences. The driver must be present and the officer will require him to produce his driving licence for examination. If the driver is not liable to disqualification because he will not have accumulated 12 or more penalty points, the officer may offer him the option of a fixed penalty and invite him to surrender his licence in exchange for a receipt which he may use as evidence that he is a licence holder. It is then for the driver to decide whether to accept the offer of a fixed penalty.

C[8.7] If the driver does not have his driving licence with him, the procedure is modified in that he may be required to produce his driving licence within seven days at a chosen police station where it will be inspected and, if appropriate, a fixed penalty offered.

Where the offence carries obligatory endorsement and the offender is not the holder of a driving licence, a fixed penalty may only be given if the officer is satisfied, on accessing the offender's driving record, that he would not be liable to points disqualification for the offence.

C[8.8] Note. There are no fixed penalties for endorsable offences when the driver is not present (but see 'Conditional offer of fixed penalty', below), nor where he is present but declines the offer. Also the police have a discretion whether to offer a fixed penalty so that, for example, a constable might decline to offer it for an isolated offence which is serious in nature.

From a date to be appointed s 3 of the **Road Safety Act 2006,** will amend s 53 of the Road Traffic Offenders Act 1988, to cater for the introduction of graduated fixed penalties. Similarly s 4 of the **Road Safety Act 2006** will likewise introduce a graduated fixed penalty points scheme.

Paying the fixed penalty

C[8.9] The defendant has to pay the fixed penalty within 21 days (or such longer period as is allowed by the ticket) to the court responsible for fixed penalties.

Offences	Fixed penalty
A fixed penalty offence under section 3 of the Road Traffic Act 1988	£100
A fixed penalty offence under s 143 of the RTA 1988	£300
A fixed penalty offence under s 172 of the RTA 1988	£200
Any other fixed penalty offence involving obligatory endorsement	£100
A fixed penalty parking offence committed in Greater London on a red route	£60
Any other fixed penalty parking offence committed in Greater London	£40
A fixed penalty offence under s 14 (seat belts: adults) of the RTA 1988	£100
A fixed penalty offence under s 15(2) or 15(4) of the RTA 1988 (restrictions on carrying children not wearing seat belts in motor vehicles)	£100
A fixed penalty offence under s 47 of the RTA 1988	£100
A fixed penalty offence under s 42(1) of the Vehicle Excise and Registration Act 1994 (driving or keeping a vehicle without required registration mark)	£100
A fixed penalty offence under s 43(1) of the Vehicle Excise and Registration Act 1994 (driving or keeping a vehicle with registration mark obscured etc)	£100
A fixed penalty offence under s 59 of VERA 1994 (failure to fit prescribed registration mark to a vehicle in accordance with regulations made under s 23(4)(a) of that Act)	£100
A fixed penalty offence under s 98(4) of the TA 1968	£300
A fixed penalty offence under s 99(4) of the TA 1968	£300
A fixed penalty offence under s 99ZD(1) of the TA 1968	£300
A fixed penalty offence under s 99C of the TA 1968	£300
A fixed penalty offence under s 3(1) of the Road Traffic (Foreign Vehicles) Act 1972	£300
A fixed penalty offence under s 12(5) of the Public Passenger Vehicles Act, 1981	£300
A fixed penalty offence under s 71(1) of the RTA 1988	£300
A fixed penalty offence under s 90D(6) of the RTOA 1988	£300
A fixed penalty offence under s 2(5) of the Goods Vehicles (Licensing of Operators) Act 1995	£300
A fixed penalty offence under reg 3 of the Goods Vehicles (Community Authorisations) Regulations 1992	£100
A fixed penalty offence under reg 3 of the Public Service Vehicles (Community Licences) Regulations 1999	£100
A fixed penalty offence under reg 3(1) of the Road Transport (Passenger Vehicles Cabotage) Regulations 1999	£100

Offences	Fixed penalty
A fixed penalty offence under reg 4(1) of the Road Transport (Passenger Vehicle Cabotage) Regulations 1999	£100
Any other fixed penalty offence except for a fixed penalty parking offence	£50
Any other fixed penalty parking offence	£30

C[8.10]–[8.15] For the purpose of the higher parking penalties, London is regarded as the Metropolitan Police District. The licence that was surrendered to the police is sent to the fixed penalty clerk who places the endorsement on it and returns it to the defendant when the penalty has been paid.

Instituting proceedings

C[8.16] In any case where a fixed penalty has been offered the defendant can at any time before the time for payment has expired, request a hearing before the magistrates and plead guilty or not guilty as he thinks fit.

Where the fixed penalty is not paid

C[8.17] In the case of an endorsable offence, the defendant's licence will already be in the possession of the police who will have forwarded it to the clerk responsible for fixed penalties. If the penalty is unpaid at the end of the required period, the police will register the penalty at the court for the area in which the defendant lives and the clerk who already holds the licence will endorse it and return it to the defendant. Unfortunately for him the penalty is registered as a fine 50% above the fixed penalty. Similar provisions apply to non-endorsable offences where the ticket is given to the driver.

C[8.18] Where the offence is non-endorsable and the ticket was affixed to the vehicle, the police send a notice to the person they believe to be the owner requesting him either to pay the penalty or to inform them who is the actual owner. If he fails to co-operate by not replying at all, he will have the enhanced penalty registered against him. He is similarly liable if he replies and admits he was the owner unless either (a) he pays the penalty, or (b) persuades the actual driver to pay it for him, or (c) he returns a form signed by the person who was actually driving and who requests a court hearing.

Enforcement of payment

C[8.19] Once a penalty has been registered, it is regarded as a fine. Non-payment of the registered penalty will result in enforcement proceedings being taken in the manner described at B[33.96].

Penalty points

C[8.20] If the accused has committed several endorsable offences on the *same occasion*, and one is dealt with under the fixed penalty procedure and his licence is to be endorsed, the penalty points for those offences dealt with at a court hearing are to be treated as being reduced by those points to be endorsed under the fixed penalty procedure.

Conditional offer of fixed penalty

C[8.21] The Road Traffic Act 1988, s 172 provides for the police to issue a notice to the keeper of the vehicle requiring information as to the identity of the driver. If the keeper fails to give the information he will be guilty of an endorsable offence deemed to have taken place in the place to where the reply ought to have been sent (*Kennet District Council v Young* [1999] RTR 235, 163 JP 622). Any reply must be in writing and signed (*DPP v Broomfield* [2002] EWHC 1962 (Admin), [2003] RTR 108). A telephone call will not be sufficient compliance with the section but a letter accompanying the form and disclosing the required information will be (*Jones v DPP* [2004] EWHC 236 (Admin), [2004] All ER (D) 319 (Jan)) but not if it is left unsigned (*Francis v DPP* [2004] EWHC 591 (Admin), [2004] All ER (D) 443 (Mar)). In *R (on the application of Flegg) v Southampton and New Forest Justices* [2006] EWHC 396 (Admin), 170 JP 373 the defendant returned a section 172 request with a covering note stating that he could not say who the driver was. The conviction was upheld on the basis that the information given was both misleading and inaccurate. The defendant as the owner or keeper of the vehicle has a duty to name potential drivers not just actual drivers.

Where the driver is identified, a conditional offer of a fixed penalty is sent to him and if he wishes to accept the offer he will send his driving licence and payment to the fixed penalty office within 28 days of the issue of the offer. The fixed penalty will be accepted unless the details of the licence disclose that the offender is liable to be disqualified under the penalty points provisions. In this case the police will be notified and a summons issued in the normal way.

In *DPP v Holden* [2006] All ER (D) 363 (Feb), the notice sent to the defendant stated that the response to the police had to be returned within 28 days but failed to specify the period during which a speeding offence could be commenced (see s 75(7)(c) RTOA 1988). In the absence of bad faith this was not a matter which directly affected the fairness of the trial; further, the delay in instituting proceedings was not so exceptional as to warrant a stay of proceedings on the ground of delay.

In *Thomson (Procurator Fiscal) v Jackson* [2010] HCJAC 96, [2011] RTR 210, the High Court of Justiciary dissented from the opinion in *Wilkinson's Road Traffic Offences* (24th edn, 2009), to the effect that there could be more than one valid requirement addressed to the same person, and in relation to the same incident under RTA 1988, s 172. There is nothing in the legislation to suggest that there can only be one requirement. The relevance of the argument goes to questions of statutory time limits and/or issues of abuse of process based on delay. The above decision is of *persuasive* authority only and it is open to question whether it would be followed in England and Wales.

Note, where a defendant is convicted of an offence under s 172, the penalty has been increased to allow for an endorsement with 6 penalty points for offences committed on or after 24 September 2007 (Road Safety Act 2006 (Commencement No 2) Order 2007 (SI 2007/2472 (C 91)).

C[8.22] This procedure would appear not to breach the rule against self-incrimination contained in Art 6 of the ECHR: see *Tora Tolinos v Spain* (No 23816/94) (17 May 1995, unreported), ECtHR, *Brown v Stott* [2001] 2 All ER 97, [2001] 2 WLR 817, PC and *Hayes v DPP* [2004] EWHC 277 (Admin), [2004] All ER (D) 55 (Feb). In *O'Halloran v United Kingdom* [2007] All ER (D) 7 (Jul), [2007] ECHR 15809/02 it was decided:

The right to remain silent and the right not to incriminate oneself were not absolute rights and the right to require an actual or potential suspect to provide information which contributed or might contribute to his conviction by direct compulsion would not cumulatively result in a violation of article 6 of the Convention. While the right to a fair trial was an unqualified right, what constituted a fair trial could not be the subject of a single unvarying rule, but had to depend on the circumstances of the particular case. In order to determine whether the essence of the applicant's right to remain silent and privilege against self-incrimination had been infringed, it was necessary to focus on the nature and degree of compulsion used to obtain the evidence, the existence of any relevant safeguards in the procedure, and the use to which any material so obtained was put.

Looking at s 172(2)(a) the ECHR noted that it was not an offence of strict liability; certain defences were still available. The essence of the applicant's right to remain silent and the privilege against self-incrimination had not been destroyed. Hence, it decided there was no violation of Art 6.

The prosecution should annex to s 9 statements proving service, a notice of intended prosecution and the requirement to provide details. If the defence fail to raise the issue, that the requirement was not lawfully made, before the end of the prosecution case the court should permit the prosecution to re open their case to prove the point (*Mohindra v DPP* [2004] EWHC 490 (Admin), [2004] All ER (D) 269 (Mar)).

C[9]

Brakes defective

Charge

C[9.1] Using, causing or permitting to be used on a road a motor vehicle or trailer with defective brakes

Road Vehicles (Construction and Use) Regulations 1986, reg 18; Road Traffic Act 1988, s 41A(b)

Maximum penalty – For goods vehicles fine level 5. Other motor vehicles or trailers fine level 4 (for fines see para **B[33]**). For endorsement and disqualification-see below, and under 'Sentencing'.

'Goods vehicles' for this purpose includes vehicles adapted to carry more than eight passengers; as to whether this includes the driver, consult the clerk.

If the defendant can satisfy the court that he did not know and had no reasonable cause to suspect the deficiency of the brakes then disqualification and endorsement cannot be ordered. The defendant does not have to establish this point beyond reasonable doubt but merely that it is true on the balance of probabilities.

Penalty points – 3.

Fixed penalty – £60.

Legal notes and definitions

C[9.2] Goods vehicle. Means a motor vehicle or trailer constructed or adapted for the carrying or hauling of goods or burden.

C[9.3] The law requires that every part of every braking system and of the means of operating the braking system must be maintained in good and efficient working order and must be properly adjusted. The offence is an absolute one and the vehicle must have proper brakes at all times. If the charge is using the prosecution need not prove that the defendant knew of the defect. If the vehicle had no brakes at all then he will be charged under a different regulation.

C[9.4] Using. This does not mean only driving along a road; mere presence on a road, even in a useless condition, may constitute using (*Pumbien v Vines* [1996] RTR 37, [1996] Crim LR 124). The term means 'to have the use of the vehicle on the road'. The test to be applied is whether or not such steps had been taken as would make it impossible for anyone to use the car. 'Use' involves an element of control, management or operation as a vehicle. Therefore, an accused who was in the driving seat of a 'vehicle' where the steering was locked, there was no ignition key, the brakes were seized on and the engine could not be started was not 'using' it when it was being towed along the road. It was an inanimate hunk of metal. It would be different if there was a possibility of control, ie its steering could be operated and its brakes were working, even if its engine were not working. In doubtful cases the legal adviser should be consulted. A person, limited company or corporate body which owns a vehicle that is being driven in the course of the owner's business is using the vehicle (*West Yorkshire Trading Standards Service v Lex Vehicle Leasing Ltd* [1996] RTR 70). Knowledge of the facts which constitute the offence is not necessary. For a recent judgment where the High Court were unable to agree on whether knowledge on the part of the employer company was required (s 5 RTRA 1984) see *Cambridgeshire County Council v Associated Lead Mills Ltd* [2005] EWHC 1627 (Admin), [2006] RTR 82.

A passenger in a car knowing the driver to be uninsured and allowing himself to be carried in it in pursuance of a joint enterprise is a person using the vehicle for insurance purposes (*Stinton v Stinton* [1995] RTR 167, [1995] 01 LS Gaz R 37, sub nom Stinton v Motor Insurers Bureau 159 JP 656, [1999] Lloyd's Rep IR 305, CA).

C[9.5] **Causing.** This implies some express or positive mandate from the person causing the vehicle to be used or some authority from him and knowledge of the *fact* which constitutes the offence (but there need be no *intention* to commit an offence). Acquiescence could amount to permission (see below) but falls short of a positive mandate (*Redhead Freight Ltd v Shulman* [1989] RTR 1, [1988] Crim LR 696).

C[9.6] **Permitting.** This includes express permission and also circumstances in which permission may be inferred. If the defendant is a limited company or corporate body it must be proved that some person for whose criminal act the company is responsible permitted the offence. A defendant charged with permitting must be shown to have known that the vehicle was being used or it must be shown that he shut his eyes to something that made it obvious to him that the vehicle was being used on a road (*Roper v Taylor's Central Garages Ltd* [1951] 2 TLR 284). In other road traffic offences permitting in the case of an employer may mean failing to take reasonable steps to prevent a contravention of the transport regulations (*Vehicle Inspectorate v Nuttall (t/a Redline Coaches)* [1999] 3 All ER 833, [1999] 1 WLR 629, HL).

C[9.7] **Motor vehicle.** Means a mechanically propelled vehicle intended or adapted for use on roads. 'Intended' does not mean intended by the user of the vehicle either at the moment of the alleged offence or for the future nor the intention of the manufacturer or the wholesaler or the retailer. The test is whether a reasonable person looking at the vehicle would say that one of its users would be a road user. If a reasonable man applying the test would say 'Yes, this vehicle might well be used on a road' then the vehicle was intended or adapted for such use. For example a Go-Ped requires both a driving licence and insurance (*DPP v Saddington* [2001] RTR 227, sub nom Chief Constable of North Yorkshire Police v Saddington (2001) 165 JP 122, [2001] Crim LR 41). If that were the case then it is nothing to the point if the individual defendant says that he normally used the vehicle for scrambling and was only pushing it home on this occasion because there was no other means of taking it home, or something of that sort (*Chief Constable of Avon and Somerset v Fleming* [1987] 1 All ER 318, [1987] RTR 378, 84 Cr App Rep 345).

C[9.8] For 'mechanically propelled' see the note at C[47.9].

C[9.9] **A trailer.** Means any vehicle being drawn by a motor vehicle.

C[9.10]–[9.15] **A road.** Means any highway (including footpaths and bridleways) and any other road to which the public has access and includes bridges but not a car park the purpose of which is to enable cars to stand and wait rather than move along it to a destination (*Cutter v Eagle Star Insurance Co Ltd* [1998] 4 All ER 417, [1998] 1 WLR 1647, HL).

Sentencing
SC Guideline – Brakes defective

C[9.16] Starting point – Band B fine (driver); Band B fine (owner-driver but consider an uplift of 25% of at least 25% on the driver's fine); Band C fine (owner-company)

C[9.16A] If the defendant proves that he did not know, and had no reasonable cause to suspect, that the brakes were deficient, endorsement and disqualification cannot be ordered. The defendant only has to prove that it is more probable than not that this was the case. Otherwise he can be disqualified and the licence **must** be endorsed unless there are 'special reasons'; see C[5.2].

C[9.17] It may sometimes be appropriate to grant a conditional or absolute discharge but if this course is adopted then a disqualification can still be imposed. Endorsement must still be ordered unless 'special reasons' exist.

C[9.18] If it appears to the court that the accused suffers from some disease or physical disability likely to cause his driving to be a source of danger to the public then the court shall notify the licensing authority (see C[5.49]).

C[9.19] When the vehicle concerned is a goods vehicle the fine will reflect the potential danger to the public and to the driver of the vehicle, and the gross weight and nature of the load may well be relevant.

C[9.20] For fines see B[33].

Dangerous condition/bodywork

Charge

C[10.1] Using, causing or permitting to be used a motor vehicle or trailer on a road when

[the condition of the motor vehicle or trailer, or of its accessories or equipment]

[the purpose for which it is used]

[the number of passengers carried by it, or the manner in which they are carried]

[the weight, position or distribution of its load, or the manner in which it is secured]

is such that the use of the motor vehicle or trailer involves a danger of injury to another person

Road Traffic Act 1988, s 40A

Maximum penalty-For goods vehicle or vehicle adapted to carry more than eight passengers fine level 5. For other vehicles or trailers fine level 4 (for fines see B[33]).

Licence must be endorsed unless special reasons exist. *May be disqualified for any period and/or until he passes a driving test. Endorsement and disqualification cannot be ordered if defendant can satisfy the court that he did not know of, and he had no reasonable cause to suspect, the dangerous condition. The defendant does not have to prove this beyond reasonable doubt. He need only prove that on the balance of probabilities it is true.

Must disqualify for at least 6 months where the offence under s 40A has been committed within three years of a previous conviction of the offender under the same section; otherwise, disqualification is discretionary: Road Safety Act 2006 (Commencement No 2) Order 2007 (SI 2007/2472 (C 91)).

Penalty points – 3.

Fixed penalty – £60.

Legal notes and definitions

C[10.2] Goods vehicle. Means a motor vehicle or trailer constructed or adapted for the carriage of goods or burden. The clerk should be consulted if there is a question whether a vehicle is a goods vehicle.

C[10.3] Using, causing, permitting. See the notes under these headings for the offence of defective brakes at C[9.4]–C[9.6].

C[10.4] Road. Means any highway (including footpaths and bridleways) and any other road to which the public has access and includes bridges.

Motor vehicle. See C[9.7].

C[10.5] The offence is an absolute one. It is no defence that the defect was latent, and only became apparent during the journey. The section requires that the vehicle (or trailer) and all its parts and accessories are both in good repair and efficient working order.

C[10.6] The wording of the summons or charge should specify the exact part or accessory which is said to be dangerous. The court can allow the prosecution to amend the wording to remedy such an omission and to offer the defence an adjournment if it needs further time to prepare its case.

Sentencing
SC Guideline – Dangerous condition/bodywork

C[10.7] Starting point – Band B fine (driver); Band B fine (owner-driver but consider an uplift of 25% of at least 25% on the driver's fine); Band C fine (owner-company)

C[10.7A] If the defendant can establish that he did not know and he had no reason to suspect the dangerous condition, in this case endorsement and disqualification cannot be ordered. The defendant does not have to prove this beyond reasonable doubt. He need only prove that on the balance of probabilities it is true.

C[10.8] If it appears to the court that the accused suffers from some disease or physical disability likely to cause his driving to be a source of danger to the public then the court shall notify the licensing authority (see C[5.49]).

C[10.9] For fines see B[33].

C[16]

Dangerous driving

Charge

C[16.1] Driving a mechanically propelled vehicle dangerously on a road or other public place

Road Traffic Act 1988, s 2 (as substituted by the Road Traffic Act 1991)

Maximum penalty – Fine level 5 and 6 months (for fines see **B[33]**). Triable either way. Must disqualify for at least one year unless special reasons. The disqualification may be for any period exceeding a year. If disqualified he *must* also be ordered to pass an extended driving test. Must endorse licence unless special reasons exist.

Crown Court – 2 years' imprisonment and unlimited fine.

Penalty points – 3–11.

Mode of trial

C[16.2] Consider the SC guideline at **C[16.7]** below.

Legal notes and definitions

C[16.3] Driving. See the note under the offence of no driving licence at C[18.8].

C[16.4] Mechanically propelled vehicle. See C[47.9].

C[16.5] Dangerously. Means that the defendant's driving falls far below what would be expected of a competent and careful driver *and* it would be obvious to a competent and careful driver that driving in that way would be dangerous.

A person is also to be regarded as driving dangerously if it would be obvious to a competent and careful driver that driving the vehicle in its current state would be dangerous. The unintentional pressing of the wrong pedal is not a defence to dangerous driving (*A-G's Reference (No 4 of 2000)* (2001)).

C[16.6] Aid and Abet. In *R v Webster* [2006] EWCA Crim 415, (2005) Times, 15 March, the defendant allowed a friend to drive his vehicle while drunk. It was held that whilst the condition of the driver could be relevant to the manner in which the vehicle was driven on the facts this had not been established by the Crown. In this case there was no evidence that the defendant had been given the opportunity to intervene once he became aware the defendant was driving in a dangerous manner.

C[16.7] Dangerous refers to danger either of injury to any person or of serious damage to property.

C[16.8] In determining what would be expected of, or obvious to, a competent and careful driver in a particular case, regard shall be had not only to the circumstances of which he could be expected to be aware but also to any circumstances shown to have been within the knowledge of the accused. The effect of s 2A(3) of the 1988 Act was not to offend against the rule that the test for dangerous driving was objective; it simply refined the objective test by reference to existing circumstances. By enacting s 2A(3) Parliament directed the court to have regard to any circumstances shown to have been within the knowledge of the accused. Subjective considerations, such as what the driver thought about the situation were irrelevant, but in so far as circumstances relevant to the issue of dangerousness was capable of being established as being within the knowledge of the accused, the fact finder had to have regard to it.

In *Milton v DPP* [2007] EWHC 532 (Admin), [2007] All ER (D) 285 (Mar), it was decided the fact that the defendant was an advanced police driver was a circumstance to which regard had to be had pursuant to s 2A(3). *Milton v DPP* has recently been overruled by *R v Bannister* [2009] EWCA Crim 1571, (2009) Times, 24 August. In the latter case the Court of Appeal reconsidered the position of a police officer who claimed specialist driving skills should be taken into account when judging the standard of driving. The Court of Appeal held: ' . . . the special skill (or indeed lack of skill) of a driver is an irrelevant circumstance when considering whether the driving is dangerous'.

C[16.9] In determining the state of the vehicle regard may be had to anything attached to or carried on or in it and to the manner in which it is attached or carried.

C[16.10]–[16.14] Road. See C[10.4] and C[22.5].

C[16.15] Public place. See C[20.7]–C[20.8].

C[16.16] Warning of proceedings. If the defence claim that notice should have been given within 14 days of intention to prosecute, consult the legal adviser.

Sentencing
SC Guideline – Dangerous Driving

C[16.17] Must endorse and disqualify for at least 12 months

Must disqualify for **at least** 2 years if offender has had two or more disqualifications for periods of 56 days or more in preceding 3 years – consult your legal adviser for further guidance

If there is a delay in sentencing after conviction, consider interim disqualification

OFFENCE SERIOUSNESS (CULPABILITY AND HARM)		
A. IDENTIFY THE APPROPRIATE STARTING POINT		
Starting points based on first time offender pleading not guilty		
Examples of nature of activity	**Starting point**	**Range**
Single incident where little or no damage or risk of personal injury	Medium level community penalty	Low level community order to high level community order

		Disqualify 12 – 15 months
Incident(s) involving excessive speed or showing off, especially on busy roads or in built-up area; OR	12 weeks custody	High level community order to 26 weeks custody
Single incident where little or no damage or risk of personal injury but offender was disqualified driver		Disqualify 15 – 24 months
Prolonged bad driving involving deliberate disregard for safety of others; OR	Crown Court	Crown Court*
Incident(s) involving excessive speed or showing off, especially on busy roads or in built-up area, by disqualified driver; OR		*Consider interim disqualification
Driving as described in box above while being pursued by the police		

OFFENCE SERIOUSNESS (CULPABILITY AND HARM)

B. CONSIDER THE EFFECT OF AGGRAVATING AND MITIGATING FACTORS (OTHER THAN THOSE WITHIN EXAMPLES ABOVE)

Common aggravating and mitigating factors are identified at B[5.2A]. The following may be particularly relevant but **these lists are not exhaustive**

Factors indicating higher culpability	*Factors indicating lower culpability*
1. Disregarding warnings of others	1. Genuine emergency
2. Evidence of alcohol or drugs	2. Speed not excessive
3. Carrying out other tasks while driving	3. Offence due to inexperience rather than irresponsibility of driver
4. Carrying passengers or heavy load	
5. Tiredness	
6. Aggressive driving, such as driving much too close to vehicle in front, racing, inappropriate attempts to overtake, or cutting in after overtaking	
7.Driving when knowingly suffering from a medical condition which significantly impairs the offender's driving skills	
8. Driving a poorly maintained or dangerously loaded vehicle, especially where motivated by commercial concerns	
Factors indicating greater degree of harm	
1. Injury to others	
2. Damage to other vehicles or property	

FORM A PRELIMINARY VIEW OF THE APPROPRIATE SENTENCE, THEN CONSIDER OFFENDER MITIGATION

Common factors are identified at B[5.2A]
CONSIDER A REDUCTION FOR A GUILTY PLEA
CONSIDER ANCILLARY ORDERS, INCLUDING COMPENSATION AND DEPRIVATION OF PROPERTY Refer to B[18] for guidance on compensation and Part B for available ancillary orders
DECIDE SENTENCE GIVE REASONS

C[16.18] See Table A at B[4.1] for available sentences.

C[16.19] If the prosecution have not brought an alternative charge of careless driving and the court finds the defendant not guilty of dangerous driving but the allegations amount to an offence of careless driving or inconsiderate driving, he may be convicted of one of these offences. For the procedure see *R v Gloucester Magistrates' Court, ex p Chung* (1989) 153 JP 75.

C[16.20] If convicted of dangerous driving the defendant's licence must be endorsed and he must be disqualified from holding a licence for at least one year (two years if the defendant has had two or more disqualifications of 56 days or more imposed three years immediately preceding the commission of the latest offence). If special reasons are found (at C[5.2]) he may avoid endorsement or a disqualification. If he is not disqualified the court must determine the number of penalty points to be recorded on any endorsement.

C[16.21]–[16.30] Forfeiture of vehicle. See B[34].

C[16A]

Causing death by careless, or inconsiderate driving

Charge

C[16A.1] Being the driver of a mechanically propelled motor vehicle on a road or other public place did cause the death of another person by driving the said vehicle without due care and attention, or without reasonable consideration for other persons using the road or place.

Road Traffic Act 1988, s 2B (as inserted by the Road Safety Act 2006 from 18 August 2008 by virtue of the Road Safety Act (Commencement No 4) Order 2008, SI 2008/1918)

Maximum penalty – Fine level 5 and 12 months (for fines see B[33]). Triable either way. Must disqualify for at least 12 months unless special reasons. The disqualification may be for any period exceeding one year. If disqualified he *must* also be ordered to pass an extended driving test. Must endorse licence unless special reasons exist.

Crown Court – 5 years' imprisonment and unlimited fine.

Penalty points – 3–11.

Mode of trial

C[16A.2] Consider the SC Guideline at C[16A.10] below. In general, offences of causing death by careless or inconsiderate driving should be tried summarily except for the presence of one or more of the aggravating factors (a)–(e), outlined under 'Sentencing' at C[16.18].

Legal notes and definitions

C[16A.3] Driving. See the note under the offence of no driving licence at C[18.8].

Mechanically propelled vehicle. See C[47.9].

C[16A.4] Road. See C[22.5].

C[16A.5] Public Place. See [C20.7]-C[20.8]. The car park of a dealership has been found to be a public place (*May v DPP* [2005] EWHC 1280 (Admin), [2005] All ER (D) 182 (Apr)).

C[16A.6] Cause. The contribution of the driving to the death must be more than minute: *R v Hennigan* [1971] 3 All ER 133, 55 Cr App Rep 262, 135 JP 504. The term 'substantial cause' may imply a larger meaning whilst reference to more than a 'slight or trifling' link is a useful way to avoid the term 'de minimis': *R v Kimsey* [1996] Crim LR 35. The driving does not need to be coterminous with the impact causing death. The question is simply whether the driving played a part in causing death, and not simply creating the occasion of the fatality: also *R v Skelton* [1995] Crim LR 635,

CA. See also *R v Jenkins* [2012] EWCA Crim 2909, [2013] RTR 21.

Due care and attention. See the detailed notes at C[25]-C[30].

Reasonable consideration. See the detailed notes at C[46] onwards.

C[16A.7] Where magistrates see fit, they may allow separate informations for an offence under s 2B and s 3 to be heard together. In this event, if the defendant is convicted of one offence, the second information may be adjourned *sine die* or the justices may make *"no adjudication"*. Should the driver successfully appeal against conviction, he can later be tried on the second information.

C[16A.8] Alternatively, where there is a single information alleging causing death by careless driving or causing death by inconsiderate driving and the magistrates do not find this proved, they may convict of careless or inconsiderate driving in the alternative (s 24 RTOA 1988 as amended by s 20 of the Road Safety Act 2006).

C[16A.9] **Warning of proceedings.** If the defence claim that notice should have been given within 14 days of intention to prosecute, consult the legal adviser.

Sentencing
SC Guideline – Causing death by careless or inconsiderate driving

C[16A.10] This guideline applies only to offenders aged 18 or over. The advice and full guideline are available on sentencingcouncil.judiciary.gov.uk.

Road Traffic Act 1988 (s 2B)

Maximum penalty. 5 years' imprisonment; minimum disqualification of 12 months, discretionary re-test

This guideline and accompanying notes are taken from the SGC's definitive guideline *Causing Death by Driving*, published 15 July 2008 and coming into force on 18 August 2008.

Key factors

(a)   It is unavoidable that some cases will be on the borderline between *dangerous* and *careless* driving, or may involve a number of factors that significantly increase the seriousness of the offence. As a result, the guideline for this offence identifies three levels of seriousness, the range for the highest of which overlaps with ranges for the lower levels of seriousness for *causing death by dangerous driving*.

(b)   The three levels of seriousness are defined by the degree of carelessness involved in the standard of driving:

•   the most serious level for this offence is where the offender's driving fell not that far short of dangerous;

•   the least serious group of offences relates to those cases where the level of culpability is low – for example in a case involving an offender who misjudges the speed of another vehicle, or turns without seeing an oncoming vehicle because of restricted visibility;

- other cases will fall into the intermediate level.

(c) Where the level of carelessness is low and there are no aggravating factors, even the fact that death was caused is not sufficient to justify a prison sentence.

(d) A fine is unlikely to be an appropriate sentence for this offence; where a non-custodial sentence is considered appropriate, this should be a community order. The nature of the requirements will be determined by the **purpose** (CJA 2003, s 142(1)) identified by the court as of primary importance. Requirements most likely to be relevant include unpaid work requirement, programme requirement and curfew requirement.

(e) Offender mitigation particularly relevant to this offence includes conduct after the offence such as where the offender gave direct, positive, assistance at the scene of a collision to victim(s). It may also include remorse – whilst it can be expected that anyone who has caused a death by driving would be remorseful, this cannot undermine its importance for sentencing purposes. It is for the court to determine whether an expression of remorse is genuine.

(f) Where an offender has a good driving record, this is not a factor that automatically should be treated as mitigation, especially now that the presence of previous convictions is a statutory aggravating factor. However, any evidence to show that an offender has previously been an exemplary driver, for example, having driven an ambulance, police vehicle, bus, taxi or similar vehicle conscientiously and without incident for many years, is a fact that the courts may well wish to take into account by way of offender mitigation. This is likely to have even greater effect where the offender is driving on public duty (for example, on ambulance, fire services or police duties) and was responding to an emergency.

(g) Disqualification of the offender from driving and endorsement of the offender's driving licence are mandatory, and the offence carries between 3 and 11 points when the court finds special reasons for not imposing disqualification. There is a discretionary power to order an extended driving test/re-test where a person is convicted of an offence: s 36(4) of the Road Traffic Offenders Act 1988.

NB: In *R v Campbell* [2009] EWCA Crim 2459 a case which could be described as a single incident of misjudgement (as opposed to momentary inattention) fell into category 2 of the guidelines as opposed to category 1.

OFFENCE SERIOUSNESS (CULPABILITY AND HARM)
A. IDENTIFY THE APPROPRIATE STARTING POINT
Starting points based on first time offender pleading not guilty

Nature of offence	Starting point	Sentencing range
Careless or inconsiderate driving arising from momentary inattention with no aggravating factors	Medium level community order	Low level community order to high level community order
Other cases of careless or inconsiderate driving	Crown Court	High level community order to Crown Court

Careless or inconsiderate driving falling not far short of dangerous driving	Crown Court	Crown Court

OFFENCE SERIOUSNESS (CULPABILITY AND HARM)

B. CONSIDER THE EFFECT OF AGGRAVATING AND MITIGATING FACTORS (OTHER THAN THOSE WITHIN EXAMPLES ABOVE)

Common aggravating and mitigating factors are identified at B[5.2A]. The following may be particularly relevant but **these lists are not exhaustive**

Factors indicating higher culpability	*Factors indicating lower culpability*
1. Other offences committed at the same time, such as driving other than in accordance with the terms of a valid licence; driving while disqualified; driving without insurance; taking a motor vehicle without consent; driving a stolen vehicle	1. Offender seriously injured in collision
2. Previous convictions for motoring offences, particularly offences that involve bad driving	2. The victim was a close friend or relative
3. Irresponsible behaviour, such as failing to stop or falsely claiming that one of the victims was responsible for the collision	3. The actions of the victim or a third party contributed to the commission of the offence
	4. The offender's lack of driving experience contributed significantly to the likelihood of a collision occurring and/or death resulting
	5. The driving was in response to a proven and genuine emergency falling short of a defence
Factors indicating greater degree of harm	
1. More than one person was killed as a result of the offence	
2. Serious injury to one or more persons in addition to death(s)	

FORM A PRELIMINARY VIEW OF THE APPROPRIATE SENTENCE, THEN CONSIDER OFFENDER MITIGATION

Common factors are identified at B[5.2A]

CONSIDER A REDUCTION FOR A GUILTY PLEA

CONSIDER ANCILLARY ORDERS, INCLUDING COMPENSATION AND DEPRIVATION OF PROPERTY

Refer to B[18] for guidance on compensation and **Part B** for available ancillary orders

DECIDE SENTENCE

GIVE REASONS

C[16A.11] Forfeiture of vehicle. See B[34].

C[16B]

Causing death by driving: unlicensed, disqualified or uninsured drivers

C[16B.1] Did cause the death of another person by driving a motor vehicle on a road, and at the time when he was driving, the circumstances are such that he was committing an offence under – s 87(1) of the Road Traffic Act 1988 (driving otherwise than in accordance with a licence), s 103(1)(b) of the Road Traffic Act 1988 (driving while disqualified), or s 143 of the said Act (driving while uninsured or unsecured against third party risks).

Road Traffic Act 1988, s 3ZB (as inserted by the Road Safety Act 2006 from 18 August 2008 by virtue of the Road Safety Act (Commencement No 4) Order 2008, SI 2008/1918).

Maximum penalty – Fine level 5 and 12 months (6 months in Scotland). For fines see B[33]. Triable either way. Must disqualify for at least one year unless special reasons. The disqualification may be for any period exceeding one year. If disqualified he *may* be ordered to pass an extended driving test. Must endorse licence unless special reasons exist.

Crown Court – 2 years' imprisonment and unlimited fine.

Penalty points – 3–11.

Mode of trial

C[16B.2] Consider first the guidance notes at D[4]. In general, offences of causing death by unlicensed, disqualified or uninsured drivers should be tried summarily except for the presence of one or more of the aggravating factors (a)–(e), outlined under 'Sentencing' at C[16.8].

C[16B.3] Driving. See the note under the offence of no driving licence at C[18.8].

C[16B.4] Motor vehicle. See the definition at A[60.4].

C[16B.5] Driving otherwise than in accordance with the conditions of a driving licence. See the notes at C[18] onwards.

Driving while disqualified. See the notes at C[19] onwards.

Driving while uninsured. See the notes at C[33] onwards.

C[16B.5A] Cause. It was held in *R v Williams* [2010] EWCA Crim 2552, [2011] 3 All ER 969, [2011] 1 WLR 588, 174 JP 606, [2011] Crim LR 471, 174 CL&J 75 that no fault or blameworthy conduct on the part of the defendant was required to commit an offence under s 3ZB; it was sufficient that driving was a cause. *Williams* was followed in *Prosecution Appeal; R v H* [2011] EWCA Crim 1508, [2011] 4 All ER 761, but the decision of the Court of Appeal was reversed by the Supreme Court on further appeal in *R v Hughes* [2013] UKSC 56, [2013] 1 WLR 2461.

'[33] Juries should thus be directed that it is not necessary for the Crown to prove careless or inconsiderate driving, but that there must be something open to proper criticism in the driving of the Defendant, beyond the mere presence of the vehicle on the road, and which contributed in some more than minimal way to the death. How much this offence will in practice add to the other offences of causing death by driving will have to be worked out as factual scenarios present themselves . . .

[36] For the reasons set out, enquiry into apportionment of liability in civil terms is not appropriate to a criminal trial. But it must follow from the use of the expression "causes ... death ... by driving" that s 3ZB requires at least some act or omission in the control of the car, which involves some element of fault, whether amounting to careless/inconsiderate driving or not, and which contributes in some more than minimal way to the death. It is not necessary that such act or omission be the principal cause of the death. In which circumstances the offence under s 3ZB will then add to the other offences of causing death by driving must remain to be worked out as factual scenarios are presented to the courts . . . ' (per Lords Hughes and Toulson)

Sentencing
SC Guideline – Causing death by driving: unlicensed, disqualified or uninsured drivers

C[16B.6] This guideline applies only to offenders aged 18 or over. The advice and full guideline are available on sentencingcouncil.judiciary.gov.uk.

Road Traffic Act 1988 (s 3ZB)

Maximum penalty. 2 years' imprisonment; minimum disqualification of 12 months, discretionary re-test

This guideline and accompanying notes are taken from the SGC's definitive guideline *Causing Death by Driving*, published 15 July 2008 and coming into force on 18 August 2008.

Key factors

(a)   Culpability arises from the offender driving a vehicle on a road or other public place when, by law, not allowed to do so; the offence does not involve any fault in the standard of driving.

(b)   Since driving while disqualified is more culpable that driving while unlicensed or uninsured, a higher starting point is proposed when the offender.

(c)   Being uninsured, unlicensed or disqualified are the only determinants of the seriousness for this offence, as there are no factors relating to th standard of driving. The list of aggravating factors identified is slightly different as the emphasis is on the decision to drive by an offender who is not permitted by the law to do so.

(d)   A fine is unlikely to be an appropriate sentence for this offence; where a non-custodial sentence is considered appropriate, this should be a community order.

(e)   Where the decision to drive was brought about by a genuine and proven emergency, that may mitigate offence seriousness and so it is included as an additional mitigating factor.

(f)   Offender mitigation particularly relevant to this offence includes conduct after the offence such as where the offender gave direct, positive, assistance at the scene of a collision to victim(s). It may also include remorse – whilst it can be expected that anyone who has caused a death by driving would be remorseful, this cannot undermine its importance for sentencing purposes. It is for the court to determine whether an expression of remorse is genuine.

(g)   Where an offender has a good driving record, this is not a factor that automatically should be treated as mitigation, especially now that the presence of previous convictions is a statutory aggravating factor. However, any evidence to show that an offender has previously been an exemplary driver, for example, having driven an ambulance, police vehicle, bus, taxi or similar vehicle conscientiously and without incident for many years, is a fact that the courts may well wish to take into account by way of offender mitigation. This is likely to have even greater effect where the offender is driving on public duty (for example, on ambulance, fire services or police duties) and was responding to an emergency.

(h)   Disqualification of the offender from driving and endorsement of the offender's driving licence are mandatory, and the offence carries between 3 and 11 points when the court finds special reasons for not imposing disqualification. There is a discretionary power to order an extended driving test/re-test where a person is convicted of an offence: s 36 (4) Road Traffic Offenders Act 1988.

OFFENCE SERIOUSNESS (CULPABILITY AND HARM) A. IDENTIFY THE APPROPRIATE STARTING POINT Starting points based on first time offender pleading not guilty		
Nature of offence	Starting point	Sentencing range
The offender was disqualified from driving OR	12 months custody	36 weeks – 2 years custody
The offender was unlicensed or uninsured plus 2 or more aggravating factors from the list below		
The offender was unlicensed or uninsured plus at least 1 aggravating factor from the list below	26 weeks custody	High level community order to 36 weeks custody
The offender was unlicensed or uninsured – no aggravating factors	Medium level community order	Low level community order to High level community order
Additional aggravating factors		Additional mitigating factors
Previous convictions for motoring offences, whether involving bad driving or involving an offence of the same kind that forms part of the present conviction (i.e. unlicensed, disqualified or uninsured driving)		The decision to drive was brought about by a proven and genuine emergency falling short of a defence

More than one person was killed as a result of the offence	The offender genuinely believed that he or she was insured or licensed to drive
Serious injury to one or more persons in addition to the death(s)	The offender was seriously injured as a result of the collision
Irresponsible behaviour such as failing to stop or falsely claiming that someone else was driving	The victim was a close friend or relative

C[16B.7] Forfeiture. See B[34].

C[16C]

Causing serious injury by dangerous driving

Charge

Being the driver of a mechanically propelled vehicle on a road or other public place, did cause serious injury to another person by driving the said vehicle dangerously

Road Traffic Act 1988, s 1A

Maximum penalty – Fine level 5 and 12 months (for fines see B[33]). Triable either way. Must disqualify for at least 12 months unless special reasons. The disqualification may be for any period exceeding one year. If disqualified he must also be ordered to pass an extended driving test. Must endorse licence unless special reasons exist.

Crown Court – 5 years' imprisonment and unlimited fine.

Penalty points – 3–11.

Mode of trial

C[16C.2] No SC guidance at the time of writing.

Legal notes and definitions

C[16C.3] The offence differs from the offence of dangerous driving only by the added element of causing serious injury.

'Serious injury' means, in England and Wales, physical harm which amounts to grievous bodily harm for the purposes of the Offences Against the Person Act 1861, and, in Scotland, severe physical injury. 'Grievous bodily harm' has been interpreted to mean no more than 'serious bodily harm': *DPP v Smith* [1961] AC 290, HL. The totality of the injuries may be taken into consideration: *R v Grundy* [1977] Crim LR 543, CA. The injury does not need to be permanent or life threatening. 'Grievous' is a matter of objective assessment, but the characteristics of the victim may be relevant. For example, what is grievous bodily harm to a child might not be for an adult: *R v Bollom* [2003] EWCA Crim 2846, [2004] 2 Cr App R 50, (2003) Times, 15 December.

The Crown Prosecution Service has drawn up guidance on what might amount to grievous bodily harm for the purposes of the Offences Act the Person Act 1861.

Sentencing
SC Guideline – causing serious injury by dangerous driving: unlicensed

C[16C.4] No SC guideline has been published at the time of writing.

C[17]

Failing to produce driving licence, insurance certificate or test certificate

Charge

C[17.1] 1 Being the driver of a motor vehicle on a road,

OR

C[17.2] 2 Being a person whom a police constable reasonably believed to have driven a motor vehicle when an accident occurred owing to its presence on a road, or other public place.

OR

C[17.3] 3 Being a person whom a police constable reasonably believed had committed an offence in relation to the use on a road or other public place of a motor vehicle, failed on being so required by a police constable to produce (his driving licence) (the relevant certificate of insurance) (the relevant test certificate) for examination.

Road Traffic Act 1988, s 164 (driving licence); s 165 (insurance and test certificates)

Maximum penalty– Fine level 3 (for fines see B[33]). No power to disqualify or endorse.

Legal notes and definitions

C[17.4] Right to demand production. Before the police officer is entitled to require the defendant to produce his driving licence or certificate of insurance the defendant must:

(a)   be driving a motor vehicle on a road or other public place; or

(b)   have been reasonably believed by the police to be the driver of a motor vehicle which was on a road or other public place and involved in an accident; or

(c)   have been reasonably believed by the police to have committed a motor vehicle offence on a road or other public place;

in addition, where a requirement is made to produce a test certificate, the vehicle must require a test certificate.

C[17.5] Purpose of production. In the case of a driving licence, to enable the constable to ascertain inter alia the holder's name and address; in the case of test and insurance certificates the person must give his name and address and those of the owner where required. Additionally, if a driver fails to produce his insurance/licence when required and the constable has reasonable grounds to believe that he doesn't have a licence/insurance, or he fails to stop for long enough for enquiries to be made, and the constable believes that he has no licence or insurance, the constable may seize and remove the vehicle, and may enter premises by force to do so (but not a private dwelling). The constable must first warn the driver unless it is impracticable to do so.

C[17.6] Driver. See the notes under the heading 'driving' for the offence of driving without a licence C[18.8].

C[17.7] Person supervising a learner driver. In the circumstances (a)–(c) outlined above the supervisor may be required to produce his driving licence.

C[17.8] Motor vehicle. See C[9.7].

C[17.9] Road. Means any highway (including footpaths and bridleways) and any other road to which the public has access and includes bridges.

Other public place. Will exclude private property but will normally include such places as car parks.

C[17.10]–[17.15] Constable. Includes a police constable of any rank. Traffic wardens also have power to require production of a driving licence and the giving of a name and address in certain, very limited, circumstances. Certain vehicle examiners may also require production of documents.

C[17.16] Insurance certificate. The law requires that the insurance certificate be produced and not the policy or a premium receipt, unless the vehicle is covered by a certificate of security instead of a conventional insurance policy. Instead of an insurance policy the compulsory insurance of a motor vehicle can be covered by depositing £500,000 with the Accountant-General of the Supreme Court and a duplicate copy of this certificate will suffice instead of an insurance certificate. It will also be acceptable to produce a certificate in the prescribed form signed by the vehicle's owner (or by an agent on his behalf) stating that he has £500,000 on deposit with the Accountant-General of the Supreme Court.

C[17.17] If the vehicle is subject to a hire-purchase agreement either party to that agreement can be the 'owner'.

C[17.18] If the motor vehicle is owned by a local authority or a police authority then that authority may issue a 'Certificate of Ownership' in a prescribed form which makes an insurance certificate unnecessary.

Defences

C[17.19] There are several defences that the defendant can use:

(a)   If the defendant is unable to produce his documents at the time, he can elect to produce them at some police station of his own choosing within seven days. Although it is not compulsory, the constable will issue the defendant with a special form (HORT1) requiring him to produce the documents. A driving licence has to be produced in *person*; insurance and test certificates merely have to be *produced*.

(b)   If the documents were not produced within the seven days it is a defence if they were produced (in person for a driving licence) at the specified police station as soon as was reasonably practicable.

Or

(c) It is also a defence if it was not reasonably practicable for the documents to be produced in the required manner before the day on which the proceedings for non-production were commenced by the laying of an information. A defendant may instead produce a *current* receipt for a licence surrendered for a fixed penalty.

C[17.20] The burden of proof to establish any of these defences rests with the defendant, however he does not have to prove his point beyond reasonable doubt but only on the balance of probabilities.

Sentencing
SC Guideline – failing to produce documents

C[17.21] Starting point – Band A fine (special considerations: fine per offence, not per document).

C[17.22] For fines see B[33].

C[18]

Driving licence offences

Charges

C[18.1] Driving on a road a motor vehicle otherwise than in accordance with a licence to drive a vehicle of that class

Road Traffic Act 1988, s 87

Maximum penalty-Fine level 3. May disqualify for any period and must endorse, unless special reasons exist (except where the driving of the accused was in accordance with any licence that could have been granted to him).

Penalty points – 3–6 (fixed penalty 3).

Fixed penalty – £60.

Legal notes and definitions

C[18.2] On an appropriate application the Secretary of State may grant a provisional licence with a view to the applicant passing a test of competence to drive. A provisional licence is subject to conditions and restrictions such as to class of vehicle which may be driven, or, in the case of motor cycles, the power of the engine. Breach of any of these conditions or restrictions is an offence (Road Traffic Act 1988, s 87 and the Motor Vehicles (Driving Licences) Regulations 1987).

C[18.3] For driving a motor car a provisional licence holder must comply with the following conditions:

(a)   *Learner plates*. He must clearly display front and rear in a conspicuous position a red letter 'L' of regulation size (102mm x 89mm x 38mm) on a white background (178mm × 178mm; the corners may be rounded off).

(b)   *Supervision*. He must be supervised by a qualified driver. This offence applies to three-wheeled cars.

C[18.4] From July 1999 all driving licence applications are in the form of the new photocard type licence.

C[18.5] Supervised. Means that the supervisor must have been in a suitable part of the vehicle for supervising. For example, if the supervisor was in a rear seat from which it was difficult to supervise, the court may decide the defendant was not supervised. If a supervised driver is convicted of an offence, eg driving without due care, the supervisor can be convicted of aiding and abetting.

C[18.6] Qualified driver. Means that the supervisor must have held a full licence to drive the same type of vehicle for at least three years and be at least 21 years of age (exemption is provided for the military).

C[18.7] Motor cyclists who are learners must not drive or ride a motorcycle to which a sidecar is not attached and carry a passenger. A motor cycle which has a bare chassis or framework attached to its side does not have a side car.

C[18.8] Driving. A person steering a car whilst another person pushes the vehicle is driving. A person who walks alongside his car, pushing it and steering it with one hand is not driving it. A motor cyclist sitting on his machine and propelling it along with his feet is driving but he is not driving it if he walks beside it pushing it [but he may be "riding" the vehicle] (*Gunnell v DPP* [1993] Crim LR 619). A person sitting in the driver's seat of a car, stationary but with the engine running, was found to be driving. (*Planton v DPP* [2001] EWHC 450 (Admin), (2001) 166 JP 324). In *DPP v Alderton* [2003] EWHC 2917 (Admin), [2003] All ER (D) 360 (Nov) the defendant was driving even though the car was stationary on the verge as the wheels were spinning and he was exercising control over the vehicle by use of the handbrake. In *R (on the application of Traves) v DPP* [2005] EWHC 1482 (Admin), 169 JP 421, applying the brakes to a vehicle being towed was held to be "driving".

C[18.9] A person pushed a motor cycle along a road, its lights were on and he had used the brakes. At some point he had turned the ignition on for long enough to warm up the exhaust pipe. When apprehended he was astride the machine and was wearing a crash helmet. It was held to be within the magistrates' discretion to find that he was driving (*McKoen v Ellis* [1987] RTR 26, 151 JP 60, [1987] Crim LR 54). A person is driving who steers and brakes a vehicle being towed by a rope or chain. The position with regard to a vehicle drawn by a rigid tow bar has not been authoritatively decided but a case decided in 1985 implies that a person in the driving seat of the towed vehicle in such a case is not driving. The nature of the force used to put or keep a vehicle in motion is irrelevant in determining whether a person is driving. The essence of driving is the use of the driver's controls in order to direct the movement, however that movement is produced (*Traves v DPP* [2005] EWHC 1482 (Admin), 169 JP 421, sub nom Traves v DPP [2005] All ER (D) 381 (Jun)). An important test in deciding whether a person is driving is whether he was in a substantial sense controlling the movement and direction of the vehicle. If he is, then the question has to be answered whether his actions fall within the ordinary meaning of the word 'driving'. It is also helpful to consider whether the defendant himself deliberately set the vehicle in motion and also the length of time that he was handling the controls. A person who knelt on the driving seat of a vehicle, released the handbrake and thereafter attempted to reapply the handbrake to stop the movement of the vehicle was held to be driving the vehicle. However a momentary seizing of the steering wheel causing the vehicle to swerve cannot properly be said to be driving (*DPP v Hastings* [1993] RTR 205, 158 JP 118). In *Cawthorn v DPP* [2000] RTR 45, sub nom Cawthorn v Newcastle upon Tyne Crown Court (1994) 164 JP 527 a man who had left his vehicle briefly to post a letter, leaving the hazard warning lights on, was held to be the driver responsible for reporting an accident when the vehicle rolled down a hill and into a wall.

C[18.10]–[18.15] Motor vehicle. See C[9.7].

C[18.16] A road. Is any highway (including footpaths and bridleways) and any other road to which the public has access and includes bridges. However it will not normally include a car park (*Clarke v Kato* [1998] 4 All ER 417, [1998] 1 WLR 1647, sub nom Clarke v General Accident Fire and Life Assurance Corpn plc [1999] RTR 153, 163 JP 502, HL).

C[18.17] Burden of proof. Proof that the driver held the appropriate driving licence rests with the defendant. The prosecution does not have to prove that the defendant did not hold a licence. As with all document offences there is not statutory requirement that the prosecution issue the defendant with a production notice; it is sufficient that they show he drove the vehicle on a road (*DPP v Hay* [2005] EWHC 1395 (Admin), [2005] All ER (D) 90 (Jun)).

C[18.18] The driver does not have to prove this beyond reasonable doubt. He need only prove that on the balance of probabilities he did hold a licence.

C[18.19] Employers. No employer shall let an employee drive unless the employee holds the appropriate driving licence, and it is his responsibility to make the necessary check that the employee has such a licence. Thus the employer is liable for permitting unless he can prove that his employee was licensed. Being misled by the employee is probably not a defence though the court might consider it a mitigating circumstance.

C[18.20] A partner is neither the employee nor employer of another partner in the same firm.

Sentencing
SC Guideline – No driving licence

C[18.21] Starting point – Band A fine (Special considerations: Aggravating factor if no licence ever held).

C[18.22] If it appears to the court that the accused suffers from some disease or physical disability likely to cause his driving to be a source of danger to the public, then the court shall notify the licensing authority. Even if the accused has never obtained a licence, the court may consider it appropriate to bring the disease or disability to the attention of the licensing authority in case the accused should apply for a licence at some future date (see C[5.49]).

C[18.23] A defendant will generally not have a licence because he has not passed a test. Therefore, the case is serious and may attract a high fine and compulsory endorsement.

C[18.24] For fines see B[33].

Large goods vehicles

C[18.24A] It is an offence to drive a large goods vehicle (or to employ a person to do so) unless the driver holds a large goods vehicle driving licence authorising him to drive large goods vehicles of that class. The LGV licence is an additional entitlement to the ordinary licence.

C[18.25]–[18.30] Penalty. Same as for an ordinary licence. For definition of large goods vehicle consult the legal adviser.

C[18.31] Under the provisions of the Road Traffic (Driver Licensing and Information Systems) Act 1989 existing Heavy Goods Vehicle Licences will be phased out. Instead a driver who passes an appropriate test of competency and who satisfies the Secretary of State that he is a fit person may be granted a 'large goods vehicle licence' which is in effect an ordinary driving licence which authorises the holder to drive vehicles of the classes formerly covered by a Heavy Goods Vehicle Licence. The penalty for driving without a licence is the same as for an ordinary licence.

C[18.32] The new style licences were issued from 1 October 1990 for licences commencing on or after 1 January 1991 and as existing HGV licences become due for renewal.

C[19]

Driving whilst disqualified

Charge

C[19.1] Driving a motor vehicle on a road when disqualified for holding or obtaining a driving licence

Road Traffic Act 1988, s 103

Maximum penalty-Fine level 5 and 6 months' imprisonment (for fines see B[33]). May disqualify for any period and/or until a driving test has been passed. Must endorse unless special reasons. Triable only by magistrates.

Penalty points – 6.

Legal notes and definitions

C[19.2] Time limit. Subject to overall maximum of three years, proceedings may be brought within six months from when, in the prosecutor's opinion, he had sufficient evidence to warrant proceedings. A certificate signed by or on behalf of the prosecutor, as to when that date was, is conclusive evidence on that point.

C[19.3] Driving. See the notes under the offence of driving without a licence at C[18.8]–C[18.9]. Once it is established that a person was driving, he may continue to be the driver of a vehicle although his conduct has changed and he no longer fulfils the test mentioned on that page.

C[19.4] Motor vehicle. See C[9.7].

C[19.5] Road. Means any highway (including footpaths and bridleways) and any other road to which the public has access and includes bridges.

C[19.6] Disqualified. The prosecution must prove the defendant was driving and that the record of disqualification relates to that defendant, although there are a number of ways in which this can be done (*R v Derwentside Magistrates' Court, ex p Swift* [1997] RTR 89, 160 JP 468). It is the prosecution's task to prove all the elements of the offence and it is therefore not for the court to consult its own records to show that the defendant was in fact a disqualified driver (*Kingsnorth v DPP* [2003] All ER (D) 235 (Mar)). In *R (on the application of Howe) v South Durham Justices* [2004] EWHC 362 (Admin), 168 JP 424, [2004] All ER (D) 226 (Feb) a court permitted the defendant's solicitor to be a witness summoned for the purposes of identifying the disqualified person. A defendant disqualified in his absence and subsequently arrested for driving whilst disqualified may make a statutory declaration to the effect that he did not know of the proceedings. However this will make the earlier proceedings void but not void ab initio leaving the disqualification as valid at the time he was driving (*Singh v DPP* [1999] RTR 424, 164 JP 82, [1999] Crim LR 914).

In *Pattison v DPP* [2005] EWHC 2938 (Admin), [2006] 2 All ER 317, it was held that evidence of identity could be proved by admission (formal or otherwise), fingerprints, a witness who was present in court, or a match between the personal details of the accused and a certificate of conviction. Even where the personal details were not uncommon eg the name, address and date of birth of the accused, that might be sufficient to found a prima facie case. See also *Mills v DPP* [2008] EWHC 3304 (Admin), [2009] RTR 143.

C[19.7] Knowledge. It is not necessary to prove that the defendant knew he was disqualified, nor that he knew he was on a road. When disqualified until a test is passed the onus is on the defendant to show that he held a provisional licence and was complying with the conditions of that licence at the time he was driving (*DPP v Baker* (2004) 168 JP 140, [2004] All ER (D) 28 (Nov), DC).

Sentencing
SC Guideline – Driving while Disqualified

C[19.8] Must endorse and may disqualify. If no disqualification, impose 6 points.

OFFENCE SERIOUSNESS (CULPABILITY AND HARM)		
A. IDENTIFY THE APPROPRIATE STARTING POINT		
Starting points based on first time offender pleading not guilty		
Examples of nature of activity	**Starting point**	**Range**
Full period expired but retest not taken	Low level community penalty	Band C fine to medium level community order
		6 points or lengthen disqualify for 3–6 months
Lengthy period of ban already served	High level community order	Medium level community order to 12 weeks custody
		Lengthen disqualification for 6–12 months beyond expiry of current ban
Recently imposed ban	12 weeks custody	High level community order to 26 weeks custody
		Lengthen disqualification for 12–18 months beyond expiry of current ban
OFFENCE SERIOUSNESS (CULPABILITY AND HARM)		
B. CONSIDER THE EFFECT OF AGGRAVATING AND MITIGATING FACTORS (OTHER THAN THOSE WITHIN EXAMPLES ABOVE)		
Common aggravating and mitigating factors are identified at B[5.2A]. The following may be particularly relevant but **these lists are not exhaustive**		
Factors indicating higher culpability	*Factors indicating lower culpability*	
1. Never passed test	1. Defendant not present when disqualification imposed and genuine reason why unaware of ban	
2. Planned long-term evasion	2. Genuine emergency established	

3. Vehicle obtained during ban 4. Driving for remuneration	
Factors indicating greater degree of harm 1. Distance driven 2. Evidence of associated bad driving 3. Offender caused accident	
FORM A PRELIMINARY VIEW OF THE APPROPRIATE SENTENCE, THEN CONSIDER OFFENDER MITIGATION Common factors are identified at B[5.2A]	
CONSIDER A REDUCTION FOR A GUILTY PLEA	
CONSIDER ANCILLARY ORDERS, INCLUDING DEPRIVATION OF PROPERTY Refer to B[18] for guidance on compensation and **Part B** for available ancillary orders	
DECIDE SENTENCE **GIVE REASONS**	

Note: An offender convicted of this offence will always have at least one relevant previous conviction for the offence that resulted in disqualification. The starting points and ranges take this into account. Any other previous convictions should be considered in the usual way – consult the legal adviser for guidance.

C[19.9] See Table B at B[4.2] for available sentences.

C[19.10] If it appears to the magistrates that the accused suffers from a disease or physical disability likely to cause his driving to be a source of danger to the public, they must notify the licensing authority in case the accused applies for a licence at some future date (see C[5.49]).

C[19.11]–[19.17] The offence does not apply to offenders who are driving under age. They are guilty of driving otherwise than in accordance with a licence, see C[18].

'Unfit through drink or drugs' (drive/attempt drive)

Charge

C[20.1] Driving or attempting to drive a mechanically propelled vehicle on a road (or public place) when unfit through drink or drugs

Road Traffic Act 1988, s 4(1), as amended

Maximum penalty-Fine level 5 and 6 months' imprisonment (for fines see B[33]). Must disqualify for at least one year unless special reasons. The disqualification may be for any period exceeding a year. He may also be ordered to pass a driving test. Must endorse licence unless special reasons exist.

Previous convictions-Where there is a previous conviction during the ten years preceding the current offence, the compulsory disqualification must be for at least three years unless special reasons exist.

A previous conviction for driving (or attempting to drive) a motor vehicle with alcohol over the prescribed limit or a previous conviction for refusing a blood etc specimen in such circumstances counts as a previous conviction for this offence.

Penalty points – 3–11.

Legal notes and definitions

C[20.2] The charge may allege either driving or attempting to drive. It must not allege both.

C[20.3] The court must be satisfied that the defendant drove (or attempted to drive) a mechanically propelled vehicle on a road or public place when his ability to drive properly was impaired by drink or drugs. The offence is one of strict liability and therefore the defence of insanity is not available (*DPP v H* [1997] 1 WLR 1406, [1998] RTR 200, sub nom DPP v Harper (1997) 161 JP 697).

C[20.4] Driving. See the notes under this heading for the offence of driving without a licence at C[18.9].

C[20.5] Mechanically propelled vehicle. See C[47.9].

C[20.6] Road. Means any highway (including footpaths and bridleways) and any other road to which the public has access and includes bridges.

C[20.7] Public place. Need not be a road. A field or enclosure at the rear of licensed premises for parking cars has been held to be a public place. In *Lewis v DPP* [2004] EWHC 3081 (Admin), [2005] All ER (D) 66 (Jan), it was decided that magistrates were entitled to infer that a public house car park was a public place and that the prosecution did not need to adduce evidence of public utilisation. See also *May v DPP* [2005] EWHC 1280

(Admin), [2005] All ER (D) 182 (Apr).

C[20.8] Whether the scene of the charge is a road or public place is a question of fact for the court to decide (such as a car park in (*R v Spence* [1999] RTR 353, 163 JP 754, [1999] Crim LR 975, CA; or the parking area of a privately owned tyre and exhaust centre: *Filmer v DPP* [2006] EWHC 3450 (Admin), [2006] All ER (D) 08 (Nov)). See *Hallett v DPP* [2011] EWHC 488 (Admin) in which the key question was whether there was before the justices evidence of public use of an unmade service road. Any road might be regarded as open to which the public had access if the public was there without overcoming physical obstruction or in defiance of a prohibition. Whether a place was public would generally be a question of fact and degree. Help might also be derived from asking whether access was only for a special class of members of the public, including guests of residents, postmen and milkmen. A sign or barrier lent weight to restriction of the area to a special class and thus to it being private, but the absence of a sign or barrier was not determinative.

In *Cowan v DPP* [2013] EWHC 192 (Admin), (2013) 177 JP 474 the appellant was driving on an internal roadway at the Kingston Hill Campus of Kingston University when the car left the road. He was later breathalysed and found to be over the limit. The justices convicted the appellant. However, they did not identify which members of the public had access to the site and for what purpose. This resulted in the quashing of the conviction. There were no doubt university campuses which provided a means of passage for ordinary members of the public. However, in the present case, there was simply no evidence of such use. What was required was a finding that the public did use the roadway on the campus as members of the public. Students were not to be treated as members of the public; they had a right to occupy their rooms and make use of the facilities not as members of the public, but in their status as students. As to their visitors, in gaining access to the site, they were not doing so as ordinary members of the public, but for the purposes of the occupier of the site. However, the court emphasised that it would not have taken much additional evidence to establish that members of the public did have access to the site and the result did not mean that anyone could drive against the law on the scores of university campuses in the United Kingdom.

C[20.9] Unfit. A person is taken to be unfit to drive if his ability to drive properly is for the time being impaired. It need not be proved that the defendant was *incapable* of driving.

C[20.10] The court may take note of such evidence as, for example, where there is evidence of drink or drugs:

(a)   driving erratically;
(b)   colliding with a stationary object for no apparent reason;
(c)   the defendant's condition-slurred speech, staggering, mental confusion. Also account may be taken of evidence of an analyst's certificate where the accused has given a sample of blood/breath/urine.

C[20.11]–[20.15] Even where the defendant has taken a drink subsequent to the incident the certificate may be evidence of the amount of alcohol consumed at the time of the incident unless the accused proves on the balance of probabilities that had he not consumed the subsequent drink his ability to drive would not have been impaired.

C[20.16] A witness who is not an expert can give his impressions as to whether an accused had taken drink but he may not give evidence whether the accused was fit to drive.

C[20.17] **Drink or drugs.** Drink means an alcoholic drink. Drugs can refer to medicine, ie something given to cure, alleviate or assist an ailing body, or it can be something which, when consumed, affected the control of the body. Accordingly, 'glue sniffing' would come within the ambit of this offence.

C[20.18] **Alternative verdict.** If the allegation is 'driving' the court may convict on the basis of attempting to drive. Where the defendant is found not guilty of an offence under s 4(1) but the allegations amount to or include an offence under the Road Traffic Act 1988, s 4(2) (being in charge when unfit to drive through drink or drugs) the court may convict him of that offence (Road Traffic Offenders Act 1988, s 24 as substituted by the Road Traffic Act 1991, s 24).

Sentencing
SC Guideline – Unfit through drink or drugs (drive/attempt to drive)

C[20.19] Must endorse and disqualify for at least 12 months.

Must disqualify for **at least** 2 years if offender has had two or more disqualifications for periods of 56 days or more in preceding 3 years – consult your legal adviser for further guidance.

Must disqualify for **at least** 3 years if offender has been convicted of a relevant drink/drive offence in preceding 10 years – consult your legal adviser for further guidance.

If there is a delay in sentencing after conviction, consider interim disqualification.

Note: the first column below provides guidance regarding the length of disqualification that may be appropriate in case to which the 3 year minimum applies. The period to be imposed in any individual case will depend on an assessment of all the relevant circumstances, including the length of time since the earlier ban was imposed and the gravity of the current offence.

OFFENCE SERIOUSNESS (CULPABILITY AND HARM)				
A. IDENTIFY THE APPROPRIATE STARTING POINT				
Starting points based on first time offender pleading not guilty				
Examples of nature of activity	Starting point	Range	Disqualification	Disqualification. 2nd offence in 10 years
Evidence of moderate level of impairment and no aggravating factors	Band C fine	Band C fine	12–16 months	36–40 months

Evidence of moderate level of impairment and presence of one or more aggravating factors listed below	Band C fine	Band C fine	17–22 months	36–46 months
Evidence of high level of impairment and no aggravating factors	Medium level community order	Low level community order to high level community order	23–28 months	36–52 months
Evidence of high level of impairment and presence of one or more aggravating factors listed below	12 weeks custody	High level community order to 26 weeks custody	29–36 months	36–60 months

OFFENCE SERIOUSNESS (CULPABILITY AND HARM)

B. CONSIDER THE EFFECT OF AGGRAVATING AND MITIGATING FACTORS (OTHER THAN THOSE WITHIN EXAMPLES ABOVE)

Common aggravating and mitigating factors are identified at B[5.2A]. The following may be particularly relevant but **these lists are not exhaustive**

Factors indicating higher culpability	*Factors indicating lower culpability*
1. LGV, HGV, PSV etc	1. Genuine emergency established*
2. Poor road or weather conditions	2. Spiked drinks*
3. Carrying passengers	3. Very short distance driven*
4. Driving for hire or reward	* Even where not amounting to special reasons
5. Evidence of unacceptable standard of driving	
Factors indicating greater degree of harm	
1. Involved in accident	
2. Location eg near school	
3. High level of traffic or pedestrians in vicinity	

FORM A PRELIMINARY VIEW OF THE APPROPRIATE SENTENCE, THEN CONSIDER OFFENDER MITIGATION

Common factors are identified at B[5.2A]

CONSIDER A REDUCTION FOR A GUILTY PLEA

CONSIDER OFFERING DRINK/DRIVE REHABILITATION COURSE

CONSIDER ANCILLARY ORDERS

Refer to B[18] for guidance on compensation and **Part B** for available ancillary orders

DECIDE SENTENCE

GIVE REASONS

C[20.20] See Table B at B[4.2] for available sentences and the notes to the offence of 'Alcohol over the prescribed limit' at C[22.2] and C[22.56] for rehabilitation courses and their effect upon disqualifications.

C[21]

'Unfit through drink or drugs (in charge)'

Charge

C[21.1] Being in charge of a mechanically propelled vehicle on a road (or public place) when unfit through drink or drugs

Road Traffic Act 1988, s 4(2), as amended

Maximum penalty – Fine level 4 and 3 months' imprisonment (for fines see B[33]). May disqualify for any period and/or until a driving test has been passed. Must endorse unless there are special reasons.

Penalty points – 10.

Legal notes and definitions

C[21.2] See the notes for the offence of 'drunken driving' at C[20.2].

C[21.3] In charge. This is a potentially wide concept. There must be proof of some connection, which can be less than attempting to drive, between the defendant and a motor vehicle on a road or public place. The owner or a person who had recently driven the vehicle would be 'in charge' unless he put the vehicle in someone else's charge or unless there was no realistic possibility of his resuming actual control, eg where he was at home in bed or a great distance from the car (*DPP v Watkins* [1989] QB 821, [1989] 1 All ER 1126 where there is further guidance in respect of defendants who are not the owner or have not recently driven the vehicle). A qualified driver supervising a provisional licence holder is 'in charge'.

C[21.4] A person is deemed not to be in charge if he can demonstrate from the evidence that at the material time the circumstances were such that there was no likelihood of his driving the vehicle so long as he remained unfit to drive through drink or drugs but in determining whether there was such a likelihood the court may disregard any injury to him and any damage to the vehicle. A supervisor of a learner driver is in charge and may need to take over at any time (*DPP v Janman* [2004] EWHC 101 (Admin), [2004] Crim LR 478, [2004] All ER (D) 171 (Jan)).

C[21.4A] ECHR. The House of Lords held that this was a reasonable and legitimate burden on the defendant (*Sheldrake v DPP* [2003] EWHC 273 (Admin), [2004] QB 487; revsd [2004] UKHL 43, [2004] 3 WLR 976).

Sentencing
SC Guideline – Unfit through drink or drugs (in charge)

C[21.5] Must endorse and may disqualify. If no disqualification, impose 10 points.

OFFENCE SERIOUSNESS (CULPABILITY AND HARM)
A. IDENTIFY THE APPROPRIATE STARTING POINT

Starting points based on first time offender pleading not guilty		
Examples of nature of activity	**Starting point**	**Range**
Evidence of moderate level of impairment and no aggravating factors	Band B fine	Band B fine 10 points
Evidence of moderate level of impairment and presence of one or more aggravating factors listed below	Band B fine	Band B fine 10 points or consider disqualification
Evidence of high level of impairment and no aggravating factors	Band C fine	Band C fine to medium level community order 10 points or consider disqualification
Evidence of high level of impairment and presence of one or more aggravating factors listed below	High level community order	Medium level community order to 12 weeks custody Consider disqualification OR 10 points
OFFENCE SERIOUSNESS (CULPABILITY AND HARM)		
B. CONSIDER THE EFFECT OF AGGRAVATING AND MITIGATING FACTORS (OTHER THAN THOSE WITHIN EXAMPLES ABOVE)		
Common aggravating and mitigating factors are identified at B[5.2A]. The following may be particularly relevant but **these lists are not exhaustive**		

Factors indicating higher culpability	*Factor indicating lower culpability*
1. LGV, HGV, PSV etc	1. Low likelihood of driving
2. High likelihood of driving	
3. Driving for hire or reward	

FORM A PRELIMINARY VIEW OF THE APPROPRIATE SENTENCE, THEN CONSIDER OFFENDER MITIGATION
Common factors are identified at B[5.2A]
CONSIDER A REDUCTION FOR A GUILTY PLEA
CONSIDER ANCILLARY ORDERS
Refer to B[18] for guidance on compensation and **Part B** for available ancillary orders
DECIDE SENTENCE
GIVE REASONS

C[21.6] See Table B at B[4.2] for available sentences and the notes to the offence of 'Alcohol over the prescribed limit' at C[22.2].

C[22]

Excess alcohol (drive/attempt to drive or in charge)

Charge 1

C[22.1] Driving (or attempting to drive) a motor vehicle on a road (or public place) with alcohol above the prescribed limit

Road Traffic Act 1988, s 5(1)(a)

Maximum penalty-Fine level 5 and 6 months' imprisonment (for fines see B[33]). Must disqualify for at least one year unless special reasons. The disqualification may be for any period exceeding a year. The defendant may also be ordered to take a test again. Must endorse licence unless special reasons.

It is not a special reason that the defendant's driving was not impaired.

Previous convictions-Where there is a previous conviction during the ten years preceding the current offence, the compulsory disqualification must be for at least three years unless special reasons.

A previous conviction for driving (or attempting to drive) a motor vehicle when unfit through drink or a previous conviction for refusing a blood or urine specimen in such circumstances counts as a previous conviction for this offence.

Penalty points – 3–11.

Legal notes and definitions

C[22.2] The charge may allege either driving or attempting to drive. It is important to note that it must not allege both. The prosecution need not prove that the defendant's ability to drive was impaired.

C[22.3] Driving. See the notes under the offence of no driving licence at C[18.2].

C[22.4] Motor vehicle. See C[9.7].

C[22.5] Road. Means any highway (including footpaths and bridleways) and any other road to which the public has access and includes bridges. The information may read 'road or other public place', but if it does not the specific allegation must be proved (*Plunkett v DPP* [2004] EWHC 1937 (Admin), [2004] All ER (D) 82 (Jul)).

C[22.6] Public place. Need not be a road. A field or enclosure at the rear of licensed premises for parking cars has been held to be a public place (see C[20.7]).

C[22.7] Whether the scene of the charge is a road or public place is a question of fact for the court to decide. It is basically a question of whether at the relevant time the public enjoyed access to the place where the offence was committed.

C[22.8] Prescribed limit. If a blood specimen was provided by the defendant the prescribed limit is 80 mg of alcohol in 100 ml of blood; if a urine specimen, 107 mg of alcohol in 100 ml of urine; if breath, 35 µg of alcohol in 100 ml of breath. Comparison of these levels is achieved by multiplying a breath/alcohol level by 2.3 and rounding up to convert to blood alcohol. The following conversion table relates blood, urine and breath levels.

C[22.9]

Blood	Urine	Breath	Blood	Urine	Breath
80	107	35	110	147	48
83	110	36	113	150	49
85	113	37	115	153	50
87	116	38	117	156	51
90	119	39	120	159	52
92	122	40	122	162	53
94	125	41	124	165	54
97	129	42	126	168	55
99	132	43	129	171	56
101	135	44	131	174	57
103	138	45	133	177	58
106	141	46	136	181	59
108	144	47	138	184	60
140	187	61	163	217	71
143	190	62	166	220	72
145	193	63	168	223	73
147	196	64	170	226	74
147	199	65	172	230	75
152	154	205	175	233	76
154	205	67	178	236	77
156	208	68	180	239	78
159	211	69	182	242	79
161	214	70	184	245	80

C[22.10]–[22.15] Breath tests. A constable in uniform may require a person to submit to a breath test if the constable reasonably suspects him to have alcohol in his body or to have committed a traffic offence while the vehicle was in motion. The test may also be required in these circumstances after a person has ceased to be a driver. If the test indicates the presence of alcohol the driver need not, but may be, arrested and taken to a police station where he will be required to offer a specimen of blood, urine or breath at the choice of the police. The roadside breath test may be taken by blowing into a bag or into a machine, but these devices are a preliminary test and the sample of breath used in these tests is not the one which is analysed to determine its alcohol content.

Once a negative breath test has been given, the police lose the power of arrest under the Road Traffic Act 1988, s 6, but may in appropriate circumstances arrest under s 4 of the Act (*DPP v Robertson* [2002] 15 LS Gaz R 33).

Breath is not confined to deep lung air but includes all that is exhaled (*Zafar v DPP* (2004) Times, 1 November).

C[22.16] If the police require a breath sample for analysis it will be analysed in a machine approved by the Secretary of State such as a Lion Intoxilyzer 6000 UK. It works by, analysing the level of alcohol in the breath by the absorption of infra red radiation and giving a printed record of the result of two samples of breath given within a short time. The lower reading is the one which will be used to determine whether a prosecution will follow. Each machine works with a simulator, a device enabling the machine to check itself for accuracy. If for any reason the police decide not to use the machine they may ask for a sample of blood or urine.

The modification of a device, which did not affect its operation, did not take it out of the approved category (*Breckon v DPP* [2007] EWHC 2013 (Admin)); whether a modification to an intoxyliser machine took it out of a type approved under the Breath Analysis Devices Approval Order 2005 required a common sense consideration of whether the function of the modified device still had the character, essence and identity of the device with type approval: *R (on the application of Coxon v Manchester City Magistrates' Court* [2010] EWHC 712 (Admin), 174 CL&J 221.

C[22.17] The form of print-out from the machine will give the subject's name and the time and date of the test. They will show the results of each of two samples given by the subject and the results of each of two checks which the machine carries out to prove its accuracy. These calibration checks must show a reading within a range of 32–38 µg; figures outside this range on either check will render the test void.

C[22.18] The print-out will be signed by the operator and by the subject and a machine-produced copy will be handed to the driver, the other copy being retained by the police. It is unlikely that a prosecution will follow if the lowest reading is less than 40, but if it is 50 or less the driver is entitled to ask for an analysis of a sample of blood or urine. In the absence of any suggestion that the machine was not used properly and providing the calibration checks show readings within the parameters mentioned above, the print-out from the machine is evidence of the level of alcohol in the breath without further proof provided that a print-out was handed to the accused at the time it was produced, or served on him more than seven days before the hearing, either personally or by registered or recorded post.

C[22.19] Evidence by certificate. A certificate signed by an authorised analyst stating the proportion of alcohol in the specimen is admissible without the analyst being called as a witness: the same applies to a certificate signed by a doctor who took a blood specimen from the defendant.

C[22.20] The defendant is entitled to insist on the attendance at court of the analyst or doctor. As the police were bound to provide the defendant with specimens of blood or urine taken at the same time, it is possible that sometimes a defendant may call his own analyst to give evidence as to the proportion of alcohol.

C[22.21] If difficulty arises about the provision of a specimen to a defendant, or about the admissibility of a certificate, the legal adviser should be consulted. The police are entitled to divide the specimen into three parts and not two.

C[22.22] The High Court has quashed a conviction because a pathologist declared the blood specimen handed to the defendant to be inadequate for examination: *Earl v Roy* [1969] 2 All ER 684, 133 JP 520.

C[22.23] The defendant is entitled to be acquitted if he can raise a reasonable doubt about the accuracy of the machine. However the prosecution do not have to prove a specific alcohol content, but that the alcohol content exceeded the prescribed limit so that where an accused called expert evidence to show that the variation in readings on the breath machine was unacceptable but where it was conceded that the readings must have been 5 microgrammes above the limit, he was convicted. In some circumstances it may not be necessary for the defendant to call expert evidence in order to rebut the presumption that the machine is reliable (*DPP v Spurrier* [2000] RTR 60, sub nom R v Crown Prosecution Service, ex p Spurrier 164 JP 369), but such evidence should relate to a particular fault relevant to the issues in the case (*DPP v Teixeira* (2002) 166 JP 1). For further case law on the statutory presumption and reliability of breath testing equipment see *DPP v Memery* (2003) 167 JP 238; *Skinner v DPP* [2004] EWHC 2914 (Admin); *Rose v DPP* [2010] EWHC 462 (Admin).

C[22.24] Special reasons. It is not a defence to the charge that unknown to him the defendant's drink had been laced. If this is put forward as a reason for not disqualifying the question must be answered whether the extra drink by itself is what took the level of alcohol in the blood over the limit and the defendant, if there is any doubt, should be invited to call expert evidence. Note that even if special reasons are proved this only gives the justices a discretion not to disqualify. They may still do so depending on the circumstances of the case (*R v Crown Court at St Albans, ex p O'Donovan* [2000] 1 Cr App Rep (S) 344).

A motorist drove 350 metres to his home address fearing the loss of valuable work tools in his van. Held, not special reasons: *DPP v Oram* [2005] EWHC 964 (Admin), [2005] All ER (D) 57 (May).

C[22.25]–[22.29] Driving in an emergency may amount to a special reason not to disqualify, but only where a sober, reasonable and responsible friend of the defendant present at the time, but unable to drive, would have advised the defendant to drive (*DPP v Bristow* [1998] RTR 100, 161 JP 35). Shortness of distance driven may be a special reason but not where the defendant's intention was to drive a longer distance than he in fact managed (*DPP v Humphries* [2000] RTR 52, sub nom Crown Prosecution Service v Humphries [2000] 2 Cr App Rep (S) 1, 164 JP 502). No specific reasons could be argued by a defendant who assumed without enquiry that a drink he consumed contained no alcohol (*Lloyd Robinson v DPP* [2003] EWHC 2718 (Admin), (2004) 168 JP 522, [2004] Crim LR 670, [2003] All ER (D) 05 (Nov)); nor where the defendant drove to the scene of an accident involving his son, having failed to wake his wife who could have legally driven (*Khan v DPP* [2004] EWHC 2505 (Admin), sub nom Khan v DPP [2004] All ER (D) 134 (Oct)).

In *Ng v DPP* [2007] EWHC 36 (Admin), the defendant contended that his breath reading had been affected by eructation (belching) during the procedure. It was decided that the evidence on which the defendant had sought to rely went directly to the commission of the offence. If accepted it could provide an explanation as to why the level of alcohol exceeded the prescribed limit. It was capable therefore of amounting a special reason.

Driving a short distance to avoid car park charges was held not to be a special reason because, on the facts, there was danger of the defendant coming into contact with other road users (*DPP v Cove* [2008] EWHC 441 (Admin), [2008] All ER (D) 199 (Feb).

C[22.30] Drinking after driving. If the accused claims that the alcohol level was increased because he had taken drink after ceasing to drive then he must prove on the balance of probabilities that the post-driving drink took him over the limit and that he was not over the limit while he was driving. This is because the law requires the court to assume that the alcohol level at the time of the driving was not less than that at the time of the test (*Griffiths v DPP* [2002] EWHC 792 (Admin), 166 JP 629, [2002] All ER (D) 132 (Apr)). If an accused wishes to raise this defence he will almost certainly have to call medical or scientific evidence.

C[22.31] Alternative verdict. If the allegation is 'driving' the court may convict him on the basis of attempting to drive. Where the defendant is found not guilty of an offence under the Road Traffic Act 1988, s 5(1)(a) but the allegations amount to or include an offence under s 5(1)(b) (being in charge of a vehicle with excess alcohol in breath, blood or urine) the court may convict him of that offence (RTOA 1988, s 24).

Sentencing
SC Guideline – Excess Alcohol (drive/attempt to drive)

C[22.32] Must endorse and disqualify for at least 12 months.

Must disqualify for **at least** 2 years if offender has had two or more disqualifications for periods of 56 days or more in preceding 3 years – consult your legal adviser for further guidance.

Must disqualify for **at least** 3 years if offender has been convicted of a relevant drink/drive offence in preceding 10 years – consult your legal adviser for further guidance.

If there is a delay in sentencing after conviction, consider interim disqualification.

Note: the first column below provides guidance regarding the length of disqualification that may be appropriate in case to which the 3 year minimum applies. The period to be imposed in any individual case will depend on an assessment of all the relevant circumstances, including the length of time since the earlier ban was imposed and the gravity of the current offence.

OFFENCE SERIOUSNESS (CULPABILITY AND HARM)				
A. IDENTIFY THE APPROPRIATE STARTING POINT				
Starting points based on first time offender pleading not guilty				
Level of alcohol Breath (mg) Blood (ml) Urine (ml)	Starting point	Range	Disqualification	Disqualification. 2nd offence in 10 years
36–59 mg (breath) or 81–137 ml (blood) or 108– 183 ml (urine)	Band C fine	Band C fine	12–16 months	36–40 months
60–89 mg (breath) or 138–206 ml (blood) or 184–274 ml (urine)	Band C fine	Band C fine	17–22 months	36–46 months
90–119 mg (breath) or 207–275 ml (blood) or 275–388 ml (urine)	Medium level community order	Low level community order to high level community order	23–28 months	36–52 months
120–150 mg (breath) and above or 276–345 ml (blood) and above or 367–459 (urine) and above	12 weeks custody	High level community order to 26 weeks custody	29–36 months	36–60 months

OFFENCE SERIOUSNESS (CULPABILITY AND HARM)

B. CONSIDER THE EFFECT OF AGGRAVATING AND MITIGATING FACTORS (OTHER THAN THOSE WITHIN EXAMPLES ABOVE)

Common aggravating and mitigating factors are identified at B[5.2A]. The following may be particularly relevant but **these lists are not exhaustive**

Factors indicating higher culpability	Factors indicating lower culpability
1. LGV, HGV, PSV etc	1. Genuine emergency established*
2. Poor road or weather conditions	2. Spiked drinks*
3. Carrying passengers	3. Very short distance driven*
4. Driving for hire or reward	* Even where not amounting to special reasons

5. Evidence of unacceptable standard of driving	
Factors indicating greater degree of harm	
1. Involved in accident	
2. Location eg near school	
3. High level of traffic or pedestrians in vicinity	

FORM A PRELIMINARY VIEW OF THE APPROPRIATE SENTENCE, THEN CONSIDER OFFENDER MITIGATION

Common factors are identified at B[5.2A]

CONSIDER A REDUCTION FOR A GUILTY PLEA

CONSIDER OFFERING DRINK/DRIVE REHABILITATION COURSE

CONSIDER ANCILLARY ORDERS, INCLUDING FORFEITURE OR SUSPENSION OF PERSONAL LIQUOR LICENCE

Refer to B[18] for guidance on compensation and **Part B** for available ancillary orders

DECIDE SENTENCE

GIVE REASONS

C[22.33] Structure of the sentencing decision. See B[3.7].

C[22.34] Available sentences. See Table B at B[4.2].

C[22.35]–[22.40] Custodial sentence. See B[2].

C[22.41] Community sentence. See B[3].

C[22.42] Fine. See B[33].

C[22.43] Forfeiture of vehicle. See B[34].

C[22.44] Disqualification. See C[5].

C[22.45] High risk offenders. An offender is a 'high risk offender' if he falls within any of the following categories, which are prescribed by reg 74 of the Motor Vehicles (Driving Licences) Regulations 1999, SI 1999/286, namely he:

(a)   has been disqualified by an order of a court by reason that the proportion of alcohol in his body equalled or exceeded—

(i)   87.5 microgrammes per 100 millilitres of breath, or

(ii)   200 milligrammes per 100 millilitres of blood, or

(iii)   267.5 milligrammes per 100 millilitres of urine;

(b)   has been disqualified by order of a court by reason that he has failed, without reasonable excuse, to provide a specimen when required to do so pursuant to section 7 of the Traffic Act; ...

(bb)   has been disqualified by order of a court by reason of failure, without reasonable excuse, to give permission for a laboratory test of a specimen of blood taken pursuant to section 7A of the Traffic Act; or

(c) has been disqualified by order of a court on two or more
    occasions within any period of 10 years by reason that—

    (i) the proportion of alcohol in his breath, blood or urine
        exceeded the limit prescribed by virtue of section 5 of the
        Traffic Act, or

    (ii) he was unfit to drive through drink contrary to section 4
        of that Act.

For the purposes of paragraph (a) and (b) a court order shall not be taken
into account unless it was made on or after 1 June 1990 and paragraph (c)
shall not apply to a person unless the last such order was made on or after
1 June 1990.

For the purposes of paragraph (bb) a court order shall not be taken into
account unless it was made on or after 1 June 2013.

C[22.46] The DVLA will write to a high risk offender and explain that
the disqualification is considered to be an indication of a drink problem.
Shortly before the expiry of the disqualification, a further letter will be sent
explaining what must be done to apply for the return of the licence. The
applicant will have to submit to a medical examination and pay an
administration fee and medical fees to the examining doctor.

C[22.47] If it appears to the court that the accused suffers from a disease
or physical disability likely to cause his driving to be a source of danger to
the public, it must notify the licensing authority (see C[5.49]).

C[22.48] The fact that the amount of alcohol is only slightly over the
statutory limit is **not** a special reason for avoiding imposing disqualification
and endorsement.

C[22.49] The 12 months' mandatory disqualification is to be regarded as
a minimum and not as a tariff and should be increased in appropriate cases.
The national sentencing guidelines suggest an increased disqualification for
cases between 56mg and 70mg.

C[22.50]–[22.55] If the defendant submits as a special reason for not
disqualifying him that he was obliged to drive by some sudden crisis or
emergency he must show that he acted responsibly and that the crisis or
emergency was not one which arose through his own irresponsibility or
lack of reasonable foresight. The driving must have been only to the extent
occasioned by the emergency.

C[22.56] Reduced disqualification for attendance on courses. Reduced
disqualification for attendance on a course may be offered to an offender
convicted of a 'relevant drink offence' (or, when s 35 of the Road Safety Act
2006 is brought fully into force, a 'specified offence') who is disqualified by
the court under s 34 of the RTOA 1988 for at least 12 months.

C[22.57] A 'relevant drink offence' means:

(a) an offence under s 3A(1)(a) of the RTA1988 (causing death by
    careless driving when unfit to drive through drink) committed when
    unfit to drive through drink,

(b) an offence under paragraph (b) of that subsection (causing death by
    careless driving with excess alcohol),

(c)   an offence under paragraph (c) of that subsection (failing to provide a specimen) where the specimen is required in connection with drink or consumption of alcohol,

(d)   an offence under s 4 of that Act (driving or being in charge when under influence of drink) committed by reason of unfitness through drink,

(e)   an offence under s 5(1) of that Act (driving or being in charge with excess alcohol),

(f)   an offence under s 7(6) of that Act (failing to provide a specimen) committed in the course of an investigation into an offence within any of the preceding paragraphs, or

(g)   an offence under s 7A(6) of that Act (failing to allow a specimen to be subjected to a laboratory test) in the course of an investigation into an offence within any of the preceding paragraphs.

RTA 1988, s 34A(3).

Offenders who come within the criteria for High Risk Offenders (HRO) may be referred to a rehabilitation scheme, but will still have to meet the requirements of the HRO scheme before their licence will be returned to them by the Secretary of State. Although referral to a rehabilitation scheme is not precluded, training courses for drink-drive offenders as a condition of a community order may be more appropriate for offenders where a higher degree of intervention is necessary to match the seriousness of the offence (DETR Guide issued in respect of the former scheme).

C[22.58] The court must have made an order for disqualification for not less than 12 months.

C[22.59] The reduction specified must be not less than three months and not more than one quarter of the original period (ie 9 months' disqualification must remain where the original unreduced period was 12 months). The reduction should be announced in open court.

C[22.60] Criteria. The court should decide whether or not to offer the offender an opportunity to participate. It must then check that:

(a)   a place on the course is available;
(b)   the offender is aged 17 years or more;
(c)   the court has explained the effect of the order in ordinary language, the amount of fees payable and that they must be paid before beginning the course;
(d)   the offender consents.

The course must be completed at least two months before the end of the reduced period of disqualification. The scheme is voluntary after referral. There is no additional penalty if the offender fails to attend the course but the full period of disqualification applies.

C[22.61] On completion, the organiser of the course will give the offender a certificate for presentation to the court.

Charge 2

C[22.62] Being in charge of a motor vehicle on a road (or public place) having consumed alcohol over the prescribed limit

Road Traffic Act 1988, s 5(1)(b)

Maximum penalty-Fine on level 4 and 3 months' imprisonment (for fines see **B[33]**). May disqualify for any period and/or until a driving test has been passed. Must endorse unless there are special reasons.

Penalty points – 10.

Legal notes and definitions

C[22.63] In charge. See notes at C[21.3].

C[22.64] ECHR. The defendant is entitled to be acquitted if he can establish from the evidence that there was no likelihood of his driving whilst he probably had an excessive proportion of alcohol in his blood. He only has to prove this on the balance of probabilities and the House of Lords held that the burden on the defendant was both reasonable and legitimate (*Sheldrake v DPP* [2003] EWHC 273 (Admin), [2004] QB 487; revsd [2004] UKHL 43, [2004] 3 WLR 976). Note that a passenger supervising a learner driver who has been drinking may be in charge for the purposes of this section (*DPP v Janman* [2004] EWHC 101 (Admin), [2004] All ER (D) 171 (Jan)).

See also the legal and sentencing notes for the previous offence, at **C[21.2]**.

Sentencing
SC Guideline – Excess Alcohol (in charge)

C[22.65] Must endorse and may disqualify. If no disqualification, impose 10 points.

OFFENCE SERIOUSNESS (CULPABILITY AND HARM)		
A. IDENTIFY THE APPROPRIATE STARTING POINT		
Starting points based on first time offender pleading not guilty		
Level of alcohol Breath (mg) Blood (ml) Urine (ml)	Starting point	Range
36–59 mg (breath) or 81–137 ml (blood) or 108–183 ml (urine)	Band B fine	Band B fine 10 points
60–89 mg (breath) or 138–206 ml (blood) or 184–274 ml (urine)	Band B fine	Band B fine 10 points OR consider disqualification
90–119 mg (breath) or 207–275 ml (blood) or 275–388 ml (urine)	Band C fine	Band C fine to medium level community order Consider disqualification up to 6 months OR 10 points
120–150 mg (breath) and above or 276–345 ml (blood)and above or	Medium level community order	Low level community order to 6 weeks custody Disqualify 6–12 months

367–459 (urine) and above		

OFFENCE SERIOUSNESS (CULPABILITY AND HARM)

B. CONSIDER THE EFFECT OF AGGRAVATING AND MITIGATING FACTORS (OTHER THAN THOSE WITHIN EXAMPLES ABOVE)

Common aggravating and mitigating factors are identified at B[5.2A]. The following may be particularly relevant but **these lists are not exhaustive**

Factors indicating higher culpability	Factor indicating lower culpability
1. LGV, HGV, PSV etc	1. Low likelihood of driving
2. Ability to drive seriously impaired	
3. High likelihood of driving	
4. Driving for hire or reward	

FORM A PRELIMINARY VIEW OF THE APPROPRIATE SENTENCE, THEN CONSIDER OFFENDER MITIGATION

Common factors are identified at B[5.2A]

CONSIDER A REDUCTION FOR A GUILTY PLEA

CONSIDER ANCILLARY ORDERS, INCLUDING FORFEITURE OR SUSPENSION OF PERSONAL LIQUOR LICENCE

Refer to B[18] for guidance on compensation and **Part B** for available ancillary orders

DECIDE SENTENCE

GIVE REASONS

C[22.66]–[22.71] See Table B at B[4.2] for available sentences and the notes for the previous offence.

Fail to provide specimen for analysis (drive/ attempt to drive)

Charge

C[23.1] Failing, without reasonable excuse, to provide a specimen of blood, urine or breath for analysis –

Road Traffic Act 1988, s 7(6) and s 7A

Maximum penalty – This varies according to whether it is alleged the defendant was driving or in charge. Accordingly the summons should make clear which of the alternative offences at C[21] and C[22], is alleged.

(a)   If the defendant drove or attempted to drive a motor vehicle on a road or public place fine on level 5 and 6 months' imprisonment. Must disqualify for at least one year (the guideline penalty is **two years**) unless special reasons. The disqualification may be for any period exceeding a year. The defendant may also be ordered to take a test again. Must endorse licence unless special reasons.

For a subsequent offence committed within ten years of a previous conviction must disqualify for at least three years and must endorse unless special reasons. The minimum ban is two years if the defendant has been disqualified for more than 56 days on at least two occasions, three years immediately preceding the commission of the current offence (s 34(4) RTOA 1988).

A previous conviction for driving (or attempting to drive) a motor vehicle when unfit through drink (see C[20]) or a previous conviction for driving (or attempting to drive) with alcohol over prescribed limit (see C[21]) count as a previous conviction for this offence.

Penalty points – 3–11.

(b)   If the defendant was in charge of a motor vehicle on a road or a public place fine level 4 and 3 months' imprisonment. May disqualify for any period and/or until a driving test has been passed. Must endorse unless there are special reasons.

Penalty points – 10.

Legal notes and definitions

C[23.2] A constable, in the course of an investigation into whether a person has committed an offence under the Road Traffic Act 1988, s 3A (causing death by careless driving where under the influence of drink or drugs) the Road Traffic Act 1988, s 4 or s 5, may require him to provide two specimens of breath or a specimen of blood or urine for analysis.

C[23.3] **Fails to provide.** If the case concerns a refusal to provide a blood specimen, an offence is committed if the defendant would only allow blood to be taken from an inappropriate part of the body (toe, penis, etc). In one case a woman refused to provide a blood or urine specimen and claimed embarrassment, there being no doctor or policewoman present. The High Court ruled this amounted to refusal. An agreement to provide a specimen which is conditional will generally be treated as a refusal. In the case of a sample of breath being required for analysis it must be provided in such a way as to make that analysis possible, that is, the required quantity at the required pressure. If a driver has a phobia/medical condition he must inform the police officer so that the police officer can require an alternative specimen (*Martiner v DPP* [2004] EWHC 2484 (Admin), [2004] All ER (D) 122 (Oct)).

In *DPP v Karamouzis* [2006] All ER (D) 109 (Oct), the defendant provided a positive roadside breath test. She was arrested and taken to a police station where she was required to provide specimens of breath for analysis. She argued that she had already been required to provide an evidential breath test under s 7 and accordingly there was no power to arrest and convey her to a police station. It was held that the roadside test was a preliminary test under s 6 and that the defendant had failed to provide specimens as required under s 7.

There must be sufficient breath to enable a test to be carried out although deep lung breath is not a legal requirement. Where an officer had requested a specimen from a Lion Intoxilyser device and requested the defendant blow into the machine and the defendant had removed the mouthpiece on eight occasions, where the device registered there was an insufficient specimen an offence under s 7(6) was made out (*DPP v Darwin* [2007] EWHC 337 (Admin). See also *DPP v Heywood* [1997] RTR 1; *Zafar v DPP* [2004] All ER (D) 6 (Nov)).

In *Rweikiza v DPP* [2008] EWHC 396 (Admin), [2008] All ER (D) 259 (Jan) the defendant's conviction was upheld because he had been properly instructed on how to use the intoxilyser and had deliberately failed to comply with those instructions and had deliberately frustrated the objectives of the test. In those circumstances the court had been correct to find that the specimen was not sufficient to enable the test or analysis to be carried out or the objective to be satisfactorily achieved.

C[23.4] Reasonable excuse. The Court of Appeal has said: 'In our judgment no excuse can be adjudged a reasonable one unless the person from whom the specimen is required is physically or mentally unable to provide it, or the provision of the specimen would entail a substantial risk to health.' The fact that a driver has not consumed alcohol at all, or that he has consumed alcohol since being involved in an accident, does not amount to a reasonable excuse for not providing a specimen. Nor can he demand to see a law book before complying (*DPP v Noe* [2000] RTR 351, [2000] 20 LS Gaz R 43), or refuse to take a test until legal advice has been received (*Kirkup v DPP* [2003] EWHC 2354 (Admin), [2003] All ER (D) 53 (Oct)).

Once the defendant had raised the issue a reasonable excuse, eg by expert medical evidence, it is for the prosecution to prove the absence of a reasonable excuse beyond a reasonable doubt (*McKeon v DPP* [2007] EWHC 3216 (Admin), [2007] All ER (D) 314 (Dec)).

Defendant must have been warned of consequences of refusing a specimen

C[23.5] The Act expressly directs a policeman requesting a specimen to warn the defendant that a failure to provide such a specimen may make the defendant liable to prosecution. If this warning has not been given, the magistrates can dismiss the charge. If the driver is incapable of understanding the warning (for example, because he does not understand English sufficiently) he may not be convicted if he refuses to provide a sample. Separate procedures apply under s 7A where the defendant is unable to give consent due to a medical condition following an accident. In such circumstances the police surgeon may take a sample of blood. The defendant must be told that the sample has been taken when he is conscious and his permission for a lab test has been obtained. Failure to give consent is an offence with the same penalties as failure to supply a sample.

C[23.6] There are three possible ways of providing a specimen: breath, blood or urine. The current law places the choice entirely in the hands of the police who will use the breath-analysis machine, only offering the defendant blood or urine if the machine is broken or unavailable, or where there are medical reasons for not requiring a sample of breath. Where the police require a specimen of blood for analysis they are not required to offer the motorist a preference but must ask whether there are any reasons why a specimen cannot or should not be taken by a medical practitioner (*DPP v Warren* [1993] AC 319, [1992] 4 All ER 865, HL). The officer must act reasonably in his choice and not ignore for example a defendant's assertions that he could not give blood due to religious reasons (*Joseph v DPP* [2003] EWHC 3078 (Admin), [2003] All ER (D) 326 (Nov)).

There was nothing in the legislation to state that where a driver failed to provide a specimen of breath and the custody sergeant sought a blood test it was not possible to abandon the blood testing procedure and prosecute the driver under s 7 (6) (*Longstaff v DPP* [2008 EWHC 303 (Admin), [2008] All ER (D) 276 (Jan)); see also *McNeil v DPP* [2008] EWHC 1254 (Admin), [2008] All ER (D) 375 (Apr).

C[23.6A] **Legal Advice.** A police officer does not have to delay the procedures to permit the suspect to consult a solicitor. As a matter of principle, however, once a police officer had decided to give a person the opportunity to consult a solicitor in respect of the requirement to provide two specimens of breath, it would be incumbent on the officer to allow that person the benefit of a full cycle on an approved device despite an earlier refusal (*Plackett v DPP* [2008] EWHC 1335 (Admin), [2008] All ER (D) 194 (May)).

Sentencing

C[23.7] Where either the defendant was driving or attempting to drive or where he was in charge see Table B at **B[4.2]** and see the notes to the offence of 'Alcohol over the prescribed limit' at C[22].

SC Guideline – Failure to Provide Evidential Specimen (drive/attempt to drive)

See C[23.9] for SC Guideline (in charge)

C[23.8] Must endorse and disqualify for at least 12 months.

Must disqualify for **at least** 2 years if offender has had two or more disqualifications for periods of 56 days or more in preceding 3 years – consult your legal adviser for further guidance.

Must disqualify for **at least** 3 years if offender has been convicted of a relevant drink/drive offence in preceding 10 years – consult your legal adviser for further guidance.

If there is a delay in sentencing after conviction, consider interim disqualification.

Note: the first column below provides guidance regarding the length of disqualification that may be appropriate in case to which the 3 year minimum applies. The period to be imposed in any individual case will depend on an assessment of all the relevant circumstances, including the length of time since the earlier ban was imposed and the gravity of the current offence.

OFFENCE SERIOUSNESS (CULPABILITY AND HARM) A. IDENTIFY THE APPROPRIATE STARTING POINT Starting points based on first time offender pleading not guilty				
Examples of nature of activity	Starting point	Range	Disqualification	Disqualification. 2nd offence in 10 years
Defendant refused test when had honestly held but unreasonable excuse	Band C fine	Band C fine	12–16 months	36–40 months
Deliberate refusal or deliberate failure	Low level community order	Band C fine to high level community order	17–28 months	36–52 months
Deliberate refusal or deliberate failure where evidence of serious impairment	12 weeks custody	High level community order to 26 weeks custody	29–36 months	36–60 months

OFFENCE SERIOUSNESS (CULPABILITY AND HARM)

B. CONSIDER THE EFFECT OF AGGRAVATING AND MITIGATING FACTORS (OTHER THAN THOSE WITHIN EXAMPLES ABOVE)

Common aggravating and mitigating factors are identified at B[5.2A]. The following may be particularly relevant but **these lists are not exhaustive**

Factors indicating higher culpability	Factors indicating lower culpability
1. Evidence of unacceptable nature of driving	1. Genuine but unsuccessful attempt to provide specimen
2. LGV, HGV, PSV etc	
3. Obvious state of intoxication	
4. Driving for hire or reward	
Factor indicating greater degree of harm	
1. Involved in accident	

FORM A PRELIMINARY VIEW OF THE APPROPRIATE SENTENCE, THEN CONSIDER OFFENDER MITIGATION

Common factors are identified at B[5.2A]

CONSIDER A REDUCTION FOR A GUILTY PLEA

CONSIDER OFFERING DRINK/DRIVE REHABILITATION COURSE; CONSIDER ANCILLARY ORDERS

Refer to B[18] for guidance on compensation and **Part B** for available ancillary orders

DECIDE SENTENCE

GIVE REASONS

*SC Guideline – Failure to Provide Evidential Specimen (in charge) See
C[23.8] for SC Guideline (drive/attempt to drive)*

C[23.9] Must endorse and may disqualify. If no disqualification, impose
10 points.

OFFENCE SERIOUSNESS (CULPABILITY AND HARM)		
A. IDENTIFY THE APPROPRIATE STARTING POINT		
Starting points based on first time offender pleading not guilty		
Examples of nature of activity	**Starting point**	**Range**
Defendant refused test when had honestly held but unreasonable excuse	Band B fine	Band B fine
Deliberate refusal or deliberate failure	Band C fine	10 points
		Band C fine to medium level community order
Deliberate refusal or deliberate failure where evidence of serious impairment	Medium level community order	Consider disqualification OR 10 points
		Low level community order to 6 weeks custody
		Disqualify 6–12 months
OFFENCE SERIOUSNESS (CULPABILITY AND HARM)		
B. CONSIDER THE EFFECT OF AGGRAVATING AND MITIGATING FACTORS (OTHER THAN THOSE WITHIN EXAMPLES ABOVE)		
Common aggravating and mitigating factors are identified at B[5.2A]. The following may be particularly relevant but **these lists are not exhaustive**		
Factors indicating higher culpability	*Factors indicating lower culpability*	
1. Obvious state of intoxication	1. Genuine but unsuccessful attempt to provide specimen	
2. LGV, HGV, PSV etc	2. Low likelihood of driving	
3. High likelihood of driving		
4. Driving for hire or reward		
FORM A PRELIMINARY VIEW OF THE APPROPRIATE SENTENCE, THEN CONSIDER OFFENDER MITIGATION		
Common factors are identified at B[5.2A]		
CONSIDER A REDUCTION FOR A GUILTY PLEA		
CONSIDER ANCILLARY ORDERS		
Refer to B[18] for guidance on compensation and **Part B** for available ancillary orders		
DECIDE SENTENCE		
GIVE REASONS		

C[24]

Failure to co-operate with roadside breath test

Charge

C[24.1] Failing, without reasonable excuse, to provide a specimen of breath for a breath test when required to do so by a policeman in uniform

Road Traffic Act 1988, s 6(4)

Maximum penalty-Fine of level 3. Must endorse unless special reasons. Disqualification is discretionary.

Penalty points – 4.

Legal notes and definitions

C[24.2] The policeman must have been in uniform at the time he requested the defendant to take a breath test and used a Home Office approved breathalyser.

C[24.3] A defendant can only be required to take this test by a constable in uniform who has reasonable cause for suspecting:

(a)   the defendant *is* driving or attempting to drive a motor vehicle on a road or other public place and has alcohol in his body or has committed a traffic offence whilst the vehicle was in motion; or

(b)   he *has been* driving or attempting to drive on a road or other public place with alcohol in his body and he still has alcohol in his body; or

(c)   he *has been* driving or attempting to drive a motor vehicle on a road or other public place and has committed a traffic offence whilst the vehicle was in motion.

For these purposes 'driving' includes being 'in charge'.

C[24.4] In addition, where there has been an accident, a constable (whether in uniform or not) may require any person who he has reasonable cause to believe was driving or attempting to drive or in charge of the vehicle at the time of the accident to provide a breath test.

C[24.5] The instructions on the breath test device need not be strictly observed. If the constable had no reason to suspect that the motorist had drunk alcohol in the previous 20 minutes he can be required to take the test immediately.

See also C[23.3].

C[24.6] Motorist in hospital. If a motorist is in a hospital as a patient, he can still be required to take a breath test, provided that the doctor in immediate charge of him is notified and does not object.

C[24.7] Reasonable excuse. If the defendant satisfies the magistrates that he had a reasonable excuse for failing to take a breath test he is entitled to be acquitted. Such a defendant will probably be rare. One example may be that the defendant was hurrying to get a doctor to deal with an emergency. The degree of proof required of the defendant is to prove that this point is probably true. He does not have to establish it beyond reasonable doubt.

C[24.8] The legal adviser should be consulted if the defence raise this point.

Sentencing
SC Guideline – Failing to co-operate with roadside
breath test

C[24.9] Starting point – Band B fine.

Since 'reasonable excuse' is a defence (see above) a conviction implies that the defendant had no excuse and therefore this is not a trivial offence and carries an endorsement.

Careless driving (drive without due care and attention)

Charge

C[25.1] Driving a mechanically propelled vehicle on a road or other public place without due care and attention

Road Traffic Act 1988, s 3, as amended

Maximum penalty – Fine level 5 for offences committed on or after 24/9/07. For fines see **B[33]**). May disqualify for any period and/or until a driving test has been passed. Must endorse unless special reasons.

Penalty points – 3–9.

Fixed penalty – £100/3 penalty points. The police are also able to offer educational training as an alternative to endorsement.

ACPO has given the following guidance:

Fixed penalty. Fixed penalty and/or educational training can be offered in situations of officer-observed, low level careless, aggressive and inconsiderate driving where other drivers are not unduly affected such as:

- driving too close to the vehicle in front;
- failing to give way at a junction (no evasive action by another driver);
- overtaking and forcing into a queue of traffic;
- wrong lane at a roundabout;
- ignoring a lane closed sign and forcing into an orderly queue;
- lane discipline such as remaining in lane two or three when lane one is empty and there is no other vehicle to overtake;
- inappropriate speed;
- wheel spins and hand brake turns.

Summons. A summons will continue to be issued in situations of aggressive driving where other drivers are endangered. These may be officer observed, witnessed or involve collisions and include:

- fast overtakes and lane hopping/weaving with other drivers having to evade;
- pulling out in front of other moving vehicle that needs to brake;
- overtaking and causing the approaching vehicle to brake or take evading action or pulling in causing the overtaken vehicle to brake or swerve;
- wrong lane at roundabout causing another vehicle on the roundabout to brake or swerve;
- staying in lane two or three with vehicles behind being held up or forced to pass on nearside.

Legal notes and definitions

C[25.2] Mechanically propelled vehicle. See C[47.9].

C[25.3] Road. See C[22.5].

C[25.4] Public place. See C[20.7]–C[20.8]. The car park of a dealership has been found to be a public place (*May v DPP* [2005] EWHC 1280 (Admin), [2005] All ER (D) 182 (Apr)).

C[25.5] Due care and attention. The standard of driving expected by the law is that of the degree of care and attention to be exercised by a reasonable and prudent driver in the circumstances. The standard of careful driving expected in law from a motorist is the same for all, even the holder of a provisional licence.

Definition: For offences committed or after 24 September 2007 the **Road Safety Act 2006** inserts after s 3 of the Road Traffic Act 1988, a new s 3ZA which provides a statutory meaning of careless, or inconsiderate, driving as follows:

(1)   This section has effect for the purposes of sections 2B and 3 above and section 3A below.

(2)   A person is to be regarded as driving without due care and attention if (and only if) the way he drives falls below what would be expected of a competent and careful driver.

(3)   In determining for the purposes of subsection (2) above what would be expected of a competent and careful driver in a particular case, regard shall be had not only to the circumstances of which he could be expected to be aware but also to any circumstances shown to have been within the knowledge of the accused.

(4)   A person is to be regarded as driving without reasonable consideration for other persons only if those persons are inconvenienced by his driving.

C[25.6] A skid may or may not be due to lack of care, but being overcome by sleep is not a defence.

C[25.7] Where a motorist is confronted by an emergency during the course of driving, he should be judged by the test of whether it was reasonable for him to have acted as he did and not according to the standard of perfection yielded by hindsight.

C[25.8] If the driving complained of was due to a mechanical defect in the vehicle, that is a defence unless the defendant knew of the defect, or he could have discovered it by exercising prudence; but the burden of proof remains on the prosecution to establish beyond reasonable doubt a lack of due care and attention.

C[25.9] Observance or non-observance of the Highway Code can be used to establish or disprove guilt. General impressions formed by a witness as to the speed of a vehicle may be admitted (*Blake v DPP* [2002] EWHC 2014 (Admin), [2002] All ER (D) 125 (Sep)).

C[25.10] Warning of proceedings. If the defence claim that notice should have been given within 14 days of intention to prosecute, consult the clerk.

Evidence will not be excluded because of the failure of a police officer to issue a caution before asking a driver if he was driving a particular vehicle involved in an accident (*Kemsley v DPP* [2005] 169 JP 148).

C[25.11]–[25.15] Death. As a matter of practice justices should not proceed with a summary trial until the inquest has been held (*Smith v DPP* [2000] RTR 36, 164 JP 96).

C[25.16] Careless or inconsiderate driving (Road Traffic Act 1988, s 3) and dangerous driving (s 2). Where the magistrates see fit, they may allow information for an offence under s 3 and s 2 to be heard together. In this event, if the defendant is convicted of one offence, the second information may be adjourned *sine die* or the justices may make "*no adjudication*". Should the driver successfully appeal against conviction, he can later be tried on the second information.

C[25.17] Alternatively, where there is a single information alleging dangerous driving and the magistrates do not find this proved, they may convict of careless driving in the alternative (s 24 RTOA 1988).

C[25.18] Emergency vehicles. The same standard of care and attention is required of the drivers of fire engines, ambulances, coastguard and police vehicles as of any other driver. That standard is that the driver takes 'due' care and pays 'due' attention.

C[25.19] Driving. See the note under the offence of no driving licence at C[18.2].

Sentencing
SC Guideline – Careless driving (drive without due care and attention)

C[25.20] Must endorse and may disqualify. If no disqualification, impose 3–9 points.

OFFENCE SERIOUSNESS (CULPABILITY AND HARM)		
A. IDENTIFY THE APPROPRIATE STARTING POINT		
Starting points based on first time offender pleading not guilty		
Examples of nature of activity	**Starting point**	**Range**
Momentary lapse of concentration or misjudgement at low speed	Band A fine	Band A fine 3–4 points
Loss of control due to speed, mishandling or insufficient attention to road conditions, or carelessly turning right across on-coming traffic	Band B fine	Band B fine 5–6 points

Overtaking manoeuvre at speed resulting in collision of vehicles, or driving bordering on the dangerous	Band C fine	Band C fine
		Consider disqualification OR
		7–9 points

OFFENCE SERIOUSNESS (CULPABILITY AND HARM)

B. CONSIDER THE EFFECT OF AGGRAVATING AND MITIGATING FACTORS (OTHER THAN THOSE WITHIN EXAMPLES ABOVE)

Common aggravating and mitigating factors are identified at B[5.2A]. The following may be particularly relevant but **these lists are not exhaustive**

Factors indicating higher culpability	*Factors indicating lower culpability*
1. Excessive speed	1. Minor risk
2. Carrying out other tasks while driving	2. Inexperience of driver
3. Carrying passengers or heavy load	3. Sudden change in road or weather conditions
4. Tiredness	
Factors indicating greater degree of harm	
1. Injury to others	
2. Damage to other vehicles or property	
3. High level of traffic or pedestrians in vicinity	
4. Location eg near school when children are likely to be present	

FORM A PRELIMINARY VIEW OF THE APPROPRIATE SENTENCE, THEN CONSIDER OFFENDER MITIGATION

Common factors are identified at B[5.2A]

CONSIDER A REDUCTION FOR A GUILTY PLEA

CONSIDER ORDERING DISQUALIFICATION UNTIL APPROPRIATE DRIVING TEST PASSED

CONSIDER ANCILLARY ORDERS, INCLUDING COMPENSATION

Refer to B[18] for guidance on compensation and Part B for available ancillary orders

DECIDE SENTENCE

GIVE REASONS

C[25.21] If it appears to the court that the offender suffers from a disease or physical disability likely to cause his driving to be a source of danger to the public, then the court shall notify the licensing authority who may take steps to withdraw the driving licence (see **C[5.49]**).

C[31]

Failing to stop and give details
after accident

Charge

C[31.1] As a driver of a mechanically propelled vehicle, owing to the presence of which on a road or other public place, an accident occurred whereby injury was caused to another person (or damage caused to another vehicle or to roadside property or injury to an animal)

[failed to stop]

[upon being reasonably required to give his name and address, the name and address of the owner of the vehicle and the number of the vehicle, failing to do so]

Road Traffic Act 1988, s 170 (4), as amended

Maximum penalty-Fine level 5 and 6 months' imprisonment. May disqualify for any period and/or until a driving test has been passed. Must endorse unless there are special reasons.

Penalty points – 5–10.

Legal notes and definitions

C[31.2] Charge. The one charge may include both factual situations without offending the rule against duplicity (*DPP v Bennett* [1993] RTR 175, 157 JP 493).

C[31.3] Relationship between the offences of failing to stop and give details and failing to report an accident. Where an accident has occurred in the circumstances described above, there is an obligation on the driver to stop at the scene of the accident. If he does not do so immediately and as soon as he could safely and conveniently, he commits the offence described here (*Hallinan v DPP* [1998] Crim LR 754). Having stopped at the scene of the accident, he has a duty to give his name and address, the name and address of the owner of the vehicle and the identification marks of the vehicle to any person having reasonable grounds for such a request. If he fails to do so, he has also committed the offence described here. Unless he has actually given his particulars to such other person, he must report the accident at a police station or to a police constable *as soon as reasonably practicable*, and in any case within 24 hours of the accident, otherwise he commits the offence at C[32.18].

C[31.4] Mechanically propelled vehicle. See C[47.9].

C[31.5] A road or other public place. See C[22.5].

C[31.6] An animal. Means any horse, cattle, ass, mule, sheep, pig, goat or dog.

C[31.7] **Roadside property.** Means any property constructed on, fixed to, growing in or otherwise forming part of the land on which the road in question is situated, or land adjacent thereto.

C[31.8] The law requires the driver to give the appropriate particulars upon being reasonably required to do so. It is acceptable to give a business address or a lawyer's office where one can be contacted *(DPP v McCarthy* [1999] RTR 323, 163 JP 585). It is not sufficient to report the incident to the police within 24 hours. Where the defendant was the driver of the vehicle involved in the accident, there is a rebuttable presumption that the defendant knew that he had been involved in the accident. If the defendant can satisfy the court that he was unaware of any accident he must be acquitted *(Selby v Chief Constable of Avon and Somerset* [1988] RTR 216).

C[31.9] The degree of proof required of the defendant is to satisfy the court that this was probably true; he does not have to prove this beyond reasonable doubt.

C[31.10]–[31.15] **Driver.** The notes under the heading 'driving' for the offence of driving without a licence at **C[18.2]** may be of assistance. A person may continue to be the driver of a motor vehicle if having fulfilled the requirements mentioned on that page he ceases to do so by reason of a change of activity.

C[31.16] Accidents involving personal injury (to a person other than the driver). The driver must at the time produce his certificate of insurance to a constable or other person having reasonable cause to require it. If he does not do so, he must report the accident as described above and produce his insurance certificate. Otherwise he commits an offence under the Road Traffic Act 1988, s 170(7)-maximum penalty a fine of up to level 3. There is a defence if the certificate is produced within seven days of the accident at a police station specified by him at the time when the accident was reported. This provision does not apply to the driver of an invalid carriage.

Sentencing
SC Guideline – Failing to stop/report accident

C[31.17]

OFFENCE SERIOUSNESS (CULPABILITY AND HARM)		
A. IDENTIFY THE APPROPRIATE STARTING POINT		
Starting points based on first time offender pleading not guilty		
Examples of nature of activity	**Starting point**	**Range**
Minor damage/injury or stopped at scene but failed to exchange particulars or report	Band B fine	Band B fine 5–6 points
Moderate damage/injury or failed to stop and failed to report	Band C fine	Band C fine 7–8 points Consider disqualification

Serious damage/injury and/or evidence of bad driving	High level community order	Band C fine to 26 weeks custody
		Disqualify 6–12 months OR
		9–10 points

OFFENCE SERIOUSNESS (CULPABILITY AND HARM)

B. CONSIDER THE EFFECT OF AGGRAVATING AND MITIGATING FACTORS (OTHER THAN THOSE WITHIN EXAMPLES ABOVE)

Common aggravating and mitigating factors are identified at B[5.2A]. The following may be particularly relevant but **these lists are not exhaustive**

Factors indicating higher culpability	Factors indicating lower culpability
1. Evidence of drink or drugs/ evasion of test	1. Believed identity known
2. Knowledge/suspicion that personal injury caused (where not an element of the offence)	2. Genuine fear of retribution
3. Leaving injured party at scene	3. Subsequently reported
4. Giving false details	

FORM A PRELIMINARY VIEW OF THE APPROPRIATE SENTENCE, THEN CONSIDER OFFENDER MITIGATION

Common factors are identified at B[5.2A]

CONSIDER A REDUCTION FOR A GUILTY PLEA

CONSIDER ANCILLARY ORDERS, INCLUDING COMPENSATION

Refer to B[18] for guidance on compensation and **Part B** for available ancillary orders

DECIDE SENTENCE

GIVE REASONS

C[31.18] If it appears to the court that the accused suffers from a disease or physical disability likely to cause his driving to be a source of danger to the public, then the court shall notify the licensing authority who may take steps to withdraw the driving licence (see C[5.49]).

C[31.19] For fines see B[33].

C[32]

Failing to report after accident

Charge

C[32.1] As a driver of a mechanically propelled vehicle, owing to the presence of which on a road or other public place an accident occurred whereby injury was caused to another person (or damage caused to another vehicle or to roadside property or to an animal), not giving his name and address to any person having reasonable grounds for requiring this information, failing to report to the police as soon as reasonably practicable and in any case within 24 hours

Road Traffic Act 1988, s 170(4), as amended

Maximum penalty – Fine level 5 and 6 months' imprisonment. May disqualify for any period and/or until a driving test has been passed. Must endorse unless there are special reasons.

Penalty points – 5–10.

Legal notes and definitions

C[32.2] Relationship between the offences of failing to stop and give details and failing to report an accident. See C[31].

C[32.3] Mechanically propelled vehicle. See C[47.9].

C[32.4] A road or other public place. See C[22.5].

C[32.5] An animal. Means any horse, cattle, ass, mule, sheep, pig, goat or dog.

C[32.6] Report. Means approaching the police oneself as soon as reasonably practicable, even if no one else was present at the scene of the accident and therefore there was nobody present to ask for the driver's particulars.

C[32.7] If the defendant were approached by a police officer within 24 hours of the accident, that would not constitute reporting the accident.

C[32.8] If the defendant can satisfy the court that he was unaware that an accident had occurred, he must be acquitted of this charge.

C[32.9] The degree of proof is to satisfy the court that this was probably true. The defendant need not prove this beyond reasonable doubt.

C[32.10]–[32.15] If the defendant gave his name and address to the other party he need not report the accident to the police.

C[32.16] Roadside property. Means any property constructed on, fixed to, growing in or otherwise forming part of the land on which the road in question is situated or land adjacent thereto.

C[32.17] Driver. See note under the offence of no driving licence at

C[18.8]. A person does not necessarily cease to be a driver if having met the requirements mentioned on that page, he ceased to do so by reason of a change of activity.

C[32.18] Reasonably practicable. A driver is not saved from conviction because he reported the accident within 24 hours if he could reasonably have reported it sooner. If, for example, he continued his journey after the accident and drove past a police station he would need a very strong reason for not reporting at that station. It appears that he is not obliged to go in search of a public telephone in order to telephone the police. It is for the court to decide what is 'reasonably practicable' in the particular circumstances of each case and the test is not 'Is it reasonable for the defendant to have reported the accident earlier?' but 'Did he report it as soon as practicable?'

In *DPP v Hay* [2005] EWHC 1395 (Admin), (2005) Times, 13 July, it was decided that, after discharging himself from hospital, a driver was still under an obligation to report an accident despite the fact that the police had seen the motorist at the hospital and despite the fact that the police did not issue the driver with an HORT 1 notice to produce the relevant documents such as insurance within 7 days.

Sentencing

C[32.19] See SC guideline and sentencing notes to previous offence at C[31.17].

No insurance (using, causing, or permitting)

Charge

C[33.1] Using (or causing or permitting to be used) a motor vehicle on a road or other public place when there is not in force a policy of insurance or security against third party risks

Road Traffic Act 1988, s 143

Maximum penalty-Fine level 5. May disqualify for any period and/or until defendant has passed a driving test. Must endorse unless special reasons.

Penalty points – 6–8.

Fixed penalty – £300/6 points

Legal notes and definitions

C[33.2] Motor vehicle. See C[9.7].

Other public place. Not private property but can include such places as car parks.

C[33.3] A road. Means any highway (including footpaths and bridleways) and any other road to which the public has access and includes bridges.

C[33.4] Security in respect of third party risks. The requirement to have insurance or a security does not apply to a vehicle owned by a person who has deposited with the Accountant General of the Supreme Court the sum of £500,000, at a time when the vehicle is being driven under the owner's control. Nor does it apply to vehicles owned by bodies such as local authorities or the police. Certain other undertakings may have instead of insurance a security given by an insurer that the undertaking will meet any liability it may incur.

C[33.5] Time limit. Subject to an overall maximum of three years, proceedings may be brought within 6 months from when, in the prosecutor's opinion, he had sufficient evidence to warrant proceedings. A certificate signed by or on behalf of the prosecutor as to when that date was constitutes conclusive evidence on that point.

C[33.6] Burden of proof. If the prosecution prove that the defendant used a motor vehicle on a road or other public place, the burden of proof shifts to the defendant to establish that he was insured. The defendant does not have to prove beyond reasonable doubt; he need only prove that he was probably insured.

C[33.7] Insurance certificate. This is in law the main item of proof of insurance and until it has been delivered to the insured he is held not to be insured. Mere proof that he has paid the premium or holds an actual policy is not sufficient.

C[33.8] Using on a road or other public place. This expression does not in law only mean driving the vehicle along the road; its mere presence on a road, jacked up and without a battery, may constitute using on a road (*Pumbien v Vines* [1996] RTR 37, [1996] Crim LR 124). A vehicle which is being towed is being used. In any given case where doubt exists consult the legal adviser. See also at C[9] (Brakes).

C[33.9] A person, limited company or body corporate which owns a vehicle that is being driven in the course of the owner's business is using the vehicle.

C[33.10]–[33.15] Causing involves an express or positive mandate from the defendant to the driver.

C[33.16] Permitting. Permission must be given by someone able to permit or withhold permissions but may be express or inferred. See further the note under this heading at C[9.6] in the section on Brakes.

C[33.17] Defence open to employed drivers. An employed driver cannot be convicted if he can prove that:

(a) the vehicle did not belong to him; and
(b) it was not in his possession under a hiring contract or on loan to him; and
(c) he was using it in the course of his employment; and
(d) he did not know and had no reason to believe he was not insured. The degree of proof required from the defendant is to prove that this defence is probably true; he does not have to prove beyond reasonable doubt.

C[33.18] The Motor Insurers' Bureau is a company funded by insurers transacting compulsory motor insurance. Under an agreement with the Secretary of State for Transport the Bureau, subject to certain limitations and exceptions, will compensate the victims of uninsured motorists. A brief outline of the scheme is given here (for the full details see the text of the agreement which is published by HMSO).

C[33.19] To obtain compensation the victim must obtain judgment in a civil court against the uninsured driver, having given the MIB notice within seven days of starting the proceedings. If the judgment is not met within seven days the victim will be entitled to be compensated by the MIB.

C[33.20] Compensation is payable for personal injury or for damage to property (except for the first £300 of the claim in respect of property damage and this figure will be the relevant limit of a compensation order made against an uninsured driver in the magistrates' court).

C[33.21] There are exceptions to claims against the MIB such as claims in relation to Crown vehicles but more particularly where damage is to the claimant's own vehicle which he himself has failed to insure as required by the Road Traffic Act or where the claimant is the passenger in a vehicle which he knew had been stolen or unlawfully taken or was being used without insurance.

C[33.22] A separate agreement covers the case of victims of untraced drivers.

Sentencing
SC Guideline – No insurance

C[33.23] Must endorse and may disqualify. If no disqualification, impose 6–8 points – see notes below.

OFFENCE SERIOUSNESS (CULPABILITY AND HARM)		
A. IDENTIFY THE APPROPRIATE STARTING POINT		
Starting points based on first time offender pleading not guilty		
Examples of nature of activity	**Starting point**	**Range**
Using a motor vehicle on a road or other public place without insurance	Band C fine	Band C fine
		6 points – 12 months disqualification – see notes below

OFFENCE SERIOUSNESS (CULPABILITY AND HARM)	
B. CONSIDER THE EFFECT OF AGGRAVATING AND MITIGATING FACTORS (OTHER THAN THOSE WITHIN EXAMPLES ABOVE)	
Common aggravating and mitigating factors are identified at B[5.2A]. The following may be particularly relevant but **these lists are not exhaustive**	
Factors indicating higher culpability	*Factors indicating lower culpability*
1. Never passed test	1. Responsibility for providing insurance rests with another
2. Giving false details	2. Genuine misunderstanding
3. Driving LGV, HGV, PSV etc	3. Recent failure to renew or failure to transfer vehicle details where insurance was in existence
4. Driving for hire or reward	4. Vehicle not being driven
5. Evidence of sustained uninsured use	
Factors indicating greater degree of harm	
1. Involved in accident	
2. Accident resulting in injury	

FORM A PRELIMINARY VIEW OF THE APPROPRIATE SENTENCE, THEN CON-SIDER OFFENDER MITIGATION
Common factors are identified at B[5.2A]
CONSIDER A REDUCTION FOR A GUILTY PLEA
CONSIDER ANCILLARY ORDERS
Refer to B[18] for guidance on compensation and **Part B** for available ancillary orders
DECIDE SENTENCE
GIVE REASONS

Notes. Consider range from 7 points – 2 months disqualification where vehicle was being driven and no evidence that the offender held insurance.

Consider disqualification of 6 – 12 months if evidence of sustained uninsured use and/or involvement in accident.

C[33.23A] Endorsement must be ordered unless special reasons exist. A short distance driven can amount to a special reason. In *DPP v Heritage* [2002] EWHC 2139 (Admin), 166 JP 772 a car was pushed onto the road to be cleaned and a vehicle collided with it.

C[33.24] If it appears to the court that the accused suffers from some disease or physical disability likely to cause his driving to be a source of danger to the public, then the court shall notify the licensing authority who may take steps to withdraw the driving licence (see C[5.49]).

C[33.25]–[33.30] Clearly a lower level of fine may be appropriate for the vehicle sitting unused outside the owner's house, whereas deliberate driving around without insurance cover aggravates the seriousness considerably.

C[33.31] For fines see B[33].

C[34]

Lights defective

Charge

C[34.1] 1 Using or causing or permitting to be used on a road a vehicle without every front position lamp, rear position lamp, headlamp, rear registration plate lamp, side marker lamp, end-outline marker lamp, rear fog lamp, retro reflector and rear marking with which it is required to be fitted by the Regulations, and every stop lamp and direction indicator, running lamp, dim- dip device, headlamp levelling device and hazard warning signal device with which it is fitted in good working order and, in the case of a lamp, clean

C[34.2] 2 Using, causing or permitting to be used on a road any vehicle with a headlamp, front fog lamp, or rear fog lamp so as to cause undue dazzle or discomfort to other persons using the road

C[34.3] 3 Using or causing or permitting to be used on a road a vehicle which is in motion between sunset and sunrise (or between sunrise and sunset in seriously reduced visibility), (or allowing to remain at rest, or causing or permitting to be allowed to remain at rest, on a road any vehicle between sunset and sunrise) unless every front position lamp, rear position lamp, rear registration plate lamp, side marker lamp and end-outline marker lamp with which the vehicle is required by the Regulations to be fitted is kept lit and unobscured

C[34.4] 4 Using, or causing or permitting to be used on a road a vehicle which is fitted with obligatory dipped beam headlamps without such lamps being lit during the hours of darkness (or in seriously reduced visibility)

Road Vehicles Lighting Regulations 1989, reg 23(1) (charge 1); reg 27 (charge 2); reg 24(1) (charge 3); reg 25(1) (charge 4);

Road Traffic Act 1988, s 42

Maximum penalty – Fine level 4 (goods vehicles etc), level 3 (private vehicles) (for fines see **B[33]**). No power to disqualify or endorse.

Fixed penalty – £50.

Legal notes and definitions

C[34.5] **Using, causing or permitting.** The charge should allege only one of these. For 'using', 'causing' and 'permitting' see **C[9.4]–C[9.6]**.

C[34.6] The obligatory minimum requirements for an ordinary motor car are two front position lights, two headlights (with a dipped beam facility), direction indicators, hazard warning lights, two rear position lamps, one rear fog lamp (vehicles first used after 1 April 1980), two stop lamps, a rear registration plate lamp and two rear reflex reflectors.

C[34.7] These requirements vary according to the category of vehicle concerned. If the matter is in dispute the legal adviser will be able to provide a list of the requirements.

C[34.8] Vehicle. Means a vehicle of any description and includes a machine or implement of any kind drawn or propelled along roads whether by animal or mechanical power.

C[34.9] Road. Means any road or highway to which the public has access and includes bridges and footways.

C[34.10]–[34.15] Front position lamp. Means a lamp used to indicate the presence and width of a vehicle when viewed from the front.

C[34.16] Hours of darkness. Means the time between half an hour after sunset and half an hour before sunrise. An almanac can be produced to establish this period if it is in dispute.

C[34.17] Exempted vehicles include

(a)   Pedal cycles and hand drawn vehicles are not required to be fitted with lamps between sunrise and sunset.
(b)   Vehicles temporarily imported or proceeding to port for export provided they comply with international Conventions.
(c)   Military vehicles which comply with certain requirements.
(d)   Vehicles drawn or propelled by hand which have an overall width (including load) not exceeding 800 millimetres are not required to be fitted with lamps and reflectors except when they are used on a carriageway between sunset and sunrise (unless they are close to the near side or are crossing the road).

Possible defences include

C[34.18] Offence 1 where a defective lamp or reflector is fitted to the vehicle which is in use between sunrise and sunset if the lamp etc becomes defective during the journey or if arrangements have been made to remedy the defect with all reasonable expedition.

C[34.19] Offence 3 where the vehicle is a car or does not exceed 1,525 kilograms and is parked on a road with a speed limit of 30 miles per hour or less in force and the vehicle is parked in a designated parking place or lay-by or is parked parallel to the kerb, close to it and facing the direction of traffic and is not less than 10 metres from a junction.

C[34.20] Offence 4. Except where there is seriously reduced visibility, the car is on a road restricted to 30 miles per hour by virtue of a system of street lighting which is lit at the time of the alleged offence.

Sentencing
SC Guideline – Lights defective

C[34.21] Starting point – Band A fine (driver); Band A fine (owner-driver but consider an uplift of at least 25% on the driver's fine); Band B fine (owner-company).

C[34.22] For fines see B[33].

Motor cyclist not wearing helmet

Charge

C[35.1] Being a person driving (or riding on) a motor cycle on a road, did not wear protective headgear

Motor Cycles (Protective Helmets) Regulations 1980, reg 4; Road Traffic Act 1988, s 16(4)

Maximum penalty – Fine level 3 (for fines see B[33]). There is no power to endorse or disqualify.

Fixed penalty – £50.

Legal notes and definitions

C[35.2] Where the person actually in breach of the regulations by not wearing a helmet is over 16, there can be no prosecution of another person for aiding and abetting. However, aiders and abettors of defendants under 16 can be prosecuted.

C[35.3] Riding on. This includes a pillion rider but not a passenger in a side-car.

C[35.4] Protective headgear is defined in the regulations as being that which complies with a certain British Standard. Headgear manufactured for use by persons on motorcycles which appears to afford the same or a greater degree of protection than laid down by the Standard is also included. But before any helmet satisfies the definition it must also be securely fastened to the head of the wearer by the straps or fastenings provided on the helmet. An unfastened helmet, therefore, would not suffice.

C[35.5] Driving. See the notes under this heading for the offence of driving without a licence at C[18.8]–C[18.9] but bear in mind the exemption mentioned at (b) below.

C[35.6] Exemptions. There is no requirement to wear a helmet:

(a)   if the motor cycle is a mowing machine;
(b)   if the motor cycle is being propelled by a person on foot;
(c)   if the driver is a Sikh and is wearing a turban.

Sentencing

C[35.7] No SC Guideline.

Starting point – Band A fine suggested.

C[35.8] For fines see B[33].

C[36]

Obstruction

Charge 1

C[36.1] Causing unnecessary obstruction of a road by a person in charge of a motor vehicle or trailer

Road Vehicles (Construction and Use) Regulations 1986, reg 103; Road Traffic Act 1988, s 42

Maximum penalty – Fine level 4 (goods vehicle etc), level 3 (otherwise) (for fines see **B[33]**). No power to disqualify or endorse.

Fixed penalty – £50.

Charge 2

C[36.1A] Did without lawful authority or excuse wilfully obstruct the free passage along a highway.

Highways Act 1980, s 137

Maximum penalty – Fine level 3

Legal notes and definitions

C[36.2] **Unnecessary obstruction.** There need be no notice or sign displayed as is the case where a driver is charged in parking offences. This offence can be committed on a road to which local parking regulations are applicable.

Wilful. If anyone does something by exercise of their free will which causes an obstruction, an offence is committed (*Arrowsmith v Jenkins* [1963] 2 QB 561, [1963] 2 All ER 210). See further **A[85]**

C[36.3] If the vehicle is parked in a lawfully designated parking place then there can be no charge of obstruction.

C[36.4] The High Court has ruled that a motorist who left his car on a road 24 ft wide for 75 minutes did not commit this offence (*Evans v Barker* [1971] RTR 453). An obstruction was not committed by a reasonable protest taking up 2 ft of an 11ft-wide path (*Westminster City Council v Haw* [2002] All ER (D) 59 (Oct)).

C[36.5] A taxi-driver was held by the High Court to have committed this offence in waiting in the road to turn right, thereby holding up heavy traffic.

C[36.6] The question is one for the justices to decide on the facts of each case. An obstruction caused by a doctor answering an emergency call may, for example, be necessary.

C[36.7] **A road.** Means any highway (including footpaths and bridleways) and any other road to which the public has access and includes bridges. A road is provided as a means of transit from one place to another and not as a place to park motor vehicles.

C[36.8] Trailer. Means any vehicle drawn by a motor vehicle.

C[36.9] A motor vehicle. See C[9.7]. If left on a road for an unreasonable time may constitute an unnecessary obstruction.

Power to order the removal of the obstruction rests with the magistrates when recording a conviction under the Highways Act 1980, s 137. Failure to comply with the order without reasonable excuse is an offence punishable by a fine not exceeding level 5 and a daily fine thereafter.

Sentencing

C[36.10]–[36.15] No SC Guideline.

Starting point – Band A fine suggested.

An average case will not usually attract more than a small fine; where there is a complete disregard for the convenience or safety of others (eg access of fire appliances or ambulances) a heavier fine is called for.

C[36.16] For fines see B[33].

C[37]

Opening door

Charge

C[37.1] Opening a door of a motor vehicle or trailer on a road so as to cause injury or danger

Road Vehicles (Construction and Use) Regulations 1986, reg 105; Road Traffic Act 1988, s 42

Maximum penalty – Fine level 4 (goods vehicle etc), level 3 (otherwise) (for fines see B[33]). No power to disqualify or endorse.

Fixed penalty – £50.

Legal notes and definitions

C[37.2] Motor vehicle. See C[9.7].

C[37.3] Trailer. Means any vehicle drawn by a motor vehicle.

C[37.4] Road. Means any highway (including footpaths and bridleways) and any other road to which the public has access and includes bridges.

C[37.5] The offence. Consists of opening or causing or permitting a door to be opened so as to cause injury or danger to any person. The offence can be committed by a passenger as well as the driver. If a child opened the door and his parent was present and knew the child was about to open the door, then the parent could be charged with permitting. If the child opened the door on the instructions of a parent then the latter could be guilty of causing the offence. Door opening, permitting or causing are all identical offences for the purpose of the penalties that may be inflicted. Only one of the offences should be alleged.

C[37.6] The prosecution does not have to prove carelessness; nor that someone was actually struck or injured. It is enough if the act caused danger.

Sentencing

C[37.7] No SC Guideline.

Starting point – Band A fine suggested.

The amount of the fine will vary according to the circumstances. It will rarely be appropriate to impose a fine less than the fixed penalty. When the offence is very dangerous, eg where it causes a motor cyclist to swerve to the offside of a busy main road, this will aggravate the seriousness. Where actual injury is caused a similar level of penalty should apply.

C[37.8] If it appears to the court that a driver suffers from some disease or physical disability likely to cause his driving to be a source of danger to the public, then the court shall notify the licensing authority who may take steps to withdraw his driving licence (see **C[5.49]**).

C[37.9] For fines see B[33].

C[38]

Overloading/exceeding axle weight

Charge

C[38.1] Using, causing or permitting to be used on a road a vehicle which equals or exceeds* the maximum (gross weight) (train weight) (weight for specified axle) shown on the (plating certificate) (manufacturer's plate fitted to the vehicle)

Road Vehicles (Construction and Use) Regulations 1986, reg 80; Road Traffic Act 1988, s 41B

Maximum penalty – Fine level 5 (for fines see B[33]). Not endorsable.

Fixed penalty – £100.

* Note the Road Vehicles (Construction and Use) (Amendment) Regulations 2014, SI 2014/264, amended reg 80 of the Construction and Use Regulations 1986 as to the way in which weight band limits are expressed. The purpose was to remove an historic difference in terminology between Directive 1999/62/EC and the Regulations, which affects vehicles on those limits. This has been achieved by inserting 'equalled or' or 'equal or' before, respectively, 'exceeded' and 'exceed'. The subsequent text should be read accordingly.

Legal notes and definitions

C[38.2] Certain vehicles specified in the Road Vehicles (Construction and Use) Regulations 1986, reg 66 must be fitted with a plate which contains information prescribed in Sch 8 or the relevant EC Directives. In particular the plate must show the maximum gross weight, train weight and weight for each axle. The weights may be specified by the manufacturer and are the limits at or below which the vehicle is considered fit for use, having regard to its design, construction and equipment and the stresses to which it is likely to be subjected in use. Further, the weights must also be specified at which the use of the vehicle will be legal in the UK having regard, inter alia, to the maximum weights set out in regs 75–79. This is a 'manufacturer's plate'.

C[38.3] In addition, goods vehicles are now covered by the compulsory 'type approval' system whereby the Secretary of State issues a certificate that a type of vehicle conforms with the appropriate requirements and the manufacturer issues a Certificate of Conformity that the vehicle conforms with the approved type. This certificate is *treated* as a 'plating certificate' and a plate (which is in fact a piece of paper) is affixed to the vehicle, which is *deemed* to be a 'ministry plate' (for this and 'plating certificate' see below).

C[38.4] After one year and annually thereafter goods vehicles must be submitted for a goods vehicle test and at the *first* test the vehicle will also be examined for the purpose of issuing a 'plating certificate'. The examiner will issue a certificate containing information similar to that on the plate previously affixed to the vehicle. If the vehicle passes its goods vehicle test the ministry plate will remain affixed in a conspicuous and readily accessible position on the vehicle and in the cab. Only one plating certificate is issued, but it will be amended where there has been a 'notifiable alteration' to the vehicle.

C[38.5] Using; causing; permitting. See C[9.4]–C[9.6].

C[38.6] Road. See C[9.10].

C[38.7] Vehicle. The provisions concerning manufacturers' plates cover such vehicles as non-agricultural tractors of various weights which do not carry loads, buses and various trailers. This article is concerned with offences committed by goods vehicles, being the most commonly encountered in the magistrates' court.

C[38.8] Maximum gross weight. The sum of the weights to be transmitted to the road surface by all the wheels of the motor vehicle (including any load imposed by a trailer on the vehicle).

C[38.9] Maximum train weight. The maximum gross weight and the weight transmitted to the road surface by any trailer drawn.

C[38.10]–[38.15] Maximum axle weight. The sum of the weights to be transmitted to the road surface by all the wheels of that axle.

C[38.16] Multiple charges. Under the former regulations 'gross', 'train' or 'axle' weight were the subject of separate charges and not combined into one. It was not oppressive for there to be a charge in respect of each axle that was overweight and for exceeding the gross weight. The new regulations are worded slightly differently but it is still permissible to prefer several charges where appropriate (*Travel-Gas (Midlands) Ltd v Reynolds* [1989] RTR 75).

C[38.17] Evidence. Unless proved to the contrary the weight indicated on a ministry plate is presumed to be the weight recorded on the relevant plating certificate.

C[38.18] Defences. In the case of a goods vehicle it is a defence for the accused to prove:

(a)   that at the time when the vehicle was being used on the road it was proceeding to a weighbridge which was the nearest available one to the place where the loading of the vehicle was completed for the purpose of being weighed, or was proceeding from a weighbridge after being weighed to the nearest point at which it was reasonably practicable to reduce the weight to the relevant limit without causing an obstruction on any road; or

(b)   in a case where the limit of that weight was not exceeded by more than 5%, that limit was not exceeded at the time the loading of the vehicle was originally completed and that since that time no person has made any addition to the load (eg a load which becomes wet owing to falling rain).

C[38.18A] 'Nearest available weighbridge' means the nearest available weighbridge that was actually available as a matter of objective fact regardless of the knowledge of the driver (*Vehicle and Operator Services Agency v F & S Gibbs Transport Services Ltd* [2006] EWHC 1109 (Admin), 170 JP 586.

C[38.19] The degree of proof required from the defendant is to prove that the defence is probably true; he does not have to prove beyond reasonable doubt.

Sentencing
SC Guideline – Overloading/exceeding axle weight

C[38.20] Starting point – Mechanically propelled vehicle-Band A fine (driver); Band A fine (owner-driver but consider an uplift of at least 25% on the driver's fine); Band B fine (owner-company). The starting point presumes an excess overload etc of no more than 10%. A further uplift of 1% for every 1% more than 10% is permissible but the total fine must not be out of proportion to the offence and the means of the defendant may be relevant.

Starting point – HGV, LGV or PSV – Band B fine (driver); Band B fine (owner-driver but consider an uplift of at least 25% on the driver's fine); Band C fine (owner-company). A further uplift of 1% for every 1% more than 10% is permissible but the total fine must not be out of proportion to the offence and the means of the defendant may be relevant.

C[38.21] For fines see B[33].

C[38A]

Breach of requirement as to speed assessment equipment detection devices

Charge

C[38A.1] A person who –

(a)   contravenes or fails to comply with a construction or use requirement as to speed assessment equipment detection devices, or

(b)   uses on a road a motor vehicle or trailer which does not comply with such a requirement, or causes or permits a motor vehicle or trailer to be so used, is guilty of an offence.

Road Traffic Act 1988, s 41C as inserted (from a date to be appointed) by s 18 **Road Safety Act 2006.**

Maximum penalty – Fine level 4 if committed on a special road otherwise level 3. Must endorse unless special reasons.

Penalty points – 3–6 (fixed penalty 3).

Fixed penalty– £100.

Legal notes and definitions

C[38A.2] Motor vehicle. See C[9.7] for definition.

Trailer. See C[9.9] for definition.

Road. See C[9.10]–C[9.15] for definition.

Sentencing

C[38A.3] Awaiting SC Guidance.

C[39]

Pelican/zebra crossing contravention

Charge

C[39.1] Failure of a driver of any vehicle to accord precedence to a pedestrian within the limits of an uncontrolled pedestrian crossing

'Zebra' Pedestrian Crossings Regulations 1971, reg 8 (or 'Pelican' Pedestrian Crossings Regulations 1987, reg 17); Road Traffic Regulation Act 1984, s 25(5)

Maximum penalty – Fine of level 3 (for fines see B[33]). If the offence was committed in a motor vehicle, the court may disqualify for any period and/or until a driving test has been passed. Must endorse unless special reasons exist.

Penalty points – 3.

Fixed penalty – £100 (3PP)

Legal notes and definitions

C[39.2] Vehicle. A bicycle is a vehicle (but not in the case of offences of stopping in an area *adjacent* to a zebra crossing, see C[40.7]–C[40.9]).

C[39.3] Zebra crossing. A driver should approach such a crossing in a manner that enables him to stop before reaching it, unless he can see there is no pedestrian on the crossing.

C[39.4] The law imposes a very strict duty on the driver and the prosecution has the advantage of not having to prove any negligence or want of care. It would, however, be a sufficient defence to satisfy the magistrates that the failure to accord precedence was due to circumstances over which the defendant had no control (eg being attacked by a swarm of bees, or a sudden brake failure).

C[39.5] The High Court in Scotland has held that where a woman was pushing her child in a pram and the pram was on the crossing but she herself had not actually stepped on to the crossing, the mother had the right of way.

C[39.6] The limits of the crossing are marked by studs bordering the striped lines. The broken white line along the striped crossing is to indicate where vehicles should give way.

C[39.7] The sections of pedestrian crossings on each side of a dual carriageway, central street refuge or reservation are considered to be two separate crossings.

C[39.8] A crossing may still legally remain a crossing even if one or more of its stripes are missing, discoloured or imperfect, or if a globe or one of its lights is missing, or even if some of the studs have disappeared. The magistrates should consult the legal adviser if a submission is made on any of these matters.

C[39.9] The regulations require pedestrians to cross 'with reasonable dispatch'.

C[39.10]–[39.15] On each side of crossings are zigzag lines parallel to the carriageway. These indicate the 'area controlled by the crossing'. On the approach side of the crossing it is an offence for a vehicle to overtake another vehicle in that area if that vehicle is either the only other vehicle in the area or is the nearest vehicle of several to the crossing. 'Overtaking' includes allowing part of the rearmost vehicle to pass the front of the overtaken vehicle, a complete passing is not necessary. The prohibition on overtaking does not apply if the overtaken vehicle is stationary otherwise than to allow pedestrians to cross (eg if it is waiting to turn left or right) or if the crossing is for the time being controlled by a policeman or traffic warden, but it applies where a vehicle has stopped to wait for pedestrians to step on to the crossing, for example as a courtesy. It also applies when the pedestrians have passed the stationary vehicle which is overtaken.

Vehicles which are waiting to proceed are not, by definition, 'proceeding'. The only circumstances in which overtaking a stationary vehicle in an approach to a crossing can amount to an offence are those set out in reg 24(1)(b), namely passing ahead of a vehicle which is stationary because: (a) of a red light; (b) it has stopped to give precedence to a pedestrian at a zebra crossing; or (c) it has stopped to give precedence to a pedestrian at a pedestrian crossing: *Brooks v Blackpool Borough Council* [2013] EWHC 3735 (Admin), (2014) 178 JP 79.

C[39.16] Pelican crossings. Similar provisions apply. A vehicle approaching such a crossing shall proceed with due regard to the safety of other users of the road. When a red light shows the vehicle must stop, similarly where a constant amber light shows, a vehicle must stop except where the vehicle cannot safely be stopped in line with the signal. Where there is a flashing amber light, a vehicle must accord precedence to pedestrians already on the crossing. Failure to comply with any of the regulations is an offence with a maximum penalty of a fine on level 3.

C[39.17] Pedestrian. A person walking and pushing a bicycle is a pedestrian. He ceases to be a pedestrian if he uses the bicycle to carry him, for example, by placing one foot on a pedal and pushing himself along with the other.

C[39.18] Precedence means allowing the pedestrian to go before the vehicle. Once the pedestrian has safely passed the vehicle's line of travel the vehicle may proceed even though the pedestrian is still on the crossing.

Sentencing
SC Guideline – Pelican/zebra crossing contravention

C[39.19] Starting point – Band A fine.

C[39.20] If it appears to the court that the defendant driver of a motor vehicle suffers from some disease or physical disability likely to cause his driving to be a source of danger to the public, then the court shall notify the licensing authority who may take steps to withdraw the driving licence (see C[5.49]).

C[39.21] For fines see B[33].

Stopping on pedestrian crossing

Charge

C[40.1] That a driver of a vehicle caused it or any part of it to stop within the limits of zebra crossing

'Zebra' Pedestrian Crossings Regulations 1971, reg 9; Road Traffic Regulation Act 1984, s 25(5)

Maximum penalty – Fine level 3 (for fines see **B[33]**). If the offence was committed in a motor vehicle, the court may disqualify for any period and/or until the defendant has passed a driving test. Must endorse unless special reasons exist.

Penalty points – 3.

Fixed penalty – £100 (3PP).

Legal notes and definitions

C[40.2] The defendant must be acquitted if he establishes any of the following:

(a)   that circumstances beyond his control compelled him to stop;
(b)   that he had to stop to avoid an accident (see **C[40.9]**).

C[40.3] The degree of proof required from the defendant is to prove that one of these is probably true; he does not have to prove one of them beyond reasonable doubt.

C[40.4] The term 'vehicle' includes a pedal cycle.

C[40.5] This charge does not apply to a push-button controlled crossing which is subject to special regulations.

C[40.6] A crossing may still legally remain a crossing even if one or more stripes are missing, discoloured or imperfect, or if a globe or its light is missing or even if some of the studs have disappeared. Consult the legal adviser.

C[40.7] Stopping in area adjacent to zebra crossing. It is also an offence to stop in a zebra-controlled area, ie the part of a road indicated by zig-zag lines at either side of the crossing ('Zebra' Pedestrian Crossings Regulations 1971, reg 12).

C[40.8] For the purposes of this regulation 'vehicle' does *not* include a pedal cycle.

C[40.9] Defences are:

(a)   that circumstances beyond his control compelled him to stop;
(b)   that he had to stop to avoid an accident;

(c)   that the stopping was for the purpose of allowing free passage to pedestrians on the crossing;

(d)   that he had to stop for fire brigade, ambulance or police purposes, because of demolitions, repairs to road, gas, water, electricity services etc;

(e)   that he stopped for the purpose of making a left or right turn;

(f)   a stage carriage or express carriage vehicle (not on a trip or excursion) in the controlled area beyond the zebra crossing for the purposes of picking up or setting down passengers.

Sentencing
SC Guideline – Pelican/zebra crossing contravention

C[40.10]–[40.15]   Starting point – Band A fine.

C[40.16]   If it appears to the court that the defendant driver of a motor vehicle suffers from some disease or physical disability likely to cause his driving to be a source of danger to the public, then the court shall notify the licensing authority who may take steps to withdraw the driving licence (see C[5.49]).

C[40.17]   For fines see B[33].

Reasonable consideration

Charge

C[46.1] Driving a mechanically propelled vehicle on a road or other public place without reasonable consideration for other persons using the road or place

Road Traffic Act 1988, s 3, as amended

Maximum penalty – Fine level 4 [level 5 for offences committed on or after 24/9/07] (for fines see **B[33]**). May disqualify for any period and/or until a driving test has been passed. Must endorse unless special reasons exist.

Penalty points – 3–9.

Fixed penalty – £100/3 penalty points. The police are also able to offer educational training as an alternative to endorsement. See further **C[25.1]**, above.

Legal notes and definitions

C[46.2] **Reasonable consideration.** At the time of the offence there must have been other people also using the road. They could be passengers in the defendant's vehicle. Another example of this offence is driving the vehicle through a muddy puddle and splashing pedestrians.

Definition: See **C[25.5]** for a new statutory definition which has been added to s 3ZA of the Road Traffic Act 1988 by the Road Safety Act 2006.

C[46.3] If no other person but the driver is using the road then this charge fails.

C[46.4] Observance or non-observance of the Highway Code can be used to establish or disprove liability.

C[46.5] The driver alleged to have committed this offence must give his name and address on request to any person having reasonable grounds for requiring it, otherwise he commits an offence under the Road Traffic Act 1988, s 168, maximum penalty fine on level 3.

C[46.6] Mechanically propelled vehicle. See C[47.9].

C[46.7] Road. See C[22.5].

C[46.8] Public place. See C[20.7]–C[20.8].

C[46.9] **Warning of prosecution.** If the defence claim that notice should have been given within 14 days of intention to prosecute, consult the legal adviser.

C[46.10]–[46.15] Other persons using the road. May include passengers in the defendant's vehicle. There must be evidence that another road user was inconvenienced by the manner of driving adopted by the accused.

C[46.16] Careless or inconsiderate driving (Road Traffic Act 1988, s 3) and dangerous driving (s 2). Where the magistrates see fit, they may allow informations for an offence under s 3 and s 2 to be heard together. In this event, if the defendant is convicted of one offence, the second information can either be adjourned *sine die* or the justices may make *"no adjudication"*. Should the driver successfully appeal against conviction for dangerous driving, he can later be tried on the second information.

C[46.17] Alternatively, where there is a single information alleging dangerous driving and the magistrates do not find this proved, they may convict of driving without reasonable consideration in the alternative (s 24 RTOA 1988).

C[46.18] Driving. See the note under the offence of no driving licence at C[18.8]–C[18.9].

Sentencing

C[46.19] SC Guideline – Careless (or inconsiderate) driving – see C[25.20].

C[46.20] In rare cases it may be appropriate to grant an absolute discharge; if this course is adopted disqualification can be imposed but this would be an unusual course to take. Endorsement must be ordered unless special reasons exist.

C[46.21] If it appears to the court that the accused suffers from some disease or physical disability likely to cause his driving to be a source of danger to the public then the court shall notify the licensing authority who may take steps to withdraw the driving licence (see C[5.49]).

C[46.22] It is the lack of consideration rather than the consequences of it which normally determines the punishment.

C[46.23] For fines see B[33].

No excise licence

Charge 1

C[47.1] Using or keeping on a public road a mechanically propelled vehicle when no excise licence is in force and doing so when a SORN is in force

Vehicle Excise and Registration Act 1994, s 29 and s 29(3A)

C[47.2] Maximum penalty-A fine of level 3 (s 29(3)) or level 4 (s 29(3A)) or 5 times the value of the licence, whichever is the greater. No power to disqualify or endorse.

Charge 2

Keeping an unlicensed vehicle while the registered keeper

Vehicle Excise and Registration Act 1994, s 31A

Maximum penalty –A fine of level 3 or 5 times the annual duty. Additional penalty of a least £1,000 if the vehicle remains unlicensed from the date of offence to the start of proceedings.

C[47.3] In addition to a fine the court is compelled, in certain cases, to order the defendant to pay loss of duty. See C[47.18] under 'Sentencing'.

Legal notes and definitions

C[47.4] The charge must stipulate whether the defendant is being charged with using or keeping. One charge cannot allege both.

C[47.5] Prosecutor and time limit. Only the Secretary of State, the police acting with his approval, or a person or authority authorised by that Secretary of State can conduct the prosecution. Proceedings must start within 6 months of their receiving sufficient evidence to warrant proceedings; subject to an overall limit of three years from the offence.

C[47.6] Using. In law means not only driving the vehicle but can also include the vehicle's mere presence on the road. The owner is not liable to be charged with using the vehicle if he allowed some other person to have the vehicle and who used it outside the scope of the authority given by the owner.

C[47.7] Keeping. Means causing the vehicle to be on a public road for any period, however short, when the vehicle is not in use. See *Secretary of State for the Environment, Transport and the Regions v Holt* [2000] RTR 309, where the High Court ruled that proof that the defendant was the registered keeper together with the adverse inference drawn from his failure to give information as to the identity of the driver was sufficient to prove he was the keeper on the day in question.

C[47.8] Public road. Refers to a road repairable at the public expense. This is different from the more usual definition of a road which means any highway (including footpaths and bridleways) and any other road to which the public has access and includes bridges.

C[47.9] Mechanically propelled vehicle. Means a vehicle with some form of engine; thus even a motor assisted pedal cycle comes within the legal definition even if the rider is just pedalling the machine without the use of the engine. A car does not cease to be a mechanically propelled vehicle after removal of its engine, nor if there is some temporary defect which prevents the engine working. If the condition of the vehicle is such that there is no reasonable prospect of it ever being made mobile again, then it ceases to be a mechanically propelled vehicle.

C[47.10]–[47.15] Employees, drivers, chauffeurs. It has been decided that it is oppressive to prosecute an employee who was not responsible for licensing the vehicle.

C[47.16] A dishonoured cheque. If offered in payment of the licensing fee renders the licence void. The licensing authority will send a notice requiring the excise licence to be delivered up within seven days of the posting of the notice. Failure to comply is an offence punishable with a maximum fine of level 3 or 5 times the annual rate of duty applicable (Customs and Excise Management Act 1979, s 102). For liability for back duty see below.

C[47.17] Exempted vehicles. Certain vehicles are exempt from duty and the clerk can supply a list: ambulances, fire engines, military vehicles, some agricultural vehicles; vehicles going for a *pre-arranged* test and some vehicles acquired by overseas residents, vehicles more than 25 years old, calculated from the 31 December of the year of first registration. This latter class of vehicles must still be licensed annually and display a VED disc. See Sch 2 of the 1994 Act. A vehicle kept off the public road may be subject to a Statutory Off-Road Notification (SORN). A SORN declaration is valid for 12 months. Failure to make or renew a SORN may be subject to a level 3 fine.

Sentencing
SC Guideline – No excise licence

C[47.18] Starting point – Band A fine (1–3 months unpaid); Band B fine (4–6 months unpaid); Band C fine (7–12 months lost).

(Special considerations: in all cases add duty lost).

The fine and the arrears of duty should be announced as separate items; we do not recommend the practice of some courts of announcing a single sum and stipulating that it includes the back duty.

Liability for back duty

C[47.19] If the defendant was the person who *kept* the vehicle at the time of the offence the court must order him to pay an amount to cover the loss of duty. Such order is in addition to a fine and the chairman of the court must announce two amounts, namely the amount of the fine and the amount of the lost duty.

C[47.20] If the court decides not to impose a fine but to grant an absolute or conditional discharge the court must still order the payment of the lost duty as well and this must be announced. It must be stressed that this provision applies only if the defendant is the person who *kept* the vehicle at the time of the offence. Thus this provision would not apply to an employed lorry driver but would apply to a private motorist who kept and used his own vehicle. It would also apply to a company which kept and used its own vehicles.

C[47.21] Dishonoured cheques. In relation to licences taken out on or after 27 July 1989 the court must, in addition to any penalty it may impose under the Customs and Excise Management Act 1979, s 102, order the defendant to pay an amount to cover the loss of duty incurred for the period for which he had the benefit of the licence.

C[47.22] Calculating back duty. This period will usually commence with the date of the expiry of the expired licence, or when the defendant notified his acquisition of the vehicle to the appropriate authority. It will terminate with the date of offence. If there is doubt about the length of the 'relevant period' consult the legal adviser. Back duty is calculated for each month or part thereof. Use on one day in a month will render him liable for back duty for the whole month.

C[47.23] Previous convictions. If the defendant has a previous conviction in respect of the same vehicle for a similar offence for which the court made an order for lost revenue then in the present proceedings the relevant period will commence with the day after the date of the previous offence.

C[47.24] Costs can be ordered as well as a fine and back duty.

C[47.25]–[47.30] Defence against back duty. If the defendant can prove any one of the following in respect of any part of the relevant period back duty cannot be ordered against him for that part of the relevant period:

(a)   the vehicle was not kept by him; or
(b)   he paid duty in respect of the vehicle for any month or part of a month (where relevant) whether or not on a licence. The defendant does not have to establish this beyond reasonable doubt but only that his contention is probably true.

Defences for a registered keeper (s 31B). The burden is on the defendant to show either:

(i)   he is no longer the keeper and has complied with the requirements under the Act;
(ii)   the vehicle was not kept on a public road and the requirements have been complied with;
(iii)   the vehicle was stolen and not recovered and the notification requirements complied with.

Note that it is an offence to use a vehicle in public if it is not properly registered; defence of no reasonable opportunity or reasonable grounds for believing that registration details were correct – level 3 fine (fixed penalty offence). A constable or authorised person may require production of vehicle registration certificate – level 2 fine for failure to do so.

C[47.31] A person is liable for all the periods when he kept a vehicle without a current tax whether it was on a public road or not. It is not obligatory for a person to tax a car that is kept off the road for the whole of that period. However since 31 January 1998 keepers of vehicles which become unlicensed and are to be kept off the public road are required to provide a declaration to the DVLA. If he ventures onto the road without tax he may find himself with a liability extending back over the time when it was not taxed or to the date when he notified his acquisition of the vehicle.

Seat belt offences

Charge

C[48.1] Unlawfully did drive or ride in a motor vehicle of a class specified in the Motor Vehicles (Wearing of Seat Belts) Regulations 1993 otherwise than in accordance with the provisions of those Regulations

Road Traffic Act 1988, s 14

Maximum penalty – Fine level 2 (for fines see B[33]). No power to endorse or disqualify.

Fixed penalty – £100

C[48.2] Unlawfully did drive a motor vehicle with a child in the front seat not wearing a seat belt

OR

C[48.3] Unlawfully did drive a motor vehicle with a child in the rear seat not wearing a seat belt

Motor Vehicles (Wearing of Seat Belts by Children in Front Seats) Regulations 1993

Road Traffic Act, s 15

Maximum penalty   — (Front seat) level 2
                        — (Rear seat) level 2 for offence (child)

No endorsement or disqualification.

Fixed penalty – £100.

Legal notes and definitions

C[48.4] **Criminal liability.** Only the person actually committing the contravention can be prosecuted. There are no provisions for another person to be prosecuted for aiding and abetting etc and causing or permitting.

C[48.5] **Specified passenger's seat** is the front seat alongside the driver's seat, or, if there is more than one such seat, the one furthest from the driver's seat. If there is no seat alongside the driver's seat, then the specified passenger's seat is the foremost forward facing seat furthest from the driver's seat, unless there is a fixed partition separating it from the space in front of it and alongside the driver's seat as, for example, in a London type taxi cab.

C[48.6] **Class of vehicle.** Every motor car registered on or after 1 January 1965, every three-wheeled vehicle not weighing more than 225 kg manufactured on or after 1 March 1970 and first used on or after 1 September 1970 and heavy motor cars first used on or after 1 October 1988, eg goods vehicles and minibuses.

C[48.7] Seat belt. The seat belt must comply with the requirements of the relevant regulations, about which the legal adviser will clarify.

C[48.8] Exemptions. Every driver and every person occupying the specified passenger's seat, as defined above, must wear a seat belt when in the vehicle, even when the vehicle is stationary, except a person who is:

(a)   using a vehicle constructed or adapted for the delivery or collection of goods or mail to consumers or addressees, as the case may be, whilst engaged in making local rounds of deliveries or collections;

(b)   driving the vehicle while performing a manoeuvre which includes reversing;

(c)   a qualified driver, and is supervising a provisional licence holder while that person is performing a manoeuvre which includes reversing;

(d)   the holder of a valid certificate in a form supplied by the Secretary of State, containing the information required by it, and signed by a registered medical practitioner to the effect that it is inadvisable on medical grounds for him to wear a seat belt;

(e)   a constable protecting or escorting another person;

(f)   not a constable, but is protecting or escorting another person by virtue of powers the same as or similar to those of a constable for that person;

(g)   in the service of a fire brigade and is donning operational clothing or equipment;

(h)   the driver of:
     (i)   a taxi which is being used for seeking hire, or answering a call for hire, or carrying a passenger for hire; or
     (ii)   a private hire vehicle which is being so used to carry a passenger for hire;

(i)   a person by whom a test of competence to drive is being conducted and his wearing a seat belt would endanger himself or any other person;

(j)   occupying a seat for which the seat belt either:
     (i)   does not comply with the relevant standards; or
     (ii)   has an inertia reel mechanism which is locked as a result of the vehicle being, or having been, on a steep incline;

(k)   riding in a vehicle being used under a trade licence, for the purpose of investigating or remedying a mechanical fault in the vehicle.

C[48.9] Children under 14 years. The above regulations do not apply but it is an offence under the Road Traffic Act 1988, s 15(2) punishable with a maximum fine on level 2 for a person without reasonable excuse to drive on a road with a child under 14 years in the front of a motor vehicle who is not wearing a seat belt.

C[48.10]–[48.15] The seat belt must conform to the Motor Vehicles (Wearing of Seat Belts by Children in Front Seats) Regulations 1993 which provide for the use of special child restraining devices, or, according to age, adult seat belts for use in the front passenger seat.

C[48.16] Exemptions similar to those at (d) and (j) apply. Generally it is now unlawful to drive a vehicle with a small child in the front unless he is wearing a suitable restraint.

C[48.17] **Rear seat belts.** It is also compulsory for both adults and children in the rear seats of a vehicle fitted with seat belts to wear them. If a child (ie a person under 14 years) on the rear seat is not wearing a seat belt (with a booster cushion where necessary, or a child restraint), the driver of the vehicle will incur liability (maximum penalty a fine on level 1) [level 2 for offences committed on or after 24/9/07]. In the case of a passenger aged 14 years or more, only he will be liable (maximum penalty a fine on level 2), there are no provisions for the driver to be guilty of aiding and abetting the offence. There is no liability where all available seat belts are in use.

C[48.18] The following table summarises the main legal requirements for wearing seat belts.

	Front seat	Rear seat	Whose responsibility
Driver	Must be worn if fitted	—	Driver
child under 3 years of age	Appropriate child restraint must be worn	Appropriate child restraint must be worn	Driver
child aged 3–11 and under 1.5 metres (about 5 feet) in height	Appropriate child restraint must be worn if available. If not an adult seat belt must be worn	Appropriate child restraint must be worn if available. If not an adult seat belt must be worn	Driver
child aged 12 or 13 or younger 1.5 metres or more in height	Adult seat belt must be worn if available	Adult seat belt must be worn if available	Driver
adult passengers	must be worn if available	must be worn if available	Passenger

Sentencing
SC Guideline – Seat belt offences

C[48.19] Starting point – Band A fine.

Speeding

Charge

C[49.1] Driving a motor vehicle on a road at a speed exceeding a statutory limit

Road Traffic Regulation Act 1984, ss 81 (84 or 86) and 89

Maximum penalty – Fine level 3 (for fines see B[33]). May disqualify for any period and/or until a driving test has been passed. Must endorse unless there are special reasons.

Note – Speeding on a motorway may be charged under the Road Traffic Regulation Act 1984, s 17 in which case the maximum penalty is a fine on level 4.

Penalty points – 3–6. [from a date to be appointed 2–6 under the **Road Safety Act 2006**] (Fixed penalty – 3.)

Fixed penalty – £100

Legal notes and definitions

C[49.2] Speeding can be considered under five main headings:

(A)   Speeding on restricted roads (Road Traffic Regulation Act 1984, s 16).
(B)   Speeding on motorways (s 17).
(C)   Breaking the speed limit imposed by the Secretary of State for the Environment or highway authorities on roads other than restricted roads (s 84).
(D)   Driving a vehicle at a speed in excess of that permitted for that class of vehicle (s 86).
(E)   Breaking a temporary or experimental speed limit imposed by the Secretary of State for the Environment on certain specified roads (s 88), or by the highway authority because of road works, etc (s 14).

These classes of speeding are dealt with in the above order on the following pages.

C[49.3] Warning of prosecution must have been given to the defendant except in circumstances prescribed in the Road Traffic Offenders Act 1988, s 2, as amended (eg following an 'accident'). Section 2 required only that there was a sufficiently causal link between the relevant offence and the offender, so that the driver need not be warned of the risk of prosecution (*R v Myers* [2007] All ER [D] 241 (Feb)). The word 'accident' in s 2 had to be given a common sense meaning and was not restricted to untoward or unintended consequences having an adverse physical effect (*R v Currie* [2007] EWCA Crim 926).

C[49.4] Evidence. The Road Traffic Offenders Act 1988, s 20 (as substituted by the Road Traffic Act 1991) provides that it will be sufficient for evidence of an offence of speeding or contravening a red traffic light to be obtained by approved devices, such as a Gatso camera, which also records speeds and times as appropriate. The record must be signed by the police and the defendant given seven days notice of its intended use. The accused may require the attendance of the person who signed the document not less than three days before the trial.

In *DPP v Thornley* [2006] EWHC 312 (Admin), [2006] 09 LS Gaz R 32, it was held that s 20(8) of the RTOA 1988 was permissive in its terms and therefore the prosecution were entitled to admit the record of speeding as a species of "real evidence". *DPP v Thornley* has since been applied and followed in *Griffiths v DPP* [2007] EWHC 619 (Admin).

A police officer was entitled to corroborate his opinion that a motorist had travelled at an excessive speed by reference to the speed reading given by a speed measuring device that was a prescribed device but which was not of an approved type. Section 20 of the Road Traffic Offenders Act 1988 was a self-contained code which did not apply to a prosecution brought under s 89 of the Road Traffic Regulation Act 1984: *Connell v DPP* [2011] EWHC 158 (Admin), 175 JP 151.

See 'Conditional offer of fixed penalty' at C[8.21]–C[8.22].

C[49.5] If the evidence merely consists of one witness's opinion that the defendant was exceeding the speed limit there cannot be a conviction. If the single witness is supported by a speedometer, stop watch, radar meter or Vascar, then there can be a conviction.

C[49.6] The evidence of two witnesses estimating the speed at the same time can result in a conviction, but if their estimates refer to speeds at different parts of the road then that will not suffice.

C[49.7] If a vehicle was being used for the purpose of the fire brigade, the police, or the ambulance services, and the driver can establish that observing the speed limit would have hindered him in the execution of his official duties, then that could be accepted as a successful line of defence by the court. It is for the court to decide this issue as there is no inherent right for all such vehicles to exceed the speed limit, for instance an empty ambulance merely returning to its garage or a fire engine out on routine test carry no exemption from a speed limit. The defence of necessity is also available to a private person and is not confined to circumstances where there is a risk to life: *Pipe v DPP* [2012] EWHC 1821 (Admin), [2012] All ER (D) 238 (May). A police officer using a vehicle to 'hone' his skills may be guilty of speeding (see **C[16]** and *DPP v Milton* [2006] EWHC 242 (Admin), (2006) 170 JP 319).

C[49.8] The defendant merely has to prove that this defence is probably true; he need not prove it beyond reasonable doubt.

C[49.9] Although the driver must be identified, the fact that he was driving when stopped is prima facie evidence that he drove over the whole distance for which he was timed.

C[49.10]–[49.15] Speed limit signs. The ordinary meaning of the words in s 85(4) of the Road Traffic Regulation Act 1984 meant that two tests had to be satisfied before the defendant could be convicted. The first was that at the time the offence was being committed there were such signs as were mentioned in s 85(1) or (2). The second was that those signs indicated the relevant speed limit. Accordingly, no offence was committed where speed signs were obscured by hedgerows (*Coombe v DPP* [2006] EWHC 3263 (Admin), [2007] RTR 383); further, in *DPP v Butler* (unreported) 4/3/10, DC, it was held that a magistrates' court was entitled to find that a terminal speed limit located within 50 metres of a street lamp did not comply with the Traffic Signs Directions and Regulations 2002, Sch 17, item 10, as it was not illuminated in darkness. Accordingly, on the facts found no offence of speeding was made out. However, see *Peake v DPP* immediately below.

In *Peake v DPP* [2010] EWHC 286 (Admin) the High Court adopted a **purposive approach** and rejected the argument that the enforcement of a speed limit was dependent upon every sign within a 40 mph area having to be compliant with the Traffic Signs Directions and Regulations 2002. On the facts found the argument was rejected because there were no deficiencies in the road along which the defendant had driven or they were de minimis (minor).

If the defendant submits that the speed sign was unlawful because of its size, composition, character or colour, etc, the legal adviser should be consulted.

On a natural reading of the relevant primary and secondary legislation and adopting a purposive approach to interpretation to the relevant provisions, if at the point of enforcement there are signs complying with the directions of the Secretary of State which in fact provide adequate guidance of the speed limit at that point, this satisfies the requirements of s 85(4) of the Road Traffic Regulation Act 1984. If the prosecution can establish the route taken by the defendant, it will only have to show that compliant signs provide adequate guidance at the point of enforcement for a motorist taking that route. If the prosecution cannot establish the route, they would have to show compliant signs on all routes the driver may have taken (*Coombes v DPP* and *Peake v DPP* considered): *Jones v DPP* [2011] EWHC 50 (Admin), 175 JP 129.

Category A – speeding on restricted roads (Road Traffic Regulation Act 1984, s 81)
Legal notes and definitions

C[49.16] Restricted road. A road becomes a restricted road in one of two ways:

(a)   it has a system of street lamps placed not more than two hundred yards apart, in which case the speed limit is 30 miles per hour; or
(b)   it is directed by the relevant authority that it becomes a restricted road, in which case the speed limit is again 30 miles per hour.

A road restricted by (a) above need not display 'repeater' signs but a road in category (b) does have to display the repeater '30' signs.

C[49.17] The relevant authority may direct that an (a) category road may be derestricted. 'Restricted road' is a term of art referring to a road having a 30 mile per hour limit because of the above provisions. Confusingly, restricted road is commonly, but erroneously, used to refer to any road having a speed limit less than the overall maxima of 70 miles per hour for motorways and dual carriageways and 60 miles per hour for single carriageways.

C[49.18] The limit on a restricted road of 30 mph can be altered by the Secretary of State for the Environment and the Home Secretary acting jointly.

C[49.19] A vehicle which is limited to a lower speed than the limit for the road must always conform to its own scheduled speed limit, for example, a lorry drawing more than one trailer is limited to 20 mph and must keep to that limit even on a restricted road where a 30 mph limit is in force.

Category B – speeding on motorways (Road Traffic Regulation Act 1984, s 17)

C[49.20] Motorway. The legal adviser can provide a detailed definition if it should be necessary. The motorway includes the hard shoulder and access and exit roads.

C[49.21] The general speed limit on a motorway is 70 miles per hour although there are lower speed limits on certain stretches of motorway.

C[49.22] Contraventions of certain temporary restrictions on motorways (eg for roadworks) are offences under s 16 and also carry an endorsement.

Category C – driving a motor vehicle at a speed in excess of a limit imposed on a road, other than a restricted road, by the highway authority (Road Traffic Regulation Act 1984, s 84)
Legal notes and definitions

C[49.23] For the purposes of this offence the appropriate highway authority for trunk roads is the Secretary of State for the Environment. For non-trunk roads the appropriate authority is either the Secretary of State for the Environment or the local authority (for instance a county council or, in London, the relevant London borough) but the local authority has to have his consent.

C[49.24] These speed limits can be ordered to be in general use or merely during specified periods.

C[49.25]–[49.30] This is the provision which enables a 40 or 50 (or whatever) miles per hour limit to be imposed on a specified road. If the road would otherwise be a 'restricted' (ie having a limit of 30 miles per hour) road, eg because of having lamp posts not more than 200 yards apart, it ceases to be a 'restricted' road when an order is made imposing a limit under this provision.

Category D – driving a motor vehicle at a speed exceeding the limit prescribed for that class of vehicle (Road Traffic Regulation Act 1984, s 86)
Legal notes and definitions

C[49.31] Permitted speed limits for restricted classes of vehicles include:

	Motor-way	Dual car-riageway	Other road
Coach or motor caravan having an unladen weight exceeding 3.05 tonnes or adapted to carry more than 8 passengers			

	Motor-way	Dual car-riageway	Other road
(a) if not exceeding 12 metres in overall length	70	60	50
(b) if exceeding 12 metres in overall length	60	60	50
Car, motor caravan, car-derived van drawing one trailer, eg a caravan	60	60	50
Goods vehicle maximum laden weight not exceeding 7.5 tonnes (except car-derived van and articulated vehicles)	70	60	50
Goods vehicle maximum laden weight exceeding 7.5 tonnes	60	50	40
Articulated goods vehicles			
(a) maximum laden weight not ex-ceeding 7.5 tonnes	60	50	50
(b) maximum laden weight exceeding 7.5 tonnes	60	50	40

Category E – where temporary or experimental speed limits have been imposed by the Ministry of Transport (Road Traffic Regulation Act 1984, s 88) or by the Highway Authority during road works, etc (RTRA 1984, s 14)
Legal notes and definitions

C[49.32] The Secretary of State for the Environment may, for a period of up to 18 months, impose a speed limit on all roads or on certain specified roads in the interests of safety or traffic flow. The limit may be general or apply only at specified times.

C[49.33] Unless such an order directs otherwise, it will not interfere with existing speed limits on restricted roads or roads which are already the subject of an order. It is an order under this provision which has imposed a general speed limit of 70 miles per hour on dual carriageways and 60 miles per hour on single carriageways. Originally of a temporary nature, the order has now been made indefinite.

C[49.34] A speed limit may be imposed on a stretch of road for a temporary period to prevent danger from works on or near the highway.

C[49.35] These provisions do not apply to motorways.

C[49.35A] The RTRA 1984, s 14 provides that if the traffic authority for a road are satisfied that traffic on the road should be restricted or prohibited—

(a)   because works are being or are proposed to be executed on or near the road; or

(b)   because of the likelihood of danger to the public, or of serious damage to the road, which is not attributable to such works; or

(c)   for the purpose of enabling the duty imposed by section 89(1)(a) or (2) of the Environmental Protection Act 1990 (litter clearing and cleaning) to be discharged, the authority may by order restrict or prohibit temporarily the use of that road, or of any part of it, by vehicles, or vehicles of any class, or by pedestrians, to such extent and subject to such conditions or exceptions as they may consider necessary.

It is an offence under s 16 to use or permitting the use of a vehicle in contravention of an order made under s 14.

In *Castle v Wakefield and Pontefract Magistrates' Court* [2014] EWHC 587 (Admin), [2014] RTR 268, 178 JP 285 the appellant challenged the *vires* of an order which provided for speed limits of 60 or 50 mph on certain designated stretches of road, during such times and to such extent as would from time to time be indicated by traffic signs. It was contended that this fell outside the scope of the enabling legislation. There were further *vires* arguments as to the legality of the order being signed by a team leader in the Highways Agency and as to the ability to delegate to the Agency whether the limit should be 60 or 50 mph.

The Divisional Court rejected all the challenges. Section 14 conferred wide powers and enabled the imposition of variable speed limits. The Secretary of State was accountable to Parliament for the Agency. Therefore, the signing of the order and setting of speed restrictions were acts lawfully performed by the Agency acting on behalf of the Secretary of State.

Sentencing
SC Guideline – Speeding

C[49.36] Must endorse or may disqualify. If no disqualification, impose 3–6 points.

OFFENCE SERIOUSNESS (CULPABILITY AND HARM)			
A. IDENTIFY THE APPROPRIATE STARTING POINT			
Starting points based on first time offender pleading not guilty			
Speed limit (mph)	Recorded speed limit	Recorded speed limit	Recorded speed limit
20 mph	21–30	31–40	41–50
30 mph	31–40	41–50	51–60
40 mph	41–55	56–65	66–75
50 mph	51–65	66–75	76–85
60 mph	61–80	81–90	91–100
70 mph	71–90	91–100	100–110
Starting point	Band A fine	Band B fine	Band B fine
Range	Band A fine	Band B fine	Band B fine
Points/disqualification	3 points	4–6 points OR Disqualify 7–28 days	Disqualify 7–56 days OR 6 points

OFFENCE SERIOUSNESS (CULPABILITY AND HARM)
B. CONSIDER THE EFFECT OF AGGRAVATING AND MITIGATING FACTORS (OTHER THAN THOSE WITHIN EXAMPLES ABOVE)

Common aggravating and mitigating factors are identified at B[5.2A]. The following may be particularly relevant but **these lists are not exhaustive**

Factors indicating higher culpability	Factor indicating lower culpability
1. Poor road or weather conditions	1. Genuine emergency established
2. LGV, HGV, PSV etc	
3. Towing caravan/trailer	
4. Carrying passengers or heavy load	
5. Driving for hire or reward	
6. Evidence of unacceptable standard of driving over and above speed	
Factors indicating greater degree of harm	
1. Location eg near school	
2. High level of traffic or pedestrians in vicinity	

FORM A PRELIMINARY VIEW OF THE APPROPRIATE SENTENCE, THEN CONSIDER OFFENDER MITIGATION
Common factors are identified at B[5.2A]
CONSIDER A REDUCTION FOR A GUILTY PLEA
CONSIDER ANCILLARY ORDERS
Refer to B[18] for guidance on compensation and **Part B** for available ancillary orders
DECIDE SENTENCE
GIVE REASONS

C[49.37] If it appears to the court that the accused suffers from some disease or physical disability likely to cause his driving to be a source of danger to the public, then the court shall notify the licensing authority who may take steps to withdraw the driving licence (see C[5.49]).

C[50]

Steering defective

Charge

C[50.1] Using, causing or permitting to be used on a road a motor vehicle with defective steering

Road Vehicles (Construction and Use) Regulations 1986, reg 29; Road Traffic Act 1988, s 41A(b)

Maximum penalty – For a goods vehicle, fine on level 5, otherwise level 4 (for fines see B[33]).

Penalty points – 3.

Fixed penalty – £100 (3PP).

Legal notes and definitions

C[50.2] All the details as to maximum penalty, legal notes, exemption from endorsement and disqualification, and definitions and sentencing set out at C[9] for defective brakes apply to this charge of defective steering.

C[50.3] As with brakes, the law demands that the steering fitted to a motor vehicle on a road shall at all times be maintained in good and efficient working order and properly adjusted.

Sentencing
SGC Guideline – Steering defective

C[50.4] Starting point – either mechanically propelled vehicle or HGV, LGV or PSV – Band B fine (driver); Band B fine (owner-driver but consider an uplift of at least 25% on the driver's fine); Band C fine (owner-company)

C[51]

No test certificate

Charge

C[51.1] Using, causing or permitting a motor vehicle to be on the road first registered 3 or more years previously without having a test certificate in force

Road Traffic Act 1988, s 47(1)

Maximum penalty – Fine level 3. Vehicles adapted to carry more than eight passengers, level 4 (for fines see B[33]). No power to endorse or disqualify.

Fixed penalty – £100

Legal notes and definitions

C[51.2] Passenger vehicles carrying more than eight passengers. These vehicles and some taxis and ambulances must be tested after one year.

C[51.3] Motor vehicle. See C[9.7].

C[51.4] Road. Means any highway (including footpaths and bridleways) and any other road to which the public has access and includes bridges.

C[51.5] Using. This does not in law only mean driving a vehicle along a road; its mere presence on a road, even in a useless condition may constitute using (*Pumbien v Vines* [1996] RTR 37, [1996] Crim LR 124). The test is whether steps had been taken to make it impossible for a driver to drive the vehicle. Where doubt exists consult the legal adviser. A person, limited company, a corporate body which owns a vehicle that is driven in the course of the owner's business is using the vehicle. See C[9.4].

C[51.6] Causing. This implies some express or positive mandate from the person causing the vehicle to be used; or some authority from him and knowledge of the facts which constitute the offence.

C[51.7] Permitting. This includes express permission and also circumstances in which permission may be inferred.

C[51.8] If the defendant is a limited company, it must be proved that some person for whose criminal act the company is responsible permitted the offence. A defendant charged with permitting must be shown to have known the vehicle was being used or that he shut his eyes to something that would have made the use obvious to him.

C[51.9] Examples of exempted vehicles include:

Goods vehicles the design gross weight of which exceeds 3,500 kg.

Motor tractors.

Articulated vehicles, and their several parts.

Works trucks.

Pedestrian-controlled vehicles.

Invalid vehicles.

Some taxis.

Certain vehicles from abroad and Northern Ireland only here temporarily.

Vehicles en route for export.

Agricultural motor vehicles.

C[51.10]–[51.15] Examples of exempted uses include:

(a) that by a previous arrangement the vehicle was being used for the purpose of taking it for a test or for bringing it back from a test *(Williams v Richards* (1997) Times, 29 July);

(b) that the examiner or a person under his personal direction was using the vehicle in the course of or in connection with a test;

(c) that following an unsuccessful test the vehicle was being used by being towed to a place where it could be broken up; or

(d) that by a previous arrangement the vehicle was being taken to or from a place where it was to be or had been taken to remedy defects on the ground of which a test certificate had been refused.

C[51.16] The defendant need not prove either kind of exemption (ie exempted vehicle or exempted use) beyond reasonable doubt; he need only prove this defence is probably true.

C[51.17] Renewal of certificate. A certificate lasts for one year. Within one month from the expiry of the certificate, the vehicle may be retested and a further certificate issued to commence on the expiry of the existing certificate.

Sentencing
SC Guideline – (1) No test certificate (2) No goods vehicle test certificate

C[51.18] Starting point – mechanically propelled vehicle – Band A fine (driver); Band A fine (owner-driver but consider an uplift of at least 25% on the driver's fine); Band B fine (owner-company).

Starting point – goods vehicle – Band B fine (driver); Band B fine (owner-driver but consider an uplift of at least 25% on the driver's fine); Band C fine (owner-company).

Traffic signs

Charge

C[52.1] Failing to comply with the indication given by a traffic sign

Road Traffic Act 1988, s 36

Maximum penalty – Fine level 3 (for fines see B[33]). Endorsement and disqualification can only be ordered if the vehicle was a motor vehicle and the traffic sign was one of the following: **Stop, Traffic Lights** (including portable traffic lights and green filter arrows), **No Entry Sign** or **Double White Lines.** For these signs disqualification can be for any period or until the accused has passed a driving test. Must endorse for these signs unless there are special reasons.

Endorsement and disqualification also apply to drivers of 'abnormal loads' at railway level crossings who fail to phone the signalman before crossing and to drivers of vehicles which contravene relevant height restrictions.

Penalty points – 3 (only for endorsable offences).

Fixed penalty – £100 (endorsable offences); £50 (otherwise).

Legal notes and definitions

C[52.2] It is not a defence that the sign was not seen.

C[52.3] The defendant can only be convicted if at the time of the offence he was warned of possible prosecution, or a summons or a notice of intended prosecution was served within 14 days upon the registered owner of the vehicle. It will be presumed that this requirement was complied with unless the contrary is proved by the defendant on the balance of probabilities.

C[52.4] The offence applies to all vehicles including pedal cycles and is not limited to mechanically propelled vehicles.

C[52.5] Even wheeling a pedal cycle in contravention of the sign is an offence.

C[52.6] A traffic sign. This is presumed to be of correct size, colour and type unless proved to the contrary by the defence.

C[52.7] Automatic traffic lights are presumed to be in proper working order unless the contrary is proved by the defence.

C[52.8] Traffic lights. It is an offence if any part of the vehicle crosses the 'stop' line when the light is red, for example, if the front part of the vehicle is already over the line and the light turns red an offence is committed if the rear part of the vehicle then crosses the line with the light still at red.

C[52.9] Double white lines. It is an offence to overtake or park in contravention of double white lines in the middle of the road. There are certain exceptions, however, such as passing a slow moving road sweeper or a taxi stopping to allow a passenger to alight or board. Ask the legal adviser for details.

C[52.10]–[52.15] A road. Means any highway (including footpaths and bridleways) and any other road to which the public has access and includes bridges.

C[52.16] Signs to which the offence applies. These include:

Emergency traffic signs placed by a constable on the instructions of a chief officer of police.

[1] Stop at major road ahead.

Give way at major road ahead.

Stop one way working.

[1] No entry.

Arrow indicating direction to be followed.

Arrow indicating keep left or right.

[1] Red light including portable light signals and at automatic level crossings.

[1] Double white lines.

Keep left dual carriageway.

Turn left at dual carriageway.

[1] Drivers of 'abnormal loads' at railway level crossings.

[1] Prohibition on vehicles exceeding specified height.

[1] Green arrow traffic signals.

No 'U' turn.

Mini roundabout sign.

---

[1]   Only these offences qualify for endorsement and disqualification. See reg 10 of the Traffic Signs Regulations and General Directions 2002.

Sentencing
SC Guideline – Failing to comply with traffic sign

C[52.17] Starting point – Band A fine (Endorsement and disqualification can only be ordered if the vehicle was a motor vehicle and the traffic sign was one of those mentioned under 'Maximum penalty').

C[52.18] If it appears to the court that the accused suffers from some disease or physical disability likely to cause his driving to be a source of danger to the public, then the court shall notify the licensing authority who may take steps to withdraw the driving licence (see **C[5.49]**).

Tyres defective

Charge

C[53.1] Using, causing or permitting to be used on a road a motor vehicle or trailer with defective tyres

Road Vehicles (Construction and Use) Regulations 1986, reg 27; Road Traffic Act 1988, s 41A(b)

Maximum penalty – For a goods vehicle, fine level 5, otherwise level 4 (for fines see B[33]). May disqualify for any period and/or until a driving test has been passed. Must endorse unless special reasons exist.

For 'special reasons', see C[5.2].

Penalty points – 3

Fixed penalty – £100 (3PP)

Legal notes and definitions

C[53.2] All the details as to legal notes, exemption from endorsement and disqualification, definitions and sentencing set out on at C[9] for defective brakes also apply to these charges.

C[53.3] It is an offence for a tyre on a car or light van (gross weight not exceeding 3,500 kg) and their trailers to be in any of the following conditions:

(a)   tyre being unsuitable having regard to the use to which the vehicle is put;
(b)   tyre being unsuitable having regard to types of tyres on other wheels;
(c)   tyre not so inflated as to make it fit for use to which vehicle is being put;
(d)   break in fabric of tyre;
(e)   ply or cord structure exposed;
(f)   the grooves of the tread pattern of the tyre do not have a depth of at least 1 millimetre throughout a continuous band comprising the central three-quarters of the breadth of the tread and round the entire outer circumference of the tyre;
(g)   tyre must be free from any defect which might damage the road surface or cause danger to persons in the vehicle or on the road.

Consult the legal adviser for the complete list.

C[53.4] The law requires all tyres of a motor vehicle or trailer on a road to be free from any defect which might in any way cause damage to the road surface or cause danger to persons in or on a vehicle or to other persons using the road.

C[53.5] If no tyre is fitted at all the offence will be brought under a different regulation.

C[53.6] Two or more defective tyres. If a vehicle has two or more defective tyres, a separate charge should be alleged for each.

Sentencing
SC Guideline – Tyres defective

C[53.7] Starting point – mechanically propelled vehicle – Band A fine (driver); Band A fine (owner-driver but consider an uplift of at least 25% on the driver's fine); Band B fine (owner-company).

Starting point – goods vehicle – Band B fine (driver); Band B fine (owner-driver but consider an uplift of at least 25% on the driver's fine); Band C fine (owner-company).

C[53.8] As for 'brakes' see C[9.16]. A vehicle with two defective tyres is much more dangerous than a vehicle with only one defective tyre. Where the means of the offender permit the penalty should usually ensure that it is cheaper to keep the vehicle in good condition than to risk a fine. A short disqualification can also be considered.

Section D

Procedure

The Human Rights Act

D[1.1] The purpose of the Human Rights Act 1998 is to allow citizens of the United Kingdom to enforce their rights under the Human Rights Convention in the domestic courts.

The Act requires all courts and tribunals to give effect to Convention rights by interpreting existing legislation and laws, where possible, compatibly with the Convention.

D[1.2] With regard to statute (primary legislation) the courts are required to interpret the legislation so as to uphold the Convention rights unless legislation is so clearly incompatible with the Convention that it is impossible to do so. If a Convention right is contravened by a provision in primary legislation which the court is unable to interpret compatibly it must give effect to the will of Parliament. However, in such circumstances an appeal may be made to the High Court for a *declaration of incompatibility* which leads to a fast track procedure in Parliament for the passing of a *remedial order* to cure the apparent incompatibility.

In the case of secondary legislation or precedent the court's duty is to give effect to Convention rights; firstly through the medium of interpretation or secondly through disapplying the relevant domestic law.

D[1.3] Additionally, courts must take into account judgments, decisions and opinions of the European Court of Human Rights and the Commission. All public authorities have a positive obligation to act compatibly with the Convention. This includes magistrates' courts, local authorities, the Probation Service and justices' clerks.

D[1.4] Advocates wishing to raise a Convention point in magistrates' courts should be prepared to identify the article of the Convention which it is suggested may be breached, the reason for the breach and the remedy required of the courts. Court may give directions requiring the parties to file skeleton arguments in support of any Convention arguments.

Procedural steps

D[1.5] Step 1 Ask if a Convention right is engaged.

If no Convention right is engaged, the case must be decided on the basis of domestic law.

If the Convention is engaged move to step 2

Step 2 Identify the relevant article and its class

* Absolute Rights:
  Article 3: prohibition of torture, inhuman or degrading treatment
  Article 4(1): prohibition of slavery or servitude
  Article 7: prohibition of punishment without law
* Limited Rights:
  Article 2: right to life

Article 4(2): prohibition of forced or compulsory labour
Article 5: right to liberty
Article 6: right to a fair trial
* Qualified Rights:
Article 8: right to respect for private and family life
Article 9: freedom of thought, conscience and religion
Article 10: freedom of expression
Article 11: freedom of assembly
* Parts of Article 6 such as art 6(1) confer limited rights. Other parts, such as art 6(3) confer qualified rights.

D[1.6] The threshold is high for breach of an *absolute right* but once breached for any reason, a violation is established.

Limited rights contain definitive statements of the circumstances which *permit* a breach of the right. If the restrictions are not complied with, there has been a violation of the Article.

Qualified Rights *may* be breached if:

* the breach is prescribed by domestic law
* the law is clear and accessible
* the breach pursues a legitimate aim which is set out in the Article
* the measure is a proportional response

If these provisions do not apply there is likely to be a violation of the convention.

D[1.7] A magistrates' court which finds a breach or potential breach of the Convention may grant such relief or remedy, or make that order within its powers and it considers just and appropriate. In essence this may mean a simple adjournment to provide more time to prepare for a trial or it may involve the exclusion of evidence which would have had an unfair effect on the trial itself.

In *R (Laporte) v Chief Constable of Gloucestershire* [2004] EWCA Civ 1639, [2005] 1 All ER 473 the High Court found that the police acted reasonably in stopping a coach party, in apprehension of a breach of the peace and did not violate their Article 10 rights. However their actions in forcibly returning the coach to London breached Article 5.

D[1.8] **Burden of Proof.** Where a statutory provision imposes a burden of proof on a defendant the court must first ascertain if it is an evidential or a legal burden. An evidential burden can be discharged by some evidence which could result in a decision in the defendant's favour. A legal burden on the other hand may breach the presumption of innocence in Article 6 (*R v Johnstone* [2003] UKHL 28, [2003] All ER (D) 323 (May), HL and *A-G's Reference No 1 (2004)*).

D[1A]

Reasons for decision

D[1A.1] There are many statutory requirements to give reasons in court. Examples are the imposition of imprisonment or where a court orders the removal of press restriction normally applicable in court. Such requirements are outlined in the text of this work. Article 6(1) states: ' . . . everyone is entitled to a fair and public hearing within a reasonable time by an independent and impartial tribunal established by law. Judgment shall be pronounced publicly . . . '.

D[1A.2] The giving of reasons enables an aggrieved person to understand the decision and make an informed decision on the right to appeal. It also provides an explanation for the public at large and those observing the proceedings in court. Reasons need not be elaborate (*McKerry v Teesdale and Wear Valley Justices* (2000) 164 JP 355, [2000] Crim LR 594, CA).

D[1A.3] However, a reasoned judgment at the end of a trial should cover the major issues in dispute, and any legal submissions, together with the findings of fact. In *Ruiz Torija v Spain* (1994) 19 EHRR 542, ECtHR the European Court stated: 'The court reiterates that Article 6(1) obliges the courts to give reasons for their judgments, but cannot be understood as requiring a detailed answer to every argument. The extent to which this duty to give reasons applies may vary according to the nature of the decision'. One area where it is clear the court will have to give reasons is where there is any suggestion that an inference from the exercise of the right to silence is to be drawn: see *Condron v United Kingdom* [2000] Crim LR 679, 8 BHRC 290, ECtHR.

D[1A.4] One other area that would appear to be clear is that the courts must not resort to formatted or standard reasons. In *Yagci and Sargin v Turkey* (1995) 20 EHRR 505, ECtHR the European Court disapproved of the use of stereotyped reasons by a court when refusing bail.

D[1A.5] The court, like all other tribunals and public authorities, must act compatibly with the European Convention. In general a rigorous approach to giving reasons for a decision will normally alert the court to any human rights issues. A structured approach to those issues should lead to a successful resolution of human rights problems in court.

Proceedings to be in open court

D[1B.1] Magistrates conducting a summary trial must generally sit in open court (Magistrates' Courts Act 1980, s 121) and comply with the provisions of Art 6 of the ECHR that everyone is entitled to a fair and public hearing. See r 37 of the Criminal Procedure Rules 2014 (Trial and Sentence in a Magistrates' Court).

D[1B.2] There may be exceptions such as governing the conduct of proceedings in a youth court (at E[2]). Also, statute provides for a court to sit in camera when considering evidence in proceedings under the Official Secrets Act 1920. All these may be read into Art 6(1) of the Convention and are unlikely to be subject to challenge.

D[1B.3] **Power to clear court while child or young person is giving evidence in certain cases.** Where, in any proceedings in relation to an offence against or any conduct contrary to decency or morality, a juvenile is called as a witness, the court may be cleared of persons other than members or officers of the court, parties to the case, their counsel or solicitors, and persons otherwise directly concerned with the case, but bona fide representatives of the press may not be excluded (Children and Young Persons Act 1933, s 37).

D[1B.4] Apart from the statutory exceptions evidence must be given in open court except where it may be necessary to depart from this principle where the nature or circumstances of the particular proceedings are such that the application of the general rule in its entirety would frustrate or render impracticable the administration of justice (*A-G v Leveller Magazines Ltd* [1979] AC 440, [1979] 1 All ER 745, HL).

D[1B.5] The High Court has commented on the magistrates' decision to hear mitigation in camera because embarrassing and intimate details of the defendant's personal life would have to be given by her and she had an overwhelming fear of revealing them publicly. The judges felt the magistrates' exercise of their discretion was unsustainable and out of accord with principle (*R v Malvern Justices, ex p Evans* [1988] QB 553, [1988] 1 All ER 371).

D[1B.6] **Non-disclosure of evidence given in open court.** Sometimes where the court decides not to sit in camera there is a request that a witness may write down his name on a piece of paper or use a pseudonym. In criminal cases at least this should only be done where the criteria for sitting in camera are met and such a device is normally only encountered in blackmail cases. Such a power is not designed for the benefit of the comfort and feelings of defendants such as where publication of a defendant's address might cause him to be harassed by his former wife (*R v Evesham Justices, ex p McDonagh* [1988] QB 553, [1988] 1 All ER 371).

Reporting of court proceedings

D[1B.7] Apart from the special provisions governing the youth and family proceedings courts referred to above, the press may report all legal proceedings held in public (Contempt of Court Act 1981, s 4(1)). There are certain exceptions to the general rule:

(a) *Children and young persons:* The court may direct that any press, radio or television report of the case must not reveal the name, address, school or identity of any child or young person concerned in the proceedings including the defendant (CYPA 1933, s 39).

This legislation seeks to capture, in wide language, at least the central participants in proceedings whether civil or criminal. It is therefore wide enough to include a child who is the 'victim' of an offence of a person being drunk in a public place whilst having the charge of a child under the age of seven years (Licensing Act 1902, s 2(1)): *R (on the application of A) v Lowestoft Magistrates' Court* [2013] EWHC 659 (Admin), (2013) 177 JP 377, [2013] Crim L R 763. Note, however, there is a clear distinction between the position in the youth court, where under the CYPA 1933, s 49 publication of the identity of the child or young person is prohibited subject to certain exceptions, and s 39 where the court has to exercise a discretion whether or not to make an order restricting publicity.

An order under s 39 must be clear as to precisely what is prohibited: *Briffet v DPP* [2001] EWHC Admin 841, 166 JP 66, [2002] EMLR 203 (sub nom *Briffett and Bradshaw v Crown Prosecution Service*), and should be in writing: *Re BBC Litigation Department* [2002] All ER (D) 69 (Apr), CA.

Great care should be taken by magistrates' courts when making an order under s 39. Before making such an order the court should generally ask members of the press whether they had any submissions so the court fully understood the issues, given the great importance of making these orders. Orders are not to be made as a matter of routine, and require a careful balance of matters relating to the public interest, after submissions have been made: *C v CPS* [2008] EWHC 854 (Admin), 172 JP 273, (2008) Times, 20 February (any embarrassment that might flow to the children was an unfortunate consequence of a parent being convicted of a crime). Unless there were exceptional circumstances the balance between arts 8 and 10 of the ECHR fell firmly in favour of removing the s 39 prohibition: *C v CPS*, above; *Re Trinity Mirror plc* [2008] EWCA Crim 50, [2008] 2 All ER 1159.

It has been doubted whether an order under s 39 can embrace reporting in digitised or other form not in existence when s 39 was enacted: *MXB v East Sussex Hospitals NHS Trust* [2012] EWHC 32769, (2012) 177 JP 177.

An order made under s 39 cannot extend to reports of proceedings after the subject of the order has attained the age of 18: *R (on the application of JC and another) v Central Criminal Court* [2014] EWHC (Admin), (2014) 178 JP 188.

A decision to vary reporting restrictions in relation to a young offender pursuant to the Children and Young Persons Act 1933, s 39 was quashed as the proper test had not been applied and inadequate reasons had been given to justify the variation. In deciding whether to impose reporting restrictions under s 39, a court had to balance the welfare of the child, the public interest and the requirements of the ECHR, art 10, and to restrict publication if the factors were evenly balanced. Prior to conviction, the former is likely to prevail. After conviction, the defendant's age and the gravity of the crime are likely to be particularly relevant: *R (on the application of Y) v Aylesbury Crown Court, Crown Prosecution Service and Newsquest.*

(b)   After an allegation of rape and other sexual offences (eg see **A[53]**) has been made the general statutory rule is that no material likely to lead to the identification by the public of the complainant may be published or broadcast (Sexual Offences (Amendment) Act 1992).

(c)   *Publication of matters exempted from disclosure in court:* Where a court has allowed a name or other matter to be withheld from the public in proceedings before the court, the court may give such directions prohibiting the publication of that name or matter in connection with the proceedings as appear to the court to be necessary for the purpose for which it was so withheld (Contempt of Court Act 1981, s 11). The order must be in writing and must state with precision its exact terms, extent and purpose. There has to be a very compelling reason to withhold the addresses of serving police officers charged with criminal offences: see *R (on the application of Harper) v Aldershot Magistrates' Court* [2010] EWHC 1319 (Admin), 174 JP 410, 174 CL&J 383.

(d)   *Power to postpone publication of reports of court proceedings:* Where it appears to be necessary for avoiding a substantial risk of prejudice to the administration of justice in those proceedings or in any other proceedings pending or imminent the court may order that the publication of any report of the proceedings or any part of the proceedings be postponed for such period as the court thinks necessary for that purpose (Contempt of Court Act 1981, s 4(2)). The order should be no wider than is necessary for the prevention of prejudice to the administration of justice (*R v Horsham Justices, ex p Farquharson* [1982] QB 762, [1982] 2 All ER 269, CA) and must be in writing and must state with precision its exact terms, extent and purpose.

(e)   Under s 46 of the Youth Justice and Criminal Evidence Act 1999 the court may prevent publication of any matter which may lead to the identification of an adult witness for the duration of that person's life, if it is satisfied that the quality of their evidence or their participation would be diminished by fear or distress related to public information.

(f)   Note, that by virtue of the Coroners and Justice Act 2009, Chapter 2, Part 3, witness anonymity is available in criminal proceedings including summary proceedings. Recourse to the relevant provisions in the magistrates' court should prove rare. Where the issue is canvassed justices should consult their legal adviser. See Part 29, Section 5 of the CPR 2012.

D[1B.8] **Twitter and other live, text-based communications.** The Lord Chief Justice in 2012 has issued guidance on the use of live, text-based communications such as mobile email, social media (including Twitter) and internet-enabled laptops in open court. This guidance replaces interim guidance issued in 2010.

The new guidance makes clear that:

•   There is no longer any need for representatives of the media/legal commentators to make an application to use text-based devices to communicate from court.

•   Members of the public should make a formal or informal application if they wish to use these devices.

•   Use of the devices should not cause a disturbance or distraction.

•   The court always retains full discretion to prohibit live, text-based communications from court, in the interests of justice. The 'paramount question' for the court in deciding whether to allow live text-based communications is whether it may interfere with the administration of justice. 'The danger . . . is likely to be at its most acute in the context of criminal trials, eg where witnesses who are out of court may be informed of what has already happened in court and so coached or briefed before they then give evidence . . . '

- Anyone using electronic text is strictly bound by the existing restrictions on reporting court proceedings under the Contempt of Court Act 1981.
- Photography in court remains strictly forbidden under the Criminal Justice Act 1925.

D[1B.9] Photographs and sketches in court. No person shall take or attempt to take a photograph, or make or attempt to make any portrait or sketch of a justice or party or witness to proceedings, in a court room or in a court building or precincts or entering or leaving them (Criminal Justice Act 1925, s 41).

D[1B.10] Tape recorders. It is a contempt of court to use a tape recorder (other than for the purpose of making an official transcript) in a court without the leave of the court (Contempt of Court Act 1981, s 9). Guidelines for the decision whether to grant leave were given in a Practice Direction by the Lord Chief Justice in 1982 which may be summarised thus:

- Has the applicant a reasonable need to use the tape recorder?
- Is there a risk of a recording being used to brief witnesses?
- What is the possibility of distracting proceedings or distracting or worrying witnesses?

D[1B.11] Abuse of the process. The jurisdiction exercised by magistrates, to protect the court's process from abuse is confined to matters directly affecting the fairness of the trial of the accused, and it does not extend to the wider supervisory jurisdiction for upholding the rule of law which is vested in the High Court (*R v Horseferry Road Magistrates, ex p Bennett* [1994] AC 42, [1993] 3 WLR 90, sub nom *Bennett v Horseferry Road Magistrates' Court* [1993] 3 All ER 138, HL). It must not be used, therefore, to exercise a disciplinary function over eg executive decisions made by a prosecuting authority.

The parameters of this power are narrowly drawn. Justices may only stay proceedings where it would be unfair to try the defendant or where the defendant cannot receive a fair trial. It may be an abuse of process if either (a) the prosecution have manipulated or misused the process of the court so as to deprive the defendant of a protection provided by the law or to take unfair advantage of a technicality, or (b) the defendant has been, or will be, prejudiced in the preparation or conduct of his defence by delay on the part of the prosecution which is unjustifiable.

The defence should give advance notice of such application. Where notice is not given magistrates should look favourably on an adjournment application by the prosecution. In addition, the court should give directions for the filing of skeleton arguments by the parties. A skeleton argument should focus on the issues arising in the case and the relevant principles. An excessive citation of authorities is to be deprecated.

D[1B.12] Principles. May be summarised as follows:

(1)   The discretionary decision as to whether or not to grant a stay as an abuse is an exercise in judicial assessment dependent on judgement, rather than on any conclusion as to fact based on evidence.

Accordingly, in cases of delay it is potentially misleading to apply to the exercise of that discretion the language of burden and standard of proof, which is more apt to an evidence-based, fact-finding process (*R v S* [2006] EWCA Crim 756, (2006) 170 JP 434).

(2)   The applicant must identify the ground or grounds upon which he relies eg delay, manipulation of the proceedings or destruction of evidence.

(3)   Where there is no fault attributable to, or the prosecution have acted in good faith, it will be very rare for a stay to be granted.

(4)   Is there serious prejudice to the accused? No stay should be granted in the absence of serious prejudice to the accused. When assessing possible serious prejudice, the court should consider its powers to regulate the admissibility of evidence, and that the trial process itself should ensure that all relevant factual issues arising from eg delay or the destruction of evidence, are placed before the court for its consideration.

(5)   When assessing possible serious prejudice, the court can take into account its powers in relation to sentence, assuming there is a conviction or a guilty plea.

(6)   A permanent stay should be the exception rather than the rule.

(7)   If having considered all the relevant factors, the court's assessment is that a fair trial will be possible, a stay should not be granted.

Abuse of the process – long delay – relevant principles: *R v F* [2011] EWCA Crim 726, [2011] 2 Cr App Rep 145, 175 CL&J 213.

The Court of Appeal derived from a review of authority five propositions concerning the treatment of criminal proceedings brought after a long delay. Those propositions were:

•   Proceedings should be stayed only if the court was satisfied that delay precluded a fair trial.

•   An application for a stay should *normally* be made at trial after all the evidence has been heard.

•   In assessing [serious] prejudice to the defendant, the court had to balance evidence that had survived the delay against missing evidence and critically examine the importance of the missing evidence.

•   Having identified [serious] prejudice, the court had to consider whether it could come compensate for the prejudice by special [jury] directions.

•   Unjustified delay by a complainant in coming forward was relevant to whether a fair trial could be achieved, but it had to be firmly borne in mind that sexual abuse victims were often unwilling to talk about their experiences for some time and for good reason.

Disclosure – delay – abuse of the process – test to be applied: *Brants v DPP* [2011] EWHC 754 (Admin), 175 JP 246.

A positive decision not to disclose relevant material culminating in delay may amount to an abuse of the process. In the case of *Brants*, the appellant, a driver of a heavy goods vehicle, was stopped by a police constable and required to produce his digital driver card. The officer downloaded the material held on the card onto his laptop. From this he produced reports and a list of offences under the Transport Act 1968, s 96. An information was laid alleging four contraventions relating to drivers' hours and rest periods. On 16 March 2009, solicitors for the appellant requested disclosure of the digital material downloaded by the police officer. It was first directed by the magistrates' court to be handed over on 14 May 2009. The material was not disclosed until 26 July 2009. At a later date, and as a preliminary issue, it was submitted that the proceedings were an abuse of the process by reason of delay. The justices ruled against the appellant and he changed his plea to guilty.

On appeal by way of case stated, the Queen's Bench Division decided this was not a case where the prosecution had positively refused to comply with a direction of the court. The prosecution did ultimately comply. However, there was a long delay before the material was disclosed. Whilst the court strongly disapproved of the failure to disclosure, the delay in this case was attributable to the inefficiency or incompetence of the prosecution: *R R (L)* [2010] EWCA Crim 924, [2011] 1 WLR 359, [2010] 2 Cr App Rep 63 distinguished.

It is submitted that the justices in *Brants* could have inferred a deliberate decision not to disclose the relevant material, having regard to the lapse of time and the number of adjourned hearings after a direction to disclose the material was given.

It was affirmed in *DPP v Gowing* [2013] EWHC 4614 (Admin), (2014) 178 JP 181 that the jurisdiction to stay proceedings as an abuse of process is exceptional and there must be a firm basis for its exercise, either bad faith or inability to hold a fair trial. The power to stay should not be used to punish prosecution inefficiency where a fair trial was still possible, Courts have a duty to investigate carefully any claims of prejudice or unfairness arising from non-compliance with disclosure duties.

D[2]

Misbehaviour in court

D[2.1] Misbehaviour by members of the public:

(a) Where persons misbehave in court the first approach should be to attempt to calm down offenders by an appeal to reason and good manners. A court can also consider putting the case back for a 'cooling off' period and the chairman may also make mention in very general terms of the court's powers to maintain order.

(b) If this is not successful a court has power to order persons disrupting the court to leave the court room. If they refuse, and their removal is necessary to enable justice to be administered properly, the court may order a court security officer or the police to remove such persons using reasonable force if necessary.

(c) Where persons are misbehaving in court the magistrates should not exercise their power to **bind over**). For procedure on binding over, see **B[10.20]**, **[10.21]**.

D[3]

Contempt of court

Charges

D[3.1]–[3.3] Contempt of court

(a) Wilfully did insult AB being a justice of the peace (or a witness before the court, or an officer of the court, or a solicitor or counsel having business before the court) during his sitting or attendance in court or when he was going to or returning from the court; or
(b) wilfully interrupted the proceedings of a magistrates' court; or
(c) wilfully misbehaved in a magistrates' court.

Contempt of Court Act 1981, s 12.

D[3.4] Maximum penalty. Fine of level 4 and one month. Proceedings under s 12: offender may be ordered to be taken into custody by an officer of the court or a constable and detained until the rising of the court in addition to or instead of the penalty mentioned above. A person under 18 years may not be committed for contempt. A substantial prison sentence (12 months) was upheld in *R v D (contempt of court: illegal photography)* (2004) Times, 13 May where the defendant had photographed the interior of the Crown Court (see **D[1B.8]**).

Legal notes

D[3.5] Wilfully insult. The word 'insult' has to be given its ordinary English meaning. A person who had *threatened* a defendant had not 'insulted' him and was not in breach of s 12 (*R v Havant Justices, ex p Palmer* (1985) 149 JP 609, [1985] Crim LR 658).

D[3.6] Officer of the court. This term is not defined in the Act. It will apply to the justices' clerk and his staff, presumably whether or not they are concerned in the particular proceedings in which the insult occurs. If there is any doubt, the matter could certainly be resolved by simply alleging misbehaviour in court.

D[3.7] Procedure. This is governed by Part 62 of the Criminal Procedure Rules 2014. This provides, so far as is relevant to magistrates' courts:

'SECTION 2: CONTEMPT OF COURT BY OBSTRUCTION, DIS-RUPTION, ETC

62.5 Initial procedure on obstruction, disruption, etc

(1) This rule applies where the court observes, or someone reports to the court—
    (c) in a magistrates' court, a contravention of—
        (i) section 97(4) of the Magistrates' Courts Act 1980 (refusing to give evidence), or
        (ii) section 12 of the Contempt of Court Act 1981 (insulting or interrupting the court, etc);

(d)   a contravention of section 9 of the Contempt of Court Act 1981 (without the court's permission, recording the proceedings, etc);

(e)   any other conduct with which the court can deal as, or as if it were, a criminal contempt of court, except failure to surrender to bail under section 6 of the Bail Act 1976.

(2)   Unless the respondent's behaviour makes it impracticable to do so, the court must—

   (a)   explain, in terms the respondent can understand (with help, if necessary)—

      (i)   the conduct that is in question,

      (ii)   that the court can impose imprisonment, or a fine, or both, for such conduct,

      (iii)   (where relevant) that the court has power to order the respondent's immediate temporary detention, if in the court's opinion that is required,

      (iv)   that the respondent may explain the conduct,

      (v)   that the respondent may apologise, if he or she so wishes, and that this may persuade the court to take no further action, and

      (vi)   that the respondent may take legal advice; and

   (b)   allow the respondent a reasonable opportunity to reflect, take advice, explain and, if he or she so wishes, apologise.

(3)   The court may then—

   (a)   take no further action in respect of that conduct;

   (b)   enquire into the conduct there and then; or

   (c)   postpone that enquiry (if a magistrates' court, only until later the same day).

[Note The conduct to which this rule applies is sometimes described as 'criminal' contempt of court.]

...

. . . Under section 97(4) of the Magistrates' Courts Act 1980, and under sections 12 and 14 of the Contempt of Court Act 1981, a magistrates' court can imprison (for a maximum of 1 month), or fine (to a maximum of £2,500), or both, a respondent who contravenes a provision listed in paragraph (1)(c) or (d). Section 12(1) of the 1981 Act allows the court to deal with any person who—

(a)   wilfully insults the justice or justices, any witness before or officer of the court or any solicitor or counsel having business in the court, during his or their sitting or attendance in court or in going to or returning from the court; or

(b)   wilfully interrupts the proceedings of the court or otherwise misbehaves in court. Under section 89 of the Powers of Criminal Courts (Sentencing) Act 2000, no respondent who is under 21 may be imprisoned for contempt of court. Under section 108 of that Act, a respondent who is at least 18 but under 21 may be detained if the court is of the opinion that no other method of dealing with him or her is appropriate. Under section 14(2A) of the Contempt of Court Act 1981, a respondent who is under 17 may not be ordered to attend an attendance centre.

Under section 258 of the Criminal Justice Act 2003, a respondent who is imprisoned for contempt of court must be released unconditionally after serving half the term.

Under sections 14, 15 and 16 of the Legal Aid, Sentencing and Punishment of Offenders Act 2012, the respondent may receive advice and representation in "proceedings for contempt committed, or alleged to have been committed, by an individual in the face of the court".

. . . Under s 12(2) of the Contempt of Court Act 1981, a magistrates' court can temporarily detain a respondent until later the same day on a contravention of that section.

[Part 19 contains rules about bail.]

62.6 Review after temporary detention

(1)   This rule applies in a case in which the court has ordered the respondent's immediate temporary detention for conduct to which rule 62.5 applies.

(2)   The court must review the case—
     (a)   if a magistrates' court, later the same day . . .

(3)   On the review, the court must—
     (a)   unless the respondent is absent, repeat the explanations required by rule 62.5(2)(a); and
     (b)   allow the respondent a reasonable opportunity to reflect, take advice, explain and, if he or she so wishes, apologise.

(4)   The court may then—
     (a)   take no further action in respect of the conduct;
     (b)   if a magistrates' court, enquire into the conduct there and then . . . '

D[3.8] Unauthorised use of disclosed prosecution material under s 17 of the CPIA 1996 Section 3 of Part 62 of the Criminal Procedure Rules 2014 (not reproduced) deals with the procedure for such contempt, which is punishable in the magistrates' court by imprisonment for six months, or a fine of £5,000, or both.

D[3.9] Witnesses. In addition to the powers outlined above, where a witness refuses to take the oath or to answer a question, he may be committed to prison for a period of up to one month (and ordered to pay a fine on level 4). He may be released immediately he changes his mind and decides to co-operate with the court. This advice may ensure his compliance.

D[3.10]–[3.14] Defendants. Disorderly defendants may be dealt with as outlined above. However, a court is naturally reluctant to deal with the case in the absence of a defendant. Accordingly, if the defendant has to be ejected the court should carefully consider adjourning the case for a 'cooling off' period. The more serious the case the less appropriate it will be to proceed in the defendant's absence. The defendant should be informed that he will be readmitted to the court any time he is prepared to conduct himself properly.

D[3.15] Taking a photograph in court with a mobile phone is a contempt of court and has resulted in immediate prison sentences in the Crown Court (*R v D* (2004) Times, 13 May). See D[1B.8].

D[3.16] Appeal. An appeal against conviction and/or sentence under s 108 Magistrates' Courts Act 1980 lies to the Crown Court pursuant to s 12(5) of the 1981 Act (*Haw and Tucker v City of Westminster Magistrates' Court* [2007] EWHC 2960 (Admin), [2008] 2 All ER 326). Procedure on appeals is governed by Part 63 of the Criminal Procedure Rules 2014.

New allocation and sending provisions

D[4.1] The mode of trial and committal for sentence provisions of Sch 3 to the Criminal Justice Act 2003 were brought into force on 28 May 2013. These provisions are intricate and often complicated.

Order of consideration – adult offenders charged with offences triable either way (except certain low value either way offences)

D[4.2] The court must first proceed in accordance with s 50A of the Crime and Disorder Act 1998, as follows.

If notice is given in respect of the either way offence under s 51B (notices in serious or complex fraud cases) or s 51C (notices in certain cases involving children) of the 1998 Act, the court must send deal with the offence by sending it to the Crown Court under s 51 of the 1998 Act.

Otherwise:

(a)   (Offences relating to a purely indictable or notice sending)
        (i)   if the adult (or another adult with whom the adult is jointly charged with the relevant offence) is sent for trial for an indictable offence or in consequence of a notice issued under s 51B or 51C and the either way offence appears to be a 'related' offence, the court must also send forthwith the either way offence (and any summary offence related to the sent offence or to the either way offence, provided the summary offence carries imprisonment or obligatory/discretionary disqualification) to the Crown Court;
        (ii)   if the adult (or another adult with whom the adult is jointly charged with the relevant offence) has previously been sent for trial for an indictable offence or in consequence of a notice issued under s 51B or 51C and the either way offence appears to be a 'related' offence, the power to send as above (together with any summary offence as described above) is discretionary, not mandatory. If the court does not send the adult for trial it shall proceed to deal with the relevant offence in accordance with ss 17A–23 of the Magistrates' Courts Act 1980.
(b)   In all other cases:
        (i)   the court must first consider the relevant offence under ss 17A–20 of the Magistrates' Courts Act 1980 (excluding s 20(8) and (9))*;
        (ii)   if a guilty plea is indicated under s 17A(6), (17(B)(2) or 20(7), the court shall proceed as consequently required by the relevant provision;
        (iii)   in any other case the court shall consider the relevant offence under the sending provisions of ss 51 and 51A of the Crime and Disorder Act 1998 and, if the adult is not then sent to the

Crown Court for trial the court shall ask the adult if he consents to summary trial and proceed thereafter in accordance with the adult's election.

(*The excluded provisions provide for the case where an accused has not indicated a guilty plea, the court determines summary trial to be suitable and the defendant does not thereafter indicate that he wishes to plead guilty. The accused must then be asked whether or not he consents to summary trial and the case must thereafter proceed in accordance with the election the accused makes. The reason for the exclusion is to ensure that, if a co-accused has elected Crown Court trial, it will no longer be the case that the other accused must be tried summarily if that is his wish. The other accused must now to be sent to the Crown Court if the two accused are appearing together, or may be sent if he appears on a subsequent occasion.)

Multiple defendant cases involving youths and adults are considered subsequently.

Offences triable either way: plea before venue

D[4.3] The court must then explain to the accused in ordinary language that he may indicate whether, if the offence were to proceed to trial, he would plead guilty or not guilty. The court must further explain to the accused that if he indicates he would plead guilty:

(a)   the court will proceed as if he had pleaded guilty to an information which was being tried summarily; and

(b)   that he may be committed for sentence to the Crown Court if the court is of opinion that greater punishment should be inflicted for the offence than the court has power to impose, or that the offender meets the criteria for the imposition of a dangerous offender sentence.

The court shall then ask the accused whether (if the offence were to proceed to trial) he would plead guilty or not guilty. If the accused indicates a guilty plea the court will then hear the prosecution case against him, listen to his mitigation and either determine sentence or commit to the Crown Court for sentence. If the accused indicates he would plead not guilty, or if he fails to indicate how he would plead, he shall be taken to indicate he would plead not guilty, and the procedure described below (mode of trial) will apply.

Committal to the Crown Court for sentence is dealt with in Section B.

Offences triable either way (except where a notice is received under ss 51B or 51C of the Crime and Disorder Act 1998): mode of trial

D[4.4] The following procedure applies where an adult is charged with an either way offence and either he or his representative indicates that if the offence were to proceed to trial he would plead not guilty.

The court shall decide whether the offence appears to it more suitable for summary trial or for trial on indictment. Before making this decision the court:

(a) shall give the prosecution an opportunity to inform the court of the accused's previous convictions (if any) (defined to include foreign convictions which would constitute an offence in the UK if committed here and service convictions); and

(b) shall give the prosecution and the accused an opportunity to make representations as to whether summary trial or trial on indictment would be more suitable.

In making its decision the court shall consider:

(a) whether the sentence which a magistrates' court would have power to impose for the offence would be adequate; and

(b) any representations made by the prosecution or the accused under subsection (2)(b) above,

and shall have regard to any allocation guidelines (or revised allocation guidelines) issued as definitive guidelines under s 122 of the Coroners and Justice Act 2009.

Where:

(a) the accused is charged with two or more offences; and

(b) it appears to the court that the charges for the offences could be joined in the same indictment or that the offences arise out of the same or connected circumstances,

references to the sentence which a magistrates' court would have power to impose refer to the maximum aggregate sentence which a magistrates' court would have power to impose for all of the offences taken together.

Procedure where summary trial appears more suitable

D[4.5] The court shall explain to the accused in ordinary language:

(a) that it appears to the court more suitable for him to be tried summarily for the offence;

(b) that he can either consent to be so tried or, if he wishes, be tried on indictment; and

(c) that if he is tried summarily and is convicted by the court, he may be committed for sentence to the Crown Court under s 3 or (if applicable) s 3A of the Powers of Criminal Courts (Sentencing) Act 2000 if the court is of such opinion as is mentioned in subsection (2) of the applicable section.

The accused may then request an indication ('an indication of sentence') of whether a custodial sentence or non-custodial sentence would be more likely to be imposed if he were to be tried summarily for the offence and to plead guilty.

If the accused requests an indication of sentence, the court may, but need not, give such an indication. If the accused requests and the court gives an indication of sentence, the court shall ask the accused whether he wishes, on the basis of the indication, to reconsider the indication of plea which he previously gave, and if the accused indicates that he wishes to reconsider that indication, the court shall ask the accused whether (if the offence were to proceed to trial) he would plead guilty or not guilty.

If the accused indicates that he would plead guilty the court shall proceed to deal with the case as a summary trial in which the accused has pleaded guilty.

If no indication is sought, or, if sought, no indication is given by the court, or the defendant does not indicate following an indication that he would plead guilty, the court shall ask the accused whether he consents to be tried summarily or wishes to be tried on indictment. If the defendant consents to be tried summarily, the court shall proceed to the summary trial of the information; and if he does not so consent, shall proceed in relation to the offence in accordance with s 51(1) of the Crime and Disorder Act 1998 (ie by sending the case to the Crown Court.

Absence of legally represented accused

D[4.6] Where:

(a)   the accused is represented by a legal representative who in his absence signifies to the court the accused's consent to the proceedings for determining how he is to be tried for the offence being conducted in his absence; and

(b)   the court is satisfied that there is good reason for proceeding in the absence of the accused,

the following procedure shall apply.

The court may proceed in the absence of the accused in accordance with such of the provisions of ss 19 to 22 of the Magistrates Courts Act 1980 as are applicable in the circumstances.

If the offence is one of those listed in Sch 2 to the Magistrates' Courts Act 1980 (certain either way offences where the value involved is relevant to mode of trial), and it is unclear to the court whether or not the value exceeds the relevant sum (currently £5,000), if the accused's consent to be tried summarily has been or is signified by the person representing him, the court shall proceed as if the offence were triable only summarily in accordance with subsection (2) of that section as if that subsection applied. If such consent is not signified, the court shall deal with mode of trial in the normal way.

If the court decides that the offence appears to be more suitable for summary trial, then:

(a)   if the accused's consent to be tried summarily has been or is signified by the person representing him, the court shall proceed without further ado to the summary trial of the information; or

(b)   if that consent has not been and is not so signified, the court shall proceed, again without further ado, in accordance with the sending provisions of s 51(1) of the Crime and Disorder Act 1998.

If the court decides under s 19 that the offence appears to it more suitable for trial on indictment, the court shall proceed, again without further ado, in accordance with the sending provisions of s 51(1) of the Crime and Disorder Act 1998.

Joint adult defendants

D[4.7] For cases where two or more adults are charged together, see para D[4.2], above. One of the key purposes of the changes made by the allocation and mode of trial provisions of Sch 3 to the Criminal Justice Act 2003 was to bring to an end the requirement to hold separate trials in the

Crown Court and the magistrates' courts where two or more defendants made conflicting choices on venue.

Adults jointly charged with youths

D[4.8] This topic is considered in detail at para E[3.18A], above, and the following is a summary only.

The legislative policy is that youths should be tried summarily wherever possible. Certain offences must, however, be sent to the Crown Court. Where this applies and an adult offender, jointly charged with an either way offence or charged with a related either way offence, appears before the court he *must* if it is the same occasion, or *may* if he appears on a subsequent occasion, be sent forthwith to the Crown Court, unless a guilty plea has been indicated by or on behalf of the adult.

Offences of criminal damage where the value is low

D[4.9] If the offence charged is criminal damage, excluding arson, or aggravated vehicle-taking (where only damage is alleged), the court will as a preliminary ask the prosecutor and the accused the value of the damage; if it appears to be £5,000 or under, the court will proceed to summary trial. If it is unclear whether the value is £5,000 or under, the court will read the charge to the accused and then say to him:

> 'If you consent now to be tried by this court, you will be so tried, and the maximum imprisonment and fine this court will inflict if it finds you guilty will be three months and £2,500 (or 6 months and/or £5,000 in a case of aggravated vehicle-taking); nor will you be liable to be sent to the Crown court for a heavier sentence. Do you consent to be tried by this court?'

If the accused refuses, the court will proceed to the plea before venue procedure described in D[4.3] and, if the accused then indicates a plea of not guilty or gives no indication as to plea, the court will proceed to the mode of trial procedure described in D[4.4].

These provisions relating to such an offence where the value is small create an absolute obligation on the court to deal with the matter as a summary offence and the procedures for plea before venue and mode of trial do not apply: *R v Kelly* [2001] RTR 45, CA. The court's task is to identify the value of the damage itself and it is not concerned with determining what, if any, consequential losses may have been sustained as a result of the damage; thus, where genetically modified crops were damaged, the farmer valued the damage at £750 but there were also wasted research costs making the overall loss somewhere between £3,250 and £14,650, it was impossible to criticise the justices for concluding that the value for mode of trial purposes was clearly less than £5,000: *R v Colchester Magistrates' Court, ex p Abbott* (2001)165 JP 386, [2001] Crim LR 564, DC. The difficulty of assessing the value in respect of damaged crops is that there is no open market for sale of damaged genetically modified crops grown for research not sale. In the circumstances of the case a court was justified in concluding that, as the crops in question had a value for research purposes, it was more than the market value of ordinary maize, but as there was no realistic way of putting a price on it, it was justified in holding that it was not clear whether the value was above or below £5,000: *R (DPP) v Prestatyn Magistrates' Court* [2002] EWHC 1177 (Admin), [2002] Crim LR 924.

Low value shoplifting

D[4.9A] Section 176 of the Anti-social Behaviour, Crime and Policing Act 2014 inserted new s 22A of the Magistrates' Court Act 1980 to make 'low value shoplifting' triable only summarily, but where the accused is an adult and appears before the court before the summary trial of the offence begins, the court must give him the opportunity to elect Crown Court trial and, if he so elects, he must be sent to the Crown Court for trial. The preservation of the right to elect may lead one to question the administrative benefits of this reform; only in very rare circumstances would magistrates decline jurisdiction. The answer, however, appears to be this. The right to elect applies only where the accused appears before the summary trial begins. Otherwise, the offence is summary for all purposes (save those mentioned below). Thus, the written plea of guilty procedure under the Magistrates' Courts Act 1980, s 12, can be invoked; or the court can proceed to try the defendant in his absence without a prior mode of trial procedure (thereby avoiding the need to issue an arrest warrant before conviction).

'Low-value shoplifting' is defined as theft of goods where the value does not exceed £200, the goods were being offered for sale in shop or any other premises, stall, vehicle or place from which there is carried on a trade or business, and at the time the accused was or was purporting to be a customer or potential customer of the person offering the goods for sale.

The value of the goods is defined as the price at which they were being offered for sale at the time. (In our view this requires a clear verbal or written representation as to the price.) Where a person is charged on the same occasion with two or more offences of low-value shoplifting the reference to the value is a reference to the aggregate of the values involved.

A person convicted of low-value shoplifting may not appeal against conviction to the Crown Court on the ground that the convicting court was mistaken as to whether the offence was one of low-value shoplifting.

These provisions apply to secondary parties as well as principal offenders.

Amendments to the Criminal Attempts Act 1981 and the Police and Criminal Evidence Act 1984 preserve, respectively, the ability to charge an offence of attempt and the inclusion of low-value shoplifting in any reference to an 'indictable offence'.

Power to change from summary trial to sending for trial

D[4.10] Where an adult defendant has proceeded to summary trial, the prosecution may, before the trial begins and before any other issue has been determined, apply for the offence to be tried on indictment instead. The court may grant this application, but only if it is satisfied that its sentencing powers, or aggregate sentencing powers, would be inadequate.

Abuse of process

D[4.11] Prior to sending an indictable offence to the Crown Court under the Crime and Disorder Act 1998, s 51, a magistrates' court has jurisdiction to stay criminal proceedings as an abuse of the process: *R (on the application of Craik, Chief Constable of Northumbria Police) v Newcastle Upon Tyne Magistrates' Court (Price, interested party)* [2010] EWHC 935

(Admin), 174 CL&J 334, [2010] 5 Archbold Review, 2. However, it will rarely be appropriate to do so. The rule seems analogous to committal proceedings, ie such matters should normally be left to the Crown Court Judge to determine. See *R v Belmarsh Magistrates' Court, ex p Watts* [1999] 2 Cr App Rep 188.

Sending for trial – indictable only offences: Procedure

D[5.1] Section 52 of the Crime and Disorder Act 1998 provides (subject as therein stated) for the remand in custody or on bail of a person sent to the Crown Court under ss 51 or 51A of that Act. It further provides (in subsection (5)) that the court may adjourn proceedings under ss 51 and 51A and, if it does so, it shall remand the accused.

Section 51D of the Crime and Disorder Act 1998 deals with the notices which the court must serve on the accused and the Crown Court as to the offences which have been sent under s 51 or, in the case of a youth, s 51A. Where more than one offence has been sent, the notice must specify the relevant subsection under which each offence has been sent. If it is a 'related offence', the offence to which it is related must also be specified. Where the court selects the place of trial, s 51D specifies the matters to which the court shall have regard.

Schedule 3 to the Crime and Disorder Act makes further provision as to persons sent to the Crown Court under ss 51 or 51A of the Act. The key features are these:

- Copies of the prosecution evidence must be served on the accused and the court within prescribed time limits.
- Prior to arraignment, the accused may apply for the dismissal of the charge or any of the charges on the ground that the evidence is insufficient for the accused to be properly convicted of that charge, and if the charged is so dismissed by the judge no further proceedings may be brought on that charge except by the preferment of a voluntary bill of indictment.
- Reporting restrictions apply to applications for dismissal.
- There is provision for a justice to take a deposition from a person who is likely to be able to give or to produce material evidence on a sent charge, and for the issue of a summons or warrant to require that person's attendance before the justice for that purpose.
- Provision is made, following conviction on indictment, for the Crown Court to deal with any summary offences which were included in the sending provided they are related and the defendant pleads guilty or the prosecution offers no evidence.
- Provision is made to cover the case where no 'main offence' (ie the offence which caused the defendant to be sent) remains before arraignment. If the defendant is an adult, the Crown Court must follow procedures which mirror those for mode of trial in the magistrates' court. If the defendant is a youth, he must be remitted to the magistrates' court.

Joinder of certain summary offences in an indictment

D[5.2] Section 40 of the Criminal Justice Act 1988 enables certain offences – for example, common assault and driving while disqualified – to be included in an indictment where the offence is founded on the same facts or evidence as a count charging an indictable offence, or is part of a series of offences of the same or similar character as such a count. The offence will then be tried in the same manner as an indictable offence, but the powers of the Crown Court on conviction will be limited to those of the magistrates' court.

Summary proceedings

1 Criminal Procedural Rules (CPR)

D[6.1] Increasingly the higher courts (see for example *R v L* [2007] EWCA Crim 764) are emphasising the importance of both the courts and the parties to criminal proceedings discharging their obligations under the Criminal Procedure Rules 2014, particularly those rules dealing with case management (Part 3). In *Narinder Malcolm v DPP* [2007] EWHC 363 (QB), reference was made by the High Court to the overriding objective of Part I of the Criminal Procedure Rules 2014 (per Stanley Brunton J at para 31):

> Criminal trials are no longer to be treated as a game, in which any move is final and any omissions by the prosecution leads to its failure. It is the duty of the defence to make its defence and the issues it raises clear to the prosecution and to the court at an early stage. The duty is implicit in r 3.3 of the CPR, which requires the parties actively to assist the exercise by the courts of its case management powers, the exercise of which requires early identification of the real issues.

CPR, Part 1 – Overriding objective:

D[6.2] 1.1 To ensure that criminal cases are dealt with **justly**.

1.2 The duty of participants in a criminal case:

(a)   Prepare and conduct the case in accordance with the overriding objective.

(b)   Comply with the Criminal Procedure Rules 2014, Practice Directions and any directions given by the court.

(c)   Inform the court and parties of any significant failure to take any procedural step as required in (b) above.

Anyone involved in any way with a criminal case is a **participant** in its conduct for the purposes of this rule.

Notification of intention to call defence witnesses. Section 6C of the Criminal Procedure and Investigations Act 1996 was brought into force on 1 May 2010. The section provides that the accused must give to the court and the prosecutor a notice indicating whether he intends to call any persons (other than himself) as witnesses at his trial and, if so, the name, address and date of birth of each such proposed witness, or as many of those details as are known to the accused when the notice is given; and provide any information in the accused's possession which might be of material assistance in identifying or finding any such proposed witness. The provision of the witness' details must be given within 14 days of the service or purported service of initial disclosure (subject to an application to extend for good reason within the 14 day period).

The revised legislation reverses in effect the decision in *R (on the application of Kelly) v Warley Magistrates' Court and the Law Society* [2007] EWHC 1836 (Admin).

The requirement to provide the relevant details applies on or after the operative date, irrespective of the fact that the prosecution commenced before 1 May. A revised section 11 of the 1996 Act permits a party to comment on the failure of the accused to comply with any provision of s 6C and/or for the court to draw such inferences as appear proper from that failure. The court may not convict solely on inferences drawn under s 11, similar to ss 34–38 of the Criminal Justice and Public Order Act 1994 (inferences from silence etc).

NB: Part 3 of the CPR 2014 sets out the general duties and powers of the court, and the duties of the parties, relevant to the pre-trial preparation of a criminal case. However, the CPR contained no sanctions for a party's failure to comply with a procedural rule or with a case management direction made by the court. The court's powers to make a costs order in consequence of such a failure, to adjourn the case or, in some circumstances, to exclude evidence or to draw adverse inferences from a late introduction of an issue or evidence, are powers that are conferred by other legislation and under some other procedural rules. Having considered the *Kelly* judgment the Criminal Procedure Rules Committee introduced what is now CPR 2013, rr 3.5 and 3.10 to make the court's powers to impose sanctions for failure to comply with a procedural rule or procedural direction explicit (see **D[6.3]** below).

In addition, further changes were introduced by the Criminal Justice and Immigration Act (Commencement No 3 and Transitional Provisions) Order 2008 from 3 November 2008. Section 6A(1) of the Criminal Procedure and Investigations Act 1996 has been amended to provide that a defence statement:

> (ca) set out particulars of the matters of fact on which he intends to rely for the purposes of his defence.

Section 11(2)(f)(ii) (defaults in disclosure by accused) has also been amended to reflect subsection (ca) above.

CPR, Part 3.2 – The duty of the court

D[6.3] The court must further the overriding objective by actively managing the case.

Active case management includes –

(a)   early identification of the real issues;
(b)   early identification of the needs of witnesses;
(c)   setting a timetable (see immediately below);
(d)   monitoring the progress of the case and compliance with directions;
(e)   discouraging delay;
(f)   making use of technology;
(g)   the facilitation of the attendance of witnesses when they are needed.

In setting the timetable, the court should scrutinise the reasons why it is said a witness is necessary and the time examination and cross-examination would take. It is also important in setting a timetable to have regard to the nature of the issues and the fact that the trial is a summary trial; any estimate of more than a day in the Magistrates' Courts should be scrutinised with the utmost rigour. Parties must realise that a summary trial requires a proportionate approach. If a timetable for the trial is not set, it is difficult to have any real confidence that the estimate is accurate. At the commencement of the trial, the

Magistrates' Court should check with the parties that the timetable and the estimates remain valid. If there is any variation which lengthens the estimate, the court should make every effort to see if the trial can still be accommodated that day by sitting late or otherwise. Once the trial has started, the court must actively manage the trial, keeping an eye on progress in relation to the timetable.

(*R (on the application of Drinkwater) v Solihull Magistrates' Court and CPS* [2012] EWHC 765 (Admin), 176 JP 401.)

CPR, Part 3.3 – The duty of the parties

D[6.4] Each party must –

(a)   actively assist the court in fulfilling its duty under Part 3.2 without or if necessary with a direction; and
(b)   apply for a direction if needed to further the overriding objective.

A person or organisation directly involved in a criminal case, either as prosecutor or defendant is a party (see the glossary to the CPR).

For the responsibility of a solicitor involved in criminal litigation under CPR, Part 3, see *R (on the application of Robinson) v Abergavenny Magistrates' Court* [2007] EWHC 2005 (Admin), 171 JP 683, 172 JPN 188.

In *R (on the application of Martin) v Harrow Crown Court* [2007] EWHC 3193 (Admin), [2007] All ER (D) 106 (Dec), it was decided that in order to avoid an adjournment in a speeding case where measurements of the distances between street lamps was required for the purpose of determining whether a road was a 'restricted road' within the meaning of s 82(1)(a) of the Road Traffic Regulation Act 1984, good practice dictated that the defendant notify the prosecution in advance that the latter would be put to proof on the matter at trial.

A **Practice Note** for guidance to **solicitors** entitled '*Criminal Procedure Rules 2005: impact on solicitors; duties to the client*' was issued by the Law Society on 16 August 2007. A revised Practice Note to solicitors entitled "Criminal plea in absence of full disclosure" was issued on 3 October 2013. A copy of this Practice Note can be accessed via lawsociety.org.uk/advice/p ractice-notes/plea-in-absence-disclosure/.

Adjournment applications

D[6.5] Examination of a number of decisions of the superior courts suggests that the judges in those courts will be prepared to uphold pre-trial decisions of magistrates including applications for adjournments (whether pre-trial or on the day of hearing), provided the magistrates, through their reasons, can demonstrate that they have properly identified and taken into account the relevant factors and exercised their discretion appropriately: see for example, *R (on the application of Khan) v Waltham Forest Magistrates' Court* [2007] EWHC 1801 (Admin), [2007] All ER (D) 29 (Jul).

The following will hopefully assist magistrates in identifying the relevant factors when faced with an adjournment application.

Adjournment applications – checklist

D[6.6] The following checklist applies to adjournment applications:

- CPR 2014, Part 1: Overriding duty on court to ensure criminal cases are dealt with justly
- ECHR, Article 6: The accused is entitled to a trial within a reasonable period of time
- ECHR, Article 6: The accused is entitled to a reasonable period of time in order to prepare his case

The 'overriding duty' does not mean that the court must adjourn on application, even where both parties seek an adjournment.

Broad approach to adjournment applications

D[6.7] The following broad approach should be taken to adjournment applications:

- What is the full (or relevant) history of the case?
- Has there been any pre-trial correspondence? – What was the court's response?
- Is it just or fair to depart from that pre-trial decision (reasons needed)? (see *Robinson v Abergavenny Magistrates' Court* [2007] EWHC 2005 (Admin)).

A.   First Hearing

D[6.8] Establish whether any issues that might affect jurisdiction eg such as dangerousness or under the Proceeds of Crime Act 2002.

Clarify whether any issues such as special measures, expert evidence or pre-trial issues such as bad character or hearsay (see **D[6.13]** below).

Does the defendant require the services of an interpreter?

Plea

D[6.9] Has the defendant received **initial details** (formerly advance disclosure) of the prosecution case? The prosecutor's duty is to serve those details on the court officer and make those details available to the defendant at, or before, the beginning of the day of the first hearing – if yes, proceed to take plea.

If no, are the details on file? – How detailed is the information? (Consider standing back the case for the defence to take instructions.) A revised Practice Note to solicitors entitled "Criminal plea in absence of full disclosure" was issued on 3 October 2013. A copy of the Practice note can be accessed at lawsociety.org.uk/advice/practice-notes/plea-in-absence-dis closure/.

CCTV: Is the prosecution relying on CCTV to prove its case? Does the CCTV evidence form part of the details disclosed? If available stand back for defence to view. If not, proceed to plea.

Initial details: A summary of the prosecution case in documentary form. By definition does not normally include CCTV or video evidence.

NB: There is a common misconception that initial details (formerly known as advance disclosure) includes CCTV (see CPR 2011, Part 21). This was based on a generous concession made by counsel in *R v Calderdale*

Magistrates' Court, ex p Donahue and Cutler [2001] Crim LR 141, that 'document' included a video. This concession was doubted in *DPP v Croydon Magistrates' Court* [2001] EWHC 552 (Admin).

NB: The prosecutor's obligation to furnish details (primary disclosure) was initially aimed at offences 'triable either way'. Given the obligations under the ECHR, the prosecutor's duty is wider and can extend to summary only cases. However, the extent and nature of the disclosure will depend on factors such as the seriousness of the charge (*R v Stratford Magistrates' Court, ex p Imbert* [1999] 2 Cr App R 276.

Defence advocates should, save in exceptional circumstances, go through the details with the defendant and advise on such matters as venue and plea without the need for an adjournment.

Having put the case back, proceed to take a plea or indication of plea and/or mode of trial.

Legal Aid

D[6.10] Has the defendant submitted an application? When? Why any delay in submission? – If defendant in receipt of benefits or paid employment stand back in the list for a decision by the court administration.

If the defendant is self-employed, has he attached accounts to the legal aid application? If not, why not? Put back to clarify the position with the court administration.

Seek clarification as to when a decision as to legal representation can be made. If necessary to adjourn, list on the earliest practicable date.

Prosecution Evidence (initial disclosure)

D[6.11] This duty only arises <u>after</u> a not guilty plea has been entered. Do not adjourn before plea. After a not guilty plea has been entered give directions on the service of the evidence eg within 14 days.

<u>Initial disclosure</u>: All material in the prosecutor's possession to be used to prove the case against the accused.

As to a failure to make disclosure following a direction of the court see D[1B.11] above.

B.   First or Subsequent Hearing

D[6.12] Disclosure of unused prosecution material. The duty on the prosecutor arises <u>only</u> after a not guilty plea has been entered.

<u>Unused material</u>: Any prosecution material which might reasonably be considered capable of undermining the case for the prosecution against the accused or of assisting the case for the accused.

Has the CPS fully complied with its legal duties (see below)?

Has the defence filed a voluntary defence statement? If not, the accused <u>cannot</u> make an application for disclosure of unused material.

Any voluntary defence statement should normally be served <u>within 14 days</u> of the date upon which the prosecution has complied with its duty to provide initial disclosure.

Has the accused in his defence statement set out particulars of the matters of fact on which he intends to rely for the purposes of his defence?

Any defence application to extend the timeframe must be in writing and must be made before the time limit expires.

The late service of a defence statement does not formally preclude the court from considering a proper application.

Where there is late service of a defence statement, any application to adjourn for further disclosure or to adjourn the trial, must be scrutinised closely (see immediately below).

If it is just to adjourn the case, the court should immediately consider the question of wasted costs (see ss 19, 19A and 19B Prosecution of Offences Act 1985 and regulations made thereunder); or, where the defendant is publicly funded, to notify the Legal Services Commission. The court must give reasons for its decision.

C.   Pre-trial Issues

D[6.13] **General.** Magistrates are often called upon to deal with applications either pre-trial or on the date of trial. Examples include bad character and hearsay applications.

- What are the issues?
- Is the evidence and/or testimony of live witnesses material?
- Could a section 9 (CJA 1967) statement cover the relevant ground?
- Can the parties formally agree the evidence under s 10 CJA 1967?
- Are court directions necessary eg filing of evidence or skeleton arguments?

See further the Criminal Practice Directions 2014, 3D: Vulnerable people in the courts.

D[6.13A] **Power to make, vary or discharge pre-trial rulings.** Section 8A of the Magistrates' Courts Act 1980 authorises a magistrates' court to make binding pre-trial rulings. That ruling remains binding upon the parties and the court unless a party applies to the court to discharge or vary that ruling on the grounds that there has been a material change of circumstances since the ruling was made (MCA 1980, s 8B).

It is open to a court of its own motion to vary or discharge a previous ruling of the magistrates' court but not solely on the basis that it would have reached a different conclusion; there must be a compelling reason such as changed circumstances or fresh evidence (*R (on the application of the CPS) v Gloucester Justices* [2008] EWHC 1488 (Admin), 172 JP 406).

In *Jones v South East Surrey Local Justice Area* [2010] EWHC 916 (Admin), 174 JP 342 it was recognised at common law that a lower court had limited power to reverse and to revoke a previously made order. It could so in the interests of justice, in particular, in changed circumstances. However, the parameters of the interests of justice test were to be measured not simply by reference to a "change of circumstances" but by reference to ss 8A and 8B of the Magistrates' Courts Act 1980 and the overriding objective of the Criminal Procedure Rules. As a result each case had to be decided in the light of it own particular circumstances. In the instant case, the justices had been right to grant the adjournment sought. There had been a "change of circumstances". For one it was clear on the day of trial, unlike the previous day, that the error for the delay lay with the police and not the Crown Prosecution Service. That may have influenced the decision that the magistrates made to refuse the adjournment.

Per Cranston J: "None of what I have said is to give encouragement to poor initial applications, which have to be supplemented later by applications to remedy the defect".

Special measures for vulnerable and intimidated witnesses

Definition: In the case of certain witnesses in criminal proceedings (other than the accused), a magistrates' court may make a "special measures direction" for the purpose of improving the quality of a witness's evidence. The statutory test or emphasis is designed to improve "the quality of a witness's evidence".

Special measures can take one of a number of forms:

- Screening the witness from the accused
- The giving of evidence by live link
- The giving of evidence in private
- Removal of wigs and gowns (arises normally only in the Crown Court)
- Video recorded evidence in chief
- Video recorded cross-examination and re-examination
- Examination of a witness through an intermediary
- Aids to communication

Other protection afforded to a witness can include:

- Protection from cross-examination by the accused in person
- Restrictions on evidence and questions about the complainant's bad character and more important (in a sexual case), sexual behaviour
- Restrictions on reporting

Inherent powers to protect a witness (as well as the accused) continue to apply:

— Provision of an interpreter (including an intermediary): see *R (on the application of AS) v Great Yarmouth Youth Court* [2011] EWHC 2059 (Admin); and *R (on the application of OP) v Secretary of State for Justice, Cheltenham Magistrates' Court and CPS (Interested Parties), Just for Kids (Intervener)* [2014] EWHC 1944 (Admin), (2014) 178 JP 377 where the court dealt with the distinction between giving general support during a trial to a defendant – normally readily achievable by an adult of appropriate experience – and giving skill support and intervention associated with the defendant giving evidence, which requires developed skills of the sort contemplated by inclusion within the Witness Intermediary Scheme.
— Use of screens

Eligibility for assistance: All persons aged under 18 years (as opposed to 17 years above) will automatically qualify as witnesses eligible for assistance.

Automatic eligibility for complainants in sexual cases has been extended to cover witnesses in specified gun and knife crimes which are listed in a new Sch 1A to the Youth Justice and Criminal Evidence Act 1999. A witness can still continue to inform the court that he/she does not wish to be eligible for assistance.

The Coroners and Justice Act 2009 removed the special category of child witnesses who are "in need of special protection". The effect is to place all child witnesses on the same footing, regardless of the offence to which the proceedings relate. There are further provisions allowing the child witness to opt out of giving evidence by a combination of video recorded and live link. The provisions are quite involved and magistrates should consult their legal adviser before giving further directions as to the conduct of the trial.

Evidence by live link: The court is able to give a direction allowing a witness to give evidence by live link. The court can also direct that a person specified by the court can accompany the witness when he/she is giving evidence by live link. The court must take the witness's wishes into account when it determines who is to accompany the witness.

Protected witness: Section 35 of the 1999 Act prevents the cross-examination of a "protected witness" by an accused in person. The definition of a protected witness includes a child. The definition of "child" has been amended to mean a person under the age of 18 years (as opposed to 17 years).

Quality of evidence: Special measures may only be authorised where the court considers that they would improve the quality of a witness's evidence, ie in terms of completeness, coherence and accuracy. Coherence refers to a witness's ability in giving evidence to give answers which address the questions put to the witness and can be understood both individually and collectively.

Procedure: The Criminal Procedure Rules 2014 govern the process. In broad terms the application for special measures must normally be made within a specific time frame and address the matters canvassed above; notably, the application must identify what sort of measures are sought and how those measures will improve the quality of the witness's evidence. It is good practice for the prosecution to attach a statement from the witness where it is being asserted that he/she is in fear or distress (not necessarily of the accused but of the court process).

If another party (usually the defence) object to the application they should normally object in writing within a given time frame. The notice of objection should address the points raised in the application for special measures.

Decision: It is for the court to determine and weigh the application in the light of the representations or evidence put before it. Be careful not to attach too much weight to assertions unsupported by evidence. The fact that there is some suggestion from the defence that there has been contact between the witness and defence during the court proceedings is not in itself sufficient to rebut the application. If there is a statement from a witness saying that he/she is in fear of giving evidence in front of the defendant without special measures, the court should attach some weight to this evidence when assessing whether it would be likely to improve the quality of the witness's evidence.

The Criminal Law Review (Issue No 7, 2012) recently reported two cases which may be of substantial benefit to the work of the court: *R v Edwards* [2011] EWCA Crim 3028, [2012] Crim LR 563 and *R v Wills* [2011] EWCA Crim 1938, [2012] 1 Cr App Rep 16, [2012] Crim LR 565.

If you read the judgments you will see in the Commentaries that the Judicial College accepted the invitation of the Court of Appeal in *Wills* and subsequently issued a Bench Checklist for Young Witness cases now

available at: www.judiciary.gov.uk/publications-and-reports/guidance/
2012/jc-bench-checklist-young-wit-cases.

This guidance, inter alia, instructs both advocates at 'ground rules' discussions to adapt their questions to a child's developmental stage enabling the child to give his/her best evidence. Consistent with the CPR it will also enable the court to control the conduct of the case and the manner in which the advocates conduct their cases, notably, the defence advocate's cross-examination of the witness.

Judging by the observation in the Commentary to *R v E* it seems to me there may be merit in the court directing the appointment of an intermediary who can be of real value in privately advising the prosecution or defence on how to formulate particular questions for a very young witness or one with learning difficulties

D[6.14] CPR, Part 35 – bad character – defendant. Has the prosecutor complied with the notice requirements? – If not, is there an acceptable reason for not complying with the rules?

Applications made very late or on the date of trial without good reason should be dealt with robustly, including a refusal of the application if its primary effect is to prejudice the fair trial of the accused.

Check that the application is not caught by s 98 of the CJA 2003 (definition of the term 'bad character'). [See *R v Chopra* [2006] EWCA Crim 2133, [2006] All ER (D) 44 (Dec); *R v Wallace* [2007] EWCA Crim 1760, 171 JP 543.]

Under which gateway or gateways is the application made (see s 101 CJA 2003)? The application should identify the gateway and its relevance.

In some cases (seek legal advice), the court is entitled to exclude the bad character evidence on the grounds that its prejudicial effect outweighs its probative value (s 101(1)(d), (g) CJA 2003).

Reasons needed.

Case law: see *R v Hanson* [2005] EWCA Crim 824, (2005) 1 WLR 3169.

D[6.15] CPR, Part 35 – bad character – non-defendant (witness). Have the notice requirements been complied with? If not, is there an acceptable reason for not complying with the rules?

Has a certificate of readiness for trial already been filed by the party seeking to make the application?

Applications made very late or on the day of trial without good reason should be dealt with robustly, including a refusal of the application, having regard to the statutory assumption (see below) and if its primary effect is to prejudice a fair trial.

What is the relevance of the non-defendant's bad character? Assume the evidence is not admissible unless under s 100 of the CJA 2003 it is –

(a) important explanatory evidence,
(b) it has substantial probative value in relation to a matter which –
     (i)   is a matter in issue in the proceedings, and
     (ii) is of substantial importance in the context of the case as a whole, or

(c)   all the parties to the proceedings agree to the evidence being admissible.

- Ask the parties to define 'important explanatory evidence'.
- Ask the parties to define 'substantial probative value'.
- Except where paragraph (c) above applies, evidence of the bad character of a witness may not be given without the leave of the court.
- Court must give reasons for its decision.

D[6.16] CPR, Part 34 – hearsay evidence. Have the notice requirements been complied with? If not, is there an acceptable reason for not complying with the rules?

Has a certificate of readiness for trial already been filed by the party seeking to make the application?

Applications made very late or on the day of trial without good reason should be dealt with robustly, including a refusal of the application, if its primary affect is to prejudice a fair trial.

Does the application identify the nature and type of hearsay evidence to be adduced (see s 114 CJA 2003 onwards)?

How important is the hearsay evidence in the context of the case a whole?

Weigh the relevant factors and other considerations prescribed by s 114(2) CJA 2003 (see *R v Cole* [2007] EWCA Crim 1924).

Court to reach a determination and give reasons for its decision.

D.   Trial

D[6.17] See 'Broad approach to adjournment applications' at D[6.7] above.

Was a certificate of readiness for trial filed either by both parties or a party? In the absence of a compelling reason, be prepared to refuse an application to adjourn the trial.

Be prepared to proceed in absence.

Remember r 3.8(4) (Case preparation and progression): 'In order to prepare for the trial, the court must take every reasonable step to encourage and to facilitate the attendance of witnesses when they are needed'.

Evidence eg sick notes, must state unfit to attend court.

Start promptly, unless there is a very good reason to the contrary.

If unable to start the trial, consider reading section 9 statements and the record of taped interview while waiting.

If the court deems it necessary for the s 9 statements etc to be read out, ask the parties to summarise the contents, where appropriate.

Do not delay the trial to allow for the editing of statements. This can be done later in the day.

Prioritise and call on as soon as practicable those witnesses available to give live evidence. Take their evidence out of order where that is feasible and will not affect the fairness or outcome of the trial.

Give reasons for your decision to proceed and/or your verdict.

E.   Guilty plea entered

D[6.18] Where possible proceed to sentence.

*   How serious is the offence?
*   What is the guideline or starting point?
*   Does the court need a psychiatric report? Would it materially affect the sentence?
*   Does the court need more information? Would it materially affect the sentence?
*   How long would it take to obtain a psychiatric report?
*   Is a full pre-sentence report necessary? Would an oral or fast-delivery report suffice?

2 Not guilty plea

D[6.19] See **section 1** above and in particular issues associated with pre-trial disclosure and pre-trial issues eg bad character applications.

At the commencement of the trial, the Magistrates' Court should check with the parties that the timetable and the estimates remain valid. If there is any variation which lengthens the estimate, the court should make every effort to see if the trial can still be accommodated that day by sitting late or otherwise. Once the trial has started, the court must actively manage the trial, keeping an eye on progress in relation to the timetable: *R (on the application of Drinkwater) v Solihull Magistrates' Court and CPS* [2012] EWHC 765 (Admin), 176 JP 401.

Trial in absence. Subject to the qualifications set out below, where at the time and place appointed for the trial or adjourned trial of an information the prosecutor appears but the accused does not:

(a)   if the accused is under 18 years of age, the court *may* proceed in his absence: and

(b)   if the accused has attained the age of 18 years, the court *shall* proceed in his absence unless it appears to the court to be contrary to the interests of justice to do so, and if the court decides not to proceed in an adult case it must state its reasons and cause those reasons to be entered in the court register.

Magistrates' Courts Act 1980, s 11(1) and (7).

The qualifications referred to above are these:

(a)   where a summons has been issued it must be proved in the prescribed manner to the satisfaction of the court that the summons was served within a reasonable time of the trial or adjourned trial or the accused appeared on a previous occasion to answer the information: Magistrates' Courts Act 1980 (MCA 1980), s 11(2);

(b)   the court shall not proceed if it considers that there is an acceptable reason for the failure to appear: MCA 1980, s 11(2A);

(c)   if the proceedings were instituted by an information followed by summons, or by a written charge, the court shall not in absence impose a custodial sentence or order that a suspended sentence shall take effect; in any other case, where such a sentence or order is imposed or made, the offender must be brought before the court before he begins to serve the sentence and the sentence will not be effective until this happens: MCA 1980, s 11(3), (3A) and (5);

(d)   if the proceedings were instituted by laying an information followed by a summons, or by a written charge, the court shall not in absence impose any disqualification on the accused except following an adjournment the notice of which must include the reason for the adjournment: MCA 1980, s 11(5).

Nothing in the above requires the court to inquire into the reasons for the accused's failure to appear before deciding whether or not to proceed in his absence: MCA 1980, s 11(6).

When bailing an accused to a trial date, it should be made clear that if he fails to attend the trial will proceed in his absence: *R v O'Hare* [2006] EWCA Crim 471, [2006] Crim LR 950.

Proceedings not covered by the above

The above narrative states the position relating to summary, adult criminal proceedings only. In the case of trial on indictment, the relevant considerations were set out in *R v Jones* [2002] UKHL 5, [2003] AC 1, [2002] 2 All ER 113, [2002] 2 WLR 524. The same principles are relevant to summary proceedings where the presumption of proceeding does not apply (see *R (Moresby) v Tower Bridge Magistrates' Court* [2007] EWHC 2766, (2008) 172 JP 155) and to civil proceedings in magistrates' courts, especially those which involve allegations of misbehaviour (eg ABSO applications) (see *R (on the application of M) v Burnley, Pendle & Rossendale Magistrates' Court* [2009] EWHC 2874, (2010) 174 JP 102).

D[6.20] Whatever the reason the accused chooses to enter a not guilty plea, once he has entered the plea all the facts relevant to the proof of guilt are said to be 'in issue' which means that the prosecutor must either prove those facts beyond reasonable doubt or (in some few cases) must establish facts which then place the burden of proving his innocence on the accused. An example of this last situation occurs where the police allege the uninsured use of a motor vehicle. Once they establish that the accused used a motor vehicle on a road it becomes the responsibility of the accused to satisfy the court that his use of the vehicle was insured. The prosecutor will establish his facts by the oral testimony of witnesses who may then be cross-examined, and/or by the production of witness statements of which the accused will have had prior notice in order to object to them if he wishes, and/or by formal admissions from the accused which should be written down and signed by him. If the accused wishes to give evidence he may use all or any of these methods of doing so.

D[6.21] No case to answer. There must be a sufficient case for the defendant to answer by the end of the prosecution case. If the prosecution have failed to prove an essential ingredient of the offence or the evidence adduced has been so discredited by cross- examination or is shown to be manifestly unreliable then if no reasonable tribunal could convict at that stage the case should be dismissed (*R v Galbraith* [1981] 2 All ER 1060, [1981] 1 WLR 1039 CA).

Where the court dismisses the case it must give reasons for its decision. The converse does not normally apply ie the court is not usually required to give reasons if it finds a case to answer (*Moran v DPP* [2002] EWHC 89 (Admin), (2002) 166 JP 467).

For a recent decision where it was held that the justices' decision that the case could not proceed beyond the half-way stage, in the light of weaknesses and inconsistencies in the accounts of prosecution witnesses, was perverse see *DPP v S* [2007] All ER (D) 148 (Dec).

A submission of no case to answer may not be made and/or considered prior to the close of the prosecution case (*Prosecution Appeal (No 32 of 2007; R v N Ltd* [2008] EWCA Crim 1223).

In *R (on the application of the Crown Prosecution Service) v Norwich Magistrates' Court* [2011] EWHC 82 (Admin), the High Court ruled that the justices erred by not permitting the Crown to re-open or to call additional evidence after the closure of its case. The prosecution had not appreciated there was any issue over identification until it had closed its case. The justices' refusal to exercise their discretion ran contrary to the overriding objective of the Criminal Procedure Rules 2010, was plainly contrary to the interests of justice and lacked any reasonable basis.

D[6.22] Inferences from silence.

(a) Accused's failure to mention facts when questioned or charged

(1)   Are there legal proceedings against the accused for an offence?
(2)   Did the alleged failure to mention a fact or facts occur before the accused was charged?
(3)   Did the alleged failure to mention a fact or facts occur while under caution by a constable or other investigating officer?
(4)   Was the constable's or other officer's questioning directed towards trying to discover whether or by whom the alleged offence had been committed?
(5)   Was the alleged fact or facts (not mentioned before charge) relied upon by the accused in his defence in these proceedings?
(6)   Was the accused's failure to mention the alleged fact or facts something which he/she could reasonably have been expected to mention when so questioned?
(7)   Can the accused's failure to mention the alleged fact or facts only be sensibly explained in that he had no answer at the time of his interview or none that would stand up to scrutiny?
(8)   Apart from the failure to mention that fact or facts is the prosecution's case sufficiently strong to amount to a case to answer against the accused?

Only if the court is sure as to 1–8 above may it draw an inference. The court may draw such inference as it deems appropriate. The inference itself may be one solely as to credit, credibility or an inference as to guilt. However, the court may not convict solely on the basis of the inferences it has drawn (see *R v Argent* (1996) 161 JP 190; *Condron v UK* (2001) 21 EHRR 1; *R v Beckles* [2005] 1 All ER 705).

In *R v Hackett* [2011] EWCA Crim 380, [2011] 2 Cr App Rep 35, the Court of Appeal held that it was wrong to give both a s 34 and a *Lucas* direction (lies as corroboration): *R v Rana* [2007] EWCA Crim 2261 applied. The Judge should have confined his directions to a s 34 direction whilst reminding the jury that unless they rejected H's explanation for not revealing his trip to the petrol station and its purpose at the first interview then no adverse inference could be drawn.

R v Rana did not decide that a s 34 direction should always be given in place of a *Lucas* direction. *Rana* decided that it had been appropriate for the trial judge to modify his directions under s 34 to take account of lies allegedly given by R in his account to the police. The principle flowing from the judgment applies equally to magistrates' courts; that is, a suitably modified direction under s 34 should be given in any advice to the justices, or, they should be invited to focus solely on whether the lies support the prosecution case in accordance with the principles laid down in *R v Lucas*.

(b) Accused's failure or refusal to account for objects, substances or marks (s 36 Criminal Justice and Public Order Act 1994)

(1) When the accused was arrested by a police constable did the accused have with him, or in or on his clothing, or on his footwear (delete as appropriate); or was there at the place he was arrested an object, substance or mark concerned (delete as appropriate)?

(2) Did the constable reasonably believe, for example, that the accused may have eg used the object to commit the crime for which he is being tried?

(3) Did the officer inform the accused of his reasonable belief and ask him/her to account for the presence of eg the object/substance/mark (delete as appropriate)?

(4) Did the officer warn the accused that if he did not account eg for the presence of the object, a court may later ask why?

(5) Did the accused fail or refuse to account eg for the presence of the object?

(6) Was the accused's failure or refusal to account eg for the presence of the object, one which he/she could reasonably have been expected to mention when arrested?

(7) Was the accused's failure or refusal to account eg for the presence of an object, because he/she had no innocent explanation to give or none that would stand up to scrutiny?

(8) Apart from the failure or refusal to account for eg the presence of an object, is the prosecution's case sufficiently strong to amount to a case to answer against the accused?

Only if the court is sure as to 1–8 above may it draw an inference. The court may draw such inference as it deems appropriate. The inference itself may be one solely as to credit, credibility or an inference as to guilt. However, the court may not convict solely on the basis of the inferences it has drawn.

(c) Accused's failure or refusal to account for presence at a particular place (s 37 Criminal Justice and Public Order Act 1994)

(1) When the accused was arrested by a police constable (or Revenue and Customs officer) was he found at or near the place (at or about the time the offence for which he was arrested was alleged to have been committed)?

(2) Was the 'place' any building or part of a building, any vehicle, vessel, aircraft, hovercraft or any other place whatsoever?

(3) Did the officer or an officer investigating the offence reasonably believe that the accused was participating in the crime for which he was arrested?

(4) Did the officer tell the accused of his belief and ask him to account for his presence?

(5) Did the accused fail or refuse to account for his presence?

(6) Was the accused's failure or refusal one which he could reasonably have been expected to account for?

(7) Was the accused's failure or refusal because he/she had no innocent explanation to give or none that would stand up to scrutiny?

(8) Apart from the failure or refusal to account for presence at a particular place, is the prosecution's case sufficiently strong to amount to a case to answer against the accused?

Only if the court is sure as to 1–8 above may it draw an inference. The court may draw such inference as it deems appropriate. The inference itself may be one solely as to credit, credibility or an inference as to guilt. However, the court may not convict solely on the basis of the inferences it has drawn.

(d) Accused's silence at trial (s 35 Criminal Justice and Public Order Act 1994)

If the accused is **legally represented,** at the conclusion of the evidence for the prosecution (assuming there is a case to answer), if the court is informed that the accused does not intend to give evidence, the legal adviser should, in the presence of the magistrates, inquire of the representative in these terms:

Have you advised your client that the stage has now been reached at which he may give evidence and, if he chooses not to do so, or having been sworn, without good cause refuses to answer any question, the court may draw such inferences as appear proper from his failure to do so?

If the reply is that the accused has been so advised the trial may proceed. If the answer is in the negative the court must direct the representative to advise his client and the consequences of such a failure.

If the accused is **not legally represented,** at the conclusion of the evidence for the prosecution (assuming there is a case to answer), the legal adviser should, in the presence of the magistrates, say to the accused:

You have heard the evidence against you. Now is the time to make your defence. You may give evidence on oath, and be cross-examined like any other witness. If you do not give evidence, or having been sworn, without good cause refuse to answer any question, the court may draw such inferences as appear proper. That means they may hold it against you. You may also call any witness or witnesses whom you have arranged to attend court [today]. Afterwards, you may also, if you wish, address the court by arguing your case from the dock. But you cannot at that stage give evidence. Do you now intend to give evidence?

(Practice Direction (Criminal: Consolidated) [2002] 3 All ER 90 (as subsequently revised).

(1) Is there a prima facie case?
(2) Has the defendant declined to give evidence or failed to answer any question properly put to him/her?
(3) Has the accused given any reason for not giving evidence or answering any question properly put to him/her?
(4) Despite the explanation given by the accused in 3 above, is the accused's failure to testify or answer any question properly put to him/her because he/she has no answer to the prosecution's case or none that would stand up to cross-examination?

Only if the court is sure as to 1–4 above may it draw an inference. The court may draw such inference as it deems appropriate. The inference itself may be one solely as to credit, credibility or an inference as to guilt. However, the court may not convict solely on the basis of the inferences it has drawn

(*R v Cowan* [1996] QB 373, [1995] 4 All ER 939, (1996) 160 JP 165; *R v Condron and Condron* [1997] 1 WLR 827, [1997] 1 Cr App Rep 185, CA; *Radford v Kent County Council* (1998) 162 JP 697; *R v Gough* (2001) 165 JPN 895; *R v Becouarn* [2005] UKHL 55, [2005] 1 WLR 2589).

A magistrates' court may not draw an inference from the defendant's failure to give evidence under s 35 of the CJPOA 1994 on account of his absence. However, a magistrates' court may draw an inference under s 35 from the defendant's failure to give evidence where he is present but a co-accused is not. There may be occasions where, in the interests of being seen to be even-handed to both defendants, the court will decline to draw an inference: *R v Hamidi* [2010] EWCA Crim 66, [2010] Crim LR 578.

D[6.23] **Amendment of charge or information.** Justices have a discretion to allow the amendment of a charge or information under the Magistrates' Courts Act 1980, s 123. This may even allege a different summary offence after the 6 month limitation period and even as late as the close of the prosecution case, but only where they are satisfied the allegation arises out of the same facts and it is in the interests of justice to allow the amendment (see *DPP v Everest* [2005] EWHC 1124 (Admin), [2005] All ER (D) 363 (May)).

In *DPP v Hammerton* [2009] EWHC 921 (Admin), [2009] 2 Cr App Rep 322, the Administrative Court stated that the CPS could not assume that they would be permitted to substitute or amend charges as a matter of course. The court retained a discretion to permit such a course of action but the overriding objective of the CPR 2005 (now CPR 2014), that a criminal case is dealt with justly, must be also be borne in mind. See also *Williams v DPP* [2009] EWHC 2354 (Admin), [2009] All ER (D) 292 (Jul)).

It is impermissible to amend an information by substituting a different defendant where the six-month statutory time limit has expired (*R (on the application of Sainsbury's Supermarkets Ltd) v Plymouth Magistrates' Court and R (on the application of J Sainsbury's Supermarkets Ltd) v Plymouth Magistrates' Court* [2006] EWHC 1749 (Admin), [2006] All ER (D) 137 (Jun)).

There are limitations on the power to amend an information. In *Shaw v DPP* [2007] EWHC 207 (Admin), a new charge was introduced in the defendant's absence after the expiry of the six-month time limit under s 127 MCA 1980, rendering him liable to imprisonment when he had not been before. In the circumstances it was not an appropriate course to take. Even if the justices had been justified in allowing the amendment, the term 'misled' in s 123(2) bore a very wide meaning and they should have adjourned to give the defendant a further opportunity to attend.

In *R (on the application of Thornhill) v Uxbridge Magistrates' Court* [2008] EWHC 508 (Admin), 172 JP 297, 172 JPN 580 the Divisional Court held that magistrates were wrong to allow the prosecution to amend an information alleging a failure to provide a specimen of breath to one of failure to provide a specimen of urine pursuant to s 7(6) of the Road Traffic Act 1988. The Divisional Court said that there was a distinct difference between the two offences and accordingly there was no need to consider if the amendment was 'in the interests of justice'. The procedures may be different but s 7(6) creates one offence of 'failing to provide a specimen'. This judgment does not sit well with previous judgments and by analogy *DPP v Butterworth* [1995] 1 AC 381, HL.

3 Guilty plea

D[6.24]–[6.25] A guilty plea must be unequivocal; when an accused purports to admit an offence but then adds words or offers an explanation redolent of a defence the legal adviser should normally be left to clarify the plea. If the defendant is unrepresented it might be advisable for the case to be stood back for the accused to seek independent legal advice from a solicitor. If the court concludes that the plea is equivocal it has no discretion but to substitute a plea of not guilty.

A guilty plea, however, is an admission of the offence charged and not necessarily of every fact which the prosecutor may allege as a circumstance of it. A guilty plea to assault, for example, would not indicate an acceptance of the prosecution's allegations of the number of blows struck or their severity. Where there is a dispute about an important circumstance of the offence either side may call evidence notwithstanding the guilty plea. The court can also decline to sentence until the matter has been resolved by evidence. This procedure is known as a **Newton hearing**. There are one or two exceptions. Evidence may also be called if there is a dispute relating to an ancillary matter, such as the amount of compensation or liability for back duty. The evidence should be confined solely to deciding the issue in question and, if the prosecution cannot establish its version of the facts beyond a reasonable doubt, the defence version must be accepted.

See generally The Criminal Practice Directions 2014 Sentencing B: Determining the factual basis of sentence.

The other aspect of the question is that the court must sentence only on the basis of the case put forward by the prosecution and not on the basis of conclusions it might draw that the case is in reality more serious. For example, if a person is accused of two cases of theft from his employer the court must not infer that in fact this was a common occurrence and sentence accordingly. Sometimes the inference might be inescapable. The important thing is that it does not affect the sentence for the offence charged. There are exceptions to the above rule eg in the case of sample or specimen charges or offences admitted and taken into consideration. Magistrates should clarify the legal principles with their legal adviser.

D[6.26] **Application to change a plea of guilty to not guilty.** A magistrates' court may allow a defendant to withdrawn his plea of guilty at any time up to sentence being passed (*S (an infant) v Manchester City Recorder* [1971] AC 481, HL). The onus lies on a party seeking to vacate a guilty plea to demonstrate that justice requires that this should be permitted.

Where the defendant pleads guilty by post under s 12 of the MCA 1980 and the plea is accepted by the court, at an adjourned hearing the accused would have to seek leave to change his plea, in accordance with the CPR outlined immediately below: see *Rymer v DPP* [2010] EWHC 1848 (Admin), 174 CL&J 526.

For the principles and procedures governing the exercise of the discretion see *R v South Tameside Magistrates' Court, ex p Rowland* (1984) 148 JP 202. For a more recent authority see *DPP v Revitt* [2006] EWHC 2266 (Admin), [2006] NLJR 1476, (2006) 170 JP 729.

D[6.27] **Application to withdraw a guilty plea.** CPR, Part 37.9 provides:

    (2)   The defendant must apply to do so –

    (a)   as soon as practicable after becoming aware of the reasons for doing so; and

    (b)   before sentence.

(3)   Unless the court otherwise directs, the application must be in writing and the defendant must serve it on –

    (a)   the court officer; and

    (b)   the prosecutor.

(4)   The application must –

    (a)   explain why it would be unjust not to allow the defendant to withdraw the guilty plea;

    (b)   identify –

        (i)   any witness that the defendant wishes to call, and

        (ii)   any other proposed witness; and

    (c)   say whether the defendant waives legal professional privilege, giving any relevant name and date.

4 Legal Advice

D[6.28] The legal adviser has a duty to advise on matters of law and matters of mixed law and fact. Justices who refuse to act on his advice in a straightforward matter (eg a driver's liability to disqualification) may run the risk of being ordered to pay the costs of a consequent appeal. The justices are entitled to invite the legal adviser to retire with them if they think that a matter may arise on which they will seek his advice. In a case of any complexity it is wise to invite the legal adviser to retire at an early stage in order that he can give such advice as the occasion may require during the justices' discussions. If the legal adviser has taken a full note of the evidence he may be called upon to refresh the justices' memory from it. However, so far as it is practical to do so, the legal adviser should be asked to give his advice openly in court. This will not always be a practical way to give advice, especially in complicated matters, or where reference to books may be necessary, or where a discussion with one or more of the justices may be involved. The justices' clerk has the right to advise the justices even though he is not sitting with them in court so that, if he is available, he may always be sent for if necessary. It should be noted, however, where representations have been made to the court which the justices' clerk has not heard they should be repeated in the presence of the justices' clerk before he gives his advice to the bench. It is especially useful to bear this in mind when sitting with an inexperienced legal adviser. Equally, where the legal adviser finds it necessary to give advice in the retiring room on a point not canvassed with the advocates then the legal adviser should return to court telling them of the advice given and allowing them to address the bench if they have anything additional to contribute.

D[6.29] For a fuller account of the role of the justices' clerk and his staff see **Section F**.

5 Consideration of guilt

D[6.30] The question for justices to ask themselves at this stage is, 'Has the prosecutor satisfied the majority of us beyond reasonable doubt that the accused committed the offence with which he has been charged?' A reasonable doubt must not be a fanciful doubt nurtured by prejudice. The burden of proof, that is the degree to which a court should be convinced of guilt, is a matter of law and one on which the legal adviser can assist.

D[6.31] When announcing the decision in court it is generally better to avoid using a reference to 'the case'. It is better to say, 'We find you guilty of theft' or as the case may be, rather than, 'We find the case proved'. The accused feels he has 'a case' too, and the latter expression of the decision sometimes creates the impression that 'the case' which the court has been concerned with has been the prosecution case. The former method of announcing the decision leaves nothing to doubt or prejudice and is especially to be recommended when there has been more than one charge or accused.

6 Reports etc

D[6.32] Irrespective the plea, once the guilt of the accused has been established the court may hear further information about him relevant to sentence. The prosecutor will give information about previous convictions or the fact that there are none. He will also indicate if the accused has admitted other similar offences which he wishes the court to take into consideration when determining the sentence. These will have been written down and should be put one by one by the clerk and the accused should be asked to signify his admission of each such offence separately. This is important because offences admitted and taken into consideration ('TICs' as these offences are usually known) may be significant in the sentencing decision and because (especially if there is a long list) it is very easy for the police to include in a list of outstanding offences some which a prisoner will admit through not giving the matter proper thought. Compensation may be ordered in respect of offences taken into consideration and this is another reason for being procedurally correct when dealing with them. The maximum amount of compensation depends on the number of substantive charges eg a plea of guilty to two charges of theft and 24 TICs means that the magistrates' powers to award compensation are limited to £10,000 (£5,000 per offence).

D[6.33] Also at this stage the prosecutor will ask for any appropriate ancillary orders such as costs or the forfeiture of a weapon or drugs, etc. The chairman should make a written note of such matters so that they are not overlooked when the final sentencing decision is made. See *Nicholas v Chester Magistrates' Court* [2009] EWHC 1504 (Admin). As a general proposition, magistrates adjourning for a full pre-sentence report cannot bind the sentencing court as to the general level of sentence, unless the same magistrates return to deal with the offender. Magistrates must also have regard to the SC Magistrates' Courts Sentencing Guidelines under s 172(1)(b) of the Criminal Justice Act 2003 when giving an indication as to the level of sentence proposed: see *Thornton v CPS* [2010] EWHC 346 (Admin), 174 JP 121.

D[6.34] Pre-sentence report. The court may at this stage consider a pre-sentence report and if one is not available the question of an adjournment in order to obtain one should not be overlooked. Although they need not do so if they are of the opinion that it is unnecessary, it is still a statutory requirement for a magistrates' court to consider a pre-sentence report before imposing any custodial sentence or a community sentence (except a probation order with no additional requirements, although the obtaining of a pre-sentence report is nevertheless still strongly advised).

D[6.35] The pre-sentence report is to assist the court in determining the most suitable method of dealing with an offender. The responsibility for determining the seriousness of an offence remains solely with the magistrates. However, the pre-sentence report will contain impartial advice and information and will balance the aggravating and mitigating factors in the case and report on the nature of the defendants offending: *R v Salisbury Magistrates' Court, ex p Gray* [2000] 1 Cr App Rep (S) 267, 163 JP 732. The report may give advice in support of a particular sentence although it will bear in mind the ultimate responsibility of the sentencer. The Crown prosecutor may make representations on matters contained in the pre-sentence report.

D[6.36] **Short or fast-delivery reports.** It is now common for the probation service to offer either to interview the defendant at court that day, or on a date in the near future, with the report being given either orally or in writing shortly after the interview. 'Fast delivery' reports are not offered, however, in cases of domestic violence or where more detailed investigation is necessary, eg as to a mental health or a substance abuse problems.

Suitability for a curfew or unpaid work can often be assessed by way of a stand down and short interview.

D[6.37] **Medical report.** Where the offender is, or appears to be, mentally disordered, the court must, if it is considering a custodial sentence, obtain a medical report. Such a report is made orally or in writing by a doctor approved under the Mental Health Act 1983 as having experience in the diagnosis or treatment of mental disorder.

D[6.38] Reports from other sources may be available, for example, a reference from an offender's employer or educational establishment etc. In any case where the court thinks fit it may adjourn and call upon the maker of a report to attend for questioning upon its contents.

D[6.39] The court must give the accused or his solicitor and the Crown Prosecutor a copy of the pre-sentence report. In the youth court the report will be given to a parent or guardian. It is very important, however, that the accused is aware of the contents of any written report submitted to the court. It is not considered entirely satisfactory simply to hand a written report to an unrepresented defendant in court. He may have difficulty in reading, especially in the stressful situation of court proceedings, so that he may not absorb the contents of the report at all, or he may not have finished reading it by the time he is invited to comment on it. Furthermore, he may not understand the meaning of everything he reads and he almost certainly will have had inadequate time to gather his thoughts and to express a useful opinion about anything contained in the report. The better practice, therefore, is that the probation officer (or youth offending officer) has discussed the contents of the pre-sentence report and especially the implications of any proposal therein, with the offender before the case is dealt with in court.

7 Guilty plea by post procedure

D[6.40] This is a quick and effective procedure for dealing with summary cases, in the absence of the accused (specified proceedings). The procedures outlined below only apply to offences dealt with in the adult court and those offences which do not carry a term of imprisonment of more than three months.

D[6.41] A summons is served on the defendant along with a witness statement of evidence. The defendant may plead guilty in absence on the basis of the evidence supplied and the clerk to the court reads the statement (or if directed by the court a summary) in open court before the court decides to accept the plea.

D[6.42] The legal adviser will then read any statement in mitigation from the defendant and any statement of means is considered along with the driving licence, in endorsable cases. The court may then pass sentence or adjourn if it requires the defendant's attendance, for example if it is considering a disqualification. This may be done in the absence of a prosecutor.

D[6.43] Failure to respond. If the summons and statements are properly served but the defendant fails to respond the proceedings become non-specified and the prosecution may use the evidence in the statements to prove the case against the defendant at the first hearing.

D[6.44] Not guilty plea. Where the defendant indicates in writing that he wishes to plead not guilty but attends court to give evidence the statement may be used at an adjourned trial date unless the defendant has indicated he wishes any of the prosecution witnesses to attend court. Note that the police will be able to ask for costs in writing against a defendant who has either pleaded guilty or been convicted on the statements served. There is also a hybrid procedure of serving the defendant with a statement of facts, upon which he may enter a guilty plea, and witness statements which will be used if he fails to enter a plea.

8 Appeals

D[6.45] There are three common forms of appeal from the Magistrates' Courts.

D[6.46] Appeal against conviction and or sentence to the Crown Court. Notice for such an appeal must be lodged within 21 days of the date of sentence. This time limit may be extended with the consent of the Crown Court (s 108 MCA 1980).

D[6.47] Appeal by way of case stated to the High Court on a point of law. The justices may be asked to state a case within 21 days of their decision. There is no power to extend this period. Once an application for a case stated is made the right to appeal to the Crown Court normally ceases (s 111 MCA 1980).

D[6.48] Application for judicial review. This application must be lodged with the High Court as soon as practicable and in any event within 3 months of the grounds for the appeal arising (Senior Courts Act 1981, ss 29, 31; Civil Procedure Rules 1998, Part 54). If successful the High Court may make quashing, prohibiting and mandatory orders to correct or prevent an error in law or a failure to exercise jurisdiction. See for example *R (on the application of Durham County Council) v North Durham Justices* [2004] EWHC 1073 (Admin), [2004] All ER (D) 260 (Apr).

D[7]

Publicly funded representation

Introduction and civil legal aid

D[7.1] Part 1 of the Legal Aid, Sentencing and Punishment of Offenders Act 2012 (LASPOA 2012) established an entirely new framework for the provision of publicly funded legal services.

The Act abolished the Legal Services Commission and established a Director of Legal Aid Casework who leads an executive agency within the Ministry of Justice which administers the delivery of legal aid services in England and Wales. The Lord Chancellor has broad powers to issue directions and guidance, but may not do so in individual cases.

The Act fundamentally changed the nature of civil legal aid by making it available only for those areas of law which are expressly included, which are listed in Sch 1 (provision for exceptional cases is made by s 10).

The Civil Legal Aid (Procedure) Regulations 2012, SI 2012/3098, have been made about the making and withdrawal of determinations that an individual qualifies for civil legal services under the Act.

The Civil Legal Aid (Merits Criteria) Regulations 2013, SI 2013/104 have also been made to prescribe the criteria the Director of Legal Aid Casework must apply when determining whether or not an individual or legal person qualifies for such services.

Criminal legal aid

D[7.2] The scheme for criminal legal aid (other than as to the administrative framework) remains substantially the same, though there are two changes of note. The first is that provision is made (by LASPOA 2012, s 20) for the Director or a court to make a provisional determination that an individual qualifies for representation in criminal proceedings where the individual is involved in an investigation which may result in such proceedings. The second is that Sch 3 to the Act enables the grant of legal aid to 'legal persons' other than individuals.

D[7.3] The Criminal Legal Aid (General) Regulations 2013, SI 2013/9, have been made to deal with the scope, making and withdrawal of applications, appeals, etc. The principal features are described below.

Scope

D[7.4] Advice and assistance is provided for people under arrest and held in custody. The application for initial advice and assistance must be made to the Defence Solicitor Call Centre and in accordance with the requirements set out in the 2010 Standard Crime Contract for the Unit of Work which is the subject of the application (LASPOA 2012, s 13 and The Criminal Legal Aid (General) Regulations 2013, Pt 2). Police station work is not means tested.

'Criminal proceedings' includes: proceedings in magistrates' courts for failure to pay a sum due or to obey an order of the court where such failure carries a risk of imprisonment; and proceedings in relation to various kinds of behaviour orders, eg ASBOs, football banning orders, restraining orders on acquittal (LASPOA 2012, s 14 and the Criminal Legal Aid (General) Regulations 2013, reg 9).

Prescribed advice and assistance is made available to individuals falling within certain categories where one of the prescribed conditions (listed in the Criminal Legal Aid (General) Regulations 2013, reg 12) is met and the Director has determined that the individual qualifies for advice and assistance having regard to the interests of justice and subject to financial eligibility. The latter is governed by the Criminal Legal Aid (Financial Resources) Regulations 2013, SI 2013/471. The client must pass both the income and capital tests, but persons in receipt of certain kinds of benefits automatically qualify. Income from certain sources is excepted, eg disability living allowance, but the income and capital of any partner are taken into account. Capital includes all assets and resources, but, where the client owns property, disregarding the first £100,000 of any equity.

The application must be made in accordance with the requirements of the 2010 Standard Crime Contract for the Unit of Work which is the subject of the application. If the Director determines not to grant the application on interests of justice grounds or because the qualifying criteria of the 2010 Contract are not met, an appeal may be made to the Independent Funding Adjudicator.

Advice and assistance covers all necessary work, other than police station work up to the point of charge or summons. Costs are limited to £300, though this can be extended on application.

Qualification for representation post charge or summons – representation orders

D[7.5] Qualification for representation in criminal proceedings is determined in accordance with the financial resources of the individual and the interests of justice (LASPOA 2012, s 17(1)).

In determining what the interests of justice consist of certain factors (LASPOA 2012, s 17(2) must be taken into account, namely:

(a) whether the applicant would be likely to lose his or her liberty or livelihood or to suffer serious damage to his or her reputation;
(b) whether consideration may need to be given to a substantial question of law;
(c) whether the applicant may be unable to understand the proceedings or to state his or her own case;
(d) whether the proceedings may involve the tracing, interviewing or expert cross examination of witnesses on behalf of the applicant; and
(e) whether it is in the interests of another person that the applicant be represented.

Guidance on the merits test will be found at http://www.justice.gov.uk/legal-aid/assess-your-clients-eligibility/crime-eligibility/interests-of-justice-test.

D[7.6] The Criminal Legal Aid (General) Regulations 2013 further provide as follows. Proceedings (other than appeals) in the Crown Court,

High Court, Court of Appeal and the Supreme Court automatically meet the interest of justice test. A determination in relation to proceedings before the magistrates' court automatically includes representation in the Crown Court following sending or committal for trial or sentence, but not in relation to appeals.

Where legal aid has been refused on interest of justice grounds, or withdrawn on those grounds, an appeal lies to the magistrates' court (which for this purpose includes a single justice or District Judge (magistrates' courts)), which must either affirm the determination or decide that the interests of justice require representation to be available or to continue to be available. If an appeal succeeds, legal aid must be granted if the individual's financial circumstances have not changed so as to make him financially ineligible.

As to the application of the regulations to 'legal persons' other than individuals, see Part 6 of the Regulations.

Financial eligibility

D[7.7] Representation orders (ROs) are means tested. Applications are made to the administrative centre for the court where the case is to be heard, which will apply the means test. (Complex financial cases are referred to the Legal Aid Agency's National Courts Team.)

Details of the test and eligibility limits will be found in the Criminal Legal Aid (Financial Resources) Regulations 2013, SI 2013/471.

Certain benefits are 'passported', ie confer automatic eligibility, namely:

• income support;
• income-based jobseeker's allowance;
• guarantee state pension credit;
• income related employment and support allowance; and
• universal credit.

This includes being a dependant in another person's claim to such a benefit.

If the applicant's gross income (defined below) is below the initial threshold, currently £12,475 pa, eligibility is again automatic. If gross income is over £22,325 pa the converse applies. Between these figures, a full means test to determine disposable income will be necessary. If this is found to be less than £3,398 pa the applicant will be eligible.

Assistance for assessing financial eligibility can be found at: www.justice.gov. uk/legal-aid/assess-your-clients-eligibility/criminal-eligibility-calculator.

'Gross income' is income from all sources, excluding certain benefits. It includes income received by the applicant's partner, unless the partner has a 'contrary interest' in the proceedings, eg is a prosecution witness. It also includes financial resources and maintenance received from another person.

Allowance is made for the applicant's partner and children by giving each such family member a weighting, adding one to 1 and then dividing the gross income by the resultant total. For example, the weighting for a partner is 0.64 and, for a child 2-4 years, 0.3. Thus, if the applicant has a partner and two such children the divider will be 1 + 0.64 + 0.3 + 0.3 = 2.24.

'Disposable income' is gross income minus:

- tax and NI;
- council tax;
- rent, mortgage, etc;
- childcare costs;
- maintenance payments; and
- living expenses allowance.

Living expenses allowance is increased using the same weighting scale for family members. The current base figure is £5.676. So, using the above example of an applicant with a partner and two small children, this will be multiplied by 2.24 = £12,714.

Proof of means is always necessary unless the applicant is in custody, in which case a statement of truth must be signed instead.

D[7.8] An RO is deemed to be granted on the date that a proper application was received. As a general rule, there can be no claim for prior work, but an order can be back-dated where urgent work was necessary (defined as a hearing within ten working days of taking initial instructions), and there was no undue delay in making the application (it was submitted no more than five days after taking initial instructions).

Where legal aid is refused on means an 'early cover' fixed fee of £75 may be claimed if certain conditions are met. Where legal aid is refused on the merits a 'pre-order cover' claim, limited to one hour's preparation at preparation rates, may be made if a qualified solicitor states on the file why it was believed the interests of justice test was passed, and not claim for early cover is made.

D[7.9] Where an individual is not financially eligible, but can demonstrate that to pay privately would cause hardship, an application can be made for hardship funding. The application is made to the Legal Aid Authority rather than the courts.

Choice of legal representative

D[7.10] The Criminal Legal Aid (Determinations by a Court and Choice of Representative) Regulations 2013, SI 2013/614, deal in Part 3 with the selection of representatives, changes of representation and level of representation. The position in the magistrates' court is summarised below.

Where there is a co-defendant, the same provider must be selected unless the relevant court or the Director determines that there is or is likely to be a conflict of interest.

There is no right to change providers unless there has been a breakdown in the relationship between the defendant and the original provider, or there is some other compelling reason why the latter cannot continue to act, or the latter considers that he is professionally obliged to withdraw or can no longer represent the defendant for reasons beyond the provider's control and the court has been provided with the relevant details. It has been held that, if it is the litigator's view that there has been no breakdown, the defendant cannot rely on the absence of details of the nature of the breakdown for the purpose of contending 'some other compelling reason': *R v Iqbal (Naseem)* [2011] EWCA Crim 1294, [2011] 2 Cr App Rep 250, (2011) Times, 21 April.

Where representation has been withdrawn and there is a subsequent determination that the defendant qualifies for representation, the original provider must be selected unless the relevant court determines there are good reasons why a different provider should be selected.

Representation may not include an advocate unless the proceedings relate to an extradition hearing under the Extradition Act 2003 or an indictable offence, and the relevant court determines that because there are circumstances which make the proceedings unusually grave or difficult, representation by an advocate would be desirable. Where these criteria are met in an extradition case, the court may determine that representation may consist of Queen's counsel or more than one advocate if the relevant court determines that the defendant could not otherwise be adequately represented.

Contribution orders

D[7.11] The Criminal Legal Aid (Contribution Orders) Regulations 2013, I 2013/483 make provision for the liability of individuals to make a payment in connection with the provision of representation, based on an assessment of the financial resources of the individual. The Regulations apply to Crown Court trials (Part 2) and appeals to the Crown Court (Part 3). Part 4 of the Regulations deals with the enforcement of contribution orders. Overdue sums payable under the Regulations are recoverable summarily as a civil debt.

Duty solicitor work

D[7.12] A solicitor who has passed both the Police Station Qualification and the Magistrates' Court Qualification and has registered as a duty solicitor with the LAA is entitled to apply to join the duty solicitor rota of his/her local court.

Duty solicitors advise and assist persons who would otherwise be unrepresented.

Court duty advice is available to those who qualify for assistance without regard to means. The duty solicitor scheme covers a wide area of representation, but excludes conducting trials or acting in cases where the client has had the services of a duty solicitor at a previous hearing.

A duty solicitor may, with the client's permission, apply for a representation order, but this should not be done where the case concludes on the day of the duty.

Remands in custody and on bail

'Remand'

D[8.1] When a case is adjourned to a fresh date the defendant may be remanded to ensure his attendance at the next hearing. The accused may be remanded in custody or released on bail.

Bail and the Human Rights Act 1998

D[8.2] Some sections of the Bail Act 1976 have been subject to challenge under the ECHR, for example the power to remove bail based solely on a police officer's belief that a defendant will breach a bail condition (Sch 1, Part 1, para 6). It is now established that while there is no need for a full inquiry following an arrest for breach of bail conditions, Art 5 does apply to any remand in custody (*R v Havering Magistrates' Court, ex p DPP* [2001] 3 All ER 997, [2000] All ER (D) 2307).

However, the Bail Act as outlined before should comply with Convention requirements if the overall concepts of fairness and proportionality are borne in mind. For example, a defendant may be remanded in custody on substantial grounds that he will commit a further offence, but that must relate to a serious offence based solely on the facts of the individual case. See *HB v Switzerland* (Application No 26899/95) (2001) 37 EHRR 1000, [2001] ECHR 26899/95, ECtHR for the application of Article 5 to the defendant's rights on arrest and production before a court.

D[8.3] **Remand on unconditional bail.** The accused is released with an obligation to surrender to the custody of the court on a certain day at a specified time. If he fails to do so, there are two consequences: the court can immediately issue a warrant for his arrest and he may be prosecuted for the criminal offence of failing to answer his bail.

D[8.4] **Remand on conditional bail.** The accused is on bail but with conditions attached to that bail, to ensure that he appears at court on the appointed day at the appropriate time or does not commit offences in the meantime or does not interfere with the witnesses in the case.

D[8.5] **Remand in custody.** Where bail is refused, the defendant is detained in prison or in police cells until his next appearance in court.

D[8.6] **Youths.** For the remands of children and young persons aged under 18, see E[3.3]–[3.18].

When must the court remand?

D[8.7] Where the court is acting with a view to committal for trial or sending an accused to the Crown Court for trial the accused must always be remanded on bail or in custody.

D[8.8] If the offence is triable either way, the court must always remand where the accused was initially arrested by the police and brought to court in custody or bailed for his appearance, or he has previously been remanded in the proceedings.

D[8.9] Where the offence is purely summary, the court always has a discretion whether to remand or simply adjourn the case.

D[8.10]–[8.15] In the case of juveniles (under 18) the court may remand if it thinks it is necessary to do so in those cases where it must do so when the defendant is 18 or over.

Length of the remand – before conviction

D[8.16] **In custody.** A remand in custody is not normally for longer than 8 clear days, ie the day when the decision to remand is made and the day when the defendant is next due to appear in court, are excluded. Therefore a remand in custody may be from the Monday of one week to the Wednesday of the next.

D[8.17] There are three major exceptions:

(a)   If the defendant is to be kept in police cells, the maximum period is 3 clear days or 24 hours in the case of a juvenile.

(b)   Where the accused is already serving a custodial sentence and will not be released in the intervening period, he may be remanded for up to 28 days.

(c)   The court may remand a defendant present before the court who has previously been remanded in custody for a period not exceeding when the next stage of the proceedings is reached or 28 days, whichever is the less. In exercising this power the court will have to have regard to the total length of time which the accused would spend in custody if it were to exercise the power. This would not affect the right of the defendant to apply for bail during this period.

D[8.18] **On bail.** Unless the accused consents, a remand on bail cannot be for more than 8 clear days. However, defendants always do consent to longer remands and that is why, as mentioned above, it is important for the magistrates to exercise control over the granting of adjournments. It should be remembered that bail is always granted to a fixed date and so it is not possible to adjourn a case *sine die* where the accused is remanded. An exception to this rule is a send to the Crown Court although a plea and directions hearing may be specified.

Length of remand – after conviction

D[8.19] A remand after conviction (for further inquiries and pre-sentence reports) cannot be for longer than 3 weeks if in custody, or should not be for longer than 4 weeks on bail.

Send to the Crown Court

D[8.20] When a magistrates' court commit or sends proceedings to the Crown Court for trial (or commits for sentence) the court may order the accused to be kept in custody until his trial (or sentence) or it may grant him bail.

Remands in the absence of the accused

D[8.21] An application for a remand for not more than 8 clear days may in prescribed circumstances be heard in the absence of the accused. The conditions to be complied with before this is possible are as follows:

(a) the court is adjourning a case before conviction; and
(b) the accused is present before the court;
(c) he is legally represented before the court (although his solicitor need not necessarily be present in court).

D[8.22] The accused must be asked whether he consents to future remands being determined in his absence. If he does, the court may remand him for up to three occasions in his absence. This means that the defendant must be brought before the court every four weeks. If the accused withdraws his consent or for any reason ceases to be legally represented, arrangements will be made by the justices' clerk to bring him before the court at the earliest opportunity, even though the period of his remand has not expired.

D[8.22A] Video remands. The Crime and Disorder Act 1998, s 57 provides for the use of video conferencing between the prison and the court for defendants previously refused bail in person. No consent is required and the defendant's next physical appearance before either the magistrates' court or the Crown Court will be for trial or plea and sentence.

Section 57 has had new sections added by s 45 of the Police and Justice Act 2006. The 2006 Act has extended a video remand hearing to include eg youths remanded to local authority accommodation or youth detention accommodation; and live video links are available for the sentencing hearing of adult and youths remanded to local authority accommodation or youth detention accommodation where the defendant consents. The new provisions came into force on **15 January 2007**. Further amendments have since been made by the Coroners and Justice Act 2009 from **14 December 2009**.

Justices are advised to consult their legal adviser before making an order.

D[8.22B] Vulnerable accused – live video links. From **15 January 2007** the Youth Justice and Criminal Evidence Act 1999 was amended to permit a direction for a vulnerable accused to give evidence by a live link. A court may give a direction on the application of the accused for the accused to give evidence via live video link where –

(1) the accused is aged *under 18*; his ability to participate effectively is compromised by his level of intellectual ability or social functioning; and the live link would enable him to participate more effectively in proceedings; or
(2) the accused has *attained the age of 18*; is suffering from a mental disorder and for that reason is unable to participate effectively; and that the live link would enable more effective participation.

D[8.22C] Live links in criminal proceedings – witnesses. From **26 April 2010** the Criminal Justice Act 2003, s 51, provides that if a magistrates' court so directs, a witness may give evidence through a live link at suitable premises other than court premises. The direction may be given in relation either to a trial or where the accused has pleaded guilty eg a "Newton hearing". A direction may be given on the application by a party to the proceedings or of the court's own motion. A direction may not be given unless the court is satisfied that it is in the interests of the efficient or effective administration of justice for the person concerned to give evidence in the proceedings through a live link. There is provision for the court to review and rescind a live video link direction: CJA 2003, s 52.

D[8.23] If the defendant has been remanded on bail or in custody and cannot appear because of accident or illness, the court may further remand him in absence. A court can always further remand in absence an accused who is on bail. *R (on the application of Grimshaw) v Leeds Magistrates' Court* [2001] EWHC Admin 880, [2001] All ER (D) 350 (Oct) is authority for a remand in the absence of the accused where he has not been produced due to a mistake.

The decision whether to remand in custody or on bail

D[8.24] **Presumption of liberty.** The general principle is that an accused man has a right to be released on bail where he has not been convicted of the charge or where his case has been adjourned for pre-sentence reports. This means that the accused never has to apply for bail, it is up to the prosecution to object to his right to bail (although in practice the defence are referred to as making an application for bail). Therefore, it is no reason for remanding an accused in custody that he has not applied for bail. However this right to bail does not apply to a committal to the Crown Court for sentence.

D[8.25] **Grant of opposed bail.** Where the court grants bail following a prosecution objection to bail the court must state its reasons for doing so.

Exceptions to the right to bail

Disapplication of exceptions to the right to bail where there is no real prospect that the defendant will be sentenced to a custodial sentence

D[8.26] The Legal Aid, Sentencing and Punishment of Offenders Act 2012 made significant amendments to the Bail Act 1976 with the aim of increasing the availability of bail. Of particular note, *certain* exceptions to the right to bail do not apply to bail in non extradition proceedings where:

(a)   the defendant has attained the age of 18;
(b)   the defendant has not been convicted of an offence in those proceedings; and
(c)   it appears to the court that there is no real prospect that the defendant will be sentenced to a custodial sentence in the proceedings.

The exceptions in the narrative below which are not disapplied are marked ***.

Imprisonable offences other than summary only offences and low value criminal damage, etc

D[8.27] The defendant need not be granted bail in the following cases (which are listed in the order in which they appear in Part 1 of Schedule 1 to the Bail Act 1976).

(1)   The court is satisfied that there are substantial grounds for believing that the defendant, if released on bail (whether subject to conditions or not) would:

(a)   fail to surrender to custody; or
(b)   commit an offence while on bail; or
(c)   interfere with witnesses or otherwise obstruct the course of justice, whether in relation to himself or any other person.

In taking the decisions required by this exception the court shall have regard to such of the following considerations as appear to it to be relevant, namely:

(i)   the nature and seriousness of the offence or default (and the probable method of dealing with the defendant for it);

(ii)   the character, antecedents, associations and community ties of the defendant;

(iii) the defendant's record as respects the fulfilment of his obligations under previous grants of bail in criminal proceedings;

(iv)   except in the case of a defendant whose case is adjourned for inquiries or a report, the strength of the evidence of his having committed the offence or having defaulted;

(v)   if the court is satisfied that there are substantial grounds for believing that the defendant, if released on bail (whether subject to conditions or not), would commit an offence while on bail, the risk that the defendant may do so by engaging in conduct that would, or would be likely to, cause physical or mental injury to any person other than the defendant,

as well as to any others which appear to be relevant.

(2)   The court is satisfied that there are substantial grounds for believing that the defendant, if released on bail conditionally or unconditionally, would commit an offence on bail by engaging in conduct that would, or would be likely to, cause:

(a)   physical or mental injury to an associated person (this means a person who is associated with the defendant within the meaning of s 62 of the Family Law Act 1996); or

(b)   an associated person to fear physical or mental injury.***

(3)   Where:

(a)   the offence is an indictable offence or an offence triable either way; and

(b)   it appears to the court that the defendant was on bail in criminal proceedings on the date of the offence.

(4)   The court is satisfied that the defendant should be kept in custody for his own protection or, if he is a child or young person, for his own welfare.***

(5)   The defendant is serving a custodial sentence.***

(6)   The court is satisfied that it has not been practicable to obtain sufficient information for the purpose of taking the decisions required by this Part of this Schedule for want of time since the institution of the proceedings against him.***

(7)   Where, having previously been released on bail in, or in connection with, the proceedings, the defendant has been arrested in pursuance of s 7 of the Bail Act 1976 (absconding or breaking bail conditions).

(8)   (This relates to defendants charged with murder, but in such cases bail decisions must be made by a Crown Court judge.)***

(9)   In relation only to a defendant whose case is adjourned for inquires or a report, the defendant need not be granted bail if it appears to the court that it would be impracticable to complete the inquiries or make the report without keeping the defendant in custody.***

*** This exception is not subject to the 'no real prospect of a custodial sentence' qualification: see para D[8.26], above.

Exceptions to the right to bail: summary-only imprisonable offences and low value criminal damage, etc

The no real prospect of a custodial sentence disapplication (see D[8.26], above) applies to the exceptions listed below other than those marked***.

D[8.28] The defendant need not be granted bail in the following cases (which are listed in the order in which they appear in Part 1A of Schedule 1 to the Bail Act 1976):

(1)   Where:
        (a)   it appears to the court that, having been previously granted bail in criminal proceedings, he has failed to surrender to custody in accordance with his obligations under the grant of bail; and
        (b)   the court believes, in view of that failure, that the defendant, if released on bail (whether subject to conditions or not) would fail to surrender to custody.

(2)   Where:
        (a)   it appears to the court that the defendant was on bail in criminal proceedings on the date of the offence; and
        (b)   the court is satisfied that there are substantial grounds for believing that the defendant, if released on bail (whether subject to conditions or not) would commit an offence while on bail.

(3)   If the court is satisfied that there are substantial grounds for believing that the defendant, if released on bail (whether subject to conditions or not), would commit an offence while on bail by engaging in conduct that would, or would be likely to, cause:
        (a)   physical or mental injury to an associated person (within the meaning of s 62 of the Family Law Act 1996); or
        (b)   an associated person to fear physical or mental injury.***

(4)   If the court is satisfied that the defendant should be kept in custody for his own protection or, if he is a child or young person, for his own welfare.***

(5)   Where the defendant is a serving prisoner.***

(6)   Where:
        (a)   having previously been released on bail in, or in connection with, the proceedings, the defendant has been arrested in pursuance of s 7 of the Bail Act 1976 (absconding or breaking bail conditions); and
        (b)   the court is satisfied that there are substantial grounds for believing that the defendant, if released on bail (whether subject to conditions or not) would fail to surrender to custody, commit an offence while on bail or interfere with witnesses or otherwise obstruct the course of justice (whether in relation to himself or any other person).

(7)   The defendant need not be granted bail where the court is satisfied that it has not been practicable to obtain sufficient information for the purpose of taking the decisions required by this Part of this Schedule for want of time since the institution of the proceedings against him.***

Exceptions to the right to bail: non-imprisonable offences

D[8.29] The defendant need not be granted bail in the following cases (which are listed in the order in which they appear in Part II of Schedule 1 to the Bail Act 1976).

(1)   Where defendant is a child or young person or has been convicted in the proceedings of an offence and:

    (a)   it appears to the court that, having been previously granted bail in criminal proceedings, he has failed to surrender to custody in accordance with his obligations under the grant of bail; and

    (b)   the court believes, in view of that failure, that the defendant, if released on bail (whether subject to conditions or not) would fail to surrender to custody.

(2)   If the court is satisfied that the defendant should be kept in custody for his own protection or, if he is a child or young person, for his own welfare.

(3)   Where the defendant is a serving prisoner.

(4)   Where the defendant is a child or young person or has been convicted in the proceedings of an offence and:

    (a)   having been released on bail in or in connection with the proceedings for the offence, he has been arrested in pursuance of s 7 of this Act (absconding or breaking bail conditions); and

    (b)   the court is satisfied that there are substantial grounds for believing that the defendant, if released on bail (whether subject to conditions or not) would fail to surrender to custody, commit an offence on bail or interfere with witnesses or otherwise obstruct the course of justice (whether in relation to himself or any other person).

(5)   Where:

    (a)   having been released on bail in, or in connection with, the proceedings for the offence, the defendant has been arrested in pursuance of s 7 (absconding or breaking bail conditions), and

    (b)   the court is satisfied that there are substantial grounds for believing that the defendant, if released on bail (whether subject to conditions or not), would commit an offence while on bail by engaging in conduct that would, or would be likely to, cause:

        (i)   physical or mental injury to an associated person (within the meaning of s 62 of the Family Law Act 1996); or

        (ii)   an associated person to fear physical or mental injury.

Special provision for drug users

D[8.30] Subject to the proviso stated below, a defendant who meets the following conditions may not be granted bail unless the court is of the opinion that that there is no significant risk of his committing an offence while on bail (whether subject to conditions or not). This exception does not apply to non-imprisonable offences, but applies in all other cases.

The conditions are:

(a)   the defendant is aged 18 or over;

(b)   a sample taken:

    (i)   under s 63B of the Police and Criminal Evidence Act 1984 (testing for presence of Class A drugs) in connection with the offence; or

    (ii)   under s 161 of the Criminal Justice Act 2003 (drug testing after conviction of an offence but before sentence),

has revealed the presence in his body of a specified Class A drug;

(c) either the offence is one under s 5(2) or (3) of the Misuse of Drugs Act 1971 and relates to a specified Class A drug, or the court is satisfied that there are substantial grounds for believing:

(i) that misuse by him of any specified Class A drug caused or contributed to the offence; or

(ii) (even if it did not) that the offence was motivated wholly or partly by his intended misuse of such a drug; and

(d) the condition set out in (e) below is satisfied or (if the court is considering on a second or subsequent occasion whether or not to grant bail) has been, and continues to be, satisfied;

(e) the condition referred to above is that after the taking and analysis of the sample:

(i) a relevant assessment has been offered to the defendant but he does not agree to undergo it; or

(ii) he has undergone a relevant assessment, and relevant follow-up has been proposed to him, but he does not agree to participate in it.

The proviso referred to above is the court has been notified by the Secretary of State that arrangements for conducting a relevant assessment or, as the case may be, providing relevant follow-up have been made for the local justice area in which it appears to the court that the defendant would reside if granted bail and the notice has not been withdrawn.

Conditions to be imposed where bail is granted

D[8.31] This is subject to the proviso set out above as to arrangements for conducting assessments, etc, where the defendant:

(a) after analysis of the sample referred to in paragraph (b)above, has been offered a relevant assessment or, if a relevant assessment has been carried out, the defendant has had relevant follow-up proposed to him; and

(b) the defendant has agreed to undergo the relevant assessment or, as the case may be, to participate in the relevant follow-up,

the court, if it grants bail, must impose as a condition of bail that the defendant both undergo the relevant assessment and participate in any relevant follow-up proposed to him or, if a relevant assessment has been carried out, that the defendant participate in the relevant follow-up.

Bail in cases of homicide or rape after a previous conviction of such offences

D[8.32] A person who in any proceedings has been charged with or convicted of an offence to which s 25 of the Criminal Justice and Public Order Act 1994 applies, in circumstances to which it applies, shall be granted bail in those proceedings only if the court considering the grant of bail is satisfied that there are exceptional circumstances which justify it.

The offences to which s 25 of the 1994 Act applies are as follows:

(a) murder;
(b) attempted murder;
(c) manslaughter;
(d) rape and other serious sexual offences and attempts.

Section 25 applies to a person charged with or convicted of any of the above offences only if he has been previously convicted by or before a court in any part of the United Kingdom of any such offence or of culpable homicide, or of a comparable offence or culpable homicide within a Member State of the EU, and, in the case of a previous conviction of manslaughter or of culpable homicide, if he was then sentenced to imprisonment or detention (detention in the case of an EU conviction) or, if he was then a child or young person, to long-term detention (in the case of an EU conviction, to a term of detention of at least two years.

Prosecution right of appeal

D[8.33]–[8.50] The Bail Amendment Act 1993 enables the prosecution to appeal against the grant of bail, subject to the conditions stated below.

Where a magistrates' court grants bail to a person who is charged with, or convicted of, an offence punishable by imprisonment the prosecution may appeal to a judge of the Crown Court against the granting of bail. Such an appeal may be made only where the prosecution is conducted by the Director of Public Prosecutions or other person falling within a class prescribed by order of the Secretary of State and it may be made only if the prosecution made representations that bail should not be granted, and the representations were made before it was granted.

In the event of the prosecution wishing to exercise this right of appeal, oral notice of appeal must be given to the magistrates' court at the conclusion of the proceedings in which bail has been granted and before the release from custody of the person concerned. Written notice of appeal must then be served on the magistrates' court and the person concerned within two hours of the conclusion of the proceedings.

The hearing of an appeal against a decision to grant bail must be commenced within 48 hours, excluding weekends and any public holiday (ie Christmas Day, Good Friday or a bank holiday) from the date on which oral notice of appeal is given. The appeal shall be by way of re-hearing and the judge may remand the person concerned in custody or may grant bail subject to such conditions, if any, as he thinks fit. While the provisions of ss 128 and 128A of the Magistrates' Courts Act 1980 do not apply to the Crown Court, if that Court upholds a prosecution appeal it should remand in custody consonantly with those provisions.

This right of appeal applies to a child or young person as if for the reference above to a remand in custody there were substituted a reference to a remand to local authority accommodation.

General considerations

D[8.51] Custody time limits. The Prosecution of Offences Act 1985, s 22 provides for restrictions on the period for which a person charged with an either way, indictable or summary offence may be remanded in custody. The maximum period of a custodial remand is 70 days between his first appearance and the start of a summary trial or committal proceedings, as appropriate. Where, in the case of an either way offence, summary trial is decided upon within 56 days the summary trial must commence within 56 days of the first appearance. Time limits also apply to proceedings before the Crown Court.

NB: An offence 'triable either way' includes an offence which, although triable only on indictment in the case of an adult, is in the case of a juvenile person under 18 years of age triable summarily or on indictment under s 24 of the Magistrates' Courts Act 1980 (grave crimes procedure) (*R v Stratford Youth Court, ex p S* (1998) 162 JP 552).

D[8.52] The court may extend the custody time limits on receipt of an application either orally or in writing but the court must not grant an extension *unless* satisfied that the need for it is justified by virtue of one of three criteria:

(a)   illness or absence of the accused, a necessary witness, a judge or magistrate; or

(b)   a postponement occasioned by the ordering by the court of separate trials in the case of two or more accused or two or more offences; or

(c)   some other good and sufficient cause.

The procedure for an application to extend time limits may be informal but the prosecution must still satisfy the court and the defendant be given an opportunity to test the application (*Wildman v DPP* [2001] EWHC 14 (Admin), (2001) 165 JP 453).

The unavailability of a suitable judge or a suitable courtroom within the maximum period specified in the CTL regulations may, in special cases and on appropriate facts, amount to good and sufficient cause for granting an extension of custody time limits. However, the CPS must provide evidence to support an extension. The court was reliant on information provided by HMCTS staff. That was wholly inadequate. The case was not given that intense level of scrutiny required. If the court had been provided with the correct information he would not have extended the CTL. The President of the Queen's Bench Division then proceeded to lay down guidance on the approach the Crown Court should take in a routine case where an extension to the CTL is sought because of a lack of resources: *R (on the application of McAuley (Clarke)) v Coventry Magistrates' Court and CPS* [2012] EWHC 680 (Admin), [2012] 3 All ER 519, [2012] 1 WLR 2766.

A successful application to vacate the trial by the defence is relevant to a reconsideration of a refusal to extend custody limits (*R (on the application of the DPP) v Blackfriars Crown Court* [2001] EWHC Admin 56, [2001] All ER (D) 205).

However, custody time limits were not extended when the defence requested an adjournment to consider disclosure which was two months late as the fault was that of the prosecution (*R (on the application of Holland) v Leeds Crown Court* [2002] EWHC 1862 (Admin), [2003] Crim LR 272).

D[8.53] The court must also be satisfied the prosecution has acted with all due diligence as well as expedition. See *R v Central Criminal Court, ex p Johnson* [1999] 2 Cr App Rep 51. The fact that a trial could not proceed because of the illness of a victim is irrelevant if the prosecution have failed otherwise to act with due diligence (*R v Central Criminal Court, ex p Bennett* (1999) Times, 25 January). This approach was rejected by the High Court in *R v Leeds Crown Court, ex p Bagoutie* (1999) Times, 31 May as leading to absurd results so that it does not matter that the prosecution has not acted with all due diligence if there is good and sufficient cause in the eyes of the court. However, in complex matters where the defendant is asking for extensive disclosure the prosecution could expect reasonable notice of such enquiries to enable it to comply (*R (on the application of Smith) v Crown Court at Woolwich* [2002] EWHC 995 (Admin), [2002] All ER (D) 05 (May)).

D[8.54] Where a custody time limit has expired the accused must be released on bail with or without conditions. However, a new charge will attract its own custody time limit (*R v Leeds Crown Court, ex p Wardle* [2001] UKHL 12, [2002] 1 AC 754, [2001] 2 All ER 1).

Conditional bail

Bail granted by the police

Police street bail

D[8.55] Section 30A of PACE (inserted by the CJA 2003) gave the police power to release on bail an arrested person at 'any time before he arrives at a police station'. From April 1, 2007 the Police and Justice Act 2006 amended PACE to allow conditions to be imposed by a constable where they are necessary:

(a)   to secure that person's surrender to custody;
(b)   to secure that person does not commit an offence;
(c)   to secure that person does not interfere with witnesses or otherwise obstruct the course of justice;
(d)   for the person's protection/welfare.

Those conditions, however, cannot include:

(a)   a recognisance;
(b)   a security;
(c)   a surety;
(d)   residence at a bail hostel.

A bail notice given to the arrested person must specify:

(i)   the requirements imposed by the condition;
(ii) the process for applying to vary those conditions.

Application to vary can be made either to the police or to a magistrates' court. A magistrates' court may consider an application to vary police street bail conditions where:

(a)   the street conditions have previously been varied by the police,
(b)   a request for variation by the police has been made and refused, or
(c)   a request was made and more than 48 hours has elapsed and the application has neither been withdrawn nor granted (PACE, s 30CB as inserted by Police and Justice Act 2006, s 6 and Sch 10).

A constable may arrest without warrant a person released on conditional bail granted on the street if he has reasonable grounds for suspecting the person has broken any of the conditions imposed by the police. A person arrested for breach of street bail conditions must be taken to a police station as soon as is practicable after the arrest.

Police bail before charge

D[8.56] Any grant of bail before charge may now have attached to it the full range of conditions similar to those outlined at D[8.55]. Applications to vary these conditions are dealt with under s 47(1E) of PACE and in accordance with r 19.6 of the Criminal Procedure Rules 2012. For variation of court bail see D[8.81A].

Police bail after charge

D[8.57]–[8.60] A custody sergeant at the police station may grant an accused conditional bail and may do so for the same reasons as a bench of magistrates who may decide that the defendant cannot be released on unconditional bail. It is only if conditional bail would be inadequate that custody should be contemplated.

Court bail

D[8.61] Conditions are only to be attached to bail where it appears to the bench necessary to do so for the purpose of preventing the accused:

(a)   failing to surrender to custody; or
(b)   committing an offence while on bail; or
(c)   interfering with witnesses or obstructing the course of justice; or
(d)   from being harmed, ie for his own protection or in the case of a juvenile for his welfare.

D[8.62] Conditions may also be imposed to enable a pre-sentence report to be prepared, or requiring a defendant to attend an interview with a legal representative before the next court hearing. The court must give its reasons for imposing conditions on the bail.

See para D[8.29] as to special provision for drug users.

D[8.63] Commonly imposed conditions are:

* residence (absconding);
* curfew (fresh offences);
* reporting to a police station (absconding);
* non-association with specified people (interference with the course of justice);
* a security or surety (absconding).

Other conditions may be imposed provided they are reasonable and are enforceable, including a 'doorstep' condition for those on a curfew condition (*R v Chorley Justices* [2002] EWHC 2162 (Admin), 166 JP 764, sub nom *R (DPP) v Chorley Justices* [2002] 43 LS Gaz R 34).

See r 19.11 of the CPR 2014. The defendant should give notice of any proposed address at which he/she would reside if granted bail to enable the court to assess its suitability.

D[8.64] It must be emphasised that conditions are not to be imposed as a matter of course; they can only be imposed to prevent one of the occurrences mentioned above. If a condition is imposed it must relate to the mischief which is feared (a *guide* is given by the words in brackets above). Conditions must not be imposed which have no relevance to the reason given by the court, eg a surety because the bench fears fresh offences.

D[8.65] Conditions may also be imposed to require defendants to comply with hostel rules where residing at a bail or probation hostel on remand or for assessment. Electronic monitoring of defendants on bail to enforce a curfew is also permitted. Electronic monitoring of children over the age of 12 is also permitted subject to the same restrictions imposed on the use of secure accommodation: s 3AA of the Bail Act 1976 (see D[8.6])*.

*When LASPOA 2012, s 151(1) is brought into force, the criteria for remanding children on bail with an electronic monitoring condition will be modified.

D[8.66] Sureties. With one exception, mentioned below, no one has to deposit money or valuables to secure a person's release in remand proceedings. However, a third party may agree to stand as surety for an accused. A

2

surety is a person who agrees to forfeit a sum of money fixed by the court (called a recognisance and pronounced 'reconnaissance') if the accused fails to surrender to custody. A surety's obligations are to ensure that the accused surrenders to custody; he is not there to ensure that the accused complies with the conditions of his bail. The court should specify that the person standing surety is to secure the accused's attendance at the next hearing or for each occasion to which the case may, from time to time, be adjourned.

A surety cannot be required for the purpose of ensuring compliance with a bail condition designed to prevent further offending: *R (on the application of Shea) v Winchester Crown Court* [2013] EWHC 1050, DC.

D[8.67] In deciding whether to accept a person as a surety, the court should in particular have regard to:

(a) the surety's financial resources;
(b) his character and any previous convictions of his;
(c) his proximity (whether in point of kinship, place or otherwise) to the person for whom he is to be surety.

D[8.68] Forfeiting the recognisance of a surety. If the accused fails to answer to his bail, the surety should be informed by the court that it is considering forfeiting his recognisance. Standing surety is a solemn obligation. The court will start from the basis that the whole amount is to be forfeited. The culpability of the surety will be investigated to see what steps he took to ensure the defendant's attendance. However, a surety should not forfeit his recognisance if he is not to blame for the defendant's failure to surrender when required to do so. When forfeiting a recognisance the court must take into account the surety's ability to pay.

D[8.69] Depositing a security. An exception to the rule that an accused does not have to deposit money or valuables is where the court believes a security is necessary to ensure the defendant surrenders to custody. The usual security is money, but it could be a valuable item such as motor car, provided it is readily convertible into money.

In the case of a security the law presumes that the sum deposited by way of security should be forfeited and it is for the person who deposited the security – on receipt of a court notice – to show cause why the sum should not remain forfeited.

D[8.70]–[8.76] The effectiveness of conditions. The usefulness of some conditions is questionable. A condition of reporting to the police at anything longer than 24-hour intervals is generally of little value and such a condition should be not imposed to make the accused more readily available for questioning. Nor should a condition be imposed for its nuisance value to the accused. A condition of depositing a passport is of little value, especially where the accused can travel within the EU without a passport.

Where bail is refused

D[8.77] Making a further application. At the first hearing after that at which the court decided not to grant the defendant bail (which normally would have been the first time the case was remanded) he is entitled to apply for bail as of right. At any subsequent hearings the court need not hear any arguments as to fact or law which it has heard previously: see *R (on the application of B) v Brent Youth Court* [2010] All ER (D) 76 (Jul).

D[8.78] The court must, however, always consider the matter of bail on each occasion on which the case is remanded. As the liberty of the accused is at stake, it is suggested that any doubt whether to allow a fresh application should be resolved in the accused's favour.

D[8.79] Appeals. The defendant may appeal to the Crown Court against the imposition of bail conditions relating to residence (other than to a bail hostel), sureties and securities, curfew and contact with other persons. Such an application may only be made following the determination of an application to vary the bail conditions made in the magistrates' court. There is no concurrent power to appeal to the High Court.

Application to a Crown Court Judge in chambers. Where the magistrates have heard a full application and refused bail, their legal adviser will supply the accused with a certificate to that effect. He then has a right to make a bail application to a Crown Court Judge in chambers.

Application to vary bail conditions imposed by the court

D[8.80]–[8.81] Advance notice (24 hours minimum) must be given by the defence of an application to vary conditions of bail, including a change of address. A new rule 19.11 has been added to the Criminal Procedure Rules 2013 whereby the defence must give notice of the address at which the defendant would reside if the court granted or varied bail, to enable the court to assess the suitability of the address proposed.

Prosecution for failing to surrender to custody

D[8.82] The law is that the accused is released on bail with a duty to turn up at court on the appointed day at the appointed time. If he fails to do so the first consequence is that a warrant may be issued for his arrest. Second, he may be prosecuted for the criminal offence of failing to surrender to custody. See D[8.85] below.

D[8.83] Where bail has been granted by a police officer for an accused to surrender either to a police station or a magistrates' court, any failure to surrender to custody should be initiated by charging the accused or laying an information. On the other hand, an accused who fails to answer to bail granted by the magistrates themselves should be brought before the court following his arrest. The court will then initiate proceedings following an express invitation by the prosecutor. The prosecutor will conduct the proceedings and, where the matter is contested, call the evidence. Any trial should normally take place immediately. In the meantime the defendant can expect to have bail revoked. In cases which cannot or are unlikely to result in custodial sentences a trial in the absence of the defendant may be a pragmatic solution. The bail offence should be dealt with immediately in normal circumstances (Revised Practice Direction (2004)).

D[8.84] Section 6 of the Bail Act 1976 creates two offences. The first offence is failing without reasonable cause to surrender to custody: Bail Act 1976, s 6(1); the second offence arises where there was reasonable cause for the failure to surrender, but the accused then failed to surrender to custody at the appointed place as soon after the appointed time as was reasonably practicable: Bail Act 1976, s 6(2).

The offences are triable only summarily where bail was granted by magistrates and proceedings are begun on the invitation of the prosecution.

The accused must be asked whether he pleads guilty or not guilty. Where a prosecution is contemplated the legal adviser should be consulted to ensure the correct procedure is followed.

D[8.85]–[8.90] Defence. It is a defence to such a charge if he proves (that it is more probable than not) that he had a reasonable cause for not answering his bail, or that having a reasonable cause for failing to surrender to custody at the appointed time and place, he surrendered to custody at the appointed place as soon after the appointed time as was reasonably practicable. It is not a defence that the accused was not given a copy of the decision to grant him bail.

'Surrender to custody' means 'at the appointed time and place' and the mere fact that the defendant is eg half an hour late cannot afford him a defence (*R v Scott (Casim)* [2007] EWCA Crim 2757, 172 JP 149).

It has been held that: 'if a court provides a procedure which, by some form of direction, by notice or orally, instructs a person surrendering to bail to report to a particular office or to a particular official, when he complies with that direction he surrenders to his bail. Thereafter, albeit he may not be physically restrained, albeit he may be allowed to sit in the court concourse and visit the court canteen, he is in the custody of the court. I have already suggested that he is under an implied, if not an express obligation, not to leave the building without consent until the case is called on. The argument that section 7(2) would have no meaning if that were not the correct construction is one which seems to me to be correct. I emphasise that if a person simply goes to the courthouse and does not report to anybody he has not surrendered to his bail. That is not enough. He has to report to somebody and do whatever he is directed to do, but when he does comply with the procedure which he is directed to follow by the court, then I emphasise that he has surrendered' (per Glidewell LJ in *DPP v Richards* [1988] QB 701). As to the position in the Crown Court, see *R v Evans* [2011] EWCA Crim 2842, [2012] 1 WLR 1192, [2012] 2 Cr App Rep 279, 176 JP 139. In the absence of special arrangements either particular to the court or to the individual case, surrender is accomplished when the defendant presents himself to the custody officers by entering the dock.

It is suggested that, when granting bail, the court should state and record that surrender to custody requires the defendant to arrive at court by the appointed time, to report his arrival in accordance with the practice of the court, to remain in court until his case is called and then to present himself to the custody officers by entering the dock (or such other part of the court as accords with its practice).

D[8.91] Penalty. A maximum penalty of 3 months' imprisonment and a fine on level 5 in the magistrates' court or the accused may be committed for sentence to the Crown Court, where the maximum penalty is 12 months' imprisonment and an unlimited fine. In *R v Clarke* [2000] 1 Cr App Rep (S) 224, CA the Court of Appeal upheld a prison sentence for the offence. Any such sentence will normally be consecutive to the sentence for the substantive offence (*R v White* (2002) Times, 9 December).

D[8.92] Failing to comply with a condition. Failing to comply with a condition of bail is not an offence (see *R v Ashley* [2003] EWCA Crim 2571, [2003] All ER (D) 106 (Aug)). It does mean, however, that a police officer can arrest the accused forthwith and bring him before the court. His failure to comply with the condition may in itself constitute an exception to the general 'right to bail'. If a defendant is arrested in breach of a bail condition the court should ask if he admits or denies the breach. If a denial is recorded the magistrates should hear evidence or a statement of the arresting officer's 'reasonable grounds' for arrest.

In determining whether the accused has broken a condition of his bail, the court is entitled to apply the civil standard of proof i.e. a balance of probabilities. The court is entitled to receive written hearsay evidence eg the statement of the arresting officer; the court's duty is to then weigh the evidence having regard to the hearsay nature of the evidence and the fact that the evidence cannot be tested by cross-examination: see *R (on the application of Thomas) v Greenwich Magistrates' Court* [2009] EWHC 1180 (Admin), 173 JP 345).

If the court is of the opinion that the defendant was in breach of his bail conditions he may be further remanded either in custody or on bail. If there is no breach of condition there is an entitlement to bail on the same conditions. Only after a finding of breach does the consideration of the reasons for breach become relevant (*R (Vickers) v West London Magistrates Court* [2003] EWHC 1809 (Admin), [2003] All ER (D) 211 (Jul)).

Note that the breach of bail exception to the right to bail is subject to the real prospect of a custodial sentence qualification (see **D[8.26]**); ie, unless there is such a prospect the defendant must be re-bailed.

Such hearing must be within 24 hours of arrest although there is power for the case to be put back in the list during that time period (*R (Hussain) v Derby Magistrates' Court* [2001] EWHC 507 (Admin), [2001] 1 WLR 2454). In *R (on the application of Culley) v Dorchester Crown Court* [2007] EWHC 109 (Admin), 172 JP 373, it was decided that:

(1)   Following the arrest of a person for breach of a bail condition, under s 7(4) Bail Act 1976 that person must be brought before a magistrates' court as soon as practicable and in any case within 24 hours of the arrest.

(2)   After the arrest of that person the court is required to complete the investigation and make a decision on whether there has been a breach of bail and, if there is a breach to remand in custody or to re-admit that person to bail.

(3)   Once 24 hours has elapsed after the arrest of that person, a magistrates' court no longer has jurisdiction under s 7(5) to deal with the breach of bail.

Bail pending appeal

D[8.93] The policy of the Court of Appeal has for long been against the granting of bail pending the hearing of an appeal against a custodial sentence, unless there are exceptional circumstances. The appellant's remedy is to apply for an expedited appeal. It is generally felt to be unsatisfactory that a person sentenced to custody is released in the hope of a successful appeal and is subsequently required to return to prison to serve his sentence. Therefore, only exceptional circumstances will lead to the granting of bail (*R v Watton* (1978) 68 Cr App Rep 293, [1979] Crim LR 246, CA). The court considering the application is not concerned with whether it would have imposed the same sentence, but only whether the sentence was reasonable. Where the sentence is clearly appropriate for the offence, then personal matters which are the basis for an appeal for clemency should not influence the court considering the bail application.

The justices' clerk

D[9.1] Some justices' clerks continue to hold independent public office. They may not be dismissed without the approval of the Lord Chancellor, who must in turn consider any representations made to him by the magistrates for the local justice area concerned. Although more recently some justices' clerks are appointed on a fixed-term contract they are still the holder of an independent public office.

D[9.2] The justices' clerk must be distinguished from those of his assistants ('legal advisers') who on his behalf give advice to justices in court when the justices' clerk is not personally in attendance. Both however are obliged to act compatibly with the ECHR.

Functions of the justices' clerk

D[9.3] Some of the functions of the justices' clerk will be seen from the following extract from the Courts Act 2003, which is not an exhaustive statement:

> The functions of a justices' clerk include giving advice to any or all of the justices to whom he is clerk about matters of law (including procedure or practice) on questions arising in connection with the discharge of their functions, including questions arising when the clerk is not personally attending on them . . . The powers of a justices' clerk include, at any time when he thinks he should do so, bringing to the attention of any or all of the justices of the peace to whom he is clerk any point of law (including procedure or practice) that is or may be involved in any question so arising.

D[9.4] The Courts Act 2003 uses the titles 'justices' clerk' and 'assistant clerk ', the latter as shorthand for 'assistant to a justices' clerk'. The latter is not subject to the direction of any person other than a justices' clerk: Courts Act 2003, s 29.

The Courts Service and Structure

D[9.5] The office of justices' chief executive was abolished by the Courts Act 2003. The Courts Act 2003 unified the court structure by abolishing magistrates' courts committees and bringing magistrates' courts within the Courts Service ('Her Majesty's Courts Service'). The Head of the Courts Service responsible for administration locally is the cluster manager but the head of the Service for the relevant region is the Delivery Director. The Delivery Director line manages both the cluster manager and the justices' clerk, although the judicial independence of the magistracy and justices' clerks (including legal advisers, whose advice in individual cases the justices' clerk is responsible for) is preserved by s 29 of the Courts Act 2003.

Advice in court

D[9.6] Although the extract from the Courts Act 2003 above refers solely to the justices' clerk himself, it is recognised that in practice he may delegate his advisory functions to legal advisers who are either professionally qualified as barristers or solicitors or are qualified under the Justices' Clerks (Qualification of Assistants) Rules 1979 as amended. Part 37A of the Criminal Practice Directions 2014 deals with the duties and responsibilities of bench legal advisers.

'CPD Trial 37A: ROLE OF THE JUSTICES' CLERK/LEGAL ADVISER

37A.1 The role of the justices' clerk/legal adviser is a unique one, which carries with it independence from direction when undertaking a judicial function and when advising magistrates. These functions must be carried out in accordance with the Bangalore Principles of Judicial Conduct (judicial independence, impartiality, integrity, propriety, ensuring fair treatment and competence and diligence). More specifically, duties must be discharged in accordance with the relevant professional Code of Conduct and the Legal Adviser Competence Framework.

37A.2 A justices' clerk is responsible for:

(a)   the legal advice tendered to the justices within the area;
(b)   the performance of any of the functions set out below by any member of his staff acting as justices' legal adviser;
(c)   ensuring that competent advice is available to justices when the justices' clerk is not personally present in court; and
(d)   ensuring that advice given at all stages of proceedings and powers exercised (including those delegated to justices' legal advisers) take into account the court's duty to deal with cases justly and actively to manage the case.

37A.3 Where a person other than the justices' clerk (a justices' legal adviser), who is authorised to do so, performs any of the functions referred to in this direction, he or she will have the same duties, powers and responsibilities as the justices' clerk. The justices' legal adviser may consult the justices' clerk, or other person authorised by the justices' clerk for that purpose, before tendering advice to the bench. If the justices' clerk or that person gives any advice directly to the bench, he or she should give the parties or their advocates an opportunity of repeating any relevant submissions, prior to the advice being given.

37A.4 When exercising judicial powers, a justices' clerk or legal adviser is acting in exactly the same capacity as a magistrate. The justices' clerk may delegate powers to a justices' legal adviser in accordance with the relevant statutory authority. The scheme of delegation must be clear and in writing, so that all justices' legal advisers are certain of the extent of their powers. Once a power is delegated, judicial discretion in an individual case lies with the justices' legal adviser exercising the power. When exercise of a power does not require the consent of the parties, a justices' clerk or legal adviser may deal with and decide a contested issue or may refer that issue to the court.

37A.5 It shall be the responsibility of the justices' clerk or legal adviser to provide the justices with any advice they require to perform their functions justly, whether or not the advice has been requested, on:

(a)   questions of law;

(b)   questions of mixed law and fact;

(c)   matters of practice and procedure;

(d)   the process to be followed at sentence and the matters to be taken into account, together with the range of penalties and ancillary orders available, in accordance with the relevant sentencing guidelines;

(e)   any relevant decisions of the superior courts or other guidelines;

(f)   the appropriate decision-making structure to be applied in any given case; and

(g)   other issues relevant to the matter before the court.

37A.6 In addition to advising the justices, it shall be the justices' legal adviser's responsibility to assist the court, where appropriate, as to the formulation of reasons and the recording of those reasons.

37A.7 The justices' legal adviser has a duty to assist an unrepresented defendant, see Rule 9.4(3)(a), in particular when the court is making a decision on allocation, bail, at trial and on sentence.

37A.8 Where the court must determine allocation, the legal adviser may deal with any aspect of the allocation hearing save for the decision on allocation, indication of sentence and sentence.

37A.9 When a defendant acting in person indicates a guilty plea, the legal adviser must explain the procedure and inform the defendant of their right to address the court on the facts and to provide details of their personal circumstances in order that the court can decide the appropriate sentence.

37A.10 When a defendant indicates a not guilty plea but has not completed the relevant sections of the Magistrates' Courts Trial Preparation Form, the legal adviser must either ensure that the Form is completed or, in appropriate cases, assist the court to obtain and record the essential information on the form.

37A.11 Immediately prior to the commencement of a trial, the legal adviser must summarise for the court the agreed and disputed issues, together with the way in which the parties propose to present their cases. If this is done by way of pre-court briefing, it should be confirmed in court or agreed with the parties.

37A.12 A justices' clerk or legal adviser must not play any part in making findings of fact, but may assist the bench by reminding them of the evidence, using any notes of the proceedings for this purpose, and clarifying the issues which are agreed and those which are to be determined.

37A.13 A justices' clerk or legal adviser may ask questions of witnesses and the parties in order to clarify the evidence and any issues in the case. A legal adviser has a duty to ensure that every case is conducted justly.

37A.14 When advising the justices, the justices' clerk or legal adviser, whether or not previously in court, should:

(a)   ensure that he is aware of the relevant facts; and
(b)   provide the parties with an opportunity to respond to any advice given.

37A.15 At any time, justices are entitled to receive advice to assist them in discharging their responsibilities. If they are in any doubt as to the evidence which has been given, they should seek the aid of their legal adviser, referring to his notes as appropriate. This should ordinarily be done in open court. Where the justices request their adviser to join them in the retiring room, this request should be made in the presence of the parties in court. Any legal advice given to the justices other than in open court should be clearly stated to be provisional; and the adviser should subsequently repeat the substance of the advice in open court and give the parties the opportunity to make any representations they wish on that provisional advice. The legal adviser should then state in open court whether the provisional advice is confirmed or, if it is varied, the nature of the variation.

37A.16 The legal adviser is under a duty to assist unrepresented parties, whether defendants or not, to present their case, but must do so without appearing to become an advocate for the party concerned. The legal adviser should also ensure that members of the court are aware of obligations under the Victims' Code.

37A.17 The role of legal advisers in fine default proceedings, or any other proceedings for the enforcement of financial orders, obligations or penalties, is to assist the court. They must not act in an adversarial or partisan manner, such as by attempting to establish wilful refusal or neglect or any other type of culpable behaviour, to offer an opinion on the facts, or to urge a particular course of action upon the justices. The expectation is that a legal adviser will ask questions of the defaulter to elicit information which the justices will require to make an adjudication, such as the explanation for the default. A legal adviser may also advise the justices as to the options open to them in dealing with the case.

37A.18 The performance of a legal adviser is subject to regular appraisal. For that purpose the appraiser may be present in the justices' retiring room. The content of the appraisal is confidential, but the fact that an appraisal has taken place, and the presence of the appraiser in the retiring room, should be briefly explained in open court.'

D[9.7] In court the legal adviser's duties are both advisory and executive. He may, if the justices so desire, perform those many tasks which ensure the smooth progress of the court's business. For example, he may decide the order in which cases are called, identify, caution and charge defendants, take their pleas and put to them other offences for the court to take into consideration. He may deal with the swearing of witnesses, he may deal with such matters as the explanation of a sentence such as a supervision requirement and confirm the defendant's consent to the requirement. He is empowered to take recognisances which have been fixed by the court, dealing with the arrangements for paying monetary penalties and the questioning of witnesses or defendants on the justices' behalf, including the conduct of a means inquiry. When the justices' clerk (or one of his legal advisers) performs these or any other similar tasks, he carries out those functions on behalf of the justices. There are at least three good reasons why he should carry out most, if not all of these executive functions: his legal knowledge, experience and professional ethics will usually mean that he can perform these functions more effectively than a justice can; there will be more uniformity of procedure if these functions are left to the legal adviser; the less the chairman has to worry about procedural tasks, the more of his attention he can give to listening and decision making.

D[9.8] The extent to which the legal adviser exercises these tasks, however, varies from court to court and even in the same place it may change according to which chairman is sitting or whether the justices' clerk himself or one of his staff is in court. Whatever the legal adviser does he should be careful to avoid giving to the general public the impression that he and not the chairman is in charge of the court's affairs. The conduct of the court is always the responsibility of the chairman in consultation with his colleagues on the bench; but a wise chairman will usually leave the general conduct of business in court to the legal adviser.

D[9.9] The Lord Chief Justice has warned that justices who fail to take the clerk's advice on a legal point may be ordered to pay the costs of any resulting appeal. This warning arose in a case where justices insisted on finding 'special reasons' in spite of advice given to them in court by the clerk and later in writing.

D[9.10]–[9.15] If the justices retire the legal adviser should not retire with them as a matter of course: either the chairman should specifically and audibly invite him to join the justices or the legal adviser should remain in court and be seen to have been sent for. NB: There is not the same prohibition on the legal adviser retiring immediately to join the justices in family proceedings eg in order to assist in the drawing up of the justices' reasons.

D[9.16] If the justices retire the legal adviser may join them. All too often justices are themselves unaware that a point has arisen in their discussion upon which they need advice, and unless the legal adviser is with them to hear their discussion he too will be unaware that they need advice. Moreover, if he is present during their discussion the legal adviser may be able to help by reminding them of parts of the evidence they may have overlooked, or by explaining the legal significance of particular evidence, or by correcting errors of recollection. In the event that the justices are later asked to state a case the clerk will find it a considerable advantage to have listened to the justices' discussion in the retiring room. Once the legal adviser is satisfied that he can be of no further assistance to the justices he should return to his place in court.

D[9.17] If the justices do not send for the clerk when they retire, he is entitled to go to advise them if he considers it necessary to do so, but will inform the parties as to what he is going to say to the justices, giving them an opportunity of making representations before that [provisional] advice is given. See *Clark (Procurator Fiscal, Kirkcaldy) v Kelly* [2003] UKPC D1, [2004] 1 AC 681, [2003] 1 All ER 1106 on the legality of the justices' clerk's advice and its compatibility with Article 6 of the ECHR.

Delegation

D[9.18]   Apart from his duty to provide justices with advice when they sit in court, the justices' clerk may perform those judicial functions of a single justice which are prescribed by the Justices' Clerks Rules 1999. Amongst the more important judicial functions which a justices' clerk can perform are: the issue of a summons, a witness summons, a distress warrant or a warrant for arrest following a defendant's failure to appear at court so long as no objection is raised on behalf of the accused. The justices' clerk may adjourn a case and grant bail to an accused in his absence with the consent of the prosecution and in the same terms as previously imposed.

D[9.19]   The justices' clerk may take a plea and fix a trial date where the defendant is on bail. He may authorise a legal adviser to exercise these functions and under the Children Act 1989 to conduct directions appointments and appoint guardians ad litem. Delegation should be by specific authorisation and in writing.

Delegation in relation to the grant of legal representation in criminal proceedings is currently governed by the Access to Justice Act 1999 and regulations made thereunder. The Criminal Defence Service Act 2006, from a date to be appointed, envisages that responsibility for the grant of representation will ultimately shift to the Legal Services Commission. However, in the first instance it is anticipated that magistrates' courts will retain the power to grant or refuse representation. The Act and regulations envisage that those functions are administrative in nature and will be delegated to court staff via the Area Director.

D[9.20]   The justices' clerk and those of his assistants with delegated powers have case management powers which can be exercised as if by a single justice. Often referred to as 'Narey Courts' the justices' clerk may sit alone in an early first hearing court where simple cases can be listed and a guilty plea is anticipated. Where the case is more complex or a not guilty plea is anticipated the case can be listed for an early administrative hearing where the justices' clerk can deal with trial listing, conditional bail variation (with the consent of the prosecution and the defence) and warrants of arrest in the event of a non-appearance by the accused.

The youth court

E[1]

Juveniles

(Children and Young Persons Acts 1933, 1963 and 1969)

E[1.1] Children (10–13) and young persons (14–17) are juveniles. Cases involving juveniles are heard in the youth court apart from exceptional cases in criminal proceedings where the juvenile appears before the adult magistrates' court charged with an adult defendant. The adult court may also remand a juvenile, when no youth court is sitting.

Determining the age of the defendant

E[1.2] Where anyone is brought before any court except as a witness and it appears that he is a child or young person, the court must make enquiry as to his age, and the age presumed or declared by the court is deemed to be his true age: Children and Young Persons Act 1933, s 99. This applies generally to determining whether a person appearing before any court is an adult or young person, and to establishing an age for the purposes of the proceedings. The statutory provisions for sentencing also make express reference to the age of the defendant. The effect of these is that the age of the offender will be deemed to be that which it appears to the court to be after considering any available evidence: see Powers of Criminal Courts (Sentencing) Act 2000, s 164(1). An order will be made on this basis. Where it is subsequently established that the defendant is of an age which precludes the sentence imposed on him, the sentence is not invalidated: *R v Brown* (1989) 11 Cr App Rep (S) 263, [1989] Crim LR 750, CA.

Where there is a dispute as to age which is material, it is better for the court to adjourn for more detailed inquiries if there is any doubt about the matter: *R v Steed* [1990] Crim LR 816.

When making an order in respect of young offenders it is generally the date of the finding of guilt that is relevant when determining the age of the offender for the purpose of the availability of orders: *R v Danga* (1991) 13 Cr App Rep (S) 408; *R v Hahn* [2003] EWCA Crim 825, [2003] 2 Cr App R (S) 106. See, however, *Aldis v DPP* [2002] EWHC 403 (Admin), [2002] 2 Cr App Rep (S) 400, [2002] Crim LR 434 where it was held, in relation to a defendant aged 17 at the time of mode of trial, at which hearing it must have been plain to all present that the possibility of a two-year detention and training order was a factor in the court's decision to try the case summarily, that the attainment of 18 before the trial and conviction did not prevent the justices from imposing a detention and training order; Parliament's intention must have been that s 100 of the Powers of Criminal Courts (Sentencing) Act 2000 should be interpreted as subject to s 29 of the Children and Young Persons Act 1963. The latter provides that where a young person attains 18 before the conclusion of the proceedings the court may deal with the case and make any order it could have made if he had not attained that age.

The youth court retains its jurisdiction concurrently with the adult court to deal with a breach of a conditional discharge where the defendant has attained 18 years: Children and Young Persons Act 1933, s 48(2). Proceedings for breach of a supervision order where a person has attained 18 years are heard in the adult magistrates' court: Powers of Criminal Courts (Sentencing) Act 2000, Sch 7, para 1.

In *R v Ghafoor* [2002] EWCA Crim 1857, [2003] Cr App R (S) 428 it was held that the starting point for sentencing was the age of the defendant at the date of the offence.

Children and young persons generally to be tried in the youth court

E[1.3] The basic principle is that a charge against a child or young person must be heard by a youth court: Children and Young Persons Act 1933, s 46. In some circumstances, however, proceedings must be commenced in an adult magistrates' court and certain cases must be sent for trial to the Crown Court.

The exceptions to the basic principle are:

(a) the child or young person is jointly charged with an adult: CYPA 1933, s 46(1); or

(b) the child or young person is charged with an offence arising out of circumstances which are the same as, or connected with, those giving rise to an offence with which a person who had attained the age of 18 is charged at the same time: CYPA 1963, s 18; or

(c) an adult is charged with aiding, abetting, counselling, procuring, allowing or permitting the offence by the child or young person: CYPA 1933, s 46(1); or

(d) the child or young person is charged with aiding and abetting, counselling, procuring, allowing, or permitting the offence by the adult: CYPA 1963, s 18; or

(e) proceedings against the child or young person are started in the adult court and it only becomes apparent later that the defendant is a child or young person: CYPA 1933, s 46(1) (and see *R v Tottenham Youth Court, ex p Fawzy* [1998] 1 All ER 365, [1999] 1 WLR 1350); or

(f) a written plea of guilty has been received and the court has no reason to believe that the accused is a child or young person. If it then transpires that the accused is a child or young person he shall nonetheless be deemed to have attained the age of 18;

(g) the court is conducting remand proceedings: CYPA 1933, s 46(1).

Where exception (a) (joint charge with adult) applies the case shall be heard in the adult magistrates' court, but where any of the other exceptions (b)–(d) apply the decision is discretionary. Exception (g) enables an adult court, where necessary, to hear a remand of a child or young person: CYPA 1933, s 46(2).

Whether an adult and a youth are jointly charged depends on a present state of affairs and it is not sufficient to embrace the situation where an adult was originally charged with the youth but has subsequently dropped out of the case.

As to sending youths to the Crown Court for trial and committing youths to the Crown Court for sentence, see E[3], below.

The youth court

E[2.1] Under s 50 of the Courts Act 2003, responsibility for the selection and authorisation of magistrates to sit in youth courts passed to the Lord Chief Justice. Through rules of court he has delegated that function to Bench Training and Development Committees (BTDC). From 13 September 2007, authorisation for winger and chairmanship selection is undertaken by BTDCs for the relevant local justice area (see the Justices of the Peace (Training and Development Committee) Rules 2007 (SI 2007/1609) and the Youth Courts (Constitution of Committees and Right to Preside) Rules 2007 (SI 2007/1611 (L9)). Copies of these rules can be viewed and downloaded from www.opsi.gov.uk.

E[2.2] Each youth court should (except in unforeseen circumstances) consist of three such magistrates, at least one of whom should be male and one female and the court should be presided over by the chairman or a deputy chairman of the panel. In *R v Birmingham Justices, ex p F* (2000) 164 JP 523, [2000] Crim LR 588 it was made clear that the court should consider representations before proceeding with a single sex bench. A district judge may sit alone in the youth court.

E[2.3] **Persons present during the hearing.** Only the following are allowed to be present:

* members and officers of the court;
* parties to the case before the court, their solicitors and counsel, and witnesses and other persons directly concerned with that case;
* bona fide representatives of newspapers or news agencies;
* such other persons as the court may specially authorise to be present.

E[2.4] **Restrictions on reporting.** The press may not report details of the name, address or school of a juvenile who is a defendant or witness in any proceedings before the youth court or any other details including the printing of a photograph which would identify him. An exception to this is when the court is dealing with an anti-social behaviour order. In such case the court may make an order under s 39 Children and Young Persons Act 1933 and give its reasons. For the principles governing a s 39 order see A[52.12].

E[2.5] These restrictions may be lifted:

* in order to avoid an injustice to a juvenile or in certain circumstances where a juvenile is unlawfully at large on application of the Director of Public Prosecutions; or
* the juvenile is convicted and the court, having listened to representations of the parties, believes it is in the public interest to do so.

Publication leading to the identification of an adult witness may also be prohibited under s 49 Youth Justice and Criminal Evidence Act 1999: see D[1B.7].

Criminal proceedings

E[3.1] It shall be the principal aim of the youth justice system to prevent offending by children and young persons. Youth courts must have regard to this aim.

Age of criminal responsibility

E[3.2] A child under the age of ten cannot be guilty of any offence (Children and Young Persons Act 1933, s 50).

In relation to offenders aged 10–14 years, the presumption and the defence of 'doli incapax' (mischievous discretion) was abolished by s 34 of the Crime and Disorder Act 1998 (*R v T* [2008] EWCA Crim 815, [2008] 3 WLR 923; affd sub nom R v JTB [2009] UKHL 20, [2009] 3 All ER 1).

Attendance of parent

E[3.3] Unless the court considers it unreasonable to do so, it must insist on the attendance of the parent or guardian of a child or young person under 16 years. In respect of those who are 16 and 17 years' old, the court has a discretion. 'Parent' will include a local authority where the juvenile is in their care. At all stages of the proceedings, if a parent refuses to attend a warrant can be issued against him or her.

Remands of children and young persons

E[3.4] When proceedings are adjourned the court may adjourn the case or remand the accused. A child (defined for these purposes as any person aged under 18) may be remanded on bail, or to local authority accommodation, or to youth detention accommodation. Remand hearings may take place in the adult court or the youth court: Children and Young Persons Act 1933, s 46.

The Bail Act 1976 applies, with some differences from the exceptions to the right to bail and the power to impose bail conditions which apply to adult offenders.

Where bail is refused, a child or young person will usually be remanded to local authority accommodation. The exceptions are:

(a)   in certain circumstances the remand may be to the custody of a constable for a period of up to 24 hours: Magistrates' Courts Act 1980, s 128(7);

(b)   where either of the prescribed sets of conditions is met, the remand may be to youth detention accommodation (see below).

Where a child is remanded to local authority accommodation, the court can impose conditions with which the child must comply and can impose requirements on the local authority to secure compliance with those conditions.

A child charged with murder cannot be granted bail by a magistrates' court and must be committed to the Crown Court either in local authority accommodation or youth detention accommodation: Coroners and Justice Act 2009, s 115. The relevant provisions are to be applied as they would be in any other case: *R (A) v Lewisham Crown Court* [2011] EWHC 1193 (Admin), (2011) 175 JP 321.

Remands and committals to local authority accommodation

E[3.5] Chapter 3 of Part 3 of the Legal Aid, Sentencing and Punishment of Offenders Act 2012 makes provision for remands and committal to local authority accommodation. Section 91 provides that where a child (ie a person aged under 18) is charged or convicted of an offence and the court remands the child, including where the court sends the child for trial or commits the child for sentence, and the child is not released on bail, the court must generally remand the child to local authority accommodation in accordance with s 92, subject to the exceptions stated in E[3.4] above (remands to police detention or to youth detention accommodation).

Section 92 provides that a remand to local authority accommodation is a remand to accommodation provided by or on behalf of a local authority. The court must designate the local authority concerned. In the case a looked after child, this will be the local authority which is looking after the child; in any other case, it will the local authority in whose area it appears to the court that the child habitually resides, or in whose area the offence or one of the offence was committed.

Section 93 provides that a court remanding a child to local authority accommodation may require the child to comply with any conditions that could be imposed if the court were granting conditional bail under s 3(6) of the Bail Act 1976. Subject to s 94 (requirements for electronic monitoring), the court may also require the child to comply with any conditions imposed for electronic monitoring for the purpose of securing compliance with the conditions imposed as above. The court may also impose on the designated local authority requirements for the purpose of securing compliance with either of the types of conditions described above. None of the above mentioned conditions or requirements can be imposed without prior consultation with the designated authority. This refers to such consultation (if any) as is reasonably practicable in all the circumstances of the case. There is provision for a relevant court to add any of the above mentioned conditions or requirements where a child has been remanded to local authority accommodation on the application of the designated authority. A relevant court may also vary or revoke any of the conditions or requirements on the application of the designated authority or the child.

Section 97 provides for liability to arrest for breaking remand conditions. Where a constable has reasonable grounds for suspecting such a breach, he may arrest the child and the child must then be brought before a court as soon as is reasonably practicable and in any event within 24 hours. If the court is of the opinion that the child has broken any of the remand conditions, it must remand him either to local authority accommodation or, if either set of conditions of remand to youth detention accommodation is met, to youth detention accommodation. If the court is not of this opinion, it must remand the child on the same conditions as before.

Remands to youth detention accommodation

E[3.6] The *first set of conditions* of the Legal Aid, Sentencing and Punishment of Offenders Act 2012, s 98:

(a)   the child must have reached the age of 12;

(b)   the offence must be a 'violent' or 'sexual offence' (defined in the Legal Aid, Sentencing and Punishment of Offenders Act 2012, s 94(8)) or an offence punishable in the case of an adult with imprisonment for a term of at least 14 years;

(c)   the court must be of the opinion, after considering all of the remand options, that only a remand to youth detention accommodation would be adequate:

     (i)   to protect the public form death or serious personal injury (whether physical or psychological) occasioned by further offences committed by the child; or

     (ii)   to prevent the commission by the child of imprisonable offences; and

(d)   the child is legal represented, or such representation has been withdrawn because of the child's conduct or financial ineligibility, or an application for such representation has been refused owing to financial ineligibility, or the child has refused or failed to take up the opportunity to apply for such representation despite being informed of his right to do so.

The *second set of conditions* of the Legal Aid, Sentencing and Punishment of Offenders Act 2012, s 99:

(a)   the child must have reached the age of 12;

(b)   it must appear to the court that there is a real prospect that the child will be sentenced to a custodial sentence for the offence or any one of them;

(c)   the offence or any one of them is an imprisonable offence;

(d)   either of the following 'history' conditions must be met:

     (i)   the child has a recent history of absconding while subject to a custodial remand, and the offence or any one of them is alleged to be or has been found to have been committed while the child was remanded to local authority accommodation; or

     (ii)   the offence or any one of them, together with any other imprisonable offences of which the child has been convicted in any proceedings, amount or would, if the child were convicted of that offence or offences, amount to a recent history of committing imprisonable offences while on bail or subject to a custodial remand;

(e)   the court must be of the opinion, after considering all of the remand options, that only a remand to youth detention accommodation would be adequate:

     (i)   to protect the public form death or serious personal injury (whether physical or psychological) occasioned by further offences committed by the child; or

     (ii)   to prevent the commission by the child of imprisonable offences; and

(f)   the child is legally represented, or such representation has been withdrawn because of the child's or financial ineligibility, or an application for such representation has been refused owing to financial ineligibility, or the child has refused or failed to take up the opportunity to apply for such representation despite being informed of his right to do so.

A remand to youth detention accommodation is a remand to such accommodation of one of the kinds listed below as the Secretary of State, after consultation with the designated local authority, directs in the child's case:

(a)   a secure children's home;
(b)   a secure training centre;
(c)   a young offender institution; and
(d)   youth detention accommodation for the purposes of the detention and training order provisions.

The designated local authority, which the court must specify, will be either:

(a)   in the case of a child looked after by a local authority, that authority; or
(b)   in any other case, the local authority in whose area it appears to the court that the child habitually resides or the offence or one of the offence was committed.

Secure accommodation

E[3.7] A local authority may not use secure accommodation, ie accommodation provided for the purpose of restricting liberty, for a period of more than 72 hours whether consecutively or in aggregate, in any period of 28 consecutive days without an order of the court authorising the use of secure accommodation. There are exemptions for public holidays and Sundays and for disregarding periods prior to a court authorisation. These provisions apply to all children accommodated by a local authority by virtue of a warrant under the Children and Young Persons Act 1969.

The primary statutory provision, s 25 of the Children Act 1989, which is supplemented by the Secure Accommodation Regulations 1991 and the Secure Accommodation (No 2) Regulations 1991, relates to both the family and criminal jurisdictions. The terminology of the family courts is used, ie the subject of any application is a 'child' defined by the Children Act 1989, s 105(1) as a person under 18.

It is the restriction of liberty which is the essential factor in determining what is secure accommodation; accordingly, a hospital ward may be 'secure accommodation': *A Metropolitan Borough Council v DB* [1997] 1 FLR 767.

In determining an application for a secure accommodation order the 'welfare principle' and the 'no order' principles of the Children Act 1989 do not apply. Where the court has found any of the criteria in the Children Act or the regulations is satisfied, it is bound to make a secure accommodation order: *Re M (a minor) (secure accommodation order)* [1995] 3 All ER 407, [1995] 2 FCR 373, [1995] 2 WLR 302, [1995] 1 FLR 418, CA and the Children Act 1989, s 25(4).

Secure accommodation – criteria

E[3.8]–[3.16] The criteria for placing/keeping a child in secure accommodation are modified in relation to children who are being looked after by a local authority and are aged 12 or over but under 17 and are being detained by the police under the Police and Criminal Evidence Act 1984, s 38(6). In such a case it must appear to the court that any other accommodation is inappropriate because:

(a)   the child is likely to abscond from such other accommodation; or
(b)   the child is likely to injure himself or other people if he is kept in any such other accommodation: Regulation 6 of the Children (Secure Accommodation) Regulations 1991, SI 1991/1505, reg 16.

In all other cases, the criteria are those applicable to family cases, namely:

(a)   the child has a history of absconding and is likely to abscond form any other description of accommodation; and
(b)   if he absconds, he is likely to suffer significant harm: Children Act 1989, s 25(1).

No court shall exercise its powers relating to secure accommodation in respect of a child who is not legally represented unless, having been informed of his right to apply for legal aid and having had the opportunity to do so, he refused or failed to apply: Children Act 1989, s 25(6).

The welfare of the child is relevant, but not paramount, in a remand situation: *Re M (a minor) (secure accommodation)* [1995] Fam 108, [1995] 3 All ER 407, CA.

The procedure is prescribed by the Magistrates' Courts (Children and Young Person) Rules 1992, SI 1992/2071.

E[3.17] The maximum period for which a court may from time to time authorise a child who has been remanded to local authority accommodation under s 91(3) of the Legal Aid, Sentencing and Punishment of Offenders Act 2012 is the period of the remand, subject to maximum of 28 days without further authorisation.

Youths and sending for trial – Crime and Disorder Act 1998, ss 51A–51E

E[3.18] The legislative policy is that youths should be tried summarily wherever possible. Certain offences must, however, be sent forthwith to the Crown Court. These are listed below. In the case of b), sending is subject to ss 24A and 24B of the Magistrates' Courts 1980 (indication of plea to be sought prior to making the relevant determination).

(a)   The offence is an offence of homicide, or each of the requirements of s 51A(1) of the Firearms Act 1968 would be satisfied with respect to the offence and the person charged with it if he were convicted of the offence, or s 29(3) of the Violent Crime Reduction Act 2006 (minimum sentences in certain cases of using someone to mind a weapon) would apply if her were convicted of the offence.
(b)   The offence is one of the serious offences mentioned in s 91 of the Powers of Criminal Courts (Sentencing) Act 2000 (other than one mentioned in d) below which appears to meet the criteria for the imposition of a dangerous offender sentence on conviction) and the court considers that if the offender is found guilty it ought to be possible to sentence him in accordance with subsection (3) of that section.

(c) Notice is given in respect of an either way offence under s 51B (notices in serious or complex fraud cases) or s 51C (notices in certain cases involving children) of the 1998 Act.

(d) The offence is a specified offence within the meaning of s 224 of the Criminal Justice Act 2003 and it appears to the court that if the offender is found guilty of the offence the criteria for a sentence under s 226B of that Act (extended sentence for certain violent or sexual offences) would be met.

Sending further offences on the same or on a subsequent occasion

E[3.18A] Where a youth is sent as per the above the court may at the same time send him to the Crown Court for trial for any indictable offence which is related to the sent offence, or for any summary offence which is imprisonable in the case of an adult or carries obligatory or discretionary disqualification and which appears to be related to the sent offence or to the indictable offence (subject, again, to indication of plea, unless the sent offence is one within s 51A(12) of the Crime and Disorder Act 1998 (ie homicide, etc, see (a) above) – s 24A of the Magistrates' Courts Act 1980 excepts this case from the indication of plea provisions the section proceeds to prescribe). (The term 'related' is defined by s 51E of the Crime and Disorder Act 1998.) There is like power to send forthwith where the youth has been sent as per the above and subsequently appears before the court charged with such a related indictable offence or summary offence (subject again to indication of plea, except where the sent offence was one within s 51A(12) of the Crime and Disorder Act 1998 as above).

Youths jointly charged with adults

E[3.18B] Where an *adult* is sent to the Crown Court and a youth is brought before the court on the same or on a subsequent occasion charged jointly with the adult with any indictable offence for which the adult is sent for trial, or an indictable offence which appears to be related to that offence, the court shall, *if it considers it necessary in the interest of justice (see below) to do so*, send the youth forthwith to the Crown Court for trial in respect of the indictable offence together with any indictable offence related to it, and any summary offence related to the sent offence or to the indictable offence which is imprisonable or carries obligatory or discretionary carrying disqualification. This is, again, subject to indication of plea under s 24A or s 24B of the Magistrates' Courts Act 1980, unless the sent offence is one within s 51A(12) of the Crime and Disorder Act 1998 – s 24A of the Magistrates' Courts Act 1980 excepts this case from the indication of plea provisions the section proceeds to prescribe.

This power to send the youth arises only after consideration has been to such of the sending conditions mentioned in **E[13.18]** *above as may apply* to the case. For example, if the adult and youth are jointly charged with robbery, the adult must be sent, consideration must then be given in the case of the youth to 'dangerousness' (indication of plea does not apply) and then, if the dangerousness criteria are not met, to the punishment of grave crimes, prior to the determination of which an indication of plea must be sought. It is only where the indication is 'not guilty' and the court determines that its powers are sufficient that the 'interests of justice' test will be considered. If the court determines that it is not in the interests of justice to send the youth to the Crown Court for trial it will remit the youth to the youth court.

Where a *youth* is sent to the Crown Court and an adult offender, jointly charged with an either way offence or charged with a related either way offence, appears before the court he *must* if it is the same occasion, or *may* if he appears on a subsequent occasion, be sent forthwith to the Crown Court, unless a guilty plea has been indicated by or on behalf of the adult. If the adult is so sent, the court shall at the time send him to the Crown Court for trial for any related either way offence (again, unless a guilty plea has been indicated), and any summary offence which is related to either of the former and which is punishable with imprisonment or carries obligatory or discretionary disqualification.

'Jointly charged' does not acquire a restricted meaning, but must be given its natural meaning. The phrase 'jointly charged' normally means two persons named in the same charge or series of charges; thus, while only one person can drive a vehicle, where two persons were charged with driving and allowing themselves to be carried in a vehicle taken without the owner's consent, they were properly considered to be 'jointly charged': *R v Peterborough Magistrates' Court, ex p Allgood* (1995) 159 JP 627, [1996] RTR 26.

Dangerous offenders and offenders accused of grave crimes

E[3.18C] **Dangerous offenders.** Where the offence is a specified offence within the meaning of s 224 of the Criminal Justice Act 2003 and it appears to the court that if the youth is found guilty of the offence the criteria for a sentence under s 226B of that Act (extended sentence for certain violent or sexual offences) would be met, the youth must be sent for trial. *Indication of plea before venue does not apply to this case.* The criteria for the imposition of an extended sentence are:

(a) the offence is a specified offence;
(b) the court considers that there is a significant risk to members of the public of serious harm occasioned by the commission by the offender of further specified offences;
(c) the court is not required by s 226(2) to impose a sentence of detention for life under s 91 of the PCVC(S)A 2000; and
(d) if the court were to impose an extended sentence, the term that it would specify as the appropriate custodial term would be at least four years.

In practice, the magistrates' court will rarely be in a position, at the stage of considering venue for the trial of the youth, to make the relevant determination on dangerousness owing to lack of reports, etc. Such cases are likely, therefore, to come before the Crown Court by sending under another power or on committal for sentence under s 3C of the Powers of Criminal Courts (Sentencing) Act 2000.

Offenders liable to be sentenced to long-term detention. If the offence is one of the serious offences mentioned in s 91 Powers of Criminal Courts (Sentencing) Act 2000, other than one which appears to meet the criteria for the imposition of a dangerous offender sentence on conviction, and the court considers that if the offender is found guilty it ought to be possible to sentence him in accordance with subsection (3) of that section, the youth must be sent for trial, *but in this case only if he indicates a not guilty plea.*

The offences to which s 91(3) applies are:

(a)   an offence punishable in the case of an adult with imprisonment for 14 years or more, not being an offence the sentence for which is fixed by law;
(b)   an offence under s 3, 13, 25 or 26 of the Sexual Offences Act 2003;
(c)   certain offences under the Firearms Act 1968 which carry a minimum sentence, but the court is of the opinion that there are exceptional circumstances which justify its not imposing the required custodial sentence;
(d)   offences under s 28 of the Violent Crime Reduction Act 2006, which attract a minimum sentence under s 29, but the court is of the opinion that there are exceptional circumstances which justify its not imposing the required custodial sentence.

The power to send (previously commit for trial) youths under the 'grave crime' provisions was formerly exercisable under s 24 of the Magistrates' Courts 1980, and a substantial body of case law arose from challenges to decisions to commit for trial. These authorities continue to have relevance.

The proper approach for the magistrates' court is to ask itself whether it would be proper for the Crown Court sentencing the defendant for the offence of which he is charged to exercise its powers under s 91 of the Powers of Criminal Courts (Sentencing) Act 2000: *R v Inner London Youth Court, ex p DPP* (1996) 161 JP 178, [1996] Crim LR 834. Magistrates should not decline jurisdiction unless the offence and the circumstances surrounding it and the offender are such as to make it 'more than a vague or theoretical possibility', a 'real possibility' or a 'real prospect' that a sentence of at least two years will be imposed: see *R (CPS) v Redbridge Youth Court* [2005] EWHC 1390 (Admin), 169 JP 393.

The Divisional Court has been concerned at the number of inappropriate committals for trial of juveniles who have not attained 15 years and has emphasised that such committals should be rare in *R (on the application of D) v Manchester City Youth Court* [2001] EWHC 860 (Admin), 166 JP 15 and in a number of authorities cited below. In *R (on the application of H) v Southampton Youth Court* [2004] EWHC 2912 (Admin), 169 JP 37, [2005] Crim LR 395 Leveson J, with the approval of the Vice President of the Court of Appeal (Criminal Division) summarised the position for the assistance of magistrates:

'[33] 1. The general policy of the legislature is that those who are under 18 years of age and in particular children under 15 years of age should, wherever possible, be tried in the youth court. It is that court which is best designed to meet their specific needs. A trial in the Crown Court with the inevitably greater formality and greatly increased number of people involved (including a jury and the public) should be reserved for the most serious cases.

[34] 2. It is further policy of the legislature that, generally speaking, first-time offenders aged 12 to 14 and all offenders under 12 should not be detained in custody and decisions as to jurisdiction should have regard to the fact that the exceptional power to detain for grave offences should not be used to water down the general principle. Those under '15 will rarely attract a period of detention and, even more rarely, those who are under 12.

[35] 3. In each case the court should ask itself whether there is a real prospect, having regard to his or her age, that this defendant whose case they are considering might require a sentence of, or in excess of, two years or, alternatively, whether although the sentence might be less than two years, there is some unusual feature of the case which justifies declining jurisdiction, bearing in mind that the absence of a power to impose a detention and training order because the defendant is under 15 is not an unusual feature.'

If, however, the conditions expressly laid down (now for sending) are met, the court must send the accused for trial; the suitability of the Crown Court for the trial of a young person is not a separate consideration to take into account by the youth court in making this decision: R *(on the application of C and D) v Sheffield Youth Court* [2003] EWHC 35 (Admin), 167 JP 159, [2003] 12 LS Gaz R 29 – not following R *(on the application of R) v Balham Youth Court Justices* [2002] EWHC 2426 (Admin), [2002] All ER (D) 73 (Sep) on this point; see also *R v Devizes Youth Court, ex p A* (2000) 164 JP 330.

Previous authorities where detention of less than two years was imposed were generally decided before the advent of detention and training orders and should now be read in this light: *R (M) v Waltham Forest Youth Court and the DPP* [2002] EWHC 1252 (Admin), 166 JP 453, [2002] Crim LR 681. See *R (W) v Southampton Youth Court, R (K) v Wirral Borough Magistrates' Court* [2002] EWHC 1640 (Admin), 166 JP 569, [2002] Crim LR 750 (W 14 years no previous convictions was a 'borderline' case for committal for robbery of a bike using a broken bottle to make threats; K 13 years, should not have been committed for indecent assault on a child aged six). See also *C v Balham Youth Court* [2003] EWHC 1332 (Admin), (2003) 167 JP 525, [2003] Crim LR 636 (committal for trial of a 14-year-old youth charged with robbery who was not a persistent offender quashed); followed in *H v Balham Youth Court* [2003] EWHC Admin 3267, (2004) 168 JP 177. Where, however, an offender under the age of 15, who is ineligible for a detention and training order because he/she is not a 'persistent offender', is sent to the Crown Court there is nothing to prevent the imposition of detention under s 91 of the Powers of Criminal Courts (Sentencing) Act 2000 for a term of less than two years: *R v Q* [2012] EWCA Crim 296, [2012] Crim LR 555.

It had been stated that a magistrates' court dealing with a minor charged with rape should never accept jurisdiction to deal with the case itself, but should invariably commit the case to the Crown Court for trial to ensure that the power under s 91 of the 2000 Act was available: *R v Billam* [1986] 1 All ER 985, 82 Cr App Rep 347; applied in *R v Fareham Youth Court, ex p M* [1999] Crim LR 325, [1999] Crim LR 325, 163 JP 812. However, at the time of that statement rape could not be committed by a person under the age of 14 years, and there may well be cases where is not appropriate to send a defendant charged with rape but aged under 14 to the Crown Court (per Smith LJ in *R (on the application of W) v Brent Youth Court and the Crown Prosecution Service (Interested Party), R (on the application of S) v Enfield Youth Court and the Crown Prosecution Service (Interested Party, R (on the application of B) v Richmond-on-Thames Youth Court and the Crown Prosecution Service (Interested Party)* [2006] EWHC Admin 95, (2006) 170 JP 198.

As to sexual activity with a child family member by an offender aged under

18, see *R v C* [2009] EWCA Crim 2231, [2010] 1 Cr App R (S) 616 (two years' DTO reduced to a supervision order where the appellant, 14, had committed four offences of causing a child under 18 to engage in sexual activity and one offence of attempted rape in relation to his eight-year-old cousin); and *A-G's Reference No 67 of 2009 (DP)* [2009] EWCA Crim 2221, [2010] 1 Cr App R (S) 676 (12 months' DTO not varied where the appellant had committed offences of rape and sexual activity with a family member, his sister, and the offences occurred when he was 14–16 and she was 11–13). In *R v S* [2011] EWCA Crim 1238, [2012] 1 Cr App Rep (S) 67, a youth aged 16 began a sexual relationship with a girl when she was one week short of her 13th birthday. The sexual relationship ended five weeks after she attained 13, when she discovered she was pregnant. The majority of the sexual behaviour (all but two of the 20 acts of sexual intercourse), which the girl admitted to police she had initiated, was not, therefore, rape, and the Court of Appeal accordingly reduced the sentence from six years' detention to two years and three months.

For a case where the Court of Appeal was critical of the decision to commit a 14-year-old to the Crown Court on charges of indecent assault and gross indecency, see *R v B (child) (mode of trial)* [2001] EWCA Crim 194, [2001] 3 FCR 341. See also *R (H, A and O) v Southampton Youth Court* [2004] EWHC 2912 (Admin), 169 JP 37, [2005] 2 Cr App R (S) 30 (committal for trial quashed of three boys under 13 years with no previous convictions for indecent assault on youth of similar age); and *R (on the application of BH (a child)) v Llandudno Youth Court* [2014] EWHC 1833 (Admin), 178 JP 305 (BH then aged 11 faced a single charge of causing or inciting a boy aged under 13 to engage in sexual activity of a non-penetrative nature – committal for trial quashed; the judge had wrongly taken as his starting point the range of sentences that an adult offender might have received).

The offence under s 13 of the Sexual Offences Act 2003 is one for which detention can be imposed under s 91 of the Powers of Criminal Courts (Sentencing) Act 2000, but it is significant that the maximum sentence on indictment for this offence is five years, indicating that there will be a range of sentences for offences against this section some way below the maximum, particularly in the case of young offenders of good character: *R (on the application of G) v Burnley Magistrates' Court* [2007] EWHC 1033 (Admin), (2007) 171 JP 445 (committal for trial quashed).

In *R v North Hampshire Youth Court, ex p DPP* (2000) 164 JP 377, DC, it was held that the justices should have committed for trial a case where two girls, aged 15, were charged with wounding another girl with intent to do her grievous bodily harm. The attack involved repeated kicking to the head and body and also use of a shoe as a weapon, though there was a lack of permanent injury to the aggrieved. See also *A-G's Ref No 48 of 2008* [2008] EWCA Crim 2514, [2009] 2 Cr App R (S) 1, where the sentence was increased from a DTO of 24 months to four years' detention; the offender (15 and of previous good character), stabbed the victim (16) in the leg as he lay defenceless, causing a near fatal injury and leaving the victim with a continuing disability.

In *R v T* [2009] EWCA Crim 1441, [2010] 1 Cr App Rep (S) 347 terms of detention of four, three and two years imposed on young offenders aged, respectively, 16, 15 and 13, were upheld for offences of damaging property being reckless as to whether life would be endangered; the offenders had thrown stones and bricks at vehicles travelling on a busy road and as a result a fatal accident had occurred.

For offences of robberies on buses by large groups of youths involving violence against passengers, see *R v McIntosh* [2011] EWCA Crim 2398, [2012] 1 Cr App Rep (S) 574 (sentences of four years and four-and-a-half years' detention upheld). Courts should nonetheless think long and hard, however, before sentencing young offenders aged 15-17 to sentences exceeding 24 months' detention, and it was inappropriate to do so where a 17-year-old male, with only one previous conviction (for theft), snatched a mobile phone from a 15-year-old male in the street and no violence was used over and above that which was necessary to extract the telephone: *R v H* [2003] 167 JPN 62 (30 months reduced to 18 months). However, a robbery committed at night by a group of youths involving gratuitous violence, including stamping, merits a term substantially in excess of two years: see *A-G's reference (No 98 of 2004)* [2004] EWCA Crim 2311, [2005] 1 Cr App R (S) 125, in which a sentence of 30 months' detention was increased to four years.

The appropriate way to challenge a decision to commit (now send) to the Crown Court for trial is to apply for judicial review and not to apply to the Crown to stay the proceedings as an abuse of process: *R v AH* [2002] EWCA Crim 2938, (2003) 167 JP 30. If the Director of Public Prosecutions is concerned about a decision of a youth court to retain jurisdiction he can either seek judicial review or apply for a voluntary bill of indictment; but the defendant's rights are better safeguarded in judicial review and that is the course which should normally be followed: *R (on the application of DPP) v Camberwell Youth Court* and *R (on the application of H) v Camberwell Youth Court* [2004] EWHC Admin 1805, [2005] 1 All ER 999, [2005] 1 WLR 810, (2005) 169 JP 105, [2005] Crim LR 165.

Plea before venue procedure

E[3.18D] Where the power to send a youth to the Crown Court for trial arises from one of the following cases the youth must be sent forthwith.

(a) it is an offence of homicide, or each of the requirements of s 51A(1) of the Firearms Act 1968 would be satisfied with respect to the offence and the person charged with it if he were convicted of the offence, or s 29(3) of the Violent Crime Reduction Act 2006 (minimum sentences in certain cases of using someone to mind a weapon) would apply if he were convicted of the offence;

(b) notice is given in respect of an either way offence under s 51B (notices in serious or complex fraud cases) or s 51C (notices in certain cases involving children) of the 1998 Act;

(c) the offence is a specified offence within the meaning of s 224 of the Criminal Justice Act 20031 and it appears to the court that if the offender is found guilty of the offence the criteria for a sentence under s 226B of that Act (extended sentence for certain violent or sexual offences) would be met.

In all other cases where the court would be required to determine, in relation to the offence, whether to send the youth to the Crown Court, or to determine any matter the effect of which would be to determine whether the youth is sent for trial, the indication of plea provisions of ss 24A and 24B of the Magistrates' Courts Act 1980 apply.

Procedure where the accused is present

E[3.18E] The procedure is as follows.

(a) The court shall cause the charge to be written down, if this has not already been done, and to be read to the accused.

(b)   The court shall then explain to the accused in ordinary language that he may indicate whether (if the offence were to proceed to trial) he would plead guilty or not guilty, and that if he indicates that he would plead guilty:

    (i)   the court must proceed as mentioned in subsection (d) below; and

    (ii)   in cases where the offence is one mentioned in s 91(1) of the Powers of Criminal Courts (Sentencing) Act 2000) he may be sent to the Crown Court for sentencing under section 3B or (if applicable) 3C of that Act if the court is of such opinion as is mentioned in subsection (2) of the applicable section.

(c)   The court shall then ask the accused whether (if the offence were to proceed to trial) he would plead guilty or not guilty.

(d)   If the accused indicates that he would plead guilty, the court shall proceed as if:

    (i)   the proceedings constituted from the beginning the summary trial of the information; and

    (ii)   s 9(1) above was complied with and he pleaded guilty under it,

    and, accordingly, the court shall not (and shall not be required to) proceed to make the relevant determination or to proceed further under s 51 or (as the case may be) s 51A of the 1998 Act in relation to the offence.

(e)   If the accused indicates that he would plead not guilty, the court shall proceed to make the relevant determination and this section shall cease to apply.

(f)   If the accused in fact fails to indicate how he would plead, for the purposes of this section he shall be taken to indicate that he would plead not guilty.

(g)   Subject to subsection (d) above, the following shall not for any purpose be taken to constitute the taking of a plea:

    (i)   asking the accused under this section whether (if the offence were to proceed to trial) he would plead guilty or not guilty;

    (ii)   an indication by the accused under this section of how he would plead.

Procedure where the youth is absent

E[3.18F] Section 24B of the Magistrates' Courts Act 1980 has effect where the indication of plea provisions of s 24A apply, the youth is represented by a legal representative, and the court considers that by reason of the youth's disorderly conduct before the court it is not practicable for proceedings under s 24A to be conducted in the youth's presence and that it should proceed in the youth's absence. In such a case:

(a)   the court shall cause the charge to be written down, if this has not already been done, and to be read to the representative;

(b)   the court shall ask the representative whether (if the offence were to proceed to trial) the accused would plead guilty or not guilty;

(c)   if the representative indicates that the accused would plead guilty the court shall proceed as if the proceedings constituted from the beginning the summary trial of the information, and as if s 9(1) of the Magistrates' Courts Act 1980 was complied with and the accused pleaded guilty under it;

(d)   if the representative indicates that the accused would plead not guilty the court shall proceed to make the relevant determination and this section shall cease to apply;

(e)   if the representative in fact fails to indicate how the accused would plead, for the purposes of this section he shall be taken to indicate that the accused would plead not guilty;

(f)   subject to (c) above, the following shall not for any purpose be taken to constitute the taking of a plea:

(i)   asking the representative under this section whether (if the offence were to proceed to trial) the accused would plead guilty or not guilty;

(ii)   an indication by the representative under this section of how the accused would plead.

Crown Court sitting as a youth court to deal with summary only matters

E[3.18G]   The following observations were made by Walker J in *R v Iles* [2012] EWCA Crim 1610, (2012) 176 JP 601:

> '3. Second, the complexities are such that there appears to have developed a practice under which the magistrates' courts adjourn summary-only matters, knowing the offender is due to appear at a Crown Court on other matters, and invite the Crown Court to enable the summary cases to be dealt with at the same time by the expedient of arranging for a Circuit Judge to sit as a District Judge. Such a practice has advantages, but there are dangers. Therefore, before this practice is followed, the magistrates' court must carefully consider whether this is in the interests of justice and ensure that there is power to do so. A Crown Court Judge who is invited to deal with two sets of proceedings in this way must decide whether it is appropriate in the light of submissions from both the prosecution and the defence. For this purpose it must be kept firmly in mind that, when sentencing as a District Judge, the sentence is imposed by the magistrates' court, and consideration must be given not only to advantages but also to dangers that may arise because (1) the Judge would, as regards the magistrates' court matters, be limited to the powers of a magistrates' court, powers which must be carefully checked by counsel and the court; and (2) sentences that the Judge imposes when sitting as a magistrates' court would have a different route of appeal from that applicable to sentences imposed by the Judge when sitting in the Crown Court. If the invitation is accepted, then consideration must again be given to these dangers at the stage of deciding what sentence should be imposed by the Judge when sitting as a magistrates' court.'

Committal to the Crown Court for sentence

E[3.18H]–[3.19]   There are three powers of committal for sentence:

(a)   where a guilty plea has been indicated to an offence which is one of those listed in s 91(1) of the PCC(S)A 2000 and the court is of the opinion that the offence, or the combination of the offence and one or more offences associated with it, is such that the sentencing powers of s 91 of the PCC(S)A 2000 should be available: PCC(S)A 2000, s 3B (see E[3.18C]);

(b)   where the offence is a specified offence and the court forms the opinion (subsequent to mode of trial) that the criteria for the imposition of an extended sentence are met (see **E[3.18C]**): PCC(S)A 2000, s 3C; and

(c)   where the offence is one of those listed in s 91(1) of the PCC(S)A 2000, a guilty plea has been indicated and the court has sent the offender for trial for one or more related offences (ie if both the offences were prosecuted in the Crown Court they could be joined in the same indictment): PCC(S)A 2000, s 4A.

Where any of the above powers is used, the court may additionally commit for sentence any other offence under PCC(S)A 2000, s 6.

In case(a) and (b) above the Crown Court has the same sentencing powers as if the offender had just been of the offence on indictment before the court: PCC(S)A 2000, s 5A. In case (c), however, if the court does not state that, in its opinion, it has the power to commit under either (a) or (b), and the offender is not convicted in the Crown Court of the or any of the related offences sent there for trial, the Crown Court's powers of sentencing are limited to those of the youth court: PCC(S)A 2000, ss 4A(4) and (5), 5A(2). Only youth court powers are available for offences committed for sentence under s 6: PCC(S)A 2000, s 7.

Procedure

E[3.20] The court has to consider two general duties, the welfare of the child and the principal aim of the youth justice system to prevent offending by juveniles.

E[3.21] The court must take care to ensure that he understands the proceedings and the charge should be explained in simple terms appropriate to his age and understanding. If not represented, his parents should be allowed to assist him in his defence.

E[3.22] Oath. In the youth court, the evidence of children under 14 years must be given unsworn, otherwise the defendant and all the witnesses use a modified form of oath which commences 'I promise before Almighty God to tell the truth' etc. This oath is also used by a juvenile who gives evidence in the adult court (Children and Young Persons Act 1963, s 28).

Evidence from a witness in need of special protection (a child victim of a violent or sexual offence) will give evidence via a live video link (*R v Camberwell Green Youth Court, ex p G* [2005] UKHL 4, [2005] All ER (D) 259 (Jan)). For vulnerable accused see **D[8.22B]**. For witnesses other than the accused see **D[8.22C]**.

E[3.23] Remission to a local court. Where the court before which a juvenile appears is not the youth court for the area in which he resides it may (and if it is an adult magistrates' court, it must unless it exercises its limited powers of sentence) remit him to be dealt with by his local youth court. This would normally be done, for example, where reports are required and the case has to be adjourned in order to obtain them. The court may give directions as to whether the defendant should be bailed or kept in custody until he appears before the local court.

E[3.24] Remission to the adult court. Where a juvenile attains the age of 18 before conviction or after conviction but before sentencing he may be remitted on bail or in custody to be dealt with in the adult court, but not for an indictable offence (*R (on the application of Denny) v Acton Youth Court* (2004) Independent, 24 May).

E[3.25] Abuse of Process – for general principles consult D[1B.11]–[1B.12].

Abuse of Process – youth incapable of following proceedings. Guidance was given in *DPP v P* [2007] EWHC 946 (Admin) as follows:

(1) Although the youth court had an inherent jurisdiction to stay proceedings as an abuse of the process, the jurisdiction was limited directly to matters affecting the fairness of the trial of the particular defendant concerned, and should only be exercised in exceptional circumstances, on the ground of one or more of the capacity issues, before any evidence was heard.

(2) The fact that a higher authority had previously held that a person was unfit to plead did not make it an abuse to try that person for subsequent criminal acts. The issue of the child's capacity to participate effectively had to be decided afresh.

(3) A child in early adolescence might well develop significantly over a relatively short period. However, where the medical evidence suggested that the child's condition had not changed since his appearance before that higher court, the decisions of that previous court would be relevant matters to be considered, although not determinative or binding.

(4) Medical evidence should be considered as part of the evidence in the case and not as the sole evidence in a [preliminary] application. It was the court's opinion of the child's level of understanding which had to determine whether a trial was to proceed.

(5) Although the medical evidence might be of great importance, it had always to be set in the context of other evidence relating to the child, which might bear upon the issues of his understanding, mental capacity and ability to participate effectively in a trial. Medical evidence on its own might appear quite strong, but when other matters were considered the court might conclude that the defendant's understanding and ability to take part in the trial were greater than was suggested by the doctors and that, with proper assistance from his legal adviser and suitable adjustments to the procedure of the court, the trial could properly proceed to a conclusion.

(6) Other factors might also be relevant to the decision that the court had to take. If a trial began, the court would wish to ensure that the child understood each stage of the process. That might involve some direct exchanges between the bench and the child (engagement). The child's responses might assist the court in deciding the child's level of understanding. Further, it might become apparent from the way in which the trial was conducted that the child's representative did not have adequate instructions on which to cross-examine witnesses.

(7) The court had a duty to keep under continuing review the question of whether the criminal trial ought to continue. If at any stage the court concluded that the child was unable to participate effectively in the trial, it might decide to call a halt. Nevertheless, the court might consider that it was in the best interests of the child that the trial should continue. If the prosecution evidence was weak, there might be no case to answer. It might be that the defendant's representative would invite the court to acquit on the ground that the child did not know that what he had done was seriously wrong: *R (on the application of P) v West London Youth Court* [2005] EWHC 2583 (Admin), [2006] 1 All ER 447 applied.

(8) If the court decided it should call a halt to the criminal trial on the ground that the child could not take an effective part in the proceedings, it should then consider whether to switch to a consid-

eration of whether the child had done the acts alleged. That decision was one for the discretion of the court, but the proceedings should be stayed as an abuse of process before fact finding only if no useful purpose could be served by finding the facts. The court would wish to consider the possibility that it might be appropriate to make a hospital [or guardianship] order, but even if such an order appeared unlikely, there might be other advantages in continuing to complete the fact finding process. If the court found that the child had done the acts alleged, it might be appropriate to alert the local authority to the position with a view to the consideration of care proceedings. If the court found that the child had not done the acts alleged, the proceedings would be brought to an end by a finding of not guilty: *R (on the application of P) v Barking Youth Court* [2002] All ER (D) 93 (Apr) applied.

(9)   It would be right for a court to stay proceedings at the outset if the child was so severely impaired as to be unable to participate in the trial and where there would be no useful purpose in finding the facts.

Vulnerable accused. Where it is said that the accused is vulnerable and may not be able to participate effectively in the proceedings the court should bear in mind that it has the power to direct that the accused can give evidence via a live video link. See D[8.22B].

Abuse of Process – delay. A stay of proceedings even on the grounds of unjustifiable delay will not normally be acceptable in a Youth Court (*R (on the application of DPP) v Croydon Youth Court* (2001) 165 JP 181, 165 JPN 34) but see *R (on the application of Knight) v West Dorset Magistrates' Court* [2002] EWHC 2152 (Admin), 166 JP 705. See I[1B.10]–D[1B.11]–[1B.12].

E[4]

Possible orders for juveniles

E[4.1] See the Process of sentencing at B[5], and also the notes on each type of sentence in the 'Sentencing' section at B[8]–B[47].

E[4.2] In the following list of orders available to courts in dealing with a minor (age 10–17 inclusive), only those marked with an asterisk * may be used by a magistrates' court that is not a youth court: Powers of Criminal Courts (Sentencing) Act 2000, s 8(6).

- *Referral order: Powers of Criminal Courts (Sentencing) Act 2000, s 16;
- *Absolute and conditional discharge: Powers of Criminal Courts (Sentencing) Act 2000, ss 12–15;
- Compensation: Powers of Criminal Courts (Sentencing) Act 2000, ss 130–134;
- Order made under s 1C of the Crime and Disorder Act 1998 (Anti-social Behaviour): Crime and Disorder Act 1998, s 1C;
- *Fine: Powers of Criminal Courts (Sentencing) Act 2000, s 135;
- *Binding over parent or guardian: Powers of Criminal Courts (Sentencing) Act 2000, s 150;
- Reparation order: Powers of Criminal Courts (Sentencing) Act 2000, ss 73–75, Sch 8;
- Attendance centre: Powers of Criminal Courts (Sentencing) Act 2000, ss 60–62, Sch 5;
- Youth rehabilitation order: Criminal Justice and Immigration Act 2008, ss 1–7 and Schs 1–4.
- Detention and training order: Powers of Criminal Courts (Sentencing) Act 2000, s 89;
- Punishment of certain grave crimes (Crown Court only): Powers of Criminal Courts (Sentencing) Act 2000, ss 90, 91;
- Committal for sentence of dangerous young offenders: Powers of Criminal Courts (Sentencing) Act 2000, s 3C.

These disposals are considered in detail in Section B Sentencing, except for punishment of grave crimes and committal for sentence of dangerous offences, which are dealt with in the immediately preceding part of this section.

Before finally disposing of the case or before remitting the case to another court, unless it considers it undesirable to do so, the court shall inform the child or young person and his parent or guardian if present, or any person assisting him in his defence, of the manner in which it proposes to deal with the case, and allow any of those persons so informed to make representations: Criminal Procedure Rules 2013, Pt 44.

Section F
Civil and miscellaneous matters

Property in possession of police

Police (Property) Act 1897

F[1.1] Application for an order for the delivery of property in possession of the police in connection with their investigation of a suspected offence under s 1 of the Act.

Legal notes and definitions

F[1.2] While this proceeding is a civil case of a kind that is more usually dealt with at a county court, nevertheless it can be dealt with at a magistrates' court. Clearly it will be cheaper and more expeditious if a magistrates' court deals with the matter fairly soon after the hearing of a criminal charge, thus saving a hearing in the county court or High Court. Sufficient notice of the date of hearing should be given to each claimant of the property to enable him to prepare for the hearing before the magistrates.

F[1.3] **When applicable.** This procedure applies when the police have in their possession property which has come into their hands during investigation into a suspected offence. It is not necessary that the person has been charged with any offence.

The powers of the executive to seize and retain goods were carefully circumscribed both at common law and by statute. As a matter of principle the police must not keep an article, or prevent its removal, for any longer than is reasonably necessary to complete their investigations or preserve it for evidence. If a copy will suffice, it should be made and the original returned. As soon as the case is over, or it is decided not to go on with it, the article should be returned. The terms of s 22(2)–(4) of PACE were directed to the retention of the article for use as evidence at trial or for investigation in connection with an offence. There was nothing in s 22 which suggested that the power of retention can be for any purpose other than a purpose for which it was originally seized: *Chief Constable of Merseyside Police v Owens* [2012] EWHC 1515 (Admin), 176 JP 688, 176 CL&J 353).

F[1.4] Often there is no such difficulty as stolen property can be restored direct to the rightful owner. In other cases where the defendant has been convicted for several offences eg theft, at the end of the case the police may be in possession of a large sum of money taken from the defendant. The various losers may each claim part or all of this money as being stolen from them or arising from the sale by the thief of the stolen property.

F[1.5] The police, any claimant or even the defendant can lay a complaint or make an application asking the magistrates to decide the ownership of property and/or to whom the property should be delivered.

F[1.6] At the hearing the police or a claimant has the right to call witnesses, cross-examine the other party's witnesses and to address the magistrates. The hearing can be expedited by the filing of written evidence which can include hearsay evidence.

F[1.7] Powers of the magistrates. Having heard all the parties the magistrates may make an order for delivery of the property to the person who appears to the court to be the owner or if he cannot be ascertained they may make such order as they think fit. The court could only decline to return the property to its owner where it was satisfied that the use of its process would in fact indirectly assist in or encourage a crime: *Chief Constable of Merseyside Police v Owens* [2012] EWHC 1515 (Admin), 176 JP 688, 176 CL&J 353).

F[1.8] This gives the magistrates wide powers of discretion. If, for instance, the magistrates are not impressed by any of the claims then they can order the money or the monies the police obtain from selling the stolen property (eg a stolen motor vehicle) to be paid to the Police Property Act Fund which is administered by the Police Authority. The money is invested and the income is used (a) to defray the expenses in handling and storing such property; (b) for compensating the persons who deliver such property to the police; (c) for charitable purposes.

F[1.9] If there are several claimants, magistrates might find in favour of one claimant and order his claim to be paid and find against the other claimants and then order the balance of the money to be delivered to the fund.

F[1.10]–[1.16] Deliver. It is to be noted that the word used in disposing of the property is 'delivered'. This means that an unsuccessful claimant can sue in the county court the authority or person to whom the magistrates order delivery, but must do so within six months from the date of the hearing, or his/her right ceases.

F[1.17] Case unsuitable for magistrates' courts. The High Court has ruled that magistrates should hesitate to deal with a claim of a similar kind if the value of the property is substantial or if difficult matters of law are likely to arise. For example, a motor car which was stolen whilst subject to a hire-purchase agreement led to there being several claimants. See *Gough v Chief Constable of West Midlands* [2004] EWCA Civ 206, [2004] All ER (D) 45 (Mar) for the interaction with civil proceedings.

F[1.18] If the magistrates decide that if either of the above points arise the best course is to adjourn the hearing *sine die* and to invite the claimant or claimants to commence proceedings in the county court or the High Court. Alternatively, the magistrates can decline to exercise their jurisdiction. A magistrates' court is not obliged to make an order.

F[1.19] Criminal Damage Act 1971. The above provisions also apply if the police have possession of property following the execution of a search warrant granted under the Criminal Damage Act 1971, s 6.

F[1.20] Costs. Proceedings should be commenced by way of complaint because in magistrates' courts there is no power to award costs where proceedings have been commenced by way of "application" (see for example, *R v Salisbury and Tisbury and Mere Combined Juvenile Court, ex p Ball* (1985) 149 JP 346. Where proceedings have begun by way of a complaint it is inappropriate to order costs against the police where they do not object to the order sought (*R v Uxbridge Justices, ex p Metropolitan Police Comr* [1981] 1 All ER 940, [1981] 1 WLR 112; affd [1981] QB 829, [1981] 3 All ER 129, CA).

Modification of the 1897 Act following the making of a deprivation order

F[1.21] Section 144(1) of the Powers of Criminal Courts (Sentencing) Act 2000 provides that:

(a)   no application shall be made under s 1(1) of the 1897 Act by any claimant of the property after the end of six months from the date on which the order in respect of the property was made under s 143 above; and

(b)   no such application shall succeed unless the claimant satisfies the court either:

    (i)   that he had not consented to the offender having possession of the property; or

    (ii)   where an order is made under subsection (1) of s 143 (property used for the purpose of committing, etc, an offence) above, that he did not know, and had no reason to suspect, that the property was likely to be used for the purpose mentioned in that subsection.

In *O'Leary International Ltd v Chief Constable of North Wales Police and Crown Prosecution Service (interested party)* [2012] EWHC 1516 (Admin), 176 JP 514, 176 CL&J 370, the appellant company owned a fleet of lorries. As a result of offences committed by drivers employed by the company four lorries and trailers were seized by the police, and in subsequent criminal proceedings against the drivers, deprivation orders were made under s 143. The company sought the return of the lorries and trailers under s 1(1) of the Police (property) Act 1897, but, applying s 144(1)(b), and despite the substantial loss to the company, the magistrates' court declined to order the return of the vehicles to the company. On appeal by way of case stated the view was expressed that the orders under s 143 would probably not have been made if the attention of the magistrates had been drawn to the relevant case law (which is set out in para 14 of the judgment). Since, however, the Divisional Court had no power to set those orders aside in the current appeal their Lordships had to proceed on the basis that the orders were extant.

It was held that s 144 did not provide exclusive statutory machinery for the owner to recover the goods. The appellant retained the full rights of the true owner, including the right to possession. The orders provided no defence to the police to that right, unless there was a public policy defence, the continued availability of which had been considered in *Chief Constable of Merseyside Police v Owens* [2012] EWHC 1515 (Admin), 176 JP 688, 176 CL&J 353. No such defence could have advanced by the police and the Court ordered the return of the lorries.

Though this disposed of the appeal, the Court proceeded to consider whether s 144 should be 'read down' by adding as a ground for return that 'deprivation would be disproportionate' (which was factually conceded). Case law concerning art 1 of the First Protocol to the ECHR was considered. It was held that it would be disproportionate for a court to have no power to consider the value of the property, the degree of culpability of the owner and the financial effect on the owner of deprivation of his goods. In considering whether or not to make an order of deprivation against the offender the court was entitled to take into account the value of the goods and the financial effect on the offender. It was, therefore, necessary to 'read down' s 144(1)(b), so that it contained the additional exception 'or (iii) deprivation would be disproportionate'.

Liquor licensing

Appeals under the Licensing Act 2003

Background

F[2.1] The Licensing Act 2003 makes provision for the grant of both personal and premises licences by local authorities.

F[2.2] A personal licence is granted under section 111 to an individual and authorises that person to supply alcohol for a period of ten years.

NB: The Licensing Act 2003 (Premises licences and club premises certificates) (Amendment) Regulations 2012 (SI 2012/955) came into force on 25 April 2012. These Regulations amend the Licensing Act 2003 (Premises licences and club premises certificates) Regulations 2005 to give effect to certain amendments made to the Licensing Act 2003 by the Police Reform and Social Responsibility Act 2011. For example, the category of 'interested party' is removed from the 2003 Act to enable any person to participate in the various processes set out in that Act, regardless of their physical proximity to the premises concerned. Moreover, the Secretary of State must by regulations require licensing authorities to advertise certain applications in a prescribed form and in a prescribed manner which is likely to bring the application to the attention of persons likely to be affected by it.

F[2.3] A premises licence under section 11 and may be granted in respect of any premises and authorises the premises to be used for one or more licensable activities.

F[2.4] The licensable activities are defined in section 1 as,

(a)   sale by retail of alcohol
(b)   supply of alcohol by club
(c)   provision of regulated entertainment and
(d)   provision of late-night refreshment.

F[2.5] The local authority will determine the application or licence under section 120 and must grant where the applicant is 18 all over, possesses a described licensing qualification, has not forfeited his personal licence within the previous five-year period nor been convicted of any relevant offence. In the case of the first three criteria the local authority must reject the application where they are not met.

Appeals

F[2.6] In respect of any of the local authority's functions outlined above or variation or imposition of conditions the applicant has a right to appeal to a magistrates' court. Schedule 5 of the Licensing Act 2003 set out in detail the decisions against which an appeal from the local authority may be made.

F[2.7]–[2.11] When the appellant considers the local authorities licensing policy to be incompatible or 'ultra vires' the provisions of the statute, an appeal to the High Court by way of judicial review may be appropriate

Notices

F[2.12] An appeal is commenced by way of written notice being given to a magistrates' court, in the case of a personal licence to the court for the area in which the local authority concerned is situated and in the case of a premises licence, the magistrates' court for the area in which premises are situated.

Period of notice

F[2.13] Notice of appeal must be lodged within the period of 21 days beginning with the date on which the appellant is notified of the local authority's decision. It is the appellant's responsibility to serve notice on all respondents and prove to the court that such notice has been given.

The hearing

F[2.14] Whilst any justice of a local magistrates' court may hear and determine an appeal most courts will have appointed an appeals panel in accordance with guidance issued by the Justices' Clerk's Society. In potentially complex appeals the court may hold a pre-hearing review to identify the issues, the numbers of witnesses and a time estimate for the hearing together with other preliminary matters. At such a hearing the justices may make directions regarding disclosure by the parties to each other (*Rushmoor Borough Council v Richards* (1996) 160 LG Rev 460). The proceedings are civil proceedings and therefore hearsay evidence may be admitted. To shorten proceedings justices or their legal adviser may give directions as to the conduct of the case – including the filing of evidence and any skeleton legal arguments.

F[2.15] The court's powers (section 181). On hearing the application the court may:

(i)   dismiss the appeal; or
(ii)   uphold the appeal and make any other decision which could have been made by the licensing authority; or
(iii)   remit the case to the licensing authority to dispose of in accordance with the direction of the court, if, for example, the local authority has simply failed to process an application.

Procedure

F[2.16] The appellant's case may be presented in person or by a representative qualified under the provisions of the Courts and Legal Services Act 1990. The appeal is by way of a rehearing on the merits of the case and is neither a review of the local authority's decision nor an appeal on a point of law. The court is, therefore, able to hear all the evidence that was before the local authority committee and any relevant evidence, which has arisen subsequent to the local authority's decision.

Order of speeches

F[2.17] As the appeal is commenced by way of a complaint the order of proceedings is governed by the Magistrates' Courts Rules 1981 (rule 14). This means that the appellant will open the case and call evidence in support of the appeal. Any respondent will be permitted to cross-examine witnesses called by the appellant and the appellant may re-examine any of those witnesses.

F[2.18] Subject to any questions the justices may have, at the end of the appellant's case the respondent will outline his case and call witnesses in support. Such witnesses may be cross-examined and re-examined and the respondent may make a closing speech leaving the appellant with the final address to the court.

The Magistrates' Courts Rules 1981, r 34 provides that where a statutory appeal lies to a magistrates' court against a decision of a local authority the appeal shall be made by way of complaint, the procedure for which involves calling evidence. Such an appeal takes the form of a fresh hearing at which the parties are free to adduce whatever evidence they think fit, subject to the control of the court. Section 181(2)(b) does not restrict the evidence which may be laid before the justices but simply makes clear that the justices have the power to make any order of the kind that the licensing authority could have made, without saying anything about the grounds on which such an order might be made. The justices' function is to consider the application by reference to the statutory licensing objectives untrammelled by any of the regulations that govern the procedure for a review under s 51. The justices are therefore entitled to consider evidence of events occurring before the application to the licensing authority as well as evidence of events occurring since its decision. Whilst it is right that a person whose licence is under threat ought to have notice of the nature of the case against him so that he has a fair chance of meeting it, this can be achieved without limiting the hearing before the magistrates to the allegations that were made before the licensing authority. The magistrates, therefore, are not limited to considering only those grounds of complaint that were raised in the notice of application or the representations before the licensing authority: *R (on the application of Khan) v Coventry Magistrates' Court* [2011] EWCA Civ 751.

The decision

F[2.19] In *R (on the application of Raphael trading as Orleans) v Highbury Corner Magistrates Court* [2011] EWCA Civ 462, the Court of Appeal decided that at a Licensing Committee's meeting, a resolution was passed establishing and empowering sub-committees for the future discharge of licensing functions. That resolution was passed after ss 7 and 10 of the Licensing Act 2003 came into force. Accordingly, the sub-committee had jurisdiction to amend the conditions of the appellant's nightclub licence and the justices (on appeal from the local authority) had been correct to reject that ground of appeal.

The court will have regard to the licensing authority's statement of licensing policy and any guidance issued by the Secretary of State under s 182 of the Act. The court will also make its decision with the aim of promoting the licensing objectives set out in the Act namely:

(i)   the prevention of crime and disorder,
(ii)   public safety,
(iii)   the prevention of public nuisance, and
(iv)   the protection of children from harm.

The court will give reasons for its decision and if the court departs from either the statutory guidance or the licensing statement it will give reasons for doing so. Justices hearing an appeal should not consider or engage in planning matters which fell properly within the jurisdiction of the licensing authority (*R (on the application of Blackwood) v Birmingham Magistrates' Court* [2006] All ER (D) 324 (Jun)). Except in the case of a closure order there is no further statutory entitlement to appeal the decision of the magistrates' court.

For more up to date guidance on the relevance of the Licensing Act's objectives when justices are hearing an appeal see (*R (on the application of Daniel Thwaites plc) v Wirral Borough Magistrates' Court* [2008] EWHC 838 (Admin), 172 JP 301).

When dealing with an appeal against a decision of a local licensing authority, the magistrates' court had to pay careful attention to the licensing committee's reasons and exercise its own judgement as to how much weight to accord to them. The fuller and clearer the reasons, the more force they were likely to carry. The appellant bore the burden of persuading the appellate court that the committee ought to have exercised its discretion differently, rather than the court being required to exercise the discretion afresh: *Stepney Borough Council v Joffe* [1949] 1 KB 599, [1949] 1 All ER 256, DC considered; *Sagnata Investments Ltd v Norwich Corporation* [1971] 2 QB 614, [1971] 2 All ER 1441, CA applied: *R (on the application of Hope and Glory Public House) v City of Westminster Magistrates' Court (Lord Mayor and Citizens of the City of Westminster, interested party)* [2011] EWCA Civ 31, [2011] 3 All ER 579, [2011] PTSR 868.

In *R (on the application of Developing Retail Ltd) v East Hampshire Magistrates' Court* [2011] EWHC 618 (Admin), on an appeal against the grant of a provisional premises licence, in accordance with s 29 of the LA 2003, the justices had sought to impose two conditions. Analogous to bail conditions, the High Court stressed the need for conditions to be clear, precise and enforceable.

The first condition modified an original condition to ensure that an external seating area was vacated by customers at 11pm. That condition was directed at late night noise emanating from the premises. The justices added to the condition by including a balcony on the premises. It was held that the justices had been entitled to regard the condition as preventative rather than reactive like the regulatory conditions preventing noise. The condition was clear and proportionate and was tailored to the activities intended to take place at the premises.

However, the justices had imposed a second condition, namely that all noise from regulated entertainment at the premises should be inaudible one metre outside any noise sensitive premises. Although a condition was justified by reference to a decibel level to protect local residents, the condition was quashed and the matter remitted to the justices to consider an alternative condition. The original condition was so vague as to be unenforceable. There was no clarity as to the premises or location intended to be protected and the meaning of 'inaudible', in that context, was unclear.

Costs

F[2.20] The court may make such order for costs as it thinks fit under s 181 of the Licensing Act 2003. Case law such as *Bradford Metropolitan District Council v Booth* (2002) suggests that public authorities need to be able to make honest, reasonable and sound administrative decisions in the public interest without fear of exposure to undue financial prejudice if they are successfully appealed.

In *Crawley Borough Council v Attenborough* [2006] EWHC 1278 (Admin), (2006) 170 JP 593, the justices varied conditions imposed by the Borough Council in relation to licensed premises run by the respondent. The justices ordered the local authority to pay all of the costs of the respondent. On appeal it was agreed that there was no practical distinction between the terms of s 64 of the MCA 1980 (civil proceedings) and s 181 of the Licensing Act 2003. The Divisional Court upheld the justices' decision to award costs having regard to the fact that they had considered all of the circumstances including the facts and the history of the case and bearing in mind the order was varied on appeal by the justices.

Just over one week later, in *Cambridge City Council v Alex Nestling Ltd* [2006] EWHC 1374 (Admin), (2006) 170 JP 539, 170 JPN 975 it was decided that although as a matter of strict law the power of the appellate court in such circumstances to award costs is not confined to cases where the local authority acted unreasonably or in bad faith, the fact that the local authority has acted reasonably and in good faith in the discharge of its public function is plainly a most important factor. In ordinary civil litigation the principle that costs follow the event does not apply in this type of case. Therefore, an award of costs should not routinely follow in favour of a successful appellant in this type of case, if anything, quite the contrary.

It is submitted that if there is a perceived conflict between the two authorities above, there was fuller argument in the latter case and therefore the approach adopted in *Alex Nesting Ltd* is to be preferred.

Note that the principles outlined in *Bradford Metropolitan District Council v Booth* above, apply equally to costs sought in forfeiture proceedings brought under s 298(2) of the Proceeds of Crime Act 2002. See F[5.47].

Closure Orders: police powers

F[2.21] Power. On licensed premises only

- closure for a period not exceeding 24 hours
- no entry to members of the public during closure
- purchases or supplies prohibited during closure
- contravention without reasonable excuse is liable to a fine not exceeding £20,000 or to imprisonment for a term not exceeding 3 months, or to both.

F[2.22] Grounds. Requires authorisation by a senior police officer who believes that:

- likely to be disorder in or near premises and that closure is necessary in the interests of public safety, or
- disorder already taking place and that closure is necessary in the interests of public safety, or
- public nuisance is being caused by noise from the premises and that closure is necessary to prevent nuisance.

F[2.23] Duration.

- up to 24 hours (notice must be given in writing);
- may be cancelled by police at any time after the order has been made (notice must be given in writing);
- order may be extended by responsible senior police officer if he/she believes grounds continue to apply and that magistrates will not have considered the order by end of closure period;

- no such extension shall come into force unless notice is given by end of previous closure period.

F[2.24] Consideration hearing by magistrates (ss 164–165).

- as soon as reasonably practicable (must have written notice);
- must be in 'open court';
- powers may be exercised by a magistrates' court (which can be exercised by a single justice);
- evidence given must be on oath.

F[2.25] Powers. The court may:

- revoke the order and any extension of it if the order or extension is still in force; or
- order the relevant premises to remain, or to be, closed until the matter is dealt with by the licensing authority. In considering whether to exercise this power the magistrates will have regard to s 161 in determining whether the grounds for making the order are continuing, or are likely to continue;
- order the premises to remain or be closed until dealt with by the licensing authority under s 167 but subject to specified exceptions;
- order the premises to remain or be closed until determination by the licensing authority unless conditions specified in the order are satisfied.

F[2.26] Appeal from the Justices. Any person aggrieved by the decision of the magistrates may appeal to the Crown Court (Licensing Act 2003, s 166).

F[2.27] Closure notices for persistently selling alcohol to children under s 147A Licensing Act 2003.

Power. Applies to any premises:

- prohibition for a period not exceeding 48 hours of sales of alcohol;
- offers the opportunity to discharge all criminal liability.

For more detail see s 169A of the Licensing Act 2003 as added by s 24 of the Violent Crime Reduction Act 2006. This legislation came into force on 6 April 2007.

The Licensing Act 2003 (Persistent Selling of Alcohol to Children) (Prescribed Form of Closure Notice) Regulations 2012 (SI 2012/963) came into force on 25 April 2012.

These Regulations revoke the Licensing Act 2003 (Persistent Selling of Alcohol to Children) (Prescribed Form of Closure Notice) Regulations 2007 and prescribe the form of a closure notice given under s 169A of the Licensing Act 2003 ('the 2003 Act') to give effect to certain amendments made to that Act by the Police Reform and Social Responsibility Act 2011.

A closure notice represents an alternative to prosecution under s 147A of the 2003 Act for the offence of persistently selling alcohol to children. The offence may be committed by the holder of a premises licence if on two or more occasions within three consecutive months alcohol is sold unlawfully to an individual aged under 18 on the premises to which the licence relates.

Previously, the effect of a closure notice was that alcohol sales at the licensed premises to which it relates could be prohibited for a period of up to 48 hours. Following the amendment to the 2003 Act, a closure notice may prohibit alcohol sales from the premises to which it relates for a period of between 48 and 336 hours. These Regulations prescribe the form of a closure notice which contains reference to the period for which premises may be prohibited from making sales of alcohol in accordance with the amendment to the 2003 Act.

Offence of fraudulently receiving programmes
(Copyright, Designs and Patents Act 1988, s 297)

F[2.28] Prosecution of designated premises supervisors and premises licence holders. The Federation Against Copyright Theft is engaged in the private prosecution of designated premises supervisors and premises licence holders throughout England and Wales for offences contrary to s 297(1). This is a relevant offence for *personal licence holders* as defined by Sch 4 to the Licensing Act 2003 and magistrates have certain powers and obligations when dealing with personal licence holders, namely:

•   The requirement for a personal licence holder to produce his licence on his first appearance in court (s 128(1)).
•   The power to order forfeiture or suspension of the personal licence (s 129).
•   The notification of a conviction for a relevant offence to the licensing authority that issued the personal licence (s 131(2)(a)).

Betting and gaming licensing

Gambling Act 2005

F[3.1] The Gambling Act 2005 contains a new regulatory system to govern the provision of all forms of gambling in Great Britain, other than the National lottery and spread betting. From **1 September 2007** the Act repealed the Betting, Gaming and Lotteries Act 1963, the Gaming Act 1968 and the Lotteries and Amusements Act 1976 respectively (see the Gambling Act 2005 (Commencement No 6 and Transitional) Provisions Order 2006 (2006/3272) (C119) as modified by several amending orders.

The following is a brief summary of the changes in procedure and jurisdiction.

General changes

F[3.2] The following general changes have been made:

* Creation of a Gambling Commission.
* A two-tier jurisdiction with local authorities dealing with premises.
* The Act removes all responsibility from licensing, betting and gaming justices for granting betting and gaming permissions, which they exercised previously.
* Decisions of the licensing authority, ie the relevant local authority, may be the subject of an appeal to the local magistrates' court. Decisions of the Gambling Commission may be the subject of an appeal to the Gambling Appeals Tribunal (but not a magistrates' court).

Appeals under the Gambling Act 2005 from local authorities

Background

F[3.3] Operating and personal licences fall under the jurisdiction of the Gambling Commission by virtue of Part 7 (s 140 onwards) of the Gambling Act 2005. Appeals lie to the Gambling Appeal Tribunal.

Premises licences fall under the licensing authority's jurisdiction ie the relevant local authority under Part 8 (s 153 onwards).

Appeals in respect of premises licences are governed by ss 206 and 207 of the Gambling Act 2005.

Appeals

F[3.4] Section 206 stipulates who is entitled to appeal.

Section 207 states that an appeal under s 206 in relation to premises must be instituted:

(a)   in the magistrates' court for a local justice area in which the premises are wholly or mainly situated

(b)   by notice of appeal given to the designated officer; and

(c) within the period of 21 days beginning with the day on which the appellant receives notice of the decision against which the appeal is brought (**NB**: there does not appear to be a power to extend the 21 day period);

(d) a fee will be payable to the magistrates' court hearing the appeal.

Section 207 prescribes who the respondent is.

Section 207(3) states that on hearing the appeal the **magistrates may**:

(a) dismiss the appeal;

(b) substitute for the decision appealed against any decision that the licensing authority could have made;

(c) remit the case to the local authority to decide in accordance with the direction of the court;

(d) make an order about costs.

Section 208 permits a stay of the order pending appeal.

There is no appeal from the decision of the magistrates' court to the Crown Court. An aggrieved party may appeal on a point of law to the High Court.

NB: As these are essentially civil proceedings, the hearing, procedure, order of speeches and the discretion to award costs are to all intents and purposes the same as in licensing appeals, see F[2] above.

Council tax

Background

F[4.1] The administration and enforcement of the council tax is regulated by the Council Tax (Administration and Enforcement) Regulations 1992.

Recovery and enforcement

F[4.2] The first action the courts are involved in is the issue of a summons by a single justice or a justices' clerk against the alleged debtor following a complaint by a local authority of non-payment. Section 127(1) of the Magistrates' Courts Act 1980 (time limit for instituting proceedings) is disapplied by the regulations; the application may be made up to six years from the date that the sum became due, which is the date when the demand was served and not when the amount of tax was set by the billing authority: *Regentford Ltd v Thanet District Council* [2004] EWHC 246 (Admin), [2004] RA 113, [2004] 11 LS Gaz R 35. Prior to this the local authority will have served a demand notice on the liable person and when payment has not been forthcoming the authority must serve a reminder notice. If payment is not made within seven days of the issue of the reminder notice the whole amount outstanding becomes due after a further seven-day period. The final step the local authority takes before making a complaint for a liability order is the issue of a final notice. Such notice will state the sum outstanding and the amount of any costs reasonably incurred in obtaining the liability order. The court will fix a date when the applications for the liability order will be heard.

F[4.3] A summons may be served on a person by delivering it to him; leaving it in his usual or last known place of abode; sending it to him by post to that address or leaving it or sending it by post to an address given by the person as an address at which the service of the summons will be accepted (eg a solicitor's office). In the case of a company service can be effected at the company's registered office.

The court hearing

F[4.4] The court hearing is conducted as a complaint and the complainant council may make out their case for a liability order on the balance of probabilities, whether or not the non-payer appears in court. In order to be successful the council must satisfy the court that:

(a) council tax has been set by resolution of the authority;
(b) a sum due has been demanded in accordance with the regulations as set out above; and
(c) a summons has been served.

F[4.5] It follows that if the amount has not been demanded in accordance with the regulations or has been duly paid then this will amount to a defence.

F[4.6] Reopening

It is noteworthy that the power to reopen and rehear a case under s 142 of the Magistrates' Courts Act 1980 does not apply to this type of civil proceedings (*R (on the application of Mathialagan) v Southwark London Borough Council* [2004] EWCA Civ 1689, [2004] All ER (D) 179 (Dec)).

Nor can the power be used when a case has been dismissed (*Verderers of the New Forest v Young* [2004] EWHC 2954 (Admin), [2004] All ER (D) 14 (Dec)). However, reg 36A of the Council Tax (Administration and Enforcement) Regulations 1992 permits a liability order to be rescinded on the application of the local authority; further, there does appear to be a limited power to review civil orders in exceptional circumstances: see case law under B[7.5].

Evidential requirements

F[4.7] Much of the evidence may be produced by way of certificate, for example, a certified copy signed by the appropriate officer showing the council's resolution setting the amount of the council tax for the given local authority area. In addition:

(a) computer generated documents are admissible under the Civil Evidence Act 1995 so long as the document constitutes or forms part of a record compiled by the authority;

(b) direct oral evidence of any facts stated would have been admissible; and

(c) where the document has been produced by a computer it is accompanied by a certificate which:

    (i) must identify the document and the computer by which it was produced;

    (ii) give appropriate explanations to the contents of the document; and

    (iii) be signed by a person occupying a responsible position in relation to the operation of the computer.

F[4.8] The only legitimate defences against the making of the liability order are outlined above and such matters as pending appeals at the valuation tribunal as to the correct banding, or disputes as to the amount owed, will not amount to a reason for the court to decline to issue a liability order. The justices are obliged to prevent the claimant from putting forward irrelevant matters such as whether the defendant should have received council tax benefit (*R (on application of Williams) v Pontefract Magistrates' Court* [2002] All ER (D) 465 (May)).

The liability order

F[4.9] Where magistrates are satisfied that the local authority has made out its case then they have no further discretion but to issue a liability order. This order will include an order for reasonable costs. A liability order gives the local authority the power to take enforcement action such as an attachment of earnings order, distress or deductions from income support. Matters which may be raised at a valuation tribunal are not relevant in liability order proceedings.

Committal proceedings

F[4.10] Following the failure of liability or other enforcement methods the local authority may apply to the court for a means inquiry to be held with a view to a committal to prison in default of payment of the outstanding council tax. A warrant of commitment may only be applied for if the local authority has first attempted to levy distress and have received a report that the bailiffs were unable to find sufficient goods on which to levy the amount outstanding. In order to secure the debtor's attendance the court may issue a summons or a warrant for his arrest. At the committal hearing the court will inquire into the defaulter's means and may impose a period of three months maximum to be served in imprisonment where they are satisfied that failure to pay is due to the person's wilful refusal or culpable neglect. Justices using this power should be satisfied of the criteria on a criminal standard of proof or a high civil standard (*R v South Tyneside Justices, ex p Martin* (1995) Independent, 20 September). The defaulter must be present before the court and although local authorities are not under a statutory obligation to exhaust all other remedies before making an application for committal, it may well be advisable for them to do so. Courts will therefore be keen to see such action being tried as clearer evidence that the defendant is culpable in his neglect to pay and not just unable to pay through impecuniosity or mismanagement.

F[4.11] When dealing with a committal application then the magistrates may:

(a) issue a warrant for commitment;
(b) fix a term of imprisonment and postpone the issue of the warrant until such time and on such conditions as the court thinks fit; note that where a warrant is issued after postponement and, since the term of imprisonment was fixed, part-payments have been made, these payments will reduce the imprisonment in a proportion to the full amount outstanding;
(c) adjourn the application;
(d) dismiss the application;
(e) remit all or part of the sum owing. As a guideline payments should be able to be made within a three-year period (*R (on the application of Broadhurst) v Sheffield Justices* (2000) 164 JP 870). Previous case law points to the fact that, as with rates enforcement, this may only be appropriate if the debtor cannot afford to pay; remission remains an option only up to the point at which a term of imprisonment has been fixed (*Harrogate Borough Council v Barker* (1995) 159 LG Rev 889, 159 JP 809);
(f) theoretically the court might find wilful refusal or culpable neglect but not issue a commitment warrant as the matter does rest within its discretion: once a warrant of commitment has been issued or a term of imprisonment fixed, a charging authority may not take further steps to recover the debt under the liability order (Council Tax (Administration and Enforcement) Regulations 1992, reg 52).

F[4.12] The Council Tax (Administration and Enforcement) Regulations 1992, regulation 47(2) makes it clear that on an application for commitment to prison being made the court shall, in the debtor's presence, inquire into his means and inquire whether the failure to pay which has led to *the application* is due to his wilful refusal or culpable neglect. In other words, the court's inquiries concern the period of time after the issue of the liability order but before the application for a commitment to prison. This in fact makes it even more important that local authorities pursue all available options to them under the authority's liability order before coming into court to ask for a commitment warrant to be issued.

There must be a separate enquiry by the magistrates into the circumstances relevant under reg 47 of the Council Tax (Administration and Enforcement)

Regulations 1992, SI 1992/613, for each of the separate years of liability. Otherwise this will be fatal to the decision of the magistrates: *R v Leeds Justices, ex p Kennett* [1996] RVR 53.

In *R (on the application of Aldous) v Dartford Magistrates' Court* [2011] EWHC 1919 (Admin), it was held that the form of enquiry as to means was hopelessly inadequate and did not meet the requirements of reg 47. The claimant was invited to fill in a standard means form, but it was deficient in terms of discovering how the claimant could meet her liability for payment in excess of £7,000. There did not appear to have been anything like an adequate number of questions posed to discover what the claimant's means were. Accordingly, there was nothing which could properly be called an enquiry. Further, the period of any imprisonment imposed under reg 47(3) must vary according to the culpability of the person in question. It was less serious to fail to pay rates through culpable neglect rather than through wilful refusal. In order to fix the amount of any term of committal it was necessary to determine whether it was due to wilful refusal or culpable neglect which had led to the failure to pay. The magistrates in the present case failed to distinguish between the two statutory criteria and failed to make a finding which was a necessary precondition to fixing a term of imprisonment in default: *R v Highbury Corner Magistrates' Court, ex p Uchendu* (1994) 158 LGR 481, [1994] RA 51, (1994) 158 JP 409 considered.

F[4.13] Although the council may only deduct 5% of debtors' benefit payments direct from income support a magistrates' court may order a payment in excess of this figure in appropriate circumstances (*R v Felixstowe, Ipswich and Woodbridge Magistrates' Court and Ipswich Borough Council, ex p Herridge* [1993] RA 83, 158 JP 307).

Suspended commitments

F[4.14] Where a commitment to prison is issued but postponed on terms it appears that the court must hold a further inquiry before the commitment warrant is issued to take the defaulter to prison. This was considered in *R v Faversham and Sittingbourne Justices, ex p Ursell* [1992] RA 99, 156 JP 765. The court considered that a further inquiry into a commitment warrant postponed on terms was necessary before that warrant could be issued. This was a further opportunity to enable the court to be satisfied that the conditions had not been met by the debtor as well as giving the debtor a further opportunity to explain his default.

F[4.15] The role of a defaulter was considered in *R v Wolverhampton Stipendiary Magistrate, ex p Mould* (1992) Times, 16 November. This was a case under the community charge legislation. The role of the defaulter was defined as going beyond the mere giving of evidence. He could also:

(a) challenge the evidence given by the charging authority as to indebtedness and any steps to levy distress;
(b) challenge the information given about his means;
(c) submit that failure to pay was not due to wilful refusal or culpable neglect; and
(d) even if it was, that a warrant of commitment postponed on suitable conditions was to be preferred to immediate custody.

F[4.16] Where the defaulter fails to attend the magistrates must be satisfied that he has received notice of the hearing and must carry out an appropriate inquiry to make sure that the notice must have come into his hands. Accordingly the notice should be sent by recorded delivery: see *R v Newcastle upon Tyne Justices, ex p Devine* (1998) 162 JP 602, DC (a case decided under the similarly worded reg 41 of the Community Charge (Administration and Enforcement) Regulations 1989, SI 1989/712).

F[4.17] A number of cases have emphasised that before committing a debtor to prison the court must have considered all available alternatives to attempt recovery of the sum due (*R v Newcastle under Lyme Justices, ex p Massey* [1995] 1 All ER 120, 158 JP 1037, [1994] NLJR 1444, sub nom R v Stoke-on-Trent Justices, ex p Knight [1994] 1 WLR 1684).

Applications to a justice

Warrants to enter premises

1 The applicant

F[5.1] Usually such applications are made by a police officer. If not, the magistrate should check whether any authority is needed by the applicant, eg in the case of an official from a supplier of Gas or Electricity (see F[5.31]). As a sensible precaution, a police officer should be asked to produce his warrant card, and anyone else evidence of his identity, and where appropriate, his authority to bring proceedings.

The obligation on an applicant is the same as that imposed on any person making a 'without notice' application, namely one of full and frank disclosure. The applicant should, for example, disclose that a private prosecution is expected to follow the issue of the warrant: *R v Zinga* [2012] EWCA Crim 2357, [2013] Crim L R 226, and ordinarily the fact that the occupant of the premises is a solicitor, especially if he is a duty solicitor and will thus be likely to keep work based devices at his home: (*R (on the application of AB) v Huddersfield Magistrates' Court* [2014] EWHC 1089 (Admin), [2014] 4 All ER 500, [2014] 2 Cr App Rep 409. The disclosure must be as full and frank as the circumstances of each case requires. For a summary of the relevant principles, see *R (on the application of Rawlinson and Hunter Trustees) v Central Criminal Court* [2012] EWHC 2254 (Admin), [2013] 1 WLR 1634. See also *R (Golfrate Property Management Ltd and Another) v Southwark Crown Court and Others* [2014] EWHC 840 (Admin), [2014] 2 Cr App R 12; and *R (on the application of S,F and L) v Chief Constable of the British Transport Police* [2013] EWHC 2189 (Admin), [2014] 1 All ER 268, [2014] 1 WLR 1647.

2 Authority for issuing a warrant

F[5.2] A warrant of entry may only be issued where a statute gives authority to do so. When considering an application the magistrate should ask the applicant under what Act and section he is applying for a warrant. The warrant and supporting paperwork should indicate the Act and section. Note that the Justices' Clerks' Society has produced a checklist (dated October 2011) and any magistrate who may be asked to deal with search warrant applications should be afforded access to that checklist.

F[5.3] Applications by the police generally fall into one of two categories:

F[5.4] Search for unlawful articles. These are powers of search for goods which generally it is an offence knowingly to possess, eg warrants to enter and search for:

- stolen goods – Theft Act 1968, s 26;
- drugs – Misuse of Drugs Act 1971, s 23;
- obscene articles – Obscene Publications Act 1959, s 3;
- firearm or ammunition – Firearms Act 1968, s 46.

Under the MDA 1971, s 23(4), a forcible search may be justified where the suspect refuses to submit to a request to spit out drugs which he was concealing in his mouth: see *James v DPP* [2012] EWHC 1317 (Admin), 176 JP 346, 176 CL&J 291.

F[5.5] **Search for evidence.** Until the Police and Criminal Evidence Act 1984, there was no power to issue a warrant to search for *evidence*, eg of a murder, unless the object of the search was also an 'unlawful article' so that a warrant could be issued under the powers described above. The Police and Criminal Evidence Act 1984, s 8 (as amended by the Serious Organised Crime and Police Act 2005) now provides a general power to search for evidence of an offence. However since the Police and Criminal Evidence Act 1984 also gives the police considerable powers of search without a warrant in connection with the arrest of a defendant, an application for a warrant to search for evidence will very often entail the power to enter the premises of a possibly innocent third party to look for evidence implicating the accused.

Issuing a warrant to search for evidence of an indictable offence (Police and Criminal Evidence Act 1984, s 8)

F[5.6] The application must be made by the police and the magistrate must have reasonable grounds for believing:

(a)   that an indictable offence has been committed; and
(b)   that there is material on premises specified in the application which is likely to be of substantial value (whether by itself or together with other material) to the investigation of the offence; and
(c)   that the material is likely to be relevant evidence; and
(d)   that it does not consist of or include items subject to legal privilege, excluded material or special procedure material; and
(e)   that any of the following applies:
       (i)   that it is not practicable to communicate with any person entitled to grant entry to the premises;
      (ii)   that it is practicable to communicate with a person entitled to grant access to the premises but it is not practicable to communicate with any person entitled to grant access to the evidence;
     (iii)   that entry to the premises will not be granted unless a warrant is produced;
     (iv)   that the purpose of a search may be frustrated or seriously prejudiced unless a constable arriving at the premises can secure immediate entry to them.

In *R (on the application of Wood) v North Avon Magistrates' Court* [2009] EWHC 3614 (Admin), 174 JP 157 the High Court suggested that, save in exceptional circumstances, the officer applying for the warrant and giving evidence on oath must be an officer directly involved in the investigation.

F[5.7] **Reasonable grounds for believing.** The magistrate himself must have reasonable grounds for believing etc and his judgment will be based on the information supplied by the officer. It is advisable for a short note to be kept by the magistrate of the reasons for granting or refusing a warrant (which can be attached to the application). In the Code of Practice issued for guidance to the police, the officer must take reasonable steps to check that the information is accurate, recent and has not been provided maliciously or irresponsibly. An application may not be made on the basis of information from an anonymous source unless corroboration is sought. The identity of an informant need not be disclosed but the officer should be prepared to deal with any questions from the magistrate about the accuracy of previous information provided by that source or other related matters. 'Belief' is something more than suspicion and implies an acceptance that something is true even though formal, admissible evidence may be lacking. It may be helpful to consider the reference to this matter made when considering the offence of handling stolen goods at A[49].

There was nothing in the 1984 Act which required the court to give reasons why it was satisfied that there were reasonable grounds for believing the matters set out in s 8(1)(a)–(e) was satisfied. In some cases it might be unnecessary to do so, such as where the written information was compelling as to the grounds for a belief and clearly addressed the specific matters in s 8(1)(a)–(d): *Glenn & Co (Essex) Ltd v Her Majesty's Commissioners for Revenues and Customs and East Berkshire Magistrates' Court* [2011] EWHC 2998 (Admin), [2012] 1 Cr App Rep 291, 176 JP 65.

Reasonable suspicion. Some legislation requires only 'reasonable suspicion' as opposed to 'reasonable grounds for belief'. In *R (on the application of Eastenders Barking Ltd) v South Western Magistrates' Court* 22 March 2011, QBD, it was held that the grant of a search warrant under s 46 of the Firearms Act 1968 required only reasonable suspicion that an offence had or might have been committed under the Act as opposed to the higher threshold of reasonable belief (see *R v Central Criminal Court, ex p Bright* [2001] 2 All ER 244, [2001]1 WLR 662, DC; *R v Windsor* [2011] EWCA Crim 143, [2011] 2 Cr App Rep 71, 175 CL&J 110.

The test for establishing reasonable suspicion was a two-fold test which comprised a subjective and objective element The issue was whether (a) the Judge or magistrate was satisfied that there were reasonable grounds for suspecting an offence had been committed under the Act; and (b) if he/she was, whether there was material before him/her on which he/she was entitled to be satisfied.

In the present case there were reasonable grounds to satisfy the objective test because intelligence existed which was reliable. The source of the evidence had been given to the Judge. The fact that more information could have been elicited did not mean there was insufficient evidence to give rise to reasonable suspicion, the threshold of which was relatively low.

F[5.8] Indictable offence means an offence which, if committed by an adult, is triable on indictment, whether it is exclusively so or triable either way. The definition also includes a 'relevant offence' as defined in s 28D(4) of the Immigration Act 1971: s 8(5) PACE 1984.

F[5.9] Relevant evidence means anything that would be admissible in evidence at a trial for the offence. The application (information) and the warrant should identify, so far as is practicable, the articles or persons to be sought: see s 15(6)(b) of PACE and *Power-Hynes v Norwich Magistrates' Court* [2009] EWHC 1512 (Admin), (2009) 173 JP 573.

F[5.10] Premises. The premises referred to above are:

- one or more sets of premises specified in the application (a '*specific premises warrant*'); or
- any premises occupied or controlled by a person specified in the application, including such sets of premises as are so specified (an '*all premises warrant*').

If the application is for an '*all premises warrant*', the magistrate must also be satisfied:

- that because of the particulars of the offence referred to in the application, there are reasonable grounds for believing that it is necessary to search premises occupied or controlled by the person in question which are not specified in the application in order to find the material referred to in the application; and
- that it is not reasonably practicable to specify in the application all the premises which he occupies or controls and which might need to be searched.

The warrant may authorise entry to and search of premises on more than one occasion if, on the application, the magistrate is satisfied that it is necessary to authorise multiple entries in order to achieve for which he issues the warrant.

A copy of the search warrant issued under PACE, s 8 had, on its face, to record the address being searched so that when the occupier was served with a copy he would know for certain that the warrant as issued did indeed cover his premises: *R (on the application of Bhatti) v Croydon Magistrates' Court* [2010] EWHC 522 (Admin)., [2010] 3 All ER 671, [2011] 1 WLR 948.

F[5.11]–[5.15] Legal privilege means in essence communications between a legal adviser and his client or communications between them and a third party in contemplation of legal proceedings. The legal adviser can supply a full definition.

F[5.16] Excluded and special procedure material. This includes material held in confidence such as personal or business records, human tissues or fluids taken for the purpose of diagnosis or treatment and journalistic material. A magistrate cannot issue a warrant in respect of excluded or special procedure material; application can only be made, where applicable, to a circuit Judge: see *R (on the application of Bates) v Chief Constable of the Avon and Somerset Police* [2009] EWHC 942 (Admin), 173 JP 313.

F[5.17] May issue. Even where all the criteria have been fulfilled, the magistrate still has a discretion.

3 *Procedure (for search warrants issued to the police for evidence under the Police and Criminal Evidence Act 1984, s 8 and under other statutes)*

F[5.18] (1) The application may be made by a constable but it must have been authorised by an inspector or more senior officer, or in a case of urgency, the senior officer on duty. Where application is made by a member of the Serious and Organised Crime Agency authorisation by a Grade 3 Officer or above is sufficient. Where the officer is not known to the magistrate, a warrant card may be produced to establish identity.

F[5.19] (2) Except in a case of emergency, if there is reason to believe that a search might have an adverse effect on relations between the police and the community, the local Police Community Liaison Officer should have been consulted.

F[5.20] (3) The application must be supported by an information in writing stating:

(a)   the ground on which he makes the application;
(b)   the enactment under which the warrant would be issued; and

(c)   if the application is for a warrant authorising entry and search on more than one occasion, the ground on which he applies for such a warrant, and whether he seeks a warrant authorising an unlimited number of entries, or (if not) the maximum number of entries desired;

(d)   to identify, so far as is practicable, the articles or persons to be sought; and

(e)   to specify the matters set out in F[5.20A] below.

F[5.20A] The matters which must be specified as in (d) above are:

(a)   if the application relates to one or more sets of premises specified in the application, each set of premises which it is desired to search and enter;

(b)   if the application relates to any premises occupied or controlled by a person specified in the application:

(i)   as many sets of premises which it is desired to enter and search as it is reasonable practicable to specify;

(ii)   the person who is in occupation or control of those premises and any others which it is desired to enter and search;

(iii)   why it is necessary to search more premises than those specified under (i) above; and

(iv)   why it is not reasonably practicable to specify all the premises which it is desired to enter and search.

In *Redknapp v Comr of the City of London Police Department* [2008] EWHC 1177 (Admin) it was stressed that all the necessary material to justify the grant of a search warrant should be contained in the information provided in the relevant pro forma. If the magistrate, on an application under s 8 requires any further information in order to satisfy himself that the warrant was justified, a note should be made of the additional information so that there was a proper record of the full basis upon which the warrant has been granted.

F[5.21] (4) The constable must answer on oath any questions which the magistrate may ask him. Apart from questions designed to ensure that the grounds for the application have been made out, eg under the Theft Act 1968, s 26, the magistrate might usefully inquire whether the officer has had the same application previously refused by another magistrate. The police cannot 'shop around' for a magistrate willing to sign the warrant. A second application can only be made where it is based on additional grounds. Finally, there is a discretion whether to issue a warrant.

F[5.22] (5) The police will usually have prepared a warrant and two copies beforehand. If he is prepared to issue the warrant, the magistrate should read it carefully and check that it covers the matters referred to in (3) above.

F[5.23] (6) The justices' clerk should retain the information and the police must forward to him, after three months at the latest, the warrant either unexecuted or endorsed as to whether the articles or persons sought were found; and whether any articles were seized, other than the articles which were sought.

F[5.24] (7) A note of reasons for grant or refusal should be retained

Subsequent applications for disclosure of material used to
obtain warrant

F[5.24A] In *Metropolitan Police Comr v B* [2014] EWHC 546 (Admin),
(2014) 178 JP 158 a person aggrieved by the issue of a search warrant
(under s 23 of the Misuse of Drugs 1971) sought disclosure of the
Information and supporting evidence laid before the court. The appellant
objected on the ground of public interest immunity. The Administrative Court dealt with a number of procedural matters. These have now been
effectively codified in Part 5 of the Criminal Procedure Rules 2014. As to
the correct tests to apply and balancing the competing interests where PII is
claimed, see paragraphs 36 to 58 of the judgment.

4 *Procedure for warrants issued to persons other than police officers*

F[5.25] The provisions outlined above might usefully be taken into
account where relevant. For non-police warrants the information is laid on
oath. The applicant will usually produce a prepared information and swear
to it in the following words: 'I swear by Almighty God that this is my
information and that the contents thereof are true to the best of my
knowledge and belief.' If he prefers it, he may substitute for the words, 'I
swear by Almighty God . . . ' the words, 'I solemnly and sincerely declare
and affirm . . . '. If the wording on the information is not sufficient a
further written statement should be appended to the information.

F[5.26] As a matter of practice the informant signs the information and
the magistrate should retain this and forward it to the justices' clerk.

Search warrants under section 161A Customs and Excise Management
Act 1979

F[5.27]–[5.30] The Justices' Clerks' Society was contacted by HM
Revenue and Customs with regard to the above. There is a concern that the
police are applying for search warrants when it should be an officer of HM
Revenue and Customs.

The section states:

161A Power to search premises: search warrant

(1)   If a justice of the peace is satisfied by information upon oath
given by an officer that there are reasonable grounds to suspect
that anything liable to forfeiture under the customs and excise
Acts is kept or concealed in any building or place, he may by
warrant under his hand authorise any officer, and any person
accompanying an officer, to enter and search the building or place
named in the warrant.

(2)   An officer or other person so authorised has power—

(a)   to enter the building or place at any time, whether by day
or night, on any day, and search for, seize, and detain or
remove any such thing, and

(b)   so far as is necessary for the purpose of such entry, search,
seizure, detention or removal, to break open any door,
window or container and force and remove any other
impediment or obstruction.

(3)   Where there are reasonable grounds to suspect that any still, vessel, utensil, spirits or materials for the manufacture of spirits is or are unlawfully kept or deposited in any building or place, subsections (1) and (2) above apply in relation to any constable as they would apply in relation to an officer.

(4)   The powers conferred by a warrant under this section are exercisable until the end of the period of one month beginning with the day on which the warrant is issued.

(5)   A person other than a constable shall not exercise the power of entry conferred by this section by night unless accompanied by a constable

Section 161A(1) allows an 'Officer' to make the application. 'Officer" is defined in s 1(1) of the Act as 'a person commissioned by the Commissioners' for Revenue and Customs. Section 8(2) qualifies this to allow other persons to act as and be given the powers of 'officers' when 'engaged by the orders or with the concurrence of the Commissioners'. Section 161A(3) gives powers to a police constable to make the application for a search warrant under this section but only where there are reasonable grounds to suspect that any 'still, vessel, utensil, spirits or materials for the manufacture of spirits is or are unlawfully kept or deposited in any building or place'.

There is a concern that the police are applying for search warrants where articles not listed in s 161A(3) are being searched for. The JCS believes the legislation is clear that the power is only available to the police where the conditions of sub-section (3) are satisfied; ie that an alcohol still or vessel etc is being searched for (dated 10 February 2012).

Warrants of entry for gas and electricity suppliers

F[5.31] The provisions are complex and are summarised below. It is good practice for all such applications to be considered at a courthouse in the presence of a legal adviser from whom advice may be obtained. Those subject to the application should receive notification of the date and venue of the application.

F[5.32] Applications may be made, for example, for entry to read a meter or to cut off the supply following non-payment of a bill. An electricity supplier may cut off the supply where the customer has not paid within 20 working days of a demand in writing and after two working days' notice of the supplier's intention to do so. However this power is not available where there is a genuine dispute about the amount owed. (Note – this procedure only applies to a bill for electricity supplied and not include monies owed on an article supplied by way of a credit sale such as a cooker. Nor is it relevant that there is a genuine dispute about the quality of service since the customer may use a separate procedure to obtain compensation.) The relevant periods where a gas supply is concerned are 28 days after the demand in writing and seven days' notice of intent to cut off the supply.

F[5.33] Right of entry. An officer of the supplier after one working day's notice (electricity) 24 hours' notice (gas) may at all reasonable times, on production of some duly authenticated document showing his authority, enter the premises for the purpose of cutting off the supply. No notice is required for entry to read a meter except where a warrant is to be applied for.

F[5.34] **Warrant of entry.** No right of entry may be exercised except with the consent of the occupier of the premises or under the authority of a justice's warrant (except in cases of emergency).

F[5.35] **Requirements.** There must be a sworn information in writing and the applicant must satisfy the justice:

(a)   that admission to the premises is reasonably required for the specified purpose;
(b)   the applicant has a right of entry to the premises;
(c)   the requirements of any relevant enactment have been complied with; and in particular
(d)   the relevant notices have been given, including notice of the hearing.

F[5.36] The justice might also ensure that:

(e)   there is no genuine dispute about the amount owed; and
(f)   the amount owed is in respect of the supply of gas or electricity.

F[5.37] **Code of practice.** Gas and electricity suppliers operate a Code of Practice (of which the clerk of the justices may be able to supply a copy) under which it is undertaken to provide assistance to domestic customers to meet their bills and the suppliers may refrain from cutting off the supply from those who are particularly vulnerable during the winter months; nevertheless where default has occurred, the suppliers may resort to the procedure outlined above.

F[5.38] **Duty to repair damage etc.** Where a right of entry has been exercised the supplier must ensure that the premises concerned are left no less secure by reason of the entry and must make good or pay compensation for any damage caused in entering the premises or making them secure.

5 The warrant

F[5.39] If the magistrate is satisfied with the application he will sign the warrant (which will normally have been prepared in advance by the applicant). This is handed back to the applicant and is his authority to enter and search etc. A magistrate who has issued a search warrant should say nothing to anyone about it, not even to a member of his own family. This is so that no suspicion falls on him in the event that it may appear that the occupier of the premises was expecting a search.

6 Who may sign

F[5.40]–[5.45] Any magistrate may sign a search warrant provided he is not on the Supplemental List (ie retired from active work on the bench).

Warrants of arrest

F[5.46] Magistrates will frequently have encountered these during sittings at court, eg for failing to answer bail. The procedure is very similar to that for issuing warrants of entry. However, it is virtually inconceivable that it should be necessary to approach a magistrate at home. The Police and Criminal Evidence Act 1984 provides wide powers of arrest without warrant even for minor offences where there is doubt about the identity of the arrested person or an arrest is necessary to prevent harm to him or the public. Accordingly, a magistrate would be unwise to issue such a warrant unless he has the advice of his justices' clerk or a legal adviser. Such applications should, as a matter of practice, be heard at the courthouse.

Proceeds of Crime Act 2002

F[5.47] Minimum amount. Section 294 of the 2002 Act allows a customs officer or constable to seize and apply for forfeiture of cash which is not less than £1,000 and is obtained through or intended to be used in unlawful conduct (see the Proceeds of Crime Act 2002 (Recovery of Cash in Summary Proceedings: Minimum amount) Order 2006, SI 2006/1699).

Search power. The police or customs may search a person or premises for tainted cash. An authorisation may be given by a single justice ex parte. A search warrant under this provision does not authorise entry to premises.

Detention of seized cash. Application may be made to any magistrate in England and Wales who may extend the officers right to detain cash for 48 hours, for up to three months. In calculating the 48 hours for which seized cash may initially be held, Saturdays, Sundays, Christmas Day, Good Friday and bank holidays should be ignored. The applicant must serve notice on anyone from whom the cash was seized, sent to or by. Service of the notice need not be proved.

Grounds for detention order. A magistrate may make the order for six months detention if he is satisfied that there are reasonable grounds for the officer's suspicion and the continued detention is justified for the purposes of investigation of its origins or use. Further extensions which may be for a total period of two years, must be made by a full court. Application for the release of detained money may also be made.

Forfeiture. The police or customs may apply for detained cash to be forfeited and a magistrates' court can make an order if it is satisfied that the cash is recoverable property or intended for use in unlawful conduct: s 298(2). A costs order may be made under s 64(1) of the Magistrates' Courts Act 1980. This includes the situation where the complaint is not proceeded with by virtue of s 52 of the Courts Act 1971 (see *Chief Constable of Cleveland Police v Vaughan* [2009] EWHC 2831 (Admin)). As to the principles, see F[2.20]. In *R (on the application of Stone) v Camberwell Magistrates' Court* [2010] EWHC 2333 (Admin), the High Court declined to consider whether there was jurisdiction to award costs in forfeiture proceedings pursuant to either s 52 (3) of the Courts Act 1971 or s 64 of the Magistrates' Courts Act 1980 describing the legal position as 'difficult'.

Legal Notes

Cash. Means notes and coins, postal orders, cheques or traveller's cheques, bankers drafts and bearer bonds and shares.

Minimum amount. Cash is only subject to the act if it is a minimum sum of £1,000, singly or as part of a larger sum. The amount may be estimated to preserve evidence.

Notice of forfeiture proceedings. In *R (on the application of Harrison) v Birmingham Magistrates' Court* [2011] EWCA Civ 332, [2011] 14 LS Gaz R 21, a forfeiture order made in respect of cash confiscated by the police when searching the house of a person arrested on suspicion of fraud was quashed where her unchallenged evidence was that she had not received a notice of the forfeiture hearing. The appellant had appealed to the Crown Court against the forfeiture order which held that by virtue of s 299(2) it had no jurisdiction to hear the appeal out of time. The Court invited the Lord Chief Justice to consider an amendment to the Magistrates' Courts (Detention and Forfeiture of Cash) Rules 2002 to permit a person to show that, notwithstanding ostensible service, the purported recipient had not in fact received notice.

The guidance handed down was that pending any amendment to the 2002 Rules, magistrates should be particularly prudent about continuing with an application for a forfeiture order in the absence of a person with a claim to the money. If criminal proceedings were still ongoing, it might be worthwhile to give notice of the hearing to the solicitors dealing with the criminal case; albeit, those solicitors had not been instructed in the civil proceedings for forfeiture.

Following that judgment, the Magistrates' Courts (Detention and Forfeiture of Cash) (Amendment) Rules 2012, SI 2012/1275 have been made. These Rules amend the 2002 Rules to allow for effective service of documents to be assumed unless the contrary is shown. The amended rules came into force on 2 July 2012.

Unlawful conduct. Includes conduct which is unlawful under the criminal law in the UK and conduct which occurs outside the UK if it would have been unlawful in the UK.

In *Angus v United Kingdom Border Agency* [2011] EWHC 461 (Admin), the appellant had been stopped at a British airport and £40,000 was found to be in her handbag, some of it wrapped in casino wrappings. She claimed that the monies represented repayment of a loan to her uncle. She later revised her story and said that the sums represented the repayment of loans made by her mother to two other individuals, repaid through their winnings obtained at casinos. An application for forfeiture was made pursuant to s 298 of the Proceeds of Crime Act 2002. The magistrates' court and on appeal, the Crown Court, found that the cash seized may well have been the proceeds of money laundering and that there was an irresistible inference that it was obtained through unlawful conduct. The appellant challenged the Crown Court's decision by way of case stated.

The Administrative Court held that irrespective of whether the litigation was High Court civil recovery proceedings or magistrates' court or Crown Court forfeiture proceedings, the test was the same. Applying the provisions of s 242(2)(b) of the PCA 2002, although it was not necessary to allege the commission of any specific offence, the matters that were alleged to constitute the particular kind or kinds of unlawful conduct by or in return for which the property was obtained had to be set out: *Director of Assets Recovery Agency v Green* [2005] EWHC 3168 (Admin), (2006) Times, 27 February considered. Accordingly, the answer to the question posed was that, in a case of cash forfeiture, a customs officer did have to show that the property seized was obtained through conduct of one of a number of kinds each of which would have been unlawful conduct.

In *Christopher Hendrik Weise v UK Border Agency* (2012) 29th June, CA, a forfeiture order made under the Proceeds of Crime Act 2002, s 298 was revoked as the Judge had not given adequate reasons for concluding that forfeited money which had been carried by a South African businessman in hand luggage and in the hold of an aeroplane constituted the proceeds of money laundering. Further, in *Begum v West Midlands Police* [2012] EWHC 2304 (Admin), it was held that a magistrates' court had erred in ordering the forfeiture of cash under s 298(2) by an offender who had failed to declare the extent of her savings in order to obtain benefits, since the undeclared cash had not been intended for use in unlawful conduct.

Legal aid. A criminal legal representation order is not available. Civil legal aid may apply subject to means.

Recoverable property. The police are not required to show that the apparent criminality of a company rendered the whole of its business unlawful. The police as claimant only had to show that there were 'reasonable grounds to suspect' that the property [cash] was in the company's hands because illegal labour had made a contribution to its acquisition *R (on the application of the Chief Constable of Greater Manchester Police) v City of Salford Magistrates' Court*, [2008] EWHC 1651 (Admin), [2009] 1 WLR 1023, [2008] EWHC 1651 (Admin), 172 JP 497.

Right of Appeal. May be made against the decision of a magistrates' court ordering forfeiture of cash by either party whether the application is dismissed or approved. In this case an appeal lies to the Crown Court: s 299.

Miscellaneous

Recognisance

F[5.48] A recognisance of a surety for bail should not be taken unless the proposed surety produces a certificate stating the amount and conditions of bail. The surety should be questioned so as to satisfy the magistrate that he has, or can easily obtain, the sum mentioned in the certificate. If the certificate states that a specific person is to be surety, evidence of identity should be required. The clerk or an officer in charge of a police station may take a recognisance and, in any case of doubt, the surety should be referred to one of these persons.

Certificate of good repute

F[5.49] A magistrate should not sign a certificate of good reputation or good character. If approached to do so he should refer the applicant to a legal adviser.

Passports and driving licences

F[5.50] A magistrate should neither endorse an application for a passport, nor sign the photograph therewith unless he knows the applicant sufficiently well to meet the criteria on the form. Similar considerations apply to applications for a photocard licence.

Removal to suitable premises of persons in need of care and attention (National Assistance Act 1948, s 47 and National Assistance (Amendment) Act 1951, s 1)

F[5.51] The following provisions are for the purposes of securing the necessary care and attention for persons who:

(a) are suffering from grave chronic disease or, being aged, infirm or physically incapacitated, are living in insanitary conditions; and

(b) are unable to devote to themselves, and are not receiving from other persons, proper care and attention.

F[5.52] Where the proper officer (formerly the medical officer of health) certifies in writing to the local authority that he is satisfied after thorough inquiry and consideration that in the interests of any such person residing in the local authority's area or for preventing injury to the health of, or serious nuisance to other persons, it is necessary to remove him from his residence, the local authority may apply to a court for an order of removal.

F[5.53] If the proper officer and another registered medical practitioner certify that in their opinion it is necessary in the interests of that person to remove him without delay, the local authority or the proper officer where duly authorised may make an application to a single justice having jurisdiction for the place where the person resides. The justice being satisfied on oral evidence under oath of the allegations in the certificate and that it is expedient so to do, may order his removal to a hospital where one is available or to some other place in, or within convenient distance of, the local authority area. If the justice thinks it necessary, the order can be made without notifying or hearing the person concerned.

F[5.54] Duration of the order. The order may be for a period of up to three weeks. After it has expired the local authority would have to make a full application to a court.

F[5.55] It should be noted, however, that as an emergency ex parte application can also be made to a magistrate sitting in a courthouse; accordingly, applications should normally be considered there except where circumstances dictate otherwise.

Statutory declarations

F[5.56] It is necessary to make sure that the clause at the end of the form is properly completed and dated. It is not necessary to read the document, nor need the magistrate be concerned to establish in his own mind the truth of the contents of it. His signature on the document simply attests that he was present and heard the maker of the document declare that the contents are true.

F[5.57]–[5.62] The words for a statutory declaration are:

> **I, AB, do solemnly and sincerely declare and affirm that the contents of this declaration are true to the best of my knowledge and belief, and I make this solemn declaration conscientiously believing the same to be true and by virtue of the provisions of the Statutory Declarations Act 1835.**

F[5.63] A Holy Book is not required for a statutory declaration.

F[5.64] Any magistrate, including those on the Supplemental List, may sign a statutory declaration.

Warrants to search for and remove mental patients

(Mental Health Act 1983, s 135)

F[5.65] A justice to whom it appears that there is reasonable cause to suspect that a person believed to be suffering from mental disorder:

(a)   has been, or is being, ill-treated, neglected or kept otherwise than under proper control in any place within the jurisdiction of the justice; or

(b)   being unable to care for himself, is living alone in any such place;

may issue a warrant authorising his removal to a place of safety with a view to making an application under the Mental Health Act 1983 or other arrangements for his treatment or care.

F[5.66] **Application** is by way of an information laid on oath by a social worker specially approved by the local authority for the purposes of the Mental Health Act 1983. The patient need not be named in the information.

F[5.67] **Warrant** authorises a constable to enter (if need be by force) any premises specified in the warrant and if thought fit to remove him to a place of safety.

F[5.68] **Place of safety** means residential accommodation provided by a local authority or a hospital, police station, mental nursing home, or residential home for mentally disturbed persons or any other suitable place where the occupier is willing to receive the patient.

F[5.69] **Duration.** The detention in a place of safety may not be for more than 72 hours.

Administration of oaths etc in certain probate business

F[5.70] Justices of the peace are empowered by the Courts and Legal Services Act 1990, s 56 to administer oaths and take affidavits in non-contentious probate matters. The Judicial Studies Board has issued the following guidance for the assistance of magistrates' courts:

(a)   The oaths envisaged in this Act are those which are non-contentious and of a probate nature, ie, civil proceedings, and should not therefore be of great urgency requiring their administration out of court hours. Each court should therefore publish set hours during which these oaths will be administered.

(b)   Justices should be discouraged from administering these oaths outside court hours and away from supervision by suitably qualified court staff.

(c)   Justices should not administer oaths for documents which are to be used in court proceedings [including civil proceedings], and court staff should look at document headings with great care, to ensure that there is no court name or reference number thereon which might indicate a current court action.

(d)   The wording of the oath to be taken is different from a court witness oath and is 'I swear by Almighty God that the contents of this my [affidavit] [and the exhibits annexed thereto] are true'.

(e)   Be prepared for the oath to be sworn by members of all religions in the appropriate form – another reason why 'out of hours oaths' should be discouraged.

(f)   An interpreter may be needed and he should be sworn first, taking the appropriate oath.

(g)   A deponent may wish to affirm, in which case he will do so in the appropriate form – again a reason for oaths to be administered in the court setting, as justices will not necessarily know the correct wording.

(h)   Every alteration to the document has to be initialled by the administering justice.

(i)   Any exhibit has to be dated and signed and must clearly indicate that it is the exhibit annexed to the affidavit produced and sworn by the deponent on that same occasion.

(j)   The jurat or attestation shall state the date and place the oath or affidavit is taken or made [Courts and Legal Services Act 1990, s 56(2)].

(k)   No justice shall exercise the powers conferred in any proceedings in which he is interested [Courts and Legal Services Act 1990, s 56(3)].

(l)   In the event of any person being sufficiently handicapped to make it impossible for him or her to attend court to swear a document, arrangement could be made by the clerk to the justices for a justice and member of the court staff to attend upon that person at their home, or a mutually convenient place. This should not occur frequently, but should be provided for by courts.

Index

Custodial sentences – *cont.*
enforcement of
    fine B33.41–B33.51,
    B33.70
immediate sentence for shortest
    time B2.17
imprisonment *see* Imprisonment
intermittent custody B2.1,
    B26.0, B26.1
legal representation
    defendant's right to, young
      offenders B2.8, B26.21
    right to B2.8, B36.2, B37.19
length B2.18–B2.20,
    B37.35–B37.39
mentally disordered
    defendant B2.23–B2.24,
    B37.18
pre-sentence reports *see* Pre-
    sentence reports
previous convictions, taking into
    account B2.10
proportionality B5.49
restrictions on
    imposing B2.8–B2.9
seriousness of offence
    determining B5.7–B5.16
    'first time offender' B5.7
    generally B5.3
    'range' B5.7
    'starting point' B5.7
see also Imprisonment;
    Sentencing; Young offender
    institution
Custody
see Custodial sentences; Remand
   in custody
Custody plus
generally B2.1
Custody time limits
application to extend D8.52
expiry D8.54
generally D8.51–D8.54
Customs and excise duty
see Revenue and Customs

D

Damage to property
see also **Criminal damage**
arson A18
criminal damage A18
possessing anything with intent
    to destroy or damage
    property A18B
threatening to destroy or
    damage property A18A
Dangerous adult offenders
committal to Crown Court for
    sentence B11.1
Dangerous dogs
age of owner A72.2
change of ownership A72.25
contingent destruction
    order A72.15
control or destruction
    order A72.10,
    A72.21–A72.38
    additional powers A72.16
    appeal A72.19, A72.38
    disqualification and A72.17
    fighting dogs A72.20
    procedure at hearing A72.31
dangerously out of control,
    meaning A72.3
disqualification from keeping
    contravention A72.18,
    A72.37
    generally A72.17, A72.20,
    A72.34–A72.35
escape from enclosed
    area A72.4
fighting dogs A72.20
Japanese Tosas A72.20
offence committed by
    omission A72.4
owner A72.2
parked car, in A72.7
physical control of dog A72.4
pit bull terriers A72.20
public place A72.5–A72.7
sentencing A72.8–A72.19

European Convention on Human
  Rights (ECHR) – *cont.*
restraining orders A41.13
self-incrimination C8.22
sentencing B5.53
silence C8.22
threatening behaviour A21.5A
Evidence
CCTV D6.9
children and young persons, by
  Bench Checklist for Young
  Witness cases D6.13A
clearing the court A52.10,
  D1B.3–D1B.5
competence A52.8
live video link E3.22, D8.22B
reporting
  restrictions E2.4–E2.5,
  D1B.7
sexual offences, as
  to A52.8–A52.9, D1B.7
unsworn evidence A52.6,
  E3.22
youth court D1B.7
council tax recovery and
  enforcement f4.7–f4.8
hearsay *see* Hearsay evidence
inference drawn from failure to
  give D6.22
live video link *see* Live video
  link
open court, in
  non-disclosure D1B.6
restitution orders B39.6
Excessive noise*see* Noise
Excise licence
keeping of unlicensed
  vehicle C47.3–C47.17
liability for back
  duty C47.19–47.31
payment by dishonoured
  cheque C47.16
Statutory Off Road Notification
  (SORN) C47.17
using vehicle without C47
Exclusion order B32
actual bodily harm, in case
  of A8.33

Exclusion order – *cont.*
football banning order *see*
  Football banning order
licensed premises B32.1–B32.2
  assault A8.33
  assaulting a constable A9.11
  expelling persons from B32.2
  wounding/grievous bodily
    harm A70.20
period B32.1
see also Community orders;
  Drinking banning order
Exclusion from school
parenting order B37A.3
Exposure A30
Extended sentences for dangerous
  adult offenders B11.1

F

Failing to disclose information
dishonesty A36.8
gain and loss A36.8
generally A36.8
legal duty A36.8
mode of trial A36.5
penalty A36.4
statutory wording A36.2
Failing to report after
  accident C31.3, C32
reasonably practicable C32.18
Failing to stop and give details
  after accident C31
Failure to surrender to
  custody A10
defence D8.85
penalty D8.91
prosecution D8.82–D8.91
sentencing A10.3
'surrender to custody' A10.2
False accounting A31
False identity documents A32
False representation
fraud, and
  dishonesty A36.7
  gain and loss A36.7